Rereading America

Cultural Contexts for
Critical Thinking and Writing

Rereading America

Cultural Contexts for Critical Thinking and Writing

Sixth Edition

Edited by

Gary Colombo
LOS ANGELES CITY COLLEGE

Robert Cullen
SAN JOSE STATE UNIVERSITY

Bonnie Lisle
UNIVERSITY OF CALIFORNIA, LOS ANGELES

Bedford/St. Martin's   Boston   •   New York

For Bedford/St. Martin's

Developmental Editor: John Sullivan
Production Editor: Ara Salibian
Senior Production Supervisor: Joe Ford
Editorial Assistant: Sarah Whitesel
Production Assistant: Kristen Merrill
Copyeditor: Alison Greene
Cover Design: Donna Lee Dennison
Cover Art: © Joseph Sohm; ChromoSohm Inc./CORBIS
Composition: Pine Tree Composition, Inc.
Printing and Binding: Haddon Craftsmen, Inc., an R. R. Donnelley & Sons
  Company

President: Joan E. Feinberg
Editorial Director: Denise B. Wydra
Editor in Chief: Karen S. Henry
Director of Marketing: Karen Melton Soeltz
Director of Editing, Design, and Production: Marcia Cohen
Managing Editor: Elizabeth M. Schaaf

Library of Congress Control Number: 2003114537

9 8 7
j i h

For information, write: Bedford/St. Martin's, 75 Arlington Street, Boston,
MA 02116 (617-399-4000)

ISBN: 0–312–40554–5

Preface for Instructors

About *Rereading America*

Designed for first-year writing and critical thinking courses, *Rereading America* anthologizes a diverse set of readings focused on the myths that dominate U.S. culture. This central theme brings together thought-provoking selections on a broad range of topics — family, education, success, gender roles, race, and America seen from a global perspective — topics that raise controversial issues meaningful to college students of all backgrounds. We've drawn these readings from many sources, both within the academy and outside of it; the selections are both multicultural and cross-curricular and thus represent an unusual variety of voices, styles, and subjects.

The readings in this anthology speak directly to students' experiences and concerns. Every college student has had some brush with prejudice, and most have something to say about education, the family, or the gender stereotypes they see in films and on television. The issues raised here help students link their personal experiences with broader cultural perspectives and lead them to analyze, or "read," the cultural forces that have shaped and continue to shape their lives. By linking the personal and the cultural, students begin to recognize that they are not academic outsiders — they too have knowledge, assumptions, and intellectual frameworks that give them authority in academic culture. Connecting personal knowledge and academic discourse helps students see that they are able to think, speak, and write academically and that they don't have to absorb passively what the "experts" say.

Features of the Sixth Edition

A Cultural Approach to Critical Thinking   Like its predecessors, the sixth edition of *Rereading America* is committed to the premise that learning to think critically means learning to identify and see beyond dominant cultural myths — collective and often unconsciously held beliefs that influence our thinking, reading, and writing. Instead of treating cultural diversity as just another topic to be studied or "appreciated," *Rereading America* encourages students to grapple with the real differences in perspective that arise in a pluralistic society like ours. This method helps students to break through conventional assumptions and patterns of thought that hinder fresh critical responses and inhibit dialogue. It helps them recognize that even the most apparently "natural" fact or obvious idea results from a process of social construction. And it helps them to develop the intellectual independence essential to critical thinking, reading, and writing.

Classic and Conservative Perspectives   To provide students with the historical context they often need, each chapter in this edition of *Rereading America* begins with a "classic" expression of the myth under examination. Approaching the myth of success, for example, by way of Horatio Alger's *Ragged Dick*—or the myth of racial superiority by way of Thomas Jefferson's infamous diatribe against "race mixing"—gives students a better sense of the myth's origins and impact. We've also included at least one contemporary conservative revision of the myth in each chapter, so you'll find in this edition more readings by cultural critics who stand to the right of center, writers like Christina Hoff Sommers, Shelby Steele, Ken Hamblin, Dinesh D'Souza, and Michael Medved.

New Issues   The events of September 11, 2001, changed the way we live in the United States and the way we think of ourselves in relation to the world around us. This edition of *Rereading America* dedicates a new chapter that invites students to reflect on America's mission and meaning in a global context. The selections in "Land of Liberty: American Mythology in a New World Order," challenge students to explore the notion of American "exceptionalism"—the idea that the United States has a special destiny to fulfill among the nations of the world, a destiny closely tied to the ideal of personal freedom. Classic and contemporary readings by authors like Albert C. Beveridge, Dinesh D'Souza, Mark Hertsgaard, Walter Mosley, June Jordan, Jerry Spence, and Patricia Williams offer students the chance to think critically about America's sense of national destiny and about the sources of the anti-Americanism that has become so apparent since 9/11. Together with a provocative "graphic novel" exposé by Joel Andreas, these selections encourage students to consider whether we are, in fact, a beacon of liberty for the rest of the world—or an "oblivious empire" that has become hopelessly "addicted to war." The chapter's visual portfolio features images dramatizing America's global influence—from a Rambo poster in the bedroom of a young Palestinian to the highly publicized photo of a U.S. Marine tenderly cradling a wounded Iraqi girl. "Land of Liberty" also invites students to question whether the very freedoms that we are fighting for abroad aren't being sacrificed as the result of increased surveillance and racial profiling in post–Patriot Act America. By placing American mythology in a global context, and by providing insight into the way we as a nation appear through "other" eyes, this new chapter offers a dramatic example of how powerfully America's cultural mythology shapes our values and attitudes. It also provides *Rereading America* with a potent new theme that is sure to engage students personally and to evoke passionate classroom debate.

Timely New Readings   To keep *Rereading America* up to date, we've worked hard to bring you the best new voices speaking on issues of race, gender, class, family, and education. As in past editions, we've retained old favorites like Malcolm X, Richard Rodriguez, Shelby Steele, Jamaica Kincaid, Paula Gunn Allen, Toni Cade Bambara, Gary Soto, Bebe Moore Campbell, Judith Ortiz Cofer, and Mike Rose. But you'll also find a host of new selections by such authors as Judy Root Aulette, Joshua Gamson, Michael Moore, Francesca Delbanco, Benjamin R. Barber, Dan Rather, Randall Robinson, and June Jordan. And like earlier versions, this edition of *Rereading America* includes a healthy mix of personal and academic writing, representing a wide variety of genres, styles, and rhetorical strategies.

Visual Portfolios   In addition to frontispieces and cartoons, we've included a Visual Portfolio of myth-related images in every chapter of *Rereading America*. These collections of photographs, advertisements, and reproductions of famous paintings invite students to examine how visual "texts" are constructed and how, like written texts, they are susceptible to multiple readings and rereadings. Each portfolio is accompanied by a series of questions that encourage critical analysis and connect portfolio images to ideas and themes in chapter reading selections. As in earlier editions, the visual frontispieces that open each chapter are integrated into the prereading assignments found in the chapter introductions. The cartoons, offered as a bit of comic relief and as opportunities for visual thinking, are paired with appropriate readings thoughout the text.

Focus on Media   We've continued the practice of including one or more selections focusing on the media in each chapter of *Rereading America*. This distribution of media pieces throughout the book allows you to discuss media representations in the context of the specific myths your class addresses. In the first chapter, Joshua Gamson examines how TV talk shows depict gay, lesbian, and transgender families. Chapter Four offers several analyses of gender issues in the media, including Jean Kilbourne on images of women in advertising, Michael A. Messner on the "manhood formula" of televised sports, Susan Faludi on teen masculinity and the culture of celebrity, and Joan Morgan on black feminism and hip-hop culture. "Created Equal: The Myth of the Melting Pot" introduces the notion of media-created "virtual integration" and discusses transracial advertising. "Land of Liberty: American Mythology in a New World Order" presents readings by media critics Michael Medved and Todd Gitlin—essays that offer sharply contrasting perspectives on the way that Hollywood portrays American life and that raise questions about the impact of American culture on more traditional societies around the world.

Focus on Struggle and Resistance   Most multicultural readers approach diversity in one of two ways: either they adopt a pluralist approach and conceive of American society as a kind of salad bowl of cultures, or, in response to recent worries about the lack of "objectivity" in the multicultural curriculum, they take what might be called the "talk show" approach and present American culture as a series of pro-and-con debates on a number of social issues. The sixth edition of *Rereading America*, like its predecessors, follows neither of these approaches. Pluralist readers, we feel, make a promise that's impossible to keep: no single text, and no single course, can do justice to the many complex cultures that inhabit the United States. Thus, the materials selected for *Rereading America* aren't meant to offer a taste of what "family" means for Native Americans, or the flavor of gender relations among immigrants. Instead, we've included selections like Melvin Dixon's "Aunt Ida Pieces a Quilt" or Harlon Dalton's "Horatio Alger," because they offer us fresh critical perspectives on the common myths that shape our ideas, values, and beliefs. Rather than seeing this anthology as a mosaic or kaleidoscope of cultural fragments that combine to form a beautiful picture, it's more accurate to think of *Rereading America* as a handbook that helps students explore the ways that the dominant culture shapes their ideas, values, and beliefs.

This notion of cultural dominance is studiously avoided in most recent multicultural anthologies. "Salad bowl" readers generally sidestep the issue of cultural dynamics: intent on celebrating America's cultural diversity, they offer a relatively static picture of a nation fragmented into a kind of cultural archipelago. "Talk show" readers admit the idea of conflict, but they distort the reality of cultural dynamics by presenting cultural conflicts as a matter of rational—and equally balanced—debate. All of the materials anthologized in *Rereading America* address the cultural struggles that animate American society—the tensions that result from the expectations established by our dominant cultural myths and the diverse realities that these myths often contradict.

Ultimately, *Rereading America* is about resistance. In this new edition we continue to include readings that offer positive alternatives to the dilemmas of cultural conflict. To make this commitment to resistance as visible as possible, we've tried to conclude every chapter of this new edition with a suite of readings offering creative and, we hope, empowering examples of Americans who work together to redefine our national myths.

Extensive Apparatus   *Rereading America* offers a wealth of features to help students hone their analytic abilities and to aid instructors as they plan class discussions, critical thinking activities, and writing assignments. These include:

- A *Comprehensive Introductory Essay*   The book begins with a comprehensive essay, "Thinking Critically, Challenging Cultural Myths," that introduces students to the relationships between thinking, cultural diversity, and the notion of dominant cultural myths, and shows how such myths can influence their academic performance. We've also included a section devoted to active reading, which offers suggestions for prereading, prewriting, note taking, text marking, and keeping a reading journal. A section helps students work with the many visual images included in the book.

- *Detailed Chapter Introductions*   An introductory essay at the beginning of each chapter offers students a thorough overview of each cultural myth, placing it in historical context, raising some of the chapter's central questions, and orienting students to the chapter's internal structure.

- *Prereading Activities*   Following each chapter introduction you'll find prereading activities designed to encourage students to reflect on what they already know about the cultural myth in question. Often connected to the images that open every chapter, these prereading activities help students to engage the topic even before they begin to read.

- *Questions to Stimulate Critical Thinking*   Three groups of questions following each selection encourage students to consider the reading carefully in several contexts: "Engaging the Text" focuses on close reading of the selection itself; "Exploring Connections" puts the selection into dialogue with other selections throughout the book; "Extending the Critical Context" invites students to connect the ideas they read about here with sources of knowledge outside the anthology, including library research, personal experience, interviews, ethnographic-style observations, and so forth. As in past editions, we've included a number of questions linking readings with contemporary television shows and feature films for instructors who want to address the interplay of cultural myths and the mass media.

- *An Extensive Instructor's Manual*   *Resources for Teaching* REREADING AMERICA provides detailed advice about ways to make the most of both the readings and the questions; it also offers further ideas for discussion, class activities, and writing assignments, as well as practical hints and suggestions that we've garnered from our own classroom experiences.

- *Online Resources*   The TopLinks Web site for *Rereading America* contains annotated research links. For more information, visit bedfordstmartins.com/rereadingamerica to explore this site and other helpful electronic resources for both students and instructors.

Acknowledgments

Critical thinking is always a collaborative activity, and the kind of critical thinking involved in the creation of an anthology like *Rereading America* represents collegial collaboration at its very best. Since publication of the last edition, we've heard from instructors across the country who have generously offered suggestions for new classroom activities and comments for further refinements and improvements. Among the many instructors who shared their insights with us as we reworked this edition, we'd particularly like to thank the following: Andrea Beaudin, Southern Connecticut State University; Nancy C. Botkin, Indiana University South Bend; Deborah Brink, Lower Columbia College; Blythe Creamer, University of California, Davis; Stephen F. Evans, University of Kansas; Kathy A. Fedorko, Middlesex County College; Julie Hirsch, University of Arizona, Tucson; Jennifer Lynn Holley, Southern Connecticut State University; Deborah Kirkman, University of Kentucky; Anna Leahy, Missouri Western State College; Kelly Mayhew, San Diego City College; Julie Nash, Merrimack College; Deirdre Neilen, SUNY Upstate Medical University; Hector Perez, University of the Incarnate Word; Josephine Perry, Los Medanos College; Margaret B. Racin, West Virginia University; Daniela Ragusa, University of Rhode Island; Marguerite Regan, Southwestern College; Elizabeth Rich, Saginaw Valley State University; Kim Robeson, MiraCosta Community College; Renée Ruderman, Metropolitan State College of Denver; Tereza M. Szeghi, University of Arizona; Karen Toloui, Diablo Valley College; Lisa Toner, University of Kentucky; Alberto S. Vitale, Indiana University South Bend; James Ray Watkins, Jr., Eastern Illinois University; James M. Welch, Wittenberg University; and Terry Williams, San Diego State University.

For their help with the fifth edition of *Rereading America,* we'd like to thank the following: Etta C. Abrahams, Michigan State University; Richard L. Arthur, Miami University of Ohio; Scott E. Ash, Nassau Community College; Michael Augsperger, University of Iowa; Larry Cain, Chabot College; Rosann M. Cook, Purdue University at Calumet; Mary Jean Corbett, Miami University of Ohio; Stephen Curley, Texas A&M University at Galveston; Ann M. DeDad, Gannon University; Florence Emch, California State University, Los Angeles; Juan F. Flores, Del Mar College; Nancy Gonchar, The College of New Rochelle; Tara Hart, Howard Community College; Sue Ellen Holbrook, Southern Connecticut State University; Stephen Horvath, Howard Community College; Irwin J. Koplik, Hofstra University; Michael Lewis, University of Iowa; Linda Maitland, University of Houston; Doug Merrell, University of Washington; Robert Murray, St. Thomas Aquinas College; Kathleen O'Brien, Boston University; Renée Ruderman, Metropolitan State College of Denver; Karen Ryan-Engel, Gannon University; Amy Sileven, Southern Illinois University at Carbondale; Jane E. Simonsen, University of Iowa; Juliet Sloger, University of Rochester; Ken Smith,

Indiana University, South Bend; Judith A. Stainbrook, Gannon University; Douglas Steward, University of Kansas.

For their help with the fourth edition of *Rereading America*, we'd like to thank the following: Dan Armstrong, Lane Community College; H. Inness Asher, University of Louisiana, Lafayette; Margot Gayle Backis, St. John Fisher College; Marlow Belschner, Southern Illinois University; Nancy Botkin, Indiana University, South Bend; Carol Brown, South Puget Sound Community College; William Carroll, Norfolk State University; Dolores Crim, Purdue University, Hammond; Linda L. Danielson, Lane Community College; Emily Detiner, Miami University; Kathy Doherty, Bentley College; Melinda M. Fiala, University of Missouri, Kansas City; Sara Gogol, Portland Community College; Joyce Huff, George Washington University; Kim Lang, Shippensburg University; Uvieja Leighton, The Union Institute; Elizabeth L. Lewis, Vermilion Community College; Jennifer Lowood, Vista Community College; Brij Lurine, University of New Mexico; Eunice M. Madison, Purdue University, Calumet; Kenneth K. Martin, Community College of Philadelphia; James McWard, University of Kansas; Kevin A. Moberg, University of North Dakota; John G. Morris, Cameron University; Craig J. Nauman, University of Wisconsin, Madison; Bruce Ouderkirk, University of Nebraska, Lincoln; E. Suzanne Owens, Lorain County Community College; Elizabeth Paulson, California State University; Amy Sapowith, University of California, Los Angeles; Jurgen Schlunk, West Virginia University; Tony Slagle, The Ohio State University; Penny L. Smith, Gannon University; Sharon Snyder, Purdue University, Calumet; Deborah Tenneg, Yale University; Ruthe Thompson, University of Arizona; Lorraine Threadgill, Community College of Philadelphia; Steve Turnwall, Los Medanos College; Riley Vann, West Virginia University; Nancy Wallace, Temple University; Ellen Weinauer, University of Southern Mississippi; Claudia L. Whitling, South Puget Sound Community College; Judy Wilkinson, Skyline College; Mark Wollarges, Vanderbilt University; Phyllis Zrzuay, Franklin Pierce College.

We are also grateful to those reviewers who helped shape previous editions.

As always, we'd also like to thank all the kind folks at Bedford/ St. Martin's, who do their best to make the effort of producing a book like this a genuine pleasure. Our publishers, Charles Christensen and Joan Feinberg, deserve special praise for the support they've shown us over the years and for the wise counsel they've offered in the occasional hour of need. Our editor, John Sullivan, has been a true partner in the development of this edition and has again demonstrated the kind of style and grace we've come to expect from him as the consummate professional. We also want to thank Ara Salibian, who served as production editor on this edition; Alison Greene, who expertly copyedited the manuscript; Donna Dennison, who produced our new cover; Sandy Schechter, for clearing text permissions; Rose Corbett Gordon, for researching and tracking down art; and editorial assistant Sarah Whitesel, who helped out with many of the hundreds of details that go into a project such as this. Finally, we'd like to acknowledge Elena Barcia, Liz Silver, and Roy Weitz, who, after these many years, have mastered the art of ignoring us completely while we put our shoulders to the task of revision one more time.

Contents

1

Harmony at Home:
The Myth of the Model Family   *17*

realize the world may not appreciate their poetry or science-fair projects as much as they themselves do."

"Students see the hypocrisy of a society that talks about the importance of education and knowledge and information while its very educational institutions are selling their own souls for a buck. . . ."

3

Money and Success:
The Myth of Individual Opportunity   293

". . . Ragged Dick. You must drop that name, and think of yourself now as' — 'Richard Hunter, Esq.; said our hero, smiling.
'A young gentleman on the way to fame and fortune. . . .'"

". . . the Alger myth . . . serves to maintain the racial pecking order. It does so by mentally bypassing the role of race in American society."

"There's always more opportunity. There's never a lack of opportunity. That's what I love about this country. So many opportunities."

"I had gone into this venture in the spirit of science, to test a mathematical proposition, but somewhere along the line, in the tunnel vision imposed by long shifts and relentless concentration, it became a test of myself, and clearly I have failed."

"From cradle to grave, class standing has a signficant impact on our chances for survival."

"The real crime of which white America is now most guilty is not
racism. It is indifference. Understanding the difference between the
two is a crucial step in liberating ourselves from the sterile and unproductive impasse that has characterized the dialogue on race relations
in recent years."

"Four basic conceptions of how ethnic or racial groups should relate to
each other have been predominant in the history of American thought
about group relations—ethnic hierarchy, one-way assimilation, cultural pluralism, and group separatism."

"By its very nature television creates imaginary or virtual relationships
among people. What makes its impact on race unique is that for most
whites their television contact with blacks is the closest they will ever
come to crossing the color line."

"I never asked to be white. I am not literally white. . . . But like so
many other Asian Americans of the second generation, I find myself
now the bearer of a strange new status: white, by acclamation."

". . . Mary Lynn wanted to have sex with any man other than her husband. . . . She was a Coeur d'Alene Indian married to a white man; she
was a wife who wanted to have sex with an indigenous stranger."

"Transracial America, in the marketplace, is a vision of the American
dream in which we are liberated from the politics of race to openly

Rereading America

Cultural Contexts for
Critical Thinking and Writing

Thinking Critically, Challenging Cultural Myths

Becoming a College Student

Beginning college can be a disconcerting experience. It may be the first time you've lived away from home and had to deal with the stresses and pleasures of independence. There's increased academic competition, increased temptation, and a whole new set of peer pressures. In the dorms you may find yourself among people whose backgrounds make them seem foreign and unapproachable. If you commute, you may be struggling against a feeling of isolation that you've never faced before. And then there are increased expectations. For an introductory history class you may read as many books as you covered in a year of high school coursework. In anthropology, you might be asked to conduct ethnographic research — when you've barely heard of an ethnography before, much less written one. In English you may tackle more formal analytic writing in a single semester than you've ever done in your life.

College typically imposes fewer rules than high school, but also gives you less guidance and makes greater demands — demands that affect the quality as well as the quantity of your work. By your first midterm exam, you may suspect that your previous academic experience is irrelevant, that nothing you've done in school has prepared you to think, read, or write in the ways your professors expect. Your sociology instructor says she doesn't care whether you can remember all the examples in the textbook as long as you can apply the theoretical concepts to real situations. In your composition class, the perfect five-paragraph essay you turn in for your first assignment is dismissed as "superficial, mechanical, and dull." Meanwhile, the lecturer in your political science or psychology course is rejecting ideas about country, religion, family, and self that have always been a part of your deepest beliefs. How can you cope with these new expectations and challenges?

There is no simple solution, no infallible five-step method that works for everyone. As you meet the personal challenges of college, you'll grow as a human being. You'll begin to look critically at your old habits, beliefs, and values, to see them in relation to the new world you're entering. You may have to re-examine your relationships to family, friends, neighborhood, and heritage. You'll have to sort out your strengths from your weaknesses and make tough choices about who you are and who you want to become. Your

1

academic work demands the same process of serious self-examination. To excel in college work you need to grow intellectually — to become a critical thinker.

What Is Critical Thinking?

What do instructors mean when they tell you to think critically? Most would say that it involves asking questions rather than memorizing information. Instead of simply collecting the "facts," a critical thinker probes them, looking for underlying assumptions and ideas. Instead of focusing on dates and events in history or symptoms in psychology, she probes for motives, causes — an explanation of how these things came to be. A critical thinker cultivates the ability to imagine and value points of view different from her own — then strengthens, refines, enlarges, or reshapes her ideas in light of those other perspectives. She is at once open and skeptical: receptive to new ideas yet careful to test them against previous experience and knowledge. In short, a critical thinker is an active learner, someone with the ability to shape, not merely absorb, knowledge.

All this is difficult to put into practice, because it requires getting outside your own skin and seeing the world from multiple perspectives. To see why critical thinking doesn't come naturally, take another look at the cover of this book. Many would scan the title, *Rereading America*, take in the surface meaning — to reconsider America — and go on to page one. There isn't much to question here; it just "makes sense." But what happens with the student who brings a different perspective? For example, a student from El Salvador might justly complain that the title reflects an ethnocentric view of what it means to be an American. After all, since America encompasses all the countries of North, South, and Central America, he lived in "America" long before arriving in the United States. When this student reads the title, then, he actually does *reread* it; he reads it once in the "commonsense" way but also from the perspective of someone who has lived in a country dominated by U.S. intervention and interests. This double vision or double perspective frees him to look beyond the "obvious" meaning of the book and to question its assumptions.

Of course, you don't have to be bicultural to become a proficient critical thinker. You can develop a genuine sensitivity to alternative perspectives even if you've never lived outside your hometown. But to do so you need to recognize that there are no "obvious meanings." The automatic equation that the native-born student makes between "America" and the United States seems to make sense only because our culture has traditionally endorsed the idea that the United States *is* America and, by implication, that other countries in this hemisphere are somehow inferior — not the genuine article. We tend to accept this equation and its unfortunate implications because we are products of our culture.

The Power of Cultural Myths

Culture shapes the way we think; it tells us what "makes sense." It holds people together by providing us with a shared set of customs, values, ideas, and beliefs, as well as a common language. We live enmeshed in this cultural web: it influences the way we relate to others, the way we look, our tastes, our habits; it enters our dreams and desires. But as culture binds us together it also selectively blinds us. As we grow up, we accept ways of looking at the world, ways of thinking and being that might best be characterized as cultural frames of reference or cultural myths. These myths help us understand our place in the world — our place as prescribed by our culture. They define our relationships to friends and lovers, to the past and future, to nature, to power, and to nation. Becoming a critical thinker means learning how to look beyond these cultural myths and the assumptions embedded in them.

You may associate the word "myth" primarily with the myths of the ancient Greeks. The legends of gods and heroes like Athena, Zeus, and Oedipus embodied the central ideals and values of Greek civilization — notions like civic responsibility, the primacy of male authority, and humility before the gods. The stories were "true" not in a literal sense but as reflections of important cultural beliefs. These myths assured the Greeks of the nobility of their origins; they provided models for the roles that Greeks would play in their public and private lives; they justified inequities in Greek society; they helped the Greeks understand human life and destiny in terms that "made sense" within the framework of that culture.

Our cultural myths do much the same. Take, for example, the American dream of success. Since the first European colonists came to the "New World" some four centuries ago, America has been synonymous with the idea of individual opportunity. For generations, immigrants have been lured across the ocean to make their fortunes in a land where the streets were said to be paved with gold. Of course, we don't always agree on what success means or how it should be measured. Some calculate the meaning of success in terms of multi-digit salaries or the acreage of their country estates. Others discover success in the attainment of a dream — whether it's graduating from college, achieving excellence on the playing field, or winning new rights and opportunities for less-fortunate fellow citizens. For some Americans, the dream of success is the very foundation of everything that's right about life in the United States. For others, the American dream is a cultural mirage that keeps workers happy in low-paying jobs while their bosses pocket the profits of an unfair system. But whether you embrace or reject the dream of success, you can't escape its influence. As Americans, we are steeped in a culture that prizes individual achievement; growing up in the United States, we are told again and again by parents, teachers, advertisers, Hollywood writers, politicians, and opinion makers that we, too, can achieve our dream — that we, too, can "Just Do It" if we try. You might aspire to become an Internet tycoon, or you might rebel and opt for a simple life, but you can't ignore the impact of the myth. We each define success in our own way, but, ultimately, the myth of success defines who we are and what we think, feel, and believe.

Cultural myths gain such enormous power over us by insinuating themselves into our thinking before we're aware of them. Most are learned at a deep, even unconscious level. Gender roles are a good example. As children we get gender role models from our families, our schools, our churches, and other important institutions. We see them acted out in the relationships between family members or portrayed on television, in the movies, or in song lyrics. Before long, the culturally determined roles we see for women and men appear to us as "self-evident": it seems "natural" for a man to be strong, responsible, competitive, and heterosexual, just as it may seem "unnatural" for a man to shun competitive activity or to take a romantic interest in other men. Our most dominant cultural myths shape the way we perceive the world and blind us to alternative ways of seeing and being. When something violates the expectations that such myths create, it may even be called unnatural, immoral, or perverse.

Cultural Myths as Obstacles to Critical Thinking

Cultural myths can have more subtle effects as well. In academic work they can reduce the complexity of our reading and thinking. A few years ago, for example, a professor at Los Angeles City College noted that he and his students couldn't agree in their interpretations of the following poem by Theodore Roethke:

My Papa's Waltz

The whiskey on your breath
Could make a small boy dizzy;
But I hung on like death:
Such waltzing was not easy.

We romped until the pans
Slid from the kitchen shelf;
My mother's countenance
Could not unfrown itself.

The hand that held my wrist
Was battered on one knuckle;
At every step you missed
My right ear scraped a buckle.

You beat time on my head
With a palm caked hard by dirt,
Then waltzed me off to bed
Still clinging to your shirt.

The instructor read this poem as a clear expression of a child's love for his blue-collar father, a rough-and-tumble man who had worked hard all his life ("a palm caked hard by dirt"), who was not above taking a drink of whiskey to ease his mind, but who also found the time to "waltz" his son off to bed. The students didn't see this at all. They saw the poem as a story about an abusive father and heavy drinker. They seemed unwilling to look beyond the father's roughness and the whiskey on his breath, equating these with drunken violence. Although the poem does suggest an element of fear mingled with the boy's excitement ("I hung on like death"), the class ignored its complexity — the mixture of fear, love, and boisterous fun that colors the son's memory of his father. It's possible that some students might overlook the positive traits in the father in this poem because they have suffered child abuse themselves. But this couldn't be true for all the students in the class. The difference between these interpretations lies, instead, in the influence of cultural myths. After all, in a culture now dominated by images of the family that emphasize "positive" parenting, middle-class values, and sensitive fathers, it's no wonder that students refused to see this father sympathetically. Our culture simply doesn't associate good, loving families with drinking or with even the suggestion of physical roughness.

Years of acculturation — the process of internalizing cultural values — leave us with a set of rigid categories for "good" and "bad" parents, narrow conceptions of how parents should look, talk, and behave toward their children. These cultural categories work like mental pigeonholes: they help us sort out and evaluate our experiences rapidly, almost before we're consciously aware of them. They give us a helpful shorthand for interpreting the world; after all, we can't stop to ponder every new situation we meet as if it were a puzzle or a philosophical problem. But while cultural categories help us make practical decisions in everyday life, they also impose their inherent rigidity on our thinking and thus limit our ability to understand the complexity of our experience. They reduce the world to dichotomies — simplified either/or choices: either women or men, either heterosexuals or homosexuals, either nature or culture, either animal or human, either "alien" or American, either them or us.

Rigid cultural beliefs can present serious obstacles to success for first-year college students. In a psychology class, for example, students' cultural myths may so color their thinking that they find it nearly impossible to comprehend Freud's ideas about infant sexuality. Ingrained assumptions about childhood innocence and sexual guilt may make it impossible for them to see children as sexual beings — a concept absolutely basic to an understanding of the history of psychoanalytic theory. Yet college-level critical inquiry thrives on exactly this kind of revision of common sense: academics prize the unusual, the subtle, the ambiguous, the complex — and expect students to appreciate them as well. Good critical thinkers in all academic disciplines welcome the opportunity to challenge conventional ways of seeing the world; they seem to take delight in questioning everything that appears clear and self-evident.

Questioning: The Basis of Critical Thinking

By questioning the myths that dominate our culture, we can begin to resist the limits they impose on our vision. In fact, they invite such questioning. Often our personal experience fails to fit the images the myths project: a young woman's ambition to be a test pilot may clash with the ideal of femininity our culture promotes; a Cambodian immigrant who has suffered from racism in the United States may question our professed commitment to equality; a student in the vocational track may not see education as the road to success that we assume it is; and few of our families these days fit the mythic model of husband, wife, two kids, a dog, and a house in the suburbs.

Moreover, because cultural myths serve such large and varied needs, they're not always coherent or consistent. Powerful contradictory myths coexist in our society and our own minds. For example, while the myth of "the melting pot" celebrates equality, the myth of individual success pushes us to strive for inequality — to "get ahead" of everyone else. Likewise, our attitudes toward education are deeply paradoxical: on one level Americans tend to see schooling as a valuable experience that unites us in a common culture and helps us bring out the best in ourselves; yet at the same time we suspect that formal classroom instruction stifles creativity and chokes off natural intelligence and enthusiasm. These contradictions infuse our history, literature, and popular culture; they're so much a part of our thinking that we tend to take them for granted, unaware of their inconsistencies.

Learning to recognize contradictions lies at the very heart of critical thinking, for intellectual conflict inevitably generates questions. Can both (or all) perspectives be true? What evidence do I have for the validity of each? Is there some way to reconcile them? Are there still other alternatives? Questions like these represent the beginning of serious academic analysis. They stimulate the reflection, discussion, and research that are the essence of good scholarship. Thus, whether we find contradictions between myth and lived experience, or between opposing myths, the wealth of powerful, conflicting material generated by our cultural mythology offers a particularly rich context for critical inquiry.

The Structure of *Rereading America*

We've designed this book to help you develop the habits of mind you'll need to become a critical thinker — someone who recognizes the way that cultural myths shape thinking and can move beyond them to evaluate issues from multiple perspectives. Each of the book's six chapters addresses one of the dominant myths of American culture. We begin with the myth that's literally closest to home — the myth of the model family. In "Harmony at

Home" we look at the impact that the idea of the nuclear family has had on generations of Americans, including those who don't fit comfortably within its limitations. We also present some serious challenges to this time-honored definition of American family life. Next we turn to a topic that every student should have a lot to say about — the myth of educational empowerment. "Learning Power" gives you the chance to reflect on how the "hidden curriculum" of schooling has shaped your own attitudes toward learning. We begin our exploration of American cultural myths by focusing on home and education because most students find it easy to make personal connections with these topics and because they both involve institutions — families and schools — that are surrounded by a rich legacy of cultural stories and myths. These two introductory chapters are followed by consideration of what is perhaps the most famous of all American myths, the American Dream. Chapter Three, "Money and Success," addresses the idea of unlimited personal opportunity that brought millions of immigrants to our shores and set the story of America in motion. It invites you to weigh some of the human costs of the dream and to reconsider your own definition of a successful life.

The second half of the book focuses on three cultural myths that offer greater intellectual and emotional challenges, in part because they are so intertwined with every American's personal identity and because they touch on highly charged social issues. "True Women and Real Men" considers the socially constructed categories of gender — the traditional roles that enforce differences between women and men. This chapter also explores the perspectives of Americans who defy conventional gender boundaries. The book's fifth chapter, "Created Equal," examines two myths that have powerfully shaped racial and ethnic relations in the United States: the myth of the melting pot, which celebrates cultural homogenization, and the myth of racial and ethnic superiority, which promotes separateness and inequality. This chapter probes the nature of prejudice, explores the ways that prejudicial attitudes are created, and examines ethnic identities within a race-divided society. Each of these two chapters questions how our culture divides and defines our world, how it artificially channels our experience into oppositions like black and white, male and female, straight and gay. The book concludes by addressing a subject that has assumed critical importance in the past few years — America's meaning in a changing world. The events of September 11, 2001, have forced us to reassess our relationships with other countries and to consider what we as a nation represent to people the world over. In "Land of Liberty: American Mythology in a 'New World Order'" we examine how one of our most prized cultural ideals, the myth of freedom, has shaped our sense of national destiny and how our belief in our own "exceptionalism" as a nation has contributed to growing anti-Americanism in other lands. This final chapter also invites you to consider whether the ideal of individual liberty can survive in a world that is increasingly obsessed with security and dominated by powerful political and economic forces.

The Selections

Our identities — who we are and how we relate to others — are deeply entangled with the cultural values we have internalized since infancy. Cultural myths become so closely identified with our personal beliefs that rereading them actually means rereading ourselves, rethinking the way we see the world. Questioning long-held assumptions can be an exhilarating experience, but it can be distressing too. Thus, you may find certain selections in *Rereading America* difficult, controversial, or even downright offensive. They are meant to challenge you and to provoke classroom debate. But as you discuss the ideas you encounter in this book, remind yourself that your classmates may bring with them very different, and equally profound, beliefs. Keep an open mind, listen carefully, and treat other perspectives with the same respect you'd expect other people to show for your own. It's by encountering new ideas and engaging with others in open dialogue that we learn to grow.

Because *Rereading America* explores cultural myths that shape our thinking, it doesn't focus on the kind of well-defined public issues you might expect to find in a traditional composition anthology. You won't be reading arguments for and against affirmative action, bilingual education, or the death penalty here. Although we do include conservative as well as liberal — and even radical — perspectives, we've deliberately avoided the traditional pro-and-con approach because we want you to aim deeper than that; we want you to focus on the subtle cultural beliefs that underlie, and frequently determine, the debates that are waged on public issues. We've also steered clear of the "issues approach" because we feel it reinforces simplistic either/or thinking. Polarizing American culture into a series of debates doesn't encourage you to examine your own beliefs or explore how they've been shaped by the cultures you're part of. To begin to appreciate the influence of your own cultural myths, you need new perspectives: you need to stand outside the ideological machinery that makes American culture run to begin to appreciate its power. That's why we've included many strongly dissenting views: there are works by community activists, gay-rights activists, socialists, libertarians, and more. You may find that their views confirm your own experience of what it means to be an American, or you may find that you bitterly disagree with them. We only hope that you will use the materials here to gain some insight into the values and beliefs that shape our thinking and our national identity. This book is meant to complicate the mental categories that our cultural myths have established for us. Our intention is not to present a new "truth" to replace the old but to expand the range of ideas you bring to all your reading and writing in college. We believe that learning to see and value other perspectives will enable you to think more critically — to question, for yourself, the truth of any statement.

You may also note that several selections in *Rereading America* challenge the way you think writing is supposed to look or sound. You won't find many "classic" essays in this book, the finely crafted reflective essays on general topics that are often held up as models of "good writing." It's not that we reject this type of essay in principle. It's just that most writers who stand outside mainstream culture seem to have little use for it.

Our selections, instead, come from a wide variety of sources: professional books and journals from many disciplines, popular magazines, college textbooks, autobiographies, oral histories, and literary works. We've included this variety partly for the very practical reason that you're likely to encounter texts like these in your college coursework. But we also see textual diversity, like ethnic and political diversity, as a way to multiply perspectives and stimulate critical analysis. For example, an academic article like Jean Anyon's study of social class and school curriculum might give you a new way of understanding Mike Rose's personal narrative about his classroom experiences. On the other hand, you may find that some of the teachers Rose encounters don't neatly fit Anyon's theoretical model. Do such discrepancies mean that Anyon's argument is invalid? That her analysis needs to be modified to account for these teachers? That the teachers are simply exceptions to the rule? You'll probably want to consider your own classroom experience as you wrestle with such questions. Throughout the book, we've chosen readings that "talk to each other" in this way and that draw on the cultural knowledge you bring with you. These readings invite you to join the conversation; we hope they raise difficult questions, prompt lively discussion, and stimulate critical inquiry.

The Power of Dialogue

Good thinking, like good writing and good reading, is an intensely social activity. Thinking, reading, and writing are all forms of relationship — when you read, you enter into dialogue with an author about the subject at hand; when you write, you address an imaginary reader, testing your ideas against probable responses, reservations, and arguments. Thus, you can't become an accomplished writer simply by declaring your right to speak or by criticizing as an act of principle: real authority comes when you enter into the discipline of an active exchange of opinions and interpretations. Critical thinking, then, is always a matter of dialogue and debate — discovering relationships between apparently unrelated ideas, finding parallels between your own experiences and the ideas you read about, exploring points of agreement and conflict between yourself and other people.

We've designed the readings and questions in this text to encourage you to make just these kinds of connections. You'll notice, for example, that we often ask you to divide into small groups to discuss readings, and we frequently suggest that you take part in projects that require you to collaborate with your classmates. We're convinced that the only way you can learn critical reading, thinking, and writing is by actively engaging others in an intellectual exchange. So we've built into the text many opportunities for listening, discussion, and debate.

The questions that follow each selection should guide you in critical thinking. Like the readings, they're intended to get you started, not to set limits; we strongly recommend that you also devise your own questions and pursue them either individually or in study groups. We've divided our questions into three categories. Here's what to expect from each:

- Those labeled "Engaging the Text" focus on the individual selection they follow. They're designed to highlight important issues in the reading, to help you begin questioning and evaluating what you've read, and sometimes to remind you to consider the author's choices of language, evidence, structure, and style.

- The questions labeled "Exploring Connections" will lead you from the selection you've just finished to one or more other readings in this book. It's hard to make sparks fly from just one stone; if you think hard about these connecting questions, though, you'll see some real collisions of ideas and perspectives, not just polite and predictable "differences of opinion."

- The final questions for each reading, "Extending the Critical Context," invite you to extend your thinking beyond the book — to your family, your community, your college, the media, or the more traditional research environment of the library. The emphasis here is on creating new knowledge by applying ideas from this book to the world around you and by testing these ideas in your world.

Active Reading

You've undoubtedly read many textbooks, but it's unlikely that you've had to deal with the kind of analytic, argumentative, and scholarly writing you'll find in college and in *Rereading America*. These different writing styles require a different approach to reading as well. In high school you probably read to "take in" information, often for the sole purpose of reproducing it later on a test. In college you'll also be expected to recognize larger issues, such as the author's theoretical slant, her goals and methods, her assumptions, and her relationship to other writers and researchers. These expectations can be especially difficult in the first two years of college, when you take introductory courses that survey large, complex fields of knowledge. With all these demands on your attention, you'll need to read actively to keep your bearings. Think of active reading as a conversation between you and the text: instead of listening passively as the writer talks, respond to what she says with questions and comments of your own. Here are some specific techniques you can practice to become a more active reader.

Prereading and Prewriting

It's best with most college reading to "preread" the text. In prereading, you briefly look over whatever information you have on the author and the selection itself. Reading chapter introductions and headnotes like those provided in this book can save you time and effort by giving you information about the author's background and concerns, the subject or thesis of the selection, and its place in the chapter as a whole. Also take a look at the title and at any headings or subheadings in the piece. These will give you further clues about an article's general scope and organization. Next, quickly skim the entire selection, paying a bit more attention to the first few paragraphs and the conclusion. Now you should have a pretty good sense of the author's position — what she's trying to say in this piece of writing.

At this point you may do one of several things before you settle down to in-depth reading. You may want to jot down in a few lines what you think the author is doing. Or you may want to make a list of questions you can ask about this topic based on your prereading. Or you may want to freewrite a page or so on the subject. Informally writing out your own ideas will prepare you for more in-depth reading by recalling what you already know about the topic.

We emphasize writing about what you've read because reading and writing are complementary activities: being an avid reader will help you as a writer by familiarizing you with a wide range of ideas and styles to draw on; likewise, writing about what you've read will give you a deeper understanding of your reading. In fact, the more actively you "process" or reshape what you've read, the better you'll comprehend and remember it. So you'll learn more effectively by marking a text as you read than by simply reading; taking notes as you read is even more effective than marking, and writing about the material for your own purposes (putting it in your own words and connecting it with what you already know) is better still.

Marking the Text and Taking Notes

After prereading and prewriting, you're ready to begin critical reading in earnest. As you read, be sure to highlight ideas and phrases that strike you as especially significant — those that seem to capture the gist of a particular paragraph or section, or those that relate directly to the author's purpose or argument. While prereading can help you identify central ideas, you may find that you need to reread difficult sections or flip back and skim an earlier passage if you feel yourself getting lost. Many students think of themselves as poor readers if they can't whip through an article at high speed without pausing. However, the best readers read recursively — that is, they shuttle back and forth, browsing, skimming, and rereading as necessary, depending on their interest, their familiarity with the subject, and the difficulty of the material. This shuttling actually parallels what goes on in your mind when you read actively, as you alternately recall prior knowledge or experience and predict or look for clues about where the writer is going next.

Keep a record of your mental shuttling by writing comments in the margins as you read. It's often useful to gloss the contents of each paragraph or section, to summarize it in a word or two written alongside the text. This note will serve as a reminder or key to the section when you return to it for further thinking, discussion, or writing. You may also want to note passages that puzzled you. Or you may want to write down personal reactions or questions stimulated by the reading. Take time to ponder why you felt confused or annoyed or affirmed by a particular passage. Let yourself wonder "out loud" in the margins as you read.

The following section illustrates one student's notes on a few stanzas of Inés Hernández-Ávila's "Para Teresa" (p. 227). In this example, you can see that the reader puts glosses or summary comments to the left of the poem and questions or personal responses to the right. You should experiment and create your own system of note taking, one that works best for the way you read. Just remember that your main goals in taking notes are to help you understand the author's overall position, to deepen and refine your responses to the selection, and to create a permanent record of those responses.

Para Teresa[1]

INÉS HERNÁNDEZ-ÁVILA

This poem explores and attempts to resolve an old conflict between its speaker and her schoolmate, two Chicanas at "Alamo which-had-to-be-its-name" Elementary School who have radically different ideas about what education means and does. Inés Hernández-Ávila (b. 1947) is an associate professor of Native American Studies at the University of California, Davis. This poem appeared in her collection Con Razón, Corazón *(1987).*

Writes ⌈ A tí-Teresa — *Why in Spanish?*
to | Te dedico las palabras estás
Teresa ⌊ que (explotan) de mi corazón[2] — *Why do her words explode?*
       ⌈ That day during lunch hour
       | at Alamo which-had-to-be-its-name   *!Why?*

---

[1] *Para Teresa:* For Teresa. [All notes are the author's.]
[2] *A . . . corazón:* To you, Teresa, I dedicate these words that explode from my heart.

The day of their confrontation

Elementary
my dear raza — *Feels close to T. (?)*
That day in the bathroom
Door guarded
Myself cornered
I was accused by you, Teresa
Tú y las demás de tus amigas
Pachucas todas
Eran Uds. cinco.[3]

T.'s accusation

Me gritaban que porque me creía tan grande[4]
What was I trying to do, you growled
Show you up?
Make the teachers like me, pet me, — *Teachers must be white / Anglo.*
Tell me what a credit (to my people) I was?
I was playing right into their hands, you challenged
And you would have none of it.
I was to stop. — *Speaker is a "good student."*

Keeping a Reading Journal

You may also want (or be required) to keep a reading journal in response to the selections you cover in *Rereading America.* In such a journal you'd keep all the freewriting that you do either before or after reading. Some students find it helpful to keep a double-entry journal, writing initial responses on the left side of the page and adding later reflections and reconsiderations on the right. You may want to use your journal as a place to explore personal reactions to your reading. You can do this by writing out imaginary dialogues — between two writers who address the same subject, between yourself and the writer of the selection, or between two parts of yourself. You can use the journal as a place to rewrite passages from a poem or essay in your own voice and from your own point of view. You can write letters to an author you particularly like or dislike or to a character in a story or poem. You might even draw a cartoon that comments on one of the reading selections.

Many students don't write as well as they could because they're afraid to take risks. They may have been repeatedly penalized for breaking "rules" of grammar or essay form; their main concern in writing becomes avoiding trouble rather than exploring ideas or experimenting with style. But without risk and experimentation, there's little possibility of growth. One of the benefits of journal writing is that it gives you a place to experiment with ideas, free from worries about "correctness." Here are two examples of student journal entries, in response to "Para Teresa" (we reprint the entries as they were written):

[3]*Tú . . . cinco:* You and the rest of your friends, all Pachucas, there were five of you.
[4]*Me . . . grande:* You were screaming at me, asking me why I thought I was so hot.

Entry 1: Internal Dialogue

> ME 1: I agree with Inés Hernández-Ávila's speaker. Her actions were justifiable in a way that if you can't fight 'em, join 'em. After all, Teresa is just making the situation worse for her because not only is she sabotaging the teacher-student relationship, she's also destroying her chance for a good education.
>
> ME 2: Hey, Teresa's action was justifiable. Why else would the speaker admit at the end of the poem that what Teresa did was fine thus she respects Teresa more?
>
> ME 1: The reason the speaker respected Teresa was because she (Teresa) was still keeping her culture alive, although through different means. It wasn't her action that the speaker respected, it was the representation of it.
>
> ME 2: The reason I think Teresa acted the way she did was because she felt she had something to prove to society. She wanted to show that no one could push her people around; that her people were tough.

Entry 2: Personal Response

> "Con cố gắng học gioi, cho Bá Má,
> Rồi sau nây dồi sống cua con sẽ thõai mái lắm."[5]
> What if I don't want to?
> What if I can't?
> Sometimes I feel my parents don't understand what
> I'm going through.
> To them, education is money.
> And money is success.
> They don't see beyond that.
> Sometimes I want to fail my classes purposely to
> See their reaction, but that is too cruel.
> They have taught me to value education.
> Education makes you a person, makes you somebody, they say.
> I agree.
> They are proud I am going to UCLA.
> They brag to their friends, our Vietnamese community, people
> I don't even know.
>   . . .
> They believe in me, but I doubt myself. . . .

You'll notice that neither of these students talks directly about "Para Teresa" as a poem. Instead, each uses it as a point of departure for her own reflections on ethnicity, identity, and education. Although we've included a number of literary works in *Rereading America*, we don't expect you to do literary analysis. We want you to use these pieces to stimulate your own thinking about the cultural myths they address. So don't feel you have to

---

[5]"*Con . . . lắm*": "Daughter, study hard (for us, your Mom and Dad), so your future will be bright and easy."

discuss imagery in Inés Hernández-Ávila's "Para Teresa" or characterization in Toni Cade Bambara's "The Lesson" in order to understand and appreciate them.

Working with Visual Images

The myths we examine in *Rereading America* make their presence felt not only in the world of print — essays, stories, poems, memoirs — but in every aspect of our culture. Consider, for example, the myth of "the American family." If you want to design a minivan, a restaurant, a cineplex, a park, a synagogue, a personal computer, or a tax code, you had better have some idea of what families are like and how they behave. Most important, you need a good grasp of what Americans *believe* about families, about the mythology of the American family. The Visual Portfolio in each chapter, while it maintains our focus on myths, also carries you beyond the medium of print and thus lets you practice your analytical skills in a different arena.

Although we are all surrounded by visual stimuli, we don't always think critically about what we see. Perhaps we are numbed by constant exposure to a barrage of images on TV, in magazines and newspapers, in video games and films. In any case, here are a few tips on how to get the most out of the images we have collected for this book. Take the time to look at the images carefully; first impressions are important, but many of the photographs contain details that might not strike you immediately. Once you have noted the immediate impact of an image, try focusing on separate elements such as background, foreground, facial expressions, and body language. Read any text that appears in the photograph, even if it's on a T-shirt or a belt buckle. Remember that many photographs are carefully *constructed*, no matter how "natural" they may look. In a photo for a magazine advertisement, for example, everything is meticulously chosen and arranged: certain actors or models are cast for their roles; they wear makeup; their clothes are really costumes; the location or setting of the ad is designed to reinforce its message; lighting is artificial; and someone is trying to sell you something.

Also be sure to consider the visual images contextually, not in isolation. How does each resemble or differ from its neighbors in the portfolio? How does it reinforce or challenge cultural beliefs or stereotypes? Put another way, how can it be understood in the context of the myths examined in *Rereading America?* Each portfolio is accompanied by a few questions to help you begin this type of analysis. You can also build a broader context for our visual images by collecting your own, then working in small groups to create a portfolio or collage.

Finally, remember that both readings and visual images are just starting points for discussion. You have access to a wealth of other perspectives and ideas among your family, friends, classmates; in your college library; in your personal experience; and in your imagination. We urge you to consult them all as you grapple with the perspectives you encounter in this text.

1

Harmony at Home

The Myth of the Model Family

The Donna Reed Show.

What would an American political campaign be without wholesome photographs of the candidates kissing babies and posing with their loving families? Politicians understand the cultural power of these symbols; they appreciate the family as one of our most sacred American institutions. The vision of the ideal nuclear family — Dad, Mom, a couple of kids, maybe a dog, and a spacious suburban home — is a cliché but also a potent myth, a dream that millions of Americans work to fulfill. The image is so compelling that it's easy to forget what a short time it's been around, especially compared with the long history of the family itself.

In fact, what we call the "traditional" family, headed by a breadwinner-father and a housewife-mother, has existed for little more than two hundred years, and the suburbs only came into being in the 1950s. But the family as a social institution was legally recognized in Western culture at least as far back as the Code of Hammurabi, created in ancient Mesopotamia some four thousand years ago. To appreciate how profoundly concepts of family life have changed, consider the absolute power of the Mesopotamian father, the patriarch: the law allowed him to use any of his dependents, including his wife, as collateral for loans or even to sell family members outright to pay his debts.

Although patriarchal authority was less absolute in Puritan America, fathers remained the undisputed heads of families. Seventeenth-century Connecticut, Massachusetts, and New Hampshire enacted laws condemning rebellious children to severe punishment and, in extreme cases, to death. In the early years of the American colonies, as in Western culture stretching back to Hammurabi's time, unquestioned authority within the family served as both the model for and the basis of state authority. Just as family members owed complete obedience to the father, so all citizens owed unquestioned loyalty to the king and his legal representatives. In his influential volume *Democracy in America* (1835), French aristocrat Alexis de Tocqueville describes the relationship between the traditional European family and the old political order:

> Among aristocratic nations, social institutions recognize, in truth, no one in the family but the father; children are received by society at his hands; society governs him, he governs them. Thus, the parent not only has a natural right, but acquires a political right to command them; he is the author and the support of his family; but he is also its constituted ruler.

By the mid-eighteenth century, however, new ideas about individual freedom and democracy were stirring the colonies. And by the time Tocqueville visited the United States in 1831, they had evidently worked a revolution in the family as well as in the nation's political structure: he observes, "When the condition of society becomes democratic, and men adopt as their general principle that it is good and lawful to judge of all things for one's self, . . . the power which the opinions of a father exercise over those of his sons diminishes, as well as his legal power." To Tocqueville, this shift away from strict patriarchal rule signaled a change in the emotional climate of families: "as manners and laws become more democratic, the relation of father and son becomes more intimate and more affectionate; rules and authority are less talked of, confidence and tenderness are oftentimes increased, and it would seem that the natural bond is drawn closer." In his view, the American family heralded a new era in human relations. Freed from the rigid hierarchy of the past, parents and children could meet as near equals, joined by "filial love and fraternal affection."

This vision of the democratic family — a harmonious association of parents and children united by love and trust — has mesmerized popular culture in the United States. From the nineteenth century to the present, popular novels, magazines, music, and advertising images have glorified the comforts of loving domesticity. In recent years, we've probably absorbed our strongest impressions of the ideal family from television situation comedies. In the 1950s we had the Andersons on *Father Knows Best,* the Stones on *The Donna Reed Show,* and the real-life Nelson family on *The Adventures of Ozzie & Harriet.* Over the next three decades, the model stretched to include single parents, second marriages, and interracial adoptions on *My Three Sons, The Brady Bunch,* and *Diff'rent Strokes,* but the underlying ideal of wise, loving parents and harmonious, happy families remained unchanged. But today, America has begun to worry about the health of its families: even the families on TV no longer reflect the domestic tranquility of the Anderson clan. America is becoming increasingly ambivalent about the future of family life, and perhaps with good reason. The myth of the family scarcely reflects the complexities of modern American life. High divorce rates, the rise of the single-parent household, the impact of remarriage, and a growing frankness about domestic violence are transforming the way we see family life; many families must also contend with the stresses of urban life and economic hardship. Such pressures on and within the family can be particularly devastating to young people, as the high suicide rate for teens grimly attests. In our world it's no longer clear whether the family is a blessing to be cherished or an ordeal to be survived.

This chapter examines the myth of the model family and explores alternative visions of family life. It opens with three paintings by Norman Rockwell that express the meaning of "family values" circa 1950, an era some consider the heyday of American family life. The subsequent readings immediately challenge the ideal of the harmonious nuclear family. In "Looking for Work," Gary Soto recalls his boyhood desire to live the myth and recounts his humorous attempts to transform his working-class Chicano family into a facsimile of the Cleavers on *Leave It to Beaver.* Stephanie Coontz then takes a close analytical look at the 1950s family, explaining its lasting appeal to some Americans but also documenting its dark side.

The core of the chapter offers diverse contemporary perspectives on the meaning of family and its relation to our broader culture. In her essay

"About Marriage," conservative commentator Danielle Crittenden defends traditional family values, suggesting that their decline accounts for many of the problems she sees in society. Next *Ann* Crittenden — no relation — addresses a different kind of family value, namely the economic value of the work mothers do, which she claims is systematically and unjustly ignored. Sociologist Judy Root Aulette shows how the dynamics of race, class, and gender — key issues throughout *Rereading America* — play out within the American family. Extending themes introduced by Aulette, the chapter's Visual Portfolio offers you a chance to practice your hand at interpreting images; the photographs in this collection suggest some of the complex ways the contemporary American family intersects with issues of gender, ethnicity, and media. Concluding the middle section, Joshua Gamson's "Talking Freaks" shows traditional ideas colliding with new realities in the intriguing arena of daytime talk shows.

The chapter concludes with three readings that explore alternative family structures and show families functioning well under trying circumstances. In "An Indian Story," Roger Jack paints a warm, magical portrait of the bond between a Native American boy and his caretaker aunt. Bebe Moore Campbell's "Envy" is a fascinating personal account of growing up father-hungry in a female-dominated African American family. Finally, Melvin Dixon's poem "Aunt Ida Pieces a Quilt" celebrates a woman who rises above prejudice to commemorate a nephew lost to AIDS. These closing selections affirm the continuing power of families as sources of acceptance, love, and support.

Sources

Gerda Lerner, *The Creation of Patriarchy.* New York: Oxford University Press, 1986.

Steven Mintz and Susan Kellogg, *Domestic Revolutions: A Social History of American Family Life.* New York: Free Press, 1988.

Alexis de Tocqueville, *Democracy in America.* 1835; New York: Vintage Books, 1990.

BEFORE READING

- Spend ten minutes or so jotting down every word, phrase, or image you associate with the idea of "family." Write as freely as possible, without censoring your thoughts or worrying about grammatical correctness. Working in small groups, compare lists and try to categorize your responses. What assumptions about families do they reveal?

- Draw a visual representation of your family. This could take the form of a graph, chart, diagram, map, cartoon, symbolic picture, or literal portrait. Don't worry if you're not a skillful artist: the main point is to convey an idea, and even stick figures can speak eloquently. When you're finished, write a journal entry about your drawing. Was it easier to depict some feelings or ideas visually than it would have been to describe them in words? Did you find some things about your family difficult or impossible to convey visually? Does your drawing "say" anything that surprises you?

- Do a brief freewrite about the television family — from *The Donna Reed Show* — pictured on the title page of this chapter (p. 17). What can you tell about their relationship? What does this image suggest to you about the ideals and realities of American family life?

A *Family Tree, Freedom from Want,* and *Freedom from Fear*

NORMAN ROCKWELL

The first "reading" for this book consists of three paintings by Norman Rockwell (1894–1978), one of America's most prolific and popular artists. Together they capture what the idea of family meant to the nation half a century ago, a time some consider the golden age of American family life. A Family Tree *(1959) is an oil painting that, like hundreds of Rockwell's images, became cover art for the* Saturday Evening Post. Freedom from Want *and* Freedom from Fear *are part of Rockwell's* Four Freedoms *series (1943). Their appearance in the* Post, *along with* Freedom of Speech *and* Freedom of Worship, *generated millions of requests for reprints.*

A Family Tree, by Norman Rockwell.

Freedom from Want, by Norman Rockwell.

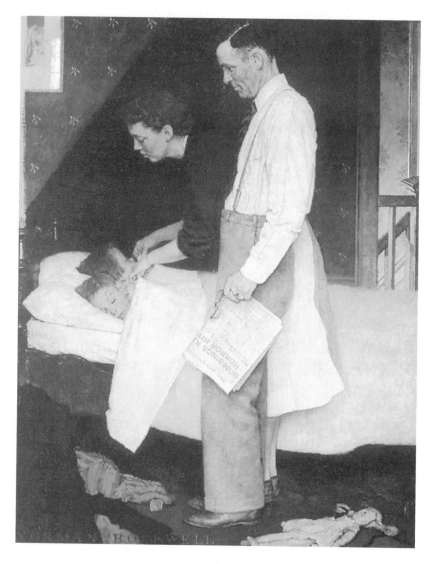

Freedom from Fear, by Norman Rockwell.

ENGAGING THE TEXT

1. What is the usual purpose of family trees? Why do you think they are important to many Americans? How significant is a family tree to you or others in your family?

2. Discuss the details of *A Family Tree* and their significance. For example, identify each figure and explain what it contributes to Rockwell's composite picture of America.

3. How does Rockwell's painting differ from your image of a typical family tree? What is its basic message? How accurate do you consider its portrayal of the American family?

4. What is the appeal of *Freedom from Want?* What ideas about family does it assume or promote? What's your own reaction to Rockwell's image? Support your answers with reference to details of the painting.

5. In *Freedom from Fear*, why did Rockwell choose this moment to paint? What can you guess about the relationships within the family? What about its relationship to the rest of the world?

EXPLORING CONNECTIONS

6. Compare Rockwell's paintings to the frontispiece photo for this chapter (p. 17). How does Rockwell's vision of family life differ from that depicted by the photo?

EXTENDING THE CRITICAL CONTEXT

7. Research your family tree and make your own drawing of it. How does it compare to the family tree Rockwell has created? Write a journal entry or short essay about your family tree.

8. Discuss how well the idea of a tree can represent what you know about families. Are there ways in which the tree image or metaphor might be misleading or inaccurate? What other analogies or metaphors can you suggest for depicting family histories? Draw either an updated version of Rockwell's family tree or an image based on a fresh metaphor or analogy.

9. What might pictures entitled *Freedom from Want* and *Freedom from Fear* look like if they were painted today? Describe in detail a scene or image to fit each of these titles; if possible, draw, paint, or photograph your image.

Looking for Work

GARY SOTO

*"Looking for Work" is the narrative of a nine-year-old Mexican Ameri-
can boy who wants his family to imitate the "perfect families" he sees on TV.
Much of the humor in this essay comes from the author's perspective as an
adult looking back at his childhood self, but Soto also respects the child's
point of view. In the marvelous details of this midsummer day, Soto captures the interplay of seductive myth and complex reality. Gary Soto
(b. 1952) grew up "on the industrial side of Fresno, right smack against a
junkyard and the junkyard's cross-eyed German shepherd." Having discovered poetry almost by chance in a city college library, he has now published
several volumes of his own; his* New and Selected Poems *(1995) was a finalist for both the* Los Angeles Times *Book Award and the National Book
Award. He has also published essays, prose memoirs, novels for young readers, short stories, and the libretto for an opera titled* Nerdlandia.

One July, while killing ants on the kitchen sink with a rolled newspaper,
I had a nine-year-old's vision of wealth that would save us from ourselves.
For weeks I had drunk Kool-Aid and watched morning reruns of *Father
Knows Best*, whose family was so uncomplicated in its routine that I very
much wanted to imitate it. The first step was to get my brother and sister to
wear shoes at dinner.

"Come on, Rick — come on, Deb," I whined. But Rick mimicked me
and the same day that I asked him to wear shoes he came to the dinner
table in only his swim trunks. My mother didn't notice, nor did my sister, as
we sat to eat our beans and tortillas in the stifling heat of our kitchen. We all
gleamed like cellophane, wiping the sweat from our brows with the backs of
our hands as we talked about the day: Frankie our neighbor was beat up by
Faustino; the swimming pool at the playground would be closed for a day
because the pump was broken.

Such was our life. So that morning, while doing-in the train of ants
which arrived each day, I decided to become wealthy, and right away! After
downing a bowl of cereal, I took a rake from the garage and started up the
block to look for work.

We lived on an ordinary block of mostly working class people: ware-
housemen, egg candlers,[1] welders, mechanics, and a union plumber. And
there were many retired people who kept their lawns green and the gutters

[1] *egg candler:* One who inspects eggs by holding them up to a light.

uncluttered of the chewing gum wrappers we dropped as we rode by on our bikes. They bent down to gather our litter, muttering at our evilness.

At the corner house I rapped the screen door and a very large woman in a muu-muu answered. She sized me up and then asked what I could do.

"Rake leaves," I answered smiling.

"It's summer, and there ain't no leaves," she countered. Her face was pinched with lines; fat jiggled under her chin. She pointed to the lawn, then the flower bed, and said: "You see any leaves there — or there?" I followed her pointing arm, stupidly. But she had a job for me and that was to get her a Coke at the liquor store. She gave me twenty cents, and after ditching my rake in a bush, off I ran. I returned with an unbagged Pepsi, for which she thanked me and gave me a nickel from her apron.

I skipped off her porch, fetched my rake, and crossed the street to the next block where Mrs. Moore, mother of Earl the retarded man, let me weed a flower bed. She handed me a trowel and for a good part of the morning my fingers dipped into the moist dirt, ripping up runners of Bermuda grass. Worms surfaced in my search for deep roots, and I cut them in halves, tossing them to Mrs. Moore's cat who pawed them playfully as they dried in the sun. I made out Earl whose face was pressed to the back window of the house, and although he was calling to me I couldn't understand what he was trying to say. Embarrassed, I worked without looking up, but I imagined his contorted mouth and the ring of keys attached to his belt — keys that jingled with each palsied step. He scared me and I worked quickly to finish the flower bed. When I did finish Mrs. Moore gave me a quarter and two peaches from her tree, which I washed there but ate in the alley behind my house.

I was sucking on the second one, a bit of juice staining the front of my T-shirt, when Little John, my best friend, came walking down the alley with a baseball bat over his shoulder, knocking over trash cans as he made his way toward me.

Little John and I went to St. John's Catholic School, where we sat among the "stupids." Miss Marino, our teacher, alternated the rows of good students with the bad, hoping that by sitting side-by-side with the bright students the stupids might become more intelligent, as though intelligence were contagious. But we didn't progress as she had hoped. She grew frustrated when one day, while dismissing class for recess, Little John couldn't get up because his arms were stuck in the slats of the chair's backrest. She scolded us with a shaking finger when we knocked over the globe, denting the already troubled Africa. She muttered curses when Leroy White, a real stupid but a great softball player with the gift to hit to all fields, openly chewed his host[2] when he made his First Communion; his hands swung at his sides as he returned to the pew looking around with a big smile.

5

10

---

[2]*his host:* The wafer that embodies, in the Catholic sacrament of Communion, the bread of the Last Supper and the body of Christ.

Little John asked what I was doing, and I told him that I was taking a break from work, as I sat comfortably among high weeds. He wanted to join me, but I reminded him that the last time he'd gone door-to-door asking for work his mother had whipped him. I was with him when his mother, a New Jersey Italian who could rise up in anger one moment and love the next, told me in a polite but matter-of-fact voice that I had to leave because she was going to beat her son. She gave me a homemade popsicle, ushered me to the door, and said that I could see Little John the next day. But it was sooner than that. I went around to his bedroom window to suck my popsicle and watch Little John dodge his mother's blows, a few hitting their mark but many whirring air.

It was midday when Little John and I converged in the alley, the sun blazing in the high nineties, and he suggested that we go to Roosevelt High School to swim. He needed five cents to make fifteen, the cost of admission, and I lent him a nickel. We ran home for my bike and when my sister found out that we were going swimming, she started to cry because she didn't have the fifteen cents but only an empty Coke bottle. I waved for her to come and three of us mounted the bike — Debra on the cross bar, Little John on the handle bars and holding the Coke bottle which we would cash for a nickel and make up the difference that would allow all of us to get in, and me pumping up the crooked streets, dodging cars and pot holes. We spent the day swimming under the afternoon sun, so that when we got home our mom asked us what was darker, the floor or us? She feigned a stern posture, her hands on her hips and her mouth puckered. We played along. Looking down, Debbie and I said in unison, "Us."

That evening at dinner we all sat down in our bathing suits to eat our beans, laughing and chewing loudly. Our mom was in a good mood, so I took a risk and asked her if sometime we could have turtle soup. A few days before I had watched a television program in which a Polynesian tribe killed a large turtle, gutted it, and then stewed it over an open fire. The turtle, basted in a sugary sauce, looked delicious as I ate an afternoon bowl of cereal, but my sister, who was watching the program with a glass of Kool-Aid between her knees, said, "Caca."

My mother looked at me in bewilderment. "Boy, are you a crazy Mexican. Where did you get the idea that people eat turtles?"

"On television," I said, explaining the program. Then I took it a step   15
further. "Mom, do you think we could get dressed up for dinner one of these days? David King does."

"Ay, Dios," my mother laughed. She started collecting the dinner plates, but my brother wouldn't let go of his. He was still drawing a picture in the bean sauce. Giggling, he said it was me, but I didn't want to listen because I wanted an answer from Mom. This was the summer when I spent the mornings in front of the television that showed the comfortable lives of white kids. There were no beatings, no rifts in the family. They wore bright clothes; toys tumbled from their closets. They hopped into bed with kisses and woke to glasses of fresh orange juice, and to a father sitting before his morning coffee while the mother buttered his toast. They hurried through the day making friends and gobs of money, returning home to a warmly lit living room, and then dinner. *Leave It to Beaver* was the program I re-played in my mind:

"May I have the mashed potatoes?" asks Beaver with a smile.

"Sure, Beav," replies Wally as he taps the corners of his mouth with a starched napkin.

The father looks on in his suit. The mother, decked out in earrings and a pearl necklace, cuts into her steak and blushes. Their conversation is po-litely clipped.

"Swell," says Beaver, his cheeks puffed with food.   20

Our own talk at dinner was loud with belly laughs and marked by our pointing forks at one another. The subjects were commonplace.

"Gary, let's go to the ditch tomorrow," my brother suggests. He ex-plains that he has made a life preserver out of four empty detergent bottles strung together with twine and that he will make me one if I can find more bottles. "No way are we going to drown."

"Yeah, then we could have a dirt clod fight," I reply, so happy to be alive.

Whereas the Beaver's family enjoyed dessert in dishes at the table, our mom sent us outside, and more often than not I went into the alley to peek over the neighbor's fences and spy out fruit, apricots or peaches.

I had asked my mom and again she laughed that I was a crazy *chavalo*[3]   25
as she stood in front of the sink, her arms rising and falling with suds, face glistening from the heat. She sent me outside where my brother and sister were sitting in the shade that the fence threw out like a blanket. They were talking about me when I plopped down next to them. They looked at one another and then Debbie, my eight-year-old sister, started in.

"What's this crap about getting dressed up?"

She had entered her *profanity* stage. A year later she would give up such words and slip into her Catholic uniform, and into squealing on my brother and me when we "cussed this" and "cussed that."

I tried to convince them that if we improved the way we looked we might get along better in life. White people would like us more. They might invite us to places, like their homes or front yards. They might not hate us so much.

My sister called me a "craphead," and got up to leave with a stalk of grass dangling from her mouth. "They'll never like us."

My brother's mood lightened as he talked about the ditch — the white   30
water, the broken pieces of glass, and the rusted car fenders that awaited our knees. There would be toads, and rocks to smash them.

[3]*chavalo:* Kid.

David King, the only person we knew who resembled the middle class, called from over the fence. David was Catholic, of Armenian and French descent, and his closet was filled with toys. A bear-shaped cookie jar, like the ones on television, sat on the kitchen counter. His mother was remarkably kind while she put up with the racket we made on the street. Evenings, she often watered the front yard and it must have upset her to see us — my brother and I and others — jump from trees laughing, the unkillable kids of the very poor, who got up unshaken, brushed off, and climbed into another one to try again.

David called again. Rick got up and slapped grass from his pants. When I asked if I could come along he said no. David said no. They were two years older so their affairs were different from mine. They greeted one another with foul names and took off down the alley to look for trouble.

I went inside the house, turned on the television, and was about to sit down with a glass of Kool-Aid when Mom shooed me outside.

"It's still light," she said. "Later you'll bug me to let you stay out longer. So go on."

I downed my Kool-Aid and went outside to the front yard. No one was around. The day had cooled and a breeze rustled the trees. Mr. Jackson, the plumber, was watering his lawn and when he saw me he turned away to wash off his front steps. There was more than an hour of light left, so I took advantage of it and decided to look for work. I felt suddenly alive as I skipped down the block in search of an overgrown flower bed and the dime that would end the day right.

35

ENGAGING THE TEXT

1. Why is the narrator attracted to the kind of family life depicted on TV? What, if anything, does he think is wrong with his life? Why do his desires apparently have so little impact on his family?

2. Why does the narrator first go looking for work? How has the meaning of work changed by the end of the story, when he goes out again "in search of an overgrown flower bed and the dime that would end the day right"? Explain.

3. As Soto looks back on his nine-year-old self, he has a different perspective on things than he had as a child. How would you characterize the mature Soto's thoughts about his childhood family life? (Was it "a good family"? What was wrong with Soto's thinking as a nine-year-old?) Back up your remarks with specific references to the narrative.

4. Review the story to find each mention of food or drink. Explain the role these references play.

5. Review the cast of "supporting characters" in this narrative — the mother, sister, brother, friends, and neighbors. What does each contribute to the story and in particular to the meaning of family within the story?

EXPLORING CONNECTIONS

6. Read Bebe Moore Campbell's "Envy" (p. 18) or Roger Jack's "An Indian Story" (p. 109) and compare Soto's family to one of the families portrayed in these selections. In particular, consider gender roles, the household atmosphere, and the expectations placed on children and parents.

7. Compare and contrast the relationship of school and family in this narrative to that described by Mike Rose (p. 182), Richard Rodriguez (p. 214), or Inés Hernández-Ávila (p. 227).

8. Like Soto's story, the cartoon on page 35 attests to the power of the media to shape our ideas about family. Write a journal entry describing the media family that most accurately reflects your image of family life. Discuss these entries, and the impact of media on your image of the family, with your classmates.

EXTENDING THE CRITICAL CONTEXT

9. Write a journal entry about a time when you wished your family were somehow different. What caused your dissatisfaction? What did you want your family to be like? Was your dissatisfaction ever resolved?

10. "Looking for Work" is essentially the story of a single day. Write a narrative of one day when you were eight or nine or ten; use details as Soto does to give the events of the day broader significance.

What We Really Miss About the 1950s

STEPHANIE COONTZ

. Popular myth has it that the 1950s were the ideal decade for the American family. In this example of academic writing at its best, Stephanie Coontz provides a clear, well-documented, and insightful analysis of what was really going on and suggests that our nostalgia for the 1950s could mislead us today. Stephanie Coontz teaches history and family studies at The Evergreen State College in Olympia, Washington. An award-winning writer and nationally recognized expert on the family, she has published her work in books, popular magazines, and academic journals; she has also testified before a House Select Committee on families and appeared in several television documentaries. Her books include The Social Origins of Private Life: A History of American Families, 1600–1900 *(1988),* The Way We Never Were: American Families and the Nostalgia Trap *(new edition, 2000), and*

The Way We Really Are: Coming to Terms with America's Changing Families (1997), from which this selection is taken.

In a 1996 poll by the Knight-Ridder news agency, more Americans chose the 1950s than any other single decade as the best time for children to grow up.[1] And despite the research I've done on the underside of 1950s families, I don't think it's crazy for people to feel nostalgic about the period. For one thing, it's easy to see why people might look back fondly to a decade when real wages grew more in any single year than in the entire ten years of the 1980s combined, a time when the average 30-year-old man could buy a median-priced home on only 15–18 percent of his salary.[2]

But it's more than just a financial issue. When I talk with modern parents, even ones who grew up in unhappy families, they associate the 1950s with a yearning they feel for a time when there were fewer complicated choices for kids or parents to grapple with, when there was more predictability in how people formed and maintained families, and when there was a coherent "moral order" in their community to serve as a reference point for family norms. Even people who found that moral order grossly unfair or repressive often say that its presence provided them with something concrete to push against.

I can sympathize entirely. One of my most empowering moments occurred the summer I turned 12, when my mother marched down to the library with me to confront a librarian who'd curtly refused to let me check out a book that was "not appropriate" for my age. "Don't you *ever* tell my daughter what she can and can't read," fumed my mom. "She's a mature young lady and she can make her own choices." In recent years I've often thought back to the gratitude I felt toward my mother for that act of trust in me. I wish I had some way of earning similar points from my own son. But much as I've always respected his values, I certainly wouldn't have walked into my local video store when he was 12 and demanded that he be allowed to check out absolutely anything he wanted!

Still, I have no illusions that I'd actually like to go back to the 1950s, and neither do most people who express such occasional nostalgia. For example, although the 1950s got more votes than any other decade in

[1]Steven Thomma, "Nostalgia for '50s Surfaces," *Philadelphia Inquirer,* Feb. 4, 1996. [All notes are the author's.]

[2]Frank Levy, *Dollars and Dreams: The Changing American Income Distribution* (New York: Russell Sage, 1987), p. 6; Frank Levy, "Incomes and Income Inequality," in Reynolds Farley, ed., *State of the Union: America in the 1990s,* vol. 1 (New York: Russell Sage, 1995), pp. 1–57; Richard May and Kathryn Porter, "Poverty and Income Trends, 1994," Washington, D.C.: Center on Budget and Policy Priorities, March 1996; Rob Nelson and Jon Cowan, "Buster Power," *USA Weekend,* October 14–16, 1994, p. 10.

the Knight-Ridder poll, it did not win an outright majority: 38 percent of respondents picked the 1950s; 27 percent picked the 1960s or the 1970s. Voters between the ages of 50 and 64 were most likely to choose the 1950s, the decade in which they themselves came of age, as the best time for kids; voters under 30 were more likely to choose the 1970s. African Americans differed over whether the 1960s, 1970s, or 1980s were best, but all age groups of blacks agreed that later decades were definitely preferable to the 1950s.

Nostalgia for the 1950s is real and deserves to be taken seriously, but it usually shouldn't be taken literally. Even people who *do* pick the 1950s as the best decade generally end up saying, once they start discussing their feelings in depth, that it's not the family arrangements in and of themselves that they want to revive. They don't miss the way women used to be treated, they sure wouldn't want to live with most of the fathers they knew in their neighborhoods, and "come to think of it" — I don't know how many times I've recorded these exact words — "I communicate with my kids *much* better than my parents or grandparents did." When Judith Wallerstein recently interviewed 100 spouses in "happy" marriages, she found that only five "wanted a marriage like their parents'." The husbands "consciously rejected the role models provided by their fathers. The women said they could never be happy living as their mothers did."[3]

People today understandably feel that their lives are out of balance, but they yearn for something totally *new* — a more equal distribution of work, family, and community time for both men and women, children and adults. If the 1990s are lopsided in one direction, the 1950s were equally lopsided in the opposite direction.

What most people really feel nostalgic about has little to do with the internal structure of 1950s families. It is the belief that the 1950s provided a more family-friendly economic and social environment, an easier climate in which to keep kids on the straight and narrow, and above all, a greater feeling of hope for a family's long-term future, especially for its young. The contrast between the perceived hopefulness of the fifties and our own misgivings about the future is key to contemporary nostalgia for the period. Greater optimism *did* exist then, even among many individuals and groups who were in terrible circumstances. But if we are to take people's sense of loss seriously, rather than merely to capitalize on it for a hidden political agenda, we need to develop a historical perspective on where that hope came from.

Part of it came from families comparing their prospects in the 1950s to their unstable, often grindingly uncomfortable pasts, especially the two horrible decades just before. In the 1920s, after two centuries of child labor and income insecurity, and for the first time in American history, a bare

[3]Judith Wallerstein and Sandra Blakeslee, *The Good Marriage: How and Why Love Lasts* (Boston: Houghton Mifflin, 1995), p. 15.

majority of children had come to live in a family with a male breadwinner, a female homemaker, and a chance at a high school education. Yet no sooner did the ideals associated with such a family begin to blossom than they were buried by the stock market crash of 1929 and the Great Depression of the 1930s. During the 1930s domestic violence soared; divorce rates fell, but informal separations jumped; fertility plummeted. Murder rates were higher in 1933 than they were in the 1980s. Families were uprooted or torn apart. Thousands of young people left home to seek work, often riding the rails across the country.[4]

World War II brought the beginning of economic recovery, and people's renewed interest in forming families resulted in a marriage and childbearing boom, but stability was still beyond most people's grasp. Postwar communities were rocked by racial tensions, labor strife, and a right-wing backlash against the radical union movement of the 1930s. Many women resented being fired from wartime jobs they had grown to enjoy. Veterans often came home to find that they had to elbow their way back into their families, with wives and children resisting their attempts to reassert domestic authority. In one recent study of fathers who returned from the war, four times as many reported painful, even traumatic, reunions as remembered happy ones.[5]

By 1946 one in every three marriages was ending in divorce. Even couples who stayed together went through rough times, as an acute housing shortage forced families to double up with relatives or friends. Tempers frayed and generational relations grew strained. "No home is big enough to house two families, particularly two of different generations, with opposite theories on child training," warned a 1948 film on the problems of modern marriage.[6]

So after the widespread domestic strife, family disruptions, and violence of the 1930s and the instability of the World War II period, people were ready to try something new. The postwar economic boom gave them the chance. The 1950s was the first time that a majority of Americans could even *dream* of creating a secure oasis in their immediate nuclear families. There they could focus their emotional and financial investments, reduce obligations to others that might keep them from seizing their own chance at a new start, and escape the interference of an older generation of neighbors or relatives who tried to tell them how to run their lives and raise their kids.

10

---

[4]Donald Hernandez, *America's Children: Resources from Family, Government and the Economy* (New York: Russell Sage, 1993), pp. 99, 102; James Morone, "The Corrosive Politics of Virtue," *American Prospect* 26 (May–June 1996), p. 37; "Study Finds U.S. No. 1 in Violence," *Olympian*, November 13, 1992. See also Stephen Mintz and Susan Kellogg, *Domestic Revolutions: A Social History of American Family Life* (New York: The Free Press, 1988).

[5]William Tuttle, Jr., *"Daddy's Gone to War": The Second World War in the Lives of America's Children* (New York: Oxford University Press, 1993).

[6]"Marriage and Divorce," *March of Time*, film series 14 (1948).

ROGER REALIZES A CHERISHED CHILDHOOD
MEMORY IS ACTUALLY A SCENE FROM AN
OLD MOVIE.

Oral histories of the postwar period resound with the theme of escaping from in-laws, maiden aunts, older parents, even needy siblings.

The private family also provided a refuge from the anxieties of the new nuclear age and the cold war, as well as a place to get away from the political witch-hunts led by Senator Joe McCarthy and his allies. When having the wrong friends at the wrong time or belonging to any "suspicious" organization could ruin your career and reputation, it was safer to pull out of groups you might have joined earlier and to focus on your family. On a more positive note, the nuclear family was where people could try to satisfy their long-pent-up desires for a more stable marriage, a decent home, and the chance to really enjoy their children.

The 1950s Family Experiment

The key to understanding the successes, failures, and comparatively short life of 1950s family forms and values is to understand the period as one of *experimentation* with the possibilities of a new kind of family, not as the expression of some longstanding tradition. At the end of the 1940s, the divorce rate, which had been rising steadily since the 1890s, dropped sharply; the age of marriage fell to a 100-year low; and the birth rate soared. Women who had worked during the Depression or World War II quit their jobs as soon as they became pregnant, which meant quite a few women were specializing in child raising; fewer women remained childless during the 1950s than in any decade since the late nineteenth century. The timing and spacing of childbearing became far more compressed, so that young mothers were likely to have two or more children in diapers at once, with no older sibling to help in their care. At the same time, again for the first time in 100 years, the educational gap between young middle-class women and men increased, while job segregation for working men and women seems to have peaked. These demographic changes increased the dependence of women on marriage, in contrast to gradual trends in the opposite direction since the early twentieth century.[7]

The result was that family life and gender roles became much more predictable, orderly, and settled in the 1950s than they were either twenty years earlier or would be twenty years later. Only slightly more than one in four marriages ended in divorce during the 1950s. Very few young people spent any extended period of time in a nonfamily setting: They moved from their parents' family into their own family, after just a brief experience with independent living, and they started having children soon after marriage. Whereas two-thirds of women aged 20 to 24 were not yet married in 1990, only 28 percent of women this age were still single in 1960.[8]

Ninety percent of all the households in the country were families in the 1950s, in comparison with only 71 percent by 1990. Eighty-six percent of all children lived in two-parent homes in 1950, as opposed to just 72 percent in

15

[7]Arlene Skolnick and Stacey Rosencrantz, "The New Crusade for the Old Family," *American Prospect,* Summer 1994, p. 65; Hernandez, *America's Children,* pp. 128–32; Andrew Cherlin, "Changing Family and Household: Contemporary Lessons from Historical Research," *Annual Review of Sociology* 9 (1983), pp. 54–58; Sam Roberts, *Who We Are: A Portrait of America Based on the Latest Census* (New York: Times Books, 1995), p. 45.

[8]Levy, "Incomes and Income Inequality," p. 20; Arthur Norton and Louisa Miller, *Marriage, Divorce, and Remarriage in the 1990s,* Current Population Reports Series P23–180 (Washington, D.C.: Bureau of the Census, October 1992); Roberts, *Who We Are* (1995 ed.), pp. 50–53.

1990. And the percentage living with both biological parents — rather than, say, a parent and stepparent — was dramatically higher than it had been at the turn of the century or is today: seventy percent in 1950, compared with only 50 percent in 1990. Nearly 60 percent of kids — an all-time high — were born into male breadwinner–female homemaker families; only a minority of the rest had mothers who worked in the paid labor force.[9]

If the organization and uniformity of family life in the 1950s were new, so were the values, especially the emphasis on putting all one's emotional and financial eggs in the small basket of the immediate nuclear family. Right up through the 1940s, ties of work, friendship, neighborhood, ethnicity, extended kin, and voluntary organizations were as important a source of identity for most Americans, and sometimes a *more* important source of obligation, than marriage and the nuclear family. All this changed in the postwar era. The spread of suburbs and automobiles, combined with the destruction of older ethnic neighborhoods in many cities, led to the decline of the neighborhood social club. Young couples moved away from parents and kin, cutting ties with traditional extrafamilial networks that might compete for their attention. A critical factor in this trend was the emergence of a group of family sociologists and marriage counselors who followed Talcott Parsons in claiming that the nuclear family, built on a sharp division of labor between husband and wife, was the cornerstone of modern society.

The new family experts tended to advocate views such as those first raised in a 1946 book, *Their Mothers' Sons*, by psychiatrist Edward Strecker. Strecker and his followers argued that American boys were infantilized and emasculated by women who were old-fashioned "moms" instead of modern "mothers." One sign that you might be that dreaded "mom," Strecker warned women, was if you felt you should take your aging parents into your own home, rather than putting them in "a good institution . . . where they will receive adequate care and comfort." Modern "mothers" placed their parents in nursing homes and poured all their energies into their nuclear family. They were discouraged from diluting their wifely and maternal commitments by maintaining "competing" interests in friends, jobs, or extended family networks, yet they were also supposed to cheerfully grant early independence to their (male) children — an emotional double bind that may explain why so many women who took this advice to heart ended up abusing alcohol or tranquilizers over the course of the decade.[10]

[9]Dennis Hogan and Daniel Lichter, "Children and Youth: Living Arrangements and Welfare," in Farley, ed., *State of the Union*, vol. 2, p. 99; Richard Gelles, *Contemporary Families: A Sociological View* (Thousand Oaks, Calif.: Sage, 1995), p. 115; Hernandez, *America's Children*, p. 102. The fact that only a small percentage of children had mothers in the paid labor force, though a full 40 percent did not live in male breadwinner–female homemaker families, was because some children had mothers who worked, unpaid, in farms or family businesses, or fathers who were unemployed, or the children were not living with both parents.

[10]Edward Strecker, *Their Mothers' Sons: The Psychiatrist Examines an American Problem* (Philadelphia: J. B. Lippincott, 1946), p. 209.

The call for young couples to break from their parents and youthful friends was a consistent theme in 1950s popular culture. In *Marty,* one of the most highly praised TV plays and movies of the 1950s, the hero almost loses his chance at love by listening to the carping of his mother and aunt and letting himself be influenced by old friends who resent the time he spends with his new girlfriend. In the end, he turns his back on mother, aunt, and friends to get his new marriage and a little business of his own off to a good start. Other movies, novels, and popular psychology tracts portrayed the dreadful things that happened when women became more interested in careers than marriage or men resisted domestic conformity.

Yet many people felt guilty about moving away from older parents and relatives; "modern mothers" worried that fostering independence in their kids could lead to defiance or even juvenile delinquency (the recurring nightmare of the age); there was considerable confusion about how men and women could maintain clear breadwinner-homemaker distinctions in a period of expanding education, job openings, and consumer aspirations. People clamored for advice. They got it from the new family education specialists and marriage counselors, from columns in women's magazines, from government pamphlets, and above all from television. While 1950s TV melodramas warned against letting anything dilute the commitment to getting married and having kids, the new family sitcoms gave people nightly lessons on how to make their marriage or rapidly expanding family work — or, in the case of *I Love Lucy,* probably the most popular show of the era, how *not* to make their marriage and family work. Lucy and Ricky gave weekly comic reminders of how much trouble a woman could get into by wanting a career or hatching some hare-brained scheme behind her husband's back.

At the time, everyone knew that shows such as *Donna Reed, Ozzie and Harriet, Leave It to Beaver,* and *Father Knows Best* were not the way families really were. People didn't watch those shows to see their own lives reflected back at them. They watched them to see how families were *supposed* to live — and also to get a little reassurance that they were headed in the right direction. The sitcoms were simultaneously advertisements, etiquette manuals, and how-to lessons for a new way of organizing marriage and child raising. I have studied the scripts of these shows for years, since I often use them in my classes on family history, but it wasn't until I became a parent that I felt their extraordinary pull. The secret of their appeal, I suddenly realized, was that they offered 1950s viewers, wracked with the same feelings of parental inadequacy as was I, the promise that there were easy answers and surefire techniques for raising kids.

Ever since, I have found it useful to think of the sitcoms as the 1950s equivalent of today's beer ads. As most people know, beer ads are consciously aimed at men who *aren't* as strong and sexy as the models in the commercials, guys who are uneasily aware of the gap between the ideal masculine pursuits and their own achievements. The promise is that if the viewers on the couch will just drink brand X, they too will be able to run 10 miles without gasping for breath. Their bodies will firm up, their complexions will clear up, and maybe the Swedish bikini team will come over and hang out at their place.

Similarly, the 1950s sitcoms were aimed at young couples who had married in haste, women who had tasted new freedoms during World War II and given up their jobs with regret, veterans whose children resented their attempts to reassert paternal authority, and individuals disturbed by the changing racial and ethnic mix of postwar America. The message was clear: Buy these ranch houses, Hotpoint appliances, and child-raising ideals; relate to your spouse like this; get a new car to wash with your kids on Sunday afternoons; organize your dinners like that — and you too can escape from the conflicts of race, class, and political witch-hunts into harmonious families where father knows best, mothers are never bored or irritated, and teenagers rush to the dinner table each night, eager to get their latest dose of parental wisdom.

Many families found it possible to put together a good imitation of this way of living during the 1950s and 1960s. Couples were often able to construct marriages that were much more harmonious than those in which they had grown up, and to devote far more time to their children. Even when marriages were deeply unhappy, as many were, the new stability, economic security, and educational advantages parents were able to offer their kids counted for a lot in people's assessment of their life satisfaction. And in some matters, ignorance could be bliss: The lack of media coverage of problems such as abuse or incest was terribly hard on the casualties, but it protected more fortunate families from knowledge and fear of many social ills.[11]

There was tremendous hostility to people who could be defined as "others": Jews, African Americans, Puerto Ricans, the poor, gays or lesbians, and "the red menace." Yet on a day-to-day basis, the civility that prevailed in homogeneous neighborhoods allowed people to ignore larger patterns of racial and political repression. Racial clashes were ever-present in the 1950s, sometimes escalating into full-scale antiblack riots, but individual homicide rates fell to almost half the levels of the 1930s. As nuclear families moved into the suburbs, they retreated from social activism but entered voluntary relationships with people who had children the same age; they became involved in PTAs together, joined bridge clubs, went bowling. There does seem to have been a stronger sense of neighborly commonalities than many of us feel today. Even though this local community was often the product of exclusion or repression, it sometimes looks attractive to modern

[11]For discussion of the discontents, and often searing misery, that were considered normal in a "good-enough" marriage in the 1950s and 1960s, see Lillian Rubin, *Worlds of Pain: Life in the Working-Class Family* (New York: Basic Books, 1976); Mirra Komarovsky, *Blue Collar Marriage* (New Haven, Conn.: Vintage, 1962); Elaine Tyler May, *Homeward Bound: American Families in the Cold War Era* (New York: Basic Books, 1988).

Americans whose commutes are getting longer and whose family or work patterns give them little in common with their neighbors.[12]

The optimism that allowed many families to rise above their internal difficulties and to put limits on their individualistic values during the 1950s came from the sense that America was on a dramatically different trajectory than it had been in the past, an upward and expansionary path that had already taken people to better places than they had ever seen before and would certainly take their children even further. This confidence that almost everyone could look forward to a better future stands in sharp contrast to how most contemporary Americans feel, and it explains why a period in which many people were much worse off than today sometimes still looks like a better period for families than our own.

Throughout the 1950s, poverty was higher than it is today, but it was less concentrated in pockets of blight existing side-by-side with extremes of wealth, and, unlike today, it was falling rather than rising. At the end of the 1930s, almost two-thirds of the population had incomes below the poverty standards of the day, while only one in eight had a middle-class income (defined as two to five times the poverty line). By 1960, a majority of the population had climbed into the middle-income range.[13]

Unmarried people were hardly sexually abstinent in the 1950s, but the age of first intercourse was somewhat higher than it is now, and despite a tripling of nonmarital birth rates between 1940 and 1958, more than 70 percent of nonmarital pregnancies led to weddings before the child was born. Teenage birth rates were almost twice as high in 1957 as in the 1990s, but most teen births were to married couples, and the effect of teen pregnancy in reducing further schooling for young people did not hurt their life prospects the way it does today. High school graduation rates were lower in the 1950s than they are today, and minority students had far worse test scores, but there were jobs for people who dropped out of high school or

[12]See Robert Putnam, "The Strange Disappearance of Civic America," *American Prospect*, Winter 1996. For a glowing if somewhat lopsided picture of 1950s community solidarities, see Alan Ehrenhalt, *The Lost City: Discovering the Forgotten Virtues of Community in the Chicago of the 1950s* (New York: Basic Books, 1995). For a chilling account of communities uniting against perceived outsiders, in the same city, see Arnold Hirsch, *Making the Second Ghetto: Race and Housing in Chicago, 1940–1960* (Cambridge, Mass.: Harvard University Press, 1983). On homicide rates, see "Study Finds United States No. 1 in Violence," *Olympian*, November 13, 1992; *New York Times*, November 13, 1992, p. A9; and Douglas Lee Eckberg, "Estimates of Early Twentieth-Century U.S. Homicide Rates: An Econometric Forecasting Approach," *Demography* 32 (1995), p. 14. On lengthening commutes, see "It's Taking Longer to Get to Work," *Olympian*, December 6, 1995.

[13]The figures in this and the following paragraph come from Levy, "Incomes and Income Inequality," pp. 1–57; May and Porter, "Poverty and Income Trends, 1994"; Reynolds Farley, *The New American Reality: Who We Are, How We Got Here, Where We Are Going* (New York: Russell Sage, 1996), pp. 83–85; Gelles, *Contemporary Families*, p. 115; David Grissmer, Sheila Nataraj Kirby, Mark Bender, and Stephanie Williamson, *Student Achievement and the Changing American Family*, Rand Institute on Education and Training (Santa Monica, Calif: Rand, 1994), p. 106.

graduated without good reading skills — jobs that actually had a future. People entering the job market in the 1950s had no way of knowing that they would be the last generation to have a good shot at reaching middle-class status without the benefit of postsecondary schooling.

Millions of men from impoverished, rural, unemployed, or poorly educated family backgrounds found steady jobs in the steel, auto, appliance, construction, and shipping industries. Lower-middle-class men went further on in college during the 1950s than they would have been able to expect in earlier decades, enabling them to make the transition to secure white-collar work. The experience of shared sacrifices in the Depression and war, reinforced by a New Deal–inspired belief in the ability of government to make life better, gave people a sense of hope for the future. Confidence in government, business, education, and other institutions was on the rise. This general optimism affected people's experience and assessment of family life. It is no wonder modern Americans yearn for a similar sense of hope.

But before we sign on to any attempts to turn the family clock back to the 1950s we should note that the family successes and community solidarities of the 1950s rested on a totally different set of political and economic conditions than we have today. Contrary to widespread belief, the 1950s was not an age of laissez-faire government and free market competition. A major cause of the social mobility of young families in the 1950s was that federal assistance programs were much more generous and widespread than they are today.

In the most ambitious and successful affirmative action program ever   30
adopted in America, 40 percent of young men were eligible for veterans' benefits, and these benefits were far more extensive than those available to Vietnam-era vets. Financed in part by a federal income tax on the rich that went up to 87 percent and a corporate tax rate of 52 percent, such benefits provided quite a jump start for a generation of young families. The GI bill paid most tuition costs for vets who attended college, doubling the percentage of college students from prewar levels. At the other end of the life span, Social Security began to build up a significant safety net for the elderly, formerly the poorest segment of the population. Starting in 1950, the federal government regularly mandated raises in the minimum wage to keep pace with inflation. The minimum wage may have been only $1.40 as late as 1968, but a person who worked for that amount full-time, year-round, earned 118 percent of the poverty figure for a family of three. By 1995, a full-time minimum-wage worker could earn only 72 percent of the poverty level.[14]

---

[14]William Chafe, *The Unfinished Journey: America Since World War II* (New York: Oxford University Press, 1986), pp. 113, 143; Marc Linder, "Eisenhower-Era Marxist-Confiscatory Taxation: Requiem for the Rhetoric of Rate Reduction for the Rich," *Tulane Law Review* 70 (1996), p. 917; Barry Bluestone and Teresa Ghilarducci, "Rewarding Work: Feasible Antipoverty Policy," *American Prospect* 28 (1996), p. 42; Theda Skocpol, "Delivering for Young Families," *American Prospect* 28 (1996), p. 67.

An important source of the economic expansion of the 1950s was that public works spending at all levels of government comprised nearly 20 percent of total expenditures in 1950, as compared to less than 7 percent in 1984. Between 1950 and 1960, nonmilitary, nonresidential public construction rose by 58 percent. Construction expenditures for new schools (in dollar amounts adjusted for inflation) rose by 72 percent; funding on sewers and waterworks rose by 46 percent. Government paid 90 percent of the costs of building the new Interstate Highway System. These programs opened up suburbia to growing numbers of middle-class Americans and created secure, well-paying jobs for blue-collar workers.[15]

Government also reorganized home financing, underwriting low down payments and long-term mortgages that had been rejected as bad business by private industry. To do this, government put public assets behind housing lending programs, created two new national financial institutions to facilitate home loans, allowed veterans to put down payments as low as a dollar on a house, and offered tax breaks to people who bought homes. The National Education Defense Act funded the socioeconomic mobility of thousands of young men who trained themselves for well-paying jobs in such fields as engineering.[16]

Unlike contemporary welfare programs, government investment in 1950s families was not just for immediate subsistence but encouraged long-term asset development, rewarding people for increasing their investment in homes and education. Thus it was far less likely that such families or individuals would ever fall back to where they started, even after a string of bad luck. Subsidies for higher education were greater the longer people stayed in school and the more expensive the school they selected. Mortgage deductions got bigger as people traded up to better houses.[17]

These social and political support systems magnified the impact of the postwar economic boom. "In the years between 1947 and 1973," reports economist Robert Kuttner, "the median paycheck more than doubled, and the bottom 20 percent enjoyed the greatest gains." High rates of unionization meant that blue-collar workers were making much more financial progress than most of their counterparts today. In 1952, when eager home buyers flocked to the opening of Levittown, Pennsylvania, the largest

[15]Joel Tarr, "The Evolution of the Urban Infrastructure in the Nineteenth and Twentieth Centuries," in Royce Hanson, ed., *Perspectives on Urban Infrastructure* (Washington, D.C.: National Academy Press, 1984); Mark Aldrich, *A History of Public Works Investment in the United States,* report prepared by the CPNSAD Research Corporation for the U.S. Department of Commerce, April 1980.

[16]For more information on this government financing, see Kenneth Jackson, *Crabgrass Frontier: The Suburbanization of the United States* (New York: Oxford University Press, 1985); and *The Way We Never Were,* chapter 4.

[17]John Cook and Laura Sherman, "Economic Security Among America's Poor: The Impact of State Welfare Waivers on Asset Accumulation," Center on Hunger, Poverty, and Nutrition Policy, Tufts University, May 1996.

planned community yet constructed, "it took a factory worker one day to earn enough money to pay the closing costs on a new Levittown house, then selling for $10,000." By 1991, such a home was selling for $100,000 or more, and it took a factory worker *eighteen weeks* to earn enough money for just the closing costs.[18]

The legacy of the union struggle of the 1930s and 1940s, combined with government support for raising people's living standards, set limits on corporations that have disappeared in recent decades. Corporations paid 23 percent of federal income taxes in the 1950s, as compared to just 9.2 percent in 1991. Big companies earned higher profit margins than smaller firms, partly due to their dominance of the market, partly to America's post-war economic advantage. They chose (or were forced) to share these extra earnings, which economists call "rents," with employees. Economists at the Brookings Institution and Harvard University estimate that 70 percent of such corporate rents were passed on to workers at all levels of the firm, ben-efiting secretaries and janitors as well as CEOs. Corporations routinely retained workers even in slack periods, as a way of ensuring workplace stability. Although they often received more generous tax breaks from com-munities than they gave back in investment, at least they kept their plants and employment offices in the same place. AT&T, for example, received much of the technology it used to finance its postwar expansion from pub-licly funded communications research conducted as part of the war effort, and, as current AT&T Chairman Robert Allen puts it, there "used to be a lifelong commitment on the employee's part and on our part." Today, how-ever, he admits, "the contract doesn't exist anymore."[19]

Television trivia experts still argue over exactly what the fathers in many 1950s sitcoms did for a living. Whatever it was, though, they obviously didn't have to worry about downsizing. If most married people stayed in long-term relationships during the 1950s, so did most corporations, sticking with the communities they grew up in and the employees they originally hired. Corporations were not constantly relocating in search of cheap labor during the 1950s; unlike today, increases in worker productivity usually led to increases in wages. The number of workers covered by corporate pension plans and health benefits increased steadily. So did limits on the work week. There is good reason that people look back to the 1950s as a less hurried

---

[18]Robert Kuttner, "The Incredible Shrinking American Paycheck," *Washington Post National Weekly Edition*, November 6–12, 1995, p. 23; Donald Bartlett and James Steele, *America: What Went Wrong?* (Kansas City: Andrews McMeel, 1992), p. 20.

[19]Richard Barnet, "Lords of the Global Economy," *Nation*, December 19, 1994, p. 756; Clay Chandler, "U.S. Corporations: Good Citizens or Bad?" *Washington Post National Weekly Edition*, May 20–26, 1996, p. 16; Steven Pearlstein, "No More Mr. Nice Guy: Corporate Amer-ica Has Done an About-Face in How It Pays and Treats Employees," *Washington Post National Weekly Edition*, December 18–24, 1995, p. 10; Robert Kuttner, "Ducking Class War-fare," *Washington Post National Weekly Edition*, March 11–17, 1996, p. 5; Henry Allen, "Ha! So Much for Loyalty," *Washington Post National Weekly Edition*, March 4–10, 1996, p. 11.

age: The average American was working a shorter workday in the 1950s than his or her counterpart today, when a quarter of the workforce puts in 49 or more hours a week.[20]

So politicians are practicing quite a double standard when they tell us to return to the family forms of the 1950s while they do nothing to restore the job programs and family subsidies of that era, the limits on corporate relocation and financial wheeling-dealing, the much higher share of taxes paid by corporations then, the availability of union jobs for noncollege youth, and the subsidies for higher education such as the National Defense Education Act loans. Furthermore, they're not telling the whole story when they claim that the 1950s was the most prosperous time for families and the most secure decade for children. Instead, playing to our understandable nostalgia for a time when things seemed to be getting better, not worse, they engage in a tricky chronological shell game with their figures, diverting our attention from two important points. First, many individuals, families, and groups were excluded from the economic prosperity, family optimism, and social civility of the 1950s. Second, the all-time high point of child well-being and family economic security came not during the 1950s but *at the end of the 1960s*.

We now know that 1950s family culture was not only nontraditional; it was also not idyllic. In important ways, the stability of family and community life during the 1950s rested on pervasive discrimination against women, gays, political dissidents, non-Christians, and racial or ethnic minorities, as well as on a systematic cover-up of the underside of many families. Families that were harmonious and fair of their own free will may have been able to function more easily in the fifties, but few alternatives existed for members of discordant or oppressive families. Victims of child abuse, incest, alcoholism, spousal rape, and wife battering had no recourse, no place to go, until well into the 1960s.[21]

At the end of the 1950s, despite ten years of economic growth, 27.3 percent of the nation's children were poor, including those in white "underclass" communities such as Appalachia. Almost 50 percent of married-couple African-American families were impoverished — a figure far higher than today. It's no wonder African Americans are not likely to pick the 1950s as a golden age, even in comparison with the setbacks they experienced in the 1980s. When blacks moved north to find jobs in the postwar urban manufacturing boom they met vicious harassment and violence, first to prevent them from moving out of the central cities, then to exclude them from public space such as parks or beaches.

[20]Ehrenhalt, *The Lost City*, pp. 11–12; Jeremy Rifken, *The End of Work: The Decline of the Global Labor Force and the Dawn of the Post-Market Era* (New York: G. P. Putnam's Sons, 1995), pp. 169, 170, 231; Juliet Schorr, *The Overworked American: The Unexpected Decline of Leisure* (New York: Basic Books, 1991).

[21]For documentation that these problems existed, see chapter 2 of *The Way We Never Were*.

In Philadelphia, for example, the City of Brotherly Love, there were   40
more than 200 racial incidents over housing in the first six months of 1955
alone. The Federal Housing Authority, such a boon to white working-class
families, refused to insure homes in all-black or in racially mixed neighborhoods. Two-thirds of the city dwellers evicted by the urban renewal projects
of the decade were African Americans and Latinos; government did almost
nothing to help such displaced families find substitute housing.[22]

Women were unable to take out loans or even credit cards in their own
names. They were excluded from juries in many states. A lack of options
outside marriage led some women to remain in desperately unhappy unions
that were often not in the best interests of their children or themselves.
Even women in happy marriages often felt humiliated by the constant
messages they received that their whole lives had to revolve around a man.
"You are not ready when he calls — miss one turn," was a rule in the Barbie
game marketed to 1950s girls; "he criticizes your hairdo — go to the beauty
shop." Episodes of *Father Knows Best* advised young women: "The worst
thing you can do is to try to beat a man at his own game. You just beat the
women at theirs." One character on the show told women to always ask
themselves, "Are you after a job or a man? You can't have both."[23]

The Fifties Experiment Comes to an End

The social stability of the 1950s, then, was a response to the stick of
racism, sexism, and repression as well as to the carrot of economic opportunity and government aid. Because social protest mounted in the 1960s and
unsettling challenges were posed to the gender roles and sexual mores of
the previous decade, many people forget that families continued to make
gains throughout the 1960s and into the first few years of the 1970s. By
1969, child poverty was down to 14 percent, its lowest level ever; it hovered
just above that marker until 1975, when it began its steady climb up to contemporary figures (22 percent in 1993; 21.2 percent in 1994). The high
point of health and nutrition for poor children was reached in the early
1970s.[24]

So commentators are being misleading when they claim that the 1950s
was the golden age of American families. They are disregarding the number
of people who were excluded during that decade and ignoring the socio-

[22]The poverty figures come from census data collected in *The State of America's Children
Yearbook, 1996* (Washington, D.C.: Children's Defense Fund, 1996), p. 77. See also Hirsch,
Making the Second Ghetto; Raymond Mohl, "Making the Second Ghetto in Metropolitan
Miami, 1940–1960," *Journal of Urban History* 25 (1995), p. 396; Micaela di Leonardo, "Boys
on the Hood," *Nation*, August 17–24, 1992, p. 180; Jackson, *Crabgrass Frontier*, pp. 226–227.

[23]Susan Douglas, *Where the Girls Are: Growing Up Female with the Mass Media* (New
York: Times Books, 1994), pp. 25, 37.

[24]*The State of America's Children Yearbook, 1966*, p. 77; May and Porter, "Poverty and
Income Trends: 1994," p. 23; Sara McLanahan et al., *Losing Ground: A Critique*, University of
Wisconsin Institute for Research on Poverty, Special Report No. 38, 1985.

economic gains that continued to be made through the 1960s. But they are quite right to note that the improvements of the 1950s and 1960s came to an end at some point in the 1970s (though not for the elderly, who continued to make progress).

Ironically, it was the children of those stable, enduring, supposedly idyllic 1950s families, the recipients of so much maternal time and attention, that pioneered the sharp break with their parents' family forms and gender roles in the 1970s. This was not because they were led astray by some youthful Murphy Brown in her student rebel days or inadvertently spoiled by parents who read too many of Dr. Spock's child-raising manuals.

Partly, the departure from 1950s family arrangements was a logical extension of trends and beliefs pioneered in the 1950s, or of inherent contradictions in those patterns. For example, early and close-spaced childbearing freed more wives up to join the labor force, and married women began to flock to work. By 1960, more than 40 percent of women over the age of 16 held a job, and working mothers were the fastest growing component of the labor force. The educational aspirations and opportunities that opened up for kids of the baby boom could not be confined to males, and many tight-knit, male-breadwinner, nuclear families in the 1950s instilled in their daughters the ambition to be something other than a homemaker.[25]

Another part of the transformation was a shift in values. Most people would probably agree that some changes in values were urgently needed: the extension of civil rights to racial minorities and to women; a rejection of property rights in children by parents and in women by husbands; a reaction against the political intolerance and the wasteful materialism of 1950s culture. Other changes in values remain more controversial: opposition to American intervention abroad; repudiation of the traditional sexual double standard; rebellion against what many young people saw as the hypocrisy of parents who preached sexual morality but ignored social immorality such as racism and militarism.

Still other developments, such as the growth of me-first individualism, are widely regarded as problematic by people on all points along the political spectrum. It's worth noting, though, that the origins of antisocial individualism and self-indulgent consumerism lay at least as much in the family values of the 1950s as in the youth rebellion of the 1960s. The marketing experts who never allowed the kids in *Ozzie and Harriet* sitcoms to be shown drinking milk, for fear of offending soft-drink companies that might sponsor the show in syndication, were ultimately the same people who slightly later invested billions of dollars to channel sexual rebelliousness and a depoliticized individualism into mainstream culture.

---

[25]For studies of how both middle-class and working-class women in the 1950s quickly departed from, or never quite accepted, the predominant image of women, see Joanne Meyerowitz, ed., *Not June Cleaver: Women and Gender in Postwar America, 1945–1960* (Philadelphia: Temple University Press, 1994).

There were big cultural changes brewing by the beginning of the 1970s, and tremendous upheavals in social, sexual, and family values. And yes, there were sometimes reckless or simply laughable excesses in some of the early experiments with new gender roles, family forms, and personal expression. But the excesses of 1950s gender roles and family forms were every bit as repellent and stupid as the excesses of the sixties: Just watch a dating etiquette film of the time period, or recall that therapists of the day often told victims of incest that they were merely having unconscious oedipal fantasies.

Ultimately, though, changes in values were not what brought the 1950s family experiment to an end. The postwar family compacts between husbands and wives, parents and children, young and old, were based on the postwar social compact between government, corporations, and workers. While there was some discontent with those family bargains among women and youth, the old relations did not really start to unravel until people began to face the erosion of the corporate wage bargain and government broke its tacit societal bargain that it would continue to invest in jobs and education for the younger generation.

In the 1970s, new economic trends began to clash with all the social ex-   50
pectations that 1950s families had instilled in their children. That clash, not the willful abandonment of responsibility and commitment, has been the primary cause of both family rearrangements and the growing social problems that are usually attributed to such family changes, but in fact have *separate* origins.

ENGAGING THE TEXT

1. According to Coontz, what do we really miss about the 1950s? In addition, what *don't* we miss?

2. In Coontz's view, what was the role of the government in making the 1950s in America what they were? What part did broader historical forces or other circumstances play?

3. Although she concentrates on the 1950s, Coontz also describes the other decades from the 1920s to the present. Use her information to create a brief chart naming the key characteristics of each decade. Then consider your own family history and see how well it fits the pattern Coontz outlines. Discuss the results with classmates or write a journal entry reflecting on what you learn.

EXPLORING CONNECTIONS

4. Compare Norman Rockwell's enormously popular portrayals of family life (pp. 22–24) with the account provided by Coontz. Do you think she would call Rockwell's paintings "nostalgic"? What do we mean by this word?

5. Review "Looking for Work" by Gary Soto (p. 26). How does this narrative evoke nostalgia for a simpler, better era for families? Does it reveal any of the problems with the 1950s that Coontz describes?

EXTENDING THE CRITICAL CONTEXT

6. Coontz suggests that an uninformed nostalgia for the 1950s could promote harmful political agendas today. (See, for example, paras. 7 and 37.) What evidence, if any, do you see in contemporary media that nostalgia for the 1950s is on the rise? Do you agree with Coontz that such nostalgia can be dangerous? Why or why not?

7. Watch an episode of a 1950s sitcom (if possible, videotape it) such as *Father Knows Best, The Donna Reed Show, Leave It to Beaver,* or *I Love Lucy.* Analyze the extent to which it reveals both positive and negative aspects of the 1950s that Coontz discusses (for example, an authoritarian father figure, limited roles for wives, economic prosperity, or a sense of a secure community).

About Marriage

DANIELLE CRITTENDEN

When the modern feminist movement was getting under way in the 1960s and 1970s, many feminist leaders scorned the nuclear family as an institution that bound women to oppressive gender roles. Freeing women, in this analysis, meant rejecting or redefining the family. Danielle Crittenden objects to such views in this selection from What Our Mothers Didn't Tell Us: Why Happiness Eludes the Modern Woman *(1999). Crittenden argues that feminism, which has challenged traditional views of marriage and family, has actually hurt many women by cheapening wedding vows, discounting the value of women's traditional roles within the family, and making it easy for husbands to abandon their duties. From Crittenden's vantage point, stereotypical 1950s suburban marriages — ones feminists consider restrictive and sexist — look "peaceful and affluent." A former columnist for the* New York Post, *Crittenden (b. 1963) is the founder of* Women's Quarterly *and the author of the novel* Amanda Bright@Home *(1999).*

Despite having suffered through the highest divorce rate in the nation's history, despite the casualness with which people are often accused of seeking divorce, nearly three quarters of Americans persist in believing that "marriage is a lifelong commitment that should not be broken except under extreme circumstances." If this is true, then we have to seriously reexamine our opinions toward the so-called traditional marriage that we rejected in favor of the more egalitarian but less enduring modern one.

The many feminist critics of marriage insist that traditional marriage is incompatible with modern women's lives: that very few women would be willing to return to marriages in which the wives confine themselves largely to home and family while their husbands go to work. These critics damn any attempt to salvage, or reexamine, traditional marriage as a pointless exercise in nostalgia — when not an actively subversive attempt to "turn back the clock" on women's achievements outside the home. Indeed, feminists mistrust marriage so profoundly that their response to the harm done to women by divorce has been to urge women to avoid it entirely, and they resent all efforts to preserve it. Like disciples of Le Corbusier[1] surveying a row of Victorian houses, they think there is nothing wrong with marriage that could not be solved by bulldozers and dynamite. As Barbara Ehrenreich wrote in *Time,* "Yes, divorce is bad — but so is the institution that generates it: marriage." Ideally, such critics believe, relationships should be formed and dissolved at whim, and there should be no assigned roles for either sex. There are thinkers, too, like Barbara Dafoe Whitehead, who recognize the harsh consequences of divorce upon women and children but who are equally reluctant to see any return to the division of labor according to sex. As she notes in the conclusion of her 1997 book, *The Divorce Culture,* "If men and women are to *find a way to share the tasks of parenthood in marriage,* that way can come about only through a change of heart and mind, a new consciousness about the meaning of commitment itself . . ." [italics mine].

Yet this quest for perfect parity in marriage will never liberate women from our duties and cravings as mothers. What it can do — what it has done for nearly half the men in America — is provide an excuse for shirking the duties of fatherhood. If men are told they are not needed to support their wives and children, if they are made to understand that their role as father is interchangeable with the mother's — or, for that matter, with the babysitter's, or the day-care worker's — what compelling reason do men have to remain with their families? To open sticky jar lids and move heavy furniture? Hardly an incentive for lifelong commitment or inspiration for enduring romance. What the feminist vision of marriage amounts to is that every marriage should resemble a gay marriage, without husbands or wives or fathers or mothers. Instead, both "partners" or "spouses" should occupy the same roles within and outside the home. And all of this may sound fine, even attractive, in a science fiction sort of way, and it will last precisely as long as the romantic attraction between the two partners lasts. But what happens then? The female partner doesn't really *need* her male partner in this unisex utopia: She has her job and her day-care center and (for a while, anyway) a succession of available lovers. Nor does the male partner really *need* his female partner. He can get take-out Chinese food and (for rather longer) girlfriends and the new line of Hallmark divorced-dad cards to send

---

[1]*Le Corbusier:* Swiss architect Charles Edouard Jenneret (1887–1965).

"So, are you still with the same parents?"

to his offspring. All but the happiest marriages are held together for *reasons:* because husbands and wives seek different, supportive roles within marriage, because they rely upon each other for different things. And marriages are held together even more by *opinion* — the opinion of society that marriage is good and laudable, that separation is a calamity and a failure, and by the opinion of the husband and wife themselves that only the gravest incompatibility can justify divorce. But we have, step by step, weakened these reasons and discarded these opinions.

There is nothing now left to bind a man to his wife and children — or a wife to her husband — but the very tenuous bonds of affection and sexual attraction. If a man is decent and loves his wife and would never abandon her, well, lucky her — she's found, by today's standards, a rare gem. But what if his sense of duty and obligation is not so strong? What if he's feeling resentful or trapped or bored or sexually listless or financially overburdened? His children might be passing through some sullen and unrewarding phase, his house might be constantly messy, his wallet may feel as if it is being consumed daily by piranhas, and his wife may be cranky and tired all the time because of the pressure *she's* facing. What holds him there? Certainly not the cost of divorce — he'll be able to escape that. He will not face banishment from his church (if he goes to church), or ostracism by his friends, or disapproving looks from his neighbors, or, if he acts civilized about it, even a harsh word from his in-laws. It's not the Dark Ages, after all, he might tell himself. And then there's that smart, attractive, and, above all, *unencumbered* young woman down the hall from his office. Hey, it could be great — for *him.* He might feel guilty for a while, sure, particularly those first few weekends when the kids come around looking all mopey-eyed, but guilt is easily the most short-lived emotion, especially when the society around you tells you that you are foolish for putting up with what doesn't make you happy. For what doesn't feel right for you. For what threatens your identity as an individual. For what, above all, doesn't seem *fair*.

So how *should* women today approach marriage? 5

For all the scorn that has been leveled against the marriages of the 1950s, those of us who are too young to have experienced them can only read about them with a kind of awe and — dare I say it? — wistfulness. Compared to today's frantic two-career households, the suburban married life that was deemed so stifling and unfulfilling a generation ago seems blissfully peaceful and affluent. The loyal, responsible, hardworking dads of that era, long ridiculed as insensitive drones, look like pure catnip to women fed up with the inconstant, immature men of our time.

Yet the feminists are probably right in believing that very few women — and very few men — could envision themselves returning to the starkly defined roles of the past. And that's not only because these roles feel, to a modern sensibility, thwarting and unfair. It's also because it would actually make no sense today for a woman to surrender her ambitions in order to run her home and raise her children. The reason it makes no sense, however, has less to do with women's attainment of sexual equality than it does with the fact that we live in an age when we can even consider lives unhampered by our biology. Until relatively recently, no woman — unless she was very poor — would wish to face working outside the home on top of everything else. True, ironing clothes with a red-hot piece of metal and cooking meals over a wood stove was not a very attractive destiny. But coal-mining in an unventilated shaft, or pulling wheat from the ground, or riveting girders thirty storeys up was, if anything, even worse. It's no accident that the most forceful and successful push for women in the workforce occurred at the same historical moment that the birth-control pill became available, childbirth was at last safe, antibiotics and healthier diets increased the average life span, and technological advances produced hundreds of thousands of jobs that could be described as pleasant or interesting, let alone "fulfilling." Today, no woman has to be "trapped" at home and confined to her role as mother — even if, in fact, she's traditionally minded and *does* decide to take five, ten, or even twenty years out of the workforce. Not only will she emerge from the experience a more youthful and fit person than her grandmother was, with many years of life ahead of her, but the advent of personal computers and the increasing flexibility of our economy are creating jobs she will be able to do from her living room or on a part-time basis when her children start school.

Perhaps we can't have — or don't want — the marriages of the past, but that doesn't mean that the basic centuries-old principles upon which marriage was founded have ceased to apply. As Tolstoy[2] reminds us, "If the purpose of marriage is the family, the person who wishes to have several wives or husbands may perhaps receive a great deal of pleasure, but in that case will not have a family." The different roles we assume as mothers and fathers, the different deals we wish to cut with each other in order to sustain these roles — these have persisted through thirty years of social revolution and beyond. What has not persisted is the society that recognized the mutual sacrifices husbands and wives make for each other, that understood marriage as an arrangement of give-and-take rather than quid pro quo.[3] A woman who had been happily married for fifty-two years told a *Washington Post* reporter that when she was wed, at twenty-one, "Divorce was not an option. You know, in those days, you couldn't say cancer out loud, you said the 'Big C.' Divorce was the same thing, you said the 'Big D,' you would never discuss it. It was a disgrace in the family. When you got married, we never said, 'Well, if it doesn't work out we could always end it.' People got married and that was that. After more than a half-century of marriage, I can also tell you that it is important to realize early on that no one person can give you everything that you want or need."

Unfortunately, there is no contemporary model for a marriage in which our modern belief in sexual equality could be reconciled with the inherent differences of our sexual natures. This is why, I suppose, women are so fearful about "going back": The only alternative to the obsessively egalitarian marriage of today that they can imagine is the rejected inegalitarian one of the past. They enter into their marriages clinging to their newfound identities and newly gained territories as tenaciously as break-away republics cling to theirs, fearful of surrendering a scrap of their independence lest the old country move in and take over again.

But it may be that in order for modern women to have the marriages   10
we want, we will have to stop being so preoccupied about our identities, and instead develop an appreciation for the mutual, if differing, contributions we make to marriage as men and women. Maybe what we should expect from our marriages is not so much an equality in kind but an equality in spirit. We want our husbands to love and respect us, to see us as their equal in all aspects of the mind and soul, but that doesn't mean we have to do exactly the same things in our day-to-day lives or to occupy identical roles. We must also understand that family has never been about the promotion of rights but about the surrender of them — by *both* the man and the woman. A wife and husband give up their sexual freedom, their financial freedom, their right to "pursue happiness" entirely on their own terms the moment they leave the altar. No matter what may come of their marriage, they have tied their identities — and fates — together. Through the act of having chil-

---

[2]*Tolstoy:* Leo Tolstoy (1828–1910), Russian novelist, author of *War and Peace.*
[3]*quid pro quo:* Latin phrase meaning "one thing in return for another." The phrase often has a negative connotation, as it does here, implying selfish and amoral bartering.

dren, they seal them. And this is what a woman today who takes her husband's name acknowledges with that symbolic act. She is hardly declaring herself his chattel. She is asserting, rather, that she and her husband have formed a new family, distinct from all their previous ties, both permanent and total in its commitment. It may seem arbitrary that they take the man's name instead of making up a new one or hyphenating both names like English nobles. But that is our custom, and it is by now a harmless one. (Matrilineal societies do exist, but this doesn't mean they necessarily have a superior record in the treatment-of-women department — ask the Spanish.) The husband's name, in any case, ceases to refer to just him and now reflects the combined personality of the family itself, like a newly merged corporation.

Alas, by withholding ourselves, or pieces of ourselves, instead of giving to our marriages wholeheartedly, we can't expect our husbands to do so, either. After all, it's not as if postponing marriage and going into it with our eyes more wide-open has made marriage any more stable than it was when men and women went into it practically blind. A young man I know told me that he'd "at last" moved in with his girlfriend of a few years. "We're more serious now," he said proudly. And I thought, No you're not. For marriage, as the married know, is about more than signing a lease, splitting bills, sharing chores, and professing a vague sort of long-term commitment; it's about more than being home in the evenings or spending weekends together or deciding what color to paint the walls; it's about more, even, than happiness and contentment and compatibility. It is about life and death, blood and sacrifice, about this generation and the next, and one's connection to eternity.

It is not nostalgic to wonder why this very obvious truth now seems to escape us; why so many men don't understand that it's wrong to walk out on their children and wives — or why so many women feel so nervous, so insecure, and so frightened about "losing themselves" the moment they marry. What is strange is that for so long we could be persuaded otherwise, that we could grow up mistrusting and steeling ourselves against so essential a human condition as love.

ENGAGING THE TEXT

1. This reading selection begins with Crittenden's claim that "nearly three quarters of Americans persist in believing that 'marriage is a lifelong commitment that should not be broken except under extreme circumstances.'" Explain why you do or do not share this belief yourself.

2. Discuss what grounds, if any, you believe a person should need to divorce her or his spouse. Don't worry about current law; focus instead on how you think things *should* work.

3. What is the feminist view of marriage, according to Crittenden, and what does she think is wrong with this view?

4. Summarize how Crittenden thinks women should approach marriage, then discuss the merits of this philosophy.

5. Crittenden refers to "the inherent differences of our sexual natures" (para. 9). What do you think she means by this phrase, and to what extent do you believe in such differences?

6. What is symbolized, according to Crittenden, by a wife taking her husband's name? What is your own view of this traditional custom?

EXPLORING CONNECTIONS

7. Near the end of this reading selection, Crittenden lists what marriage is and is not about (para. 11). Examine the paintings of Norman Rockwell (pp. 22–24) and discuss which ideas in Crittenden's list also show up in the paintings. For example, do any details in Rockwell's images suggest "blood and sacrifice"? Overall, how well does Crittenden's concept of family appear to mesh with Rockwell's?

8. Compare Crittenden's description of the 1950s family to that of Stephanie Coontz (p. 31). For example, how do they differ in emphasis? Are they ever flatly contradictory? Which description of family life in the 1950s do you find more sensible, plausible, or compelling?

EXTENDING THE CRITICAL CONTEXT

9. Think of a current TV show — soap opera, sitcom, or drama — in which marriage figures prominently. Examine how marriage is portrayed in this show, supporting your analysis with specific examples from several episodes. To extend the assignment, pool your response with those of other students to see if TV seems to reflect a cultural consensus about what marriage is or should be.

10. Create a questionnaire designed to probe current student ideas about marriage; focus on ideas you consider most interesting, controversial, or important. Respondents should be anonymous, but they should probably indicate their gender. If possible, give the questionnaire to another class taught by your instructor, then tabulate and analyze the results.

The Truly Invisible Hand

ANN CRITTENDEN

Who has the most to do with creating American wealth — entrepreneurs, CEOs, politicians, laborers, small business owners, investors — or is it perhaps mothers? Ann Crittenden argues that while Americans may love Mom (and apple pie), we don't begin to understand the true economic value of mothers' work, in part because traditional economic models wholly ignore it. Crittenden wants more than respect: she advocates changes in social and economic policy that would fundamentally challenge what she sees as the systematic exploitation of mothers. Crittenden (b. 1937) has written on fi-nancial issues for the New York Times, Newsweek, The Nation, *and many other publications. A Pulitzer Prize nominee, she is author of* Killing the Sa-cred Cows: Bold Ideas for a New Economy *(1993) and* The Price of Moth-erhood: Why the Most Important Job in the World Is Still the Least Valued *(2001), from which this selection is taken.*

> How did we ever come to believe that it was more important for some-body to have a meaningless job than to raise their children well? This doesn't make sense even in simple accounting terms.
> — ROBERT THEOBALD, in *Reworking Success*

The invention of the "unproductive housewife" still has tremendously negative consequences for women, and for our understanding of the true origins of our prosperity. If the creation of human capital that takes place in the home is not accorded any monetary value, then it is unlikely that it will be supported, or encouraged, or rewarded as it should be. And for that, everyone, not just caregivers and children, is the loser.

The assumption that the unpaid labor of child-rearing has nothing to do with the real economy was cast in stone as early as the 1920s. By that time the official decision had been made to include in measures of the United States' output only transactions in which money changed hands. When the first prototype of what later became the Gross National Product was devel-oped in the early 1930s, its calculations were limited to the total monetary value of goods and services that were sold. Services provided under any other terms did not, by definition, add to the national wealth and were therefore excluded from the GNP. Thus almost all of the activities of mar-ried women were omitted from the scorecard of capitalism.

Simon Kuznets, the statistician who developed the GNP (and won a Nobel prize for his efforts), clearly saw the limitations of his handiwork. In his very first report to Congress in 1934, Kuznets warned that "the welfare of a nation" can "scarcely be inferred" from the measurement system that was emerging.[1] The system could only measure *tangible* things, like tons of steel or bushels of grain, the number of fish caught or trees cut. *Intangibles*, such as improvements in a surgical technique, the value of clean water, or the care provided by a family member, could not be quantified. Social sci-ence had not progressed enough to be able to measure some of the most important things in life.

---

[1]Clifford Cobb, Ted Halstead, and Jonathan Rowe, "If the GNP Is Up, Why Is America Down?" *Atlantic Monthly*, October 1995, p. 67.

But the concept of the GNP was seductively simple, and by 1950 all of the world had adopted the same guidelines, later enshrined in the United Nations System of National Accounts. Sir Richard Stone, the man who was instrumental in developing the international system, was also subsequently awarded a Nobel prize, the only Nobel, ironically, that has never gone to a woman. The GNP (officially renamed the Gross Domestic Product in 1991) became the world's economic measuring stick. Today countries are competitively ranked according to their growth in GDP; that is, by their volume of *monetary* transactions.

Thus the great part of women's work does not figure. Nothing counts   5
unless it is bought and sold. This produces absurd perversities: a nurse feeding formula to a baby counts as a productive activity, but a mother's breastfeeding doesn't; care for an aging relative in a nursing home counts, while at-home care by an unpaid family member doesn't; paying bills and taxes and planning family investments counts when done by an accountant, but not when done by a spouse; charitable contributions of money are tax-deductible, but volunteer donations of time are not,[2] teaching twenty children in a classroom counts, while home schooling one's own children doesn't.

I once heard Marilyn Waring, New Zealand activist and the world's foremost advocate of putting unpaid work in the GDP, give a speech in which she asked the audience what kind of system would count a soldier sitting eight hours a day in a missile silo as usefully employed, but consider a mother taking care of two preschoolers "unoccupied." The answer was obvious: a system that devalues women.

Women have always had a hard time being "counted." The verb "to count" has several meanings: "to matter," "to make a difference," "to enumerate." Women have long been regarded as deficient in all of these ways, including the idea that they are not very good at math. But in the days when men were still the undisputed heads of the household, there was great respect for the activity that takes place in the home — and a recognition that it did, in fact, generate wealth. The very word "economics" derives from the Greek root *oikonomia,* the management of the household. Aristotle had the highest regard for oikonomia and made an important distinction between it and *chrematistics.* Oikonomia referred to the management of a household so as to increase its use value to all of its members over the long run. Chrematistics was the manipulation of property and wealth so as to maximize short-term exchange values.[3] The man who planted olive trees and built olive presses was practicing oikonomia; the man who leased all the olive groves in the winter and charged monopoly rates for renting them out at harvest time was practicing chrematistics. One activity enhanced future

---

[2]These examples are cited by Gloria Steinem in her book *Moving Beyond Words* (New York: Simon & Schuster, 1994).

[3] Herman Daly and John B. Cobb, Jr., *For the Common Good* (Boston: Beacon Press, 1989), p. 138.

productivity to the ultimate benefit of the community, while the other sought short-term gain for the individual. The man who practiced oiko-nomia was highly respected, whereas the chrematistic speculator was held in low esteem.[4]

These attitudes have been turned upside down. Much of what passes for economic activity in capitalism, from the seventeenth-century specula-tion in tulip bulbs to twenty-first-century stock market churning, is chrema-tistics. And what was once condemned as the vice of shortsighted self-aggrandizement has been transformed into a virtue.

Chrematistics found its rationale in classical economic theory, which casts "economic man" as the chief actor in the drama of wealth creation. Economic man is both the one who plants the olive trees *and* the one who rents them out, but in this new theory the moral differences between the two become irrelevant. The individual's pursuit of personal gain theoreti-cally adds to the sum total of riches. No matter how self-interested he may be, economic man's strivings to garner wealth for himself will be guided as if by an invisible hand to produce more resources than could ever be gener-ated by the well-meaning plans of government or the community.

This is what is called the "magic of the marketplace." The beauty of the   10 free market, according to Charles L. Schultze, economic adviser to Presi-dent Lyndon B. Johnson, is that it reduces "the need for compassion, patrio-tism, brotherly love, and cultural solidarity as motivating forces behind social improvement. . . . Harnessing the 'base' motive of material self-interest to promote the common good is perhaps the most important social invention mankind has achieved."[5]

But this satisfying scenario, assuring us that we can all be as selfish as we like and still be doing good, is only half of the story — the second half. In the beginning, we are all helpless babies, and another economic actor, "con-scientious mother," holds center stage. Without conscientious mother, there would be no economic man.

Here is another way the story of wealth creation might begin: Consci-entious mothers, motivated by feelings of compassion and love, nurture, protect, and train children for adulthood. Fathers, other female caregivers, and relatives may play a part in this process, but mothers have the primary role. Their altruism, and willingness to do all that they can for their off-spring, left unfettered, will be guided as if by an invisible hand to produce healthy children who will become the productive, enterprising economic men and women of the future.

Conscientious mothers, in other words, are the contemporary practi-tioners of oikonomia: the building and preservation of long term communal value that used to be the essence of economics.

---

[4]I am indebted to Rita Brock, director of the Bunting Institute in Cambridge, Massachu-setts, for calling my attention to the Aristotelian distinction between *oikonomia* and *chrematis-tics.*

[5]Quoted in Daly and Cobb, *op. cit.,* p. 139.

When I first met Virginia Williams in November of 1998, she was decked out in a colorful print dress, purple sweater, and a black stole covered with glittering musical notes. Her ample bosom was draped with necklaces, crosses, and a Star of David, tokens of her Catholic faith and a reminder of a great-grandfather who was Jewish. As I soon discovered, Virginia, a seventy-two-year-old African-American, was a one-woman rainbow coalition, if not a one-woman band. (Her business card identified her as "evangelist, singer, community activist.")

She and her late husband, Lewis, a fellow postal service worker, had raised eight children, including Anthony, who at that time was the Democratic candidate for mayor of Washington, D.C. Tony had been adopted at age three. As Virginia tells the story, a white postal office coworker kept bringing in pictures of his little foster son. "I looked at those pictures and I said, 'That's not a white child!' We later found out the boy's mother was white, an unmarried seventeen-year-old, and the father was black. Her family wouldn't let the girl keep the baby, and she had put him into foster care.

"I believe the foster father loved that child dearly. But I think his wife may have neglected him," she continued. "I worried about that, and about a black child growing up in a poor white neighborhood. I sent his picture around to all of my black friends who didn't have children, but not one would adopt him; they all had one reason or another. His head was a little bit disfigured from lying in the crib . . . and although he was three years old, he hadn't said a word yet. The foster parents had him tested, and the father told me they were going to send him to a home for retarded children.

"I knew that child wasn't retarded. I told my husband that I felt like God wanted us to have this child. Tony was exactly two years younger than my oldest, Lewis, and two years older than my second child, Virginia. I firmly believed that God had left that space for Tony.

"My husband thought I was crazy. We already had two young kids, and I was pregnant again. Our priest said I shouldn't do it; that it wouldn't be fair to our other children, who had very high IQs, to bring a retarded child into the house. But my husband said if you can get the money to adopt him, you can."

Virginia sang professional light opera whenever she could, and she raised money for the adoption by recording for the sound track of the film *Carmen Jones*. Only a couple of weeks after Tony came to live with the family, she had an inkling of what he had been through.

"I was changing the bed with the kids and the phone rang," she said. "I told them all to wait a minute in the hall, and I went to talk, and when I finally got back, about an hour later, the other two were long gone, but Tony was still standing there, alone, in the hall. That's when I knew that someone had abused that child. I got down on my knees and held him and cried. I never would let them test him after that."

The Williamses brought their children up as Catholics, and all attended parochial school. There never was any doubt that they would all go to college — "it was always *when* you finish college, never *if,*" she said — and they all did. Lewis is a graduate of MIT and a professor of economics at the University of California at Redlands. Tony, the "retarded" child, attended both Harvard and Yale and went on to acquire a reputation as a brilliant manager in several city governments, including Washington, D.C., where as chief financial officer he steered the city away from fiscal collapse.

Virginia, who throughout our interview answered her endlessly ringing telephone with a chirpy "Tony Williams's mother," readily admitted that her influence alone did not turn a mistreated orphan into one of the country's most prominent African-Americans. "I had plenty of help," she confided. Her own mother pitched in, as did her sister Myrtle, who had no children.

She was also blessed with a job that allowed her to take time off whenever she had to, even to travel on short singing engagements. And above all, she had a husband who worked nights and stayed home during the day, allowing him to be deeply involved with his family.

"When I married Lewis, in 1947, he said he wanted three things in life: to have six kids, to be married fifty years, and to live to be eighty. He got all three," she told me. Her husband, who died in 1998, was a strong moral influence. She described an incident that occurred when Tony was in the eighth grade. The boy had come home bruised and scratched, and told his parents that he had been hit by a car that had suddenly come barreling out of an alley. They subsequently learned from one of Tony's teachers that he was the one who had come barreling out of the alley, right into the path of the car.

Her husband sat Tony down and said, "I want you to tell the truth about how the accident happened." When the boy admitted that he had caused the accident, his parents asked why he had lied. "Kids told me we could get a lot of insurance money if it was the driver's fault," he explained, "and I know we can always use more money."

Lewis said nothing, but as Virginia tells it, the next day the insurance agent arrived, papers were signed, and the insurer turned over a check of several thousand dollars to her husband. He dramatically tore it up. "When we start needing money that bad, I'll let you know," he told his son. "You'll never lie to get anything and think that I'll appreciate it."

"That showed character," Virginia declared emphatically.

On the day of our conversation, the voters in the nation's capital, tired of a mayor who took drugs and let every basic city service deteriorate, essentially decided an election on the issue of character. Two-thirds of the voters cast their ballot for Tony Williams for mayor of Washington, D.C. It was quite a victory for a onetime retarded child, who had been headed for institutionalization as a ward of the state before Virginia Williams saw his picture.

This is not the kind of story you will read in an economics textbook. And Virginia Williams is not the kind of person who is celebrated as a source of national wealth. But her story suggests that something fundamental has been left out of conventional economics. She reminds us that altruism is a driving force in human betterment, and that "irrational" mother love, backed by steadfast fathers and supportive kin, makes the material world go round.

Human Capital

The quality of early care is one of the most important determinants of human intellectual and emotional capabilities. This is as clear as a summer sky over Texas. A large and growing body of research in child development has shown that care and guidance of the young child lays the essential groundwork for the formation of human knowledge, skills, creativity, and entrepreneurship.

Economics are also beginning to realize that human capital — or human capabilities — is an even more important component of a nation's riches than natural capital (land, minerals, water) or physical capital (bricks and mortar, machines, roads). In 1995, when the World Bank started to include estimates of human capital in measuring countries' wealth, the bank's first rough estimates turned up the surprising finding that 59 percent of the wealth in developed countries is embodied in human and social capital (that is, educational levels, skills, a culture of entrepreneurship). The remainder consists of natural resources (25 percent) and manufactured capital (16 percent). Since most natural resources are a given — you can't create more oil or arable land — this means that *in the wealthiest countries, human capital accounts for three-quarters of the producible forms of wealth.*[6]

Human capital is more important today than it has ever been. Skilled human beings are the raw material of the new economy, the key ingredient in the recipe for prosperity in the postindustrial age. Harris Miller, president of the Information Technology Association of America, has said that "running out of IT workers today is like running out of iron ore in the Industrial Revolution." Or as Wall Street economist Roger Kubarych once remarked, "Human capital is everything; look at Singapore" — a small and prosperous city-state whose only resource is its industrious population.[7]

If most of our national prosperity reflects the productivity of our human capital, then the people who provide primary care to children are the single most important source of our most valuable economic assets. Put another way, conscientious mothers are key players in the drama of economic growth, the stars who never receive top billing. This is the back story, still largely untold by the economics profession.

The profession remains stubbornly reluctant to think about the maternal contribution to the economy, prompting Shirley Burggraf to joke that most economists don't know where babies come from. The prevailing assumption is that the formation of productive skills *begins* with formal education, when a

[6]World Bank, *Monitoring Environmental Progress,* Washington, D.C., 1995.
[7]Roger Kubarych, personal communication, May 1996.

child goes off to school.[8] Somehow, in the abstract world of economics, curious babies spontaneously evolve into eager students, ready to read and write.

One of the most popular economics textbooks for college undergradu-   35 ates, for example, acknowledges that "recent research on economic growth has emphasized that human capital is at least as important as physical in explaining international differences in standards of living." But then the author, a Harvard professor, defines human capital as "the knowledge and skills that workers acquire through education, from early childhood programs such as Head Start to on-the-job training for adults."[9] Thus, with one stroke, he deletes thirty years of infant research showing that before formal learning can begin, there have to be years of nurturing, confidence building, creative play, and curious exploration, all under the guidance of caring mentors. Utterly undigested is the harsh truth, in the words of one child psychologist, that "beginning education at age five is too late."[10]

Even when psychologists identify some of the mechanisms by which mothers produce human capital, their findings are ignored by economists. In the 1950s, Harvard psychologist David C. McClelland became interested in the cultural and psychological underpinnings of economic growth and decline. In his 1961 book, *The Achieving Society,* McClelland described how child-rearing practices can inculcate the traits that make individuals and societies entrepreneurial.

He cited a group of studies that pinpointed what some mothers did to produce in their sons a drive for achievement, the principal character trait that has fueled the rise of modern capitalism. (Daughters were not included in any of these 1950s studies.) In one particular study of twenty-nine white middle-class families in the American Midwest, researcher Marion Winterbottom identified the child-rearing practices that explained why some boys had a notable drive for achievement by the age of eight, while others showed little or none. The mothers of the "high" achievement-oriented sons expected them to have more independence and mastery of various tasks. The boys were expected to do more for themselves, to make their own friends, to try harder in competitions. The mothers of the other boys reported putting more restrictions on their sons at the same age; that is, on playmates, entertainment, and on such decisions as how to spend their allowance and what books to read.[11]

---

[8]See, for example, Dale Jorgenson and Barbara Frameni, "The Accumulation of Human and Nonhuman Capital, 1948–84," in Robert Lipsey and Helen Stone, eds., *The Measurement of Saving, Investment, and Wealth* (Chicago: University of Chicago Press, 1989), pp. 227–85.

[9]N. Gregory Mankiw, *Macroeconomics* (New York: Worth Publishers, 1997), p. 109.

[10]Craig Ramey, quoted in Sandra Blakeslee, "Studies Show Talking with Infants Shapes Basis of Ability to Think," *New York Times,* April 17, 1997.

[11]Marion R. Winterbottom, "The Relation of the Need for Achievement to Learning Experiences in Independence and Mastery," in J. W. Atkinson, ed., *Motives in Fantasy, Action, and Society* (Princeton, N.J.: D. Van Nostrand Co., Inc. 1958), pp. 453–78; cited in David C. McClelland, *The Achieving Society* (Princeton, N.J.: D. Van Nostrand Co., Inc., 1961), pp. 46–49, 342–45.

Subsequent investigations confirmed Winterbottom's conclusions on the essential role of primary caregivers in instilling ambition, but these provocative findings have never been integrated into the study of economic growth.

The one economic theory to treat parents as serious economic producers is the "New Home Economics" developed by Gary S. Becker of the University of Chicago. Recognizing that a steady supply of skilled workers cannot simply be taken for granted, Becker decided to look deeper into the all-important question of how human capital is formed. He concluded what every parent knows: that families do the bulk of the work. He estimated that direct investments by families account for more than three-quarters of all investment in human capital.[12] Parental investments in their offsprings' "skills, health, learning, motivation, 'credentials,' and many other characteristics," he wrote, are even more important than schools or specialized training.[13]

But this pioneering effort to analyze the family as a serious economic enterprise became the butt of jokes within the profession. For years the New Home Economics was not taken any more seriously than the old home economics had been. (One earlier male writer on the family's economic contribution was condescendingly dismissed as a "potty chair" economist.) Becker was virtually ostracized by other economists, not because his portrayal of family dynamics was unrealistic but because he took activities within the family seriously at all. He finally earned the respect of his peers and was awarded a Nobel Prize in 1992. But many of his colleagues continue to brush off the issue of women's unpaid labor like a piece of lint on a fine dark suit.

40

ENGAGING THE TEXT

1. As long as mothers raise their children well, does it matter to you if the work is included in the gross domestic product? Why is it essential, in Crittenden's view, to assign mothers' work monetary, economic value even though mothers are not paid wages?

2. Explain the distinction Crittenden draws between "oikonomia" and "chrematistics," demonstrating your understanding of the terms by applying them to a few examples beyond those the author provides in paragraphs 7–9. Do you agree that the prevailing attitude in the United States today is opposite to the classical Greek ideal?

[12]Gary S. Becker, *Human Capital* (3rd edition) (Chicago: University of Chicago Press, 1994), p. 209.

[13]Shirley Burggraf has estimated that 95 percent of the costs of raising a child in the United States are borne by parents. This is why she calls the family the "greatest investment institution" in the country. [Shirley Burggraf, *The Feminine Economy and Economic Man: Reviving The Role of Family in the Post-industrial Age* (Reading, Mass.: Addison-Wesley, 1997) p. 64.]

Gary S. Becker and Nigel Tomes, "Human Capital and the Rise and Fall of Families," *Journal of Labor Economics* 43, pt. 2 (July 1986): S5.

3. What is the "magic of the marketplace," and what problems does Critten-den see with this paradigm?

4. Write a help-wanted ad specifying hours, duties, salary, and benefits for two parents. (To see such a hypothetical ad crafted by economist Shirley Burggraf, see p. 81 of Crittenden's book.)

5. Salaried workers often gain more than just wages from their jobs: they may get health or life insurance; they are entitled to set up tax-deferred retire-ment accounts; they can establish a good credit history; they earn Social Se-curity benefits. Discuss the justice and feasibility of extending any or all such benefits to unsalaried mothers.

EXPLORING CONNECTIONS

6. Read or review one or more of the selections listed below. Describe the child-rearing work women do in these pieces, evaluate how well they do it, and discuss how it could and should be valued.

> Gary Soto, "Looking for Work" (p. 26)
> Bebe Moore Campbell, "Envy" (p. 118)
> Melvin Dixon, "Aunt Ida Pieces a Quilt" (p. 131)
> Tony Cade Bambara, "The Lesson" (p. 404)
> Jamaica Kincaid, "Girl" (p. 421)
> Judith Ortiz Cofer, "The Story of My Body" (p. 433)
> Paula Gunn Allen, "Where I Come From Is Like This" (p. 443)

EXTENDING THE CRITICAL CONTEXT

7. Interview a mother — not necessarily your own — to get a rough idea of the work she did during one recent week. Explain what you learned to the class and assign a dollar amount to represent the value of the mother's work.

8. Drawing if possible on information from question 7 above, work in small groups to devise a plan to assign an economic value to mothering. (For ex-ample, should the value be based on hours worked or "on call," or perhaps on wages that could have been earned if not for child-rearing duties, or on results, or on what it would cost to hire someone else to do the work?) Re-port to the class on what progress you made and on what problems you en-countered.

9. In the concluding chapter of *The Price of Motherhood* (not reprinted here), Crittenden lists several steps that she thinks husbands, communities, busi-nesses, and the government should take to treat mothers more justly. Read her final chapter and summarize Crittenden's recommendations for the class.

From *Changing American Families*
Judy Root Aulette

Imagine that you had spent the last several years studying everything written about the American family in terms of gender, race, and social class. Many of the key things you would have learned are summarized in this selection. Author Judy Root Aulette synthesizes the conclusions of dozens of studies by other researchers, offering an extremely informative overview of how American families both reflect and help maintain social stratification according to race, class, and gender. Professor Aulette teaches at the University of North Carolina at Charlotte, in the Department of Sociology and Anthropology. This reading is taken from her book Changing American Families *(2002).*

Social Class, Race Ethnicity, and Gender and Family Life

The stratification systems of class, race ethnicity, and gender constitute a major feature of the macro level of social organization in our society. They exist beyond the control of any individual and are so pervasive they sometimes become invisible. But they weave in and out of our lives, sometimes overlapping, and sometimes contradicting each other, but always defining and shaping our lives and our relationships with others.

In this section, we will examine the way in which class, race, and gender create different experiences within families. The emphasis will be on the effect that the macro organization of our society, which includes these three systems of stratification, has on the micro level of society, the everyday experience of families. We will also observe the ways in which families respond to the macro system by helping to preserve inequality, attempting to survive in spite of inequality, and creating ways in which to resist inequality and thereby alter the institutions of inequality.

This section investigates different social classes and racial ethnic groups. Gender is also covered, as the section discusses how women and men relate to each other in families in various social classes and racial ethnic groups.

Upper-Class Families: Gatekeepers

Life in an upper-class family is not often open to scrutiny by the public or by researchers. As a result, less is known about the private lives of the members of this social class than of others. Rich people, however, know a lot about each other. Their preoccupation with maintaining boundaries between themselves and others has been noted by a number of scholars who have studied the elite (Domhoff, 1970; Eitzen, 1985; Mills, 1956). Families are a key way in which "membership" is identified. Being from a "good family" is essential and sometimes even overrides financial status. For example, when one of the "best families" loses its fortune, family members may be still counted as upper class, at least for a time, because of their ancestry (Bedard, 1992).

Georg Simmel (1907/1978) wrote that "Aristocrats would get to know   5 each other better in an evening than the middle class would in a month." He meant that wealthy people identify themselves by membership and background, while middle-class people identify themselves by individual achievement. Therefore, a person who knows the meaning of various memberships and connections among the upper class can draw a complete picture of a person. An essential piece of information in determining membership is family lineage.

Families play a critical role in keeping an individual in the upper class:

> The most important single predictor of a son's occupational status is his father's occupational status. A man born into the top 5% of family income had a 63% chance of earning over $25,000 a year in 1976 (being in the top 17.8% of family income). But a man born into the bottom 10% of family income had only a 1% chance of attaining this level (Braun, 1991).

Women in elite families play a special role in maintaining boundaries. "Women serve as gatekeepers of many of the institutions of the very rich. They launch children, serve as board members at private schools, run clubs, and facilitate marriage pools through events like debuts and charity balls" (Rapp, 1982).

Families also help maintain an individual's social standing among the wealthy class by teaching family members how to maintain their class position. For example, upper-class children learn not to "spend down capital" (Millman, 1991). This means that they should use only the interest, not the principal, of an inherited estate. The wealth that has been accumulated may have taken generations to acquire and is thought of as belonging to the family line, not to individuals.

Tax laws reinforce the idea that wealth belongs to all generations of a family rather than to individuals. Inheritance taxes can be reduced if the inheritance of an estate skips generations. When the inheritance is claimed only every other generation, taxes must be paid only every other generation. For example, if a wealthy person wills his or her estate to grandchildren rather than to children, one tax is paid rather than two (Millman, 1991). This increases the motivation to teach children to live on the interest and not to touch the principal and that the family fortune should be shared only within a small circle of kin.

Volunteer work is an especially important activity in the production and   10 maintenance of social status (Daniels, 1988). Susan Ostrander (1984) interviewed thirty-six upper-class women about their activities "to uphold the power and privilege of their class in the social order of things" (Ostrander, 1984, p. 3).

Marriage was one issue about which they spoke. One woman explained, "A compatible marriage first and foremost is a marriage within one's class" (Ostrander, 1984, p. 86). The women talked about debuts as critical events to ensure that their children met the proper prospective mates. Social clubs were also cited as places to keep themselves away from those the women referred to as "anybodies."

Athletic games and activities were also mentioned as important. The women believed that these activities enhanced the ability of their children to stay in their class. They spoke of the lessons of "discipline, confidence, competition, and a sense of control" (Ostrander, 1984, p. 94).

A good education in a prestigious upper-class school was another goal because of both the academic training and the social networks it afforded their children. The women spent much time planning and orchestrating all of these activities.

Upper-class families are largely responsible for maintaining their own position within the stratification system. They pass wealth down within families. They teach their children how to maintain their position, and they bring their children into the social institutions such as elite schools and clubs that further reinforce their membership in the class. Women play a special role in maintaining the class and especially the boundaries around the class.

Along with the maintenance of individual families within the class or the maintenance of the class itself is the maintenance of the system of inequality. In a system of finite resources where some have control over a large proportion of those resources, others have control over less. Resources are not distributed equally. Families are essential to the constant work of retaining those resources and creating relationships of difference and inequality between themselves and other classes. "The family as an institution ensures the continuity of the have-nots as well as entrenching the power and privilege of the haves" (Morgan, 1985, p. 214).

Middle-Class Families

Four factors characterize middle-class families: (1) geographical mobility resulting in residence away from kin; (2) replacement of kin with other institutions for economic support; (3) reliance on friendship rather than kinship for affective support and exchange; and (4) investment of resources lineally (Rapp, 1982).

In order to maintain their income, middle-class families may have to move around. For example, people in middle-class occupations are frequently asked to move when their company needs them to work at another site. Middle-class professionals may find that to get a raise or further their career they must take a job with another company in another state.

These moves remove them from extended family ties, and when economic help is needed middle-class people may rely on nonfamily sources. For example, a middle-class family that needs money for a down payment on a house would go to a bank for a loan. Both upper-class and working-class families might be more likely to seek assistance from their kin.

Middle-class families may also replace kin with friends in seeking emotional and social support. In the discussion of working-class families that follows, we will see how working-class people convert friends into kin in order to facilitate sharing material goods (Stack, 1974). Rayna Rapp (1982) argues that middle-class people do just the opposite. She states that middle-class people refrain from sharing with extended kin and maintain friendships that do not include sharing resources. In this way, middle-class families are better able to accumulate material wealth rather than dispersing it. Middle-class families stress upward mobility based on not sharing what they have accumulated (Millman, 1991).

The wealth that each relatively independent middle-class household is   20 able to accumulate is invested lineally — between parents and children — rather than laterally among extended family and close friends, as is the case in working-class households. Investing in education for their children and in extravagant wedding gifts are examples of the ways middle-class families share lineally (Rapp, 1982).

Geographic Mobility.   Americans have always been a mobile community, although today we are somewhat less mobile than in previous years. In the nineteenth century, 50 to 75 percent of the residents in any given town were likely to not be there ten years later. People born in the twentieth century were more likely to live near their birthplace than people born in the nineteenth century (Coontz, 1992). Nevertheless, one of the sources of the independence and isolation of contemporary middle-class families is the geographic mobility that accompanies their occupations. Every year about 45 million Americans move. More than half of these moves are for a job. Of interstate moves, 22 percent are for a job transfer, 19 percent are for a new job, 6 percent are to look for a job, and 3 percent are for what the Census Bureau calls "unspecified employment related reasons" (Hendershott, 1995).

Most researchers have looked at this issue as it exists in families where the husband needs to move because men are much more likely than women, especially married women, to move for work. The "typical" relocated corporate employee is a thirty-seven-year-old married man who owns his home, has two children, and works in sales and marketing (Hendershott, 1995).

These moves are experienced differently for women and men in families. The moves enhance the career of the husband for whom the move is being made, and many men seem to feel that moving is not a problem. Almost half of the men in one survey said that family ties pose no obstacle to their possible relocation (Harrison, 1991). When a man must move because his wife has found another job, however, his response is somewhat different. Research shows that a man will follow his wife only if she earns 25 percent to 40 percent more than he does (Lee, 1986). Although the moves are rewarding for men and the household they support, they also create hardship for wives and children. "Very few women do not suffer some losses as the result of a family move. These may include giving up friends, community and sense of self-worth and identity, close contact with relatives and often, a job or career possibility" (Gaylord, 1984). Children, especially those between the ages of three and five and the ages of fourteen and sixteen, also report emotional difficulties with moving (Seidenberg, 1973).

Much of the research on the "trailing wife" and the difficulty that relocation for a man's job causes for his family was done in the 1970s and 1980s. Hendershott (1995) reviewed relocation policies and surveys of more than five hundred companies in the 1990s and found that some factors have been altered more recently. She found that moving is not without stress, but that the focus of the older research on the disruption and loss caused by relocation overshadows the ways in which mobility creates improved economic opportunities for the moving families and at times even for the trailing spouse and children. In addition to the greater opportunities of the new job, some companies offer incentives for the move itself. For example, the FBI has given 25 percent cost-of-living increases and $20,000 bonuses to agents who move (Hendershott, 1995).

Hendershott (1995) also compared relocaters with "stayers," people who did not agree to relocate. She found that the stress of declining an opportunity that involved moving can be equal to the stress of accepting a move.

Another area of change Hendershott (1995) observed was an increase in the importance of elder care concerns. In a large 1993 survey of corporations, 25 percent said they believed that concern for employees about their older parents was growing in importance in decisions about relocation.

The Black Middle Class. Black middle-class families are similar to white ones in the focus of their lives on home and family (Bedard, 1992). Charles Willie's (1983) research on black middle-class families shows them to be achievement oriented, upwardly mobile, immersed in work, and with little time for leisure. Education, hard work, and thrift are perceived to be the means to achievement.

There are also some interesting differences between black middle-class and working-class families and white middle-class and working-class families. Attitudes about education are one example. Middle-class and working-class black families place an enormous amount of emphasis on education for their children because they perceive education to be the road to success and a way to overcome racial discrimination (Wilkinson, 1984). Lower-middle-class black families prioritize education and encourage their daughters to choose education over marriage (Higgenbotham, 1981).

In contrast working-class white families are more ambivalent and sometimes even negative about education for their children (Willie, 1985). They "worry that highly educated children will no longer honor family customs and maintain cohesion with their relatives" (Anderson, 1988, p. 177).

A second racial ethnic difference is the perception by black middle-class families of cultivating community responsibility: 30

> Middle-class black parents insist that their children get a good education not only to escape possible deprivations but to serve as symbols of achievement for the family as well as for the race. Each generation is expected to stand on the shoulders of the past generation and to do more. All achievement by members in black middle-class families is for the purpose of group advancement as well as individual enhancement. (Willie, 1988, p. 183)

In contrast, white families emphasize freedom, autonomy, and individualism. The negative feature of this emphasis is that individualism can shatter family solidarity and can lead individuals to display narcissistic attitudes and hedonistic behavior (Willie, 1988).

In the black middle-class family, "Individual fulfillment is seen as self-centered activity and therefore is less valued. What counts in the black middle class is how the family is faring" (Willie, 1988, p. 184). The down side of the emphasis on solidarity is that it stifles experimentation. Risk-taking is discouraged, and individuals may hesitate to try more experimental and creative activities.

Willie (1988) concludes that blacks and whites can learn from each other on this question. "Too much creativity has been stifled in middle-class blacks who have been trained to put family needs above personal needs. And too many individuals have drifted aimlessly in middle-class white families who have been taught to put individual freedom before collective concern" (Willie, 1988, p. 184).

The third difference concerns the question of gender equality. A number of studies have found a greater level of equality between husbands and wives in black families than in white families (Morgan, 1985; Middleton & Putney, 1960; Willie, 1983, 1985, 1988; TenHouten, 1970; Mack, 1978). . . . Black women are more likely to have been in the labor force than white women. Egalitarian ideologies are stronger among blacks than whites (Hunter & Sellers, 1998). Black men are more likely to share in housework and child care than white men (Anderson, 1988). Willie (1988) asserts that gender equality is a worthy goal and that black families have been pioneers in this effort. Therefore, he concludes, "the egalitarian family form is a major contribution by blacks to American society" (Willie, 1988, p. 186).

Working-Class White Families

White working-class families are characterized by three factors: (1) the ideological commitment to marry for love, not money; (2) the importance of extended kin and other networks to economic and emotional survival; and (3) the appearance of separation of work and family. Within each of these factors is a contrast between what people believe and what they really experience (Rapp, 1982).   35

Working-class couples marry for love. Person after person in Lillian Rubin's (1976) interviews of blue-collar couples said they had married for love and that love provided a way to escape from the difficulties of their parents' homes. One young woman recalled: "We just knew right away that we were in love. We met at a school dance, and that was it. I knew who he was before. He was real popular; everybody liked him. I was so excited when he asked me to dance, I just melted" (Rubin, 1976, p. 52).

In contrast, upper-class couples recognize their marriages as a way to preserve their class identity (Millman, 1991). Upper-class couples may marry for love, but they are conscious that love should only occur between themselves and others of their class. Middle-class people may also marry for love, but as we saw in the discussion above of middle-class families, the overriding task of middle-class families is also an economic one, to enhance the earning power of the breadwinner.

Working-class people are also affected by the economic realities of their lives. Working-class families must operate as economic units. The economic tasks of families are less a part of their dreams about marriage than they are a part of the reality of their married lives. "The economic realities that so quickly confronted the young working-class couples of this study ricocheted through the marriage dominating every aspect of experience, coloring every facet of their early adjustment. The women finding their dreams disappointed felt somehow that their men had betrayed the promise implicit in their union" (Rubin, 1976, p. 75).

The second characteristic of working-class families is the reliance on extended kin and others "to bridge the gap between what a household's resources really are and what a family's position is supposed to be" (Rapp, 1982, p. 175). Rapp (1982) says that working-class families are normatively nuclear. By this she means that they believe that independent autonomous families are the best form and that for the most part their families are independent and autonomous.

Observations of their real behavior, however, reveal much sharing of baby-sitting, meals, and small amounts of money, especially among extended kin (Rubin, 1976; Stacey, 1990). Sometimes these extended kin relationships became problematic, and half of the women Rubin (1976) interviewed said that the struggle over who comes first, a man's wife or his mother, was a source of contention between themselves and their husbands. For example, one woman told Rubin: "He used to stop off there at his mother's house on his way home from work and that used to make me furi-   40 ous. On top of that they eat supper earlier than we do, so a lot of times, he'd eat with them. Then he'd come home and I'd have a nice meal fixed, and he'd say he wasn't hungry. Boy did that make me mad" (Rubin, 1976, p. 88).

The third characteristic of working-class families is the appearance that work and family are completely separate. Blue-collar jobs do not include bringing work home, and one's occupation does not carry over into one's identity in the way a middle-class professional's might. But work and family are not entirely separate in the working class, where work affects family life and family affects the workplace. . . .

Working-Class African American Families:
The Moynihan Report and Its Historical Context
    . . . From the days of slavery up to the middle of the twentieth century . . . black families were a focus of the struggle of African Americans for equality. During slavery, African American people fought plantation owners and the slave system for the right to marry and live with their spouses and children. During the sharecropping period, black families struggled for the right for wives and mothers to devote time to their families instead of working for whites. As industrialization developed, African American women moved from the farms to the cities to take jobs as domestics. Here they challenged their employers for the right to work shorter hours to spend time with their husbands and children.

In the last half of the twentieth century and into the twenty-first, African American families continue to be a volatile political issue. Some have blamed African American families for a myriad of urban problems. . . . Advocates of African American families have fought back, expressing an alternative point of view. They argue that black families have been scapegoats and are not to blame for poverty and civil unrest. Furthermore, they argue, black families have been the victims of poverty and inequality caused by structural problems.

One important event in this history was the publication of a U.S. Labor Department report entitled *The Negro Family: A Case for National Action* (Moynihan, 1965), commonly called the Moynihan Report after its author, Daniel Patrick Moynihan, the senator from the state of New York.

The 1950s and 1960s were an important period in American history   45
because of one of the most significant social movements in the twentieth century, the Civil Rights Movement, which protested the unequal treatment of African Americans in the United States. Civil rights activists argued that socially powerful institutions like the legal system, government, schools, businesses, and landlords had created poverty and injustice in the black community. In 1965 the Moynihan Report appeared with an alternative point of view.

The Moynihan Report blamed the dilapidated housing, poverty, unemployment, and inferior education experienced by African Americans on the organization of black families. Where the civil rights movement saw these same problems and found their cause in the racism of the most powerful sectors of society, Moynihan blamed the victims.

Moynihan argued that black families were disorganized and female dominated. He maintained that black men were humiliated and emasculated by domineering black women. According to Moynihan, the only hope for saving the black family and therefore the community was to reestablish black men as the rightful heads of their families (Giddings, 1984). Moynihan wrote: "Ours is a society which presumes male leadership in private and public affairs, a subculture such as that of the Negro American, in which this is not the pattern, is placed at a distinct disadvantage" (quoted in Gresham, 1989, p. 118). In order to overcome this disadvantage, the Moynihan Report advised "that jobs had primacy and the government should not rest until every able-bodied Negro man was working even if it meant that some women's jobs had to be redesigned to enable men to fulfill them" (Giddings, 1984, p. 328).

The Moynihan Report also suggested that if black men were to take their rightful place as head of the family and community, they would need to bolster their skills in behaving in a properly masculine manner. Moynihan suggested they join the army: "There is another special quality about military service for Negro men: it is an utterly masculine world. Given the strains of the disorganized and matrifocal family life in which so many Negro youth come of age, the Armed Forces are a dramatic and desperately needed change: a world away from women, a world run by strong men of unquestioned authority" (Moynihan, 1965, p. 42).

Moynihan reframed the debate around civil rights so that the opposing sides were no longer African Americans versus an unrepresentative government or poor people versus the power structure. New lines were drawn by the Moynihan Report between black men and black women over who would have access to scarce jobs and who would dominate in families.

Several scholars and the African American community in general re- 50 acted critically to the Moynihan Report. People like Joyce Ladner (1971), Andrew Billingsley (1968), and William Ryan (1971) led the debate against Moynihan's assertions (Giddings, 1984; Rainwater & Yancey, 1967).

One of the most controversial features of the report concerned the so-called "black matriarchy." The term *matriarchy* means rule by the mother. At the core of Moynihan's argument was the characterization of African American women as dominant authoritarian figures, matriarchs. Robert Staples (1981) actively attacked this idea, calling black matriarchy a myth. He asked, if black women are so dominant and powerful, why do we not see great numbers of black women in Congress, and why do we continue to see black women earning less than white men and women and black men?

Staples argued, furthermore, that when we see black women actively working to ensure that their children are fed and when we see black women fighting shoulder to shoulder with black men for integration, education, and civil rights, we should be proud, not critical. Staples commented: "While white women have entered the history books for making flags and engaging in social work, black women have participated in the total black liberation struggle" (Staples, 1981, p. 32).

Carol Stack (1974), an anthropologist, decided to systematically investigate Moynihan's thesis by doing fieldwork in a low-income black neighborhood she called the Flats. Her work became one of the most influential alternative views of poor black families (Katz, 1989).

The Flats.   Were African American families in the Flats disorganized matriarchies? This was the question with which Stack began her research. After two years of observing and interviewing the residents of the Flats, Stack (1974) concluded that the families there were neither nuclear nor male dominated. Nor were they disintegrating, nonexistent, or matriarchal. Instead, Stack found families that were complex organized networks characterized by five factors: (1) kin and nonkin membership, (2) swapping, (3) shared child raising, (4) fluid physical boundaries, and (5) domestic authority of women.

Networks were composed of both kin and nonkin — parents, siblings, 55 cousins, aunts, uncles, and grandparents, as well as nonkin who became "like family" because of their extended interaction and support of network members. After living in the Flats for two years and sharing rides and child care, even Carol Stack was integrated into the network as a member of the family and began to be called sister by one of the women in the Flats. When people change friends into family, as the people in the Flats did with Carol Stack, sociologists call them fictive kin (Gittens, 1998).

The stereotypical middle-class white family is bound together through blood or legal relationships of marriage and adoption. In the Flats, people recognized these ties. More importantly, however, familial networks in the Flats were also bound together by social relationships based on swapping.

Swapping.   *Swapping* refers to the borrowing and trading of resources, possessions, and services. In times of need, a member of the network could rely on other members for money, food, clothes, a ride, or child care. In return the member was obligated to share what he or she had with those in need. Because resources were scarce, people in the Flats constantly redistributed them in order to survive.

Stack describes an example of a swapping network. The description illustrates the many different kinds of resources that are swapped and the complex system that keeps those resources moving in an efficient and fair manner:

> Cecil (35) lives in the Flats with his mother Willie Mae, his oldest sister and her two children, and his younger brother. Cecil's younger sister Lily lives with their mother's sister Bessie. Bessie has three children and Lily has two. Cecil and his mother have part-time jobs in a cafe and Lily's children are on aid. In July of 1970 Cecil and his

mother had just put together enough money to cover their rent. Lily paid her utilities, but she did not have enough money to buy food stamps for herself and her children. Cecil and Willie Mae knew that after they paid their rent they would not have any money for food for the family. They helped Lily by buying her food stamps, and then the two households shared meals together until Willie Mae was paid two weeks later. A week later Lily received her second ADC check and Bessie got some spending money from her boyfriends. They gave some of this money to Cecil and Willie Mae to pay their rent, and gave Willie Mae money to cover her insurance and pay a small sum on a living room suite at the local furniture store. Willie Mae reciprocated later on by buying dresses for Bessie and Lily's daughters and by caring for all the children when Bessie got a temporary job. (Stack, 1974, p. 37)

Bloodmothers and Other Mothers.   Child keeping is a special form of swapping in the Flats and other black communities (Collins, 1990). Poverty makes it difficult for parents to care for children alone. In addition, the value of community responsibility is historically rooted in the culture of West Africa and the slave community of the South. Sharing child care in the black community is common, with various adults in addition to the parents sharing or entirely taking over the responsibility for raising a child.

Sometimes child keeping may be shared among parents and other adults for a short time. In other cases it may be for an extended period of years. Sometimes the child lives with one adult at a time. In other cases the child is literally shared, staying in one residence one night and another the next, or eating with one adult and sleeping in the home of another. 60

Children do not see this as being without a real parent but rather as having a number of real parents. Adults, likewise, do not treat their children differently depending on whether they are their natural children or network children. Rather, among many African Americans, adults feel a sense of responsibility for all children in the community (Collins, 1990)).

Household and Family.   The domestic networks that comprise the families in the Flats are often spread over several addresses. On the other hand, people who are not nuclear family members may "double up" within a household. Where people sleep and eat and where they contribute money for the rent or spend their time is not necessarily concentrated in one physical location. The physical boundaries of families in the Flats are fluid. They range over several addresses; they change; and they overlap.

In middle-class nuclear families, in contrast, households and families tend to be the same. Nuclear family members live in a single family home, and other people do not live with them. A person who assumes that nuclear families are the only possible way in which to organize a family might look at families in the Flats and conclude that no family existed. A more careful examination, however, reveals that a family form does exist, although it is quite different from that of the middle-class nuclear family.

Extended Network Families in Racial Ethnic Communities. Child sharing among an extended network family is not unique to African American communities. John Red Horse (1980) describes this kind of family organization in some Native American societies. He explains: "An Indian family, therefore, is an active kinship system inclusive of parents, children, aunts, uncles, cousins and grandparents and is accompanied by the incorporation of significant non-kin who become family members" (Red Horse, 1980, p. 463).

Red Horse notes that sharing in the Native American community is 65 sometimes informal, as it is for African Americans in the Flats, but also may be formally marked by naming rituals. In naming ceremonies, which may occur immediately after birth or later in a child's life, the child is given a name and an adult is chosen as the namesake. After the ceremony, the adult is responsible for the child and is obligated to set a good example and to help care for the child or to take over child care completely if the parent is unable to care for the child.

In the Chicano community, a similar system of shared child raising occurs, called *compadrazgo* (Dill, 1986). Many parents designate nonkin, *compadres*, as godparents (*padrinos* and *madrinas*). Godparents celebrate holidays and important rites of passage like first communion and marriage with their godchildren. They are also relied on for economic and social support in times of need to substitute in case of the death of a parent (Camarillo, 1979).

Asian American families, especially those that are recent immigrants to the United States, also rely on networks of kin and nonkin (Hein, 1993; Lockery, 1998). Jon Matsuoka (1990) explains that among Vietnamese and other Southeast Asian immigrants, a quickly expanding population, extended family includes not only those who are currently alive but ancestors and families of the future. Children are taught that their primary duty is to their family lineage. The dominant American ideology that emphasizes the individual and his or her place in a nuclear family has been problematic for Asian immigrants who believe that one's connections are much broader (Kitano & Daniels, 1988). Asian families illustrate the way in which child sharing not only implies a broad range of people who are responsible for children but also a range of people to whom children are obligated.

Women's Domestic Authority. This description of life in the Flats indicates that Moynihan's (1965) portrayal of the black community as one in which families were disrupted or chaotic was false. The families in the Flats were quite different from the stereotypical middle-class white family. But they were highly organized and provided a source of survival in an impoverished community.

Moynihan (1965) also proposed that black families were matriarchal. Stack (1974) investigated this issue as well and concluded that women in the Flats were not matriarchal.

In a matriarchal society, power over households and the community as   70
a whole is controlled by older women. . . . The Flats was not matriarchal
because women were not powerful in the community. Power in the Flats
was wielded by landlords, employers, and especially the government
through the welfare office.

Stack found that women in the Flats also did not have matriarchal relationships with the men in their network families. Women had more authority relative to men than women in white middle-class, male-dominated nuclear families. But decisions in the Flats tended to be made by groups of
people that included both women and men in the network. In more general
overviews of the question of the black matriarchy, no empirical data have
been shown to support its existence (McAdoo, 1988).

Immigrant Families

The percentage of the population living in the United States that was
born in another country was highest, about 14 percent, at the turn of the
nineteenth century. It fell steadily to a low of about 4.5 percent in 1970,
when it began to rise, reaching 8 percent in 1990. The proportion has never
been huge, but immigrants have been and continue to be an important part
of our population.

Earlier in the century, most immigrants came from Europe. Today
most come from Latin America and Asia. Mexico represents the largest
source country, with 13 percent of immigrants. It is followed by the Philippines (7 percent), Vietnam (6 percent), Dominican Republic (5 percent),
China (5 percent), and India (5 percent). Most immigrants are concentrated
in the following states: California (23 percent), New York (18 percent),
Florida (9 percent), Texas (7 percent), New Jersey (6 percent), and Illinois
(5 percent) (Littman, 1998).

Mexican Americans.   Until the middle of the nineteenth century, the
areas that we now call the states of New Mexico, California, Nevada, Utah,
Arizona, as well as most of Texas, half of Colorado, and a little bit of Oklahoma, Kansas, and Wyoming were part of Mexico. The Texas War of Independence and the Mexican-American War resulted in 814,145 square miles
of land becoming part of the Untied States (Russell, 1994). The people who
lived in those areas included many Mexicans and Native Americans as well
as Anglos who had migrated there before annexation. Since then, many
Mexican people born in the currently Mexican area have migrated into the
formerly Mexican area.

. . . Through births and continued immigration, the proportion of the   75
population that is Hispanic is predicted to grow from about 12.5 in 2000 to
about 25 percent in 2050. These data include people from many other Latin
American nations besides Mexico, but . . . , Mexican Americans make up a
significant percentage of the total Latino population.

Immigrant families face special kinds of problems. Julia Rodriguez (1988; see also Zavella, 1987) studied women who came north both to follow their husbands who were seeking work and to find jobs themselves. Their emigration from Mexico depended on their ability to obtain support from relatives and friends in Mexico who could help them obtain documents, pay for travel, and arrange for child care. In addition, some had to find child care for children they left temporarily in Mexico while they moved to the United States.

Once they arrived in the United States, the women quickly worked to become familiar with their new communities and to establish new networks to exchange goods. They also needed to establish information networks because of their special needs as new immigrants or undocumented workers so as to find employment, housing, health care, and schools in a new environment.

This kind of migration, which takes place in steps with some members following others, is called family stage migration (Hondagneu-Sotelo, 1997). Hondagneu-Sotelo (1997) has found that the process of migration creates change in gender relations within families. She reviews two periods of migration: pre-1965 and post-1965. In the 1950s and 1960s, ideas about what is properly masculine gave men the authority to act autonomously to decide to migrate. Gender expectations also told men that they were supposed to be good providers and therefore had to choose to leave their families. Properly gendered women had to accept their husband's decision, remain chaste, and stay behind to take care of the children despite their fears of becoming *mujer abandonada* (an abandoned woman) or being unable to handle the financial and social burdens of raising a family alone. After the 1970s, expectations about gender changed, and women were more likely to follow their husbands rather than stay behind.

Before 1965, men had come mostly unaccompanied and had stayed for long periods of time in bachelor communities in which many men shared households. Men learned to do work that had been reserved for women, like cooking, cleaning, and shopping. One man explained:

> Back in Mexico, I didn't know how to prepare food, iron a shirt, or wash my clothes. I only knew how to work, how to harvest. But when I found myself with certain urgencies here, I learned how to do everything that a woman can do to keep a man comfortable. And the custom stayed with me. . . . I now know how to prepare American food and Mexican food, while back in my country I didn't know to cook at all. Necessity forced me to do things which I had previously ignored. (Hondagneu-Sotelo, 1997, p. 480)

The men expressed pride in their newfound talents and continued to share these tasks when their wives joined them. At the same time, the long periods during which wives had been forced to take charge while their

MORE NONTRADITIONAL FAMILY UNITS

Guy, Chair, Three-Way Lamp

A Woman, Her Daughter, Forty-four My Little Ponies

The Troy Triplets and Their Personal Trainer

Two Guys, Two Gals, Two Phones, a Fax, and a Blender

R. Chast

Drawing by R. Chast © 1992, The New Yorker Magazine, Inc.

husbands were away changed them as well, making them more assertive and less subservient. One woman explained:

> When he came here [to the United States], everything changed. It was different. It was me who took the responsibility for putting food on the table, for keeping the children clothed, for tending the animals. I did

all of these things alone, and in this way, I discovered my capacities. And do you know, these accomplishments gave me satisfaction. (Hondagneu-Sotelo, 1997, p. 479)

In households where the men had migrated after 1965 and their wives   80 had quickly joined them, these kind of gender transitions had not occurred. The pre-1965 migrants' households were strikingly more egalitarian than the post-1965 households (Hondagneu-Sotelo, 1997).

Vietnamese Immigrant Families.   Vietnamese families have described similar experiences (Kibria, 1996). Traditional Vietnamese families were modeled on Confucian principles that organized extended families around a patriarch. Young brides joined their husbands' households, where they had little status and were subordinate and dependent on their husbands (Kandiyoti, 1988). If the wife lived long enough, however, she could expect in her old age to take her place at a higher level in the household hierarchy and enjoy deference and allegiance from younger members. This model began to change in Vietnam in the 1950s and 1960s as a result of the war.

Migration to the United States further challenged the traditional model for two reasons. First, Vietnamese women were more likely to find employment in the United States than men were, which created a shift in power that benefited women. Second, women began to organize social networks to help them survive in their new communities. They exchanged food, information, and strategies to use to negotiate institutions like social services, hospitals, and schools. The networks also became useful ways to control men inside households. For example, if men were abusive or tried to keep their wives from working outside the home, network members would intervene by mobilizing community opinion against them.

Kibria (1996) argues that these changes altered the patriarchal relations but did not transform them. Gender inequality remained intact despite immigration, although it was renegotiated. Access to economic resources improved for women, but such resources were too limited to provide independence. In addition, women themselves often wanted to maintain the old system because it allotted authority over children to them in their old age, which they did not wish to give up.

References

Anderson, Margaret. 1988. *Thinking about women: Sociological perspectives on sex and gender.* 2d ed. New York: Macmillan.

Bedard, Marcia. 1992. *Breaking with tradition: Diversity, conflict and change in contemporary American families.* Dix Hills, NY: General Hall.

Billingsley, Andrew. 1968. *Black families in white America.* Englewood Cliffs, NJ: Prentice-Hall.

Braun, Denny. 1991. *The rich get richer: The rise of income inequality in the U.S. and the world.* Chicago: Nelson Hall.

Camarillo, Albert. 1979. *Chicanos in a changing society: From Mexican pueblos to American barrios in Santa Barbara and Southern California, 1848–1930.* Cambridge, MA: Harvard University Press.

Collins, Patricia Hill. 1990. *Black feminist thought: Knowledge, consciousness and the politics of empowerment.* New York: Harper Collins.

Coontz, Stephanie. 1992. *The way we never were: American families and the nostalgia trap.* New York: Basic Books.

Dill, Bonnie Thornton. 1986. *Our mother's grief: Racial ethnic women and the maintenance of families.* Memphis, TN: MSU Center for Research on Women.

Domhoff, William. 1970. *The higher circles: The governing class in America.* New York: Random House.

Eitzen, D. Stanley. 1985. *In conflict and order: Understanding society.* 3d ed. Boston: Allyn and Bacon.

Gaylord, Maxine. 1984. Relocation and the corporate family. In R. Voydanoff (ed.), *Work and family: Changing roles of women and men* (pp. 144–152). Palo Alto, CA: Mayfield.

Giddings, Paula. 1984. *When and where I enter: The impact of black women on race and sex in America.* New York: Bantam Books.

Gittens, Diane. 1998. The family in question: Is it universal? In S. Ferguson (ed.), *Shifting the center: Understanding contemporary families* (pp. 1–12). Mountain View, CA: Mayfield.

Gresham, Jewell. 1989. White patriarchal supremacy: The politics of family in America. *Nation* 249 (4):116–121.

Harrison, Lee. 1991. California report. *Personnel Journal* 70 (October):26.

Hein, Jeremy. 1993. *States and international migrants: The incorporation of Indochinese refugees in the U.S. and France.* San Francisco: Westview.

Hendershott, Anne. 1995. *Moving for work: The sociology of relocating in the 1990s.* New York: University Press of America.

Higgenbotham, Elizabeth. 1981. Is marriage a priority? Class differences in marital options of educated black women. In P. Stein (ed.), *Single life: Unmarried adults in social context* (pp. 259–267). New York: St. Martin's Press.

Hondagneu-Sotelo, Pierrette. 1997. Overcoming patriarchal constraints: The reconstruction of gender relations among Mexican immigrant women and men. In M. Baca Zinn, P. Hondagneu-Sotelo, and M. Messner (eds.), *Through the prism of difference: Readings on sex and gender* (pp. 477–485). Boston: Allyn and Bacon.

Hunter, Andrea, and Sherrill Sellers. 1998. Feminist attitudes among African American women and men. *Gender and Society* 12 (1):81–99.

Kandiyoti, D. 1988. Bargaining with patriarchy. *Gender and Society* 2:274–291.

Katz, Michael. 1989. *The undeserving poor: From the war on poverty to the war on welfare.* New York: Pantheon.

Kibria, Nazlia. 1996. Power, patriarchy and gender conflict in the Vietnamese immigrant community. In E. Chow, D. Wilkinson, and M. Baca Zinn (eds.), *Race, class and gender: Common bonds, different voices* (pp. 206–222). Thousand Oaks, CA: Sage.

Kitano, Harry, and Roger Daniels. 1988. *Asian Americans: Emerging minorities.* Englewood Cliffs, NJ: Prentice Hall.

Ladner, Joyce. 1971. *Tomorrow's tomorrow: The black woman,* Garden City, NY: Doubleday.

Lee, Dwight. 1986. Government policy and the distortions in family housing. In J. Peden and F. Glahe (eds.), *American family and the state* (pp. 310–320). San Francisco: Pacific Research Institute.

Littman, Mark, ed. 1998. *Statistical portrait of U.S.: Social conditions and trends, 1998.* Lanham, MD: Bernan Press.

Lockery, Shirley. 1998. Caregiving among racial and ethnic minority elders: Family and social supports. In E. Stanford and F. Torres-Gil (eds.), *Diversity: New approaches to ethnic minority aging* (pp. 113–122). Amityville, NY: Baywood.

Mack, Delores. 1978. The power relations in black families and white families. In R. Staples (ed.), *The black family* (pp. 144–149). Belmont, CA: Wadsworth.

Matsuoka, Jon. 1990. Differential acculturation among Vietnamese refugees. *Social Work* 35:341–345.

McAdoo, John. 1988. Roles of black fathers in the socialization of black children. In H. McAdoo (ed.), *Black families.* Newbury Park, CA: Sage.

Middleton, R., and S. Putney. 1960. Dominance in decisions in the family: Race and class differences. *American Journal of Sociology* 65 (6):605–609.

Millman, Marcia. 1991. *Warm hearts and cold cash: The intimate dynamics of families and money.* New York: Free Press.

Mills, C. Wright. 1956. *The power elite.* London: Oxford University Press.

Morgan, David. 1985. *The family, politics and social theory.* Boston: Routledge and Kegan Paul.

Moynihan, Daniel. 1965. *The Negro family: The case for national action.* Office of Policy Planning and Research, U.S. Department of Labor. Washington, DC: GPO.

Ostrander, Susan. 1984. *Women of the upper class.* Philadelphia: Temple University Press.

Rainwater, Lee, and William Yancey. 1967. *The Moynihan Report and the politics of the controversy.* Cambridge, MA: MIT Press.

Rapp, Rayna. 1982. Family and class in contemporary America: Notes toward an understanding of ideology. In B. Thorne with M. Yalom (eds.), *Rethinking the family: Some feminist questions* (pp. 168–187). New York: Longman.

Red Horse, John. 1980. Family structure and value orientation in American Indians. *Social Casework: The Journal of Contemporary Social Work* 59:462–467.

Rodriguez, Julia. 1988. Labor migration and familial responsibilities: Experience of Mexican women. In M. Melville (ed.), *Mexicanas at work in the U.S.* (pp. 47–63). Houston: University of Houston Press.

Rubin, Lillian. 1976. *Worlds of pain: Life in working class families.* New York: Basic Books.

Russell, James. 1994. *After the fifth sun: Class and race in North America.* Englewood Cliff, NJ: Prentice Hall.

Ryan, William. 1971. *Blaming the victim.* New York: Random House.

Seidenberg, R. 1973. *Corporate wives — corporate casualties?* New York: Amacon.

Simmel, Georg. (1907/1978). *The philosophy of money*. London: Routledge and Kegan Paul.

Stacey, Judith. 1990. *Brave new families: Stories of domestic upheaval in late twentieth century America*. New York: Basic Books.

Stack, Carol. 1974. *All our kin: Strategies for survival in the black community*. New York: Harper and Row.

Staples, Robert. 1981. The myth of the black matriarchy. *Black Scholar*, December, 32.

TenHouten, W. 1970. The black family: Myth and reality. *Psychiatry* 25:145–173.

Wilkinson, Doris. 1984. Afro-American women and their families. *Marriage and Family Review* 7 (Fall): 459–467.

Willie, Charles. 1983. *Race, ethnicity and socioeconomic status: A theoretical analysis of their interrelationship*. Dix Hills, NY: General Hall.

Willie, Charles. 1985. *Black and white families: A study in complementarity*. Bayside, NY: General Hall.

Willie, Charles. 1988. *A new look at black families*. 3d ed. Bayside, NY: General Hall.

Zavella, Patricia. 1987. *Women's work and Chicano families: Cannery workers of the Santa Clara Valley*. Ithaca: Cornell University Press.

ENGAGING THE TEXT

1. Review the distinguishing characteristics Aulette associates with upper-class families — for example, volunteering and learning not to spend down capital. Explain how these practices function to mark and maintain social status. Also discuss how well these characteristics match your own impressions of upper-class families — based on personal experience or on portrayals of the wealthy in books, TV, and movies.

2. In paragraph 16, Aulette associates four factors with middle-class American families. If possible, test these four factors against the family histories of your classmates. For example, do you find "geographical mobility resulting in residences away from kin"? Taken as a whole, does the students' experience support the significance of the four factors Aulette identifies?

3. Working in groups, make a large version of the chart below and fill in the rows and columns with the characteristics Aulette says researchers have discovered.

	Middle Class	*Working Class*
White Families	**(Example)** Huge emphasis on education	Ambivalence about education
Black Families		

What evidence can you find in your reading or personal experience to support or challenge these generalizations? What useful purpose, if any, is served by such generalizations about family, class, and race?

4. Describe the significance of the Moynihan Report, and summarize the problems or errors Aulette identifies in the report. (Note in particular Aulette's extensive summary of research carried out by Carol Stack in "the Flats.") Then discuss how Moynihan's analysis of black families could be so influential if it was indeed so seriously flawed.

EXPLORING CONNECTIONS

5. Read "Envy" by Bebe Moore Campbell (p. 118). How closely does the family depicted there resemble the families in the Flats as described by Carol Stack (paras. 54–71)? What details in "Envy" suggest that Campbell's family was or was not a low-income family like those Stack studied?

6. Read "An Indian Story" (p. 109). Cite specific ways in which the family described in Roger Jack's narrative fits or fails to fit Aulette's brief description of Native American families (paras. 64–65).

7. Look at the photo "Affluence" on page 293. List a dozen or more details that Aulette would say marks the man's upper-class status. To what extent can you connect these details to the man's family life?

EXTENDING THE CRITICAL CONTEXT

8. Aulette describes many family types in the selection above. Which type or types offer the best fit to your own family? Explain how Aulette's generalizations reflect your individual family, and describe any ways in which your family is unlike the pattern researchers see.

Visual Portfolio

READING IMAGES OF AMERICAN FAMILIES

HDTV. It's A Joy.

Simply from Samsung. For the digital generation. High-Definition Television. The ultimate viewing experience from the world leader in extrasensory reception. Picture and sound so clear, you won't believe your eyes and ears. Samsung's Tantus HDTV is the finest high-definition (1080i resolution), 55" widescreen (16:9 display design), fully-integrated system you can buy. Samsung circuitry transforms your regular television signal into absolute clarity. And the 45-watt Dolby Digital* system makes it sound-sational. A dreamlike experience: reality will never seem the same. Tantus HDTV. The beginning of a new era in home entertainment. For more information on Samsung's full line of digital televisions, call 1 800 SAMSUNG or visit our web site at www.samsungdigital.com

SAMSUNG
DIGITAL

Visual Portfolio
Reading Images of American Families

1. The first image in the portfolio shows a family posing for a group photo-graph. What might be the occasion for this photo? Who do you think the people are, and what are their relationships? What impressions do you get about them from their facial expressions, their clothing, and the room and its furnishings? In terms of its messages about family, how closely does this image resemble those painted by Norman Rockwell that appear on pages 22–24?

2. The photograph of Thomas Jefferson's descendants is clearly posed. Ex-plain in detail why you think photographer Erica Burger constructed the image as she did.

3. The photograph on page 85 encompasses more than 250 years of American history, from Thomas Jefferson's birth in 1743 to 1999. What parts of American history can you link to specific details in the photo? What does the photo say to you about the next century of American history?

4. What ideas and emotions do you think are most strongly projected by the image of the gay fathers on page 86? What elements of the photograph help convey these ideas and emotions? Compare this image to "Freedom from Fear" by Norman Rockwell (p. 24) in terms of its portrayal of mar-riage and parenting.

5. First, describe your initial reaction to the photograph of the lesbian brides; for example, did it surprise you or work against your expectations? Next, tell the story of this picture: discuss what's happening and find out if your classmates "read" the photo in the same way you do. Explain the signifi-cance of as many details in the image as possible — for example, gowns, fa-cial expression, setting, and background. This photograph was published with the caption, "Love and Marriage"; explain why you think it is or is not a good title for the image.

6. What is the emotional impact of the photograph of a woman bathing her child in a washtub in the kitchen? What do you feel when you see this image, and why? Why does the photographer consider this moment worthy of our attention?

7. One of Samsung's objectives (p. 89) is to grab your attention with a dra-matic and unusual image: you have presumably never seen a 55-inch TV atop a baby carriage. But why does the company choose, of all things in the world, a baby carriage? Analyze Samsung's strategy and explain what the image and the strategy imply about the American family. Also discuss the caption, "HDTV. It's A Joy."

8. Compare any of these contemporary images to one or more of the Norman Rockwell paintings that opened this chapter (pp. 22–24). What questions does this comparison raise?

Talking Freaks: Lesbian, Gay, Bisexual, and Transgender Families on Daytime Talk TV

JOSHUA GAMSON

As previous selections have shown, the mythical "model family" carries with it a number of powerful cultural messages. One of the most important of these messages is that families are founded on heterosexual relationships; the myth is not well equipped to accommodate gay marriage or lesbian parenting, for example. In "Talking Freaks," this chapter's media selection, Joshua Gamson studies the cultural battles over family and sexuality that are waged on daytime talk shows. Gamson (b. 1962) is a professor of sociology at the University of San Francisco and the author of Claims to Fame: Celebrity in Contemporary America *(1994) and* Freaks Talk Back: Tabloid Talk Shows and Sexual Nonconformity *(1998). His work has also appeared in numerous academic publications and in* The Nation, *the* Utne Reader, *and the* New Yorker. *"Talking Freaks" appeared in* Queer Families, Queer Politics: Challenging Culture and the State *(2001), edited by Mary Bernstein and Renate Reimann.*

The thing we constantly ask ourselves is, "Is this something our audience can relate to?" So whereas lesbian issues aren't something that maybe middle America, you know, maybe the housewife with three kids who's in Kansas City isn't that related to, but yet she can understand a mother-son relationship. I think that people can kind of relate to what it must be like to be going through something like that and have to deal with your children. Or like coming out to your parents and friends. It's not necessary that everyone can relate to being homosexual, but people can relate to having to reveal something to your parents, reveal something to your friends, that's going to potentially cause problems.

—*Leeza* executive producer NANCY ALSPAUGH[1]

Springer had a person who had a sex change, and they dragged his family on there. His two sons saying, "We ain't going to talk to him

---

[1]This chapter works from transcript, video, and interview data collected for a book-length study, *Freaks Talk Back* (Gamson 1998). Although only a small portion is discussed here, the data consist of the following: in-depth, semi-structured interview with twenty talk-show production staff and forty-four talk-show guests; quantitative and qualitative content analysis of the 160 available transcripts in which lesbian, gay, bisexual, and gender-crossing subjects made a significant appearance, for the years 1984–86 and 1994–95; and interpretive analysis of about one hundred hours of talk-show videotapes. The data cover experiences on nearly every topic-driven daytime talk show that has had a life. Unless otherwise noted, quotations are from interviews conducted by the author in 1995 and 1996.

anymore." And his little eleven-year-old daughter stands up in the audience, says, "I don't want to ever see him again." And Springer stands up with his last five-minute little comment and says, "If you're thinking about having one of these things and you brought kids into the world, why don't you just keep your pants on until they're grown up and out of the house and then do what you're going to do." That was an outright attack on our community and we are desperately trying to dry up his supply of transgenders. They'll still find people. They're going to have to find an awful lot of rogue people, though, people that aren't connected, because anybody who's connected with anything, we're going to basically say, "This show is quarantined."

—transsexual activist and former talk-show guest CHERYL-ANN COSTA

Queer parents, parents of lesbians, cross-dressing teenagers and their mothers, married gay couples adopting children, drag queens and their sisters: queer family relationships, while emerging in a strained and limited way in the political arena, are all over daytime television. Family politics, in fact, are emerging not in an arena of cultural silence in daytime entertainment genres but in one of exploding cultural visibility, of ongoing chatter, testimony, and display. Now that Ellen's coming-out episode[2] is already a distant memory, and drag queen Ru Paul holds court on *The Hollywood Squares,* and prime-time sitcom *Will and Grace* boasts the first gay male title character, and both gay-male "best-friend" characters and chic lesbian bars are becoming movie clichés, it is time to revisit the politics of visibility. We are clearly in the midst of an explosion of visibility for gay, lesbian, bisexual, and transgender people in commercial-media culture. Even though plenty of Hollywood stars remain closeted (Signorile 1993), much of what is happening seems to be right in line with what many of us have craved personally for years, and organizations such as the Gay and Lesbian Alliance Against Defamation (GLAAD) have pursued politically for years. It has been something of a sacred cow[3] in gay-media studies and politics that more exposure is the goal (Fejes and Petrich 1993; Gross 1989; Russo 1987), and now we are getting that. But looking at representations of lesbian, gay, bisexual, and transgender families on daytime television talk shows complicates the question of visibility just a bit — and now is an especially important time to do so.

On a collective level, the desire for visibility is especially powerful for marginalized groups, whose public images are often minimal or wildly distorted. Since contemporary lesbian and gay identities began forming earlier in this century, cultural visibility has been a central concern for lesbian, gay, bisexual, and transgender people, who have been subject to the charge that they do not exist, and many of whom, since queerness is not marked on the

[2]*Ellen's coming-out episode:* On April 30, 1997, the leading character of the TV comedy *Ellen* (played by Ellen DeGeneres) came out of the closet.

[3]*Sacred cow:* Something accepted as beyond criticism, often without good reason.

body, can and do choose to be invisible. The positive effects of visibility are quite plain: "Cultural visibility can prepare the ground for gay civil rights protection," as Rosemary Hennessy sums it up, and "affirmative images of lesbians and gays in the mainstream media . . . can be empowering for those of us who have lived most of our lives with no validation at all from the dominant culture" (1994/95:31–32). In the case of political struggle for the recognition of a diversity of lesbian, gay, bisexual, and transgender family forms, for instance, the fact that such families *exist* on their own terms, and the stories that get widely told about where sex- and gender-nonconformists fit in "the family," are clearly important. The desire to be recognized, affirmed, validated, and to lay the cultural groundwork for political change, in fact, is so strong it has tended to inhibit careful analysis of the dynamics of becoming visible.

A number of things recommend talk shows as a place to look at visibility processes. For one, in a sense they paved the way for the kinds of publicity we are seeing now: they have been really the one place in commercial media where we, since the 1970s, have been consistently visible. It is no accident that Oprah Winfrey played Ellen-the-character's therapist in the famous 1996 coming-out episode, and that Ellen-the-star chose Winfrey's show as the one on which to first appear with then-girlfriend Anne Heche. On a certain level, "queers" rule these shows (Gamson 1998a; Shattuc 1997). More important, they offer a case in which transgendered people, lesbians, bisexuals, and gay men are, at least partially and potentially, *agents* in their own visibility. Beyond their obvious exploitative and sensationalist nature, that is the twist talk shows provide: people playing themselves. A close look appropriately messes up conventional thinking about visibility. What kinds of visibility does television provide, and for whom exactly, and on what terms? Might "positive" images also be "negative" ones? Just what kind of cultural environment underwrites the politics of the family?

It is with these more general questions in mind—what is, can, and should be going on with cultural visibility—that I turn to the representation of families in the talk-show genre. As anyone who has watched one of these shows knows, "family" is a topic of particular interest to talk shows. One dominant format, especially now, is programming that features families in conflict; more generally, producers, aiming primarily at women for whom everyday marriage and family relationships are central, routinely produce their programs by putting such family issues at the center. In the culture at large, put simply, sexual "deviants" have been seen as aliens within families or outcasts from them, biologically incapable of reproducing (Weston 1991); on talk shows, families with queers in them, and queer families, can usually be counted upon for a certain amount of conflict, and are thus constants.

In fact, "family" is the firm, beating heart of daytime talk TV. As a genre   5
that is highly domestic, in which chattering people in pseudo-living rooms make their way into actual living rooms, and a genre targeting primarily

women at home, there is a constant return to the concerns of family life. "In the end," as Jane Shattuc has argued, "the shows depend on the nuclear family as their mainstay. . . . Almost every show plays upon the fear and loss and the triumph and return of the nuclear family" (1997:45). That mainstay is and has been an opening for sexually nonconforming people — who are parts of families and make trouble for them — one major source of lesbian, gay, bisexual, and transgender visibility on these shows, a visibility that simultaneously gives voice and exploits. It is also the source of a major tension on the shows: between promoting "acceptance" and "tolerance" of different sorts of family members and protecting the underpinnings of the heterosexual, monogamous, nuclear family, in which people of "opposite" sexes make exclusive emotional and sexual commitments to one another, divide up tasks (at least loosely) along gender lines, and rear children together.

As I move into the details of this picture, I want to expand on this tension between "normalizing" and "freakifying" our families. Talk shows do this, I will argue, by on the one hand working with a loosely liberal ideology while on the other hand establishing a new, updated, culturally conservative version of "normal" families that includes gays and lesbians while programming transgendered and bisexual people as too selfish and monstrous for the family. This is another important reminder that our visibility is shot through with a politics of division (Gamson 1998b; Schacter 1997). The cultural visibility strategies to which family politics are attached must take these divisions carefully into account.

Talk Shows, Class, and Families

> The show was about people who can't accept their gay relatives, and my job was to sort through all of the things that had just been seen on the air and try to come to some sort of understanding. . . . So it's about five minutes into the show, and I realize that they have on a collection of the most incredibly dysfunctional people from rural parts of the United States. People who have never been on television before and are saying the most horrific, hateful things to each other. Mother to daughter, lesbian lover to the mother-in-law, half-brother to brother. And I'm watching this thinking, "How am I ever going to go out there and make any sense of any of this?" One guy yelled, "The only pussy you've ever seen is the cat that crawled across the floor in your house," and "my fucking daughter this and that." Every other word was "fuck." Then they introduced a mother and her straight daughter and they interviewed the lesbian daughter — they haven't seen each other in I don't know how long — and her lover. There was screaming back and forth. "You're not my child. They must have mixed up the babies at the hospital." And the sister says, "She's ruined her life. They took the children away because of the lover." Terrible things back and forth. Then they brought out a sister and brother, Hispanic sister and brother. And, "fucking this," and "fuck that," and "he borrows my clothes and I'm going to get AIDS from the clothes." And

then Sally introduced two boys, sixteen and nineteen, straight kids from the mountains of Tennessee, who had the most horrible things to say about gay people. They were there because their brother was going to be on the show. Well, they introduced the brother and the lover. They came out holding hands, swish onto the stage, throw themselves in their chairs and tongue kiss. But they were worked up too, they were angry and they were told to do whatever, and they're not going on with any particular agendas. And I thought, "We're in great shape now."

—Writer and *Sally* guest ERIC MARCUS

   The recent history of the TV-talk genre offers the first indicators of the kinds of divisions on which talk-show visibility depends. The talk-show genre has always combined the rational, "propriety"-oriented styles of public participation associated with the middle classes with the more emotional, "irreverent" public culture associated with American lower classes. There is nothing inherent in class background, of course, that dictates how one behaves in public, nothing inherently rational about middle-class people or inherently emotional about working-class ones. Yet historically, to boil it down to its simplest, class cultures developed — typically by defining themselves against one another — such that rationality became the more common middle-class public participatory strategy and emotionality became the stronger base of working-class public participation (see DiMaggio 1991; Habermas 1991; Levine 1988; Peiss 1986).

   Talk shows joined the two, exaggerating each through various strategies and routines (guest and audience recruitment, programming frames, guest and audience coaching, host styles, and so on). In the earlier days of the genre, when the *Donahue*[4] model dominated, and continuing in some programs today, primarily white, middle-class, highly educated, organizationally affiliated guests came on to talk "rationally" about issues, either in debate or testimonial format. More recently, beginning in the 1990s with *Ricki Lake, Jerry Springer,* and their imitators — who targeted a younger, more racially and socioeconomically diverse audience — primarily unaffiliated, working-class and poor people of many colors with little education come on TV mainly to argue emotionally about interpersonal relationships (Gamson 1998a; Grindstaff 1997; Shattuc 1997). The genre has thus more or less split into two subgenres: one dependent on an exaggerated middle-class "social controversy" and "service" culture, the other on an exaggerated working-class and underclass "interpersonal conflict" culture; one relatively polite and taking itself quite seriously, the other unapologetically and playfully rowdy.

   "Class" takes its place on TV-talk shows not so much through explicit discussion — a rarity in American popular culture in general — but through its embodiment, often amplified by the programs, in both studio audiences and guests. Occupational markers may be provided (a guest presented and labeled as "lawyer" or "truck-lift operator"), but class backgrounds mostly

---

[4]*Donahue:* One of the first and longest running (1967–1996) daytime TV talk shows, hosted by Phil Donahue.

come across through widely recognized markers such as their language use, levels of emotional effusiveness, gestures, the conditions of their bodies and teeth, and their clothing and hair styles. There may be occasional ambiguity, and we are not talking about class in any strict sociological sense, but for the most part it is safe to say that viewers know that on programs such as *Leeza* they are encountering middle-class people and discourses and on programs such as *Springer* they are encountering working-class or poverty-class people and discourses (Grindstaff 1997). These class-based divisions are the foundation on which talk-show representations of the family are constructed — and it is typically the "trashy" shows (read: the shows with guests and audiences who are not middle-class) that are criticized for giving lesbians, gay men, bisexuals, and transgendered people, among others, a bad name (Gamson 1998b).

For a taste of the differences, compare two 1995 programs on gay and lesbian parenting. The first, in the middle-class salon style, is hosted by former *Taxi* star Marilu Henner, whose guests — presumably recruited, as on this brand of shows they tend to be, through organizational networks — are various lesbians and gay men raising kids. No one is there to oppose them, no right-wing bigot to argue about recruitment and seduction and America's vulnerable children, and both host and audience are politely supportive. The guests are dressed in professional suitlike garb, the audience members are generally quiet, showing themselves through applause and asking informational questions; very little slang is used, and everyone speaks in the words and cadences of the college educated.

Everyone at this *Marilu* show pretty much agrees that loving families are a good thing. The implicit and sometimes explicit model of family offered, not surprisingly, is the one exemplified by the chosen guests: a liberal revision of the "normal" (and normative) mainstream, two-parent, middle-class nuclear family. Good parenting takes love, Henner suggests in her opening, and "it really shouldn't matter what color skin a parent has, or what religion they are, or even what their sexual orientation is, as long as a parent can raise a child with love and understanding." The rest of the show is structured to back up that thesis. Jeff, a white gay man in a suit and tie, an amiable cantor, talks about his adopted daughter ("a little Gemini," crows Marilu) and the women who help raise her and makes jokes about prejudice ("I don't make eggs in a gay way"). Debra, a blonde lesbian professional in a smart suit and pearls, talks about finding a "darling guy" in a Beverly Hills hair salon to donate sperm, quotes Thoreau, and praises her children's school ("the parents know we're gay, and nobody cares, and that's beautiful"), explaining that the "only negativity I feel is from Lou Sheldon[5] and Newt Gingrich,"[6] and so on. The parents talk of spiritual paths and praying

[5]*Lou Sheldon:* The Rev. Louis P. Sheldon, founder of the Traditional Values Coalition.
[6]*Newt Gingrich:* Republican congressman from Georgia, a prominent conservative spokesman in the 1990s.

before dinner and "normal families" and "journeys of learning." Debra explains how when she began looking for "alternatives to how I could have children," it was still a pioneering area. "You probably made it easier for a lot of the people who were doing it," Marilu observes, to which Debra responds:

> Yes, I did. It was very scary to get into that, but one of the reasons I'm on this show twelve years later to discuss it is because it's worked out in such a positive way, and my children are wonderful and they're happy and they're thriving. So it was an experiment that's worked out in a very positive manner. So I think it's important that we share that with the world, when the radical right is trying to actually talk to us about family values and their family values.

"Mmm hmm," Marilu says, smiling and nodding. "Cause this looks like a family to me." There's a brief pause, and then the camera pans a calmly applauding audience—applauding, apparently, for the integration of lesbians into standard middle-class family forms, for a lesbian family that still "looks like a family to me" (Perpetual Notion 1995). This show, with its unthreatening, professional, woman-in-pearls/man-in-suit, clean-talking, articulate guests (and host, and audience) could have been scripted by GLAAD. But are these "positive" images?

The newer breed of shows, on the other hand, routinely recruits guests through toll-free numbers rather than through organizations, and attracts a crowd with little familiarity with a movement agenda; different kinds of queer families show up here. Consider, for instance, the class and ethnic markers in Eric Marcus's description, quoted in the epigraph to this section, of the rather typical *Sally* show on which he appeared as the middle-class, mainstream counterpoint: the bleeped-out swearing, the "Hispanic sister and brother," the "dysfunctional" guests from "the mountains of Tennessee," the public display of tongue kissing. Or consider a 1995 *Ricki Lake* show, which, despite the various markers announcing that the guests are not middle-class professionals (a straight-woman-versus-lesbian-mothers set from Arkansas, facing off in indelicate language about whether "a child of gay parents can grow up normal"), at first appears to be only a slight, personalized adaptation of the bigotry-is-bad programming of the *Donahue* years. When a panelist complains that the lesbians' kid will not know what is normal, Lake, in a sharp navy pants suit, gets a serious, slightly impatient look on her face, as though she is speaking to a small, somewhat bratty child. "But that's just it, what *is* normal, Lorraine?" Asked by Lake why straight couples can sit on the same sofa and hold hands at her house while the lesbians cannot, Lorraine says she is not ready to explain it to her kids. "What is the difference?" says Ricki. "They love each other. It's not like they're spewing hate everywhere. What *you're* doing is spewing hate telling them it's wrong to love someone." Applause from the audience. Bigots bad, lesbians good.

That is, until a "bad" lesbian mother shows up. Karen, a fifteen-year-old heterosexual African American, is there to tell her mother, Helen ("bartender, Illinois," says her caption) and her mother's Latina lover, Marie ("I'm a mechanic, I work in construction," she says to audience applause) that she thinks "being gay or lesbian is disgusting." Helen, in black leggings, big earrings, and a sparkly blazer, reports that she has seven kids, and speaks angrily, unapologetically, and colloquially — she is about as far as you can get from the middle-class lesbians on *Marilu* — about how this is "something Karen has to deal with," and how "her opinion doesn't matter to me, I'm happy, I made a choice to be with a woman and I'm not ashamed of it." The sympathy, not surprisingly, quickly moves toward the daughter, who confesses to Ricki that she was so bothered by her mother's lesbianism that she once tried to take her own life. The audience responds with cooing sympathy, and Helen becomes a lightning rod for audience hostility during the rest of the program, while various other guests do their shtick: a lesbian who doesn't think gay people should parent; a white gay man with discolored teeth who wants children bickering with a large straight woman who complains that he goes through his lovers like he changes his underwear; circuit-conservative Paul Cameron (a discredited psychologist from the right-wing Family Research Institute) who trades "facts" with certified homosexual Gabriel Rotello — the latter two, in professional outfits, clearly representing middle-class expertise. Helen spars with guests ("What society tell her to feel, I don't care"), with Lorraine ("How many daddies have your kids had?"), with her own daughter, and most of all with Cameron ("We up here to talk about *why* are peoples against it"). "Just because you got on a suit and tie and you got what they got a manhood down there," she spits at Cameron, "what make you so *normal?*"

One does not often see or hear from working-class lesbians of color raising children in American mass culture; on TV-talk shows, however, they make regular appearances. And Helen's arguments are not much different from those of white, college-educated gay activists — "normal" is often a synonym for "in power," homophobia not homosexuality is the social problem, lesbians and gays are as entitled to fulfillment as straight people, and so on — albeit in a different language, and in brief, hard-to-catch outbursts. Yet Helen herself is booed largely because of her presentational style, is not sympathetic, has a bad attitude, and most of all is a *"bad mother,"* (Paramount Pictures 1995a), lacking the "enlightened" parenting techniques advocated by middle-class experts. In the terms encouraged by the program, Helen lacks "class"; indeed, her status as a relatively poor, relatively uneducated woman of color makes it quite easy for class and racial hostilities to attach to hostilities toward nonnormative family forms, the whole package dismissed as selfish, unfair, inhumane.

Now, are these negative images? The newer, rowdier type of talk show, 15 with its anyone-can-be-a-star recruitment strategies and its strategy of giving the stage to people from marginalized class and racial positions (in order to exploit them, of course), has meant, for instance, a tremendous diversification in the available images of families on these shows. It is no longer just white and middle-class people who are shown creating queer families or dealing with lesbian, gay, bisexual, or transgender family members. For another thing, it has meant that a much more aggressive, noisy, challenging, "in your face" approach to families of origin — *What makes you so normal?* — and to gay, bisexual, transgender, and lesbian people's roles in families and as parents has taken the stage. Activists interested in establishing the similarity of gay families to "normal" ones through their closeness to the middle-class mainstream, that is, have lost control of the discourse. The model of the lesbian or gay family that makes its way onto the screens on these kinds of shows thus includes, on the one hand, a much wider range of classes and races within it than one finds almost anywhere in American media culture, and these guests from marginalized class, ethnic, and racial statuses often present themselves with extraordinary strength, articulateness, and power; on the other hand, the lower status of the guests as poor, often not white, *and* queer, their heavily marked class positioning in a world where middle class is normative, their setting-off against representatives of middle-class family values, means that they and their families are easily dismissed as "dysfunctional" and not "respectable." The class division of talk shows has made the question of "positive" and "negative" family images harder to answer, in large part because it amplifies the question of just whose version of lesbian mother, or gay father, or transsexual daughter, or bisexual son is going to get air time. Whether one thinks the changes in the genre are good or not, they provide another important reminder of the divisions playing out as our visibility increases. Just whose families get to be seen as "ours"? Just whose "family values" get to be presented as ours? Any path to visibility must face down these questions.

Therapeutic Liberalism and the Vulnerable Child

These people are going to repeat the same thing, that if God wanted to create Adam and Steve he would have, blah blah blah. It's all been said and done before, so how are we going to advance it? You never get anywhere. You're never going to change the Bible thumpers. Never. No matter what you do. So why make that the issue of an hour show? It is one of those issues that people are so entrenched religiously, emotionally. How are we going to *maybe* change some of their minds? How are we going to *maybe* create tolerance? The only way you do it is not inherently make that the focus of the hour, not making it a right or wrong issue. It's not like it's right or wrong, it's more like, "Can this mother accept her son's gay lover?" It's like we're taking the assumption that the mother is accepting the son is gay. What you do is take real people that have real family concerns and they in particular want to try to get over it. Or they themselves within the two of them, the son and the mother, want to have some sort of peace. Like, "My mom kicked me out because I'm gay," okay. We're talking about individuals now. We're not talking about the issue of gayness. We're talking about an issue where a son wants to be able to go back into the house because he loves his mother. The mother can't accept the fact that he's gay. That goes beyond saying, "Is gay right or wrong?" We have a family in a crisis.

— Daytime talk show executive producer

Representations of gay, bisexual, lesbian, and transgender parents and family members are shaped not just by these two talk-show models but also by a more general ideological tension inherent in the genre: between a liberal-sexual ideology that eschews secrets and a conservative-gender ideology expressed in a concern for the creation of gender-normal boys and girls. On the one hand, talk shows — whether the older, more sedate *Donahue*-style or the newer, hipper *Ricki* style — are very receptive to the argument that family members must love and accept their homosexual children. This is in part because the shows operate with a loose ideology of liberal pluralism: we are all different, live and let live, tolerate and respect the rights of others to be who they are (Carbaugh 1989). This pluralist tone gets wedded, moreover, to therapeutic values — disseminated by hosts such as Oprah Winfrey — which give an extra push toward tolerance (White 1992). Speech and disclosure are cleansing and healthy, confession is good for the soul; at all costs, talk, you'll feel better. Given the profit-making strategies of the shows, this liberal, therapeutic ideology (once again, a feature of what can loosely be called bourgeois culture) makes good sense: for TV talk to work, everyone must be allowed to speak, or yell, regardless of their position; appeals in the name of tolerance, understanding, free speech, and mental health give this talk at least the appearance of a purpose.

Crass and cynical as it can be, this therapeutic-pluralism-turned-entertainment is much more sympathetic to liberal approaches to gay and lesbian families and family members (and sometimes to transgender and bisexual ones) than to conservative condemnations of it. The result, in fact, is often that the bigot who can't accept a family member becomes the pariah, and the accepting family member becomes the hero. *Donahue,* for instance, programmed a show on gay teens by bringing on a young man whose father tried to kill him after discovering his son was gay; a sixteen-year-old whose mother put him in a mental hospital because he's gay, along with the boy's mother and stepmother; and a nineteen-year-old lesbian and her mother. "We got to get rid of this closet," Donahue declares, typically. One boy, rejected by his biological family, talks about how he has "developed my own family," his surrogate parents, two men. The next tells how his mother called him a "little faggot" and then institutionalized him; she, contrite and ashamed, talks about how "I would say terrible things to him like that and I didn't realize the pressure he was going through," and the grandmother steps in to say "it's a matter of unconditional love." The young lesbian's mother, the last of the family guests, talks about how "you can either reject your child, you can tolerate your child, or you can accept your child," and gets in a plug for Parents and Friends of Lesbians and Gays (PFLAG) just before a brief interview with the associate executive director of Hetrick Martin, a New York City organization serving gay, lesbian, bisexual, and transgender youth. The audience is courteous and sympathetic. The show is quite explicitly programmed to model "acceptance" of gay and lesbian kids and even to give information about how to go about it (Multimedia Entertainment 1994).

Ricki Lake has taken this kind of show to its extreme, often by programming class-inflected lessons in tolerance. Writer and ACT UP[7] veteran Michelangelo Signorile, for instance, took the role usually given to a therapist, holding forth from a thronelike chair on a show whose title, "I'm Gay, Get Over It!" even recalls Queer Nation's[8] "We're here, we're queer, get used to it!" Various family members denounce their gay relatives, refusing, in Lake's terms, "to accept you for who you are": Tammy tells her sister Pam, a butch lift-truck operator from Georgia, that Pam doesn't know what she's missing ("I know what I'm missin', but I know what I'm a-gittin', too," Pam responds); a grandmother says she knew there was something wrong with her grandson when he was born ("Not wrong, just different," corrects Lake). "Michelangelo, can you educate her?" Lake says, turning to Signorile. "Michelangelo, enlighten us," which he does, telling this one to love her child and that one that there's nothing she can do about it. Not only was there no antigay, don't-accept-your-children "other side" but, in a twist that has some of the sweetness of just desserts, the militant gay activist had become the one dispensing advice to unloving family members, the gay son elevated to the therapist's throne (Paramount Pictures 1995c). "Remember," Lake says to the camera in her final word, sitting casually on the steps of the stooplike stage, after a series of people have been blasted by the audience and other panelists for objecting to gays coming near their kids, "children are not born to hate and fear, they are *taught* to hate and fear" (Paramount Pictures 1995b). Any moral condemnation of gayness that takes place within this kind of "love and accept your gay children" show is at a distinct disadvantage.

A general, self-interested constitutional hostility toward closets, toward secrets that are left unrevealed, leads many talk shows to tilt, regardless of their class compositions and class strategies, toward a welcoming of lesbian and gay family members. Yet, on the other hand, despite the repeated

---

[7]*ACT UP:* The AIDS Coalition to Unleash Power, an activist group "united in anger and committed to direct action to end the AIDS crisis."

[8]*Queer Nation:* Activist group of the 1990s that protested homophobia and promoted gay and lesbian visibility.

attacks the shows facilitate on the myth that homosexuals recruit children, or ruin them, or are never found in preadult forms, a ubiquitous concern for the fate of "the children" of gays and lesbians also continuously shows up and competes for primacy. Again, this is as much a production-driven concern as an ideological one: the shows target primarily a female audience, often presumed to be mothers (middle-class or not), by programming from the point of view of a generic, heterosexual "mother." The arguments that queer kids should be accepted just like any other, and that children should not be taught to hate and fear gay people, are, in fact, just particular versions of the more general argument that children need parental protection and that families ought to provide safety rather than threat. Often, such a logic is turned against lesbians, gay men, bisexuals, and gender-crossers — especially when the issue of gay parenting comes up anywhere on the shows — triggering repeated expressions of worry by audiences for "the children." Significantly, although much of it is fueled by religiously based opposition to homosexuality in general, and in some cases simply repeats the charge that children of gay people will turn out to be gay themselves (and that such a fate is undesirable), the underlying worry seems to be how these children will learn to be "normal" *men and women* — that is, conventionally masculine or feminine.

So, for example, on a 1993 Oprah show on "The Lesbian and Gay   20
Baby Boom," a mixed-race panel offers testimonials on the experience of being lesbian or gay and raising children, joined by expert testimony from lesbian researchers Charlotte Patterson and April Martin. Roberta and Jacqué, an African American couple, are joined by their kids Nabiway and Eqion, and John and Ron, a white gay couple who are both lawyers and parents, and another lesbian couple and their adult children. By the applause it seems the audience is on the side of tolerance, but when Oprah goes to the audience the program heats up. Hostile audience members object, some on the grounds that homosexuality is immoral and others on the grounds that subjecting children to the hardship and ridicule of having lesbian or gay parents is — as Paul Cameron, attacking Helen the bartender, would argue later on *Ricki* — "selfish." Oprah then hands the microphone to an African American man who seems dying to speak and who reveals the concern that often seems to underwrite the objection to lesbian and gay parenting. "How [are] these two gentlemen," he says, pointing at the lawyers, "going to teach a little girl to be a girl? And how can you people, how can you teach this boy to be a man, and he's a fruitcake?" (King World 1993). While TV-talk shows are often programmed to celebrate tolerance of lesbian and gay *children* by their straight parents, their "what about the children?" mantra also encourages attacks on lesbian and gay *parents* for undermining the life chances — the chance to be a "normal" man or woman, especially in terms of gender presentation — of their presumed-to-be-heterosexual children.

Bisexuals, Transgenders, and the Conditional Acceptance of Queer Families

This concern with "the children" is in part a knee-jerk habit, but the underlying concern with conformity to basic norms of gender and monogamy holds important clues. In many ways, bisexuals and transgendered people pay the price for daytime television's progay moral cheerleading. The push for accepting gay family members and gay families, in fact, is predicted upon the frequent dismissal of transgendered and bisexual people on TV talk. The ideology the talk-show field seems structured to protect is no longer so much the moral superiority of heterosexual families; rather, it is that of the moral inferiority of unconventional gender presentation and sexual nonmonogamy (see Ringer, chapter 9). This is an advance for *some* gay and lesbian families, but a severely compromised one.

To begin with, bisexuals appear much more rarely than homosexuals in family-focused talk-show formats in which their role as siblings or children or parents is central; instead, they are disproportionately programmed through the format of "relationship troubles." That is, they are positioned almost exclusively as those who make family life impossible, largely through the reliance on familiar, moldy stereotypes: as people who can't decide (caught in love triangles, or married bisexuals), who are sexually voracious (rarely do you find a monogamous bisexual), and so on (Hutchins and Ka'ahumanu 1990). Bisexuals are routinely attacked on these shows for their inability "to commit" and for wanting to "have their cake and eat it too." Although they sometimes get to talk about their families, bisexuals on talk shows for the most part appear as an external *threat* to monogamous family relationships taking place around them, be they heterosexual or homosexual. By comparison, monogamous homosexuals, in fact, look like relatively unthreatening, more easily accepted — more easily *absorbed* — family members. If homosexuals are often invited into the institution of the family on these programs, it is on the condition that they do not bring with them these stereotyped characteristics that TV-talk shows on bisexuals are structured to emphasize: multiple partnering, undisciplined sexuality, indecisiveness, and selfishness.

Transgendered people get much more air play, much of it in bikinis. But they are also very frequently programmed in "family conflict" dramas: confronting their own children, parents, and siblings. If they have children, they are routinely criticized for the gender "confusion" they are alleged to cause: "Do they call you mother or father?" is as standard a question as "Which bathroom do you use?," and both tend to elicit audience laughter. On the short-lived *Gabrielle* show, for example, activist and historian Susan Stryker is attacked by a young man asking her, "Do you think it's fair to your son that he calls you mother considering he has no father figure to play catch and teach him the manly things in life?" The audience explodes into applause and cheers (Twentieth Century Fox 1995). "When you bring a child into the world," Jerry Springer argues on another similar show, "until the child is grown, you have his or her life to live as well. And the trauma of having a young child see Dad become Mom is probably too much to lay on any kid. Until your kids are grown, let Mom wear the dress" (Multimedia Entertainment 1995a). What goes for gay families, obviously, does not go for transgendered ones here.

When they are dealing with their own parents, transgendered people fare a tiny bit better. For one thing, they get some sympathy for being "diseased": they should be accepted, Springer repeats on his many trans shows, just like you would accept a child born with a birth defect. For another thing, if their parents are particularly brutal, they get the same tolerance line offered lesbian and gay "victims." But they are still regularly attacked for disrupting their families with their "selfishness": if they would only act "normal," everything would be just fine. As one audience member put it to a cross-dressing teenager on *Sally*, "You don't think you're selfish to put your mother and brother on national TV looking like a freak?" (Multimedia Entertainment 1995c).

Gender-crossing, in fact, is often treated as homosexuality gone hay- 25 wire, the nutty extreme of a sexual difference that is acceptable in gender-normative form. On a *Jerry Springer* show nicely titled "Please Act Straight!" — the coercive command phrased as a polite request — a series of transgendered kids are pelted with ridicule and attacks, mainly on the grounds that by cross-dressing they "flaunt" their homosexuality in ways that humiliate their families. They are unwilling, that is, to do *gender* the way others want them to do it, and thus they forfeit their place in the family. Springer asks a guest, the sister of a teenager waiting in the wings, what she thinks about his effeminacy. "I don't want my kids around that," she says. "I be wanting him to play football with them." When the young man emerges, deliberately and smilingly flouncing onto the stage wearing red high heels below an otherwise relatively conventional man's outfit, the crowd hoots and hollers its disapproval. "No," says his mother, simply, shaking her hand. "No way." Later, she flatly announces her plan of action should her son get a sex-change operation: "I'll kill him" (Multimedia Entertainment 1995b). The price for acceptance into the family, here, is gender conformity. With transgendered youth, or gay youth straying outside the bounds of gender norms, the repeated worry about children takes a different shape: it is the pained parent whose kid has "gone too far," who refuses to "*act* straight," who gets the sympathy of the victimized, not the child.

This is a rather stark contrast to the representation of lesbian and gay families, and a vivid, if somewhat unsurprising, example of the ideological barter going on here. An adjustment is made, as the family is shown to be open not just to heterosexuals but also to *certain* homosexuals. Unaccepting family members are vilified when their kids are run-of-the-mill, gender-normative gays and lesbians, but applauded when they cut off, publicly disown, or threaten to kill their transgendered kids. A new, postcloset kind of normalization pattern is at work here: the acceptability of lesbian and gay families, and of lesbian and gay people into their birth families, is predicted on their *not* exhibiting the "selfish" sexuality of bisexuals or the "freakish" gender of transgendered people.

Familial Divisions

"At their worst," Jane Shattuc suggests, daytime TV-talk shows "ostracize difference as antithetical to the morals of the familial structure. And at their best, they make difference permissible as the nation attempts to redefine the family in the late twentieth century" (1997:45). The lesson of talk-show visibility is thus perhaps not so much that we are faced with a choice between "positive" and "negative" imagery but that we are faced with a continual drawing of lines in and through the boom of cultural visibility for gay men, lesbians, transgendered people, and bisexuals in which we now find ourselves. TV-talk shows plant land mines in the ideological ground on which redefinitions of the family are taking shape. That is not of course something they do alone, but they are central to the process, partly because they help it along in such unintentional, entertaining ways and partly because they mix it so effectively with pleas for tolerance, enlightenment, and love.

The *kinds* of lines they emphasize, the kinds of differences that are allowed, in their protection of conventional family structures are telling: they set apart potentially powerful sets of political and cultural partners, helping to cut the threads linking various dissident family types and family members. They enact, in their profit-oriented attempt to capture audiences of various kinds through differing class-predicted programming formats, a class-based struggle over control of gay, lesbian, bisexual, and transgender family discourse. Activist guests seeking to establish the acceptable middle-classness of gay and lesbian families are set off against, and increasingly displaced by, working- and poverty-class guests (usually without an explicit political agenda), whose distance from middle-class acceptability offers a strikingly diverse, often more challenging, yet more easily dismissed, version of lesbian, gay, bisexual, and transgender family forms and values. The class lines cutting through queer family politics are exacerbated.

The alliance between those whose sexual object choice makes them "queer" and those whose gender nonconformity does so — always a tenuous alliance, and a longstanding fault line in sex and gender politics — is also aggravated. The talk show distaste for secrets, expressed routinely in calls for healing and tolerance, is undercut by the "what about the children?" refrain, but not so much, or at least not primarily, because of a worry that children are going to be raised gay. Healing and tolerance calls are instead rescinded primarily because of a concern for the "normal" *gender* future of the children; the temptation, often put into words, is for those gay people who can to emphasize gender normality, distancing themselves from gender-nonconforming "others." Moreover, the awkward, somewhat contorted steps taken on these programs toward the acceptance of lesbian and gay families (lesbian and gay children should be loved just like everyone else, lesbians and gay men have the right to raise their own children just like everyone else) are met by a heightened, quasi-systematic, often vicious treatment of transgendered and bisexual people as the more serious threats to the family structure. As gay and lesbian families move inside, that is, bisexual and transgendered ones move further toward the freaky; indeed, it is arguably through the positioning of transgenders and bisexuals as not-assimilable that homosexual families are rendered acceptable.

Here again, those who might share an interest in the transformation of   30 the family structure are, through the process of talk-show visibility, pushed further and further apart. This line drawing, this exaggerated division of the "classy" from the "trashy" family, the "normal" from the "freaky" child, which conserves even as it revises the familial structure, is the biggest lesson for family politics from the weird world of daytime talk television.

References

Carbaugh, Donal. 1989. *Talking American: Cultural Discourses on Donahue.* Norwood, N.J.: Ablex.

DiMaggio, Paul. 1991. "Cultural Entrepreneurship in Nineteenth-Century Boston: The Creation of an Organizational Base for High Culture in America." In Chandra Mukerji and Michael Schudson, eds., *Rethinking Popular Culture: Contemporary Perspectives in Cultural Studies,* pp. 374–97. Berkeley: University of California Press.

Fejes, Fred, and Kevin Petrich. 1993. "Invisibility, Homophobia, and Heterosexism: Lesbians, Gays, and the Media." *Critical Studies in Mass Communication* 10 (December 4): 396–422.

Gamson, Joshua. 1998a. *Freaks Talk Back: Tabloid Talk Shows and Sexual Nonconformity.* Chicago: University of Chicago Press.

———. 1998b. "Publicity Traps: Television Talk Shows and Lesbian, Gay, Bisexual, and Transgender Visibility." *Sexualities* I: 11–41.

Grindstaff, Laura. 1997. "Producing Trash, Class, and the Money Shot: A Behind the Scenes Account of Daytime TV Talkshows." In James Lull and Stephen Hinerman, eds., *Media Scandals,* pp. 164–202. New York: Columbia University Press.

Gross, Larry. 1989. "Out of the Mainstream: Sexual Minorities and the Mass Media." In Ellen Seiter, ed., *Remote Control: Television, Audiences, and Cultural Power,* pp. 130–49. New York: Routledge.

Habermas, Jurgen. 1991. *The Structural Transformation of the Public Sphere.* Cambridge: MIT Press.

Hennessy, Rosemary. 1994–95. "Queer Visibility in Commodity Culture." *Cultural Critique* (Winter): 31–75.

Hutchins, Loraine, and Lani Ka'ahumanu. 1990. *Bi Any Other Name: Bisexual People Speak Out.* Boston: Alyson.

King World. 1993. *Oprah* ("Lesbian and Gay Baby Boom"). Livingston, N.J.: Burrelle's Information Services. May 10.

Levine, Lawrence W. 1988. *Highbrow/Lowbrow: The Emergence of Cultural Hierarchy in America*. Cambridge: Harvard University Press.

Multimedia Entertainment. 1994. *Donahue* ("Gay Teens"). Denver, Colo.: Journal Graphics, June 3.

———. 1995a. *The Jerry Springer Show* ("My Dad Is a Woman!"). Livingston, N.J.: Burrelle's Information Services. August 4.

———. 1995b. *The Jerry Springer Show* ("Please Act Straight!"). Livingston, N.J.: Burrelle's Information Services. October 23.

———. 1995c. *Sally Jessy Raphael* ("My Teen Son Wants to Be a Woman"). Livingston, N.J.: Burrelle's Information Services. June 27.

Paramount Pictures. 1995a. *Ricki Lake* ("You're Gay, How Dare You Raise a Child"). April 27.

———. 1995b. *Ricki Lake* ("Get It Straight: I Don't Want Gays Around My Kids"). June 15.

———. 1995c. *Ricki Lake* ("Listen, Family, I'm Gay . . . It's Not a Phase . . . Get Over It!"). November 20.

Peiss, Kathy. 1986. *Cheap Amusements: Working Women and Leisure in Turn-of-the-Century New York*. Philadelphia: Temple University Press.

Perpetual Notion Inc. 1995. *Marilu* ("Gay and Lesbian Parents"). April 4.

Russo, Vito. 1987. *The Celluloid Closet: Homosexuality in the Movies*. New York: Harper & Row.

Schacter, Jane S. 1997. "Skepticism, Culture, and the Gay Civil Rights Debate in Post-Civil-Rights Era." *Harvard Law Review* 110: 684–731.

Shattuc, Jane. 1997. *The Talking Cure: TV Talk Shows and Women*. New York: Routledge.

Signorile, Michelangelo. 1993. *Queer in America: Sex, the Media, and the Closets of Power*. New York: Anchor Books.

Twentieth Century Fox. 1995. *Gabrielle* ("Switching Sexes"). October 5.

Weston, Kath. 1991. *Families We Choose: Lesbians, Gays, Kinship*. New York: Columbia University Press.

White, Mimi. 1992. *Tele-Advising: Therapeutic Discourse in American Television*. Chapel Hill: University of North Carolina Press.

ENGAGING THE TEXT

1. Why, in Gamson's view, are "queer family relationships" such an important element in daytime talk TV? Why, for example, do straight people tune in to talk shows about queer families? What role does the mythical nuclear family play in daytime TV?

2. Explain Gamson's contention that talk shows can both normalize and "freakify" queer families. Have the talk shows you have seen done more to normalize or freakify nontraditional families? Overall, do you think daytime talk TV tends to challenge or reinforce long-standing myths about family? What about other kinds of TV shows, like soap operas, sit-coms, and "reality" TV?

3. Explain the importance of social class in the recipe for compelling daytime TV. What messages about family and social class are viewers receiving?

4. What does Gamson mean by "therapeutic liberalism"? Do you agree that therapeutic liberalism is a staple of talk shows?

5. Review Gamson's argument that daytime talk TV is shaped in significant ways by ideological agendas, and explain why you do or do not find his argument persuasive.

EXPLORING CONNECTIONS

6. Look back at the images of gay parents and lesbian brides on pages 86 and 87. Do you think Gamson would consider these images "normalizing," or would he claim that they "freakify" their subjects in some way? Support your observations by citing specific details in the photographs.
7. To what extent does Gamson's analysis of the "freakifying" tendencies of daytime TV talk shows support Michael Medved's claim (p. 769) that American mass media presents a distorted image of American society to the world? How might Gamson respond to Medved's account of the motives behind this distortion?

EXTENDING THE CRITICAL CONTEXT

8. Make sure that you understand each of the ideas listed below, reviewing "Talking Freaks" as needed. Then watch one or more daytime talk shows, looking for evidence to support or challenge what Gamson writes about these four topics. (Both online and print resources may help you identify specific shows that deal with issues of family or sexual orientation; note also that videotaping makes this work much easier.)

> normalizing vs. "freakifying"
> therapeutic liberalism
> social class and daytime talk TV
> conditional acceptance of queer families

Report your findings to the class orally or in an essay.

An Indian Story
ROGER JACK

This narrative concerns growing up away from one's father in one of the Indian cultures of the Pacific Northwest. It's also an intimate view of a nonnuclear family; the author is interested in the family not as a static set of defined relationships but as a social network that adapts to the ever-changing circumstances and needs of its members. Roger Jack works as a counselor and instructor for the American Indian Studies Program at Eastern Washington University. His work has been published in several journals and anthologies, including Spawning the Medicine River, Earth Power Coming, *and* The Clouds Threw This Light. *"An Indian Story" appeared in* Dancing on the Rim of the World: An Anthology of Contemporary Northwest Native American Writing *(1990), edited by Andrea Lerner.*

Aunt Greta was always a slow person. Grandpa used to say she was like an old lady out of the old days who never hurried herself for anything, no matter what. She was only forty-five, heavyset, dark-complexioned, and very knowledgeable of the old ways, which made her seem even older. Most of the time she wore her hair straight up or in a ponytail that hung below her beltline. At home she wore pants and big, baggy shirts, but at ritual gatherings she wore her light blue calico dress, beaded moccasins, hair braided and clasped with beaded barrettes. Sometimes she wore a scarf on her head like ladies older than she. She said we emulate those we love and care for. I liked seeing her dressed for ceremonials. Even more, I liked seeing her stand before crowds of tribal members and guests translating the old language to the new for our elders, or speaking on behalf of the younger people who had no understanding of the Indian language. It made me proud to be her nephew and her son.

My mom died when I was little. Dad took care of me as best he could after that. He worked hard and earned good money as an accountant at the agency. But about a year after Mom died he married a half-breed Indian and this made me feel very uncomfortable. Besides, she had a child of her own who was white. We fought a lot — me and Jeffrey Pine — and then I'd get into trouble because I was older and was supposed to know better than to misbehave.

I ran away from home one day when everyone was gone — actually, I walked to Aunt Greta's and asked if I could move in with her since I had already spent so much time with her anyway. Then after I had gone to bed that night, Dad came looking for me and Aunt Greta told him what I had told her about my wanting to move in with her. He said it would be all right for a while, then we would decide what to do about it later. That was a long time ago. Now I am out of high school and going to college. Meanwhile, Jeffrey Pine is a high-school dropout and living with the folks.

Aunt Greta was married a long time ago. She married a guy named Mathew who made her very happy. They never had children, but when persistent people asked either of them what was wrong, they would simply reply they were working on it. Then Mathew died during their fifth year of marriage. No children. No legacy. After that Aunt Greta took care of Grandpa, who had moved in with them earlier when Grandma died. Grandpa wasn't too old, but sometimes he acted like it. I guess it came from that long, drawn-out transition from horse riding and breeding out in the wild country to reservation life in buggies, dirt roads, and cars. He walked slowly everywhere he went; he and Aunt Greta complemented each other that way.

Eventually, Aunt Greta became interested in tribal politics and threat-   5
ened to run for tribal council, so Grandpa changed her Indian name from Little Girl Heart to Old Woman Walking, which he had called Grandma when she was alive. Aunt Greta didn't mind. In fact, she was proud of her new name. Little Girl Heart was her baby name, she said. When Grandpa died a couple of years later she was all alone. She decided tribal politics wasn't for her but began teaching Indian culture and language classes. That's when I walked into her life like a newborn Mathew or Grandpa or the baby she never had. She had so much love and knowledge to share, which she passed on to me naturally and freely; she received wages for teaching others. But that was gesticulation, she said.

My home and academic life improved a lot after I had moved in with Aunt Greta. Dad and his wife had a baby boy, and then a girl, but I didn't see too much of them. It was like we were strangers living a quarter mile from one another. Aunt Greta and I went on vacations together from the time I graduated from the eighth grade. We were trailblazers, she said, because our ancestors never traveled very far from the homeland.

The first year we went to Maryhill, Washington, which is about a ten-hour drive from our reservation home in Park City, and saw the imitation Stonehenge Monument. We arrived there late in the evening because we had to stop off in every other town along the road to eat, whether or not we were hungry, because that was Aunt Greta's way and Grandma's and all the other old ladies of the tribe. You have to eat to survive, they would say. It was almost dark when we arrived at the park. We saw the huge outlines of the massive hewn stones placed in a circular position and towering well over our heads. We stood small and in awe of their magnificence, especially seeing darkness fall upon us. Stars grew brighter and we saw them more keenly as time passed. Then they started falling, dropping out of the sky to meet us where we stood. I could see the power of Aunt Greta protruding through her eyes; if I had power I wouldn't have to explore, physically, the sensation

I imagined her feeling. She said nothing for a long time. Then, barely audible, she murmured something like, "I have no teepee. I need no cover. This moment has been waiting for me here all this time." She paused. Then, "I wasn't sure what I would find here, but I'm glad we came. I was going to say something goofy like 'we should have brought the teepee and we could call upon Coyote to come and knock over these poles so we could drape our canvas over the skeleton and camp!' But I won't. I'm just glad we came here."

"Oh no, you aren't flipping out on me, are you?" I ribbed her. She always said good Indians remember two things: their humor and their history. These are the elements that dictate our culture and our survival in this crazy world. If these are somehow destroyed or forgotten, we would be doomed to extinction. Our power gone. And she had the biggest, silliest grin on her face. She said, "I want to camp right here!" and I knew she was serious.

We camped in the car, in the parking lot, that night. But neither of us slept until nearly daybreak. She told me Coyote stories and Indian stories and asked me what I planned to do with my life. "I want to be like you," I told her. Then she reminded me that I had a Dad to think about, too, and that maybe I should think about taking up his trade. I thought about a lot of stories I had heard about boys following in their father's footsteps — good or bad — and I told Aunt Greta that I wasn't too sure about living on the reservation and working at the agency all my life. Then I tried to sleep, keeping in mind everything we had talked about. I was young, but my Indian memory was good and strong.

On our way home from Maryhill we stopped off at Coyote's Sweat- house down by Soap Lake. I crawled inside the small cavernous stone struc- ture and Aunt Greta said to make a wish for something good. She tossed a coin inside before we left the site. Then we drove through miles of desert country and basalt cliffs and canyons, but we knew we were getting closer to home when the pine trees starting weeding out the sagebrush, and the mountains overrode the flatland.

Our annual treks after that brought us to the Olympic Peninsula on the coast and the Redwood Forest in northern California; Yellowstone National Park in Wyoming and Glacier Park in Montana; and the Crazy Horse / Mount Rushmore Monuments in South Dakota. We were careful in coordi- nating our trips with pow-wows too. Then we talked about going all the way to Washington, D.C., and New York City to see the sights and how the other half lived, but we never did.

After high-school graduation we went to Calgary for a pow-wow and I got into trouble for drinking and fighting with some local Indians I had met. They talked me into it. The fight occurred when a girlfriend of one of the guys started acting very friendly toward me. Her boyfriend got jealous and started pushing me around and calling me names; only after I defended my- self did the others join in the fight. Three of us were thrown into the tribe's makeshift jail. Aunt Greta was not happy when she came to pay my bail. As a matter of fact, I had never seen her angry before. Our neighbors at the campground thought it was funny that I had been arrested and thrown into jail and treated the incident as an everyday occurrence. I sat in the car imagining my own untimely death. I was so sick.

After dropping the ear poles, I watched Aunt Greta take down the rest of the teepee with the same meticulousness with which we had set it up. She went around the radius of the teepee removing wooden stakes from the ground that held fast the teepee's body to the earth. Then she stood on a folding chair to reach the pins that held the face of the teepee together. She folded the teepee into halves as it hung, still, on the center pole. She folded it again and again until it grew clumsy and uneven, then she motioned for me to come and drop the pole so she could untie the fastener that made the teepee our home. Meanwhile, I had to drop all skeletal poles from the sky and all that remained were a few holes in the ground and flattened patches of grass that said we had been there. I stood looking over the crowd. Lots of people had come from throughout Canada and the northern states for the pow-wow. Hundreds of people sat watching the war dance. Other people watched the stick-games and card games. But what caught my attention were the obvious drunks in the crowd. I was "one of them" now.

Aunt Greta didn't talk much while we drove home. It was a long, lonely drive. We stopped only twice to eat cold, tasteless meals. Once in Canada and once stateside. When we finally got home, Aunt Greta said, "Good night," and went to bed. It was only eight o'clock in the evening. I felt a heavy calling to go talk to Dad about what had happened. So I did.

He was alone when I arrived at his house. As usual I walked through the front door without knocking, but immediately heard him call out, "Son?" 15

"Yeah," I said as I went to sit on a couch facing him. "How did you know it was me?"

He smiled, said hello, and told me a father is always tuned in to his son. Then he sensed my hesitation to speak and asked, "What's wrong?"

"I got drunk in Calgary." My voice cracked. "I got into a fight and thrown in jail too. Aunt Greta had to bail me out. Now she's mad at me. She hasn't said much since we packed to come home."

"Did you tell her you were sorry for screwing up?" Dad asked.

"Yeah. I tried to tell her. But she clammed up on me." 20

"I wouldn't worry about it," Dad said. "This was bound to happen sooner or later. You really feel guilty when you take that first drink and get caught doing it. Hell, when I got drunk the first time, my Mom and Dad took turns preaching to me about the evils of drinking, fornication, and loose living. It didn't stop me though. I was one of those smart asses who had to have his own way. What you have to do is come up with some sort of reparation. Something that will get you back on Greta's good side."

"I guess that's what got to me. She didn't holler or preach to me. All the while I was driving I could feel her staring at me." My voice strengthened, "But she wouldn't say anything."

"Well, Son. You have to try to imagine what's going through her mind too. As much as I love you, you have been Greta's boy since you were knee-high to a grasshopper. She has done nothing but try to provide all the love and proper caring that she can for you. Maybe she thinks she has done something wrong in your upbringing. She probably feels more guilty about what happened than you. Maybe she hasn't said anything because she isn't handling this very well either." Dad became a little less serious before adding, "Of course, Greta's been around the block a time or two herself."

Stunned, I asked, "What do you mean?"

"Son, as much as Greta's life has changed, there are some of us who re-   25
member her younger days. She liked drinking, partying, and loud music along with war dancing, stick-games, and pow-wows. She got along wherever she went looking for a good time. She was one of the few who could do that. The rest of us either took to drinking all the time, or we hit the pow-wow circuit all straight-faced and sober, never mixing up the two. Another good thing about Greta was that when she found her mate and decided to settle down, she did it right. After she married Mathew she quit running around." Dad smiled, "Of course, Mathew may have had some influence on her behavior, since he worked for the alcohol program."

"I wonder why she never remarried?" I asked.

"Some women just don't," Dad said authoritatively. "But she never had a shortage of men to take care of. She had your Grandpa — and YOU!" We laughed. Then he continued, "Greta could have had her pick of any man on the reservation. A lot of men chased after her before she married, and a lot of them chased after her after Mathew died. But she never had time for them."

"I wonder if she would have gotten married again if I hadn't moved in on her?"

"That's a question only Greta can answer. You know, she may work in tribal programs and college programs, but if she had to give it all up for one reason in the world, it would be you." Dad became intent, "You are her bloodline. You know that? Otherwise I wouldn't have let you stay with her all these years. The way her family believes is that two sisters coming from the same mother and father are the same. Especially blood. After your Mother died and you asked to go and live with your Aunt, that was all right. As a matter of fact, according to her way, we were supposed to have gotten married after our period of mourning was over."

"You — married to Aunt Greta!" I half-bellowed and again we laughed.   30

"Yeah. We could have made a hell of a family, don't you think?" Dad tried steadying his mood. "But, you know, maybe Greta's afraid of losing you too. Maybe she's afraid that you're entering manhood and that you'll be leaving her. Like when you go away to college. You are still going to college, aren't you?"

"Yeah. But I never thought of it as leaving her. I thought it more like going out and doing what's expected of me. Ain't I supposed to strike out on my own one day?"

"Yeah. Your leaving your family and friends behind may be expected, but like I said, 'you are everything to Greta,' and maybe she has other plans for you." Dad looked down to the floor and I caught a glimpse of graying streaks of hair on top of his head. Then he asked me which college I planned on attending.

"One in Spokane," I answered. "I ain't decided which one yet."

Then we talked about other things and before we knew it his missus   35
and the kids were home. Junior was nine, Anna Lee eight; they had gone to the last day of the tribe's celebration and carnival in Nespelem, which was what Aunt Greta and I had gone to Calgary to get away from for once. I sat quietly and wondered what Aunt Greta must have felt for my wrongdoing. The kids got louder as they told Dad about their carnival rides and games and prizes they had won. They shared their goodies with him and he looked to be having a good time eating popcorn and cotton candy.

I remembered a time when Mom and Dad brought me to the carnival. Grandpa and Grandma were with us. Mom and Dad stuck me on a big, black merry-go-round horse with flaming red nostrils and fiery eyes. Its long, dangling tongue hung out of its mouth. I didn't really want to ride that horse, but I felt I had to because Grandpa kept telling Mom and Dad that I belonged on a real horse and not some wooden thing. I didn't like the horse, when it hit certain angles it jolted and scared me even more. Mom and Dad offered me another ride on it, but I refused.

"Want some cotton candy?" Junior brought me back to reality. "We had fun going on the rides and trying to win some prizes. Here, you can have this one." He handed me one of his prizes. And, "Are you gonna stay with us tonight?"

I didn't realize it was after eleven o'clock.

"You can sleep in my bed," Junior offered.

"Yeah. Maybe I will, Little Brother." Junior smiled. I bade everyone   40
good night and went to his room and pulled back his top blanket revealing his Star Wars sheets. I chuckled at the sight of them before lying down and trying to sleep on them. This would be my first time sleeping away from Aunt Greta in a long time. I still felt tired from my drinking and the long drive home, but I was glad to have talked to Dad. I smiled in thinking that he said he loved me, because Indian men hardly ever verbalize their emotions. I went to sleep thinking how alone Aunt Greta must have felt after I had left home and promised myself to return there as early as I could.

I ate breakfast with the family before leaving. Dad told me one last thing that he and Aunt Greta had talked about sometime before. "You know, she talked about giving you an Indian name. She asked me if you had one and I said 'no.' She talked about it and I thought maybe she would go ahead and do it too, but her way of doing this is: boys are named for their father's side and girls are named for their mother's. Maybe she's still waiting for me to give you a name. I don't know."

"I remember when Grandpa named her, but I never thought of having a name myself. What was the name?" I asked.

"I don't remember. Something about stars."

Aunt Greta was sitting at the kitchen table drinking coffee and listening to an Elvis album when I got home. Elvis always made her lonesome for the old days or it cheered her up when she felt down. I didn't know what to say, but showed her the toy totem pole Junior had given me.

"That's cute," she said. "So you spent the night at the carnival?"   45

"No. Junior gave it to me," I explained. "I camped at Dad's."

"Are you hungry?" she was about to get up from the table.

"No. I've eaten." I saw a stack of pancakes on the stove. I hesitated another moment before asking, "What's with Elvis?"

"He's dead!" she said and smiled, because that's what I usually said to her. "Oh well, I just needed a little cheering up, I guess."

I remember hearing a story about Aunt Greta that happened a long time   50 ago. She was a teenager when the Elvis craze hit the reservation. Back then hardly any families had television sets, so they couldn't see Elvis. But when his songs hit the airwaves on the radio the girls went crazy. The guys went kind of crazy too — but they were pissed off crazy. A guy can't be that good looking and talented too, they claimed. They were jealous of Elvis. Elvis had a concert in Seattle and my Mom and Aunt Greta and a couple other girls went to it. Legend said that Elvis kissed Aunt Greta on the cheek during his performance and she took to heart the old "ain't never going to wash that cheek again" promissory and never washed her cheek for a long time and it got chapped and cracked until Grandpa and Grandma finally had to order her to go to the clinic to get some medicine to clean up her face. She hated them for a while, still swearing Elvis would be her number one man forever.

"How's your Dad?"

"He's all right. The kids were at the carnival when I got to his house, so we had a nice, long visit." I paused momentarily before adding, "And he told me some stories about you too."

"Oh?" she acted concerned even though her crow's feet showed.

"Yeah. He said you were quite a fox when you were young. And he said you probably could have had any man you wanted before you married Uncle Mathew, and you could have had any man after Uncle Mathew died. So, how come you never snagged yourself another husband?"

Aunt Greta sat quietly for a moment. I could see her slumping into the   55 old way of doing things which said you thought things through before saying them. "I suppose I could have had my pick of the litter. It's just that after my old man died I didn't want anyone else. He was so good to me that I didn't think I could find any better. Besides, I had you and Grandpa to care for, didn't I? Have I ever complained about that?"

"Yeah," I persisted, "but haven't you ever thought about what might have happened if you had gotten married again? You might have done like Dad and started a whole new family. Babies, even!"

Aunt Greta was truly embarrassed. "Will you get away from here with talk like that. I don't need babies. Probably won't be long now and you'll be bringing them home for me to take care of anyhow."

Now I was embarrassed. We got along great after that initial conversation. It was like we had never gone to Calgary and I had never gotten on to her wrong side at all. We were like kids rediscovering what it was worth to have a real good friend go away for a while and then come back. To be appreciative of each other, I imagined Aunt Greta might have said.

Our trip to Calgary happened in July. August and September found me dumbfounded as to what to do with myself college-wise. I felt grateful that Indian parents don't throw out their offspring when they reach a certain age. Aunt Greta said it was too late for fall term and that I should rest my brain for a while and think about going to college after Christmas. So I explored different schools in the area and talked to people who had gone to them. Meanwhile, some of my friends were going to Haskell Indian Junior College in Kansas. Aunt Greta frowned upon my going there. She said it was too far away from home, people die of malaria there, and if you're not drunk, you're just crazy. So I stuck with the Spokane plan.

That fall Aunt Greta was invited to attend a language seminar in Port-   60 land. She taught Indian language classes when asked to. So we decided to take a side trip to our old campsite at Stonehenge. This time we arrived early in the morning and it was foggy and drizzling rain. The sight of the stones didn't provide the feeling we had experienced earlier. To us, the sight seemed to be just a bunch of rocks standing, overlooking the Columbia River, a lot of sagebrush, and two state highways. It didn't offer us feelings of mysticism and power anymore. Unhappy with the mood, Aunt Greta said we might as well leave; her words hung heavy on the air.

We stayed in Portland for a week and then made it a special point to leave late in the afternoon so we could stop by Stonehenge again at dusk. So with careful planning we arrived with just enough light to take a couple pictures and then darkness began settling in. We sat in the car eating baloney sandwiches and potato chips and drinking pop because we were tired of restaurant food and we didn't want people staring at us when we ate. That's where we were when an early evening star fell. Aunt Greta's mouth fell open, potato chip crumbs clung to the sides of her mouth. "This is it!" she squealed in English, Indian, and English again. "Get out of the car, Son," and she half pushed me out the door. "Go and stand in the middle of the circle and pray for something good to happen to you." I ran out and stood waiting and wondering what was supposed to happen. I knew better than to doubt Aunt Greta's wishes or superstitions. Then the moment came to pass.

"Did you feel it?" she asked as she led me back to the car.

"I don't know," I told her because I didn't think anything had happened.

"I guess it just takes some people a little longer to realize," she said.

I never quite understood what was supposed to have happened that day. 65
A couple months later I was packing up to move to Spokane. I decided to go
into the accounting business, like Dad. Aunt Greta quizzed me hourly before
I was to leave whether I was all right and if I would be all right in the city.
"Yeah, yeah," I heard myself repeating. So by the time I really was to leave she
clued me in on her new philosophy: it wasn't that I was leaving her, it was just
that she wouldn't be around to take care of me much anymore. She told me,
"Good Indians stick together," and that I should search out our people who
were already there, but not forget those who were still at home.

After I arrived in Spokane and settled down I went home all too frequently to actually experience what Aunt Greta and everyone told me. Then
my studies got so intense that I didn't think I could travel home as much anymore. So I stayed in Spokane a lot more than before. Finally it got so I didn't
worry as much about the folks at home. I would be out walking in the evening
and know someone's presence was with me. I never bothered telephoning
Dad at his office at the agency; and I never knew where or when Aunt Greta
worked. She might have been at the agency or school. Then one day Dad telephoned me at school. After asking how I was doing, he told me why he was
calling. "Your Aunt Greta is sick. The doctors don't know what's wrong with
her yet. They just told me to advise her family of the possibility that it could be
serious." I only half heard what he was saying, "Son, are you there?"

"Yeah."

"Did you hear me? Did you hear what I said?"

"Yeah. I don't think you have to worry about Aunt Greta though. She'll
be all right. Like the old timers used to say, 'she might go away for a while,
but she'll be back,'" and I hung up the telephone unalarmed.

ENGAGING THE TEXT

1. Give specific examples of how the narrator's extended family or kinship
   structure works to solve family problems. What problems does it seem to
   create or make worse?

2. What key choices does the narrator make in this story? How are these
   choices influenced by family members or family considerations?

3. Is the family portrayed here matriarchal, patriarchal, egalitarian, or something else? Explain. To what extent is parenting influenced by gender
   roles?

4. What events narrated in this story might threaten the survival of a nuclear
   family? How well does the extended family manage these crises?

5. How strong an influence does the narrator's father have on him? How can
   you explain the father's influence given how rarely the two see each other?

6. How do you interpret the narrator's reaction when he hears about Aunt
   Greta's failing health? What is implied in the story's closing lines?

EXPLORING CONNECTIONS

7. Review what Judy Root Aulette writes in "Working-Class African American Families" on pages 71–74. What characteristics of these African American families can you also find in "An Indian Story"? How would you account for the similarities and differences you see?

8. Imagine you are Judy Root Aulette (p. 64) or Carol Stack, whose work Aulette summarizes — that is, you are a sociologist studying the family. Imagine further that you have been granted interviews with the narrator of "An Indian Story," with his father, and with Aunt Greta. Make a brief list of the topics you would want to discuss with each. Then role-play or write up one of these interviews.

9. Compare and contrast "Looking for Work" (p. 26) and "An Indian Story" in terms of what each narrator learns about family and how they learn it.

EXTENDING THE CRITICAL CONTEXT

10. This story celebrates the power of stories to connect people and to shape or affirm one's identity. Throughout, the narrator relates family stories about his father and his aunt that give him a clearer sense of himself and his relationship to those he loves. In a journal entry or essay, relate one or two family stories that are important to you and explain how they help you define who you are.

Envy

BEBE MOORE CAMPBELL

What would make a schoolgirl who is afraid to chew gum in class threaten to stab her teacher? In this narrative, at least, it's not grammar drills or sentence diagrams — it's anger, frustration, and envy caused by an absentee father. Like Gary Soto's "Looking for Work" (p. 26), this personal recollection of childhood combines the authenticity of actual experience with the artistry of expert storytelling. Bebe Moore Campbell (b. 1950) is the author of several books, three of which have been New York Times *bestsellers:* Brothers and Sisters *(1994),* Singing in the Comeback Choir *(1998), and* What You Owe Me *(2001). She has also published articles in many national newspapers and magazines, including the* New York Times, *the* Washington Post, *the* Los Angeles Times, Ms., Ebony, *and* Essence. *"Envy" is taken from her memoir* Sweet Summer: Growing Up With and Without My Dad *(1989).*

The red bricks of 2239 North 16th Street melded into the uniformity of look-alike doors, windows, and brownstone-steps. From the outside our rowhouse looked the same as any other. When I was a toddler, the similarity was unsettling. The family story was that my mother and I were out walking on the street one day when panic rumbled through me. "Where's our house? Where's our house?" I cried, grabbing my mother's hand.

My mother walked me to our house, pointed to the numbers painted next to the door. "Twenty-two thirty-nine," she said, slapping the wall. "This is our house."

Much later I learned that the real difference was inside.

In my house there was no morning stubble, no long johns or Fruit of the Loom on the clothesline, no baritone hollering for keys that were sitting on the table. There was no beer in the refrigerator, no ball game on TV, no loud cussing. After dark the snores that emanated from the bedrooms were subtle, ladylike, little moans really.

Growing up, I could have died from overexposure to femininity. 5 Women ruled at 2239. A grandmother, a mother, occasionally an aunt, grown-up girlfriends from at least two generations, all the time rubbing up against me, fixing my food, running my bathwater, telling me to sit still and be good in those grown-up, girly-girl voices. Chanel and Prince Matchabelli wafting through the bedrooms. Bubble bath and Jergens came from the bathroom, scents unbroken by aftershave, macho beer breath, a good he-man funk. I remember a house full of 'do rags and rollers, the soft, sweet allure of Dixie peach and bergamot;[1] brown-skinned queens wearing pastel housecoats and worn-out size six-and-a-half flip-flops that slapped softly against the wood as the royal women climbed the stairs at night carrying their paperbacks to bed.

The outside world offered no retreat. School was taught by stern, old-maid white women with age spots and merciless gray eyes; ballet lessons, piano lessons, Sunday school, and choir were all led by colored sisters with a hands-on-their-hips attitude who cajoled and screeched in distaff[2] tongues.

And what did they want from me, these Bosoms? Achievement! This desire had nothing to do with the pittance they collected from the Philadelphia Board of Education or the few dollars my mother paid them. Pushing little colored girls forward was in their blood. They made it clear: a life of white picket fences and teas was for other girls to aspire to. I was to *do* something. And if I didn't climb willingly up their ladder, they'd drag me to the top. Rap my knuckles hard for not practicing. Make me lift my leg until I wanted to die. Stay after school and write "I will listen to the teacher" five hundred times. They were not playing. "Obey them," my mother commanded.

[1]*bergamot:* A citrus tree with a fragrant fruit.
[2]*distaff:* Female, maternal.

When I entered 2B — the Philadelphia school system divided grades into A and B — in September 1957, I sensed immediately that Miss Bradley was not a woman to be challenged. She looked like one of those evil old spinsters Shirley Temple[3] was always getting shipped off to live with; she was kind of hefty, but so tightly corseted that if she happened to grab you or if you fell against her during recess, it felt as if you were bouncing into a steel wall. In reality she was a sweet lady who was probably a good five years past her retirement age when I wound up in her class. Miss Bradley remained at Logan for one reason and one reason only: she was dedicated. She wanted her students to learn! learn! learn! Miss Bradley was halfway sick, hacking and coughing her lungs out through every lesson, spitting the phlegm into fluffy white tissues from the box on her desk, but she was *never* absent. Each day at three o'clock she kissed each one of her "little pupils" on the cheek, sending a faint scent of Emeraude home with us. Her rules for teaching children seemed to be: love them; discipline them; reward them; and make sure they are clean.

Every morning she ran a hygiene check on the entire class. She marched down the aisle like a stormtrooper, rummaging through the ears of hapless students, checking for embedded wax. She looked under our fingernails for dirt. Too bad on you if she found any. Once she made David, a stringy-haired white boy who thought Elvis Presley was a living deity and who was the most notorious booger-eater in the entire school, go to the nurse's office to have the dirt cleaned from under his fingernails. Everybody knew that what was under David's fingernails was most likely dried-up boogies and not dirt, but nobody said anything.

If she was death on dirt and earwax, Miss Bradley's specialty was head-lice patrol. Down the aisles she stomped in her black Enna Jettick shoes,[4] stopping at each student to part strands of blond, brown, or dark hair, looking for cooties. Miss Bradley would flip through plaits, curls, kinks — the woman was relentless. I always passed inspection. Nana put enough Nu Nile in my hair to suffocate any living creature that had the nerve to come tipping up on my scalp. Nu Nile was the official cootie killer. I was clean, wax-free, bug-free, and smart. The folder inside my desk contained a stack of spelling and arithmetic papers with A's emblazoned across the top, gold stars in the corner. Miss Bradley always called on me. She sent me to run errands for her too. I was her pet.

When Mrs. Clark, my piano teacher and my mother's good friend, told my mother that Logan Elementary School was accepting children who didn't live in the neighborhood, my mother immediately enrolled Michael and later me. "It's not crowded and it's mixed," she told a nodding, smiling Nana. The fact that Logan was integrated was the main reason Michael and

10

---

[3]*Shirley Temple:* Famous child actor (b. 1928); later, Shirley Temple Black, U.S. ambassador.

[4]*Enna Jettick shoes:* Brand name of "sensible" women's shoes.

I were sent there. Nana and Mommy, like most upwardly mobile colored women, believed that to have the same education as a white child was the first step up the rocky road to success. This viewpoint was buttressed by the fact that George Washington Carver, my neighborhood school, was severely overcrowded. Logan was just barely integrated, with only a handful of black kids thrown in with hordes of square-jawed, pale-eyed second-generation Ukrainians whose immigrant parents and grandparents populated the neighborhood near the school. There were a few dark-haired Jews and aristocratic-looking WASPs too. My first day in kindergarten it was Nana who enthusiastically grabbed Michael's and my hands, pulling us away from North Philly's stacked-up rowhouses, from the hucksters whose wagons bounced down the streets with trucks full of ripe fruits and vegetables, from the street-corner singers and jitterbugs who filled my block with all-day doo-wahs. It was Nana who resolutely walked me past the early-morning hordes of colored kids heading two blocks away to Carver Elementary School, Nana who pulled me by the hand and led me in another direction.

We went underground at the Susquehanna and Dauphin subway station, leaving behind the unremitting asphalt and bricks and the bits of paper strewn in the streets above us. We emerged at Logan station, where sunlight, brilliant red and pink roses and yellow chrysanthemums, and neatly clipped lawns and clean streets startled me. There were robins and blue jays flying overhead. The only birds in my neighborhood were sparrows and pigeons. Delivering me at the schoolyard, Nana firmly cupped my chin with her hand as she bent down to instruct me. "Your mother's sending you up here to learn, so you do everything your teacher tells you to, okay?" To Michael she turned and said, "You're not up here to be a monkey on a stick." Then to both of us: "Don't talk. Listen. Act like you've got some home training. You've got as much brains as anybody up here. Do you know that? All right now. Make Nana proud of you."

A month after I returned from Pasquotank County,[5] I sat in Miss Bradley's classroom on a rainy Monday watching her write spelling words on the blackboard. The harsh sccurr, sccurr of Miss Bradley's chalk and the tinny sound the rain made against the window took my mind to faraway places. I couldn't get as far away as I wanted. Wallace, the bane of the whole class, had only moments earlier laid the most gigunda fart in history, one in a never-ending series, and the air was just clearing. His farts were silent wonders. Not a hint, not the slightest sound. You could be in the middle of a sentence and then wham! bam! Mystery Funk would knock you down.

Two seats ahead of me was Leonard, a lean colored boy from West Philly who always wore suits and ties to school, waving his hand like a crazy man. A showoff if ever there was one.

---

[5]*Pasquotank County:* County in North Carolina where Campbell's father lived; she visited him there every summer.

I was bored that day. I looked around at the walls. Miss Bradley had 15
decorated the room with pictures of the ABCs in cursive. Portraits of the
presidents were hanging in a row on one wall above the blackboard. On
the bulletin board there was a display of the Russian satellite, *Sputnik I,* and
the American satellite, *Explorer I.* Miss Bradley was satellite-crazy. She
thought it was just wonderful that America was in the "space race" and she
constantly filled our heads with space fantasies. "Boys and girls," she told us,
"one day man will walk on the moon." In the far corner on another bulletin
board there was a Thanksgiving scene of turkeys and pilgrims. And stuck in
the corner was a picture of Sacajawea.[6] Sacajawea, Indian Woman Guide. I
preferred looking at Sacajawea over satellites any day.

Thinking about the bubble gum that lay in my pocket, I decided to
sneak a piece, even though gum chewing was strictly forbidden. I rarely
broke the rules. Could anyone hear the loud drumming of my heart, I wondered, as I slid my hand into my skirt pocket and felt for the Double Bubble? I peeked cautiously to either side of me. Then I managed to unwrap it
without even rustling the paper; I drew my hands to my lips, coughed, and
popped the gum in my mouth. Ahhh! Miss Bradley's back was to the class. I
chomped down hard on the Double Bubble. Miss Bradley turned around. I
quickly packed the gum under my tongue. My hands were folded on top of
my desk. "Who can give me a sentence for 'birthday'?" Leonard just about
went nuts. Miss Bradley ignored him, which she did a lot. "Sandra," Miss
Bradley called.

A petite white girl rose obediently. I liked Sandra. She had shared her
crayons with me once when I left mine at home. I remember her drawing: a
white house with smoke coming out of the chimney, a little girl with yellow
hair like hers, a mommy, a daddy, a little boy, and a dog standing in front of
the house in a yard full of flowers. Her voice was crystal clear when she
spoke. There were smiles in that voice. She said, "My father made me a
beautiful dollhouse for my birthday."

The lump under my tongue was suddenly a stone and when I swallowed,
the taste was bitter. I coughed into a piece of tablet paper, spit out the bubble
gum, and crumpled up the wad and pushed it inside my desk. The center of
my chest was burning. I breathed deeply and slowly. Sandra sat down as de-
murely as a princess. She crossed her ankles. Her words came back to me in a
rush. "Muuuy fatha made me a bee-yoo-tee-ful dollhouse." Miss Bradley said,
"Very good," and moved on to the next word. Around me hands were waving,
waving. Pick me! Pick me! Behind me I could hear David softly crooning,
"You ain't nothin' but a hound dog, cryin' all the time." Sometimes he would
stick his head inside his desk, sing Elvis songs, and pick his boogies at the
same time. Somebody was jabbing pins in my chest. Ping! Ping! Ping! I
wanted to holler, "Yowee! Stop!" as loud as I could, but I pressed my lips together hard.

[6]*Sacajawea:* A Shoshone Indian woman (1786–1812), captured and sold to a white man;
she became the famous guide of the 1804 Lewis and Clark expedition.

"Now who can give me a sentence?" Miss Bradley asked. I put my head down on my desk and when Miss Bradley asked me what was wrong I told her that I didn't feel well and that I didn't want to be chosen. When Leonard collected the homework, I shoved mine at him so hard all the papers he was carrying fell on the floor.

Bile was still clogging my throat when Miss Bradley sent me into the cloakroom to get my lunchbox. The rule was, only one student in the cloakroom at a time. When the second one came in, the first one had to leave. I was still rummaging around in my bookbag when I saw Sandra.

"Miss Bradley said for you to come out," she said. She was smiling. That dollhouse girl was always smiling. I glared at her.

"Leave when I get ready to," I said, my words full of venom.

Sandra's eyes darted around in confusion. "Miss Bradley said . . ." she began again, still trying to smile as if she expected somebody to crown her Miss America or something and come take her picture any minute.

In my head a dam broke. Terrible waters rushed out. "I don't care about any Miss Bradley. If she messes with me I'll, I'll . . . I'll take my butcher knife and stab her until she bleeds." What I lacked in props I made up for in drama. My balled-up hand swung menacingly in the air. I aimed the invisible dagger toward Sandra. Her Miss America smile faded instantly. Her eyes grew round and frightened as she blinked rapidly. "Think I won't, huh? Huh?" I whispered, enjoying my meanness, liking the scared look on Sandra's face. Scaredy cat! Scaredy cat! Muuuy fatha made me a bee-yoo-tee-full dollhouse. "What do you think about that?" I added viciously, looking into her eyes to see the total effect of my daring words.

But Sandra wasn't looking at me. Upon closer inspection, I realized that she was looking *over* me with sudden relief in her face. I turned to see what was so interesting, and my chin jammed smack into the Emeraude-scented iron bosom of Miss Bradley. Even as my mind scrambled for an excuse, I knew I was lost.

Miss Bradley had a look of horror on her face. For a minute she didn't say anything, just stood there looking as though someone had slapped her across the face. Sandra didn't say anything. I didn't move. Finally, "Would you mind repeating what you just said, Bebe."

"I didn't say anything, Miss Bradley." I could feel my dress sticking to my body.

"Sandra, what did Bebe say?"

Sandra was crying softly, little delicate tears streaming down her face. For just a second she paused, giving a tiny shudder. I rubbed my ear vigorously, thinking, "Oh, please . . ."

"She said, she said, if you bothered with her she would cut you with her knife."

"Unh unh, Miss Bradley, I didn't say that. I didn't. I didn't say anything like that."

Miss Bradley's gray eyes penetrated mine. She locked me into her gaze until I looked down at the floor. Then she looked at Sandra.

"Bebe, you and I had better go see the principal."

The floor blurred. The principal!! Jennie G., the students called her with awe and fear. As Miss Bradley wrapped her thick knuckles around my forearm and dutifully steered me from the cloakroom and out the classroom door, I completely lost what little cool I had left. I began to cry, a jerky, hiccuping, snot-filled cry for mercy. "I didn't say it. I didn't say it," I moaned.

Miss Bradley was nonplussed. Dedication and duty overruled compassion. Always. "Too late for that now," she said grimly.   35

Jennie G.'s office was small, neat, and dim. The principal was dwarfed by the large brown desk she sat behind, and when she stood up she wasn't much bigger than I. But she was big enough to make me tremble as I stood in front of her, listening to Miss Bradley recount the sordid details of my downfall. Jennie G. was one of those pale, pale vein-showing white women. She had a vocabulary of about six horrible phrases, designed to send chills of despair down the spine of any young transgressor. Phrases like "We'll just see about that" or "come with me, young lady," spoken ominously. Her face was impassive as she listened to Miss Bradley. I'd been told that she had a six-foot paddle in her office used solely to beat young transgressors. Suppose she tried to beat me? My heart gave a lurch. I tugged rapidly at my ears. I longed to suck my thumb.

"Well, Bebe, I think we'll have to call your mother."

My mother! I wanted the floor to swallow me up and take me whole. My mother! As Jennie G. dialed the number, I envisioned my mother's face, clouded with disappointment and shame. I started crying again as I listened to the principal telling my mother what had happened. They talked for a pretty long time. When she hung up, ole Jennie G. flipped through some paper on her desk before looking at me sternly.

"You go back to class and watch your mouth, young lady."

As I was closing the door to her office I heard her say to Miss Bradley,   40
"What can you expect?"

"Ooooh, you're gonna get it girl," is how Michael greeted me after school. Logan's colored world was small, and news of my demise had blazed its way through hallways and classrooms, via the brown-skinned grapevine. Everyone from North Philly, West Philly, and Germantown knew about my crime. The subway ride home was depressing. My fellow commuters kept coming up to me and asking, "Are you gonna get in trouble?" Did they think my mother would give me a reward or something? I stared at the floor for most of the ride, looking up only when the train came to a stop and the doors hissed open. Logan. Wyoming. Hunting Park. Each station drew me closer to my doom, whatever that was going to be. "What can you expect?" I mulled over those words. What did she mean? My mother rarely spanked, although Nana would give Michael or me, usually Michael, a whack across the butt from time to time. My mother's social-worker instincts were too strong for such undignified displays; Doris believed in talking things out, which was sometimes worse than a thousand beatings. As the train drew closer to Susquehanna and

Dauphin I thought of how much I hated for my mother to be disappointed in me. And now she would be. "What can you expect?"

Of me? Didn't Jennie G. know that I was riding a subway halfway across town as opposed to walking around the corner to Carver Elementary School, for a reason: the same reason I was dragged away from Saturday cartoons and pulled from museum to museum, to Judimar School of Dance for ballet (art class for Michael), to Mrs. Clark for piano. The Bosoms wanted me to Be Somebody, to be the second generation to live out my life as far away from a mop and scrub brush and Miss Ann's floors as possible.

My mother had won a full scholarship to the University of Pennsylvania. The story of that miracle was a treasured family heirloom. Sometimes Nana told the tale and sometimes my mother described how the old Jewish counselor at William Penn High School approached her and asked why a girl with straight E's (for "excellent") was taking the commercial course. My mother replied that Nana couldn't afford to send her to college, that she planned to become a secretary. "Sweetheart, you switch to academic," the woman told her. "You'll get to college." When her graduation day approached, the counselor pulled her aside. "I have two scholarships for you. One to Cheyney State Teacher's College and the other to the University of Pennsylvania." Cheyney was a small black school outside of Philadelphia. My mother chose Penn. I had been born to a family of hopeful women. One miracle had already taken place. They expected more. And now I'd thrown away my chance. Michael, who was seated next to me on the subway and whose generosity of spirit had lasted a record five subway stops, poked me in my arm. "Bebe," he told me gleefully, "your ass is grass."

Nana took one look at my guilty face, scowled at me, and sucked her teeth until they whistled. My mother had called her and told her what happened and now she was possessed by a legion of demons. I had barely entered the room when she exploded. "Don't. Come. In. Here. Crying," Nana said, her voice booming, her lips quivering and puffy with anger. When Nana talked in staccato language she was beyond pissed off. Waaaay beyond. "What. Could. Possess. You. To. Say. Such. A. Thing? Embarrassingyourmotherlikethatinfrontof *those people!*" Before I could answer she started singing some Dinah Washington[7] song, real loud. Volume all the way up. With every word she sang I sank deeper and deeper into gloom.

Later that evening, when my mother got home and Aunt Ruth, 45 Michael's mother, came to visit, the three women lectured me in unison. The room was full of flying feathers. Three hens clucking away at me, their breasts heaving with emotion. Cluck! Cluck! Cluck! How could I have said such a thing? What on earth was I thinking about? Cluck! Cluck! Cluck! A knife, such a *colored* weapon.

---

[7]*Dinah Washington:* Blues singer, born Ruth Jones (1924–1963).

"But I didn't do anything," I wailed, the tears that had been trickling all day now falling in full force.

"Umph, umph, umph," Nana said, and started singing. Billie Holiday[8] this time.

"You call threatening somebody with a knife nothing?" Aunt Ruth asked. Ruth was Nana's middle girl. She was the family beauty, as pretty as Dorothy Dandridge[9] or Lena Horne.[10] Now her coral lips were curled up in disdain and her Maybelline eyebrows were raised in judgment against me. "They expect us to act like animals and you have to go and say that. My God."

Animals. Oh. Oh. Oh.

My mother glared at her sister, but I looked at Aunt Ruth in momen- 50 tary wonder and appreciation. Now I understood. The unspoken rule that I had sensed all my life was that a colored child had to be on her best behavior whenever she visited the white world. Otherwise, whatever opportunity was being presented would be snatched away. I had broken the rule. I had committed the unpardonable sin of embarrassing my family in front of *them*. Sensing my remorse and shame, Mommy led me out of the kitchen. We sat down on the living room sofa; my mother took my hand, "Bebe, I want you to go to your room and think about what you've done. I don't understand your behavior. It was very hard for me to get you in Logan." She drew a breath. I drew a breath and looked into the eyes of a social worker. "I'm extremely disappointed in you."

I didn't go straight to my room. Instead I sneaked into Michael's room, which overlooked Mole Street, the tiny, one-sided alley of narrow rowhouses that faced the backyards of 16th Street. Michael and I usually played on the "back street." Alone in Michael's room with the window open, I could hear Mr. Watson, our neighbor, hollering at one of his kids. Why had I said what I said? What had possessed me? Then I remembered. "Muuuy fatha made me a bee-yoo-tee-ful dollhouse for muuuuy birthday." Something pinched me inside my chest when I heard those words. Pain oozed from my heart like a tube of toothpaste bursting open, going every whichaway. Blue-eyes kept yapping away with her golden hair and her goofy little smile. Who cared what her fatha did? Who cared? I couldn't help it. When she came into the cloakroom I got mad all over again. When I said I had a knife, she looked just like Grandma Mary's chickens. Scared. And my chest stopped hurting. Just stopped.

Mr. Watson's baritone voice was a seismic rumble echoing with the threat of upheaval, violence. His words floated over Mole Street and into the bedroom window. Whoever was in trouble over there was really gonna

[8]*Billie Holiday:* Celebrated jazz singer (1915–1959).

[9]*Dorothy Dandridge:* Glamorous film star (1923–1965).

[10]*Lena Horne:* Singer, actor (b. 1917); first black woman vocalist to be featured with a white band.

get it. None of this "go to your room" stuff. None of this corny "I'm disappointed in you" stuff. Mr. Watson was getting ready to beat somebody's ass.

Adam's. He was the youngest and one of my playmates. I could tell by his pleading voice. "Please, Daddy. I won't do it anymore, Daddy. I'm sorry, Daddy."

Michael came into the room. "What are you doing?" he whispered.

"Shhh. Adam's getting a whipping." 55

"You better go to your room before Aunt Doris comes upstairs."

"Shhhh."

My playmate's misery took my mind off my own. His father's exotic yelling hypnotized me. From downstairs I could hear the hens, still clucking away. Michael and I sat quietly, not making a sound. Mr. Watson's voice sounded so foreign coming into our house. For a moment I pretended that his anger was emanating from Michael's bedroom, and I remembered how only last year he got mad and ran after all of us kids — Jackie, Jane, and Adam, his own three, and me. His face was covered with shaving cream and he held a razor in one hand and a thick leather belt in the other. I don't recall what we had done, but I remember him chasing us and yelling ferociously, "This belt's got your name on it too, Miss Bebe!" And I recall that I was thrilled when the leather grazed my hiney with the vengeance of a father's wrath.

My mind drifted back a few years. The memory was vague and fuzzy. When I was four or five I was playing on Mole Street when my ten-year-old neighbor, a boy named Buddy, asked me to come inside his yard. He was sitting on an old soda crate. "Come closer," he told me. "Wanna play doctor?"

"Uh huh." 60

"You can examine me."

I told my mother, prattling on about the "game" I had played. She sat me down on her bed. "Did he touch your private parts?"

"Nope." Why was Mommy's face so serious?

"Did you touch his?"

"I touched his zipper." Had I done something wrong? 65

Nana went into hysterics, singing and screeching like a wild woman. "Mother, just calm down," Mommy told her.

Mommy was cool, every inch the social worker; she took my hand and we walked down the street to Buddy's house. He was in his yard making a scooter out of the crate. "Buddy," my mother said softly. When he saw the two of us, he dropped his hammer. "Buddy, I want to talk with you."

My mother questioned him. Calmly put the fear of God in him. Warned him of penalties for a repeat performance. And that was that. Not quite. Weeks, maybe months later, my father came to visit me, one of his pop-in, no-real-occasion visits. My mother, my father, and I were sitting in his car and she told him about my playing doctor. His leg shot out in wild, uncontrollable spasms. His face became contorted and he started yelling.

Nana's screeching paled in contrast. This was rage that my mother and Nana could not even begin to muster. And it was in my honor. This energy was for my avengement, my protection. Or should have been. But the sound of his fury frightened me. I remember angling away from my father, this man who was yelling like an animal in pain. I leaned toward my mother, and she put one arm around me and with her other hand tried to pat my father's shoulder, only he snatched [it] away. He leaned forward and started reaching for his chair.[11] "I may not be able to walk, goddammit, but I can tear that little son of a bitch's ass up."

My mother kept talking very softly, saying, "No, no, no. It's all right. He's just a kid. I took care of it. It's okay." I leaned away from my father's anger, his determination. He frightened me. But the rage was fascinating too. And after a while, when my father was shouting only a little, I moved closer to him. I wanted to see the natural progression of his hot words. If he snatched his wheelchair out of the backseat and rolled up to Buddy's house, what would he do? What should he do in my honor? My mother calmed my father. His shouting subsided. I was relieved. I was disappointed.

"Hey" — I suddenly heard Michael's persistent voice — "ain't you glad   70
Mr. Watson ain't your father?" I felt Michael's hands, shaking my shoulder. "Ain't you?"

I didn't answer. I was thinking about Miss Bradley, Jennie G., Aunt Ruth, Nana, and Mommy. All these women with power over me. I could hear Mrs. Watson telling her husband that enough was enough and then the baritone telling her he knew when to stop and Adam letting out another feeble little yelp. "Muuuy fatha made me a bee-yoo-tee-ful dollhouse." Maybe my mother would write my daddy and tell him how bad I had been. Maybe he would get so mad he would get into his car and drive all the way to Philly just to whip my behind. Or tell me he was disappointed in me. Either one.

The Bosoms decided to forgive me. My mother woke me up with a kiss and a snuggle and then a crisp, "All right, Bebe. It's a brand-new day. Forget about yesterday." When I went to get a bowl of cereal that morning, my Aunt Ruth was sitting in the kitchen drinking coffee and reading the newspaper. She had spent the night. "Did you comb your hair?" she asked me.

I nodded.

"That's not what I call combed. Go get me the comb and brush."

She combed out my hair and braided it all over again. This time there   75
were no wispy little ends sticking out. "Now you look nice," she said. "Now you look like a pretty girl, and when you go to school today, act like a pretty girl. All right?"

I nodded.

---

[11]*his chair:* Campbell's father had lost the use of his legs in an automobile accident.

Last night Nana had hissed at me between her teeth. "If you want to behave like a little *heathen,* if you want go up there acting like a, a . . . *monkey on a stick* . . . well, thenyoucangotoschoolrightaroundthecornerand I'llwalkyoubackhomeandI'llcomeandgetyouforlunchnowyou*behave*yourself!" But today she was sanguine, even jovial, as she fixed my lunch. She kissed me when I left for school.

On my way out the door my mother handed me two elegant letters, one to Miss Bradley and the other to Jennie G., assuring them that I had an overactive imagination, that I had no access to butcher knives or weapons of any kind, that she had spoken to me at length about my unfortunate outburst, and that henceforth my behavior would be exemplary. These letters were written on her very best personalized stationery. The paper was light pink and had "D.C.M." in embossed letters across the top. Doris C. knew lots of big words and she had used every single one of them in those letters. I knew that all of her *i*'s were dotted and all of her *t*'s were crossed. I knew the letters were extremely dignified. My mother was very big on personal dignity. Anyone who messed with her dignity was in serious trouble.

I was only five when an unfortunate teller at her bank called her by her first name loud enough for the other customers to hear. My mother's body stiffened when she heard, "Doris, oh Doris," coming from a girl almost young enough to be her child.

"Are you talking to *me,* dear?" Her English was so clipped, her words so 80 razor sharp she could have taken one, stabbed the teller, and drawn blood. The girl nodded, her speckled green eyes wide and gaping, aware that something was going on, not quite sure what, and speechless because she was no match at all for this imperious little brown-skinned woman. "The people in *my* office all call me *Mrs. Moore.*"

And she grabbed me by the hand and we swept out of the bank. Me and Bette Davis.[12] Me and Claudia McNeil.[13] People stepped aside to let us pass.

So I knew my mother's letters not only would impress Miss Bradley and Jennie G. but also would go a long way toward redeeming me. After Miss Bradley read the note she told me I have a very nice mother and let me know that if I was willing to be exemplary she would let bygones be bygones and I could get back into her good graces. She was, after all, a dedicated teacher. And I had learned my lesson.

My mother wrote my father about the knife incident. I waited anxiously to hear from him. Would he suddenly appear? I searched the street in front of the school every afternoon. At home I jumped up nervously whenever I heard a horn beep. Finally, a letter from my dad arrived — one page of southpaw scribble.

---

[12]*Bette Davis:* Actor (1908–1989) known for her portrayals of strong, beautiful, intelligent women.

[13]*Claudia McNeil:* Emmy-winning actor (1917–1993).

Dear Bebe,
Your mother told me what happened in school about the knife. That wasn't a good thing to say. I think maybe you were joking. Remember, a lot of times white people don't understand how colored people joke, so you have to be careful what you say around them. Be a good girl.

Lots of love,
Daddy.

The crumpled letter hit the edge of the wastepaper basket in my mother's room and landed in front of her bureau. I picked it up and slammed it into the basket, hitting my hand in the process. I flung myself across the bed, buried my face into my pillow, and howled with pain, rage, and sadness. "It's not fair," I wailed. Ole Blondie had her dollhouse-making daddy whenever she wanted him. "Muuuy fatha . . ." Jackie, Jane, and Adam had their wild, ass-whipping daddy. All they had to do was walk outside their house, look under a car, and there he was, tinkering away. Ole ugly grease-monkey man. Why couldn't I have my daddy all the time too? I didn't want a letter signed "Lots of love," I wanted my father to come and yell at me for acting like a monkey on a stick. I wanted him to come and beat my butt or shake his finger in my face, or tell me that what I did wasn't so bad after all. Anything, I just wanted him to come.

ENGAGING THE TEXT

1. Why does Sandra's sentence in Miss Bradley's class so upset Bebe?
2. The family in "Envy" is clearly matriarchal: "Women ruled at 2239" (para. 5). What positive and negative effects did this matriarchal family have on the author when she was a child?
3. How did the matriarchs groom young Bebe for success? What lessons were taught in this family? Do you think the women's methods of raising the child were the best possible?
4. What does the young Bebe think she is missing with her father's absence? What might he provide that the women do not? Do you think the mature author sees the situation much differently than she did as a child?
5. What traditionally male roles do the women in Bebe's family play? How well do you think they perform these roles?

EXPLORING CONNECTIONS

6. Compare Campbell's family life with Roger Jack's in "An Indian Story" (p. 109). In what ways and for what reasons does each depart from the structure of the Western European nuclear family?
7. Referring to "Envy" (p. 118), "An Indian Story" (p. 109), Rockwell's paintings (pp. 22–24), and this chapter's Visual Portfolio (p. 84), discuss the meaning of the phrase "a close family." For example, is a "close family" syn-

onymous with a "good family" or a "happy family"? Also consider whether
the meaning of "a close family" has shifted since the 1950s, when Rockwell
painted *A Family Tree.*

EXTENDING THE CRITICAL CONTEXT

8. If you have ever felt the lack of a father, mother, sister, brother, or grand-
   parent in your family, write a journal entry or narrative memoir exploring
   your memories and emotions.

9. At the end of *Sweet Summer,* Campbell decides that, while she saw her father only during the summer, her extended family, including uncles, board-
   ers, and family friends, had provided her with plenty of healthy male influences. Read the rest of the book and report to the class on Campbell's
   portrayal of her relationship with her immediate and extended family.

Aunt Ida Pieces a Quilt

MELVIN DIXON

*This is an extraordinary poem about AIDS, love, and family life. Its au-
thor, Melvin Dixon (b. 1950), received his Ph.D. from Brown University; in
addition to teaching English at Queens College in New York, he published
poetry, literary criticism, translations, and two novels. "Aunt Ida" appeared
in* Brother to Brother: New Writings by Black Gay Men *(1991). Dixon died
of complications from AIDS in 1992.*

> You are right, but your patch isn't big enough.
> — JESSE JACKSON

> *When a cure is found and the last panel is
> sewn into place, the Quilt will be displayed
> in a permanent home as a national monument
> to the individual, irreplaceable people lost to AIDS —
> and the people who knew and loved them most.*
> — CLEVE JONES, *founder, The NAMES Project*

They brought me some of his clothes. The hospital gown,
those too-tight dungarees, his blue choir robe
with the gold sash. How that boy could sing!
His favorite color in a necktie. A Sunday shirt.
What I'm gonna do with all this stuff?   5
I can remember Junie without this business.

My niece Francine say they quilting all over the country.
So many good boys like her boy, gone.

At my age I ain't studying no needle and thread.
My eyes ain't so good now and my fingers lock in a fist,   10
they so eaten up with arthritis. This old back
don't take kindly to bending over a frame no more.
Francine say ain't I a mess carrying on like this.
I could make two quilts the time I spend running my mouth.

Just cut his name out the cloths, stitch something nice   15
about him. Something to bring him back. You can do it,
Francine say. Best sewing our family ever had.
Quilting ain't that easy, I say. Never was easy.
Y'all got to help me remember him good.

Most of my quilts was made down South. My mama   20
And my mama's mama taught me. Popped me on the tail
if I missed a stitch or threw the pattern out of line.
I did "Bright Star" and "Lonesome Square" and "Rally Round,"
what many folks don't bother with nowadays. Then Elmo and me
married and came North where the cold in Connecticut   25
cuts you like a knife. We was warm, though.
We had sackcloth and calico and cotton, 100% pure.
What they got now but polyester rayon. Factory made.

Let me tell you something. In all my quilts there's a secret
nobody knows. Every last one of them got my name Ida   30
stitched on the back side in red thread.
That's where Junie got his flair. Don't let nobody fool you.
When he got the Youth Choir standing up and singing
the whole church would rock. He'd throw up his hands
from them wide blue sleeves and the church would hush   35
right down to the funeral parlor fans whisking the air.
He'd toss his head back and holler and we'd all cry holy.

And nevermind his too-tight dungarees.
I caught him switching down the street one Saturday night,
and I seen him more than once. I said, Junie,   40
you ain't got to let the world know all your business.
Who cared where he went when he wanted to have fun.
He'd be singing his heart out come Sunday morning.

When Francine say she gonna hang this quilt in the church
I like to fall out. A quilt ain't no showpiece,   45
it's to keep you warm. Francine say it can do both.
Now I ain't so old-fashioned I can't change,

but I made Francine come over and bring her daughter
Belinda. We cut and tacked his name, *JUNIE.*
Just plain and simple, *"JUNIE, our boy."*   50
Cut the *J* in blue, the *U* in gold. *N* in dungarees
just as tight as you please. The *I* from the hospital gown
and the white shirt he wore First Sunday. Belinda
put the necktie in *E* in the cross stitch I showed her.

Wouldn't you know we got to talking about Junie.   55
We could smell him in the cloth.
Underarm. Afro Sheen pomade.[1] Gravy stains.
I forgot all about my arthritis.
When Francine left me to finish up, I swear
I heard Junie giggling right along with me   60
as I stitched Ida on the back side in red thread.

Francine say she gonna send this quilt to Washington
like folks doing from all 'cross the country,
so many good people gone. Babies, mothers, fathers
and boys like our Junie. Francine say   65
they gonna piece this quilt to another one,
another name and another patch
all in a larger quilt getting larger and larger.

Maybe we all like that, patches waiting to be pieced.
Well, I don't know about Washington.   70
We need Junie here with us. And Maxine,
she cousin May's husband's sister's people,
she having a baby and here comes winter already.
The cold cutting like knives. Now where did I put that needle?

ENGAGING THE TEXT

1. Identify all of the characters and their relationships in the poem. Then
   retell the story of the poem in your own words.
2. Discuss the movement of Aunt Ida's mind and her emotions as we move
   from stanza to stanza. What happens to Aunt Ida in the poem? What is the
   dominant feeling at the end of the poem?
3. Junie's clothes take on symbolic weight in the quilt and, of course, in the
   poem as well. What do the hospital gown, the dungarees, the choir robe,
   and the white shirt and necktie represent?
4. What is Aunt Ida about to make at the end of the poem, and what is its significance?

[1]*Afro Sheen pomade:* Hair-care product for African Americans.

Exploring Connections

5. Discuss the actions of the women in this poem in light of Judy Root
   Aulette's discussion of working-class African American families (p. 64). To
   what extent do the authors seem to share similar perspectives on black
   families?

6. Review the paintings by Norman Rockwell (p. 21–24) and the photographs
   in this chapter's Visual Portfolio (p. 84). Discuss how you might tell the
   story of "Aunt Ida Pieces a Quilt" visually instead of verbally — for example, as a painting, a mural, a photograph, or a photo essay. Sketch or draw
   an image based on the poem and share it with classmates.

Extending the Critical Context

7. Write a screenplay or dramatic script to "translate" the story of "Aunt Ida
   Pieces a Quilt" into dramatic form. Time permitting, organize a group to
   read or perform the piece for the class.

8. Through this chapter, families have been portrayed through a variety of
   metaphors: they have appeared as a nuclear unit, a tree, a network of relationships, and a quilt with many parts. What are the implications of each of
   these metaphors? How do they affect our view of family? What other
   metaphors might capture your vision of American family life?

9. Watch the documentary *Common Threads: Stories from the Quilt* and
   write a poem based on the life of one of the people profiled in this film.

Learning Power

The Myth of Education and Empowerment

Skeptical Student, photo by Charles Agel.

Broke out of Chester gaol,[1] last night, one James Rockett, a very short well set fellow, pretends to be a schoolmaster, of a fair complexion, and smooth fac'd; Had on when he went away, a light colored camblet coat, a blue cloth jacket, without sleeves, a check shirt, a pair of old dy'd leather breaches, gray worsted stockings, a pair of half worn pumps, and an almost new beaver hat; his hair is cut off, and wears a cap; he is a great taker of snuff, and very apt to get drunk; he has with him two certificates, one from some inhabitants in Burlington county, Jersey, which he will no doubt produce as a pass. Who ever takes up and secures said Rockett in any gaol, shall have two Pistoles reward, paid by October 27, 1756. — SAMUEL SMITH, Gaoler

— Advertisement for a "runaway schoolmaster"
Pennsylvania Gazette, November 25, 1756

Americans have always had mixed feelings about schooling. Today, most Americans tend to see education as something intrinsically valuable or important. After all, education is the engine that drives the American Dream. The chance to learn, better oneself, and gain the skills that pay off in upward mobility has sustained the hope of millions of Americans. As a nation we look up to figures like Abraham Lincoln and Frederick Douglass, who learned to see beyond poverty and slavery by learning to read. Education tells us that the American Dream can work for everyone. It reassures us that we are, in fact, "created equal" and that the path to achievement lies through individual effort and hard work, not blind luck or birth.

But as the advertisement quoted above suggests, American attitudes toward teachers and teaching haven't always been overwhelmingly positive. The Puritans who established the Massachusetts Bay Colony viewed education with respectful skepticism. Schooling in Puritan society was a force for spiritual rather than worldly advancement. Lessons were designed to reinforce moral and religious training and to teach children to read the Bible for themselves. Education was important to the Puritan "Divines" because it was a source of order, control, and discipline. But when education aimed at more worldly goals or was undertaken for self-improvement, it was seen as a menacing, sinful luxury. Little wonder, then, that the Puritans often viewed teaching as something less than an ennobling profession. In fact, teachers in the early colonies were commonly treated as menial employees by the families and communities they served. The following list of the "Duties of a Schoolmaster" gives you some idea of the status of American educators in the year 1661:

1. Act as court-messenger
2. Serve summonses
3. Conduct certain ceremonial church services

---

[1]*gaol:* Jail.

4. Lead Sunday choir
5. Ring bell for public worship
6. Dig graves
7. Take charge of school
8. Perform other occasional duties

Colonial American teachers were frequently indentured servants who had sold themselves for five to ten years, often for the price of passage to the New World. Once here, they drilled their masters' children in spiritual exercises until they earned their freedom — or escaped.

The reputation of education in America began to improve with the onset of the Revolutionary War. Following the overthrow of British rule, leaders sought to create a spirit of nationalism that would unify the former colonies. Differences were to be set aside, for, as George Washington pointed out, "the more homogeneous our citizens can be made . . . the greater will be our prospect of permanent union." The goal of schooling became the creation of uniformly loyal, patriotic Americans. In the words of Benjamin Rush, one of the signers of the Declaration of Independence, "Our schools of learning, by producing one general and uniform system of education, will render the mass of people more homogeneous and thereby fit them more easily for uniform and peaceable government."

Thomas Jefferson saw school as a training ground for citizenship and democratic leadership. Recognizing that an illiterate and ill-informed population would be unable to assume the responsibilities of self-government, Jefferson laid out a comprehensive plan in 1781 for public education in the state of Virginia. According to Jefferson's blueprint, all children would be eligible for three years of free public instruction. Of those who could not afford further schooling, one promising "genius" from each school was to be "raked from the rubbish" and given six more years of free education. At the end of that time, ten boys would be selected to attend college at public expense. Jeffersonian Virginia may have been the first place in the United States where education so clearly offered the penniless boy a path to self-improvement. However, this path was open to very few, and Jefferson, like Washington and Rush, was more concerned with benefiting the state than serving the individual student: "We hope to avail the state of those talents which nature has sown as liberally among the poor as the rich, but which perish without use, if not sought for and cultivated." For leaders of the American Revolution, education was seen as a tool for nation-building, not personal development.

Perhaps that's why Native American leaders remained lukewarm to the idea of formal education despite its growing popularity with their colonial neighbors. When, according to Ben Franklin's report, the government of Virginia offered to provide six American Indian youths with the best college education it could afford in 1744, the tribal leaders of the Six Nations politely declined, pointing out that our ideas of this kind of education happen not to be the same with yours. We have had some experience of it; several of our young people were formerly brought up at the colleges of the northern provinces; they were instructed in all your sciences; but when they came back to us, they were bad runners; ignorant of every means of living in the woods; unable to bear either cold or hunger; knew neither how to build a cabin, take a deer, or kill an enemy; spoke our language imperfectly; were therefore neither fit for hunters, warriors, or counselors: they were totally good for nothing.

It's not surprising that these tribal leaders saw American education as useless. Education works to socialize young people — to teach them the values, beliefs, and skills central to their society; the same schooling that prepared students for life in Anglo-American culture made them singularly unfit for tribal life. As people who stood outside the dominant society, Native Americans were quick to realize education's potential as a tool for enforcing cultural conformity. But despite their resistance, by the 1880s the U.S. government had established special "Indian schools" dedicated to assimilating Indian children into Anglo-American culture and destroying tribal knowledge and tribal ways.

In the nineteenth century two great historical forces — industrialization and immigration — combined to exert even greater pressure for the "homogenization" of young Americans. Massive immigration from Ireland and Eastern and Central Europe led to fears that "nonnative" peoples would undermine the cultural identity of the United States. Many saw school as the first line of defense against this perceived threat, a place where the children of "foreigners" could become Americanized. In a meeting of educators in 1836, one college professor stated the problem as bluntly as possible:

> Let us now be reminded, that unless we educate our immigrants, they will be our ruin. It is no longer a mere question of benevolence, of duty, or of enlightened self-interest, but the intellectual and religious training of our foreign population has become essential to our own safety; we are prompted to it by the instinct of self-preservation.

Industrialization gave rise to another kind of uniformity in nineteenth-century public education. Factory work didn't require the kind of educational preparation needed to transform a child into a craftsman or merchant. So, for the first time in American history, school systems began to categorize students into different educational "tracks" that offered qualitatively different kinds of education to different groups. Some — typically students from well-to-do homes — were prepared for professional and managerial positions. But most were consigned to education for life "on the line." Increasing demand for factory workers put a premium on young people who were obedient and able to work in large groups according to fixed schedules. As a result, leading educators in 1874 proposed a system of schooling that would meet the needs of the "modern industrial community" by stressing "punctuality, regularity, attention, and silence, as habits necessary through life." History complicates the myth of education as a source of personal empowerment. School can bind as effectively as it can liberate; it can enforce conformity and limit life chances as well as foster individual talent.

But history also supplies examples of education serving the idealistic goals of democracy, equality, and self-improvement. Nineteenth-century educator and reformer Horace Mann worked to expand educational opportunity to all Americans. Mann believed that genuine democratic self-government would become a reality only if every citizen were sufficiently educated to make reasoned judgments about even the thorniest public issues. "Education," according to Mann, "must prepare our citizens to become municipal officers, intelligent jurors, honest witnesses, legislators, or competent judges of legislation — in fine, to fill all the manifold relations of life." In Mann's conception, the "common school," offering educational opportunity to anyone with the will to learn, would make good on the central promise of American democracy; it would become "the great equalizer of the conditions of men."

At the turn of the century, philosopher and educational theorist John Dewey made even greater claims for educational empowerment. A fierce opponent of the kind of "tracking" associated with industrial education, Dewey proposed that schools should strive to produce thinking citizens rather than obedient workers. As members of a democracy, all men and women, according to Dewey, are entitled to an education that helps them make the best of their natural talents and enables them to participate as fully as possible in the life of their community: "only by being true to the full growth of the individuals who make it up, can society by any chance be true to itself." Most of our current myths of education echo the optimism of Mann and Dewey. Guided by their ideas, most Americans still believe that education leads to self-improvement and can help us empower ourselves — and perhaps even transform our society.

Does education empower us? Or does it stifle personal growth by squeezing us into prefabricated cultural molds? This chapter takes a critical look at American education: what it can do and how it shapes or enhances our identities. The first set of readings provides a starting point for exploring the myth of educational empowerment. We begin with a classic statement of the goals of American education — Horace Mann's 1848 "Report of the Massachusetts Board of Education." Mann's optimistic view of education as a means of social mobility in a democratic state provides a clear statement of the myth of personal empowerment through education. For a quick update on where we stand a century and a half later, we turn to documentary filmmaker Michael Moore's scathing assessment of the current state of American education in "Idiot Nation." Next, veteran teacher and libertarian John Taylor Gatto offers his own conservative analysis of the debilitating "hidden curriculum" of American schooling. In

"'I Just Wanna Be Average,'" Mike Rose provides a moving personal account of the dream of educational success and pays tribute to an inner-city teacher who never loses sight of what can be achieved in a classroom. An excerpt from Jean Anyon's "Social Class and the Hidden Curriculum of Work" rounds off the section by suggesting that schools virtually program students for success or failure according to their socioeconomic status.

Following these initial readings, the chapter's Visual Portfolio presents three paintings by Norman Rockwell that reflect some of America's most hallowed cultural memories of the classroom experience. The reproductions include *The Spirit of Education, The Graduate,* and Rockwell's famous civil-rights-movement portrait of Ruby Bridges as she was escorted to the schoolhouse door. They offer you the chance to consider the place of education in America's cultural mythology and to imagine how a contemporary artist might update the story of educational success for the twenty-first century.

The next group of readings offers a closer look at the tensions experienced by so-called nontraditional students as they struggle with the complexities — and prejudices — of a deeply traditional educational system. The section begins with a classic autobiographical selection by Richard Rodriguez, which raises questions about the ambivalent role schooling plays in the lives of many Americans who come from families new to the world of higher education. In her dramatic narrative poem "Para Teresa," Inés Hernández-Ávila asks whether academic achievement demands cultural conformity or whether it can become a form of protest against oppression and racism. Claude M. Steele's "Thin Ice: 'Stereotype Threat' and Black College Students" presents research suggesting that the academic performance of many minority college students is limited by persistent negative cultural stereotypes and not, as some have argued, by genetics or inherited intelligence. "Learning to Read" closes the section with the moving story of Malcolm X's spiritual and political rebirth through his self-made and highly untraditional education in prison.

The last selections in the chapter round off our examination of the nature of American education by considering some alternatives to the traditional classroom. Deborah Tannen's "The Roots of Debate in Education and the Hope of Dialogue" suggests that the combative intellectual style of American higher education works against the interests of female students. Francesca Delbanco follows Tannen's call for a more dialogical approach to education by reassessing the vices and virtues of alternative schooling in "The Progressive Basics." The chapter closes with renowned social scientist Benjamin R. Barber's critique of the "corporatization" of education and the "privatization" of knowledge in "The Educated Student: Global Citizen or Global Consumer?" In this selection, Barber argues passionately for a return to citizenship as the goal of democratic education in post–9/11 America — but citizenship with a distinctly global twist.

Sources

John Hardin Best and Robert T. Sidwell, eds., *The American Legacy of Learning: Readings in the History of Education.* Philadelphia: J. B. Lippincott Co., 1966.

Sol Cohen, ed., *Education in the United States: A Documentary History,* 5 vols. New York: Random House, 1974.

John Dewey, "The School and Society" (1899) and "My Pedagogic Creed" (1897). In *John Dewey on Education.* New York: Modern Library, 1964.

Benjamin Franklin, "Remarks Concerning the Savages of North America." In *The Works of Dr. Benjamin Franklin.* Hartford: S. Andrus and Son, 1849.

Thomas Jefferson, *Notes on the State of Virginia.* Chapel Hill: University of North Carolina Press, 1955.

Lorraine Smith Pangle and Thomas L. Pangle, *The Learning of Liberty: The Educational Ideas of the American Founders.* Lawrence: University Press of Kansas, 1993.

Leonard Pitt, *We Americans,* vol. 2, 3rd ed. Dubuque: Kendall/Hunt, 1987.

Edward Stevens and George H. Wood, *Justice, Ideology, and Education: An Introduction to the Social Foundations of Education.* New York: Random House, 1987.

Elizabeth Vallance, "Hiding the Hidden Curriculum: An Interpretation of the Language of Justification in Nineteenth-Century Educational Reform." *Curriculum Theory Network,* vol. 4. no. 1 (1973–74), pp. 5–21.

Robert B. Westbrook, "Public Schooling and American Democracy." In *Democracy, Education, and the Schools,* Roger Soder, ed. San Francisco: Jossey-Bass Publishers, 1996.

BEFORE READING

- Freewrite for fifteen or twenty minutes about your best and worst educational experiences. Then, working in groups, compare notes to see if you can find recurring themes or ideas in what you've written. What aspects of school seem to stand out most clearly in your memories? Do the best experiences have anything in common? How about the worst? What aspects of your school experience didn't show up in the freewriting?

- Work in small groups to draw a collective picture that expresses your experience of high school or college. Don't worry about your drawing skill — just load the page with imagery, feelings, and ideas. Then show your work to other class members and let them try to interpret it.

- Write a journal entry from the point of view of the girl pictured on the title page of this chapter (p. 135). Try to capture the thoughts that are going through her head. What has her day in school been like? What is she looking forward to? What is she dreading? Share your entries with your classmates and discuss your responses.

From *Report of the Massachusetts Board of Education, 1848*

HORACE MANN

If you check a list of schools in your home state, you'll probably discover at least a few dedicated to the memory of Horace Mann. We memorialize Mann today in school systems across the country because he may have done more than any other American to codify the myth of empowerment through education. Born on a farm in Franklin, Massachusetts, in 1796, Mann raised himself out of rural poverty to a position of national eminence through hard work and study. His first personal educational experiences, however, were far from pleasurable: the ill-trained and often brutal schoolmasters he first encountered in rural Massachusetts made rote memorization and the power of the rod the focus of their educational approach. After graduating from Brown University in 1819, Mann pursued a career in law and politics and eventually served as president of the Massachusetts State Senate. Discouraged by the condition of the state's public schools, Mann abandoned his political career to become secretary of the Massachusetts Board of Education in 1837. Mann's vision of "the common school," the centerpiece of his approach to democratic education, grew out of research he conducted on the Prussian school system during his tour of Europe in 1843. Presented originally as an address to the Massachusetts State Legislature, the report of 1848 has had a lasting impact on the goals and content of American education.

Without undervaluing any other human agency, it may be safely affirmed that the common school, improved and energized as it can easily be, may become the most effective and benignant of all the forces of civilization. Two reasons sustain this position. In the first place, there is a universality in its operation, which can be affirmed of no other institution whatever. If administered in the spirit of justice and conciliation, all the rising generation may be brought within the circle of its reformatory and elevating influences. And, in the second place, the materials upon which it operates are so pliant and ductile as to be susceptible of assuming a greater variety of forms than any other earthly work of the Creator. The inflexibility and ruggedness of the oak, when compared with the lithe sapling or the tender germ, are but feeble emblems to typify the docility of childhood when contrasted with the obduracy and intractableness of man. It is these inherent advantages of the common school, which, in our own State, have produced results so striking, from a system so imperfect, and an administration so feeble. In teaching the blind and the deaf and dumb, in kindling the latent spark of intelligence that lurks in an idiot's mind, and in the more holy work of reforming abandoned and outcast children, education has proved what it can do by glorious experiments. These wonders it has done in its infancy, and with the lights of a limited experience; but when its faculties shall be fully developed, when it shall be trained to wield its mighty energies for the protection of society against the giant vices which now invade and torment it, — against intemperance, avarice, war, slavery, bigotry, the woes of want, and the wickedness of waste, — then there will not be a height to which these enemies of the race can escape which it will not scale, nor a Titan among them all whom it will not slay.

I proceed, then, in endeavoring to show how the true business of the schoolroom connects itself, and becomes identical, with the great interests of society. The former is the infant, immature state of those interests; the latter their developed, adult state. As "the child is father to the man," so may the training of the schoolroom expand into the institutions and fortunes of the State.

Physical Education

In the worldly prosperity of mankind, health and strength are indispensable ingredients. . . .

Leaving out, then, for the present purpose, all consideration of the pains of sickness and the anguish of bereavement, the momentous truth still remains, that sickness and premature death are positive evils for the statesman and political economist to cope with. The earth, as a hospital for the diseased, would soon wear out the love of life; and, if but the half of mankind were sick, famine, from non-production, would speedily threaten the whole.

Now, modern science has made nothing more certain than that both good and ill health are the direct result of causes mainly within our own control. In other words, the health of the race is dependent upon the conduct of the race. The health of the individual is determined primarily by his parents, secondarily by himself. The vigorous growth of the body, its strength and its activity, its powers of endurance, and its length of life, on the one hand; and dwarfishness, sluggishness, infirmity, and premature death on the other, — are all the subjects of unchangeable laws. These laws are ordained of God; but the knowledge of them is left to our diligence, and the observance of them to our free agency. . . .

My general conclusion, then, under this head, is, that it is the duty of all the governing minds in society — whether in office or out of it — to diffuse a knowledge of these beautiful and beneficent laws of health and life throughout the length and breadth of the State; to popularize them; to make them, in the first place, the common acquisition of all, and, through education and custom, the common inheritance of all, so that the healthful habits naturally growing out of their observance shall be inbred in the people, exemplified in the personal regimen of each individual, incorporated into the economy of every household, observable in all private dwellings, and in all public edifices, especially in those buildings which are erected by capitalists for the residence of their work-people, or for renting to the poorer classes; obeyed, by supplying cities with pure water; by providing public baths, public walks, and public squares; by rural cemeteries; by the drainage and sewerage of populous towns, and by whatever else may promote the general salubrity of the atmosphere: in fine, by a religious observance of all those sanitary regulations with which modern science has blessed the world.

For this thorough diffusion of sanitary intelligence, the common school is the only agency. It is, however, an adequate agency. . . .

Intellectual Education as a Means of Removing Poverty, and Securing Abundance

. . . According to the European theory, men are divided into classes, — some to toil and earn, others to seize and enjoy. According to the Massachusetts theory, all are to have an equal chance for earning, and equal security in the enjoyment of what they earn. The latter tends to equality of condition; the former, to the grossest inequalities. . . .

But is it not true that Massachusetts, in some respects, instead of adhering more and more closely to her own theory, is becoming emulous of the baneful examples of Europe? The distance between the two extremes of society is lengthening, instead of being abridged. With every generation, fortunes increase on the one hand, and some new privation is added to poverty on the other. We are verging towards those extremes of opulence and of penury, each of which unhumanizes the human mind. A perpetual struggle for the bare necessaries of life, without the ability to obtain them, makes men wolfish. Avarice, on the other hand, sees, in all the victims of misery around it, not objects for pity and succor, but only crude materials to be worked up into more money.

I suppose it to be the universal sentiment of all those who mingle any ingredient of benevolence with their notions on political economy, that vast and overshadowing private fortunes are among the greatest dangers to which the happiness of the people in a republic can be subjected. Such fortunes would create a feudalism of a new kind, but one more oppressive and unrelenting than that of the middle ages. The feudal lords in England and on the Continent never held their retainers in a more abject condition of servitude than the great majority of foreign manufacturers and capitalists hold their operatives and laborers at the present day. The means employed are different; but the similarity in results is striking. What force did then, money does now. The villein of the middle ages had no spot of earth on which he could live, unless one were granted to him by his lord. The operative or laborer of the present day has no employment, and therefore no bread, unless the capitalist will accept his services. The vassal had no shelter but such as his master provided for him. Not one in five thousand of English operatives or farm-laborers is able to build or own even a hovel; and therefore they must accept such shelter as capital offers them. The baron prescribed his own terms to his retainers: those terms were peremptory, and the serf must submit or perish. The British manufacturer or farmer prescribes the rate of wages he will give to his work-people; he reduces these wages under whatever pretext he pleases; and they, too, have no alternative but submission or starvation. In some respects, indeed, the condition of the modern dependant is more forlorn than that of the corresponding serf class in former times. Some attributes of the patriarchal relation did spring up between the lord and his lieges to soften the harsh relations subsisting between them. Hence came some oversight of the condition of children, some relief in sickness, some protection and support in the decrepitude of age. But only in instances comparatively few have kindly offices smoothed the rugged relation between British capital and British labor. The children of the work-people are abandoned to their fate; and notwithstanding the privations they suffer, and the dangers they threaten, no power in the realm has yet been able to secure them an education; and when the adult laborer is prostrated by sickness, or eventually worn out by toil and age, the poor-house, which has all along been his destination, becomes his destiny. . . .

Now, surely nothing but universal education can counterwork this tendency to the domination of capital and servility of labor. If one class possesses all the wealth and the education, while the residue of society is ignorant and poor, it matters not by what name the relation between them may be called: the latter, in fact and in truth, will be the servile dependants and subjects of the former. But, if education be equably diffused, it will draw property after it by the strongest of all attractions, for such a thing never did happen, and never can happen, as that an intelligent and practical body of men should be permanently poor. Property and labor in different classes are essentially antagonistic; but property and labor in the same class are essentially fraternal. The people of Massachusetts have, in some degree, appreciated the truth, that the unexampled prosperity of the State — its comfort, its competence, its general intelligence and virtue — is attributable to the education, more or less perfect, which all its people have received: but are they sensible of a fact equally important; namely, that it is to this same education that two-thirds of the people are indebted for not being to-day the vassals of as severe a tyranny, in the form of capital, as the lower classes of Europe are bound to in the form of brute force?

Education, then, beyond all other devices of human origin, is the great equalizer of the conditions of men, — the balance-wheel of the social machinery. I do not here mean that it so elevates the moral nature as to make men disdain and abhor the oppression of their fellow-men. This idea pertains to another of its attributes. But I mean that it gives each man the independence and the means by which he can resist the selfishness of other men. It does better than to disarm the poor of their hostility towards the rich: it prevents being poor. Agrarianism is the revenge of poverty against wealth. The wanton destruction of the property of others — the burning of hay-ricks and corn-ricks, the demolition of machinery because it supersedes hand-labor, the sprinkling of vitriol on rich dresses — is only agrarianism run mad. Education prevents both the revenge and the madness. On the other hand, a fellow-feeling for one's class or caste is the common instinct of hearts not wholly sunk in selfish regards for person or for family. The spread of education, by enlarging the cultivated class or caste, will open a wider area over which the social feelings will expand; and, if this education should be universal and complete, it would do more than all things else to obliterate factitious distinctions in society. . . .

For the creation of wealth, then, — for the existence of a wealthy people and a wealthy nation, — intelligence is the grand condition. The number of improvers will increase as the intellectual constituency, if I may call it, increases. In former times, and in most parts of the world even at the present day, not one man in a million has ever had such a development of mind as made it possible for him to become a contributor to art or science. Let this development precede, and contributions, numberless, and of inestimable value, will be sure to follow. That political economy, therefore, which busies itself about capital and labor, supply and demand, interest and rents, favorable and unfavorable balances of trade, but leaves out of account the element of a widespread mental development, is nought but stupendous folly. The greatest of all the arts in political economy is to change a consumer into a producer; and the next greatest is to increase the producer's producing power, — an end to be directly attained by increasing his intelligence. For mere delving, an ignorant man is but little better than a swine, whom he so much resembles in his appetites, and surpasses in his powers of mischief. . . .

Political Education

The necessity of general intelligence, — that is, of education (for I use the terms as substantially synonymous, because general intelligence can never exist without general education, and general education will be sure to produce general intelligence), — the necessity of general intelligence under a republican form of government, like most other very important truths, has become a very trite one. It is so trite, indeed, as to have lost much of its force by its familiarity. Almost all the champions of education seize upon this argument first of all, because it is so simple as to be understood by the ignorant, and so strong as to convince the sceptical. Nothing would be easier than to follow in the train of so many writers, and to demonstrate by logic, by history, and by the nature of the case, that a republican form of government, without intelligence in the people, must be, on a vast scale, what a madhouse, without superintendent or keepers, would be on a small one, — the despotism of a few succeeded by universal anarchy, and anarchy by despotism, with no change but from bad to worse. . . .

However elevated the moral character of a constituency may be, however well informed in matters of general science or history, yet they must, if citizens of a republic, understand something of the true nature and functions of the government under which they live. That any one, who is to participate in the government of a country when he becomes a man, should receive no instruction respecting the nature and functions of the government he is afterwards to administer, is a political solecism. In all nations, hardly excepting the most rude and barbarous, the future sovereign receives some training which is supposed to fit him for the exercise of the powers and duties of his anticipated station. Where, by force of law, the government devolves upon the heir while yet in a state of legal infancy, some regency, or other substitute, is appointed to act in his stead until his arrival at mature age; and, in the mean time, he is subjected to such a course of study and discipline as will tend to prepare him, according to the political theory of the time and the place, to assume the reins of authority at the appointed age. If in England, or in the most enlightened European monarchies, it would be a proof of restored barbarism to permit the future sovereign to grow up without any knowledge of his duties, — and who can doubt that it would be such a proof? — then, surely, it would be not less a proof of restored or of never-removed barbarism amongst us to empower any individual to use the elective franchise without preparing him for so momentous a trust. Hence the Constitution of the United States, and of our own State, should be made a study in our public schools. The partition of the powers of government into the three co-ordinate branches, — legislative, judicial, and executive — with the duties appropriately devolving upon each; the mode of electing or of appointing all officers, with the reasons on which it was founded; and, especially, the duty of every citizen, in a government of laws, to appeal to the courts for redress in all cases of alleged wrong, instead of undertaking to vindicate his own rights by his own arm; and, in a government where the people are the acknowledged sources of power, the duty of changing laws and rulers by an appeal to the ballot, and not by rebellion, — should be taught to all the children until they are fully understood.

Had the obligations of the future citizen been sedulously inculcated upon all the children of this Republic, would the patriot have had to mourn over so many instances where the voter, not being able to accomplish his purpose by voting, has proceeded to accomplish it by violence; where, agreeing with his fellow-citizens to use the machinery of the ballot, he makes a tacit reservation, that, if that machinery does not move according to his pleasure, he will wrest or break it? If the responsibleness and value of the elective franchise were duly appreciated, the day of our state and national elections would be among the most solemn and religious days in the calendar. Men would approach them, not only with preparation and solicitude, but with the sobriety and solemnity with which discreet and religious-minded men meet the great crises of life. No man would throw away his vote through caprice or wantonness, any more than he would throw away his estate, or sell his family into bondage. No man would cast his vote through malice or revenge, any more than a good surgeon would amputate a limb, or a good navigator sail through perilous straits, under the same criminal passions.

But perhaps it will be objected, that the Constitution is subject to different readings, or that the policy of different administrations has become the subject of party strife; and, therefore, if any thing of constitutional or political law is introduced into our schools, there is danger that teachers will be chosen on account of their affinities to this or that political party, or that teachers will feign affinities which they do not feel in order that they may be chosen; and so each schoolroom will at length become a miniature political club-room, exploding with political resolves, or flaming out with political addresses, prepared by beardless boys in scarcely legible hand-writing and in worse grammar.

With the most limited exercise of discretion, all apprehensions of this kind are wholly groundless. There are different readings of the Constitution, it is true; and there are partisan topics which agitate the country from side to side: but the controverted points, compared with those about which there is no dispute, do not bear the proportion of one to a hundred. And, what is more, no man is qualified, or can be qualified, to discuss the disputable questions, unless previously and thoroughly versed in those questions about which there is no dispute. In the terms and principles common to all, and recognized by all, is to be found the only common medium of language and of idea by which the parties can become intelligible to each other; and there, too, is the only common ground whence the arguments of the disputants can be drawn. . . .

. . . Thus may all the children of the Commonwealth receive instruction in all the great essentials of political knowledge, — in those elementary ideas without which they will never be able to investigate more recondite and debatable questions; thus will the only practicable method be adopted for discovering new truths, and for discarding, instead of perpetuating, old errors; and thus, too, will that pernicious race of intolerant zealots, whose whole faith may be summed up in two articles, — that they themselves are always infallibly right, and that all dissenters are certainly wrong, — be extinguished, — extinguished, not by violence, nor by proscription, but by the more copious inflowing of the light of truth.

Moral Education

Moral education is a primal necessity of social existence. The unrestrained passions of men are not only homicidal, but suicidal; and a community without a conscience would soon extinguish itself. Even with a natural conscience, how often has evil triumphed over good! From the beginning of time, wrong has followed right, as the shadow the substance. . . .   20

But to all doubters, disbelievers, or despairers in human progress, it may still be said, there is one experiment which has never yet been tried. It is an experiment, which, even before its inception, offers the highest authority for its ultimate success. Its formula is intelligible to all; and it is as legible as though written in starry letters on an azure sky. It is expressed in these few and simple words: *"Train up a child in the way he should go; and, when he is old, he will not depart from it."* This declaration is positive. If the conditions are complied with, it makes no provision for a failure. Though pertaining to morals, yet, if the terms of the direction are observed, there is no more reason to doubt the result than there would be in an optical or a chemical experiment.

But this experiment has never yet been tried. Education has never yet been brought to bear with one-hundredth part of its potential force upon the natures of children, and, through them, upon the character of men and of the race. In all the attempts to reform mankind which have hitherto been made, whether by changing the frame of government, by aggravating or softening the severity of the penal code, or by substituting a government-created for a God-created religion, — in all these attempts, the infantile and youthful mind, its amenability to influences, and the enduring and self-operating character of the influences it receives, have been almost wholly unrecognized. Here, then, is a new agency, whose powers are but just beginning to be understood, and whose mighty energies hitherto have been but feebly invoked; and yet, from our experience, limited and imperfect as it is, we do know, that, far beyond any other earthly instrumentality, it is comprehensive and decisive. . . .

. . . So far as human instrumentalities are concerned, we have abundant means for surrounding every child in the State with preservative and moral influences as extensive and as efficient as those under which the present industrious, worthy, and virtuous members of the community were reared. And as to all those things in regard to which we are directly dependent upon the divine favor, have we not the promise, explicit and unconditional, that the men SHALL NOT depart from the way in which they should go, if the children are trained up in it? It has been overlooked that this promise is not restricted to parents, but seems to be addressed indiscriminately to all, whether parents, communities, states, or mankind. . . .

Religious Education

But it will be said that this grand result in practical morals is a consummation of blessedness that can never be attained without religion, and that no community will ever be religious without a religious education. Both these propositions I regard as eternal and immutable truths. Devoid of religious principles and religious affections, the race can never fall so low but that it may sink still lower; animated and sanctified by them, it can never rise so high but that it may ascend still higher. And is it not at least as presumptuous to expect that mankind will attain to the knowledge of truth, without being instructed in truth, and without that general expansion and development of faculty which will enable them to recognize and comprehend truth in any other department of human interest as in the department of religion? . . .

. . . That our public schools are not theological seminaries, is admitted. That they are debarred by law from inculcating the peculiar and distinctive doctrines of any one religious denomination amongst us, is claimed; and that they are also prohibited from ever teaching that what they do teach is the whole of religion, or all that is essential to religion or to salvation, is equally certain. But our system earnestly inculcates all Christian morals; it founds its morals on the basis of religion; it welcomes the religion of the Bible; and, in receiving the Bible, it allows it to do what it is allowed to do in no other system, — *to speak for itself.* But here it stops, not because it claims to have compassed all truth, but because it disclaims to act as an umpire between hostile religious opinions.

The very terms "public school" and "common school" bear upon their face that they are schools which the children of the entire community may attend. Every man not on the pauper-list is taxed for their support; but he is not taxed to support them as special religious institutions: if he were, it would satisfy at once the largest definition of a religious establishment. But he is taxed to support them as a *preventive* means against dishonesty, against fraud, and against violence, on the same principle that he is taxed to support criminal courts as a *punitive* means against the same offences. He is taxed to support schools, on the same principle that he is taxed to support paupers, — because a child without education is poorer and more wretched than a man without bread. He is taxed to support schools, on the same principle that he would be taxed to defend the nation against foreign invasion, or against rapine committed by a foreign foe, — because the general prevalence of ignorance, superstition, and vice, will breed Goth and Vandal at home more fatal to the public well-being than any Goth or Vandal from abroad. And, finally, he is taxed to support schools, because they are the most effective means of developing and training those powers and faculties in a child, by which, when he becomes a man, he may understand what his highest interests and his highest duties are, and may be in fact, and not in name only, a free agent. The elements of a political education are not bestowed upon any school child for the purpose of making him vote with this or that political party when he becomes of age, but for the purpose of enabling him to choose for himself with which party he will vote. So the religious education which a child receives at school is not imparted to him for the purpose of making him join this or that denomination when he arrives at years of discretion, but for the purpose of enabling him to judge for himself, according to the dictates of his own reason and conscience, what his religious obligations are, and whither they lead. . . .

Such, then, in a religious point of view, is the Massachusetts system of common schools. Reverently it recognizes and affirms the sovereign rights of

the Creator, sedulously and sacredly it guards the religious rights of the creature; while it seeks to remove all hinderances, and to supply all furtherances,
to a filial and paternal communion between man and his Maker. In a social
and political sense, it is a *free* school-system. It knows no distinction of rich
and poor, of bond and free, or between those, who, in the imperfect light of
this world, are seeking, through different avenues, to reach the gate of
heaven. Without money and without price, it throws open its doors, and
spreads the table of its bounty, for all the children of the State. Like the sun,
it shines not only upon the good, but upon the evil, that they may become
good; and, like the rain, its blessings descend not only upon the just, but upon
the unjust, that their injustice may depart from them, and be known no more.

Engaging the Text

1. What is Mann's view of the powers of education? What does he see as education's role in society? To what extent would you agree that education successfully carries out these functions today?

2. What does Mann mean by "sanitary intelligence" (para. 7)? Why did he feel
   that the development of this kind of intelligence was such an important aspect of schooling? In what ways has your own education stressed the development of sanitary intelligence? How valuable has this nonacademic
   instruction been?

3. How does Mann view the role of education in relation to wealth and
   poverty? How do you think such views would be received today if advocated by a school-board candidate or contender for the presidency? In your
   estimation, how effective has education been in addressing economic differences in American society?

4. Mann suggests that education plays a special role in preparing citizens to
   become active participants in a republican form of government. In what
   ways has your education prepared you to participate in democratic decision
   making? How effective has this preparation been? What could be done to
   improve the way that schools currently prepare students for their role as
   citizens?

5. What, according to Mann, is the proper relationship of public education to
   issues of morality and religion? What specific moral or ethical principles
   should public schools attempt to teach?

Exploring Connections

6. Read "Class in America: Myths and Realities (2000)" by Gregory Mantsios
   (p. 331), "Stephen Cruz" by Studs Terkel (p. 348), and "Race at the End of
   History" by Ronald Takaki (p. 393) and write an essay in which you discuss
   how class differences in American society complicate the educational program outlined by Mann.

Troubletown

BY LLOYD DANGLE

GOOD MORNING CLASS. BEFORE WE BEGIN, PATTY WILL RECITE THE PLEDGE OF ALLEGIANCE, HENRY WILL LEAD MORNING PRAYER SERVICE, PHILLIP WILL WHISTLE THE CONFEDERATE ANTHEM, KIMBERLY WILL INSPECT UNIFORMS, DEAN WILL STAMP EVERYONE'S VOUCHERS, AND LUCY WILL CRUISE THE NETWORK FOR BUGS AND EVIDENCE OF TAMPERING WITH OUR OBSCENITY-BLOCKING SOFTWARE!

IF ALL THE "EDUCATION REFORMS" HAPPENED AT ONCE,

7. Review the cartoon "If All the 'Education Reforms' Happened at Once," which appears at the top of this page. As a class, debate whether or not American education is trying to do too much today.

EXTENDING THE CRITICAL CONTEXT

8. Research recent court decisions and legislative initiatives on the issue of prayer in school. How do prevailing views of the separation of church and state compare with the ideas presented in Mann's assessment of the goals of public education in 1848? Then, as a class, debate the proper role of moral and religious instruction in public education.

9. Working in small groups, draft a list of what you think the proper goals of public education in a democracy should be. Exchange these lists, then compare and discuss your results. How does your class's view of the powers of education differ from that offered by Mann?

Idiot Nation

MICHAEL MOORE

When Michael Moore (b. 1954) held up his Oscar for best documentary during the 2002 Academy Awards show and shouted "Shame on you, Mr. Bush" to a chorus of boos from the audience, no one who knew his work would have been shocked. A social gadfly and cinematic activist without equal for the past two decades, Moore isn't the type to shy away from telling the president what he thinks of him on national TV; nor is he the type to disguise his contempt for the general level of idiocy he sees in American society. In this selection from Stupid White Men . . . and Other Sorry Excuses for the State of the Nation, *his best-selling 2002 diatribe against our collective cluelessness, Moore zeroes in on the sorry state of American education. Serving up generous examples from his own less-than-stellar educational career, Moore takes us on a tour of the failings of America's schoolrooms — from libraries without books to commanders in chief who can't distinguish between countries and continents. Along the way, he touches on topics like the cultural illiteracy of television talk show hosts, the growing movement for educational "accountability," and the corporate takeover of America's classrooms. He even offers a list of things every student can do to fight back against educational subservience. Before winning the Oscar in 2002 for his* Bowling for Columbine, *Moore directed* Roger and Me *(1989), which chronicled his attempts to question then-General-Motors-chairman Roger Smith about a series of factory closures that devastated the economy of Flint, Michigan, Moore's hometown. He is also the creator of the feature film* Canadian Bacon *(1995) and the experimental Emmy-award-winning 1995 television series* TV Nation.

Do you feel like you live in a nation of idiots?

I used to console myself about the state of stupidity in this country by repeating this to myself: *Even if there are two hundred million stone-cold idiots in this country, that leaves at least eighty million who'll get what I'm saying — and that's still more than the populations of the United Kingdom and Iceland combined!*

Then came the day I found myself sharing an office with the ESPN game show *Two-Minute Drill.* This is the show that tests your knowledge of not only who plays what position for which team, but who hit what where in a 1925 game between Boston and New York, who was rookie of the year in 1965 in the old American Basketball Association, and what Jake Wood had for breakfast the morning of May 12, 1967.

I don't know the answer to any of those questions — but for some reason I do remember Jake Wood's uniform number: 2. Why on earth am I retaining that useless fact?

I don't know, but after watching scores of guys waiting to audition for that ESPN show, I think I do know something about intelligence and the American mind. Hordes of these jocks and lunkheads hang out in our hallway awaiting their big moment, going over hundreds of facts and statistics in their heads and challenging each other with questions I can't see why anyone would be able to answer other than God Almighty Himself. To look at these testosterone-loaded bruisers you would guess that they were a bunch of illiterates who would be lucky if they could read the label on a Bud.

In fact, they are geniuses. They can answer all thirty obscure trivia questions in less than 120 seconds. That's four seconds a question — including the time used by the slow-reading celebrity athletes who ask the questions.

I once heard the linguist and political writer Noam Chomsky say that if you want proof the American people aren't stupid, just turn on any sports talk radio show and listen to the incredible retention of facts. It is amazing — and it's proof that the American mind is alive and well. It just isn't challenged with anything interesting or exciting. *Our* challenge, Chomsky said, was to find a way to make politics as gripping and engaging as sports. When we do that, watch how Americans will do nothing but talk about who did what to whom at the WTO.[1]

But first, they have to be able to read the letters *WTO*.

There are forty-four million Americans who cannot read and write above a fourth-grade level — in other words, who are functional illiterates.

How did I learn this statistic? Well, I *read* it. And now you've read it. So we've already eaten into the mere 99 hours a *year* an average American adult spends reading a book — compared with 1,460 hours watching television.

I've also read that only 11 percent of the American public bothers to *read* a daily newspaper, beyond the funny pages or the used car ads.

So if you live in a country where forty-four million can't read — and perhaps close to another two hundred million can read but usually don't — well, friends, you and I are living in one very scary place. A nation that not only churns out illiterate students BUT GOES OUT OF ITS WAY TO REMAIN IGNORANT AND STUPID is a nation that should not be running the world — at least not until a majority of its citizens can locate Kosovo[2] (or any other country it has bombed) on the map.

It comes as no surprise to foreigners that Americans, who love to revel in their stupidity, would "elect" a president who rarely reads *anything* —

---

[1]*WTO:* World Trade Organization.

[2]*Kosovo:* Province that precipitated the 1999 NATO invasion of Serbia after it demanded increased autonomy.

including his own briefing papers—and thinks Africa is a nation, not a continent. An idiot leader of an idiot nation. In our glorious land of plenty, less is always more when it comes to taxing any lobe of the brain with the intake of facts and numbers, critical thinking, or the comprehension of anything that isn't . . . well, sports.

Our Idiot-in-Chief does nothing to hide his ignorance — he even brags about it. During his commencement address to the Yale Class of 2001, George W. Bush spoke proudly of having been a mediocre student at Yale. "And to the C students, I say you, too, can be President of the United States!" The part where you also need an ex-President father, a brother as governor of a state with missing ballots, and a Supreme Court full of your dad's buddies must have been too complicated to bother with in a short speech.

As Americans, we have quite a proud tradition of being represented by ignorant high-ranking officials. In 1956 President Dwight D. Eisenhower's nominee as ambassador to Ceylon (now Sri Lanka) was unable to identify either the country's prime minister or its capital during his Senate confirmation hearing. Not a problem — Maxwell Gluck was confirmed anyway. In 1981 President Ronald Reagan's nominee for deputy secretary of state, William Clark, admitted to a wide-ranging lack of knowledge about foreign affairs at his confirmation hearing. Clark had no idea how our allies in Western Europe felt about having American nuclear missiles based there, and didn't know the names of the prime ministers of South Africa or Zimbabwe. Not to worry — he was confirmed, too. All this just paved the way for Baby Bush, who hadn't quite absorbed the names of the leaders of India or Pakistan, two of the seven nations that possess the atomic bomb.

And Bush went to Yale *and* Harvard.

Recently a group of 556 seniors at fifty-five prestigious American universities (e.g., Harvard, Yale, Stanford) were given a multiple-choice test consisting of questions that were described as "high school level." Thirty-four questions were asked. These top students could only answer 53 percent of them correctly. And only one student got them all right.

A whopping 40 percent of these students did not know when the Civil War took place — even when given a wide range of choices: A. 1750–1800; B. 1800–1850; C. 1850–1900; D. 1900–1950; or E. after 1950. (*The answer is C, guys.*) The two questions the college seniors scored highest on were (1) Who is Snoop Doggy Dog? (98 percent got that one right), and (2) Who are Beavis and Butt-head? (99 percent knew). For my money, Beavis and Butt-head represented some of the best American satire of the nineties, and Snoop and his fellow rappers have much to say about America's social ills, so I'm not going down the road of blaming MTV.

What I *am* concerned with is why politicians like Senators Joe Lieberman of Connecticut and Herbert Kohl of Wisconsin want to go after MTV when *they* are the ones responsible for the massive failure of American education. Walk into any public school, and the odds are good that you'll find overflowing classrooms, leaking ceilings, and demoralized teachers. In 1 out of 4 schools, you'll find students "learning" from textbooks published in the 1980s — or earlier.

Why is this? Because the political leaders — and the people who vote for them — have decided it's a bigger priority to build another bomber than to educate our children. They would rather hold hearings about the depravity of a television show called *Jackass* than about their own depravity in neglecting our schools and children and maintaining our title as Dumbest Country on Earth.   20

I hate writing these words. I *love* this big lug of a country and the crazy people in it. But when I can travel to some backwater village in Central America, as I did back in the eighties, and listen to a bunch of twelve-year-olds tell me their concerns about the World Bank, I get the feeling that *something* is lacking in the United States of America.

Our problem isn't just that our kids don't know nothin' but that the adults who pay their tuition are no better. I wonder what would happen if we tested the U.S. Congress to see just how much our representatives know. What if we were to give a pop quiz to the commentators who cram our TVs and radios with all their nonstop nonsense? How many would *they* get right?

A while back, I decided to find out. It was one of those Sunday mornings when the choice on TV was the *Parade of Homes* real estate show or *The McLaughlin Group*. If you like the sound of hyenas on Dexedrine, of course, you go with *McLaughlin*. On this particular Sunday morning, perhaps as my punishment for not being at Mass, I was forced to listen to magazine columnist Fred Barnes (now an editor at the right-wing *Weekly Standard* and co-host of the Fox News show *The Beltway Boys*) whine on and on about the sorry state of American education, blaming the teachers and their evil union for why students are doing so poorly.

"These kids don't even know what *The Iliad* and *The Odyssey* are!" he bellowed, as the other panelists nodded in admiration at Fred's noble lament.

The next morning I called Fred Barnes at his Washington office.   25
"Fred," I said, "tell me what *The Iliad* and *The Odyssey* are."

He started hemming and hawing. "Well, they're . . . uh . . . you know . . . uh . . . okay, fine, you got me — I don't know what they're about. Happy now?"

No, not really. You're one of the top TV pundits in America, seen every week on your own show and plenty of others. You gladly hawk your "wisdom" to hundreds of thousands of unsuspecting citizens, gleefully scorning others for their ignorance. Yet you and your guests know little or nothing yourselves. Grow up, get some books, and go to your room.

Yale and Harvard. Princeton and Dartmouth. Stanford and Berkeley. Get a degree from one of those universities, and you're set for life. So what if, on that test of the college seniors I previously mentioned, 70 percent of the students at those fine schools had never heard of the Voting Rights Act[3] or President Lyndon Johnson's Great Society initiatives?[4] Who needs to know stuff like that as you sit in your Tuscan villa watching the sunset and checking how well your portfolio did today?

So what if *not one* of these top universities that the ignorant students attend requires that they take even one course in American history to graduate? Who needs history when you are going to be tomorrow's master of the universe?

Who cares if 70 percent of those who graduate from America's colleges are not required to learn a foreign language? Isn't the rest of the world speaking English now? And if they aren't, hadn't all those damn foreigners better GET WITH THE PROGRAM? 30

And who gives a rat's ass if, out of the seventy English Literature programs at seventy major American universities, only twenty-three now require English majors to take a course in Shakespeare? Can somebody please explain to me what Shakespeare and English have to do with each other? What good are some moldy old plays going to be in the business world, anyway?

Maybe I'm just jealous because I don't have a college degree. Yes, I, Michael Moore, am a college dropout.

Well, I never *officially* dropped out. One day in my sophomore year, I drove around and around the various parking lots of our commuter campus in Flint, searching desperately for a parking space. There simply was no place to park — every spot was full, and no one was leaving. After a frustrating hour spent circling around in my '69 Chevy Impala, I shouted out the window, "That's it, I'm dropping out!" I drove home and told my parents I was no longer in college.

"Why?" they asked.

"Couldn't find a parking spot," I replied, grabbing a Redpop and moving on with the rest of my life. I haven't sat at a school desk since. 35

My dislike of school started somewhere around the second month of first grade. My parents — and God Bless Them Forever for doing this — had taught me to read and write by the time I was four. So when I entered St. John's Elementary School, I had to sit and feign interest while the other kids, like robots, sang, "A-B-C-D-E-F-G . . . Now I know my ABCs, tell me what you think of me!" Every time I heard that line, I wanted to scream out, "Here's what I think of you — quit singing that damn song! Somebody get me a Twinkie!"

---

[3]*Voting Rights Act:* 1965 legislation that guaranteed equal voting rights for African Americans.

[4]*Lyndon Johnson's Great Society initiatives:* 1964–65 program of economic and social welfare legislation designed by Lyndon Johnson, thirty-sixth president of the United States, to eradicate poverty.

I was bored beyond belief. The nuns, to their credit, recognized this, and one day Sister John Catherine took me aside and said that they had decided to skip me up to second grade, effective immediately. I was thrilled. When I got home I excitedly announced to my parents that I had already advanced a grade in my first month of school. They seemed underwhelmed by this new evidence of my genius. Instead they let out a "WHAT THE —," then went into the kitchen and closed the door. I could hear my mother on the phone explaining to the Mother Superior that there was *no way* her little Michael was going to be attending class with kids bigger and older than him, so please, Sister, put him back in first grade.

I was crushed. My mother explained to me that if I skipped first grade I'd always be the youngest and littlest kid in class all through my school years (well, inertia and fast food eventually proved her wrong on that count). There would be no appeals to my father, who left most education decisions to my mother, the valedictorian of her high school class. I tried to explain that if I was sent back to first grade it would appear that I'd *flunked* second grade on my first day — putting myself at risk of having the crap beaten out of me by the first graders I'd left behind with a rousing "See ya, suckers!" But Mom wasn't falling for it; it was then I learned that the only person with higher authority than Mother Superior was Mother Moore.

The next day I decided to ignore all instructions from my parents to go back to first grade. In the morning, before the opening bell, all the students had to line up outside the school with their classmates and then march into the building in single file. Quietly, but defiantly, I went and stood in the second graders' line, praying that God would strike the nuns blind so they wouldn't see which line I was in. The bell rang — and no one had spotted me! The second grade line started to move, and I went with it. *Yes!* I thought. *If I can pull this off, if I can just get into that second grade classroom and take my seat, then nobody will be able to get me out of there.* Just as I was about to enter the door of the school, I felt a hand grab me by the collar of my coat. It was Sister John Catherine.

"I think you're in the wrong line, Michael," she said firmly. "You are now in first grade again." I began to protest: my parents had it "all wrong," or "those weren't *really* my parents," or . . .   40

For the next twelve years I sat in class, did my work, and remained constantly preoccupied, looking for ways to bust out. I started an underground school paper in fourth grade. It was shut down. I started it again in sixth. It was shut down. In eighth grade I not only started the paper again, I convinced the good sisters to let me write a play for our class to perform at the Christmas pageant. The play had something to do with how many rats occupied the parish hall and how all the rats in the country had descended on St. John's Parish Hall to have their annual "rat convention." The priest put a stop to that one — and shut down the paper again. Instead, my friends and I were told to go up on stage and sing three Christmas carols and then leave the stage without uttering a word. I organized half the class to go up there and utter nothing. So we stood there and refused to sing the carols, our silent protest against censorship. By the second song, intimidated by the stern looks from their parents in the audience, most of the protesters joined in on the singing — and by the third song, I too, had capitulated, joining in on "O Holy Night," and promising myself to live to fight another day.

High school, as we all know, is some sort of sick, sadistic punishment of kids by adults seeking vengeance because they can no longer lead the responsibility-free, screwing-around-24/7 lives young people enjoy. What other explanation could there be for those four brutal years of degrading comments, physical abuse, and the belief that you're the only one not having sex?

As soon as I entered high school — and the public school system — all the grousing I'd done about the repression of the Sisters of St. Joseph was forgotten; suddenly they all looked like scholars and saints. I was now walking the halls of a two-thousand-plus-inmate holding pen. Where the nuns had devoted their lives to teaching for no earthly reward, those running the public high school had one simple mission: "Hunt these little pricks down like dogs, then cage them until we can either break their will or ship them off to the glue factory!" Do this, don't do that, tuck your shirt in, wipe that smile off your face, where's your hall pass, THAT'S THE WRONG PASS! *YOU — DETENTION!!*

One day I came home from school and picked up the paper. The headline read: "26th Amendment Passes — Voting Age Lowered to 18." Below that was another headline: "School Board President to Retire, Seat Up for Election."

Hmm. I called the county clerk. 45

"Uh, I'm gonna be eighteen in a few weeks. If I can vote, does that I mean I can also run for office?"

"Let me see," the lady replied. "That's a new question!"

She ruffled through some papers and came back on the phone. "Yes," she said, "you can run. All you need to do is gather twenty signatures to place your name on the ballot."

Twenty signatures? That's it? I had no idea running for elective office required so little work. I got the twenty signatures, submitted my petition, and started campaigning. My platform? "Fire the high school principal and the assistant principal!"

Alarmed at the idea that a high school student might actually find a 50 legal means to remove the very administrators he was being paddled by, five local "adults" took out petitions and got themselves added to the ballot, too.

Of course, they ended up splitting the older adult vote five ways — and I won, getting the vote of every single stoner between the ages of eighteen and twenty-five (who, though many would probably never vote again, relished the thought of sending their high school wardens to the gallows).

The day after I won, I was walking down the hall at school (I had one more week to serve out as a student), and I passed the assistant principal, my shirt tail proudly untucked.

"Good morning, Mr. Moore," he said tersely. The day before, my name had been "Hey-You!" Now I was his boss.

Within nine months after I took my seat on the school board, the principal and assistant principal had submitted their "letters of resignation," a face-saving device employed when one is "asked" to step down. A couple of years later the principal suffered a heart attack and died.

I had known this man, the principal, for many years. When I was eight years old, he used to let me and my friends skate and play hockey on this little pond beside his house. He was kind and generous, and always left the door to his house open in case any of us needed to change into our skates or if we got cold and just wanted to get warm. Years later, I was asked to play bass in a band that was forming, but I didn't own a bass. He let me borrow his son's.

I offer this to remind myself that all people are actually good at their core, and to remember that someone with whom I grew to have serious disputes was also someone with a free cup of hot chocolate for us shivering little brats from the neighborhood.

Teachers are now the politicians' favorite punching bag. To listen to the likes of Chester Finn, a former assistant secretary of education in Bush the Elder's administration, you'd think all that has crumbled in our society can be traced back to lax, lazy, and incompetent teachers. "If you put out a Ten-Most-Wanted list of who's killing American education, I'm not sure who you would have higher on the list: the teachers' union or the education school faculties," Finn said.

Sure, there are a lot of teachers who suck, and they'd be better suited to making telemarketing calls for Amway. But the vast majority are dedicated educators who have chosen a profession that pays them less than what some of their students earn selling Ecstasy, and for that sacrifice we seek to punish them. I don't know about you, but I want the people who have the direct attention of my child more hours a day than I do treated with tender loving care. Those are my kids they're "preparing" for this world, so why on earth would I want to piss them off?

You would think society's attitude would be something like this:

Teachers, thank you so much for devoting your life to my child. Is there ANYTHING I can do to help you? Is there ANYTHING you need? I am here for you. Why? Because you are helping my child — MY BABY — learn and grow. Not only will you be largely responsible for her ability to make a living, but your influence will greatly affect how she views the world, what she knows about other people in this world, and how she will feel about herself. I want her to believe she can attempt anything—that no doors are closed and that no dreams are too distant. I am entrusting the most valuable person in my life to you for seven hours each day. You are thus one of the most important people in my life! Thank you.

No, instead, this is what teachers hear: 60

- "You've got to wonder about teachers who claim to put the interests of children first — and then look to milk the system dry through wage hikes." (*New York Post,* 12/26/00)
- "Estimates of the number of bad teachers range from 5 percent to 18 percent of the 2.6 million total." (Michael Chapman, *Investor's Business Daily,* 9/21/98)
- "Most education professionals belong to a closed community of devotees . . . who follow popular philosophies rather than research on what works." (Douglas Carminen, quoted in the *Montreal Gazette,* 1/6/01)
- "Teachers unions have gone to bat for felons and teachers who have had sex with students, as well as those who simply couldn't teach." (Peter Schweizen, *National Review,* 8/17/98)

What kind of priority do we place on education in America? Oh, it's on the funding list — somewhere down between OSHA[5] and meat inspectors. The person who cares for our child every day receives an average of $41,351 annually. A Congressman who cares only about which tobacco lobbyist is taking him to dinner tonight receives $145,100.

Considering the face-slapping society gives our teachers on a daily basis, is it any wonder so few choose the profession? The national teacher shortage is so big that some school systems are recruiting teachers outside the United States. Chicago recently recruited and hired teachers from twenty-eight foreign countries, including China, France, and Hungary. By the time the new term begins in New York City, seven thousand veteran teachers will have retired — and 60 percent of the new teachers hired to replace them are uncertified.

But here's the kicker for me: 163 New York City schools opened the 2000–2001 school year *without a principal!* You heard right — school, with *no one in charge.* Apparently the mayor and the school board are experimenting with chaos theory — throw five hundred poor kids into a crumbling building, and watch nature take its course! In the city from which most of the wealth in the world is controlled, where there are more millionaires per square foot than there is gum on the sidewalk, we somehow can't find the money to pay a starting teacher more than $31,900 a year. And we act surprised when we can't get results.

And it's not just teachers who have been neglected — American schools are *literally* falling apart. In 1999 one-quarter of U.S. public schools reported that the condition of at least one of their buildings was inadequate. In 1997 the entire Washington, D.C., school system had to delay the start of school for three weeks because nearly *one-third* of the schools were found to be unsafe.

[5]*OSHA:* Occupational Safety and Health Administration.

Almost 10 percent of U.S. public schools have enrollments that are more   65
than 25 percent greater than the capacity of their permanent buildings.
Classes have to be held in the hallways, outdoors, in the gym, in the cafeteria; one school I visited even held classes in a janitor's closet. It's not as if the
janitor's closets are being used for anything related to cleaning, anyway — in
New York almost 15 percent of the eleven hundred public schools are without full-time custodians, forcing teachers to mop their own floors and students to do without toilet paper. We already send our kids out into the street
to hawk candy bars so their schools can buy band instruments — what's
next? Car washes to raise money for toilet paper?

Further proof of just how special our little offspring are is the number
of public and even school libraries that have been shut down or had their
hours cut back. The last thing we need is a bunch of kids hanging out
around a bunch of books!

Apparently "President" Bush agrees: in his first budget he proposed cutting federal spending on libraries by $39 million, down to $168 million — a
nearly 19 percent reduction. Just the week before, his wife, former school librarian Laura Bush, kicked off a national campaign for America's libraries,
calling them "community treasure chests, loaded with a wealth of information available to everyone, equally." The President's mother, Barbara Bush,
heads the Foundation for Family Literacy. Well, there's nothing like having
firsthand experience with illiteracy in the family to motivate one into acts of
charity.

For kids who are exposed to books at home, the loss of a library is sad.
But for kids who come from environments where people don't read, the loss
of a library is a tragedy that might keep them from ever discovering the joys
of reading — or from gathering the kind of information that will decide
their lot in life. Jonathan Kozol, for decades an advocate for disadvantaged
children, has observed that school libraries "remain the clearest window to a
world of noncommercial satisfactions and enticements that most children in
poor neighborhoods will ever know."

Kids deprived of access to good libraries are also being kept from developing the information skills they need to keep up in workplaces that are
increasingly dependent on rapidly changing information. The ability to conduct research is "probably the most essential skill [today's students] can
have," says Julie Walker, executive director of the American Association of
School Librarians. "The knowledge [students] acquire in school is not going
to serve them throughout their lifetimes. Many of them will have four to
five careers in a lifetime. It will be their ability to navigate information that
will matter."

Who's to blame for the decline in libraries? Well, when it comes to   70
school libraries, you can start by pointing the finger (yes, *that* finger) at
Richard Nixon. From the 1960s until 1974, school libraries received specific
funding from the government. But in 1974 the Nixon administration
changed the rules, stipulating that federal education money be doled out in

"block grants" to be spent by states however they chose. Few states chose to spend the money on libraries, and the downslide began. This is one reason that materials in many school libraries today date from the 1960s and early 1970s, before funding was diverted. ("No, Sally, the Soviet Union isn't our enemy. The Soviet Union has been kaput for ten years. . . .")

This 1999 account by an *Education Week* reporter about the "library" at a Philadelphia elementary school could apply to any number of similarly neglected schools:

> Even the best books in the library at T. M. Pierce Elementary School are dated, tattered, and discolored. The worst — many in a latter state of disintegration — are dirty and fetid and leave a moldy residue on hands and clothing. Chairs and tables are old, mismatched, or broken. There isn't a computer in sight. . . . Outdated facts and theories and offensive stereotypes leap from the authoritative pages of encyclopedias and biographies, fiction and nonfiction tomes. Among the volumes on these shelves a student would find it all but impossible to locate accurate information on AIDS or other contemporary diseases, explorations of the moon and Mars, or the past five U.S. presidents.

The ultimate irony in all of this is that the very politicians who refuse to fund education in America adequately are the same ones who go ballistic over how our kids have fallen behind the Germans, the Japanese, and just about every other country with running water and an economy not based on the sale of Chiclets. Suddenly they want "accountability." They want the teachers held responsible and to be tested. And they want the kids to be tested — over and over and over.

There's nothing terribly wrong with the concept of using standardized testing to determine whether kids are learning to read and write and do math. But too many politicians and education bureaucrats have created a national obsession with testing, as if everything that's wrong with the educational system in this country would be magically fixed if we could just raise those scores.

The people who really should be tested (besides the yammering pundits) are the so-called political leaders. Next time you see your state representative or congressman, give him this pop quiz — and remind him that any future pay raises will be based on how well he scores:

1. What is the annual pay of your average constituent?
2. What percent of welfare recipients are children?
3. How many known species of plants and animals are on the brink of extinction?
4. How big is the hole in the ozone layer?
5. Which African countries have a lower infant mortality rate than Detroit?
6. How many American cities still have two competing newspapers?

7. How many ounces in a gallon?
8. Which do I stand a greater chance of being killed by: a gun shot in school or a bolt of lightning?
9. What's the only state capital without a McDonald's?
10. Describe the story of either *The Iliad* or *The Odyssey*.

Answers

1. $28,548
2. 67 percent
3. 11,046
4. 10.5 million square miles
5. Libya, Mauritius, Seychelles
6. 34
7. 128 ounces
8. You're twice as likely to be killed by lightning as by a gunshot in school.
9. Montpelier, Vermont
10. *The Iliad* is an ancient Greek epic poem by Homer about the Trojan War. *The Odyssey* is another epic poem by Homer recounting the ten-year journey home from the Trojan War made by Odysseus, the king of Ithaca.

Chances are, the genius representing you in the legislature won't score 50 percent on the above test. The good news is that you get to flunk him within a year or two.

There is one group in the country that isn't just sitting around carping about all them lamebrain teachers — a group that cares deeply about what kinds of students will enter the adult world. You could say they have a vested interest in this captive audience of millions of young people . . . or in the billions of dollars they spend each year. (Teenagers alone spent more than $150 billion last year.) Yes, it's Corporate America, whose generosity to our nation's schools is just one more example of their continuing patriotic service.

Just how committed are these companies to our children's schools?

According to numbers collected by the Center for the Analysis of Commercialism in Education (CACE), their selfless charity has seen a tremendous boom since 1990. Over the past ten years, school programs and activities have seen corporate sponsorship increase by 248 percent. In exchange for this sponsorship, schools allow the corporation to associate its name with the events.

For example, Eddie Bauer sponsors the final round of the National Geography Bee. Book covers featuring Calvin Klein and Nike ads are distributed to students. Nike and other shoemakers, looking for early access to tomorrow's stars, sponsor inner-city high school basketball teams.

Pizza Hut set up its "Book-It!" program to encourage children to read.   80
When students meet the monthly reading goal, they are rewarded with a certificate for a Pizza Hut personal pan pizza. At the restaurant, the store manager personally congratulates the children and gives them each a sticker and a certificate. Pizza Hut suggests school principals place a "Pizza Hut Book-It!" honor roll list in the school for everyone to see.

General Mills and Campbell's Soup thought up a better plan. Instead of giving free rewards, they both have programs rewarding schools for getting parents to buy their products. Under General Mills's "Box Tops for Education" program, schools get ten cents for each box top logo they send in, and can earn up to $10,000 a year. That's 100,000 General Mills products sold. Campbell's Soup's "Labels for Education" program is no better. It touts itself as "Providing America's children with FREE school equipment!" Schools can earn one "free" Apple iMac computer for only 94,950 soup labels. Campbell's suggests setting a goal of a label a day from each student. With Campbell's conservative estimate of five labels per week per child, all you need is a school of 528 kids to get that free computer.

It's not just this kind of sponsorship that brings these schools and corporations together. The 1990s saw a phenomenal 1,384 percent increase in exclusive agreements between schools and soft-drink bottlers. Two hundred and forty school districts in thirty-one states have sold exclusive rights to one of the big three soda companies (Coca-Cola, Pepsi, Dr. Pepper) to push their products in schools. Anybody wonder why there are more overweight kids than ever before? Or more young women with calcium deficiencies because they're drinking less milk? And even though federal law prohibits the sale of soft drinks in schools until lunch periods begin, in some overcrowded schools "lunch" begins in midmorning. Artificially flavored carbonated sugar water — the breakfast of champions! (In March 2001 Coke responded to public pressure, announcing that it would add water, juice, and other sugar-free, caffeine-free, and calcium-rich alternatives to soda to its school vending machines.)

I guess they can afford such concessions when you consider their deal with the Colorado Springs school district. Colorado has been a trailblazer when it comes to tie-ins between the schools and soft drink companies. In Colorado Springs, the district will receive $8.4 million over ten years from its deal with Coca-Cola — and more if it exceeds its "requirement" of selling seventy thousand cases of Coke products a year. To ensure the levels are met, school district officials urged principals to allow students unlimited access to Coke machines and allow students to drink Coke in the classroom.

But Coke isn't alone. In the Jefferson County, Colorado, school district (home of Columbine High School), Pepsi contributed $1.5 million to help build a new sports stadium. Some county schools tested a science course, developed in part by Pepsi, called "The Carbonated Beverage Company."

166LEARNING POWER

Students taste-tested colas, analyzed cola samples, watched a video tour of a
Pepsi bottling plant, and visited a local plant.

The school district in Wylie, Texas, signed a deal in 1996 that shared   85
the rights to sell soft drinks in the schools between Coke and Dr. Pepper.
Each company paid $31,000 a year. Then, in 1998, the county changed its
mind and signed a deal with Coke worth $1.2 million over fifteen years. Dr.
Pepper sued the county for breach of contract. The school district bought
out Dr. Pepper's contract, costing them $160,000 — plus another $20,000
in legal fees.

It's not just the companies that sometimes get sent packing. Students
who lack the proper corporate school spirit do so at considerable risk. When
Mike Cameron wore a Pepsi shirt on "Coke Day" at Greenbrier High
School in Evans, Georgia, he was suspended for a day. "Coke Day" was part
of the school's entry in a national "Team Up With Coca-Cola" contest,
which awards $10,000 to the high school that comes up with the best plan
for distributing Coke discount cards. Greenbrier school officials said
Cameron was suspended for "being disruptive and trying to destroy the
school picture" when he removed an outer shirt and revealed the Pepsi shirt
as a photograph was being taken of students posed to spell out the word
Coke. Cameron said the shirt was visible all day, but he didn't get in trouble
until posing for the picture. No slouch in the marketing department, Pepsi
quickly sent the high school senior a box of Pepsi shirts and hats.

If turning the students into billboards isn't enough, schools and corporations sometimes turn the school itself into one giant neon sign for corporate
America. Appropriation of school space, including scoreboards, rooftops,
walls, and textbooks, for corporate logos and advertising is up 539 percent.

Colorado Springs, not satisfied to sell its soul only to Coca-Cola, has
plastered its school buses with advertisements for Burger King, Wendy's,
and other big companies. Free book covers and school planners with ads for
Kellogg's Pop-Tarts and pictures of FOX TV personalities were also handed
out to the students.

After members of the Grapevine-Colleyville Independent School District in Texas decided they didn't want advertisements in the classrooms,
they allowed Dr. Pepper and 7-Up logos to be painted on the rooftops of
two high schools. The two high schools, not coincidentally, lie under the
Dallas airport flight path.

The schools aren't just looking for ways to advertise; they're also con-   90
cerned with the students' perceptions of various products. That's why, in
some schools, companies conduct market research in classrooms during
school hours. Education Market Resources of Kansas reports that "children
respond openly and easily to questions and stimuli" in the classroom setting.
(Of course, that's what they're *supposed* to be doing in a classroom—but for
their own benefit, not that of some corporate pollsters.) Filling out marketing surveys instead of learning, however, is probably *not* what they should
be doing.

Companies have also learned they can reach this confined audience by "sponsoring" educational materials. This practice, like the others, has exploded as well, increasing 1,875 percent since 1990.

Teachers have shown a Shell Oil video that teaches students that the way to experience nature is by driving there — after filling your Jeep's gas tank at a Shell station. ExxonMobil prepared lesson plans about the flourishing wildlife in Prince William Sound, site of the ecological disaster caused by the oil spill from the Exxon *Valdez.* A third-grade math book features exercises involving counting Tootsie Rolls. A Hershey's-sponsored curriculum used in many schools features "The Chocolate Dream Machine," including lessons in math, science, geography — and nutrition.

In a number of high schools, the economics course is supplied by General Motors. GM writes and provides the textbooks and the course outline. Students learn from GM's example the benefits of capitalism and how to operate a company — like GM.

And what better way to imprint a corporate logo on the country's children than through television and the Internet beamed directly into the classroom. Electronic marketing, where a company provides programming or equipment to schools for the right to advertise to their students, is up 139 percent.

One example is the ZapMe! Corporation, which provides schools with a free computer lab and access to pre-selected Web sites. In return, schools must promise that the lab will be in use at least four hours a day. The catch? The ZapMe! Web browser has constantly scrolling advertisements — and the company gets to collect information on students' browsing habits, information they can then sell to other companies.

Perhaps the worst of the electronic marketers is Channel One Television. Eight million students in 12,000 classrooms watch Channel One, an in-school news *and advertising* program, every day. (That's right: EVERY day.) Kids are spending the equivalent of six full school days a year watching Channel One in almost 40 percent of U.S. middle and high schools. Instructional time lost to the ads alone? One entire day per year. That translates into an annual cost to taxpayers of more than $1.8 billion.

Sure, doctors and educators agree that our kids can never watch enough TV. And there's probably a place in school for some television programs — I have fond memories of watching astronauts blasting off on the television rolled into my grade school auditorium. But out of the daily twelve-minute Channel One broadcasts, only 20 percent of the airtime is devoted to stories about politics, the economy, and cultural and social issues. That leaves a whopping 80 percent for advertising, sports, weather, features, and Channel One promotions.

Channel One is disproportionately shown in schools in low income communities with large minority populations, where the least money is available for education, and where the least amount is spent on textbooks and other academic materials. Once these districts receive corporate handouts, government's failure to provide adequate school funding tends to remain unaddressed.

For most of us, the only time we enter an American high school is to vote at our local precinct. (There's an irony if there ever was one — going to participate in democracy's sacred ritual while two thousand students in the same building live under some sort of totalitarian dictatorship.) The halls are packed with burned-out teenagers shuffling from class to class, dazed and confused, wondering what the hell they're doing there. They learn how to regurgitate answers the state wants them to give, and any attempt to be an individual is now grounds for being suspected to be a member of the trench coat mafia.[6] I visited a school recently, and some students asked me if I noticed that they and the other students in the school were all wearing white or some neutral color. Nobody dares wear black, or anything else wild and distinct. That's a sure ticket to the principal's office — where the school psychologist will be waiting to ascertain whether that Limp Bizkit shirt you have on means that you intend to shoot up Miss Nelson's fourth hour geometry class.

So the kids learn to submerge any personal expression. They learn that   100
it's better to go along so that you get along. They learn that to rock the boat could get them rocked right out of the school. Don't question authority. Do as you're told. Don't think, just do as I say.

Oh, and have a good and productive life as an active, well-adjusted participant in our thriving democracy!

Are You a Potential School Shooter?

The following is a list of traits the FBI has identified as "risk factors" among students who may commit violent acts. Stay away from any student showing signs of:

- Poor coping skills
- Access to weapons
- Depression
- Drug and alcohol abuse
- Alienation
- Narcissism
- Inappropriate humor
- Unlimited, unmonitored television and Internet use

Since this includes all of you, drop out of school immediately. Home schooling is not a viable option, because you must also stay away from yourself.

---

[6]*trench coat mafia:* Name of a self-styled group of students that included Columbine High School shooters Eric Harris and Dylan Klebold; hence, any potentially violent group of students.

How To Be a Student Subversive Instead of a Student Subservient

There are many ways you can fight back at your high school — and have fun while doing it. The key thing is to learn what all the rules are, and what your rights are by law and by school district policy. This will help to prevent you getting in the kinds of trouble you don't need.

It may also get you some cool perks. David Schankula, a college student who has helped me on this book, recalls that when he was in high school in Kentucky, he and his buddies found some obscure state law that said any student who requests a day off to go to the state fair must be given the day off. The state legislature probably passed this law years ago to help some farm kid take his prize hog to the fair without being penalized at school. But the law was still on the books, and it gave any student the right to request the state fair day off — regardless of the reason. So you can imagine the look on the principal's face when David and his city friends submitted their request for their free day off from school — and there was nothing the principal could do.

Here's a few more things you can do:

1. *Mock the Vote.*

Student council and class elections are the biggest smokescreen the   105 school throws up, fostering the illusion that you actually have any say in the running of the school. Most students who run for these offices either take the charade too seriously — or they just think it'll look good on their college applications.

So why not run yourself? Run just to ridicule the whole ridiculous exercise. Form your own party, with its own stupid name. Campaign on wild promises: *If elected, I'll change the school mascot to an amoeba,* or *If elected, I'll insist that the principal must first eat the school lunch each day before it is fed to the students.* Put up banners with cool slogans: "Vote for me — a real loser!"

If you get elected, you can devote your energies to accomplishing things that will drive the administration crazy, but help out your fellow students (demands for free condoms, student evaluations of teachers, less homework so you can get to bed by midnight, etc).

2. *Start a School Club.*

You have a right to do this. Find a sympathetic teacher to sponsor it. The Pro-Choice Club. The Free Speech Club. The Integrate Our Town Club. Make every member a "president" of the club, so they all can claim it on their college applications. One student I know tried to start a Feminist Club, but the principal wouldn't allow it because then they'd be obliged to give equal time to a Male Chauvinist Club. That's the kind of idiot thinking you'll encounter, but don't give up. (Heck, if you find yourself in that situation, just say *fine* — and suggest the that principal could sponsor the Chauvinist Club.)

3. Launch Your Own Newspaper or Webzine.

You have a constitutionally protected right to do this. If you take care not to be obscene, or libelous, or give them any reason to shut you down, this can be a great way to get the truth out about what's happening at your school. Use humor. The students will love it.

4. Get Involved in the Community.

Go to the school board meetings and inform them what's going on in   110 the school. Petition them to change things. They will try to ignore you or make you sit through a long, boring meeting before they let you speak, but they have to let you speak. Write letters to the editor of your local paper. Adults don't have a clue about what goes on in your high school. Fill them in. More than likely you'll find someone there who'll support you.

Any or all of this will raise quite a ruckus, but there's help out there if you need it. Contact the local American Civil Liberties Union if the school retaliates. Threaten lawsuits — school administrators HATE to hear that word. Just remember: there's no greater satisfaction than seeing the look on your principal's face when you have the upper hand. Use it.

And Never Forget This:

There Is No Permanent Record!

ENGAGING THE TEXT

1. What evidence does Moore offer to support his contention that America is a nation of idiots? To what extent would you agree with this blunt assessment of American intelligence? Why? What limitations, if any, do you see in the "question/answer" approach that Moore takes to gauging intelligence?

2. Moore shares a number of personal experiences in this selection to dramatize his disgust with formal education. How do your own elementary and high school memories compare with Moore's school experiences? Overall, how would you characterize his attitude towards schools and schooling? To what extent would you agree with him?

3. How accurate is the grim picture of American schools that Moore offers in this selection? Would you agree with his assessment of the typical classroom, the quality of the average school library, and the general ability of American teachers and of the staff who support them?

4. Who, in Moore's view, is responsible for the sorry state of America's schools? To what extent would you agree? What reforms do you think

Moore would like to see, and what changes, if any, would you recommend?

5. How does Moore feel about corporate involvement in public education? Why? What possible conflicts of interest or ethical questions do you see arising in relation to the following kinds of corporate/school collaboration:

   - Sponsorship of sports teams and clubs
   - Exclusive contracts for soda and snack vending machines
   - Fast-food franchise "food courts"
   - Sponsorship of libraries, computer labs, etc.
   - Commercial instruction via cable TV
   - Free books with inserted advertising
   - Free courses on history or economics with business or corporate content
   - Volunteer "teachers" and tutors from corporate ranks

   What role, if any, do you think corporations should play in support of American public schools? Why?

6. What does Moore suggest that individual students do to "fight back" against the deadening effects of the educational system? What did you do when you were in elementary and secondary school to make your own experience more meaningful? Now that you're in college, what can you do to be a "student subversive instead of a student subservient"?

EXPLORING CONNECTIONS

7. How does Moore's portrayal of the current state of American education compare with the image of the American school as described by Horace Mann (p. 142)? What seems to be the mission or goal of public schooling, according to Moore? How would you expect him to react to the goals that Mann envisions for the school? Why? Would you agree with Moore?

8. To what extent does Moore's assessment of education support or challenge John Taylor Gatto's critique of "The Seven-Lesson Schoolteacher" (p. 173)? Do you think that Moore would agree with Gatto's claim that mandatory public schooling amounts to the "compulsory subordination of all"? Which of these two views of teachers and teaching do you find more persuasive? Why?

EXTENDING THE CRITICAL CONTEXT

9. Test Moore's central thesis about the idiocy of the average American by working in groups to devise and administer your own general information test. You can borrow questions from the many bits of information that Moore offers throughout this selection, or simply pool your own knowledge supplemented with additional library research. Administer your questionnaire to groups of fellow students, professors, family, friends, or members of the community at large. Then compare your results to see if Americans really are as uninformed as Moore suggests.

10. As Moore suggests, even some top American universities no longer require students to take basic courses in subjects like history or foreign language. How comprehensive are the general education requirements at your col-

lege? Do you think that they provide the average student with a well-rounded education? What additional courses or requirements, if any, would you include? Why?

From *School Is Hell* © 1987 Matt Groening. All rights reserved. Reprinted by permission of Pantheon Books, a division of Random House Publishers, Inc., New York.

The Seven-Lesson Schoolteacher

John Taylor Gatto

There's no doubt that America's schools are meant to benefit the students they serve; they're intended to transmit a body of knowledge — a curriculum — that equips students with all the ideas, skills, and attitudes necessary to help them lead happy and productive lives. But even the best intentions can go awry; as John Taylor Gatto (b. 1935) argues in this selection, education in the United States may harbor a "hidden curriculum" — an unwritten, unacknowledged set of lessons about self and society that schooling inflicts on every student from kindergarten to graduate school. An award-winning educator and ardent libertarian, Gatto suggests that what school does best is to inculcate seven such unconscious and debilitating lessons. Gatto has taught in New York City public schools for more than two decades. In 1990 he was named New York City Teacher of the Year. This selection comes from Dumbing Us Down: The Hidden Curriculum of Compulsory Schooling *(1992). His most recent book is* The Underground History of American Education *(2001).*

I

Call me Mr. Gatto, please. Twenty-six years ago, having nothing better to do with myself at the time, I tried my hand at schoolteaching. The license I have certifies that I am an instructor of English language and English literature, but that isn't what I do at all. I don't teach English, I teach school — and I win awards doing it.

Teaching means different things in different places, but seven lessons are universally taught from Harlem to Hollywood Hills. They constitute a national curriculum you pay for in more ways than you can imagine, so you might as well know what it is. You are at liberty, of course, to regard these lessons any way you like, but believe me when I say I intend no irony in this presentation. These are the things I teach, these are the things you pay me to teach. Make of them what you will.

1. Confusion

A lady named Kathy wrote this to me from Dubois, Indiana, the other day:

> What big ideas are important to little kids? Well, the biggest idea I think they need is that what they are learning isn't idiosyncratic — that there is some system to it all and it's not just raining down on them as they helplessly absorb. That's the task, to understand, to make coherent.

Kathy has it wrong. *The first lesson I teach is confusion. Everything* I teach is out of context. I teach the un-relating of everything. I teach disconnections. I teach too much: the orbiting of planets, the law of large numbers, slavery, adjectives, architectural drawing, dance, gymnasium, choral singing, assemblies, surprise guests, fire drills, computer languages, parents' nights, staff-development days, pull-out programs, guidance with strangers my students may never see again, standardized tests, age-segregation unlike anything seen in the outside world. . . . What do any of these things have to do with each other?

Even in the best schools a close examination of curriculum and its se-   5
quences turns up a lack of coherence, full of internal contradictions. Fortunately the children have no words to define the panic and anger they feel *at constant violations of natural order and sequence* fobbed off on them as quality in education. The logic of the school-mind is that it is better to leave school with a tool kit of superficial jargon derived from economics, sociology, natural science, and so on, than with one genuine enthusiasm. But quality in education entails learning about something in depth. Confusion is thrust upon kids by too many strange adults, each working alone with only the thinnest relationship with each other, pretending, for the most part, to an expertise they do not possess.

Meaning, not disconnected facts, is what sane human beings seek, and education is a set of codes for processing raw data into meaning. Behind the patchwork quilt of school sequences and the school obsession with facts and theories, the age-old human search for meaning lies well concealed. This is harder to see in elementary school where the hierarchy of school experience seems to make better sense because the good-natured simple relationship between "let's do this" and "let's do that" is just assumed to mean something and the clientele has not yet consciously discerned how little substance is behind the play and pretense.

Think of the great natural sequences — like learning to walk and learning to talk; the progression of light from sunrise to sunset; the ancient procedures of a farmer, a smithy, or a shoemaker; or the preparation of a Thanksgiving feast — all of the parts are in perfect harmony with each other, each action justifies itself and illuminates the past and the future. School sequences aren't like that, not inside a single class and not among the total menu of daily classes. School sequences are crazy. There is no particular reason for any of them, nothing that bears close scrutiny. Few teachers would dare to teach the tools whereby dogmas of a school or a teacher could be criticized, since everything must be accepted. School subjects are learned, if they *can* be learned, like children learn the catechism or memorize the Thirty-nine Articles of Anglicanism.

I teach the un-relating of everything, an infinite fragmentation the opposite of cohesion; what I do is more related to television programming than to making a scheme of order. In a world where home is only a ghost, because both parents work, or because of too many moves or too many job changes or too much ambition, or because something else has left everybody too confused to maintain a family relation, I teach you how to accept confusion as your destiny. That's the first lesson I teach.

2. Class Position

The second lesson I teach is class position. I teach that students must stay in the class where they belong. I don't know who decides my kids belong there but that's not my business. The children are numbered so that if any get away they can be returned to the right class. Over the years the variety of ways children are numbered by schools has increased dramatically, until it is hard to see the human beings plainly under the weight of numbers they carry. Numbering children is a big and very profitable undertaking, though what the strategy is designed to accomplish is elusive. I don't even know why parents would, without a fight, allow it to be done to their kids.

In any case, that's not my business. My job is to make them like being   10
locked together with children who bear numbers like their own. Or at the least to endure it like good sports. If I do my job well, the kids can't even *imagine* themselves somewhere else, because I've shown them how to envy and fear the better classes and how to have contempt for the dumb classes. Under this efficient discipline the class mostly polices itself into good marching order. That's the real lesson of any rigged competition like school. You come to know your place.

In spite of the overall class blueprint, which assumes that ninety-nine percent of the kids are in their class to stay, I nevertheless make a public effort to exhort children to higher levels of test success, hinting at eventual transfer from the lower class as a reward. I frequently insinuate the day will come when an employer will hire them on the basis of test scores and grades, even though my own experience is that employers are rightly indifferent to such things. I never lie outright, but I've come to see that truth and schoolteaching are, at bottom, incompatible, just as Socrates said thousands of years ago. The lesson of numbered classes is that everyone has a proper place in the pyramid and there is no way out of your class except by number magic. Failing that, you must stay where you are put.

3. Indifference

The third lesson I teach is indifference. I teach children not to care too much about anything, even though they want to make it appear that they do. How I do this is very subtle. I do it by demanding that they become totally involved in my lessons, jumping up and down in their seats with anticipation, competing vigorously with each other for my favor. It's heartwarming when they do that; it impresses everyone, even me. When I'm at my best I plan lessons very carefully in order to produce this show of enthusiasm. But when the bell rings I insist they drop whatever it is we have been doing and proceed quickly to the next work station. They must turn on and off like a light switch. Nothing important is ever finished in my class nor in any class I know of. Students never have a complete experience except on the installment plan.

Indeed, the lesson of bells is that no work is worth finishing, so why care too deeply about anything? Years of bells will condition all but the strongest to a world that can no longer offer important work to do. Bells are the secret logic of schooltime; their logic is inexorable. Bells destroy the past and future, rendering every interval the same as any other, as the abstraction of a map renders every living mountain and river the same, even though they are not. Bells inoculate each undertaking with indifference.

4. Emotional Dependency

The fourth lesson I teach is emotional dependency. By stars and red checks, smiles and frowns, prizes, honors, and disgraces, I teach kids to surrender their will to the predestinated chain of command. Rights may be granted or withheld by any authority without appeal, because rights do not exist inside a school — not even the right of free speech, as the Supreme Court has ruled — unless school authorities say they do. As a schoolteacher, I intervene in many personal decisions, issuing a pass for those I deem legitimate, or initiating a disciplinary confrontation for behavior that threatens my control. Individuality is constantly trying to assert itself among children and teenagers, so my judgments come thick and fast. Individuality is a contradiction of class theory, a curse to all systems of classification.

Here are some common ways it shows up: children sneak away for a private moment in the toilet on the pretext of moving their bowels, or they steal a private instant in the hallway on the grounds they need water. I know they don't, but I allow them to "deceive" me because this conditions them to depend on my favors. Sometimes free will appears right in front of me in pockets of children angry, depressed, or unhappy about things outside my ken; rights in such matters cannot be recognized by schoolteachers, only privileges that can be withdrawn, hostages to good behavior.

5. Intellectual Dependency

The fifth lesson I teach is intellectual dependency. Good students wait for a teacher to tell them what to do. It is the most important lesson, that we must wait for other people, better trained than ourselves, to make the meanings of our lives. The expert makes all the important choices; only I, the teacher, can determine what my kids must study, or rather, only the people who pay me can make those decisions, which I then enforce. If I'm told that evolution is a fact instead of a theory, I transmit that as ordered, punishing deviants who resist what I have been told to tell them to think. This power to control what children will think lets me separate successful students from failures very easily.

Successful children do the thinking I assign them with a minimum of resistance and a decent show of enthusiasm. Of the millions of things of value to study, I decide what few we have time for, or actually it is decided by my faceless employers. The choices are theirs, why should I argue? Curiosity has no important place in my work, only conformity.

Bad kids fight this, of course, even though they lack the concepts to know what they are fighting, struggling to make decisions for themselves about what they will learn and when they will learn it. How can we allow that and survive as schoolteachers? Fortunately there are tested procedures to break the will of those who resist; it is more difficult, naturally, if the kids have respectable parents who come to their aid, but that happens less and less in spite of the bad reputation of schools. No middle-class parents I have ever met actually believe that *their* kid's school is one of the bad ones. Not one single parent in twenty-six years of teaching. That's amazing, and probably the best testimony to what happens to families when mother and father have been well-schooled themselves, learning the seven lessons.

Good people wait for an expert to tell them what to do. It is hardly an exaggeration to say that our entire economy depends upon this lesson being learned. Think of what might fall apart if children weren't trained to be dependent: the social services could hardly survive; they would vanish, I think, into the recent historical limbo out of which they arose. Counselors and therapists would look on in horror as the supply of psychic invalids vanished. Commercial entertainment of all sorts, including television, would wither as people learned again how to make their own fun. Restaurants, the prepared-food industry, and a whole host of other assorted food services would be drastically down-sized if people returned to making their own meals rather than depending on strangers to plant, pick, chop, and cook for them. Much of modern law, medicine, and engineering would go too, the clothing business and schoolteaching as well, unless a guaranteed supply of helpless people continued to pour out of our schools each year.

Don't be too quick to vote for radical school reform if you want to continue getting a paycheck. We've built a way of life that depends on people doing what they are told because they don't know how to tell *themselves* what to do. It's one of the biggest lessons I teach.

6. Provisional Self-Esteem

The sixth lesson I teach is provisional self-esteem. If you've ever tried to wrestle into line kids whose parents have convinced them to believe they'll be loved in spite of anything, you know how impossible it is to make self-confident spirits conform. Our world wouldn't survive a flood of confident people very long, so I teach that a kid's self-respect should depend on expert opinion. My kids are constantly evaluated and judged.

A monthly report, impressive in its provision, is sent into a student's home to elicit approval or mark exactly, down to a single percentage point, how dissatisfied with the child a parent should be. The ecology of "good" schooling depends on perpetuating dissatisfaction, just as the commercial economy depends on the same fertilizer. Although some people might be surprised how little time or reflection goes into making up these mathematical records, the cumulative weight of these objective-seeming documents establishes a profile that compels children to arrive at certain decisions about themselves and their futures based on the casual judgment of strangers. Self-evaluation, the staple of every major philosophical system that ever appeared on the planet, is never considered a factor. The lesson of report cards, grades, and tests is that children should not trust themselves or their parents but should instead rely on the evaluation of certified officials. People need to be told what they are worth.

7. One Can't Hide

The seventh lesson I teach is that one can't hide. I teach students they are always watched, that each is under constant surveillance by myself and my colleagues. There are no private spaces for children, there is no private time. Class change lasts exactly three hundred seconds to keep promiscuous fraternization at low levels. Students are encouraged to tattle on each other or even to tattle on their own parents. Of course, I encourage parents to file reports about their own child's waywardness too. A family trained to snitch on itself isn't likely to conceal any dangerous secrets.

I assign a type of extended schooling called "homework," so that the effect of surveillance, if not that surveillance itself, travels into private households, where students might otherwise use free time to learn something unauthorized from a father or mother, by exploration, or by apprenticing to some wise person in the neighborhood. Disloyalty to the idea of schooling is a devil always ready to find work for idle hands.

The meaning of constant surveillance and denial of privacy is that no one can be trusted, that privacy is not legitimate. Surveillance is an ancient imperative, espoused by certain influential thinkers, a central prescription set down in *The Republic*, in *The City of God*, in the *Institutes of the Christian Religion*, in *New Atlantis*, in *Leviathan*,[1] and in a host of other places. All these childless men who wrote these books discovered the same thing: children must be closely watched if you want to keep a society under tight central control. Children will follow a private drummer if you can't get them into a uniformed marching band.   25

II

It is the great triumph of compulsory government monopoly mass-schooling that among even the best of my fellow teachers, and among even the best of my students' parents, only a small number can imagine a different way to do things. "The kids have to know how to read and write, don't

---

[1]*The Republic*, in *The City of God . . . Leviathan:* Famous political and philosophical writings by authors like Plato, St. Augustine, and Thomas Hobbes.

they?" "They have to know how to add and subtract, don't they?" "They have to learn to follow orders if they ever expect to keep a job."

Only a few lifetimes ago things were very different in the United States. Originality and variety were common currency; our freedom from regimentation made us the miracle of the world; social-class boundaries were relatively easy to cross; our citizenry was marvelously confident, inventive, and able to do much for themselves independently, and to think for themselves. We were something special, we Americans, all by ourselves, without government sticking its nose into and measuring every aspect of our lives, without institutions and social agencies telling us how to think and feel. We were something special, as individuals, as Americans.

But we've had a society essentially under central control in the United States since just before the Civil War, and such a society requires compulsory schooling, government monopoly schooling, to maintain itself. Before this development schooling wasn't very important anywhere. We had it, but not too much of it, and only as much as an individual *wanted*. People learned to read, write, and do arithmetic just fine anyway; there are some studies that suggest literacy at the time of the American Revolution, at least for non-slaves on the Eastern seaboard, was close to total. Thomas Paine's *Common Sense*[2] sold 600,000 copies to a population of 3,000,000, 20 percent of whom were slaves, and 50 percent indentured servants.

Were the colonists geniuses? No, the truth is that reading, writing, and arithmetic only take about one hundred hours to transmit as long as the audience is eager and willing to learn. The trick is to wait until someone asks and then move fast while the mood is on. Millions of people teach themselves these things, it really isn't very hard. Pick up a fifth-grade math or rhetoric textbook from 1850 and you'll see that the texts were pitched then on what would today be considered college level. The continuing cry for "basic skills" practice is a smoke screen behind which schools preempt the time of children for twelve years and teach them the seven lessons I've just described to you.

The society that has come increasingly under central control since just   30
before the Civil War shows itself in the lives we lead, the clothes we wear, the food we eat, and the green highway signs we drive by from coast to coast, all of which are the products of this control. So too, I think, are the epidemics of drugs, suicide, divorce, violence, cruelty, and hardening of class into caste in the United States products of the dehumanization of our lives, the lessening of individual, family, and community importance, a diminishment that proceeds from central control. The character of large compulsory institutions is inevitable; they want more and more until there isn't any more to give. School takes our children away from any possibility of an active role in community life — in fact it destroys communities by relegating the training of children to

---

[2]*Common Sense:* Paine's fifty-page pamphlet, published January 10, 1776, was recognized as the war-cry of the American revolutionary movement.

the hands of certified experts — and by doing so it ensures our children cannot grow up fully human. Aristotle taught that without a fully active role in community life one could not hope to become a healthy human being. Surely he was right. Look around you the next time you are near a school or an old people's reservation if you wish a demonstration.

School as it was built is an essential support system for a model of social engineering that condemns most people to be subordinate stones in a pyramid that narrows as it ascends to a terminal of control. School is an artifice that makes such a pyramidical social order seem inevitable, although such a premise is a fundamental betrayal of the American Revolution. From Colonial days through the period of the Republic we had no schools to speak of — read Benjamin Franklin's *Autobiography* for an example of a man who had no time to waste in school — and yet the promise of democracy was beginning to be realized. We turned our backs on this promise by bringing to life the ancient pharaonic dream of Egypt: compulsory subordination for all. That was the secret Plato reluctantly transmitted in *The Republic* when Glaucon and Adeimantus extort from Socrates the plan for total state control of human life, a plan necessary to maintain a society where some people take more than their share. "I will show you," says Socrates, "how to bring about such a feverish city, but you will not like what I am going to say." And so the blueprint of the seven-lesson school was first sketched.

The current debate about whether we should have a national curriculum is phony. We already have a national curriculum locked up in the seven lessons I have just outlined. Such a curriculum produces physical, moral, and intellectual paralysis, and no curriculum of content will be sufficient to reverse its hideous effects. What is currently under discussion in our national hysteria about failing academic performance misses the point. Schools teach exactly what they are intended to teach and they do it well: how to be a good Egyptian and remain in your place in the pyramid.

ENGAGING THE TEXT

1. Working in groups, try to summarize each of the seven lessons that Gatto claims are taught as part of the hidden curriculum in all American schools. To what extent does the collective experience of your group support or challenge Gatto's claims?

2. Working together in small groups, construct an imaginary profile of the kind of student that Gatto's seven-lesson teacher would be likely to produce. How accurately does this portrait describe most high school graduates intellectually, socially, and emotionally?

3. Freewrite for a page or two about a particular teacher you had who didn't fit Gatto's description of the seven-lesson teacher. What set this teacher apart or made her stand out for you? To what extent did she teach any or all of the lessons outlined by Gatto?

4. What does Gatto mean when he says that "truth and schoolteaching are, at bottom, incompatible" (para. 11)? Given his concerns about the impact of public education, why do you think Gatto continues to teach?

EXPLORING CONNECTIONS

5. How might Gatto assess the vision of education presented in the excerpt from Horace Mann's report of 1848 (p. 142)? How might you account for

the gulf between Gatto's views of the function of education and those for-warded by Mann?

6. Compare the "lessons" taught in the Matt Groening cartoons (pictured on pp. 172 and 181) with those described by Gatto. To what extent is Gatto's indictment of education simply a matter of perspective?

7. Look ahead to Jean Anyon's excerpt from "Social Class and the Hidden Curriculum of Work" (p. 194) and compare Anyon's analysis of the hidden agenda of American education with that described by Gatto. Which of Gatto's seven lessons might be explained by differences of social class? Which, if any, seem unrelated to issues of status or class position?

EXTENDING THE CRITICAL CONTEXT

8. Evaluate the hidden curriculum of the college courses you've taken or are currently enrolled in. To what extent do they reinforce or counter the lessons that Gatto describes?

9. Working in groups, brainstorm a design for a school that would make it *impossible* to teach the hidden curriculum that Gatto describes. How would classes be structured in such a school? What roles would teachers and students play? What would students study? How would they be graded?

"I Just Wanna Be Average"
MIKE ROSE

Mike Rose is anything but average: he has published poetry, scholarly research, a textbook, and two widely praised books on education in America. A professor in the School of Education at UCLA, Rose (b.1944) has won awards from the National Academy of Education, the National Council of Teachers of English, and the John Simon Guggenheim Memorial Foundation. Below you'll read the story of how this highly successful teacher and writer started high school in the "vocational education" track, learning dead-end skills from teachers who were often underprepared or incompetent. Rose shows that students whom the system has written off can have tremendous unrealized potential, and his critique of the school system specifies several reasons for the "failure" of students who go through high school belligerent, fearful, stoned, frustrated, or just plain bored. This selection comes from Lives on the Boundary (1989), *Rose's exploration of America's educationally underprivileged. His most recent book,* Possible Lives (1996), *offers a nationwide tour of creative classrooms and innovative educational programs. Rose is currently a professor at the UCLA Graduate School of Education and Information Studies.*

It took two buses to get to Our Lady of Mercy. The first started deep in South Los Angeles and caught me at midpoint. The second drifted through neighborhoods with trees, parks, big lawns, and lots of flowers. The rides were long but were livened up by a group of South L.A. veterans whose parents also thought that Hope had set up shop in the west end of the county. There was Christy Biggars, who, at sixteen, was dealing and was, according to rumor, a pimp as well. There were Bill Cobb and Johnny Gonzales, grease-pencil artists extraordinaire, who left Nembutal-enhanced[1] swirls of "Cobb" and "Johnny" on the corrugated walls of the bus. And then there was Tyrrell Wilson. Tyrrell was the coolest kid I knew. He ran the dozens[2] like a metric halfback, laid down a rap that outrhymed and outpointed Cobb, whose rap was good but not great — the curse of a moderately soulful kid trapped in white skin. But it was Cobb who would sneak a radio onto the bus, and thus underwrote his patter with Little Richard, Fats Domino, Chuck Berry, the Coasters, and Ernie K. Doe's[3] mother-in-law, an awful woman who was "sent from down below." And so it was that Christy and Cobb and Johnny G. and Tyrrell and I and assorted others picked up along the way passed our days in the back of the bus, a funny mix brought together by geography and parental desire.

Entrance to school brings with it forms and releases and assessments. Mercy relied on a series of tests, mostly the Stanford-Binet,[4] for placement, and somehow the results of my tests got confused with those of another student named Rose. The other Rose apparently didn't do very well, for I was placed in the vocational track, a euphemism for the bottom level. Neither I nor my parents realized what this meant. We had no sense that Business Math, Typing, and English–Level D were dead ends. The current spate of reports on the schools criticizes parents for not involving themselves in the education of their children. But how would someone like Tommy Rose, with his two years of Italian schooling, know what to ask? And what sort of pressure could an exhausted waitress apply? The error went undetected, and I remained in the vocational track for two years. What a place.

My homeroom was supervised by Brother Dill, a troubled and unstable man who also taught freshman English. When his class drifted away from him, which was often, his voice would rise in paranoid accusations, and occasionally he would lose control and shake or smack us. I hadn't been there two months when one of his brisk, face-turning slaps had my glasses sliding down the aisle. Physical education was also pretty harsh. Our teacher was a stubby ex-lineman who had played old-time pro ball in the Midwest. He routinely had us grabbing our ankles to receive his stinging paddle across

[1]*Nembutal:* Trade name for pentobarbital, a sedative drug.
[2]*the dozens:* A verbal game of African origin in which competitors try to top each other's insults.
[3]*Little Richard, Fats Domino, Chuck Berry, the Coasters, and Ernie K. Doe:* Popular black musicians of the 1950s.
[4]*Stanford-Binet:* An IQ test.

our butts. He did that, he said, to make men of us. "Rose," he bellowed on our first encounter; me standing geeky in line in my baggy shorts. "'Rose' ? What the hell kind of name is that?"

"Italian, sir," I squeaked.

"Italian! Ho. Rose, do you know the sound a bag of shit makes when it   5
hits the wall?"

"No, sir."

"Wop!"[5]

Sophomore English was taught by Mr. Mitropetros. He was a large, be-jeweled man who managed the parking lot at the Shrine Auditorium. He would crow and preen and list for us the stars he'd brushed against. We'd ask questions and glance knowingly and snicker, and all that fueled the poor guy to brag some more. Parking cars was his night job. He had little training in English, so his lesson plan for his day work had us reading the district's required text, *Julius Caesar,* aloud for the semester. We'd finished the play way before the twenty weeks was up, so he'd have us switch parts again and again and start again: Dave Snyder, the fastest guy at Mercy, muscling through Caesar to the breathless squeals of Calpurnia, as interpreted by Steve Fusco, a surfer who owned the school's most envied paneled wagon. Week ten and Dave and Steve would take on new roles, as would we all, and render a water-logged Cassius and a Brutus that are beyond my powers of description.

Spanish I — taken in the second year — fell into the hands of a new re-cruit. Mr. Montez was a tiny man, slight, five foot six at the most, soft-spoken and delicate. Spanish was a particularly rowdy class, and Mr. Montez was as prepared for it as a doily maker at a hammer throw. He would tap his pencil to a room in which Steve Fusco was propelling spitballs from his heavy lips, in which Mike Dweetz was taunting Billy Hawk, a half-Indian, half-Spanish, reed-thin, quietly explosive boy. The vocational track at Our Lady of Mercy mixed kids traveling in from South L.A. with South Bay surfers and a few Slavs and Chicanos from the harbors of San Pedro. This was a dangerous miscellany: surfers and hodads[6] and South-Central blacks all ablaze to the metronomic tapping of Hector Montez's pencil.

One day Billy lost it. Out of the corner of my eye I saw him strike out   10
with his right arm and catch Dweetz across the neck. Quick as a spasm, Dweetz was out of his seat, scattering desks, cracking Billy on the side of the head, right behind the eye. Snyder and Fusco and others broke it up, but the room felt hot and close and naked. Mr. Montez's tenuous authority was fi-nally ripped to shreds, and I think everyone felt a little strange about that. The charade was over, and when it came down to it, I don't think any of the kids really wanted it to end this way. They had pushed and pushed and bul-lied their way into a freedom that both scared and embarrassed them.

[5]*Wop:* Derogatory term for Italian.
[6]*hodads:* Nonsurfers.

Students will float to the mark you set. I and the others in the vocational classes were bobbing in pretty shallow water. Vocational education has aimed at increasing the economic opportunities of students who do not do well in our schools. Some serious programs succeed in doing that, and through exceptional teachers — like Mr. Gross in *Horace's Compromise*[7] — students learn to develop hypotheses and troubleshoot, reason through a problem, and communicate effectively — the true job skills. The vocational track, however, is most often a place for those who are just not making it, a dumping ground for the disaffected. There were a few teachers who worked hard at education; young Brother Slattery, for example, combined a stern voice with weekly quizzes to try to pass along to us a skeletal outline of world history. But mostly the teachers had no idea of how to engage the imaginations of us kids who were scuttling along at the bottom of the pond.

And the teachers would have needed some inventiveness, for none of us was groomed for the classroom. It wasn't just that I didn't know things — didn't know how to simplify algebraic fractions, couldn't identify different kinds of clauses, bungled Spanish translations — but that I had developed various faulty and inadequate ways of doing algebra and making sense of Spanish. Worse yet, the years of defensive tuning out in elementary school had given me a way to escape quickly while seeming at least half alert. During my time in Voc. Ed., I developed further into a mediocre student and a somnambulant problem solver, and that affected the subjects I did have the wherewithal to handle: I detested Shakespeare; I got bored with history. My attention flitted here and there. I fooled around in class and read my books indifferently — the intellectual equivalent of playing with your food. I did what I had to do to get by, and I did it with half a mind.

But I did learn things about people and eventually came into my own socially. I liked the guys in Voc. Ed. Growing up where I did, I understood and admired physical prowess, and there was an abundance of muscle here. There was Dave Snyder, a sprinter and halfback of true quality. Dave's ability and his quick wit gave him a natural appeal, and he was welcome in any clique, though he always kept a little independent. He enjoyed acting the fool and could care less about studies, but he possessed a certain maturity and never caused the faculty much trouble. It was a testament to his independence that he included me among his friends — I eventually went out for track, but I was no jock. Owing to the Latin alphabet and a dearth of *R*s and *S*s, Snyder sat behind Rose, and we started exchanging one-liners and became friends.

There was Ted Richard, a much-touted Little League pitcher. He was chunky and had a baby face and came to Our Lady of Mercy as a seasoned street fighter. Ted was quick to laugh and he had a loud, jolly laugh, but when he got angry he'd smile a little smile, the kind that simply raises the corner of the mouth a quarter of an inch. For those who knew, it was an

---

[7]*Horace's Compromise:* A book on American education by Theodore Sizer.

eerie signal. Those who didn't found themselves in big trouble, for Ted was very quick. He loved to carry on what we would come to call philosophical discussions: What is courage? Does God exist? He also loved words, enjoyed picking up big ones like *salubrious* and *equivocal* and using them in our conversations — laughing at himself as the word hit a chuckhole rolling off his tongue. Ted didn't do all that well in school — baseball and parties and testing the courage he'd speculated about took up his time. His textbooks were *Argosy* and *Field and Stream,* whatever newspapers he'd find on the bus stop — from the *Daily Worker* to pornography — conversations with uncles or hobos or businessmen he'd meet in a coffee shop, *The Old Man and the Sea.* With hindsight, I can see that Ted was developing into one of those rough-hewn intellectuals whose sources are a mix of the learned and the apocryphal, whose discussions are both assured and sad.

And then there was Ken Harvey. Ken was good-looking in a puffy way   15
and had a full and oily ducktail and was a car enthusiast . . . a hodad. One day in religion class, he said the sentence that turned out to be one of the most memorable of the hundreds of thousands I heard in those Voc. Ed. years. We were talking about the parable of the talents, about achievement, working hard, doing the best you can do, blah-blah-blah, when the teacher called on the restive Ken Harvey for an opinion. Ken thought about it, but just for a second, and said (with studied, minimal affect), "I just wanna be average." That woke me up. Average? Who wants to be average? Then the athletes chimed in with the clichés that make you want to laryngectomize them, and the exchange became a platitudinous melee. At the time, I thought Ken's assertion was stupid, and I wrote him off. But his sentence has stayed with me all these years, and I think I am finally coming to understand it.

Ken Harvey was gasping for air. School can be a tremendously disorienting place. No matter how bad the school, you're going to encounter notions that don't fit with the assumptions and beliefs that you grew up with — maybe you'll hear these dissonant notions from teachers, maybe from the other students, and maybe you'll read them. You'll also be thrown in with all kinds of kids from all kinds of backgrounds, and that can be unsettling — this is especially true in places of rich ethnic and linguistic mix, like the L.A. basin. You'll see a handful of students far excel you in courses that sound exotic and that are only in the curriculum of the elite: French, physics, trigonometry. And all this is happening while you're trying to shape an identity, your body is changing, and your emotions are running wild. If you're a working-class kid in the vocational track, the options you'll have to deal with this will be constrained in certain ways: you're defined by your school as "slow"; you're placed in a curriculum that isn't designed to liberate you but to occupy you, or, if you're lucky, train you, though the training is for work the society does not esteem; other students are picking up the cues from your school and your curriculum and interacting with you in particular ways. If you're a kid like Ted Richard, you turn your back on all this and let your mind roam where it may. But youngsters like Ted are rare. What Ken and so many others do is protect themselves from such suffocating madness by taking on with a vengeance the identity implied in the vocational track. Reject the confusion and frustration by openly defining yourself as the Common Joe. Champion the average. Rely on your own good sense. Fuck this bullshit. Bullshit, of course, is everything you — and the others — fear is beyond you: books, essays, tests, academic scrambling, complexity, scientific reasoning, philosophical inquiry.

The tragedy is that you have to twist the knife in your own gray matter to make this defense work. You'll have to shut down, have to reject intellectual stimuli or diffuse them with sarcasm, have to cultivate stupidity, have to convert boredom from a malady into a way of confronting the world. Keep your vocabulary simple, act stoned when you're not or act more stoned than you are, flaunt ignorance, materialize your dreams. It is a powerful and effective defense — it neutralizes the insult and the frustration of being a vocational kid and, when perfected, it drives teachers up the wall, a delightful secondary effect. But like all strong magic, it exacts a price.

My own deliverance from the Voc. Ed. world began with sophomore biology. Every student, college prep to vocational, had to take biology, and unlike the other courses, the same person taught all sections. When teaching the vocational group, Brother Clint probably slowed down a bit or omitted a little of the fundamental biochemistry, but he used the same book and more or less the same syllabus across the board. If one class got tough, he could get tougher. He was young and powerful and very handsome, and looks and physical strength were high currency. No one gave him any trouble.

I was pretty bad at the dissecting table, but the lectures and the textbook were interesting: plastic overlays that, with each turned page, peeled away skin, then veins and muscle, then organs, down to the very bones that Brother Clint, pointer in hand, would tap out on our hanging skeleton. Dave Snyder was in big trouble, for the study of life — versus the living of it — was sticking in his craw. We worked out a code for our multiple-choice exams. He'd poke me in the back: once for the answer under *A*, twice for *B*, and so on; and when he'd hit the right one, I'd look up to the ceiling as though I were lost in thought. Poke: cytoplasm. Poke, poke: methane. Poke, poke, poke: William Harvey. Poke, poke, poke, poke: islets of Langerhans. This didn't work out perfectly, but Dave passed the course, and I mastered the dreamy look of a guy on a record jacket. And something else happened. Brother Clint puzzled over this Voc. Ed. kid who was racking up 98s and 99s on his tests. He checked the school's records and discovered the error. He recommended that I begin my junior year in the College Prep program. According to all I've read since, such a shift, as one report put it, is virtually impossible. Kids at that level rarely cross tracks. The telling thing is how chancy both my placement into and exit from Voc. Ed. was; neither I nor my parents had anything to do with it. I lived in one world during spring semester, and when I came back to school in the fall, I was living in another.

Switching to College Prep was a mixed blessing. I was an erratic student. I was undisciplined. And I hadn't caught onto the rules of the game: 20

why work hard in a class that didn't grab my fancy? I was also hopelessly behind in math. Chemistry was hard; toying with my chemistry set years before hadn't prepared me for the chemist's equations. Fortunately, the priest who taught both chemistry and second-year algebra was also the school's athletic director. Membership on the track team covered me; I knew I wouldn't get lower than a C. U.S. history was taught pretty well, and I did okay. But civics was taken over by a football coach who had trouble reading the textbook aloud — and reading aloud was the centerpiece of his pedagogy. College Prep at Mercy was certainly an improvement over the vocational program — at least it carried some status — but the social science curriculum was weak, and the mathematics and physical sciences were simply beyond me. I had a miserable quantitative background and ended up copying some assignments and finessing the rest as best I could. Let me try to explain how it feels to see again and again material you should once have learned but didn't.

You are given a problem. It requires you to simplify algebraic fractions or to multiply expressions containing square roots. You know this is pretty basic material because you've seen it for years. Once a teacher took some time with you, and you learned how to carry out these operations. Simple versions, anyway. But that was a year or two or more in the past, and these are more complex versions, and now you're not sure. And this, you keep telling yourself, is ninth- or even eighth-grade stuff.

Next it's a word problem. This is also old hat. The basic elements are as familiar as story characters: trains speeding so many miles per hour or shadows of buildings angling so many degrees. Maybe you know enough, have sat through enough explanations, to be able to begin setting up the problem: "If one train is going this fast . . ." or "This shadow is really one line of a triangle . . ." Then: "Let's see . . ." "How did Jones do this?" "Hmmmm." "No." "No, that won't work." Your attention wavers. You wonder about other things: a football game, a dance, that cute new checker at the market. You try to focus on the problem again. You scribble on paper for a while, but the tension wins out and your attention flits elsewhere. You crumple the paper and begin daydreaming to ease the frustration.

The particulars will vary, but in essence this is what a number of students go through, especially those in so-called remedial classes. They open their textbooks and see once again the familiar and impenetrable formulas and diagrams and terms that have stumped them for years. There is no excitement here. *No* excitement. Regardless of what the teacher says, this is not a new challenge. There is, rather, embarrassment and frustration and, not surprisingly, some anger in being reminded once again of long-standing inadequacies. No wonder so many students finally attribute their difficulties to something inborn, organic: "That part of my brain just doesn't work." Given the troubling histories many of these students have, it's miraculous that any of them can lift the shroud of hopelessness sufficiently to make deliverance from these classes possible.

Through this entire period, my father's health was deteriorating with cruel momentum. His arteriosclerosis progressed to the point where a simple nick on his shin wouldn't heal. Eventually it ulcerated and widened. Lou Minton would come by daily to change the dressing. We tried renting an oscillating bed — which we placed in the front room — to force blood through the constricted arteries in my father's legs. The bed hummed through the night, moving in place to ward off the inevitable. The ulcer continued to spread, and the doctors finally had to amputate. My grandfather had lost his leg in a stockyard accident. Now my father too was crippled. His convalescence was slow but steady, and the doctors placed him in the Santa Monica Rehabilitation Center, a sun-bleached building that opened out onto the warm spray of the Pacific. The place gave him some strength and some color and some training in walking with an artificial leg. He did pretty well for a year or so until he slipped and broke his hip. He was confined to a wheelchair after that, and the confinement contributed to the diminishing of his body and spirit.

I am holding a picture of him. He is sitting in his wheelchair and smiling   25
at the camera. The smile appears forced, unsteady, seems to quaver, though it is frozen in silver nitrate. He is in his mid-sixties and looks eighty. Late in my junior year, he had a stroke and never came out of the resulting coma. After that, I would see him only in dreams, and to this day that is how I join him. Sometimes the dreams are sad and grisly and primal: my father lying in a bed soaked with his suppuration,[8] holding me, rocking me. But sometimes the dreams bring him back to me healthy: him talking to me on an empty street, or buying some pictures to decorate our old house, or transformed somehow into someone strong and adept with tools and the physical.

Jack MacFarland couldn't have come into my life at a better time. My father was dead, and I had logged up too many years of scholastic indifference. Mr. MacFarland had a master's degree from Columbia and decided, at twenty-six, to find a little school and teach his heart out. He never took any credentialing courses, couldn't bear to, he said, so he had to find employment in a private system. He ended up at Our Lady of Mercy teaching five sections of senior English. He was a beatnik who was born too late. His teeth were stained, he tucked his sorry tie in between the third and fourth buttons of his shirt, and his pants were chronically wrinkled. At first, we couldn't believe this guy, thought he slept in his car. But within no time, he had us so startled with work that we didn't much worry about where he slept or if he slept at all. We wrote three or four essays a month. We read a book every two to three weeks, starting with the *Iliad* and ending up with Hemingway. He gave us a quiz on the reading every other day. He brought a prep school curriculum to Mercy High.

MacFarland's lectures were crafted, and as he delivered them he would pace the room jiggling a piece of chalk in his cupped hand, using it to

[8]*suppuration:* Discharge from wounds.

scribble on the board the names of all the writers and philosophers and plays and novels he was weaving into his discussion. He asked questions often, raised everything from Zeno's paradox to the repeated last line of Frost's "Stopping by Woods on a Snowy Evening." He slowly and carefully built up our knowledge of Western intellectual history — with facts, with connections, with speculations. We learned about Greek philosophy, about Dante, the Elizabethan world view, the Age of Reason, existentialism. He analyzed poems with us, had us reading sections from John Ciardi's *How Does a Poem Mean?*, making a potentially difficult book accessible with his own explanations. We gave oral reports on poems Ciardi didn't cover. We imitated the styles of Conrad, Hemingway, and *Time* magazine. We wrote and talked, wrote and talked. The man immersed us in language.

Even MacFarland's barbs were literary. If Jim Fitzsimmons, hung over and irritable, tried to smart-ass him, he'd rejoin with a flourish that would spark the indomitable Skip Madison — who'd lost his front teeth in a hapless tackle — to flick his tongue through the gap and opine, "good chop," drawing out the single "o" in stinging indictment. Jack MacFarland, this tobacco-stained intellectual, brandished linguistic weapons of a kind I hadn't encountered before. Here was this *egghead,* for God's sake, keeping some pretty difficult people in line. And from what I heard, Mike Dweetz and Steve Fusco and all the notorious Voc. Ed. crowd settled down as well when MacFarland took the podium. Though a lot of guys groused in the schoolyard, it just seemed that giving trouble to this particular teacher was a silly thing to do. Tomfoolery, not to mention assault, had no place in the world he was trying to create for us, and instinctively everyone knew that. If nothing else, we all recognized MacFarland's considerable intelligence and respected the hours he put into his work. It came to this: the troublemaker would look foolish rather than daring. Even Jim Fitzsimmons was reading *On the Road* and turning his incipient alcoholism to literary ends.

There were some lives that were already beyond Jack MacFarland's ministrations, but mine was not. I started reading again as I hadn't since elementary school. I would go into our gloomy little bedroom or sit at the dinner table while, on the television, Danny McShane was paralyzing Mr. Moto with the atomic drop, and work slowly back through *Heart of Darkness,* trying to catch the words in Conrad's sentences. I certainly was not MacFarland's best student; most of the other guys in College Prep, even my fellow slackers, had better backgrounds than I did. But I worked very hard, for MacFarland had hooked me. He tapped my old interest in reading and creating stories. He gave me a way to feel special by using my mind. And he provided a role model that wasn't shaped on physical prowess alone, and something inside me that I wasn't quite aware of responded to that. Jack MacFarland established a literacy club, to borrow a phrase of Frank Smith's, and invited me — invited all of us — to join.

There's been a good deal of research and speculation suggesting that 30 the acknowledgment of school performance with extrinsic rewards — smiling faces, stars, numbers, grades — diminishes the intrinsic satisfaction children experience by engaging in reading or writing or problem solving. While it's certainly true that we've created an educational system that encourages our best and brightest to become cynical grade collectors and, in general, have developed an obsession with evaluation and assessment, I must tell you that venal though it may have been, I loved getting good grades from MacFarland. I now know how subjective grades can be, but then they came tucked in the back of essays like bits of scientific data, some sort of spectroscopic readout that said, objectively and publicly, that I had made something of value. I suppose I'd been mediocre for too long and enjoyed a public redefinition. And I suppose the workings of my mind, such as they were, had been private for too long. My linguistic play moved into the world; . . . these papers with their circled, red B-pluses and A-minuses linked my mind to something outside it. I carried them around like a club emblem.

One day in the December of my senior year, Mr. MacFarland asked me where I was going to go to college. I hadn't thought much about it. Many of the students I teach today spent their last year in high school with a physics text in one hand and the Stanford catalog in the other, but I wasn't even aware of what "entrance requirements" were. My folks would say that they wanted me to go to college and be a doctor, but I don't know how seriously I ever took that; it seemed a sweet thing to say, a bit of supportive family chatter, like telling a gangly daughter she's graceful. The reality of higher education wasn't in my scheme of things: no one in the family had gone to college; only two of my uncles had completed high school. I figured I'd get a night job and go to the local junior college because I knew that Snyder and Company were going there to play ball. But I hadn't even prepared for that. When I finally said, "I don't know," MacFarland looked down at me — I was seated in his office — and said, "Listen, you can write."

My grades stank. I had A's in biology and a handful of B's in a few English and social science classes. All the rest were C's — or worse. MacFarland said I would do well in his class and laid down the law about doing well in the others. Still, the record for my first three years wouldn't have been acceptable to any four-year school. To nobody's surprise, I was turned down flat by USC and UCLA. But Jack MacFarland was on the case. He had received his bachelor's degree from Loyola University, so he made calls to old professors and talked to somebody in admissions and wrote me a strong letter. Loyola finally accepted me as a probationary student. I would be on trial for the first year, and if I did okay, I would be granted regular status. MacFarland also intervened to get me a loan, for I could never have afforded a private college without it. Four more years of religion classes and four more years of boys at one school, girls at another. But at least I was going to college. Amazing.

In my last semester of high school, I elected a special English course fashioned by Mr. MacFarland, and it was through this elective that there arose at Mercy a fledgling literati. Art Mitz, the editor of the school newspaper and a very smart guy, was the kingpin. He was joined by me and by Mark Dever, a quiet boy who wrote beautifully and who would die before he was forty. MacFarland occasionally invited us to his apartment, and those visits became the high point of our apprenticeship: we'd clamp on our training wheels and drive to his salon.

He lived in a cramped and cluttered place near the airport, tucked away in the kind of building that architectural critic Reyner Banham calls a *dingbat.* Books were all over: stacked, piled, tossed, and crated, underlined and dog eared, well worn and new. Cigarette ashes crusted with coffee in saucers or spilling over the sides of motel ashtrays. The little bedroom had, along two of its walls, bricks and boards loaded with notes, magazines, and oversized books. The kitchen joined the living room, and there was a stack of German newspapers under the sink. I had never seen anything like it: a great flophouse of language furnished by City Lights and Café le Metro. I read every title. I flipped through paperbacks and scanned jackets and memorized names: Gogol, *Finnegans Wake,* Djuna Barnes, Jackson Pollock, *A Coney Island of the Mind,* F. O. Matthiessen's *American Renaissance,* all sorts of Freud, *Troubled Sleep,* Man Ray, *The Education of Henry Adams,* Richard Wright, *Film as Art,* William Butler Yeats, Marguerite Duras, *Redburn, A Season in Hell, Kapital.* On the cover of Alain-Fournier's *The Wanderer* was an Edward Gorey drawing of a young man on a road winding into dark trees. By the hotplate sat a strange Kafka novel called *Amerika,* in which an adolescent hero crosses the Atlantic to find the Nature Theater of Oklahoma. Art and Mark would be talking about a movie or the school newspaper, and I would be consuming my English teacher's library. It was heady stuff. I felt like a Pop Warner[9] athlete on steroids.

Art, Mark, and I would buy stogies and triangulate from MacFarland's apartment to the Cinema, which now shows X-rated films but was then L.A.'s premier art theater, and then to the musty Cherokee Bookstore in Hollywood to hobnob with beatnik homosexuals — smoking, drinking bourbon and coffee, and trying out awkward phrases we'd gleaned from our mentor's bookshelves. I was happy and precocious and a little scared as well, for Hollywood Boulevard was thick with a kind of decadence that was foreign to the South Side. After the Cherokee, we would head back to the security of MacFarland's apartment, slaphappy with hipness.

Let me be the first to admit that there was a good deal of adolescent passion in this embrace of the avant-garde: self-absorption, sexually charged pedantry, an elevation of the odd and abandoned. Still it was a time during which I absorbed an awful lot of information: long lists of titles, images from expressionist paintings, new wave shibboleths,[10] snippets of philosophy, and names that read like Steve Fusco's misspellings — Goethe, Nietzsche,

35

---

[9]*Pop Warner:* A nationwide youth athletics organization.

[10]*new wave shibboleths:* Trendy phrases or jargon.

Kierkegaard. Now this is hardly the stuff of deep understanding. But it was an introduction, a phrase book, a Baedeker[11] to a vocabulary of ideas, and it felt good at the time to know all these words. With hindsight I realize how layered and important that knowledge was.

It enabled me to do things in the world. I could browse bohemian bookstores in far-off, mysterious Hollywood; I could go to the Cinema and see events through the lenses of European directors; and, most of all, I could share an evening, talk that talk, with Jack MacFarland, the man I most admired at the time. Knowledge was becoming a bonding agent. Within a year or two, the persona of the disaffected hipster would prove too cynical, too alienated to last. But for a time it was new and exciting: it provided a critical perspective on society, and it allowed me to act as though I were living beyond the limiting boundaries of South Vermont.[12]

ENGAGING THE TEXT

1. Describe Rose's life in Voc. Ed. What were his teachers like? Have you ever had experience with teachers like these?

2. What did Voc. Ed. do to Rose and his fellow students? How did it affect them intellectually, emotionally, and socially? Why was it subsequently so hard for Rose to catch up in math?

3. Why is high school so disorienting to students like Ken Harvey? How does he cope with it? What other strategies do students use to cope with the pressures and judgments they encounter in school?

4. What does Jack MacFarland offer Rose that finally helps him learn? Do you think it was inevitable that someone with Rose's intelligence would eventually succeed?

EXPLORING CONNECTIONS

5. To what extent do Rose's experiences challenge or confirm John Taylor Gatto's critique of public education in "The Seven-Lesson Schoolteacher" (p. 173)?

6. How does Michael Moore's assessment of the general state of intelligence in America in "Idiot Nation" (p. 153) help to explain the attitudes of Rose's friends toward education? How would you account for the fact that many American teens seem to feel it's OK to be "average" intellectually even as they strive for other kinds of excellence?

7. Draw a Groening-style cartoon (see pp. 172 and 181) or comic strip of Rose in the vocational track, or of Rose before and after his liberation from Voc. Ed.

8. Read Gregory Mantsios's "Class in America: Myths and Realities (2000)" (p. 331) and write an imaginary dialogue between Rose and Mantsios about why some students, like Rose, seem to be able to break through social class barriers and others, like Dave Snyder, Ted Richard, and Ken Harvey, do not.

[11]*Baedeker:* Travel guide.
[12]*South Vermont:* A street in an economically depressed area of Los Angeles.

Extending the Critical Context

9. Rose explains that high school can be a "tremendously disorienting place" (para. 16). What, if anything, do you find disorienting about college? What steps can students at your school take to lessen feelings of disorientation? What could the college do to help them?

10. Review one or more of Rose's descriptions of his high school classmates; then write a description of one of your own high school classmates, trying to capture in a nutshell how that person coped or failed to cope with the educational system.

11. Watch on videotape any one of the many films that have been made about charismatic teachers (for example, *Dangerous Minds, Renaissance Man, Stand and Deliver,* or *Dead Poets Society*) and compare Hollywood's depiction of a dynamic teacher to Rose's portrayal of Jack MacFarland. What do such charismatic teachers offer their students personally and intellectually? Do you see any disadvantages to classes taught by teachers like these?

From *Social Class and the Hidden Curriculum of Work*

Jean Anyon

It's no surprise that schools in wealthy communities are better than those in poor communities, or that they better prepare their students for desirable jobs. It may be shocking, however, to learn how vast the differences in schools are — not so much in resources as in teaching methods and philosophies of education. Jean Anyon observed five elementary schools over the course of a full school year and concluded that fifth graders of different economic backgrounds are already being prepared to occupy particular rungs on the social ladder. In a sense, some whole schools are on the vocational education track, while others are geared to produce future doctors, lawyers, and business leaders. Anyon's main audience is professional educators, so you may find her style and vocabulary challenging, but, once you've read her descriptions of specific classroom activities, the more analytic parts of the essay should prove easier to understand. Anyon is chairperson of the Department of Education at Rutgers University, Newark. Her most recent book is Ghetto Schooling: A Political Economy of Urban Educational Reform *(1997). This essay first appeared in the* Journal of Education *in 1980.*

Scholars in political economy and the sociology of knowledge have recently argued that public schools in complex industrial societies like our own make available different types of educational experience and curriculum knowledge to students in different social classes. Bowles and Gintis[1] for example, have argued that students in different social-class backgrounds are rewarded for classroom behaviors that correspond to personality traits allegedly rewarded in the different occupational strata — the working classes for docility and obedience, the managerial classes for initiative and personal assertiveness. Basil Bernstein, Pierre Bourdieu, and Michael W. Apple,[2] focusing on school knowledge, have argued that knowledge and skills leading to social power and regard (medical, legal, managerial) are made available to the advantaged social groups but are withheld from the working classes, to whom a more "practical" curriculum is offered (manual skills, clerical knowledge). While there has been considerable argumentation of these points regarding education in England, France, and North America, there has been little or no attempt to investigate these ideas empirically in elementary or secondary schools and classrooms in this country.[3]

This article offers tentative empirical support (and qualification) of the above arguments by providing illustrative examples of differences in student *work* in classrooms in contrasting social-class communities. The examples were gathered as part of an ethnographical[4] study of curricular, pedagogical, and pupil evaluation practices in five elementary schools. The article attempts a theoretical contribution as well and assesses student work in the light of a theoretical approach to social-class analysis. . . . It will be suggested that there is a "hidden curriculum" in schoolwork that has profound implications for the theory — and consequence — of everyday activity in education. . . .

The Sample of Schools

. . . The social-class designation of each of the five schools will be identified, and the income, occupation, and other relevant available social characteristics of the students and their parents will be described. The first three

---

[1]S. Bowles and H. Gintis, *Schooling in Capitalist America: Educational Reform and the Contradictions of Economic Life* (New York: Basic Books, 1976). [All notes are the author's, except 4 and 11.]

[2]B. Bernstein, *Class, Codes and Control,* Vol. 3. *Towards a Theory of Educational Transmission,* 2d ed. (London: Routledge & Kegan Paul, 1977); P. Bourdieu and J. Passeron, *Reproduction in Education, Society and Culture* (Beverly Hills, Calif.: Sage, 1977); M. W. Apple, *Ideology and Curriculum* (Boston: Routledge & Kegan Paul, 1979).

[3]But see, in a related vein, M. W. Apple and N. King, "What Do Schools Teach?" *Curriculum Inquiry* 6 (1977): 341–58; R. C. Rist, *The Urban School: A Factory for Failure* (Cambridge, Mass.: MIT Press, 1973).

[4]*ethnographical:* Based on an anthropological study of cultures or subcultures — the "cultures" in this case being the five schools observed.

schools are in a medium-sized city district in northern New Jersey, and the other two are in a nearby New Jersey suburb.

The first two schools I will call *working-class schools.* Most of the parents have blue-collar jobs. Less than a third of the fathers are skilled, while the majority are in unskilled or semiskilled jobs. During the period of the study (1978–1979), approximately 15 percent of the fathers were unemployed. The large majority (85 percent) of the families are white. The following occupations are typical: platform, storeroom, and stockroom workers; foundrymen, pipe welders, and boilermakers; semiskilled and unskilled assemblyline operatives; gas station attendants, auto mechanics, maintenance workers, and security guards. Less than 30 percent of the women work, some part-time and some full-time, on assembly lines, in storerooms and stockrooms, as waitresses, barmaids, or sales clerks. Of the fifth-grade parents, none of the wives of the skilled workers had jobs. Approximately 15 percent of the families in each school are at or below the federal "poverty" level;[5] most of the rest of the family incomes are at or below $12,000, except some of the skilled workers whose incomes are higher. The incomes of the majority of the families in these two schools (at or below $12,000) are typical of 38.6 percent of the families in the United States.[6]

The third school is called the *middle-class school,* although because of   5
neighborhood residence patterns, the population is a mixture of several social classes. The parents' occupations can be divided into three groups: a small group of blue-collar "rich," who are skilled, well-paid workers such as printers, carpenters, plumbers, and construction workers. The second group is composed of parents in working-class and middle-class white-collar jobs: women in office jobs, technicians, supervisors in industry, and parents employed by the city (such as firemen, policemen, and several of the school's teachers). The third group is composed of occupations such as personnel directors in local firms, accountants, "middle management," and a few small capitalists (owners of shops in the area). The children of several local doctors attend this school. Most family incomes are between $13,000 and $25,000, with a few higher. This income range is typical of 38.9 percent of the families in the United States.[7]

The fourth school has a parent population that is at the upper income level of the upper middle class and is predominantly professional. This school will be called the *affluent professional school.* Typical jobs are: cardiologist, interior designer, corporate lawyer or engineer, executive in advertising or television. There are some families who are not as affluent as the

---

[5]The U.S. Bureau of the Census defines *poverty* for a nonfarm family of four as a yearly income of $6,191 a year or less. U.S. Bureau of the Census, *Statistical Abstract of the United States: 1978* (Washington, D.C.: U.S. Government Printing Office, 1978), 465, table 754.

[6]U.S. Bureau of the Census, "Money Income in 1977 of Families and Persons in the United States," *Current Population Reports* Series P-60, no. 118 (Washington, D.C.: U.S. Government Printing Office, 1979), p. 2, table A.

[7]Ibid.

majority (the family of the superintendent of the district's schools, and the one or two families in which the fathers are skilled workers). In addition, a few of the families are more affluent than the majority and can be classified in the capitalist class (a partner in a prestigious Wall Street stock brokerage firm). Approximately 90 percent of the children in this school are white. Most family incomes are between $40,000 and $80,000. This income span represents approximately 7 percent of the families in the United States.[8]

In the fifth school the majority of the families belong to the capitalist class. This school will be called the *executive elite school* because most of the fathers are top executives (for example, presidents and vice-presidents) in major United States–based multinational corporations — for example, AT&T, RCA, Citibank, American Express, U.S. Steel. A sizable group of fathers are top executives in financial firms on Wall Street. There are also a number of fathers who list their occupations as "general counsel" to a particular corporation, and these corporations are also among the large multinationals. Many of the mothers do volunteer work in the Junior League, Junior Fortnightly, or other service groups; some are intricately involved in town politics; and some are themselves in well-paid occupations. There are no minority children in the school. Almost all the family incomes are over $100,000, with some in the $500,000 range. The incomes in this school represent less than 1 percent of the families in the United States.[9]

Since each of the five schools is only one instance of elementary education in a particular social-class context, I will not generalize beyond the sample. However, the examples of schoolwork which follow will suggest characteristics of education in each social setting that appear to have theoretical and social significance and to be worth investigation in a larger number of schools. . . .

The Working-Class Schools

In the two working-class schools, work is following the steps of a procedure. The procedure is usually mechanical, involving rote behavior and very little decision making or choice. The teachers rarely explain why the work is being assigned, how it might connect to other assignments, or what the idea is that lies behind the procedure or gives it coherence and perhaps meaning or significance. Available textbooks are not always used, and the teachers often prepare their own dittos or put work examples on the board. Most of the rules regarding work are designations of what the children are to do; the rules are steps to follow. These steps are told to the children by the teachers and are often written on the board. The children are usually told to copy the

---

[8]This figure is an estimate. According to the Bureau of the Census, only 2.6 percent of families in the United States have money income of $50,000 or over. U.S. Bureau of the Census, *Current Population Reports* Series P-60. For figures on income at these higher levels, see J. D. Smith and S. Franklin, "The Concentration of Personal Wealth, 1922–1969," *American Economic Review* 64 (1974): 162–67.

[9]Smith and Franklin, "The Concentration of Personal Wealth."

steps as notes. These notes are to be studied. Work is often evaluated not according to whether it is right or wrong but according to whether the children followed the right steps.

The following examples illustrate these points. In math, when two-digit division was introduced, the teacher in one school gave a four-minute lecture on what the terms are called (which number is the divisor, dividend, quotient, and remainder). The children were told to copy these names in their notebooks. Then the teacher told them the steps to follow to do the problems, saying, "This is how you do them." The teacher listed the steps on the board, and they appeared several days later as a chart hung in the middle of the front wall: "Divide, Multiply, Subtract, Bring Down." The children often did examples of two-digit division. When the teacher went over the examples with them, he told them what the procedure was for each problem, rarely asking them to conceptualize or explain it themselves: "Three into twenty-two is seven; do your subtraction and one is left over." During the week that two-digit division was introduced (or at any other time), the investigator did not observe any discussion of the idea of grouping involved in division, any use of manipulables, or any attempt to relate two-digit division to any other mathematical process. Nor was there any attempt to relate the steps to an actual or possible thought process of the children. The observer did not hear the terms *dividend, quotient,* and so on, used again. The math teacher in the other working-class school followed similar procedures regarding two-digit division and at one point her class seemed confused. She said, "You're confusing yourselves. You're tensing up. Remember, when you do this, it's the same steps over and over again — and that's the way division always is." Several weeks later, after a test, a group of her children "still didn't get it," and she made no attempt to explain the concept of dividing things into groups or to give them manipulables for their own investigation. Rather, she went over the steps with them again and told them that they "needed more practice."

In other areas of math, work is also carrying out often unexplained fragmented procedures. For example, one of the teachers led the children through a series of steps to make a 1-inch grid on their paper *without* telling them that they were making a 1-inch grid or that it would be used to study scale. She said, "Take your ruler. Put it across the top. Make a mark at every number. Then move your ruler down to the bottom. No, put it across the bottom. Now make a mark on top of every number. Now draw a line from . . ." At this point a girl said that she had a faster way to do it and the teacher said, "No, you don't; you don't even know what I'm making yet. Do it this way or it's wrong." After they had made the lines up and down and across, the teacher told them she wanted them to make a figure by connecting some dots and to measure that, using the scale of 1 inch equals 1 mile. Then they were to cut it out. She said, "Don't cut it until I check it."

In both working-class schools, work in language arts is mechanics of punctuation (commas, periods, question marks, exclamation points), capitalization, and the four kinds of sentences. One teacher explained to me, "Simple punctuation is all they'll ever use." Regarding punctuation, either a teacher or a ditto stated the rules for where, for example, to put commas. The investigator heard no classroom discussion of the aural context of punctuation (which, of course, is what gives each mark its meaning). Nor did the investigator hear any statement or inference that placing a punctuation mark could be a decision-making process, depending, for example, on one's intended meaning. Rather, the children were told to follow the rules. Language arts did not involve creative writing. There were several writing assignments throughout the year, but in each instance the children were given a ditto, and they wrote answers to questions on the sheet. For example, they wrote their "autobiography" by answering such questions as "Where were you born?" "What is your favorite animal?" on a sheet entitled "All About Me."

In one of the working-class schools, the class had a science period several times a week. On the three occasions observed, the children were not called upon to set up experiments or to give explanations for facts or concepts. Rather, on each occasion the teacher told them in his own words what the book said. The children copied the teacher's sentences from the board. Each day that preceded the day they were to do a science experiment, the teacher told them to copy the directions from the book for the procedure they would carry out the next day and to study the list at home that night. The day after each experiment, the teacher went over what they had "found" (they did the experiments as a class, and each was actually a class demonstration led by the teacher). Then the teacher wrote what they "found" on the board, and the children copied that in their notebooks. Once or twice a year there are science projects. The project is chosen and assigned by the teacher from a box of 3-by-5-inch cards. On the card the teacher has written the question to be answered, the books to use, and how much to write. Explaining the cards to the observer, the teacher said, "It tells them exactly what to do, or they couldn't do it."

Social studies in the working-class schools is also largely mechanical, rote work that was given little explanation or connection to larger contexts. In one school, for example, although there was a book available, social studies work was to copy the teacher's notes from the board. Several times a week for a period of several months the children copied these notes. The fifth grades in the district were to study United States history. The teacher used a booklet she had purchased called "The Fabulous Fifty States." Each day she put information from the booklet in outline form on the board and the children copied it. The type of information did not vary: the name of the state, its abbreviation, state capital, nickname of the state, its main products, main business, and a "Fabulous Fact" ("Idaho grew twenty-seven billion potatoes in one year. That's enough potatoes for each man, woman, and . . ."). As the children finished copying the sentences, the teacher erased them and wrote more. Children would occasionally go to the front to pull down the wall map in order to locate the states they were copying, and the teacher did not dissuade them. But the observer never saw her refer to the map; nor did the observer ever hear her make other than perfunctory remarks concerning the information the children were copying. Occasionally the children colored in a ditto and cut it out to make a stand-up figure (representing, for example, a man roping a cow in the Southwest). These were referred to by the teacher as their social studies "projects."

Rote behavior was often called for in classroom work. When going over   15
math and language arts skills sheets, for example, as the teacher asked for the answer to each problem, he fired the questions rapidly, staccato, and the scene reminded the observer of a sergeant drilling recruits: above all, the questions demanded that you stay at attention: "The next one? What do I put here? . . . Here? Give us the next." Or "How many commas in this sentence? Where do I put them . . . The next one?"

The four fifth-grade teachers observed in the working-class schools attempted to control classroom time and space by making decisions without consulting the children and without explaining the basis for their decisions. The teacher's control thus often seemed capricious. Teachers, for instance, very often ignored the bells to switch classes — deciding among themselves to keep the children after the period was officially over to continue with the work or for disciplinary reasons or so they (the teachers) could stand in the hall and talk. There were no clocks in the rooms in either school, and the children often asked, "What period is this?" "When do we go to gym?" The children had no access to materials. These were handed out by teachers and closely guarded. Things in the room "belonged" to the teacher: "Bob, bring me my garbage can." The teachers continually gave the children orders. Only three times did the investigator hear a teacher in either working-class school preface a directive with an unsarcastic "please," or "let's," or "would you." Instead, the teachers said, "Shut up," "Shut your mouth," "Open your books," "Throw your gum away — if you want to rot your teeth, do it on your own time." Teachers made every effort to control the movement of the children, and often shouted, "Why are you out of your seat??!!" If the children got permission to leave the room, they had to take a written pass with the date and time. . . .

Middle-Class School

In the middle-class school, work is getting the right answer. If one accumulates enough right answers, one gets a good grade. One must follow the directions in order to get the right answers, but the directions often call for some figuring, some choice, some decision making. For example, the children must often figure out by themselves what the directions ask them to do and how to get the answer: what do you do first, second, and perhaps third? Answers are usually found in books or by listening to the teacher. Answers are usually words, sentences, numbers, or facts and dates; one writes them on paper, and one should be neat. Answers must be given in the right order, and one cannot make them up.

The following activities are illustrative. Math involves some choice: one may do two-digit division the long way or the short way, and there are some math problems that can be done "in your head." When the teacher explains how to do two-digit division, there is recognition that a cognitive process is involved; she gives you several ways and says, "I want to make sure you understand what you're doing — so you get it right"; and, when they go over the homework, she asks the *children* to tell how they did the problem and what answer they got.

In social studies the daily work is to read the assigned pages in the textbook and to answer the teacher's questions. The questions are almost always designed to check on whether the students have read the assignment and understood it: who did so-and-so; what happened after that; when did it happen, where, and sometimes, why did it happen? The answers are in the book and in one's understanding of the book; the teacher's hints when one doesn't know the answers are to "read it again" or to look at the picture or at the rest of the paragraph. One is to search for the answer in the "context," in what is given.

Language arts is "simple grammar, what they need for everyday life." 20 The language arts teacher says, "They should learn to speak properly, to write business letters and thank-you letters, and to understand what nouns and verbs and simple subjects are." Here, as well, actual work is to choose the right answers, to understand what is given. The teacher often says, "Please read the next sentence and then I'll question you about it." One teacher said in some exasperation to a boy who was fooling around in class, "If you don't know the answers to the questions I ask, then you can't stay in this *class!* [pause] You *never* know the answers to the questions I ask, and it's not fair to me — and certainly not to you!"

Most lessons are based on the textbook. This does not involve a critical perspective on what is given there. For example, a critical perspective in social studies is perceived as dangerous by these teachers because it may lead to controversial topics; the parents might complain. The children, however, are often curious, especially in social studies. Their questions are tolerated and usually answered perfunctorily. But after a few minutes the teacher will say, "All right, we're not going any farther. Please open your social studies workbook." While the teachers spend a lot of time explaining and expanding on what the textbooks say, there is little attempt to analyze how or why things happen, or to give thought to how pieces of a culture, or, say, a system of numbers or elements of a language fit together or can be analyzed. What has happened in the past and what exists now may not be equitable or fair, but (shrug) that is the way things are and one does not confront such matters in school. For example, in social studies after a child is called on to read a passage about the pilgrims, the teacher summarizes the paragraph and then says, "So you can see how strict they were about everything." A child asks, "Why?" "Well, because they felt that if you weren't busy you'd get into trouble." Another child asks, "Is it true that they burned women at the stake?" The teacher says, "Yes, if a woman did anything strange, they hanged them. [*sic*] What would a woman do, do you think, to make them burn them? [*sic*] See if you can come up with better answers than my other [social studies] class." Several children offer suggestions, to which the teacher nods but does not comment. Then she says, "Okay, good," and calls on the next child to read.

Work tasks do not usually request creativity. Serious attention is rarely given in school work on *how* the children develop or express their own feelings and ideas, either linguistically or in graphic form. On the occasions when creativity or self-expression is requested, it is peripheral to the main activity or it is "enrichment" or "for fun." During a lesson on what similes are, for example, the teacher explains what they are, puts several on the board, gives some other examples herself, and then asks the children if they can "make some up." She calls on three children who give similes, two of which are actually in the book they have open before them. The teacher does not comment on this and then asks several others to choose similes from the list of phrases in the book. Several do so correctly, and she says, "Oh good! You're picking them out! See how good we are?" Their homework is to pick out the rest of the similes from the list.

Creativity is not often requested in social studies and science projects, either. Social studies projects, for example, are given with directions to "find information on your topic" and write it up. The children are not supposed to copy but to "put it in your own words." Although a number of the projects subsequently went beyond the teacher's direction to find information and had quite expressive covers and inside illustrations, the teacher's evaluative comments had to do with the amount of information, whether they had "copied," and if their work was neat.

The style of control of the three fifth-grade teachers observed in this school varied from somewhat easygoing to strict, but in contrast to the working-class schools, the teachers' decisions were usually based on external rules and regulations — for example, on criteria that were known or available to the children. Thus, the teachers always honor the bells for changing classes, and they usually evaluate children's work by what is in the textbooks and answer booklets.

There is little excitement in schoolwork for the children, and the assignments are perceived as having little to do with their interests and feelings. As one child said, what you do is "store facts up in your head like cold storage — until you need it later for a test or your job." Thus, doing well is important because there are thought to be *other*, likely rewards: a good job or college.[10]

25

---

[10]A dominant feeling, expressed directly and indirectly by teachers in this school, was boredom with their work. They did, however, in contrast to the working-class schools, almost always carry out lessons during class times.

Affluent Professional School

In the affluent professional school, work is creative activity carried out independently. The students are continually asked to express and apply ideas and concepts. Work involves individual thought and expressiveness, expansion and illustration of ideas, and choice of appropriate method and material. (The class is not considered an open classroom, and the principal explained that because of the large number of discipline problems in the fifth grade this year they did not departmentalize. The teacher who agreed to take part in the study said she is "more structured" this year than she usually is.) The products of work in this class are often written stories, editorials and essays, or representations of ideas in mural, graph, or craft form. The products of work should not be like everybody else's and should show individuality. They should exhibit good design, and (this is important) they must also fit empirical reality. Moreover, one's work should attempt to interpret or "make sense" of reality. The relatively few rules to be followed regarding work are usually criteria for, or limits on, individual activity. One's product is usually evaluated for the quality of its expression and for the appropriateness of its conception to the task. In many cases, one's own satisfaction with the product is an important criterion for its evaluation. When right answers are called for, as in commercial materials like SRA (Science Research Associates) and math, it is important that the children decide on an answer as a result of thinking about the idea involved in what they're being asked to do. Teacher's hints are to "think about it some more."

The following activities are illustrative. The class takes home a sheet requesting each child's parents to fill in the number of cars they have, the number of television sets, refrigerators, games, or rooms in the house, and so on. Each child is to figure the average number of a type of possession owned by the fifth grade. Each child must compile the "data" from all the sheets. A calculator is available in the classroom to do the mechanics of finding the average. Some children decide to send sheets to the fourth-grade families for comparison. Their work should be "verified" by a classmate before it is handed in.

Each child and his or her family has made a geoboard. The teacher asks the class to get their geoboards from the side cabinet, to take a handful of rubber bands, and then to listen to what she would like them to do. She says, "I would like you to design a figure and then find the perimeter and area. When you have it, check with your neighbor. After you've done that, please transfer it to graph paper and tomorrow I'll ask you to make up a question about it for someone. When you hand it in, please let me know whose it is and who verified it. Then I have something else for you to do that's really fun. [pause] Find the average number of chocolate chips in three cookies. I'll give you three cookies, and you'll have to *eat* your way through, I'm afraid!" Then she goes around the room and gives help, suggestions, praise, and admonitions that they are getting noisy. They work sitting, or standing up at their desks, at benches in the back, or on the floor. A child hands the teacher his paper and she comments, "I'm not accepting this paper. Do a better design." To another child she says, "That's fantastic! But you'll never find the area. Why don't you draw a figure inside [the big one] and subtract to get the area?"

The school district requires the fifth grade to study ancient civilization (in particular, Egypt, Athens, and Sumer). In this classroom, the emphasis is on illustrating and re-creating the culture of the people of ancient times. The following are typical activities: the children made an 8mm film on Egypt, which one of the parents edited. A girl in the class wrote the script, and the class acted it out. They put the sound on themselves. They read stories of those days. They wrote essays and stories depicting the lives of the people and the societal and occupational divisions. They chose from a list of projects, all of which involved graphic representations of ideas: for example, "Make a mural depicting the division of labor in Egyptian society."

Each child wrote and exchanged a letter in hieroglyphics with a fifth 30
grader in another class, and they also exchanged stories they wrote in cuneiform. They made a scroll and singed the edges so it looked authentic. They each chose an occupation and made an Egyptian plaque representing that occupation, simulating the appropriate Egyptian design. They carved their design on a cylinder of wax, pressed the wax into clay, and then baked the clay. Although one girl did not choose an occupation but carved instead a series of gods and slaves, the teacher said, "That's all right, Amber, it's beautiful." As they were working the teacher said, "Don't cut into your clay until you're satisfied with your design."

Social studies also involves almost daily presentation by the children of some event from the news. The teacher's questions ask the children to expand what they say, to give more details, and to be more specific. Occasionally she adds some remarks to help them see connections between events.

The emphasis on expressing and illustrating ideas in social studies is accompanied in language arts by an emphasis on creative writing. Each child wrote a rebus story for a first grader whom they had interviewed to see what kind of story the child liked best. They wrote editorials on pending decisions by the school board and radio plays, some of which were read over the school intercom from the office and one of which was performed in the auditorium. There is no language arts textbook because, the teacher said, "The principal wants us to be creative." There is not much grammar, but there is punctuation. One morning when the observer arrived, the class was doing a punctuation ditto. The teacher later apologized for using the ditto. "It's just for review," she said. "I don't teach punctuation that way. We use their language." The ditto had three unambiguous rules for where to put commas in a sentence. As the teacher was going around to help the children with the ditto, she repeated several times, "Where you put commas depends on how you say the sentence; it depends on the situation and what you want to say." Several weeks later the observer saw another punctuation activity. The teacher had printed a five-paragraph story on an oak tag and then cut it into phrases. She read the whole story to the class from the book, then passed out the phrases. The group had to decide how the phrases could best be put together again. (They arranged the phrases on the floor.) The point was not to replicate the story, although that was not irrelevant, but to "decide what you think the best way is." Punctuation marks on cardboard pieces were then handed out, and the children discussed and then decided what mark was best at each place they thought one was needed. At the end of each paragraph the teacher asked, "Are you satisfied with the way the paragraphs are now? Read it to yourself and see how it sounds." Then she read the original story again, and they compared the two.

Describing her goals in science to the investigator, the teacher said, "We use ESS (Elementary Science Study). It's very good because it gives a hands-on experience — so they can make *sense* out of it. It doesn't matter whether it [what they find] is right or wrong. I bring them together and there's value in discussing their ideas."

The products of work in this class are often highly valued by the children and the teacher. In fact, this was the only school in which the investigator was not allowed to take original pieces of the children's work for her files. If the work was small enough, however, and was on paper, the investigator could duplicate it on the copying machine in the office.

The teacher's attempt to control the class involves constant negotiation. 35 She does not give direct orders unless she is angry because the children have been too noisy. Normally, she tries to get them to foresee the consequences of their actions and to decide accordingly. For example, lining them up to go see a play written by the sixth graders, she says, "I presume you're lined up by someone with whom you want to sit. I hope you're lined up by someone you won't get in trouble with." . . .

One of the few rules governing the children's movement is that no more than three children may be out of the room at once. There is a school rule that anyone can go to the library at any time to get a book. In the fifth grade I observed, they sign their name on the chalkboard and leave. There are no passes. Finally, the children have a fair amount of officially sanctioned say over what happens in the class. For example, they often negotiate what work is to be done. If the teacher wants to move on to the next subject, but the children say they are not ready, they want to work on their present projects some more, she very often lets them do it.

Executive Elite School

In the executive elite school, work is developing one's analytical intellectual powers. Children are continually asked to reason through a problem, to produce intellectual products that are both logically sound and of top academic quality. A primary goal of thought is to conceptualize rules by which elements may fit together in systems and then to apply these rules in solving a problem. Schoolwork helps one to achieve, to excel, to prepare for life.

The following are illustrative. The math teacher teaches area and perimeter by having the children derive formulas for each. First she helps them, through discussion at the board, to arrive at A = W × L as a formula (not *the* formula) for area. After discussing several, she says, "Can anyone make up a formula for perimeter? Can you figure that out yourselves? [pause] Knowing what we know, can we think of a formula?" She works out three children's suggestions at the board, saying to two, "Yes, that's a good one," and then asks the class if they can think of any more. No one volunteers. To prod them, she says, "If you use rules and good reasoning, you get many ways. Chris, can you think up a formula?"

She discusses two-digit division with the children as a decision-making process. Presenting a new type of problem to them, she asks, "What's the *first* decision you'd make if presented with this kind of example? What is the first thing you'd *think?* Craig?" Craig says, "To find my first partial quotient." She responds, "Yes, that would be your first decision. How would you do that?" Craig explains, and then the teacher says, "OK, we'll see how that works for you." The class tries his way. Subsequently, she comments on the merits and shortcomings of several other children's decisions. Later, she tells the investigator that her goals in math are to develop their reasoning and mathematical thinking and that, unfortunately, "there's no *time* for manipulables."

While right answers are important in math, they are not "given" by the book or by the teacher but may be challenged by the children. Going over some problems in late September the teacher says, "Raise your hand if you do not agree." A child says, "I don't agree with sixty-four." The teacher responds, "OK, there's a question about sixty-four. [to class] Please check it. Owen, they're disagreeing with you. Kristen, they're checking yours." The teacher emphasized this repeatedly during September and October with statements like "Don't be afraid to say you disagree. In the last [math] class, somebody disagreed, and they were right. Before you disagree, check yours, and if you still think we're wrong, then we'll check it out." By Thanksgiving, the children did not often speak in terms of right and wrong math problems but of whether they agreed with the answer that had been given. 40

There are complicated math mimeos with many word problems. Whenever they go over the examples, they discuss how each child has set up the problem. The children must explain it precisely. On one occasion the teacher said, "I'm more — just as interested in *how* you set up the problem as in what answer you find. If you set up a problem in a good way, the answer is *easy* to find."

Social studies work is most often reading and discussion of concepts and independent research. There are only occasional artistic, expressive, or illustrative projects. Ancient Athens and Sumer are, rather, societies to analyze. The following questions are typical of those that guide the children's independent research. "What mistakes did Pericles make after the war?" "What mistakes did the citizens of Athens make?" "What are the elements of a civilization?" "How did Greece build an economic empire?" "Compare the way Athens chose its leaders with the way we choose ours." Occasionally the children are asked to make up sample questions for their social studies tests. On an occasion when the investigator was present, the social studies teacher rejected a child's question by saying, "That's just fact. If I asked you that question on a test, you'd complain it was just memory! Good questions ask for concepts."

In social studies — but also in reading, science, and health — the teachers initiate classroom discussions of current social issues and problems. These discussions occurred on every one of the investigator's visits, and a teacher told me, "These children's opinions are important — it's important that they learn to reason things through." The classroom discussions always struck the observer as quite realistic and analytical, dealing with concrete social issues like the following: "Why do workers strike?" "Is that right or wrong?" "Why do we have inflation, and what can be done to stop it?" "Why do companies put chemicals in food when the natural ingredients are available?" and so on. Usually the children did not have to be prodded to give their opinions. In fact, their statements and the interchanges between them struck the observer as quite sophisticated conceptually and verbally, and well-informed. Occasionally the teachers would prod with statements such as, "Even if you don't know [the answers], if you think logically about it, you can figure it out." And "I'm asking you [these] questions to help you think this through."

Language arts emphasizes language as a complex system, one that should be mastered. The children are asked to diagram sentences of complex grammatical construction, to memorize irregular verb conjugations (he lay, he has lain, and so on . . .), and to use the proper participles, conjunctions, and interjections in their speech. The teacher (the same one who teaches social studies) told them, "It is not enough to get these right on tests; you must use what you learn [in grammar classes] in your written and oral work. I will grade you on that."

Most writing assignments are either research reports and essays for social studies or experiment analyses and write-ups for science. There is only an occasional story or other "creative writing" assignment. On the occasion observed by the investigator (the writing of a Halloween story), the points the teacher stressed in preparing the children to write involved the structural aspects of a story rather than the expression of feelings or other ideas. The teacher showed them a filmstrip, "The Seven Parts of a Story," and lectured them on plot development, mood setting, character development, consistency, and the use of a logical or appropriate ending. The stories they subsequently wrote were, in fact, well-structured, but many were also personal and expressive. The teacher's evaluative comments, however, did not refer to the expressiveness or artistry but were all directed toward whether they had "developed" the story well.

Language arts work also involved a large amount of practice in presentation of the self and in managing situations where the child was expected to

45

be in charge. For example, there was a series of assignments in which each child had to be a "student teacher." The child had to plan a lesson in grammar, outlining, punctuation, or other language arts topic and explain the concept to the class. Each child was to prepare a worksheet or game and a homework assignment as well. After each presentation, the teacher and other children gave a critical appraisal of the "student teacher's" performance. Their criteria were: whether the student spoke clearly, whether the lesson was interesting, whether the student made any mistakes, and whether he or she kept control of the class. On an occasion when a child did not maintain control, the teacher said, "When you're up there, you have authority and you have to use it. I'll back you up." . . .

The executive elite school is the only school where bells do not demarcate the periods of time. The two fifth-grade teachers were very strict about changing classes on schedule, however, as specific plans for each session had been made. The teachers attempted to keep tight control over the children during lessons, and the children were sometimes flippant, boisterous, and occasionally rude. However, the children may be brought into line by reminding them that "It is up to you," "You must control yourself," "You are responsible for your work," you must "set your own priorities." One teacher told a child, "You are the only driver of your car — and only you can regulate your speed." A new teacher complained to the observer that she had thought "these children" would have more control.

While strict attention to the lesson at hand is required, the teachers make relatively little attempt to regulate the movement of the children at other times. For example, except for the kindergartners the children in this school do not have to wait for the bell to ring in the morning; they may go to their classroom when they arrive at school. Fifth graders often came early to read, to finish work, or to catch up. After the first two months of school, the fifth-grade teachers did not line the children up to change classes or to go to gym, and so on, but, when the children were ready and quiet, they were told they could go — sometimes without the teachers.

In the classroom, the children could get materials when they needed them and took what they needed from closets and from the teacher's desk. They were in charge of the office at lunchtime. During class they did not have to sign out or ask permission to leave the room; they just got up and left. Because of the pressure to get work done, however, they did not leave the room very often. The teachers were very polite to the children, and the investigator heard no sarcasm, no nasty remarks, and few direct orders. The teachers never called the children "honey" or "dear" but always called them by name. The teachers were expected to be available before school, after school, and for part of their lunchtime to provide extra help if needed. . . .

The foregoing analysis of differences in schoolwork in contrasting 50 social-class contexts suggests the following conclusion: the "hidden curriculum" of schoolwork is tacit preparation for relating to the process of production in a particular way. Differing curricular, pedagogical, and pupil evaluation practices emphasize different cognitive and behavioral skills in each social setting and thus contribute to the development in the children of certain potential relationships to physical and symbolic capital,[11] to authority, and to the process of work. School experience, in the sample of schools discussed here, differed qualitatively by social class. These differences may not only contribute to the development in the children in each social class of certain types of economically significant relationships and not others but would thereby help to *reproduce* this system of relations in society. In the contribution to the reproduction of unequal social relations lies a theoretical meaning and social consequence of classroom practice.

The identification of different emphases in classrooms in a sample of contrasting social-class contexts implies that further research should be conducted in a large number of schools to investigate the types of work tasks and interactions in each to see if they differ in the ways discussed here and to see if similar potential relationships are uncovered. Such research could have as a product the further elucidation of complex but not readily apparent connections between everyday activity in schools and classrooms and the unequal structure of economic relationships in which we work and live.

ENGAGING THE TEXT

1. Examine the ways any single subject is taught in the four types of schools Anyon describes. What differences in teaching methods and in the student-teacher relationship do they reflect? What other differences do you note in the schools? What schools in your geographic region would closely approximate the working-class, middle-class, affluent professional, and executive elite schools of her article?

2. What attitudes toward knowledge and work are the four types of schools teaching their students? What kinds of jobs are students being prepared to do? Do you see any evidence that the schools in your community are producing particular kinds of workers?

3. What is the "hidden curriculum" of Anyon's title? How is this curriculum taught, and what social, cultural, or political purposes does it serve?

EXPLORING CONNECTIONS

4. Which of the four types of schools that Anyon describes do you think Michael Moore attended, given the experiences he offers from his own education in "Idiot Nation" (p. 153)? Why? Do you think his attitude toward the state of schooling in America would be different if he had attended a different kind of school?

---

[11]*physical and symbolic capital:* Elsewhere Anyon defines *capital* as "property that is used to produce profit, interest, or rent"; she defines *symbolic capital* as the knowledge and skills that "may yield social and cultural power."

5. Contrast Anyon's depiction of the "hidden curriculum" of American education with that proposed by John Taylor Gatto (p. 173). How common would you expect the "Seven-Lesson Schoolteacher" to be in each of the four types of schools Anyon mentions?

6. Draw a Groening-like (see pp. 172 and 181) cartoon or comic strip about a classroom situation in a working-class, middle-class, professional, or elite school (but do not identify the type of school explicitly). Pool all the cartoons from the class. In small groups, sort the comics according to the type of school they represent.

7. Analyze the teaching styles that Mike Rose encounters at Our Lady of Mercy (p. 182). Which of Anyon's categories would they fit best? Do Rose's experiences at his high school tend to confirm or complicate Anyon's analysis?

EXTENDING THE CRITICAL CONTEXT

8. Should all schools be run like professional or elite schools? What would be the advantages of making these schools models for all social classes? Do you see any possible disadvantages?

9. Choose a common elementary school task or skill that Anyon does not mention. Outline four ways it might be taught in the four types of schools.

Visual Portfolio

READING IMAGES OF EDUCATION AND EMPOWERMENT

The Spirit of Education (1934), by Norman Rockwell.

The Graduate (1959), by Norman Rockwell.

The Problem We All Live With (1964), by Norman Rockwell.

Visual Portfolio

READING IMAGES OF EDUCATION AND EMPOWERMENT

1. What is happening in *The Spirit of Education?* What is Norman Rockwell saying about the situation — and about education — through the attitudes of the boy and the seated woman?

2. What meaning can you find in the elements that make up the boy's costume? What significance is there in the book, the torch, the laurel crown, the toga and sandals? What are these symbols supposed to suggest about education? If you were to costume someone to represent education today, how would you do it?

3. In *The Graduate,* why has Rockwell chosen to place his subject in front of a newspaper? To what extent are the headlines of the paper relevant? What is Rockwell suggesting through the young man's posture and attitude?

4. Plan an updated version of the portrait on page 212, featuring a twenty-first-century graduate and a more contemporary background.

5. What is the setting of *The Problem We All Live With?* What event does it commemorate? How do you interpret the painting's title?

6. What does Rockwell suggest about the relationship of education, society, power, and violence through the visual details included in this painting? What significance do you see, for example, in the absence of the men's faces, the position of their hands and arms, the rhythm of their strides, the smallness of the girl, her attitude, the materials she carries, and so forth?

The Achievement of Desire

RICHARD RODRIGUEZ

Hunger of Memory, the autobiography of Richard Rodriguez and the source of the following selection, set off a storm of controversy in the Chicano community when it appeared in 1981. Some hailed it as an uncompromising portrayal of the difficulties of growing up between two cultures; others condemned it because it seemed to blame Mexican Americans for the difficulties they encountered assimilating into mainstream American society. Rodriguez was born in 1944 into an immigrant family outside San Francisco. Though he was unable to speak English when he entered school, his educational career can only be described as brilliant: undergraduate work at Stanford University, graduate study at Berkeley and Columbia, a Fulbright fellowship to study English literature in London, a subsequent grant from the National Endowment for the Humanities. In this selection, Rodriguez analyzes the motives that led him to abandon his study of Renaissance literature and return to live with his parents. He is currently an associate editor with the Pacific News Service in San Francisco, an essayist for the Newshour with Jim Lehrer, *and a contributing editor for* Harper's *magazine and for the Opinion section of the* Los Angeles Times. *His other books include* Mexico's Children *(1991)*, Days of Obligation: An Argument with My Mexican Father *(1993), which was nominated for the Pulitzer Prize in nonfiction, and* Brown: The Last Discovery of America *(2002).*

I stand in the ghetto classroom — "the guest speaker" — attempting to lecture on the mystery of the sounds of our words to rows of diffident students. "Don't you hear it? Listen! The music of our words. *'Sumer is i-cumen in.*[1] . . .' And songs on the car radio. We need Aretha Franklin's voice to fill plain words with music — her life." In the face of their empty stares, I try to create an enthusiasm. But the girls in the back row turn to watch some boy passing outside. There are flutters of smiles, waves. And someone's mouth elongates heavy, silent words through the barrier of glass. Silent words — the lips straining to shape each voiceless syllable: *"Meet meee late errr."* By the door, the instructor smiles at me, apparently hoping that I will be able to spark some enthusiasm in the class. But only one student seems to be listening. A girl, maybe fourteen. In this gray room her eyes shine with ambition. She keeps nodding and nodding at all that I say; she even takes notes. And each time I ask a question, she jerks up and down in her desk like a marionette, while her hand waves over the bowed heads of her classmates. It is myself (as a boy) I see as she faces me now (a man in my thirties).

The boy who first entered a classroom barely able to speak English, twenty years later concluded his studies in the stately quiet of the reading room in the British Museum. Thus with one sentence I can summarize my academic career. It will be harder to summarize what sort of life connects the boy to the man.

With every award, each graduation from one level of education to the next, people I'd meet would congratulate me. Their refrain always the same: "Your parents must be very proud." Sometimes then they'd ask me how I managed it — my "success." (How?) After a while, I had several quick answers to give in reply. I'd admit, for one thing, that I went to an excellent grammar school. (My earliest teachers, the nuns, made my success their ambition.) And my brother and both my sisters were very good students. (They often brought home the shiny school trophies I came to want.) And my mother and father always encouraged me. (At every graduation they were behind the stunning flash of the camera when I turned to look at the crowd.)

---

[1]*Sumer is i-cumen in:* Opening line of a Middle English poem ("Summer has come").

As important as these factors were, however, they account inadequately for my academic advance. Nor do they suggest what an odd success I managed. For although I was a very good student, I was also a very bad student. I was a "scholarship boy," a certain kind of scholarship boy. Always successful, I was always unconfident. Exhilarated by my progress. Sad. I became the prized student — anxious and eager to learn. Too eager, too anxious — an imitative and unoriginal pupil. My brother and two sisters enjoyed the advantages I did, and they grew to be as successful as I, but none of them ever seemed so anxious about their schooling. A second-grade student, I was the one who came home and corrected the "simple" grammatical mistakes of our parents. ("Two negatives make a positive.") Proudly I announced — to my family's startled silence — that a teacher had said I was losing all trace of a Spanish accent. I was oddly annoyed when I was unable to get parental help with a homework assignment. The night my father tried to help me with an arithmetic exercise, he kept reading the instructions, each time more deliberately, until I pried the textbook out of his hands, saying, "I'll try to figure it out some more by myself."

When I reached the third grade, I outgrew such behavior. I became   5
more tactful, careful to keep separate the two very different worlds of my day. But then, with ever-increasing intensity, I devoted myself to my studies. I became bookish, puzzling to all my family. Ambition set me apart. When my brother saw me struggling home with stacks of library books, he would laugh, shouting: "Hey, Four Eyes!" My father opened a closet one day and was startled to find me inside, reading a novel. My mother would find me reading when I was supposed to be asleep or helping around the house or playing outside. In a voice angry or worried or just curious, she'd ask: "What do you see in your books?" It became the family's joke. When I was called and wouldn't reply, someone would say I must be hiding under my bed with a book.

(How did I manage my success?)

What I am about to say to you has taken me more than twenty years to admit: *A primary reason for my success in the classroom was that I couldn't forget that schooling was changing me and separating me from the life I enjoyed before becoming a student.* That simple realization! For years I never spoke to anyone about it. Never mentioned a thing to my family or my teachers or classmates. From a very early age, I understood enough, just enough about my classroom experiences to keep what I knew repressed, hidden beneath layers of embarrassment. Not until my last months as a graduate student, nearly thirty years old, was it possible for me to think much about the reasons for my academic success. Only then. At the end of my schooling, I needed to determine how far I had moved from my past. The adult finally confronted, and now must publicly say, what the child shuddered from knowing and could never admit to himself or to those many faces that smiled at his every success. ("Your parents must be very proud. . . .")

At the end, in the British Museum (too distracted to finish my dissertation) for weeks I read, speed-read, books by modern educational theorists, only to find infrequent and slight mention of students like me. (Much more is written about the more typical case, the lower-class student who barely is helped by his schooling.) Then one day, leafing through Richard Hoggart's *The Uses of Literacy,* I found, in his description of the scholarship boy, myself. For the first time I realized that there were other students like me, and so I was able to frame the meaning of my academic success, its consequent price — the loss.

Hoggart's description is distinguished, at least initially, by deep understanding. What he grasps very well is that the scholarship boy must move between environments, his home and the classroom, which are at cultural extremes, opposed. With his family, the boy has the intense pleasure of intimacy, the family's consolation in feeling public alienation. Lavish emotions texture home life. *Then,* at school, the instruction bids him to trust lonely reason primarily. Immediate needs set the pace of his parents' lives. From his mother and father the boy learns to trust spontaneity and nonrational ways of knowing. *Then,* at school, there is mental calm. Teachers emphasize the value of a reflectiveness that opens a space between thinking and immediate action.

Years of schooling must pass before the boy will be able to sketch the   10
cultural differences in his day as abstractly as this. But he senses those differences early. Perhaps as early as the night he brings home an assignment from school and finds the house too noisy for study.

> He has to be more and more alone, if he is going to "get on." He will have, probably unconsciously, to oppose the ethos[2] of the hearth, the intense gregariousness of the working-class family group. Since everything centres upon the living-room, there is unlikely to be a room of his own; the bedrooms are cold and inhospitable, and to warm them or the front room, if there is one, would not only be expensive, but would require an imaginative leap — out of the tradition — which most families are not capable of making. There is a corner of the living-room table. On the other side Mother is ironing, the wireless is on, someone is singing a snatch of song or Father says intermittently whatever comes into his head. The boy has to cut himself off mentally, so as to do his homework, as well as he can.[3]

The next day, the lesson is as apparent at school. There are even rows of desks. Discussion is ordered. The boy must rehearse his thoughts and raise his hand before speaking out in a loud voice to an audience of classmates. And there is time enough, and silence, to think about ideas (big ideas) never considered at home by his parents.

Not for the working-class child alone is adjustment to the classroom difficult. Good schooling requires that any student alter early childhood

---

[2]*ethos:* The fundamental spirit or character of a thing.
[3]All quotations are from Richard Hoggart, *The Uses of Literacy* (London: Chatto and Windus, 1957), Chapter 10. [Author's note]

habits. But the working-class child is usually least prepared for the change. And, unlike many middle-class children, he goes home and sees in his parents a way of life not only different but starkly opposed to that of the classroom. (He enters the house and hears his parents talking in ways his teachers discourage.)

Without extraordinary determination and the great assistance of others — at home and at school — there is little chance for success. Typically most working-class children are barely changed by the classroom. The exception succeeds. The relative few become scholarship students. Of these, Richard Hoggart estimates, most manage a fairly graceful transition. Somehow they learn to live in the two very different worlds of their day. There are some others, however, those Hoggart pejoratively terms "scholarship boys," for whom success comes with special anxiety. Scholarship boy: good student, troubled son. The child is "moderately endowed," intellectually mediocre, Hoggart supposes — though it may be more pertinent to note the special qualities of temperament in the child. High-strung child. Brooding. Sensitive. Haunted by the knowledge that one *chooses* to become a student. (Education is not an inevitable or natural step in growing up.) Here is a child who cannot forget that his academic success distances him from a life he loved, even from his own memory of himself.

Initially, he wavers, balances allegiance. ("The boy is himself [until he reaches, say, the upper forms[4]] very much of *both* the worlds of home and school. He is enormously obedient to the dictates of the world of school, but emotionally still strongly wants to continue as part of the family circle.") Gradually, necessarily, the balance is lost. The boy needs to spend more and more time studying, each night enclosing himself in the silence permitted and required by intense concentration. He takes his first step toward academic success, away from his family.

From the very first days, through the years following, it will be with his parents — the figures of lost authority, the persons toward whom he feels deepest love — that the change will be most powerfully measured. A separation will unravel between them. Advancing in his studies, the boy notices that his mother and father have not changed as much as he. Rather, when he sees them, they often remind him of the person he once was and the life he earlier shared with them. He realizes what some Romantics[5] also know when they praise the working class for the capacity for human closeness, qualities of passion and spontaneity, that the rest of us experience in like measure only in the earliest part of our youth. For the Romantic, this doesn't make working-class life childish. Working-class life challenges precisely because it is an *adult* way of life.

[4]*upper forms:* Upper grades or classes in British secondary schools.

[5]*Romantics:* Adherents of the principles of romanticism — a literary and philosophical movement that emphasized the imagination, freedom, nature, the return to a simple life, and the ordinary individual.

The scholarship boy reaches a different conclusion. He cannot afford to admire his parents. (How could he and still pursue such a contrary life?) He permits himself embarrassment at their lack of education. And to evade nostalgia for the life he has lost, he concentrates on the benefits education will bestow upon him. He becomes especially ambitious. Without the support of old certainties and consolations, almost mechanically, he assumes the procedures and doctrines of the classroom. The kind of allegiance the young student might have given his mother and father only days earlier, he transfers to the teacher, the new figure of authority. "[The scholarship boy] tends to make a father-figure of his form-master,"[6] Hoggart observes.

But Hoggart's calm prose only makes me recall the urgency with which I came to idolize my grammar school teachers. I began by imitating their accents, using their diction, trusting their every direction. The very first facts they dispensed, I grasped with awe. Any book they told me to read, I read — then waited for them to tell me which books I enjoyed. Their every casual opinion I came to adopt and to trumpet when I returned home. I stayed after school "to help" — to get my teacher's undivided attention. It was the nun's encouragement that mattered most to me. (She understood exactly what — my parents never seemed to appraise so well — all my achievements entailed.) Memory gently caressed each word of praise bestowed in the classroom so that compliments teachers paid me years ago come quickly to mind even today.

The enthusiasm I felt in second-grade classes I flaunted before both my parents. The docile, obedient student came home a shrill and precocious son who insisted on correcting and teaching his parents with the remark: "My teacher told us. . . ."

I intended to hurt my mother and father. I was still angry at them for having encouraged me toward classroom English. But gradually this anger was exhausted, replaced by guilt as school grew more and more attractive to me. I grew increasingly successful, a talkative student. My hand was raised in the classroom; I yearned to answer any question. At home, life was less noisy than it had been. (I spoke to classmates and teachers more often each day than to family members.) Quiet at home, I sat with my papers for hours each night. I never forgot that schooling had irretrievably changed my family's life. That knowledge, however, did not weaken ambition. Instead, it strengthened resolve. Those times I remembered the loss of my past with regret, I quickly reminded myself of all the things my teachers could give me. (They could make me an educated man.) I tightened my grip on pencil and books. I evaded nostalgia. Tried hard to forget. But one does not forget by trying to forget. One only remembers. I remembered too well that education had changed my family's life. I would not have become a scholarship boy had I not so often remembered.

---

[6]*form-master:* A teacher in a British secondary school.

Once she was sure that her children knew English, my mother would   20
tell us, "You should keep up your Spanish." Voices playfully groaned in response. "¡*Pochos!*"[7] my mother would tease. I listened silently.

After a while, I grew more calm at home. I developed tact. A fourth-
grade student, I was no longer the show-off in front of my parents. I became a conventionally dutiful son, politely affectionate, cheerful enough,
even — for reasons beyond choosing — my father's favorite. And much
about my family life was easy then, comfortable, happy in the rhythm of our
living together: hearing my father getting ready for work; eating the breakfast my mother had made me; looking up from a novel to hear my brother
or one of my sisters playing with friends in the backyard; in winter, coming
upon the house all lighted up after dark.

But withheld from my mother and father was any mention of what
most mattered to me: the extraordinary experience of first-learning. Late
afternoon: in the midst of preparing dinner, my mother would come up
behind me while I was trying to read. Her head just over mine, her breath
warmly scented with food. "What are you reading?" Or, "Tell me about your
new courses." I would barely respond, "Just the usual things, nothing
special." (A half smile, then silence. Her head moving back in the silence.
Silence! Instead of the flood of intimate sounds that had once flowed
smoothly between us, there was this silence.) After dinner, I would rush
to a bedroom with papers and books. As often as possible, I resisted
parental pleas to "save lights" by coming to the kitchen to work. I kept
so much, so often, to myself. Sad. Enthusiastic. Troubled by the excitement of coming upon new ideas. Eager. Fascinated by the promising texture of a brand-new book. I hoarded the pleasures of learning.
Alone for hours. Enthralled. Nervous. I rarely looked away from my
books — or back on my memories. Nights when relatives visited and
the front rooms were warmed by Spanish sounds, I slipped quietly out of
the house.

It mattered that education was changing me. It never ceased to matter.
My brother and sisters would giggle at our mother's mispronounced words.
They'd correct her gently. My mother laughed girlishly one night, trying not
to pronounce *sheep* as *ship*. From a distance I listened sullenly. From that
distance, pretending not to notice on another occasion, I saw my father
looking at the title pages of my library books. That was the scene on my
mind when I walked home with a fourth-grade companion and heard him
say that his parents read to him every night. (A strange-sounding book —
Winnie the Pooh.) Immediately, I wanted to know, "What is it like?" My
companion, however, thought I wanted to know about the plot of the book.
Another day, my mother surprised me by asking for a "nice" book to read.
"Something not too hard you think I might like." Carefully I chose one,

---

[7]*Pocho:* A derogatory Spanish word for a Mexican American who has adopted the attitudes, values, and lifestyle of Anglo culture.

Willa Cather's[8] *My Àntonia*. But when, several weeks later, I happened to see it next to her bed unread except for the first few pages, I was furious and suddenly wanted to cry. I grabbed up the book and took it back to my room and placed it in its place, alphabetically on my shelf.

"Your parents must be very proud of you." People began to say that to me about the time I was in sixth grade. To answer affirmatively, I'd smile. Shyly I'd smile, never betraying my sense of the irony: I was not proud of my mother and father. I was embarrassed by their lack of education. It was not that I ever thought they were stupid, though stupidly I took for granted their enormous native intelligence. Simply, what mattered to me was that they were not like my teachers.

But, "Why didn't you tell us about the award?" my mother demanded,   25
her frown weakened by pride. At the grammar school ceremony several weeks after, her eyes were brighter than the trophy I'd won. Pushing back the hair from my forehead, she whispered that I had "shown" the *gringos*.[9] A few minutes later, I heard my father speak to my teacher and felt ashamed of his labored, accented words. Then guilty for the shame. I felt such contrary feelings. (There is no simple roadmap through the heart of the scholarship boy.) My teacher was so soft-spoken and her words were edged sharp and clean. I admired her until it seemed to me that she spoke too carefully. Sensing that she was condescending to them, I became nervous. Resentful. Protective. I tried to move my parents away. "You both must be very proud of Richard," the nun said. They responded quickly. (They were proud.) "We are proud of all our children." Then this afterthought: "They sure didn't get their brains from us." They all laughed. I smiled.

In fourth grade I embarked upon a grandiose reading program. "Give me the names of important books," I would say to startled teachers. They soon found out that I had in mind "adult books." I ignored their suggestion of anything I suspected was written for children. (Not until I was in college, as a result, did I read *Huckleberry Finn* or *Alice's Adventures in Wonderland*.) Instead, I read *The Scarlet Letter* and Franklin's *Autobiography*. And whatever I read I read for extra credit. Each time I finished a book, I reported the achievement to a teacher and basked in the praise my effort earned. Despite my best efforts, however, there seemed to be more and more books I needed to read. At the library I would literally tremble as I came upon whole shelves of books I hadn't read. So I read and I read and I read: *Great Expectations;* all the short stories of Kipling; *The Babe Ruth Story;* the entire first volume of the *Encyclopaedia Britannica* (A–ANSTEY); the *Iliad; Moby Dick; Gone with the Wind; The Good Earth; Ramona; Forever Amber; The Lives of the Saints; Crime and Punishment; The Pearl*. . . .

---

[8]*Willa Cather:* American novelist (1876–1947).
[9]*gringos:* Anglos.

Librarians who initially frowned when I checked out the maximum ten books at a time started saving books they thought I might like. Teachers would say to the rest of the class, "I only wish the rest of you took reading as seriously as Richard obviously does."

But at home I would hear my mother wondering, "What do you see in your books?" (Was reading a hobby like her knitting? Was so much reading even healthy for a boy? Was it the sign of "brains"? Or was it just a convenient excuse for not helping around the house on Saturday mornings?) Always, "What do you see . . . ?"

What *did* I see in my books? I had the idea that they were crucial for my academic success, though I couldn't have said exactly how or why. In the sixth grade I simply concluded that what gave a book its value was some major idea or theme it contained. If that core essence could be mined and memorized, I would become learned like my teachers. I decided to record in a notebook the themes of the books that I read. After reading *Robinson Crusoe,* I wrote that its theme was "the value of learning to live by oneself." When I completed *Wuthering Heights,* I noted the danger of "letting emotions get out of control." Rereading these brief moralistic appraisals usually left me disheartened. I couldn't believe that they were really the source of reading's value. But for many more years, they constituted the only means I had of describing to myself the educational value of books.

I entered high school having read hundreds of books. My habit of reading made me a confident speaker and writer of English. Reading also enabled me to sense something of the shape, the major concerns, of Western thought. (I was able to say something about Dante[10] and Descartes[11] and Engels[12] and James Baldwin[13] in my high school term papers.) In these various ways, books brought me academic success as I hoped that they would. But I was not a good reader. Merely bookish, I lacked a point of view when I read. Rather, I read in order to acquire a point of view. I vacuumed books for epigrams, scraps of information, ideas, themes — anything to fill the hollow within me and make me feel educated. When one of my teachers suggested to his drowsy tenth-grade English class that a person could not have a "complicated idea" until he had read at least two thousand books, I heard the remark without detecting either its irony or its very complicated truth. I merely determined to compile a list of all the books I had ever read. Harsh with myself, I included only once a title I might have read several times. (How, after all, could one read a book more than once?) And I included only those books over a hundred pages in length. (Could anything shorter be a book?)

---

[10]*Dante:* Dante Alighieri, Italian poet (1265–1321); author of the *Divine Comedy.*

[11]*Descartes:* René Descartes, French philosopher and mathematician (1596–1650).

[12]*Engels:* Friedrich Engels, German socialist (1820–1895); coauthor with Karl Marx of the *Communist Manifesto* in 1848.

[13]*James Baldwin:* American novelist and essayist (1924–1987).

There was yet another high school list I compiled. One day I came   30
across a newspaper article about the retirement of an English professor at a
nearby state college. The article was accompanied by a list of the "hundred
most important books of Western Civilization." "More than anything else in
my life," the professor told the reporter with finality, "these books have
made me all that I am." That was the kind of remark I couldn't ignore. I
clipped out the list and kept it for the several months it took me to read all
of the titles. Most books, of course, I barely understood. While reading
Plato's *Republic,* for instance, I needed to keep looking at the book jacket
comments to remind myself what the text was about. Nevertheless, with the
special patience and superstition of a scholarship boy, I looked at every
word of the text. And by the time I reached the last word, relieved, I convinced myself that I had read *The Republic.* In a ceremony of great pride, I
solemnly crossed Plato off my list.

    . . . The scholarship boy does not straddle, cannot reconcile, the two
great opposing cultures of his life. His success is unromantic and plain. He
sits in the classroom and offers those sitting beside him no calming reassurance about their own lives. He sits in the seminar room — a man with
brown skin, the son of working-class Mexican immigrant parents. (Addressing the professor at the head of the table, his voice catches with nervousness.) There is no trace of his parents' accent in his speech. Instead he ap-
proximates the accents of teachers and classmates. Coming from *him* those
sounds seem suddenly odd. Odd too is the effect produced when *he* uses
academic jargon — bubbles at the tip of his tongue: "*Topos* . . . negative capability . . . vegetation imagery in Shakespearean comedy."[14] He lifts an
opinion from Coleridge, takes something else from Frye or Empson or
Leavis.[15] He even repeats exactly his professor's earlier comment. All his
ideas are clearly borrowed. He seems to have no thought of his own. He
chatters while his listeners smile — their look one of disdain.

    When he is older and thus when so little of the person he was survives,
the scholarship boy makes only too apparent his profound lack of *self-*
confidence. This is the conventional assessment that even Richard Hoggart
repeats:

> [The scholarship boy] tends to over-stress the importance of examina-
> tions, of the piling-up of knowledge and of received opinions. He dis-
> covers a technique of apparent learning, of the acquiring of facts
> rather than of the handling and use of facts. He learns how to receive a
> purely literate education, one using only a small part of the personality
> and challenging only a limited area of his being. He begins to see life
> as a ladder, as a permanent examination with some praise and some
> further exhortation at each stage. He becomes an expert imbiber and

---

[14]*topos . . . negative capability . . .* : Technical terms associated with the study of literary
criticism.

[15]*Coleridge . . . Frye . . . Empson . . . Leavis:* Important literary critics.

dolerout; his competence will vary, but will rarely be accompanied by genuine enthusiasms. He rarely feels the reality of knowledge, of other men's thoughts and imaginings, on his own pulses. . . . He has something of the blinkered pony about him. . . .

But this is criticism more accurate than fair. The scholarship boy is a very bad student. He is the great mimic; a collector of thoughts, not a thinker; the very last person in class who ever feels obliged to have an opinion of his own. In large part, however, the reason he is such a bad student is because he realizes more often and more acutely than most other students — than Hoggart himself — that education requires radical self-reformation. As a very young boy, regarding his parents, as he struggles with an early homework assignment, he knows this too well. That is why he lacks self-assurance. He does not forget that the classroom is responsible for remaking him. He relies on his teacher, depends on all that he hears in the classroom and reads in his books. He becomes in every obvious way the worst student, a dummy mouthing the opinions of others. But he would not be so bad — nor would he become so successful, a *scholarship* boy — if he did not accurately perceive that the best synonym for primary "education" is "imitation."

Like me, Hoggart's imagined scholarship boy spends most of his years in the classroom afraid to long for his past. Only at the very end of his schooling does the boy-man become nostalgic. In this sudden change of heart, Richard Hoggart notes:

> He longs for the membership he lost, "he pines for some Nameless Eden where he never was." The nostalgia is the stronger and the more ambiguous because he is really "in quest of his own absconded self yet scared to find it." He both wants to go back and yet thinks he has gone beyond his class, feels himself weighted with knowledge of his own and their situation, which hereafter forbids him the simpler pleasures of his father and mother. . . .

According to Hoggart, the scholarship boy grows nostalgic because he   35
remains the uncertain scholar, bright enough to have moved from his past, yet unable to feel easy, a part of a community of academics.

This analysis, however, only partially suggests what happened to me in my last years as a graduate student. When I traveled to London to write a dissertation on English Renaissance literature, I was finally confident of membership in a "community of scholars." But the pleasure that confidence gave me faded rapidly. After only two or three months in the reading room of the British Museum, it became clear that I had joined a lonely community. Around me each day were dour faces eclipsed by large piles of books. There were the regulars, like the old couple who arrived every morning, each holding a loop of the shopping bag which contained all their notes. And there was the historian who chattered madly to herself. ("Oh dear! Oh!

Now, what's this? What? Oh, my!") There were also the faces of young men and women worn by long study. And everywhere eyes turned away the moment our glance accidentally met. Some persons I sat beside day after day, yet we passed silently at the end of the day, strangers. Still, we were united by a common respect for the written word and for scholarship. We did form a union, though one in which we remained distant from one another.

More profound and unsettling was the bond I recognized with those writers whose books I consulted. Whenever I opened a text that hadn't been used for years, I realized that my special interests and skills united me to a mere handful of academics. We formed an exclusive — eccentric! — society, separated from others who would never care or be able to share our concerns. (The pages I turned were stiff like layers of dead skin.) I began to wonder: Who, beside my dissertation director and a few faculty members, would ever read what I wrote? and: Was my dissertation much more than an act of social withdrawal? These questions went unanswered in the silence of the Museum reading room. They remained to trouble me after I'd leave the library each afternoon and feel myself shy — unsteady, speaking simple sentences at the grocer's or the butcher's on my way back to my bed-sitter.[16]

Meanwhile my file cards accumulated. A professional, I knew exactly how to search a book for pertinent information. I could quickly assess and summarize the usability of the many books I consulted. But whenever I started to write, I knew too much (and not enough) to be able to write anything but sentences that were overly cautious, timid, strained brittle under the heavy weight of footnotes and qualifications. I seemed unable to dare a passionate statement. I felt drawn by professionalism to the edge of sterility, capable of no more than pedantic, lifeless, unassailable prose.

Then nostalgia began.

After years spent unwilling to admit its attractions, I gestured nostalgi-   40
cally toward the past. I yearned for that time when I had not been so alone. I became impatient with books. I wanted experience more immediate. I feared the library's silence. I silently scorned the gray, timid faces around me. I grew to hate the growing pages of my dissertation on genre[17] and Renaissance literature. (In my mind I heard relatives laughing as they tried to make sense of its title.) I wanted something — I couldn't say exactly what. I told myself that I wanted a more passionate life. And a life less thoughtful. And above all, I wanted to be less alone. One day I heard some Spanish academics whispering back and forth to each other, and their sounds seemed ghostly voices recalling my life. Yearning became preoccupation then. Boyhood memories beckoned, flooded my mind. (Laughing intimate voices. Bounding up the front steps of the porch. A sudden embrace inside the door.)

---

[16]*bed-sitter:* A one-room apartment.

[17]*genre:* A class or category of artistic work; e.g., the genre of poetry.

For weeks after, I turned to books by educational experts. I needed to learn how far I had moved from my past — to determine how fast I would be able to recover something of it once again. But I found little. Only a chapter in a book by Richard Hoggart . . . I left the reading room and the circle of faces.

I came home. After the year in England, I spent three summer months living with my mother and father, relieved by how easy it was to be home. It no longer seemed very important to me that we had little to say. I felt easy sitting and eating and walking with them. I watched them, nevertheless, looking for evidence of those elastic, sturdy strands that bind generations in a web of inheritance. I thought as I watched my mother one night: of course a friend had been right when she told me that I gestured and laughed just like my mother. Another time I saw for myself: my father's eyes were much like my own, constantly watchful.

But after the early relief, this return, came suspicion, nagging until I realized that I had not neatly sidestepped the impact of schooling. My desire to do so was precisely the measure of how much I remained an academic. *Negatively* (for that is how this idea first occurred to me): my need to think so much and so abstractly about my parents and our relationship was in itself an indication of my long education. My father and mother did not pass their time thinking about the cultural meanings of their experience. It was I who described their daily lives with airy ideas. And yet, *positively:* the ability to consider experience so abstractly allowed me to shape into desire what would otherwise have remained indefinite, meaningless longing in the British Museum. If, because of my schooling, I had grown culturally separated from my parents, my education finally had given me ways of speaking and caring about that fact.

My best teachers in college and graduate school, years before, had tried to prepare me for this conclusion, I think, when they discussed texts of aristocratic pastoral literature. Faithfully, I wrote down all that they said. I memorized it: "The praise of the unlettered by the highly educated is one of the primary themes of 'elitist' literature." But, "the importance of the praise given the unsolitary, richly passionate and spontaneous life is that it simultaneously reflects the value of a reflective life." I heard it all. But there was no way for any of it to mean very much to me. I was a scholarship boy at the time, busily laddering my way up the rungs of education. To pass an examination, I copied down exactly what my teachers told me. It would require many more years of schooling (an inevitable miseducation) in which I came to trust the silence of reading and the habit of abstracting from immediate experience — moving away from a life of closeness and immediacy I remembered with my parents, growing older — before I turned unafraid to desire the past, and thereby achieved what had eluded me for so long — the end of education.

ENGAGING THE TEXT

1. How does education affect Rodriguez's relationship to his family, his past, and his culture? Do you agree with him that education requires "radical self-reformation" (para. 33)?
2. What is a "scholarship boy"? Why does Rodriguez consider himself a bad student despite his academic success?
3. What happens to Rodriguez in London? Why does he ultimately abandon his studies there?
4. What drives Rodriguez to succeed? What does education represent to him? To his father and mother?
5. What is Rodriguez's final assessment of what he has gained and lost through his education? Do you agree with his analysis?

EXPLORING CONNECTIONS

6. Compare Rodriguez's attitude toward education and success with that of Mike Rose (p. 182) in "'I Just Wanna Be Average.'"
7. To what extent do Rodriguez's experiences as a "scholarship boy" confirm or complicate Jean Anyon's analysis (p. 194) of the relationship between social class, education, and success?
8. Read "Stephen Cruz" (p. 348) and compare his attitudes toward education and success with those of Rodriguez.

EXTENDING THE CRITICAL CONTEXT

9. What are your personal motives for academic success? How do they compare with those of Rodriguez?
10. Today many college students find that they're following in the footsteps of family members — not breaking ground as Rodriguez did. What special difficulties do such second- or third-generation college students face?

Para Teresa[1]
INÉS HERNÁNDEZ-ÁVILA

This poem explores and attempts to resolve an old conflict between its speaker and her schoolmate, two Chicanas at "Alamo which-had-to-be-its-name" Elementary School who have radically different ideas about what education means and does. Inés Hernández-Ávila (b. 1947) is an associate

[1]*Para Teresa:* For Teresa. [All notes are the author's.]

professor of Native American studies at the University of California, Davis.
This poem appeared in her collection Con Razón, Corazón *(1987).*

A tí-Teresa
Te dedico las palabras estás
que explotan de mi corazón[2]

That day during lunch hour
at Alamo which-had-to-be-its-name   5
Elementary
my dear raza
That day in the bathroom
Door guarded
Myself cornered   10
I was accused by you, Teresa
Tú y las demás de tus amigas
Pachucas todas
Eran Uds. cinco.[3]

                                                                     15
Me gritaban que porque me creía tan grande[4]
What was I trying to do, you growled
Show you up?
Make the teachers like me, pet me,
Tell me what a credit to my people I was?
I was playing right into their hands, you challenged   20
And you would have none of it.
I was to stop.

I was to be like you
I was to play your game of deadly defiance
Arrogance, refusal to submit.   25
The game in which the winner takes nothing
Asks for nothing
Never lets his weaknesses show.

But I didn't understand.
My fear salted with confusion   30
Charged me to explain to you
I did nothing *for the teachers.*
I studied for my parents and for my grandparents
Who cut out honor roll lists

[2] *A . . . corazón:* To you, Teresa, I dedicate these words that explode from my heart.
[3] *Tú . . . cinco:* You and the rest of your friends, all Pachucas, there were five of you.
[4] *Me . . . grande:* You were screaming at me, asking me why I thought I was so hot.

Whenever their nietos'[5] names appeared   35
For my shy mother who mastered her terror
to demand her place in mother's clubs
For my carpenter-father who helped me patiently with my math.
For my abuelos que me regalaron lápices en la Navidad[6]
And for myself.   40

Porque reconocí en aquel entonces
una verdad tremenda
que me hizo a mi un rebelde
Aunque tú no te habías dadocuenta[7]
We were not inferior   45
You and I, y las demás de tus amigas
Y los demás de nuestra gente[8]
I knew it the way I knew I was alive
We were good, honorable, brave
Genuine, loyal, strong   50
And smart.
Mine was a deadly game of defiance, also.
My contest was to prove
beyond any doubt
that we were not only equal but superior to them.   55
That was why I studied.
If I could do it, we all could.

You let me go then.
Your friends unblocked the way
I who-did-not-know-how-to-fight   60
was not made to engage with you-who-grew-up-fighting
Tu y yo,[9] Teresa
We went in different directions
Pero fuimos juntas.[10]

                                                              65
In sixth grade we did not understand
Uds. with the teased, dyed-black-but-reddening hair,
Full petticoats, red lipsticks
and sweaters with the sleeves
pushed up

[5] *nietos':* Grandchildren's.

[6] *abuelos... Navidad:* Grandparents who gave me gifts of pencils at Christmas.

[7] *Porque... dadocuenta:* Because I recognized a great truth then that made me a rebel, even though you didn't realize it.

[8] *Y... gente:* And the rest of your friends / And the rest of our people.

[9] *Tu y yo:* You and I.

[10] *Pero fuimos juntas:* But we were together.

Y yo conformándome con lo que deseaba mi mamá[11]   70
Certainly never allowed to dye, to tease, to paint myself
I did not accept your way of anger,
Your judgements
You did not accept mine.

But now in 1975, when I am twenty-eight   75
Teresa
I remember you.
Y sabes —
Te comprendo,
Es más, te respeto.   80
Y si me permites,
Te nombro — "hermana."[12]

ENGAGING THE TEXT

1. The speaker says that she didn't understand Teresa at the time of the incident she describes. What didn't she understand, and why? How have her views of Teresa and of herself changed since then? What seems to have brought about this change?

2. What attitudes toward school and the majority culture do Teresa and the speaker represent? What about the speaker's family? In what way are both girls playing a game of "deadly defiance"? What arguments can you make for each form of rebellion?

3. Why do you think Hernández-Ávila wrote this poem in both Spanish and English? What does doing so say about the speaker's life? About her change of attitude toward Teresa?

EXPLORING CONNECTIONS

4. Compare the speaker's attitude toward school and family with those of Richard Rodriguez (p. 214). What motivates each of them? What tensions do they feel?

5. Write a dialogue between the speaker of this poem, who wants to excel, and Ken Harvey, the boy whom Mike Rose said just wanted to be average (p. 182). Explore the uncertainties, pressures, and desires that these students felt. In what ways are these two apparently contrasting students actually similar?

EXTENDING THE CRITICAL CONTEXT

6. Was there a person or group you disliked, feared, or fought with in elementary school? Has your understanding of your adversary or of your own motives changed since then? If so, what brought about this change?

[11] Y...mamá: And I conforming to my mother's wishes.
[12] Y sabes..."hermana": And do you know what, I understand you. Even more, I respect you. And, if you permit me, I name you my sister.

Thin Ice: "Stereotype Threat" and Black College Students

CLAUDE M. STEELE

In 1994 Richard Herrnstein and Charles Murray rocked the world of higher education by publishing The Bell Curve: Intelligence and Class Structure in American Life. *In this highly controversial book, the authors argued that differences in performance on standardized tests are due primarily to genetics and not to differences of opportunity or cultural background. Minority groups, the authors claimed, score lower on aptitude tests and have lower GPAs in college than their white counterparts because of inherited intelligence and not because of historical factors like racism or unequal access to educational resources. This selection by noted African American psychologist Claude M. Steele (b. 1946) suggests that even the best minority students may encounter academic difficulties in American colleges, not because of genetics but because of persistent negative stereotypes — stereotypes that books like* The Bell Curve *perpetuate. According to Steele, differences in minority student performance can be eliminated if colleges take positive steps to minimize these subtle forms of discrimination. Steele is a professor and chair of the Department of Psychology at Stanford University. This selection first appeared in* Atlantic Monthly *in 1999.*

The buildings had hardly changed in the thirty years since I'd been there. "There" was a small liberal-arts school quite near the college that I attended. In my student days I had visited it many times to see friends. This time I was there to give a speech about how racial and gender stereotypes, floating and abstract though they might seem, can affect concrete things like grades, test scores, and academic identity. My talk was received warmly, and the next morning I met with a small group of African-American students. I have done this on many campuses. But this time, perhaps cued by the familiarity of the place, I had an experience of déjà vu. The students expressed a litany of complaints that could have come straight from the mouths of the black friends I had visited there thirty years earlier: the curriculum was too white, they heard too little black music, they were ignored in class, and too often they felt slighted by faculty members and other students. Despite the school's recruitment efforts, they were a small minority. The core of their social life was their own group. To relieve the dysphoria, they went home a lot on weekends.

I found myself giving them the same advice my father gave me when I was in college: lighten up on the politics, get the best education you can, and move on. But then I surprised myself by saying, "To do this you have to learn from people who part of yourself tells you are difficult to trust."

Over the past four decades African-American college students have been more in the spotlight than any other American students. This is because they aren't just college students; they are a cutting edge in America's effort to integrate itself in the thirty-five years since the passage of the Civil Rights Act. These students have borne much of the burden for our national experiment in racial integration. And to a significant degree the success of the experiment will be determined by their success.

Nonetheless, throughout the 1990s the national college-dropout rate for African-Americans has been 20 to 25 percent higher than that for whites. Among those who finish college, the grade-point average of black students is two-thirds of a grade below that of whites.

A recent study by William Bowen and Derek Bok, reported in their 5
book *The Shape of the River,* brings some happy news: despite this underachievement in college, black students who attend the most selective schools in the country go on to do just as well in postgraduate programs and professional attainment as other students from those schools. This is a telling fact in support of affirmative action, since only these schools use affirmative action in admissions. Still, the underperformance of black undergraduates is an unsettling problem, one that may alter or hamper career development, especially among blacks not attending the most selective schools.

Attempts to explain the problem can sound like a debate about whether America is a good society, at least by the standard of racial fairness, and maybe even about whether racial integration is possible. It is an uncomfortably finger-pointing debate. Does the problem stem from something about black students themselves, such as poor motivation, a distracting peer culture, lack of family values, or — the unsettling suggestion of *The Bell Curve* — genes? Or does it stem from the conditions of blacks' lives: social and economic deprivation, a society that views blacks through the lens of diminishing stereotypes and low expectations, too much coddling, or too much neglect?

In recent years this debate has acquired a finer focus: the fate of middle-class black students. Americans have come to view the disadvantages associated with being black as disadvantages primarily of social and economic resources and opportunity. This assumption is often taken to imply that if you are black and come from a socioeconomically middle-class home, you no longer suffer a significant disadvantage of race. "Why should the son of a black physician be given an advantage in college admission over the son of a white delivery-truck driver?" This is a standard question in the controversy over affirmative action. And the assumption behind it is that surely in today's society the disadvantages of race are overcome when lower socioeconomic status is overcome.

But virtually all aspects of underperformance — lower standardized-test scores, lower college grades, lower graduation rates — persist among students from the African-American middle class. This situation forces on us an uncomfortable recognition: that beyond class, something racial is depressing the academic performance of these students.

Some time ago I and two colleagues, Joshua Aronson and Steven Spencer, tried to see the world from the standpoint of these students, concerning ourselves less with features of theirs that might explain their troubles than with features of the world they see. A story I was told recently depicts some of these. The storyteller was worried about his friend, a normally energetic black student who had broken up with his longtime girlfriend and had since learned that she, a Hispanic, was now dating a white student. This hit him hard. Not long after hearing about his girlfriend, he sat through an hour's discussion of *The Bell Curve*[1] in his psychology class, during which the possible genetic inferiority of his race was openly considered. Then he overheard students at lunch arguing that affirmative action allowed in too many underqualified blacks. By his own account, this young man had experienced very little of what he thought of as racial discrimination on campus. Still, these were features of his world. Could they have a bearing on his academic life?

My colleagues and I have called such features "stereotype threat"— the [10] threat of being viewed through the lens of a negative stereotype, or the fear of doing something that would inadvertently confirm that stereotype. Everyone experiences stereotype threat. We are all members of some group about which negative stereotypes exist, from white males and Methodists to women and the elderly. And in a situation where one of those stereotypes applies — a man talking to women about pay equity, for example, or an aging faculty member trying to remember a number sequence in the middle of a lecture — we know that we may be judged by it.

Like the young man in the story, we can feel mistrustful and apprehensive in such situations. For him, as for African-American students generally, negative stereotypes apply in many situations, even personal ones. Why was that old roommate unfriendly to him? Did that young white woman who has been so nice to him in class not return his phone call because she's afraid he'll ask her for a date? Is it because of his race or something else about him? He cannot know the answers, but neither can his rational self fully dismiss the questions. Together they raise a deeper question: Will his race be a boundary to his experience, to his emotions, to his relationships?

With time he may weary of the extra vigilance these situations require and of what the psychologists Jennifer Crocker and Brenda Major have called the "attributional ambiguity" of being on the receiving end of negative stereotypes. To reduce this stress he may learn to care less about the situations and activities that bring it about — to realign his self-regard so that it no longer depends on how he does in the situation. We have called this psychic adjustment "disidentification." Pain is lessened by ceasing to identify with the part of life in which the pain occurs. This withdrawal of

---

[1]*The Bell Curve:* See headnote (p. 231).

psychic investment may be supported by other members of the stereotype-threatened group — even to the point of its becoming a group norm. But not caring can mean not being motivated. And this can have real costs. When stereotype threat affects school life, disidentification is a high price to pay for psychic comfort. Still, it is a price that groups contending with powerful negative stereotypes about their abilities — women in advanced math, African-Americans in all academic areas — may too often pay.

Stereotype Threat Versus Self-Fulfilling Prophecy

Another question arises: Do the effects of stereotype threat come entirely from the fear of being stereotyped, or do they come from something internal to black students — self-doubt, for example?

Beginning with George Herbert Mead's[2] idea of the "looking-glass self," social psychology has assumed that one's self-image derives in large part from how one is viewed by others — family, school, and the broader society. When those views are negative, people may internalize them, resulting in lower self-esteem — or self-hatred, as it has been called. This theory was first applied to the experience of Jews, by Sigmund Freud and Bruno Bettelheim, but it was also soon applied to the experience of African-Americans, by Gordon Allport, Frantz Fanon, Kenneth Clark, and others.[3] According to the theory, black students internalize negative stereotypes as performance anxiety and low expectations for achievement, which they then fulfill. The "self-fulfilling prophecy" has become a commonplace about these students. Stereotype threat, however, is something different, something external: the situational threat of being negatively stereotyped. Which of these two processes, then, caused the results of our experiments?

Joshua Aronson, Michael Lustina, Kelli Keough, Joseph Brown, Catherine Good, and I devised a way to find out. Suppose we told white male students who were strong in math that a difficult math test they were about to take was one on which Asians generally did better than whites. White males should not have a sense of group inferiority about math, since no societal stereotype alleges such an inferiority. Yet this comment would put them under a form of stereotype threat: any faltering on the test could cause them to be seen negatively from the standpoint of the positive stereotype about Asians and math ability. If stereotype threat alone — in the absence of any internalized self-doubt — was capable of disrupting test performance, then white males taking the test after this comment should perform less well than white males taking the test without hearing the comment. That is just what happened. Stereotype threat impaired intellectual functioning in a group unlikely to have any sense of group inferiority.

15

---

[2]*George Herbert Mead:* Noted early-twentieth-century American philosopher (1863–1931).

[3]*Sigmund Freud . . . Kenneth Clark:* Famous psychologists and social critics.

In science, as in the rest of life, few things are definitive. But these results are pretty good evidence that stereotype threat's impairment of standardized-test performance does not depend on cueing a pre-existing anxiety. Steven Spencer, Diane Quinn, and I have shown how stereotype threat depresses the performance of accomplished female math students on a difficult math test, and how that performance improves dramatically when the threat is lifted. Jean-Claude Croizet, working in France with a stereotype that links poor verbal skills with lower-class status, found analogous results: lower-class college students performed less well than upper-class college students under the threat of a stereotype-based judgment, but performed as well when the threat was removed.

Is everyone equally threatened and disrupted by a stereotype? One might expect, for example, that it would affect the weakest students most. But in all our research the most achievement-oriented students, who were also the most skilled, motivated, and confident, were the most impaired by stereotype threat. This fact had been under our noses all along — in our data and even in our theory. A person has to care about a domain in order to be disturbed by the prospect of being stereotyped in it. That is the whole idea of disidentification — protecting against stereotype threat by ceasing to care about the domain in which the stereotype applies. Our earlier experiments had selected black students who identified with verbal skills and women who identified with math. But when we tested participants who identified less with these domains, what had been under our noses hit us in the face. None of them showed any effect of stereotype threat whatsoever.

These weakly identified students did not perform well on the test: once they discovered its difficulty, they stopped trying very hard and got a low score. But their performance did not differ depending on whether they felt they were at risk of being judged stereotypically.

Why Strong Students Are Stereotype-Threatened

This finding, I believe, tells us two important things. The first is that the poorer college performance of black students may have another source in addition to the one — lack of good preparation and, perhaps, of identification with school achievement — that is commonly understood. This additional source — the threat of being negatively stereotyped in the environment — has not been well understood. The distinction has important policy implications: different kinds of students may require different pedagogies of improvement.

The second thing is poignant: what exposes students to the pressure of stereotype threat is not weaker academic identity and skills but stronger academic identity and skills. They may have long seen themselves as good students — better than most. But led into the domain by their strengths, they pay an extra tax on their investment — vigilant worry that their future will be compromised by society's perception and treatment of their group.   20

This tax has a long tradition in the black community. The Jackie Robinson story[4] is a central narrative of black life, literature, and journalism. *Ebony* magazine has run a page for fifty years featuring people who have broken down one or another racial barrier. Surely the academic vanguard among black college students today knows this tradition — and knows, therefore, that the thing to do, as my father told me, is to buckle down, pay whatever tax is required, and disprove the damn stereotype.

That, however, seems to be precisely what these students are trying to do. In some of our experiments we administered the test of ability by computer, so that we could see how long participants spent looking at different parts of the test questions. Black students taking the test under stereotype threat seemed to be trying too hard rather than not hard enough. They reread the questions, reread the multiple choices, rechecked their answers, more than when they were not under stereotype threat. The threat made them inefficient on a test that, like most standardized tests, is set up so that thinking long often means thinking wrong, especially on difficult items like the ones we used.

Philip Uri Treisman, an innovator in math workshops for minority students who is based at the University of Texas, saw something similar in his black calculus students at the University of California at Berkeley: they worked long hours alone but they worked inefficiently — for example, checking and rechecking their calculations against the correct answers at the back of the book, rather than focusing on the concepts involved. Of course, trying extra hard helps with some school tasks. But under stereotype threat this effort may be misdirected. Achievement at the frontier of one's skills may be furthered more by a relaxed, open concentration than by a strong desire to disprove a stereotype by not making mistakes.

Sadly, the effort that accompanies stereotype threat exacts an additional price. Led by James Blascovich, of the University of California at Santa Barbara, we found that the blood pressure of black students performing a difficult cognitive task under stereotype threat was elevated compared with that of black students not under stereotype threat or white students in either situation.

In the old song about the "steel-drivin' man," John Henry races the new   25
steam-driven drill to see who can dig a hole faster. When the race is over, John Henry has prevailed by digging the deeper hole — only to drop dead. The social psychologist Sherman James uses the term "John Henryism" to describe a psychological syndrome that he found to be associated with hypertension in several samples of North Carolina blacks: holding too rigidly to the faith that discrimination and disadvantage can be overcome with hard work and persistence. Certainly this is the right attitude. But taken to extremes, it can backfire. A deterioration of performance under stereotype

---

[4]*The Jackie Robinson story:* In 1947, Jackie Robinson (1919–1972) was the first African American baseball player to join a white major-league team.

threat by the skilled, confident black students in our experiments may be rooted in John Henryism.

This last point can be disheartening. Our research, however, offers an interesting suggestion about what can be done to overcome stereotype threat and its detrimental effects. The success of black students may depend less on expectations and motivation — things that are thought to drive academic performance — than on trust that stereotypes about their group will not have a limiting effect in their school world.

How to Reduce Stereotype Threat

Putting this idea to the test, Joseph Brown and I asked, How can the usual detrimental effect of stereotype threat on the standardized-test performance of these students be reduced? By strengthening students' expectations and confidence, or by strengthening their trust that they are not at risk of being judged on the basis of stereotypes? In the ensuing experiment we strengthened or weakened participants' confidence in their verbal skills, by arranging for them to have either an impressive success or an impressive failure on a test of verbal skills, just before they took the same difficult verbal test we had used in our earlier research. When the second test was presented as a test of ability, the boosting or weakening of confidence in their verbal skills had no effect on performance: black participants performed less well than equally skilled white participants. What does this say about the commonsense idea that black students' academic problems are rooted in lack of self-confidence?

What did raise the level of black students' performance to that of equally qualified whites was reducing stereotype threat — in this case by explicitly presenting the test as racially fair. When this was done, blacks performed at the same high level as whites even if their self-confidence had been weakened by a prior failure.

These results suggest something that I think has not been made clear elsewhere: when strong black students sit down to take a difficult standardized test, the extra apprehension they feel in comparison with whites is less about their own ability than it is about having to perform on a test and in a situation that may be primed to treat them stereotypically. We discovered the extent of this apprehension when we tried to develop procedures that would make our black participants see the test as "race-fair." It wasn't easy. African-Americans have endured so much bad press about test scores for so long that, in our experience, they are instinctively wary about the tests' fairness. We were able to convince them that our test was race-fair only when we implied that the research generating the test had been done by blacks. When they felt trust, they performed well regardless of whether we had weakened their self-confidence beforehand. And when they didn't feel trust, no amount of bolstering of self-confidence helped.

Policies for helping black students rest in significant part on assump-   30
tions about their psychology. As noted, they are typically assumed to lack
confidence, which spawns a policy of confidence-building. This may be useful for students at the academic rearguard of the group. But the psychology
of the academic vanguard appears different — underperformance appears
to be rooted less in self-doubt than in social mistrust.

Education policy relevant to non-Asian minorities might fruitfully shift
its focus forward fostering racial trust in the schooling situation — at least
among students who come to school with good skills and high expectations.
But how should this be done? Without particulars this conclusion can fade
into banality, suggesting, as Alan Ryan has wryly put it in *Liberal Anxieties
and Liberal Education,* that these students "will hardly be able to work at all
unless everyone else exercises the utmost sensitivity to [their] anxieties."
Sensitivity is nice, but it is an awful lot to expect, and even then, would it instill trust?

That is exactly what Geoffrey Cohen, Lee Rosa, and I wondered as we
took up the question of how a teacher or a mentor could give critical feedback across the "racial divide" and have that feedback be trusted. We reasoned that an answer to this question might yield insights about how to instill trust more broadly in the schooling environment. Cohen's hunch was
that niceness alone wouldn't be enough. But the first question had to be
whether there was in fact a racial divide between teachers and students, especially in the elite college environment in which we worked.

We set up a simple experiment. Cohen asked black and white Stanford
students one at a time to write essays about their favorite teachers, for possible publication in a journal on teaching. They were asked to return several
days later for feedback on their essays. Before each student left the first
writing session, Cohen put a Polaroid snapshot of the student on top of his
or her essay. His ostensible purpose was to publish the picture if the essay
was published. His real purpose was to let the essay writers know that the
evaluator of their writing would be aware of their race. When they returned
days later, they were given constructive but critical feedback. We looked at
whether different ways of giving this feedback engendered different degrees of trust in it.

We found that neither straight feedback nor feedback preceded by the
"niceness" of a cushioning statement ("There were many good things about
your essay") was trusted by black students. They saw these criticisms as
probably biased, and they were less motivated than white students to improve their essays. White students took the criticism at face value — even as
an indication of interest in them. Black students, however, faced a different
meaning: the "ambiguating" possibility that the criticism was motivated by
negative stereotypes about their group as much as by the work itself. Herein
lies the power of race to make one's world insecure — quite apart from
whatever actual discrimination one may experience.

But this experiment also revealed a way to be critical across the racial   35
divide: tell the students that you are using high standards (this signals that
the criticism reflects standards rather than race), and that your reading of
their essays leads you to believe that they can meet those standards (this signals that you do not view them stereotypically). This shouldn't be faked.
High standards, at least in a relative sense, should be an inherent part of
teaching, and critical feedback should be given in the belief that the recipient can reach those standards. These things go without saying for many students. But they have to be made explicit for students under stereotype
threat. The good news of this study is that when they *are* made explicit, the
students trust and respond to criticism. Black students who got this kind of
feedback saw it as unbiased and were motivated to take their essays home
and work on them even though this was not a class for credit. They were
more motivated than any other group of students in the study — as if this
combination of high standards and assurance was like water on parched
land, a much needed but seldom received balm.

Reassessing the Test-Score Gap

There is, of course, another explanation for why black college students
haven't fared well on predominantly white campuses: they aren't prepared
for the competition. This has become an assumption of those who oppose
affirmative action in college admissions. Racial preference, the argument
goes, brings black students onto campuses where they simply aren't prepared to compete.

The fact most often cited in support of the underpreparation explanation is the lower SAT scores of black students, which sometimes average
200 points below those of other students on the same campus. The test-
score gap has become shorthand for black students' achievement problems.
But the gap must be assessed cautiously.

First, black students have better skills than the gap suggests. Most of
the gap exists because the proportion of blacks with very high SAT scores is
smaller than the corresponding proportions of whites and Asians. Thus
when each group's scores are averaged, the black average will be lower than
the white and Asian averages. This would be true even if the same admissions cut-off score were used for each group — even if, for example, affirmative action were eliminated entirely. Why a smaller proportion of blacks
have very high scores is, of course, a complex question with multiple answers, involving, among other things, the effects of race on educational access and experience as well as the processes dwelt on in this article. The
point, though, is that blacks' test-score deficits are taken as a sign of underpreparation, whereas in fact virtually all black students on a given campus
have tested skills within the same range as the tested skills of other students
on the campus.

In any case, the skills and preparation measured by these tests also turn out not to be good determinants of college success. As the makers of the SAT themselves tell us, although this test is among the best of its kind, it measures only about 18 percent of the skills that influence first-year grades, and even less of what influences subsequent grades, graduation rates, and professional success.

Indulge a basketball analogy that my colleagues Jay Rosner and Lee Ross 40 and I have developed. Suppose that you were obliged to select a basketball team on the basis of how many of ten free throws a player makes. You'd regret having to select players on the basis of a single criterion. You'd know that free-throw shooting involves only a few of the skills that go into basketball — and, worse, you'd know that you'd never pick a Shaquille O'Neal.[5]

You'd also wonder how to interpret a player's score. If he made ten out of ten or zero out of ten, you'd be fairly confident about making a judgment. But what about the kid who makes five, six, or seven? Middling scores like these could be influenced by many things other than underlying potential for free-throw shooting or basketball playing. How much practice was involved? Was the kid having a good or a bad day? Roughly the same is true, I suggest, for standardized-test scores. Are they inflated by middle-class advantages such as prep courses, private schools, and tours of European cathedrals? Are they deflated by race-linked experiences such as social segregation and being consistently assigned to the lower tracks in school?

In sum, black college students are not as underprepared in academic skills as their group score deficit is taken to suggest. The deficit can appear large, but it is not likely to be the sole cause of the troubles they have once they get on campus.

Showing the insufficiency of one cause, of course, does not prove the sufficiency of another. My colleagues and I believed that our laboratory experiments had brought to light an overlooked cause of poor college performance among non-Asian minorities: the threat to social trust brought about by the stereotypes of the larger society. But to know the real-life importance of this threat would require testing *in situ*, in the buzz of everyday life.

To this end Steven Spencer, Richard Nisbett, Kent Harber, Mary Hummel, and I undertook a program aimed at incoming first-year students at the University of Michigan. Like virtually all other institutions of higher learning, Michigan had evidence of black students' underachievement. Our mission was clear: to see if we could improve their achievement by focusing on their transition into college life.

We also wanted to see how little we could get away with — that is, to 45 develop a program that would succeed broadly without special efforts. The

[5]*Shaquille O'Neal:* Outstanding center (b. 1972) on the Los Angeles Lakers basketball team.

program (which started in 1991 and is ongoing) created a racially integrated "living and learning" community in a 250-student wing of a large dormitory. It focused students on academic work (through weekly "challenge" workshops), provided an outlet for discussing the personal side of college life (through weekly rap sessions), and affirmed the students' abilities (through, for example, reminding them that their admission was a vote of confidence). The program lasted just one semester, although most students remained in the dormitory wing for the rest of their first year.

Still, it worked: it gave black students a significant academic jump start. Those in the program (about 15 percent of the entering class) got better first-year grades than black students outside the program, even after controlling for differences between these groups in the skills with which they entered college. Equally important, the program greatly reduced underperformance: black students in the program got first-year grades almost as high as those of white students in the general Michigan population who entered with comparable test scores. This result signaled the achievement of an academic climate nearly as favorable to black students as to white students. And it was achieved through a concert of simple things that enabled black students to feel racially secure.

One tactic that worked surprisingly well was the weekly rap sessions — black and white students talking to one another in an informal dormitory setting, over pizza, about the personal side of their new lives in college. Participation in these sessions reduced students' feelings of stereotype threat and improved grades. Why? Perhaps when members of one racial group hear members of another racial group express the same concerns they have, the concerns seem less racial. Students may also learn that racial and gender stereotypes are either less at play than they might have feared or don't reflect the worst-feared prejudicial intent. Talking at a personal level across group lines can thus build trust in the larger campus community. The racial segregation besetting most college campuses can block this experience, allowing mistrust to build where cross-group communication would discourage it.

Our research bears a practical message: even though the stereotypes held by the larger society may be difficult to change, it is possible to create niches in which negative stereotypes are not felt to apply. In specific classrooms, within specific programs, even in the climate of entire schools, it is possible to weaken a group's sense of being threatened by negative stereotypes, to allow its members a trust that would otherwise be difficult to sustain. Thus when schools try to decide how important black-white test-score gaps are in determining the fate of black students on their campuses, they should keep something in mind: for the greatest portion of black students — those with strong academic identities — the degree of racial trust they feel in their campus life, rather than a few ticks on a standardized test, may be the key to their success.

ENGAGING THE TEXT

1. According to Steele, how does stereotype threat affect minority students in terms of their performance on standardized tests and their attitudes toward education? Why does Steele reject arguments that black students perform less successfully than other groups because of poor preparation?

2. What difference does Steele see between the impact of stereotype threat and the effect of "self-fulfilling prophecies" of minority-student failure? Why is this distinction important to his argument?

3. What is "John Henryism" and how is it involved with the phenomenon of stereotype threat? To what extent do you think these problems affect members of other groups, such as Asian Americans, Latinos, women, and gays?

4. In Steele's view, what can instructors do to minimize stereotype threat in testing situations or when critiquing student work? What can colleges do to discourage it throughout the campus community? How effective do you think these approaches would be in practice? Why?

EXPLORING CONNECTIONS

5. To what extent might the concept of stereotype threat be used to account for the difficulties encountered by Mike Rose in "'I Just Wanna Be Average'" (p. 182) and Richard Rodriguez in "The Achievement of Desire" (p. 214)?

6. How might Malcolm X (p. 243) respond to Steele's claim that black students need to be able to trust their teachers in order to cope with stereotype threat?

7. Read the experiences of Trung Dung (p. 310), Stephen Cruz (p. 348), and Cora Tucker (p. 353). What do these differing perspectives on success suggest about the impact of John Henryism?

EXTENDING THE CRITICAL CONTEXT

8. Working in groups, draft a list of actions students, teachers, and administrators might engage in to build trust across racial boundaries and minimize stereotype threat on your college campus.

9. Steele describes two styles of instructor comments in response to student papers: one that attempts to cushion criticism with a few gentle introductory remarks of praise, and a second that offers more direct criticism in the name of high standards. In small groups, discuss the kinds of responses you've received from instructors on past writing assignments. Is there any one style you've found to be particularly helpful? Do male and female students or students from different ethnic or economic backgrounds tend to prefer one style of response over another?

10. Form your class into small "application review committees" to determine standards for granting admission to your college. What criteria would you

use, in addition to or in place of standardized test scores, in making admission decisions? Why?

11. Some critics of *Rereading America* might argue that essays like Steele's actually increase the likelihood of stereotype threat by focusing on the academic performance of different student groups. To what extent do you agree that discussing issues like stereotypes and stereotype threat may place additional pressures on minority students in their college classes? Would it be better to avoid such topics? Why or why not?

Learning to Read
MALCOLM X

Born Malcolm Little on May 19, 1925, Malcolm X was one of the most articulate and powerful leaders of black America during the 1960s. A street hustler convicted of robbery in 1946, he spent seven years in prison, where he educated himself and became a disciple of Elijah Muhammad, founder of the Nation of Islam. In the days of the civil rights movement, Malcolm X emerged as the leading spokesman for black separatism, a philosophy that urged black Americans to cut political, social, and economic ties with the white community. After a pilgrimage to Mecca, the capital of the Muslim world, in 1964, he became an orthodox Muslim, adopted the Muslim name El Hajj Malik El-Shabazz, and distanced himself from the teachings of the black Muslims. He was assassinated in 1965. In the following excerpt from his autobiography (1965), coauthored with Alex Haley and published the year of his death, Malcolm X describes his self-education.

It was because of my letters that I happened to stumble upon starting to acquire some kind of a homemade education.

I became increasingly frustrated at not being able to express what I wanted to convey in letters that I wrote, especially those to Mr. Elijah Muhammad.[1] In the street, I had been the most articulate hustler out there — I had commanded attention when I said something. But now, trying to write simple English, I not only wasn't articulate, I wasn't even functional. How would I sound writing in slang, the way I would *say* it, something such as, "Look, daddy, let me pull your coat about a cat, Elijah Muhammad — "

---

[1] *Elijah Muhammad:* American clergyman (1897–1975); leader of the Nation of Islam, 1935–1975.

Many who today hear me somewhere in person, or on television, or those who read something I've said, will think I went to school far beyond the eighth grade. This impression is due entirely to my prison studies.

It had really begun back in the Charlestown Prison, when Bimbi[2] first made me feel envy of his stock of knowledge. Bimbi had always taken charge of any conversations he was in, and I had tried to emulate him. But every book I picked up had few sentences which didn't contain anywhere from one to nearly all of the words that might as well have been in Chinese. When I just skipped those words, of course, I really ended up with little idea of what the book said. So I had come to the Norfolk Prison Colony still going through only book-reading motions. Pretty soon, I would have quit even these motions, unless I had received the motivation that I did.

I saw that the best thing I could do was get hold of a dictionary — to study, to learn some words. I was lucky enough to reason also that I should try to improve my penmanship. It was sad. I couldn't even write in a straight line. It was both ideas together that moved me to request a dictionary along with some tablets and pencils from the Norfolk Prison Colony school.

I spent two days just riffling uncertainly through the dictionary's pages. I'd never realized so many words existed! I didn't know *which* words I needed to learn. Finally, just to start some kind of action, I began copying.

In my slow, painstaking, ragged handwriting, I copied into my tablet everything printed on that first page, down to the punctuation marks.

I believe it took me a day. Then, aloud, I read back, to myself, everything I'd written on the tablet. Over and over, aloud, to myself, I read my own handwriting.

I woke up the next morning, thinking about those words — immensely proud to realize that not only had I written so much at one time, but I'd written words that I never knew were in the world. Moreover, with a little effort, I also could remember what many of these words meant. I reviewed the words whose meanings I didn't remember. Funny thing, from the dictionary first page right now, that "aardvark" springs to my mind. The dictionary had a picture of it, a long-tailed, long-eared, burrowing African mammal, which lives off termites caught by sticking out its tongue as an anteater does for ants.

I was so fascinated that I went on — I copied the dictionary's next page. And the same experience came when I studied that. With every succeeding page, I also learned of people and places and events from history. Actually the dictionary is like a miniature encyclopedia. Finally the dictionary's A section had filled a whole tablet — and I went on into the B's. That was the way I started copying what eventually became the entire dictionary. It went a lot faster after so much practice helped me to pick up handwriting speed. Between what I wrote in my tablet, and writing letters, during the rest of my time in prison I would guess I wrote a million words.

[2]*Bimbi:* A fellow inmate whose encyclopedic learning and verbal facility greatly impressed Malcolm X.

I suppose it was inevitable that as my word-base broadened, I could for the first time pick up a book and read and now begin to understand what the book was saying. Anyone who has read a great deal can imagine the new world that opened. Let me tell you something: from then until I left that prison, in every free moment I had, if I was not reading in the library, I was reading on my bunk. You couldn't have gotten me out of books with a wedge. Between Mr. Muhammad's teachings, my correspondence, my visitors, . . . and my reading of books, months passed without my even thinking about being imprisoned. In fact, up to then, I never had been so truly free in my life.

The Norfolk Prison Colony's library was in the school building. A variety of classes was taught there by instructors who came from such places as Harvard and Boston universities. The weekly debates between inmate teams were also held in the school building. You would be astonished to know how worked up convict debaters and audiences would get over subjects like "Should Babies Be Fed Milk?"

Available on the prison library's shelves were books on just about every general subject. Much of the big private collection that Parkhurst[3] had willed to the prison was still in crates and boxes in the back of the library — thousands of old books. Some of them looked ancient: covers faded, old-time parchment-looking binding. Parkhurst . . . seemed to have been principally interested in history and religion. He had the money and the special interest to have a lot of books that you wouldn't have in a general circulation. Any college library would have been lucky to get that collection.

As you can imagine, especially in a prison where there was heavy emphasis on rehabilitation, an inmate was smiled upon if he demonstrated an unusually intense interest in books. There was a sizable number of well-read inmates, especially the popular debaters. Some were said by many to be practically walking encyclopedias. They were almost celebrities. No university would ask any student to devour literature as I did when this new world opened to me, of being able to read and *understand*.

I read more in my room than in the library itself. An inmate who was   15 known to read a lot could check out more than the permitted maximum number of books. I preferred reading in the total isolation of my own room.

When I had progressed to really serious reading, every night at about ten P.M. I would be outraged with the "lights out." It always seemed to catch me right in the middle of something engrossing.

Fortunately, right outside my door was a corridor light that cast a glow into my room. The glow was enough to read by, once my eyes adjusted to it. So when "lights out" came, I would sit on the floor where I could continue reading in that glow.

At one-hour intervals at night guards paced past every room. Each time I heard the approaching footsteps, I jumped into bed and feigned sleep.

---

[3]*Parkhurst:* Charles Henry Parkhurst (1842–1933); American clergyman, reformer, and president of the Society for the Prevention of Crime.

And as soon as the guard passed, I got back out of bed onto the floor area of that light-glow, where I would read for another fifty-eight minutes until the guard approached again. That went on until three or four every morning. Three or four hours of sleep a night was enough for me. Often in the years in the streets I had slept less than that.

The teachings of Mr. Muhammad stressed how history had been "whitened" — when white men had written history books, the black man simply had been left out. Mr. Muhammad couldn't have said anything that would have struck me much harder. I had never forgotten how when my class, me and all of those whites, had studied seventh-grade United States history back in Mason, the history of the Negro had been covered in one paragraph, and the teacher had gotten a big laugh with his joke, "Negroes' feet are so big that when they walk, they leave a hole in the ground."

This is one reason why Mr. Muhammad's teachings spread so swiftly all over the United States, among *all* Negroes, whether or not they became followers of Mr. Muhammad. The teachings ring true — to every Negro. You can hardly show me a black adult in America — or a white one, for that matter — who knows from the history books anything like the truth about the black man's role. In my own case, once I heard of the "glorious history of the black man," I took special pains to hunt in the library for books that would inform me on details about black history. 20

I can remember accurately the very first set of books that really impressed me. I have since bought that set of books and I have it at home for my children to read as they grow up. It's called *Wonders of the World*. It's full of pictures of archeological finds, statues that depict, usually, non-European people.

I found books like Will Durant's[4] *Story of Civilization*. I read H. G. Wells'[5] *Outline of History. Souls of Black Folk* by W. E. B. Du Bois[6] gave me a glimpse into the black people's history before they came to this country. Carter G. Woodson's[7] *Negro History* opened my eyes about black empires before the black slave was brought to the United States, and the early Negro struggles for freedom.

J. A. Rogers'[8] three volumes of *Sex and Race* told about race-mixing before Christ's time; and Aesop being a black man who told fables; about Egypt's Pharaohs; about the great Coptic Christian Empire;[9] about Ethi-

[4]*Will Durant:* American author and historian (1885–1981).

[5]*H. G. Wells:* English novelist and historian (1866–1946).

[6]*W. E. B. Du Bois:* William Edward Burghardt Du Bois, distinguished black scholar, author, and activist (1868–1963). Du Bois was the first director of the NAACP and was an important figure in the Harlem Renaissance; his best-known book is *Souls of Black Folk.*

[7]*Carter G. Woodson:* Distinguished African American historian (1875–1950); considered the father of black history.

[8]*J. A. Rogers:* African American historian and journalist (1883–1965).

[9]*Coptic Christian Empire:* The domain of the Coptic Church, a native Egyptian Christian church that retains elements of its African origins.

opia, the earth's oldest continuous black civilization, as China is the oldest continuous civilization.

Mr. Muhammad's teaching about how the white man had been created led me to *Findings in Genetics*, by Gregor Mendel.[10] (The dictionary's G section was where I had learned what "genetics" meant.) I really studied this book by the Austrian monk. Reading it over and over, especially certain sections, helped me to understand that if you started with a black man, a white man could be produced; but starting with a white man, you never could produce a black man — because the white chromosome is recessive. And since no one disputes that there was but one Original Man, the conclusion is clear.

During the last year or so, in the *New York Times*, Arnold Toynbee[11]   25 used the word "bleached" in describing the white man. His words were: "White (i.e., bleached) human beings of North European origin...." Toynbee also referred to the European geographic area as only a peninsula of Asia. He said there was no such thing as Europe. And if you look at the globe, you will see for yourself that America is only an extension of Asia. (But at the same time Toynbee is among those who have helped to bleach history. He has written that Africa was the only continent that produced no history. He won't write that again. Every day now, the truth is coming to light.)

I never will forget how shocked I was when I began reading about slavery's total horror. It made such an impact upon me that it later became one of my favorite subjects when I became a minister of Mr. Muhammad's. The world's most monstrous crime, the sin and the blood on the white man's hands, are almost impossible to believe. Books like the one by Frederick Olmsted[12] opened my eyes to the horrors suffered when the slave was landed in the United States. The European woman, Fanny Kemble,[13] who had married a Southern white slaveowner, described how human beings were degraded. Of course I read *Uncle Tom's Cabin*.[14] In fact, I believe that's the only novel I have ever read since I started serious reading.

Parkhurst's collection also contained some bound pamphlets of the Abolitionist[15] Anti-Slavery Society of New England. I read descriptions of atrocities, saw those illustrations of black slave women tied up and flogged with whips; of black mothers watching their babies being dragged off, never to be seen by their mothers again; of dogs after slaves, and of the fugitive

---

[10]*Gregor Mendel:* Austrian monk, botanist, and pioneer in genetic research (1822–1884).

[11]*Arnold Toynbee:* English historian (1889–1975).

[12]*Frederick Olmsted:* Frederick Law Olmsted (1822–1903), American landscape architect, city planner, and opponent of slavery.

[13]*Fanny Kemble:* Frances Anne Kemble, English actress and author (1809–1893); best known for her autobiographical *Journal of a Residence on a Georgia Plantation,* published in 1863 to win support in Britain for the abolitionist cause.

[14]*Uncle Tom's Cabin:* Harriet Beecher Stowe's 1852 antislavery novel.

[15]*Abolitionist:* Advocating the prohibition of slavery.

slave catchers, evil white men with whips and clubs and chains and guns. I read about the slave preacher Nat Turner, who put the fear of God into the white slavemaster. Nat Turner wasn't going around preaching pie-in-the-sky and "non-violent" freedom for the black man. There in Virginia one night in 1831, Nat and seven other slaves started out at his master's home and through the night they went from one plantation "big house" to the next, killing, until by the next morning 57 white people were dead and Nat had about 70 slaves following him. White people, terrified for their lives, fled from their homes, locked themselves up in public buildings, hid in the woods, and some even left the state. A small army of soldiers took two months to catch and hang Nat Turner. Somewhere I have read where Nat Turner's example is said to have inspired John Brown[16] to invade Virginia and attack Harpers Ferry nearly thirty years later, with thirteen white men and five Negroes.

I read Herodotus,[17] "the father of History," or, rather, I read about him. And I read the histories of various nations, which opened my eyes gradually, then wider and wider, to how the whole world's white men had indeed acted like devils, pillaging and raping and bleeding and draining the whole world's non-white people. I remember, for instance, books such as Will Durant's *The Story of Oriental Civilization*, and Mahatma Gandhi's[18] accounts of the struggle to drive the British out of India.

Book after book showed me how the white man had brought upon the world's black, brown, red, and yellow peoples every variety of the suffering of exploitation. I saw how since the sixteenth century, the so-called "Christian trader" white man began to ply the seas in his lust for Asian and African empires, and plunder, and power. I read, I saw, how the white man never has gone among the non-white peoples bearing the Cross in the true manner and spirit of Christ's teachings — meek, humble, and Christlike.

I perceived, as I read, how the collective white man had been actually   30
nothing but a piratical opportunist who used Faustian machinations[19] to make his own Christianity his initial wedge in criminal conquests. First, always "religiously," he branded "heathen" and "pagan" labels upon ancient non-white cultures and civilizations. The stage thus set, he then turned upon his non-white victims his weapons of war.

I read how, entering India — half a *billion* deeply religious brown people — the British white man, by 1759, through promises, trickery, and manipulations, controlled much of India through Great Britain's East India Company. The parasitical British administration kept tentacling out to half

---

[16]*John Brown:* American abolitionist (1800–1859); leader of an attack on Harpers Ferry, West Virginia, in 1859.

[17]*Herodotus:* Early Greek historian (484?–425? B.C.).

[18]*Mahatma Gandhi:* Hindu religious leader, social reformer, and advocate of nonviolence (1869–1948).

[19]*Faustian machinations:* Evil plots or schemes. Faust was a legendary character who sold his soul to the devil for knowledge and power.

of the sub-continent. In 1857, some of the desperate people of India finally mutinied — and, excepting the African slave trade, nowhere has history recorded any more unnecessary bestial and ruthless human carnage than the British suppression of the non-white Indian people.

Over 115 million African blacks — close to the 1930's population of the United States — were murdered or enslaved during the slave trade. And I read how when the slave market was glutted, the cannibalistic white powers of Europe next carved up, as their colonies, the richest areas of the black continent. And Europe's chancelleries for the next century played a chess game of naked exploitation and power from Cape Horn to Cairo.

Ten guards and the warden couldn't have torn me out of those books. Not even Elijah Muhammad could have been more eloquent than those books were in providing indisputable proof that the collective white man had acted like a devil in virtually every contact he had with the world's collective non-white man. I listen today to the radio, and watch television, and read the headlines about the collective white man's fear and tension concerning China. When the white man professes ignorance about why the Chinese hate him so, my mind can't help flashing back to what I read, there in prison, about how the blood forebears of this same white man raped China at a time when China was trusting and helpless. Those original white "Christian traders" sent into China millions of pounds of opium. By 1839, so many of the Chinese were addicts that China's desperate government destroyed twenty thousand chests of opium. The first Opium War[20] was promptly declared by the white man. Imagine! Declaring *war* upon someone who objects to being narcotized! The Chinese were severely beaten, with Chinese-invented gunpowder.

The Treaty of Nanking made China pay the British white man for the destroyed opium; forced open China's major ports to British trade; forced China to abandon Hong Kong; fixed China's import tariffs so low that cheap British articles soon flooded in, maiming China's industrial development.

After a second Opium War, the Tientsin Treaties legalized the ravaging opium trade, legalized a British-French-American control of China's customs. China tried delaying that Treaty's ratification; Peking was looted and burned.

"Kill the foreign white devils!" was the 1901 Chinese war cry in the Boxer Rebellion.[21] Losing again, this time the Chinese were driven from Peking's choicest areas. The vicious, arrogant white man put up the famous signs, "Chinese and dogs not allowed."

Red China after World War II closed its doors to the Western white world. Massive Chinese agricultural, scientific, and industrial efforts are

35

---

[20]*Opium War:* 1839–1842 war between Britain and China that ended with China's cession of Hong Kong to British rule.
[21]*Boxer Rebellion:* The 1898–1900 uprising by members of a secret Chinese society who opposed foreign influence in Chinese affairs.

described in a book that *Life* magazine recently published. Some observers inside Red China have reported that the world never has known such a hate-white campaign as is now going on in this non-white country where, present birth-rates continuing, in fifty more years Chinese will be half the earth's population. And it seems that some Chinese chickens will soon come home to roost, with China's recent successful nuclear tests.

Let us face reality. We can see in the United Nations a new world order being shaped, along color lines — an alliance among the non-white nations. America's U.N. Ambassador Adlai Stevenson[22] complained not long ago that in the United Nations "a skin game"[23] was being played. He was right. He was facing reality. A "skin game" *is* being played. But Ambassador Stevenson sounded like Jesse James accusing the marshal of carrying a gun. Because who in the world's history ever has played a worse "skin game" than the white man?

Mr. Muhammad, to whom I was writing daily, had no idea of what a new world had opened up to me through my efforts to document his teachings in books.

When I discovered philosophy, I tried to touch all the landmarks of   40
philosophical development. Gradually, I read most of the old philosophers, Occidental and Oriental. The Oriental philosophers were the ones I came to prefer; finally, my impression was that most Occidental philosophy had largely been borrowed from the Oriental thinkers. Socrates, for instance, traveled in Egypt. Some sources even say that Socrates was initiated into some of the Egyptian mysteries. Obviously Socrates got some of his wisdom among the East's wise men.

I have often reflected upon the new vistas that reading opened to me. I knew right there in prison that reading had changed forever the course of my life. As I see it today, the ability to read awoke inside me some long dormant craving to be mentally alive. I certainly wasn't seeking any degree, the way a college confers a status symbol upon its students. My homemade education gave me, with every additional book that I read, a little bit more sensitivity to the deafness, dumbness, and blindness that was afflicting the black race in America. Not long ago, an English writer telephoned me from London, asking questions. One was, "What's your alma mater?" I told him, "Books." You will never catch me with a free fifteen minutes in which I'm not studying something I feel might be able to help the black man.

Yesterday I spoke in London, and both ways on the plane across the Atlantic I was studying a document about how the United Nations proposes to insure the human rights of the oppressed minorities of the world. The American black man is the world's most shameful case of minority oppres-

---

[22]*Adlai Stevenson:* American politician (1900–1965); Democratic candidate for the presidency in 1952 and 1956.

[23]*skin game:* A dishonest or fraudulent scheme, business operation, or trick, with the added reference in this instance to skin color.

sion. What makes the black man think of himself as only an internal United States issue is just a catch-phrase, two words, "civil rights." How is the black man going to get "civil rights" before first he wins his *human* rights? If the American black man will start thinking about his *human* rights, and then start thinking of himself as part of one of the world's great peoples, he will see he has a case for the United Nations.

I can't think of a better case! Four hundred years of black blood and sweat invested here in America, and the white man still has the black man begging for what every immigrant fresh off the ship can take for granted the minute he walks down the gangplank.

But I'm digressing. I told the Englishman that my alma mater was books, a good library. Every time I catch a plane, I have with me a book that I want to read — and that's a lot of books these days. If I weren't out here every day battling the white man, I could spend the rest of my life reading, just satisfying my curiosity — because you can hardly mention anything I'm not curious about. I don't think anybody ever got more out of going to prison than I did. In fact, prison enabled me to study far more intensively than I would have if my life had gone differently and I had attended some college. I imagine that one of the biggest troubles with colleges is there are too many distractions, too much panty-raiding, fraternities, and boola-boola and all of that. Where else but in a prison could I have attacked my ignorance by being able to study intensely sometimes as much as fifteen hours a day?

ENGAGING THE TEXT

1. What motivated Malcolm X to educate himself?

2. What kind of knowledge did Malcolm X gain by learning to read? How did this knowledge free or empower him?

3. Would it be possible for public schools to empower students in the way that Malcolm X's self-education empowered him? If so, how? If not, why not?

4. Some readers are offended by the strength of Malcolm X's accusations and by his grouping of all members of a given race into "collectives." Given the history of racial injustice he recounts here, do you feel he is justified in taking such a position?

EXPLORING CONNECTIONS

5. Compare and contrast Malcolm X's views on the meaning and purpose of education — or on the value and nature of reading — with those of Richard Rodriguez (p. 214). How can you account for the differences in their attitudes?

6. Imagine that John Taylor Gatto (p. 173), Mike Rose (p. 182), Richard Rodriguez (p. 214), and Malcolm X have been appointed to redesign American education. Working in groups, role-play a meeting in which the

THE BOONDOCKS   by **AARON MCGRUDER**

committee attempts to reach consensus on its recommendations. Report to
the class the results of the committee's deliberations and discuss them.

7. Given his experience of self-education, how might Malcolm X respond to
    Claude M. Steele's concerns (p. 231) about the impact of stereotype threat
    and John Henryism on the best minority students today?

8. What does the *Boondocks* cartoon on this page suggest about the possibility
    of teaching and learning "revolutionary" ideas within the setting of a public
    school system?

EXTENDING THE CRITICAL CONTEXT

9. Survey some typical elementary or secondary school textbooks to test the
    currency of Malcolm X's charge that the educational establishment pre-
    sents a "whitened" view of America. What view of America is presently
    being projected in public school history and social science texts?

10. Go to the library and read one page of the dictionary chosen at random.
    Study the meanings of any unfamiliar words and follow up on the informa-
    tion on your page by consulting encyclopedias, books, or articles. Let your-
    self be guided by chance and by your interests. After you've tried this ex-
    periment, discuss in class the benefits and drawbacks of an unsystematic
    self-education like Malcolm X's.

The Roots of Debate in Education and the Hope of Dialogue

DEBORAH TANNEN

From the perspective of the twenty-first century, it's hard to imagine a time when women were excluded from institutions of higher education. Although many American colleges began admitting women in significant numbers little more than a century ago, female students now outnumber males on almost every co-educational campus in the nation. But as Deborah Tannen reminds us, the history of higher education stretches back far earlier than the founding of the United States. The college as an institution grew up in the male-dominated cultures of ancient Greece and medieval Europe and continues to this day to value an "agonistic," or conflict-based, mode of intellectual inquiry that, in Tannen's view, undermines the performance of many female students. A professor of linguistics at Georgetown University and a regular guest and commentator on television news shows like 20/20 *and* The McNeil/Lehrer News Hour, *Tannen (b. 1945) has authored sixteen books on issues of interpersonal and crossgender communication. Her publications include* That's Not What I Meant: How Conversational Style Makes or Breaks Relationships *(1986),* You Just Don't Understand: Women and Men in Conversation *(1990), and the source of this selection,* The Argument Culture: Stopping America's War of Words *(1999).*

The teacher sits at the head of the classroom, feeling pleased with herself and her class. The students are engaged in a heated debate. The very noise level reassures the teacher that the students are participating, taking responsibility for their own learning. Education is going on. The class is a success.

But look again, cautions Patricia Rosof, a high school history teacher who admits to having experienced that wave of satisfaction with herself and the job she is doing. On closer inspection, you notice that only a few students are participating in the debate; the majority of the class is sitting silently, maybe attentive but perhaps either indifferent or actively turned off. And the students who are arguing are not addressing the subtleties, nuances, or complexities of the points they are making or disputing. They do not have that luxury because they want to win the argument — so they must go for the most gross and dramatic statements they can muster. They will not concede an opponent's point, even if they can see its validity, because that would weaken their position. Anyone tempted to synthesize the varying views would not dare to do so because it would look like a "cop-out," an inability to take a stand.

One reason so many teachers use the debate format to promote student involvement is that it is relatively easy to set up and the rewards are quick and obvious: the decibel level of noise, the excitement of those who are taking part. Showing students how to integrate ideas and explore subtleties and complexities is much harder. And the rewards are quieter — but more lasting.

Our schools and universities, our ways of doing science and approaching knowledge, are deeply agonistic. We all pass through our country's educational system, and it is there that the seeds of our adversarial culture are planted. Seeing how these seeds develop, and where they came from, is a key to understanding the argument culture and a necessary foundation for determining what changes we would like to make.

Roots of the Adversarial
Approach to Knowledge

The argument culture, with its tendency to approach issues as a polarized debate, and the culture of critique, with its inclination to regard criticism and attack as the best if not the only type of rigorous thinking, are deeply rooted in Western tradition, going back to the ancient Greeks.[1] This point is made by Walter Ong, a Jesuit professor at Saint Louis University, in his book *Fighting for Life.* Ong credits the ancient Greeks with a fascination with adversativeness in language and thought.[2] He also connects the adver-   5

---

[1]This does not mean it goes back in an unbroken chain. David Noble, in *A World Without Women,* claims that Aristotle was all but lost to the West during the early Christian era and was rediscovered in the medieval era, when universities were first established. This is significant for his observation that many early Christian monasteries welcomed both women and men who could equally aspire to an androgynous ideal, in contrast to the Middle Ages, when the female was stigmatized, unmarried women were consigned to convents, priests were required to be celibate, and women were excluded from spiritual authority. [All notes are the author's, except 6, 15, 18, 20, and 21.]

[2]There is a fascinating parallel in the evolution of the early Christian Church and the Southern Baptist Church: Noble shows that the early Christian Church regarded women as equally beloved of Jesus and equally capable of devoting their lives to religious study, so women comprised a majority of early converts to Christianity, some of them leaving their husbands — or bringing their husbands along — to join monastic communities. It was later, leading up to the medieval period, that the clerical movement gained ascendancy in part by systematically separating women, confining them in either marriage or convents, stigmatizing them, and barring them from positions of power within the church. Christine Leigh Heyrman, in *Southern Cross: The Beginnings of the Bible Belt,* shows that a similar trajectory characterized the Southern Baptist movement. At first, young Baptist and Methodist preachers (in the 1740s to 1830s) preached that both women and blacks were equally God's children, deserving of spiritual authority — with the result that the majority of converts were women and slaves. To counteract this distressing demography, the message was changed: antislavery rhetoric faded, and women's roles were narrowed to domesticity and subservience. With these shifts, the evangelical movement swept the South. At the same time, Heyrman shows, military imagery took over: The ideal man of God was transformed from a "willing martyr" to a "formidable fighter" led by "warrior preachers."

sarial tradition of educational institutions to their all-male character. To attend the earliest universities, in the Middle Ages, young men were torn from their families and deposited in cloistered environments where corporal, even brutal, punishment was rampant. Their suffering drove them to bond with each other in opposition to their keepers — the teachers who were their symbolic enemies. Similar in many ways to puberty rites in traditional cultures, this secret society to which young men were confined also had a private language, Latin, in which students read about military exploits. Knowledge was gleaned through public oral disputation and tested by combative oral performance, which carried with it the risk of public humiliation. Students at these institutions were trained not to discover the truth but to argue either side of an argument — in other words, to debate. Ong points out that the Latin term for school, *ludus,* also referred to play or games, but it derived from the military sense of the word — training exercises for war.

If debate seems self-evidently the appropriate or even the only path to insight and knowledge, says Ong, consider the Chinese approach. Disputation was rejected in ancient China as "incompatible with the decorum and harmony cultivated by the true sage."[3] During the Classical periods in both China and India, according to Robert T. Oliver, the preferred mode of rhetoric was exposition rather than argument. The aim was to "enlighten an inquirer," not to "overwhelm an opponent." And the preferred style reflected "the earnestness of investigation" rather than "the fervor of conviction." In contrast to Aristotle's trust of logic and mistrust of emotion, in ancient Asia intuitive insight was considered the superior means of perceiving truth. Asian rhetoric was devoted not to devising logical arguments but to explicating widely accepted propositions. Furthermore, the search for abstract truth that we assume is the goal of philosophy, while taken for granted in the West, was not found in the East, where philosophy was concerned with observation and experience.

If Aristotelian philosophy, with its emphasis on formal logic, was based on the assumption that truth is gained by opposition, Chinese philosophy offers an alternative view. With its emphasis on harmony, says anthropologist Linda Young, Chinese philosophy sees a diverse universe in precarious balance that is maintained by talk. This translates into methods of investigation that focus more on integrating ideas and exploring relations among them than on opposing ideas and fighting over them.

Onward, Christian Soldiers

The military-like culture of early universities is also described by historian David Noble, who describes how young men attending medieval universities were like marauding soldiers: The students — all seminarians —

---

[3]Ong, *Fighting for Life,* p. 122. Ong's source, on which I also rely, is Oliver, *Communication and Culture in Ancient India and China.* My own quotations from Oliver are from p. 259.

roamed the streets bearing arms, assaulting women, and generally creating mayhem. Noble traces the history of Western science and of universities to joint origins in the Christian Church. The scientific revolution, he shows, was created by religious devotees setting up monastery-like institutions devoted to learning. Early universities were seminaries, and early scientists were either clergy or devoutly religious individuals who led monk-like lives. (Until as recently as 1888, fellows at Oxford were expected to be unmarried.)

That Western science is rooted in the Christian Church helps explain why our approach to knowledge tends to be conceived as a metaphorical battle: The Christian Church, Noble shows, has origins and early forms rooted in the military. Many early monks had actually been soldiers before becoming monks.[4] Not only were obedience and strict military-like discipline required, but monks saw themselves as serving "in God's knighthood," warriors in a battle against evil. In later centuries, the Crusades brought actual warrior-monks.

The history of science in the Church holds the key to understanding   10
our tradition of regarding the search for truth as an enterprise of oral disputation in which positions are propounded, defended, and attacked without regard to the debater's personal conviction. It is a notion of truth as objective, best captured by formal logic, that Ong traces to Aristotle. Aristotle regarded logic as the only trustworthy means for human judgment; emotions get in the way: "The man who is to judge would not have his judgment warped by speakers arousing him to anger, jealousy, or compassion. One might as well make a carpenter's tool crooked before using it as a measure."[5]

This assumption explains why Plato wanted to ban poets from education in his ideal community. As a lover of poetry, I can still recall my surprise and distress on reading this in *The Republic*[6] when I was in high school. Not until much later did I understand what it was all about.[7] Poets in ancient Greece were wandering bards who traveled from place to place performing oral poetry that persuaded audiences by moving them emotionally. They were like what we think of as demagogues: people with a danger-

[4]Pachomius, for example, "the father of communal monasticism . . . and organizer of the first monastic community, had been a soldier under Constantine" and modeled his community on the military, emphasizing order, efficiency, and military obedience. Cassian, a fourth-century proselytizer, "'likened the monk's discipline to that of the soldier,' and Chrysostom, another great champion of the movement, 'sternly reminded the monks that Christ had armed them to be soldiers in a noble fight'" (Noble, *A World Without Women*, p. 54).

[5]Aristotle, quoted in Oliver, *Communication and Culture in Ancient India and China*, p. 259.

[6]*The Republic*: Plato's utopian vision of the ideal state.

[7]I came to understand the different meaning of "poet" in Classical Greece from reading Ong and also *Preface to Plato* by Eric Havelock. These insights informed many articles I wrote about oral and literate tradition in Western culture, including "Oral and Literate Strategies in Spoken and Written Narratives" and "The Oral/Literate Continuum in Discourse."

ous power to persuade others by getting them all worked up. Ong likens this to our discomfort with advertising in schools, which we see as places where children should learn to think logically, not be influenced by "teachers" with ulterior motives who use unfair persuasive tactics.

Sharing Time: Early Training in School

A commitment to formal logic as the truest form of intellectual pursuit remains with us today. Our glorification of opposition as the path to truth is related to the development of formal logic, which encourages thinkers to regard truth seeking as a step-by-step alternation of claims and counterclaims.[8] Truth, in this schema, is an abstract notion that tends to be taken out of context. This formal approach to learning is taught in our schools, often indirectly.

Educational researcher James Wertsch shows that schools place great emphasis on formal representation of knowledge. The common elementary school practice of "sharing time" (or, as it used to be called, "show-and-tell") is a prime arena for such training. Wertsch gives the example of a kindergarten pupil named Danny who took a piece of lava to class.[9] Danny told his classmates, "My mom went to the volcano and got it." When the teacher asked what he wanted to tell about it, he said, "I've always been taking care of it." This placed the rock at the center of his feelings and his family: the rock's connection to his mother, who gave it to him, and the attention and care he has lavished on it. The teacher reframed the children's interest in the rock as informational: "Is it rough or smooth?" "Is it heavy or light?" She also suggested they look up "volcano" and "lava" in the dictionary. This is not to imply that the teacher harmed the child; she built on his personal attachment to the rock to teach him a new way of thinking about it. But the example shows the focus of education on formal rather than relational knowledge — information about the rock that has meaning out of context, rather than information tied to the context: Who got the rock for him? How did she get it? What is his relation to it?

Here's another example of how a teacher uses sharing time to train children to speak and think formally. Sarah Michaels spent time watching and tape-recording in a first-grade classroom. During sharing time, a little girl named Mindy held up two candles and told her classmates, "When I was in day camp we made these candles. And I tried it with different colors with both of them but one just came out, this one just came out blue and I don't know what this color is." The teacher responded, "That's neat-o. Tell the kids how you do it from the very start. Pretend we don't know a thing about candles. OK, what did you do first? What did you use?" She

---

[8]Moulton, "A Paradigm of Philosophy"; Ong, *Fighting for Life.*
[9]The example of Danny and the lava: Wertsch, *Voices of the Mind,* pp. 113–14.

continued to prompt: "What makes it have a shape?" and "Who knows what the string is for?" By encouraging Mindy to give information in a sequential manner, even if it might not seem the most important to her and if the children might already know some of it, the teacher was training her to talk in a focused, explicit way.

The tendency to value formal, objective knowledge over relational, in-   15
tuitive knowledge grows out of our notion of education as training for de-
bate. It is a legacy of the agonistic heritage. There are many other traces as well. Many Ph.D. programs still require public "defenses" of dissertations or dissertation proposals, and oral performance of knowledge in comprehensive exams. Throughout our educational system, the most pervasive inheritance is the conviction that issues have two sides, that knowledge is best gained through debate, that ideas should be presented orally to an audience that does its best to poke holes and find weaknesses, and that to get recognition, one has to "stake out a position" in opposition to another.

Integrating Women in the Classroom Army

If Ong is right, the adversarial character of our educational institutions is inseparable from their all-male heritage. I wondered whether teaching techniques still tend to be adversarial today and whether, if they are, this may hold a clue to a dilemma that has received much recent attention: that girls often receive less attention and speak up less in class.[10] One term I taught a large lecture class of 140 students and decided to take advantage of this army (as it were) of researchers to answer these questions. Becoming observers in their own classrooms, my students found plenty of support for Ong's ideas.

I asked the students to note how relatively adversarial the teaching methods were in their other classes and how the students responded. Gabrielle DeRouen-Hawkins's description of a theology class was typical:

> The class is in the format of lecture with class discussion and participation. There are thirteen boys and eleven girls in the class.[11] In a fifty-minute class:
>   Number of times a male student spoke: 8
>   Number of times a female student spoke: 3
>   . . . In our readings, theologians present their theories surrounding G–D, life, spirituality, and sacredness. As the professor (a male) outlined the main ideas about the readings, he posed questions like "And what is the fault with / Smith's / basis that the sacred is individualistic?" The only hands that went up were male. Not one female <u>dared</u> challenge or refute an author's writings. The only questions that

[10]See David and Myra Sadker, *Failing at Fairness*.

[11]Although my colleagues and I make efforts to refer to our students — all over the age of eighteen — as "women" and "men" and some students in my classes do the same, the majority refer to each other and themselves as "girls" and "boys" or "girls" and "guys."

the females asked (and all female comments were questions) involved a problem they had with the content of the reading. The males, on the other hand, openly questioned, criticized, and refuted the readings on five separate occasions. The three other times that males spoke involved them saying something like: "/ Smith / is very vague in her theory of XX. Can you explain it further?" They were openly argumentative.

This description raises a number of fascinating issues. First, it gives concrete evidence that at least college classrooms proceed on the assumption that the educational process should be adversarial: The teacher invited students to criticize the reading. (Theology, a required course at Georgetown, was a subject where my students most often found adversarial methods — interestingly, given the background I laid out earlier.) Again, there is nothing inherently wrong with using such methods. Clearly, they are very effective in many ways. However, among the potential liabilities is the risk that women students may be less likely to take part in classroom discussions that are framed as arguments between opposing sides — that is, debate — or as attacks on the authors — that is, critique. (The vast majority of students' observations revealed that men tended to speak more than women in their classes — which is not to say that individual women did not speak more than individual men.)

Gabrielle commented that since class participation counted for 10 percent of students' grades, it might not be fair to women students that the agonistic style is more congenial to men. Not only might women's grades suffer because they speak up less, but they might be evaluated as less intelligent or prepared because when they did speak, they asked questions rather than challenging the readings.

I was intrigued by the student's comment "/Smith/ is very vague in her theory of XX. Can you explain it further?" It could have been phrased "I didn't understand the author's theory. Can you explain it to me?" By beginning "The author is vague in her theory," the questioner blamed the author for his failure to understand. A student who asks a question in class risks appearing ignorant. Prefacing the question this way was an excellent way to minimize that risk. 20

In her description of this class, Gabrielle wrote that not a single woman "dared challenge or refute" an author. She herself underlined the word "dared." But in reading this I wondered whether "dared" was necessarily the right word. It implies that the women in the class wished to challenge the author but did not have the courage. It is possible that not a single woman *cared* to challenge the author. Criticizing or challenging might not be something that appealed to them or seemed worth their efforts. Going back to the childhoods of boys and girls, it seems possible that the boys had had more experiences, from the time they were small, that encouraged them to challenge and argue with authority figures than the girls had.

This is not to say that classrooms are more congenial to boys than girls in every way. Especially in the lowest grades, the requirement that children sit quietly in their seats seems clearly to be easier for girls to fulfill than boys, since many girls frequently sit fairly quietly for long periods of time when they play, while most boys' idea of play involves at least running around, if not also jumping and roughhousing. And researchers have pointed out that some of the extra attention boys receive is aimed at controlling such physical exuberance. The adversarial aspect of educational traditions is just one small piece of the pie, but it seems to reflect boys' experiences and predilections more than girls'.

A colleague commented that he had always taken for granted that the best way to deal with students' comments is to challenge them; he took it to be self-evident that this technique sharpens their minds and helps them develop debating skills. But he noticed that women were relatively silent in his classes. He decided to try beginning discussion with relatively open questions and letting comments go unchallenged. He found, to his amazement and satisfaction, that more women began to speak up in class.

Clearly, women can learn to perform in adversarial ways. Anyone who doubts this need only attend an academic conference in the field of women's studies or feminist studies — or read Duke University professor Jane Tompkins's essay showing how a conference in these fields can be like a Western shoot-out. My point is rather about the roots of the tradition and the tendency of the style to appeal initially to more men than women in the Western cultural context. Ong and Noble show that the adversarial culture of Western science and its exclusion of women were part and parcel of the same historical roots — not that individual women may not learn to practice and enjoy agonistic debate or that individual men may not recoil from it. There are many people, women as well as men, who assume a discussion must be contentious to be interesting. Author Mary Catherine Bateson recalls that when her mother, the anthropologist Margaret Mead, said, "I had an argument with" someone, it was a positive comment. "An argument," to her, meant a spirited intellectual interchange, not a rancorous conflict. The same assumption emerged in an obituary for Diana Trilling, called "one of the very last of the great midcentury New York intellectuals."[12] She and her friends had tried to live what they called "a life of significant contention"— the contention apparently enhancing rather than undercutting the significance.

Learning by Fighting

Although there are patterns that tend to typify women and men in a given culture, there is an even greater range among members of widely divergent cultural backgrounds. In addition to observing adversarial encoun-   25

[12]Jonathan Alter, "The End of the Journey," *Newsweek,* Nov. 4, 1996, p. 61. Trilling died at the age of ninety-one.

ters in their current classrooms, many students recalled having spent a junior year in Germany or France and commented that American classrooms seemed very placid compared to what they had experienced abroad. One student, Zach Tyler, described his impressions this way:

> I have very vivid memories of my junior year of high school, which I spent in Germany as an exchange student. The classroom was very debate-oriented and agonistic. One particular instance I remember well was in physics class, when a very confrontational friend of mine had a heated debate with the teacher about solving a problem. My friend ran to the board and scribbled out how he would have solved the problem, completely different from the teacher's, which also gave my friend the right answer and made the teacher wrong.
>
> STUDENT: "You see! This is how it should be, and you are wrong!"
> TEACHER: "No! No! No! You are absolutely wrong in every respect! Just look at how you did this!" (He goes over my friend's solution and shows that it does not work.) "Your solution has no base, as I just showed you!"
> STUDENT: "You can't prove that. Mine works just as well!"
> TEACHER: "My God, if the world were full of technical idiots like yourself! Look again!" (And he clearly shows how my friend's approach was wrong, after which my friend shut up.)

In Zach's opinion, the teacher encouraged this type of argument. The student learned he was wrong, but he got practice in arguing his point of view.

This incident occurred in high school. But European classrooms can be adversarial even at the elementary school level, according to another student, Megan Smyth, who reported on a videotape she saw in her French class:

> Today in French class we watched an excerpt of a classroom scene of fifth-graders. One at a time, each student was asked to stand up and recite a poem that they were supposed to have memorized. The teacher screamed at the students if they forgot a line or if they didn't speak with enough emotion. They were reprimanded and asked to repeat the task until they did it perfectly and passed the "oral test."

There is probably little question about how Americans would view this way of teaching, but the students put it into words:

> After watching this scene, my French teacher asked the class what our opinion was. The various responses included: French schools are very strict, the professor was "mean" and didn't have respect for the students, and there's too much emphasis on memorization, which is pointless.

If teaching methods can be more openly adversarial in European than American elementary and high schools, academic debate can be more openly adversarial there as well. For example, Alice Kaplan, a professor of

French at Duke University, describes a colloquium on the French writer
Céline that she attended in Paris:

> After the first speech, people started yelling at each other. "Are you
> suggesting that Céline was fascist!" "You call that evidence!" "I will not
> accept ignorance in the place of argument!" I was scared.[13]

These examples dramatize that many individuals can thrive in an adversarial
atmosphere. And those who learn to participate effectively in any verbal
game eventually enjoy it, if nothing else than for the pleasure of exercising
that learned skill. It is important to keep these examples in mind in order to
avoid the impression that adversarial tactics are always destructive. Clearly,
such tactics sometimes admirably serve the purpose of intellectual inquiry.
In addition to individual predilection, cultural learning plays a role in
whether or not someone enjoys the game played this way.

Graduate School as Boot Camp

Although the invective Kaplan heard at a scholarly meeting in Paris is
more extreme than what is typical at American conferences, the assumption
that challenge and attack are the best modes of scholarly inquiry is pervasive in American scholarly communities as well. Graduate education is a
training ground not only for teaching but also for scientific research. Many
graduate programs are geared to training young scholars in rigorous thinking, defined as the ability to launch and field verbal attacks.

Communications researchers Karen Tracy and Sheryl Baratz tapped
into some of the ethics that lead to this atmosphere in a study of weekly
symposia attended by faculty and graduate students at a major research university. When they asked participants about the purpose of the symposia,
they were told it was to "trade ideas" and "learn things." But it didn't take
too much discussion to uncover the participants' deeper concern: to be seen
as intellectually competent. And here's the rub: to be seen as competent, a
student had to ask "tough and challenging questions."

One faculty member commented, when asked about who participated
actively in a symposium,

> Among the graduate students, the people I think about are Jess, Tim,
> uh let's see, Felicia will ask a question but it'll be a nice little support-
> ive question.[14]

"A nice little supportive question" diminished the value of Felicia's participation and her intelligence — the sort of judgment a student would wish to
avoid. Just as with White House correspondents, there is value placed on

---

[13]Kaplan, *French Lessons,* p. 119.
[14]Tracy and Baratz, "Intellectual Discussion in the Academy as Situated Discourse,"
p. 309.

asking "tough questions." Those who want to impress their peers and superiors (as most, if not all, do) are motivated to ask the sorts of questions that
gain approval.

Valuing attack as a sign of respect is part of the argument culture of   30
academia — our conception of intellectual interchange as a metaphorical
battle. As one colleague put it, "In order to play with the big boys, you have
to be willing to get into the ring and wrestle with them." Yet many graduate
students (and quite a few established scholars) remain ambivalent about
this ethic, especially when they are on the receiving rather than the distribution end. Sociolinguist Winnie Or tape-recorded a symposium at which a
graduate student presented her fledgling research to other students and
graduate faculty. The student later told Or that she left the symposium feeling that a truck had rolled over her. She did not say she regretted having
taken part; she felt she had received valuable feedback. But she also mentioned that she had not looked at her research project once since the symposium several weeks before. This is telling. Shouldn't an opportunity to
discuss your research with peers and experts fire you up and send you back
to the isolation of research renewed and reinspired? Isn't something awry if
it leaves you not wanting to face your research project at all?

This young scholar persevered, but others drop out of graduate school,
in some cases because they are turned off by the atmosphere of critique.
One woman who wrote to me said she had been encouraged to enroll in
graduate school by her college professors, but she lasted only one year in a
major midwest university's doctoral program in art history. This is how she
described her experience and her decision not to continue.

> Grad school was the nightmare I never knew existed. . . . Into the den
> of wolves I go, like a lamb to slaughter. . . . When, at the end of my
> first year (masters) I was offered a job as a curator for a private collec-
> tion, I jumped at the chance. I wasn't cut out for academia — better
> try the "real world."

Reading this I thought, is it that she was not cut out for academia, or is it
that academia as it was practiced in that university is not cut out for people
like her. It is cut out for those who enjoy, or can tolerate, a contentious environment.

(These examples remind us again of the gender dynamic. The graduate
student who left academia for museum work was a woman. The student
who asked a "nice little supportive question" instead of a "tough, challenging one" was a woman. More than one commentator has wondered aloud if
part of the reason women drop out of science courses and degree programs
is their discomfort with the agonistic culture of Western science. And Lani
Guinier[15] has recently shown that discomfort with the agonistic procedures

---

[15]*Lani Guinier:* Legal scholar (b. 1950) whose 1993 nomination to the Supreme Court
was defeated in Congress.

of law school is partly responsible for women's lower grade point averages in law school, since the women arrive at law school with records as strong as the men's.)

The Culture of Critique: Attack in the Academy

The standard way of writing an academic paper is to position your work in opposition to someone else's, which you prove wrong. This creates a *need* to make others wrong, which is quite a different matter from reading something with an open mind and discovering that you disagree with it. Students are taught that they must disprove others' arguments in order to be original, make a contribution, and demonstrate their intellectual ability. When there is a *need* to make others wrong, the temptation is great to oversimplify at best, and at worst to distort or even misrepresent others' positions, the better to refute them — to search for the most foolish statement in a generally reasonable treatise, seize upon the weakest examples, ignore facts that support your opponent's views, and focus only on those that support yours. Straw men spring up like scarecrows in a cornfield.

Sometimes it seems as if there is a maxim driving academic discourse that counsels, "If you can't find something bad to say, don't say anything." As a result, any work that gets a lot of attention is immediately opposed. There is an advantage to this approach: Weaknesses are exposed, and that is surely good. But another result is that it is difficult for those outside the field (or even inside) to know what is "true." Like two expert witnesses hired by opposing attorneys, academics can seem to be canceling each other out. In the words of policy analysts David Greenberg and Philip Robins:

> The process of scientific inquiry almost ensures that competing sets of results will be obtained. . . . Once the first set of findings are published, other researchers eager to make a name for themselves must come up with different approaches and results to get their studies published.[16]

How are outsiders (or insiders, for that matter) to know which "side" to believe? As a result, it is extremely difficult for research to influence public policy.

A leading researcher in psychology commented that he knew of two young colleagues who had achieved tenure by writing articles attacking him. One of them told him, in confidence, that he actually agreed with him, but of course he could not get tenure by writing articles simply supporting someone else's work; he had to stake out a position in opposition. Attacking an established scholar has particular appeal because it demonstrates originality and independence of thought without requiring true innovation. After

35

---

[16]Greenberg and Robins, "The Changing Role of Social Experiments in Policy Analysis," p. 350.

all, the domain of inquiry and the terms of debate have already been established. The critic has only to say, like the child who wants to pick a fight, "Is not!" Younger or less prominent scholars can achieve a level of attention otherwise denied or eluding them by stepping into the ring with someone who has already attracted the spotlight.

The young psychologist who confessed his motives to the established one was unusual, I suspect, only in his self-awareness and willingness to articulate it. More commonly, younger scholars, or less prominent ones, convince themselves that they are fighting for truth, that they are among the few who see that the emperor has no clothes. In the essay mentioned earlier, Jane Tompkins describes how a young scholar-critic can work herself into a passionate conviction that she is morally obligated to attack, because she is fighting on the side of good against the side of evil. Like the reluctant hero in the film *High Noon,* she feels she has no choice but to strap on her holster and shoot. Tompkins recalls that her own career was launched by an essay that

> began with a frontal assault on another woman scholar. When I wrote it I felt the way the hero does in a Western. Not only had this critic argued *a, b,* and *c,* she had held *x, y,* and *z!* It was a clear case of outrageous provocation.[17]

Because her attack was aimed at someone with an established career ("She was famous and I was not. She was teaching at a prestigious university and I was not. She had published a major book and I had not."), it was a "David and Goliath situation" that made her feel she was "justified in hitting her with everything I had." (This is analogous to what William Safire[18] describes as his philosophy in the sphere of political journalism: "Kick 'em when they're up.")[19]

The claim of objectivity is belied by Tompkins's account of the spirit in which attack is often launched: the many motivations, other than the search for truth, that drive a critic to pick a fight with another scholar. Objectivity would entail a disinterested evaluation of all claims. But there is nothing disinterested about it when scholars set out with the need to make others wrong and transform them not only into opponents but into villains.

In academia, as in other walks of life, anonymity breeds contempt. Some of the nastiest rhetoric shows up in "blind" reviews — of articles submitted to journals or book proposals submitted to publishers. "Peer review" is the cornerstone of academic life. When someone submits an article to a journal, a book to a publisher, or a proposal to a funding institution, the

---

[17]These and other quotes from Tompkins appear in her essay "Fighting Words," pp. 588–89.

[18]*William Safire:* Political commentator (b. 1929).

[19]Safire is quoted in Howard Kurtz, "Safire Made No Secret of Dislike for Inman," *The Washington Post,* Jan. 19, 1994, p. A6.

work is sent to established scholars for evaluation. To enable reviewers to be honest, they remain anonymous. But anonymous reviewers often take a tone of derision such as people tend to use only when talking about some-one who is not there — after all, the evaluation is not addressed to the au-thor. But authors typically receive copies of the evaluations, especially if their work is rejected. This can be particularly destructive to young scholars just starting out. For example, one sociolinguist wrote her dissertation in a firmly established tradition: She tape-recorded conversations at the com-pany where she worked part-time. Experts in our field believe it is best to examine conversations in which the researcher is a natural participant, because when strangers appear asking to tape-record, people get nervous and may change their behavior. The publisher sent the manuscript to a re-viewer who was used to different research methods. In rejecting the pro-posal, she referred to the young scholar "using the audiotaped detritus from an old job." Ouch. What could justify the sneering term "detritus"? What is added by appending "old" to "job," other than hurting the author? Like Heathcliff,[20] the target hears only the negative and — like Heathcliff —may respond by fleeing the field altogether.

One reason the argument culture is so widespread is that arguing is so easy to do. Lynne Hewitt, Judith Duchan, and Erwin Segal came up with a fascinating finding: Speakers with language disabilities who had trouble tak-ing part in other types of verbal interaction were able to participate in argu-ments. Observing adults with mental retardation who lived in a group home, the researchers found that the residents often engaged in verbal con-flicts as a means of prolonging interaction. It was a form of sociability. Most surprising, this was equally true of two residents who had severe language and comprehension disorders yet were able to take part in the verbal dis-putes, because arguments have a predictable structure.

Academics, too, know that it is easy to ask challenging questions with-out listening, reading, or thinking very carefully. Critics can always com-plain about research methods, sample size, and what has been left out. To study anything, a researcher must isolate a piece of the subject and narrow the scope of vision in order to focus. An entire tree cannot be placed under a microscope; a tiny bit has to be separated to be examined closely. This gives critics the handle of a weapon with which to strike an easy blow: They can point out all the bits that were not studied. Like family members or partners in a close relationship, anyone looking for things to pick on will have no trouble finding them.

All of this is not to imply that scholars should not criticize each other or disagree. In the words of poet William Blake,[21] "Without contraries is no

---

[20]*Heathcliff:* The male protagonist of Emily Brontë's nineteenth-century novel *Wuther-ing Heights.* He overreacts when he hears the novel's heroine criticize him.

[21]*William Blake:* English Romantic poet (1757–1827).

progression."[22] The point is to distinguish constructive ways of doing so from nonconstructive ones. Criticizing a colleague on empirical grounds is the beginning of a discussion; if researchers come up with different findings, they can engage in a dialogue: What is it about their methods, data, or means of analysis that explains the different results? In some cases, those who set out to disprove another's claims end up proving them instead — something that is highly unlikely to happen in fields that deal in argumentation alone.

A stunning example in which opponents attempting to disprove a heretical claim ended up proving it involves the cause and treatment of ulcers. It is now widely known and accepted that ulcers are caused by bacteria in the stomach and can be cured by massive doses of antibiotics. For years, however, the cure and treatment of ulcers remained elusive, as all the experts agreed that ulcers were the classic psychogenic illness caused by stress. The stomach, experts further agreed, was a sterile environment: No bacteria could live there. So pathologists did not look for bacteria in the stomachs of ailing or deceased patients, and those who came across them simply ignored them, in effect not seeing what was before their eyes because they did not believe it could be there. When Dr. Barry Marshall, an Australian resident in internal medicine, presented evidence that ulcers are caused by bacteria, no one believed him. His findings were ultimately confirmed by researchers intent on proving him wrong.[23]

The case of ulcers shows that setting out to prove others wrong can be constructive — when it is driven by genuine differences and when it motivates others to undertake new research. But if seeking to prove others wrong becomes a habit, an end in itself, the sole line of inquiry, the results can be far less rewarding.

Believing as Thinking

"The doubting game" is the name English professor Peter Elbow gives   45
to what educators are trained to do. In playing the doubting game, you approach others' work by looking for what's wrong, much as the press corps follows the president hoping to catch him stumble or an attorney pores over an opposing witness's deposition looking for inconsistencies that can be challenged on the stand. It is an attorney's job to discredit opposing witnesses, but is it a scholar's job to approach colleagues like an opposing attorney?

Elbow recommends learning to approach new ideas, and ideas different from your own, in a different spirit — what he calls a "believing game." This does not mean accepting everything anyone says or writes in an

[22]I've borrowed the William Blake quote from Peter Elbow, who used it to open his book *Embracing Contraries.*

[23]Terence Monmaney, "Marshall's Hunch," *The New Yorker,* Sept. 20, 1993, pp. 64–72.

unthinking way. That would be just as superficial as rejecting everything without thinking deeply about it. The believing game is still a game. It simply asks you to give it a whirl: Read *as if* you believed, and see where it takes you. Then you can go back and ask whether you want to accept or reject elements in the argument or the whole argument or idea. Elbow is not recommending that we stop doubting altogether. He is telling us to stop doubting exclusively. We need a systematic and respected way to detect and expose strengths, just as we have a systematic and respected way of detecting faults.

Americans need little encouragement to play the doubting game because we regard it as synonymous with intellectual inquiry, a sign of intelligence. In Elbow's words, "We tend to assume that the ability to criticize a claim we disagree with counts as more serious intellectual work than the ability to enter into it and temporarily assent."[24] It is the believing game that needs to be encouraged and recognized as an equally serious intellectual pursuit.

Although criticizing is surely part of critical thinking, it is not synonymous with it. Again, limiting critical response to critique means not doing the other kinds of critical thinking that could be helpful: looking for new insights, new perspectives, new ways of thinking, new knowledge. Critiquing relieves you of the responsibility of doing integrative thinking. It also has the advantage of making the critics feel smart, smarter than the ill-fated author whose work is being picked apart like carrion. But it has the disadvantage of making them less likely to learn from the author's work.

The Socratic Method — or Is It?

Another scholar who questions the usefulness of opposition as the sole path to truth is philosopher Janice Moulton. Philosophy, she shows, equates logical reasoning with the Adversary Paradigm, a matter of making claims and then trying to find, and argue against, counterexamples to that claim. The result is a debate between adversaries trying to defend their ideas against counterexamples and to come up with counterexamples that refute the opponent's ideas. In this paradigm, the best way to evaluate someone's work is to "subject it to the strongest or most extreme opposition."[25]

But if you parry individual points — a negative and defensive enter-   50
prise — you never step back and actively imagine a world in which a different system of ideas could be true — a positive act. And you never ask how larger systems of thought relate to each other. According to Moulton, our devotion to the Adversary Paradigm has led us to misinterpret the type of argumentation that Socrates favored: We think of the Socratic method as

---

[24]Elbow, *Embracing Contraries*, p. 258.
[25]Moulton, "A Paradigm of Philosophy," p. 153.

systematically leading an opponent into admitting error. This is primarily a way of showing up an adversary as wrong. Moulton shows that the original Socratic method — the *elenchus* — was designed to convince others, to shake them out of their habitual mode of thought and lead them to new insight. Our version of the Socratic method — an adversarial public debate — is unlikely to result in opponents changing their minds. Someone who loses a debate usually attributes that loss to poor performance or to an adversary's unfair tactics. . . .

Getting Beyond Dualism

At the heart of the argument culture is our habit of seeing issues and ideas as absolute and irreconcilable principles continually at war. To move beyond this static and limiting view, we can remember the Chinese approach to yin and yang. They are two principles, yes, but they are conceived not as irreconcilable polar opposites but as elements that coexist and should be brought into balance as much as possible. As sociolinguist Suzanne Wong Scollon notes, "Yin is always present in and changing into yang and vice versa."[26] How can we translate this abstract idea into daily practice?

To overcome our bias toward dualism, we can make special efforts not to think in twos. Mary Catherine Bateson, an author and anthropologist who teaches at George Mason University, makes a point of having her class compare *three* cultures, not two. If students compare two cultures, she finds, they are inclined to polarize them, to think of the two as opposite to each other. But if they compare three cultures, they are more likely to think about each on its own terms.[27]

As a goal, we could all try to catch ourselves when we talk about "both sides" of an issue — and talk instead about "all sides." And people in any field can try to resist the temptation to pick on details when they see a chance to score a point. If the detail really does not speak to the main issue, bite your tongue. Draw back and consider the whole picture. After asking, "Where is this wrong?" make an effort to ask, "What is right about this?"— not necessarily *instead*, but *in addition*. . . .

Perhaps, too, it is time to question our glorification of debate as the best, if not the only, means of inquiry. The debate format leads us to regard those doing different kinds of research as belonging to warring camps. There is something very appealing about conceptualizing differing approaches in this way, because dichotomies appeal to our sense of how knowledge should be organized.

Well, what's wrong with that? 55

What's wrong is that it obscures aspects of disparate work that overlap and can enlighten each other.

---

[26]Suzanne Wong Scollon, personal communication.
[27]Mary Catherine Bateson, personal communication.

What's wrong is that it obscures the complexity of research. Fitting ideas into a particular camp requires you to oversimplify them. Again, disinformation and distortion can result. Less knowledge is gained, not more. And time spent attacking an opponent or defending against attacks is not spent doing something else — like original research.

What's wrong is that it implies that only one framework can apply, when in most cases many can. As a colleague put it, "Most theories are wrong not in what they assert but in what they deny."[28] Clinging to the elephant's leg, they loudly proclaim that the person describing the elephant's tail is wrong. This is not going to help them — or their readers — understand an elephant. Again, there are parallels in personal relationships. I recall a man who had just returned from a weekend human-development seminar. Full of enthusiasm, he explained the main lesson he had learned: "I don't have to make others wrong to prove that I'm right." He experienced this revelation as a liberation; it relieved him of the burden of trying to prove others wrong.

If you limit your view of a problem to choosing between two sides, you inevitably reject much that is true, and you narrow your field of vision to the limits of those two sides, making it unlikely you'll pull back, widen your field of vision, and discover the paradigm shift that will permit truly new understanding.

In moving away from a narrow view of debate, we need not give up conflict and criticism altogether. Quite the contrary, we can develop more varied — and more constructive — ways of expressing opposition and negotiating disagreement. 60

We need to use our imaginations and ingenuity to find different ways to seek truth and gain knowledge, and add them to our arsenal — or, should I say, to the ingredients for our stew. It will take creativity to find ways to blunt the most dangerous blades of the argument culture. It's a challenge we must undertake, because our public and private lives are at stake.

References

Bateson, Mary Catherine. *With a Daughter's Eye: A Memoir of Margaret Mead and Gregory Bateson* (New York: William Morrow, 1984).
Elbow, Peter. *Embracing Contraries: Explorations in Learning and Teaching* (New York and Oxford: Oxford University Press, 1986).
Greenberg, David H., and Philip K. Robins. "The Changing Role of Social Experiments in Policy Analysis." *Journal of Policy Analysis and Management* 5:2 (1986), pp. 340–62.
Guinier, Lani, Michelle Fine, and Jane Balin, with Ann Bartow and Deborah Lee Stachel. "Becoming Gentlemen: Women's Experiences at One Ivy League Law School." 143 *University of Pennsylvania Law Review* (Nov. 1994), pp. 1–110.

[28]I got this from A. L. Becker, who got it from Kenneth Pike, who got it from . . .

Havelock, Eric A. *Preface to Plato* (Cambridge, Mass.: Belknap Press, Harvard University Press, 1963).

Hewitt, Lynne E., Judith F. Duchan, and Erwin M. Segal. "Structure and Function of Verbal Conflicts Among Adults with Mental Retardation." *Discourse Processes* 16(4) (1993), pp. 525–43.

Heyrman, Christine Leigh. *Southern Cross: The Beginnings of the Bible Belt* (New York: Knopf, 1997).

Kaplan, Alice. *French Lessons: A Memoir* (Chicago: University of Chicago Press, 1993).

Kurtz, Howard. *Hot Air: All Talk, All the Time* (New York: Times Books, 1996).

Michaels, Sarah. "'Sharing Time': Children's Narrative Styles and Differential Access to Literacy." *Language in Society* 10:3 (1981), pp. 423–42.

Moulton, Janice. "A Paradigm of Philosophy: The Adversary Method." In *Discovering Reality*, Sandra Harding and Merrill B. Hintikka, eds. (Dordrecht, Holland: Reidel, 1983), pp. 149–64.

Noble, David. *A World Without Women: The Christian Clerical Culture of Western Science* (New York and Oxford: Oxford University Press, 1992).

Oliver, Robert T. *Communication and Culture in Ancient India and China* (Syracuse, N.Y.: Syracuse University Press, 1971).

Ong, Walter J. *Fighting for Life: Contest, Sexuality, and Consciousness* (Ithaca, N.Y.: Cornell University Press, 1981).

Or, Winnie Wing Fung. "Agonism in Academic Discussion." Paper presented at the 96th Annual Meeting of the American Anthropological Association, Nov. 19–23, 1997, Washington, D.C.

Rosof, Patricia J. F. "Beyond Rhetoric." *The History Teacher* 26(4) (1993), pp. 493–97.

Sadker, Myra, and David Sadker. *Failing at Fairness: How America's Schools Cheat Girls* (New York: Scribner's, 1994).

Tompkins, Jane. "Fighting Words: Unlearning to Write the Critical Essay." *Georgia Review* 42 (1988), pp. 585–90.

Tracy, Karen, and Sheryl Baratz. "Intellectual Discussion in the Academy as Situated Discourse." *Communication Monographs* 60 (1993), pp. 300–20.

Wertsch, James V. *Voices of the Mind: A Sociocultural Approach to Mediated Action* (Cambridge, Mass.: Harvard University Press, 1991).

Young, Linda W. L. *Crosswalk and Culture in Sino-American Communication* (Cambridge, England: Cambridge University Press, 1994).

ENGAGING THE TEXT

1. How, according to Tannen, do today's classrooms reflect their origin in Greek philosophy and the Christian universities of the medieval era? What

relationship does Tannen see between the thinking of the early Christian Church and Western science?

2. Explain the distinction that Tannen makes between "formal, objective knowledge" and "relational, intuitive knowledge" (paras. 12–15). How, according to Tannen, do these different understandings of knowledge affect the experiences of male and female students in contemporary college classrooms?

3. What is the "culture of critique" that, in Tannen's view, dominates higher education? To what extent does your experience of schooling support the claim that critical, or Socratic, thinking is taught within an "Adversary Paradigm" in American colleges? Do you agree that "the argument culture" has become so widespread in our society because arguing is "easy to do"?

4. What's wrong, according to Tannen, with the argumentative, or "agonistic," intellectual culture of higher education? How does Tannen suggest we move beyond it? Does Tannen herself move beyond an argumentative approach to critical thinking in this analysis of higher education?

EXPLORING CONNECTIONS

5. Compare Tannen's evaluation of the culture of schooling with that offered by John Taylor Gatto in "The Seven-Lesson Schoolteacher" (p. 173). Which of these views of education and its impact on students more nearly agrees with the experiences you've had in school? How might you account for the differences in Tannen's and Gatto's views of the culture of education?

6. In examining the educational cultures of schools serving students from differing social classes, Jean Anyon (p. 194) describes a "hidden curriculum" that reinforces social class position. Compare Anyon's notion of a hidden curriculum with the one revealed by Tannen in her analysis of education's culture of argument.

7. Explain the *Doonesbury* cartoon on this page in terms of Tannen's discussion of the male-centeredness of American education.

Doonesbury

BY GARRY TRUDEAU

EXTENDING THE CRITICAL CONTEXT

8. Replicate the informal research Tannen assigns her students by observing how frequently adversarial teaching methods are employed in the other classes you are taking. In your observations, describe the type of conflict involved as well as the way that students respond to it. Do your conclusions support or challenge Tannen's analysis of the culture of higher education?

9. In recent years, there has been growing interest in returning to same-sex schooling at all educational levels. Working in groups, debate the advantages and disadvantages of same-sex schools.

10. Read "Girls Rule" by Christina Hoff Sommers in the May 2000 issue of the *Atlantic Monthly* magazine, an article that disputes the claim that the culture of American classrooms encourages educational inequality. Report to the class on Sommers's objections to the position that schools and teachers tend to favor boys over girls. To what extent do you think that teachers and teaching styles generally favor either male or female students in American schools?

The Progressive Basics

FRANCESCA DELBANCO

Nowadays, the idea of "free schools" might seem as dated as the notion of 1960s "love-ins," tie-dyed T-shirts, and Grateful Dead concerts. But as Francesca Delbanco reminds us, the basic principles of progressive education are still alive and well in some of America's top private prep schools. In this bittersweet memoir of her return to the world of experimental education as an up-and-coming reporter for Seventeen Magazine *(January 1999), Delbanco reflects on the vices and virtues of progressive schooling and on the values of the corporate world that it ultimately opposes. Delbanco (b. 1974) graduated from Harvard in 1995 and received her M.F.A. from the University of Michigan in 2000. She currently lives in New York where she continues to write a regular column for* Seventeen. *Her first novel,* Ask Me Anything, *is scheduled for publication in 2004.*

I was raised during the 1970s in a small town in southern Vermont, populated largely by mill workers who lived in trailers and hippies who lived in lean-tos. My parents, who didn't belong comfortably to either category, moved there from New York City to teach at the college that shares the town's name, Bennington. Life in Bennington was a bohemian affair: the town selectman played in the local orchestra, the campus green featured art installations starring students and professors in various states of undress, and the college president grew prize-winning tubers in his patch of community garden. I have a photograph of my mother and father from that era, lying next to each other in a banana-shaped hammock, wearing matching hand-woven serapes. I keep it as proof that even the sanest, most grounded people are susceptible to the occasional vogue.

Anyone who has lived in a university town knows that the prevailing ethos of campus life, whatever it may be, has a trickle-down effect on the rest of the community. There were few residents of Bennington who remained untouched by the creative, avant-garde esprit of the college — even our next-door neighbor, the town pediatrician, converted her garage into a metal-working studio and displayed her work in the waiting room of her office. It was only natural that those liberal ideals of higher learning, the educational values that made "Composition for Nonmusical Sound" and "Body Parts Art" viable concentrations at a degree-granting institution, would filter down to those of us at more elementary stages of our academic careers. When the time came for me to lace up my red Keds and hoist on my first backpack, I reported for duty to the Prospect School, a tiny private school in a three-room farmhouse that billed itself as "an experiment in progressive learning." I have often wondered, in the two decades since that day, what might prompt parents to gamble several thousand dollars and their own child's future on "an experiment."

Here are some of the disciplines on the list of educational priorities at Prospect: woodworking, painting, cooking, sewing, gardening, weaving, small worlds (blocks and dollhouses), animal rearing — practical, pioneer-inspired skills I've come to think of as the "progressive basics." The theory behind the Prospect philosophy was that students learn best when they study what interests them most. Functionally speaking, this was a very sweet deal. I was intensely interested in becoming a professional ballerina at that time, an ambition that my teacher, Dirck, encouraged wholeheartedly, though no one else seemed dazzled by my talent. Dirck seized upon my interest in dance as a natural avenue for me to learn about rhythm (progressive math), choreography (progressive composition), and physical discipline (progressive sports). For me, the main dividend was the right to wear a tutu and ballet slippers to school. Now, in a more strictly regimented environment, such clothing choices might have been discouraged as distracting or disrespectful, but freedom of expression was a cherished value at Prospect. In fact, a boy in my class wore his Halloween costume, a plastic monster mask with a built-in electronic death groan, for six straight weeks.

An average day at Prospect: you arrived in the morning and reported to your group meeting. ("Grades," naturally, were too hierarchical; group divisions were supposedly based on temperament and learning style.) After group meeting came indoor time, followed by snack, then outdoor time and, finally, free play. Alone time was also a prized elective. We were always allowed, at any given moment, to cease whatever we were doing and retreat into the "private room," a closet furnished with pillows, afghans, and an anthology of multicultural fairy tales. Of course, it would have been difficult to evaluate our performance in such abstract subjects as "Dream Sharing," so every semester the teachers sent our parents extensive written comments in lieu of assigning letter grades. (For the record, chilly personality analysis can be just as damning as a mediocre letter grade. Dirck had a way of suggesting that while I excelled in all competitive arenas, I was not the most adept sharer in group one. This critique has haunted me for the past twenty years, and in some small way I feel that I am proving myself to Dirck every time I offer up a bite of my sandwich, or a quarter to make a telephone call.)

The few rules we were required to follow (no bossing anyone around, no shouting, generous use of *please* and *thank you*) Dirck pledged to follow as well, resulting in such gently and grammatically problematic passive-aggressive statements as "Francesca, the bathroom faucet needs to be turned off." Dirck was a mild-mannered believer in absolute democracy. For every unit he taught us, we were invited to teach him something, a practice he gave a Sanskrit name which translated into English as "learning exchange." I spent a good deal of time working with him on arabesques; by the time I moved on to group two, we had worked up a graceful pas de deux.

While our brothers and sisters at Bennington Elementary School had multiplication tables drilled into their brains by rote repetition, we subjects of the Prospect experiment practiced whittling different types of wood. They memorized state capitals; we made artwork out of nonperishables from the school kitchen. They conjugated verb tenses and diagrammed sentences; we learned to feed baby goats from EvenFlo bottles. On the rare occasions where our public school and private school worlds collided, such as the annual Recreation Center Youth Athletic Tournament, we routinely got our asses kicked ("athletics" at Prospect generally required a leotard and a Philip Glass[1] accompaniment). Anyway, competition was not valued or encouraged at our school. Wanting to win was a sign of bad character. We were content just to sit outside and sketch the different varieties of clouds hovering over the playing fields, and to pick edible clover for the next day's snack.

The party ended when I was eight years old. I don't know exactly what spawned my parents' change of heart, but I do remember sitting on my bunk bed one spring night, weaving a God's eye out of Popsicle sticks and yarn, when my mother came into my room and asked me to help her with some long division. I, of course, had never heard of division, much less long division, and what followed was an ugly scene exposing my arithmetical inadequacies. The next fall I was dressed in a kilt and a sweater vest, sitting on a school bus headed across the state border into Massachusetts, to begin my new existence as a prep school girl.

[1] *Philip Glass:* Famous contemporary American composer (b. 1937).

Though I was far behind my new classmates in certain basic skills (such as telling time on a nondigital clock), apparently I had learned something at Prospect, after all: I tested into the grade ahead of my age group, and the administration encouraged my parents to let me skip up. (Incidentally, this was true of the majority of my peers who left Prospect during elementary school: we were almost all invited to skip grades or join the advanced tracks at our new schools.) The transition was disorienting at first — not because of the academic demands so much as the unfamiliar environments of home-work, exams, scores. But Dirck's analysis proved right: I thrived on competi-tion, that black sin of progressivism, and fell in line quickly on the brick paths of my new school campus. I traded in my handmade journal for a college-ruled notebook, wore my hair in a ponytail, gave up ballet, and joined the field hockey team. I learned to speak French, to recite the order of the American presidents, to identify the periodic elements by their sym-bols, and to perform long division. Eventually I matriculated at an Ivy League college and wrote an honors thesis on the Civil War.

The Prospect School shut its doors before I finished college. Just as "the experiment" was perfectly suited to the seventies culture of free-form creativity, it was ill suited to the eighties culture of status-consciousness and demonstrable achievement. Enrollment dwindled, tuition went up, and soon the only people in our town who could afford to send their children there could also afford the fanciest private schools in New England. I felt real regret reading the alumni report that contained the news of closure. While it's easy to tally the tangible opportunities I've gained from my more "prestigious" degrees, part of me has always felt I owe the greatest debt to Prospect.

Those first years of schools are formative ones, and though I can't claim   10
to remember much about stained-glass smelting or chick incubation, I know that my confidence and desire to learn flourished under the vaguely super-visory presence of teachers like Dirck, who believed in standing back and letting us discover our own best talents.

After college, I moved to New York City and got hired as a reporter for *Seventeen,* the monthly magazine read by some 2.5 million teenage girls. The editors sized me up quickly and assigned me to the only beat that had nothing to do with fashion or beauty: a regular feature story called "School Zone." Every month, I traveled with a photographer to a different American high school, interviewed fifty or so kids, and then returned to the office to compose my article about life, school, and culture in such exotic locales at Salt Lake City and Little Rock.

What I discovered, after the initial thrill of striding through the nation's largest schools without a hall pass wore off, is that most American high schools are extraordinarily similar. One town's Mardi Gras Society may be another's Young Farm Association, but the basic curricula, activities, clubs, and social cliques don't vary all that much from place to place, at least not in a way which can be adequately conveyed in an eight-hundred-word column. That broad-spectrum continuity makes sense — after all, we have national educational standards, and national magazines like the one I work for to dictate taste and trends on a countrywide level.

But since my job was to churn out fresh copy for every issue, copy that made tenth grade life in St. Louis, Missouri, seem glamorous and intriguing and worth reading about (and also worth my first-class plane ticket and generous per diem expense account), I began to worry. Month after month, my editor slouched into my office, "School Zone" proofs and grease pencil in hand, begging for something sexier to lead with than yet another state athletic championship or outstanding A.P. program. The solution, I argued to the editor in chief when she summoned me into her office to apprise me of "School Zone"'s flagging ratings was to start profiling different kinds of schools. She looked at me doubtfully, unable to imagine a school sufficiently different from the ones we already covered to breathe life back into the ailing column. Apparently, she hadn't been to Vermont.

My own alma mater may have folded, but plenty of schools around the country still churn out enlightened, self-reliant teenagers who know how to chop firewood *and* multiply fractions, and as soon as I walked out of that meeting, I set about finding one. A short afternoon of research led me to the Putney School, a boarding academy in southern Vermont which is one of the most famous progressive schools in America. Sons and daughters of our nation's intellectual and artistic elite have been bunking in the shabby wooden cabins on the Putney campus since 1935, receiving outstanding educations both inside and outside the classroom. The public relations officer I spoke with seemed thrilled at the prospect of our story, and she sent stacks of glossy brochures featuring Putney students looking through telescopes, riding tractors, working at blackboards, slopping in cow barns, and making sculpture in the metal-working studio. The metal-working studio! Ah, youth!

I should add here that producing a "School Zone" feature — or any   15
multiple-page spread for a commercial magazine — is an elaborate, costly endeavor. Our crews, counting producers, assistants, hairstylists, and makeup artists, never included fewer than six people, and our production budgets climbed easily to five digits every month. For these reasons, the senior members of *Seventeen's* staff were reluctant to green-light any proposal that smacked remotely of "a gamble"; "School Zone" simply cost too much and required too much advance planning to be anything but a guaranteed hit. Which is why I prepared a particularly cogent editorial argument for Putney, emphasizing the intellectual and spiritual rewards I myself had reaped from a similar academic environment, and fervently expressing my desire to share that joy with our readers.

As our crew hauled equipment from commuter plane to rental car, across two-lane New England highways packed bumper to bumper with leaf-peeping tourists, I orated unceasingly on the merits of progressive education. Eyes may have glazed over while I sang the Prospect campfire songs, but nothing could temper my enthusiasm on the homeward-headed pilgrimage. Eventually the landscape, ablaze in its autumnal glory, dulled even the rumblings of urban dissent emanating from the backseat; so did our pit stop for apple cider at the general store in Brattleboro. Pulling up the long dirt drive to the cluster of white farmhouses and red barns on the Putney campus, I felt as if I were being reunited with a dear old friend. I leaped out of the car and went to the main building to announce our arrival. The public relations officer, our administrative contact, greeted me warmly and offered us a tour.

"I should tell you," she said, snapping her down vest as we headed back outside, "some of our students are a bit anxious about your arrival."

This was par for the course, I reassured her. Our school visits always generated a frenzy of adolescent excitement; in Chicago, our car had been surrounded by fans of the magazine hoping for a glimpse of someone famous.

She looked at me placidly. "That won't happen here."

The entrance hall of the first building she led us to, the dining complex,   20
was plastered in pages photocopied from *Seventeen*. Scrawled across each of them, in brightly colored magic marker, were angry slogans: Seventeen Hurts Women; Take Your Superficiality Back to New York; This Magazine Is Capitalist Poison! My eyes widened.

"Something's always being protested around here," she said, waving her hand dismissively.

Inside the dining room, students stood gathered around a table, clad in white T-shirts spray-painted with the words Fuck Seventeen. Some of them had decorated their shirts very creatively indeed, with dyes and beads and interesting bits of collage — probably neat little tailoring tricks they'd learned in sewing class. They turned toward us and stared. After a few moments of mutual gaping, I asked the public relations officer if my producer and I might have a word with her, back in the foyer. We needed to know how much of the student body was against our being there.

"The freedom to express opinions is a right we take very seriously here at Putney," she explained to us in a maddeningly calm voice. More kids in Fuck Seventeen T-shirts paraded to lunch. "Some of our students feel that your magazine's content is in conflict with their ideals. And we value open debate as one of the most fruitful methods of education."

I redefined *value* for her in the terms of the magazine industry, and asked how she suggested we get the cheerful, upbeat story she'd promised us out of a hostile crowd. Fortunately, she'd convened an all-school assembly for that night, at which time we would explain *Seventeen's* mission to the concerned student body.

I bit my tongue. The idea of defending our jobs to a group of wealthy   25
private schoolers caught up in adolescent Marxism would not appeal to the crew. It did not appeal to me, alleged booster of the progressive method.

But there seemed to be no alternative way to proceed. We piled back into our cars and checked into our inn early. I did not call the office to report.

That evening, as kids sprawled all over the couches and floors of the main meeting room, our "open forum" on the Putney story commenced. The students voiced their concerns about fashion magazines, the familiar litany of dangers and damages such publications could inflict on girls' self-esteem. We argued back, citing our intent to include all of them, their real pictures and real words, as proof that we were interested in more than just models and celebrities. It was a debate I'd had many times before, and in truth my own feelings on this subject are more conflicted than they are re-solved. But sitting on my metal folding chair that night, fielding suggestions from a bunch of self-righteous, privileged teenagers on how to make my work more palatable to their tastes, I vowed that my own children, should I ever have any, would attend military school. Faculty members beamed proudly as their intellectual progeny questioned mainstream authority, stu-dents applauded each other for sharing their thoughts and fears, and I re-treated into an elaborate fantasy about the day each of them would get a first job, and have to wear a tie or panty hose and respond politely when commanded to fax out their boss's lunch reservations. The conventions of the real world, of discipline and hierarchy, do not receive much respect or regard in the progressive philosophy. The result is charming in a six-year-old who contributes her own opinion at a dinner table full of adults. It is moderately charming in a twelve-year-old who insists on making her par-ents observe vegetarianism because of her political beliefs. And it is patently uncharming in a group of eighteen-year-olds who do not understand that their talents at sheepshearing and tractor riding are luxuries underwritten by their parents.

We ended the assembly by promising not to harass anyone who didn't want to participate in the story, and immediately the goodwill engendered by compromise surged around the room. Over the next days, every student we approached *did* want to participate in the story — either because we'd defended our mission so articulately, or because at some level *all* teenagers, even the most staunchly antiestablishment ones, can't resist an offer to be interviewed and photographed. The result was a fabulously interesting three days on campus: we heard a choral concert, a cello recital, and a rock band practice, toured the student art galleries, watched a play rehearsal, and ate homemade meals in the dining room. And following in the tradition of the learning exchange, we made our contribution to school life, too: our photographer taught an informal clinic on portraits, the hair and makeup as-sistants let students groom themselves, and I milked a cow for the first time in fifteen years.

By the time we left Putney, I felt more exhausted than I had at the end of any other "School Zone." Partly that was due to the round-the-clock schedule we had to follow in order to capture boarding school life; there was no three P.M. bell to release us to the comfort of our hotel rooms. But mostly, I think, my exhaustion came from spending three straight days with a thorny, intense crowd of teenagers who questioned every choice I made, every quote I wrote down. That degree of intrusive self-confidence never wore off during our visit, and I found myself longing for a dose of the submissive, respectful treatment I was accustomed to receiving at other schools. Self-professed liberal that I am, the seeds of conservatism already blossomed in my twenty-five-year-old heart; apparently I'd spent enough years calling my own teachers "Mr." and "Mrs." to begin to see some merit in those conventions.

Perhaps it's inconsistent to be both an appreciative product of progressivism and a critic of it, but returning to New York to write my column, I felt exactly that way. All that focused, individual attention on each student, all those teachers believing every child who passes through their class might be the artistic or intellectual flower of the next generation, all those exhibits and performances and adult-endorsed shrines to blossoming creativity, can combine to create a class of self-important, coddled adolescents who have no idea what will hit them the minute they leave school. At the risk of sounding like a young old fogy, I do believe a certain amount of competition — even discouragement — can be healthy. I was a terrible ballerina, and while I'm grateful to Dirck for indulging my childhood hobby and boosting my fledgling confidence, I'm equally grateful to the subsequent ballet teacher who blew the whistle on my artless, clumsy form and spared me another decade of believing I could be the next Pavlova. There comes a time when kids need to know the score, need to know they deserve a C in a subject in which they don't pass muster, need to realize the world may not appreciate their poetry or science-fair projects as much as they themselves do. I only began to learn those lessons after I left Prospect but, in moderation, they have served me well. I found it alarming at Putney to meet a group of high school seniors who had been so indulged, and had so little recognition of their own privilege.

But then again, the value of all that attentive indulgence is perfectly evident: the Putney students were confident and curious and well-spoken, they had a strong sense of themselves and a strong sense of what they believed. Once I got over feeling irked by their protest, I admired the way they chose to question *Seventeen*. I've been all across the country on my "School Zone" travels; one rarely encounters teenagers who have the courage to challenge the glossy standards set by fashion magazines. More important, and perhaps more to the point, finding an *administration* that encourages those kinds of challenges is nearly impossible. At any other school I visited, an organized movement to wear profane T-shirts to class would have been squelched with the zeal of a SWAT team. For the most part, large public schools don't have the means or resources to nurture independent thinking of that potentially inconvenient sort: classrooms are

30

crowded, teachers have predetermined material they have to get through in order to meet school requirements, and the kid who wants to take time out to ask why, or to disagree, or to approach work from a different angle is a big pain in the ass. I have, of course, met artistic, unconventional students — the very sort who would flourish at Putney — all over the country, and by and large, they are either reluctantly tolerated, ignored, or, worse, harassed and treated as a threat to institutional order. The urge to drum kids into uniformity has gotten particularly fierce in the recent response to school violence: the rash of strictly regimented dress codes, for example, seems to suggest that every boy in a black coat might be the next Dylan Klebold or Eric Harris.[2] Big schools prize homogeneity for its convenience; the best way to control a crowd is to ensure that it's a like-minded, well-behaved one, and while that's a valuable policy for teachers and administrators, I'm not sure how valuable it is for students. Not every child who wants to wear a black coat, or a hat, or even a profane T-shirt, is in danger of becoming a mass murderer. And even if he were, would forbidding such clothing choices really be the best way to go about saving him?

The progressive system may at times veer too far in the opposite direction, but nurturing the individual *does* deliver intellectual dividends. Kids blossom when they're taught to believe their own ideas count, that they can do more than merely regurgitate facts and ace standardized tests. Those first few years of dancing and singing and exploring led a disproportionate number of my classmates from Prospect to pursue creative careers of one sort or anther — which may account for the paltry alumni contributions that doomed the possibility of a substantial endowment. But what a gift it was, truly, to be paid so much attention as a child, to go to school and have a teacher want *you* to teach *him* something, to have a say in what you're most interested in learning. A certain amount of flakiness may be the inevitable result of such a system, but again, so many of the classrooms I've visited on my "School Zone" route suffer from the opposite: an excess of dull, tired material, an uninspired teacher droning on and on, row after row of glassy-eyed teenagers who can't wait for the bell to ring so they can check their pagers and go to each other's houses to play video games. I read and hear constant laments for the ubiquitousness of teen culture, the hollow pastimes of our nation's youth, their lack of decent values. But mightn't it be the culture of public education that's running our schools down, at least as much as the alleged superficiality of teen culture? Huge public high schools have a ubiquitous, national culture of their own. I've seen it. It's not the best environment for producing creative and reflective young people. And it doesn't do much more than *Seventeen* to encourage individualism, intellectualism, and tolerance of difference. All kids could profit from exposure to the sort of positive, supportive, hands-on school environment that comes

---

[2]*Dylan Klebold or Eric Harris:* Student shooters who killed 13 and then committed suicide at Columbine High School on April 20, 1999, in Littleton, Colorado.

with the progressive philosophy. I understand now, rather better, why my own parents took a gamble on experimental education. When and if my turn comes to bet, I'd place my marker on it, too.

ENGAGING THE TEXT

1. How do the subjects that Delbanco studied at the Prospect School compare with those you encountered in your own elementary education? To what extent would you agree that a student's education should be structured around his or her own personal interests and talents and not around a set body of knowledge or skills that everyone should know?

2. Why was Delbanco shocked by the reception she received when she visited the Putney School for *Seventeen Magazine?* What do you think she and her corporate editors expected? In your view was the response of the Putney students and administration appropriate? Why or why not?

3. How would you characterize Delbanco's attitude toward progressive education? What are its strengths and weaknesses, from her point of view? What features of the Prospect and Putney Schools, if any, would you like to see in all American classrooms? Would you agree that public schools simply don't have the resources to encourage genuine "independent thinking"?

EXPLORING CONNECTIONS

4. How might Michael Moore (p. 153) or John Taylor Gatto (p. 173) respond to the kind of progressive education practiced at the Prospect or Putney Schools? What "lessons" did Delbanco learn from her own progressive school experiences? What lessons does she seem to fear that the relatively privileged students at Putney are learning?

5. To what extent do the progressive schools that Delbanco describes in this selection reflect the features of "executive elite" education as defined by Jean Anyon (p. 194)? Why do you think that many of the wealthiest and most powerful families in America send their children to schools that deemphasize formal instruction and academic competition, and that focus instead on activities like handicrafts and animal husbandry?

6. How do you think Mike Rose (p. 182) or Richard Rodriguez (p. 214) would have fared if they had been sent to either the Prospect or Putney Schools? Would they have thrived as Delbanco did? What factors might have made the transition to progressive schooling difficult for them?

7. Write a brief dialogue between Delbanco and Deborah Tannen (p. 253) on the role of competition and the "culture of critique" in the classroom. How might Tannen assess the level of conflict in the progressive schools that Delbanco describes? To what extent might she see these schools as fostering the kind of intellectual dialogue she hopes will eventually replace the culture of debate? How might Delbanco respond to Tannen's critique of competition in the academy?

EXTENDING THE CRITICAL CONTEXT

8. Do additional research to learn more about the history of the progressive education movement and about other examples of well-known progressive or experimental schools. When did the first progressive schools arise? What philosophical and pedagogical principles are common to most experiments in progressive education? Overall, what's your own assessment of the effectiveness of progressive educational theory?

9. Working in small groups, locate and visit one or more schools in your community that have established a reputation for their progressive principles. To what extent do they resemble the schools Delbanco describes in terms of subject matter, teaching techniques, and attitudes of students, faculty, and administrative staff?

10. Survey popular teen magazines, like *Seventeen Magazine* or *YM*, for regular columns or features on education. In general, how do these magazines depict American schools and student life? What aspects of the classroom experience do they focus on? What messages do they send to their readers about school and schooling? How accurate are the "lessons" that they teach young readers?

The Educated Student: Global Citizen or Global Consumer?

BENJAMIN R. BARBER

Before the terrorist attacks on the World Trade Center and the Pentagon, Benjamin Barber was a respected social scientist with a series of well-received scholarly and popular publications to his credit. After the attacks, he was trumpeted in the media as a prophet who had predicted the inevitable conflict between the "post-modern" culture of Western global capitalism and the more traditional tribal cultures that still dominate much of the Middle East, Asia, and Africa. In the aftermath of 9/11, Barber's Jihad vs. McWorld *(1995) became a touchstone for interpreting the motives behind the al-Qaeda assault on the most famous symbols of American corporate and military power. In this selection written a year later, Barber reflects on how the events of 9/11 have forced us to rethink basic ideas like citizenship and independence and, ultimately, how American schools should respond to the challenges associated with life in a "globalized" world. Barber is the Gershon and Carol Kekst Professor of Civil Society at the University or Maryland and principal of the Democracy Collaborative in New York. His fifteen major publications include* Strong Democracy: Paticipatory Politics for a New Age *and* The Truth of Power: Intellectual Affairs in the Clinton White House *(2001). This selection was excerpted from an address Barber originally delivered to the American Association of Colleges and Universities at its annual meeting in 2002.*

I want to trace a quick trajectory from July 4, 1776 to Sept. 11, 2001. It takes us from the Declaration of Independence to the declaration of interdependence — not one that is actually yet proclaimed but one that we educators need to begin to proclaim from the pulpits of our classrooms and administrative suites across America.

In 1776 it was all pretty simple for people who cared about both education and democracy. There was nobody among the extraordinary group of men who founded this nation who did not know that democracy — then an inventive, challenging, experimental new system of government — was dependent for its success not just on constitutions, laws, and institutions, but dependent for its success on the quality of citizens who would constitute the new republic. Because democracy depends on citizenship, the emphasis then was to think about what and how to constitute a competent and virtuous citizen body. That led directly, in almost every one of the founders' minds, to the connection between citizenship and education.

Whether you look at Thomas Jefferson in Virginia or John Adams in Massachusetts, there was widespread agreement that the new republic, for all of the cunning of its inventive and experimental new Constitution, could not succeed unless the citizenry was well educated. That meant that in the period after the Revolution but before the ratification of the Constitution, John Adams argued hard for schools for every young man in Massachusetts (it being the case, of course, that only men could be citizens). And in Virginia, Thomas Jefferson made the same argument for public schooling for every potential citizen in America, founding the first great public university there. Those were arguments that were uncontested.

By the beginning of the nineteenth century this logic was clear in the common school movement and later, in the land grant colleges. It was clear in the founding documents of every religious, private, and public higher ed-ucation institution in this country. Colleges and universities had to be com-mitted above all to the constituting of citizens. That's what education was about. The other aspects of it — literacy, knowledge, and research — were in themselves important. Equally important as dimensions of education and citizenship was education that would make the Bill of Rights real, education that would make democracy succeed.

It was no accident that in subsequent years, African Americans and then women struggled for a place and a voice in this system, and the key was always seen as education. If women were to be citizens, then women's education would have to become central to suffragism.[1] After the Civil War, African Americans were given technical liberty but remained in many ways in economic servitude. Education again was seen as the key. The struggle over education went on, through Plessy vs. Ferguson[2] in 1896 — separate, but equal — right down to the 1954 Brown vs. Board of Education,[3] which declared separate but equal unconstitutional.

In a way our first 200 years were a clear lesson in the relationship be-tween democracy, citizenship, and education, the triangle on which the freedom of America depended. But sometime after the Civil War with the emergence of great corporations and of an economic system organized around private capital, private labor, and private markets, and with the im-port from Europe of models of higher education devoted to scientific re-search, we began to see a gradual change in the character of American edu-cation generally and particularly the character of higher education in America's colleges and universities. From the founding of Johns Hopkins at the end of the nineteenth century through today we have witnessed the pro-fessionalization, the bureaucratization, the privatization, the commercializa-tion, and the individualization of education. Civics stopped being the enve-lope in which education was put and became instead a footnote on the letter that went inside and nothing more than that.

With the rise of industry, capitalism, and a market society, it came to pass that young people were exposed more and more to tutors other than teachers in their classrooms or even those who were in their churches, their synagogues — and today, their mosques as well. They were increasingly ex-posed to the informal education of popular opinion, of advertising, of mer-chandising, of the entertainment industry. Today it is a world whose mes-sages come at our young people from those ubiquitous screens that define modern society and have little to do with anything that you teach. The large

[1]*suffragism:* The movement to gain women the right to vote.
[2]*Plessy vs. Ferguson:* 1896 Supreme Court case that established the "separate but equal" doctrine of legal discrimination practiced in the South in the form of "Jim Crow" laws until the 1950s.
[3]*Brown vs. Board of Education:* The 1954 Supreme Court case that reversed *Plessy v. Ferguson.*

screens of the multiplex promote content determined not just by Hollywood but by multinational corporations that control information, technology, communication, sports, and entertainment. About ten of those corporations control over 60 to 70 percent of what appears on those screens.

Then, too, there are those medium-sized screens, the television sets that peek from every room of our homes. That's where our children receive not the twenty-eight to thirty hours a week of instruction they might receive in primary and secondary school, or the six or nine hours a week of classroom instruction they might get in college, but where they get anywhere from forty to seventy hours a week of ongoing "information," "knowledge," and above all, entertainment. The barriers between these very categories of information and entertainment are themselves largely vanished.

Then, there are those little screens, our computer screens, hooked up to the Internet. Just fifteen years ago they were thought to be a potential new electronic frontier for democracy. But today very clearly they are one more mirror of a commercialized, privatized society where everything is for sale. The Internet which our children use is now a steady stream of advertising, mass marketing, a virtual mall, a place where the violence, the values — for better or worse — of these same universal corporations reappear in video games and sales messages. Ninety-five to 97 percent of the hits on the Internet are commercial. Of those, 25 to 30 percent are hits on pornographic sites. Most of our political leaders are deeply proud that they have hooked up American schools to the Internet, and that we are a "wired nation." We have, however, in effect hooked up our schools to what in many ways is a national sewer.

In the nineteenth century, Alexis de Tocqueville[4] talked about the "immense tutelary power" of that other source of learning, not education, but public opinion. Now public opinion has come under the control of corporate conglomerates whose primary interest is profit. They are willing to put anything out there that will sell and make a profit.

We have watched this commercialization and privatization, a distortion of the education mission and its content, going to the heart of our schools themselves. Most American colleges and universities now are participants — and in some ways beneficiaries — but ultimately victims of the cola wars. Is your college a Pepsi college or a Coke college? Which do you have a contract with? And which monopoly do your kids have to drink the goods of? While you are busy teaching them the importance of critical choices, they can only drink one cola beverage on this campus. Choice ends at the cafeteria door.

Go to what used to be the food services cafeteria of your local college or university and in many cases you will now find a food court indistinguishable from the local mall featuring Taco Bell, Starbucks, McDonalds, and Burger King. Yes, they are feeding students, but more importantly, they are

10

---

[4]*Alexis de Tocqueville:* French politician and writer (1805–1859), famed for his reflections on American society and culture in *Democracy in America* (volume 1, 1835 and volume 11, 1840).

creating a venue in the middle of campus for what is not education, but an acquisition-of-brands learning. Brand learning means getting young people on board: any merchandiser will tell you, "If we can get the kids when they are in high school and college to buy into our brand, we've got them for life."

Consequences of De-funding

Part of privatization means the de-funding of public institutions, of culture and education, and the de-funding of universities, and so these institutions make a pact with the devil. A real mischief of the modern world (one that colleges haven't yet encountered) is Channel One, which goes into our nation's junior high schools and high schools — particularly the poor ones, those in the inner-city that can't afford their own technology or their own equipment. It makes this promise: "We're not going to give it to you, but we'll lease you some equipment: television sets, maybe a satellite dish, some modems, maybe even a few computers, if you do one thing. Once a day make sure that every student in this school sits in the classroom and watches a very nice little twelve-minute program. Only three minutes of it will be advertising. Let us feed advertising to your kids during a history or a social studies class, and we will lend you some technology."

Most states — New York state is the only one that has held out — in America have accepted Channel One, which is now in over twelve or thirteen thousand high schools around the nation. Our students sit during class time, possibly a social studies or history class, and watch advertising. I dare say, if somebody said they were going to give you some equipment as long as you watch the message of Christ or the church of Christ for three minutes a day, or said they were going to give you some equipment as long as you listen to the message of the Communist Party or the Democratic party during class for three out of twelve minutes, there would be an outcry and an uproar. Totalitarianism! State propaganda! Theocracy! But because they have been so degradingly de-funded, we have allowed our schools to be left without the resources to resist this deal with the devil.

Tell me why it is in the modern world that when a political party or a   15 state takes over the schools and spews its propaganda into them and takes over every sector of society, we call that political totalitarianism and oppose it as the denial of liberty. And when a church or a religion takes over every sector of society and spews its propaganda forth in its schools, we call it theocratic and totalitarian and go to war against it. But when the market comes in with its brands and advertising and takes over every sector of society and spews its propaganda in our schools, we call it an excellent bargain on the road to liberty. I don't understand that, and I don't think we should put up with it, and I don't think America should put up with it. I know the people who sell it would not sit for a minute if their own children, sitting in private schools somewhere, were exposed to that commercial advertising.

They're not paying $25,000 a year to have their kids watch advertising in the classroom. But, of course, it's not their children's schools that are at risk; it's mostly the schools of children of families who don't have much of a say about these things.

Imagine how far Channel One has come from Jefferson's dream, from John Adams's dream, the dream of the common school. And how low we have sunk as a society where we turn our heads and say, "Well, it's not so bad, its not really, it's just advertising." Advertisers know how valuable the legitimizing venue of the classroom is and pay double the rates of prime time to advertise on Channel One, not because the audience is so broad but because it is the perfect target audience and because it gets that extraordinary legitimization of the American classroom where what kids believe you "learn" in your classroom has to be true.

Commercialization and privatization go right across the board. You see them in every part of our society. You see cultural institutions increasingly dependent on corporate handouts. Because we will not fund the arts, the arts, too, like education have to make a profit. In our universities and colleges, scientists are now selling patents and making deals that the research they do will benefit not humanity and their students, but the shareholders of corporations, and so their research will otherwise be kept private. Again, most administrators welcome that because they don't have to raise faculty research budgets. The corporate world will take care of that.

These practices change the nature of knowledge and information. They privatize, making research a part of commercial enterprise. That's the kind of bargain we have made with our colleges and universities. We hope that somehow the faculty will remain insulated from it. We hope the students won't notice, but then when they're cynical about politics and about the administration, and cynical about their own education, and when they look to their own education as a passport to a hot job and big money — and nothing else — we wonder what's going on with them.

But of course students see everything; they have noses for hypocrisy. Students see the hypocrisy of a society that talks about the importance of education and knowledge and information while its very educational institutions are selling their own souls for a buck, and they're doing it because the society otherwise won't support them adequately, is unwilling to tax itself, is unwilling to ask itself for sufficient funds to support quality education. That's where we are. That's where we were on September 10.

What We've Learned

On September 11 a dreadful, pathological act occurred, which nonetheless may act in a brutal way as a kind of tutorial for America and for its educators. On that day, it suddenly became apparent to many people who'd forgotten it that America was no longer a land of independence or sovereignty, a land that could "go it alone." America was no longer capable of surviving as a free democracy unless it began to deal in different terms with a world that for 200 years it had largely ignored and in the last fifty or seventy-five years had treated in terms of that sad phrase "collateral damage." Foreign policy was about dealing with the collateral damage of America being America, America being commercialized, America being prosperous, America "doing well" in the economic sense — if necessary, at everybody else's expense.

September 11 was a brutal and perverse lesson in the inevitability of interdependence in the modern world — and of the end of independence, where America could simply go it alone. It was the end of the time in which making a buck for individuals would, for those that were doing all right, be enough; somehow the fact that the rest of the world was in trouble and that much of America was in trouble — particularly its children (one out of five in poverty) — was incidental. After thirty years of privatization and commercialization, the growing strength of the ideology that said the era not just of government, but of big government was over; that said, this was to be the era of markets, and markets will solve every problem: education, culture, you name it, the markets can do it.

On September 11 it became clear that there were areas in which the market could do nothing: terrorism, poverty, injustice, war. The tragedy pointed to issues of democracy and equality and culture, and revealed a foreign policy that had been paying no attention. In the early morning of September 12, nobody called Bill Gates at Microsoft or Michel Eisner at Disney and said "Help us, would you? You market guys have good solutions. Help us get the terrorists." Indeed, the heroes of September 11 were public officials, public safety officers: policemen, firemen, administrators, even a mayor who found his soul during that period. Those were the ones we turned to and suddenly understood that they played a public role representing all of us.

Suddenly, Americans recognized that its citizens were the heroes. Not the pop singers, fast-ball pitchers, and the guys who make all the money in the NBA; not those who've figured out how to make a fast buck by the time they're thirty, the Internet entrepreneurs. In the aftermath of 9/11, it was particularly those public-official-citizens. All citizens because in what they do, they are committed to the welfare of their neighbors, their children, to future generations. That's what citizens are supposed to do: think about the communities to which they belong and pledge themselves to the public good of those communities.

Hence the importance of the civic professions like teaching. In most countries, in fact, teachers and professors are public officials. They are seen, like firemen and policemen, as guardians of the public good, of the res publica[5], those things of the public that we all care about. On September 11 and the days afterwards, it became clear how important those folks were. As a consequence, a kind of closing of a door occasioned by the fall of the towers became an opening of a window of new opportunities, new possibilities,

---

[5]*res publica:* Latin for "the common good."

new citizenship: an opportunity to explore interdependence. Interdependence is another word for citizenship.

Citizenship in the World

The citizen is the person who acknowledges and recognizes his or her   25
interdependence in a neighborhood, a town, a state, in a nation — and
today, in the world. Anyone with eyes wide open during the last thirty to
forty years has known that the world has become interdependent in in-
eluctable and significant ways. AIDS and the West Nile Virus don't carry
passports. They go where they will. The Internet doesn't stop at national
boundaries; it's a worldwide phenomenon. Today's telecommunications
technologies define communications and entertainment all over the world
without regard to borders. Global warming recognizes no sovereignty, and
nobody can say he or she won't have to suffer the consequences of polluted
air. Ecology, technology, and of course economics and markets are global in
character, and no nation can pretend that its own destiny is any longer in its
own hands in the manner of eighteenth and nineteenth century nations.

In particular, this nation was the special land where independence had
been declared, and our two oceans would protect us from the world. We
went for several hundred years thinking America was immune to the problems and tumult and prejudices of the wars of the world beyond the oceans.
And then 9/11 — and suddenly it became clear that no American could ever
rest comfortably in bed at night if somewhere, someone else in the world
was starving or someone's children were at risk. With 9/11 it became apparent that whatever boundaries once protected us and whatever new borders
we were trying to build including the missile shield (a new technological
"virtual ocean" that would protect us from the world) were irrelevant.

Multilateralism becomes a new mandate of national security, a necessity.
There are no oceans wide enough, there are no walls high enough to protect
America from the rest of our world. What does that say about education? It
means that for the first time a lot of people who didn't care about civic education — the education of citizens, the soundness of our own democracy, the
ability of our children to understand the world — now suddenly recognize
this is key, that education counts. Multicultural education counts because we
have to understand the cultures of other worlds. Language education counts
because language is a window on other cultures and histories.

Citizenship is now the crucial identity. We need to think about what an
adequate civic education means today, and what it means to be a citizen.
We need education-based community service programs. We need experien-
tial learning, not just talking about citizenship but exercises in doing it. We
need to strongly support the programs around the country that over the '80s
and '90s sprang up but have recently been in decline.

But we also need new programs in media literacy. I talked about the
way in which a handful of global corporations control the information chan-

nels of television, the Internet, and Hollywood. We need young people who are sophisticated in media, who understand how media work, how media affect them, how to resist, how to control, how to become immune to media. Media literacy and media studies from my point of view become a key part of how we create a new civic education. Of course history, the arts, sociology, and anthropology, and all of those fields that make young people aware of the rest of the world in a comparative fashion are more important than ever before.

We are a strange place because we are one of the most multicultural   30
nations on Earth with people in our schools from all over the world, and yet we know less than most nations about the world from which those people come. At one and the same time, we are truly multicultural, we represent the globe, and yet we know little about it.

Coming Full Circle

In coming full circle, the trajectory from the Declaration of Independence 200 years ago to the declaration of interdependence that was sounded on September 11 opens an opportunity for us as educators to seize the initiative to make civic education central again. The opportunity to free education from the commercializers and privatizers, to take it back for civic education and for our children, and to make the schools of America and the world the engines of democracy and liberty and freedom that they were supposed to be. And that's not just an abstraction. That starts with addressing commercialization directly: confronting Channel One and the food court at your local college, the malling of your cafeterias, and the sellout of corporate research.

There are things that every one of us can do inside our own colleges and universities. If we do, our students will notice. And if we really make our colleges and universities democratic, civic, independent, autonomous, international, and multilateral again, we will no longer even need civics classes. Our students will take one look at what we've done in the university and understand the relationship between education and democracy. That must be our mission. I hope that as individual citizens, teachers, administrators, you will take this mission seriously. I certainly do, and I know that as before, the future of liberty, the future of democracy in both America and around the world, depends most of all on its educational institutions and on the teachers and administrators who control them. Which means we really are in a position to determine what our future will be.

Engaging the Text

1. What, according to Barber, did the men who founded the United States believe about the role of education in a democratic society? In what ways might education be seen as preparing a person for democratic citizenship?

How effectively has your own education prepared you to participate in democratic government?

2. How did the rise of corporate capitalism change American education, in Barber's view? What has the "corporatization" of higher education done to America's colleges? Would you agree with Barber that we should resist what he calls the "privatization" of knowledge? Why or why not?

3. Why does Barber object to the presence of Channel One in American secondary schools? Would you agree that the presence of advertising in schools amounts to a kind of "corporate totalitarianism"?

4. What does Barber seem to mean by the concept of "citizenship" in this essay? Why has the idea of the citizen become so important to Barber in a post–9/11 world? Would you agree that the events of 9/11 have forced us to replace pride in our independence with the recognition of what Barber terms our "interdependence"? Why or why not?

EXPLORING CONNECTIONS

5. Freewrite an imaginary conversation involving Benjamin Barber, John Taylor Gatto (p. 173), Michael Moore (p. 153), and Francesca Delbanco (p. 273), on the topic of corporate America's influence on education. To what extent would these authors agree on the way that corporations have shaped America's educational institutions and educational culture? Would they likely see this influence as a positive or negative development? Why?

6. To what extent might it be possible to view Malcolm X's self-education (p. 243) as an example of the kind of global education for world citizenship that Barber calls for in this selection? How might Malcolm X's education have prepared him to interpret and even anticipate the events of 9/11?

7. How might Mark Hertsgaard's analysis of U.S. foreign policy (p. 728) challenge Barber's belief that the 9/11 terror attacks have brought about the "end of independence" for America?

EXTENDING THE CRITICAL CONTEXT

8. Research the extent of your college's dependency on corporate capitalism. What evidence of corporate presence can you see around you when you walk through your campus? What corporations provide funding and other forms of support for your college's science labs, arts facilities, or endowed faculty positions? How has the ratio of public to private funding changed for your college over the past fifty years? Overall, would you agree with Barber that your college has been "corporatized" and that it has been "left without the resources to resist this deal with the devil"? Why or why not?

9. Working in groups, make a rough outline of the courses you feel should be required in college to prepare students for participation in a global society. To what extent do you expect your own college education to include this global emphasis?

3

Money and Success

The Myth of Individual Opportunity

Affluence, photo by Steven Weinrebe.

In some ways the world of money and success has been turned upside down in the past few years. At the turn of the century, the American economy was roaring along, dot-com millionaires were a dime a dozen, and the "New Economy" promised continued prosperity without painful recessions. Since then we've witnessed the burst of the Internet bubble, the meltdown of the giant corporation Enron, an old-fashioned recession, and countless personal and corporate bankruptcies. The NASDAQ stock index plummeted 75 percent in three years, wiping out billions of dollars of wealth. Martha Stewart, one of the most spectacularly successful businesswomen in American history, has been indicted for securities fraud, conspiracy, obstruction of justice, and other charges.

Dramatic as these reversals have been, however, the American Dream of individual success has perhaps changed very little: cultural myths about success have deep roots and a long history. Indeed, the dream of individual opportunity has been at home in America since Europeans discovered a "new world" in the Western Hemisphere. Early immigrants like J. Hector St. John de Crèvecoeur extolled the freedom and opportunity to be found in this new land. His glowing descriptions of a classless society where anyone could attain success through honesty and hard work fired the imaginations of many European readers: in *Letters from an American Farmer* (1782) he wrote, "We are all animated with the spirit of an industry which is unfettered and unrestrained, because each person works for himself. . . . We have no princes, for whom we toil, starve, and bleed: we are the most perfect society now existing in the world." The promise of a land where "the rewards of [a man's] industry follow with equal steps the progress of his labor" drew poor immigrants from Europe and fueled national expansion into the western territories.

Our national mythology abounds with illustrations of the American success story. There's Benjamin Franklin, the very model of the self-educated, self-made man, who rose from modest origins to become a renowned scientist, philosopher, and statesman. In the nineteenth century, Horatio Alger, a writer of pulp fiction for young boys—fiction that you will get to sample below—became America's best-selling author with rags-to-riches tales like *Struggling Upward* (1886) and *Bound to Rise* (1873). The notion of success haunts us: we spend millions every year reading about the rich and famous, learning how to "make a fortune in real estate with no money down," and "dressing for success." The myth of success has even invaded our personal relationships: today it's as important to be "successful" in marriage or parenthood as it is to come out on top in business.

But dreams easily turn into nightmares. Every American who hopes to "make it" also knows the fear of failure, because the myth of success inevitably implies comparison between the haves and the have-nots, the achievers and the drones, the stars and the anonymous crowd. Under pressure of the myth, we become engrossed in status symbols: we try to live in the "right" neighborhoods, wear the "right" clothes, eat the "right" foods.

These emblems of distinction assure us and others that we are different, that we stand out from the crowd. It is one of the great paradoxes of our culture that we believe passionately in the fundamental equality of all yet strive as hard as we can to separate ourselves from our fellow citizens.

Steeped in a Puritan theology that vigorously preached the individual's responsibility to the larger community, colonial America balanced the drive for individual gain with concern for the common good. To Franklin, the way to wealth lay in practicing the virtues of honesty, hard work, and thrift: "Without industry and frugality nothing will do, and with them every thing. He that gets all he can honestly, and saves all he gets . . . will certainly become RICH" ("Advice to a Young Tradesman," 1748). And Alger's heroes were as concerned with moral rectitude as they were with financial gain: a benefactor advises Ragged Dick, "If you'll try to be somebody, and grow up into a respectable member of society, you will. You may not become rich,— it isn't everybody that becomes rich, you know,— but you can obtain a good position and be respected." But in the twentieth century the mood of the myth changed. Contemporary guides to success, like Robert Ringer's enormously popular *Looking Out for Number One* (1977), urge readers to "forget foundationless traditions, forget the 'moral' standards others may have tried to cram down your throat . . . and, most important, think of yourself— Number One. . . . You and you alone will be responsible for your success or failure." The myth of success may have been responsible for making the United States what it is today, but it also seems to be pulling us apart. Can we exist as a living community if our greatest value can be summed up by the slogan "Me first"?

The chapter begins with a reading that unambiguously promotes the myth of individual success—an excerpt from Horatio Alger's *Ragged Dick,* a classic nineteenth-century rags-to-riches novel. Next, Harlon Dalton's "Horatio Alger" examines the myth that Alger made popular and finds it not just misleading but "socially destructive." The profile of "Trung Dung" by Dan Rather shows the American Dream in action in the Internet age, as a poor Vietnamese immigrant soars to a level of wealth Ragged Dick never would have imagined.

The next several readings explore the meaning of money, social class, and success from both personal and analytical perspectives. In "Serving in Florida," Barbara Ehrenreich immerses us in working-class life as she recounts her struggle to get by on waitressing wages. "Class in America (2000)," by Gregory Mantsios, points to the overwhelming importance of social class in the United States; what we may want to believe about upward mobility and equal opportunity is everywhere contradicted by Mantsios's stark portrayal of a social and economic system that serves the powerful and wealthy. Next, the oral history of Stephen Cruz, a successful Mexican American engineer, reveals a man pursuing the Dream but gradually becoming disillusioned with it. The Dream is radically redefined in Anne Witte Garland's "Good Noise: Cora Tucker," which presents the story of an

African American activist who measures success in terms of lives saved instead of dollars spent. Finally, psychologist Tim Kasser presents evidence from his book *The High Price of Materialism* that the material goods so many Americans are eagerly pursuing are associated with *reduced* feelings of happiness and well-being.

Kasser's eye-opening argument is followed by the chapter's Visual Portfolio and two short poems. The portfolio captures many of the themes that have been previously introduced—dreams of success, fear of failure, the reality of social class. The poem "From Seven Floors Up," by Sharon Olds, examines a similar idea, namely the distance between affluence and homelessness. Dana Gioia's poem "Money" demonstrates the importance of money in our daily lives by highlighting our obsession with the language of cold, hard cash.

The chapter's final three readings all deal with race and success, but they are remarkably different otherwise. "The Black Avenger," by conservative talk show host Ken Hamblin, downplays the importance of race and celebrates the vitality of the American Dream, specifically its openness to black Americans willing to seize their opportunities. In contrast, Ronald Takaki's "Race at the End of History," as its title indicates, sees race as a fundamental component of myths of success; Takaki challenges the media-created stereotype of the successful Asian American, the "model minority." The chapter closes with Toni Cade Bambara's "The Lesson," a lively story that dramatizes economic inequality by presenting it through the eyes of a group of kids from Harlem who venture uptown to see how the rich live and spend.

Sources

Peter Baida, *Poor Richard's Legacy: American Business Values from Benjamin Franklin to Donald Trump.* New York: William Morrow, 1990.

J. Hector St. John de Crèvecoeur, *Letters from an American Farmer.* New York: Dolphin Books, 1961. First published in London, 1782.

BEFORE READING

- Working alone or in groups, make a list of people who best represent your idea of success. (You may want to consider public and political figures, leaders in government, entertainment, sports, education, or other fields.) List the specific qualities or accomplishments that make these people successful. Compare notes with your classmates, then freewrite about the meaning of success: What does it mean to you? To the class as a whole?

- Keep your list and your definition. As you work through this chapter, reread and reflect on what you've written, comparing your ideas with those of the authors included here.

- Write a journal entry that captures the thoughts of the man pictured in the photo at the beginning of this chapter (p. 293). What feelings or attitudes can you read in his expression, his dress, and his body language? How do you think he got where he is today?

From *Ragged Dick*

HORATIO ALGER

The choice of Horatio Alger to exemplify the myth of individual opportunity is almost automatic. Alger's rags-to-riches stories have become synonymous with the notion that anyone can succeed—even to generations of Americans who have never read one of the books that were best-sellers a century ago. The excerpt below is typical of Alger's work in that it focuses on a young man's progress from a poor background toward "fame and fortune." Alger (1832–1899) published over a hundred such stories; most observers agree that their popularity depended less on their literary accomplishments than on the promises they made about opportunity in America and the rewards of hard work.

Dick now began to look about for a position in a store or counting-room. Until he should obtain one he determined to devote half the day to blacking boots, not being willing to break in upon his small capital. He found that he could earn enough in half a day to pay all his necessary expenses, including the entire rent of the room. Fosdick desired to pay his half; but Dick steadily refused, insisting upon paying so much as compensation for his friend's services as instructor.

It should be added that Dick's peculiar way of speaking and use of slang terms had been somewhat modified by his education and his intimacy with Henry Fosdick. Still he continued to indulge in them to some extent, especially when he felt like joking, and it was natural to Dick to joke, as my readers have probably found out by this time. Still his manners were considerably improved, so that he was more likely to obtain a situation than when first introduced to our notice.

Just now, however, business was very dull, and merchants, instead of hiring new assistants, were disposed to part with those already in their employ. After making several ineffectual applications, Dick began to think he should be obliged to stick to his profession until the next season. But about this time something occurred which considerably improved his chances of preferment.

This is the way it happened.

As Dick, with a balance of more than a hundred dollars in the savings   5
bank, might fairly consider himself a young man of property, he thought himself justified in occasionally taking a half holiday from business, and going on
an excursion. On Wednesday afternoon Henry Fosdick was sent by his employer on an errand to that part of Brooklyn near Greenwood Cemetery. Dick
hastily dressed himself in his best, and determined to accompany him.

The two boys walked down to the South Ferry, and, paying their two
cents each, entered the ferry-boat. They remained at the stern, and stood by
the railing, watching the great city, with its crowded wharves, receding from
view. Beside them was a gentleman with two children,—a girl of eight and
a little boy of six. The children were talking gayly to their father. While he
was pointing out some object of interest to the little girl, the boy managed
to creep, unobserved, beneath the chain that extends across the boat, for
the protection of passengers, and, stepping incautiously to the edge of the
boat, fell over into the foaming water.

At the child's scream, the father looked up, and, with a cry of horror,
sprang to the edge of the boat. He would have plunged in, but, being unable to swim, would only have endangered his own life, without being able
to save his child.

"My child!" he exclaimed in anguish,—"who will save my child? A
thousand—ten thousand dollars to any one who will save him!"

There chanced to be but few passengers on board at the time, and
nearly all these were either in the cabins or standing forward. Among the
few who saw the child fall was our hero.

Now Dick was an expert swimmer. It was an accomplishment which he   10
had possessed for years, and he no sooner saw the boy fall than he resolved
to rescue him. His determination was formed before he heard the liberal
offer made by the boy's father. Indeed, I must do Dick the justice to say
that, in the excitement of the moment, he did not hear it at all, nor would it
have stimulated the alacrity with which he sprang to the rescue of the little
boy.

Little Johnny had already risen once, and gone under for the second
time, when our hero plunged in. He was obliged to strike out for the boy,
and this took time. He reached him none too soon. Just as he was sinking
for the third and last time, he caught him by the jacket. Dick was stout and
strong, but Johnny clung to him so tightly, that it was with great difficulty he
was able to sustain himself.

"Put your arms round my neck," said Dick.

The little boy mechanically obeyed, and clung with a grasp strengthened by his terror. In this position Dick could bear his weight better. But
the ferry-boat was receding fast. It was quite impossible to reach it. The
father, his face pale with terror and anguish, and his hands clasped in sus-
pense, saw the brave boy's struggles, and prayed with agonizing fervor that
he might be successful. But it is probable, for they were now midway of the
river, that both Dick and the little boy whom he had bravely undertaken to

rescue would have been drowned, had not a row-boat been fortunately near. The two men who were in it witnessed the accident, and hastened to the rescue of our hero.

"Keep up a little longer," they shouted, bending to their oars, "and we will save you."

Dick heard the shout, and it put fresh strength into him. He battled   15
manfully with the treacherous sea, his eyes fixed longingly upon the approaching boat.

"Hold on tight, little boy," he said. "There's a boat coming."

The little boy did not see the boat. His eyes were closed to shut out the fearful water, but he clung the closer to his young preserver. Six long, steady strokes, and the boat dashed along side. Strong hands seized Dick and his youthful burden, and drew them into the boat, both dripping with water.

"God be thanked!" exclaimed the father, as from the steamer he saw the child's rescue. "That brave boy shall be rewarded, if I sacrifice my whole fortune to compass it."

"You've had a pretty narrow escape, young chap," said one of the boatmen to Dick. "It was a pretty tough job you undertook."

"Yes," said Dick. "That's what I thought when I was in the water. If it   20
hadn't been for you, I don't know what would have 'come of us."

"Anyhow you're a plucky boy, or you wouldn't have dared to jump into the water after this little chap. It was a risky thing to do."

"I'm used to the water," said Dick, modestly. "I didn't stop to think of the danger, but I wasn't going to see that little fellow drown without tryin' to save him."

The boat at once headed for the ferry wharf on the Brooklyn side. The captain of the ferry-boat, seeing the rescue, did not think it necessary to stop his boat, but kept on his way. The whole occurrence took place in less time than I have occupied in telling it.

The father was waiting on the wharf to receive his little boy, with what feeling of gratitude and joy can be easily understood. With a burst of happy tears he clasped him to his arms. Dick was about to withdraw modestly, but the gentleman perceived the movement, and, putting down the child, came forward, and, clasping his hand, said with emotion, "My brave boy, I owe you a debt I can never repay. But for your timely service I should now be plunged into an anguish which I cannot think of without a shudder."

Our hero was ready enough to speak on most occasions, but always felt   25
awkward when he was praised.

"It wasn't any trouble," he said, modestly. "I can swim like a top."

"But not many boys would have risked their lives for a stranger," said the gentleman. "But," he added with a sudden thought, as his glance rested on Dick's dripping garments, "both you and my little boy will take cold in wet clothes. Fortunately I have a friend living close at hand, at whose house you will have an opportunity of taking off your clothes, and having them dried."

Dick protested that he never took cold; but Fosdick, who had now joined them, and who, it is needless to say, had been greatly alarmed at Dick's danger, joined in urging compliance with the gentleman's proposal, and in the end our hero had to yield. His new friend secured a hack, the driver of which agreed for extra recompense to receive the dripping boys into his carriage, and they were whirled rapidly to a pleasant house in a side street, where matters were quickly explained, and both boys were put to bed.

"I aint used to goin' to bed quite so early," thought Dick. "This is the queerest excursion I ever took."

Like most active boys Dick did not enjoy the prospect of spending half 30
a day in bed; but his confinement did not last as long as he anticipated.

In about an hour the door of his chamber was opened, and a servant appeared, bringing a new and handsome suit of clothes throughout.

"You are to put on these," said the servant to Dick; "but you needn't get up till you feel like it."

"Whose clothes are they?" asked Dick.

"They are yours."

"Mine! Where did they come from?" 35

"Mr. Rockwell sent out and bought them for you. They are the same size as your wet ones."

"Is he here now?"

"No. He bought another suit for the little boy, and has gone back to New York. Here's a note he asked me to give you."

Dick opened the paper, and read as follows, —

"Please accept this outfit of clothes as the first instalment of a debt 40
which I can never repay. I have asked to have your wet suit dried, when you can reclaim it. Will you oblige me by calling to-morrow at my counting room, No. —, Pearl Street.

"Your friend,
"JAMES ROCKWELL."

When Dick was dressed in his new suit, he surveyed his figure with pardonable complacency. It was the best he had ever worn, and fitted him as well as if it had been made expressly for him.

"He's done the handsome thing," said Dick to himself; "but there wasn't no 'casion for his givin' me these clothes. My lucky stars are shinin' pretty bright now. Jumpin' into the water pays better than shinin' boots; but I don't think I'd like to try it more'n once a week."

About eleven o'clock the next morning Dick repaired to Mr. Rockwell's counting-room on Pearl Street. He found himself in front of a large and handsome warehouse. The counting-room was on the lower floor. Our hero entered, and found Mr. Rockwell sitting at a desk. No sooner did that gentleman see him than he arose, and, advancing, shook Dick by the hand in the most friendly manner.

"My young friend," he said, "you have done me so great a service that I wish to be of some service to you in return. Tell me about yourself, and what plans or wishes you have formed for the future."

Dick frankly related his past history, and told Mr. Rockwell of his desire to get into a store or counting-room, and of the failure of all his applications thus far. The merchant listened attentively to Dick's statement, and, when he had finished, placed a sheet of paper before him, and, handing him a pen, said, "Will you write your name on this piece of paper?"

Dick wrote, in a free, bold hand, the name Richard Hunter. He had very much improved his penmanship, as has already been mentioned, and now had no cause to be ashamed of it.

Mr. Rockwell surveyed it approvingly.

"How would you like to enter my counting-room as clerk, Richard?" he asked.

Dick was about to say "Bully," when he recollected himself, and answered, "Very much."

"I suppose you know something of arithmetic, do you not?"

"Yes, sir."

"Then you may consider yourself engaged at a salary of ten dollars a week. You may come next Monday morning."

"Ten dollars!" repeated Dick, thinking he must have misunderstood.

"Yes; will that be sufficient?"

"It's more than I can earn," said Dick, honestly.

"Perhaps it is at first," said Mr. Rockwell, smiling; "but I am willing to pay you that. I will besides advance you as fast as your progress will justify it."

Dick was so elated that he hardly restrained himself from some demonstration which would have astonished the merchant; but he exercised self-control, and only said, "I'll try to serve you so faithfully, sir, that you won't repent having taken me into your service."

"And I think you will succeed," said Mr. Rockwell, encouragingly. "I will not detain you any longer, for I have some important business to attend to. I shall expect to see you on Monday morning."

Dick left the counting-room, hardly knowing whether he stood on his head or his heels, so overjoyed was he at the sudden change in his fortunes. Ten dollars a week was to him a fortune, and three times as much as he had expected to obtain at first. Indeed he would have been glad, only the day before, to get a place at three dollars a week. He reflected that with the stock of clothes which he had now on hand, he could save up at least half of it, and even then live better than he had been accustomed to do; so that his little fund in the savings bank, instead of being diminished, would be steadily increasing. Then he was to be advanced if he deserved it. It was indeed a bright prospect for a boy who, only a year before, could neither read nor write, and depended for a night's lodging upon the chance hospitality of an alley-way or old wagon. Dick's great ambition to "grow up 'spectable" seemed likely to be accomplished after all.

"I wish Fosdick was as well off as I am," he thought generously. But he   60
determined to help his less fortunate friend, and assist him up the ladder as
he advanced himself.

When Dick entered his room on Mott Street, he discovered that some
one else had been there before him, and two articles of wearing apparel had
disappeared.

"By gracious!" he exclaimed; "somebody's stole my Washington coat
and Napoleon pants. Maybe it's an agent of Barnum's, who expects to make
a fortun' by exhibitin' the valooable wardrobe of a gentleman of fashion."

Dick did not shed many tears over his loss, as, in his present circumstances, he never expected to have any further use for the well-worn garments. It may be stated that he afterwards saw them adorning the figure of
Micky Maguire; but whether that estimable young man stole them himself,
he never ascertained. As to the loss, Dick was rather pleased that it had occurred. It seemed to cut him off from the old vagabond life which he hoped
never to resume. Henceforward he meant to press onward, and rise as high
as possible.

Although it was yet only noon, Dick did not go out again with his brush.
He felt that it was time to retire from business. He would leave his share of
the public patronage to other boys less fortunate than himself. That evening
Dick and Fosdick had a long conversation. Fosdick rejoiced heartily in his
friend's success, and on his side had the pleasant news to communicate that
his pay had been advanced to six dollars a week.

"I think we can afford to leave Mott Street now," he continued. "This   65
house isn't as neat as it might be, and I should like to live in a nicer quarter
of the city."

"All right," said Dick. "We'll hunt up a new room tomorrow. I shall
have plenty of time, having retired from business. I'll try to get my reg'lar
customers to take Johnny Nolan in my place. That boy hasn't any enterprise. He needs somebody to look out for him."

"You might give him your box and brush, too, Dick."

"No," said Dick; "I'll give him some new ones, but mine I want to keep,
to remind me of the hard times I've had, when I was an ignorant boot-black,
and never expected to be anything better."

"When, in short, you were 'Ragged Dick.' You must drop that name,
and think of yourself now as" —

"Richard Hunter, Esq.," said our hero, smiling.   70

"A young gentleman on the way to fame and fortune," added Fosdick.

ENGAGING THE TEXT

1. List the values, characteristics, and actions that help Ragged Dick succeed.
   How valuable do you consider these today? How important is virtue compared to good luck — in the story and in your own experience?

2. Skim the Alger selection to find as many mentions of money as you can. How frequent are they? What seem to be Alger's ideas about money, wealth, salaries, and other financial issues?

3. By the time we reach the end of this story, quite a few things have changed from the time Dick "was an ignorant boot-black, and never expected to be anything better" (para. 68). Working in small groups, list as many changes as you can. What seems to be Alger's attitude toward them?

4. Why is Alger careful to note that Dick does not hear Mr. Rockwell's offer of $10,000 to whoever would save Little Johnny? Is Dick being short-changed by getting a job and clothes but not a $10,000 reward?

EXPLORING CONNECTIONS

5. Look ahead to "Horatio Alger" by Harlon L. Dalton below. Does Dalton's analysis of the Alger myth change your understanding of this excerpt? Explain. What elements in this story might Dalton cite to support his claims?

6. Read "Looking for Work" by Gary Soto (p. 26). Compare and contrast Alger's ideas about work, money, and aspiration to those found in Soto's narrative.

EXTENDING THE CRITICAL CONTEXT

7. Dick considers himself a "young man of property" when he has $100 in the bank. Talk to classmates and see if you can reach any consensus about what it would take today to be a "young man or woman of property." Similarly, see if you can agree on what a good starting salary would be for a recent college graduate, or on what levels of wealth and income define the poor, the middle class, and the upper class in the United States today. Write a note summarizing your conclusions and keep it for reference as you read the rest of this chapter.

8. If you did the first "Before Reading" assignment on page 296, compare and contrast the qualities that made the people on your list successful with the qualities Alger gives to Ragged Dick.

Horatio Alger

HARLON L. DALTON

The preceding selection dramatizes the American Dream coming true in an uncomplicated if rather contrived way: the ambitious young "Ragged Dick" determines to improve himself, works hard, seizes his opportunity, and quickly makes his way to "fame and fortune." This piece by Harlon L. Dalton (b. 1947) questions that myth, calling it not only false, but worse — "socially destructive." Using Alger as his prime example, Dalton systematically explains how the rags-to-riches myth can conceal important social realities like race and class. Dalton is a professor at Yale Law School and has published extensively on AIDS and the law. He has served on the board of directors for the American Civil Liberties Union since 1995 and was a member of the National Commission on AIDS. "Horatio Alger" is taken from his book Racial Healing: Confronting the Fear Between Blacks and Whites *(1995).*

Ah, Horatio Alger, whose name more than any other is associated with the classic American hero. A writer of mediocre fiction, Alger had a formula for commercial success that was simple and straightforward: his lead characters, young boys born into poverty, invariably managed to transcend their station in life by dint of hard work, persistence, initiative, and daring.[1] Nice story line. There is just one problem — it is a myth. Not just in the sense that it is fictional, but more fundamentally because the lesson Alger conveys is a false one. To be sure, many myths are perfectly benign, and more than a few are salutary, but on balance Alger's myth is socially destructive.

The Horatio Alger myth conveys three basic messages: (1) each of us is judged solely on her or his own merits; (2) we each have a fair opportunity to develop those merits; and (3) ultimately, merit will out. Each of them is, to be charitable, problematic. The first message is a variant on the rugged individualism ethos. . . . In this form, it suggests that success in life has nothing to do with pedigree, race, class background, gender, national origin, sexual orientation — in short, with anything beyond our individual control. Those variables may exist, but they play no appreciable role in how our actions are appraised.

This simply flies in the face of reality. There are doubtless circumstances — the hiring of a letter carrier in a large metropolitan post office, for example — where none of this may matter, but that is the exception rather than the rule. Black folk certainly know what it is like to be favored, disfavored, scrutinized, and ignored all on the basis of our race. Sometimes we are judged on a different scale altogether. Stephen Carter has written movingly about what he calls "the best black syndrome," the tendency of White folk to judge successful Black people only in relation to each other rather than against all comers. Thus, when Carter earned the second-highest score in his high school on the National Merit Scholarship qualifying test, he was readily recognized as "the best Black" around, but somehow not seen as one of the best students, period.[2]

---

[1]Edwin P. Hoyt, *Horatio's Boys: The Life and Works of Horatio Alger, Jr.* (Radnor, Penn.: Chilton Book Company, 1974). [All notes are Dalton's.]

[2]Stephen L. Carter, *Reflections of an Affirmative Action Baby* (New York: Basic Books, 1991), 47–49.

Although I would like to think that things are much different now, I know better. Not long ago a student sought my advice regarding how to deal with the fact that a liberal colleague of mine (and of Stephen Carter's) had written a judicial clerkship recommendation for her in which he described her as the best Black student to have ever taken his class. Apparently the letter caused a mild stir among current law clerks in several courthouses, one of whom saw fit to inform the student. "What was the professor [whom she declined to name] thinking of?" she wondered aloud. "What does his comment mean? What is a judge supposed to make of it? 'If for some reason you think you have to hire one of them, then she's the way to go'? I could understand if he said I was one of the top ten students or even the top thousand, but what does the 'best Black' mean?"

Black folk also know what it is like to be underestimated because of the   5
color of their skin. For example, those of us who communicate in standard English are often praised unduly for how well we speak. This is, I might add, an experience all too familiar to Asian-Americans, including those born and bred in the U.S.A. And we know what it is like to be feared, pitied, admired, and scorned on account of our race, before we even have a chance to say boo! We, in turn, view White people through the prism of our own race-based expectations. I honestly am surprised every time I see a White man who can play basketball above the rim, just as Puerto Ricans and Cubans tend to be surprised to discover "Americans" who salsa truly well. All of which is to say that the notion that every individual is judged solely on personal merit, without regard for sociological wrapping, is mythical at best.

The second message conveyed by Horatio Alger is that we all have a shot at reaching our true potential. To be fair, neither Alger nor the myth he underwrote suggests that we start out equal. Nor does the myth necessarily require that we be given an equal opportunity to succeed. Rather, Alger's point is that each of us has the power to create our own opportunities. That turns out to be a difficult proposition to completely disprove, for no matter what evidence is offered up to show that a particular group of people have not fared well, it can always be argued that they did not try hard enough, or that they spent too much time wallowing in their predicament and not enough figuring out how to rise above it. Besides, there are always up-by-the-bootstraps examples to point to, like Colin Powell, whose name has so frequently been linked with that of Horatio Alger's that he must think they are related.[3] Nevertheless, it is by now generally agreed

[3]Sandy Grady, "Will He or Won't He?: Win or Lose, Presidential Pursuit by Colin Powell Would Do America a Necessary Service," *Kansas City Star,* 24 April 1995; Thomas B. Edsall, "For Powell, Timing Could be Crucial: As Gulf War Hero Hints at 1996 Bid, Associates Look into Details," *Washington Post,* 6 April 1995; J. F. O. McAllister, "The Candidate of Dreams," *Time,* 13 March 1995; Deroy Murdock, "Colin Powell: Many Things to Many People," *Washington Times,* 16 January 1995; Doug Fischer, "U.S. Politics: War Hero Well-Placed to Become First Black President," *Ottawa Citizen,* 8 October 1994; "General Nice Guy: Profile Colin Powell," *Sunday Telegraph,* 25 September 1994; Otto Kreisher, "As a Civilian, Powell's Options Are Enviable," *San Diego Union-Tribune,* 26 September 1993.

that there is a large category of Americans—some have called it the under-class—for whom upward mobility is practically impossible without massive changes in the structure of the economy and in the location of public re-sources.

As for the notion that merit will out, it assumes not only a commitment to merit-based decision making but also the existence of standards for mea-suring merit that do not unfairly favor one individual over another. Such standards, of course, must come from somewhere. They must be decided upon by somebody. And that somebody is rarely without a point of view. Ask a devotee of West Coast basketball what skills you should look for in re-cruiting talent and near the top of his list will be the ability to "get out on the break," to "be creative in the open court," and "to finish the play." On the other hand, ask someone who prefers East Coast basketball and her list will rank highly the ability "to d-up [play defense]," "to board [rebound]," and "to maintain focus and intensity."

Or, to take another example, what makes a great Supreme Court jus-tice? Brains to spare? Common sense? Proper judicial temperament? Politi-cal savvy? Extensive lawyering experience? A well-developed ability to ab-stract? Vision? Well-honed rhetorical skills? A reverence for our rich legal heritage? The capacity to adapt to changing times? Even if one is tempted to say "all of the above," how should these (or any other set of characteris-tics) be ranked? Measured? Evaluated?

The answers depend in part on whom you ask. Practicing lawyers, for example, are probably likely to rank extensive lawyering experience more highly than, say, brains. They are also likely to pay close attention to judicial temperament, which for them means whether the prospective justice would be inclined to treat them with respect during a court appearance. Sitting judges are also likely to rank judicial temperament highly, meaning whether the prospective justice would be a good colleague. In choosing among the other characteristics, they might each favor the ones that they happen to possess in abundance. Politicians might well see more merit in political savvy than would, say, academics, who could be expected to favor brains, the ability to abstract, and perhaps rhetorical skills.

All of these relevant actors might be honestly trying to come up with appropriate standards for measuring merit, but they would arrive at markedly different results. And any given result would screen out people who would succeed under another, equally plausible set of standards. Thus, if there is a genuine commitment to merit-based decision making it is pos-sible that merit will out, but only for those who have the right kind of merit.

Which brings us to the prior question: is merit all we care about in de-ciding who gets what share of life's goodies? Clearly not. Does anyone, for example, honestly believe that any Supreme Court justice in recent memory was nominated solely on the basis of merit (however defined)? Any Presi-dent? Any member of Congress? Does anyone believe that America's health-care resources are distributed solely on merit? That tax breaks are

10

THE BOONDOCKS   by **AARON MCGRUDER**

distributed solely on merit? That baseball club owners are selected solely on merit?

As I suggested earlier, the mere fact that a myth is based on false premises or conveys a false image of the world does not necessarily make it undesirable. Indeed, I place great stock in the idea that some illusions are, or at least can be, positive. As social psychologist Shelley Taylor has observed, "[normal] people who are confronted with the normal rebuffs of everyday life seem to construe their experience [so] as to develop and maintain an exaggeratedly positive view of their own attributes, an unrealistic optimism about the future, and a distorted faith in their ability to control what goes on around them."[4] Taylor's research suggests that, up to a point, such self-aggrandizement actually improves one's chances of worldly success.[5]

This may well explain the deep appeal of the Horatio Alger myth. True or not, it can help to pull people in the direction they want to go. After all, in order to succeed in life, especially when the odds are stacked against you, it is often necessary to first convince yourself that there is a reason to get up in the morning. So what is my beef? Where is the harm?

In a nutshell, my objection to the Alger myth is that it serves to maintain the racial pecking order. It does so by mentally bypassing the role of race in American society. And it does so by fostering beliefs that themselves serve to trivialize, if not erase, the social meaning of race. The Alger myth encourages people to blink at the many barriers to racial equality (historical, structural, and institutional) that litter the social landscape. Yes, slavery was built on the notion that Africans were property and not persons; yes, even after that "peculiar institution" collapsed, it continued to shape the life prospects of those who previously were enslaved; yes, the enforced illiteracy and cultural disruption of slavery, together with the collapse of Reconstruction, virtually assured that the vast majority of "freedmen" and "freedwomen" would not be successfully integrated into society; yes, Jim Crow

[4]Shelley E. Taylor, *Positive Illusions: Creative Self-Deception and the Healthy Mind* (New York: Basic Books, 1989), xi.
[5]Ibid., xi, 7, 228–46.

laws, segregation, and a separate and unequal social reality severely undermined the prospects for Black achievement; yes, these and other features of our national life created a racial caste system that persists to this day; yes, the short-lived civil rights era of the 1950s and 1960s was undone by a broad and sustained White backlash; yes, the majority of Black people in America are mired in poverty; yes, economic mobility is not what it used to be, given the decline in our manufacturing and industrial base; yes, the siting of the illicit drug industry in our inner cities has had pernicious effects on Black and Latino neighborhoods; yes, yes, yes, BUT (drumroll) "all it takes to make it in America is initiative, hard work, persistence, and pluck." After all, just look at Colin Powell!

There is a fundamental tension between the promise of opportunity enshrined in the Alger myth and the realities of a racial caste system. The main point of such a system is to promote and maintain inequality. The main point of the Alger myth is to proclaim that everyone can rise above her station in life. Despite this tension, it is possible for the myth to coexist with social reality. To quote Shelley Taylor once again:

> [T]he normal human mind is oriented toward mental health and . . . at every turn it construes events in a manner that promotes benign fictions about the self, the world, and the future. The mind is, with some significant exceptions, intrinsically adaptive, oriented toward overcoming rather than succumbing to the adverse events of life. . . . At one level, it constructs beneficent interpretations of threatening events that raise self-esteem and promote motivation; yet at another level, it recognizes the threat or challenge that is posed by these events.[6]

Not surprisingly, then, there are lots of Black folk who subscribe to the Alger myth and at the same time understand it to be deeply false. They live with the dissonance between myth and reality because both are helpful and healthful in dealing with "the adverse events of life." Many Whites, however, have a strong interest in resolving the dissonance in favor of the myth. Far from needing to be on guard against racial "threat[s] or challenge[s]," they would just as soon put the ugliness of racism out of mind. For them, the Horatio Alger myth provides them the opportunity to do just that.[7]

Quite apart from the general way in which the myth works to submerge the social realities of race, each of the messages it projects is also incompatible with the idea of race-based advantage or disadvantage. If, as the myth suggests, we are judged solely on our individual merits, then caste has little practical meaning. If we all can acquire the tools needed to reach our full potential, then how important can the disadvantage of race be? If merit will eventually carry the day, then shouldn't we be directing our energies toward

15

[6]Ibid., xi.
[7]Robert T. Carter, et al., "White Racial Identity Development and Work Values," *Journal of Vocational Behavior, Special Issue: Racial Identity and Vocational Behavior* 44, no. 2 (April 1994): 185–97.

encouraging Black initiative and follow-through rather than worrying about questions of power and privilege?

By interring the myth of Horatio Alger, or at least forcing it to coexist with social reality, we can accomplish two important goals. First, we can give the lie to the idea that Black people can simply lift themselves up by their own bootstraps. With that pesky idea out of the way, it is easier to see why White folk need to take joint ownership of the nation's race problem. Second, the realization that hard work and individual merit, while certainly critical, are not guarantors of success should lead at least some White people to reflect on whether their own achievements have been helped along by their preferred social position.

Finally, quite apart from race, it is in our national interest to give the Horatio Alger myth a rest, for it broadcasts a fourth message no less false than the first three—that we live in a land of unlimited potential. Although that belief may have served us well in the past, we live today in an era of diminished possibilities. We need to make a series of hard choices, followed by yet more hard choices regarding how to live with the promise of less. Confronting that reality is made that much harder by a mythology that assures us we can have it all.

ENGAGING THE TEXT

1. The first message communicated by the Alger myth, according to Dalton, is that "each of us is judged solely on her or his own merits" (para. 2). What does this message mean to Dalton, and why does he object to it? How does he make his case against it, and what kind of evidence does he provide? Explain why you agree or disagree with his claim that this first message "simply flies in the face of reality" (para. 3).

2. Dalton says it is "generally agreed," but do *you* agree that "there is a large category of Americans . . . for whom upward mobility is practically impossible" (para. 6)? Why or why not?

3. How persuasive do you find Dalton's claims that American society is far from operating as a strictly merit-based system?

4. Why does Dalton believe that the Alger myth is destructive? Do you think the power of the American Dream to inspire or motivate people is outweighed by the negative effects Dalton cites, or vice versa? Write a journal entry explaining your position.

EXPLORING CONNECTIONS

5. Test Dalton's claims against the actual excerpt from Horatio Alger's *Ragged Dick* (p. 297). For example, does the novel seem to match the formula Dalton summarizes in his first paragraph? Similarly, can you find in the novel any examples of the three messages Dalton identifies in his second paragraph? On balance, does the excerpt from Alger seem to promote ideas that you consider socially destructive? Why or why not?

6. What ideas and attitudes about success are expressed in the cartoon by Aaron McGruder on page 307, and how do they compare and contrast with the myth of success as embodied by Ragged Dick (p. 297)? How might Harlon Dalton explain the humor of the cartoon?

7. Look ahead to the next reading, the modern-day success story of Trung Dung below. How do you think Dalton would respond to Trung's story, which may seem to some readers to validate the Horatio Alger myth?

EXTENDING THE CRITICAL CONTEXT

8. Pick a few contemporary cultural heroes like Colin Powell, Tiger Woods, and Oprah Winfrey. Conduct a minipoll about what their success means to race relations in the United States. Do the responses you get support Dalton's contention that such heroes encourage people "to blink at the many barriers to racial equality" (para. 14)?

9. Dalton argues that the Alger myth should be buried, or, to use his word, "interred." Supposing for the moment that you agree, how could that be accomplished? How is a cultural myth challenged, revised, or robbed of its mythic power?

Trung Dung
DAN RATHER

A century ago, the hero of a Horatio Alger rags-to-riches story might be happy to get a new suit of clothes, a respectable job, and a generous wage. Trung Dung, a contemporary embodiment of the myth, rose from humble beginnings to earn a Ph.D., found his own companies, and make hundreds of millions of dollars. Trung's spectacular success was powered by some of the key elements of the American Dream—education, hard work, and ambition. Does his story validate the myth? Dan Rather (b. 1931), anchor of the CBS Evening News *and* 48 Hours, *is one of America's best-known journalists. His books include* The Camera Never Blinks: Adventures of a TV Journalist *(1977);* The Palace Guard *(1974), coauthored with Gary Paul Gates; and* The American Dream: Stories from the Heart of Our Nation *(2001), in which "Trung Dung" appears.*

The term "Internet millionaire" fast became a cliché in a society obsessed with the "new economy." Internet millionaires were for a time our hottest business heroes, their youthful image and cutting-edge, casual glamour fueling countless American dreams of avarice. But, like all stereotypes, this one obscured the individuals behind it. In San Francisco, a virtual stone's throw from Silicon Valley, there's an Internet millionaire named Trung Dung (pronounced "Young"), who doesn't at all fit the mold of the Brioni jacket–wearing man-child eternally at play.

Thirty years ago, when Saigon fell and the book closed on America's longest war, Trung Dung was an eight-year-old boy living in Vietnam. The images of those final days, of the last helicopters evacuating Americans and South Vietnamese dependents, are deeply etched into our national consciousness. Trung Dung and his family were not on one of those helicopters.

Trung's family had lived in relative stability in wartime Vietnam. His father had been a politician before the war and had served as an officer in the South Vietnamese army. Once the new regime took over in the south, however, Trung's world crumbled around him. His father was sent to a labor camp. All of the family's property was confiscated. And Trung, his mother, grandmother, and two sisters were left to fend for themselves as pariahs in the new communist state.

There was no work for the wife of a former enemy, but there was the underground economy. Trung's mother bought simple goods, such as clothing and appliances, in Saigon and sold them for a small profit in the family's hometown of Phan Thiet. In Phan Thiet, she in turn bought fish sauce for a fraction of the "official" price in Saigon and was able to sell it there; and so this former housewife gradually became a merchant. "These were very heavy things and the transportation was by bus," Trung remembers. "It was a very tough life for her, and so, being the only son in the house, I had to step up from early on to help out."

This only son was only in the fifth grade, but he still found ways to contribute. Trung caught fish after classes and sold them in the evenings. At school he sold fruit to his classmates in between classes on Marxist theory. As he got older, he built and repaired bikes with scavenged parts. Trung's small enterprises were thoroughly illegal in the new Vietnam . . . and crucial to his family's survival.

Trung's family was able to get by with a combination of hard work and ingenuity, but Trung wanted something more. He dreamed of pursuing higher education. Looking around him, he began to see that he would not be able to reach his dream in his homeland. "By '78, the height of the boat people escaping Vietnam, we realized that I can never get into school, into university, because of my background," Trung recalls. His father was still in a labor camp, and there was no sign that he would ever be released. "The only way to have a future was to get out."

The family directed its efforts toward saving for Trung's escape. If he could establish himself somewhere else, they thought, maybe the rest of the family could join him later.

In 1982, the day finally came. After selling all their furniture, jewelry, trinkets, extra clothes, and everything else not already confiscated by the government, Trung's family had five ounces of gold—enough to pay a smuggler to take him down the Tien Giang branch of the Mekong River and across the sea to a friendly country. Trung's mother sent him off with a tenth of an ounce of gold—about fifty dollars—to start a new life, and he joined a group in a shack by the river to wait for a boat that never came.

"The boat never showed up, and the local police came in the morning," Trung remembers. "They took me in for a day and questioned me about who was organizing all this stuff. I told them I ran away from home and just saw these people waiting. I didn't want to implicate my mother. They gave me a few slaps and released me."

Today Trung laughs about his unexpected homecoming, but at the time it was deadly serious. "I went back to school and went back home—normal, but now we [had] lost everything." Everything, that is, but the dream of a better life for Trung. A year later, they found a more reliable boat at a cheaper price. The few belongings they hadn't sold for the first attempt they exchanged for gold. And again Trung waited by the river. 10

The boat left on schedule, but only ten minutes into the voyage, a patrol boat appeared as if from nowhere and opened fire. "They were shooting because they didn't want anyone to jump into the river. We had to lie on the deck. It was really traumatic." To make matters worse, Trung realized as shots whizzed over his head that he wouldn't get off as easy as he had the first time. "This time I was fifteen, and so they put me in this hard-core jail, where all the hard-core criminals live, and I stayed there for a month. That was a very interesting experience in itself."

By the time he got out, Trung found that his mother had worked her way into the underworld of refugee smugglers. She was now a middleman, connecting families with boat owners. It was an incredibly risky business, as Trung's own experiences had shown. And when such arrangements go wrong, it's generally the middleman who gets caught holding the bag.

Trung's mother wasn't profiting from the risk, though. Her commissions went toward getting another place on another boat for her son. As Trung says now, with considerable gratitude, "She put her life on the line for me."

Her efforts finally paid off in 1984. Trung's third try seemed to be a charm, as he successfully boarded a boat that took him and about forty other escaping Vietnamese to an Indonesian offshore drilling rig, and from there officials took the group to a refugee camp. He was out, and he knew why: "My mother had absolute confidence in me, and I cannot even imagine what she went through. Imagine a housewife raising three young kids in a very hostile environment and then [having] to take care of the grandmother and a husband in jail. How she managed to do all that and make sure we are in school and do well in school. . . . And she's personally responsible for me getting out here. It's mind-boggling to me. I have no idea how she did it."

Once he was out, it was as if the baton had passed to Trung. Responsi- 15
bility for carving out a place for his family in a new country was entirely on
his seventeen-year-old shoulders. Luckily, he wasn't alone. One day, as he
bided his time in the refugee camp, his elder sister stepped off a boat of
new arrivals. Their mother was still at work.

It took a year for Trung and his sister to gain admittance to the United
States as children of former allies. Trung says they picked Louisiana because of the climate—reminiscent of home—but something went wrong
down the bureaucratic line. "When I got off the plane," Trung remembers,
"I realized I was in Boston." No matter. Trung knew that there were schools
in Boston as well, and that's where he went, just days after his arrival.

Trung had learned some English in Vietnam and in the camp, but not
enough to join a class of his contemporaries. A high school counselor told
him that he would need to take two to three years of classes to earn a
diploma. This was unacceptable. "I knew my mother was in pretty bad
shape, so I asked around and a counselor at the University of Massachusetts
said he could help me get admitted if I took the GED." He did and passed
by the slimmest of margins: "Pure luck. I think I did well enough on the
math and science part to pass."

Trung started to learn, slowly, that he could safely raise his expectations
in his adopted country. He could work. He could get scholarships and student loans. He could become a college student. Although his situation was
bleak—he shared an apartment with other immigrants who slept three to a
room and worked as a janitor in a hospital and a dishwasher in a restaurant
in order to send money home—he sensed opportunity in the air and
breathed deeply. "I took twice the normal load of classes, too. I don't know
how I did it, but at the same time there was so much to do."

Just months earlier, Trung had seen a computer for the first time in the
refugee camp. He even remembers the model—an old Apple II. He had
never even used a pocket calculator before he took his first computer class
at the University of Massachusetts at Boston, but he knew as soon as he
dove in that his future would be in programming.

Why was this former refugee from an undeveloped country drawn so 20
strongly to computer science? This was, remember, well before the Internet
boom. Perhaps it was a matter of control. Programming gave Trung absolute control over a complex and expensive machine—a stark contrast to
the helplessness he had felt in a childhood where others determined his
fate. But beyond that, he says, programming gave him a way to express himself clearly and unambiguously. In computers, Trung found a bridge across
the language barrier. As he puts it, "The way people program is to articulate, as if to a young child. It's very simple stuff, but you can accomplish
very complex things. That's why I enjoy it."

Trung graduated in 1988 at the top of his class. In three years he had
taken every undergraduate and almost every graduate course in computer

science that the university had to offer. He had fulfilled his childhood dream . . . and he was immediately presented with a serious choice.

"I was offered a job and also offered a chance to study for the Ph.D. program at Boston University. A Ph.D. was an unimaginable dream, because when I was in school, people who had the Ph.D. were like gods to me, beyond what I could even think of." A job, on the other hand, would have allowed Trung to send more money home. His mother and his father, still in prison, both wrote Trung urging him to take the scholarship. The slightly better life the extra money would have afforded them was not as important to his mother and father as the opportunity before their son.

Trung's parents didn't realize it at the time, but a better life was just around the corner. In 1990, as relations between the United States and Vietnam warmed, Trung's father was released from prison and the entire family was allowed to immigrate to the United States. A joyous reunion was in the making. "When I left the country, my younger sister was a little girl. Now she was almost twenty. And my father, I didn't even remember what he looked like. It was wonderful. It was the first time since 1975 that the whole family [was] together in one place. For the first few days all we did was talk.

The son they had sent abroad was already a success in his parents' eyes, but the addition of three new family members into Trung's small, run-down Dorchester apartment forced him to reconsider academic life. Just short of completing his thesis, Trung left the Ph.D. program and joined a promising e-commerce company. Before long, he had saved enough to buy his family a house.

Trung's goals were still very modest. He could see his life moving for- 25 ward methodically, in the risk-free, traditional manner favored by his father. But with the emergence of the Internet as a popular medium, Trung again found himself at a crossroads. Should he enter the high-risk, high-return world of start-ups and IPOs or stay on the steady career path that would guarantee his family's well-being?

By day, Trung dutifully performed his role as company man. But in the evenings, he played with a piece of revolutionary programming. The idea came while he was building a contact list of refugees for a local Vietnamese temple's Web site. After he got tired of searching for common Vietnamese names, cutting them from various sites, and pasting them onto the list, he automated the process. This meant that a visitor to the temple's Web site could run a complicated search with a few simple clicks, without leaving the Web site.

This technology, now common, had commercial applications that Trung could see even before "e-commerce" was a household word. Businesses don't want viewers to leave their Web site. Trung's application pulls information from other sources and organizes it in a user-friendly manner so they don't have to. That makes it extremely valuable.

But the company Trung worked for, Open Market, couldn't see that far ahead: "It was way too early. The Internet was too young for that kind of idea." Besides, this start-up didn't seem to need it. Their initial public offering in early 1996 was an early success, and Trung's stock options soared to a value of over one million dollars.

This should have been a happy time, but fate had dealt the household a heavy blow. Trung's mother was dying of cancer. "I guess a lot of the hardworking years caught up to her," he says. Her illness brought the family closer together, and Trung spent countless hours by her bed, where he told her about his idea. "She was in a lot of pain. So I kept talking to take her mind away from the pain. I talked to her about all these dreams, about the difficulty I was having persuading the Open Market people to try to adopt my idea. And maybe I should go out on my own and pursue my idea. She was always very supportive, but at the time I didn't believe I could do it."

The day Trung's mother passed away, he knew that he had to start his own company. It really didn't matter that he was leaving a million dollars in stock options behind. "I considered having a hundred thousand dollars very, very rich. But the more I talked to my mother the more she said go and do it. So I made up my mind that I had to do it. All I could think about was that idea."

A former classmate put Trung in touch with a prominent venture capitalist who found him a business partner in technology pioneer Mark Pine. Their instant rapport led to a partnership, with Mark as CEO and Trung as chief technology officer. Trung flew to California and lived in Mark's pool house while he expanded on his initial idea. After four rounds of financing, they raised $35 million. OnDisplay went public in December 1999, pushing the value of Trung's share over $100 million. Trung gave his sisters stock worth more than $20 million each.

What did $100 million mean to a man who used to fish for a living? "It's ridiculous. But I think having the money is great because my sisters and father and relatives don't have to worry." His older sister used to be an accountant who took temporary and contract assignments. Trung says, with a smile, that she's in retirement now. His younger sister recently finished optometry school and relocated to the Bay Area to be closer to her brother. And his father couldn't be more pleased. He's director of a federally funded program for Southeast Asian refugees, and will more than likely continue to do social work after his coming retirement.

With the family taken care of, Trung's attention turned to his company: "After the first few weeks of becoming public, I checked the stocks every day to see what's going on. To me right now it's more meaningful to survive, to be one of the companies that survives." Being so focused on survival doesn't give Trung much time to be extravagant. He's working fifteen-hour days, six days a week, and tutoring Vietnamese-American youth on Sundays. He did find the time to fall in love with and marry a medical student from

Vietnam. They even squeezed in a honeymoon. But the couple returned to the same modest apartment in southwest San Francisco that she had lived in before she married a multimillionaire.

Every Tet (the Vietnamese New Year) Trung looks back on the year past. This year, he says he'll be asking himself, "How did this happen?" He knows that he owes a great deal to his mother, his teachers, his financial backers, and his team. But most of his fortune, he believes, is due to something larger: "When I look back," he says, his open gaze reflecting the distance of his journey, "what I see is opportunity."

That's what Trung sees when he looks forward as well. Even if it all 35 came crashing down tomorrow, he says he would "take a few days to suffer" and then go on. "The important thing is how do you recover from the mishaps. There's always more opportunity. There's never a lack of opportunity. That's what I love about this country. So many opportunities."

ENGAGING THE TEXT

1. Why does Rather choose Trung Dung as one embodiment of the American Dream? What is your gut-level reaction to Trung's story—admiration, envy, inspiration?

2. Aside from the biographical facts about Trung, what are the primary messages about success, hard work, and race embedded in this text? To what extent do you agree or disagree with them?

3. In what ways are Trung and his experiences unique or exceptional? Do the severe challenges he faced and the huge success he achieved do more to support or to challenge the myth of individual success?

4. Rather's sketch of Trung begins in Vietnam. What elements of the Horatio Alger myth can you find in this first part of the narrative? What role do the experiences of immigrants play in the myth?

5. Review the information Rather provides about Trung's mother, father, and sisters. Explain how successful you think each of them is.

EXPLORING CONNECTIONS

6. Compare and contrast the youthful Trung Dung to Ragged Dick (p. 297), being sure to consider their circumstances, attitudes, personal attributes, and goals. Has the myth changed in any way between Dick's time and ours?

7. How well does Trung Dung's story fit the Alger formula as defined in the first paragraph of "Horatio Alger" by Harlon Dalton (p. 303)?

8. The paintings by Norman Rockwell on pages 22 and 23 show a family tree and a holiday dinner. Imagine Trung Dung's family as the subject of such paintings—how would you illustrate his family tree, and how do you visualize millionaires celebrating a holiday? Sketch or draw one such image and discuss what light it sheds on contemporary ideas about money and success.

EXTENDING THE CRITICAL CONTEXT

9. In small groups, brainstorm how you could use the Internet to update Rather's profile of Trung. What would you like to know about him, and how, specifically, might you find that information? Carry out your research and report back to the class.

Serving in Florida
BARBARA EHRENREICH

If you're considering dropping out of college and settling into a comfy minimum-wage job (or two), please read this excerpt first. As a journalist preparing to write about working-class life, Barbara Ehrenreich decided to take a series of unglamorous jobs —waitressing, housecleaning, retail sales — and to live on the meager wages these jobs paid. In this narrative, Ehrenreich describes trying to make ends meet by adding a second waitressing job (at "Jerry's") to her eight-hour shift at "The Hearthside," having discovered that $2.43 an hour plus tips doesn't add up as fast as her rent and other bills. The full account of Ehrenreich's "plunge into poverty" may be found in Nickel and Dimed: On (Not) Getting By in America *(2001). Ehrenreich (b. 1941) is the author of more than ten books, including* Fear of Falling: The Inner Life of the Middle Class, *which was nominated for a National Book Critics Circle Award. She has also published articles in* Time, Harper's, The New Republic, The Nation, *and the* New York Times Magazine.

Picture a fat person's hell, and I don't mean a place with no food. Instead there is everything you might eat if eating had no bodily consequences—the cheese fries, the chicken-fried steaks, the fudge-laden desserts—only here every bite must be paid for, one way or another, in human discomfort. The kitchen is a cavern, a stomach leading to the lower intestine that is the garbage and dishwashing area, from which issue bizarre smells combining the edible and the offal: creamy carrion, pizza barf, and that unique and enigmatic Jerry's[1] scent, citrus fart. The floor is slick with spills, forcing us to walk through the kitchen with tiny steps, like Susan McDougal in leg irons.[2] Sinks everywhere are clogged with scraps of

[1]*Jerry's:* Not the real name of the restaurant where Ehrenreich worked; the restaurant was part of a "well-known national chain."

[2]*Susan McDougal in leg irons:* McDougal refused to testify against President Bill Clinton and Hillary Clinton before the Whitewater grand jury in 1996; she spent almost twenty-two months in various prisons and eventually received a presidential pardon in 2001.

lettuce, decomposing lemon wedges, water-logged toast crusts. Put your hand down on any counter and you risk being stuck to it by the film of ancient syrup spills, and this is unfortunate because hands are utensils here, used for scooping up lettuce onto the salad plates, lifting out pie slices, and even moving hash browns from one plate to another. The regulation poster in the single unisex rest room admonishes us to wash our hands thoroughly, and even offers instructions for doing so, but there is always some vital substance missing—soap, paper towels, toilet paper—and I never found all three at once. You learn to stuff your pockets with napkins before going in there, and too bad about the customers, who must eat, although they don't realize it, almost literally out of our hands.

The break room summarizes the whole situation: there is none, because there are no breaks at Jerry's. For six to eight hours in a row, you never sit except to pee. Actually, there are three folding chairs at a table immediately adjacent to the bathroom, but hardly anyone ever sits in this, the very rectum of the gastroarchitectural system. Rather, the function of the peri-toilet area is to house the ashtrays in which servers and dishwashers leave their cigarettes burning at all times, like votive candles, so they don't have to waste time lighting up again when they dash back here for a puff. Almost everyone smokes as if their pulmonary well-being depended on it—the multinational mélange of cooks; the dishwashers, who are all Czechs here; the servers, who are American natives—creating an atmosphere in which oxygen is only an occasional pollutant. My first morning at Jerry's, when the hypoglycemic shakes set in, I complain to one of my fellow servers that I don't understand how she can go so long without food. "Well, I don't understand how *you* can go so long without a cigarette," she responds in a tone of reproach. Because work is what you do for others; smoking is what you do for yourself. I don't know why the antismoking crusaders have never grasped the element of defiant self-nurturance that makes the habit so endearing to its victims—as if, in the American workplace, the only thing people have to call their own is the tumors they are nourishing and the spare moments they devote to feeding them.

Now, the Industrial Revolution is not an easy transition, especially, in my experience, when you have to zip through it in just a couple of days. I have gone from craft work straight into the factory, from the air-conditioned morgue of the Hearthside[3] directly into the flames. Customers arrive in human waves, sometimes disgorged fifty at a time from their tour buses, puckish and whiny. Instead of two "girls" on the floor at once, there can be as many as six of us running around in our brilliant pink-and-orange Hawaiian shirts. Conversations, either with customers or with fellow employees, seldom last more than twenty seconds at a time. On my first day, in fact, I am hurt by my sister servers' coldness. My mentor for the day is a supremely competent, emotionally uninflected twenty-three-year-old, and

---

[3]*Hearthside:* The other restaurant where Ehrenreich worked.

the others, who gossip a little among themselves about the real reason someone is out sick today and the size of the bail bond someone else has had to pay, ignore me completely. On my second day, I find out why. "Well, it's good to see *you* again," one of them says in greeting. "Hardly anyone comes back after the first day." I feel powerfully vindicated—a survivor— but it would take a long time, probably months, before I could hope to be accepted into this sorority.

I start out with the beautiful, heroic idea of handling the two jobs at once, and for two days I almost do it: working the breakfast/lunch shift at Jerry's from 8:00 till 2:00, arriving at the Hearthside a few minutes late, at 2:10, and attempting to hold out until 10:00. In the few minutes I have between jobs, I pick up a spicy chicken sandwich at the Wendy's drive-through window, gobble it down in the car, and change from khaki slacks to black, from Hawaiian to rust-colored polo. There is a problem, though. When, during the 3:00–4:00 o'clock dead time, I finally sit down to wrap silver, my flesh seems to bond to the seat. I try to refuel with a purloined cup of clam chowder, as I've seen Gail and Joan do dozens of time, but Stu[4] catches me and hisses "No *eating!*" although there's not a customer around to be offended by the sight of food making contact with a server's lips. So I tell Gail I'm going to quit, and she hugs me and says she might just follow me to Jerry's herself.

But the chances of this are minuscule. She has left the flophouse and her annoying roommate and is back to living in her truck. But, guess what, she reports to me excitedly later that evening, Phillip has given her permission to park overnight in the hotel parking lot, as long as she keeps out of sight, and the parking lot should be totally safe since it's patrolled by a hotel security guard! With the Hearthside offering benefits like that, how could anyone think of leaving? This must be Phillip's theory, anyway. He accepts my resignation with a shrug, his main concern being that I return my two polo shirts and aprons.

Gail would have triumphed at Jerry's, I'm sure, but for me it's a crash course in exhaustion management. Years ago, the kindly fry cook who trained me to waitress at a Los Angeles truck stop used to say: Never make an unnecessary trip; if you don't have to walk fast, walk slow; if you don't have to walk, stand. But at Jerry's the effort of distinguishing necessary from unnecessary and urgent from whenever would itself be too much of an energy drain. The only thing to do is to treat each shift as a one-time-only emergency: you've got fifty starving people out there, lying scattered on the battlefield, so get out there and feed them! Forget that you will have to do this again tomorrow, forget that you will have to be alert enough to dodge the drunks on the drive home tonight—just burn, burn, burn! Ideally, at some point you enter what servers call a "rhythm" and psychologists term a

[4]*Gail, Joan, Stu:* Waitress, hostess, and assistant manager at the Hearthside restaurant. Philip, mentioned in the subsequent paragraph, is the top manager.

"flow state," where signals pass from the sense organs directly to the muscles, bypassing the cerebral cortex, and a Zen-like emptiness sets in. I'm on a 2:00–10:00 P.M. shift now, and a male server from the morning shift tells me about the time he "pulled a triple"—three shifts in a row, all the way around the clock—and then got off and had a drink and met this girl, and maybe he shouldn't tell me this, but they had sex right then and there and it was like *beautiful.*

But there's another capacity of the neuromuscular system, which is pain. I start tossing back drugstore-brand ibuprofens as if they were vitamin C, four before each shift, because an old mouse-related repetitive-stress injury in my upper back has come back to full-spasm strength, thanks to the tray carrying. In my ordinary life, this level of disability might justify a day of ice packs and stretching. Here I comfort myself with the Aleve commercial where the cute blue-collar guy asks: If you quit after working four hours, what would your boss say? And the not-so-cute blue-collar guy, who's lugging a metal beam on his back, answers: He'd fire me, that's what. But fortunately, the commercial tells us, we workers can exert the same kind of authority over our painkillers that our bosses exert over us. If Tylenol doesn't want to work for more than four hours, you just fire its ass and switch to Aleve.

True, I take occasional breaks from this life, going home now and then to catch up on e-mail and for conjugal visits (though I am careful to "pay" for everything I eat here, at $5 for a dinner, which I put in a jar), seeing *The Truman Show*[5] with friends and letting them buy my ticket. And I still have those what-am-I-doing-here moments at work, when I get so homesick for the printed word that I obsessively reread the six-page menu. But as the days go by, my old life is beginning to look exceedingly strange. The e-mails and phone messages addressed to my former self come from a distant race of people with exotic concerns and far too much time on their hands. The neighborly market I used to cruise for produce now looks forbiddingly like a Manhattan yuppie emporium. And when I sit down one morning in my real home to pay bills from my past life, I am dazzled by the two- and three-figure sums owed to outfits like Club Body Tech and Amazon.com.

Management at Jerry's is generally calmer and more "professional" than at the Hearthside, with two exceptions. One is Joy, a plump, blowsy woman in her early thirties who once kindly devoted several minutes of her time to instructing me in the correct one-handed method of tray carrying but whose moods change disconcertingly from shift to shift and even within one. The other is B.J., aka B.J. the Bitch, whose contribution is to stand by the kitchen counter and yell, "Nita, your order's up, move it!" or "Barbara, didn't you see you've got another table out there? Come *on,* girl!" Among other things, she is hated for having replaced the whipped cream squirt

---

[5]*The Truman Show:* 1998 film (directed by Peter Weir and starring Jim Carrey) about a man who discovers his whole life is actually a TV show.

cans with big plastic whipped-cream-filled baggies that have to be squeezed with both hands—because, reportedly, she saw or thought she saw employees trying to inhale the propellant gas from the squirt cans, in the hope that it might be nitrous oxide. On my third night, she pulls me aside abruptly and brings her face so close that it looks like she's planning to butt me with her forehead. But instead of saying "You're fired," she says, "You're doing fine." The only trouble is I'm spending time chatting with customers: "That's how they're getting you." Furthermore I am letting them "run me," which means harassment by sequential demands: you bring the catsup and they decide they want extra Thousand Island; you bring that and they announce they now need a side of fries, and so on into distraction. Finally she tells me not to take her wrong. She tries to say things in a nice way, but "you get into a mode, you know, because everything has to move so fast."[6]

I mumble thanks for the advice, feeling like I've just been stripped   10
naked by the crazed enforcer of some ancient sumptuary law:[7] No chatting for *you*, girl. No fancy service ethic allowed for the serfs. Chatting with customers is for the good-looking young college-educated servers in the downtown carpaccio and ceviche joints, the kids who can make $70–$100 a night. What had I been thinking? My job is to move orders from tables to kitchen and then trays from kitchen to tables. Customers are in fact the major obstacle to the smooth transformation of information into food and food into money—they are, in short, the enemy. And the painful thing is that I'm beginning to see it this way myself. There are the traditional asshole types—frat boys who down multiple Buds and then make a fuss because the steaks are so emaciated and the fries so sparse—as well as the variously impaired—due to age, diabetes, or literacy issues—who require patient nutritional counseling. The worst, for some reason, are the Visible Christians—like the ten-person table, all jolly and sanctified after Sunday night service, who run me mercilessly and then leave me $1 on a $92 bill. Or the guy with the crucifixion T-shirt (SOMEONE TO LOOK UP TO) who complains that his baked potato is too hard and his iced tea too icy (I cheerfully fix both) and leaves no tip at all. As a general rule, people wearing crosses or WWJD? ("What Would Jesus Do?") buttons look at us disapprovingly no matter what we do, as if they were confusing waitressing with Mary Magdalene's original profession.

I make friends, over time, with the other "girls" who work my shift: Nita, the tattooed twenty-something who taunts us by going around saying brightly, "Have we started making money yet?" Ellen, whose teenage son

---

[6]In *Workers in a Lean World: Unions in the International Economy* (Verso, 1997), Kim Moody cites studies finding an increase in stress-related workplace injuries and illness between the mid-1980s and the early 1990s. He argues that rising stress levels reflect a new system of "management by stress" in which workers in a variety of industries are being squeezed to extract maximum productivity, to the detriment of their health. [Ehrenreich's note.]

[7]*sumptuary laws:* Laws which regulate personal behavior on moral or religious grounds.

cooks on the graveyard shift and who once managed a restaurant in Massachusetts but won't try out for management here because she prefers being a
"common worker" and not "ordering people around." Easygoing fiftyish
Lucy, with the raucous laugh, who limps toward the end of the shift because
of something that has gone wrong with her leg, the exact nature of which
cannot be determined without health insurance. We talk about the usual
girl things—men, children, and the sinister allure of Jerry's chocolate
peanut-butter cream pie—though no one, I notice, ever brings up anything
potentially expensive, like shopping or movies. As at the Hearthside, the
only recreation ever referred to is partying, which requires little more than
some beer, a joint, and a few close friends. Still, no one is homeless, or cops
to it anyway, thanks usually to a working husband or boyfriend. All in all, we
form a reliable mutual-support group: if one of us is feeling sick or over-
whelmed, another one will "bev" a table or even carry trays for her. If one of
us is off sneaking a cigarette or a pee, the others will do their best to conceal
her absence from the enforcers of corporate rationality.[8]

But my saving human connection—my oxytocin receptor, as it were—
is George, the nineteen-year-old Czech dishwasher who has been in this
country exactly one week. We get talking when he asks me, tortuously, how
much cigarettes cost at Jerry's. I do my best to explain that they cost over a
dollar more here than at a regular store and suggest that he just take one
from the half-filled packs that are always lying around on the break table.
But that would be unthinkable. Except for the one tiny earring signaling his
allegiance to some vaguely alternative point of view, George is a perfect
straight arrow—crew-cut, hardworking, and hungry for eye contact. "Czech
Republic," I ask, "or Slovakia?" and he seems delighted that I know the difference. "Vaclav Havel," I try, "Velvet Revolution, Frank Zappa?" "Yes, yes,
1989," he says, and I realize that for him this is already history.

My project is to teach George English. "How are you today, George?" I
say at the start of each shift. "I am good, and how are you today, Barbara?"
I learn that he is not paid by Jerry's but by the "agent" who shipped him
over—$5 an hour, with the agent getting the dollar or so difference be-
tween that and what Jerry's pays dishwashers. I learn also that he shares an
apartment with a crowd of other Czech "dishers," as he calls them, and that

---

[8]Until April 1998, there was no federally mandated right to bathroom breaks. According
to Marc Linder and Ingrid Nygaard, authors of *Void Where Prohibited: Rest Breaks and the
Right to Urinate on Company Time* (Cornell University Press, 1997), "The right to rest and
void at work is not high on the list of social or political causes supported by professional or executive employees, who enjoy personal workplace liberties that millions of factory workers can
only dream about. . . . While we were dismayed to discover that workers lacked an acknowledged right to void at work, [the workers] were amazed by outsiders' naïve belief that their employers would permit them to perform this basic bodily function when necessary. . . . A factory
worker, not allowed a break for six-hour stretches, voided into pads worn inside her uniform;
and a kindergarten teacher in a school without aides had to take all twenty children with her to
the bathroom and line them up outside the stall door while she voided." [Ehrenreich's note.]

he cannot sleep until one of them goes off for his shift, leaving a vacant bed. We are having one of our ESL sessions late one afternoon when B.J. catches us at it and orders "Joseph" to take up the rubber mats on the floor near the dishwashing sinks and mop underneath. "I thought your name was George," I say loud enough for B.J. to hear as she strides off back to the counter. Is she embarrassed? Maybe a little, because she greets me back at the counter with "George, Joseph—there are so many of them!" I say nothing, neither nodding nor smiling, and for this I am punished later, when I think I am ready to go and she announces that I need to roll fifty more sets of silverware, and isn't it time I mixed up a fresh four-gallon batch of blue-cheese dressing? May you grow old in this place, B.J., is the curse I beam out at her when I am finally permitted to leave. May the syrup spills glue your feet to the floor.

I make the decision to move closer to Key West. First, because of the drive. Second and third, also because of the drive: gas is eating up $4–$5 a day, and although Jerry's is as high-volume as you can get, the tips average only 10 percent, and not just for a newbie like me. Between the base pay of $2.15 an hour and the obligation to share tips with the busboys and dish-washers, we're averaging only about $7.50 an hour. Then there is the $30 I had to spend on the regulation tan slacks worn by Jerry's servers—a set-back it could take weeks to absorb. (I had combed the town's two downscale department stores hoping for something cheaper but decided in the end that these marked-down Dockers, originally $49, were more likely to survive a daily washing.) Of my fellow servers, everyone who lacks a working husband or boyfriend seems to have a second job: Nita does something at a computer eight hours a day; another welds. Without the forty-five-minute commute, I can picture myself working two jobs and still having the time to shower between them.

So I take the $500 deposit I have coming from my landlord, the $400 I have earned toward the next month's rent, plus the $200 reserved for emergencies, and use the $1,100 to pay the rent and deposit on trailer number 46 in the Overseas Trailer Park, a mile from the cluster of budget hotels that constitute Key West's version of an industrial park. Number 46 is about eight feet in width and shaped like a barbell inside, with a narrow region— because of the sink and the stove—separating the bedroom from what might optimistically be called the "living" area, with its two-person table and half-sized couch. The bathroom is so small my knees rub against the shower stall when I sit on the toilet, and you can't just leap out of the bed, you have to climb down to the foot of it in order to find a patch of floor space to stand on. Outside, I am within a few yards of a liquor store, a bar that advertises "free beer tomorrow," a convenience store, and a Burger King—but no su-permarket or, alas, Laundromat. By reputation, the Overseas park is a nest of crime and crack, and I am hoping at least for some vibrant multicultural street life. But desolation rules night and day, except for a thin stream of pedestrians heading for their jobs at the Sheraton or the 7-Eleven. There

15

are not exactly people here but what amounts to canned labor, being preserved between shifts from the heat.

In line with my reduced living conditions, a new form of ugliness arises at Jerry's. First we are confronted—via an announcement on the computers through which we input orders—with the new rule that the hotel bar, the Driftwood, is henceforth off-limits to restaurant employees. The culprit, I learn through the grapevine, is the ultraefficient twenty-three-year-old who trained me—another trailer home dweller and a mother of three. Something had set her off one morning, so she slipped out for a nip and returned to the floor impaired. The restriction mostly hurts Ellen, whose habit it is to free her hair from its rubber band and drop by the Driftwood for a couple of Zins[9] before heading home at the end of her shift, but all of us feel the chill. Then the next day, when I go for straws, I find the dry-storage room locked. It's never been locked before; we go in and out of it all day—for napkins, jelly containers, Styrofoam cups for takeout. Vic, the portly assistant manager who opens it for me, explains that he caught one of the dishwashers attempting to steal something and, unfortunately, the miscreant will be with us until a replacement can be found—hence the locked door. I neglect to ask what he had been trying to steal but Vic tells me who he is—the kid with the buzz cut and the earring, you know, he's back there right now.

I wish I could say I rushed back and confronted George to get his side of the story. I wish I could say I stood up to Vic and insisted that George be given a translator and allowed to defend himself or announced that I'd find a lawyer who'd handle the case pro bono.[10] At the very least I should have testified as to the kid's honesty. The mystery to me is that there's not much worth stealing in the dry-storage room, at least not in any fenceable quantity: "Is Gyorgi here, and am having 200—maybe 250—catsup packets. What do you say?" My guess is that he had taken—if he had taken anything at all—some Saltines or a can of cherry pie mix and that the motive for taking it was hunger.

So why didn't I intervene? Certainly not because I was held back by the kind of moral paralysis that can mask as journalistic objectivity. On the contrary, something new—something loathsome and servile—had infected me, along with the kitchen odors that I could still sniff on my bra when I finally undressed at night. In real life I am moderately brave, but plenty of brave people shed their courage in POW camps, and maybe something similar goes on in the infinitely more congenial milieu of the low-wage American workplace. Maybe, in a month or two more at Jerry's, I might have regained my crusading spirit. Then again, in a month or two I might have turned into a different person altogether—say, the kind of person who would have turned George in.

---

[9]*Zins:* Glasses of zinfandel wine.
[10]*pro bono:* Free of charge.

But this is not something I was slated to find out. When my monthlong plunge into poverty was almost over, I finally landed my dream job—housekeeping. I did this by walking into the personnel office of the only place I figured I might have some credibility, the hotel attached to Jerry's, and confiding urgently that I had to have a second job if I was to pay my rent and, no, it couldn't be front-desk clerk. "All *right*," the personnel lady fairly spits, "so it's *housekeeping*," and marches me back to meet Millie, the housekeeping manager, a tiny, frenetic Hispanic woman who greets me as "babe" and hands me a pamphlet emphasizing the need for a positive attitude. The pay is $6.10 an hour and the hours are nine in the morning till "whenever," which I am hoping can be defined as a little before two. I don't have to ask about health insurance once I meet Carlotta, the middle-aged African American woman who will be training me. Carlie, as she tells me to call her, is missing all of her top front teeth.

On that first day of housekeeping and last day—although I don't yet know it's the last—of my life as a low-wage worker in Key West, Carlie is in a foul mood. We have been given nineteen rooms to clean, most of them "checkouts," as opposed to "stay-overs," and requiring the whole enchilada of bed stripping, vacuuming, and bathroom scrubbing. When one of the rooms that had been listed as a stay-over turns out to be a checkout, she calls Millie to complain, but of course to no avail. "So make up the mother-fucker," she orders me, and I do the beds while she sloshes around the bathroom. For four hours without a break I strip and remake beds, taking about four and a half minutes per queen-sized bed, which I could get down to three if there were any reason to. We try to avoid vacuuming by picking up the larger specks by hand, but often there is nothing to do but drag the monstrous vacuum cleaner—it weighs about thirty pounds—off our cart and try to wrestle it around the floor. Sometimes Carlie hands me the squirt bottle of "Bam" (an acronym for something that begins, ominously, with "butyric"—the rest of it has been worn off the label) and lets me do the bathrooms. No service ethic challenges me here to new heights of performance. I just concentrate on removing the pubic hairs from the bathtubs, or at least the dark ones that I can see.

I had looked forward to the breaking-and-entering aspect of cleaning the stay-overs, the chance to examine the secret physical existence of strangers. But the contents of the rooms are always banal and surprisingly neat—zipped-up shaving kits, shoes lined up against the wall (there are no closets), flyers for snorkeling trips, maybe an empty wine bottle or two. It is the TV that keeps us going, from Jerry to Sally to *Hawaii Five-O* and then on to the soaps. If there's something especially arresting, like "Won't Take No for an Answer" on Jerry, we sit down on the edge of a bed and giggle for a moment, as if this were a pajama party instead of a terminally dead-end job. The soaps are the best, and Carlie turns the volume up full blast so she won't miss anything from the bathroom or while the vacuum is on. In Room

20

503, Marcia confronts Jeff about Lauren. In 505, Lauren taunts poor cheated-on Marcia. In 511, Helen offers Amanda $10,000 to stop seeing Eric, prompting Carlie to emerge from the bathroom to study Amanda's troubled face. "You take it, girl," she advises. "I would for sure."

The tourists' rooms that we clean and, beyond them, the far more expensively appointed interiors in the soaps begin after a while to merge. We have entered a better world—a world of comfort where every day is a day off, waiting to be filled with sexual intrigue. We are only gate-crashers in this fantasy, however, forced to pay for our presence with backaches and perpetual thirst. The mirrors, and there are far too many of them in hotel rooms, contain the kind of person you would normally find pushing a shopping cart down a city street—bedraggled, dressed in a damp hotel polo shirt two sizes too large, and with sweat dribbling down her chin like drool. I am enormously relieved when Carlie announces a half-hour meal break, but my appetite fades when I see that the bag of hot dog rolls she has been carrying around on our cart is not trash salvaged from a checkout but what she has brought for her lunch.

Between the TV and the fact that I'm in no position, as a first dayer, to launch new topics of conversation, I don't learn much about Carlie except that she hurts, and in more than one way. She moves slowly about her work, muttering something about joint pain, and this is probably going to doom her, since the young immigrant housekeepers—Polish and Salvadoran—like to polish off their rooms by two in the afternoon, while she drags the work out till six. It doesn't make any sense to hurry, she observes, when you're being paid by the hour. Already, management has brought in a woman to do what sounds like time-motion studies and there's talk about switching to paying by the room.[11] She broods, too, about all the little evidences of disrespect that come her way, and not only from management. "They don't care about us," she tells me of the hotel guests; in fact, they don't notice us at all unless something gets stolen from a room—"then they're all over you." We're eating our lunch side by side in the break room when a white guy in a maintenance uniform walks by and Carlie calls out, "Hey you," in a friendly way, "what's your name?"

"Peter Pan," he says, his back already to us.

"That wasn't funny," Carlie says, turning to me. "That was no kind of   25 answer. Why did he have to be funny like that?" I venture that he has an attitude, and she nods as if that were an acute diagnosis. "Yeah, he got a attitude all right."

"Maybe he's a having a bad day," I elaborate, not because I feel any obligation to defend the white race but because her face is so twisted with hurt.

---

[11]A few weeks after I left, I heard ads on the radio for housekeeping jobs at this hotel at the amazing rate of "up to $9 an hour." When I inquired, I found out that the hotel had indeed started paying by the room, and I suspect that Carlie, if she lasted, was still making the equivalent of $6 an hour or quite a bit less. [Ehrenreich's note.]

When I request permission to leave at about 3:30, another housekeeper warns me that no one has so far succeeded in combining housekeeping with serving at Jerry's: "Some kid did it once for five days, and you're no kid." With that helpful information in mind, I rush back to number 46, down four Advils (the name brand this time), shower, stooping to fit into the stall, and attempt to compose myself for the oncoming shift. So much for what Marx termed the "reproduction of labor power," meaning the things a worker has to do just so she'll be ready to labor again. The only unforeseen obstacle to the smooth transition from job to job is that my tan Jerry's slacks, which had looked reasonably clean by 40-watt bulb last night when I hand washed my Hawaiian shirt, prove by daylight to be mottled with catsup and ranch-dressing stains. I spend most of my hour-long break between jobs attempting to remove the edible portions of the slacks with a sponge and then drying them over the hood of my car in the sun.

I can do this two-job thing, is my theory, if I can drink enough caffeine and avoid getting distracted by George's ever more obvious suffering.[12] The first few days after the alleged theft, he seemed not to understand the trouble he was in, and our chirpy little conversations had continued. But the last couple of shifts he's been listless and unshaven, and tonight he looks like the ghost we all know him to be, with dark half-moons hanging from his eyes. At one point, when I am briefly immobilized by the task of filling little paper cups with sour cream for baked potatoes, he comes over and looks as if he'd like to explore the limits of our shared vocabulary, but I am called to the floor for a table. I resolve to give him all my tips that night, and to hell with the experiment in low-wage money management. At eight, Ellen and I grab a snack together standing at the mephitic end of the kitchen counter, but I can only manage two or three mozzarella sticks, and lunch had been a mere handful of McNuggets. I am not tired at all, I assure myself, though it may be that there is simply no more "I" left to do the tiredness monitoring. What I would see if I were more alert to the situation is that the forces of destruction are already massing against me. There is only one cook on duty, a young man named Jesus ("Hay-Sue," that is), and he is new to the job. And there is Joy, who shows up to take over in the middle of the shift dressed in high heels and a long, clingy white dress and fuming as if she'd just been stood up in some cocktail bar.

Then it comes, the perfect storm. Four of my tables fill up at once. Four tables is nothing for me now, but only so long as they are obligingly staggered. As I bev table 27, tables 25, 28, and 24 are watching enviously. As I bev 25, 24 glowers because their bevs haven't even been ordered.

[12]In 1996 the number of persons holding two or more jobs averaged 7.8 million, or 6.2 percent of the workforce. It was about the same rate for men and for women (6.1 versus 6.2). About two-thirds of multiple jobholders work one job full-time and the other part-time. Only a heroic minority—4 percent of men and 2 percent of women—work two full-time jobs simultaneously (John F. Stinson Jr., "New Data on Multiple Jobholding Available from the CPS," *Monthly Labor Review,* March 1997). [Ehrenreich's note.]

Twenty-eight is four yuppyish types, meaning everything on the side and agonizing instructions as to the chicken Caesars. Twenty-five is a middle-aged black couple who complain, with some justice, that the iced tea isn't fresh and the tabletop is sticky. But table 24 is the meteorological event of the century: ten British tourists who seem to have made the decision to absorb the American experience entirely by mouth. Here everyone has at least two drinks—iced tea *and* milk shake, Michelob *and* water (with lemon slice in the water, please)—and a huge, promiscuous orgy of breakfast specials, mozz sticks, chicken strips, quesadillas, burgers with cheese and without, sides of hash browns with cheddar, with onions, with gravy, seasoned fries, plain fries, banana splits. Poor Jesus! Poor me! Because when I arrive with their first tray of food—after three prior trips just to refill bevs—Princess Di refuses to eat her chicken strips with her pancake and sausage special since, as she now reveals, the strips were meant to be an appetizer. Maybe the others would have accepted their meals, but Di, who is deep into her third Michelob, insists that everything else go back while they work on their starters. Meanwhile, the yuppies are waving me down for more decaf and the black couple looks ready to summon the NAACP.

Much of what happens next is lost in the fog of war. Jesus starts going under. The little printer in front of him is spewing out orders faster than he can rip them off, much less produce the meals. A menacing restlessness rises from the tables, all of which are full. Even the invincible Ellen is ashen from stress. I take table 24 their reheated main courses, which they immediately reject as either too cold or fossilized by the microwave. When I return to the kitchen with their trays (three trays in three trips) Joy confronts me with arms akimbo: "What *is* this?" She means the food—the plates of rejected pancakes, hash browns in assorted flavors, toasts, burgers, sausages, eggs. "Uh, scrambled with cheddar," I try, "and that's—" "*No,*" she screams in my face, "is it a traditional, a super-scramble, an eye-opener?" I pretend to study my check for a clue, but entropy has been up to its tricks, not only on the plates but in my head, and I have to admit that the original order is beyond reconstruction. "You don't know an eye-opener from a traditional?" she demands in outrage. All I know, in fact, is that my legs have lost interest in the current venture and have announced their intention to fold. I am saved by a yuppie (mercifully not one of mine) who chooses this moment to charge into the kitchen to bellow that his food is twenty-five minutes late. Joy screams at him to get the hell out of her kitchen, *please,* and then turns on Jesus in a fury, hurling an empty tray across the room for emphasis.

I leave. I don't walk out, I just leave. I don't finish my side work or pick up my credit card tips, if any, at the cash register or, of course, ask Joy's permission to go. And the surprising thing is that you *can* walk out without permission, that the door opens, that the thick tropical night air parts to let me pass, that my car is still parked where I left it. There is no vindication in this exit, no fuck-you surge of relief, just an overwhelming dank sense of failure pressing down on me and the entire parking lot. I had gone into this venture in the spirit of science, to test a mathematical proposition, but somewhere along the line, in the tunnel vision imposed by long shifts and relentless concentration, it became a test of myself, and clearly I have failed. Not only had I flamed out as a housekeeper/server, I had forgotten to give George my tips, and, for reasons perhaps best known to hardworking, generous people like Gail and Ellen, this hurts. I don't cry, but I am in a position to realize, for the first time in many years, that the tear ducts are still there and still capable of doing their job.

When I moved out of the trailer park, I gave the key to number 46 to Gail and arranged for my deposit to be transferred to her. She told me that Joan was still living in her van and that Stu had been fired from the Hearthside. According to the most up-to-date rumors, the drug he ordered from the restaurant was crack and he was caught dipping into the cash register to pay for it. I never found out what happened to George.

ENGAGING THE TEXT

1. What's the point of Ehrenreich's experiment? What do you think she was hoping to learn by stepping down the economic ladder, and what can you learn as her reader? Explain why you find her approach more or less effective than one that provides economic data and analysis.

2. Throughout this selection Ehrenreich seeks not merely to narrate facts but to elicit emotional and other responses from her readers. For one or more of the passages listed below, explain what response you think Ehrenreich is after and what *specific* methods she uses to evoke it:

   The opening description of Jerry's (para. 1–2)
   The description of customers (para. 10)
   George's story (paras. 12–13, 16–18)
   The description of trailer number 46 (para. 15)
   The footnotes throughout the narrative

3. Ehrenreich ordinarily lives much more comfortably than she did as a waitress, and of course she had an escape hatch from her experiment—she would not serve food or clean rooms forever and could have gone back to her usual life if necessary at any time. Explain the effect her status as a "tourist" in working-class culture has on you as a reader.

4. Write a journal entry about your worst job. How did your experience of being "nickeled and dimed" compare with Ehrenreich's? What was the worst aspect of this work experience for you?

5. The annual incomes listed below are selected form a list published by the *San Francisco Chronicle* ("What People Earn," March 3, 2002). Which, if any, strike you as unreasonably high or low, and which seem about right?

Anna Kournikova	Tennis pro	$10 million
Ray Kubik	Farmer	$18,000
Kevin Polston	Meteorologist	$60,000
Donald Rumsfeld	Sec. of Defense	$166,700
Scott McQuilkin	Private investigator	$23,510
Diane Sawyer	TV news anchor	$10 million
Angelina Tidal	Librarian	$36,000
John Grisham	Author	$28 million
Bradley Bloom	Pediatrician	$110,000
Doyle Syling	Police officer	$42,000
Getchen Richie	Jazz singer	$20,000

Is there necessarily anything wrong with a system in which one person would have to work fifteen centuries to earn as much as someone else makes in a year?

EXPLORING CONNECTIONS

6. Not everyone can be a millionaire like Trung Dung (p. 310), but what, if anything, do you think Gail, Ellen, and George could do to substantially improve their material/economic well-being? What are the greatest barriers they face? What advice might Trung Dung or Horatio Alger give them, and how do you think it would be received?

7. Using Gail, Ellen, or George as a rough model for your central character, write a detailed plot summary for a novel that would be the anti–*Ragged Dick*, a story in which someone pursues the American Dream and fails. How plausible is your story line compared to the one Horatio Alger created for Ragged Dick (p. 297)?

EXTENDING THE CRITICAL CONTEXT

8. Ehrenreich made $6.10 per hour as a housekeeper. Working in groups, sketch out a monthly budget based on this salary for *a)* an individual, *b)* a single parent with a pre-teen child, and *c)* a family of four in which one adult is ill or has been laid off. Be sure to include money for basics like rent, utilities, food, clothing, transportation, and medical care.

9. Check local want ads and shop windows to identify some of the least promising job prospects in your community. Talk to potential employers and learn as much as you can about such issues as wages, working conditions, hours, drug screening, and healthcare, retirement, or other benefits.

10. Order a meal at whichever restaurant in your community is most like "Jerry's." Study the working conditions in the restaurant, paying special attention to the kinds of problems Ehrenreich faced on her shifts. Write up an informal journal entry from the imagined point of view of a server at the restaurant.

Class in America: Myths and Realities (2000)
GREGORY MANTSIOS

Which of these gifts might a high school graduate in your family receive—a corsage, a savings bond, or a BMW? The answer indicates your social class, a key factor in American lives that many of us conspire to ignore. The selection below, however, makes it hard to deny class distinctions and their nearly universal influence on our lives. The essay's title aptly describes its method: Mantsios (b. 1950) outlines four widely held beliefs about class in the United States and then systematically refutes them with statistical evidence. Even if your eyes are already open to the existence of classes in the United States, some of the numbers the author cites are likely to surprise you. Mantsios is director of the Labor Resource Center at Queens College of the City University of New York and editor of A New Labor Movement for the New Century *(1998). The essay reprinted below appeared in* Race, Class, and Gender in the United States: An Integrated Study, *edited by Paula S. Rothenberg (2001).*

People in the United States don't like to talk about class. Or so it would seem. We don't speak about class privileges, or class oppression, or the class nature of society. These terms are not part of our everyday vocabulary, and in most circles they are associated with the language of the rhetorical fringe. Unlike people in most other parts of the world, we shrink from using words that classify along economic lines or that point to class distinctions: phrases like "working class," "upper class," and "ruling class" are rarely uttered by Americans.

For the most part, avoidance of class-laden vocabulary crosses class boundaries. There are few among the poor who speak of themselves as lower class; instead, they refer to their race, ethnic group, or geographic location. Workers are more likely to identify with their employer, industry, or occupational group than with other workers, or with the working class.[1]

---

[1] See Jay MacLead, *Ain't No Makin' It: Aspirations and Attainment in a Lower-Income Neighborhood,* Boulder, CO, Westview Press, 1995; Benjamin DeMott, *The Imperial Middle,* New York, Morrow, 1990; Ira Katznelson, *City Trenches: Urban Politics and Patterning of Class in the United States,* New York, Pantheon Books, 1981; Charles W. Tucker, "A Comparative Analysis of Subjective Social Class: 1945–1963," *Social Forces,* no. 46, June 1968, pp. 508–514; Robert Nisbet, "The Decline and Fall of Social Class," *Pacific Sociological Review,* vol. 2, Spring 1959, pp. 11–17; and Oscar Glantz, "Class Consciousness and Political Solidarity," *American Sociological Review,* vol. 23, August 1958, pp. 375–382. [All notes are author's, except 18.]

Neither are those at the other end of the economic spectrum likely to use the word "class." In her study of thirty-eight wealthy and socially prominent women, Susan Ostrander asked participants if they considered themselves members of the upper class. One participant responded, "I hate to use the word 'class.' We are responsible, fortunate people, old families, the people who have something." Another said, "I hate [the term] upper class. It is so non–upper class to use it. I just call it 'all of us,' those who are well-born."[2]

It is not that Americans, rich or poor, aren't keenly aware of class differences—those quoted above obviously are; it is that class is not in the domain of public discourse. Class is not discussed or debated in public because class identity has been stripped from popular culture. The institutions that shape mass culture and define the parameters of public debate have avoided class issues. In politics, in primary and secondary education, and in the mass media, formulating issues in terms of class is unacceptable, perhaps even un-American.

There are, however, two notable exceptions to this phenomenon. First, it is acceptable in the United States to talk about "the middle class." Interestingly enough, such references appear to be acceptable precisely because they mute class differences. References to the middle class by politicians, for example, are designed to encompass and attract the broadest possible constituency. Not only do references to the middle class gloss over differences, but these references also avoid any suggestion of conflict or exploitation.

This leads us to the second exception to the class-avoidance phenomenon. We are, on occasion, presented with glimpses of the upper class and the lower class (the language used is "the wealthy" and "the poor"). In the media, these presentations are designed to satisfy some real or imagined voyeuristic need of "the ordinary person." As curiosities, the ground-level view of street life and the inside look at the rich and the famous serve as unique models, one to avoid and one to aspire to. In either case, the two models are presented without causal relation to each other: one is not rich because the other is poor. Similarly, when social commentators or liberal politicians draw attention to the plight of the poor, they do so in a manner that obscures the class structure and denies class exploitation. Wealth and poverty are viewed as one of several natural and inevitable states of being: differences are only differences. One may even say differences are the American way, a reflection of American social diversity.

We are left with one of two possibilities: either talking about class and recognizing class distinctions are not relevant to U.S. society, or we mistakenly hold a set of beliefs that obscure the reality of class differences and their impact on people's lives.

---

[2]Susan Ostrander, "Upper-Class Women: Class Consciousness as Conduct and Meaning," in G. William Domhoff, *Power Structure Research*, Beverly Hills, CA, Sage Productions, 1980, pp. 78–79. Also see, Stephen Birmingham, *America's Secret Aristocracy*, Boston, Little Brown, 1987.

Let us look at four common, albeit contradictory, beliefs about the United States.

Myth 1: The United States is fundamentally a classless society. Class distinctions are largely irrelevant today, and whatever differences do exist in economic standing are, for the most part, insignificant. Rich or poor, we are all equal in the eyes of the law, and such basic needs as health care and education are provided to all regardless of economic standing.

Myth 2: We are, essentially, a middle-class nation. Despite some varia-   10
tions in economic status, most Americans have achieved relative affluence in what is widely recognized as a consumer society.

Myth 3: We are all getting richer. The American public as a whole is steadily moving up the economic ladder, and each generation propels itself to greater economic well-being. Despite some fluctuations, the U.S. position in the global economy has brought previously unknown prosperity to most, if not all, North Americans.

Myth 4: Everyone has an equal chance to succeed. Success in the United States requires no more than hard work, sacrifice, and perseverance: "In America, anyone can become a millionaire; it's just a matter of being in the right place at the right time."

In trying to assess the legitimacy of these beliefs, we want to ask several important questions. Are there significant class differences among Americans? If these differences do exist, are they getting bigger or smaller, and do these differences have a significant impact on the way we live? Finally, does everyone in the United States really have an equal opportunity to succeed?

The Economic Spectrum

We will begin by looking at differences. An examination of available data reveals that variations in economic well-being are in fact immense. Consider the following:

- The wealthiest 20 percent of the American population holds 85 percent of the total household wealth in the country. That is, they own nearly seven-eighths of all the consumer durables (such as houses, cars, and stereos) and financial assets (such as stocks, bonds, property, and savings accounts).[3]
- Approximately 144,000 Americans, or 0.1 percent of the adult working population, earn more than $1 million **annually,** with many of these individuals earning $10 million and some earning over $100 million annually. It would take the average American, earning $34,000 per year, more than 65 **lifetimes** to earn $100 million.[4]

---

[3]Jared Bernstein, Lawrence Hishel, and John Schmitt, *The State of Working America: 1998–99,* ILR Press, Cornell University Press, 1998, p. 262.

[4]The number of individuals filing tax returns showing a gross adjusted income of $1 million or more in 1997 was 144,459 (Internal Revenue Service, *Statistics of Income Bulletin, Summer 1999,* Washington, DC, 1999, p. 268). The total civilian employment in 1997 was 129,588,000 (U.S. Bureau of Labor Statistics, 1997).

Affluence and prosperity are clearly alive and well in certain segments 15
of the United States population. However, this abundance is in contrast to
the poverty and despair that is also prevalent in the United States. At the
other end of the spectrum:

- A total of 13 percent of the American population—that is, one of
  every eight[5]—live below the government's official poverty line (calculated in 1999 at $8,500 for an individual and $17,028 for a family
  of four).[6] These poor include a significant number of homeless
  people—approximately two million Americans.
- Approximately one out of every five children in the United States
  under the age of eighteen lives in poverty.[7]

The contrast between rich and poor is sharp, and with nearly one-third
of the American population living at one extreme or the other, it is difficult
to argue that we live in a classless society. The income gap between rich and
poor in the United States (measured as the percentage of total income held
by the wealthiest 20 percent of the population versus the poorest 20 percent) is approximately 11 to 1, one of the highest ratios in the industrialized
world. The ratio in Japan and Germany, by contrast, is 4 to 1.[8]

Reality 1: There are enormous differences in the economic status of
American citizens. A sizable proportion of the U.S. population occupies opposite ends of the economic spectrum.

In the middle range of the economic spectrum:

- Sixty percent of the American population holds less than 4 percent
  of the nation's wealth.[9]
- While the real income of the top 1 percent of U.S. families skyrocketed by 89 percent during the economic growth period from 1977 to
  1995, the income of the middle fifth of the population actually declined by 13 percent during that same period.[10] This led one prominent economist to describe economic growth as a "spectator sport
  for the majority of American families."[11]

[5]Joseph Dalaker, U.S. Bureau of the Census, "Current Population Reports," series
P60–207, *Poverty in the United States: 1998,* Washington, DC, U.S. Government Printing Office, 1999, p. v.

[6]"Preliminary Estimates of Weighted Average Poverty Thresholds in 1999," Department
of Commerce, Bureau of Census, 2000.

[7]Ibid, p. v.

[8]See The Center on Budget and Policy Priorities, Economic Policy Institute, "Pulling
Apart: State-by-State Analysis of Income Trends," January 2000, fact sheet; U.S. Department
of Commerce, "Current Population Reports: Consumer Income," Washington, DC, 1993; The
World Bank, "World Development Report: 1992," Washington, DC, International Bank for
Reconstruction and Development, 1992; The World Bank "World Development Report
1999/2000," pp. 238–239.

[9]Jared Bernstein et al., op. cit., p. 262

[10]Derived from Ibid, p. 95.

[11]Alan Blinder, quoted by Paul Krugman, in "Disparity and Despair," *U.S. News and
World Report,* March 23, 1992. p. 54.

The level of inequality is sometimes difficult to comprehend fully with dollar figures and percentages. To help his students visualize the distribution of income, the well-known economist Paul Samuelson asked them to picture an income pyramid made of children's blocks, with each layer of blocks representing $1,000. If we were to construct Samuelson's pyramid today, the peak of the pyramid would be much higher than the Eiffel Tower, yet almost all of us would be within six feet of the ground.[12] In other words, the distribution of income is heavily skewed; a small minority of families take the lion's share of national income, and the remaining income is distributed among the vast majority of middle-income and low-income families. Keep in mind that Samuelson's pyramid represents the distribution of income, not wealth. The distribution of wealth is skewed even further.

Reality 2: The middle class in the United States holds a very small share 20 of the nation's wealth, and its income — in constant dollars — is declining.

Lottery millionaires and celebrity salaries notwithstanding, evidence suggests that the level of inequality in the United States is getting higher. Census data show the gap between the rich and the poor to be the widest since the government began collecting information in 1947. Furthermore, the percentage of households earning between $25,000 and $75,000 has been falling steadily since 1969, while the percentage of households earning less than $25,000 has actually increased between 1989 and 1997.[13] And economic polarization is expected to increase over the next several decades.[14]

Reality 3: The middle class is shrinking in size, and the gap between rich and poor is bigger than it has ever been.

American Life-Styles

At last count, nearly 35 million Americans across the nation lived in unrelenting poverty.[15] Yet, as political scientist Michael Harrington once commented, "America has the best dressed poverty the world has ever known."[16] Clothing disguises much of the poverty in the United States, and this may explain, in part, its middle-class image. With increased mass marketing of "designer" clothing and with shifts in the nation's economy from blue-collar (and often better-paying) manufacturing jobs to white-collar and pink-collar jobs in the service sector, it is becoming increasingly difficult to distinguish class differences based on appearance.[17]

---

[12]Paul Samuelson, *Economics,* 10th ed., New York, McGraw-Hill, 1976, p. 84.

[13]"Money Income of Households, Families, and Persons in the United States: 1992," U.S. Department of Commerce, "Current Population Reports: Consumer Income" series P60–184, Washington, DC, 1993, p. B6. Also, Jared Bernstein et al., op. cit., p. 61.

[14]Paul Blumberg, *Inequality in an Age of Decline,* New York, Oxford University Press, 1980.

[15]U.S. Census Bureau, 1999, op. cit., p. v.

[16]Michael Harrington, *The Other America,* New York, Macmillan, 1962, p. 12–13.

[17]Stuart Ewen and Elizabeth Ewen, *Channels of Desire: Mass Images and the Shaping of American Consciousness,* New York, McGraw-Hill, 1982.

Beneath the surface, there is another reality. Let us look at some "typical" and not-so-typical life-styles.

American Profile No. 1

Name:	Harold S. Browning
Father:	manufacturer, industrialist
Mother:	prominent social figure in the community
Principal child-rearer:	governess
Primary education:	an exclusive private school on Manhattan's Upper East Side *Note:* a small, well-respected primary school where teachers and administrators have a reputation for nurturing student creativity and for providing the finest educational preparation *Ambition:* "to become President"
Supplemental tutoring:	tutors in French and mathematics
Summer camp:	sleep-away camp in northern Connecticut *Note:* camp provides instruction in the creative arts, athletics, and the natural sciences
Secondary education:	a prestigious preparatory school in Westchester County *Note:* classmates included the sons of ambassadors, doctors, attorneys, television personalities, and well-known business leaders *After-school activities:* private riding lessons *Ambition:* "to take over my father's business" *High-school graduation gift:* BMW
Family activities:	theater, recitals, museums, summer vacations in Europe, occasional winter trips to the Caribbean *Note:* as members of and donors to the local art museum, the Brownings and their children attend private receptions and exhibit openings at the invitation of the museum director.
Higher education:	an Ivy League liberal arts college in Massachusetts *Major:* economics and political science *After-class activities:* debating club, college newspaper, swim team *Ambition:* "to become a leader in business"
First full-time job (age 23):	assistant manager of operations, Browning Tool and Die, Inc. (family enterprise)

Subsequent employment:	*3 years*—executive assistant to the president, Browning Tool and Die
	Responsibilities included: purchasing (materials and equipment), personnel, and distribution networks
	4 years—advertising manager, Lackheed Manufacturing (home appliances)
	3 years—director of marketing and sales, Comerex, Inc. (business machines)
Present employment (age 38):	executive vice president, SmithBond and Co. (digital instruments)
	Typical daily activities: review financial reports and computer printouts, dictate memoranda, lunch with clients, initiate conference calls, meet with assistants, plan business trips, meet with associates
	Transportation to and from work: chauffeured company limousine
	Annual salary: $315,000
	Ambition: "to become chief executive officer of the firm, or one like it, within the next five to ten years"
Present residence:	eighteenth-floor condominium on Manhattan's Upper West Side, eleven rooms, including five spacious bedrooms and terrace overlooking river
	Interior: professionally designed and accented with elegant furnishings, valuable antiques, and expensive artwork
	Note: building management provides doorman and elevator attendant; family employs au pair[18] for children and maid for other domestic chores
Second residence:	farm in northwestern Connecticut, used for weekend retreats and for horse breeding (investment/hobby)
	Note: to maintain the farm and cater to their needs when they are there, the Brownings employ a part-time maid, groundskeeper, and horse breeder

Harold Browning was born into a world of nurses, maids, and governesses. His world today is one of airplanes and limousines, five-star restaurant, and luxurious living accommodations. The life and life-style of Harold Browning is in sharp contrast to that of Bob Farrell.   25

[18]*au pair:* A young woman from another country who works for a family, typically caring for children in exchange for room and board.

American Profile No. 2

Name:	Bob Farrell
Father:	machinist
Mother:	retail clerk
Principal child-rearer:	mother and sitter
Primary education:	a medium-size public school in Queens, New York, characterized by large class size, outmoded physical facilities, and an educational philosophy emphasizing basic skills and student discipline.
	Ambition: "to become President"
Supplemental tutoring:	none
Summer camp:	YMCA day camp
	Note: emphasis on team sports, arts and crafts
Secondary education:	large regional high school in Queens
	Note: classmates included the sons and daughters of carpenters, postal clerks, teachers, nurses, shopkeepers, mechanics, bus drivers, police officers, salespersons
	After-school activities: basketball and handball in school park
	Ambition: "to make it through college"
	High-school graduation gift: $500 savings bond
Family activities:	family gatherings around television set, bowling, an occasional trip to the movie theater, summer Sundays at the public beach
Higher education:	a two-year community college with a technical orientation
	Major: electrical technology
	After-school activities: employed as a part-time bagger in local supermarket
	Ambition: "to become an electrical engineer"
First full-time job (age 19):	service-station attendant
	Note: continued to take college classes in the evening
Subsequent employment:	mail clerk at large insurance firm, manager trainee, large retail chain
Present employment (age 38):	assistant sales manager, building supply firm
	Typical daily activities: demonstrate products, write up product orders, handle customer complaints, check inventory
	Transportation to and from work: city subway
	Annual salary: $39,261

	Ambition: "to open up my own business"
	Additional income: $6,100 in commissions from evening and weekend work as salesman in local men's clothing store
President residence:	the Farrells own their own home in a working-class neighborhood in Queens

Bob Farrell and Harold Browning live very differently: the life-style of one is privileged; that of the other is not so privileged. The differences are class differences, and these differences have a profound impact on the way they live. They are differences between playing a game of handball in the park and taking riding lessons at a private stable; watching a movie on television and going to the theater; and taking the subway to work and being driven in a limousine. More important, the difference in class determines where they live, who their friends are, how well they are educated, what they do for a living, and what they come to expect from life.

Yet, as dissimilar as their life-styles are, Harold Browning and Bob Farrell have some things in common. They live in the same city, they work long hours, and they are highly motivated. More important, they are both white males.

Let us look at someone else who works long and hard and is highly motivated. This person, however, is black and female.

American Profile No. 3

Name:	Cheryl Mitchell
Father:	janitor
Mother:	waitress
Principal child-rearer:	grandmother
Primary education:	large public school in Ocean Hill-Brownsville, Brooklyn, New York
	Note: rote teaching of basic skills and emphasis on conveying the importance of good attendance, good manners, and good work habits; school patrolled by security guards
	Ambition: "to be a teacher"
Supplemental tutoring:	none
Summer camp:	none
Secondary education:	large public school in Ocean Hill-Brownsville
	Note: classmates included sons and daughters of hairdressers, groundskeepers, painters, dressmakers, dishwashers, domestics

After-school activities: domestic chores, part-time employment as babysitter and house-keeper
Ambition: "to be a social worker"
High-school graduation gift: corsage

Family activities: church-sponsored socials

Higher education: one semester of local community college
Note: dropped out of school for financial reasons

First full-time job (age 17): counter clerk, local bakery

Subsequent employment: file clerk with temporary service agency, supermarket checker

Present employment (age 38): nurse's aide at a municipal hospital
Typical daily activities: make up hospital beds, clean out bedpans, weigh patients and assist them to the bathroom, take temperature readings, pass out and collect food trays, feed patients who need help, bathe patients, and change dressings
Annual salary: $14,024
Ambition: "to get out of the ghetto"

Present residence: three-room apartment in the South Bronx, needs painting, has poor ventilation, is in a high-crime area
Note: Cheryl Mitchell lives with her four-year-old son and her elderly mother

When we look at the lives of Cheryl Mitchell, Bob Farrell, and Harold Browning, we see life-styles that are very different. We are not looking, however, at economic extremes. Cheryl Mitchell's income as a nurse's aide puts her above the government's official poverty line.[19] Below her on the income pyramid are 35 million poverty-stricken Americans. Far from being poor, Bob Farrell has an annual income as an assistant sales manager that puts him in the fifty-first percentile of the income distribution.[20] More than 50 percent of the U.S. population earns less money than Bob Farrell. And while Harold Browning's income puts him in a high-income bracket, he stands only a fraction of the way up Samuelson's income pyramid. Well above him are the 144,000 individuals whose annual salary exceeds $1 million. Yet Harold Browning spends more money on his horses than Cheryl Mitchell earns in a year.

[19]This is based on the 1999 poverty threshold of $13,290 for a family of three.
[20]Based on a median income in 1998 of $38,885.

Reality 4: Even ignoring the extreme poles of the economic spectrum,   30
we find enormous class differences in the life-styles among the haves, the
have-nots, and the have-littles.

Class affects more than life-style and material well-being. It has a significant impact on our physical and mental well-being as well.

Researchers have found an inverse relationship between social class
and health. Lower-class standing is correlated to higher rates of infant mortality, eye and ear disease, arthritis, physical disability, diabetes, nutritional
deficiency, respiratory disease, mental illness, and heart disease.[21] In all
areas of health, poor people do not share the same life chances as those in
the social class above them. Furthermore, lower-class standing is correlated
with a lower quality of treatment for illness and disease. The results of poor
health and poor treatment are borne out in the life expectancy rates within
each class. Researchers have found that the higher your class standing, the
higher your life expectancy. Conversely, they have also found that within
each age group, the lower one's class standing, the higher the death rate; in
some age groups, the figures are as much as two and three times as high.[22]

Reality 5: From cradle to grave, class standing has a significant impact
on our chances for survival.

The lower one's class standing, the more difficult it is to secure appropriate housing, the more time is spent on the routine tasks of everyday life,
the greater is the percentage of income that goes to pay for food and other
basic necessities, and the greater is the likelihood of crime victimization.[23]
Class can predict chances for both survival and success.

Class and Educational Attainment

School performance (grades and test scores) and educational at-   35
tainment (level of schooling completed) also correlate strongly with economic class. Furthermore, despite some efforts to make testing fairer and

---

[21]E. Pamuk, D. Makuc, K. Heck, C. Reuben, and K. Lochner, *Socioeconomic Status and
Health Chartbook, Health, United States, 1998*, Hyattsville, MD, National Center for Health
Statistics, 1998, pp. 145–159; Vincente Navarro "Class, Race, and Health Care in the United
States," in, Bersh Berberoglu, *Critical Perspectives in Sociology*, 2nd ed., Dubuque, IA,
Kendall/Hunt, 1993, pp. 148–156; Melvin Krasner, *Poverty and Health in New York City*,
United Hospital Fund of New York, 1989. See also U.S. Dept. of Health and Human Services,
Health Status of Minorities and Low Income Groups, 1985; and Dan Hughes, Kay Johnson,
Sara Rosenbaum, Elizabeth Butler, and Janet Simons, *The Health of America's Children*, The
Children's Defense Fund, 1988.

[22]E. Pamuk et al., op. cit.; Kenneth Neubeck and Davita Glassberg, *Sociology; A Critical
Approach*, New York, McGraw-Hill, 1996, pp. 436–438; Aaron Antonovsky, "Social Class, Life
Expectancy, and Overall Mortality," in *The Impact of Social Class*, New York, Thomas Crowell,
1972, pp. 467–491. See also Harriet Duleep, "Measuring the Effect of Income on Adult Mortality Using Longitudinal Administrative Record Data," *Journal of Human Resources*, vol. 21,
no. 2, Spring 1986.

[23]E. Pamuk et al., op. cit., fig. 20; Dennis W. Roncek, "Dangerous Places: Crime and Residential Environment," *Social Forces*, vol. 60, no. 1, September 1981, pp. 74–96.

schooling more accessible, current data suggest that the level of inequity is staying the same or getting worse.

In his study for the Carnegie Council on Children fifteen years ago, Richard De Lone examined the test scores of over half a million students who took the College Board exams (SATs). His findings were consistent with earlier studies that showed a relationship between class and scores on standardized tests; his conclusion: "the higher the student's social status, the higher the probability that he or she will get higher grades."[24] Fifteen years after the release of the Carnegie report, College Board surveys reveal data that are no different: test scores still correlate strongly with family income.

Table 1   Average Combined Scores by Income (400 to 1600 scale)[25]

FAMILY INCOME	MEDIAN SCORE
More than $100,000	1130
$80,000 to $100,000	1082
$70,000 to $80,000	1058
$60,000 to $70,000	1043
$50,000 to $60,000	1030
$40,000 to $50,000	1011
$30,000 to $40,000	986
$20,000 to $30,000	954
$10,000 to $20,000	907
less than $10,000	871

These figures are based on the test results of 1,302,903 SAT takers in 1999.

A little more than twenty years ago, researcher William Sewell showed a positive correlation between class and overall educational achievement. In comparing the top quartile (25%) of his sample to the bottom quartile, he found that students from upper-class families were twice as likely to obtain training beyond high school and four times as likely to attain a postgraduate degree. Sewell concluded: "Socioeconomic background . . . operates independently of academic ability at every stage in the process of educational attainment."[26]

Today, the pattern persists. There are, however, two significant changes. On the one hand, the odds of getting into college have improved for the bottom quartile of the population, although they still remain relatively low compared to the top. On the other hand, the chances of completing a col-

[24]Richard De Lone, *Small Futures*, New York, Harcourt Brace Jovanovich, 1978, pp. 14–19.

[25]Derived from The College Entrance Examination Board, "1999, A Profile of College Bound Seniors: SAT Test Takers," www.collegeboard.org/sat/cbsenior/yr1999/NAT/natbk499.html#income

[26]William H. Sewell, "Inequality of Opportunity for Higher Education," *American Sociological Review*, vol. 36, no. 5, 1971, pp. 793–809.

lege degree have deteriorated markedly for the bottom quartile. Researchers estimate the chances of completing a four-year college degree (by age 24) to be nineteen times as great for the top 25 percent of the population as it is for the bottom 25 percent. "Those from the bottom quartile of family income . . . are faring worse than they have at any time in the 23 years of published Current Population Survey data."[27]

Reality 6: Class standing has a significant impact on chances for educational attainment.

Class standing, and consequently life chances, are largely determined at birth. Although examples of individuals who have gone from rags to riches abound in the mass media, statistics on class mobility show these leaps to be extremely rare. In fact, dramatic advances in class standing are relatively few. One study showed that fewer than one in five men surpass the economic status of their fathers.[28] For those whose annual income is in six figures, economic success is due in large part to the wealth and privileges bestowed on them at birth. Over 66 percent of the consumer units with incomes of $100,000 or more have some inherited assets. Of these units, over 86 percent reported that inheritances constituted a substantial portion of their total assets.[29]

Economist Harold Wachtel likens inheritance to a series of Monopoly games in which the winner of the first game refuses to relinquish his or her cash and commercial property for the second game. "After all," argues the winner, "I accumulated my wealth and income by my own wits." With such an arrangement, it is not difficult to predict the outcome of subsequent games.[30]

Reality 7: All Americans do not have an equal opportunity to succeed. Inheritance laws ensure a greater likelihood of success for the offspring of the wealthy.

Spheres of Power and Oppression

When we look at society and try to determine what it is that keeps most people down—what holds them back from realizing their potential as healthy, creative, productive individuals—we find institutionally oppressive forces that are largely beyond their individual control. Class domination is one of these forces. People do not choose to be poor or working class; instead, they are limited and confined by the opportunities afforded or denied them by a social and economic system. The class structure in the United States is a function of its economic system—capitalism, a system that is

40

[27]The Mortenson Report on Public Policy Analysis of Opportunity for Postsecondary Education, "Postsecondary Education Opportunity," Iowa City, IA, September 1993, no. 16.

[28]De Lone, op. cit., pp. 14–19.

[29]Howard Tuchman, *Economics of the Rich*, New York, Random House, 1973, p. 15.

[30]Howard Wachtel, *Labor and the Economy*, Orlando, FL, Academic Press, 1984, pp. 161–162.

based on private rather than public ownership and control of commercial enterprises, and on the class division between those who own and control and those who do not. Under capitalism, those enterprises are governed by the need to produce a profit for the owners, rather than to fulfill collective needs.

Racial and gender domination are other such forces that hold people down. Although there are significant differences in the way capitalism, racism, and sexism affect our lives, there are also a multitude of parallels. And although race, class, and gender act independently of each other, they are at the same time very much interrelated.

On the one hand, issues of race and gender oppression cut across class lines. Women experience the effects of sexism whether they are well-paid professionals or poorly paid clerks. As women, they face discrimination and male domination, as well as catcalls and stereotyping. Similarly, a black man faces racial oppression, is subjected to racial slurs, and is denied opportunities because of his color. Regardless of their class standing, women and members of minority races are confronted with oppressive forces precisely because of their gender, color, or both.

On the other hand, class oppression permeates other spheres of power and oppression, so that the oppression experienced by women and minorities is also differentiated along class lines. Although women and minorities find themselves in subordinate positions vis-à-vis white men, the particular issues they confront may be quite different, depending on their position in the class structure. Inequalities in the class structure distinguish social functions and individual power, and these distinctions carry over to race and gender categories.

Power is incremental, and class privileges can accrue to individual women and to individual members of a racial minority. At the same time, class-oppressed men, whether they are white or black, have privileges afforded them as men in a sexist society. Similarly, class-oppressed whites, whether they are men or women, have privileges afforded them as white in a racist society. Spheres of power and oppression divide us deeply in our society, and the schisms between us are often difficult to bridge.

Whereas power is incremental, oppression is cumulative, and those who are poor, black, and female have all of the forces of classism, racism, and sexism bearing down on them. This cumulative oppression is what is meant by the double and triple jeopardy of women and minorities.

Furthermore, oppression in one sphere is related to the likelihood of oppression in another. If you are black and female, for example, you are much more likely to be poor or working class than you would be as a white male. Census figures show that the incidence of poverty varies greatly by race and gender.

In other words, being female and being nonwhite are attributes in our   50
society that increase the chances of poverty and of lower-class standing.

Reality 8: Racism and sexism compound the effects of classism in society.

Table 2   Chances of Being Poor in America[31]

WHITE MALE/ FEMALE	WHITE FEMALE HEAD°	HISPANIC MALE/ FEMALE	HISPANIC FEMALE HEAD°	BLACK MALE/ FEMALE	BLACK FEMALE HEAD°
1 in 10	1 in 4	1 in 4	1 in 2	1 in 4	1 in 2

°Persons in families with female householder, no husband present.

[31]Derived from Census, 1999, op. cit., p. vi.

ENGAGING THE TEXT

1. Reexamine the four myths Mantsios identifies (para. 9–12). What does Mantsios say is wrong about each myth, and what evidence does he provide to critique each? How persuasive do you find his evidence and reasoning?

2. Does the essay make a case that the wealthy are exploiting the poor? Does it simply assume this? Are there other possible interpretations of the data Mantsios provides? Explain your position, taking into account the information in "Class in America (2000)."

3. Work out a rough budget for a family of four with an annual income of $17,000. Be sure to include costs for food, clothing, housing, transportation, healthcare, and other unavoidable expenses. Do you think this is a reasonable "poverty line," or is it too high or too low?

4. Imagine that you are Harold S. Browning, Bob Farrell, or Cheryl Mitchell. Write an entry for this person's journal after a tough day on the job. Compare and contrast your entry with those written by other students.

5. In this essay, Mantsios does not address solutions to the problems he cites. What changes do you imagine Mantsios would like to see? What changes, if any, would you recommend?

EXPLORING CONNECTIONS

6. Working in small groups, discuss which class each of the following would belong to and how this class affiliation would shape the life chances of each:

> Gary Soto in "Looking for Work" (p. 26)
> George in "Serving in Florida" (p. 317)
> The narrator of "An Indian Story" (p. 109)
> Stephen Cruz (p. 348)
> Miss Moore in "The Lesson" (p. 404)
> Cora Tucker (p. 353)
> C. P. Ellis (p. 591)
> Mike Rose (p. 182)
> Richard Rodriguez (p. 214)

7. Although Mantsios does not focus on the Horatio Alger myth as does Harlon Dalton (p. 303), both authors concern themselves with seeing beyond myths of success to underlying realities. Compare the ways these two writers challenge the American mythology of success. Do the two readings complement one another, or do you see fundamental disagreements between the two authors? Whose approach do you find more persuasive, insightful, or informative, and why?

8. Compare this essay by Mantsios to the selections from *Changing American Families* by Judy Root Aulette (p. 64). What similarities or differences do

you see in the ways they understand and write about social class, wealth, and poverty?

EXTENDING THE CRITICAL CONTEXT

9. Mantsios points out that "inheritance laws ensure a greater likelihood of success for the offspring of the wealthy" (para. 42). Explain why you think this is or is not a serious problem. Keeping in mind the difference between wealth and income, discuss how society might attempt to remedy this problem and what policies you would endorse.

10. Skim through a few recent issues of a financial magazine like *Forbes* or *Money*. Who is the audience for these publications? What kind of advice is offered, what kinds of products and services are advertised, and what levels of income and investment are discussed?

11. Study the employment pages of a major newspaper in your area. Roughly what percentage of the openings would you consider upper class, middle class, and lower class? On what basis do you make your distinctions? What do the available jobs suggest about the current levels of affluence in your area?

Stephen Cruz

STUDS TERKEL

The speaker of the following oral history is Stephen Cruz, a man who at first glance seems to be living the American Dream of success and upward mobility. He is never content, however, and he comes to question his own values and the meaning of success in the world of corporate America. Studs Terkel (b. 1912) is the best-known practitioner of oral history in the United States. Over the course of a long career he has compiled several books by interviewing widely varying people — ordinary people for the most part — about important subjects like work, race, faith, and the Great Depression. The edited versions of these interviews are often surprisingly powerful crystallizations of American social history: Terkel's subjects give voice to the frustrations and hopes of whole generations of Americans. Terkel won a Pulitzer Prize in 1985 for "The Good War": An Oral History of World War II. *This selection first appeared in his* American Dreams: Lost and Found *(1980).*

He is thirty-nine.

"The family came in stages from Mexico. Your grandparents usually came first, did a little work, found little roots, put together a few bucks, and brought the family in, one at a time. Those were the days when controls at the border didn't exist as they do now."

You just tried very hard to be whatever it is the system wanted of you. I was a good student and, as small as I was, a pretty good athlete. I was well liked, I thought. We were fairly affluent, but we lived down where all the trashy whites were. It was the only housing we could get. As kids, we never understood why. We did everything right. We didn't have those Mexican accents, we were never on welfare. Dad wouldn't be on welfare to save his soul. He woulda died first. He worked during the Depression. He carries that pride with him, even today.

Of the five children, I'm the only one who really got into the business world. We learned quickly that you have to look for opportunities and add things up very quickly. I was in liberal arts, but as soon as Sputnik[1] went up, well, golly, hell, we knew where the bucks were. I went right over to the registrar's office and signed up for engineering. I got my degree in '62. If you had a master's in business as well, they were just paying all kinds of bucks. So that's what I did. Sure enough, the market was super. I had fourteen job offers. I could have had a hundred if I wanted to look around.

---

[1]*Sputnik:* Satellite launched by the Soviet Union in 1957; this launch signaled the beginning of the "space race" between the United States and the USSR.

I never once associated these offers with my being a minority. I was   5
aware of the Civil Rights Act of 1964, but I was still self-confident enough
to feel they wanted me because of my abilities. Looking back, the reason I
got more offers than the other guys was because of the government edict.
And I thought it was because I was so goddamned brilliant. (Laughs.) In
1962, I didn't get as many offers as those who were less qualified. You have
a tendency to blame the job market. You just don't want to face the issue of
discrimination.

I went to work with Procter & Gamble. After about two years, they told
me I was one of the best supervisors they ever had and they were gonna
promote me. Okay, I went into personnel. Again, I thought it was because I
was such a brilliant guy. Now I started getting wise to the ways of the American Dream. My office was glass-enclosed, while all the other offices were
enclosed so you couldn't see into them. I was the visible man.

They made sure I interviewed most of the people that came in. I just
didn't really think there was anything wrong until we got a new plant manager, a southerner. I received instructions from him on how I should interview blacks. Just check and see if they smell, okay? That was the beginning
of my training program. I started asking: Why weren't we hiring more minorities? I realized I was the only one in a management position.

I guess as a Mexican I was more acceptable because I wasn't really black.
I was a good compromise. I was visibly good. I hired a black secretary, which
was *verboten*. When I came back from my vacation, she was gone. My boss
fired her while I was away. I asked why and never got a good reason.

Until then, I never questioned the American Dream. I was convinced if
you worked hard, you could make it. I never considered myself different.
That was the trouble. We had been discriminated against a lot, but I never
associated it with society. I considered it an individual matter. Bad people,
my mother used to say. In '68 I began to question.

I was doing fine. My very first year out of college, I was making twelve   10
thousand dollars. I left Procter & Gamble because I really saw no opportunity. They were content to leave me visible, but my thoughts were not really
solicited. I may have overreacted a bit, with the plant manager's attitude,
but I felt there's no way a Mexican could get ahead here.

I went to work for Blue Cross. It's 1969. The Great Society[2] is in full
swing. Those who never thought of being minorities before are being
turned on. Consciousness raising is going on. Black programs are popping
up in universities. Cultural identity and all that. But what about the one
issue in this country: economics? There were very few management jobs for
minorities, especially blacks.

The stereotypes popped up again. If you're Oriental, you're real good
in mathematics. If you're Mexican, you're a happy guy to have around,

---

[2]*The Great Society:* President Lyndon B. Johnson's term for the American society he
hoped to establish through social reforms, including an antipoverty program.

pleasant but emotional. Mexicans are either sleeping or laughing all the time. Life is just one big happy kind of event. *Mañana*. Good to have as part of the management team, as long as you weren't allowed to make decisions.

I was thinking there were two possibilities why minorities were not making it in business. One was deep, ingrained racism. But there was still the possibility that they were simply a bunch of bad managers who just couldn't cut it. You see, until now I believed everything I was taught about the dream: the American businessman is omnipotent and fair. If we could show these turkeys there's money to be made in hiring minorities, these businessmen—good managers, good decision makers—would respond. I naively thought American businessmen gave a damn about society, that given a choice they would do the right thing. I had that faith.

I was hungry for learning about decision-making criteria. I was still too far away from top management to see exactly how they were working. I needed to learn more. Hey, just learn more and you'll make it. That part of the dream hadn't left me yet. I was still clinging to the notion of work your ass off, learn more than anybody else, and you'll get in that sphere.

During my fifth year at Blue Cross, I discovered another flaw in the American Dream. Minorities are as bad to other minorities as whites are to minorities. The strongest weapon the white manager had is the old divide and conquer routine. My mistake was thinking we were all at the same level of consciousness.

I had attempted to bring together some blacks with the other minorities. There weren't too many of them anyway. The Orientals never really got involved. The blacks misunderstood what I was presenting, perhaps I said it badly. They were on the cultural kick: a manager should be crucified for saying "Negro" instead of "black." I said as long as the Negro or the black gets the job, it doesn't mean a damn what he's called. We got into a huge hassle. Management, of course, merely smiled. The whole struggle fell flat on its face. It crumpled from divisiveness. So I learned another lesson. People have their own agenda. It doesn't matter what group you're with, there is a tendency to put the other guy down regardless.

The American Dream began to look so damn complicated, I began to think: Hell, if I wanted, I could just back away and reap the harvest myself. By this time, I'm up to twenty-five thousand dollars a year. It's beginning to look good, and a lot of people are beginning to look good. And they're saying: "Hey, the American Dream, you got it. Why don't you lay off?" I wasn't falling in line.

My bosses were telling me I had all the "ingredients" for top management. All that was required was to "get to know our business." This term comes up all the time. If I could just warn all minorities and women whenever you hear "get to know our business," they're really saying "fall in line." Stay within that fence, and glory can be yours. I left Blue Cross disillusioned. They offered me a director's job at thirty thousand dollars before I quit.

All I had to do was behave myself. I had the "ingredients" of being a good Chicano, the equivalent of the good nigger. I was smart. I could articulate well. People didn't know by my speech patterns that I was of Mexican heritage. Some tell me I don't look Mexican, that I have a certain amount of Italian, Lebanese, or who knows. (Laughs.)

One could easily say: "Hey, what's your bitch? The American Dream has treated you beautifully. So just knock it off and quit this crap you're spreading around." It was a real problem. Every time I turned around, America seemed to be treating me very well.   20

Hell, I even thought of dropping out, the hell with it. Maybe get a job in a factory. But what happened? Offers kept coming in. I just said to myself: God, isn't this silly? You might as well take the bucks and continue looking for the answer. So I did that. But each time I took the money, the conflict in me got more intense, not less.

Wow, I'm up to thirty-five thousand a year. This is a savings and loan business. I have faith in the executive director. He was the kind of guy I was looking for in top management: understanding, humane, also looking for the formula. Until he was up for consideration as executive v.p. of the entire organization. All of a sudden everything changed. It wasn't until I saw this guy flip-flop that I realized how powerful vested interests are. Suddenly he's saying: "Don't rock the boat. Keep a low profile. Get in line." Another disappointment.

Subsequently, I went to work for a consulting firm. I said to myself: Okay, I've got to get close to the executive mind. I need to know how they work. Wow, a consulting firm.

Consulting firms are saving a lot of American businessmen. They're doing it in ways that defy the whole notion of capitalism. They're not allowing these businesses to fail. Lockheed was successful in getting U.S. funding guarantees because of the efforts of consulting firms working on their behalf, helping them look better. In this kind of work, you don't find minorities. You've got to be a proven success in business before you get there.

The American Dream, I see now, is governed not by education, opportunity, and hard work, but by power and fear. The higher up in the organization you go, the more you have to lose. The dream is *not losing*. This is the notion pervading America today: don't lose.   25

When I left the consulting business, I was making fifty thousand dollars a year. My last performance appraisal was: you can go a long way in this business, you can be a partner, but you gotta know our business. It came up again. At this point, I was incapable of being disillusioned any more. How easy it is to be swallowed up by the same set of values that governs the top guy. I was becoming that way. I was becoming concerned about losing that fifty grand or so a year. So I asked other minorities who had it made. I'd go up and ask 'em: "Look, do you owe anything to others?" The answer was: "We owe nothing to anybody." They drew from the civil rights movement but felt no debt. They've quickly forgotten how it happened. It's like I was when I first got out of college. Hey, it's really me, I'm great. I'm great. I'm as angry with these guys as I am with the top guys.

Right now, it's confused. I've had fifteen years in the business world as "a success." Many Anglos would be envious of my progress. Fifty thousand dollars a year puts you in the one or two top percent of all Americans. Plus my wife making another thirty thousand. We had lots of money. When I gave it up, my cohorts looked at me not just as strange, but as something of a traitor. "You're screwing it up for all of us. You're part of our union, we're the elite, we should govern. What the hell are you doing?" So now I'm looked at suspiciously by my peer group as well.

I'm teaching at the University of Wisconsin at Platteville. It's nice. My colleagues tell me what's on their minds. I got a farm next-door to Platteville. With farm prices being what they are (laughs), it's a losing proposition. But with university work and what money we've saved, we're gonna be all right.

The American Dream is getting more elusive. The dream is being governed by a few people's notion of what the dream is. Sometimes I feel it's a small group of financiers that gets together once a year and decides all the world's issues.

It's getting so big. The small-business venture is not there any more. 30
Business has become too big to influence. It can't be changed internally. A counterpower is needed.

ENGAGING THE TEXT

1. As Cruz moves up the economic ladder, he experiences growing conflict that keeps him from being content and proud of his accomplishments. To what do you attribute his discontent? Is his "solution" one that you would recommend?

2. Cruz says that the real force in America is the dream of "not losing" (para. 25). What does he mean by this? Do you agree?

3. What, according to Stephen Cruz, is wrong with the American Dream? Write an essay in which you first define and then either defend or critique his position.

4. Imagine a continuation of Stephen Cruz's life in which he gives up his teaching job and returns to the business world. What might his career have been like over the last twenty years? How would you expect Cruz to react to the business environment today?

EXPLORING CONNECTIONS

5. Compare Stephen Cruz to Ragged Dick (p. 297) and Trung Dung (p. 310) in terms of the American Dream and individual success. How similar are Cruz's circumstances, goals, beliefs, and values to those examples of the Dream come true? What distinguishes him from those figures?

6. Compare Stephen Cruz to Richard Rodriguez (p. 214), Gary Soto (p. 26), and Mike Rose (p. 182) in terms of their attitudes toward education and success.

Extending the Critical Context

7. According to Cruz, in 1969 few management positions were open to members of minority groups. Working in small groups, go to the library and look up current statistics on minorities in business (for example, the number of large minority-owned companies; the number of minority chief executives among major corporations; the distribution of minorities among top management, middle management, supervisory, and clerical positions). Compare notes with classmates and discuss.

Good Noise: Cora Tucker

Anne Witte Garland

When most people think about the American Dream, they don't visualize a factory job and a cluttered house right next to the railroad tracks. As you read this selection about community activist Cora Tucker, however, think about the connection of her life to core American values like democracy, progress, and individual rights. Author Anne Witte Garland is a free-lance writer covering environmental, public health, consumer, and women's issues. She is the author of The Way We Grow: Good-Sense Solutions for Protecting Our Families from Pesticides in Food *(1993). This selection comes from her 1988 book* Women Activists: Challenging the Abuse of Power.

Cora Tucker's house is so close to the railroad tracks that at night when trains thunder by, the beds shake. The house and furniture are modest, and in the kitchen there's a lingering smell of the lard Cora cooks with. There are traces of Virginia red clay on the kitchen floor, and piled up on the bedroom floor are cardboard boxes overflowing with newspaper clippings and other papers.

Cora admits she doesn't like housekeeping anymore. The plaques and photographs hanging in the kitchen and living room attest to what she does enjoy; alongside religious pictures and photos of her children and grandchildren, there are several citizenship awards, certificates acknowledging her work in civil rights, and photos of her—a pretty, smiling black woman—with various politicians. One framed picture in the kitchen was handmade for Cora by some of the inmates in a nearby prison, whom Cora has visited and helped. In it, Old English letters made of foil spell out, "God grant me the serenity to accept the things I cannot change, the courage to change the things I can, and wisdom to know the difference." Cora has plenty of all three virtues, although "serene" probably isn't the first adjective a stranger would pin on her. But then, there isn't much that Cora would say she can't change, either.

Cora Tucker is something of an institution in Halifax County, Virginia, a rural county bordering North Carolina. In more than a dozen years, she has missed only a handful of the county board of supervisors' monthly meetings. Her name appears in the letters columns of the two daily newspapers several times a week—either signed onto her own letter or, almost as often, vilified in someone else's. She seems to know and be known by every black person on the street, in the post offices, and in stores and restaurants. And she is known by white and black people alike as having taken on many of the local, white-controlled institutions. Her main concern is simply fighting for the underdog, which she does in many ways—from social work–like visits to the elderly and invalids, to legal fights against racial discrimination, registering people to vote, and lobbying on issues like health care and the environment.

Cora was born in 1941 ten miles from where she lives now, near the Halifax county seat, in the small town of South Boston. Her father was a school teacher and later a railway porter. He died when Cora was three, and her mother and the nine children became sharecroppers on white men's farms. It was as a sharecropper, Cora says, that she learned how to do community organizing. She started by trying to help other sharecroppers to get things like better heating and food stamps. "I didn't call it 'organizing,' then," she says. "I just called it 'being concerned.' When you do sharecropping, you move around a lot. So I got to know everybody in the county, and to know what people's problems were.

"Sharecropping is the worst form of drudgery; it's slavery really. You work on a man's farm, supposedly for half the profit on the crops you grow. That's what the contract says. But you pay for all the stuff that goes into the crop—seeds, fertilizer, and all. You get free housing, but most sharecroppers' housing is dilapidated and cold. It isn't insulated—it's just shacks, really. Sharecroppers are poor. I know of a family of twelve who grew fifteen acres of tobacco, and at the end of the year, they had earned just fifty dollars. And I know sharecroppers who needed food and applied for food stamps, but couldn't get them because they supposedly made too much money; the boss went to the food stamp office, and said they made such and such, so they couldn't qualify."

Cora went to work very young, planting and plowing with the others in the family. Her mother taught her to cook when she was six; Cora remembers having to stand on a crate to reach the kitchen counter. She was a curious and intelligent child who loved school and was unhappy when she had to stay out of school to clean house for the white woman on the farm where they lived.

Cora always adored her mother. Bertha Plenty Moesley was a "chief stringer"—a step in tobacco processing that involves picking the green tobacco leaves from the plants one at a time, and stringing them together three leaves to a stick, so that they can be hung to dry and cure. "My mama worked hard," Cora says. "She would plow and do all the things the men did. She was independent; she raised her children alone for eighteen years. When I was little, I felt so bad that she had to work that hard just so we could survive. There was welfare out there—all kinds of help, if only somebody had told her how to go about getting it. She had very little education, and didn't know to go down to the welfare office for help. As I got older, I was upset by that and made up my mind, when I was about eight or nine years old, that if I ever got grown, I'd make sure that everybody knew how to get everything there was to get. And I really meant it. I learned early how to get things done, and I learned it would take initiative to get what I wanted."

By the time Cora learned about welfare, her mother wouldn't take advantage of it. She was proud, and she told the children to have self-respect. "We didn't have anything else," Cora's mother says. "The kids had only themselves to be proud of." Cora took the advice to heart. There's a story she tells about growing up that has found a permanent place in community-organizing lore. In her high school, which was segregated at the time (Halifax County schools didn't integrate until 1969, under court order), Cora entered an essay contest on the topic of "what America means to me." She was taken by surprise when her bitter essay about growing up black in the South won a statewide award. But on awards night she was in for another surprise. The winners were to have their essays read, and then shake hands with the Virginia governor. Cora's mother was in the audience beaming, along with Cora's friends and teachers. But when her essay was read, Cora didn't recognize it—it had been rewritten, and the less critical sentiments weren't hers at all. She refused to greet the governor. "I disappointed everyone—my mother even cried."

The only person who supported her that night, she says, was a high school literature teacher, whom she credits as an important influence on her. "He spent a lot of time with me, encouraging me. Every time an issue came up that I felt strongly about, he'd have me write about it—letters to the editor that never got printed. He told me, 'Nobody can make you a second-class citizen but you. You should be involved in what's going on around you.'"

Instead, at seventeen she dropped out of high school to get married. As 10
she describes it, the next several years were consumed with housekeeping and having children—six of them in rapid succession. She and her husband adopted a seventh. At first, Cora says, she threw herself enthusiastically into her new role. "I just wanted to be married. My father-in-law used to tease me about making myself so busy just being married. He'd say, 'You ain't

going to keep this up for long.' But I'd say yes I would. Every morning, I put clean sheets on our beds—washed and ironed them. I ironed every diaper. I read all the housekeeping magazines; my house was immaculate. But I was beginning to find myself so bored, even then. My husband was farming then, sharecropping, and he'd get up early; I'd get up too, and feed him and the kids, and then do the cleaning. But when you clean every day, there just isn't that much to do, so I'd be finished by ten in the morning! I joined a book club, so that I would get a book every month—but I would get bored in between. I would read the book in two days—I tried to savor it, but I couldn't make it last any longer. Then, when the kids started growing up and going to school, that would occupy me a little more. I'd feed them, then take them to school, and come back and clean and then start making lunch. But just as soon as my baby started school, I went out and got a job."

Halifax County has several textile and garment factories, and Cora went to work as a seamstress for one of the largest, a knit sportswear manufacturer. It was a fairly new operation, and the mostly women employees were expected to do everything, from lifting fabric bolts weighing forty or fifty pounds each, to sitting at sewing machines for eight hour stretches. There was no union; the county boasts in promotional material that less than 5 percent of the county's workforce is unionized. "Every time I used to talk to the girls there, my boss thought I was trying to get a union started. And I sure thought there *should* be a union; there were lots of health hazards, and people were always getting hurt. People got back injuries, two people even had heart attacks in the factory, because of the working conditions. I once got a woman to come down from Baltimore to talk about forming a union, but people got frightened because the bosses warned us that if there was any union activity, we'd lose our jobs."

Cora worked at the factory for seven years. The first thing she did with the money she was earning was to buy land for a house. "We had lived in places where we were so cold," she says. "We'd have no windows, and no wood. My dream was always to grow up and build me a house—my own house, out of brick. My husband never really wanted one; he was just as happy moving around. But after I had the babies and went to work at the factory, I told him I was going to build me a house. So the first year I worked, I saved a thousand dollars. The next year I saved another thousand, and then borrowed some from the company, to buy some land. Then I started saving again, for the house. But when I went to the FHA, they said I couldn't get a house without my husband's permission. At first, he said he wasn't going to have anything to do with it, so I said I'd buy a trailer instead. When he found out, he figured I might just as well put the money into a house, so he signed the papers. We built the house; it was the first time any of us had been inside a new house. I was crazy about it; we could sit down and say exactly where we wanted things. And while I was working, I bought every stick of furniture in it."

In 1976 Cora hurt her back and had to leave her job. Over the next few years she underwent surgery several times—first for her back, and then for cancer (for which she has had to have periodic treatments ever since). In the meantime, she had become active in the community. In the 1960s, she had participated in organizations like the National Association for the Advancement of Colored People, and another group called the Assemblies, but they moved too slowly for her tastes. ("They weren't really interested in taking on the power structure," she complains.) She had also organized her own letter-writing campaign in support of the federal Voting Rights Act to make it easier for blacks to vote. She had gone around to local churches, speaking to people and encouraging them to write to their representatives in Washington. She also took advantage of knowing women who ran beauty parlors—she provided the paper and pens, so that women could write letters while they sat under the hair dryers. "People would say to me, 'What good will it do?' But I think politicians have to be responsive if enough pressure can be brought to bear on them. You can complain, I can complain, but that's just two people. A politician needs to get piles of letters saying vote for this bill, because if you don't, you won't be in office much longer!" Cora was responsible for generating about five hundred letters supporting the voting law.

She takes voting very seriously. In 1977, she campaigned for a populist candidate for Virginia governor. She was undergoing cancer treatments at the time, but they made her tired, so she stopped the treatments in order to register people to vote. She had taught herself to drive, and personally rode around the county from house to house, filling her car with everyone there who was of voting age, driving them to the court house to register, and then home again. She's credited with having registered over one thousand people this way, and on election day, she personally drove many of them to the polling place.

While Cora was growing up, her mother's house was always filled with   15
people—besides her own family, several cousins lived with them, and aunts and uncles who had moved up north and came back to visit would stay with Cora's mother. Cora's own house was the same way—always filled with neighborhood teenagers, white and black. Cora became a confidante for the young people, and she encouraged them to read about black history, and to be concerned about the community. One of the things that upset the teenagers was the fate of a county recreation center. Halifax had no recreation facilities, and the county had applied for money from the federal Department of Housing and Urban Development (HUD) to build a center. When HUD awarded the county $500,000, however, the county turned it down because, as Cora puts it, there were "too many strings attached"— meaning it would have to be integrated. At home because of her back trouble and cancer, Cora took it on herself to help steer the teenagers' anger toward research into community problems. "When I heard about the recreation center, I went to the county board meeting and raised hell," she

says. "But they went ahead and did what they wanted anyway. What I realized then was that if I had had all those kids come with me to the meeting, there would have been some changes. You need warm bodies—persons present and accounted for—if you want to get things done."

In 1975, Cora founded her own organization, Citizens for a Better America. CBA's first project was a study of black spending and employment patterns in the county. The study was based on a survey of three hundred people; it took two years to complete, with Cora's teenage friends doing much of the legwork. The findings painted a clear picture of inequality. Blacks made up nearly half the county population, and according to the survey, spent a disproportionate share of their salaries on food, cars, and furniture. But, as the study pointed out, there were very few black employees at the grocery stores where the money was spent, not a single black salesperson in the furniture stores, and no black salesperson at the auto dealerships. Blacks weren't represented at all on newspaper or radio station staffs.

Cora saw to it that the survey results were published in the local newspaper. The next step was to act on the results. The survey had uncovered problems with hiring practices and promotions of blacks in the school system, so Cora complained to the school board. After waiting in vain for the board to respond, CBA filed a complaint with what was then the federal Department of Health, Education, and Welfare. An HEW investigation confirmed the problems, and the agency threatened to cut off federal education funds to the county if the discrimination wasn't corrected. The county promised that the next principals it hired would be black.

CBA then took on other aspects of the county government. The survey had found that of all the county employees, only 7 percent were black—chiefly custodial workers or workers hired with federal Comprehensive Employment Training Administration (CETA) funds. Only one black person in the county government made over $20,000 a year. When the county refused to negotiate with Cora's organization about their hiring practices, CBA filed a complaint with the federal revenue sharing program. A Virginia state senator was successful in getting a federal investigation into the complaint stalled, but Cora went over his head, to the congressional Black Caucus and Maryland's black congressman, Parren Mitchell. Mitchell contacted Senator Edward Kennedy's office, which pressed to have the investigation completed. The findings confirmed CBA's, and the county was told to improve its hiring practices or stand to lose federal revenues.

CBA also initiated a boycott of local businesses that didn't hire minorities—Cora avoided the term "boycott," and instead called the action the "Spend Your Money Wisely Campaign." Leaflets were distributed listing the stores that hired black employees, and urging people, "Where Blacks are not HIRED, Blacks should not buy!"

Cora was developing a reputation. She started having frequent contact with the congressional Black Caucus, and would be called occasionally to   20 testify in Washington on welfare issues. "They don't usually get people like me to testify; they get all these 'experts' instead. But every once in a while, it's good for them to hear from someone who isn't a professional, whose English isn't good, and who talks from a grassroots level."

It wasn't just in Washington that her reputation was growing, but back home, too. "I have a lot of enemies," she says. "There are derogatory things in the papers about me all the time. And the county government doesn't like me, because I keep going to all those board meetings and raising hell about what they do. When I go sometimes, they say, 'Yes, what do you want now, Ms. Tucker?' But I don't care what they think—I just tell them what I want. So a lot of the white power structure don't really like me. They think I'm a troublemaker, but I'm not really. I just believe what I believe in. Then there are black people too, who think that I want too much too soon. But when you think about it, black people have been in America 360-some years, so when is the time ever going to be right? The time doesn't *get* right; you make it right. So I'm not offended by what anybody says about me."

Sometimes the problem isn't just what people say; it's what they do. Cora has had many experiences with harassment. At first it was phone calls, from people threatening to burn her house down or telling her to "go back to Africa." Once she wrote a letter to the editor saying, "This is an open letter to all the people who call me and ask, what do you niggers want now? and hang up before I can tell them....

"Blacks and poor people want to share in the economic progress of Halifax County, and when we get our children educated and motivated we would like them to come back to Halifax County and do something other than push mops and brooms. And a few of us would like our grandchildren to grow up near us, and if our children decide to make their home elsewhere it will be due to choice and not an economic necessity."

The harassment has taken other forms as well. Cora was followed and run off the highway one night, and had all four tires slashed one day when her car was parked in town. Once she was in the post office and a man recognized her, walked over, and spit on her; another time a car with out-of-state license plates pulled up next to her car as if to ask directions, and the man spat into her face. She came home from a meeting one night to find that someone had broken into her home and drenched her bed with gasoline. But Cora views the abuses with amazing equanimity: "If you stop doing things because somebody says something bad about you or does something to you," she says, "then you'll never get *anything* done."

And she wasn't making only enemies; she was also gaining a following. 25 One woman, who now works in the local legal aid office where Cora stops in frequently to get answers to legal questions, tells how she first met Cora. The woman had been born in Halifax, but had moved to New Jersey when she was a young girl. The civil rights movement progressed, and when the woman was finished with school, she moved back to Virginia, thinking that things there would be much better than they *had* been for blacks. But she found that any progress had been superficial only. When she started looking for work, she discovered that there were no blacks in responsible positions. She wore her hair in an Afro, and in hindsight thinks that it cost her jobs: at one point, it seemed she would be offered a position with the county, but when the man who was to be her boss saw her, he didn't give her the job. Another prospective employer turned her down with the flat statement that he didn't want any union people around.

She became disillusioned, and was shocked at the complacency around her. About that time, she saw Cora Tucker's name in the paper. She was impressed, and started asking around about Cora. Not too long afterwards, she went to a community action program meeting, and noticed that Cora was scheduled to speak. "I was excited. I thought, finally, I'm going to meet a black person who's alive!" But she was initially disappointed. "I had pictured her as a towering woman—a fiery, eloquent speaker, like Barbara Jordan. Instead, there she was, short, and not that articulate."

But she quickly got drawn to Cora's strengths. "Cora wouldn't be happy at home, doing housekeeping," she says. "She's just not cut out for that. She's cut out for doing exactly what she's doing—getting out and raising hell about issues that affect people. She keeps pushing. When I get burned, I back off. But when Cora gets burned, she just blows out the fire and goes on."

Even people who don't like Cora give her credit: "I'm not a Cora Tucker fan," says one South Boston resident. "But I admit that she might just be the most informed person on political issues in this county." People credit Cora with having stamina and with inspiring others. An old friend of hers who runs a corner grocery says, "She keeps people fired up; she won't let us get lazy. It's because of her that I even watch the news!" One woman who was in school with Cora and now works for the county government says, "She was always making noise at school. We knew she'd grow up noisy. But it's *good* noise. When Cora talks, she knows what she's talking about."

And although Cora thinks she'll never be much of a public speaker, others disagree. One man who has worked with Cora for several years described a dinner ceremony sponsored by a human rights coalition in Richmond. "They had asked Cora to come and be a featured speaker. The woman who spoke before her gave this very polished speech. And then Cora got up, and gave her very unpolished speech. But it was moving to everyone in the room, because it was so much from the heart. It was the contrast of day and night between her and the previous speaker. What she had to say was so honest and down to earth, that people were very touched by it. And that's just the way she is."

Cora is very religious. "I believe in God, and in the providence of   30
prayer. I go to church regularly." The churches in her area are still segregated; she attends the Crystal Hill Baptist Church, which, she points out

with a chuckle, is brick-colored, while the white congregation down the road painted their brick church white. In an essay called "Halifax County and Blacks," under a subtitle "Things Blacks Must Do to Succeed," Cora once wrote, "First, blacks must go to church. The church is the backbone of black progress." Every summer for several years Cora has organized a "Citizenship Day of Prayer" on the lawn of the county courthouse in South Boston, which attracts hundreds of people who probably wouldn't gather if the event were called a rally. At the event a list of grievances is always read off—including complaints about such things as how people are treated by the welfare system, unfair employment practices, or disproportionate suspensions of black pupils in the schools.

Problems like that—and what to do about them—are raised regularly at Citizens for a Better America meetings, held the fourth Friday of each month at a local funeral home. CBA has several hundred members, and with help from friends, Cora publishes a monthly one-page newsletter, which she decorates with American flag stickers and short religious sayings. The newsletter is a hodgepodge of useful information, including notices of food stamp law changes, regular updates on what the Virginia General Assembly is considering, board of supervisors' actions, community news, and news about other subjects that Cora is currently concerned with. One issue might have an essay on education, something on federal budget cutbacks and poor people, and a paragraph on the dangers of uranium mining. In 1986, when the federal government was considering southern Virginia, including part of Halifax County, as a possible site for a high-level nuclear waste dump, Cora and CBA fought back, using a section of the federal law requiring that the siting consideration take Indians and other minorities into account. Among other things, CBA found that blacks owned more farmland in Halifax County than in any other county in the country, and that historically, the first black-owned businesses and land in the country were on the site that would be affected by the nuclear waste dump.

Cora learns facts quickly; she can attend a meeting on the problems of family farmers one day, and the next, go to another meeting and be able to reel off facts and figures about farm foreclosures, the cost of fertilizers, trends in agribusiness, and the harmful effect of various pesticides. She reads constantly—newspapers, books, anything on an issue that interests her. "I save newspaper clippings—especially statements from politicians. That way, five years from now when they say, 'I'm definitely against that,' I can go back and say, 'But on such and such a date, you said *this*.'"

Cora stays extremely busy. Several years ago, she went back and got her graduate equivalency diploma, and took some courses at the community college. She thought she might want her degree: "I used to think I wanted to be a social worker. But I changed my mind, because you can't do as much inside the system as you can on the outside. There are so many people who become social workers, and then sit there with their hands tied. What people really need is somebody on the outside who's going to go and raise hell for them about laws and regulations."

Besides CBA gatherings, meetings of the county board of supervisors, and her usual rounds to the legal aid office and the county office building, Cora still visits elderly people, helps women without cars to do their shopping, reads and explains people's mail about food stamps and social security to them, and answers frequent letters. She takes every letter seriously. One, for instance, addressed simply to "Cora Tucker, Halifax, Virginia," read, "Dear Mrs. Tucker, Please don't let the county send us to be experimented on. We heard that they are going to take people on welfare to be experimented on." Cora remembered that there had been separate articles in the newspaper recently, on the "workfare" program to employ welfare recipients, and on a county decision to allow dogs from the animal pound to be used for medical experiments. Cora concluded that the person who wrote the letter had gotten the two issues confused—but she wasn't satisfied until she had called the county administrator and had gotten him to pledge to do a better job of explaining the issues publicly.

Cora's work goes far beyond Halifax. CBA itself has chapters in several other places, including one started in Baltimore by one of Cora's sisters. In addition, when a new coalition group, Virginia Action, was started in the state in 1980, Cora was on the founding committee and was elected its first president. She also became active on the board of its national affiliate, Citizen Action. And in 1981, on top of everything else she was doing, this woman who as a girl had refused to shake the governor's hand was talked into running as a write-in protest candidate for governor by several black groups. She didn't get many votes, but her campaign was covered in the press, and she thinks that she raised issues about black people's concerns that otherwise would have been ignored.

Cora hasn't received much support in her work from her family, except from her mother. She and her husband are estranged, and her children haven't taken an active interest in Cora's work. Cora visits her mother often, in an old house several miles away that has woodburning stoves for heat, religious pictures in the downstairs room, and, hanging in the stairway, a plastic placemat depicting Martin Luther King's tomb. Cora's mother is clearly proud of her; she emphasizes what a smart girl Cora was, and is, and how courageous.

Others agree. As a man who works with Cora at Virginia Action puts it, "All of the issues Cora has taken on—like voting rights and employment discrimination—had been problems in Halifax County for decades. But nobody was willing to fight. And the reason was that it's very, very hard to be somebody going against the mainstream in a small rural community. It's a hell of a lot easier to play the role of the gadfly when you live in an urban environment, where you have your own community of friends, and you don't have to worry about the world. In a small rural community, your community *is* your world. And it's hard to fight the people you have to face every single day. Cora's able to do it because she's got guts. There's just nothing else to it but courage. In a small community those people writing nasty letters to the editor about you are people you're going to run into at the grocery, or whose kids go to school with yours. In addition, being black in a southern rural community, and being a woman, make it that much harder. She hasn't even had the active support of a large part of the black community—they feel threatened by her; she's stolen a lot of their fire. And she's always fighting back as opposed to the blacks who always cooperate with the white power structure. She just reached a point where she decided that slow-moving efforts weren't enough for the things that needed doing—things that were clear in her mind. She recognized the dangers that would be involved, but went ahead because she knew she was right."

ENGAGING THE TEXT

1. How might Cora Tucker define success? To what extent has she achieved it?

2. What motivates Cora Tucker? How do you explain her courage and commitment? Can you think of any ways to encourage more people to emulate some of her virtues?

3. What has her experience taught Cora Tucker about "organizing"? What are her strategies for getting things done?

4. Do you think people in small towns or rural communities are better able than urban dwellers to influence political decisions that affect them? Why or why not?

EXPLORING CONNECTIONS

5. Review the stories of Ragged Dick (p. 297) and Trung Dung (p. 310) to refresh in your mind those versions of the American Dream. What, if anything, does Cora Tucker have in common with Dick or Trung? How does she differ from them?

6. In "Class in America: Myths and Realities (2000)" (p. 331), Gregory Mantsios writes, "When we look at society and try to determine what it is that keeps most people down—what holds them back from realizing their potential as healthy, creative, productive individuals—we find institutionally oppressive forces that are largely beyond their individual control." How do you think Cora Tucker might respond to this statement? Does her story challenge this or other claims by Mantsios?

EXTENDING THE CRITICAL CONTEXT

7. Research grass-roots organizations like Citizens for a Better America in your community. Choose one, attend a meeting, and interview members of the organization. Report to the class on its goals, strategies, accomplishments, and current objectives and challenges.

8. In May 2000, the American Association of Retired Persons (AARP) released "Money and the American Family," a report based on nationwide interviews. The report contains several interesting findings—for example, that 11 percent of Americans are "wealth-averse" and, like Cora Tucker, don't particularly crave money. Consult the AARP report and summarize what you find for the class. If you have Internet access, visit the AARP Web site at www.aarp.org or the *Rereading America* site: www.bedfordstmartins.com/rereadingamerica.

From *The High Price of Materialism*
TIM KASSER

Tim Kasser is certainly not the first person to argue that the pursuit of material possessions does not lead to happiness—spiritual leaders and philosophers have sounded this theme for centuries. Kasser may be the first, however, to prove it scientifically. According to a number of studies carried out by Kasser and his colleagues, those of us who place a high value on money and possessions are more prone to depression, anxiety, and other psychological problems, and even to such physical ills as headaches and sore throats. Note that one of the populations most studied was college students. Kasser (b. 1966) is a professor of psychology and a prize-winning teacher at Knox College in Galesburg, Illinois. He has authored many scientific articles and book chapters. The reading here is taken from his recent book The High Price of Materialism *(2002).*

> To continue much longer overwhelmed by business cares and with most of my thoughts wholly upon the way to make money in the shortest time must degrade me beyond hope of permanent recovery.
> —ANDREW CARNEGIE[1]

   In recent years, scientific investigators working in a variety of fields have begun to tally the costs of a materialistic lifestyle. Although the body of empirical literature on materialism is not large, especially compared with what we know about topics such as depression, stereotyping, neurons, and memory, its findings are quite consistent. Indeed, what stands out across the studies is a simple fact: people who strongly value the pursuit of wealth

---

[1]Carnegie quotation is from Hendrick (1932), pp. 146–147.

and possessions report lower psychological well-being than those who are less concerned with such aims.

Research from Our Lab

Since 1993 my colleagues and I have been publishing a series of papers in which we have been exploring how people's values and goals relate to their well-being. Our focus has been on understanding what people view as important or valuable in life, and on associating those values statistically with a variety of other aspects of their lives, such as happiness, depression, and anxiety. What people value clearly varies from one individual to another. For some, spirituality and religion are of paramount importance; for others, home life, relationships, and family are especially valued; other people focus on having fun and excitement; and others on contributing to the community.[2] In our work, we have been particularly interested in individuals for whom materialistic values are relatively important. That is, compared with other things that might be deemed central to one's life, what happens psychologically when a person feels that making money and having possessions are relatively high in the pantheon of values?

Our First Study

To obtain an answer to this question, Richard Ryan and I began by developing a questionnaire to measure people's values, which we called the Aspiration Index.[3] People who complete this questionnaire are presented with many different types of goals and asked to rate each one in terms of whether it is not at all important, somewhat important, extremely important, and so on. The current version of the Aspiration Index includes a large number of possible goals people might have, such as desires to feel safe and secure, to help the world be a better place, to have a great sex life, and to have good relationships with others. By assessing different types of goals, we can obtain a valid assessment of how important materialistic values are in the context of a person's entire system of values. Most value researchers view this as crucial and insist that we can know how much someone values a particular outcome only when that value is considered in relation to other things that might possibly be valued.[4]

Table 2.1 shows items used to assess materialistic values in our first study. Of central interest, participants reported how important several

[2]There is no real agreement in psychology as to the exact number or content of values that make up the human value system, although Shalom Schwartz (1992, 1994, 1996) has made an excellent case for a "universal" system of values. Nonetheless, a glance through a review of value measures (Braithwaite & Scott 1991) will probably impress the reader for how much disagreement exists among psychologists about what values are important to measure.

[3] This first study is Kasser and Ryan (1993).

[4]Milton Rokeach (1973), a prominent thinker in empirical value research, coined the term "relative centrality" to describe how important a value is relative to other values. His insistence on this means of measurement is relatively well accepted among value researchers.

financial success aspirations were to them. We also asked participants how much they were concerned with *self-acceptance* (desires for psychological growth, autonomy, and self-esteem), *affiliation* (desires for a good family life and friendships), and *community feeling* (desires to make the world a better place through one's own actions). From these ratings, we could determine how important, or central, the value of financial success was for each person relative to the other three values.

Ryan and I administered the Aspiration Index to a group of individuals who, second to white rats, form the backbone of much scientific research in psychology: college students. Three hundred sixteen students at the University of Rochester completed a survey packet that included the index and four questionnaires that assessed positive feelings of well-being and negative feelings of distress.

The first measure of well-being assessed self-actualization, a concept made popular by the father of humanistic psychology, Abraham Maslow. Maslow conceived of self-actualization as the pinnacle of psychological health, the state attained by people motivated by growth, meaning, and aesthetics, rather than by insecurity and the attempt to fit in with what other people expect.[5] People who score high on this measure of self-actualization generally agree with statements such as, "It is better to be yourself than to be popular," and "I do not feel ashamed of any of my emotions." Our second measure of well-being, vitality, also assesses psychological growth and the energy that goes along with authentically expressing who one really is. Vital people are likely to feel energized, alert, and overflowing with that wonderful feeling of being alive.

The last two measures assessed two of the most common psychological disorders: depression and anxiety. The depression questionnaire asked participants how frequently they had experienced common depressive symptoms such as feeling down, feeling lonely or disconnected from others, having sleep or appetite troubles, and having little energy or difficulty concentrating. The anxiety measure asked how much they generally experienced nervousness or shakiness inside, felt tense or fearful, or were suddenly scared for no reason.[6]

Table 2.1   Financial success items from Kasser and Ryan's (1993) Aspiration Index

You will buy things just because you want them.
You will be financially successful.
You will be your own boss.
You will have a job with high social status.
You will have a job that pays well.

Participants rate how important these aspirations are, from not at all to very important.
Reprinted by permission of the American Psychological Association.

[5]Maslow (1954) described this idea well.

[6]Well-being measures include self-actualization (Jones & Crandall, 1986), vitality (Ryan & Frederick, 1997), anxiety (Derogatis et al., 1974), and depression (Radloff, 1977).

5

When we used statistical analyses to examine how people's value orientations related to their well-being, the results were intriguing. Compared with students who were more oriented toward self-acceptance, affiliation, or community feeling, those who considered financial success a relatively central value reported significantly lower levels of self-actualization and vitality, as well as significantly higher levels of depression and anxiety. Notably, such a strong focus was associated with decreased psychological well-being regardless of whether participants were men or women.

These results supported the premise that materialistic values are unhealthy, but we wanted to see if they would be replicated with young adults who were not in college, and with other ways of assessing well-being besides questionnaires. We therefore gave a somewhat shorter version of the Aspiration Index to a wide-ranging group of 140 eighteen-year-olds. These adolescents varied greatly in terms of race, socioeconomic status, and their mothers' psychological health. Their current situation in life was also diverse, with some having dropped out of high school and others going on to college, some already having had children, and others in trouble with the law.

We evaluated psychological well-being in a somewhat different way in this sample. Instead of completing questionnaires, participants met with an experienced clinical psychologist who interviewed them using a set of standard questions. From these interviews ratings were made of the extent to which the teens were socially productive and of how much they exhibited symptoms of behavior disorders. A socially productive adolescent was defined as someone who was doing well in school, was holding down a job, and had hobbies and other outside interests. Behavior disorders, one of the most common of all childhood problems, involved a variety of symptoms expressing oppositional, defiant, and antisocial behavior common in unhappy teens, such as fighting, belonging to a gang, stealing, and torturing small animals. We also measured the teens' general functioning in life by rating them on a 100-point scale commonly used to assess people's level of psychiatric impairment and overall adaptation to life.[7]

Even with these differences in samples and the way we assessed well-being, the results with these teenagers revealed a pattern consistent with our earlier findings: individuals who were focused on financial success, compared with nonmaterialistic values, were not adapting to society well and were acting in rather destructive ways. Specifically, they were not functioning well in school, on the job, or in their extracurricular activities, and were likely to exhibit various symptoms of behavior disorders, such as vandalizing, skipping school, and carrying weapons.

Our first studies therefore showed that when young adults report that financial success is relatively central to their aspirations, low well-being,

10

---

[7] The scales in this study were social productivity (Ikle et al., 1983), conduct disorders (Herjanic & Reich, 1982), and global functioning (American Psychiatric Association, 1987). See Sameroff et al. (1982) for more information about the heterogeneous sample.

high distress, and difficulty adjusting to life are also evident. Although we cannot be sure from these results whether materialistic values cause unhappiness, or whether other factors are at work, the results do suggest a rather startling conclusion: the American dream has a dark side, and the pursuit of wealth and possessions might actually be undermining our well-being.

More Recent Work from Our Lab

These results raised a number of further questions in our minds. Were financial success values the only ones that were problematic for people's psychological health? What would happen if we looked at older individuals? Would similar results be found for other aspects of psychological health and distress? These were some of the issues Ryan and I tried to grapple with in our next study.[8]

We began by revising the Aspiration Index to include some other prominent goals and values of consumer culture. Although strivings for money and possessions certainly constitute the core message encouraged by consumeristic and capitalistic cultures, two other goals are also typically encouraged: having the "right" image and being well known socially. Image and fame values are entwined with those for money and possessions in at least a couple of ways. First, the media in consumeristic cultures frequently link these values by having good-looking celebrities sell products. The underlying message is that owning these products will enhance our image and ensure our popularity with others. A second way these values are connected is that image, fame, and money all share a focus of looking for a sense of worth outside of oneself, and involve striving for external rewards and the praise of others. When we focus on these values (which Ryan and I called "extrinsic"), we are seeking sources of satisfaction outside of ourselves, whether in money, in the mirror, or in admiration by others. In capitalistic, consumer cultures such as the United States, these extrinsic values are often encouraged as worthy because they seemingly convey a sense of success and power.

Table 2.2 lists the items we used in the revised version of the Aspiration Index to measure these three types of materialistic values. In several studies, we have found that people who value one of these values, such as fame, also tend to value money and image. Thus they seem to have "bought into" the prominent goals of consumer society. Notably, this cluster of goals also was found in students from both Russia and Germany, suggesting that the coexistence of money, fame, and image values can be found in cultures less consumeristic than the United States.[9]

Having expanded the Aspiration Index to measure a greater number of values relevant to the messages of consumer culture, Ryan and I set out to

[8]Further information on results from the next two samples reviewed can be found in Kasser (1994) or Kasser and Ryan (1996).

[9]See Ryan et al. (1999) and Schmuck et al. (2000).

Table 2.2   Sample items from Kasser and Ryan's (1996) revised Aspiration Index

Financial success
You will have a job with high social status.
You will have a job that pays well.
You will be financially successful.
You will have a lot of expensive possessions.
Social recognition
Your name will be known by many people.
You will do something that brings you much recognition.
You will be admired by many people.
You will be famous.
Your name will appear frequently in the media.
Appealing appearance
You will successfully hide the signs of aging.
You will have people comment often about how attractive you look.
You will keep up with fashions in hair and clothing.
You will achieve the "look" you've been after.
Your image will be one others find appealing.

determine whether our results would be the same in adults as they were in college students and teenagers. We randomly sampled a group of 100 adults living in a diverse neighborhood of Rochester, New York. The participants ranged from eighteen to seventy-nine years of age and came from lower, middle, and upper socioeconomic backgrounds. The survey packet we left at participants' doors contained the revised Aspiration Index and the four measures of well-being we used previously (self-actualization, vitality, anxiety, depression measures). Participants also reported on their physical health by noting how often they had experienced nine physical symptoms in the past week (headache, stomach aches, backaches, etc.).[10]

The findings largely corroborated those reported with young adults. Adults who focused on money, image, and fame reported less self-actualization and vitality, and more depression than those less concerned with these values. What is more, they also reported significantly more experiences of physical symptoms. That is, people who believed it is important to strive for possessions, popularity, and good looks also reported more headaches, backaches, sore muscles, and sore throats than individuals less focused on such goals. This was really one of the first indicators, to us, of the pervasive negative correlates of materialistic values—not only is people's psychological well-being worse when they focus on money, but so is their physical health.

As in our studies of college students, materialistic values were equally unhealthy for men and women. Because of the nature of this sample, we could also examine whether findings depended on age or income. Analyses

[10]Items were taken from Emmons (1991).

showed that regardless of their age or wealth, people with highly central materialistic values also reported lower well-being.

Having documented some of the problems associated with materialism in adults of different ages and backgrounds, we returned to college students and teenagers to explore further the many different ways that these values are associated with low well-being. As a start, we wanted a better sense of the daily lives of people with a strong materialistic orientation. The earlier studies asked individuals to look back on some portion of their lives and tell us about their well-being; although this is a quick method to measure how people are feeling, we wanted to change the focus and obtain a snapshot of people's daily lives. Therefore, in addition to completing our standard packet of questionnaires, we asked 192 students at the University of Rochester to keep a diary for two weeks. In the middle of each day, and then again at the end of each day, they answered several questions about their current experience: how much they had the same nine physical symptoms assessed in the adult sample and how much they felt each of nine emotions (e.g., happy, joyful, unhappy, angry).

As before, participants highly focused on materialistic values reported   20 less self-actualization and vitality and more depression than those with less interest in those values. They also experienced more physical symptoms and less in the way of positive emotions over the two weeks. Something about a strong desire for materialistic pursuits actually affected the participants' day-to-day lives and decreased the quality of their daily experience.[11]

Another new element of this study was measurement of participants' narcissistic tendencies. In psychological parlance, narcissism describes people who cover an inner feeling of emptiness and questionable self-worth with a grandiose exterior that brags of self-importance. Narcissists are typically vain, expect special treatment and admiration from others, and can be manipulative and hostile toward others. Social critics and psychologists have often suggested that consumer culture breeds a narcissistic personality by focusing individuals on the glorification of consumption (e.g., "Have it your way"; "Want it? Get it!").[12] Furthermore, narcissists' desire for external validation fits well with our conception of materialistic values as extrinsic and focused on others' praise. Thus it was not surprising to find that students

---

[11]Another important finding from this study related to an issue relevant to socially desirable responding. Psychologists are often concerned that participants' responses to certain questionnaires are clouded by the desire to answer in a way that fits with what they think society feels is "good." As a result, they may be unlikely to admit to feelings and thoughts that might be seen as deviant or less than optimal. Because a scale exists to measure socially desirable responding (Crowne & Marlowe, 1960), we examined whether this might explain why people strongly focused on materialistic values reported low well-being. Our statistical analysis found no support for this idea, as the effects remained significant even after accounting for socially desirable responses. Notably, however, Mick (1996) reached a different conclusion with other measures of materialism.

[12]See Cushman (1990) or Kanner and Gomes (1995).

with strong materialistic tendencies scored high on a standard measure of narcissism, agreeing with statements such as, "I am more capable than other people," "I like to start new fads and fashions," "I wish somebody would write my biography one day," and "I can make anybody believe anything I want them to."[13]

More recent studies expanded our measurements of psychological functioning by examining the extent to which materialism is associated with the use of substances such as tobacco, alcohol, and drugs. In one such project, Ryan and I asked 261 students at Montana State University how many cigarettes they smoked on a typical day, and how often in the last year they had "gotten drunk," "smoked marijuana," and "done hard drugs." When we averaged these four indicators, results showed that people with a strong materialistic value orientation were highly likely to use such substances frequently.[14]

These results were replicated by Geoff Williams in two groups of high school students.[15] In one study, 141 high school students were asked whether they had smoked 100 cigarettes in their lifetime, which is the National Cancer Institute's definition of a smoker. Student smokers were more oriented toward materialistic values than toward values such as self-acceptance, affiliation, and community feeling. Williams next asked 271 ninth- through twelfth-graders about an even broader list of behaviors that put teens at risk for later problems, such as use of cigarettes, chewing tobacco, alcohol, and marijuana, as well as whether they ever had sexual intercourse. Materialistic teens were more likely to engage in each of these five risk behaviors than were teens focused on other values.

References

American Psychiatric Association. (1987). *Diagnostic and statistical manual of mental disorders* (3rd ed., rev.). Washington, DC: American Psychiatric Association.

Braithwaite, V. A., & Scott, W. A. (1991). Values. In J. P. Robinson, P. R. Shaver, & L. S. Wrightsman (Eds.), *Measures of personality and social psychological attitudes* (pp. 661–753). San Diego: Academic Press.

Crowne, D. P., & Marlowe, D. (1960). A new scale of social desirability independent of psychopathology. *Journal of Consulting Psychology, 24,* 349–354.

Cushman, P. (1990). Why the self is empty: Toward a historically situated psychology. *American Psychologist, 45,* 599–611.

Derogatis, L. R., Lipman, R. S., Rickels, K., Uhlenhuth, E. H., & Covi, L. (1974). The Hopkins Symptom Checklist (HSCL): A self-report symptom inventory. *Behavioral Science, 19,* 1–15.

[13]This narcissism scale was developed by Raskin and Terry (1988).
[14]Kasser and Ryan (2001).
[15]Williams et al. (2000).

Emmons, R. A. (1991). Personal strivings, daily life events, and psychological and physical well-being. *Journal of Personality, 59,* 453–472.

Hendrick, B. J. (1932). *The life of Andrew Carnegie,* Vol. 1. Garden City, NY: Doubleday.

Herjanic, B., & Reich, W. (1982). Development of a structured psychiatric interview for children: Agreement between child and parent on individual symptoms. *Journal of Abnormal Child Psychology, 10,* 307–324.

Ikle, D. N., Lipp, D. O., Butters, E. A., & Ciarlo, J. (1983). *Development and validation of the adolescent community mental health questionnaire.* Denver, CO: Mental Systems Evaluation Project.

Jones, A., & Crandall, R. (1986). Validation of a short index of self-actualization. *Personality and Social Psychology Bulletin, 12,* 63–73.

Kanner, A. D., & Gomes, M. E. (1995). The all-consuming self. In T. Roszak, M. E. Gomes, & A. D. Kanner (Eds.), *Ecopsychology: Restoring the Earth, healing the mind* (pp. 77–91). San Francisco: Sierra Club Books.

Kasser, T. (1994). *Further dismantling the American dream: Differential well-being correlates of intrinsic and extrinsic goals.* Unpublished doctoral dissertation, University of Rochester, Rochester, NY.

Kasser, T., & Ryan, R. M. (1993). A dark side of the American dream: Correlates of financial success as a central life aspiration. *Journal of Personality and Social Psychology, 65,* 410–422.

Kasser, T., & Ryan, R. M. (1996). Further examining the American dream: Differential correlates of intrinsic and extrinsic goals. *Personality and Social Psychology Bulletin, 22,* 280–287.

Kasser, T., & Ryan R. M. (2001). Be careful what you wish for: Optimal functioning and the relative attainment of intrinsic and extrinsic goals. In P. Schmuck & K. M. Sheldon (Eds.), Life goals and well-being: *Towards a positive psychology of human striving* (pp. 116–131). Goettingen, Germany: Hogrefe & Huber.

Maslow, A. H. (1954). *Motivation and personality.* New York: Harper & Row.

Mick, D. G. (1996). Are studies of dark side variables confounded by socially desirable responding? The case of materialism. *Journal of Consumer Research, 23,* 106–119.

Radloff, L. (1977). The CES-D scale: A self-report depression scale for research in the general population. *Applied Psychological Measurement, 1,* 385–401.

Raskin, R., & Terry, H. (1988). A principal components analysis of the Narcissistic Personality Inventory and further evidence of its construct validity. *Journal of Personality and Social Psychology, 54,* 890–902.

Rokeach, M. (1973). *The nature of human values.* New York: Free Press.

Ryan, R. M., Chirkov, V. I., Little, T. D., Sheldon, K. M., Timoshina, E., & Deci, E. L. (1999). The American dream in Russia: Extrinsic aspirations and well-being in two cultures. *Personality and Social Psychology Bulletin, 25,* 1509–1524.

Ryan, R. M., & Frederick, C. (1997). On energy, personality, and health: Subjectivity vitality as a dynamic reflection of well-being. *Journal of Personality, 65,* 529–565.

Sameroff, A. J., Seifer, R., & Zax, M. (1982). Early development of children at risk for emotional disorders. *Monographs of the Society for Research in Child Development, 47* (serial no. 199).

Schmuck, P., Kasser, T., & Ryan, R. M. (2000). Intrinsic and extrinsic goals: Their structure and relationship to well-being in German and U.S. college students. *Social Indicators Research, 50,* 225–241.

Schwartz, S. H. (1992). Universals in the content and structure of values: Theoretical and empirical tests in 20 countries. In M. Zanna (Ed.), *Advances in experimental and social psychology,* Vol. 25 (pp. 1–65). Orlando, FL: Academic Press.

Schwartz, S. H. (1994). Are there universal aspects in the content and structure of values? *Journal of Social Issues, 50,* 19–45.

Schwartz, S. H. (1996). Values, priorities and behavior: Applying of theory of integrated value systems. In C. Seligman, J. M. Olson, & M. P. Zanna (Eds.), *The psychology of values: The Ontario symposium,* Vol. 8 (pp. 1–24). Hillsdale, NJ: Erlbaum.

Williams, G. C., Cox, E. M., Hedberg, V. A., & Deci, E. L. (2000). Extrinsic life goals and health risk behaviors in adolescents. *Journal of Applied Social Psychology, 30,* 1756–1771.

ENGAGING THE TEXT

1. Kasser's central message is very straightforward—"people who strongly value the pursuit of wealth and possessions report lower psychological well-being than those who are less concerned with such aims." To what extent does this claim support or challenge your own view?

2. If Kasser is right about the negative effect of materialism on personal well-being, why isn't this phenomenon more widely understood? How and why might cultural myths about the desirability of money and success thrive in the face of the negative consequences of materialism?

3. What fields of study and what careers most appeal to you, and why? How important is the prospect of material success in your attraction to these fields?

4. Jot down some notes concerning what level of material wealth and possessions you think should be "enough" for a couple and two adolescent children (e.g., living space, bathrooms, TVs (if any), cars, phones, computers, savings or investments, and so on). Compare notes with classmates and discuss. Would you be content with "enough"?

5. Make two lists:

   a. Material possessions you have purchased but could readily do without

   b. Things you would truly like to buy but can't afford (at least not yet)

   How important to you are these things compared to some of the other values Kasser mentions, such as relationships, spirituality, community involvement, or fun and excitement? To the extent that you do want certain *things*, consider precisely why you want them (e.g., convenience, status, social acceptance, and so on). Write down your ideas in a journal entry or short essay.

EXPLORING CONNECTIONS

6. Briefly review *Ragged Dick* (p. 297) to determine how "materialistic" Dick is. In small groups, brainstorm the kind of future Kasser might predict for him.

7. Review "Serving in Florida" (p. 317), looking for any correlations between materialism and levels of personal well-being. How do you think Kasser might assess the lives of the people Barbara Ehrenreich describes?

8. Look back to "An Indian Story" (p. 109), "Looking for Work" (p. 26), "Aunt Ida Pieces a Quilt" (p. 131), "Good Noise: Cora Tucker" (p. 353), or "Stephen Cruz" (p. 348). How important are material possessions to the people in these selections? Do you think these stories provide powerful support for Kasser's thesis? Why or why not?

EXTENDING THE CRITICAL CONTEXT

9. Search the Internet for a version of Kasser and Ryan's Aspiration Index. First complete the questionnaire yourself; then study how it is constructed and scored. Report to the class on how the index works and give your assessment of its usefulness.

10. In the final chapter of *The High Price of Materialism,* Kasser poses two key questions: "First, we must ask what is an alternative vision of personal and social life that is not centered on materialistic aims? Second, we must ask the even more difficult question, how do we go about implementing the changes necessary to reach a more inwardly rich vision of the good life?" [p. 97 of Kasser]. Work in groups to generate several possible answers to these questions. To extend the assignment, consult Kasser's book to find his recommendations.

Visual Portfolio

READING IMAGES OF INDIVIDUAL OPPORTUNITY

The only thing better than waking up feeling like a million dollars is waking up with a million dollars.

With a Simmons® Beautyrest® or BackCare,® you are bound to wake up feeling better rested and more refreshed. And there couldn't be a better time to check one out than now. Because you can win up to $1 million instantly in our "Million Dollar Mattress Test." Just stop by your local participating Simmons dealer and try out a Beautyrest or BackCare. These sleep systems are designed to give you a better night's sleep. Something 80% of Americans aren't getting these days. For a Simmons dealer near you, call 1-800-SIMMONS. It could be well worth the trip.

www.simmons.com

Visual Portfolio
READING IMAGES OF INDIVIDUAL OPPORTUNITY

1. When do you think the photo of the father giving cash to his family was taken, and what ideas about money, social class, family, and gender was it meant to convey at that time? Explain why you think it was or was not meant to be humorous. What meanings does the image convey to you today? Compare this photograph with Norman Rockwell's *Freedom from Fear* (p. 24) in terms of cultural messages and visual composition or structure.

2. Explain the appeal of the Simmons mattress ad. Consider in particular the different ways the idea of money is being used to sell mattresses. Also discuss such details of the photograph as its overhead perspective, the woman's posture and facial expression, and the amount of money actually pictured.

3. What's happening in the photograph of the bank meeting? Discuss such elements of the photo as the setting, the bankers' clothes, their facial expressions, and the framed portraits on the wall. What does this image tell you about money and success? Compare the women in this photo to the other females in this portfolio—the mother and daughter getting their allowance, and the woman with a million dollars. Considered as a group, what do these images say about women and money in American culture?

4. How does the urban scene with the TV fit into a portfolio of images about money and success? What ideas and emotions does it trigger in you? Explain the prominence of the broken TV: Why is a portion of the image framed by a TV rather than by one of countless alternatives (picture frame, doorway, window, etc.)?

5. In the photograph of a man repairing novelty items during vocational training, what else is going on? What is the man thinking? What is his relationship to his work, to the toys, and to his coworker? What do you make of the slogan on his T-shirt, "Freedom by any means necessary"?

6. Working in small groups, take a close look at the design of whatever coins and paper money you have handy. What information is being conveyed in their words and images?

From Seven Floors Up

SHARON OLDS

This short poem uses one of the simplest but most effective artistic methods ever devised—dramatic contrast. The figures compared here are a homeless man and the comfortable poet who observes him; the differences between the two invite you to consider why poverty and affluence coexist and what determines who succeeds. Sharon Olds (b. 1942) is author of several books of poetry, including Satan Says *(1980),* The Dead and the Living *(1983, winner of the National Book Critics Circle Award),* The Gold Cell *(1987),* The Father *(1992), and* Blood, Tin, Straw *(1999). Olds was honored as poet laureate of New York State for 1998–2000; she teaches at New York University. Her most recent volume of poetry,* The Unswept Room *(2002), was a National Book Award finalist.*

He is pushing a shopping cart up the ramp
out of the park.[1] He owns, in the world,
only what he has there—no sink, no water, no
heat. When we'd come out of the wilderness,
after the week in the desert, in tents,   5
and on the river, by canoe, and when I had my own
motel-room, I cried for humble, dreading
joy in the shower, I kneeled and put
my arms around the cold, clean
toilet. From up here, his profile looks like   10
Che Guevara's,[2] in the last picture,
the stitches like marks on a butcher's chart.
Suddenly I see that I have thought that it could not
happen to me, homelessness
—like death, by definition it would not happen.   15
And he shoulders his earth, his wheeled hovel,
north, the wind at his back—November,
the trees coming bare in earnest. November,
month of my easy birth.

ENGAGING THE TEXT

1. Why do you think Olds chose the title "From Seven Floors Up"? Why is this detail important enough to become the poem's title?

---

[1]*up the ramp / out of the park:* This suggests Central Park in New York City.
[2]*Che Guevara:* Ernesto Guevara, Argentina-born Cuban revolutionary (1928–1967).

2. Take a few moments to visualize each image in the poem. Identify those you consider most powerful or interesting.

3. What is the dominant feeling about homelessness expressed in this poem? Does it express any of your own feelings about poverty? Explain.

4. What does the speaker mean when she says that hers was an "easy birth"? The speaker seems to think she could become homeless; how likely does this seem to you?

5. Do you think homelessness could ever happen to you? Explain why or why not.

EXPLORING CONNECTIONS

6. Write a conversation among three or more of these figures as they discuss what determines success versus failure:

> The speaker of the poem "From Seven Floors Up"
> The homeless man in "From Seven Floors Up"
> Gregory Mantsios, author of "Class in America (2000)," page 331
> Barbara Ehrenreich, author of "Serving in Florida," page 317

7. Like this poem, Barbara Ehrenreich's "Serving in Florida" (p. 317) is based on a relatively privileged woman's observation of those less fortunate. Compare the relationship of this poem's speaker and the homeless man to that of Ehrenreich and her co-workers. For example, to what extent are the ideas of each piece shaped by the observer's nearness to or distance from the people she is observing? Explain the effect each author's approach has on you as a reader.

EXTENDING THE CRITICAL CONTEXT

8. Write a brief poem from the point of view of the homeless man, imagining him looking seven stories up and seeing someone gazing down at him.

Money

DANA GIOIA

Money and poetry are strange bedfellows: we rarely think of them to-gether. Dana Gioia (b. 1950) is well suited to couple them, however; he did graduate study in both comparative literature and business administration, and even when he worked as a product manager for Kool-Aid, he set aside two

*hours a day for reading and writing poetry. Gioia is chair of the National En-
dowment for the Arts. His publications include* Daily Horoscope: Poems
(1986), The Gods of Winter: Poems *(1991),* Interrogations at Noon: Poems
(2001), and Nosferatu: An Opera Libretto *(2001). In this poem, published in*
Forbes *(1999), he invites us to think about the ways we talk about money.*

> Money is a kind of poetry.
> —WALLACE STEVENS

Money, the long green,
cash, stash, rhino, jack
or just plain dough.

Chock it up, fork it over,
shell it out. Watch it   5
burn holes through pockets.

To be made of it! To have it
to burn! Greenbacks, double eagles,
megabucks and Ginnie Maes.

It greases the palm, feathers a nest,   10
holds heads above water,
makes both ends meet.

Money breeds money.
Gathering interest, compounding daily.
Always in circulation   15

Money. You don't know where it's been,
but you put it where your mouth is.
And it talks.

ENGAGING THE TEXT

1. Which words and phrases in the poem are familiar to you, which unfamiliar? Work with classmates to clarify the meanings of as many words and
   phrases as possible. As you do so, try to associate each word or phrase with
   one or more particular settings where it might be used (for example, banks,
   casinos, Wall Street, drug deals) and with any particular ideas about money
   it expresses.
2. What is the dominant attitude about money expressed in the poem? To
   what extent do you share this attitude?
3. The brevity of the last line and its placement at the poem's conclusion give
   it special emphasis. Why do you think Gioia ends his poem this way?

EXPLORING CONNECTIONS

4. Compare this poem with the one by Sharon Olds that precedes it (p. 381). Think about the tone of each poem, about each poem's speaker or voice, and about the ways each poem tries to appeal to you.

EXTENDING THE CRITICAL CONTEXT

5. An ordinary dictionary may not help you much with understanding synonyms for money like "rhino" and "jack." How might you find out more about the meanings of these words, and perhaps about their derivation or history? In other words, what resources beyond your dictionary are available to you for learning about language? Consult some of these resources and see what you can find out about the vocabulary in this poem.

6. Gioia constructs his poem by using many words and phrases either meaning "money" or associated with money. Write your own poem using the same strategy, but with a different main topic—food, music, friendship, TV, or a topic of your choice. A dictionary of quotations and a thesaurus might help you.

The Black Avenger
KEN HAMBLIN

If radio talk show hosts are paid to be controversial, Ken Hamblin earns his money. He refers to young black women who bear children out of wedlock as "brood mares"; most of their children were sired, he writes, by "black thugs." Hamblin's main theme is the vitality of the American Dream and, in particular, his belief that black Americans should embrace that dream, quit whining about white racism, forget affirmative action, and make successes of themselves in the best country on earth. "The Black Avenger" touches on many of Hamblin's most provocative ideas. It is excerpted from his book Pick a Better Country: An Unassuming Colored Guy Speaks His Mind about America *(1996). Hamblin has himself lived a version of the American Dream. Raised in a poor area of Brooklyn by West Indian immigrant parents, his work in varied media fields (photojournalism, cinematography, TV production, newspapers, talk radio) has led to national recognition and an audience of over two million for* The Ken Hamblin Show. *In 1999 he published* Plain Talk and Common Sense from the Black Avenger.*

Broad brushstrokes have been used over the last couple of years to paint a simplistic picture of the serious grievances emanating from middle America.

This picture painted and broadcast by the mainstream media is far different from the complex white backlash that I see and fear, however. The mainstream media have reduced nearly every political and social phenomenon I have written about in this book to a simple sound bite and a three-word headline: "Angry White Men."

The premise is that the black race and the white race are moving farther and farther apart because these angry white men are coming together in a collective backlash against the benefits afforded blacks through civil rights over the last three decades.

The evidence frequently cited is that these men, who for years held an unfair advantage in the workplace and in society in general, now are attacking programs such as affirmative action, which were designed to give minorities the edge to compensate for the years they were not treated as equals.

The predominantly liberal media report that these white men make up   5
the core of the growing conservative audience of talk radio. As a nationally syndicated talk radio host who is on the air for three hours five days a week, I guess this means that I should be among the first to hear from these guys.

But in actuality, that misconception is shattered regularly on *The Ken Hamblin Show*. The most interesting evidence against the stereotype comes in call after call, day after day, from white men, white southern men in particular, whom I hear crying uncle in this tired debate about race.

They are not crying uncle in the sense that they are rolling over.

What they are saying is: "Look, I personally didn't do it. I've gone through the family Bible. I haven't found one instance where we owned slaves. But I'll admit that at one time in America an injustice was committed against people of color—against black people, African Americans, Negroes. And as a white person, I am willing to atone for that."

In January of 1994 my local Denver radio program was broadcast live on C-Span and then repeated several times over the following week. On that show I addressed this guilt factor among white Americans and, as a spoof, offered to send my listeners and my viewers a copy of my very own "Certificate of Absolution."

Some months earlier, a man had called me on the air, identified himself   10
as white, and told me with candor and some degree of desperation that he was tired of feeling guilty about "my people."

That prompted me to come up with an official pardon in the form of a certificate, which only a clear-thinking black American would be authorized to issue. Soon after that, a Denver printer named Rex Kniss, who listened to my show, called and said he would be willing to print the certificate.

Rex added some "certificate" language to my thoughts and we ended up with the following:

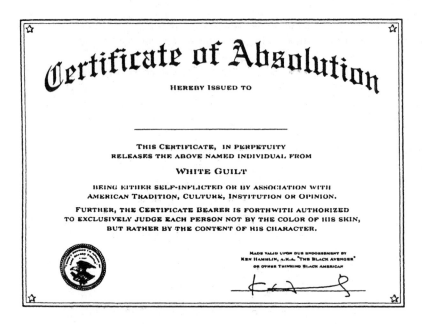

I signed the Certificate "The Black Avenger," a moniker that I use particularly with my radio listeners. The idea behind the name was that I wanted to avenge the lies and the disinformation that more than thirty years of liberalism have brought about in this country. More to the point, I wanted to present myself as living proof that America works for black people too. As the Black Avenger, I was a living, breathing challenge to the well-honed Myth of the Hobbled Black.[1]

"The Black Avenger" caught on among my fans in 1993 while I was on a local Denver radio station that also carried Rush Limbaugh. Limbaugh was hyping his newsletter by promoting an appearance in Colorado after one of his callers from Fort Collins, a man named Dan, said his wife wouldn't let him spend the money to buy a subscription. Limbaugh said he'd personally come out to Fort Collins if Dan would organize a bake sale to raise money for the subscription. The result was "Dan's Bake Sale," which drew Limbaugh fans from all over the country and raised money not only for Dan's newsletter but also for charity.

My local station got behind the event by lining up buses to take our 15
Limbaugh fans fifty miles north to Fort Collins.

Meanwhile, I had just gotten back into motorcycles—a couple of years late, I might add. As I tell my wife and all of my male friends circa fifty years of age, it's a male rite of passage to buy a motorcycle when you turn fifty. I was fifty-two, pushing fifty-three, and hadn't ridden one since I had a Honda 150 in the late 1960s.

---

[1] *Myth of the Hobbled Black:* Hamblin's name for the notions that African Americans are helplessly victimized by past and present racial discrimination, that few blacks are successful in America, that blacks can't make it without special assistance.

A fellow motorcyclist called my show and said he didn't want to go to Dan's Bake Sale by bus, but that he and I should go on our scoots. That prompted a lot of on-air bravado, and I ended up leading a cavalcade of some forty bikes in front of that many more buses to Fort Collins. On the ride, I was dressed in black leather from head to toe and wearing a black helmet with a tinted face guard—exhibiting some resemblance to Darth Vader or—you got it—the Black Avenger. After that trip, the Black Avenger moniker stuck.

Over time, when asked why I called myself the Black Avenger, I must admit I started answering a bit flippantly, mocking the comic book characters of my youth: "Truth, justice, and the American way . . . honey."[2]

I added "honey" after a black caller, in all seriousness, challenged me, claiming that "truth, justice, and the American way" were not "black" values because these American principles weren't afforded to black people. He further insinuated that I was trying to "act white." Of course, I stood my ground.

I am an American first, I replied. Don't ask me to choose between this   20
Republic and the color of my skin. If you're a Pan-Africanist or a black nationalist, you won't like that answer.

After thinking about the absurdity of this man trying to discount blacks as beneficiaries of the American Way, I decided to add "honey" with an ethnic ghetto drawl for the sole purpose of messing with self-righteous African Americans like him who still feed off the Myth of the Hobbled Black.

As a result of my appearance on C-Span, I received nearly 8,000 pieces of mail, more than 5,000 of them requesting the Certificate of Absolution. To this day I hear from people from all over America who remember the program, and my staff continues to fill orders for the certificate every week.

Needless to say, it warms my heart to know that so many white people are sleeping better at night, no longer writhing in pain brought about by their white guilt.

All joking aside, the extent of white guilt in this country is immense. It directly correlates with the endless depiction by the mass media of the profound pain that black people purportedly still suffer as a result of the years they were excluded from America's mainstream.

The constant reports of this pain and suffering that are broadcast   25
through the media, combined with the "blame whitey" syndrome that emanates from the black-trash[3] welfare culture, have caused some white Americans to suffer such a high degree of guilt that they have an almost fanatic desire to undo the injustices of slavery, perhaps beginning with guilt about not having delivered the forty acres and a mule promised to every Negro after the Civil War.

The greater majority of white Americans have passed on a nagging

---

[2]*Truth, justice, and the American way:* The values that Superman stands for.
[3]*black-trash*: Hamblin's counterpart to "white trash," these are black Americans who, in his words, are "unskilled and unemployed" and who "tend to be socially inept, possess limited education and few salable job skills."

sense of social obligation from one generation to the next. After four or five generations, however, mass amnesia has set in. The people who are haunted by this guilt—the white majority, mainstream Americans obsessed with undoing this injustice—have forgotten exactly what their crime was. In fact, they have no idea what their particular crime was.

As is the case with my southern callers, most Americans can't trace their family tree back to the equivalent of Tara, the fictitious plantation in *Gone With the Wind,* or to the ownership of slaves. So the guilt no longer arises from having once personally owned slaves, be they black people or indentured Irishmen. The guilt now is imposed just because of a lack of melanin in their skin, just because they are white. Simply by virtue of the birth of a white child, another guilty American is created. It's as if we were talking about the burden of the national debt. That baby inherits the guilt of slavery, the guilt of an injustice of long, long ago.

Because of this guilt and the ongoing stories of black oppression, white people have been conditioned to accept just about any level of black rage and the illogical demands resulting from it.

All of which brings us back around to modern-day African-American revolutionaries like welfare queen Dorothy King.

Despite her crassness, in some ways King is very sophisticated. She   30
knowingly touches a little secret in white people who have been conditioned by years of hearing about black hardships—the little secret that they are glad, they are relieved, to have been born white rather than a disenfranchised minority. These white middle-class citizens—especially the thirty- and forty-something crowd—have been inundated from the cradle with news reports about the dreadful burden of being black in America—reports of suffering the hardships of poverty, racism, and second-class citizenship.

While going through college, these white folks saw liberal administrators and professors excuse low test scores from black students because of these inherent hardships. They felt sorry for affirmative action students who obviously must have been scared, because they refused to compete. And though clearly this discrimination was self-imposed by the blacks themselves, they watched black students segregate themselves at all levels of campus life—from African-American studies to African-American student unions to African-American graduations—in essence implementing a post–civil rights version of "white only" and "colored" sections.

These white people graduated, got married, and began family life in comfortable suburbs . . . and bingo! They see Dorothy King on the nightly TV news, cataloging all the black hardships they have been conditioned to believe exist.

So when King makes absurd demands, like "give me" a house, these guilt-ridden white people shy away from standing up to her with what should be the logical American response: "Heavens no, we won't give you a house. Go out and work for it."

Nope. They stay out of it. Because they fear that X-ray vision might discern their little secret—the secret that they are eternally thankful they are white, and just having that thought makes them racists.

I have heard white Americans express so much racial guilt that, being   35
the old Catholic that I am, on some days I feel as though my radio show has become a confessional.

Because of the earnestness with which these people come to my show, it has dawned on me that if we as minority people, as black Americans, can't cut a deal with these average white Americans who are sitting at the table apologizing for the past, then we are a flawed and a lost people.

Or we are a disingenuous people who demand to prolong the negotiation with no intention of ever ending the strife and the separation, with no intention of ever doing our part to fill up the moat between the races or of getting on with the business of continuing to build a strong America that will benefit all of us.

I have a bigger, more selfish reason for wanting to avenge white guilt, however, a reason that goes beyond relieving the strain on white America. Guilt almost certainly inspires pity for the injured party—in this case black Americans. I contend that we can never stand tall as a people and expect to be treated as equals so long as we allow ourselves to be patronized in this fashion.

I also hear from white people across the country who call my radio show and say essentially, "Get over it."

They respond to the poverty pimps' demands for more and more repa-   40
rations for black people by asking what credit they get for all the taxes they have paid to support decades of Great Society programs that benefited black recipients. They want consideration for the years of affirmative action that gave black Americans a pass to automatically step to the front of the employment line.

Those kinds of queries undoubtedly contribute to the notion that there are angry white men. And I am certain there are, in fact, some white men who are angry, perhaps even racist. But the truth is that, as a black man, I ask some of the same questions, albeit from a different perspective.

When will black people recognize that we are able and willing to stand on our own? When will we acknowledge that we are able and willing to stand side by side with other Americans to compete for jobs and our piece of the American Dream? When will we get over that ugly and unjust period in our American history and evolve into healthy citizens of this great country?

I don't perceive that the majority of white Americans I talk to are saying "Get over it" sarcastically in order to dismiss the subject or to lobby for a return to the days of yore.

Rather, I think they are saying to black Americans: "Get over it, because even if we haven't paid the bill in full, we certainly have made enough of an effort to make amends that you should acknowledge some sincerity on our part."

Personally, I heartily second the call to get over it.   45

I am absolutely convinced that if we black Americans unequivocally throw in our lot with mainstream America today, we have much more to gain in the future than we have lost in the past. We have more to gain by putting our energies into the pursuit of the American Dream than we have to gain by continuing to whine about being compensated for having been kept out of the game in the past. We have an opportunity to realize all the benefits of being an American in the name of all of those who came before us, those Negroes who were kept unfairly from the full potential of this great country.

I would go so far as to say that we *owe* it to our forefathers to seize the opportunity that they helped to make available to us by their own stalwart faith in the American Dream. I know that all of my life I have felt I owed it to my mother and her sisters to make something of myself, to achieve the level of success that they only dreamed would be possible in their new homeland.

Today mainstream America has opened its full society and culture to us. The white majority has supported legislation that makes the American Dream truly accessible to all black citizens.

Oh, sure, there's still the old-guard club or the snooty neighborhood where the members or residents may look down their noses at black newcomers. But I would wager that those scenarios are few and far between.

And I am also willing to bet that in most cases the feelings of discrimi- 50 nation and exclusion are self-imposed by xenophobic quota blacks.

In fact, some of today's cries of racism have become downright ludicrous.

I wrote a column in the *Denver Post* in the summer of 1994 about a group of Denver area black women who claimed that a white shopkeeper in a Western Slope mountain town "stripped away our dignity, making us feel frustrated and powerless" by making an offhand remark when they walked into his store.

It seems one of the women was complaining about the heat, and the shopkeeper responded, "Hey! Watermelon's not served until one o'clock."

When he realized the ladies were seriously offended, he reportedly tried to make light of the situation, but alas, the oppressed travelers bustled out the door and followed up by writing a critical letter to the editor of the local newspaper.

I wrote that had I been presented with the watermelon-serving 55 schedule, I promptly would have inquired about the cantaloupe.

I don't doubt there are some angry white men. I'm still unconvinced that this shopkeeper was one of them, however.

More important is the fact that I am one black man who refuses to be shamed or made to feel powerless anymore by white bigots and racists. White folks can no longer intimidate me. I know better.

What I am constantly amazed at is how thin-skinned, how delicate, and how utterly afraid the beneficiaries of Dr. Martin Luther King's proud march for liberation have become.

Furthermore, as a black American, I am shamed by the Myth of the Hobbled Black. I am shamed that so many of my people have allowed themselves in one way or another to become part of the sham.

Someone must have the courage to kill this myth. Someone has to be 60 embarrassed that, with the opportunities available to us today, so many black Americans remain in a declining state of existence in Dark Town. Someone has to be embarrassed for the great number of middle-class black Americans who live in seclusion, apparently afraid to celebrate their success as educated and sophisticated Americans.

Someone must speak out to avenge the mythical disability of the Hobbled Black, and I think it's only logical that successful middle-class black Americans take the lead to meet this challenge.

White liberals won't do it because they continue to feed off the myth in order to further their own political and social agenda. White conservatives who speak out about ending the welfare culture have no credibility. They are summarily labeled racists.

And so I have lobbed a loud salvo by declaring myself the Black Avenger, standing tall to dispel the Myth of the Hobbled Black. I am standing up to put an end to the decades of liberal propaganda which deny that today opportunity exists for any American man or woman willing to pursue it.

I fully understand that it's not easy to be black and publicly refute the Myth of the Hobbled Black, because the quota blacks, the poverty pimps, the African Americans, will do all in their collective power to try to de-black you: "You ain't black no more. You don't understand the pain and suffering. You forgot your roots, boy."

But their admonishments have nothing to do with pain and suffering. 65 The real reason they are trying to de-black me and people like me is that we are telling the truth. And the truth is that being poor and black does not give you an excuse to gang-bang, to ruin a city, to make parks unsafe, to terrorize senior citizens, and to denounce the American Dream.

I am not a mean person. But I have run the gauntlet of ghetto life, and I have survived. I understand the value of life. And I understand that being poor is never an excuse to become a mugger or a killer.

Like a lot of black babies, I started out on the lowest social rung. I was raised by women. I grew up on welfare. I lived on the toughest streets of New York.

But I was not raised to be black trash or to be a victim. I never went through a drug rehab center. I have never been a guest of the government beyond my enlistment in the service. I have never believed—because I was never told—that because of the color of my skin I could never get the fullest measure of opportunity in America.

When you are poor, you may be so busy trying to survive that you miss the opportunity to smell the roses. You may miss the pure joy of watching your children grow up. But none of that gives you a valid reason to disregard what's right and what's wrong.

I am one American who is saying no to the myth that all people of color   70
are weak, illiterate, potentially violent, and substandard in their expectations for themselves and their children as contributors to the community.

Despite the attempted intimidation emanating from the black-trash
welfare culture, every day I hear from more and more healthy black Americans—and guilt-free white Americans—who are joining the crusade to tell
the truth about black people and their good fortune to be Americans.

My personal adventure in America is at its pinnacle today because I am
able to talk every day on my radio show with so many people from coast to
coast and from all walks of life. I hear personally from hundreds more
Americans off the air every day through the Internet and via letters to the
editors of newspapers that carry my column.

And every day I am reassured that the heartbeat of America remains
strong. I am reassured that the great majority of Americans maintain the true
American spirit, the spirit that ultimately will make it possible for us to prevail.

I draw my strength from that heartbeat of America; it gives me the
power to be the Black Avenger.

ENGAGING THE TEXT

1. Working in groups, summarize the central claims Hamblin makes about
   the United States and the American Dream. To what extent do you agree
   or disagree with these assertions, and why?

2. Assess Hamblin's assertion that some white Americans "suffer such a high
   degree of guilt that they have an almost fanatic desire to undo the injustices
   of slavery" (para. 25). Have you seen evidence of such a compulsion in the
   media, in your education or reading, in your community? Discuss.

3. Hamblin often uses language that is rhetorically daring, to say the least—
   language that is pointedly *not* politically correct. What do you think he
   means by the terms listed below? What effect does such language have on
   you as a reader?

   welfare queen (para. 29)
   poverty pimp (para. 40)
   quota blacks (para. 50)
   Dark Town (para. 60)

4. Review Hamblin's account of how he assumed his alias, "The Black
   Avenger" (paras. 13–18); note the various components of this persona, including the motorcycle and motorcycle outfit, the Darth Vader connection,
   the Superman/comic books connection, and his ghetto pronunciation of
   "honey." What impression do you think Hamblin is trying to create? How
   well do you think he succeeds?

EXPLORING CONNECTIONS

5. Review Anne Witte Garland's "Good Noise: Cora Tucker" (p. 353). Compare and contrast her ideas about success with Hamblin's. Be sure to touch

on Tucker's and Hamblin's views of poverty, welfare, and obstacles to success for African Americans.

6. Hamblin believes there are few barriers in the United States today for African Americans who are motivated to succeed. How do you think Gregory Mantsios might respond to this claim? Review "Class in America (2000)" (p. 331) for data or claims that challenge or complicate Hamblin's argument, and discuss how these two writers can come to such different conclusions about barriers to success.

7. Consider Cheryl Mitchell, the highly motivated African American woman that Gregory Mantsios profiles in "Class in America (2000)" (p. 331). Beginning with the information Mantsios provides, write Mitchell's story so that she becomes a clear success. Share stories with classmates, and discuss the plausibility of each story. Do the results of this exercise tend to support or call into question Hamblin's claims about opportunity?

EXTENDING THE CRITICAL CONTEXT

8. In paragraph 31, Hamblin offers a brief description of black students segregating themselves on college campuses. How well would his description fit your campus today: To what extent are ethnic groups segregated or self-segregated?

9. Listen to one or more broadcasts of *The Ken Hamblin Show* and analyze what you hear. What issues are being discussed? What sort of persona does Hamblin project? How would you characterize his audience? To what extent does Hamblin echo themes found in the reading selection above?

Race at the End of History

RONALD TAKAKI

According to conventional wisdom, Asian Americans offer the best evidence that the American Dream is alive and well. Publications like Time *and* Newsweek *have celebrated Asian Americans as a "super minority" that has adopted the Puritan work ethic and outshone even the Anglo majority in terms of education and financial success. In this reading selection, Ronald Takaki challenges the idea of the model minority and provides an alternative interpretation of how myths of race and myths of success intertwine. The grandson of Japanese immigrant plantation workers in Hawaii, Takaki (b. 1939) is an award-winning historian whose mission, in his own words, has been "to write a more inclusive and hence more accurate history of Americans, Chicanos, Native Americans as well as certain European immigrant groups like the Irish and Jews." His most recent in a series of influential books is titled* Double Victory: A Multicultural History of America in World War II (2000). *Takaki teaches at the University of California, Berkeley.*

Several years ago I was invited to deliver a keynote address at a national multicultural conference in Norfolk, Virginia. Once I arrived at the Norfolk airport I caught a cab, and soon was engaged in conversation with the driver. We looked at each other through the rearview mirror of the cab as we talked. At first, we discussed the weather and how this region was becoming a very important area for tourism. But it did not take long before the cab driver posed a more personal question: "How long have you been in this country?"

"All my life," I snapped; after a while, one gets impatient responding to that question. But then I calmed down and informed this white man in his forties, at whom I was looking in the rearview mirror, that my grandfather had come to the United States in 1886. I explained to him that we had been in this country as a family for more than one hundred years, and that I myself was born here. And then he looked at me in the rearview mirror and said, with a broad Southern drawl, "Well, I was wondering about you, because your English is excellent."

He did not see me as an American. I am not saying that he asked me this question because he was a Southerner, since Northerners have asked me the same question. Nor can I attribute his ignorance to economic class since, to be honest, Ph.D.s have also asked me this question. And it is not necessarily a matter of race, either, since African Americans have also questioned my nationality. I do not look American to a lot of people.

My experience in the cab mirrors a very common assumption that being "American" means being white or European in ancestry. But one need only look around the streets of just about any American city to realize how far from reality this perception is. Many of us came originally from Africa, others were already here, others came up from Latin America, and others, like my grandfather, came from a Pacific shore, and we're all Americans. Yet, despite that history, the prevailing debate about American citizenship revolves around identity: Who is an American and how does identity shape American society?

Racial and ethnic diversity is being promoted, and contested, of   5
course, on university and college campuses across the country. In 1989, my colleagues at the University of California, Berkeley, voted favorably to establish a multicultural requirement for graduation. We call it the "American cultures requirement," and it applies to every student in the university. Even students in engineering, computer science, and business administration must take a course before graduation that is designed to deepen and broaden their understanding of American society in terms of race and eth-

nicity. The course is neither a cultural diversity requirement, nor a global studies requirement. It is a requirement that focuses on diversity in the United States of America. The curriculum is designed to study comparatively—and we underline "comparatively"—five groups, which we have identified as African American, Asian American, Latino, American Indian, and European immigrant groups, particularly those groups that arrived in the late nineteenth and early twentieth centuries from Italy, Greece, Poland, Hungary, and Russia. Berkeley today offers approximately 125 courses that fulfill this requirement, fielded by faculty in almost twenty different departments.

The Berkeley faculty instituted the American cultures requirement essentially for two reasons. The first motivation was intellectual, since we believed that it would bring our students to a more accurate understanding of American society. On a more urgent note, however, we believed that we were witnessing at the time the most serious racial crisis in America since the Civil War. Those fears were confirmed only three years later when, on 29 April 1992, we saw on our television screens terrifying images beamed out of Los Angeles: Korean stores burning out of control, black smoke rising to the skies above the city, and murderous melee in the streets. The most powerful image that came out of those events was the face of Rodney King. I still remember his trembling words, "Please, people, we're stuck here for a while; we can work it out, we can get along."

But many of us, educators and students alike, wondered, "How do we get along, how do we work it out, unless we learn more about one another?" The Berkeley faculty trusted that a comparative approach to multiculturalism would help our students understand the beauty and promise of a pluralistic America.

I am often asked by faculty, deans, and provosts across the country to describe what a multicultural approach to culture looks like. Offering a theoretical description is usually less effective than providing an actual demonstration. The remainder of this essay, then, serves as a demonstration of a comparative multicultural approach to history.

Francis Fukuyama, a fellow Asian American intellectual, proclaims in his book entitled *The End of History and the Last Man* that at the turn of the twentieth century the globe is witnessing the end of history. Liberal democracy, he declares, has triumphed over communism, and the capitalist economic system has emerged as the only coherent political and economic ideology. The overriding message Fukuyama offers is celebratory—the triumph of American liberal democracy and capitalism, the end of history.

But Fukuyama's conclusion that history has come to an end relies upon a   10
very specific view of history. If we define history as the conflict between liberal democracy and capitalism on the one hand, and feudalism, monarchy, and communism on the other hand, then perhaps we would have to agree with Fukuyama that history has ended. Alternatively, if one defines history as the expansion of Europe into Africa, the Americas, Asia, and the Pacific, if one defines

history as the history of colonialism, if one defines history as a trail of racial and ethnic conflicts, then one would have to say that history has in no way ended.

Even Fukuyama would have to agree that U.S. history has not come to an end, for example, since racial inequality for Blacks is such an undeniable social fact. All the same, he does not accept any explanation that finds fault with liberal democracy for this state of affairs. He instead would frame racial inequality as a cultural problem for Blacks. In his analysis, Black poverty is a matter of cultural difference. Blacks lack middle-class values of thrift, hard work, self-reliance, and family values that they need in order to succeed, he argues. In other words, the Black problem is group specific and cultural. His remedy: the way for Blacks to make it into the mainstream is for the group to acquire the proper values.

Fukuyama's judgment of Black failure is juxtaposed with his estimation of economic success gained by other ethnic groups. In *The End of History*, for instance, he noted that Japan's economic miracle is based on the richness of its culture. He compares the Japanese cultural ethos favorably to the Protestant ethic: values rooted in hard work, thrift, industry, and family. Though Fukuyama did not develop this comparison any further in *The End of History*, in a subsequent book, entitled *Trust*, he expands this theory that links cultural values and material well-being. He confesses admiration for the gains of Asian Americans in the United States; more specifically, he lauds the broad achievements of Japanese Americans, Chinese Americans, and Korean Americans. He again attributes the success of Asian Americans to their strong family values and ethnic enterprise, and pointedly notes that Blacks are deficient in these values.

In making these comparisons and contrasts, Fukuyama continues the long and storied myth of the Asian American model minority. This myth rests on the claim that Asian Americans have made it economically, and is usually documented by statistics which show that Asian American families have incomes that even at times exceed those of white families. But statistics that measure family income make sense only in relation to the number of workers per family. A close look at these numbers reflects that Asian American families typically have more workers per family than white families, which serves to incline upward Asian American family incomes.

The myth of Asian American success also overlooks a second important reality. The majority of the Asian American population lives in three states: New York, California, and Hawaii, with the highest concentration situated in San Francisco, Los Angeles, New York City, and Honolulu. These cities annually report among the highest cost of living indexes in the entire country. So, of course, an inflated index will incline income upward. Those numbers do not necessarily suggest a higher standard of living, however.

And there is yet another problem with this myth. It lumps together all Asian Americans, whether they be Chinese, Japanese, Koreans, Hmong, Vietnamese, Cambodians, or a host of other Asian immigrant groups. Such lumping together renders invisible those Asian American groups that have not yet made it economically in this country. Even within a group that seem- 15

ingly is successful, say Chinese Americans, this myth overlooks the class het-
erogeneity within that community. In New York City, for example, wide class
divisions divide the uptown Chinese from the downtown Chinese.

I am not trying to deny that there are many successful Asian Americans
in the United States. But it is important to realize that many of them, probably the majority who are successful, are post-1965 immigrants. They often
come from the professional and highly educated classes of South Korea,
Taiwan, Hong Kong, and the Philippines. One study of Korean greengro-
cers in New York City, for example, revealed that nearly 78 percent of those
interviewed had college degrees. Hence, many relatively recent immigrants
came here already middle-class and upper-middle-class. They did not pull
themselves up by their bootstraps.

All the same, many of these professional Asian Americans complain
that they experience a "glass ceiling." In other words, even though they may
have degrees from elite universities, they find that they are not earning an
income comparable to their skill level and their level of education.

But the point of this celebration of Asian Americans as a model minority, in reality, is not sociology. The debate between Fukuyama and me is not
even about history. It is really about ideology, because embedded within
that sociology, contained within that history, is an ideology. This message is
this: The American dream still holds promise to all of us as Americans.
Everyone, regardless of race, can make it into the mainstream through hard
work and private effort.

The key word here is "private." Notice, these Asian Americans made it
not through affirmative action, not through welfare, but through private activities — business, education, and individual effort. In other words, the way
to make it into the mainstream, the way to advance oneself economically, is
in the private domain, relying on family resources, not by means of government assistance.

As a historian, I have to raise the question whether this representation   20
of Asian Americans as a model minority is a recent phenomenon. It certainly receives wide promotion from scholars such as Fukuyama, Thomas
Sowell, Dinesh D'Souza, and Nathan Glazer. But it is not a recent idea.

Looking backward into the nineteenth century to just one year —
1870 — we find two fascinating examples of how Asian Americans were used
as a model minority. The first series of events took place in the states of Mississippi and Louisiana. After the Civil War, following the emancipation of enslaved African Americans, planters in Mississippi, Louisiana, and other states
in the South were confronted with a wage-earning class of Blacks. Often, the
planters had labor conflicts with these newly freed Blacks. So in 1870, a coalition of planters transported into Mississippi and Louisiana more than five
hundred Chinese immigrant laborers whom they pitted against Black wage-
earners. A review of newspaper reports from the period as well as written correspondence among the planters themselves reveal the clear intent of this importation of Chinese labor. The planters blatantly admitted their plans to use

these Chinese immigrant laborers as examples of obedient, hard-working laborers. A model minority for whom? For the newly freed Blacks.

In 1870, another significant event occurred, but this time in the North, in a small industrial town in Massachusetts. The largely immigrant Irish working class of North Adams had organized themselves into a union called the "Knights of St. Crispins." These Irish factory workers went out on strike against a factory owned by Charles Sampson in 1870. So Sampson transported across the country about seventy-five Chinese immigrant laborers, brought them to North Adams, Massachusetts, to break the strike. Again, the local newspapers went wild, proclaiming, here we have the solution to all of our labor problems; not only cheap labor but obedient labor, industrious labor. Their statistics in fact "proved"—and this was later hailed by the mainstream media beyond North Adams—that after four months the Chinese workers were out-producing the Irish workers. In short, the Chinese were touted as more efficient workers.

The Irish workers of North Adams initially tried to build class solidarity across racial lines, even attempting to organize a Chinese Lodge of the Knights of St. Crispins. But Sampson locked the Chinese within the compounds, separated them from the Irish strikers, and broke the strike. That was in 1870. In Mississippi, Alabama, and North Adams, Massachusetts, the Chinese were used as a model minority for Black workers and as a model minority for Irish immigrant workers.

But then nearly a decade later came a nativist backlash against Chinese immigrants that culminated in the 1882 Chinese Exclusion Act. The closing of the gates to Chinese immigration occurred within a larger context, however. American industrial development had become overheated by the 1880s and production was slowing down. America "discovered" unemployment for the first time in its history.

A young historian by the name of Frederick Jackson Turner chose this important cultural moment to deliver a seminal thesis at the meeting of the American Historical Association in Chicago in 1893. The paper was entitled "The Significance of the Frontier in American History." Turner proposed that America's manifest destiny and national character were deeply shaped by the frontier experience. He hailed the westward migration of white settlers, and the expansion of what he called "the advance of civilization against savagery," a hard-fought victory won at the expense of the Native American Indians. Viewed from our present perspective, Turner's thesis could be very well retitled, "The Significance of the Frontier and Race in American History."

There stood Turner at the end of the nineteenth century, contemplating the social significance of the end of the frontier, and today we have Francis Fukuyama, contemplating the end of another century and the eclipse of that frontier he calls history. Turner idealized the triumphant advance of civilization across a continent, while Fukuyama trumpeted the advance of civilization across the entire world. In the 1870s Chinese immigrant laborers were used as a model minority against Blacks and Irish immigrant workers. The workplace—the plantation, the shoe factory—was a site of discipline, the site to create docile, obedient, efficient workers. Today, the site of discipline has shifted from the workplace to the cultural terrain. "Cultural terrain" refers to ideology and culture, to representations of minorities in the mass media, but also to representations in our scholarly and political discourse.

In the nineteenth century there was a need for Black labor. Today, we are witnessing a dramatic decline in the need for Black labor. We presently have what William Julius Wilson calls the formation and expansion of a "Black underclass" in our inner cities. Wilson identifies two very important factors behind this development in the U.S. economy. He highlights the deindustrialization of America and the emergence of a globalized economy. Now our factories can go overseas, our jobs can go to Mexico, to Indonesia, to Malaysia. This exportation of production is hollowing out the industrial inner cities.

Another development that Wilson underscores is the suburbanization of production, that is, the movement of sites of production away from our cities, that began in earnest in the early 1980s. Not just manufacturing production, but also information production thrives in suburban office parks. Downtowns are rapidly closing down, leaving the people who cannot move trapped in inner cities.

Jeremy Rifkin's study on the changing patterns of work in America adds a further perspective on the formation of an underclass that is largely Black. In his book, *The End of Work,* Rifkin shows very persuasively that while industrial and information production have both risen dramatically in the last two decades, the need for labor has remained level and in some cases even declined. Rifkin discovers these trends not only in manufacturing labor, but also in white-collar labor. In essence, our economy has less need for labor and so work is coming to an end. Rifkin claims that the creation of superfluous workers in American society will only increase in the twenty-first century, and this problem is having, and will continue to have, a disproportionate impact upon African Americans trapped in our inner cities.

In the nineteenth century the purpose of the model minority was to control labor. The function of the model minority today is not to control Black or Irish immigrant labor, and not even to create obedient, hardworking laborers. The function today is social control, a reaffirmation of the American dream directed especially to those workers, many of them White and many of them Black, who are struggling simply to make ends meet. "Be like Asian Americans, emulate their family values."

But this message had a special targeting for African Americans who feel that their future is hopeless. It says to them, "Look at those Asian Americans. They were able to make it, they're shopkeepers, they're successful, they're getting their children into schools like Berkeley and Harvard and Princeton. And how did they do it? They did it through private activities, through emphasis on education, through family values."

"Family values" have become the code words for defining the problem of poverty in terms of the family and the individual rather than the structures of our economy and the structures of our society. Blacks are told to be like Asian Americans—be law-abiding, be civil members of society, don't depend on welfare, don't try to get ahead through affirmative action.

Many Asian Americans have inadvertently joined Fukuyama in touting Asian American success; in some cases even liberal Asian American organizations have done so. They actively promote Asian American family values, releasing sociological data showing that we have low welfare dependency rates. They also regularly provide information to the media about how we're contributing as Asian Americans to the economy through shopkeeping, through connections with businesses in South Korea, Taiwan, and Hong Kong. These liberal Asian Americans say they are performing these activities to resist racism, to combat the backlash against immigrants, to show that Asian Americans are good citizens, that we're good Americans. But like the conservative Fukuyama, these liberal Asian Americans overlook the social and economic structures that produce and reproduce racial inequality. In a complicated way, the Asian American model minority representation has become part of Michel Foucault's[1] concept of the panopticon—society controlled by an ideology dividing us into distinct groups, ever being watched and compared.

There are major differences that distinguish the economy and society at the end of the nineteenth century to that we are facing at the end of the twentieth century. But, as it turns out, there are also significant similarities. Both periods represent times of economic crisis and class tensions among Whites. Consider the labor turmoils and strikes in the late nineteenth century, the 1885 Haymarket Riot in Chicago, the Homestead Riot, and the Pullman Strike. These events were eruptions that shook American society, and it was within the context of white/white class conflicts that this young historian, Frederick Jackson Turner, gave his paper. He was in Chicago, only eight years after the bloody Haymarket Riot, presenting this paper on the significance of the frontier. He was worried about his country's future, and his interpretation of the end of the frontier was informed by that larger economic context of an industrial machine slowing down, rising unemployment, and the emergence of white/white class conflict.

Turner was not the only person contemplating the meaning of the end   35
of his century. At about the same time another American, Henry George,

[1]*Michel Foucault:* Philosopher, psychiatrist, and influential French intellectual (1926–1984). His book *Discipline and Punish*—a major work on the history, psychology, and architecture of imprisonment—discusses a prison called a panopticon whose key feature is that prisoners can always be seen by guards who can't be seen.

was calling for a radical redefinition of citizenship that would include shared ownership of the continent. In his book, *Progress and Poverty,* George argued that the advance of capitalism in American civilization would inevitably lead to more intense and violent class conflicts within white society. He proposed the idea of a tax on unearned income to reduce the conflict. Once land becomes valuable due to industrial production, then there should be a tax on the added value of that land. He argued, for instance, that Leland Stanford and the Central Pacific Railroad should not be the sole beneficiary of the increase in the value of the property due to the construction of that railroad. George believed that the income derived from that tax then should be used for the benefit of the society. But not for the entire society, for George argued that the funds should only be distributed to White Americans. Chinese immigrants were not real Americans in his estimation. So although he was a visionary of more economic equality, George scapegoated the Chinese as vehemently as other American intellectuals. He in fact was a leader in the movement calling for Chinese exclusion. He saw the Chinese as the lackeys of the monopolist capitalists. In the economic crises of the late nineteenth century, the Chinese were vilified by all sides.

The end of the nineteenth century was also a period of profound cultural crisis. The frontier had come to an end. Nineteenth-century America had drawn its energies, its buoyancy, from the seemingly endless potential offered by an open frontier. So Turner was pondering, as an historian looking backward, but also peering forward, what would happen to a frontierless America.

Today, a century later, we are also experiencing a cultural crisis. This crisis is actually more complicated than that of an earlier century. Our cultural crisis manifests itself most significantly within two arenas. The first arena is our expanding racial diversity. Some time in the twenty-first century Whites will become a minority of the total U.S. population. In other words, the faces of America are changing. Already you can see the changing faces in every major city in the United States—San Francisco, Cleveland, Chicago, New York, Philadelphia, Washington, San Antonio, Los Angeles. And the question many people are asking is this: How will we define who is an American in the twenty-first century?

Fukuyama more dramatically addresses the second arena of our cultural crisis. Ever since the waning moments of World War II, the Cold War allowed us to discern our manifest destiny. America's manifest destiny was to contain communism. That would be the new frontier: the containment of communism—Vietnam, Cambodia, Laos, Cuba, Chile, Nicaragua, El Salvador, Guatemala. And now that the Soviet Union has collapsed and the Cold War is over, Francis Fukuyama encourages us to place our faith in liberal democracy and capitalism as guides to a brighter future. "History has ended."

Fukuyama's optimism is reflected in the way he ends his book, *The End of History.* He concludes with a story about a wagon train traveling west:

Mankind will seem like a long wagon train, strung out along the road. Several wagons attacked by Indians will have been set aflame and abandoned along the way. There will be a few wagoneers who, stunned by the battle, will have lost their sense of direction and are temporarily heading in the wrong direction, but the great majority of wagons will be making the journey into town and most will eventually arrive there.

Here we have embedded in Fukuyama's final story a remarkable rendition of Turner's frontier thesis. Fukuyama intends his story about the wagon train moving west to illustrate his central thesis: All along "there had been only one journey and one destination." 40

Yet the very metaphor that Fukuyama has chosen raises more questions than it resolves: "Whose" journey, "whose" destination, and "who" are "we"? Certainly, a good citizen should be able to embrace the larger narrative of what America is, the collective memory of who we are as a nation. But a good citizen must also be able to look "in a different mirror" and see the diversity that Americans reflect, to accept that we come with different faces and different names, like Garcia and Takaki. We are all American, and we should not have to explain or defend our citizenship every time we jump into a taxicab. To draw from Walt Whitman's wonderful poetry, we must all become listeners—"to hear the varied carols of America," the songs and stories of our democratic diversity.

As we approach the coming multicultural millennium, we have to remind Fukuyama and his agreeing readers of William Faulkner's insight: "The past is not even past." Indeed, history has not ended. Rather it is sedimented into our present and our future. This powerful continuance of events and developments in our history requires us to know that history inclusively and accurately. This study of the past can enable us to confront the history of the enslavement of African Americans, the dispossession of Native Americans, the exploitation of Chinese immigrant workers, and the disciplining of Irish immigrant laborers. This understanding of our history can also guide us toward a future where we might be able to work it out and get along in our diversity. After all, how many nations in the world have been founded, "dedicated," to use Lincoln's language, to the "proposition" that "all men are created equal"?

ENGAGING THE TEXT

1. Central to this reading selection is the concept of the "model minority." Working in small groups, define the concept and discuss how you learned this myth. For example, have you seen evidence of the myth's operation in the media, in your reading, or in your own family, community, church, workplace, or school? Try to draw some conclusions about how this type of cultural "knowledge" is taught.

2. What is wrong with the myth of the model minority, in Takaki's view? In what specific ways does it misrepresent or distort reality? How can the myth, which on the surface seems to celebrate the success of Asian Americans, actually harm them?

3. Takaki critiques the myth of the model minority by analyzing particular events in the past that illustrate how the myth works. How persuasive do you find this historical critique, and why? What other types of evidence might he have used?

4. Review Takaki's summary of Francis Fukuyama's ideas in paragraphs 9–13. Paraphrase Takaki's critique of Fukuyama's book and explain why Takaki refers so extensively to a point of view with which he fundamentally disagrees.

5. If you have ever had an experience like Takaki's taxicab ride, relate your story in a brief essay or journal entry.

EXPLORING CONNECTIONS

6. When Stephen Cruz (p. 348) became successful, he was seen not as a member of a model minority group but rather as a model member of a minority group. In what ways was his situation as a successful young Chicano engineer comparable to that of Asian Americans today, and in what respects did it differ?

7. Compare the idea of the model minority with the idea of the "scholarship boy" as defined by Richard Rodriguez (p. 214). On what assumptions does each concept rest? What expectations does each create? Why is each of these labels dangerous?

EXTENDING THE CRITICAL CONTEXT

8. Although the news media have been quick to extol the virtues of Asian Americans as models of achievement, representations of Asians and Asian Americans are scarce in most forms of mass entertainment. Survey movies, TV shows, music videos, song lyrics, and other forms of popular culture. How are Asian Americans represented, and how do these images compare with those implied by the myth of the model minority?

9. In paragraphs 5–7, Takaki outlines the multicultural requirement at the University of California, Berkeley. After reviewing his summary, research any multicultural requirements your school has adopted (for example, their origins, their stated purpose, the courses designed to meet them) and report your findings to the class. To extend this assignment, arrange for a teacher or administrator to visit your class to discuss the history of the requirement or to review any debates surrounding proposals of such a requirement.

The Lesson

TONI CADE BAMBARA

"The Lesson" looks at wealth through the eyes of a poor black girl whose education includes a field trip to one of the world's premier toy stores. The story speaks to serious social issues with a comic, energetic, and utterly engaging voice. Toni Cade Bambara (1939–1995) grew up in the Harlem and Bedford-Stuyvesant areas of New York City. Trained at Queens College and City College of New York in dance, drama, and literature, she is best known for her collections of stories, Gorilla, My Love *(1972) and* The Seabirds Are Still Alive and Other Stories *(1977), and for her novels,* If Blessing Comes *(1987) and* The Salt Eaters *(1980), winner of the American Book Award. Her novel* Those Bones Are Not My Child, *edited by Toni Morrison, was published posthumously in 1999. "The Lesson" is taken from* Gorilla, My Love.

Back in the days when everyone was old and stupid or young and foolish and me and Sugar were the only ones just right, this lady moved on our block with nappy hair and proper speech and no makeup. And quite naturally we laughed at her, laughed the way we did at the junk man who went about his business like he was some big-time president and his sorry-ass horse his secretary. And we kinda hated her too, hated the way we did the winos who cluttered up our parks and pissed on our handball walls and stank up our hallways and stairs so you couldn't halfway play hide-and-seek without a goddamn gas mask. Miss Moore was her name. The only woman on the block with no first name. And she was black as hell, cept for her feet, which were fish-white and spooky. And she was always planning these boring-ass things for us to do, us being my cousin, mostly, who lived on the block cause we all moved North the same time and to the same apartment then spread out gradual to breathe. And our parents would yank our heads into some kinda shape and crisp up our clothes so we'd be presentable for travel with Miss Moore, who always looked like she was going to church, though she never did. Which is just one of the things the grownups talked about when they talked behind her back like a dog. But when she came calling with some sachet[1] she'd sewed up or some gingerbread she'd made or some book, why then they'd all be too embarrassed to turn her down and we'd get handed out all spruced up. She'd been to college and said it only right that she should take responsibility for the young ones' education, and

---

[1] *sachet:* A small bag filled with a sweet-smelling substance. Sachets are often placed in drawers to scent clothes.

she not even related by marriage or blood. So they'd go for it. Specially Aunt Gretchen. She was the main gofer in the family. You got some ole dumb shit foolishness you want somebody to go for, you send for Aunt Gretchen. She been screwed into the go-along for so long, it's a blood-deep natural thing with her. Which is how she got saddled with me and Sugar and Junior in the first place while our mothers were in a la-de-da apartment up the block having a good ole time.

So this one day Miss Moore rounds us all up at the mailbox and it's puredee hot and she's knockin herself out about arithmetic. And school suppose to let up in summer I heard, but she don't never let up. And the starch in my pinafore scratching the shit outta me and I'm really hating this nappy-head bitch and her goddamn college degree. I'd much rather go to the pool or to the show where it's cool. So me and Sugar leaning on the mailbox being surly, which is a Miss Moore word. And Flyboy checking out what everybody brought for lunch. And Fat Butt already wasting his peanut-butter-and-jelly sandwich like the pig he is. And Junebug punchin on Q.T.'s arm for potato chips. And Rosie Giraffe shifting from one hip to the other waiting for somebody to step on her foot or ask her if she from Georgia so she can kick ass, preferably Mercedes'. And Miss Moore asking us do we know what money is, like we a bunch of retards. I mean real money, she say, like it's only poker chips or monopoly papers we lay on the grocer. So right away I'm tired of this and say so. And would much rather snatch Sugar and go to the Sunset and terrorize the West Indian kids and take their hair ribbons and their money too. And Miss Moore files that re-mark away for next week's lesson on brotherhood, I can tell. And finally I say we oughta get to the subway cause it's cooler and besides we might meet some cute boys. Sugar done swiped her mama's lipstick, so we ready.

So we heading down the street and she's boring us silly about what things cost and what our parents make and how much goes for rent and how money ain't divided up right in this country. And then she gets to the part about we all poor and live in the slums, which I don't feature. And I'm ready to speak on that, but she steps out in the street and hails two cabs just like that. Then she hustles half the crew in with her and hands me a five-dollar bill and tells me to calculate 10 percent tip for the driver. And we're off. Me and Sugar and Junebug and Flyboy hangin out the window and hollering to everybody, putting lipstick on each other cause Flyboy a faggot anyway, and making farts with our sweaty armpits. But I'm mostly trying to figure how to spend this money. But they all fascinated with the meter ticking and Junebug starts laying bets as to how much it'll read when Flyboy can't hold his breath no more. Then Sugar lays bets as to how much it'll be when we get there. So I'm stuck. Don't nobody want to go for my plan, which is to jump out at the next light and run off to the first bar-b-que we can find. Then the driver tells us to get the hell out cause we are there already. And the meter reads eighty-five cents. And I'm stalling to figure out the tip and Sugar say give him a dime. And I decide he don't need it bad as I do, so later for him. But then he tries to take off with Junebug foot still in the door so we talk about his mama something ferocious. Then we check out that we on Fifth Avenue[2] and everybody dressed up in stockings. One lady in a fur coat, hot as it is. White folks crazy.

"This is the place," Miss Moore say, presenting it to us in the voice she uses at the museum. "Let's look in the windows before we go in."

"Can we steal?" Sugar asks very serious like she's getting the ground rules square away before she plays. "I beg your pardon," say Miss Moore, and we fall out. So she leads us around the windows of the toy store and me and Sugar screamin, "This is mine, that's mine, I gotta have that, that was made for me, I was born for that," till Big Butt drowns us out.

"Hey, I'm goin to buy that there."

"That there? You don't even know what it is, stupid."

"I do so," he say punchin on Rosie Giraffe. "It's a microscope."

"Whatcha gonna do with a microscope, fool?"

"Look at things."

"Like what, Ronald?" ask Miss Moore. And Big Butt ain't got the first notion. So here go Miss Moore gabbing about the thousands of bacteria in a drop of water and the somethinorother in a speck of blood and the million and one living things in the air around us is invisible to the naked eye. And what she say that for? Junebug go to town on that "naked" and we rolling. Then Miss Moore ask what it cost. So we all jam into the window smudgin it up and the price tag say $300. So then she ask how long'd take for Big Butt and Junebug to save up their allowances. "Too long," I say. "Yeh," adds Sugar, "outgrown it by that time." And Miss Moore say no, you never outgrow learning instruments. "Why, even medical students and interns and," blah, blah, blah. And we ready to choke Big Butt for bringing it up in the first damn place.

"This here costs four hundred eighty dollars," say Rosie Giraffe. So we pile up all over her to see what she pointin out. My eyes tell me it's a chunk of glass cracked with something heavy, and different-color inks dripped into the splits, then the whole thing put into a oven or something. But for $480 it don't make sense.

"That's a paperweight made of semi-precious stones fused together under tremendous pressure," she explains slowly, with her hands doing the mining and all the factory work.

"So what's a paperweight?" asks Rosie Giraffe.

"To weigh paper with, dumbbell," say Flyboy, the wise man from the East.

"Not exactly," say Miss Moore, which is what she say when you warm or way off too. "It's to weigh paper down so it won't scatter and make your desk untidy." So right away me and Sugar curtsy to each other and then to Mercedes who is more the tidy type.

---

[2]*Fifth Avenue:* The street in New York most famous for its expensive stores.

"We don't keep paper on top of the desk in my class," say Junebug, figuring Miss Moore crazy or lyin one.

"At home, then," she say. "Don't you have a calendar and a pencil case and a blotter and a letter-opener on your desk at home where you do your homework?" And she know damn well what our homes look like cause she nosys around in them every chance she gets.

"I don't even have a desk," say Junebug. "Do we?"

"No. And I don't get no homework neither," say Big Butt.   20

"And I don't even have a home," say Flyboy like he do at school to keep the white folks off his back and sorry for him. Send this poor kid to camp posters, is his speciality.

"I do," say Mercedes. "I have a box of stationery on my desk and a picture of my cat. My godmother bought the stationery and the desk. There's a big rose on each sheet and the envelopes smell like roses."

"Who want to know about your smelly-ass stationery," say Rosie Giraffe fore I can get my two cents in.

"It's important to have a work area all your own so that..."

"Will you look at this sailboat, please," say Flyboy, cuttin her off and   25
pointin to the thing like it was his. So once again we tumble all over each other to gaze at this magnificent thing in the toy store which is just big enough to maybe sail two kittens across the pond if you strap them to the posts tight. We all start reciting the price tag like we in assembly. "Handcrafted sailboat of fiberglass at one thousand one hundred ninety-five dollars."

"Unbelievable," I hear myself say and am really stunned. I read it again for myself just in case the group recitation put me in a trance. Same thing. For some reason this pisses me off. We look at Miss Moore and she lookin at us, waiting for I dunno what.

"Who'd pay all that when you can buy a sailboat set for a quarter at Pop's, a tube of glue for a dime, and a ball of string for eight cents? It must have a motor and a whole lot else besides," I say. "My sailboat cost me about fifty cents."

"But will it take water?" say Mercedes with her smart ass.

"Took mine to Alley Pond Park once," say Flyboy. "String broke. Lost it. Pity."

"Sailed mine in Central Park and it keeled over and sank. Had to ask   30
my father for another dollar."

"And you got the strap," laugh Big Butt. "The jerk didn't even have a string on it. My old man wailed on his behind."

Little Q.T. was staring hard at the sailboat and you could see he wanted it bad. But he too little and somebody'd just take it from him. So what the hell. "This boat for kids, Miss Moore?"

"Parents silly to buy something like that just to get all broke up," say Rosie Giraffe.

"That much money it should last forever," I figure.

"My father'd buy it for me if I wanted it."   35

"Your father, my ass," say Rosie Giraffe getting a chance to finally push Mercedes.

"Must be rich people shop here," say Q.T.

"You are a very bright boy," say Flyboy. "What was your first clue?" And he rap him on the head with the back of his knuckles, since Q.T. the only one he could get away with. Though Q.T. liable to come up behind you years later and get his licks in when you half expect it.

"What I want to know is," I says to Miss Moore though I never talk to her, I wouldn't give the bitch that satisfaction, "is how much a real boat costs? I figure a thousand'd get you a yacht any day."

"Why don't you check that out," she says, "and report back to the group?" Which really pains my ass. If you gonna mess up a perfectly good swim day least you could do is have some answers. "Let's go in," she say like she got something up her sleeve. Only she don't lead the way. So me and Sugar turn the corner to where the entrance is, but when we get there I kinda hang back. Not that I'm scared, what's there to be afraid of, just a toy store. But I feel funny, shame. But what I got to be shamed about? Got as much right to go in as anybody. But somehow I can't seem to get hold on the door, so I step away for Sugar to lead. But she hangs back too. And I look at her and she looks at me and this is ridiculous. I mean, damn, I have never ever been shy about doing nothing or going nowhere. But then Mercedes steps up and then Rosie Giraffe and Big Butt crowd in behind and shove, and next thing we all stuffed into the doorway with only Mercedes squeezing past us, smoothing out her jumper and walking right down the aisle. Then the rest of us tumble in like a glued-together jigsaw done all wrong. And people lookin at us. And it's like the time me and Sugar crashed into the Catholic church on a dare. But once we got in there and everything so hushed and holy and the candles and the bowin and the hand-kerchiefs on all the drooping heads, I just couldn't go through with the plan. Which was for me to run up to the altar and do a tap dance while Sugar played the nose flute and messed around in the holy water. And Sugar kept givin me the elbow. Then later teased me so bad I tied her up in the shower and turned it on and locked her in. And she'd be there till this day if Aunt Gretchen hadn't finally figured I was lying about the boarder takin a shower.

Same thing in the store. We all walkin on tiptoe and hardly touchin the games and puzzles and things. And I watched Miss Moore who is steady watchin us like she waitin for a sign. Like Mama Drewery watches the sky and sniffs the air and takes note of just how much slant is in the bird forma-tion. Then me and Sugar bump smack into each other, so busy gazing at the toys, 'specially the sailboat. But we don't laugh and go into our fat-lady bump-stomach routine. We just stare at that price tag. Then Sugar run a fin-ger over the whole boat. And I'm jealous and want to hit her. Maybe not her, but I sure want to punch somebody in the mouth.

"Watcha bring us here for, Miss Moore?"

"You sound angry, Sylvia. Are you mad about something?" Give me one of them grins like she tellin a grown-up joke that never turns out to be funny. And she's lookin very closely at me like maybe she plannin to do my portrait from memory. I'm mad, but I won't give her that satisfaction. So I slouch around the store bein very bored and say, "Let's go."

Me and Sugar at the back of the train watchin' the tracks whizzin by large then small then gettin gobbled up in the dark. I'm thinkin about this tricky toy I saw in the store. A clown that somersaults on a bar then does chin-ups just cause you yank lightly at his leg. Cost $35. I could see me askin my mother for a $35 birthday clown. "You wanna who that costs what?" she'd say, cockin her head to the side to get a better view of the hole in my head. Thirty-five dollars could buy new bunk beds for Junior and Gretchen's boy. Thirty-five dollars and the whole household could go visit Granddaddy Nelson in the country. Thirty-five dollars would pay for the rent and the piano bill too. Who are these people that spend that much for performing clowns and $1,000 for toy sailboats? What kinda work they do and how they live and how come we ain't in on it? Where we are is who we are, Miss Moore always pointin out. But it don't necessarily have to be that way, she always adds then waits for somebody to say that poor people have to wake up and demand their share of the pie and don't none of us know what kind of pie she talkin about in the first damn place. But she ain't so smart cause I still got her four dollars from the taxi and she sure ain't gettin it. Messin up my day with this shit. Sugar nudges me in my pocket and winks.

Miss Moore lines us up in front of the mailbox where we started from, seem like years ago, and I got a headache for thinkin so hard. And we lean all over each other so we can hold up under the draggy-ass lecture she always finishes us off with at the end before we thank her for borin us to tears. But she just looks at us like she readin tea leaves. Finally she say, "Well, what did you think of F.A.O. Schwarz?"[3]

Rosie Giraffe mumbles, "White folks crazy."

"I'd like to go in there again when I get my birthday money," says Mercedes, and we shove her out the pack so she has to lean on the mailbox by herself.

"I'd like a shower. Tiring day," say Flyboy.

Then Sugar surprises me by saying, "You know, Miss Moore, I don't think all of us here put together eat in a year what that sailboat costs." And Miss Moore lights up like somebody goosed her. "And?" she say, urging Sugar on. Only I'm standin on her foot so she don't continue.

"Imagine for a minute what kind of society it is in which some people can spend on a toy what it would cost to feed a family of six or seven. What do you think?"

45

50

---

[3]*F.A.O. Schwarz:* The name and the toy store are real. The store, in fact, has become a tourist attraction.

"I think," say Sugar pushing me off her feet like she never done before, cause I whip her ass in a minute, "that this is not much of a democracy if you ask me. Equal chance to pursue happiness means an equal crack at the dough, don't it?" Miss Moore is besides herself and I am disgusted with Sugar's treachery. So I stand on her foot one more time to see if she'll shove me. She shuts up, and Miss Moore looks at me, sorrowfully I'm thinkin. And somethin weird is going on, I can feel it in my chest.

"Anybody else learn anything today?" lookin dead at me. I walk away and Sugar has to run to catch up and don't even seem to notice when I shrug her arm off my shoulder.

"Well, we got four dollars anyway," she says.

"Uh hunh."

"We could go to Hascombs and get half a chocolate layer and then go   55
to the Sunset and still have plenty money for potato chips and ice-cream sodas."

"Uh hunh."

"Race you to Hascombs," she say.

We start down the block and she gets ahead which is O.K. by me cause I'm goin to the West End and then over to the Drive to think this day through. She can run if she want to and even run faster. But ain't nobody gonna beat me at nuthin.

ENGAGING THE TEXT

1. What is the lesson Miss Moore is trying to teach in this story? How well is it received by Mercedes, Sugar, and the narrator, Sylvia? Why does the narrator react differently from Sugar, and what is the meaning of her last line in the story, "But ain't nobody gonna beat me at nuthin"?

2. Why did Bambara write the story from Sylvia's point of view? How would the story change if told from Miss Moore's perspective? From Sugar's? How would it change if the story were set today as opposed to thirty years ago?

3. The story mentions several expensive items: a fur coat, a microscope, a paperweight, a sailboat, and a toy clown. Why do you think the author chose each of these details?

4. In paragraph 44 Sylvia says, "Where we are is who we are, Miss Moore always pointin out. But it don't necessarily have to be that way." What does Miss Moore mean by this? Do you agree? What does Miss Moore expect the children to do to change the situation?

EXPLORING CONNECTIONS

5. Write a dialogue between Miss Moore and Gregory Mantsios, author of "Class in America (2000)" (p. 331), in which they discuss Sylvia's future and her chances for success.

6. Compare Miss Moore with the matriarchs in "Envy" by Bebe Moore Campbell (p. 118). In particular, examine the goals they set, the behavior they expect, and their means of influencing the young women in their charge.

7. Compare Miss Moore with the "Seven-Lesson Schoolteacher" described by John Taylor Gatto (p. 173). To what extent does Miss Moore's approach to education avoid the pitfalls Gatto identifies with formal schooling? Does Miss Moore's "lesson" have a hidden curriculum?

8. Compare Sylvia and Sugar's relationship here with that of Teresa and the speaker of the poem in "Para Teresa" (p. 227). Which girls stand the better chance of achieving success? Why?

EXTENDING THE CRITICAL CONTEXT

9. For the next class meeting, find the most overpriced, unnecessary item you can in a store, catalog, TV ad, or newspaper. Spend a few minutes swapping examples, then discuss the information you've gathered: Are there any lessons to be learned here about wealth, success, and status?

10. The opening lines of "The Lesson" suggest that Sylvia is now a mature woman looking back on her youth. Working in groups, write a brief biography explaining what has happened to Sylvia since the day of "The Lesson." What has she done? Who has she become? Read your profiles aloud to the class and explain your vision of Sylvia's development.

11. This chapter of *Rereading America* has been criticized by conservatives for undermining the work ethic of American college students. Rush Limbaugh, for example, claims that the chapter "presents America as a stacked deck," thus "robbing people of the ability to see the enormous opportunities directly in front of them." Do you agree? Write a journal entry in which you explain how these readings have influenced your attitudes toward work and success.

4

True Women and Real Men

Myths of Gender

Bree Scott-Hartland as Delphinia Blue, photo by Carolyn Jones. (From *Living Proof*, Abbeville Press, 1994.)

Common sense tells us that there are obvious differences between females and males: after all, biology, not culture, determines whether you're able to bear children. But culture and cultural myths do shape the roles men and women play in our public and private relationships: we may be born female and male, but we are made women and men. Sociologists distinguish between sex and gender—between one's biological identity and the conventional patterns of behavior we learn to associate with each sex. While biological sex remains relatively stable, the definition of "appropriate" gender behavior varies dramatically from one cultural group or historical period to the next. The variations show up markedly in the way we dress. For example, in Thailand, men who act and dress like women are not only socially accepted but encouraged to participate in popular, male-only beauty pageants; in contemporary Anglo-American culture, on the other hand, cross-dressers are usually seen as deviant or ridiculous. Male clothing in late-seventeenth- and early-eighteenth-century England would also have failed our current "masculinity" tests: in that period, elaborate laces, brocades, wigs, and even makeup signaled wealth, status, and sexual attractiveness for men and women alike.

History shows us how completely our gender derives from cultural myths about what is proper for men and women to think, enjoy, and do. And history is replete with examples of how the apparent "naturalness" of gender has been used to regulate political, economic, and personal relations between the sexes.

Many nineteenth-century scientists argued that it was "unnatural" for women to attend college; rigorous intellectual activity, they asserted, would draw vital energy away from a woman's reproductive organs and make her sterile. According to this line of reasoning, women who sought higher education threatened the natural order by jeopardizing their ability to bear children and perpetuate the species. Arguments based on nature were likewise used to justify women's exclusion from political life. In his classic 1832 treatise on American democracy, for instance, James Fenimore Cooper remarked that women's domestic role and "necessary" subordination to men made them unsuitable for participation in public affairs. Thus, he argued, denying women the right to vote was perfectly consistent with the principles of American democracy:

> In those countries where the suffrage is said to be universal, exceptions exist, that arise from the necessity of things.... The interests of women being thought to be so identified with those of their male relatives as to become, in a great degree, inseparable, females are, almost generally, excluded from the possession of political rights. There can be no doubt that society is greatly the gainer, by thus excluding one half its members, and the half that is best adapted to give a tone to its domestic happiness, from the strife of parties, and the fierce struggles of political controversies.... These exceptions, however, do not very materially affect the principle of political equality. (*The American Democrat*)

Resistance to gender equality has been remarkably persistent in the United States. It took over seventy years of hard political work by both black and white women's organizations to win the right to vote. But while feminists gained the vote for women in 1920 and the legal right to equal educational and employment opportunities in the 1970s, attitudes change even more slowly than laws. Contemporary antifeminist campaigns voice some of the same anxieties as their nineteenth-century counterparts over the "loss" of femininity and domesticity.

Women continue to suffer economic inequities based on cultural assumptions about gender. What's defined as "women's work"—nurturing, feeding, caring for family and home—is devalued and pays low wages or none at all. When women enter jobs traditionally held by men, they often encounter discrimination, harassment, or "glass ceilings" that limit their advancement. But men, too, pay a high price for their culturally imposed roles. Psychological research shows higher rates of depression among people of both sexes who adhere closely to traditional roles than among those who do not. Moreover, studies of men's mental and physical health suggest that social pressure to "be a man" (that is, to be emotionally controlled, powerful, and successful) can contribute to isolation, anxiety, stress, and illness, and may be partially responsible for men's shorter life spans. As sociologist Margaret Andersen observes, "traditional gender roles limit the psychological and social possibilities for human beings."

Even our assumption that there are "naturally" only two genders is a cultural invention that fails to accommodate the diversity of human experience. Some cultures have three or more gender categories. One of the best-known third genders is the American Indian *berdache,* a role that is found in as many as seventy North and South American tribes. The berdache is a biological male who takes the social role of a woman, does women's work (or in some cases both women's and men's work), and often enjoys high status in the society; the berdache has sex with men who are not themselves berdaches and in some cultures may also marry a man. Euro-American culture, by contrast, offers no socially acceptable alternative gender roles. As a result, gay men, lesbians, bisexuals, transsexuals, cross-dressers, and other gender rebels confront pervasive and often legally sanctioned discrimination similar to that once experienced by women. Just as many Americans in the past considered it "unnatural" and socially destructive for women to vote or go to college, many now consider it "unnatural" and socially destructive for gays and lesbians to marry, bear or adopt children, serve in the military, lead scout groups, or teach school.

This chapter focuses on cultural myths of gender and the influence they wield over human development and personal identity. The first three selections examine how dominant American culture defines female and male gender roles—and how those roles may define us. In "How the Americans Understand the Equality of the Sexes," Alexis de Tocqueville describes the status of American women in the early years of the Republic. Jamaica

Kincaid's "Girl," a story framed as a mother's advice to her daughter, presents a more contemporary take on what it means to be raised a woman. Aaron H. Devor's "Becoming Members of Society" examines gender as a socially constructed category and discusses the psychological processes that underlie gender role acquisition.

Next, two personal narratives and a Visual Portfolio present strong rereadings of traditional gender roles. Judith Ortiz Cofer's personal reflection, "The Story of My Body," traces the shifting meanings of gender and identity for a woman of color who moves among different social and cultural contexts. In "Where I Come From Is Like This," Paula Gunn Allen counters dominant American myths of gender with an eloquent description of the powerful roles played by women in American Indian cultures. The portfolio presents both conventional and unconventional images of women and men that provide an opportunity to think about the ways that we "read" gender visually.

The second half of the chapter opens with two essays that examine the power of media to shape our attitudes and behavior as women and men. Jean Kilbourne's "'Two Ways a Woman Can Get Hurt': Advertising and Violence" argues that the objectification of women in ads constitutes a form of cultural abuse. According to Kilbourne, ads that play with pornographic imagery and hint at sexual aggression contribute to an epidemic of real violence against women. In "Center of Attention: The Gender of Sports Media," Michael A. Messner contends that TV sports coverage promotes a conception of masculinity based on gender stereotypes, racial hierarchy, aggression, and consumerism. "Appearances," by Carmen Vázquez, introduces another kind of gendered violence: homophobic assault. Vázquez documents the penalties—from verbal harassment to murder—paid by both gay and straight people who commit "gender betrayal" by daring to cross conventional gender boundaries. "The Bridge Builder" offers a more hopeful vision of nonconformity; it relates the story of Kathleen Boatwright, a devout Christian and a lesbian who refuses to be confined by gay stereotypes or rigid attitudes toward homosexuality.

A final trio of essays addresses what it means to be male in a culture where the old rules are rapidly changing. Susan Faludi's "Girls Have All the Power: What's Troubling Troubled Boys" represents a feminist reporter's effort to comprehend the motives and psychology of the Spur Posse, a group of teenage boys who gained notoriety in the early 1990s for competing to see who could rack up the most "points" for having sex with the most girls, a number that included one ten-year-old. Christina Hoff Sommers, in "Save the Males," challenges those, like Faludi, who see sexual predators and teenage killers as evidence of a masculinity crisis in America. The problem, as she sees it, lies more with feminist researchers and "crisis writers" than with the boys and men they study. "From Fly-Girls to Bitches and Hos" concludes the chapter with reflections on the sometimes strained alliance of African American women and men. In the essay, self-described "hip-hop feminist" Joan Morgan maintains that it's necessary to look behind the violent misogyny of many rap lyrics in order to understand and heal the pain of the African American men who compose and perform such songs.

Sources

Margaret L. Andersen, *Thinking About Women: Sociological Perspectives on Gender,* 3rd ed. New York: Macmillan, 1993.

James Fenimore Cooper, *The American Democrat.* N.p.: Minerva Press, 1969.

Marilyn French, *Beyond Power: On Women, Men, and Morals.* New York: Ballantine Books, 1985.

Paula Giddings, *When and Where I Enter: The Impact of Black Women on Race and Sex in America.* New York: Bantam Books, 1984.

Ruth Hubbard, *The Politics of Women's Biology.* New Brunswick, NJ: Rutgers University Press, 1990.

Judith Lorber, *Paradoxes of Gender.* New Haven and London: Yale University Press, 1994.

James D. Weinrich and Walter L. Williams, "Strange Customs, Familiar Lives: Homosexualities in Other Cultures." *Homosexuality: Research Implications for Public Policy.* Ed. John C. Gonsiorek and James D. Weinrich. Newbury Park, CA: Sage, 1991.

BEFORE READING

- Imagine for a moment that you were born female (if you're a man) or male (if you're a woman). How would your life be different? Would any of your interests and activities change? How about your relationships with other people? Write a journal entry describing your past, present, and possible future in this alternate gender identity.

- Collect and bring to class images of girls and boys, women and men taken from popular magazines and newspapers. Working in groups, make a collage of either male or female gender images; then compare and discuss your results. What do these media images tell you about what it means to be a woman or a man in this culture?

- Do a brief freewrite focusing on the performer in the frontispiece to this chapter (p. 412). How would you describe this person's gender? In what ways does this image challenge traditional ideas about maleness and femaleness?

How the Americans Understand the Equality of the Sexes

ALEXIS DE TOCQUEVILLE

In 1831, Alexis de Tocqueville (1805–1859), a French aristocrat, left Europe to study the American penal system. The young democracy that he observed in the United States left a deep impression on Tocqueville, and in 1835 he published his reflections on this new way of life in Democracy in America—*a work that has since become the point of departure for many studies of American culture. In the following passage from* Democracy in America, *Tocqueville compares the social condition of American women to that of their European counterparts. Tocqueville's concept of equality and assumptions about women can seem foreign to modern readers, so it would be a good idea to take your time as you read this short passage.*

I have shown how democracy destroys or modifies the different inequalities which originate in society; but is that all? or does it not ultimately affect that great inequality of man and woman which has seemed, up to the present day, to be eternally based in human nature? I believe that the social changes which bring nearer to the same level the father and son, the master and servant, and, in general, superiors and inferiors, will raise woman, and make her more and more the equal of man. But here, more than ever, I feel the necessity of making myself clearly understood; for there is no subject on which the coarse and lawless fancies of our age have taken a freer range.

There are people in Europe who, confounding together the different characteristics of the sexes, would make man and woman into beings not only equal, but alike. They would give to both the same functions, impose on both the same duties, and grant to both the same rights; they would mix them in all things,—their occupations, their pleasures, their business. It may readily be conceived, that, by thus attempting to make one sex equal to the other, both are degraded; and from so preposterous a medley of the works of nature, nothing could ever result but weak men and disorderly women.

It is not thus that the Americans understand that species of democratic equality which may be established between the sexes. They admit that, as nature has appointed such wide differences between the physical and moral constitution of man and woman, her manifest design was to give a distinct employment to their various faculties; and they hold that improvement does not consist in making beings so dissimilar do pretty nearly the same things, but in causing each of them to fulfil their respective tasks in the best possible manner. The Americans have applied to the sexes the great principle of political economy which governs the manufactures of our age, by carefully dividing the duties of man from those of woman, in order that the great work of society may be the better carried on.

In no country has such constant care been taken as in America to trace two clearly distinct lines of action for the two sexes, and to make them keep pace one with the other, but in two pathways which are always different. American women never manage the outward concerns of the family, or conduct a business, or take a part in political life; nor are they, on the other hand, ever compelled to perform the rough labor of the fields, or to make any of those laborious exertions which demand the exertion of physical strength. No families are so poor as to form an exception to this rule. If, on the one hand, an American woman cannot escape from the quiet circle of domestic employments, she is never forced, on the other, to go beyond it. Hence it is, that the women of America, who often exhibit a masculine strength of understanding and a manly energy, generally preserve great delicacy of personal appearance, and always retain the manners of women, although they sometimes show that they have the hearts and minds of men.

Nor have the Americans ever supposed that one consequence of democratic principles is the subversion of marital power, or the confusion of the natural authorities in families. They hold that every association must have a head in order to accomplish its object, and that the natural head of the conjugal association is man. They do not therefore deny him the right of directing his partner; and they maintain that, in the smaller association of husband and wife, as well as in the great social community, the object of democracy is to regulate and legalize the powers which are necessary, and not to subvert all power. 5

This opinion is not peculiar to one sex, and contested by the other: I never observed that the women of America consider conjugal authority as a fortunate usurpation of their rights, nor that they thought themselves degraded by submitting to it. It appeared to me, on the contrary, that they attach a sort of pride to the voluntary surrender of their own will, and make it their boast to bend themselves to the yoke,—not to shake it off. Such, at least, is the feeling expressed by the most virtuous of their sex; the others are silent; and, in the United States, it is not the practice for a guilty wife to clamor for the rights of women, whilst she is trampling on her own holiest duties.[1]

It has often been remarked, that in Europe a certain degree of contempt lurks even in the flattery which men lavish upon women: although a European frequently affects to be the slave of woman, it may be seen that

[1] Allusion to Mary Wollstonecraft (1759–1797), English radical, political theorist, and author of *Vindication of the Rights of Woman*, who argued that women should enjoy complete political, economic, and sexual freedom; Wollstonecraft scandalized the "polite" society of her day by living according to her feminist principles.

he never sincerely thinks her his equal. In the United States, men seldom compliment women, but they daily show how much they esteem them. They constantly display an entire confidence in the understanding of a wife, and a profound respect for her freedom; they have decided that her mind is just as fitted as that of a man to discover the plain truth, and her heart as firm to embrace it; and they have never sought to place her virtue, any more than his, under the shelter of prejudice, ignorance, and fear.

It would seem that, in Europe, where man so easily submits to the despotic sway of women, they are nevertheless deprived of some of the greatest attributes of the human species, and considered as seductive but imperfect beings; and (what may well provoke astonishment) women ultimately look upon themselves in the same light, and almost consider it as a privilege that they are entitled to show themselves futile, feeble, and timid. The women of America claim no such privileges.

Again, it may be said that in our morals we have reserved strange immunities to man; so that there is, as it were, one virtue for his use, and another for the guidance of his partner; and that, according to the opinion of the public, the very same act may be punished alternately as a crime, or only as a fault. The Americans know not this iniquitous division of duties and rights; amongst them, the seducer is as much dishonored as his victim.

It is true that the Americans rarely lavish upon women those eager attentions which are commonly paid them in Europe; but their conduct to women always implies that they suppose them to be virtuous and refined; and such is the respect entertained for the moral freedom of the sex, that in the presence of a woman the most guarded language is used, lest her ear should be offended by an expression. In America, a young unmarried woman may, alone and without fear, undertake a long journey.

10

The legislators of the United States, who have mitigated almost all the penalties of criminal law, still make rape a capital offence, and no crime is visited with more inexorable severity by public opinion. This may be accounted for; as the Americans can conceive nothing more precious than a woman's honor, and nothing which ought so much to be respected as her independence, they hold that no punishment is too severe for the man who deprives her of them against her will. In France, where the same offence is visited with far milder penalties, it is frequently difficult to get a verdict from a jury against the prisoner. Is this a consequence of contempt of decency, or contempt of women? I cannot but believe that it is a contempt of both.

Thus, the Americans do not think that man and woman have either the duty or the right to perform the same offices, but they show an equal regard for both their respective parts; and though their lot is different, they consider both of them as beings of equal value. They do not give to the courage of woman the same form or the same direction as to that of man; but they never doubt her courage: and if they hold that man and his partner ought not always to exercise their intellect and understanding in the same manner, they at least believe the understanding of the one to be as sound as that of the other, and her intellect to be as clear. Thus, then, whilst they have allowed the social inferiority of woman to subsist, they have done all they could to raise her morally and intellectually to the level of man; and in this respect they appear to me to have excellently understood the true principle of democratic improvement.

As for myself, I do not hesitate to avow, that, although the women of the United States are confined within the narrow circle of domestic life, and their situation is, in some respects, one of extreme dependence, I have nowhere seen woman occupying a loftier position; and if I were asked, now that I am drawing to the close of this work, in which I have spoken of so many important things done by the Americans, to what the singular prosperity and growing strength of that people ought mainly to be attributed, I should reply, To the superiority of their women.

ENGAGING THE TEXT

1. What roles does Tocqueville assume are natural and appropriate for women? For men? Which of his assumptions, if any, seem contemporary? Which ones seem antiquated, and why?

2. How do American and European attitudes toward women differ, according to Tocqueville? In what ways, according to Tocqueville, is American democracy enabling women to become "more and more the equal of man" (para. 1)?

3. By the time Tocqueville wrote this selection, the first feminist manifesto, Wollstonecraft's *Vindication of the Rights of Woman* (1792), had been read and discussed in Europe for over forty years. Which parts of Tocqueville's essay seem to be intended as a response to feminist arguments for women's equality?

4. Tocqueville finds some forms of equality between women and men more desirable than others. Which forms does he approve of, which does he disapprove of, and why?

EXPLORING CONNECTIONS

5. Read the essay by Paula Gunn Allen (p. 443) for information on the various roles assigned to women and men in traditional tribal cultures. How are these roles similar to or different from the ones described by Tocqueville? Do they tend to support or challenge his observation that the "great inequality of man and woman" appears to be "eternally based in human nature" (para. 1)?

6. Both Tocqueville and Thomas Jefferson (p. 551) attempt to justify or rationalize a particular form of inequality. What strategies does each writer use to build his case for the subjection of women or for the enslavement of blacks? Which of their arguments appear least effective to you as a modern reader, and why?

EXTENDING THE CRITICAL CONTEXT

7. Work in groups to list the specific tasks involved in maintaining a household in the 1830s (keep in mind that electricity, indoor plumbing, ready-made clothing, and prepared foods were not available). How credible is Tocqueville's claim that no American woman is "ever compelled...to make any of those laborious exertions which demand the exertion of physical strength" (para. 4)? How do you explain his failure to acknowledge the hard physical labor routinely performed by many women during this time?

Girl

JAMAICA KINCAID

Although she now lives in New England, Jamaica Kincaid (b. 1949) retains strong ties, including citizenship, to her birthplace—the island of Antigua in the West Indies. After immigrating to the United States to attend college, she ended up educating herself instead, eventually becoming a staff writer for The New Yorker, *the author of several critically acclaimed books, and an instructor at Harvard University. About the influence of parents on children she says, "The magic is they carry so much you don't know about. They know you in a way you don't know yourself." Some of that magic is exercised in the story "Girl," which was first published in Kincaid's award-winning collection* At the Bottom of the River *(1983). She has written and edited many volumes of nonfiction on subjects ranging from colonialism to gardening and has published four novels:* Annie John *(1985),* Lucy *(1990),* The Autobiography of My Mother *(1996), and* Mr. Potter *(2002).*

Wash the white clothes on Monday and put them on the stone heap; wash the color clothes on Tuesday and put them on the clothesline to dry; don't walk barehead in the hot sun; cook pumpkin fritters[1] in very hot sweet oil; soak your little clothes right after you take them off; when buying cotton to make yourself a nice blouse, be sure that it doesn't have gum[2] on it, because that way it won't hold up well after a wash; soak salt fish overnight before you cook it; is it true that you sing benna[3] in Sunday school?; always eat

---

[1] *fritters:* Small fried cakes of batter, often containing vegetables, fruit, or other fillings.
[2] *gum:* Plant residue on cotton.
[3] *sing benna:* Sing popular music (not appropriate for Sunday school).

your food in such a way that it won't turn someone else's stomach; on Sundays try to walk like a lady and not like the slut you are so bent on becoming; don't sing benna in Sunday school; you mustn't speak to wharf-rat boys, not even to give directions; don't eat fruits on the street—flies will follow you; *but I don't sing benna on Sundays at all and never in Sunday school;* this is how to sew on a button; this is how to make a buttonhole for the button you have just sewed on; this is how to hem a dress when you see the hem coming down and so to prevent yourself from looking like the slut I know you are so bent on becoming; this is how you iron your father's khaki shirt so that it doesn't have a crease; this is how you iron your father's khaki pants so that they don't have a crease; this is how you grow okra[4]—far from the house, because okra tree harbors red ants; when you are growing dasheen,[5] make sure it gets plenty of water or else it makes your throat itch when you are eating it; this is how you sweep a corner; this is how you sweep a whole house; this is how you sweep a yard; this is how you smile to someone you don't like too much; this is how you smile to someone you don't like at all; this is how you smile to someone you like completely; this is how you set a table for tea; this is how you set a table for dinner; this is how you set a table for dinner with an important guest; this is how you set a table for lunch; this is how you set a table for breakfast; this is how to behave in the presence of men who don't know you very well, and this way they won't recognize immediately the slut I have warned you against becoming; be sure to wash every day, even if it is with your own spit; don't squat down to play marbles—you are not a boy, you know; don't pick people's flowers— you might catch something; don't throw stones at blackbirds, because it might not be a blackbird at all; this is how to make a bread pudding; this is how to make doukona;[6] this is how to make pepper pot;[7] this is how to make a good medicine for a cold; this is how to make a good medicine to throw away a child before it even becomes a child; this is how to catch a fish; this is how to throw back a fish you don't like, and that way something bad won't fall on you; this is how to bully a man; this is how a man bullies you; this is how to love a man, and if this doesn't work there are other ways, and if they don't work don't feel too bad about giving up; this is how to spit up in the air if you feel like it, and this is how to move quick so that it doesn't fall on you; this is how to make ends meet; always squeeze bread to make sure it's fresh; *but what if the baker won't let me feel the bread?;* you mean to say that after all you are really going to be the kind of woman who the baker won't let near the bread?

---

[4]*okra:* A shrub whose pods are used in soups, stews, and gumbo.
[5]*dasheen:* The taro plant, cultivated, like the potato, for its edible tuber.
[6]*doukona:* Plantain pudding; the plantain fruit is similar to the banana.
[7]*pepper pot:* A spicy West Indian stew.

ENGAGING THE TEXT

1. What are your best guesses as to the time and place of the story? Who is telling the story? What does this dialogue tell you about the relationship between the characters, their values and attitudes? What else can you surmise about these people (for instance, ages, occupation, social status)? On what evidence in the story do you base these conclusions?

2. Why does the story juxtapose advice on cooking and sewing, for example, with the repeated warning not to act like a slut?

3. Explain the meaning of the last line of the story: "you mean to say that after all you are really going to be the kind of woman who the baker won't let near the bread?"

4. What does the story tell us about male-female relationships? According to the speaker, what roles are women and men expected to play? What kinds of power, if any, does the speaker suggest that women may have?

EXPLORING CONNECTIONS

5. To what extent would Tocqueville approve of the behaviors and attitudes that the mother is trying to teach her daughter in this selection?

6. What does it mean to be a successful mother in "Girl"? How does this compare to being a good mother or parent in "Envy" (p. 118), "An Indian Story" (p. 109), or "Looking for Work" (p. 26)? Of all the parents in these narratives, which do you consider most successful, which least, and why?

EXTENDING THE CRITICAL CONTEXT

7. Write an imitation of the story. If you are a woman, record some of the advice or lessons your mother or another woman gave you; if you are a man, put down advice received from your father or from another male. Read what you have written aloud in class, alternating between male and female speakers, and discuss the results: How does parental guidance vary according to gender?

8. Write a page or two recording what the daughter might be thinking as she listens to her mother's advice; then compare notes with classmates.

Becoming Members of Society: Learning the Social Meanings of Gender

AARON H. DEVOR

*Gender is the most transparent of all social categories: we acquire gen-
der roles so early in life and so thoroughly that it's hard to see them as the
result of lessons taught and learned. Maleness and femaleness seem "natural," not the product of socialization. In this wide-ranging scholarly essay,
Aaron H. Devor suggests that many of our notions of what it means to be female or male are socially constructed. He also touches on the various ways
that different cultures define gender. A professor of sociology and Dean of
Graduate Studies at the University of Victoria in British Columbia, Devor is
a member of the International Academy of Sex Research and author of*
FTM: Female-to-Male Transsexuals in Society *(1997).* Born Holly Devor in
1951, *Devor announced in 2003 his decision to live as a man and to adopt
the name Aaron H. Devor. This selection is taken from his groundbreaking
book,* Gender Blending: Confronting the Limits of Duality *(1989).*

The Gendered Self

The task of learning to be properly gendered members of society only
begins with the establishment of gender identity. Gender identities act as
cognitive filtering devices guiding people to attend to and learn gender role
behaviors appropriate to their statuses. Learning to behave in accordance
with one's gender identity is a lifelong process. As we move through our
lives, society demands different gender performances from us and rewards,
tolerates, or punishes us differently for conformity to, or digression from,
social norms. As children, and later adults, learn the rules of membership in
society, they come to see themselves in terms they have learned from the
people around them.

Children begin to settle into a gender identity between the age of eighteen months and two years.[1] By the age of two, children usually understand
that they are members of a gender grouping and can correctly identify other

[1]Much research has been devoted to determining when gender identity becomes solidi-
fied in the sense that a child knows itself to be unequivocally either male or female. John
Money and his colleagues have proposed eighteen months of age because it is difficult or impossible to change a child's gender identity once it has been established around the age of
eighteen months. Money and Ehrhardt, p. 243. [All notes are Devor's except 12, 20, and 21.]

members of their gender.[2] By age three they have a fairly firm and consistent concept of gender. Generally, it is not until children are five to seven years old that they become convinced that they are permanent members of their gender grouping.[3]

Researchers test the establishment, depth, and tenacity of gender identity through the use of language and the concepts mediated by language. The language systems used in populations studied by most researchers in this field conceptualize gender as binary and permanent. All persons are either male or female. All males are first boys and then men; all females are first girls and then women. People are believed to be unable to change genders without sex change surgery, and those who do change sex are considered to be both disturbed and exceedingly rare.

This is by no means the only way that gender is conceived in all cultures. Many aboriginal cultures have more than two gender categories and accept the idea that, under certain circumstances, gender may be changed without changes being made to biological sex characteristics. Many North and South American native peoples had a legitimate social category for persons who wished to live according to the gender role of another sex. Such people were sometimes revered, sometimes ignored, and occasionally scorned. Each culture had its own word to describe such persons, most commonly translated into English as "berdache." Similar institutions and linguistic concepts have also been recorded in early Siberian, Madagascan, and Polynesian societies, as well as in medieval Europe.[4]

Very young children learn their culture's social definitions of gender   5
and gender identity at the same time that they learn what gender behaviors are appropriate for them. But they only gradually come to understand the meaning of gender in the same way as the adults of their society do. Very young children may learn the words which describe their gender and be able to apply them to themselves appropriately, but their comprehension of their meaning is often different from that used by adults. Five-year-olds, for example, may be able to accurately recognize their own gender and the genders of the people around them, but they will often make such ascriptions on the basis of role information, such as hair style, rather than physical

---

[2]Mary Driver Leinbach and Beverly I. Fagot, "Acquisition of Gender Labels: A Test for Toddlers," *Sex Roles* 15 (1986), pp. 655–66.

[3]Maccoby, pp. 225–29; Kohlberg and Ullian, p. 211.

[4]See Susan Baker, "Biological Influences on Human Sex and Gender," in *Women: Sex and Sexuality,* ed. Catherine R. Stimpson and Ethel S. Person (Chicago: University of Chicago Press, 1980), p. 186; Evelyn Blackwood, "Sexuality and Gender in Certain Native American Tribes: The Case of Cross-Gender Females," *Signs* 10 (1984), pp. 27–42; Vern L. Bullough, "Transvestites in the Middle Ages," *American Journal of Sociology* 79 (1974), 1381–89; J. Cl. DuBois, "Transsexualisme et Anthropologie Culturelle," *Gynecologie Practique* 6 (1969), pp. 431–40; Donald C. Forgey, "The Institution of Berdache among the North American Plains Indians," *Journal of Sex Research* 11 (Feb. 1975), pp. 1–15; Walter L. Williams, *The Spirit and the Flesh: Sexual Diversity in American Indian Culture* (Boston: Beacon, 1986).

attributes, such as genitals, even when physical cues are clearly known to them. One result of this level of understanding of gender is that children in this age group often believe that people may change their gender with a change in clothing, hair style, or activity.[5]

The characteristics most salient to young minds are the more culturally specific qualities which grow out of gender role prescriptions. In one study, young school age children, who were given dolls and asked to identify their gender, overwhelmingly identified the gender of the dolls on the basis of attributes such as hair length or clothing style, in spite of the fact that the dolls were anatomically correct. Only 17 percent of the children identified the dolls on the basis of their primary or secondary sex characteristics.[6] Children five to seven years old understand gender as a function of role rather than as a function of anatomy. Their understanding is that gender (role) is supposed to be stable but that it is possible to alter it at will. This demonstrates that although the standard social definition of gender is based on genitalia, this is not the way that young children first learn to distinguish gender. The process of learning to think about gender in an adult fashion is one prerequisite to becoming a full member of society. Thus, as children grow older, they learn to think of themselves and others in terms more like those used by adults.

Children's developing concepts of themselves as individuals are necessarily bound up in their need to understand the expectations of the society of which they are a part. As they develop concepts of themselves as individuals, they do so while observing themselves as reflected in the eyes of others. Children start to understand themselves as individuals separate from others during the years that they first acquire gender identities and gender roles. As they do so, they begin to understand that others see them and respond to them as particular people. In this way they develop concepts of themselves as individuals, as an "I" (a proactive subject) simultaneously with self-images of themselves as individuals, as a "me" (a member of society, a subjective object). Children learn that they are both as they see themselves and as others see them.[7]

To some extent, children initially acquire the values of the society around them almost indiscriminately. To the degree that children absorb the generalized standards of society into their personal concept of what is correct behavior, they can be said to hold within themselves the attitude of the "generalized other."[8] This "generalized other" functions as a sort of monitoring or measuring device with which individuals may judge their own actions against those of their generalized conceptions of how members of

[5]Maccoby, p. 255.

[6]Ibid., p. 227.

[7]George Herbert Mead, "Self," in *The Social Psychology of George Herbert Mead*, ed. Anselm Strauss (Chicago: Phoenix Books, 1962, 1934), pp. 212–60.

[8]G. H. Mead.

society are expected to act. In this way members of society have available to them a guide, or an internalized observer, to turn the more private "I" into the object of public scrutiny, the "me." In this way, people can monitor their own behavioral impulses and censor actions which might earn them social disapproval or scorn. The tension created by the constant interplay of the personal "I" and the social "me" is the creature known as the "self."

But not all others are of equal significance in our lives, and therefore not all others are of equal impact on the development of the self. Any person is available to become part of one's "generalized other," but certain individuals, by virtue of the sheer volume of time spent in interaction with someone, or by virtue of the nature of particular interactions, become more significant in the shaping of people's values. These "significant others" become prominent in the formation of one's self-image and one's ideals and goals. As such they carry disproportionate weight in one's personal "generalized other."[9] Thus, children's individualistic impulses are shaped into a socially acceptable form both by particular individuals and by a more generalized pressure to conformity exerted by innumerable faceless members of society. Gender identity is one of the most central portions of that developing sense of self. . . .

Gender Role Behaviors and Attitudes

The clusters of social definitions used to identify persons by gender are   10
collectively known as femininity and masculinity. Masculine characteristics are used to identify persons as males, while feminine ones are used as signifiers for femaleness. People use femininity or masculinity to claim and communicate their membership in their assigned, or chosen, sex or gender. Others recognize our sex or gender more on the basis of these characteristics than on the basis of sex characteristics, which are usually largely covered by clothing in daily life.

These two clusters of attributes are most commonly seen as mirror images of one another with masculinity usually characterized by dominance and aggression, and femininity by passivity and submission. A more even-handed description of the social qualities subsumed by femininity and masculinity might be to label masculinity as generally concerned with egoistic dominance and femininity as striving for cooperation or communion.[10] Characterizing femininity and masculinity in such a way does not portray the two clusters of characteristics as being in a hierarchical relationship to

[9]Hans Gerth and C. Wright Mills, *Character and Social Structure: The Psychology of Social Institutions* (New York: Harcourt, Brace and World, 1953), p. 96.

[10]Egoistic dominance is a striving for superior rewards for oneself or a competitive striving to reduce the rewards for one's competitors even if such action will not increase one's own rewards. Persons who are motivated by desires for egoistic dominance not only wish the best for themselves but also wish to diminish the advantages of others whom they may perceive as competing with them. See Maccoby, p. 217.

one another but rather as being two different approaches to the same question, that question being centrally concerned with the goals, means, and use of power. Such an alternative conception of gender roles captures the hierarchical and competitive masculine thirst for power, which can, but need not, lead to aggression, and the feminine quest for harmony and communal well-being, which can, but need not, result in passivity and dependence.

Many activities and modes of expression are recognized by most members of society as feminine. Any of these can be, and often are, displayed by persons of either gender. In some cases, cross gender behaviors are ignored by observers, and therefore do not compromise the integrity of a person's gender display. In other cases, they are labeled as inappropriate gender role behaviors. Although these behaviors are closely linked to sexual status in the minds and experiences of most people, research shows that dominant persons of either gender tend to use influence tactics and verbal styles usually associated with men and masculinity, while subordinate persons, of either gender, tend to use those considered to be the province of women.[11] Thus it seems likely that many aspects of masculinity and femininity are the result, rather than the cause, of status inequalities.

Popular conceptions of femininity and masculinity instead revolve around hierarchical appraisals of the "natural" roles of males and females. Members of both genders are believed to share many of the same human characteristics, although in different relative proportions; both males and females are popularly thought to be able to do many of the same things, but most activities are divided into suitable and unsuitable categories for each gender class. Persons who perform the activities considered appropriate for another gender will be expected to perform them poorly; if they succeed adequately, or even well, at their endeavors, they may be rewarded with ridicule or scorn for blurring the gender dividing line.

The patriarchal gender schema[12] currently in use in mainstream North American society reserves highly valued attributes for males and actively supports the high evaluation of any characteristics which might inadvertently become associated with maleness. The ideology which the schema grows out of postulates that the cultural superiority of males is a natural outgrowth of the innate predisposition of males toward aggression and dominance, which is assumed to flow inevitably from evolutionary and biological sources. Female attributes are likewise postulated to find their source in innate predispositions acquired in the evolution of the species. Feminine characteristics are thought to be intrinsic to the female facility for childbirth and breastfeeding. Hence, it is popularly believed that the social position of

---

[11]Judith Howard, Philip Blumstein, and Pepper Schwartz, "Sex, Power, and Influence Tactics in Intimate Relationships," *Journal of Personality and Social Psychology* 51 (1986), pp. 102–09; Peter Kollock, Philip Blumstein, and Pepper Schwartz, "Sex and Power in Interaction: Conversational Privileges and Duties," *American Sociological Review* 50 (1985), pp. 34–46.

[12]*schema:* A mental framework, scheme, or pattern that helps us make sense of experience.

females is biologically mandated to be intertwined with the care of children and a "natural" dependency on men for the maintenance of mother-child units. Thus the goals of femininity and, by implication, of all biological females are presumed to revolve around heterosexuality and maternity.[13]

Femininity, according to this traditional formulation, "would result in warm and continued relationships with men, a sense of maternity, interest in caring for children, and the capacity to work productively and continuously in female occupations."[14] This recipe translates into a vast number of proscriptions and prescriptions. Warm and continued relations with men and an interest in maternity require that females be heterosexually oriented. A heterosexual orientation requires women to dress, move, speak, and act in ways that men will find attractive. As patriarchy has reserved active expressions of power as a masculine attribute, femininity must be expressed through modes of dress, movement, speech, and action which communicate weakness, dependency, ineffectualness, availability for sexual or emotional service, and sensitivity to the needs of others. 15

Some, but not all, of these modes of interrelation also serve the demands of maternity and many female job ghettos. In many cases, though, femininity is not particularly useful in maternity or employment. Both mothers and workers often need to be strong, independent, and effectual in order to do their jobs well. Thus femininity, as a role, is best suited to satisfying a masculine vision of heterosexual attractiveness.

Body postures and demeanors which communicate subordinate status and vulnerability to trespass through a message of "no threat" make people appear to be feminine. They demonstrate subordination through a minimizing of spatial use: people appear feminine when they keep their arms closer to their bodies, their legs closer together, and their torsos and heads less vertical then do masculine-looking individuals. People also look feminine when they point their toes inward and use their hands in small or childlike gestures. Other people also tend to stand closer to people they see as feminine, often invading their personal space, while people who make frequent appeasement gestures, such as smiling, also give the appearance of femininity. Perhaps as an outgrowth of a subordinate status and the need to avoid conflict with more socially powerful people, women tend to excel over men at the ability to correctly interpret, and effectively display, nonverbal communication cues.[15]

[13]Chodorow, p. 134.

[14]Jon K. Meyer and John E. Hoopes, "The Gender Dysphoria Syndromes: A Position Statement on So-Called 'Transsexualism'," *Plastic and Reconstructive Surgery* 54 (Oct. 1974), pp. 444–51.

[15]Erving Goffman, *Gender Advertisements* (New York: Harper Colophon Books, 1976); Judith A. Hall, *Non-Verbal Sex Differences: Communication Accuracy and Expressive Style* (Baltimore: Johns Hopkins University Press, 1984); Nancy M. Henley, *Body Politics: Power, Sex and Non-Verbal Communication* (Englewood Cliffs, New Jersey: Prentice Hall, 1979); Marianne Wex, *"Let's Take Back Our Space": "Female" and "Male" Body Language as a Result of Patriarchal Structures* (Berlin: Frauenliteraturverlag Hermine Fees, 1979).

Speech characterized by inflections, intonations, and phrases that convey nonaggression and subordinate status also make a speaker appear more feminine. Subordinate speakers who use more polite expressions and ask more questions in conversation seem more feminine. Speech characterized by sounds of higher frequencies are often interpreted by listeners as feminine, childlike, and ineffectual.[16] Feminine styles of dress likewise display subordinate status through greater restriction of the free movement of the body, greater exposure of the bare skin, and an emphasis on sexual characteristics. The more gender distinct the dress, the more this is the case.

Masculinity, like femininity, can be demonstrated through a wide variety of cues. Pleck has argued that it is commonly expressed in North American society through the attainment of some level of proficiency at some, or all, of the following four main attitudes of masculinity. Persons who display success and high status in their social group, who exhibit "a manly air of toughness, confidence, and self-reliance" and "the aura of aggression, violence, and daring," and who conscientiously avoid anything associated with femininity are seen as exuding masculinity.[17] These requirements reflect the patriarchal ideology that masculinity results from an excess of testosterone, the assumption being that androgens supply a natural impetus toward aggression, which in turn impels males toward achievement and success. This vision of masculinity also reflects the ideological stance that ideal maleness (masculinity) must remain untainted by female (feminine) pollutants.

Masculinity, then, requires of its actors that they organize themselves   20
and their society in a hierarchical manner so as to be able to explicitly quantify the achievement of success. The achievement of high status in one's social group requires competitive and aggressive behavior from those who wish to obtain it. Competition which is motivated by a goal of individual achievement, or egoistic dominance, also requires of its participants a degree of emotional insensitivity to feelings of hurt and loss in defeated others, and a measure of emotional insularity to protect oneself from becoming vulnerable to manipulation by others. Such values lead those who subscribe to them to view feminine persons as "born losers" and to strive to eliminate any similarities to feminine people from their own personalities. In patriarchally organized societies, masculine values become the ideological structure of the society as a whole. Masculinity thus becomes "innately" valuable and femininity serves a contrapuntal function to delineate and magnify the hierarchical dominance of masculinity.

Body postures, speech patterns, and styles of dress which demonstrate and support the assumption of dominance and authority convey an impression of masculinity. Typical masculine body postures tend to be expansive

[16]Karen L. Adams, "Sexism and the English Language: The Linguistic Implications of Being a Woman," in *Women: A Feminist Perspective*, 3rd edition, ed. Jo Freeman (Palo Alto, Calif.: Mayfield, 1984), pp. 478–91; Hall, pp. 37, 130–37.

[17]Elizabeth Hafkin Pleck, *Domestic Tyranny: The Making of Social Policy Against Family Violence from Colonial Times to the Present* (Cambridge: Oxford University Press, 1989), p. 139.

and aggressive. People who hold their arms and hands in positions away from their bodies, and who stand, sit, or lie with their legs apart—thus maximizing the amount of space that they physically occupy—appear most physically masculine. Persons who communicate an air of authority or a readiness for aggression by standing erect and moving forcefully also tend to appear more masculine. Movements that are abrupt and stiff, communicating force and threat rather than flexibility and cooperation, make an actor look masculine. Masculinity can also be conveyed by stern or serious facial expressions that suggest minimal receptivity to the influence of others, a characteristic which is an important element in the attainment and maintenance of egoistic dominance.[18]

Speech and dress which likewise demonstrate or claim superior status are also seen as characteristically masculine behavior patterns. Masculine speech patterns display a tendency toward expansiveness similar to that found in masculine body postures. People who attempt to control the direction of conversations seem more masculine.[19] Those who tend to speak more loudly, use less polite and more assertive forms, and tend to interrupt the conversations of others more often also communicate masculinity to others. Styles of dress which emphasize the size of upper body musculature, allow freedom of movement, and encourage an illusion of physical power and a look of easy physicality all suggest masculinity. Such appearances of strength and readiness to action serve to create or enhance an aura of aggressiveness and intimidation central to an appearance of masculinity. Expansive postures and gestures combine with these qualities to insinuate that a position of secure dominance is a masculine one.

Gender role characteristics reflect the ideological contentions underlying the dominant gender schema in North American society. That schema leads us to believe that female and male behaviors are the result of socially directed hormonal instructions which specify that females will want to have children and will therefore find themselves relatively helpless and dependent on males for support and protection. The schema claims that males are innately aggressive and competitive and therefore will dominate over females. The social hegemony[20] of this ideology ensures that we are all raised to practice gender roles which will confirm this vision of the nature of the sexes. Fortunately, our training to gender roles is neither complete nor uniform. As a result, it is possible to point to multitudinous exceptions to, and variations on, these themes. Biological evidence is equivocal about the source of gender roles; psychological androgyny[21] is a widely accepted concept. It seems most likely that gender roles are the result of systematic power imbalances based on gender discrimination.[22]

[18]Goffman, *Gender Advertisements;* Hall; Henley; Wex.

[19]Adams; Hall, pp. 37, 130–37.

[20]*hegemony:* System of preponderant influence, authority, or dominance.

[21]*androgyny:* The state of having both male and female characteristics.

[22]Howard, Blumstein, and Schwartz; Kollock, Blumstein, and Schwartz.

"We don't believe in pressuring the children. When the time is right, they'll choose the appropriate gender."

ENGAGING THE TEXT

1. Devor charges that most languages present gender as "binary and permanent" (para. 3). Has this been your own view? How does Devor challenge this idea — that is, what's the alternative to gender being binary and permanent — and how persuasive do you find his evidence?

2. How, according to Devor, do children "acquire" gender roles? What are the functions of the "generalized other" and the "significant other" in this process?

3. Explain the distinction Devor makes between the "I" and the "me" (paras. 7 and 8). Write a journal entry describing some of the differences between your own "I" and "me."

4. Using examples from Devor and from other reading or observation, list some "activities and modes of expression" (para. 12) that society considers characteristically female and characteristically male. Which are acceptable crossgender behaviors, and which are not? Search for a "rule" that defines what types of crossgender behaviors are tolerated.

5. Do some aspects of the traditional gender roles described by Devor seem to be changing? If so, which ones, and how?

EXPLORING CONNECTIONS

6. Review Bebe Moore Campbell's "Envy" (p. 118); what evidence of gender role socialization do you find in the story? To what extent do Moore's childhood experiences complicate Devor's presentation of gender role acquisition?

7. To what extent do Alexis de Tocqueville's views of women and men (p. 417) reflect the "patriarchal gender schema" as Devor defines it?

8. Drawing on Devor's discussion of gender role formation, analyze the difference between the "I" and the "me" of the girl in Jamaica Kincaid's story (p. 421).

9. How would Devor explain the humor of the cartoon on page 432? How do the details of the cartoon—the setting, the women's appearance, the three pictures on the coffee table—contribute to its effect?

EXTENDING THE CRITICAL CONTEXT

10. As a class, identify at least half a dozen men living today who are widely admired in American culture. To what extent do they embody the "four main attitudes of masculinity" outlined by Devor (para. 19)?

11. Write an essay or journal entry analyzing your own gender role socialization. To what extent have you been pressured to conform to conventional roles? To what extent have you resisted them? What roles have "generalized others" and "significant others" played in shaping your identity?

The Story of My Body

JUDITH ORTIZ COFER

Accepting the idea that gender roles are socially constructed might not be too difficult, but it may come as a shock to realize that even the way we see our bodies is filtered through the lens of social values and beliefs. In this personal essay, Judith Ortiz Cofer reflects on the different roles her own body has assumed in different contexts and cultures—the ways that different societies have "read" the meanings of her physical appearance. The story of her body becomes, to some extent, the story of her life, and woven into the tale are intriguing comments on gender and on cross-cultural perception. A native of Puerto Rico, Ortiz Cofer (b. 1952) is the Franklin Professor of English and Creative Writing at the University of Georgia. Her publications include The Line of the Sun *(1989), a novel;* Silent Dancing *(1990), a collection of poetry and prose;* An Island Like You: Stories of the Barrio *(1996);*

and Woman in Front of the Sun: On Becoming a Writer *(2000).* "The Story of My Body" *appeared in her short story collection,* The Latin Deli *(1993).*

> Migration is the story of my body.
> —VICTOR HERNÁNDEZ CRUZ

Skin

I was born a white girl in Puerto Rico but became a brown girl when I came to live in the United States. My Puerto Rican relatives called me tall; at the American school, some of my rougher classmates called me Skinny Bones, and the Shrimp because I was the smallest member of my classes all through grammar school until high school, when the midget Gladys was given the honorary post of front row center for class pictures and score-keeper, bench warmer, in P.E. I reached my full stature of five feet in sixth grade.

I started out life as a pretty baby and learned to be a pretty girl from a pretty mother. Then at ten years of age I suffered one of the worst cases of chicken pox I have ever heard of. My entire body, including the inside of my ears and in between my toes, was covered with pustules which in a fit of panic at my appearance I scratched off my face, leaving permanent scars. A cruel school nurse told me I would always have them—tiny cuts that looked as if a mad cat had plunged its claws deep into my skin. I grew my hair long and hid behind it for the first years of my adolescence. This was when I learned to be invisible.

Color

In the animal world it indicates danger: the most colorful creatures are often the most poisonous. Color is also a way to attract and seduce a mate. In the human world color triggers many more complex and often deadly re-actions. As a Puerto Rican girl born of "white" parents, I spent the first years of my life hearing people refer to me as *blanca,* white. My mother insisted that I protect myself from the intense island sun because I was more prone to sunburn than some of my darker, *trigueño*[1] playmates. People were always commenting within my hearing about how my black hair contrasted so nicely with my "pale" skin. I did not think of the color of my skin consciously except when I heard the adults talking about complexion. It seems to me that the subject is much more common in the conversation of mixed-race peoples than in mainstream United States society, where it is a touchy and sometimes even embarrassing topic to discuss, except in a political context. In Puerto Rico I heard many conversations about skin color. A

---

[1]*trigueño:* Brown-skinned.

pregnant woman could say, "I hope my baby doesn't turn out *prieto*" (slang for "dark" or "black") "like my husband's grandmother, although she was a good-looking *negra*[2] in her time." I am a combination of both, being olive-skinned—lighter than my mother yet darker than my fair-skinned father. In America, I am a person of color, obviously a Latina. On the Island I have been called everything from a *paloma blanca*,[3] after the song (by a black suitor), to *la gringa*.[4]

My first experience of color prejudice occurred in a supermarket in Paterson, New Jersey. It was Christmastime, and I was eight or nine years old. There was a display of toys in the store where I went two or three times a day to buy things for my mother, who never made lists but sent for milk, cigarettes, a can of this or that, as she remembered from hour to hour. I enjoyed being trusted with money and walking half a city block to the new, modern grocery store. It was owned by three good-looking Italian brothers. I liked the younger one with the crew-cut blond hair. The two older ones watched me and the other Puerto Rican kids as if they thought we were going to steal something. The oldest one would sometimes even try to hurry me with my purchases, although part of my pleasure in these expeditions came from looking at everything in the well-stocked aisles. I was also teaching myself to read English by sounding out the labels on packages: L&M cigarettes, Borden's homogenized milk, Red Devil potted ham, Nestle's chocolate mix, Quaker oats, Bustelo coffee, Wonder bread, Colgate toothpaste, Ivory soap, and Goya (makers of products used in Puerto Rican dishes) everything—these are some of the brand names that taught me nouns. Several times this man had come up to me, wearing his blood-stained butcher's apron, and towering over me had asked in a harsh voice whether there was something he could help me find. On the way out I would glance at the younger brother who ran one of the registers and he would often smile and wink at me.

It was the mean brother who first referred to me as "colored." It was a few days before Christmas, and my parents had already told my brother and me that since we were in Los Estados[5] now, we would get our presents on December 25 instead of Los Reyes, Three Kings Day, when gifts are exchanged in Puerto Rico. We were to give them a wish list that they would take to Santa Claus, who apparently lived in the Macy's store downtown— at least that's where we had caught a glimpse of him when we went shopping. Since my parents were timid about entering the fancy store, we did not approach the huge man in the red suit. I was not interested in sitting on a stranger's lap anyway. But I did covet Susie, the talking schoolteacher doll that was displayed in the center aisle of the Italian brothers' supermarket.

5

[2]*negra:* Black.
[3]*paloma blanca:* White dove.
[4]*la gringa:* A white, non-Latina woman.
[5]*Los Estados:* "The States"—that is, the United States.

She talked when you pulled a string on her back. Susie had a limited reper-
toire of three sentences: I think she could say: "Hello, I'm Susie Schoolteacher," "Two plus two is four," and one other thing I cannot remember.
The day the older brother chased me away, I was reaching to touch Susie's
blond curls. I had been told many times, as most children have, not to touch
anything in the store that I was not buying. But I had been looking at Susie
for weeks. In my mind, she was my doll. After all, I had put her on my
Christmas wish list. The moment is frozen in my mind as if there were a
photograph of it on file. It was not a turning point, a disaster, or an earth-
shaking revelation. It was simply the first time I considered—if naively—
the meaning of skin color in human relations.

I reached to touch Susie's hair. It seems to me that I had to get on tip-
toe, since the toys were stacked on a table and she sat like a princess on top
of the fancy box she came in. Then I heard the booming "Hey, kid, what do
you think you're doing!" spoken very loudly from the meat counter. I felt
caught, although I knew I was not doing anything criminal. I remember not
looking at the man, but standing there, feeling humiliated because I knew
everyone in the store must have heard him yell at me. I felt him approach,
and when I knew he was behind me, I turned around to face the bloody
butcher's apron. His large chest was at my eye level. He blocked my way. I
started to run out of the place, but even as I reached the door I heard him
shout after me: "Don't come in here unless you gonna buy something. You
PR kids put your dirty hands on stuff. You always look dirty. But maybe
dirty brown is your natural color." I heard him laugh and someone else too
in the back. Outside in the sunlight I looked at my hands. My nails needed a
little cleaning as they always did, since I liked to paint with watercolors, but
I took a bath every night. I thought the man was dirtier than I was in his
stained apron. He was also always sweaty—it showed in big yellow circles
under his shirt-sleeves. I sat on the front steps of the apartment building
where we lived and looked closely at my hands, which showed the only skin
I could see, since it was bitter cold and I was wearing my quilted play coat,
dungarees, and a knitted navy cap of my father's. I was not pink like my
friend Charlene and her sister Kathy, who had blue eyes and light brown
hair. My skin is the color of the coffee my grandmother made, which was
half milk, *leche con café* rather than *café con leche*.[6] My mother is the opposite mix. She has a lot of café in her color. I could not understand how my
skin looked like dirt to the supermarket man.

I went in and washed my hands thoroughly with soap and hot water,
and borrowing my mother's nail file, I cleaned the crusted watercolors from
underneath my nails. I was pleased with the results. My skin was the same
color as before, but I knew I was clean. Clean enough to run my fingers
through Susie's fine gold hair when she came home to me.

---

[6]*leche con café…café con leche:* Milk with coffee (light brown) … coffee with milk (dark
brown).

Size

My mother is barely four feet eleven inches in height, which is average for women in her family. When I grew to five feet by age twelve, she was amazed and began to use the word tall to describe me, as in "Since you are tall, this dress will look good on you." As with the color of my skin, I didn't consciously think about my height or size until other people made an issue of it. It is around the preadolescent years that in America the games children play for fun become fierce competitions where everyone is out to "prove" they are better than others. It was in the playground and sports fields that my size-related problems began. No matter how familiar the story is, every child who is the last chosen for a team knows the torment of waiting to be called up. At the Paterson, New Jersey, public schools that I attended, the volleyball or softball game was the metaphor for the battlefield of life to the inner city kids—the black kids versus the Puerto Rican kids, the whites versus the blacks versus the Puerto Rican kids; and I was 4F,[7] skinny, short, bespectacled, and apparently impervious to the blood thirst that drove many of my classmates to play ball as if their lives depended on it. Perhaps they did. I would rather be reading a book than sweating, grunting, and running the risk of pain and injury. I simply did not see the point in competitive sports. My main form of exercise then was walking to the library, many city blocks away from my barrio.

Still, I wanted to be wanted. I wanted to be chosen for the team. Physical education was compulsory, a class where you were actually given a grade. On my mainly all A report card, the C for compassion I always received from the P.E. teachers shamed me the same as a bad grade in a real class. Invariably, my father would say: "How can you make a low grade for *playing games?*" He did not understand. Even if I had managed to make a hit (it never happened) or get the ball over that ridiculously high net, I already had a reputation as a "shrimp," a hopeless nonathlete. It was an area where the girls who didn't like me for one reason or another—mainly because I did better than they on academic subjects—could lord it over me; the playing field was the place where even the smallest girl could make me feel powerless and inferior. I instinctively understood the politics even then; how the *not* choosing me until the teacher forced one of the team captains to call my name was a coup of sorts—there, you little show-off, tomorrow you can beat us in spelling and geography, but this afternoon you are the loser. Or perhaps those were only my own bitter thoughts as I sat or stood in the sidelines while the big girls were grabbed like fish and I, the little brown tadpole, was ignored until Teacher looked over in my general direction and shouted, "Call Ortiz," or, worse, "Somebody's *got* to take her."

---

[7]*4F:* Draft-board classification meaning "unfit for military service;" hence, not physically fit.

No wonder I read Wonder Woman comics and had Legion of Super Heroes daydreams. Although I wanted to think of myself as "intellectual," my body was demanding that I notice it. I saw the little swelling around my once-flat nipples, the fine hairs growing in secret places; but my knees were still bigger than my thighs, and I always wore long- or half-sleeve blouses to hide my bony upper arms. I wanted flesh on my bones — a thick layer of it. I saw a new product advertised on TV, Wate-On. They showed skinny men and women before and after taking the stuff, and it was a transformation like the ninety-seven-pound-weakling-turned-into-Charles-Atlas ads that I saw on the back covers of my comic books. The Wate-On was very expensive. I tried to explain my need for it in Spanish to my mother, but it didn't translate very well, even to my ears — and she said with a tone of finality, eat more of my good food and you'll get fat — anybody can get fat. Right. Except me. I was going to have to join a circus someday as Skinny Bones, the woman without flesh.

Wonder Woman was stacked. She had a cleavage framed by the spread wings of a golden eagle and a muscular body that has become fashionable with women only recently. But since I wanted a body that would serve me in P.E., hers was my ideal. The breasts were an indulgence I allowed myself. Perhaps the daydreams of bigger girls were more glamorous, since our ambitions are filtered through our needs, but I wanted first a powerful body. I daydreamed of leaping up above the gray landscape of the city to where the sky was clear and blue, and in anger and self-pity, I fantasized about scooping my enemies up by their hair from the playing fields and dumping them on a barren asteroid. I would put the P.E. teachers each on their own rock in space too, where they would be the loneliest people in the universe, since I knew they had no "inner resources," no imagination, and in outer space, there would be no air for them to fill their deflated volleyballs with. In my mind all P.E. teachers have blended into one large spiky-haired woman with a whistle on a string around her neck and a volleyball under one arm. My Wonder Woman fantasies of revenge were a source of comfort to me in my early career as a shrimp.

I was saved from more years of P.E. torment by the fact that in my sophomore year of high school I transferred to a school where the midget, Gladys, was the focal point of interest for the people who must rank according to size. Because her height was considered a handicap, there was an unspoken rule about mentioning size around Gladys, but of course, there was no need to say anything. Gladys knew her place: front row center in class photographs. I gladly moved to the left or to the right of her, as far as I could without leaving the picture completely.

Looks

Many photographs were taken of me as a baby by my mother to send to my father, who was stationed overseas during the first two years of my life. With the army in Panama when I was born, he later traveled often on tours of duty with the navy. I was a healthy, pretty baby. Recently, I read that people are drawn to big-eyed round-faced creatures, like puppies, kittens, and certain other mammals and marsupials, koalas, for example, and, of course, infants. I was all eyes, since my head and body, even as I grew older, remained thin and small-boned. As a young child I got a lot of attention from my relatives and many other people we met in our barrio. My mother's beauty may have had something to do with how much attention we got from strangers in stores and on the street. I can imagine it. In the pictures I have seen of us together, she is a stunning young woman by Latino standards: long, curly black hair, and round curves in a compact frame. From her I learned how to move, smile, and talk like an attractive woman. I remember going into a bodega[8] for our groceries and being given candy by the proprietor as a reward for being *bonita,* pretty.

I can see in the photographs, and I also remember, that I was dressed in the pretty clothes, the stiff, frilly dresses, with layers of crinolines underneath, the glossy patent leather shoes, and, on special occasions, the skull-hugging little hats and the white gloves that were popular in the late fifties and early sixties. My mother was proud of my looks, although I was a bit too thin. She could dress me up like a doll and take me by the hand to visit relatives, or go to the Spanish mass at the Catholic church and show me off. How was I to know that she and the others who called me "pretty" were representatives of an aesthetic that would not apply when I went out into the mainstream world of school?

In my Paterson, New Jersey, public schools there were still quite a few   15
white children, although the demographics of the city were changing rapidly. The original waves of Italian and Irish immigrants, silk-mill workers, and laborers in the cloth industries had been "assimilated." Their children were now the middle-class parents of my peers. Many of them moved their children to the Catholic schools that proliferated enough to have leagues of basketball teams. The names I recall hearing still ring in my ears: Don Bosco High versus St. Mary's High, St. Joseph's versus St. John's. Later I too would be transferred to the safer environment of a Catholic school. But I started school at Public School Number 11. I came there from Puerto Rico, thinking myself a pretty girl, and found that the hierarchy for popularity was as follows: pretty white girl, pretty Jewish girl, pretty Puerto Rican girl, pretty black girl. Drop the last two categories; teachers were too busy to have more than one favorite per class, and it was simply understood that if there was a big part in the school play, or any competition where the main qualification was "presentability" (such as escorting a school visitor to or from the principal's office), the classroom's public address speaker would be requesting the pretty and/or nice-looking white boy or girl. By the time I was in the sixth grade, I was sometimes called by the principal to represent my class because I dressed neatly (I knew this from a progress report sent to

[8]*bodega:* Market.

my mother, which I translated for her) and because all the "presentable" white girls had moved to the Catholic schools (I later surmised this part). But I was still not one of the popular girls with the boys. I remember one incident where I stepped out into the playground in my baggy gym shorts and one Puerto Rican boy said to the other: "What do you think?" The other one answered: "Her face is OK, but look at the toothpick legs." The next best thing to a compliment I got was when my favorite male teacher, while handing out the class pictures, commented that with my long neck and delicate features I resembled the movie star Audrey Hepburn. But the Puerto Rican boys had learned to respond to a fuller figure: long necks and a perfect little nose were not what they looked for in a girl. That is when I decided I was a "brain." I did not settle into the role easily. I was nearly devastated by what the chicken pox episode had done to my self-image. But I looked into the mirror less often after I was told that I would always have scars on my face, and I hid behind my long black hair and my books.

After the problems at the public school got to the point where even nonconfrontational little me got beaten up several times, my parents enrolled me at St. Joseph's High School. I was then a minority of one among the Italian and Irish kids. But I found several good friends there—other girls who took their studies seriously. We did our homework together and talked about the Jackies. The Jackies were two popular girls, one blonde and the other red-haired, who had women's bodies. Their curves showed even in the blue jumper uniforms with straps that we all wore. The blonde Jackie would often let one of the straps fall off her shoulder, and although she, like all of us, wore a white blouse underneath, all the boys stared at her arm. My friends and I talked about this and practiced letting our straps fall off our shoulders. But it wasn't the same without breasts or hips.

My final two and a half years of high school were spent in Augusta, Georgia, where my parents moved our family in search of a more peaceful environment. There we became part of a little community of our army-connected relatives and friends. School was yet another matter. I was enrolled in a huge school of nearly two thousand students that had just that year been forced to integrate. There were two black girls and there was me. I did extremely well academically. As to my social life, it was, for the most part, uneventful—yet it is in my memory blighted by one incident. In my junior year, I became wildly infatuated with a pretty white boy. I'll call him Ted. Oh, he was pretty: yellow hair that fell over his forehead, a smile to die for—and he was a great dancer. I watched him at Teen Town, the youth center at the base where all the military brats gathered on Saturday nights. My father had retired from the navy, and we had all our base privileges—one other reason we moved to Augusta. Ted looked like an angel to me. I worked on him for a year before he asked me out. This meant maneuvering to be within the periphery of his vision at every possible occasion. I took the long way to my classes in school just to pass by his locker, I went to football games, which I detested, and I danced (I too was a good dancer) in front of him at Teen Town—this took some fancy footwork, since it involved subtly moving my partner toward the right spot on the dance floor. When Ted finally approached me, "A Million to One" was playing on the jukebox, and when he took me into his arms, the odds suddenly turned in my favor. He asked me to go to a school dance the following Saturday. I said yes, breathlessly. I said yes, but there were obstacles to surmount at home. My father did not allow me to date casually. I was allowed to go to major events like a prom or a concert with a boy who had been properly screened. There was such a boy in my life, a neighbor who wanted to be a Baptist missionary and was practicing his anthropological skills on my family. If I was desperate to go somewhere and needed a date, I'd resort to Gary. This is the type of religious nut that Gary was: when the school bus did not show up one day, he put his hands over his face and prayed to Christ to get us a way to get to school. Within ten minutes a mother in a station wagon, on her way to town, stopped to ask why we weren't in school. Gary informed her that the Lord had sent her just in time to find us a way to get there in time for roll call. He assumed that I was impressed. Gary was even good-looking in a bland sort of way, but he kissed me with his lips tightly pressed together. I think Gary probably ended up marrying a native woman from wherever he may have gone to preach the Gospel according to Paul. She probably believes that all white men pray to God for transportation and kiss with their mouths closed. But it was Ted's mouth, his whole beautiful self, that concerned me in those days. I knew my father would say no to our date, but I planned to run away from home if necessary. I told my mother how important this date was. I cajoled and pleaded with her from Sunday to Wednesday. She listened to my arguments and must have heard the note of desperation in my voice. She said very gently to me: "You better be ready for disappointment." I did not ask what she meant. I did not want her fears for me to taint my happiness. I asked her to tell my father about my date. Thursday at breakfast my father looked at me across the table with his eyebrows together. My mother looked at him with her mouth set in a straight line. I looked down at my bowl of cereal. Nobody said anything. Friday I tried on every dress in my closet. Ted would be picking me up at six on Saturday: dinner and then the sock hop at school. Friday night I was in my room doing my nails or something else in preparation for Saturday (I know I groomed myself nonstop all week) when the telephone rang. I ran to get it. It was Ted. His voice sounded funny when he said my name, so funny that I felt compelled to ask: "Is something wrong?" Ted blurted it all out without a preamble. His father had asked who he was going out with. Ted had told him my name. "Ortiz? That's Spanish, isn't it?" the father had asked. Ted had told him yes, then shown him my picture in the yearbook. Ted's father had shaken his head. No. Ted would not be taking me out. Ted's father had known Puerto Ricans in the army. He had lived in New York City while studying architecture and had seen how the spics lived. Like rats. Ted repeated his father's words to me as if I should understand *his* predicament when I heard why he was breaking our date. I don't remember what I said before hanging up. I do recall the darkness of my room that sleepless night and the heaviness of my blanket in which I wrapped myself like a shroud. And I remember my parents' respect for my pain and their gentleness toward me that weekend. My mother did not say "I warned you," and I was grateful for her understanding silence.

In college, I suddenly became an "exotic" woman to the men who had survived the popularity wars in high school, who were not practicing to be worldly: they had to act liberal in their politics, in their lifestyles, and in the women they went out with. I dated heavily for a while, then married young. I had discovered that I needed stability more than social life. I had brains for sure and some talent in writing. These facts were a constant in my life. My skin color, my size, and my appearance were variables—things that were judged according to my current self-image, the aesthetic values of the time, the places I was in, and the people I met. My studies, later my writing, the respect of people who saw me as an individual person they cared about, these were the criteria for my sense of self-worth that I would concentrate on in my adult life.

ENGAGING THE TEXT

1. Ortiz Cofer writes a good deal about how people perceived her and about how their perceptions changed according to time and place. Trace the stages Ortiz Cofer lived through, citing examples from the text, and discuss in each instance how her self-image was affected by people around her. What main point(s) do you think Ortiz Cofer may be trying to make with the narrative?

2. Which of the difficulties Ortiz Cofer faces are related specifically to gender (or made more serious by gender)? Do boys face comparable problems?

3. In your opinion, did Ortiz Cofer make the right decisions throughout her story? Is there anything she or her parents could have done to avoid or resist the various mistreatments she describes?

4. What role do media images play in Ortiz Cofer's story?

5. Does everyone have a story similar to Ortiz Cofer's, or not? Other people may be overweight, wear braces, mature very early or very late, have big noses or unusual voices, and so on. What, if anything, sets Ortiz Cofer's experience apart from the usual "traumas" of childhood?

EXPLORING CONNECTIONS

6. Review Aaron H. Devor's "Becoming Members of Society" (p. 424). How do Ortiz Cofer's experiences support and/or complicate Devor's explanation of gender role socialization?

7. Compare the childhood experiences of Ortiz Cofer and Gary Soto (p. 26). To what extent do their relationships, concerns, and behavior appear to be influenced by gender? What other social forces shape their lives?

8. Like Ortiz Cofer, Eric Liu (p. 660) must find ways to define his identity within multiple cultures. What problems do they face, what strengths or advantages do they find within each culture, and what strategies do they adopt to negotiate the tensions that arise among conflicting cultural values?

EXTENDING THE CRITICAL CONTEXT

9. In her self-analysis, Ortiz Cofer discusses the "variables" in her physical appearance—the socially determined values that influence her perception of her body. She also reflects on personal "facts" or "constants"—more durable features, like her writing and her need for stability—that contribute to her identity. Write a series of journal entries that tell the story of your own body. What "variables" have influenced your perception of your appearance? What "facts" about yourself have become "constants"?

Where I Come From Is Like This

PAULA GUNN ALLEN

Paula Gunn Allen was born in 1939 in Cubero, New Mexico, a Spanish-Mexican land grant village; where she comes from is life as a Laguna Pueblo–Sioux–Lebanese woman. In this essay she discusses some of the ways traditional images of women in American Indian cultures differ from images in mainstream American culture. Allen is widely recognized for her books of poetry and for her novel The Woman Who Owned the Shadows *(1983). Other works, including* Grandmothers of the Light *(1991) and* Women in American Indian Mythology *(1994), have focused on the female spiritual traditions of Native America. Her most recent work is a biography entitled* Pocahontas: Medicine Woman, Spy, Entrepreneur, Diplomat *(2003). This essay appeared in her essay collection,* The Sacred Hoop: Recovering the Feminine in American Indian Traditions *(1986).*

I

Modern American Indian women, like their non-Indian sisters, are deeply engaged in the struggle to redefine themselves. In their struggle they must reconcile traditional tribal definitions of women with industrial and postindustrial non-Indian definitions. Yet while these definitions seem to be more or less mutually exclusive, Indian women must somehow harmonize and integrate both in their own lives.

An American Indian woman is primarily defined by her tribal identity. In her eyes, her destiny is necessarily that of her people, and her sense of herself as a woman is first and foremost prescribed by her tribe. The definitions of woman's roles are as diverse as tribal cultures in the Americas. In some she is devalued, in others she wields considerable power. In some she is a familial/clan adjunct, in some she is as close to autonomous as her economic circumstances and psychological traits permit. But in no tribal definitions is she perceived in the same way as are women in western industrial and postindustrial cultures.

In the west, few images of women form part of the cultural mythos, and these are largely sexually charged. Among Christians, the madonna is the female prototype, and she is portrayed as essentially passive: her contribution is simply that of birthing. Little else is attributed to her and she certainly possesses few of the characteristics that are attributed to mythic figures among Indian tribes. This image is countered (rather than balanced) by the witch-goddess/whore characteristics designed to reinforce cultural beliefs about women, as well as western adversarial and dualistic perceptions of reality.

The tribes see women variously, but they do not question the power of femininity. Sometimes they see women as fearful, sometimes peaceful, sometimes omnipotent and omniscient, but they never portray women as mindless, helpless, simple, or oppressed. And while the women in a given tribe, clan, or band may be all these things, the individual woman is provided with a variety of images of women from the interconnected supernatural, natural, and social worlds she lives in.

As a half-breed American Indian woman, I cast about in my mind for   5
negative images of Indian women, and I find none that are directed to Indian women alone. The negative images I do have are of Indians in general and in fact are more often of males than of females. All these images come to me from non-Indian sources, and they are always balanced by a positive image. My ideas of womanhood, passed on largely by my mother and grandmothers, Laguna Pueblo women, are about practicality, strength, reasonableness, intelligence, wit, and competence. I also remember vividly the women who came to my father's store, the women who held me and sang to me, the women at Feast Day, at Grab Days,[1] the women in the kitchen of my Cubero home, the women I grew up with; none of them appeared weak or helpless, none of them presented herself tentatively. I remember a certain reserve on those lovely brown faces; I remember the direct gaze of eyes framed by bright-colored shawls draped over their heads and cascading down their backs. I remember the clean cotton dresses and carefully

---

[1]*Grab Days:* Laguna ritual in which women throw food and small items (like pieces of cloth) to those attending.

pressed hand-embroidered aprons they always wore; I remember laughter and good food, especially the sweet bread and the oven bread they gave us. Nowhere in my mind is there a foolish woman, a dumb woman, a vain woman, or a plastic woman, though the Indian women I have known have shown a wide range of personal style and demeanor.

My memory includes the Navajo woman who was badly beaten by her Sioux husband; but I also remember that my grandmother abandoned her Sioux husband long ago. I recall the stories about the Laguna woman beaten regularly by her husband in the presence of her children so that the children would not believe in the strength and power of femininity. And I remember the women who drank, who got into fights with other women and with the men, and who often won those battles. I have memories of tired women, partying women, stubborn women, sullen women, amicable women, selfish women, shy women, and aggressive women. Most of all I remember the women who laugh and scold and sit uncomplaining in the long sun on feast days and who cook wonderful food on wood stoves, in beehive mud ovens, and over open fires outdoors.

Among the images of women that come to me from various tribes as well as my own are White Buffalo Woman, who came to the Lakota long ago and brought them the religion of the Sacred Pipe which they still practice; Tinotzin the goddess who came to Juan Diego to remind him that she still walked the hills of her people and sent him with her message, her demand, and her proof to the Catholic bishop in the city nearby. And from Laguna I take the images of Yellow Woman, Coyote Woman, Grandmother Spider (Spider Old Woman), who brought the light, who gave us weaving and medicine, who gave us life. Among the Keres she is known as Thought Woman who created us all and who keeps us in creation even now. I remember Iyatiku, Earth Woman, Corn Woman, who guides and counsels the people to peace and who welcomes us home when we cast off this coil of flesh as huskers cast off the leaves that wrap the corn. I remember Iyatiku's sister, Sun Woman, who held metals and cattle, pigs and sheep, highways and engines and so many things in her bundle, who went away to the east saying that one day she would return.

II

Since the coming of the Anglo-Europeans beginning in the fifteenth century, the fragile web of identity that long held tribal people secure has gradually been weakened and torn. But the oral tradition has prevented the complete destruction of the web, the ultimate disruption of tribal ways. The oral tradition is vital; it heals itself and the tribal web by adapting to the flow of the present while never relinquishing its connection to the past. Its adaptability has always been required, as many generations have experienced. Certainly the modern American Indian woman bears slight resemblance to her forebears—at least on superficial examination—but she is still a tribal woman in her deepest being. Her tribal sense of relationship to all that is continues to flourish. And though she is at times beset by her knowledge of the enormous gap between the life she lives and the life she was raised to live, and while she adapts her mind and being to the circumstances of her present life, she does so in tribal ways, mending the tears in the web of being from which she takes her existence as she goes.

My mother told me stories all the time, though I often did not recognize them as that. My mother told me stories about cooking and childbearing; she told me stories about menstruation and pregnancy; she told me stories about gods and heroes, about fairies and elves, about goddesses and spirits; she told me stories about the land and the sky, about cats and dogs, about snakes and spiders; she told me stories about climbing trees and exploring the mesas; she told me stories about going to dances and getting married; she told me stories about dressing and undressing, about sleeping and waking; she told me stories about herself, about her mother, about her grandmother. She told me stories about grieving and laughing, about thinking and doing; she told me stories about school and about people; about darning and mending; she told me stories about turquoise and about gold; she told me European stories and Laguna stories; she told me Catholic stories and Presbyterian stories; she told me city stories and country stories; she told me political stories and religious stories. She told me stories about living and stories about dying. And in all of those stories she told me who I was, who I was supposed to be, whom I came from, and who would follow me. In this way she taught me the meaning of the words she said, that all life is a circle and everything has a place within it. That's what she said and what she showed me in the things she did and the way she lives.

Of course, through my formal, white, Christian education, I discovered 10 that other people had stories of their own—about women, about Indians, about fact, about reality—and I was amazed by a number of startling suppositions that others made about tribal customs and beliefs. According to the un-Indian, non-Indian view, for instance, Indians barred menstruating women from ceremonies and indeed segregated them from the rest of the people, consigning them to some space specially designed for them. This showed that Indians considered menstruating women unclean and not fit to enjoy the company of decent (nonmenstruating) people, that is, men. I was surprised and confused to hear this because my mother had taught me that white people had strange attitudes toward menstruation: they thought something was bad about it, that it meant you were sick, cursed, sinful, and weak and that you had to be very careful during that time. She taught me that menstruation was a normal occurrence, that I could go swimming or hiking or whatever else I wanted to do during my period. She actively scorned women who took to their beds, who were incapacitated by cramps, who "got the blues."

As I struggled to reconcile these very contradictory interpretations of American Indians' traditional beliefs concerning menstruation, I realized that the menstrual taboos were about power, not about sin or filth. My conclusion was later borne out by some tribes' own explanations, which, as you may well imagine, came as quite a relief to me.

The truth of the matter as many Indians see it is that women who are at the peak of their fecundity are believed to possess power that throws male power totally out of kilter. They emit such force that, in their presence, any male-owned or -dominated ritual or sacred object cannot do its usual task. For instance, the Lakota say that a menstruating woman anywhere near a yuwipi man, who is a special sort of psychic, spirit-empowered healer, for a day or so before he is to do his ceremony will effectively disempower him. Conversely, among many if not most tribes, important ceremonies cannot be held without the presence of women. Sometimes the ritual woman who empowers the ceremony must be unmarried and virginal so that the power she channels is unalloyed, unweakened by sexual arousal and penetration by a male. Other ceremonies require tumescent women, others the presence of mature women who have borne children, and still others depend for empowerment on postmenopausal women. Women may be segregated from the company of the whole band or village on certain occasions, but on certain occasions men are also segregated. In short, each ritual depends on a certain balance of power, and the positions of women within the phases of womanhood are used by tribal people to empower certain rites. This does not derive from a male-dominant view; it is not a ritual observance imposed on women by men. It derives from a tribal view of reality that distinguishes tribal people from feudal and industrial people.

Among the tribes, the occult power of women, inextricably bound to our hormonal life, is thought to be very great; many hold that we possess innately the blood-given power to kill—with a glance, with a step, or with a judicious mixing of menstrual blood into somebody's soup. Medicine women among the Pomo of California cannot practice until they are sufficiently mature; when they are immature, their power is diffuse and is likely to interfere with their practice until time and experience have it under control. So women of the tribes are not especially inclined to see themselves as poor helpless victims of male domination. Even in those tribes where something akin to male domination was present, women are perceived as powerful, socially, physically, and metaphysically. In times past, as in times present, women carried enormous burdens with aplomb. We were far indeed from the "weaker sex," the designation that white aristocratic sisters unhappily earned for us all.

I remember my mother moving furniture all over the house when she wanted it changed. She didn't wait for my father to come home and help— she just went ahead and moved the piano, a huge upright from the old days, the couch, the refrigerator. Nobody had told her she was too weak to do such things. In imitation of her, I would delight in loading trucks at my father's store with cases of pop or fifty-pound sacks of flour. Even when I was quite small I could do it, and it gave me a belief in my own physical strength that advancing middle age can't quite erase. My mother used to tell me about the Acoma Pueblo women she had seen as a child carrying huge ollas (water pots) on their heads as they wound their way up the tortuous stairwell carved into the face of the "Sky City" mesa, a feat I tried to imitate with books and tin buckets. ("Sky City" is the term used by the Chamber of Commerce for the mother village of Acoma, which is situated atop a high sandstone table mountain.) I was never very successful, but even the attempt reminded me that I was supposed to be strong and balanced to be a proper girl.

Of course, my mother's Laguna people are Keres Indian, reputed to be   15
the last extreme mother-right people on earth. So it is no wonder that I got notably nonwhite notions about the natural strength and prowess of women. Indeed, it is only when I am trying to get non-Indian approval, recognition, or acknowledgement that my "weak sister" emotional and intellectual ploys get the better of my tribal woman's good sense. At such times I forget that I just moved the piano or just wrote a competent paper or just completed a financial transaction satisfactorily or have supported myself and my children for most of my adult life.

Nor is my contradictory behavior atypical. Most Indian women I know are in the same bicultural bind: we vacillate between being dependent and strong, self-reliant and powerless, strongly motivated and hopelessly insecure. We resolve the dilemma in various ways: some of us party all the time; some of us drink to excess; some of us travel and move around a lot; some of us land good jobs and then quit them; some of us engage in violent exchanges; some of us blow our brains out. We act in these destructive ways because we suffer from the societal conflicts caused by having to identify with two hopelessly opposed cultural definitions of women. Through this destructive dissonance we are unhappy prey to the self-disparagement common to, indeed demanded of, Indians living in the United States today. Our situation is caused by the exigencies of a history of invasion, conquest, and colonization whose searing marks are probably ineradicable. A popular bumper sticker on many Indian cars proclaims: "If You're Indian You're In," to which I always find myself adding under my breath, "Trouble."

III

No Indian can grow to any age without being informed that her people were "savages" who interfered with the march of progress pursued by respectable, loving, civilized white people. We are the villains of the scenario when we are mentioned at all. We are absent from much of white history except when we are calmly, rationally, succinctly, and systematically dehumanized. On the few occasions we are noticed in any way other than as howling, bloodthirsty beings, we are acclaimed for our noble quaintness. In this definition, we are exotic curios. Our ancient arts and customs are used to draw tourist money to state coffers, into the pocketbooks and bank accounts of scholars, and into support of the American-in-Disneyland promoters' dream.

As a Roman Catholic child I was treated to bloody tales of how the savage Indians martyred the hapless priests and missionaries who went among them in an attempt to lead them to the one true path. By the time I was through high school I had the idea that Indians were people who had benefitted mightily from the advanced knowledge and superior morality of the Anglo-Europeans. At least I had, perforce, that idea to lay beside the other one that derived from my daily experience of Indian life, an idea less dehumanizing and more accurate because it came from my mother and the other Indian people who raised me. That idea was that Indians are a people who don't tell lies, who care for their children and their old people. You never see an Indian orphan, they said. You always know when you're old that someone will take care of you—one of your children will. Then they'd list the old folks who were being taken care of by this child or that. No child is ever considered illegitimate among the Indians, they said. If a girl gets pregnant, the baby is still part of the family, and the mother is too. That's what they said, and they showed me real people who lived according to those principles.

Of course the ravages of colonization have taken their toll; there are orphans in Indian country now, and abandoned, brutalized old folks; there are even illegitimate children, though the very concept still strikes me as absurd. There are battered children and neglected children, and there are battered wives and women who have been raped by Indian men. Proximity to the "civilizing" effects of white Christians has not improved the moral quality of life in Indian country, though each group, Indian and white, explains the situation differently. Nor is there much yet in the oral tradition that can enable us to adapt to these inhuman changes. But a force is growing in that direction, and it is helping Indian women reclaim their lives. Their power, their sense of direction and of self will soon be visible. It is the force of the women who speak and work and write, and it is formidable.

Through all the centuries of war and death and cultural and psychic destruction have endured the women who raise the children and tend the fires, who pass along the tales and the traditions, who weep and bury the dead, who are the dead, and who never forget. There are always the women, who make pots and weave baskets, who fashion clothes and cheer their children on at powwow, who make fry bread and piki bread, and corn soup and chili stew, who dance and sing and remember and hold within their hearts the dream of their ancient peoples—that one day the woman who thinks will speak to us again, and everywhere there will be peace. Meanwhile we tell the stories and write the books and trade tales of anger and woe and stories of fun and scandal and laugh over all manner of things that happen every day. We watch and we wait. 20

My great-grandmother told my mother: never forget you are Indian. And my mother told me the same thing. This, then, is how I have gone about remembering, so that my children will remember too.

ENGAGING THE TEXT

1. Outline how Allen's views of women differ from traditional Anglo-American views. Do you see any difference between Allen's perspective and "feminism" as you understand the term?

2. What does Allen mean by "bicultural bind" (para. 16)? How has it affected her, and how does she deal with it?

3. How does Allen represent relationships between American Indian women and men?

4. Why is remembering so important to Allen? What roles does it play in helping her live in a world dominated by an alien culture? How does it help her define herself as a woman?

5. Allen's essay includes much personal recollection. Try to "translate" some of this information into more abstract statements of theme or message. (For instance, you might write, "Women's roles in American Indian cultures are maintained through example, through oral tradition, and through ceremonial tribal practices.") What is gained, what lost in such "translations"?

6. Review how Allen uses the image of the web to explain tribal identity. In what ways is this an appropriate and effective metaphor?

EXPLORING CONNECTIONS

7. Review Aaron H. Devor's discussion of gender role socialization (p. 424), and compare the influence of "generalized others" and "significant others" in the experiences of Allen and Judith Ortiz Cofer (p. 433). What tension does each woman feel between her "I" and her "me"? How does she resolve it?

8. Read or reread Roger Jack's "An Indian Story" (p. 109). What similarities do you find in Jack's and Allen's ideas about family and tribal identity?

9. According to Allen and to Judy Root Aulette (p. 64), in what ways do many American Indian and African American women resist Anglo-European roles?

EXTENDING THE CRITICAL CONTEXT

10. Are you struggling to reconcile different definitions of what you should be? (For example, are family, friends, and school pushing you in different directions?) Write an essay or journal entry exploring this issue.

Visual Portfolio
READING IMAGES OF GENDER

1. Who is the intended audience for the Jim Beam ad? What implied difficulty does the text of the ad seek to address? How would you characterize the three young men in the photograph? How does the photo support or contradict the text of the ad? In what ways does the ad as a whole reflect or fail to reflect your own experience?

2. What does the photo of the victorious boxer suggest about her feelings at that moment? About her opponent's response to his loss? What other messages— about sports or gender or competition, for example—does the picture convey to you? Point to particular visual details that support your interpretations.

3. How would you describe the mood or feeling the photographer has captured in the picture of the father and child? How do the light, the setting, the stance, and the expression of each figure contribute to this impression?

4. Do you think that "Masculinity" would be an appropriate title for the picture of the man and child? Why or why not? Eli Reed, the photographer, titles the photo simply, "Mississippi, 1991"; why do you think he chose to identify it by place and time rather than by theme?

5. Taking the perspective of the mother or the daughter in the beauty pageant photo, freewrite about what is happening (or has just happened) and what you're thinking at that moment. Compare your response to those of classmates.

"Two Ways a Woman Can Get Hurt": Advertising and Violence
JEAN KILBOURNE

Most of us like to think of ourselves as immune to the power of ads — we know that advertisers use sex to get our attention and that they make exaggerated claims about a product's ability to make us attractive, popular, and successful. Because we can see through these subtle or not-so-subtle messages, we assume that we're too smart to be swayed by them. But Jean Kilbourne argues that ads affect us in far more profound and potentially damaging ways. The way that ads portray bodies — especially women's bodies — as objects conditions us to seeing each other in dehumanizing ways, thus "normalizing" attitudes that can lead to sexual aggression. Kilbourne (b. 1946) has spent most of her professional life teaching and lecturing about the world of advertising. She has produced award-winning documentaries on images of women in ads (Killing Us Softly, Slim Hopes) *and tobacco advertising* (Pack of Lies). *She has also been a member of the National Advisory Council on Alcohol Abuse and Alcoholism and has twice served as an adviser to the surgeon general of the United States. Currently she teaches at Wellesley College. This selection is taken from her 1999 book,* Can't Buy My Love: How Advertising Changes the Way We Think and Feel *(formerly titled* Deadly Persuasion*).*

Sex in advertising is more about disconnection and distance than connection and closeness. It is also more often about power than passion, about violence than violins. The main goal, as in pornography, is usually power over another, either by the physical dominance or preferred status of men or what is seen as the exploitative power of female beauty and female sexuality. Men conquer and women ensnare, always with the essential aid of a product. The woman is rewarded for her sexuality by the man's wealth, as in an ad for Cigarette boats in which the woman says, while lying in a man's embrace clearly after sex, "Does this mean I get a ride in your Cigarette?"

Two Ways A Woman Can Get Hurt.

(Heartbreaker)

(Soap and water shave)

Skintimate® Shave Gel Ultra Protection formula contains 75% moisturizers, including vitamin E, to protect your legs from nicks, cuts and razor burn. So while guys may continue to be a pain, shaving most definitely won't.

SKINTIMATE® SHAVE GEL
LOVE YOUR LEGS

© 1997 S.C. Johnson & Son, Inc. All rights reserved. www.skintimate.com

Sex in advertising is pornographic because it dehumanizes and objectifies people, especially women, and because it fetishizes products, imbues them with an erotic charge—which dooms us to disappointment since products never can fulfill our sexual desires or meet our emotional needs. The poses and postures of advertising are often borrowed from pornography, as are many of the themes, such as bondage, sadomasochism, and the sexual exploitation of children. When a beer ad uses the image of a man licking the high-heeled boot of a woman clad in leather, when bondage is used to sell neckties in the *New York Times*, perfume in

The right tie can make even the most casual evening more memorable

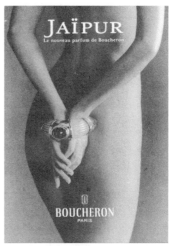

The New Yorker, and watches on city buses, and when a college magazine promotes an S&M Ball, pornography can be considered mainstream.

Most of us know all this by now and I suppose some consider it kinky good fun. Pornography is more dangerously mainstream when its glorification of rape and violence shows up in mass media, in films and television shows, in comedy and music videos, and in advertising. Male violence is subtly encouraged by ads that encourage men to be forceful and dominant, and to value sexual intimacy more than emotional intimacy. "Do you want to be the one she tells her deep, dark secrets to?" asks a three-page ad for men's cologne. "Or do you want to be her deep, dark secret?" The last page advises men, "Don't be such a good boy." There are two identical women looking adoringly at the man in the ad, but he isn't looking at either one of them. Just what is the deep, dark secret? That he's sleeping with both of them? Clearly the way to get beautiful women is to ignore them, perhaps mistreat them.

"Two ways a woman can get hurt," says an ad for shaving gel, featuring a razor and a photo of a handsome man. My first thought is that the man is a batterer or date rapist, but the ad informs us that he is merely a "heartbreaker." The gel will protect the woman so that "while guys may continue to be a pain, shaving most definitely won't." Desirable men are painful—heartbreakers at best.

Wouldn't it be wonderful if, realizing the importance of relationships in all of our lives, we could seek to learn relational skills from women and to help men develop these strengths in themselves? In fact, we so often do the opposite. The popular culture usually trivializes these abilities in women, mocks men who have real intimacy with women (it is almost always married men in ads and cartoons who are jerks), and idealizes a template for relationships between men and women that is a recipe for disaster: a template that views sex as more important than anything else, that ridicules men who are not in control of their women (who are "pussy-whipped"), and that disparages fidelity and commitment (except, of course, to brand names).

Indeed the very worst kind of man for a woman to be in an intimate relationship with, often a truly dangerous man, is the one considered most sexy and desirable in the popular culture. And the men capable of real intimacy (the ones we tell our deep, dark secrets to) constantly have their very masculinity impugned. Advertising often encourages women to be attracted to hostile and indifferent men while encouraging boys to become these men. This is especially dangerous for those of us who have suffered from "condemned isolation" in childhood: like heat-seeking missiles, we rush inevitably to mutual destruction.

Men are also encouraged to never take no for an answer. Ad after

sweat. Go all out. We'll keep up. New Old Spice® Anti-Perspirant helps stop the sweat that causes odor. The proof? You're looking at her. For great odor production, now you've got **proof** not promises.

P◌SSESSION
SHIRTS AND SHORTS
1-800-229-GRVPO

ad implies that girls and women don't really mean "no" when they say it, that women are only teasing when they resist men's advances. "NO" says an ad showing a man leaning over a woman against a wall. Is she screaming or laughing? Oh, it's an ad for deodorant and the second word, in very small print, is "sweat." Sometimes it's "all in good fun," as in the ad for Possession shirts and shorts featuring a man ripping the clothes off a woman who seems to be having a good time.

And sometimes it is more sinister. A perfume ad running in several teen magazines features a very young woman, with eyes blackened by makeup or perhaps something else, and the copy, "Apply generously to your neck so he can smell the scent as you shake your head 'no.'" In other words, he'll understand that you don't really mean it and he can respond to the scent like any other animal.

fetish
SCENT
fetish ™ib Apply generously to your neck so he can smell the scent as you shake your head "no".

Sometimes there seems to be no question but that a man should force a woman to have sex. A chilling newspaper ad for a bar in Georgetown features a closeup of a cocktail and the headline, "If your date won't listen to reason, try a Velvet Hammer." A vodka ad pictures a wolf hiding in a flock of sheep, a hideous grin on its face. We all know what wolves do to

IF YOUR DATE WON'T LISTEN TO REASON, TRY A VELVET HAMMER.

Sip exotic cocktails, dine and dance to Swing Era music at Georgetown's top nightspot. 1232 36th St., NW. Reservations, call 342-0009. Free valet parking. Jackets required.

F. SCOTT'S

sheep. A campaign for Bacardi Black rum features shadowy figures almost obliterated by darkness and captions such as "Some people embrace the night because the rules of the day do not apply." What it doesn't say is that people who are above the rules do enormous harm to other people, as well as to themselves.

These ads are particularly troublesome, given that between one-third and three-quarters of all cases of sexual assault involve alcohol consumption by the perpetrator, the victim, or both.[1] "Make strangers your friends, and your friends a lot stranger," says one of the ads in a Cuervo campaign that uses colorful cartoon beasts and emphasizes heavy drinking. This ad is especially disturbing when we consider the role of alcohol in date rape, as is another ad in the series that says, "The night began with a bottle of Cuervo and ended with a vow of silence." Over half of all reported rapes on college campuses occur when either the victim or the assailant has been drinking.[2] Alcohol's role has different meaning for men and women, however. If a man is drunk when he commits a rape, he is considered less responsible. If a woman is drunk (or has had a drink or two or simply met the man in a bar), she is considered more responsible.

In general, females are still held responsible and hold each other responsible when sex goes wrong—when they become pregnant or are the victims of rape and sexual assault or cause a scandal. Constantly exhorted to be sexy and attractive, they discover when assaulted that that very sexiness is evidence of their guilt, their lack of "inno-

PURE FANTASY. (SMIRNOFF)

---

[1]Wilsnack, Plaud, Wilsnack, and Klassen, 1997, 262. [All notes are the author's, except 5, 9, 15, and 18.]

[2]Abbey, Ross, and McDuffie, 1991. Also Martin, 1992, 230–37.

cence." Sometimes the ads play on this by "warning" women of what might happen if they use the product. "Wear it but beware it," says a perfume ad. Beware what exactly? Victoria's Secret tempts young women with blatantly sexual ads promising that their lingerie will make them irresistible. Yet when a young woman accused William Kennedy Smith of raping her, the fact that she wore Victoria's Secret panties was used against her as an indication of her immorality. A jury acquitted Smith, whose alleged history of violence against women was not permitted to be introduced at trial.

It is sadly not surprising that the jury was composed mostly of women. Women are especially cruel judges of other women's sexual behavior, mostly because we are so desperate to believe we are in control of what happens to us. It is too frightening to face the fact that male violence against women is irrational and commonplace. It is reassuring to believe that we can avoid it by being good girls, avoiding dark places, staying out of bars, dressing "innocently." An ad featuring two young women talking intimately at a coffee shop says, "Carla and Rachel considered themselves open-minded and non-judgmental people. Although they did agree Brenda was a tramp." These terrible judgments from other women are an important part of what keeps all women in line.

If indifference in a man is sexy, then violence is sometimes downright erotic. Not surprisingly, this attitude too shows up in advertising. "Push my buttons," says a young woman, "I'm looking for a man who can totally floor me." Her vulnerability is underscored by the fact that she is in an elevator, often a dangerous place for women. She is young, she is submissive (her eyes are downcast), she is in a dangerous place, and she is dressed provocatively. And she is literally asking for it.

"Wear it out and make it scream," says a jeans ad portraying a man sliding his hands under a woman's transparent blouse. This could be a seduction, but it could as easily be an attack. Although the ad that ran in the

Czech version of *Elle* portraying three men attacking a woman seems unambiguous, the terrifying image is being used to sell jeans *to women.* So someone must think that women would find this image compelling or attractive. Why would we? Perhaps it is simply designed to get our attention, by shocking us and by arousing unconscious anxiety. Or perhaps the intent is more subtle and it is designed to play into the fantasies of domination and even rape that some women use in order to maintain an illusion of being in control (we are the ones having the fantasies, after all, we are the directors).

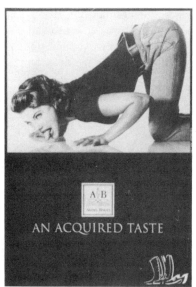

AN ACQUIRED TASTE

A camera ad features a woman's torso wrapped in plastic, her hands   15
tied behind her back. A smiling woman in a lipstick ad has a padlocked
chain around her neck. An ad for **MTV** shows a vulnerable young woman,
her breasts exposed, and the simple copy "Bitch." A perfume ad features a
man shadowboxing with what seems to be a woman.

Sometimes women are shown dead or in the process of being killed.
"Great hair never dies," says an ad featuring a female corpse lying on a bed,
her breasts exposed. An ad in the Italian version of *Vogue* shows a man aiming a gun at a nude woman wrapped in plastic, a leather briefcase covering
her face. And an ad for Bitch skateboards, for
God's sake, shows a cartoon version of a similar
scene, this time clearly targeting young people.
We believe we are not affected by these images,
but most of us experience visceral shock when we
pay conscious attention to them. Could they be
any less shocking to us on an unconscious level?

Most of us become numb to these images,
just as we become numb to the daily litany in the
news of women being raped, battered, and killed.
According to former surgeon general Antonia
Novello, battery is the single greatest cause of injury to women in America, more common than
automobile accidents, muggings, and stranger
rapes combined, and more than one-third of

La Borsa è la Vita

bitch skateboards

women slain in this country die at the hands of husbands or boyfriends.[3] Throughout the world, the biggest problem for most women is simply surviving at home. The Global Report on Women's Human Rights concluded that "Domestic violence is a leading cause of female injury in almost every country in the world and is typically ignored by the state or only erratically punished."[4] Although usually numb to these facts on a conscious level, most women live in a state of subliminal terror, a state that, according to Mary Daly,[5] keeps us divided both from each other and from our most passionate, powerful, and creative selves.[6]

Ads don't directly cause violence, of course. But the violent images contribute to the state of terror. And objectification and disconnection create a climate in which there is widespread and increasing violence. Turning a human being into a thing, an object, is almost always the first step toward justifying violence against that person. It is very difficult, perhaps impossible, to be violent to someone we think of as an equal, someone we have empathy with, but it is very easy to abuse a thing. We see this with racism,

[3]Novello, 1991. Also Blumenthal, 1995.
[4]Wright, 1995, A2.
[5]*Mary Daly:* Radical feminist scholar and author (b. 1928).
[6]Weil, 1999, 21.

with homophobia. The person becomes an object and violence is inevitable. This step is already taken with women. The violence, the abuse, is partly the chilling but logical result of the objectification.

An editorial in *Advertising Age* suggests that even some advertisers are concerned about this: "Clearly it's time to wipe out sexism in beer ads; for the brewers and their agencies to wake up and join the rest of America in realizing that sexism, sexual harassment, and the cultural portrayal of women in advertising are inextricably linked."[7] Alas, this editorial was written in 1991 and nothing has changed.

It is this link with violence that makes the objectification of women a 20 more serious issue than the objectification of men. Our economic system constantly requires the development of new markets. Not surprisingly, men's bodies are the latest territory to be exploited. Although we are growing more used to it, in the beginning the male sex object came as a surprise. In 1994 a "gender bender" television commercial in which a bevy of women office workers gather to watch a construction worker doff his shirt to quaff a Diet Coke led to so much hoopla that you'd have thought women were mugging men on Madison Avenue.[8]

There is no question that men are used as sex objects in ads now as never before. We often see nude women with fully clothed men in ads (as in art), but the reverse was unheard of, until recently. These days some ads do feature clothed and often aggressive women with nude men. And women sometimes blatantly objectify men, as in the Metroliner ad that says, "'She's reading Nietzsche,' Harris noted to himself as he walked towards the café car for a glass of cabernet. And as he passed her seat, Maureen looked up from her book and thought, 'Nice buns.'"

Although these ads are often funny, it is never a good thing for human beings to be objectified. However, there is a world of difference between the objectification of men and that of women. The most important difference is that there is no danger for most men, whereas objectified women are always at risk. In the Diet Coke ad, for instance, the women are physically separated from the shirtless man. He is the one in control. His body is powerful, not passive. Imagine a true role reversal of this ad: a group of businessmen gather to leer at a beautiful woman worker on her break, who removes her shirt before drinking her Diet Coke. This scene would be frightening, not funny, as the Diet Coke ad is. And why is the Diet Coke ad

[7]Brewers can help fight sexism, 1991, 28.
[8]Kilbourne, 1994, F13.

funny? Because we know it doesn't describe any truth. However, the ads featuring images of male violence against women do describe a truth, a truth we are all aware of, on one level or another.

When power is unequal, when one group is oppressed and discriminated against *as a group,* when there is a context of systemic and historical oppression, stereotypes and prejudice have different weight and meaning. As Anna Quindlen[9] said, writing about "reverse racism": "Hatred by the powerful, the majority, has a different weight—and often very different effects—than hatred by the powerless, the minority."[10] When men objectify women, they do so in a cultural context in which women are constantly objectified and in which there are consequences—from economic discrimination to violence—to that objectification.

For men, though, there are no such consequences. Men's bodies are not routinely judged and invaded. Men are not likely to be raped, harassed, or beaten (that is to say, men presumed to be heterosexual are not, and very few men are abused in these ways by women). How many men are frightened to be alone with a woman in an elevator? How many men cross the street when a group of women approaches? Jackson Katz, who writes and lectures on male violence, often begins his workshops by asking men to describe the things they do every day to protect themselves from sexual assault. The men are surprised, puzzled, sometimes amused by the question. The women understand the question easily and have no trouble at all coming up with a list of responses. We don't list our full names in the phone directory or on our mailboxes, we try not to be alone after dark, we carry our keys in our hands when we approach our cars, we always look in the back seat before we get in, we are wary of elevators and doorways and bushes, we carry pepper sprays, whistles, Mace.

Nonetheless, the rate of sexual assault in the United States is the highest of any industrialized nation in the world.[11] According to a 1998 study by the federal government, one in five of us has been the victim of rape or attempted rape, most often before our seventeenth birthday. And more than half of us have been physically assaulted, most often by the men we live with. In fact, three of four women in the study who responded that they had been raped or assaulted as adults said the perpetrator was a current or former husband, a cohabiting partner or a date.[12] The article reporting the results of this study was buried on page twenty-three of my local newspaper, while the front page dealt with a long story about the New England Patriots football team.

A few summers ago, a Diet Pepsi commercial featured Cindy Crawford being ogled by two boys (they seemed to be about twelve years old) as she

25

---

[9]*Anna Quindlen:* Novelist and Pulitzer Prize–winning journalist who often writes about women's issues (b. 1953).

[10]Quindlen, 1992, E17.

[11]Blumenthal, 1995, 2.

[12]Tjaden and Thoennes, 1998.

where women are women and men are roadkill.

got out of her car and bought a Pepsi from a machine. The boys made very suggestive comments, which in the end turned out to be about the Pepsi's can rather than Ms. Crawford's. There was no outcry: the boys' behavior was acceptable and ordinary enough for a soft-drink commercial.

Again, let us imagine the reverse: a sexy man gets out of a car in the countryside and two preteen girls make suggestive comments, seemingly about his body, especially his buns. We would fear for them and rightly so. But the boys already have the right to ogle, to view women's bodies as property to be looked at, commented on, touched, perhaps eventually hit and raped. The boys have also learned that men ogle primarily to impress other men (and to affirm their heterosexuality). If anyone is in potential danger in this ad, it is the woman (regardless of the age of the boys). Men are not seen as *property* in this way by women. Indeed if a woman does whistle at a man or touches his body or even makes direct eye contact, it is still *she* who is at risk and the man who has the power.

"I always lower my eyes to see if a man is worth following," says the woman in an ad for men's pants. Although the ad is offensive to everyone, the woman is endangering only herself.

"Where women are women and men are roadkill," says an ad for motor-cycle clothing featuring an angry-looking African-American woman. Women are sometimes hostile and angry in ads these days, especially women of color who are often seen as angrier and more threatening than white women. But, regardless of color, we all know that women are far more likely than men to end up as roadkill—and, when it happens, they are blamed for being on the road in the first place.

Even little girls are sometimes held responsible for the violence against them. In 1990 a male Canadian judge accused a three-year-old girl of being "sexually aggressive" and suspended the sentence of her molester, who was then free to return to his job of baby-sitter.[13] The deeply held belief that all women, regardless of age, are really temptresses in disguise, nymphets, sexually insatiable and seductive, conveniently transfers all blame and responsibility onto women.

All women are vulnerable in a culture in which there is such widespread objectification of women's bodies, such glorification of disconnection, so much violence against women, and such blaming of the victim. When everything and everyone is sexualized, it is the powerless who are most at risk. Young girls, of course, are

30

[13]Two men and a baby, 1990, 10.

especially vulnerable. In the past twenty years or so, there have been several trends in fashion and advertising that could be seen as cultural reactions to the women's movement, as perhaps unconscious fear of female power. One has been the obsession with thinness. Another has been an increase in images of violence against women. Most disturbing has been the increasing sexualization of children, especially girls. Sometimes the little girl is made up and seductively posed. Sometimes the language is suggestive. "Very cherry," says the ad featuring a sexy little African-American girl who is wearing a dress with cherries all over it. A shocking ad in a gun magazine features a smiling little girl, a toddler, in a bathing suit that is tugged up suggestively in the rear. The copy beneath the photo says, "short BUTTS from FLEMING FIREARMS."[14] Other times girls are juxtaposed with grown women, as in the ad for underpants that says "You already know the feeling."

This is not only an American phenomenon. A growing national obsession in Japan with schoolgirls dressed in uniforms is called "Loli-con," after Lolita.[15] In Tokyo hundreds of "image clubs" allow Japanese men to act out

[14]Herbert, 1999, WK 17.
[15]*Lolita:* The title character of Vladimir Nabokov's 1955 novel, Lolita is a young girl who is sexually pursued by her stepfather.

their fantasies with make-believe schoolgirls. A magazine called *V-Club* featuring pictures of naked elementary-school girls competes with another called *Anatomical Illustrations of Junior High School Girls*.[16] Masao Miyamoto, a male psychiatrist, suggests that Japanese men are turning to girls because they feel threatened by the growing sophistication of older women.[17]

In recent years, this sexualization of little girls has become even more disturbing as hints of violence enter the picture. A three-page ad for Prada clothing features a girl or very young woman with a barely pubescent body, clothed in what seem to be cotton panties and perhaps a training bra, viewed through a partially opened door. She seems surprised, startled, worried, as if she's heard a strange sound or glimpsed someone watching her. I suppose this could be a woman awaiting her lover, but it could as easily be a girl being preyed upon.

The 1996 murder of six-year-old JonBenet Ramsey[18] was a gold mine for the media, combining as it did child pornography and violence. In November of 1997 *Advertising Age* reported in an article entitled "JonBenet keeps hold on magazines" that the child had been on five magazine covers in October, "Enough to capture the Cover Story lead for the month. The pre-adolescent beauty queen, found slain in her home last Christmas, garnered 6.5 points. The case earned a *triple play* [italics mine] in the *National Enquirer,* and one-time appearances on *People* and *Star.*"[19] Imagine describing a six-year-old child as "pre-adolescent."

Sometimes the models in ads are children, other times they just look like children. Kate Moss was twenty when she said of herself, "I look

35

---

[16]Schoolgirls as sex toys, 1997, 2E.

[17]Ibid.

[18]*JonBenet Ramsey:* Six-year-old beauty-pageant winner who was sexually molested and murdered in her Boulder, Colorado, home in 1996.

[19]Johnson, 1997, 42.

twelve."[20] She epitomized the vacant, hollow-cheeked look known as "heroin chic" that was popular in the mid-nineties. She also often looked vulnerable, abused, and exploited. In one ad she is nude in the corner of a huge sofa, cringing as if braced for an impending sexual assault. In another she is lying nude on her stomach, pliant, available, androgynous enough to appeal to all kinds of pedophiles. In a music video she is dead and bound to a chair while Johnny Cash sings "Delia's Gone."

It is not surprising that Kate Moss models for Calvin Klein, the fashion designer who specializes in breaking taboos and thereby getting himself public outrage, media coverage, and more bang for his buck. In 1995 he brought the federal government down on himself by running a campaign that may have crossed the line into child pornography.[21] Very young models (and oth-

ers who just seemed young) were featured in lascivious print ads and in television commercials designed to mimic child porn. The models were awkward, self-conscious. In one commercial, a boy stands in what seems to be a finished basement. A male voiceover tells him he has a great body and asks him to take off his shirt. The boy seems embarrassed but he complies. There was a great deal of protest, which brought the issue into national consciousness but which also gave Klein the publicity and free media coverage he was looking for. He pulled the ads but, at the same time, projected that his jeans sales would almost double from $115 million to $220

---

[20]Leo, 1994, 27.
[21]Sloan, 1996, 27.

million that year, partly because of the free publicity but also because the controversy made his critics seem like prudes and thus positioned Klein as the daring rebel, a very appealing image to the majority of his customers.

Having learned from this, in 1999 Klein launched a very brief advertising campaign featuring very little children frolicking in their underpants, which included a controversial billboard in Times Square.[22] Although in some ways this campaign was less offensive than the earlier one and might have gone unnoticed had the ads come from a department store catalog rather than from Calvin Klein, there was the expected protest and Klein quickly withdrew the ads, again getting a windfall of media coverage. In my opinion, the real obscenity of this campaign is the whole idea of people buying designer underwear for their little ones, especially in a country in which at least one in five children doesn't have enough to eat.

Although boys are sometimes sexualized in an overt way, they are more often portrayed as sexually precocious, as in the Pepsi commercial featuring the young boys ogling Cindy Crawford or the jeans ad portraying a very little boy looking up a woman's skirt. It may seem that I am reading too much into this ad, but imagine if the genders were reversed. We would fear for a little girl who was unzipping a man's fly in an ad (and we would be shocked, I would hope). Boys are vulnerable to sexual abuse too, but cultural atti-

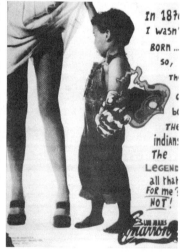

---

[22]Associated Press, 1999, February 18, A7.

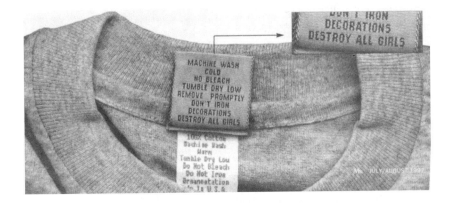

tudes make it difficult to take this seriously. As a result, boys are less likely to report abuse and to get treatment.

Many boys grow up feeling that they are unmanly if they are not always "ready for action," capable of and interested in sex with any woman who is available. Advertising doesn't cause this attitude, of course, but it contributes to it. A Levi Strauss commercial that ran in Asia features the shock of a schoolboy who discovers that the seductive young woman who has slipped a note into the jeans of an older student is his teacher. And an ad for BIC pens pictures a young boy wearing X-ray glasses while ogling the derriere of an older woman. Again, these ads would be unthinkable if the genders were reversed. It is increasingly difficult in such a toxic environment to see children, boys or girls, as *children.*

In the past few years there has been a proliferation of sexually   40 grotesque toys for boys, such as a Spider Man female action figure whose exaggerated breasts have antennae coming out of them and a female Spawn figure with carved skulls for breasts. Meantime even children have easy access to pornography in video games and on the World Wide Web, which includes explicit photographs of women having intercourse with groups of men, with dogs, donkeys, horses, and snakes; photographs of women being raped and tortured; some of these women made up to look like little girls.

It is hard for girls not to learn self-hatred in an environment in which there is such widespread and open contempt for women and girls. In 1997 a company called Senate distributed clothing with inside labels that included, in addition to the usual cleaning instructions, the line "Destroy all girls." A Senate staffer explained that he thought it was "kind of cool."[23] Given all this, it's not surprising that when boys and girls were asked in a recent study to write an essay on what it would be like to be the other gender, many boys wrote they would rather be dead. Girls had no trouble writing essays about activities, power, freedom, but boys were often stuck, could think of nothing.

[23]Wire and *Times* staff reports, 1997, D1.

It is also not surprising that, in such an environment, sexual harassment is considered normal and ordinary. According to an article in the journal *Eating Disorders:*

> In our work with young women, we have heard countless accounts of this contempt being expressed by their male peers: the girls who do not want to walk down a certain hallway in their high school because they are afraid of being publicly rated on a scale of one to ten; the girls who are subjected to barking, grunting and mooing calls and labels of "dogs, cows, or pigs" when they pass by groups of male students; those who are teased about not measuring up to buxom, bikini-clad [models]; and the girls who are grabbed, pinched, groped, and fondled as they try to make their way through the school corridors.
>
> Harassing words do not slide harmlessly away as the taunting sounds dissipate.... They are slowly absorbed into the child's identity and developing sense of self, becoming an essential part of who she sees herself to be. Harassment involves the use of words as weapons to inflict pain and assert power. Harassing words are meant to instill fear, heighten bodily discomfort, and diminish the sense of self.[24]

It is probably difficult for those of us who are older to understand how devastating and cruel and pervasive this harassment is, how different from the "teasing" some of us might remember from our own childhoods (not that that didn't hurt and do damage as well). A 1993 report by the American Association of University Women found that 76 percent of female students in grades eight to eleven and 56 percent of male students said they had been sexually harassed in school.[25] One high-school junior described a year of torment at her vocational school: "The boys call me slut, bitch. They call me a ten-timer, because they say I go with ten guys at the same time. I put up with it because I have no choice. The teachers say it's because the boys think I'm pretty."[26]

High school and junior high school have always been hell for those who were different in any way (gay teens have no doubt suffered the most, although "overweight" girls are a close second), but the harassment is more extreme and more physical these days. Many young men feel they have the right to judge and touch young women and the women often feel they have no choice but to submit. One young woman recalled that "the guys at school routinely swiped their hands across girls' legs to patrol their shaving prowess and then taunt them if they were slacking off. If I were running late, I'd protect myself by faux shaving—just doing the strip between the bottom of my jeans and the top of my cotton socks."[27]

[24]Larkin, Rice, and Russell, 1996, 5–26.
[25]Daley and Vigue, 1999, A12.
[26]Hart, 1998, A12.
[27]Mackler, 1998, 56.

Sexual battery, as well as inappropriate sexual gesturing, touching, and   45
fondling, is increasing not only in high schools but in elementary and
middle schools as well.[28] There are reports of sexual assaults by students on
other students as young as eight. A fifth-grade boy in Georgia repeatedly
touched the breasts and genitals of one of his fellow students while saying,
"I want to get in bed with you" and "I want to feel your boobs." Authorities
did nothing, although the girl complained and her grades fell. When her
parents found a suicide note she had written, they took the board of education to court.[29]

A high-school senior in an affluent suburban school in the Boston area
said she has been dragged by her arms so boys could look up her skirt and
that boys have rested their heads on her chest while making lewd comments. Another student in the same school was pinned down on a lunch
table while a boy simulated sex on top of her. Neither student reported any
of the incidents, for fear of being ostracized by their peers.[30] In another
school in the Boston area, a sixteen-year-old girl, who had been digitally
raped by a classmate, committed suicide.[31]

According to Nan Stein, a researcher at Wellesley College:

> Schools may in fact be training grounds for the insidious cycle of do-
> mestic violence.... The school's hidden curriculum teaches young
> women to suffer abuse privately, that resistance is futile. When they
> witness harassment of others and fail to respond, they absorb a differ-
> ent kind of powerlessness — that they are incapable of standing up to
> injustice or acting in solidarity with their peers. Similarly, in schools
> boys receive permission, even training, to become batterers through
> the practice of sexual harassment.[32]

This pervasive harassment of and contempt for girls and women constitute a kind of abuse. We know that addictions for women are rooted in
trauma, that girls who are sexually abused are far more likely to become addicted to one substance or another. I contend that all girls growing up in
this culture are sexually abused — abused by the pornographic images of female sexuality that surround them from birth, abused by all the violence
against women and girls, and abused by the constant harassment and threat
of violence. Abuse is a continuum, of course, and I am by no means implying that cultural abuse is as terrible as literally being raped and assaulted.
However, it hurts, it does damage, and it sets girls up for addictions and
self-destructive behavior. Many girls turn to food, alcohol, cigarettes, and
other drugs in a misguided attempt to cope.

[28]Daley and Vigue, 1999, A1, A12.
[29]Shin, 1999, 32.
[30]Daley and Vigue, 1999, A12.
[31]Daley and Abraham, 1999, B6.
[32]Stein, 1993, 316–17.

As Marian Sandmaier said in *The Invisible Alcoholics: Women and Alcohol Abuse in America*, "In a culture that cuts off women from many of their own possibilities before they barely have had a chance to sense them, that pain belongs to all women. Outlets for coping may vary widely, and may be more or less addictive, more or less self-destructive. But at some level, all women know what it is to lack access to their own power, to live with a piece of themselves unclaimed."[33]

Today, every girl is endangered, not just those who have been physically and sexually abused. If girls from supportive homes with positive role models are at risk, imagine then how vulnerable are the girls who have been violated. No wonder they so often go under for good—ending up in abusive marriages, in prison, on the streets. And those who do are almost always in the grip of one addiction or another. More than half of women in prison are addicts and most are there for crimes directly related to their addiction. Many who are there for murder killed men who had been battering them for years. Almost all of the women who are homeless or in prisons and mental institutions are the victims of male violence.[34]

Male violence exists within the same cultural and sociopolitical context that contributes to addiction. Both can be fully understood only within this context, way beyond individual psychology and family dynamics. It is a context of systemic violence and oppression, including racism, classism, heterosexism, weightism, and ageism, as well as sexism, all of which are traumatizing in and of themselves. Advertising is only one part of this cultural context, but it is an important part and thus is a part of what traumatizes.

Sources

Abbey, A., Ross, L., and McDuffie, D. (1991). Alcohol's role in sexual assault. In Watson, R., ed. *Addictive behaviors in women.* Towota, NJ: Humana Press.

Associated Press (1999, February 18). Calvin Klein retreats on ad. *Boston Globe,* A7.

Blumenthal, S. J. (1995, July). *Violence against women.* Washington, DC: Department of Health and Human Services.

Brewers can help fight sexism (1991, October 28). *Advertising Age,* 28.

Daley, B., and Vigue, D. I. (1999, February 4). Sex harassment increasing amid students, officials say. *Boston Globe,* A1, A12.

Hart, J. (1998, June 8). Northampton confronts a crime, cruelty. *Boston Globe,* A1, A12.

Herbert, B. (1999, May 2). America's littlest shooters. *New York Times,* WK 17.

Johnson, J. A. (1997, November 10). JonBenet keeps hold on magazines. *Advertising Age,* 42.

[33]Sandmaier, 1980, xviii.
[34]Snell, 1991.

Kilbourne, J. (1994, May 15). 'Gender bender' ads: Same old sexism. *New York Times,* F13.

Larkin, J., Rice, C., and Russell, V. (1996, Spring). Slipping through the cracks: Sexual harassment. *Eating Disorders: The Journal of Treatment and Prevention,* vol. 4, no. 1, 5–26.

Leo, J. (1994, June 13). Selling the woman-child. *U.S. News and World Report,* 27.

Mackler, C. (1998). Memoirs of a (sorta) ex-shaver. In Edut, O., ed. (1998). *Adios, Barbie.* Seattle, WA: Seal Press, 55–61.

Novello, A. (1991, October 18). Quoted by Associated Press, AMA to fight wife-beating. *St. Louis Post Dispatch,* 1, 15.

Quindlen, A. (1992, June 28). All of these you are. *New York Times,* E17.

Sandmaier, M. (1980). *The invisible alcoholics: Women and alcohol abuse in America.* New York: McGraw-Hill.

Schoolgirls as sex toys. *New York Times* (1997, April 16), 2E.

Shin, A. (1999, April/May). Testing Title IX. *Ms.* 32.

Sloan, P. (1996, July 8). Underwear ads caught in bind over sex appeal. *Advertising Age,* 27.

Snell, T. L. (1991). *Women in prison.* Washington, DC: U.S. Department of Justice.

Stein, N. (1993). No laughing matter: Sexual harassment in K–12 schools. In Buchwald, E., Fletcher, P. R., and Roth, M. (1993). *Transforming a rape culture.* Minneapolis, MN: Milkweed Editions, 311–31.

Tjaden, R., and Thoennes, N. (1998, November). *Prevalence, incidence, and consequences of violence against women: Findings from the National Violence Against Women Survey.* Washington, DC: U.S. Department of Justice.

Two men and a baby (1990, July/August). *Ms.* 10.

Vigue, D. J., and Abraham, Y. (1999, February 7). Harassment a daily course for students. *Boston Globe,* B1, B6.

Weil, L. (1999, March). Leaps of faith. *Women's Review of Books,* 21.

Wilsnack, S. C., Plaud, J. J., Wilsnack, R. W., and Klassen, A. D. (1997). Sexuality, gender, and alcohol use. In Wilsnack, R. W., and Wilsnack, S. C., eds. *Gender and alcohol: Individual and social perspectives.* New Brunswick, N.J.: Rutgers Center of Alcohol Studies, 262.

Wire and Times Staff Reports (1997, May 20). Orange County skate firm's 'destroy all girls' tags won't wash. *Los Angeles Times,* D1.

Wright, R. (1995, September 10). Brutality defines the lives of women around the world. *Boston Globe,* A2.

ENGAGING THE TEXT

1. What parallels does Kilbourne see between advertising and pornography? How persuasive do you find the evidence she offers? Do the photos of the ads she describes strengthen her argument? Why or why not?

2. Why is it dangerous to depict women and men as sex objects, according to Kilbourne? Why is the objectification of women *more* troubling, in her view? Do you agree?

3. How does Kilbourne explain the appeal of ads that allude to bondage, sexual aggression, and rape—particularly for female consumers? How do you respond to the ads reproduced in her essay?

476 TRUE WOMEN AND REAL MEN

4. What does Kilbourne mean when she claims that the depiction of women in advertising constitutes "cultural abuse"? How does she go about drawing connections between advertising images and social problems like sexual violence, harassment, and addiction? Which portions of her analysis do you find most and least persuasive, and why?

EXPLORING CONNECTIONS

5. Media images constitute part of the "generalized other"—the internalized sense of what is socially acceptable and unacceptable—described by Aaron H. Devor (p. 424). In addition to the violent and sexualized images Kilbourne examines, what other images or messages about gender do you encounter regularly in the media? Which ones have been most influential in the development of your "generalized other"?

6. Write an essay exploring the power of media to promote or curb violence, drawing on Kilbourne and on any or all of the selections by the following writers:

> Michael A. Messner (p. 477)
> Carmen Vázquez (p. 489)
> Joan Morgan (p. 539)
> Joshua Gamson (p. 91)
> Leon E. Wynter (p. 688)
> Michael Medved (p. 769)

EXTENDING THE CRITICAL CONTEXT

7. Kilbourne claims that popular culture idealizes dangerous, exploitative, or dysfunctional relationships between women and men. Working in small groups, discuss the romantic relationships depicted in movies you've seen recently. Does her critique seem applicable to those films? List the evidence you find for and against her argument and compare your results with those of other groups.

8. In her analysis of two ads (the Diet Pepsi commercial featuring Cindy Crawford and the Diet Coke ad with the shirtless construction worker), Kilbourne applies a gender reversal test in order to demonstrate the existence of a double standard. Try this test yourself on a commercial or ad that relies on sexual innuendo. Write a journal entry describing the ad and explaining the results of your test.

9. Working in pairs or small groups, survey the ads in two magazines—one designed to appeal to a predominantly female audience and one aimed at a largely male audience. What differences, if any, do you see in the kinds of images and appeals advertisers use in the two magazines? How often do you see the kinds of "pornographic" ads Kilbourne discusses? Do you find any ads depicting the "relational skills" that she suggests are rarely emphasized in popular culture?

Center of Attention:
The Gender of Sports Media

MICHAEL A. MESSNER

Imagine for a moment that you're an anthropologist from the distant future: you're trying to understand early twenty-first-century American culture, but the only artifacts remaining from that ancient time are videotapes of old ESPN broadcasts. What conclusions would you draw about the roles and relationships of men and women based on those tapes? Sociologist Michael A. Messner analyzes a similar body of evidence—twenty-three hours' worth of televised football, basketball, baseball, and extreme sports— and identifies a set of recurrent themes about masculinity that run throughout TV sports coverage. He dubs these themes "the televised sports manhood formula." Messner (b. 1952) is a professor of sociology and gender studies at the University of Southern California, where he chairs the Sociology Department; he has also served as president of the North American Society for the Sociology of Sport. His many publications include Power at Play: Sports and the Problem of Masculinity *(1992),* Politics of Masculinities: Men in Movements *(1997), and* Taking the Field: Women, Men, and Sports *(2002), the source of this selection.*

Reading the Center

A recent national survey found eight- to seventeen-year-old children to be avid consumers of sports media, with television most often named as the preferred medium.[1] Girls watch sports in great numbers, but boys are markedly more likely to be regular consumers of televised sports. The most popular televised sports with boys, in descending order, are pro football, men's pro basketball, pro baseball, pro wrestling, men's college basketball, college football, and extreme sports.[2] What are kids seeing and hearing when they watch these programs? In particular, what kinds of values concerning gender, race, aggression, violence, and consumerism are boys exposed to when they watch their favorite televised sports programs, with their accompanying commercials? Children Now, a children's advocacy organization, asked my colleagues Darnell Hunt and Michele Dunbar and me to shed light on these questions by analyzing these televised sports and their

---

[1]Amateur Athletic Foundation of Los Angeles, *Children and Sports Media.* [All notes are Messner's.]

[2]There are some differences and some similarities in what boys and girls prefer to watch. The top seven televised sports reported by girls are, in order, gymnastics, men's pro basketball, pro football, pro baseball, swimming/diving, men's college basketball, and women's pro or college basketball.

accompanying commercials.[3] Our analysis revealed that sports programming presents boys with narrow and stereotypical messages about race, gender, and violence. We identified ten distinct themes that, together, make up what we call the televised sports manhood formula:

White males are the voices of authority. The play-by-play and ongoing "color commentary" in National Football League (NFL), professional wrestling, National Basketball Association (NBA), extreme sports, and major league baseball (MLB) broadcasts that we examined was conducted exclusively by white male play-by-play commentators. With the exception of ESPN's *SportsCenter,* women and African American men never appeared as the main voices of authority, "in the booth," conducting play-by-play or ongoing color commentary. The NFL broadcasts occasionally cut to field-level color commentary by a white woman, but her commentary was a very brief interlude. Similarly, the NBA broadcasts used African American men and white or African American women for occasional on-court, pregame, and halftime analysis but not for play-by-play commentary. Although viewers commonly see African American male athletes, especially on televised NBA games, they rarely hear or see African American men (or any women) as voices of authority in the broadcast booth.[4] In fact, the only African American commentators that appeared on the NBA shows that we examined were former star basketball players (Cheryl Miller, Doc Rivers, and Isiah Thomas). An African American male briefly appeared to welcome the audience to open one of the extreme sports shows, but he did no play-by-play; in fact, he was used only to open the show with a cool, street, hip-hop style for what turned out to be an almost totally white show.[5]

Sport is a man's world. Images and discussion of women athletes are almost entirely absent in the sports programs that boys watch most. The baseball, basketball, wrestling, and football programs we watched were men's contests so perhaps could not have been expected to cover or mention women athletes. However, extreme sports are commonly viewed as alternative or emerging sports in which women are challenging masculine hege-

---

[3]In all, we examined about twenty-three hours of sports programming, nearly one-quarter of which was time taken up by commercials. We examined a total of 722 commercials, which spanned a large range of products and services. We collected both quantitative and qualitative data. For a more detailed discussion of this research and its documentation, see Messner, Dunbar, and Hunt, "The Televised Sports Manhood Formula."

[4]Sabo and Jansen, "Seen But Not Heard."

[5]The racial coding of extreme sports shows is especially intriguing. Though little research has yet been done on this topic, I speculate that many white, middle-class adolescent boys and young men get involved in sports like skateboarding partly as an alternative to the central sports team sports, which are viewed as dominated by African American males. Nevertheless, these alternative extreme sports liberally borrow African American street styles and codes of clothing and music. The emergent TV portrayals of these sports tend to demonstrate this hybrid coding of black cultural style in a predominantly white sport setting.

mony.[6] Despite this, the extreme sports shows we watched devoted only a single fifty-second interview segment to a woman athlete. This segment constituted about 1 percent of the total extreme sports programming and, significantly, did not show this woman athlete in action.

Perhaps this limited coverage of women athletes on the extreme sports shows we examined is evidence of what sociologist Robert Rinehart calls a "pecking order" in alternative sports, which develops when new sports are appropriated and commodified by the media. When ESPN first produced the eXtreme games, Rinehart observes, they were sponsored by Miller Lite Ice, Taco Bell, Mountain Dew, Nike's ACG brand, AT&T, and General Motors. This "coopting by corporations," Rinehart argues, is paradoxical: though now sanctioned by a governing body and by some of the largest U.S. corporations, the appeal of extreme sports to many consumers appears to be their "outlaw" nature. To be commercially successful then, extreme sports televised productions and their accompanying commercial advertisements have creatively played with this paradox, highlighting moments of symbolic (masculine) "outlaw" rebellion while constructing an audience of conformist consumers.[7]

Men are foregrounded in commercials. The gender composition and   5 imagery in commercials reinforce the idea that sport is a man's world. Women almost never appear in commercials unless they are in the company of men. Of the 722 commercials we examined, 279 portrayed only men, and only 28 showed only women. That 38.6 percent of all commercials portrayed only men actually understates the extent to which men dominated these commercials, for two reasons. First, nearly every one of the 91 commercials containing no visual portrayals of people included a male voice-over. When we include the "voice-over" group, the proportions shift to over 50 percent of commercials portraying "men only" images and/or voice-overs, and only 3.9 percent portraying only women. Moreover, when we combine the "men only" and "women and men" categories, we see that men were actually visible in 83.5 percent and present (at least in voice) in 96.1 percent of all commercials. Second, in the commercials that portrayed both women and men, women were often (though not exclusively) portrayed in stereotypical and very minor "background" roles.

Women are sexy props or prizes for men's successful sports performances or consumption choices. Though women are mostly absent from sports commentary, when they do appear, it is most often in stereotypical roles as sexy, masculinity-validating props, often cheering the men on. For instance, X-sports on Fox Sports West used a bikini-clad blond woman as a "hostess" to welcome viewers back after each commercial break while the camera moved provocatively over her body. Though she mentioned the show's sponsors, she

---

[6]Wheaton and Tomlinson, "The Changing Gender Order in Sport?"
[7]Rinehart, "Inside of the Outside."

did not narrate the actual sporting event. The wrestling shows generously utilized scantily clad women (e.g., in pink miniskirts or tight Spandex and high heels), who overtly displayed the dominant cultural signs of heterosexy attractiveness,[8] to escort the male wrestlers to the ring, often with announcers discussing the women's provocative physical appearances. Women also appeared in the wrestling shows as sexually provocative dancers (e.g., the Gorgeous Nitro Girls on TNT).

In sports-related commercials, women are numerically more evident and generally depicted in more varied roles than in the sports programming. Still, women are underrepresented and rarely appear in commercials unless they are in the company of men. A common theme in commercials aimed at boys and men is to depict women as capable either of humiliating men or of affirming men's masculine desirability. And women's supposed masculinity-validating power is clearly linked to men's consumption choices: women will ignore or humiliate the man who is incapable of buying the right product or unwilling to, but women become sexy and accessible "prizes" for men who are wise enough to make the right consumption choices. Both of these themes were rawly depicted in a commercial for Keystone Light Beer that ran on *SportsCenter.* Two white guys are attending a major league baseball game, when one of them unexpectedly appears on the stadium big screen. His buddy says, "Dude, look, you're on! *Do* something!" All the guy can think to do with his sudden ten seconds of fame is to take a drink of his beer. Immediately, the taste of this bitter beer twists and distorts his face. The stadium announcer reacts in shock to his ugliness ("Ay caramba!"), and the camera cuts to two conventionally attractive young women in the crowd, who are totally grossed out ("Eeeew!") by having to look at this man's contorted face. But then the voice-over reassuringly instructs the viewer, "Don't be a victim of bitter beer. Drink Keystone Light, America's never bitter beer, so there's always a great taste and never a bitter face." When the commercial ends, the formerly contorted and humiliated man has returned to normal, and we see him again on the big screen, now holding a Keystone Light and looking healthy, attractive, and confident with the same two young fashion-model-like women standing on either side of him, now adoring him. He says, "I hope my wife's not watching!" as the two women happily wave to the audience.

This madonna-whore juxtaposition of women—wives and girlfriends and other castrating bitches are to be avoided, but sexy dancers or models are desirable objects of consumption—is also evident in a series of

---

[8]Though images of feminine beauty shift, change, and are contested throughout history, female beauty is presented in sports programming and commercials in narrow ways. "Attractive" women look like fashion models: they are tall, thin, young, usually (though not always) white, with signs of heterosexual femininity encoded and overtly displayed through hair, makeup, sexually provocative facial and bodily gestures, large (often partly exposed) breasts, long (often exposed) legs, and so on. For a critical discussion of this kind of encoding of femininity, see Banet-Weiser, *The Most Beautiful Girl in the World.*

2000–2001 full-page magazine ads for Jim Beam whiskey that, under the umbrella theme of "Real friends. Real bourbon," pitched male bonding through alcohol consumption to a college-aged (or young college-educated) crowd of men. Against a striking red background, black-and-white photos of clean-cut, mostly white young men in bars drinking, laughing, and happily partying together were accompanied by these captions: "Unlike your girl-friend, they never ask where this relationship is going," and "You can count on them never to ask you to get in touch with your feminine side."

Women, the ads imply, demand levels of emotional commitment and expression that men are not ready or willing to submit to. Women are a pain in the ass. Life with the guys (and the booze) is comfortable, comforting, and safe. It's also exciting. The one ad in the series that included an image of a woman showed only part of her body (*Sports Illustrated* ran this one in its 2000 swimwear issue, in 3-D if you were willing to put on the glasses). The guys are drinking again together at a bar. In the foreground, we see the high-heeled legs of what appears to be a dancing female stripper. The guys drink, laugh, and seem very amused with each other. "Your lives would make a great sitcom," the caption reads. "Of course, it would have to run on cable." That the guys mostly seem to be ignoring the woman dancer affirms the strength and primacy of their bond with each other; they don't need her or any other women, it seems to say. On the other hand, her powerfully sex-ual presence appears to affirm that the bond between the men is safely within the bounds of heterosexuality.[9]

Whites are foregrounded in commercials. The racial composition of the 10 commercials is, if anything, narrower and more limited than the gender composition. African American, Latino, or Asian American people almost never appear in commercials unless the commercial also has white people in it. And when we examined the quality of the portrayals of African Ameri-cans, Latinos, and Asian Americans in the "multiracial" commercials, we found that people of color are far more often than not relegated to minor roles, literally "in the background" of scenes that feature whites, and/or they are relegated to stereotypical or negative roles. For instance, a Wendy's commercial that appeared on several of the sports programs in our sample showed white customers enjoying a sandwich with the white owner while a barely perceptible African American male walked by in the background.

Aggressive players get the prize; nice guys finish last. Viewers of tele-vised sports are continually immersed in images and commentary about the positive rewards that come to the most "aggressive" competitors and of the negative consequences of playing "soft" and lacking aggression.

[9]This mediated theme of heterosexual male bonding through alcohol reflects common practices in men's use of "sports bars." Lawrence Wenner, in his fascinating study of sports bars, observes, "Not only do public drinking and participation in sports serve as masculine rites of passage, their spaces and places often serve as refuge from women." Wenner, "In Search of the Sports Bar," 303.

Commentators consistently laud athletes who most successfully employ "physical" and "aggressive" play and "toughness." For instance, after having his toughness called into question, NBA player Brian Grant was awarded "redemption" by *SportsCenter* because he showed that he's "not afraid to take it to Karl Malone." *SportsCenter* also informed viewers that "the aggressor usually gets the calls [from the officials], and the Spurs were the ones getting them." In pro wrestling commentary, this is a constant theme. WWF announcers praised the "raw power" of wrestler Shamrock and approvingly dubbed Hardcore Holly as "the world's most dangerous man." NBA commentators suggested that it's okay to be a good guy off the court, but one must be tough and aggressive on the court: Brian Grant and Jeff Hornacek are "true gentlemen of the NBA . . . as long as you don't have to play against them. You know they're great off the court; on the court, every single guy out there *should* be a killer."

When players are not doing well, they are often described as hesitant and lacking aggression, emotion, and desire (e.g., desire for a loose ball or a rebound). For instance, commentators lamented that "the Jazz aren't going to the hoop; they're being pushed and shoved around," that Utah was responding to the Blazers' aggression "passively, in a reactive mode," and that "Utah's got to get Karl Malone toughened up." *SportsCenter* echoed this theme, opening one show with a depiction of Horace Grant elbowing Karl

In an effort to reduce injuries, the Clodpell Valley Football Conference devised the two-hand tickle tackling rule.

Malone and asking of Malone, "Is he feeble?" Similarly, NFL broadcasters waxed on about the virtues of aggression and domination. Big "hits," ball carriers who got "buried," "stuffed" or "walloped" by the defense, and players who got "cleaned out" or "wiped out" by a blocker were often shown on replays, with announcers enthusiastically describing the plays. By contrast, announcers declared that it's a very bad thing to be "passive" and to let yourself get "pushed around" and "dominated" at the line of scrimmage. Announcers also approvingly noted that "going after" an opposing player's injured body part is just smart football; in one NFL game, the Miami strategy to blitz the opposing quarterback was lauded as brilliant: "When you know your opposing quarterback is a bit nicked and something is wrong, Boomer, you got to come after him."

This injunction for boys and men to be aggressive, not passive, is reinforced in commercials, where a common formula is to play on the insecurities of young males (e.g., that they are not strong enough, tough enough, smart enough, rich enough, attractive enough, decisive enough, etc.) and then attempt to convince them to avoid, overcome, or mask their fears, embarrassments, and apparent shortcomings by buying a particular product. These commercials often portray men as potential or actual geeks, nerds, or passive schmucks who can overcome their geekiness (or avoid being a geek like the guy in the commercial) by becoming decisive and purchasing a particular product. . . .

Boys will be (violent) boys. Announcers often take a humorous "boys will be boys" attitude in discussing fights or near fights during contests, and they also commonly use a recent fight, altercation, or disagreement between two players as a "teaser" to build audience excitement. Fights, near fights, threats of fights, or other violent actions are overemphasized in sports coverage and often verbally framed in sarcastic language that suggests that this kind of action, though reprehensible, is to be expected. For instance, when *SportsCenter* showed NBA centers Robinson and O'Neal exchanging forearm shoves, the commentators said, simply, "much love." Similarly, in an NFL game, a brief scuffle between players was met with a sarcastic comment by the broadcaster that the players were simply "making their acquaintance." This is, of course, a constant theme in pro wrestling. My colleagues and I found it noteworthy that the supposedly spontaneous fights outside the wrestling ring (what we call unofficial fights) were given more coverage time and focus than the supposedly official fights inside the ring. We speculate that wrestling producers know that viewers already watch fights inside the ring with some skepticism as to their authenticity, so they stage the unofficial fights outside the ring to bring a feeling of spontaneity and authenticity to the show and to build excitement and a sense of anticipation for the fight that will later occur inside the ring.

Give up your body for the team. Athletes who are "playing with pain," "giving up their body for the team," or engaging in obviously highly dangerous plays or maneuvers are consistently portrayed as heroes; conversely, 15 those who remove themselves from games because of injuries raise questions about their character, their manhood. This theme cuts across all sports programming. For instance, *SportsCenter* asked, "Could the Dominator be soft?" when an NHL star goalie decided to sit out a game because of a groin injury. Heroically taking risks while already hurt was a constant theme in extreme sports commentary. For instance, one bike competitor was lauded for "overcoming his fear" and competing "with a busted up ankle," and another was applauded when he "popped his collarbone out in the street finals in Louisville" but came back to "his bike here in Richmond, just two weeks later!" Athletes appear especially heroic when they go against doctors' wishes not to compete. For instance, an X Games interviewer adoringly told a competitor, "Doctors said don't ride, but you went ahead and did it anyway, and escaped serious injury." Similarly, NBA player Isaiah Rider was lauded for having "heart" for "playing with that knee injury." Injury discussions in NFL games often include speculation about whether the player will be able to return to this or future games. A focus on a star player in a pregame or halftime show, such as the feature on 49er Garrison Hearst, often contains commentary about a heroic overcoming of serious injuries (in this case, a knee blowout, reconstructive surgery, and rehabilitation). When one game began, commentators noted that thirty-seven-year-old "Steve Young has remained a rock. . . . Not bad for a guy who a lotta people figured was—what?—one big hit from ending his career." It's especially impressive when an injured player is able and willing to continue to play with aggressiveness and reckless abandon: "Kurt Scrafford at right guard—bad neck and all—is just out there wiping out guys. . . ." And announcers love the team leader who plays hurt: "Drew Bledsoe gamely tried to play in loss to Rams yesterday; really admirable to try to play with that pin that was surgically implanted in his finger during the week; I don't know how a QB could do that. You know, he broke his finger the time we had him on Monday night, and he led his team to two come-from-behind victories, really gutted it out, and I think he took that team on his shoulders and showed he could play and really elevated himself in my eyes, he really did."

Sports are war. Commentators in our study consistently (an average of nearly five times during each hour of sports commentary) used martial metaphors and language of war and weaponry to describe sports action (e.g., *battle, kill, ammunition, weapons, professional sniper, depth charges, taking aim, fighting, shot in his arsenal, reloading, detonate, squeezes the trigger, attack mode, firing blanks, blast, explosion, blitz, point of attack, a lance through the heart,* etc.). Some shows went beyond commentators' use of war terminology and actually framed the contests *as* wars. For instance, one of the wrestling shows offered a continuous flow of images and commentary that reminded the viewers that "RAW is WAR!" Similarly, NFL *Monday Night Football* broadcasts were introduced with explosive graphics and an opening song that included these lyrics: "Like a rocket burning through time and space, the NFL's best will rock this place . . . the battle lines are drawn. . . ." This sort of use of sports-war metaphors has been a common practice in televised sports commentary for many years, serving to fuse (and confuse) the distinctions between values of nationalism with team identity and athletic aggression with military destruction.[10] War themes were also reinforced in many commercials, including commercials for movies, other sports programs, and the occasional commercial for the U.S. Military.

Show some guts! Commentators continually depict and replay big hits, violent crashes, and incidents of athletes engaging in reckless acts of speed or showing guts in the face of danger. This theme was evident across all of the sports programs in our study but was especially predominant in extreme sports, which continually depicted crashing vehicles or bikers in an exciting manner. For instance, when one race ended with a crash, it was showed again in slow-motion replay, with commentators approvingly dubbing it "unbelievable" and "original." Extreme sports commentators commonly raised excitement levels by saying "he's on fire!" or "he's going huge!" when a competitor was obviously taking greater risks. An athlete's ability to deal with the fear of a possible crash, in fact, is the mark of an "outstanding run": "Watch out, Richmond," an X Games announcer shouted to the crowd, "he's gonna wreck this place!" A winning competitor laughingly said, "I do what I can to smash into [my opponents] as much as I can." Another competitor said, "If I crash, no big deal; I'm just gonna go for it." NFL commentators introduced the games with images of reckless collisions, and during the game, a "fearless" player was likely to be applauded: "There's no chance that Barry Sanders won't take when he's running the football." In another game, the announcer noted that receiver "Tony Simmons plays big. And for those of you not in the NFL, playing big means you're not afraid to go across the middle and catch the ball and make a play out of it after you catch the ball." Men showing guts in the face of speed and danger was also a major theme in forty of the commercials that we analyzed.

The Televised Sports Manhood Formula

Tens of millions of people, many of them children, watch televised sports programs with their accompanying commercial advertisements. Though there are certainly differences across different kinds of sports as well as across different commercials, when my colleagues and I looked at all of the programming together, we identified ten recurrent themes, outlined above. Taken together, these themes codify a consistent and (mostly) coherent message about what it means to be a man. We call this message the televised sports manhood formula:

> *What is a real man? A real man is strong, tough, aggressive, and above all, a winner in what is still a man's world. To be a winner he has to do*

[10]Jansen and Sabo, "The Sport/War Metaphor"; Malszecki and Cavar, "Men, Masculinities, War, and Sport"; Trujillo, "Machines, Missiles, and Men."

what needs to be done. He must be willing to compromise his own long-term health by showing guts in the face of danger, by fighting other men when necessary, and by giving up his body for the team when he's injured. He must avoid being soft; he must be the aggressor, both on the "battlefields" of sports and in his consumption choices. Whether he is playing sports or making choices about which snack food or auto products to purchase, his aggressiveness will net him the ultimate prize: the adoring attention of conventionally beautiful women. He will know if and when he has arrived as a real man when the voices of authority—white males—say he is a real man. But even when he has finally managed to win the big one, has the good car and the right beer, and is surrounded by beautiful women, he will be reminded by these same voices of authority just how fragile this real manhood is: After all, he has to come out and prove himself all over again tomorrow. You're only as good as your last game (or your last purchase).

There is an ideological center to sports culture, and this is it. The major elements of the televised sports manhood formula are evident, in varying degrees, in the football, basketball, baseball, extreme sports, and *SportsCenter* programs and in their accompanying commercials. . . .

It is not possible, merely on the basis of my (or anyone else's) textual analysis of sports programs, to explicate precisely what kind of impact broadcast sports, sports in magazines, and their accompanying commercials have on audiences. Do boys and men swallow the televised sports manhood formula whole? What is the appeal of watching violent sports?[11] Does watching violent sports tend to make some boys and men accept violence, celebrate violence, and act more violently in their daily lives?[12] Do certain

---

[11]Timothy Beneke argues that the appeal of boys' and men's sports spectating, reading the sports pages, and talking sports with other men lies in "BIRGING—Basking In Reflected Glory . . . gaining esteem through showing off connections with successful others." Beneke, *Proving Manhood.* For scholarly analysis of the appeal of violent entertainment (including sports) to audiences, see Goldstein, ed., *Why We Watch;* and Briant, Zillman, and Raney, "Violence and the Enjoyment of Media Sports."

[12]This is a huge and complicated question that connects to years of research and debate about violence, media, and audiences. Though it is beyond the purview of my focus here to delve into these debates, I want to note that since the 1980s, it has been part of the "common knowledge" in the United States that rates of violence against women, especially in the home, rise on Super Bowl Sunday. In 1993, journalist Robert Lipsyte dubbed the Super Bowl the "Abuse Bowl." However, as far as I know no actual research has ever documented this relationship between watching the Super Bowl and higher rates of domestic violence. A few years back, a reporter called several women's shelters after the Super Bowl and found that there was no surge in calls from abused women during or immediately following the event. Canadian researchers studied the relationship between televised NHL playoff games and rates of domestic violence, and their findings were inconclusive. Holman, *Sports, Media and Domestic Violence.* Sabo and his colleagues took a different approach to studying this issue. They began with the assumption that any relationship between watching violent sports and acts of spousal violence is, perhaps like spousal rape rates, extremely difficult to measure accurately. So instead of try-

groups of boys and men (by age, race-ethnicity, social class, sexual orientation, etc.) derive or construct different meanings from televised sports and
their ads? . . . These kinds of questions are best approached through direct
research with audiences, very little of which has thus far been conducted in
sport studies. However, audience research in general tells us that audiences
interpret, use, and draw meanings from media variously, on the basis of factors such as social class, race-ethnicity, and gender.[13]

It is also important to go beyond my emphasis in this chapter on the   20
ways that the dominant themes at the center of the sports media reinforce
the hegemony of current race, gender, and commercial relations. In addition to these continuities, there are some identifiable discontinuities within
and among the various sports programs and within and among the accompanying commercials. For instance, television commercials are far more
varied in the ways that they present gender imagery than sports programs
themselves are. Though the dominant tendency in commercials accompanying sports programs is either to erase women or to present them as
stereotypical support- or sex-objects, a significant minority of commercials
present themes that set up boys and men as insecure and/or obnoxious
schmucks and women as secure, knowledgeable, and authoritative. In addition, a few athletes such as Dennis Rodman offer up images that are profoundly mixed and paradoxical in their gender, sexual, and racial meanings.[14] Audience research with people of all ages and backgrounds would
shed fascinating light on how people variously decode and interpret these
more complex, mixed, and paradoxical gender images against the dominant,
hegemonic image of the televised sports manhood formula.

ing to measure or document a statistical correlation, they located and interviewed eighteen
women who had been regularly beaten by male partners who were watching (or had just finished watching) televised sports (mostly, hockey, football, and basketball). Often, these men
battered the women in view of others, as a "display of power and domination" in front of an
"audience" that included "children, extended family members, and male friends." The authors
concluded that while no simple cause-effect relationship could be drawn between watching
sports and wife beating, watching the sporting event was a key part of a violent matrix. Rather
than providing a "symbolic refuge" for these male viewers, watching sports on TV "aroused
emotional and cultural associations with masculinity that, in turn, seemed to combine with aspects of life history, individual psychology, the use of drugs and alcohol, and gambling to produce violence against women." Sabo, Gray, and Moore, "Domestic Violence and Televised
Athletic Events," 145.

[13]Darnell Hunt has provided a solid example of how to study audiences' racialized interpretations of a controversial news item. Hunt, *O.J. Simpson Facts and Fictions.* In sport studies, very little audience research has been conducted so far, though some scholars have laid out
the fundamental questions that will be of use to future scholars. See Wenner and Gantz,
"Watching Sports on Television"; and Whannel, "Reading the Sports Media Audience."

[14]Sociologist Michele Dunbar argues that even though he plays with sexual and gender
codes, Dennis Rodman's image appears to constitute an individualized rebellion that is mostly
reproductive (rather than disruptive or resistant) of dominant gender and race relations. She
does note, though, that her critical reading of Rodman would be enhanced by audience studies. Dunbar, "Dennis Rodman—Do You Feel Feminine Yet?"

ENGAGING THE TEXT

1. What is the "televised sports manhood formula," according to Messner? Based on your own experience as a viewer, do you agree that "sports programming presents boys with narrow and stereotypical messages about race, gender, and violence" (para. 1)? Why or why not?

2. At the end of this selection, Messner poses a series of questions about the impact of sports coverage on fans:

> Do boys and men swallow the televised sports manhood formula whole? What is the appeal of watching violent sports? Does watching violent sports tend to make some boys and men accept violence, celebrate violence, and act more violently in their daily lives? Do certain boys and men . . . construct different meanings from televised sports and their ads? (para. 19)

   How would you answer each of these questions, and what is the basis of your opinions? Compare your views to those of your classmates: Do men and women respond to these questions differently?

3. If you played sports in high school or are currently a student athlete, have you or your teammates been pressured to play while injured? If so, how and to what extent? Do you consider it heroic to risk serious injury or permanent disability in order to win a game? Why or why not?

4. Messner cites several "identifiable discontinuities" in the ways that sports programs represent gender, including commercials that portray women as more capable than men and athletes like Dennis Rodman who violate gender stereotypes. How do you interpret these discontinuities? What other exceptions or contradictions to the "sports manhood formula" have you observed?

5. Messner calls for audience research to gauge how viewers interpret the gender images they see in TV sports broadcasts. If you were a researcher, how would you go about evaluating the responses to televised sports of a large, diverse audience?

EXPLORING CONNECTIONS

6. Play the role of Aaron H. Devor (p. 424) and write a journal entry explaining how the televised sports images descried by Messner contribute to the "social hegemony" of the "patriarchal gender schema."

7. Jean Kilbourne (p. 455), like Messner, worries about how media representations of aggression and violence may affect children. What are their specific concerns, and to what extent do you believe these concerns are justified? Do you recall how you responded to images of people being hurt or threatened when you were very young? What reactions or attitudes have you observed in younger siblings or children you've worked with? How do you respond to such images now?

8. In the cartoon on page 482, how does the artist play with our assumptions about football players, football, and fans of the sport? Is he making fun of

football itself, of people who criticize violent sports, of masculine stereo-types, of bureaucratic solutions to complex questions, or something else?

EXTENDING THE CRITICAL CONTEXT

9. Break down Messner's "sports manhood formula" into a series of simple statements (e.g., "Being a man means being strong," "Being a man means being aggressive," "Being a man means being a winner"). Create a survey that asks respondents to note the hours of sports programming they watch on average per week and to rate the degree to which they agree or disagree with each statement. Also include an open question inviting them to list any other characteristics that they believe define manhood. Do the people you surveyed generally endorse or reject Messner's formula? Is there more agreement about some items than about others? Do men's responses differ from women's? Can you draw any conclusions based on the amount of tele-vised sports a respondent watches?

10. Watch TV coverage of one or more men's sports that Messner does not dis-cuss—tennis, golf, soccer, volleyball, water polo, boxing, or figure skating, for example. To what extent do Messner's ten themes appear in the broad-casts and commercials surrounding these sports? Do you observe differ-ences in the ways that masculinity is represented by these sportscasts and their commercial sponsors? If so, how do you explain the differences?

11. Watch a televised women's basketball, soccer, or softball game and record your observations. What similarities or differences do you see in the ways that female and male athletes are portrayed in television sports coverage? Is there a televised sports womanhood formula?

Appearances
CARMEN VÁZQUEZ

Have you ever gone for a walk in the evening, ridden a city bus, or gone out dancing? Did these activities make you fear for your life? In this essay, Vázquez writes about what can happen in such everyday situations when the pedestrian, commuter, or dancer is perceived as gay or lesbian. She also discusses some possible causes of homophobia, and she pleads for change. Vázquez (b. 1949) was born in Bayamon, Puerto Rico, and grew up in Harlem, New York. She has been active in the lesbian/gay movement for many years and currently serves as Director of Public Policy for the Lesbian and Gay Community Services Center in New York City; she also codirects Promote the Vote, a registration project sponsored by community centers across the nation. She has published essays and book reviews in a number of

publications. "Appearances" comes from an anthology titled Homophobia:
How We All Pay the Price *(1992).*

   North of Market Street and east of Twin Peaks, where you can see the
white fog mushroom above San Francisco's hills, is a place called the Castro. Gay men, lesbians, and bisexuals stroll leisurely up and down the
bustling streets. They jaywalk with abandon. Night and day they fill the
cafés and bars, and on weekends they line up for a double feature of vintage
classics at their ornate and beloved Castro theater.

   The 24 bus line brings people into and out of the Castro. People from
all walks of life ride the electric-powered coaches. They come from the opulence of San Francisco's Marina and the squalor of Bayview projects. The
very gay Castro is in the middle of its route. Every day, boys in pairs or
gangs from either end of the city board the bus for a ride through the Castro and a bit of fun. Sometimes their fun is fulfilled with passionately obscene derision: "Fucking cocksucking faggots." "Dyke cunts." "Diseased
butt fuckers." Sometimes, their fun is brutal.

   Brian boarded the 24 Divisadero and handed his transfer to the driver
one late June night. Epithets were fired at him the moment he turned for a
seat. He slid his slight frame into an empty seat next to an old woman with
silver blue hair who clutched her handbag and stared straight ahead. Brian
stuffed his hands into the pockets of his worn brown bomber jacket and
stared with her. He heard the flip of a skateboard in the back. The taunting
shouts grew louder. "Faggot!" From the corner of his eye, he saw a beer
bottle hurtling past the window and crash on the street. A man in his forties,
wearing a Giants baseball cap and warmup jacket, yelled at the driver to
stop the bus and get the hoodlums off. The bus driver ignored him and
pulled out.

   Brian dug his hands deeper into his pockets and clenched his jaw. It
was just five stops to the top of the hill. When he got up to move toward the
exit, the skateboard slammed into his gut and one kick followed another
until every boy had got his kick in. Despite the plea of the passengers, the
driver never called the police.

   Brian spent a week in a hospital bed, afraid that he would never walk   5
again. A lawsuit filed by Brian against the city states, "As claimant lay
crumpled and bleeding on the floor of the bus, the bus driver tried to force
claimant off the bus so that the driver could get off work and go home.
Claimant was severely beaten by a gang of young men on the #24 Divisadero Bus who perceived that he was gay."

   On the south side of Market Street, night brings a chill wind and rough
trade. On a brisk November night, men with sculptured torsos and thighs
wrapped in leather walked with precision. The clamor of steel on the heels
of their boots echoed in the darkness. Young men and women walked by

the men in leather, who smiled in silence. They admired the studded bracelets on Mickey's wrists, the shine of his flowing hair, and the rise of his laughter. They were, each of them, eager to be among the safety of like company where they could dance with abandon to the pulse of hard rock, the hypnotism of disco, or the measured steps of country soul. They looked forward to a few drinks, flirting with strangers, finding Mr. or Ms. Right or, maybe, someone to spend the night with.

At the end of the street, a lone black street lamp shone through the mist. The men in leather walked under the light and disappeared into the next street. As they reached the corner, Mickey and his friends could hear the raucous sounds of the Garden spill onto the street. They shimmied and rocked down the block and through the doors.

The Garden was packed with men and women in sweat-stained shirts. Blue smoke stung the eyes. The sour and sweet smell of beer hung in the air. Strobe lights pulsed over the dancers. Mickey pulled off his wash-faded black denim jacket and wrapped it around his waist. An iridescent blue tank top hung easy on his shoulders. Impatient with the wait for a drink, Mickey steered his girlfriend onto the crowded dance floor.

Reeling to the music and immersed in the pleasure of his rhythms, Mickey never saw the ice pick plunge into his neck. It was just a bump with a drunk yelling, "Lame-assed faggot." "Faggot. Faggot. Faggot. Punk faggot." Mickey thought it was a punch to the neck. He ran after the roaring drunk man for seven steps, then lurched and fell on the dance floor, blood gushing everywhere. His girlfriend screamed. The dance floor spun black.

Mickey was rushed to San Francisco General Hospital, where thirty-six stitches were used by trauma staff to close the wound on his neck. Doctors said the pick used in the attack against him was millimeters away from his spinal cord. His assailant, charged with attempted murder, pleaded innocent.   10

Mickey and Brian were unfortunate stand-ins for any gay man. Mickey was thin and wiry, a great dancer clad in black denim, earrings dangling from his ear. Brian was slight of build, wore a leather jacket, and boarded a bus in the Castro. Dress like a homo, dance like a homo, must be a homo. The homophobic fury directed at lesbians, gay men, and bisexuals in America most often finds its target. Ironclad evidence of sexual orientation, however, is not necessary for someone to qualify as a potential victim of deadly fury. Appearances will do.

The incidents described above are based on actual events reported to the San Francisco Police and Community United Against Violence (CUAV), an agency serving victims of antilesbian and antigay violence where I worked for four years. The names of the victims have been changed. Both men assaulted were straight.

Incidents of antilesbian and antigay violence are not uncommon or limited to San Francisco. A *San Francisco Examiner* survey estimates that over one million hate-motivated physical assaults take place each year against lesbians, gays, and bisexuals. The National Gay and Lesbian Task Force conducted a survey in 1984 that found that 94 percent of all lesbians and gay men surveyed reported being physically assaulted, threatened, or harassed in an antigay incident at one time or another. The great majority of these incidents go unreported.

To my knowledge, no agency other than CUAV keeps track of incidents of antigay violence involving heterosexuals as victims. An average of 3 percent of the over three hundred victims seen by CUAV each year identify as heterosexuals. This may or may not be an accurate gauge of the actual prevalence of antigay violence directed at heterosexuals. Most law enforcement agencies, including those in San Francisco, have no way of documenting this form of assault other than under a generic "harassment" code. The actual incidence of violence directed at heterosexuals that is motivated by homophobia is probably much higher than CUAV's six to nine victims a year. Despite the official paucity of data, however, it is a fact that incidents of antigay and antilesbian violence in which straight men and women are victimized do occur. Shelters for battered women are filled with stories of lesbian baiting of staff and of women whose husbands and boyfriends repeatedly called them "dykes" or "whores" as they beat them.[1] I have personally experienced verbal abuse while in the company of a straight friend, who was assumed to be my lover.

Why does it happen? I have no definitive answers to that question. Understanding homophobic violence is no less complex than understanding racial violence. The institutional and ideological reinforcements of homophobia are myriad and deeply woven into our culture. I offer one perspective that I hope will contribute to a better understanding of how homophobia works and why it threatens all that we value as humane.

At the simplest level, looking or behaving like the stereotypical gay man or lesbian is reason enough to provoke a homophobic assault. Beneath the veneer of the effeminate gay male or the butch dyke, however, is a more basic trigger for homophobic violence. I call it *gender betrayal*.

The clearest expression I have heard of this sense of gender betrayal comes from Doug Barr, who was acquitted of murder in an incident of gay bashing in San Francisco that resulted in the death of John O'Connell, a gay man. Barr is currently serving a prison sentence for related assaults on the same night that O'Connell was killed. He was interviewed for a special report on homophobia produced by ABC's *20/20* (10 April 1986). When asked what he and his friends thought of gay men, he said, "We hate homosexuals. They degrade our manhood. We was brought up in a high school where guys are football players, mean and macho. Homosexuals are sissies who wear dresses. I'd rather be seen as a football player."

15

---

[1]See Suzanne Pharr, *Homophobia: A Weapon of Sexism* (Inverness, Calif.: Chardon, 1988). [All notes are Vázquez's.]

Doug Barr's perspective is one shared by many young men. I have made about three hundred presentations to high school students in San Francisco, to boards of directors and staff of nonprofit organizations, and at conferences and workshops on the topic of homophobia or "being lesbian or gay." Over and over again, I have asked, "Why do gay men and lesbians bother you?" The most popular response to the question is, "Because they act like girls," or, "Because they think they're men." I have even been told, quite explicitly, "I don't care what they do in bed, but they shouldn't act like that."

They shouldn't act like that. Women who are not identified by their relationship to a man, who value their female friendships, who like and are knowledgeable about sports, or work as blue-collar laborers and wear what they wish are very likely to be "lesbian baited" at some point in their lives. Men who are not pursuing sexual conquests of women at every available opportunity, who disdain sports, who choose to stay at home and be a house-husband, who are employed as hairdressers, designers, or housecleaners, or who dress in any way remotely resembling traditional female attire (an earring will do) are very likely to experience the taunts and sometimes the brutality of "fag bashing."

The straitjacket of gender roles suffocates many lesbians, gay men, and   20
bisexuals, forcing them into closets without an exit and threatening our very existence when we tear the closet open. It also, however, threatens all heterosexuals unwilling to be bound by their assigned gender identity. Why, then, does it persist?

Suzanne Pharr's examination of homophobia as a phenomenon based in sexism and misogyny offers a succinct and logical explanation for the virulence of homophobia in Western civilization:

> It is not by chance that when children approach puberty and increased sexual awareness they begin to taunt each other by calling these names: "queer," "faggot," "pervert." It is at puberty that the full force of society's pressure to conform to heterosexuality and prepare for marriage is brought to bear. Children know what we have taught them, and we have given clear messages that those who deviate from standard expectations are to be made to get back in line....
>
> To be named as lesbian threatens all women, not just lesbians, with great loss. And any woman who steps out of role risks being called a lesbian. To understand how this is a threat to all women, one must understand that any woman can be called a lesbian and there is no real way she can defend herself: there is no real way to credential one's sexuality. (*The Children's Hour,* a Lillian Hellman play, makes this point when a student asserts two teachers are lesbians and they have no way to disprove it.) She may be married or divorced, have children, dress in the most feminine manner, have sex with men, be celibate — but there are lesbians who do all these things. *Lesbians look like all women and all women look like lesbians.*[2]

[2]Ibid., 17–19.

I would add that gay men look like all men and all men look like gay men. There is no guaranteed method for identifying sexual orientation. Those small or outrageous deviations we sometimes take from the idealized mystique of "real men" and "real women" place all of us—lesbians, gay men, bisexuals, and heterosexuals alike—at risk of violence, derision, isolation, and hatred.

It is a frightening reality. Dorothy Ehrlich, executive director of the Northern California American Civil Liberties Union (ACLU), was the victim of a verbal assault in the Castro several years ago. Dorothy lives with her husband, Gary, and her two children, Jill and Paul, in one of those worn and comfortable Victorian homes that grace so many San Francisco neighborhoods. Their home is several blocks from the Castro, but Dorothy recalls the many times she and Gary could hear, from the safety of their bedroom, shouts of "faggot" and men running in the streets.

When Jill was an infant, Gary and Dorothy had occasion to experience for themselves how frightening even the threat of homophobic violence can be. One foggy, chilly night they decided to go for a walk in the Castro. Dorothy is a small woman whom some might call petite; she wore her hair short at the time and delights in the comfort of jeans and oversized wool jackets. Gary is very tall and lean, a bespectacled and bearded cross between a professor and a basketball player who wears jean jackets and tweed jackets with the exact same slouch. On this night they were crossing Castro Street, huddled close together with Jill in Dorothy's arms. As they reached the corner, their backs to the street, they heard a truck rev its engine and roar up Castro, the dreaded "faggot" spewing from young men they could not see in the fog. They looked around them for the intended victims, but there was no one else on the corner with them. They were the target that night: Dorothy and Gary and Jill. They were walking on "gay turf," and it was reason enough to make them a target. "It was so frightening," Dorothy said. "So frightening and unreal."

But it is real. The 20/20 report on homophobia ends with the story of Tom and Jan Matarrase, who are married, have a child, and lived in Brooklyn, New York, at the time of their encounter with homophobic violence. On camera, Tom and Jan are walking down a street in Brooklyn lined with brown townhouses and black wrought-iron gates. It is snowing, and, with hands entwined, they walk slowly down the street where they were assaulted. Tom is wearing a khaki trenchcoat, slacks, and loafers. Snowflakes melt into the tight dark curls on his head. Jan is almost his height, her short bobbed hair moving softly as she walks. She is wearing a black leather jacket, a red scarf, and burnt orange cords. The broadness of her hips and softness of her face belie the tomboy flavor of her carriage and clothes, and it is hard to believe that she was mistaken for a gay man. But she was.

They were walking home, holding hands and engrossed with each 25 other. On the other side of the street, Jan saw a group of boys moving toward them. As the gang approached, Jan heard a distinct taunt meant for her and Tom: "Aw, look at the cute gay couple." Tom and Jan quickened their step, but it was too late. Before they could say anything, Tom was being punched in the face and slammed against a car. Jan ran toward Tom and the car, screaming desperately that Tom was her husband. Fists pummeled her face as well. Outnumbered and in fear for their lives, Tom yelled at Jan to please open her jacket and show their assailants that she was a woman. The beating subsided only when Jan was able to show her breasts.

For the *20/20* interview, Jan and Tom sat in the warmth of their living room, their infant son in Jan's lap. The interviewer asked them how they felt when people said they looked like a gay couple. "We used to laugh," they said. "But now we realize how heavy the implications are. Now we know what the gay community goes through. We had no idea how widespread it was. It's on every level."

Sadly, it *is* on every level. Enforced heterosexism and the pressure to conform to aggressive masculine and passive feminine roles place fag bashers and lesbian baiters in the same psychic prison with their victims, gay or straight. Until all children are free to realize their full potential, until all women and men are free from the stigma, threats, alienation, or violence that come from stepping outside their roles, we are all at risk.

The economic and ideological underpinnings of enforced heterosexism and sexism or any other form of systematic oppression are formidable foes and far too complex for the scope of this essay. It is important to remember, however, that bigots are natural allies and that poverty or the fear of it has the power to seduce us all into conformity. In Castro graffiti, *faggot* appears right next to *nigger* and *kike*. Race betrayal or any threat to the sanctimony of light-skinned privilege engenders no less a rage than gender betrayal, most especially when we have a great stake in the elusive privilege of proper gender roles or the right skin color. *Queer lover* and *fag hag* are cut from the same mold that gave us *nigger lover,* a mold forged by fears of change and a loss of privilege.

Unfortunately, our sacrifices to conformity rarely guarantee the privilege or protection we were promised. Lesbians, gay men, and bisexuals who have tried to pass know that. Heterosexuals who have been perceived to be gay know that. Those of us with a vision of tomorrow that goes beyond tolerance to a genuine celebration of humanity's diversity have innumerable fronts to fight on. Homophobia is one of them.

But how will this front be won? With a lot of help, and not easily. Challenges to homophobia and the rigidity of gender roles must go beyond the visible lesbian and gay movement. Lesbians, gay men, and bisexuals alone cannot defuse the power of stigmatization and the license it gives to frighten, wound, or kill. Literally millions of us are needed on this front, straight and gay alike. We invite any heterosexual unwilling to live with the damage that "real men" or "real women" messages wreak on them, on their children, and on lesbians, gay men, and bisexuals to join us. We ask that you

30

not let queer jokes go unchallenged at work, at home, in the media, or anywhere. We ask that you foster in your children a genuine respect for themselves and their right to be who and what they wish to be, regardless of their gender. We ask that you embrace your daughter's desire to swing a bat or be a carpenter, that you nurture your son's efforts to express affection and sentiment. We ask that you teach your children how painful and destructive words like *faggot* or *bulldyke* are. We ask that you invite your lesbian, gay, and bisexual friends and relatives into the routine of your lives without demanding silence or discretion from them. We invite you to study our history, read the literature written by our people, patronize our businesses, come into our homes and neighborhoods. We ask that you give us your vote when we need it to protect our privacy or to elect open lesbians, gay men, and bisexuals to office. We ask that you stand with us in public demonstrations to demand our right to live as free people, without fear. We ask that you respect our dignity by acting to end the poison of homophobia.

Until individuals are free to choose their roles and be bound only by the limits of their own imagination, *faggot, dyke,* and *pervert* will continue to be playground words and adult weapons that hurt and limit far many more people than their intended victims. Whether we like it or not, the romance of virile men and dainty women, of Mother, Father, Dick, Jane, Sally, and Spot is doomed to extinction and dangerous in a world that can no longer meet the expectations conjured by history. There is much to be won and so little to lose in the realization of a world where the dignity of each person is worthy of celebration and protection. The struggle to end homophobia can and must be won, for all our sakes. Personhood is imminent.

ENGAGING THE TEXT

1. Do you think violent events like the ones described above are fairly common or quite rare? How aware of this problem are people in your community? How much attention have you seen paid to gay-bashing in the newspapers, on TV, in books or films, or in everyday conversation?

2. Vázquez waits a while to disclose that "Brian" and "Mickey" were actually straight men, but she *does* disclose this fact. Why does she wait? Why does she disclose it? Does the issue of antigay violence change in any way when we recognize that sometimes its victims are heterosexual?

3. Vázquez cites "gender betrayal" as a possible cause of antigay violence. Explain gender betrayal in your own words; discuss how it works and how well it explains the violence described in the narratives Vázquez recounts.

4. According to Vázquez, Suzanne Pharr links homophobia to misogyny, the hatred of women: the "lesbian" label, she says, can be used to threaten all women. Review and discuss this argument; then discuss how well it can be applied to men, as Vázquez suggests it might be.

5. Besides the threat of physical violence, how does homophobia place us *all* "at risk," according to Vázquez?

EXPLORING CONNECTIONS

6. To what extent does Vázquez's concept of "gender betrayal" (para. 16) explain the attitudes and behavior encountered by Kathleen Boatwright (p. 498)?

7. Read or review the essay by Joshua Gamson (p. 91). Do you think that the representations of gay, lesbian, bisexual, and transgendered people on daytime talk shows are likely to reduce, increase, or have no effect on the level of antigay violence in the United States? Explain your reasoning.

8. Vázquez suggests that we are imprisoned by "enforced heterosexism and the pressure to conform to aggressive masculine and passive feminine roles" (para. 27). How might advertising images contribute to this problem, according to the analyses of Jean Kilbourne (p. 455) and Michael A. Messner (p. 477)? What evidence, if any, do you find of ads working against conventional gender identities?

EXTENDING THE CRITICAL CONTEXT

9. Vázquez writes that "the institutional and ideological reinforcements of homophobia are myriad and deeply woven into our culture" (para. 15). Over a period of days, keep track of all references to gays, lesbians, or homosexuality in casual conversations, news reports, TV programs, and other media. To what extent do you agree with Vázquez that homophobia is deeply ingrained in our culture?

10. San Francisco, the city in which some of the incidents described took place, is known as one of the most tolerant in the United States. Research your own community's history of assaults on gay and lesbian people. You might begin by talking to gay and lesbian organizations; police or public health departments may also have pertinent information. Report to the class or write a formal paper presenting your findings.

11. Near the end of her essay, Vázquez lists a variety of ways that individuals can combat homophobia (para. 30). Write a journal entry assessing how easy or how difficult it would be for you to follow each of her suggestions, and why.

The Bridge Builder:
Kathleen Boatwright

ERIC MARCUS

> *Conservative Christian, mother of four, lesbian activist—Kathleen Boatwright cheerfully defies categories and stereotypes. "The Bridge Builder" recounts the political and spiritual journey that begins for Boatwright when she discovers her sexual orientation and makes the courageous decision to be the person God created her to be. This selection originally appeared in* Making History: The Struggle for Gay and Lesbian Equal Rights 1945–1990 (1992), *a collection of oral histories edited by Eric Marcus. A former associate producer for* CBS This Morning *and* Good Morning America, *Marcus (b. 1958) has written many books on gay and lesbian issues, including* Together Forever: Gay and Lesbian Marriage (1998) *and* What If Someone I Know Is Gay? Answers to Questions About Gay and Lesbian People (2000). *He has also coauthored two autobiographies,* Breaking the Surface (1995) *with Olympic diving champion Greg Louganis, and* Ice Breaker (1997) *with figure skater Rudy Galindo.*

> *Invariably wearing a sensible Sears dress or skirt and jacket, Kathleen Boatwright doesn't look the part of a social activist, as she describes herself. But as vice president of the Western Region of Integrity, the gay and lesbian Episcopal ministry, Kathleen uses her conventional appearance, her status as a mother of four, her Christian roots, her knowledge of the scriptures, and her disarming personal warmth to wage a gentle battle for reform in the church she loves—and to change the hearts and minds of individuals within the church. According to Kathleen, "I see myself uniquely gifted to show people what we do to each other in ignorance."*

> *Kathleen Boatwright's very difficult and painful journey from fundamentalist Christian, director of the children's choir at her local church, and pillar of her community to Episcopal lesbian activist began one day in August, 1984, when Jean, a veterinary student at Oregon State University, walked through the door of Kathleen's church in Corvallis, Oregon.*

The first time I met Jean, she was having a nice conversation with my fifteen-year-old daughter at our church. I was very impressed by the mature way in which she spoke to my daughter. Then, during the service, I sat in the front row and watched Jean sing. I was so enamored by her presence that she stuck in my mind. But then she left town and was gone until January the following year.

Come January, I was sitting in church and I looked across the room, and there was Jean, carrying her guitar, walking down the aisle with such determination. I had this incredible lump in my throat, and I said to myself, *Jean's back.* After the service, and despite my difficulty talking to new people, I just had to ask Jean where she had been. I had to talk to her.

I found out that she was back in Corvallis for five months to finish her   5
degree. She didn't have a place to live. So I said to her, "Don't worry, my parents have always wanted to take in a college student. You're redheaded like Dad. They'll love it!" I went and dragged my mother away from where she was talking and I said, "You remember Jean, she's looking for a place to stay. Why don't you and Dad take her in and board her?"

From early on my parents encouraged the friendship because they saw how much Jean meant to me. Meeting her brought me to life in a way they hadn't seen before. They knew that I used to cry for hours on end when I was a child because no girls liked me at school. My mother would come in and rub my leg or pat my hand. I was extremely intelligent and bright, but I had low self-esteem because I wasn't able to find friendship. So my parents encouraged Jean to invite me to lunch or to take me for a drive or go horseback riding. They felt that her friendship was really wonderful for me. They were glad I was happy. For a while.

My husband didn't pay much attention—at first. He was a state police-man and had always been nonparticipatory, both as a parent and a spouse.

After four months of being friends, of having this wonderful platonic relationship, Jean had to go away for a month for her externship. While she was away she met a fundamentalist couple. Well, Jean sent me a postcard and said, "Something's going on. I'm playing with fire. I can't handle it. I've got to talk to you." My heart wrenched. What was going on?

When we were finally able to meet and talk, Jean explained to me how she and this fundamentalist woman started sharing in an intimate way. My response was to put my arm through hers and say, "Don't worry. We'll get it fixed." Jean couldn't be homosexual because it was wrong. Besides, if she was homosexual, then she would be leaving my life. And I think on a deeper level, I didn't want Jean exploring these things with anyone but me.

After her externship, Jean wanted to be more sensual with me. Her at-   10
titude was, "Now I'm going to show *you*." She said, "I'll give you a back rub some night." So one night—after Bible study, no less—she was over at my house and said, "Why don't you lay down on the blanket on the floor and take off your blouse and bra and I'll rub your back?" And I was like, "Okaaay!" My husband was working all night, and this just seemed like a great setup. So this nice little Christian lady rubbed my back, and I said to myself, *Gee, this is it!*

All the little pieces, all the little feelings came together. Even com-ments my mother made to me over the years began to make sense. She'd say things like, "don't cut your hair too short." "You can't wear tailored clothes." It was then that I also realized that the neighbors I had grown up with were a lesbian couple, even though I had never thought about that before. I recalled the feeling of walking through the Waldenbooks bookstore, looking at *The Joy of Lesbian Sex* and longing for that kind of intimacy. It all came upon me at that moment, and I felt a real willingness to release myself to this person in a way I had never done before. Then the phone rang. It was my son from Bible college. I thought, *Oh, God, saved by the bell! I don't know where this would have gone.*

By the end of the month, Jean was graduating, taking her national boards, and trying to figure out what to do about her feelings toward me and what to do about the fundamentalist woman. It was Pentecostal hysteria.

Now don't forget, at this time I still had a husband and four kids. I had a nineteen-year-old son at a conservative Bible college. I had a sixteen-year-old daughter in the evangelical Christian high school, of which I was a board member. Two children were in parochial day school. My father was the worship leader at church. And I was still very bound to my parents for emotional support. I was the favorite child. And my grandparents lived in town.

Well, shit, I was in way over my head. I was really painted into a corner because there wasn't a single place I could turn for even questioning. So I started looking to some Christian sources. Some of the advice was so incredible, like, "If you feel homosexual tendencies, you can't have the person you have those feelings for over to your house in the evening." "You can never let a member of the same sex sit on your bed while you're chatting." "Meet only in a public place." I thought this advice was ridiculous, but I also thought it was my only option because my spiritual nature was more important than my physical nature. Intellectually and emotionally, I was so hungry and so turned on that I didn't know what to do with my feelings.

At this point, people pull the trigger, turn to the bottle, take drugs, leave town. But I didn't do any of those things because I was madly in love. If I had pulled the trigger, I wouldn't have been able to express the part of me I had discovered. I had found someone, someone who shared the same sort of values I had.

Everything reached a crisis point. I acknowledged to myself and to Jean that I was a lesbian and that I loved her. By this time we had already been sexually active. My husband began to get suspicious that something was going on, and he and I went into counseling. Jean was leaving for a job in Colorado and told me that I couldn't go with her because she was a responsible woman and didn't want to destroy my family. And I still hadn't yet found the spiritual guidance that I needed.

I had to get away and do some soul-searching. I needed to figure out if there was any Christian support somewhere that said I could reconcile my love for Jean and my love for my faith. I didn't feel I could build a life of love if I rejected my faith. So I packed my bags and told my parents that I was leaving to go to stay with my great-aunt in Los Angeles for ten days. I told my husband, "I am going to get away and I'm going to think about a bunch of issues, and then I'm coming back."

For the first time in my entire life, at the age of thirty-six, I was by myself with my own agenda. I had left my husband, my children, my parents, my support structures; got in a car; and started driving to West Hollywood, where I knew there was a lesbian mayor and a gay community. So surely, I thought, there had to be a spiritual gay community.

In West Hollywood I found Evangelicals Together. It's not a church, just a storefront ministry to the gay community for people coming out of an evangelical Christian background. It's led by a former American Baptist minister who talked my language. He said to me, "In order to deal with your dilemma, you have to take a step back from your relationship with Jean. Lay her aside and ask yourself, *Who did God create me to be?*"

Through our sharing, and by looking from a different perspective at the   20 gospel and what Jesus had to say, I could embrace the theology that said, "God knew me before I was born. He accepted me as I was made to be, uniquely and wholly." Ultimately, in an obedience to God, you answer that call to be all that He has created you to be. I felt firmly and wholly that what I had experienced with Jean was no demonic possession, was not Satan tempting me with sins of lust, but an intimacy and a love that was beautiful and was God given. So now I had to figure out how to deal with it.

When you're my age, you're either going to go back to the way it's always been—go for the security you've always known—or take a chance. I felt that for the love I felt for Jean I was willing to risk all. Of course, having Jean there, I was hedging my bet a bit. I was jumping off a cliff, but I was holding somebody's hand.

Jean flew down a few days later to join me in Los Angeles. She agreed to commit to me and I to her. The first Sunday after we affirmed our relationship, we worshiped at All Saints' Episcopal Church in Pasadena because I was told that the Episcopals had the framework of faith I loved, as well as an ability to use reason in light of tradition and scripture.

It was God answering the cry of my heart to send me to that worshiping place. Jean and I had never been to an Episcopal church before. We went into this beautiful place with the largest Episcopal congregation west of the Mississippi River. We sat in the fourth row. It was just this incredible Gothic wonderful place. It was All Saints' Day at All Saints' Church. They played the Mozart Requiem with a full choir and a chamber ensemble, and a female celebrant sang the liturgy. We held hands and wept and wept. We could go forward because in the Anglican tradition, the Eucharist is open for everyone. God extends himself. There are no outcasts in the Episcopal church.

When I got back to town, I met with my husband at a counselor's office. I said, "Yes, you're right. I am gay and I'm going to ask for a divorce. I'm going to take this stand. I want to meet with my older children and my parents to talk about the decisions I've made." I felt at least I had a right to make my own decisions. I went to pick up my two youngest girls at my father's house. I went to open the door and I heard a flurry of activity, and the children saw me. "Oh, Mommy's home! Mommy's home!" And my dad stepped out on the front porch and pushed the children away and slammed the door. He took me forcibly by the arm and led me down the stairs and said, "You're never seeing your children again without a court order! Just go shack up with your girlfriend!" And he forced me down to the street.

It took going to court to see my two youngest children. They hadn't   25
seen me for two weeks. They asked, "Mommy, Mommy, what's wrong?" I leaned over and whispered in their ears, "Mommy loves you." My husband wanted to know, "What are you telling the children?" I had only a minute with them, then went downstairs, and my husband told me that he wanted me to come back, that he would be my brother, not my husband.

I tell you, my whole world came down upon my ears. I wasn't allowed to see my children. I was denied access to my residence. The church had an open prayer meeting disclosing my relationship with Jean. They tried to get Jean fired from her job. And when that didn't work, they called Jean's parents, who then tried to have her committed or have me arrested. My family physically disinherited me and emotionally cut me off. My older daughter, upon the advice of her counselor-pastor, shook my hand and said, "Thank you for being my biological mother. I never want to have anything to do with you again." After that, whenever she saw me in town, she hid from me. I saw her lay flat on the asphalt in the grocery store parking lot so I wouldn't see her. People I'd known all my life avoided me like I had the plague. I was surprised that Jean didn't just say, "Hey, lady, I'm out of here!"

Fortunately, I wasn't entirely without support. I went to Parents and Friends of Lesbians and Gays and I met some wonderful loving, Christian, supportive parents and gay children who said, "You're not sick. You're not weird. Everybody's hysterical." They offered any kind of assistance possible. Through their emotional support, I felt like it was possible to survive the crush.

Living in a small rural county in Oregon, I didn't know anything about women's rights, let alone gay rights. So it's not surprising that I bought into the lie that children of lesbians or gays are better off living with the custodial heterosexual parent. I believed my husband could provide a sense of normality that I could not. So I signed away my custodial rights and became a secondary parent. After being the primary-care parent for twenty devoted years, the judge only let me see the children two days a week.

By then I'd had enough. So I packed one suitcase and a few things in grocery sacks and left my family and children behind. Jean and I just rode quietly out of town in the sunset to her job in Denver, Colorado.

As you drive into Denver, you go over this big hill about fifteen miles   30
from town. We stopped at a phone booth and called the local Parents

FLAG president to ask if there was a supportive Episcopal parish in town. She said, "Yes, go to this place, look up this person." It was getting to be evening. It was clear, and we were going over the mountain. It was a whole new adventure. It was real closure to my past and a real opening toward my future. Still, the guiding force in my life was, "The church has the answers."

Jean and I called the church and found out when services were and asked if they had an Integrity chapter. Integrity is the Episcopal ministry to the gay and lesbian community. There was one, so two nights later we walked into our first Integrity meeting. There were twelve attractive men in their thirties and the rector. They were shocked to see two women because it's unusual for women to be in Integrity. The only thing dirtier than being a lesbian in a Christian community is being a Christian in the lesbian community because it brings in so many other issues besides sexual orientation, like women's issues and patriarchy and all that stuff.

Denver Integrity was an affirming congregation. We were out as a couple. We were healed of so many things through the unconditional love and acceptance of this parish of eighty people. The rector there encouraged me to become involved. Out of his own pocket he sent me to the first regional convention I went to, in 1987 in San Francisco. Now, I'm vice president of the Western Region for Integrity, and I'm on the national board of directors, I'm one of only maybe 125 women in Integrity's membership of about 1,500.

Integrity gives me a forum for the things I want to say, both as a lesbian woman and as a committed Christian. And because of my background and experience, I can speak to the church I love on a variety of issues that others cannot. I can say, "I call you into accountability. You are bastardizing children raised in nontraditional households. You're not affirming the people that love and guide them. You say you welcome us, but on the other hand you don't affirm us. You don't give us rites of passage and ritual and celebration like you do for heterosexual families."

The church needs to change. What we're asking for are equal *rites*. We're asking the church to bless same-sex unions. I'm asking for canonical changes that affirm my wholeness as a child of Christ who is at the same time in a loving committed relationship with a woman. We're also challenging the church to make statements asking the government to legitimize our relationships and give us the same sorts of tax breaks, pension benefits, et cetera. But most importantly, we need the church to get off the dime and start affirming gay and lesbian children's lives. I never want a girl to go through what I went through. I want to spare everybody right up front.

To get my point across when I go out and talk to groups as a representative of Integrity, I personalize the issue. I personalize my political activism by speaking to people as a person, as Kathleen Boatwright. People don't need to hear dogma or doctrine or facts or theology. They need to meet people.

Here's a great example. For the first time, the women of Integrity got seated at Triennial, which is this gigantic group of very traditional women who have a convention every three years. It used to be that while the men were making the decisions, the women held their own convention. With women's issues having changed so dramatically in the Episcopal church, that's no longer true. Now that women are allowed to serve in the House of Deputies and can be ordained into the priesthood, we've become full team members in the canonical process.

Triennial was made for me. Everybody wears their Sears Roebuck dress. Everybody is a mom. Everybody lived like I had lived for twenty years. I know how to network and how to deal with those women. But I also have a new truth to tell them that will have an impact on their lives in very special ways. Gays and lesbians are 10 percent of the population. Everybody is personally affected by that issue, including these women at Triennial.

During the convention, I attended a seminar given by conservative Episcopals who said gays and lesbians have confused gender identity. Later, we had an open meeting in which we talked about human sexuality. But no one talked about sexuality. Instead, we only talked about information on biological reproduction. After about forty minutes of hearing these women drone on, I stood up in my Sears Roebuck dress and said, "OK ladies, put on your seat belts because you're going to take a trip into reality. You won't want to hear it, but I need to say it because you need to know what people's lives are really like."

I talked to them about my journey. I talked to them about the misnomers, about "confused gender identity." I was wearing this circle skirt and I said, "As you can see from my appearance," and I curtsied, "I do not have a 'confused gender identity.'" Everybody who had been really stiff started laughing—and they started listening. The key is that I take risks. I risk being vulnerable. I risk sharing the secrets of my heart. We already know what the straight people feel in their hearts. But no one talks about how the lesbian or gay person feels in his or her heart.

For the next hour and a half, people talked about where they really live. 40 They talked about their pregnant teenagers or the suicide attempts in their families. All those gut-level issues. But you have to have someone lead you to that. That's me—because I'm safe. I've also learned that instead of having all the answers, that God calls me to listen to people's pain, and not to judge it.

This one woman told me that she had been driving by her daughter's house for eight years and that her husband had never let her stop because her daughter was a lesbian. "But," she said, "I'm going to go home and I'm going to see her. My daughter's name is also Kathleen." Then she started to cry. She had never even told the women from her church about what had happened to her daughter. It's like the living dead for many Christian families. They just have a child who is lost prematurely in so many senses of the word.

Inevitably, everywhere I go I hear about parents who have made ulti-matums. This one mother said, "I've never told anybody, but I said to my son, 'I wish you were dead.' And by forcing him into the closet, I fulfilled that prophecy. Three years later, he was dead." Then there was a woman who said to me, "Kathleen, I'm questioning my sexuality at seventy. Could you send me some information?"

I think in my heart that I represent the hidden majority of lesbian women because many, many are married or have been married, have chil-dren, and have too much to risk—like I've risked and lost—to come out. And those women who are out, who are much more political and aggressive, have seen enough successes happen, enough bridges built by my approach, that they're beginning to respect the fact that I can go through doors they never can.

The first time I spoke publicly to the leadership of the women of the church, I spoke along with another lesbian. She was politically correct and a strong feminist. *Feminist* was always a dirty word for me, so I've had to overcome a lot of my own bias. I said to her, "Please don't speak about poli-tics. Don't browbeat these people. Stand up and say that you're a doctor, that you've never been in a committed relationship, that you're a feminist. Because I want to stand up and say, 'I've been a Blue Bird leader.' What that will say is that we represent the gamut of human experience, just like the heterosexual community. It's just our ability to develop intimate relationships with the same sex that makes us different."

People don't have to identify with my ideology. They identify with my person, and then the questions come from them. We don't have to tell them. They start asking us. People say to me, "What do you call your partner?" "You don't have any medical insurance?" To me that's the best sort of teaching process: answering questions rather than giving information.

My husband remarried; he married the baby-sitter. At Easter of 1987, I got a call informing me that he had removed my ten-year-old daughter from his house, accusing her of using "inappropriate touch" with his new stepsons. He wanted to unload the difficult child. Then he used that child as a weapon to try and deny me visitation for the younger one. The end result was that I had one child and he had one child. I filed suit against him without any hope or prayer of winning back custody of my other child.

I went to a lesbian minister to ask her about finding a lawyer to handle my case, and she said to me, "The best attorney in this town is Hal Harding, but he's your husband's attorney. Maybe that will prove to be a blessing." So I had to find another attorney.

As part of the custody proceedings, Jean and I eventually met with my husband's attorney. He took depositions and asked Jean and me really heartfelt questions. Then he advised his client—my ex-husband—to go ahead and have a psychological evaluation. The court had not ordered it and, in fact, would not order it because there was no precedent in that county. But my former husband agreed to go to the psychologist of his choice. That psychologist, a woman, took the time and energy to interview every person involved and recommended to the court that Jean and I become custodial parents. We now have custody of both children, sole custody. It was indeed a blessing.

We just added Jean's ninety-one-year-old grandmother to our family. So we are all-American lesbians living here in Greenacres, Washington. We are Miss and Mrs. America living together. The thing that we need in our life now that our faith doesn't give us is a community of supportive women. We have yet to find that place.

Not long ago, I went to the National Organization for Women lesbian rights agenda meeting and gave a workshop on spirituality for women, from the Christian perspective. And I took a deep breath in my Betty Crocker suit—if I ever write a book it's going to be *The Radicalization of Betty Crocker*—and thought, *I wonder what the Assemblies of God girls would say now? From their perspective, I'm walking into the total pit of hell, and I'm bringing the very gift that they should be giving.* Who would have believed it?

ENGAGING THE TEXT

1. What family, religious, and cultural bonds initially restrained Boatwright from acknowledging her sexuality? What were her options? How do you think she should have reacted when she realized that she was attracted to Jean? Why?

2. In what different ways does Boatwright's emerging lesbian identity change her and her life? What price does she pay?

3. How do Boatwright's attitudes toward the church develop during her story? How does her self-image change?

4. How do you interpret the title of this oral history? In what different senses is Boatwright a "bridge builder"?

5. From the information available about her past, write a brief character sketch of Boatwright, tracing the development of her personality from childhood through the occasion of this oral history.

EXPLORING CONNECTIONS

6. Write an imaginary conversation between Boatwright and Paula Gunn Allen (p. 443) about whether women continue to be oppressed in American society and about the role of religion in liberating or subordinating women.

7. To what extent does Boatwright's experience support Carmen Vázquez's (p. 489) assertion that "the straitjacket of gender roles suffocates many lesbians, gay men, and bisexuals, forcing them into closets without an exit and threatening our very existence when we tear the closet open" (para. 20)? What resources finally enable Boatwright to survive and thrive despite the open hostility of her family and community?

8. What flaws of logic does the cartoon on page 505 reveal in the speaker's antigay position? Why does the cartoonist depict both figures as relatively featureless?

EXTENDING THE CRITICAL CONTEXT

9. Browse the press releases and news postings about religion and lesbian/gay issues on one or more of the following Web sites:

> Parents and Friends of Lesbians and Gays (www.pflag.org)
>
> Integrity (www.integrityusa.org)
>
> Interfaith Working Group (www.iwgonline.org)
>
> Universal Fellowship of Metropolitan Community Churches
> (www.ufmcc.com)

Summarize your findings about how various religious groups are responding to questions about gay marriage, gay clergy, and violence against lesbians and gay men.

Girls Have All the Power:
What's Troubling Troubled Boys

SUSAN FALUDI

Are American men in crisis? In a culture that equates manhood with power and dominance, men in the last fifty years have had to contend with cultural forces—war, recession, corporate restructuring, suburban isola-tion, new technology, consumerism, and media hype—that seem hell-bent on demonstrating that they aren't in control of their own lives. Described as "the story of a feminist's travels through a postwar male realm," Susan Faludi's Stiffed: The Betrayal of the American Man *(1999) traces the lives of these men as they struggle to come to terms with the limits of their power. In this passage from the book, Faludi reports from "ground zero of the American masculinity crisis," the suburban home of the Spur Posse, a group of high school boys whose competitive sex games briefly attracted the atten-tion of the police and the media.* Stiffed *is in a sense a companion volume to her influential book* Backlash: The Undeclared War Against American Women *(1991). A Pulitzer Prize–winning journalist, Faludi (b. 1959) is a contributing editor for* Newsweek: *she has also written for the* Wall Street Journal, *the* New York Times, The Nation, Esquire, *and* The New Yorker.

We Could've Been Big

It was long past lunchtime on a weekday in early October, but Kris Belman had been awake for only a couple of hours. The nineteen-year-old with the dazed, shaggy surfer looks had risen, as was his custom, at noon. He had nowhere in particular to go. He had graduated from high school the pre-vious spring—the spring of 1993—though he wouldn't get his diploma until he paid a $44 fine for ripping his football jersey. "I'm only paying it if I get my jersey back," he said. He hadn't been able to find a job, except for "picking up scraps for this guy who hangs dry wall," and that only lasted three days. In Lakewood, a bedroom community built to house tens of thousands of McDonnell Douglas workers, and later workers at aerospace firms like Rock-well (now closed) and nearby Northrop and Hughes (where thousands were being laid off), not to speak of all the companies that once supplied and ser-viced them, there was little work left to justify getting out of bed.[1]

He was home alone; his father, a salesman for an aerospace vendor whose prime contractor was McDonnell Douglas, was out and his mother

[1]Patt Morrison, "Farewell to Arms," *Los Angeles Times*, Dec. 5, 1993, p. A1; James F. Peltz, "As Defense Cuts Deepen, Southern California's Aerospace Industry Is Down but Not Out," *Los Angeles Times*, Sept. 26, 1993, p. D1. [All notes are the author's, except 10 and 12.]

had moved out after his parents' separation earlier that year. His older brother was off wandering, probably in search of gambling "action." Kris Belman stepped into a pair of baggy shorts and ventured forth into the flat grid of stucco-over-chicken-wire pillbox houses and browning lawns, looking for signs of life. The sidewalks were empty, shades drawn against the hard, biscuit sun that baked this suburb southeast of Los Angeles. The nearly identical houses, their foundations only a foot deep, dug by a bucket excavator in a mere fifteen minutes, had been thrown up in a hurry to create this virtually all-white town in the early 1950s—as many as a hundred a day, 17,500 homes in under three years, the biggest housing project America had ever seen. On the day the homes went on the market in April 1950, *Time* reported thirty thousand people "stampeded" to lay their claim. Only a few furnished models had been built, but that didn't stop more than six hundred customers that week from buying one of the eight- to nine-thousand-dollar units with automatic garbage disposals, stainless-steel kitchens, and picture windows. "The City as New as Tomorrow" was the development's motto. It was a slogan that the city's founders evidently approached with some uneasiness: as Lakewood author and city official D. J. Waldie observed in *Holy Land,* his poetic, ambivalent paean to his hometown, one of the town's first ordinances declared all forms of fortune-telling illegal.[2]

Kris Belman gravitated, as did much of Lakewood's young male populace, toward the parks. As a community, Lakewood had been designed to serve the aerospace sons. A network of small parks was built so that a baseball diamond and football field would be within reach of every boy—and they could walk to them on special service roads shielded from traffic. Park sports leagues were inaugurated in the late 1950s.[3]

The aerospace fathers were at a loss to explain to their sons what they did at work, much less to pass down a "mastery" of such bureaucratic duties. The park was where father-coaches transmitted their knowledge to son-players, and where the sons got the idea that such knowledge would be useful to them on the road past childhood. By the empty bleachers, Kris ran into Jimmy Rafkin and Shad Blackman, buddies from high school; Jimmy was aimlessly swinging a strip of discarded plywood as if at an invisible ball. Kris and Jimmy had played together on the football team. Shad had only made the badminton squad. Kris said he wasn't doing anything and they said they weren't doing anything either, and after a while they decided they might as well do nothing together at the Belman house. The three trooped down the service road and up the drive, all in identical plaid shorts with elastic waistbands —"for easy access," as Shad Blackman liked to say.

[2]D. J. Waldie, *Holy Land* (New York: W. W. Norton, 1996), pp. 7, 37, 41, 62, 158; "Birth of a City," *Time,* April 17, 1950, p. 99. See also Joan Didion, "Trouble in Lakewood," *The New Yorker,* July 26, 1993, p. 46.
[3]Waldie, *Holy Land,* pp. 49, 176.

Kris headed like a homing pigeon for the television, which he liked to   5
have tuned at all times to the white noise of MTV. Jimmy had a shoebox
under his arm. He now placed it lovingly on the couch and opened the lid
with a flourish. "Check this out, dude," Shad said to Kris in a rare state of
enthusiasm. "Reeboks. Jimmy got 'em for thirty-eight bucks instead of
forty-five, because the box was marked wrong." They were all pleased with
this minor scam and the story of the mislabeled box had to be repeated several times before it was wrung dry of sweet triumph. Then they were ready
for lunch. And lucky for them, since only Jimmy had any money from
"working occasionally" at a ship-repair company where his dad was a supervisor, I was buying. Chili's, a fast-food Mexican franchise by the Lakewood
mall, was their eatery of choice.

They tumbled into the vinyl banquette, poking and elbowing each
other and talking loudly about "whipping out our fake IDs," and how "I may
be nineteen but this afternoon I'm twenty-three." An oblivious and chirpy-
voiced waitress jotted down their drink orders without comment: three
strawberry margaritas.

"She wants me, dude, I can tell," Shad said as the waitress disappeared
to get their drinks. "I could hit on her, easy."

Kris leaned toward me. "See, that's what I mean. We can have any girl
we want. Girls come daily to my friends; we don't have to *force* 'em. There's
a gang of fish in the sea." He shot me a sly look. "There's one sitting right
next to me."

"What I don't understand is why girls have so much say, you know?"
Shad put in. "They can lie, you know, and just get anybody in trouble. Like
you," he said, jabbing a butter knife in my direction. "Right now anything
could happen and you could get us in trouble."

"How exactly?" I said.   10

"Well, this is just 'for instance,' right? Say, like we're driving and just
fooling around or whatever, and say you hated the way we acted or whatever, say you totally despised us. You could go back and publish something
like 'They tried to hit on me, blah, blah, blah.' Your say is bigger than ours.
You know what I'm saying?"

Their burritos arrived and they dived in like they hadn't eaten in days.
"Could we get some more of this cheese and salsa?" Shad asked plaintively.
"Or do they charge you extra?" For all their swagger, the boys seemed a bit
shaky on the basics of restaurant dining.

Jimmy picked up Shad's point. "Like Kris went out with this girl last
night. She could say, 'Oh, he raped me,' or whatever, and no questions
asked, automatically —"

"Automatically," Shad jumped in, "they'll throw you in jail just to find
out if you did it. Girls can say whatever they want and it's believed. I just
don't understand why they have so much pull, you know?"

Kris chimed in: "Girls have the power to have sex with somebody if   15
they want to. They have the power. If you hear a girl scream, are you going

to come running? Yep. But if you hear a guy scream, who comes running? Nobody."

Shad fished a maraschino cherry from Jimmy's drained glass. He chewed on the stem, still stewing about the unjust fate of his generation. "My dad did the same thing when he was young, a couple girls, one-night stands. It was no big deal. And now it's—after the Tyson thing, you know, it's been getting worse."

"Wait a second," Kris cut in. "What Tyson did, that's rape, dude. That's what I consider it. But a girl having sex with up to seven guys a night, daily, and then she turns around and —"

Was he talking about an actual girl? I ask.

"I'm talking about this girl who gave it up with seven people a night, I heard," Kris said. "And with her dad right there in the other room."

"I think they just were out to get us," Jimmy said.   20

"I'm glad to see girls get more authority in the world," Shad said magnanimously. "But it's like they already got enough authority when it comes to, you know ..." He made a thrusting motion with his butter knife. "Girls are like, I dunno, they're going to start getting up their courage in a couple years and going head to head with the guys. Fighting 'em and shit. And girls are going to have to get knocked out. That's how it's going to be, dude."

Jimmy giggled. Shad's remarks had jogged a memory. "It's funny. This girl, she got in a fight with her boyfriend. And this guy we know, he came by and started beating up her boyfriend. And then she came and started hitting *him* and everything. So he punched her."

"Punched her in the mouth," Shad interjected.

"So what happened?" I asked.

"Nothing for publication," Jimmy said.   25

Shad jumped back in. "See? There, right there, you can say, 'Oh, they hit girls.' That's your word over our word. And your word wins every time."

We drove back to the Belmans', my car radio blasting as loud as the boys could crank it. "Hey dude, did you taste how she put more alcohol in the second round of margaritas?" Shad said. "That girl definitely liked us. We shoulda hit on her." Kris jerked his thumb out the window at a passing young woman. "There's that girl who hates me."

From the backseat, Shad made obscene grunting noises.

"She called the cops on me and shit," Kris said.

"See," Shad said, leaning over the seat and tapping me insistently on   30
the shoulder. "See what I mean? Girls have all the power."

For several years in the mid-1990s the Belman boys and their teenage friends, a.k.a. the Spur Posse, had given form to America's suspicion that its male culture was misogynistic and violent, and that its boys were running amok. Their reign in the spotlight began on March 18, 1993, when the police showed up at Lakewood High School and arrested eight Spur Posse members (and one more boy over the weekend) on suspicion of nearly twenty counts of sexual crimes, ranging from rape to unlawful sexual intercourse to lewd conduct with a ten-year-old girl. In the end, the prosecutor's office concluded that the sex was consensual and all but one count were dropped. One boy spent less than a year in a juvenile rehabilitation center on the lewd conduct charge; the other eight Spurs were released after only a week.[4] The only serious jail time was served by Kris Belman's older brother, Dana, the founder of the Spurs, but that wasn't for sexual assault. He was sentenced to ten years in state prison on thirteen burglary and fraud convictions, most notably for stealing a young woman's credit card and racking up charges during a gambling binge in the Dunes Hotel in Las Vegas.[5] Nonetheless, the subsequent strutting and bragging of the boys, as they cut as comprehensive a swath through the TV talk shows as they had through their high-school yearbook, earned their hometown the moniker of "Rapewood."[6] They mugged on the front page of the *New York Times;* they posed everywhere from *Newsweek* to *Sassy* to *Penthouse;* and for a while in the spring of 1993, it was difficult to flip the channels without running into one Spur or another chatting up a television personality. The local paper, the *Long Beach Press-Telegram,* ran boxed announcements listing their upcoming television spots, under such headlines as POSSE PREMIERE and THE SPUR POSSE ON TV.[7] Most of the Spurs interviewed on the talk shows weren't the ones arrested, but it didn't seem to matter, as long as they were willing to elaborate on (or embellish) their sexual exploits. And they were.

Tirelessly they repeated the details of a Spur Posse "game" that had riveted the media. It was a sex-for-points intramural contest in which each time you had sex with a girl, which they called "hooking up," you racked up a point. You had to achieve penetration and you could only get one point per girl. "It doesn't count if you have, like, sex with a girl, like one hundred and fifty times, two hundred—that's only *one* point," as the Spurs' Kevin Howard took pains to clarify on *The Jenny Jones Show.*"[8] When your points added up to the corresponding number on some sports star's jersey, you could then claim that player's name as your own, and the other Spurs would address you as, say, Dave Robinson of the San Antonio Spurs—the basketball player who had unwittingly inspired the posse's name. (Dana Belman was a Robinson fan, and when the Spurs signed Robinson, Belman and his

---

[4]David Ferrell, "One of 9 Students to Be Charged in Campus Sex Case," *Los Angeles Times,* March 23, 1993, p. A1; Robin Abcarian, "Spur Posse Case: The Same Old (Sad) Story," *Los Angeles Times,* April 7, 1993, p. E1.

[5]Janet Wiscombe, "Visit to a Shattered Home," *Long Beach Press-Telegram,* Feb. 3, 1994, p. 8; "Alleged Founder of Spur Posse Sentenced in Burglary," *Los Angeles Times,* Jan. 7, 1994, p. B2; Andy Rose and G. M. Bush, "Founder of Spur Posse Already Facing Numerous Charges," *Long Beach Press-Telegram,* March 21, 1993, p. A1.

[6]Amy Cunningham, "Sex in High School," *Glamour,* Sept. 1993, p. 253.

[7]"Posse Premiere," *Long Beach Press-Telegram,* April 2, 1993, p. A8; "The Spur Posse on TV," *Long Beach Press-Telegram,* April 6, 1993, p. A6.

[8]*The Jenny Jones Show,* April 7, 1993.

buddies signed up too in the only way they knew how: they went to a sporting-goods store and bought Spurs caps.) This game had only one real winner, of course, the Spur with the most points. And for four years running that was Billy Shehan, with a final score of 67....[9]

Their place in the national eye had transformed the Spurs into permanent celebrities, at least in their own minds. "You'll recognize me," Jeff Howard said as we arranged by phone to meet just before Christmas 1993. "I was on *Maury Povich.*"

When I arrived at Coco's, another of the Spurs' preferred dining establishments when someone else was picking up the bill, Howard had brought along a few of his Spur buddies—all twelve of them. The Spurs, as I was to learn, rarely traveled solo. The waitresses had to drag together four tables, and the Spurs took their places ceremonially as if attending a high-school varsity awards banquet. Only none of them were in high school anymore.

It was, in fact, almost a reunion, as Howard informed me when I first   35 walked in. He pointed out a slight boy, who at sixteen seemed barely pubescent, with scared, shadowy eyes that darted nervously around the room. He was the Spur who had been sent to the Kirby Juvenile Detention Center for lewd conduct with a ten-year-old girl. He had been released for a family visit, supposedly to the custody of relatives. But here he was, parentless in Coco's.

I passed a notebook around so the Spurs could write down their names. The nervous boy of honor perched next to me. I told him I wouldn't be identifying him because of his juvenile record, and he asked if he could go by a pseudonym of his choosing. "You could call me the Lost Boy," he said softly. I could see why. He lacked the brazen cockiness one would expect from the posse's lone decorated war hero, on leave from the juvy-hall front. "They called me 'pretty boy' at Kirby," he said in a low, flat voice. "They thought I was wimpish." He looked around furtively, then stared down at his place mat as I asked him questions. He answered passively but dutifully, in a dull monotone, describing one of his sexual encounters as if it were a story that belonged to someone else.

"She gave me oral copulation," he said bureaucratically. "Then I never saw her again." He stopped, waiting for further direction. Well, how did he happen to be in this girl's room? "I went there with two other guys," he went on in his mechanical tone, "and she sucked one of the guys' dicks and my dick."

"She's a whore," one of the boys shouted across the table.

"I heard she's been picked up for prostitution," the Lost Boy said, and then, as if that weren't outlandish enough, he added, "twice."

[9]Amy Cunningham, "Sex in High School," p. 254; Jane Gross, "Where 'Boys Will Be Boys,' and Adults Are Bewildered," *New York Times,* March 29, 1993, p. A1; Jennifer Allen, "Boys: Hanging with the Spur Posse," *Rolling Stone,* July 8–22, 1993, p. 55; "Sex for Points Scandal," *The Jane Whitney Show,* April 1, 1993.

"She was seen at parties," Jeff Howard said, then delivered the coup de   40
grâce. "She was seen drinking beer."

The Lost Boy returned to his story. "The girl was giving me oral copulation for twenty minutes. Usually, it takes me only a couple of minutes, but it
was—I guess I was feeling good, but—it wasn't..." He struggled to put a
word to the particular state of mind he had found himself in that evening. "I
was bored," he said finally. "I didn't want to sit there all night." He stopped.

So what finally happened? I asked.

"Ten minutes later, I pulled up my pants and left. I called my oldest
brother to pick me up. Dana [Belman], I mean. I call Dana 'my oldest
brother.' Another guy kept fucking her."

When I asked him about the incident with the ten-year-old girl that had
landed him in jail, he said, "If I didn't admit it, maybe nothing would've
happened to me either."

But something *did* happen, I said; he had a sexual encounter with a   45
ten-year-old.

"I didn't know how old she was. She had a body and everything. I just
seen her at parties. I didn't even know her name."

"Points" king Billy Shehan, who was the unofficial philosopher of the
Spurs, leaned across the table. "These girls are *no-names*. We've got a
name." He gestured around the table. "That's why you're talking to us. It's
all about brand names."

This seemed a strange segue from an appalling account of an appalling
sexual episode, but once the subject of developing a "name" was introduced, there was no getting off it. "We could've been big," Kris Belman
said. "If we had just got the right contacts."

"We're all into communication," Billy Shehan said.

"I want to be an actor, or a model," Jimmy Rafkin said. "I want fame   50
that way."

"I want to be a DJ at my own station," Kris Belman said. "Or a big-time
comedian. When I was little, I wanted to play sports. That was my dream.
Now, I want to move to Vegas, crack a joke at some casino and hopefully
somebody will hear me. I've seen a lot of those guys on all the shows, like
HBO—Eddie Murphy, [Andrew] Dice Clay. I just want to be up there
with the big boys. Someday I think I might."

Billy Shehan summed up the exchange. "See, brand names are very important. It's like having Guess jeans on instead of some no-name pair."

The Lost Boy sat very still next to me, soaking up the swirl of voices. He
didn't seem to mind their interrupting his story. I asked him why he'd been
lewd with a ten-year-old. "There are only so many girls," he replied. "You
had to have girls to hook up with. I had started keeping track of my points.
So, if it's three girls and three guys, and say I had sex with one, after I finish,
I'll say, 'Can we switch off?' and most of the time, the girls say yes. Sometimes they say no. And then you say, 'Can I have a phone number?' I never
forced a girl. I looked at myself highly. I looked at it like they are passing up

something great." These last remarks were delivered dully into the place mat, as if he were reading from a boilerplate script, auditioning for a character he didn't believe in.

"We tell a girl, we don't want to waste our time," he continued. "We don't want to waste time romancing."

Why have sex with girls you don't want to "waste time with" anyway,   55
girls who leave you "bored"?

He looked directly at me for the first time. "For the points," he said. "You *had* to have the points. I was developing my reputation. I was developing my *name*." It occurred to me that maybe Billy Shehan hadn't changed the subject after all.

The most fun they ever had, the Lost Boy told me, was when they would videotape themselves having sex with one of the girls. "Once, three of us were in the closet spying," he recalled. "We opened the door, and we took pictures and videos. It was funny. We could sell the video, but who would buy it?"

Billy Shehan began a story about the time he and another Spur had a porn movie playing while they took turns having sex with a girl and he began copying the moves he saw in the movie. "It felt like I was *in* the movie," he said, and that sensation was so gratifying that the next night he replayed it, this time with four Spurs in attendance. The night after that, he gathered ten Spurs—and a video camera. "We made a porn film of it," he said. "It was great."

But for all that, there was a strange affectlessness to the way he and other Spurs told their sex stories, a boredom that seemed to drop away only with the introduction of a video camera. Their sexual exploits evidently had less to do with the act itself than with being, themselves, an act.

That night, the boys would reconvene for a party at a Spur home, se-   60
lected because the parents were away. Spur parties were all the same: a blackjack game in one corner, a stereo blasting rap music (in this case, Public Enemy), and a circle of bodies collapsed around the television. But this party, like the Coco's luncheon, was a special event. They had gathered to watch themselves on *The Tonight Show*. Well, Billy Shehan conceded, they weren't really "on" the program. A few of them had managed to get passes to be in the audience for Howard Stern's appearance on the show. "We got this girl who works for KSLX to get us in.... We were yelling so hard, 'Spur Posse loves you, Howard!'" Shehan said. "I think he heard us. I know he did."

A Spur sporting a clash of logos—Spurs cap, Dodgers shirt, and Georgetown athletic shorts—sauntered up to Billy. "Hey dude, how'd you get on Jay Leno?" Billy explained. "And of course," he said, "there's the factor of our sales. It's good for marketability to have us in the audience." Advancing the Spurs "brand name" was the ultimate goal. "You gotta get your image out there. It's all about building that image on a worldwide basis."

Earlier, Kris Belman had filled me in on his fruitless efforts at Spur promotion in Hollywood. "You know Mickey Rourke, the actor? One of his roommates called us up, this guy Kizzy, I don't know his full name. And we went to visit his loft in Hollywood." (Rourke's publicist told me that while the actor does have a loft, he has no roommate named Kizzy.) "We didn't see Mickey Rourke, but I guess he told Kizzy to call us. Kizzy and some guys took us to pizza a couple of times. He took me and my two older brothers out to this club called Tatou. And he introduced us to some agents for movie deals.

"Then they decided to blow us over," Kris said of the agents and producers who had originally expressed interest in a TV movie about the Spurs. "They wanted to make us out as real bad guys, where we went to the parents' house and beat up the dad and took the daughter, that's what they wanted. We were like, no, that's not how we are." But Kris and his posse buddies quickly assented to the plotline anyway. "They were gonna pay out cash. But then all the shows, all the channels like Fox and them thought we were all *too* bad guys, rapists, and they said we don't want to make these guys rich." Kris suspected that the "female executives" were the ones who killed the project. After that, he said, Kizzy "moved out of that loft, and now we don't talk to him at all." For the first time, an emotion played across Kris Belman's face, and it was anger. "I'd like to get ahold of him, though," he said, slamming a fist on the table, "because he screwed us. He screwed us bad."

At the party that evening, I would witness several such bitter outbursts, always revolving around a media or entertainment personality who had helped advance their "name," but somehow hadn't done enough. "Maury Povich, he *lied* to us," Chris Albert shouted, kicking hard at the leg of the blackjack table. "He made it look like he was offering us a palace. Ten days in New York. Two limos. Povich is a cock-sucking bitch." Why he was so incensed he couldn't precisely say. He got his ten days, after all. In fact, eleven. He rode in a limo. But it had left him with the strong suspicion that he had been ripped off. There should have been something more, though he didn't know what.

With another hour before *The Tonight Show*, Billy Shehan went out back to smoke some dope. Lonnie Rodriguez was sitting on the stoop, idly poking a stick in the grass. They greeted each other like long-lost cellmates. Which they had been, in a way. "Lonnie and I did telemarketing together for, like, oh man, it felt like years," Billy said. They had sat in sterile cubicles in windowless rooms with nothing but a phone on a desk, dialing endless rows of numbers. "It was so stressful," said Lonnie, who had recently served six months in jail for violating probation. ("Assaults mostly," he told me when I asked why he'd been in jail, "that's what I'm known for.") He said he found incarceration at National Promotions more debilitating.

"It sucked," Billy agreed. "But you know, the first week, I was the second seller, at three hundred dollars. The second week, I was first. We'd just pitch to hook people, and we didn't care what happened after that. I would change my voice, like an act. I had ten different personalities. I was being fake with all these people. It was like, in telemarketing, even before the Spurs, we were hooking. We've been hooking for years."

Telemarketing was an important landmark in the Spurs' short history. "That's when we first started keeping track of points," Billy said. They had already been counting their rate of return on customer calls, and it seemed a natural progression to apply the same approach to their sex lives. "It's all about statistics," Billy added. As it was in the larger world they inhabited. Telemarketing and the "points system" were just two expressions of an economy in which ratings and rankings, marketing percentiles and slugging percentages, were what seemed to count most. The men who mattered were the ones who claimed the most points, whose number-one ranking in whatever category displayed a controlling dominance. As Billy Shehan told me that night, "I want to get control of the world. Well, not the world, but I want to get where they *see* me because I'm on top, where all heads turn when they say my name."

From the living room came howls of "It's on! It's on!" Billy and Lonnie leaped up and charged inside. On the carpet, the Spurs were jostling for a prime spot before the wide-screen TV, which took up much of the tiny living room. Billy and Lonnie settled in just as the show broke for commercials—Wal-Mart wishing America a very merry Christmas, followed by a promotion for an episode of a tabloid TV show on both the Menendez brothers[10] and Michael Jackson. The guys booed and moaned, barely able to contain themselves. "Get this shit off of there," one yelled. "This is our moment!"

And then, at last, Jay Leno was back, schmoozing with Howard Stern. The room went silent for the first time all evening, breaths held, eyes riveted, necks craned forward. The camera did a quick pan of the audience, nothing. Then another, and Chris Albert leaped up, thrusting his arms into the air, triumphant. "That's me! That's me! That's fucking me on the fucking *Tonight Show!*" Albert did a victory walk around the room, exchanging high fives with his compadres. Now the camera had returned to Howard Stern, and Billy Shehan nudged me. He swore he could see a glint of recognition in Stern's eyes. "See how he looked? Howard's acknowledging us."

The party dwindled after that. A few more rounds of blackjack and then Spurs began streaming out the door into the darkened grid of right-angled streets. I walked out with Billy, Lonnie, and Chris, who was still glowing from his media moment.

"Spurs is how I gained my respect," Lonnie said. "But I'm going to have to get out of it soon." He had fathered an infant son and was about to start a

70

---

[10]*the Menendez brothers*: After two highly publicized trials in 1993 and 1995, Lyle and Erik Menendez were convicted in 1996 of the brutal murder of their parents; Erik was eighteen and Lyle twenty-one at the time the crime was committed.

job of sorts, behind the counter at Baskin-Robbins 31 Flavors. "The Spurs will never die down, though," he said. "My son will carry it on. We'll always exist."

"And we *do* exist," Billy said, as if someone had suggested otherwise. "I swear to God, we do exist!" Billy threw back his head and shouted to the impassive black firmament. "Howard Stern knows we exist. They all acknowledged us, all in one night."

I got in my car and headed toward Los Angeles. I would see Billy and Lonnie again, but not Chris Albert. A year and a half later, on the Fourth of July, he went to Huntington Beach to set off firecrackers, got into a street fight, and was shot to death. His passing would be noted in a small Associated Press item. "Albert," the brief obituary stated, citing his only achievement meriting mention, "appeared on several news and talk shows, including *Dateline NBC* and *The Jenny Jones Show.*"[11] His existence on *The Tonight Show* went unnoticed.

Visible and Not Ready to Be Visible

One day in the spring of 1994, I met Billy Shehan at a Lakewood park. He was sitting on a bench watching his old Pony League baseball team practice. The thirteen-year-old boys stood around thwacking their fists in their mitts and adjusting their caps, paying no attention to Billy, the lone observer.

He was brooding about his own truncated athletic career. He had been cut a few weeks earlier from the Long Beach City College baseball team. Before Long Beach, he had played ball for Golden West College until he got into a fight in the outfield, and then at Rio Hondo College, where the team was lackluster and he had quit in disgust. His Spur celebrity had made him a standout at Long Beach (a celebrity based on media, not police, attention—Billy was never arrested). "People would call out from the stands, 'Hey, how many points did you score?'" But it also cost him a spot on the roster, or so he had convinced himself. "The coach told me, 'You didn't make the team because you were too much of a distraction. People aren't focused on the game.'" In a fury, Billy had "shredded" his Long Beach City College baseball cap.

It had all been so promising back in Pony League. "I had a good name through Pop Warner,[12] a good image," he said. "Lakewood Pop Warner never loses. My name was getting more recognized. But someone with a bigger brand name came along." That boy, whose batting stats weren't—so Billy told me—as good as his but whose father was a well-liked coach in town, got the slot on the All-Star team that Billy thought was meant for him. "I didn't get on All-Stars until later, and then it was too late. The guys who get drafted early get the brand name. It's like Pepsi."

[11]"Spur Posse Member Killed," Associated Press, July 6, 1995.
[12]*Pony League and Pop Warner*: Community-based youth sports organizations promoting baseball and football, respectively.

Billy recognized the Pony League coaches from his own playing days and went over to say hello.

"Where is everybody?" Billy said, gesturing toward the empty bleachers. His question opened up a gusher.

"Oh, I don't know, it's just not as team oriented anymore the way it used to be," Coach Al Weiner said dispiritedly. He took off his cap and ran a hand through his thinning white hair.

"It's with the mothers never being home anymore and all," Coach Art   80
Tavizon commented.

"Naah, it's this thing with the kids," Weiner said. "In the old days, the kids who didn't get on, they would show up to watch. Now, if they're not playing, they won't watch."

"And the girls don't watch anymore," Tavizon said.

Weiner nodded. "The girls aren't interested. They're more into girls' sports now."

Tavizon set his mouth in a thin line at the mention of girls' sports and looked grimly across the field as if he had just spotted a menacing thundercloud on the horizon. "Title Nine changed everything," he said, alluding to the 1972 federal law that prohibited sex discrimination at schools receiving federal money, thereby ushering girls into school athletics.... "All the big moneymakers—football, baseball—and we've got to give it all to girls' badminton! Coaches are getting out of the business because they have to spend all their time fund-raising because the money's been taken to give to girls' sports."

The coach paused, but only to take a breath. He was just getting   85
started. "We had our weight room taken away because girls needed gymnastics. We had that weight room eleven years. We got pushed outside." His voice was getting louder, his face redder, and I suddenly realized that Billy had dropped out of the picture. The coach was directing his ire at me, the representative woman. "If the women would sit down and give a little bit, instead of insisting, 'Our half of the pie is fifty-fifty.' If they'd just back off and let the big sports be funded the way they used to be. Title Nine is going to be the destruction of high-school sports."

With that, he stormed back to his thirteen-year-old boy stars. Billy and I watched him go. "That's not the problem with baseball," Billy said, and offered his own more up-to-date diagnosis. "The problem with baseball is that it's a *dad's* game." And not a glamour game. "Baseball doesn't stand out because they don't have the cheerleaders, so there isn't as much of a star thing like you have with football." I wondered at the ranking of fathers under teenage girls in his version of the sports arena. When had the opinions of the older men who coached the game stopped mattering? Billy's father had devotedly coached Pop Warner for twelve years. So had Kris and Dana Belman's father, Don, who had also been a dedicated coach of Park League, Little League, Pony League, and Colt League.

What's so bad about a "dad's game"? I asked Billy.

"My dad, he was living through me with sports. When I got in trouble, he took it like *I* fucked *him* up. My dad provided anything that produced a championship. Sports is what our dads embedded in us. It was like a disease and it contaminated the whole town." Billy's father, doubtless, wanted only what every father wanted—to pass something along to his son, and in post-war suburbia, that patrimony was athletic achievement. Yet it turned out that the lines of inheritance ran upstream. In a generational reversal, the parents were getting their "name" through their children. As Dottie Belman, Kris and Dana's mother, told a reporter: "We became stars, too. We'd walk into Little League and we were hot stuff."[13] In his gut, Billy Shehan knew that the fathers had nothing to teach him about the way the world worked—but the girls did. The Spur Posse members, after all, prayed for what women had long commanded: the camera's attention. Far more than they ever courted women, they courted women's secret access to enshrinement in the public eye. As Billy Shehan told Jane Whitney on her show, he was trying to do from Lakewood what she was doing on the studio stage. "We probably have the same concept going here," he said....[14]

The Pop Warner System

... The media misconceived the nature of the Spurs' "club," which was less like a gang or fraternity than a bunch of casual drinking buddies. "People kept calling us a gang," Kris Belman said to me. "We weren't anything like that. It was just some guys who wore hats.... And then, once we got famous, there were all these other guys claiming they were Spurs who we didn't even know." If the core group of Spurs all seemed to wear baggy plaid shorts and their caps turned backward, this was in obeisance more to consumer culture than to group bonding. "We weren't ever a real group," Billy Shehan told me one day. "We were just a few people who liked David Robinson. Once the media grouped us together, *that's* when we became more tight." And then it was for promotional, not emotional, reasons. The Spurs weren't looking for the intimacy of a close-knit group. They were looking for the celebrity that identification with a brand name like David Robinson might provide. Like their elders in aerospace, they had attached themselves not to one another but to a household label. Everybody knew the San Antonio Spurs, as everybody knew McDonnell Douglas—and by extension, they could be "known," too; Robinson's name would be theirs.

"Billy did not even really run with this group of kids," Billy's mother, Joyce Shehan, observed to me. "He went to a different high school [from a lot of the other Spurs]. It was the lure of the media, which was overwhelming for all of these boys." She recalled how it all started, the day the eight Spurs were arrested: "I came home that afternoon and Billy said, 'Gotta go,

90

[13]Janet Wiscombe, "An American Tragedy," *Los Angeles Times*, March 22, 1996, p. E1.
[14]"Sex for Points Scandal," *The Jane Whitney Show*, April 1, 1993.

Mom! *Current Affair* is at the Belmans'!' He felt like destiny was calling him." Joyce pleaded with her son, to no avail. When the door slammed shut, she sat down in her living room and wept. "I felt overtaken."

"Doing sports is up there with sexual activities," Billy Shehan explained to me, as he gave me a tour of his parents' home. The walls of the ten-by-ten-foot bedroom where he still lived then were decorated with posters of the scantily clad Bud Lite woman, Hooters women, and decals asserting BLOW ME, STAY HARD, BAD BOYS CLUB, and PUSSIES AREN'T HEROES. I was having trouble matching these sniggering mud-flap sentiments with Billy, who distinguished himself from the other Spurs by a certain capacity (albeit sometimes lost in a dope-induced fog) for self-analysis. He had been in the accelerated program for gifted students throughout school, had graduated with honors, and was one of the few Spurs in school, although his attendance at Long Beach City College was spotty. He was proud of his high SAT scores (1410 out of a possible 1600, he said). For all his weight lifting — he tried to work out every other day at the Family Fitness gym — Billy had a physical softness to him; he retained the loose-limbed downiness and padded gait of adolescence. Aside from the posters, his room could've been a kid's, with its sports pennants and discarded clumps of clothing on the floor.

The tour complete, we returned to the living room, where Billy's uncle Brian Shehan; Billy's new girlfriend, Holly Badger; and Spur Jeff Howard were watching a TV movie about baseball and eating corn chips out of a jumbo bag. "When I'm thinking of attraction to girls, I'm thinking I have to stand out," Billy said. "How else can it be done? Same thing with sports. You try for a hit. It's like a mirror." It was the first time I had heard someone equate playing sports to looking in a mirror, and I asked him what he meant.

"It's what Pop Warner is all about," Billy said, "and Lakewood was built around Pop Warner." Playing football in the Pop Warner league was one of the few continuities a Lakewood boy could count on. The city's fathers established the park sports leagues out of alarm over the vast and idle child population of the new suburb: by 1953, 45 percent of Lakewood was under the age of nineteen.[15] The leagues were supposed to keep the baby-boom progeny out of trouble; they needed something to do. But what the elaborate Lakewood regimen of Pop Warners and Pony Leagues and Colt Leagues and All-Stars became, Billy was saying, was not something to *do* but something to *be*. "Pop Warner is what made me like hooking."

His uncle leaned heavily against the wall, his lined face under a battered Pittsburgh Steelers cap, a beaten version of Billy's. He was visiting from Las Vegas, where one week before Christmas he had been laid off as head cook at a restaurant called Bubba's. He had once been a front-end-loader operator but wound up in the new economy slinging hash and

[15]Waldie, *Holy Land*, p. 40.

ringing up purchases at Fedco's. "So," he said, almost wearily, "it's the Pop Warner Sex-Orgy System?"

"It *is* a system," Billy said. "In the Pop Warner system, you learn how to stand out, you learn how to get people to recognize you. You wear your hat a certain way. Like I started wearing mine angled with the bangs showing, because it looks cute. And everybody else started doing it. I set a lot of fashion trends."

"Every guy is in Pop Warner to get attention," Holly Badger said, though from the exasperated set of her mouth it was clear she found this truth more pathetic than ennobling.

"Sports is not sports anymore," Billy told his uncle. "It's evolved to this whole other level. It's this gamble of are you going to hit it big."

"Why do you guys like to gamble?" Holly interrupted. "All you *do* is gamble." She turned to me. "Every weekend, these guys are off to Las Vegas."

"It's a rush, a fix," Billy said. "It's like Dana's fixation with stealing."

"Yeah, or like breaking and entering," Holly said pointedly. One of the Spurs arrested for sexual misconduct, she told me, had broken into her house four years earlier when she was in the ninth grade. "He forced himself down on top me and a girlfriend of mine. I kicked him and he called me a bitch. Then he took my ring off my finger and put it on his finger and ran out." Hers was not an isolated story. Some of the Spurs had been known to steal things from girls: credit cards and checkbooks and jewelry, and oddities like gym membership cards, which one of the Spurs even tried to use, in spite of the feminine face laminated on the square of plastic.

"Stealing *is* gambling," Billy said. "Gambling evolves into something else."

"Billy wastes his life pursuing baseball," his uncle told me later that day, as we stood on the front porch. He had as much chance making the pros as hitting the jackpot—and as a Las Vegas resident, Brian Shehan knew how good those chances were. As for himself, Brian said, he was considering becoming a nurse; at least society needed them. He crossed his arms and gazed out at the orderly row of houses across the street. "Baseball and celebrity. Billy promised his dad he wouldn't go on the talk shows, and a few days later, he's flying to New York City."

Holly appeared on the porch, her bag over her shoulder. She was on her way to class at a nearby junior college. Jeff and Billy, their baseball caps on backward—Jeff's said STÜSSY, Billy's said L.A.—kicked their designer sneakers at the concrete stoop and talked about job possibilities. Billy last found work as a box boy at Victoria's Secret, but it had only lasted through the Christmas rush. Holly apprised them coolly: "*I* go to school and *I* work," she said. Billy kept kicking at the stoop and said nothing. Holly leaned over to give him a distracted kiss good-bye and drove off.

We went back inside, and Billy booted up his computer to show me his "movie treatment," in which he starred as "Billy Sherwood," the one with "the most points" who "doesn't accept failure." He had quit writing after the cast list and had typed instead some notes to himself about his girlfriend troubles, in lyric form. Billy and a few Spurs formed a band a while back, and he was the songwriter.

> The girl I used to kiss used to only kiss me
> But she has changed and she is 'ho again.
> She's back to who she was.
> I thought I could make her mine ...

He had broken off there. Underneath, he had written, "But I realize by the answers to my questions, that I never needed her. What I needed was for her to need me."

The training grounds for the Spurs were supposed to be the playing fields   105
of Pony League and Pop Warner, and in a way, they were training grounds for the celebrity age. The young men who flocked to Lakewood's sports leagues certainly learned that they would be expected to climb the star ladder, that fame based on your stats would be the determining factor in modern masculinity. But they also learned how high the stakes were, how few resources they had to win the stats war. Playing ball led to stardom for a very few. For the rest, Pop Warner was ultimately a lesson in how impossible it was to be a masculine "player" today. As Spur Jimmy Rafkin told me: "Growing up, everything revolved around Pop Warner. You try and do your best in sports and try to be the best and try to become the best, but it's like one out of a million make it, by far. So what was the point? What was it all *for*?"

ENGAGING THE TEXT

1. How did the boys' experiences in telemarketing and amateur athletics (Pop Warner, Pony League) help shape their behavior and values as Spur Posse members?

2. Why is the idea of a "brand name" so important to Billy Shehan and his friends?

3. The Lakewood boys complain that "girls have all the power." What do they mean by this, and what is their perception based on? How realistic or unrealistic does their attitude seem to you, and why?

4. Faludi subtitled her book *The Betrayal of the American Man.* In what ways does she suggest that the Lakewood boys have been cheated or "betrayed"? How does her understanding of their betrayal differ from their own? Who or what is responsible for their problems according to each perspective?

5. Faludi treats Lakewood itself almost like a character in her narrative, including information about its origin, architecture, layout, economy, and social life. Why are these details important to the story of the "troubled boys" she profiles?

6. What does Faludi's language reveal about her attitude toward the Lost Boy and the other Spur Posse members she interviews? How does she seem to want readers to respond to them? How do you react to them, and why?

EXPLORING CONNECTIONS

7. Roleplay or write a script for a roundtable discussion among Michael A. Messner (p. 477), Jean Kilbourne (p. 455), Carmen Vázquez (p. 489), Joan Morgan (p. 539), and Faludi about the influence of media in shaping attitudes toward masculinity, femininity, male-female relationships, and power.

8. Faludi highlights the stark disparity between the daily lives of the Lakewood boys and their dreams of fame and wealth. How do their dreams of success differ from those of Ragged Dick (p. 297), Trung Dung (p. 310), or Stephen Cruz (p. 348)? Would you call them believers in the American Dream? Why or why not?

EXTENDING THE CRITICAL CONTEXT

9. Sensational daytime talk shows and other "reality-based" programs in which participants essentially live their lives on camera have gained tremendous popularity in recent years. What is the appeal of such shows for audiences? Why are participants willing or even eager to share intimate and sometimes humiliating details of their lives with a TV audience?

Save the Males

CHRISTINA HOFF SOMMERS

Presenting a counterpoint to the previous selection, Christina Hoff Sommers accuses writers like Susan Faludi of manufacturing nonexistent crises in order to sell books. She condemns the motives and methods of researchers who have found evidence of widespread anxiety and depression among adolescent males. Boys in general are well adjusted, she insists, and the popularity of books like Faludi's simply indicates that "Americans seem all too ready to entertain almost any suggestion that a large group of outwardly normal people are suffering from some pathological condition." Currently a resident scholar at the American Enterprise Institute, Sommers formerly taught philosophy at Clark University in Worcester, Massachusetts. She is the author of two controversial books, Who Stole Feminism? *(1994) and* The War Against Boys: How Misguided Feminism Is Harming Our Young Men *(2000), from which this passage is taken.*

On June 4, 1998, McLean Hospital, the psychiatric teaching hospital of the Harvard Medical School, issued a two-page press release announcing the results of a new study of boys.[1] The release, headlined "Adolescence Is Time of Crisis for Even 'Healthy' Boys," reported that researchers at McLean and Harvard Medical School found that "psychologically 'healthy' middle-class boys" are anxious, alienated, lonely, and isolated—"despite appearing outwardly content."[2]

The study, entitled "Listening to Boys' Voices," was conducted by Dr. William Pollack, codirector of the Center for Men at McLean Hospital and assistant clinical professor of psychiatry at Harvard Medical School. Though McLean issued the press release in June 1998, Pollack, a psychologist, had already come out with a book publicizing these dismaying findings entitled *Real Boys: Rescuing Our Sons from the Myths of Boyhood*.[3]

Real Boys had been moderately successful before the Columbine High School shootings in April 1999. But it really took off when a startled public, hungry for expert counsel on what was wrong with the nation's boys, saw in Pollack a confident authority. Pollack appeared on *Oprah, 48 Hours, CBS This Morning,* and *Dateline NBC* to tell about his research finding that a silent crisis was engulfing American boys. He joined Vice President Al Gore on CNN's *Larry King Live* for a program dedicated to understanding school violence. He spoke to principals, counselors, and PTA leaders. In May 1999, for example, he delivered a keynote address to a convention of more than fourteen hundred Texas elementary school counselors seeking to better understand the boys in their care. In June he addressed two thousand PTA leaders in Portland, Oregon.[4]

Referring to boys as "Ophelia's brothers,"[5] Pollack did for boys what Gilligan and Mary Pipher[6] had done for girls: he brought news of diminished and damaged lives to a large public. *Real Boys* stayed on *The New York Times'* best-seller list for more than six months. What sort of research findings does Pollack bring in support of his portrait of a nation of dysfunctional unhappy boys? Let's go back to the McLean announcement of Pollack's discovery.

[1]McLean Hospital press release (http://www.mcleanhospital.org/PublicAffairs/boys1998), June 4, 1998.
[2]Ibid. (In the study, as in the McLean press release, the word "healthy," when applied to boys, is invariably encased in ironic scare quotes.)
[3]William Pollack, *Real Boys: Rescuing Our Sons from the Myths of Boyhood* (New York: Random House, 1998).
[4]http://www.williampollack.com/talks, July 12, 1999.
[5]*Ophelia's brothers:* Refers to a 1994 book by Mary Pipher, entitled *Reviving Ophelia*, which deals with problems of female adolescence.
[6]*Gilligan and Mary Pipher:* Carol Gilligan is a Harvard psychologist whose research suggests that traditional models of psychological development do not account for the experiences of girls and young women; Pipher takes Gilligan's work as a starting point for her own study of adolescent girls.

The press release listed the study's major findings. Among them: 5

- "As boys mature, they feel increased pressure to conform to an aggressive dominant male stereotype, which leads to low self-esteem and high incidence of depression."
- "Boys feel significant anxiety and sadness about growing up to be men."
- "Despite appearing outwardly content, many boys feel deep feelings of loneliness and alienation."

We must bear in mind that Pollack is not talking about a small percentage of boys who are seriously disturbed and lethally dangerous. He is attributing pathology to normal boys, and his conclusions are expansive and alarming. "These findings," he said, "carry massive implications for what appears to be a larger national crisis, one that we are now seeing can occasion serious violence."[7] This national emergency called for a major social reform: "The time has come to change the way boys are raised—in our homes, in our schools and in society."[8]

It is unusual to find such sensational claims and recommendations issued from a staid research institution such as McLean. McLean is routinely ranked among the top three psychiatric hospitals in the United States, and its research program is the best endowed and largest of any private psychiatric hospital in the country. Any study bearing its imprimatur automatically and deservedly receives respectful attention. But this one strained credulity.

I requested a copy of the "Listening to Boys' Voices" study from McLean. A few days later, a thirty-page typed manuscript arrived. It had not been published, nor was it marked as about to be published. It had none of the usual properties of a professional research paper. Unlike most scientific papers, which alert readers to their limits, Pollack's paper was unabashedly extravagant, declaring that "these findings about boys are unprecedented in the literature of research psychology."[9]

Pollack said he had been moved to do his research on boys in great part because of the "startling findings" of Gilligan and others on girls, which had awakened "our nation . . . from its gender slumbers," alerting us to "the plights of adolescent girls lacking for voice and a coherent sense of self . . . many sinking into a depressive joyless existence." Except for Pollack's adulatory references to Carol Gilligan and Nancy Chodorow for their "profound insights," the manuscript contains not a single footnote referencing other research. Its conclusion, which reports on a "national crisis" centering on boys, was based on a battery of vaguely described tests administered to 150 boys. Pollack gave no explanation of how the boys had been selected or whether they constituted anything like a representative sample.

---

[7]William Pollack, "Listening to Boys' Voices," May 22, 1998, p. 28. (Available through McLean Hospital Public Affairs Office, Belmont, Massachusetts.)

[8]McLean Hospital press release, p. 2.

[9]Pollack, "Listening to Boys' Voices," p. 24.

Pollack's pronouncements on the psychic condition of America's boys   10
were grim. But even if we disregard the limitations of the database, his research came nowhere near supporting a finding of a "silent crisis" national
in scope. On several of the tests he and his group administered, most of the
150 boys showed themselves to be healthy and well adjusted. A self-esteem
test found them confident. The Beck's Depression Inventory, a widely used
psychological assessment tool, uncovered "little or no clinical depression."[10]
In private interviews the boys said they were close to their families, and enjoyed strong friendships with both males and females. Something called the
"King & King's Sex Role Egalitarian Scale" found the vast majority of them
agreeing that "there should be equal pay for equal work," "men should
share in the housework," and "men should express their feelings."[11]

Pollack, however, repeatedly warns readers not to be fooled by such
seemingly encouraging results. By interviewing boys and giving them tests
that measure "unconscious attitudes," he claims to have found a truer picture, one of forlorn, alienated, and unconfident boys: "The results of this
study of 'normal' everyday boys were deeply disturbing. They showed that
while boys on the surface pretend to be doing 'fine,' beneath the outward
bravado—what I have called the 'mask of masculinity'—many of our sons
are in crisis."[12]

In one probe of the boys' "deeper unconscious processes," Pollack used
a "modified" Thematic Apperception Test (TAT). In TAT tests, subjects are
asked to look at ambiguous drawings of people and describe them. It is assumed that subjects will project their hopes and fears into the pictures.
Pollack and his colleagues presented the boys with a series of drawings and
asked them to write stories about them. One drawing depicts a young
blond-haired boy sitting by himself in the open doorway of an old wooden
house. The sun is shining on the boy, but a shadow eclipses whatever it is
that lies inside. Pollack was alarmed by the boys' responses.

"What was shocking," he wrote, "was that *sixty percent* interpreted the
picture as that of an *abandoned boy,* an *isolated child* or a *victim* of adult
mistreatment"[13] (emphasis in the original). Pollack saw the children's stories
as corroboration of the Gilligan/Chodorow thesis about early maternal
abandonment: "The high percentage of stories featuring themes of abandonment, loneliness, and isolation, I believe, is suggestive of subconscious
memories of premature traumatic separation."[14]

Pollack called the test he administered to boys a "modified" TAT. Modified how? He did not say. Even if it were accurate to say that the boys' reactions to the picture suggested feelings of loneliness and isolation, it is

[10]Ibid., p. 10.
[11]Ibid.
[12]Ibid., p. 9.
[13]Ibid., p. 17.
[14]Ibid., p. 18.

quite a leap to attribute their response to an early separation trauma. Before concluding that the boys' stories are the effect of their premature forced independence from mothers, we need to know whether other groups — say, a group of girls or of adult female psychologists — would have similarly "shocking" reactions to Pollack's modified TAT. Pollack makes no mention of control groups. In any case, before projecting his findings onto the entire population of American boys, he would need to establish that the boys he was testing were a representative sample.

It is also worth mentioning that Pollack's claimed discovery of an early   15 and devastating separation trauma for boys contradicts findings of the American Psychiatric Association. Its official diagnostic guidebook, *DSM-IV*, says that separation anxiety disorder afflicts no more than 4 percent of children and more girls than boys. Nor does the disorder appear to be related to being prematurely separated from one's mother. "Children with [this disorder]" says *DSM-IV*, "tend to come from families that are close knit."[15]

Pollack also expressed concern about the boys' apparent confusion about masculinity. A high percentage of his boys agreed with statements such as

- "It is essential for a guy to get respect."
- "Men are always ready for sex."[16]

He pointed out that these are the very same boys who said they believed "men and women deserve equal pay" and "boys and girls should both be allowed to express feelings." Pollack took these responses as evidence that the boys are hostage to a "double standard of masculinity." He concluded, "These boys reveal a dangerous psychological fissure: a split in their sense of what it means to become a man."[17]

This is not persuasive. We might well find teenage girls telling us that "It is essential for a girl to get respect." As for "Men are always ready for sex," why should any psychologist find it startling that adolescent boys agree with that? There is massive evidence — anthropological, psychological, even endocrinological, abundantly corroborated by everyday experience — that males are, on the whole, primed for sex and more ready to engage in it casually than females. And this begins in adolescence.

One well-known experiment compared the responses of male and female college students to invitations to have casual sex from an attractive

[15]American Psychiatric Association, *Diagnostic and Statistical Manual of Mental Disorders,* 4th ed. (Washington, D.C.: American Psychiatric Association, 1994), pp. 111–12. For an excellent critique of Pollack's work on boys, see Gwen Broude, "Boys Will Be Boys," *Public Interest* 136 (Summer 1999), pp. 3–17. It was Broude's article that brought the *DSM-IV* data on separation anxiety to my attention.

[16]McLean Hospital press release, p. 2.

[17]Pollack, "Listening to Boys' Voices," p. 11.

stranger of the opposite sex. Seventy percent of males said, "Okay, let's do it," and almost all seemed comfortable with the request. Of the females, 100 percent said, "No," and a majority felt insulted by the proposal.[18]

To recognize that males tend to welcome sexual opportunities is not to say that boys endorse an exploitative promiscuity. Given the biological changes boys are undergoing, their eagerness is natural and not unhealthy. On the other hand, society correctly demands that they suppress what is natural in favor of what is moral. So most parents try to teach their sons to practice responsible restraint. Pollack regards the boys' positive response to "Men are always ready for sex" as an indication that something is very wrong with them. While this response may indicate some confusion among today's young men about right and wrong, nothing in it suggests any kind of psychological disorder. Pollack's reaction tells us more about his own limitations as a reliable guide to the nature of boys than it does about what boys are really like.

In sum, Pollack's paper does not present a single persuasive piece of evidence for a national boy crisis. I do not know whether "Listening to Boys' Voices" has been submitted for publication in a professional journal. Its sparse data and its strident and implausible conclusions render it unpublishable as a scholarly article.

Why did a research institute such as McLean give what amounts to a seal of approval to such dubious research? The press release speaks of "findings" and "correlations" and gives readers the impression that "Listening to Boys' Voices" is a study that meets McLean/Harvard standards for responsible, data-backed research. McLean requires investigators to submit research projects to a twelve-member Institutional Review Board for approval. According to Geena Murphy, a member of this board, approval is granted "on the basis of the study's scientific merit."

Pollack's study, with its outsized claims and lack of evidence, could hardly have been approved on the basis of scientific merit. How did it get past the board? In conversations with psychiatrists, I learned that because of managed care, hospitals, administrators, and staff are continuously looking for ways to generate revenue and publicity for their institutions. Members of the McLean Institutional Review Board might have decided that an attention-grabbing "boys-are-in-crisis" study produced by McLean's Center for Men, which Pollack codirects, would bring favorable attention to the hospital. If so, scientific merit, usually indispensable for a McLean study, may have been compromised.

I asked Dr. Bruce Cohen, chief psychiatrist at McLean, how Pollack's "research" had managed to receive McLean's endorsement and was told, "I prefer not to talk about this at this time." He had read Pollack's study? I asked. "I don't read every study that comes out of McLean," he answered.

---

[18]Russell D. Clark and Elaine Hatfield, "Gender Differences in Receptivity to Sexual Offers," *Journal of Psychology and Human Sexuality* 2 (1989), pp. 39–55.

I explained that this study was quite unusual. Pollack claims to have uncovered a national crisis; his findings are "unprecedented in the literature of research psychology." Surely that must have come to Dr. Cohen's notice. I asked how it was that, without having reviewed Pollack's evidence, McLean had issued a press release giving Pollack's work the cachet of genuine science. Cohen told me someone would get back to me. But before he hung up, I asked him for his opinion "as a clinician" of Pollack's description of the nation's boys as "young Hamlets who succumb to an inner state of Denmark." "That's in there?" he asked, in the worried tone of a high school principal inquiring about what seniors have put in the yearbook.

The next day, I received a call from Roberta Shaw, director of public   25
relations at McLean. She explained that the decision to issue a press release had been based on the "news value" of the study. "We ask ourselves, 'Is it of public interest?'" She also assured me that Pollack "had several journals interested in publishing his study." She didn't know what they were. She suggested I call him directly. I did, but he never returned the call.

When medical scientists and journalists see a McLean press release reporting a significant research finding, they assume that the research meets the standards for which McLean is noted. If that assumption is wrong, McLean's office of public relations should caution the public that a "McLean study" simply means a "newsworthy" finding. Alternatively and preferably, Dr. Cohen should change his institution's policy and make scientific soundness a necessary condition for McLean's stamp of approval.

Universities such as Harvard are clearly uncomfortable with the use of their names to confer prestige on dubious work. In October 1998, Harvard announced a new policy barring faculty members from labeling their work as having been sponsored or endorsed by Harvard without the express permission of the dean or provost. As the Associated Press reported, "many institutions in the Ivy League have found themselves . . . linked to disputed data or research."[19] Last year Yale faced the same problem, and now anyone who wants to use the phrase "Yale University study" must get permission from the university's director of licensing. McLean might consider establishing a similar requirement for its researchers.

The Media Blitz

Well before the shootings in Littleton, Colorado,[20] news organizations around the country were carrying stories about new research on the nation's anguished boys, citing Harvard and McLean scholars as authorities. In March 1998, *The Washington Post* ran a front-page story about the "plight of young males." It quoted Barney Brawer, Carol Gilligan's former partner

---

[19]"Harvard and Yale Restrict Use of Their Names," Associated Press, October 13, 1998. See also http://www.nytimes.com/library/national/science.

[20]*the shootings in Littleton, Colorado:* In 1998, two heavily armed male students at Columbine High School in Littleton killed twelve classmates, a teacher, and themselves.

at the Harvard Project on Women's Psychology, Boys' Development and the Culture of Manhood, who said, "An enormous crisis of men and boys is happening before our eyes without our seeing it . . . an extraordinary shift in the plate tectonics of gender."[21]

In a May 1998 *Newsweek* cover story on boys, Pollack warned readers, "Boys are in silent crisis. The only time we notice is when they pull the trigger."[22] ABC's *20/20* aired a segment on Pollack and his disturbing message, "Why Boys Hide Their Emotions."[23] *People* ran a profile of Pollack in which he explained how boys who massacre their schoolmates are the "tip of the iceberg, the extreme end of one large crisis."[24]

On July 15, 1998, Maria Shriver interviewed Pollack on the NBC *Today* show.

He informed the program's mass audience of the results of his research:

> Shriver: You say there is really a silent crisis going on with, quote, "normal boys." As a parent of a young boy, that concerns me, scares me a lot.
> Pollack: Well, absolutely. In addition to the national crisis, the boys who pick up guns, the boys who are suicidal and homicidal, the boys next door or the boy living in the room next door is also, I have found in my research, isolated, feeling lonely, can't express his feelings. And that happens because of the way we bring boys up.

Pollack's easy slide from "boys who pick up guns" to "the boy next door"—who, he assures us, is not very different inside—scared a lot of parents. This slide from abnormal boy to normal one, is, of course, illegitimate. There is not a shred of evidence in Pollack's research that justifies his "tip-of-the-iceberg," "boys-are-in-crisis" hypothesis. Yet Pollack glibly tossed it into the media echo chamber.

In an earlier interview (March 28), Jack Ford, the cohost of NBC's *Saturday Today*, asked Pollack, "Should I sit down with my eleven-year-old son and say to him, 'Look at what happened here down in Arkansas.[25] Let me tell you why. Part of it is your makeup, part of it is how we've been bringing you up. Now let's sort of work through this together,' or is it too late for that?"

---

[21]Megan Rosenfeld, "Reexamining the Plight of Young Males," *Washington Post*, March 26, 1998, p. A1.

[22]Barbara Kantrowitz and Claudia Kalb, "Boys Will Be Boys," *Newsweek*, May 11, 1998, p. 57. See also http://www.nytimes.com/library/national/science.

[23]"The Difference Between Boys and Girls: Why Boys Hide Their Emotions," ABC, June 5, 1998.

[24]Tom Duffy, "Behind the Silence," *People*, September 21, 1998, p. 175.

[25]*what happened . . . in Arkansas:* In 1998, two Jonesboro, Arkansas, boys, ages eleven and thirteen, shot and killed four girls and a female teacher at their middle school.

Pollack did not tell Ford that it would be wrong to suggest to his son that he too is capable of killing people. Instead he replied: "I think we should do that with eleven-year-old boys. I think we should start with two- and three- and four- and five-year-old boys and not push them . . . from their mothers. . . ."[26]

This is a remarkable exchange—one that would be inconceivable if the   35
children under discussion were girls. No one takes disturbed young women such as Susan Smith (who made headlines in 1994 when she drowned her two sons by pushing her car into a lake) or Melissa Drexler (the New Jersey teenager who, in 1997, gave birth to a healthy baby at her senior prom, strangled him, and threw him into a trash bin) as tip-of-the-iceberg exemplars of American young women. Girl criminals are never taken to be representative of girls in general. But when the boy reformers generalize from school killers to "our sons," they're including your son and mine as well as Jack Ford's and Maria Shriver's. Would it ever occur to Jack Ford to ask a psychologist whether he should sit down with his daughter and say to her, "Look what happened at that New Jersey prom. . . . Part of it is your makeup, part of it is how we've been bringing you up. Now let's sort of work through this together"?

Pollack sees the killer boys at the extreme end of a continuum that includes "everyday boys." However, when one reviews the individual histories of boys who perpetrated the shootings, one quickly learns that they are very unlike most "seemingly normal" boys. The Jonesboro, Arkansas, killers were members of a satanic cult. Kip Kingle, the Oregon boy who shot classmates and then killed his parents, had a history of torturing animals and setting fires. Columbine killers Eric Harris and Dylan Klebold were admirers of Hitler, choosing his birthday as the day of their Götterdämmerung.[27] Even among seriously disturbed children, Harris, Klebold, and the other school killers represent an extreme.

In putting all boys "pushed from their mothers" onto a continuum with the Littleton shooters, Pollack does not adequately distinguish between healthy and unhealthy children. Before we call for radical changes in the way we rear our male children, we ought to ask the boy reformers to tell us why there are so many seemingly healthy boys who, despite having been "pushed from their mothers," are nonviolent, morally responsible human beings. How do those who say boys are disturbed account for the fact that in any given year less than one half of 1 percent of males under eighteen are arrested for a violent crime?[28]

---

[26]*Saturday Today,* March 28, 1998.

[27]*Götterdämmerung:* Twilight of the gods (German); refers to the turbulent or violent end of an era, regime, or way of life.

[28]FBI Uniform Crime Report (http://www.fbi.gov/ucr/Cius_97/97crime). See also U.S. Department of Justice, *Juvenile Offenders and Victims: A National Report* (Washington, D.C.: U.S. Department of Justice, 1995).

Pollack's explanation for adolescent male violence in schools contributes to the national climate of prejudice against boys. That is surely not his intention. It is, however, an inevitable consequence of his sensationalizing approach to boys, treating healthy boys as if they were abnormal and abnormal, lethally violent boys as "the extreme end of one large pattern."[29]

A Nation of Hamlets and Ophelias

In regarding seemingly normal children as abnormally afflicted, Pollack was taking the well-trodden path pioneered by Carol Gilligan and Mary Pipher. Gilligan had described the nation's girls as drowning, disappearing, traumatized, and undergoing various kinds of "psychological foot-binding." Following Gilligan, Mary Pipher, in *Reviving Ophelia,* had written of the selves of girls going down in flames, "crashing and burning." Pollack's *Real Boys* continues in this vein: "Hamlet fared little better than Ophelia. . . . He grew increasingly isolated, desolate, and alone, and those who loved him were never able to get through to him. In the end he died a tragic and unnecessary death."[30]

By using Ophelia and Hamlet as symbols, Pipher and Pollack paint a picture of American children as disturbed and in need of rescue. But once one discounts the anecdotal and scientifically ineffectual reports on the inner turmoil of adolescents that have issued from the Harvard Graduate School of Education and the McLean Hospital's Center for Men, there remains no reason to believe that girls or boys are in crisis. Mainstream researchers see no evidence of it.[31] American children, boys as well as girls, are on the whole psychologically sound. They are not isolated, full of despair, or "hiding parts of themselves from the world's gaze"—no more so, at least, than any other age group in the population. 40

One wonders why the irresponsible and baseless claims that girls and boys are psychologically impaired have been so uncritically received by the

---

[29]Some passages in *Real Boys* show that Pollack has a genuine understanding of the needs of boys. There is, for example, an excellent discussion of the ways our schools neglect boys and favor girls. He notes that our "coeducational schools . . . have evolved into institutions that are better at satisfying the needs of girls than those of boys . . . not providing the kind of classroom activities that will help most to thrive." Unfortunately, such passages are rare. Most of his book is about a male culture that is harming boys, as it harms girls. The demoralization of girls is the paradigm. Even as he is pointing out that our schools are unfairly neglecting boys, Pollack treats girls as the default victims of our culture, adding only that "adolescent boys, *just like adolescent girls,* are suffering from a crisis in self-esteem" (emphasis in original) (p. 239).

[30]Pollack, *Real Boys,* p. 6.

[31]See, for example, Anne C. Petersen et al., "Depression in Adolescence," *American Psychologist* 48, no. 2 (February 1993), p. 155; and Daniel Offer and Kimberly A. Schonert-Reichl, "Debunking the Myths of Adolescence: Findings from Recent Research," *Journal of American Adolescent Psychiatry* 31, no. 6 (November 1992), pp. 1003–14. See also entry on "September Anxiety Disorders," in *Diagnostic and Statistical Manual of Mental Disorders,* 4th ed., p. 112.

media and the public. One reason, perhaps, is that Americans seem all too ready to entertain almost any suggestion that a large group of outwardly normal people are suffering from some pathological condition. By 1999, best-selling books had successively identified women, girls, and boys as being in crisis and in need of rescue. Late in 1999, Susan Faludi's *Stiffed: The Betrayal of the American Male* called our attention to yet another huge segment of the population that no one had realized was in serious trouble: adult men.[32] Faludi claims to have unmasked a "masculinity crisis" so severe and pervasive that she finds it hard to understand why men do not rise up in rebellion.

Although Faludi seems to have arrived at her view of men without having read Pollack's analysis of boys, her conclusions about men are identical to his about boys. She claims that men are suffering because the culture imposes stultifying myths and ideals of manliness on them. *Stiffed* shows us the hapless baby-boomer males, burdened "with dangerous prescriptions of manhood,"[33] trying vainly to cope with a world in which they are bound to fail. Men have been taught that "to be a man means to be at the controls and at all times to feel yourself in control."[34] They cannot live up to this stoical ideal of manliness. At the same time, our "misogynist culture" now imposes its humiliating "ornamental" demands on men as well as women. "No wonder," says Faludi, "men are in such agony."[35]

What is Faludi's evidence of an "American masculinity crisis"? She talked to dozens of unhappy men, among them wife batterers in Long Beach, California, distressed male pornography stars, teenage sex predators known as the Spur Posse (how did she miss the Menendez brothers?).[36] Most of Faludi's subjects have sad stories to tell about inadequate fathers, personal alienation, and feelings of helplessness. Unfortunately, the reader never learns why the disconsolate men Faludi selected for attention are to be regarded as representative.

If men are experiencing the agonies Faludi speaks of, they are doing so with remarkable equanimity. The National Opinion Research Center at the University of Chicago, which has been tracking levels of general happiness and life satisfaction in the general population since 1957, consistently finds that approximately 90 percent of Americans describe themselves as happy with their lives, with no significant differences between men and women.[37] I recently asked its survey director, Tom Smith, if there had been any un-

[32]Susan Faludi, *Stiffed: The Betrayal of the American Male* (New York: Morrow, 1999).
[33]Ibid., p. 358.
[34]Ibid., p. 9.
[35]Ibid., p. 39.
[36]*the Menendez brothers:* Convicted in 1996 of murdering their parents, the brothers were eighteen and twenty-one at the time they committed the crime.
[37]David Myers and Ed Diener, "Who Is Happy?" *Psychological Science* 6, no. 1 (January 1995), p. 14. For data from the National Opinion Research Center, see http://www.icpsr.umich.edu/gss99.

usual signs of distress among men in the last few decades (the years in which Faludi claims that a generation of men have seen "all their hopes and dreams burn up on the launch pad"[38]). Smith replied, "There have been no trends in a negative direction during those years." But Faludi believes otherwise and joins Gilligan, Pollack, and the others in calling for a "new paradigm" of how to be men.

Faludi cites the work of Dr. Darrel Regier, director of the Division of Epidemiology at the National Institute of Mental Health, to support her thesis that men are increasingly unhappy.[39] I asked Dr. Reiger what he thought of her men-are-in-distress claim. "I am not sure where she gets her evidence for any substantial rise in male distress," he replied. He was surprised that one of his own 1988 studies had been cited by Faludi as evidence of an increase in "anxiety, depressive disorders, suicide." "Well," Dr. Regier said, "that is a fallacy. The article shows no such thing."[40] What does he think of these false mental health scares? I asked. "I guess they sell books," he said.

Apolcalyptic alarms about looming mental health disasters do sell well. In a satirical article entitled "A Nation of Nuts," *New York Observer* editor Jim Windolf tallied the number of Americans allegedly suffering from some kind of mental disorder. He sent away for brochures and literature of dozens of advocacy agencies and mental health organizations. Then he did the math. Windolf reported, "If you believe the statistics, 77 percent of America's adult population is a mess. . . . And we haven't even thrown in alien abductees, road ragers, and internet addicts."[41] If you factor in Gilligan's and Pipher's hapless girls, Pollack's suffering and dangerous boys, and Faludi's agonized men, we seem to be a country going to Hell in a handbasket.

Perhaps this fin de siècle[42] fashion in identifying large groups as mentally infirm will soon wane—it has nothing left to feed on. With women, girls, boys, and now men all identified as stricken populations, the genre seems to have run out of victims.

Gilligan, Pollack, and Faludi are the preeminent crisis writers. Each finds abnormality and inner anguish in an outwardly normal and happy population. Each traces the malaise to the "male culture," which is blamed for forcing harmful gender stereotypes, myths, or "masks" on the population in crisis (be it women, girls, boys, or men). Girls and women, they say, are constrained to be "nice and kind"; boys and men are constrained to be "in control" and emotionally disconnected. Each writer projects an air of sympathy;

[38]Faludi, *Stiffed,* p. 27.

[39]Ibid., p. 6. Regier is one of the researchers cited in Faludi's supporting footnote (p. 612, footnote 5).

[40]*DSM-IV,* the official desk reference of the American Psychiatric Association, reports that the prevalence of clinical depression among men is 2 to 3 percent.

[41]Jim Windolf, "A Nation of Nuts," *Wall Street Journal,* October 22, 1997.

[42]*fin de siècle:* End of the century (French); the last years of a century are often associated with grim prophecies and unusual popular beliefs.

each sincerely wants to help the casualties of our patriarchal culture. Nevertheless, by taking an unhappy minority as representative of a whole group, each of these writers is less than respectful to the allegedly afflicted population. Pollack, who wants to rescue boys from the myths of boyhood, unwittingly harms them by arousing public fear, dismay, and suspicion. In characterizing boys as "Hamlets," he stigmatizes an entire sex and a particular age group. His seemingly benign project of rescuing boys from "the myths of boyhood" by reconnecting them to their nurturers puts pressure on boys to be more like girls. The unintended effect is to put boys on the defensive. Gilligan, Pipher, and Faludi portray their disconsolate multitudes sympathetically—but at the price of presenting them as pitiable.

Boys Out of Touch

I have inveighed against the large, extreme, and irresponsible claims of the crisis writers, pointing out that no credible evidence backs them up. What about their more moderate and seemingly reasonable assertions? Gilligan and Pollack speak of boys as hiding their humanity and submerging their sensitivity. They suggest that apparently healthy boys are emotionally repressed and out of touch with their feelings. Is that true?

My own fourteen-year-old son, David, sometimes shows signs of the kind of emotional disengagement that worries the boy reformers. He came to me one evening when he was in the seventh grade, utterly confused by his homework assignment. Like many contemporary English and social studies textbooks, his book, *Write Source 2000*, was chock full of exercises designed to improve children's self-esteem and draw them out emotionally.[43] "Mom, what do they want?" David asked. He had read a short story in which one character always compared himself to another. Here are the questions David had to answer:

- Do you often compare yourself with someone?
- Do you compare to make yourself feel better?
- Does your comparison ever make you feel inferior?

Another set of questions asked about profanity in the story:

- How do you feel about [the main character's] choice of words?
- Do you curse? Why? When? Why not?
- Does cursing make you feel more powerful? Are you feeling a bit uneasy about discussing cursing? Why? Why not?

The *Write Source 2000 Teacher's Guide* suggests grading students on a scale from 1 to 10: 10 for a student who is "intensely engaged," down to 1

[43]Pat Sebranek and Dave Kemper, *Write Source 2000 Teacher's Guide* (Burlington, Wis.: The Write Source/D.C. Health, 1995), p. 70. In a 1999 interview, one of the writers, Dave Kemper, told me that in future editions most of the "feeling" questions and self-esteem exercises will be eliminated.

for a student who "does not engage at all." My son did not engage at all. Here is how he answered:

- Do you often compare yourself to someone else? "Sometimes."
- Do you compare to make yourself feel better? "No. I do not."
- Do your comparisons make you feel inferior? "No."

I was amused by his terse replies, but in the spirit of Gilligan and Pollack, the authors of *Write Source 2000* might see them as signs of emotional shutdown. Toy manufacturers know about boys' reluctance to engage in social interactions. They have never been able to interest boys in the kinds of interactive social games that girls love. In the computer game "Talk with Me Barbie," Barbie develops a personal relationship with the player: she learns her name and chats with her about dating, careers, and playing house. These Barbie games are among the all-time best-selling interactive games. But boys don't buy them.

Males, whether young or old, are less interested than females in talking about feelings and personal relationships. In one experiment, researchers at Northeastern University analyzed college students' conversations at the cafeteria table. They found that young women were far more likely to discuss intimates: close friends, boyfriends, family members. "Specifically," say authors, "56 percent of the women's targets but only 25 percent of the men's targets were friends and relatives."[44] This is just one study, but it is backed up by massive evidence of distinct male and female interests and preferences. In another study, boys and girls differed in how they perceived objects and people.[45] Researchers simultaneously presented male and female college students with two images on a stereoscope: one of an object, the other of a person. Asked to say what they saw, the male subjects saw the object more often than they saw the person; the female subjects saw the person more often than they saw the object. In addition, dozens of experiments confirm that women are much better than men at judging emotions based on the expression on a stranger's face.[46]

These differences have motivated the gender specialists at the Harvard Graduate School of Education, the Wellesley Center, the Boys' Project at Tufts, and McLean Hospital's Center for Men to recommend that we all try to "reconnect" boys. But do boys need to be more emotionally connected? Would boys be more connected if they were taught to be comfortable playing with "Talk with Me Barbie"? Are their behavioral preferences and emotional attitudes signs of insensitivity and repression, or are they normal

[44]Jack Levin and Arnold Arluke, "An Exploratory Analysis of Sex Differences in Gossip," *Sex Roles* 12 (1985), pp. 281–85.

[45]Diane McGuinness and John Symonds, "Sex Differences in Choice Behavior: The Object-Person Dimension," *Perception* 6, no. 6 (1977), pp. 691–94.

[46]See, for example, Leslie Brody and Judith Hall, "Gender and Emotion," in *Handbook of Emotions*, ed. Michael Lewis and Jeannette Haviland (New York: Guilford, 1993), p. 452.

manifestations of biological structures that determine the different ways in which boys and girls function?

If, as the evidence strongly suggests, the characteristically different interests, preferences, and behaviors of males and females are expressions of innate, "hardwired" biological differences, the differences in emotional styles will be difficult or impossible to eliminate. But then why should anyone make it their business to eliminate them?

The gender experts will reply that boys' relative taciturnity puts them and   55
others in harm's way; in support they adduce their own research. But as I have tried to show, that research is flawed. There is no good reason to believe that boys as a group are emotionally endangered; nor is there reason to think that the typical male reticence is some kind of disorder in need of treatment. In fact, the boy reformers such as Pollack, Gilligan, and their acolytes need to consider the possibility that male stoicism and reserve may well be traits to be encouraged, not vices or psychological weaknesses to be overcome.

ENGAGING THE TEXT

1. What are Sommers's objections to William Pollack's ideas and research methods? Which of her criticisms seem strongest, which seem weakest, and why?

2. Although Sommers refers to Pollack's book, *Real Boys*, her criticism focuses on the unpublished manuscript of an article he wrote. What is her stated reason for this focus? What other reasons might she have for basing her argument on the manuscript rather than the book?

3. Sommers faults Pollack for contributing to "the national climate of prejudice against boys" (para. 37). What evidence, if any, have you seen of such a prejudice?

4. How does Sommers support her assertion that "the characteristically different interests, preferences, and behaviors of males and females are expressions of innate, 'hardwired' biological differences" (para. 53)? What makes the evidence she presents convincing or unconvincing? Do you agree with her claim? Why or why not?

5. Sommers suggests that "male stoicism and reserve may well be traits to be encouraged" (para. 54). List as many benefits of keeping your thoughts and feelings to yourself as you can; then list as many drawbacks as you can. Likewise, list the benefits and drawbacks of expressing yourself openly. Compare lists and discuss.

EXPLORING CONNECTIONS

6. Review the preceding essay by Susan Faludi: Based on this selection, does Sommers's characterization of Faludi's purpose and ideas seem accurate? Why or why not? Which essay do you find more persuasive, and why?

7. How might Aaron H. Devor (p. 424), Jean Kilbourne (p. 455), and Michael A. Messner (p. 477) respond to Sommers's assertion that male/female differences are biologically rather than culturally determined? Write or act

out a discussion among these four authors about the degree to which gender roles are innate or learned.

EXTENDING THE CRITICAL CONTEXT

8. Working in groups, read Pollack's *Real Boys,* with each group taking responsibility for reading one chapter and reporting back to the class. How convincing or unconvincing do you find his analysis of boys' development? Which of Sommers's criticisms, if any, seem justified?

9. Using an academic database, do some quick research on the number of scholarly articles that have been published recently on gender differences. Read the online abstracts of the articles you find: How much consensus does there seem to be on the issue of biological vs. cultural influences on gender identity?

From Fly-Girls to Bitches and Hos
JOAN MORGAN

As a music writer and fan of hip-hop, Joan Morgan loves the power of rap. As a feminist, she is troubled by the pervasive sexism of its lyrics. The misogyny of rap, she argues, is a symptom of crisis in the black community; it must be confronted and understood, not simply condemned, as a step toward healing the pain that it both expresses and inflicts. This passage comes from her collection of essays, When Chickenheads Come Home to Roost ... My Life as a Hip-Hop Feminist *(1999). Morgan is editor-at-large at* Essence *magazine and lives in Brooklyn, New York. She has also written for* The Village Voice *and* Vibe.

> Feminist criticism, like many other forms of social analysis, is widely considered part of a hostile white culture. For a black feminist to chastise misogyny in rap publicly would be viewed as divisive and counterproductive. There is a widespread perception in the black community that public criticism of black men constitutes collaborating with a racist society....
>
> — MICHELE WALLACE, "When Black Feminism
> Faces the Music, and the Music Is Rap,"
> *The New York Times*[1]

---

[1]Michele Wallace, "When Black Feminism Faces the Music, and the Music Is Rap," *The New York Times,* July 29, 1990. [All notes are Morgan's.]

Lord knows our love jones for hip-hop is understandable. Props given to rap music's artistic merits, its irrefutable impact on pop culture, its ability to be alternately beautiful, poignant, powerful, strong, irreverent, visceral, and mesmerizing—homeboy's clearly got it like that. But in between the beats, booty shaking, and hedonistic abandon, I have to wonder if there isn't something inherently unfeminist in supporting a music that repeatedly reduces me to tits and ass and encourages pimping on the regular. While it's human to occasionally fall deep into the love thang with people or situations that simply aren't good for you, feminism alerted me long ago to the dangers of romancing a misogynist (and ridiculously fine, brilliant ones with gangsta leans are no exception). Perhaps the nonbelievers were right, maybe what I'd been mistaking for love and commitment for the last twenty years was really nothing but a self-destructive obsession that made a mockery of my feminism. . . .

I guess it all depends on how you define the f-word. My feminism places the welfare of black women and the black community on its list of priorities. It also maintains that black-on-black love is essential to the survival of both.

We have come to a point in our history, however, when black-on-black love—a love that's survived slavery, lynching, segregation, poverty, and racism—is in serious danger. The stats usher in this reality like taps before the death march: According to the U.S. Census Bureau, the number of black two-parent households has decreased from 74 percent to 48 percent since 1960. The leading cause of death among black men ages fifteen to twenty-four is homicide. The majority of them will die at the hands of other black men.[2]

Women are the unsung victims of black-on-black crime. A while back, a friend of mine, a single mother of a newborn (her "babyfather"—a brother—abdicated responsibility before their child was born) was attacked by a pit bull while walking her dog in the park. The owner (a brother) trained the animal to prey on other dogs and the flesh of his fellow community members.

A few weeks later my mom called, upset, to tell me about the murder of a family friend. She was a troubled young woman with a history of substance abuse, aggravated by her son's murder two years ago. She was found beaten and burned beyond recognition. Her murderers were not "skinheads," "The Man," or "the racist white power structure." More likely than not, they were brown men whose faces resembled her own.

Clearly, we are having a very difficult time loving one another.

Any feminism that fails to acknowledge that black folks in nineties America are living and trying to love in a war zone is useless to our struggle against sexism. Though it's often portrayed as part of the problem, rap music is essential to that struggle because it takes us straight to the battlefield.

5

---

[2] Joan Morgan, "Real Love," *Vibe,* April 1996, p. 38.

My decision to expose myself to the sexism of Dr. Dre, Ice Cube, Snoop Dogg, or the Nortorious B.I.G. is really my plea to my brothers to tell me who they are. I need to know why they are so angry at me. Why is disrespecting me one of the few things that make them feel like men? What's the haps, what are you going through on the daily that's got you acting so foul?

As a black woman and a feminist I listen to the music with a willingness to see past the machismo in order to be clear about what I'm *really* dealing with. What I hear frightens me. On booming track after booming track, I hear brothers talking about spending each day high as hell on malt liquor and Chronic. Don't sleep. What passes for "40 and a blunt" good times in most of hip-hop is really alcoholism, substance abuse, and chemical dependency. When brothers can talk so cavalierly about killing each other and then reveal that they have no expectation to see their twenty-first birthday, that is straight-up depression *masquerading* as machismo.

Anyone curious about the processes and pathologies that form the psyche of the young, black, and criminal-minded needs to revisit our dearly departed Notorious B.I.G.'s first album, *Ready to Die.* Chronicling the life and times of the urban "soldier," the album is a blues-laden soul train that took us on a hustler's life journey. We boarded with the story of his birth, strategically stopped to view his dysfunctional, warring family, his first robbery, his first stint in jail, murder, drug-dealing, getting paid, partying, sexin', rappin', mayhem, and death. Biggie's player persona might have momentarily convinced the listener that he was livin' phat without a care in the world but other moments divulged his inner hell. The chorus of "Everyday Struggle": *I don't wanna live no more / Sometimes I see death knockin' at my front door* revealed that "Big Poppa" was also plagued with guilt, regret, and depression. The album ultimately ended with his suicide. 10

The seemingly impenetrable wall of sexism in rap music is really the complex mask African-Americans often wear both to hide and express the pain. At the close of this millennium, hip-hop is still one of the few forums in which young black men, even surreptitiously, are allowed to express their pain.

When it comes to the struggle against sexism and our intimate relationships with black men, some of the most on-point feminist advice I've received comes from sistas like my mother, who wouldn't dream of using the term. During our battle to resolve our complicated relationships with my equally wonderful and errant father, my mother presented me with the following gem of wisdom, "One of the most important lessons you will ever learn in life and love, is that you've got to love people for what they are — not for who you would like them to be."

This is crystal clear to me when I'm listening to hip-hop. Yeah, sistas are hurt when we hear brothers calling us bitches and hos. But the real crime isn't the name-calling, it's their failure to love us — to be our brothers in the way that we commit ourselves to being their sistas. But recognize: Any man who doesn't truly love himself is incapable of loving us in the healthy way we need to be loved. It's extremely telling that men who can only see us as "bitches" and "hos" refer to themselves only as "niggas."

In the interest of our emotional health and overall sanity, black women have got to learn to love brothers realistically, and that means differentiating between who they are and who we'd like them to be. Black men are engaged in a war where the real enemies — racism and the white power structure — are masters of camouflage. They've conditioned our men to believe the enemy is brown. The effects of this have been as wicked as they've been debilitating. Being in battle with an enemy that looks just like you makes it hard to believe in the basics every human being needs. For too many black men there is no trust, no community, no family. Just self.

Since hip-hop is the mirror in which so many brothers see themselves,   15 it's significant that one of the music's most prevalent mythologies is that black boys rarely grow into men. Instead, they remain perpetually postadolescent or die. For all the machismo and testosterone in the music, it's frighteningly clear that many brothers see themselves as powerless when it comes to facing the evils of the larger society, accepting responsibility for their lives, or the lives of their children.

So, sista friends, we gotta do what any rational, survivalist-minded person would do after finding herself in a relationship with someone whose pain makes him abusive. We've gotta continue to give up the love but *from a distance that's safe.* Emotional distance is a great enabler of unconditional love and support because it allows us to recognize that the attack, the "bitch, ho" bullshit — isn't personal but part of the illness.

And the focus of black feminists has got to change. We can't afford to keep expending energy on banal discussions of sexism in rap when sexism is only part of a huge set of problems. Continuing on our previous path is akin to demanding that a fiending, broke crackhead not rob you blind because it's *wrong* to do so.

If feminism intends to have any relevance in the lives of the majority of black women, if it intends to move past theory and become functional it has to rescue itself from the ivory towers of academia. Like it or not, hip-hop is not only the dominion of the young, black, and male, it is also the world in which young black women live and survive. A functional game plan for us, one that is going to be as helpful to Shequanna on 142nd as it is to Samantha at Sarah Lawrence, has to recognize hip-hop's ability to articulate the pain our *community* is in and use that knowledge to create a redemptive, healing space.

Notice the emphasis on "community." Hip-hop isn't only instrumental in exposing black men's pain, it brings the healing sistas need right to the surface. Sad as it may be, it's time to stop ignoring the fact that rappers meet "bitches" and "hos" daily — women who reaffirm their depiction of us on vinyl. Backstage, the road, and the 'hood are populated with women who would do anything to be with a rapper sexually for an hour if not a night. It's time to stop fronting like we don't know who rapper Jeru the Damaja was talking about when he said:

> Now a queen's a queen but a stunt's a stunt
> You can tell who's who by the things they want

Sex has long been the bartering chip that women use to gain protection, 20 material wealth, and the vicarious benefits of power. In the black community, where women are given less access to all of the above, "trickin'" becomes a means of leveling the playing field. Denying the justifiable anger of rappers—men who couldn't get the time of day from these women before a few dollars and a record deal—isn't empowering and strategic. Turning a blind eye and scampering for moral high ground diverts our attention away from the young women who are being denied access to power and are suffering for it.

It might've been more convenient to direct our sistafied rage attention to "the sexist representation of women" in those now infamous Sir Mix-A-Lot videos, to fuss over *one* sexist rapper, but wouldn't it have been more productive to address the failing self-esteem of the 150 or so half-naked young women who were willing, unpaid participants? And what about how flip we are when it comes to using the b-word to describe each other? At some point we've all been the recipients of competitive, unsisterly, "bitchiness," particularly when vying for male attention.

Since being black and a woman makes me fluent in both isms, I sometimes use racism as an illuminating analogy. Black folks have finally gotten to the point where we recognize that we sometimes engage in oppressive behaviors that white folks have little to do with. Complexion prejudices and classism are illnesses which have their *roots* in white racism but the perpetrators are certainly black.

Similarly, sistas have to confront the ways we're complicit in our own oppression. Sad to say it, but many of the ways in which men exploit our images and sexuality in hip-hop is done with our permission and cooperation. We need to be as accountable to each other as we believe "race traitors" (i.e., one hundred or so brothers in blackface cooning in a skinhead's music video) should be to our community. To acknowledge this doesn't deny our victimization but it does raise the critical issue of whose responsibility it is to end our oppression. As a feminist, I believe it is too great a responsibility to leave to men.

A few years ago, on an airplane making its way to Montego Bay, I received another gem of girlfriend wisdom from a sixty-year-old self-declared nonfeminist. She was meeting her husband to celebrate her thirty-fifth wedding anniversary. After telling her I was twenty-seven and very much single, she looked at me and shook her head sadly. "I feel sorry for your generation. You don't know how to have relationships, especially the women." Curious, I asked her why she thought this was. "The women of your generation, you want to be right. The women of my generation, we didn't care about being right. We just wanted to win."

Too much of the discussion regarding sexism and the music focuses on being right. We feel we're *right* and the rappers are wrong. The rappers feel it's their *right* to describe their "reality" in any way they see fit. The store owners feel it's their *right* to sell whatever the consumer wants to buy. The consumer feels it's his *right* to be able to decide what he wants to listen to. We may be the "rightest" of the bunch but we sure as hell ain't doing the winning.

I believe hip-hop can help us win. Let's start by recognizing that its illuminating, informative narration and its incredible ability to articulate our collective pain is an invaluable tool when examining gender relations. The information we amass can help create a redemptive, healing space for brothers and sistas.

We're all winners when a space exists for brothers to honestly state and explore the roots of their pain and subsequently their misogyny, sans judgment. It is criminal that the only space our society provided for the late Tupac Shakur to examine the pain, confusion, drug addiction, and fear that led to his arrest and his eventual assassination was in a prison cell. How can we win if a prison cell is the only space an immensely talented but troubled young black man could dare utter these words: "Even though I'm not guilty of the charges they gave me, I'm not innocent in terms of the way I was acting. I'm just as guilty for not doing things. Not with this case but with my life. I had a job to do and I never showed up. I was so scared of this responsibility that I was running away from it."[3] We have to do better than this for our men.

And we have to do better for ourselves. We desperately need a space to lovingly address the uncomfortable issues of our failing self-esteem, the ways we sexualize and objectify ourselves, our confusion about sex and love and the unhealthy, unloving, unsisterly ways we treat each other. Commitment to developing these spaces gives our community the potential for remedies based on honest, clear diagnoses.

As I'm a black woman, I am aware that this doubles my workload — that I am definitely going to have to listen to a lot of shit I won't like — but without these candid discussions, there is little to no hope of exorcising the illness that hurts and sometimes kills us.

ENGAGING THE TEXT

1. What qualities of rap music and rap artists does Morgan admire or appreciate? What fears does she have for rap's female fans and for the artists themselves? To what extent do you agree with Morgan's assessment of the misogyny, anger, and despair expressed by rap?

---

[3] Kevin Powell, "The Vibe Q: Tupac Shakur, Ready to Live," *Vibe*, April 11, 1995, p. 52.

2. What evidence does Morgan offer that "black folks in nineties America are living and trying to love in a war zone"? How does she explain the causes of the violence she describes? How persuasive do you find her analysis, and why?

3. How do you interpret Morgan's call for establishing "a redemptive, healing space" for confronting the pain expressed by rap? What kind of "space" is she talking about, and how would you go about establishing it?

4. What audience is Morgan addressing and what persuasive strategies—of both argument and style—does she use to appeal to that audience? What do you find effective or ineffective about her approach?

EXPLORING CONNECTIONS

5. Compare Jean Kilbourne's analysis of sexism and violence in advertising (p. 455) to Morgan's discussion of the same themes in rap. What are the causes and consequences of "pornographic" depictions of women in popular culture according to each writer? Do you think Kilbourne would concur with Morgan about how we should respond to these images? Why or why not?

6. Although Morgan and Susan Faludi (p. 508) argue that we need to examine the lives of young men like Notorious B.I.G. and the members of the Spur Posse in order to understand the roots of their misogyny, critics might counter that these writers are simply making excuses for intolerable behavior. Do you agree with both Morgan and Faludi, with one of them, or with neither? Write an essay explaining and supporting your position.

7. How would Morgan respond to Christina Sommers's (p. 524) assumption that American boys are, on the whole, well-adjusted and happy? How and why do these writers' views of young men differ?

EXTENDING THE CRITICAL CONTEXT

8. Survey the current issues of several magazines aimed at fans of rap music. What images do they present of women, men, and human relationships? How often do they reflect the themes that Morgan discusses? What other themes and patterns do you find, if any, and how do you explain their significance?

9. Examine the lyrics of several female rappers and compare them to those of the male rappers Morgan mentions. What similarities and differences do you find in the subjects they address and the feelings they express? If you're not a fan of rap, you may want to consult an online hip-hop dictionary for help in decoding some of the language (www.rapdict.org).

5

Created Equal

The Myth of the Melting Pot

Antiracism March, photo by Eli Reed.

The myth of the melting pot predates the drafting of the U.S. Constitution. In 1782, a year before the Peace of Paris formally ended the Revolutionary War, J. Hector St. John de Crèvecoeur envisioned the young American republic as a crucible that would forge its disparate immigrant population into a vigorous new society with a grand future:

> What, then, is the American, this new man? He is neither an European, or the descendant of an European....He is an American, who leaving behind him all his ancient prejudices and manners, receives new ones from the new mode of life he has embraced, the new government he obeys, and the new rank he holds....Here individuals of all nations are melted into a new race of men, whose labours and posterity will one day cause great changes in the world.

Crèvecoeur's metaphor has remained a powerful ideal for many generations of American scholars, politicians, artists, and ordinary citizens. Ralph Waldo Emerson, writing in his journal in 1845, celebrated the national vitality produced by the mingling of immigrant cultures: "In this continent— asylum of all nations,—the energy of...all the European tribes,—of the Africans, and of the Polynesians—will construct a new race, a new religion, a new state, a new literature." An English Jewish writer named Israel Zangwill, himself an immigrant, popularized the myth in his 1908 drama, *The Melting Pot*. In the play, the hero rhapsodizes, "Yes East and West, and North and South, the palm and the pine, the pole and the equator, the crescent and the cross—how the great Alchemist melts and fuses them with his purging flame! Here shall they all unite to build the Republic of Man and the Kingdom of God." The myth was perhaps most vividly dramatized, though, in a pageant staged by Henry Ford in the early 1920s. Decked out in the costumes of their native lands, Ford's immigrant workers sang traditional songs from their homelands as they danced their way into an enormous replica of a cast-iron pot. They then emerged from the other side wearing identical "American" business suits, waving miniature American flags, and singing "The Star-Spangled Banner."

The drama of becoming an American has deep roots: immigrants take on a new identity—and a new set of cultural myths—because they want to become members of the community, equal members with all the rights, responsibilities, and opportunities of their fellow citizens. The force of the melting pot myth lies in this implied promise that all Americans are indeed "created equal." However, the myth's promises of openness, harmony, unity, and equality were deceptive from the beginning. Crèvecoeur's exclusive concern with the mingling of *European* peoples (he lists the "English, Scotch, Irish, French, Dutch, Germans, and Swedes") utterly ignored the presence of some three-quarters of a million Africans and African Americans who then lived in this country, as well as the tribal peoples who had lived on the land for thousands of years before European contact.

Crèvecoeur's vision of a country embracing "all nations" clearly applied only to northern European nations. Benjamin Franklin, in a 1751 essay, was more blunt: since Africa, Asia, and most of America were inhabited by dark-skinned people, he argued, the American colonies should consciously try to increase the white population and keep out the rest: "Why increase the Sons of Africa, by Planting them in America, where we have so fair an opportunity, by excluding Blacks and Tawneys, of increasing the lovely White...?" If later writers like Emerson and Zangwill saw a more inclusive cultural mix as a source of hope and renewal for the United States, others throughout this country's history have, even more than Franklin, feared that mix as a threat.

The fear of difference underlies another, equally powerful American myth—the myth of racial supremacy. This is the negative counterpart of the melting pot ideal: instead of the equal and harmonious blending of cultures, it proposes a racial and ethnic hierarchy based on the "natural superiority" of Anglo-Americans. Under the sway of this myth, differences become signs of inferiority, and "inferiors" are treated as childlike or even subhuman. This myth has given rise to some of the most shameful passages in our national life: slavery, segregation, and lynching; the near extermination of tribal peoples and cultures; the denial of citizenship and constitutional rights to African Americans, American Indians, Chinese and Japanese immigrants; the brutal exploitation of Mexican and Asian laborers. The catalog of injustices is long and painful. The melting pot ideal itself has often masked the myth of racial and ethnic superiority. "Inferiors" are expected to "melt" into conformity with Anglo-American behavior and values. Henry Ford's pageant conveys the message that ethnic identity is best left behind—exchanged for something "better," more uniform, less threatening.

This chapter explores the interaction between these two related cultural myths: the myth of unity and the myth of difference and hierarchy. It examines how the categories of race and ethnicity are defined and how they operate to divide us. These issues become crucial as the population of the United States grows increasingly diverse. The selections here challenge you to reconsider the fate of the melting pot myth as we enter the era of multi-ethnic, multicultural America. Can we learn to accept and honor our differences?

The first half of the chapter focuses on the origins and lingering consequences of racism. It opens with a selection by Thomas Jefferson that unambiguously expresses the myth of racial superiority. Pondering the future of freed slaves, Jefferson concludes that because blacks "are inferior to whites in the endowments both of body and mind," they should be prevented from intermarrying and "staining the blood" of the superior race. Randall Robinson, in "Thoughts About Restitution," surveys the economic and psychological damage inflicted on African Americans by almost 400 years of racial oppression and challenges America to repay the debt it owes to blacks for the wrongs they have endured as a result of slavery and segregation. Surveying the most common psychological and sociological theories of prejudice, Vincent N. Parrillo provides a series of frameworks for understanding the roots of racial conflict. Studs Terkel's oral history "C. P. Ellis" at once reminds us of the persistence of racist beliefs and offers hope for change: this remarkable first-person account of Ellis's transformation from Klansman to union activist examines racism from the inside and shows how one man conquered his own bigotry. Next, two essays consider the difficulty—and the necessity—of dealing with race in our daily interactions. In "I'm Black, You're White, Who's Innocent?" Shelby Steele argues that the psychological need to feel innocent on the highly charged issue of race keeps us from honest dialogue; he proposes that African Americans take the initiative by ceasing to blame whites for the injustices of the past and by refusing to play the victim. Psychotherapist Paul L. Wachtel offers a different perspective, arguing that we must all directly face the problems of race in order to solve them, but that to do so we need a more nuanced vocabulary for discussing racial issues. A Visual Portfolio gives individual faces to abstractions like race and discrimination; the images challenge us to ponder the centrality of race in American culture and to rethink ways we "read" identity.

The second half of the chapter addresses the emerging myth of the "new melting pot." First, George M. Fredrickson presents an overview of ethnic relations in American history, showing how concepts of ethnic hierarchy, assimilation, pluralism, and separatism have shaped group identities and interactions over time. Leonard Steinhorn and Barbara Diggs-Brown contend that multicultural media images may in fact undermine racial progress. Television in particular—with its black superstars, multi-ethnic news teams, and diverse casting—shows us a harmoniously integrated virtual world, offering false reassurance that race is no longer a serious problem. The next two selections explore the complexities of personal identity and human relationships in an increasingly multicultural America. "Notes of a Native Speaker" is Eric Liu's autobiographical meditation on his experience as an assimilated Chinese American—a man who has become "white by acclamation." In his pointedly funny short story, "Assimilation," Sherman Alexie introduces us to a Native American woman who begins to question the meaning of her marriage to a white man. Leon E. Wynter celebrates the emergence of a transracial ideal in American consumer culture: the willingness of the public literally to "buy" diversity, he declares, heralds a new freedom from "the shackles of centuries-old political constructions of race." Finally, in her poem "Child of the Americas," Aurora Levins Morales affirms both the value of her multicultural roots and the enduring power of the melting pot myth.

Sources

John Hope Franklin, *Race and History: Selected Essays,* 1938–1988. Baton Rouge: Louisiana State University Press, 1989, pp. 321–31.

Milton M. Gordon, *Assimilation in American Life: The Role of Race, Religion, and National Origins.* New York: Oxford University Press, 1964.

Itabari Njeri, "Beyond the Melting Pot." *Los Angeles Times,* January 13, 1991, pp. E1, E8–9.

Leonard Pitt, *We Americans,* vol. 2, 3rd ed. Dubuque: Kendall/Hunt, 1987.

Ronald Takaki, "Reflections on Racial Patterns in America." In *From Different Shores: Perspectives on Race and Ethnicity in America,* Ronald Takaki, ed. New York: Oxford University Press, 1987, pp. 26–37.

BEFORE READING

- Survey images in the popular media (newspapers, magazines, TV shows, movies, and pop music) for evidence of the myth of the melting pot. Do you find any figures in popular culture who seem to endorse the idea of a "new melting pot" in the United States? How closely do these images reflect your understanding of your own and other ethnic and racial groups? Explore these questions in a journal entry, then discuss in class.

- Alternatively, you might investigate the metaphors that are being used to describe racial and ethnic group relations or interactions between members of different groups on your campus and in your community. Consult local news sources and campus publications, and keep your ears open for conversations that touch on these issues. Do some freewriting about what you discover and compare notes with classmates.

- The frontispiece photo on page 546 was taken at an antiracism march. Why do you think that these people and this particular moment of the march caught the photographer's eye? What do the positions and expressions of the four main figures suggest about their feelings and concerns and about the cause they are marching for? Jot down your impressions and note the visual details that support your "reading" of the picture. Then compare your responses in small groups: How much consistency or variation do you find in your interpretations?

From *Notes on the State of Virginia*

THOMAS JEFFERSON

Thomas Jefferson is probably best known as the author of the Declaration of Independence. *As third president of the United States (1801–1809), Thomas Jefferson (1743–1826) promoted westward expansion in the form of the Louisiana Purchase and the Lewis and Clark Expedition. In addition to his political career he was a scientist, architect, city planner (Washington, D.C.), and founder of the University of Virginia. This passage from his* Notes on the State of Virginia *(1785) reveals a very different and, for many readers, shocking side of Jefferson's character—that of a slave owner and defender of white supremacy. Here he proposes that the new state of Virginia gradually phase out slavery rather than abolish it outright. He also recommends that all newly emancipated slaves be sent out of the state to form separate colonies, in part to prevent racial conflict and in part to prevent intermarriage with whites. Jefferson was not the first and was far from the last politician to advocate solving the nation's racial problems by removing African Americans from its boundaries. In 1862, the Great Emancipator himself, Abraham Lincoln, called a delegation of black leaders to the White House to enlist their support in establishing a colony for African Americans in Central America. Congress had appropriated money for this project, but it was abandoned after the governments of Honduras, Nicaragua, and Costa Rica protested the plan.*

Many of the laws which were in force during the monarchy being relative merely to that form of government, or inculcating principles inconsistent with republicanism, the first assembly which met after the establishment of the commonwealth appointed a committee to revise the whole code, to reduce it into proper form and volume, and report it to the assembly. This work has been executed by three gentlemen,[1] and reported.... The following are the most remarkable alterations proposed:

To change the rules of descent, so as that the lands of any person dying intestate shall be divisible equally among all his children, or other representatives, in equal degree.

To make slaves distributable among the next of kin, as other movables....

---

[1]*executed by three gentlemen:* Jefferson was one of the three men who wrote this set of proposed revisions to the legal code of Virginia.

To emancipate all slaves born after the passing [of] the act. The bill reported by the revisers does not itself contain this proposition; but an amendment containing it was prepared, to be offered to the legislature whenever the bill should be taken up, and farther directing, that they should continue with their parents to a certain age, then to be brought up, at the public expense, to tillage, arts, or sciences, according to their geniuses, till the females should be eighteen, and the males twenty-one years of age, when they should be colonized to such place as the circumstances of the time should render most proper, sending them out with arms, implements of household and of the handicraft arts, seeds, pairs of the useful domestic animals, &c., to declare them a free and independent people, and extend to them our alliance and protection, till they have acquired strength; and to send vessels at the same time to other parts of the world for an equal number of white inhabitants; to induce them to migrate hither, proper encouragements were to be proposed. It will probably be asked, Why not retain and incorporate the blacks into the State, and thus save the expense of supplying by importation of white settlers, the vacancies they will leave? Deep-rooted prejudices entertained by the whites; ten thousand recollections, by the blacks, of the injuries they have sustained; new provocations; the real distinctions which nature has made; and many other circumstances, will divide us into parties, and produce convulsions, which will probably never end but in the extermination of the one or the other race. To these objections, which are political, may be added others, which are physical and moral. The first difference which strikes us is that of color. Whether the black of the negro resides in the reticular membrane between the skin and scarf-skin, or in the scarf-skin itself; whether it proceeds from the color of the blood, the color of the bile, or from that of some other secretion, the difference is fixed in nature, and is as real as if its seat and cause were better known to us. And is this difference of no importance? Is it not the foundation of a greater or less share of beauty in the two races? Are not the fine mixtures of red and white, the expressions of every passion by greater or less suffusions of color in the one, preferable to that eternal monotony, which reigns in the countenances, that immovable veil of black which covers the emotions of the other race? Add to these, flowing hair, a more elegant symmetry of form, their own judgment in favor of the whites, declared by their preference of them, as uniformly as is the preference of the Oranootan[2] for the black woman over those of his own species. The circumstance of superior beauty, is thought worthy of attention in the propagation of our horses, dogs, and other domestic animals; why not in that of man? Besides those of color, figure, and hair, there are other physical distinctions proving a difference of race. They have less hair on the face and body. They secrete less by the kidneys, and more by the glands of the skin, which gives them a very strong and disagreeable odor. This greater degree of transpira-

[2]*Oranootan:* Orangutan.

tion, renders them more tolerant of heat, and less so of cold than the whites. Perhaps, too, a difference of structure in the pulminary apparatus, which a late ingenious experimentalist has discovered to be the principal regulator of animal heat, may have disabled them from extricating, in the act of inspiration, so much of that fluid from the outer air, or obliged them in expiration, to part with more of it. They seem to require less sleep. A black after hard labor through the day, will be induced by the slightest amusements to sit up till midnight, or later, though knowing he must be out with the first dawn of the morning. They are at least as brave, and more adventuresome. But this may perhaps proceed from a want of forethought, which prevents their seeing a danger till it be present. When present, they do not go through it with more coolness or steadiness than the whites. They are more ardent after their female; but love seems with them to be more an eager desire, than a tender delicate mixture of sentiment and sensation. Their griefs are transient. Those numberless afflictions, which render it doubtful whether heaven has given life to us in mercy or in wrath, are less felt, and sooner forgotten with them. In general, their existence appears to participate more of sensation than reflection. To this must be ascribed their disposition to sleep when abstracted from their diversions, and unemployed in labor. An animal whose body is at rest, and who does not reflect, must be disposed to sleep of course. Comparing them by their faculties of memory, reason, and imagination, it appears to me that in memory they are equal to the whites; in reason much inferior, as I think one could scarcely be found capable of tracing and comprehending the investigations of Euclid; and that in imagination they are dull, tasteless, and anomalous. It would be unfair to follow them to Africa for this investigation. We will consider them here, on the same stage with the whites, and where the facts are not apochryphal on which a judgment is to be formed. It will be right to make great allowances for the difference of condition, of education, of conversation, of the sphere in which they move. Many millions of them have been brought to, and born in America. Most of them, indeed, have been confined to tillage, to their own homes, and their own society; yet many have been so situated, that they might have availed themselves of the conversation of their masters; many have been brought up to the handicraft arts, and from that circumstance have always been associated with the whites. Some have been liberally educated, and all have lived in countries where the arts and sciences are cultivated to a considerable degree, and all have had before their eyes samples of the best works from abroad. The Indians, with no advantages of this kind, will often carve figures on their pipes not destitute of design and merit. They will crayon out an animal, a plant, or a country, so as to prove the existence of a germ in their minds which only wants cultivation. They astonish you with strokes of the most sublime oratory; such as prove their reason and sentiment strong, their imagination glowing and elevated. But never yet could I find that a black had uttered a thought above the level of plain narration; never saw even an elementary trait of painting or sculpture.

In music they are more generally gifted than the whites with accurate ears for tune and time, and they have been found capable of imagining a small catch.[3] Whether they will be equal to the composition of a more extensive run of melody, or of complicated harmony, is yet to be proved. Misery is often the parent of the most affecting touches in poetry. Among the blacks is misery enough, God knows, but no poetry. Love is the peculiar œstrum of the poet. Their love is ardent, but it kindles the senses only, not the imagination. Religion, indeed, has produced a Phyllis Whately [sic];[4] but it could not produce a poet. The compositions published under her name are below the dignity of criticism. The heroes of the Dunciad[5] are to her, as Hercules to the author of that poem. Ignatius Sancho[6] has approached nearer to merit in composition; yet his letters do more honor to the heart than the head. They breathe the purest effusions of friendship and general philanthropy, and show how great a degree of the latter may be compounded with strong religious zeal. He is often happy in the turn of his compliments, and his style is easy and familiar, except when he affects a Shandean[7] fabrication of words. But his imagination is wild and extravagant, escapes incessantly from every restraint of reason and taste, and, in the course of its vagaries, leaves a tract of thought as incoherent and eccentric, as is the course of a meteor through the sky. His subjects should often have led him to a process of sober reasoning; yet we find him always substituting sentiment for demonstration. Upon the whole, though we admit him to the first place among those of his own color who have presented themselves to the public judgment, yet when we compare him with the writers of the race among whom he lived and particularly with the epistolary class in which he has taken his own stand, we are compelled to enroll him at the bottom of the column. This criticism supposes the letters published under his name to be genuine, and to have received amendment from no other hand; points which would not be of easy investigation. The improvement of the blacks in body and mind, in the first instance of their mixture with the whites, has

[3]The instrument proper to them is the Banjar, which they brought hither from Africa, and which is the original of the guitar, its chords being precisely the four lower chords of the guitar. [Author's note]

[4]*Phyllis Whately:* Phillis Wheatley (175?–1784) was born in Africa but transported to the United States and sold as a slave when she was a young child. Her *Poems on Various Subjects, Religious and Moral* (1773) was the first book of poetry to be published by an African American.

[5]*the heroes of the Dunciad:* In the mock epic poem *The Dunciad* (1728), English satirist Alexander Pope (1688–1744) lampoons his literary rivals as fools and dunces.

[6]*Ignatius Sancho:* Born on a slave ship, Ignatius Sancho (1729–1780) became a servant in the homes of several English aristocrats, where he educated himself and became acquainted with some of the leading writers and artists of the period. He later became a grocer in London and devoted himself to writing. His letters were collected and published in 1782.

[7]*Shandean:* In the style of Laurence Sterne's comic novel, *The Life and Opinions of Tristram Shandy* (1758–1766). Sancho admired Sterne's writing and corresponded regularly with him.

been observed by every one, and proves that their inferiority is not the effect merely of their condition of life....

The opinion that they are inferior in the faculties of reason and imagi-   5
nation, must be hazarded with great diffidence. To justify a general conclusion, requires many observations, even where the subject may be submitted to the anatomical knife, to optical glasses, to analysis by fire or by solvents. How much more then where it is a faculty, not a substance, we are examining; where it eludes the research of all the senses; where the conditions of its existence are various and variously combined; where the effects of those which are present or absent bid defiance to calculation; let me add too, as a circumstance of great tenderness, where our conclusion would degrade a whole race of men from the rank in the scale of beings which their Creator may perhaps have given them. To our reproach it must be said, that though for a century and a half we have had under our eyes the races of black and of red men, they have never yet been viewed by us as subjects of natural history. I advance it, therefore, as a suspicion only, that the blacks, whether originally a distinct race, or made distinct by time and circumstances, are inferior to the whites in the endowments both of body and mind. It is not against experience to suppose that different species of the same genus, or varieties of the same species, may possess different qualifications. Will not a lover of natural history then, one who views the gradations in all the races of animals with the eye of philosophy, excuse an effort to keep those in the department of man as distinct as nature has formed them? This unfortunate difference of color, and perhaps of faculty, is a powerful obstacle to the emancipation of these people. Many of their advocates, while they wish to vindicate the liberty of human nature, are anxious also to preserve its dignity and beauty. Some of these, embarrassed by the question, "What further is to be done with them?" join themselves in opposition with those who are actuated by sordid avarice only. Among the Romans emancipation required but one effort. The slave, when made free, might mix with, without staining the blood of his master. But with us a second is necessary, unknown to history. When freed, he is to be removed beyond the reach of mixture.

ENGAGING THE TEXT

1. Jefferson proposes colonizing—that is, sending away—all newly emancipated slaves and declaring them "a free and independent people" (para. 4). In what ways would their freedom and independence continue to be limited, according to this proposal?

2. Jefferson predicts that racial conflict in the United States "will probably never end but in the extermination of the one or the other race" (para. 4). Which of the divisive issues he mentions, if any, are still sources of conflict today? Given the history of race relations from Jefferson's time to our own, do you think his pessimism was justified? Why or why not?

3. Jefferson presents what seems on the surface to be a systematic and logical catalog of the differences he sees between blacks and whites; he then attempts to demonstrate the "natural" superiority of whites based on these differences. Working in pairs or small groups, look carefully at his observations and the conclusions he draws from them. What flaws do you find in his analysis?

EXPLORING CONNECTIONS

4. Consider the picture of Jefferson's descendants on page 85. Write a journal entry or essay comparing the image of Jefferson you received in American history classes to the impression you get from the photo and from the passage above. How do you account for the differences?

5. Working in groups, write scripts for an imaginary meeting between Jefferson and Malcolm X (p. 243) and present them to the class. After each group has acted out its scenario, compare the different versions of the meeting. What does each script assume about the motives and character of the two men?

EXTENDING THE CRITICAL CONTEXT

6. Read the Declaration of Independence and compare Jefferson's most famous document to the lesser-known passage reprinted here. How do the purposes of the two texts differ? What ideas and principles, if any, do they have in common, and where do they conflict? (The text of the Declaration is reprinted as an appendix in most unabridged dictionaries and is available online at http://lcweb2.loc.gov/const/declar.html.)

7. Write a letter to Jefferson responding to this selection and explaining your point of view. What would you tell him about how and why attitudes have changed between his time and ours?

8. Influenced by the heroic image of Jefferson as a champion of freedom and democracy, civic leaders have named libraries, schools, and other public institutions after him for the last two hundred years. Debate whether or not it is appropriate to honor Jefferson in this way given the opinions expressed in this passage.

Thoughts about Restitution

RANDALL ROBINSON

In the years following the Civil War, Congress debated many proposals that would have taken land from large southern plantations and redistributed it to former slaves as compensation for their unpaid labor under slavery. None of these plans was adopted. In a few states, such land grants were initially made, only to be quickly rescinded by the federal government. Since then, activists have mounted a number of unsuccessful attempts to win economic restitution for the former slaves and their descendants. The most powerful contemporary voice to address this issue has been Randall Robinson's. His book, The Debt: What America Owes to Blacks *(2000), from which this passage is taken, offers a passionately argued case for reparations. The book has generated intense controversy: critics contend that the quest for reparations is too late and too divisive to be worthwhile; proponents debate what form restitution might take and how it could be fairly distributed. A graduate of Harvard Law School, Robinson (b. 1941) is the founder and president of TransAfrica Forum, a nonprofit Washington, D.C., research institution devoted to U.S. foreign policy in Africa and the Caribbean. His other books are* Defending the Spirit: A Black Life in America *(1999) and* The Reckoning: What Blacks Owe to Each Other *(2002).*

> The world itself is stolen goods. All property is theft, and those who have stolen most of it make the laws for the rest of us.
> —JOHN UPDIKE, *Brazil*

On January 5, 1993, Congressman John Conyers, a black Democrat from Detroit, introduced in Congress a bill to "acknowledge the fundamental injustice, cruelty, brutality, and inhumanity of slavery in the United States and the 13 American colonies between 1619 and 1865 and to establish a commission to examine the institution of slavery, subsequent *de jure* and *de facto*[1] racial and economic discrimination against African Americans, and the impact of these forces on living African Americans, to make recommendations to the Congress on appropriations remedies, and for other purposes."

The bill, which did not ask for reparations for the descendants of slaves but merely a commission to study the effects of slavery, won from the 435-member U.S. House of Representatives only 28 cosponsors, 18 of whom were black.

---

[1] *de jure . . . de facto:* Contrasting terms meaning "according to law" and "in fact."

The measure was referred to the House Committee on the Judiciary and from there to the House Subcommittee on Civil and Constitutional Rights. The bill has never made it out of committee.

More than twenty years ago, black activist James Foreman interrupted the Sunday morning worship service of the largely white Riverside Church in New York City and read a *Black Manifesto* which called upon American churches and synagogues to pay $500 million as "a beginning of the reparations due us as people who have been exploited and degraded, brutalized, killed, and persecuted." Foreman followed by promising to penalize poor response with disruptions of the churches' program agency operations. Though Foreman's tactics were broadly criticized in the mainstream press, the issue of reparations itself elicited almost no thoughtful response. This had been the case by then for nearly a century, during which divergent strains of black thought had offered a variety of reparations proposals. The American white community had turned a deaf ear almost uniformly.

Gunnar Myrdal, a widely respected thinker, wrote of dividing up plantations into small parcels for sale to ex-slaves on long-term installment plans. He theorized that American society's failure to secure ex-slaves with an agrarian economic base had led ultimately to an entrenched segregated society, a racial caste system. But while Myrdal had seen white landowners being compensated for their land, he never once proposed recompense of any kind for the ex-slave he saw as in need of an economic base. In fact, in his book on the subject, *An American Dilemma*,[2] Myrdal never once uses the words: reparation, restitution, indemnity, or compensation.

In the early 1970s Boris Bittker, a Yale Law School professor, wrote a book, *The Case for Black Reparations,* which made the argument that slavery, Jim Crow,[3] and a general climate of race-based discrimination in America had combined to do grievous social and economic injury to African Americans. He further argued that sustained government-sponsored violations had rendered distinctions between *de jure* and *de facto* segregation meaningless for all practical purposes. Damages, in his view, were indicated in the form of an allocation of resources to some program that could be crafted for black reparations. The book evoked little in the way of scholarly response or follow-up.

The slim volume was sent to me by an old friend who once worked for me at TransAfrica, Ibrahim Gassama, now a law professor at the University of Oregon. I had called Ibrahim in Eugene to talk over the legal landscape for crafting arguments for a claim upon the federal and state governments for restitution or reparations to the derivative victims of slavery and the racial abuse that followed in its wake.

"It's the strangest thing," Ibrahim had said to me. "We law professors talk about every imaginable subject, but when the issue of reparations is raised among white professors, many of whom are otherwise liberal, it is

[2]*An American Dilemma:* Book published in 1941.
[3]*Jim Crow:* Collective term for Southern segregation laws.

met with silence. Clearly, there is a case to be made for this as an unpaid debt. Our claim may not be enforceable in the courts because the federal government has to agree to allow itself to be sued. In fact, this will probably have to come out of the Congress as other American reparations have. Nonetheless, there is clearly a strong case to be made. But, I tell you, the mere raising of the subject produces a deathly silence, not unlike the silence that greeted the book I'm sending you."

Derrick Bell, who was teaching at Harvard Law School while I was a student there in the late 1960s, concluded his review of Bittker's book in a way that may explain the reaction Ibrahim got from his colleagues:

> Short of a revolution, the likelihood that blacks today will obtain direct payments in compensation for their subjugation as slaves before the Emancipation Proclamation, and their exploitation as quasi-citizens since, is no better than it was in 1866, when Thaddeus Stevens recognized that his bright hope of "forty acres and a mule" for every freedman had vanished "like the baseless fabric of a vision."

If Bell is right that African Americans will not be compensated for the   10 massive wrongs and social injuries inflicted upon them by their government, during and after slavery, then there is *no* chance that America can solve its racial problems—if solving these problems means, as I believe it must, closing the yawning economic gap between blacks and whites in this country. The gap was opened by the 246-year practice of slavery. It has been resolutely nurtured since in law and public behavior. It has now ossified. It is structural. Its framing beams are disguised only by the counterfeit manners of a hypocritical governing class.

For twelve years Nazi Germany inflicted horrors upon European Jews. And Germany paid. It paid Jews individually. It paid the state of Israel. For two and a half centuries, Europe and America inflicted unimaginable horrors upon Africa and its people. Europe not only paid nothing to Africa in compensation, but followed the slave trade with the remapping of Africa for further European economic exploitation. (European governments have yet even to accede to Africa's request for the return of Africa's art treasures looted along with its natural resources during the century-long colonial era.)

While President Lincoln supported a plan during the Civil War to compensate slave owners for their loss of "property," his successor, Andrew Johnson, vetoed legislation that would have provided compensation to ex-slaves.

Under the Southern Homestead Act, ex-slaves were given six months to purchase land at reasonably low rates without competition from white southerners and northern investors. But, owing to their destitution, few ex-slaves were able to take advantage of the homesteading program. The largest number that did were concentrated in Florida, numbering little more than three thousand. The soil was generally poor and unsuitable for farming purposes. In any case, the ex-slaves had no money on which to subsist for months while waiting for crops, or the scantest wherewithal to purchase the most elementary farming implements. The program failed. In sum, the United States government provided no compensation to the victims of slavery.

Perhaps I should say a bit here about why the question of reparations is critical to finding a solution to our race problems.

This question—and how blacks gather to pose it—is a good measure 15 of our psychological readiness as a community to pull ourselves abreast here at home and around the world. I say this because no outside community can be more interested in solving our problems than we. Derrick Bell suggested in his review of Bittker's book that the white power structure would never support reparations because to do so would operate against its interests. I believe Bell is right in that view. The initiative must come from blacks, broadly, widely, implacably.

But what exactly will black enthusiasm, or lack thereof, measure? There is no linear solution to any of our problems, for our problems are not merely technical in nature. By now, after 380 years of unrelenting psychological abuse, the biggest part of our problem is inside us: in how we have come to see ourselves, in our damaged capacity to validate a course for ourselves without outside approval.

> Meanwhile, the cotton the slaves produced had become not only the United States' leading export but exceeded in value all other exports combined. After the slave trade was outlawed in 1807 approximately one million slaves were moved from the states that produced less cotton (Maryland, Virginia, the Carolinas) to those that produced more (Georgia, Alabama, Mississippi, Louisiana, Texas)—a migration almost twice as large as that from Africa to the British colonies and the United States. With the increase in cotton production, the price of slaves went up, to such an extent that by 1860 capital investment in slaves in the south—who now numbered close to four million, or one third of the population— exceeded the value of all other capital worth, including land.
> —YUVAL TAYLOR, *I Was Born a Slave*

The issue here is not whether or not we can, or will, win reparations. The issue rather is whether we will fight for reparations, because we have decided for ourselves that they are our due. In 1915, into the sharp teeth of southern Jim Crow hostility, Cornelius J. Jones filed a lawsuit against the United States Department of the Treasury in an attempt to recover sixty-eight million dollars for former slaves. He argued that, through a federal tax placed on raw cotton, the federal government had benefited financially from the sale of cotton that slave labor had produced, and for which the black men, women, and children who had produced the cotton had not been paid. Jones's was a straightforward proposition. The monetary value of slaves' labor, which he estimated to be sixty-eight million dollars, had been appropriated by the United States government. A debt existed. It had to be paid to the, by then, ex-slaves or their heirs.

Where was the money?

A federal appeals court held that the United States could not be sued without its consent and dismissed the so-called Cotton Tax case. But the court never addressed Cornelius J. Jones's question about the federal government's appropriation of property—the labor of blacks who had worked the cotton fields—that had never been compensated.

Let me try to drive the point home here: through keloids[4] of suffering, 20 through coarse veils of damaged self-belief, lost direction, misplaced compass, shit-faced resignation, racial transmutation, black people worked long, hard, killing days, years, centuries—and they were never *paid*. The value of their labor went into others' pockets—plantation owners, northern entrepreneurs, state treasuries, the United States government.

Where was the money?

Where *is* the money?

There is a debt here.

I know of no statute of limitations either legally or morally that would extinguish it. Financial quantities are nearly as indestructible as matter. Take away here, add there, interest compounding annually, over the years, over the whole of the twentieth century.

Where is the money?   25

Jews have asked this question of countries and banks and corporations and collectors and any who had been discovered at the end of the slimy line holding in secret places the gold, the art, the money that was the rightful property of European Jews before the Nazi terror. Jews have demanded what was their due and received a fair measure of it.

Clearly, how blacks respond to the challenge surrounding the simple demand for restitution will say a lot more about us *and do a lot more for us* than the demand itself would suggest. We would show ourselves to be responding as any normal people would to victimization were we to assert collectively in our demands for restitution that, for 246 years and with the complicity of the United States government, hundreds of millions of black people endured unimaginable cruelties—kidnapping, sale as livestock, deaths in the millions during terror-filled sea voyages, backbreaking toil, beatings, rapes, castrations, maimings, murders. We would begin a healing of our psyches were the most public case made that whole peoples lost religions, languages, customs, histories, cultures, children, mothers, fathers. It

---

[4]keloids: Raised, fibrous scar tissue; one well-known old photograph of a former slave shows his back as a mass of keloid scars—evidence of vicious whippings.

would make us more forgiving of ourselves, more self-approving, more self-understanding to see, *really see,* that on three continents and a string of islands, survivors had little choice but to piece together whole new cultures from the rubble shards of what theirs had once been. And they were never made whole. And never compensated. Not one red cent.

Left behind to gasp for self-regard in the vicious psychological wake of slavery are history's orphans played by the brave black shells of their ancient forebears, people so badly damaged that they cannot *see* the damage, or how their government may have been partly, if not largely, responsible for the disabling injury that by now has come to seem normal and unattributable.

Until America's white ruling class accepts the fact that the book never closes on massive unredressed social wrongs, America can have no future as one people. Questions must be raised, to American private, as well as public, institutions. Which American families and institutions, for instance, were endowed in perpetuity by the commerce of slavery? And how do we square things with slavery's modern victims from whom all natural endowments were stolen? What is a fair measure of restitution for this, the most important of all American human rights abuses?

> The founders of Brown University, Nicholas and Joseph Brown, got their wealth by manufacturing and selling slave ships and investing in the slave trade.
> *The Black Holocaust for Beginners,* S. E. ANDERSON

If one leaves aside the question of punitive damages to do a rough reckoning of what might be fair in basic compensation, we might look first at the status of today's black male.   30

For purposes of illustration, let us picture one representative individual whose dead-end crisis in contemporary America symbolizes the plight of millions. At various times in his life he will likely be in jail or unemployed or badly educated or sick from a curable ailment or dead from violence.

What happened to him? From what did he emerge?

His great-great-grandfather was born a slave and died a slave. Great-great-grandfather's labors enriched not only his white southern owner but also shipbuilders, sailors, ropemakers, caulkers, and countless other northern businesses that serviced and benefited from the cotton trade built upon slavery. Great-great-grandfather had only briefly known his mother and father before being sold off from them to a plantation miles away. He had no idea where in Africa his people had originally come from, what language they had spoken or customs they had practiced. Although certain Africanisms—falsetto singing, the ring shout,[5] and words like *yam*—had survived, he did not know that their origins were African.

He was of course compulsorily illiterate. His days were trials of backbreaking work and physical abuse with no promise of relief. He had no past and no future. He scratched along only because some biological instinct impelled him to survive.

His son, today's black male's great-grandfather, was also born into slavery and, like his father, wrenched so early from his parents that he could scarcely remember them. At the end of the Civil War, he was nineteen years old. While he was pleased to no longer be a slave, he was uncertain that the new status would yield anything in real terms that was very much different from the life (if you could call it that) that he had been living. He too was illiterate and completely without skills.

He was one of four million former slaves wandering rootlessly around in the defeated South. He trusted no whites, whether from the North or South. He had heard during the war that even President Lincoln had been urging blacks upon emancipation to leave the United States en masse for colonies that would be set up in Haiti and Liberia. In fact, Lincoln had invited a group of free blacks to the White House in August 1862 and told them: "Your race suffers greatly, many of them, by living among us, while ours suffer from your presence. In a word we suffer on each side. If this is admitted, it affords a reason why we should be separated."

Today's black male's great-grandfather knew nothing of Haiti or Liberia, although he had a good idea why Lincoln wanted to ship blacks to such places. By 1866 his life had remained a trial of instability and rootlessness. He had no money and little more than pickup work. He and other blacks in the South were faced as well with new laws that were not unlike the antebellum Slaves Codes. The new measures were called Black Codes and, as John Hope Franklin noted in *From Slavery to Freedom,* they all but guaranteed that

> the control of blacks by white employers was about as great as that which slaveholders had exercised. Blacks who quit their job could be arrested and imprisoned for breach of contract. They were not allowed to testify in court except in cases involving members of their own race. Numerous fines were imposed for seditious speeches, insulting gestures or acts, absence from work, violating curfew, and the possession of firearms. There was, of course, no enfranchisement of blacks and no indication that in the future they could look forward to full citizenship and participation in a democracy.

Although some blacks received land in the South under the Southern Homestead Act of 1866, the impression that every ex-slave would receive

[5]ring shout: West African dance performed by slaves, characterized by call-and-response singing and a circular, shuffling motion.

"forty acres and a mule" as a gift of the government never became a reality. Great-grandfather, like the vast majority of the four million former slaves, received nothing and died penniless in 1902—but not before producing a son who was born in 1890 and later became the first of his line to learn to read.

Two decades into the new century, having inherited nothing in the way of bootstraps with which to hoist himself, and faced with unremitting racial discrimination, Grandfather became a sharecropper on land leased from whites whose grandparents had owned at least one of his forebears. The year was 1925 and neither Grandfather nor his wife was allowed to vote. His son would join him in the cotton fields under the broiling sun of the early 1930s. They worked twelve hours or more a day and barely eked out a living. Grandfather had managed to finish the fifth grade before leaving school to work full time. Inasmuch as he talked like the people he knew, and like his parents and their parents before them, his syntax and pronunciation bore the mark of the unlettered. Grandfather wanted badly that his son's life not mirror his, but was failing depressingly in producing for the boy any better opportunity than that with which he himself had been presented. Not only had he no money, but he survived against the punishing strictures of southern segregation that allowed for blacks the barest leavings in education, wages, and political freedom. He was trapped and afraid to raise his voice against a system that in many respects resembled slavery, now a mere seventy years gone.

Grandfather drank and expressed his rage in beatings administered to his wife and his son. In the early 1940s Grandfather disappeared into a deep depression and never seemed the same again. 40

Grandfather's son, the father of today's black male, periodically attended segregated schools, first in a rural area near the family's leased cotton patch and later in a medium-sized segregated southern city. He learned to read passably but never finished high school. He was not stigmatized for this particular failure because the failure was not exceptional in the only world that he had ever known.

Ingrained low expectation, when consciously faced, invites impenetrable gloom. Thus, Father did not dwell on the meagerness of his life chances. Any penchant he may have had for introspection, like his father before him, he drowned in corn spirits on Friday nights. He was a middle-aged laborer and had never been on first-name terms with anyone who was not a laborer like himself. He worked for whites and, as far as he could tell, everyone in his family before him had. Whites had, to him, the best of everything—houses, cars, schools, movie theaters, neighborhoods. Black neighborhoods he could tell from simply looking at them, even before he saw the people. And it was not just that the neighborhoods were poor. No, he had subconsciously likened something inside himself, a jagged rent in his ageless black soul, to the sagging wooden tenement porches laden with old household objects—ladders, empty flowerpots, wagons—that rested on them, often wrong side up, for months at a time. The neighborhoods, lacking sidewalks, streetlights, and sewage systems, had, like Father and other blacks, preserved themselves by not caring. Hunkered down. Gone inside themselves, turning blank, sullen faces to the outside world.

The world hadn't bothered to notice.

Father died of heart disease at the age of forty-five just before the Voting Rights Act was passed in 1965. Like his ancestors who had lived and died in slavery in centuries before, he was never allowed to cast a vote in his life. Little else distinguished his life from theirs, save a subsistence wage, the freedom to walk around in certain public areas, and the ability to read a newspaper, albeit slowly.

Parallel lines never touch, no matter how far in time and space they   45
extend.

They had been declared free—four million of them. Some had simply walked off plantations during the war in search of Union forces. Others had become brazenly outspoken to their white masters toward the war's conclusion. Some had remained loyal to their masters to the end. Abandoned, penniless and unskilled, to the mercies of a humiliated and hostile South, millions of men, women, and children trudged into the false freedom of the Jim Crow South with virtually nothing in the way of recompense, preparation, or even national apology.

It is from this condition that today's black male emerged.

His social crisis is so alarming that the United States Commission on Civil Rights by the spring of 1999 had made it the subject of an unusual two-day conference. "This is a very real and serious and difficult issue," said Mary Frances Berry, chair of the commission. "The crisis has broad implications for the future of the race."

The black male is far more likely than his white counterpart to be in prison, to be murdered, to have no job, to fail in school, to become seriously ill. His life will be shorter by seven years, his chances of finishing high school smaller—74 percent as opposed to 86 percent for his white counterpart. Exacerbating an already crushing legacy of slavery-based social disabilities, he faces fresh discrimination daily in modern America. In the courts of ten states and the District of Columbia, he is ten times more likely to be imprisoned than his white male counterpart for the same offense. If convicted on a drug charge, he will likely serve a year more in prison than his white male counterpart will for the same charge. While he and his fellow black males constitute 15 percent of the nation's drug users, they make up 33 percent of those arrested for drug use and 57 percent of those convicted. And then they die sooner, and at higher rates of chronic illnesses like AIDS, hypertension, diabetes, cancer, stroke, and Father's killer, heart disease.

Saddest of all, they have no clear understanding of why such debilitat-   50
ing fates have befallen them. There were no clues in their public school education. No guideposts in the popular culture. Theirs was the "now" culture. They felt no impulse to look behind for causes.

Q: What were the five greatest human rights tragedies that occurred in the world over the last five hundred years?

Pose this question to Europeans, Africans, and Americans, and I would guess that you would get dramatically divergent answers.

My guess is that both the Americans and the Europeans would place the Jewish holocaust and Pol Pot's extermination of better than a million Cambodians at the top of the their list. Perhaps the Europeans would add the Turkish genocide against Armenians. Europe and America would then agree that Stalin's massive purges would qualify him for third, fourth, or fifth place on the list. The Europeans would omit the destruction of Native Americans, in an oversight. The Americans would omit the Native Americans as well, but more for reasons of out-of-sight than oversight. Perhaps one or both would assign fifth place to the 1994 Hutu massacre of Tutsis in Rwanda. No one outside of Africa would remember that from 1890 to 1910 the Belgian King Leopold II (who was viewed at the time in Europe and America as a "philanthropic" monarch) genocidally plundered the Congo, killing as many as ten million people.

All of these were unspeakably brutal human rights crimes that occurred over periods ranging from a few weeks to the span of an average lifetime. But in each of these cases, the cultures of those who were killed and persecuted survived the killing spasms. Inasmuch as large numbers, or even remnants of these groups, weathered the savageries with their cultural memories intact, they were able to regenerate themselves and their societies. They rebuilt their places of worship and performed again their traditional religious rituals. They rebuilt their schools and read stories and poems from books written in their traditional languages. They rebuilt stadia, theaters, and amphitheaters in which survivors raised to the heavens in ringing voices songs so old that no one knew when they had been written or who had written them. They remembered their holidays and began to observe them again. They had been trapped on an island in a burning river and many had perished. But the fire had eventually gone out and they could see again their past and future on the river's opposite banks.

The enslavement of black people was practiced in America for 246 years. In spite of and because of its longevity, it would not be placed on the list by either the Americans or the Europeans who had played a central role in slavery's business operations. Yet the black holocaust is far and away the most heinous human rights crime visited upon any group of people in the world over the last five hundred years.

There is oddly no inconsistency here.

Like slavery, other human rights crimes have resulted in the loss of millions of lives. But only slavery, with its sadistic patience, asphyxiated memory, and smothered cultures, has hulled empty a whole race of people with inter-generational efficiency. Every artifact of the victims' past cultures, every custom, every ritual, every god, every language, every trace element of a people's whole hereditary identity, wrenched from them and ground into a sharp choking dust. It is a human rights crime without parallel in the modern world. For it produces its victims *ad infinitum,* long after the active stage of the crime has ended.

Our children have no idea who they are. How can we tell them? How can we make them understand who they were before the ocean became a furnace incinerating every pedestal from which the ancient black muses had offered inspiration? What can we say to the black man on death row? The black mother alone, bitter, overburdened, and spent? Who tells them that their fate washed ashore at Jamestown with twenty slaves in 1619?

But Old Massa now, he knows what to say. Like a sexually abusing father with darting snake eyes and liquid lips he whispers—

I know this has hurt and I won't do it again, but don't you tell anybody.   60

Then on the eve of emancipation, in a wet wheedling voice, Old Massa tells the fucked-up 246-year-old spirit-dead victims with posthypnotic hopefulness—

Now y'all just forget about everything. Gwan now. Gwan.

Go where? Do what? With what? Where is my mother? My father? And theirs? And theirs? I can hear my own voice now loud in my ears.

America has covered itself with a heavy wet material that soaks up annoying complaints like mine. It listens to nothing it does not want to hear and wraps its unread citizens, white and black, in the airless garment of circumambient denial, swathing it all in a lace of fine, sweet lies that further blur everyone's understanding of "why black people are like they are."

America's is a mentality of pictorial information and physical descrip-   65
tion placed within comprehensible frames of time. We understand tragedy when buildings fall and masses of people die in cataclysmic events. We don't understand tragedy that cannot be quantified arithmetically, requiring more than a gnat's attention span.

> The Negro is an American. We know nothing of Africa.
> —MARTIN LUTHER KING JR.

Culture is the matrix on which the fragile human animal draws to remain socially healthy. As fish need the sea, culture, with its timeless reassurance and its seeming immortality, offsets for the frail human spirit the brevity, the careless accidentalness of life. An individual human life is easy to extinguish. Culture is leaned upon as eternal. It flows large and old around its children. And it is very hard to kill. Its murder must be undertaken over hundreds of years and countless generations. Pains must be taken to snuff out every traditional practice, every alien word, every heaven-sent ritual, every pride, every connection of the soul, gone behind and reaching ahead. The carriers of the doomed culture must be ridiculed and debased and humiliated. This must be done to their mothers and their fathers, their children, their children's children and their children after them. And there will come a time of mortal injury to all of their souls, and their culture will breathe no more. But they will not mourn its passing, for they will by then have forgotten that which they might have mourned.

On April 27, 1993, under the auspices of the Organization of African Unity (a body comprised of African governments), the first pan-African conference on the subject of reparations was convened in Abuja, Nigeria. Among the hundreds who attended from thirty countries and four continents were Abdou Diouf, chairman of the OAU and president of Senegal, and Salim Salim, OAU's secretary general. My fried Dudley Thompson, the Jamaican human rights lawyer, served as rapporteur[6] for the three-day conference. The delegation at the end of their deliberations drafted a declaration that was later unanimously adopted by Africa's heads of state at a summit meeting.

I should like to quote for you parts of that declaration, for it accomplishes at least two important purposes. First, it makes known the victim's (in other words, Africa's) very public witness, which has been long suppressed. Second, it introduces what I believe to be a just and legitimate claim against the United States and the countries of western Europe for restitution:

> Recalling the establishment by the Organization of African Unity of a machinery for appraising the issue of reparations in relation to the damage done to Africa and to the Diaspora[7] by enslavement, colonialism and neo-colonialism; convinced that the issue of reparations is an important question requiring the united action of Africa and its Diaspora and worthy of the active support of the rest of the international community;

> Fully persuaded that the damage sustained by the African peoples is not a theory of the past but is painfully manifested from Harare to Harlem and in the damaged economies of Africa and the black world from Guinea to Guyana, from Somalia to Surinam;

> Aware of historic precedents in reparations varying from German payments of restitution to the Jews, to the question of compensating Japanese-Americans for the injustice of internment by the Roosevelt Administration in the United States during World War II;

> Cognizant of the fact that compensation for injustice need not necessarily be paid entirely in capital transfer but could include service to the victims or other forms of restitution and re-adjustment of the relationship agreeable to both parties;

> Emphasizing that an admission of guilt is a necessary step to reverse this situation;

---

[6]*rapporteur:* Literally "reporter" (French), a rapporteur is the person responsible for producing a report for a meeting, conference, or committee.
[7]*Diaspora:* Africans scattered to other continents.

Emphatically convinced that what matters is not the guilt but the responsibility of those states whose economic evolution once depended on slave labour and colonialism and whose forebears participated either in selling and buying Africans, or in owning them, or in colonizing them;

Convinced that the pursuit of reparations by the African peoples on the continent and in the Diaspora will be a learning experience in self-discovery and in uniting political and psychological experiences;

Calls upon the international community to recognize that there is a unique and unprecedented moral debt owed to the African peoples which has yet to be paid—the debt of compensation to the Africans as the most humiliated and exploited people of the last four centuries of modern history.

The declaration was ignored by American media, and I confess that I knew nothing about it until Dudley Thompson brought it to my attention after my speech in March 1999 at the University of Technology in Kingston. I cannot say that I was surprised that American media had not covered the conference. News decision-makers no doubt decided that such deliberations were unimportant, even though they had for years heaped attention upon the appeals of other groups in the world for compensation as wronged parties. As you can see, such claims were hardly unique in the world and many had been pursued successfully, resulting in billions of dollars in compensation.

After World War I the allies made successful claims against Germany, 70 as would Jews after World War II. The Poles also laid claims against the Germans after being used by the Nazis during the Second World War as slave labor. Japanese-Americans recovered from the United States government. The Inuit recovered from the Canadian government. Aborigines recovered money and large areas of land from the Australian government. Korean women, forced into prostitution by Japan during World War II, were compensated as well.

According to Dudley Thompson, international law in this area is replete with precedents.

Not only is there a moral debt but there is clearly established precedence in law based on the principle of unjust enrichment. In law if a party unlawfully enriches himself by wrongful acts against another, then the party so wronged is entitled to recompense. There have been some 15 cases in which the highest tribunals including the International Court at the Hague have awarded large sums as reparations based on this law.

Only in this case of black people have the claims, the claimants, the crime, the law, the precedents, the awful contemporary social consequences all been roundly ignored. The thinking must be that the case that cannot be substantively answered is best not acknowledged at all. Hence, the United

States government and white society generally have opted to deal with this *debt* by forgetting that it is owed. The crime — 246 years of an enterprise murderous both of a people and their culture — is so unprecedentedly massive that it would require some form of collective insanity not to see it and its living victims.

But still many, if not most, whites cannot or will not see it (a behavior that is accommodated by all too many uncomplaining blacks). This studied white blindness may be a modern variant of a sight condition that afflicted their slaveholding forebears who concocted something called *drapetomania,* the so-called mental disorder that slaveholders seriously believed caused blacks to run away to freedom. America accepts responsibility for little that goes wrong in the world, least of all the contemporary plight of black Americans. And until America can be made to do so, it is hard to see how we can progress significantly in our race relations.

On my behalf, my old friend Ibrahim called Robert Westley, a black law professor at Tulane Law School in New Orleans. Westley had been on the verge of publishing in the *Boston College Law Review* a detailed legal analysis of the case for reparations he believes the United States government owes African Americans as a group. Within a week of Ibrahim's call to Westley, I received from Westley a one-hundred-page draft of his article, "Many Billions Gone," which measured, with quantitative data compiled by respected academic social researchers, the cumulative economic consequences to African Americans of three and a half centuries of U.S. government–backed slavery, segregation, and *de jure* racial discrimination. The moral and legal merits of Westley's arguments were compelling, particularly when measured against those of claims for reparations that have been successful. One such ground-breaking claim, which had been formulated by Jewish organizations and leaders before the end of World War II, resulted in September 1952 in the Luxemburg Agreement. The claimants were two entities: the state of Israel, on behalf of the five hundred thousand Nazi war victims who had resettled in Israel, and the Conference on Jewish Material Claims Against Germany (the Claims Conference), on behalf of victims who had settled in countries other than Israel. The Claims Conference also represented the interests of the Jewish people as a whole who were entitled to indemnification for property that had been left by those who had died without known heirs.

Westley wrote of the treaty:

> Wiedergutmachung [literally, "making good again"] was unprecedented in several respects. . . . The treaty obligation by which Israel was to receive the equivalent of one billion dollars in reparations from West Germany for crimes committed by the Third Reich against the Jewish people reflected Chancellor Konrad Adenauer's view that the German people had a moral duty to compensate the Jewish people for their material losses and suffering. Secondly, the sums paid not only to Israel but also to the Claims Conference showed a genuine desire on

the part of the Germans to make Jewish victims of Nazi persecution whole. Under Protocol No. 1 of the Luxemburg Agreement, national legislation was passed in Germany that sought to compensate Jews individually for deprivation of liberty, compulsory labor and involuntary abandonment of their homes, loss of income and professional or educational opportunities, loss of [World War I] pensions, damage to health, loss of property through discriminatory levies such as the Flight Tax, damage to economic prospects, and loss of citizenship.

Israel's prime minister, David Ben-Gurion, was to say of the agreement:

> For the first time in the history of relations between people, a precedent has been created by which a great State, as a result of moral pressure alone, takes it upon itself to pay compensation to the victims of the government that preceded it. For the first time in the history of a people that has been persecuted, oppressed, plundered, and despoiled for hundreds of years in the countries of Europe, a persecutor and despoiler has been obliged to return part of his spoils and has even undertaken to make collective reparation as partial compensation for material losses.

The principle, set forward in the agreement and amplified by Ben-Gurion for other reparation claims that would follow, was simple. When a government kills its own people or facilitates their involuntary servitude and generalized victimization based on group membership, then that government or its successor has a moral obligation to materially compensate that group in a way that would make it whole, while recognizing that material compensation alone can never adequately compensate the victims of great human rights crimes.

Some would argue that such an obligation does not obtain in the case of the black holocaust because the wrongful action took place so long ago. Such arguments are specious at best. They can be answered in at least two ways, the second more compelling than the first.

Beginning with the question of late amends-making, in 1998 President Clinton signed into law the Sand Creek Massacre National Historic Study Site Act, which officially acknowledges an 1864 attack by seven hundred U.S. soldiers on a peaceful Cheyenne village located in the territory of Colorado. Hundreds, largely women and children, were killed. The act calls for the establishment of a federally funded Historic Site at Sand Creek. While not providing for payment to the victims' heirs, the apology/restitution measure, coming 134 years after the event, does counter the "it's too late" objection.

In 1994, seventy-one years after the Rosewood massacre in which white lynch mobs, during a weeklong orgy of hate, killed six blacks and drove survivors into the swamps near a prosperous black community in Florida, Governor Lawton Chiles signed into law a bill (House Bill 591) that provided

> In the early years of the twentieth century, it was becoming clear that the Negro would be effectively disfranchised throughout the South, that he would be firmly relegated to the lower rungs of the economic ladder, and that neither equality nor aspirations for equality in any department of life were for him.
>
> The public symbols and constant reminders of his inferior position were the segregation statutes, or "Jim Crow" laws. They constituted the most elaborate and formal expression of sovereign white opinion upon the subject. In bulk and detail as well as in effectiveness of enforcement the segregation codes were comparable with the black codes of the old regime, though the laxity that mitigated the harshness of the black codes was replaced by a rigidity that was more typical of the segregation code. That code lent the sanction of law to a racial ostracism that extended to churches and schools, to housing and jobs, to eating and drinking. Whether by law or by custom, that ostracism extended to virtually all forms of public transportation, to sports and recreations, to hospitals, orphanages, prisons, and asylums, and ultimately to funeral homes, morgues, and cemeteries.
> —C. VANN WOODWARD, *The Strange Career of Jim Crow*

for the payment of $2.1 million in reparations to the descendants of the black victims at Rosewood.

Indeed, slavery itself did not end in 1865, as is commonly believed, but rather extended into the twentieth century to within a few years of the Rosewood massacre for which reparations were paid. As Yuval Taylor has pointed out in *I Was Born a Slave:*

> Although they were not called *slavery,* the post-Reconstruction Southern practices of peonage, forced convict labor, and to a lesser degree sharecropping essentially continued the institution of slavery well into the twentieth century, and were in some ways even worse. (Peonage, for example, was a complex system in which a black man would be arrested for "vagrancy," another word for unemployment, ordered to pay a fine he could not afford, and incarcerated. A plantation owner would pay his fine and "hire" him until he could afford to pay off the fine himself: The peon was then forced to work, locked up at night, and, if he ran away, chased by bloodhounds until recaptured. One important difference between peonage and slavery was that while slaves had considerable monetary value for the plantation owner, peons had almost none, and could therefore be mistreated—and even murdered— without monetary loss.)

The foregoing precedents for reparations would be less sustaining, 80 however, had the enormous human rights crime of slavery (later practiced as peonage) not been overlapped and extended by a century of government-sponsored segregation and general racial discrimination.

What slavery had firmly established in the way of debilitating psychic pain and a lopsidedly unequal economic relationship of blacks and whites, formal organs of state and federal government would cement in law for the century that followed. Thus it should surprise no one that the wealth gap (wealth defined as the net value of assets) separating blacks from whites over the twentieth century has mushroomed beyond any ability of black earned income ever to close it. This too is the fruit of long-term structural racial discrimination, government-sponsored in many cases, acquiesced to in others.

The evidence of this discrimination is so overwhelming that one hardly knows which examples to select to illustrate the point. Westley writes in "Many Billions Gone":

> Based on discrimination in home mortgage approval rates, the projected number of credit-worthy home buyers and the median white housing appreciation rate, it is estimated that the current generation of blacks will lose about $82 billion in equity due to institutional discrimination. All things being equal, the next generation of black home owners will lose $93 billion.
>
> As the cardinal means of middle class wealth accumulation, this missed opportunity for home equity due to private and governmental racial discrimination is devastating to the black community.

Of course, benefiting intergenerationally from this weather of racism were white Americans whose assets piled up like fattening snowballs over three and a half centuries' terrain of slavery and the mean racial climate that followed it.

Indeed, until 1950 the Federal Housing Authority provided subsidies to white mortgage holders who were bound by restrictive covenants to exclude blacks from any future ownership of their real property. This device alone caused blacks to miss out on billions in home equity wealth accumulation. Since 1950 American residential apartheid and middle-class wealth-building discrimination have been maintained through, among other means, the practice of redlining.[8]

It follows unavoidably from this that the black middle class would be almost wholly dependent upon the gossamer filaments of salary to suspend it over rank poverty's chasm below. Consider. College-educated whites enjoy an average annual income of $38,700, a net worth of $74,922, and net financial assets of $19,823. College-educated blacks, however, earn only $29,440 annually with a net worth of $17,437 and $175 in net financial assets.

---

[8]*redlining:* Denying a home mortgage or insurance to people based on their ethnicity or neighborhood; some companies drew red boundary lines on local maps to designate "undesirable" areas whose residents they refused to serve or whom they charged much higher rates.

Attributing the black middle class's sickly economic condition to mortgage   85
and other past and existing forms of racial discrimination, Westley reports:

> Blacks who hold white collar jobs have $0 net financial assets com-
> pared to their white counterparts who on average hold $11,952 in net
> financial assets. Black middle class status, as such figures indicate, is
> based almost entirely on income, not assets or wealth. Thus, the black
> middle class can best be described as fragile. Even blacks earning as
> much as $50,000 per year have on average net financial assets of only
> $290 compared to $6,988 for whites. Moreover black families need
> more wage earners per household to attain the living standards of
> white households of similar income. Thus whether poor or "middle
> class," black families live without assets, and compared to white fami-
> lies, black families are disproportionately dependent on the labor mar-
> ket to maintain status. In real life terms, this means that blacks could
> survive an economic crisis, such as loss of a job, for a relatively short
> time.

So you can see that an unbroken story line of evidence and logic drawn
across time from Jamestown to Appomattox to contemporary America renders the "it's too late" response to reparations for African Americans inadequate. For blacks, the destructive moral crime that began in Jamestown in
1619 has yet to end.

Let's not mince words here. The racial economic gaps in this country
have been locked open at constant intervals since the days of slavery. The
gaps will not close themselves. To close them will require, as Norman
Francis, president of Xavier University of Louisiana, has said, a counter-
force "as strong as the force that put us in chains."

During the centuries of the Atlantic slave trade, Africa was denuded of
tens of millions of its ablest people, a massive pillage from which Africa has
yet to recover. During the century-long period of colonial exploitation that
followed on the heels of slavery, Africa saw its theretofore viable social,
political, economic, and agricultural systems destroyed by the colonizing
powers of Western Europe. The magnitude of this long-running multidi-
mensional human rights crime continues to define not only the crushing
dilemmas of contemporary Africa but the here-and-now burdens borne by
the scattered descendants of her sold-off issue as well. For black people, no
human rights wrongdoing stands before slavery and what followed it.

Our lives — all of our lives, all races, all classes — have a regular course
to them. They are habit-shaped. There is habit in the way we see ourselves,
the way we see and relate to each other, as genders, as classes, as races.
Habit has to it a silence, a soothing transparency. In our cluttered modern
lives, charged with the burdens of the clock and the cool embrace of electronic socialization, habit relieves us of the myriad social decisions we've
neither the time nor the energy to make or remake. Why throw the rice at
the bridal couple? Who knows anymore? But everyone throws it. Harmless,

eh? Most customs are, and habits as well. Habit does not alleviate pain. It does, however, cause us often to forget its source.

Well before the birth of our country, Europe and the eventual United
States perpetrated a heinous wrong against the peoples of Africa—and sustained and benefited from the wrong for centuries. Europe followed the grab of Africa's people with the rape, through colonial occupation, of Africa's material resources. America followed slavery with more than a hundred combined years of legal racial segregation and legal racial discrimination of one variety or another. In 1965, after nearly 350 years of legal racial suppression, the United States enacted the *Voting Rights Act* and, virtually simultaneously, began to walk away from the social wreckage that centuries of white hegemony had wrought. The country then began to rub itself with the memory-emptying salve of contemporaneousness. (If the wrong did not *just* occur, it did not occur at all in a way that would render the living responsible.)

But when the black living suffer real and current consequences as a result of wrongs committed by a younger America, then contemporary America must be caused to shoulder responsibility for those wrongs until such wrongs have been adequately compensated and righted. The life and responsibilities of a society or nation are not circumscribed by the life spans of its mortal constituents. Social rights, wrongs, obligations, and responsibilities flow eternal.

There are many ways to begin righting America's massive wrong, some of which you must already have inferred. But let there be no doubt, it will require great resources and decades of national fortitude to resolve economic and social disparities so long in the making.

Habit is the enemy. For whites and blacks have made a habit now, beyond the long era of legal discrimination, of seeing each other (the only way they can remember seeing each other) in a certain relation of economic and social inequality.

American capitalism, which starts each child where its parents left off, is not a fair system. This is particularly the case for African Americans, whose general economic starting points have been rearmost in our society because of slavery and its long racialist aftermath. American slaves for two and a half centuries saw taken from them not just their freedom but the inestimable economic value of their labor as well, which, were it a line item in today's gross national product report, would undoubtedly run into the billions of dollars. Whether the monetary obligation is legally enforceable or not, a large debt is owed by America to the descendants of America's slaves.

Here too, habit has become our enemy, for America has made an art
form by now of grinding its past deeds, no matter how despicable, into mere ephemera. African Americans, unfortunately, have accommodated this habit of American amnesia all too well. It would behoove African Americans to remember that history forgets, first, those who forget themselves. To do

what is necessary to accomplish anything approaching psychic and economic parity in the next half century will not only require a fundamental attitude shift in American thinking but massive amounts of money as well. Before the country in general can be made to understand, African Americans themselves must come to understand that this demand is not for charity. It is simply for what they are *owed* on a debt that is old but compellingly obvious and valid still.

Sources

Anderson, S.E. *The Black Holocaust for Beginners.* New York: Writers and Readers Publishing, 1995.

Bittker, Boris. *The Case for Black Reparations.* New York: Random House, 1973.

Franklin, John Hope. *From Slavery to Freedom,* New York: Knopf, 1947.

Taylor, Yuval, ed. *I was Born a Slave* (vol. 1). Chicago: Lawrence Hill, 1999.

Updike, John. *Brazil.* New York: Knopf, 1994.

Westley, Robert, "Many Billions Gone." *Boston College Law Review,* June 1999.

ENGAGING THE TEXT

1. Outline Robinson's economic argument for reparations: What measurable monetary losses have African Americans suffered as a result of slavery and discrimination? Are there losses that cannot be measured in economic terms? If so, how might they be redressed?

2. How does Robinson counter the objection that it's too late to demand restitution for slavery? What evidence does he present to support his contention that African Americans today still feel the effects of slavery? How persuasive do you find his reasoning?

3. Why does Robinson feel that it's important for African Americans to fight for reparations even when there's little chance of success?

4. Robinson cites a number of historical and legal precedents for reparations. In what ways are these cases similar to or different from the case of slavery? To what extent do the precedents strengthen Randall's argument?

5. Debate Robinson's claim that unless the United States addresses the issue of reparations, "there is *no* chance that America can solve its racial problems" (para. 10).

EXPLORING CONNECTIONS

6. What does Robinson mean when he says that "the biggest part of our problem is inside us" (para. 16)? How might Claude M. Steele (p. 231), Ken Hamblin (p. 384), Shelby Steele (p. 602), or Walter Mosley (p. 755) respond to his analysis of the psychological damage inflicted on African Americans by slavery and discrimination?

7. Compare Robinson's discussion of "studied white blindness" (para. 72) to Paul L. Wachtel's (p. 613) analysis of white "indifference" to the problems of African Americans. How do these writers explain the reactions of whites to blacks' demands for recognition or social change? What solutions do they offer? What are the benefits and drawbacks of each approach?

EXTENDING THE CRITICAL CONTEXT

8. Research the debate about reparations for slavery. Summarize the arguments you find both for and against reparations for slavery as well as some of the specific proposals for how reparations might be distributed. In class, stage a congressional hearing on the issue, taking the roles of a variety of experts who offer testimony to the Committee on Reparations. Then write an essay evaluating the testimony and explaining how you would vote on the issue, and why.

9. In paragraph 49, Robinson cites a series of statistics on the precarious position of black males in the United States. Do some further research into the comparative status of white and black Americans: income, home ownership, education, and so forth. To what extent do your findings support Randall's contention that a "yawning economic gap between blacks and whites" (para. 10) persists in this country?

Causes of Prejudice

VINCENT N. PARRILLO

What motivates the creation of racial categories? In the following selection, Vincent Parrillo reviews several theories that seek to explain the motives for prejudiced behavior—from socialization theory to economic competition. As Parrillo indicates, prejudice cannot be linked to any single cause: a whole network of forces and frustrations underlies this complex set of feelings and behaviors. Parrillo (b. 1938) chairs the Department of Sociology at William Paterson College in New Jersey. His books include Rethinking Today's Minorities *(1991),* Diversity in America *(1996), and* Understanding Race and Ethnic Relations *(2002). He has also written and produced two award-winning documentaries for PBS television. This excerpt originally appeared in* Strangers to These Shores *(1999, 6th ed.).*

Prejudicial attitudes may be either positive or negative. Sociologists primarily study the latter, however, because only negative attitudes can lead to turbulent social relations between dominant and minority groups.

Numerous writers, therefore, have defined *prejudice* as an attitudinal "system of negative beliefs, feelings, and action-orientations regarding a certain group or groups of people."[1] The status of the strangers is an important factor in the development of a negative attitude. Prejudicial attitudes exist among members of both dominant and minority groups. Thus, in the relations between dominant and minority groups, the antipathy felt by one group for another is quite often reciprocated.

Psychological perspectives on prejudice—whether behaviorist, cognitive, or psychoanalytic—focus on the subjective states of mind of individuals. In these perspectives, a person's prejudicial attitudes may result from imitation or conditioning (behaviorist), perceived similarity–dissimilarity of beliefs (cognitive), or specific personality characteristics (psychoanalytic). In contrast, sociological perspectives focus on the objective conditions of society as the social forces behind prejudicial attitudes and behind racial and ethnic relations. Individuals do not live in a vacuum; social reality affects their states of mind.

Both perspectives are necessary to understand prejudice. As psychologist Gordon Allport argued, besides needing a close study of habits, perceptions, motivation, and personality, we need an analysis of social settings, situational forces, demographic and ecological variables, and legal and economic trends.[2] Psychological and sociological perspectives complement each other in providing a fuller explanation about intergroup relations.

The Psychology of Prejudice

We can understand more about prejudice among individuals by focusing on four areas of study: levels of prejudice, self-justification, personality, and frustration.

Levels of Prejudice. Bernard Kramer suggests that prejudice exists on three levels: cognitive, emotional, and action orientation.[3] The **cognitive level of prejudice** encompasses a person's beliefs and perceptions of a group as threatening or nonthreatening, inferior or equal (e.g., in terms of intellect, status, or biological composition), seclusive or intrusive, impulse-gratifying, acquisitive, or possessing other positive or negative characteristics. Mr. X's cognitive beliefs are that Jews are intrusive and acquisitive. Other illustrations of cognitive beliefs are that the Irish are heavy drinkers and fighters. African Americans are rhythmic and lazy, and the Poles are

5

---

[1]Reported by Daniel Wilner, Rosabelle Price Walkley, and Stuart W. Cook, "Residential Proximity and Intergroup Relations in Public Housing Projects," *Journal of Social Issues* 8 (1) (1952): 45. See also James W. Vander Zanden, *American Minority Relations,* 3d ed. (New York: Ronald Press, 1972), p. 21. [All notes are the author's.]

[2]Gordon W. Allport, "Prejudice: Is It Societal or Personal?" *Journal of Social Issues* 18 (1962): 129–30.

[3]Bernard M. Kramer, "Dimensions of Prejudice," *Journal of Psychology* 27 (April 1949): 389–451.

thick-headed and unintelligent. Generalizations shape both ethnocentric and prejudicial attitudes, but there is a difference. **Ethnocentrism** is a generalized rejection of all outgroups on the basis of an ingroup focus, whereas **prejudice** is a rejection of certain people solely on the basis of their membership in a particular group.

In many societies, members of the majority group may believe that a particular low-status minority group is dirty, immoral, violent, or law-breaking. In the United States, the Irish, Italians, African Americans, Mexicans, Chinese, Puerto Ricans, and others have at one time or another been labeled with most, if not all, of these adjectives. In most European countries and in the United States, the group lowest on the socioeconomic ladder has often been depicted in caricature as also lowest on the evolutionary ladder. The Irish and African Americans in the United States and the peasants and various ethnic groups in Europe have all been depicted in the past as apelike:

> The Victorian images of the Irish as "white Negro" and simian Celt, or a combination of the two, derived much of its force and inspiration from physiognomical beliefs ... [but] every country in Europe had its equivalent of "white Negroes" and simianized men, whether or not they happened to be stereotypes of criminals, assassins, political radicals, revolutionaries, Slavs, gypsies, Jews, or peasants.[4]

The **emotional level of prejudice** refers to the feelings that a minority group arouses in an individual. Although these feelings may be based on stereotypes from the cognitive level, they represent a more intense stage of personal involvement. The emotional attitudes may be negative or positive, such as fear/envy, distrust/trust, disgust/admiration, or contempt/empathy. These feelings, based on beliefs about the group, may be triggered by social interaction or by the possibility of interaction. For example, whites might react with fear or anger to the integration of their schools or neighborhoods, or Protestants might be jealous of the lifestyle of a highly successful Catholic business executive.

An **action-orientation level of prejudice** is the positive or negative predisposition to engage in discriminatory behavior. A person who harbors strong feelings about members of a certain racial or ethnic group may have a tendency to act for or against them—being aggressive or nonaggressive, offering assistance or withholding it. Such an individual would also be likely to want to exclude or include members of that group both in close, personal social relations and in peripheral social relations. For example, some people would want to exclude members of the disliked group from doing business with them or living in their neighborhood. Another manifestation of the action-orientation level of prejudice is the desire to change or maintain the status differential or inequality between the two groups, whether the area is

[4]L. Perry Curtis, Jr., *Apes and Angels: The Irishman in Victorian Caricature* (Washington, D.C.: Smithsonian Press, 1971).

economic, political, educational, social, or a combination. Note that an action orientation is a predisposition to act, not the action itself.

Self-Justification.   **Self-justification** involves denigrating a person or group to justify maltreatment of them. In this situation, self-justification leads to prejudice and discrimination against members of another group.

Some philosophers argue that we are not so much rational creatures as   10 we are rationalizing creatures. We require reassurance that the things we do and the lives we live are proper, that good reasons for our actions exist. If we can convince ourselves that another group is inferior, immoral, or dangerous, we may feel justified in discriminating against its members, enslaving them, or even killing them.

History is filled with examples of people who thought their maltreatment of others was just and necessary: As defenders of the "true faith," the Crusaders killed "Christ-killers" (Jews) and "infidels" (Moslems). Participants in the Spanish Inquisition imprisoned, tortured, and executed "heretics," "the disciples of the Devil." Similarly, the Puritans burned witches, whose refusal to confess "proved they were evil"; pioneers exploited or killed Native Americans who were "heathen savages"; and whites mistreated, enslaved, or killed African Americans, who were "an inferior species." According to U.S. Army officers, the civilians in the Vietnamese village of My Lai were "probably" aiding the Vietcong; so in 1968 U.S. soldiers fighting in the Vietnam War felt justified in slaughtering over 300 unarmed people there, including women, children, and the elderly.

Some sociologists believe that self-justification works the other way around. That is, instead of self-justification serving as a basis for subjugating others, the subjugation occurs first and the self-justification follows, resulting in prejudice and continued discrimination.[5] The evolution of racism as a concept after the establishment of the African slave trade would seem to support this idea. Philip Mason offers an insight into this view:

> A specialized society is likely to defeat a simpler society and provide a lower tier still of enslaved and conquered peoples. The rulers and organizers sought security for themselves and their children; to perpetuate the power, the esteem, and the comfort they had achieved, it was necessary not only that the artisans and labourers should work contentedly but that the rulers should sleep without bad dreams. No one can say with certainty how the myths originated, but it is surely relevant that when one of the founders of Western thought set himself to frame an ideal state that would embody social justice, he—like the earliest city dwellers—not only devised a society stratified in tiers but believed it would be necessary to persuade the traders and work-

---

[5]See Marvin B. Scott and Stanford M. Lyman, "Accounts," *American Sociological Review* 33 (February 1968): 40–62.

people that, by divine decree, they were made from brass and iron, while the warriors were made of silver and the rulers of gold.[6]

Another example of self-justification serving as a source of prejudice is the dominant group's assumption of an attitude of superiority over other groups. In this respect, establishing a prestige hierarchy—ranking the status of various ethnic groups—results in differential association. To enhance or maintain self-esteem, a person may avoid social contact with groups deemed inferior and associate only with those identified as being of high status. Through such behavior, self-justification may come to intensify the social distance between groups. . . . *Social distance* refers to the degree to which ingroup members do not engage in social or primary relationships with members of various outgroups.

Personality.   In 1950, in *The Authoritarian Personality*, T. W. Adorno and his colleagues reported a correlation between individuals' early childhood experiences of harsh parental discipline and their development of an **authoritarian personality** as adults.[7] If parents assume an excessively domineering posture in their relations with a child, exercising stern measures and threatening to withdraw love if the child does not respond with weakness and submission, the child tends to be insecure and to nurture much latent hostility against the parents. When such children become adults, they may demonstrate **displaced aggression,** directing their hostility against a powerless group to compensate for their feelings of insecurity and fear. Highly prejudiced individuals tend to come from families that emphasize obedience.

The authors identified authoritarianism by the use of a measuring instrument called an F scale (the *F* standing for potential fascism). Other tests included the A-S (anti-Semitism) and E (ethnocentrism) scales, the latter measuring attitudes toward various minorities. One of their major findings was that people who scored high on authoritarianism also consistently showed a high degree of prejudice against all minority groups. These highly prejudiced persons were characterized by rigidity of viewpoint, dislike for ambiguity, strict obedience to leaders, and intolerance of weakness in themselves and others.   15

No sooner did *The Authoritarian Personality* appear than controversy began. H. H. Hyman and P. B. Sheatsley challenged the methodology and analysis.[8] Solomon Asch questioned the assumptions that the F scale

[6]Philip Mason, *Patterns of Dominance* (New York: Oxford University Press, 1970), p. 7. See also Philip Mason, *Race Relations* (New York: Oxford University Press, 1970), pp. 17–29.

[7]T. W. Adorno, Else Frankel-Brunswik, Daniel J. Levinson, and R. Nevitt Sanford, *The Authoritarian Personality* (New York: Harper & Row, 1950).

[8]H. H. Hyman and P. B. Sheatsley, "The Authoritarian Personality: A Methodological Critique," in R. Christie and M. Jahoda (eds.), *Studies in the Scope and Method of "The Authoritarian Personality"* (Glencoe, Ill.: Free Press, 1954).

responses represented a belief system and that structural variables (such as ideologies, stratification, and mobility) do not play a role in shaping personality.[9] E. A. Shils argued that the authors were interested only in measuring authoritarianism of the political right while ignoring such tendencies in those at the other end of the political spectrum.[10] Other investigators sought alternative explanations for the authoritarian personality. D. Stewart and T. Hoult extended the framework beyond family childhood experiences to include other social factors.[11] H. C. Kelman and Janet Barclay pointed out that substantial evidence exists showing that lower intelligence and less education also correlate with high authoritarianism scores on the F scale.[12]

Despite the critical attacks, the underlying conceptions of *The Authoritarian Personality* were important, and research into personality as a factor in prejudice has continued. Subsequent investigators refined and modified the original study. Correcting scores for response bias, they conducted cross-cultural studies. Respondents in Germany and Near East countries, where more authoritarian social structures exist, scored higher on authoritarianism and social distance between groups. In Japan, Germany, and the United States, authoritarianism and social distance were moderately related. Other studies suggested that an inverse relationship exists between social class and F scale scores: the higher the social class, the lower the authoritarianism.[13]

Although studies of authoritarian personality have helped us understand some aspects of prejudice, they have not provided a causal explanation. Most of the findings in this area show a correlation, but the findings do not prove, for example, that harsh discipline of children causes them to become prejudiced adults. Perhaps the strict parents were themselves prejudiced, and the child learned those attitudes from them. Or as George Simpson and J. Milton Yinger say:

> One must be careful not to assume too quickly that a certain tendency — rigidity of mind, for example — that is correlated with prejudice necessarily causes that prejudice.... The sequence may be the other way around.... It is more likely that both are related to more basic factors.[14]

[9]Solomon E. Asch, *Social Psychology* (Englewood Cliffs, N.J.: Prentice-Hall, 1952), p. 545.

[10]E. A. Shils, "Authoritarianism: Right and Left," in *Studies in the Scope and Method of "The Authoritarian Personality."*

[11]D. Stewart and T. Hoult, "A Social-Psychological Theory of 'The Authoritarian Personality.'" *American Journal of Sociology* 65 (1959): 274.

[12]H. C. Kelman and Janet Barclay, "The F Scale as a Measure of Breadth of Perspective," *Journal of Abnormal and Social Psychology* 67 (1963): 608–15.

[13]For an excellent summary of authoritarian studies and literature, see John P. Kirscht and Ronald C. Dillehay, *Dimensions of Authoritarianism: A Review of Research and Theory* (Lexington: University of Kentucky Press, 1967).

[14]George E. Simpson and J. Milton Yinger, *Racial and Cultural Minorities: An Analysis of Prejudice and Discrimination* (New York: Harper & Row, 1953), p. 91.

For some people, prejudice may indeed be rooted in subconscious childhood tensions, but we simply do not know whether these tensions directly cause a high degree of prejudice in the adult or whether other powerful social forces are the determinants. Whatever the explanation, authoritarianism is a significant phenomenon worthy of continued investigation. Recent research, however, has stressed social and situational factors, rather than personality, as primary causes of prejudice and discrimination.[15]

Yet another dimension of the personality component is that people with   20
low self-esteem are more prejudiced than those who feel good about themselves. Some researchers have argued that individuals with low self-esteem deprecate others to enhance their feelings about themselves.[16] One study asserts that "low self-esteem individuals seem to have a generally negative view of themselves, their ingroup, outgroups, and perhaps the world," and thus their tendency to be more prejudiced is not due to rating the outgroup negatively in comparison to their ingroup.[17]

Frustration.   Frustration is the result of relative deprivation in which expectations remain unsatisfied. **Relative deprivation** is a lack of resources, or rewards, in one's standard of living in comparison with those of others in the society. A number of investigators have suggested that frustrations tend to increase aggression toward others.[18] Frustrated people may easily strike out against the perceived cause of their frustration. However, this reaction may not be possible because the true source of the frustration is often too nebulous to be identified or too powerful to act against. In such instances, the result may be displaced aggression; in this situation, the frustrated individual or group usually redirects anger against a more visible, vulnerable, and socially sanctioned target, one unable to strike back. Minorities meet these criteria and are thus frequently the recipients of displaced aggression by the dominant group.

Blaming others for something that is not their fault is known as **scapegoating.** The term comes from the ancient Hebrew custom of using a goat

[15]Ibid., pp. 62–79.

[16]Howard J. Ehrlich, *The Social Psychology of Prejudice* (New York: Wiley, 1974); G. Sherwood, "Self-Serving Biases in Person Perception," *Psychological Bulletin* 90 (1981): 445–59; T. A. Wills, "Downward Comparison Principles in Social Psychology," *Psychological Bulletin* 90 (1981): 245–71.

[17]Jennifer Crocker and Ian Schwartz, "Prejudice and Ingroup Favoritism in a Minimal Intergroup Situation: Effects of Self-Esteem," *Personality and Social Psychology Bulletin* 11 (4) (December 1985): 379–86.

[18]John Dollard, Leonard W. Doob, Neal E. Miller, O. H. Mowrer, and Robert P. Sears, *Frustration and Aggression* (New Haven, Conn.: Yale University Press, 1939); A. F. Henry and J. F. Short, Jr., *Suicide and Homicide* (New York: Free Press, 1954); Neal Miller and Richard Bugelski, "Minor Studies in Aggression: The Influence of Frustration Imposed by the Ingroup on Attitudes Expressed Toward Out-Groups," *Journal of Psychology* 25 (1948): 437–42; Stuart Palmer, *The Psychology of Murder* (New York: T. Y. Crowell, 1960); Brenden C. Rule and Elizabeth Percival, "The Effects of Frustration and Attack on Physical Aggression," *Journal of Experimental Research on Personality* 5 (1971): 111–88.

during the Day of Atonement as a symbol of the sins of the people. In an annual ceremony, a priest placed his hands on the head of a goat and listed the people's sins in a symbolic transference of guilt; he then chased the goat out of the community, thereby freeing the people of sin.[19] Since those times, the powerful group has usually punished the scapegoat group rather than allowing it to escape.

There have been many instances throughout world history of minority groups serving as scapegoats, including the Christians in ancient Rome, the Huguenots in France, the Jews in Europe and Russia, and the Puritans and Quakers in England. Gordon Allport suggests that certain characteristics are necessary for a group to become a suitable scapegoat. The group must be (1) highly visible in physical appearance or observable customs and actions; (2) not strong enough to strike back; (3) situated within easy access of the dominant group and, ideally, concentrated in one area; (4) a past target of hostility for whom latent hostility still exists; and (5) the symbol of an unpopular concept.[20]

Some groups fit this typology better than others, but minority racial and ethnic groups have been a perennial choice. Irish, Italians, Catholics, Jews, Quakers, Mormons, Chinese, Japanese, Blacks, Puerto Ricans, Chicanos, and Koreans have all been treated, at one time or another, as the scapegoat in the United States. Especially in times of economic hardship, societies tend to blame some group for the general conditions, which often leads to aggressive action against the group as an expression of frustration. For example, a study by Carl Hovland and Robert Sears found that, between 1882 and 1930, a definite correlation existed between a decline in the price of cotton and an increase in the number of lynchings of Blacks.[21]

In several controlled experiments, social scientists have attempted to measure the validity of the scapegoat theory. Neal Miller and Richard Bugelski tested a group of young men aged eighteen to twenty who were working in a government camp about their feelings toward various minority groups. The young men were reexamined about these feelings after experiencing frustration by being obliged to take a long, difficult test and being denied an opportunity to see a film at a local theater. This group showed some evidence of increased prejudicial feelings, whereas a control group, which did not experience any frustration, showed no change in prejudicial attitudes.[22]

Donald Weatherley conducted an experiment with a group of college students to measure the relationship between frustration and aggression against a specific disliked group.[23] After identifying students who were or

25

[19]Leviticus 16:5–22.

[20]Gordon W. Allport, *The Nature of Prejudice* (Cambridge, Mass.: Addison-Wesley, 1954), pp. 13–14.

[21]Carl I. Hovland and Robert R. Sears, "Minor Studies of Aggression: Correlation of Lynchings with Economic Indices," *Journal of Psychology* 9 (Winter 1940): 301–10.

[22]Miller and Bugelski, "Minor Studies in Aggression," pp. 437–42.

[23]Donald Weatherley, "Anti-Semitism and the Expression of Fantasy Aggression," *Journal of Abnormal and Social Psychology* 62 (1961): 454–57.

were not highly anti-Semitic and subjecting them to a strongly frustrating experience, he asked the students to write stories about pictures shown to them. Some of the students were shown pictures of people who had been given Jewish names; other students were presented with pictures of unnamed people. When the pictures were unidentified, the stories of the anti-Semitic students did not differ from those of other students. When the pictures were identified, however, the anti-Semitic students wrote stories reflecting much more aggression against the Jews in the pictures than did the other students.

For over twenty years, Leonard Berkowitz and his associates studied and experimented with aggressive behavior. They concluded that, confronted with equally frustrating situations, highly prejudiced individuals are more likely to seek scapegoats than are nonprejudiced individuals. Another intervening variable is that personal frustrations (marital failure, injury, or mental illness) make people more likely to seek scapegoats than do shared frustrations (dangers of flood or hurricane).[24]

Some experiments have shown that aggression does not increase if the frustration is understandable.[25] Other experiments have found that people become aggressive only if the aggression directly relieves their frustration.[26] Still other studies have shown that anger is a more likely result if the person responsible for the frustrating situation could have acted otherwise.[27] Clearly, the results are mixed, depending on the variables within a given social situation.

Frustration–aggression theory, although helpful, is not completely satisfactory. It ignores the role of culture and the reality of actual social conflict and fails to show any causal relationship. Most of the responses measured in these studies were of people already biased. Why did one group rather than another become the object of the aggression? Moreover, frustration does not necessarily precede aggression, and aggression does not necessarily flow from frustration.

The Sociology of Prejudice

Sociologist Talcott Parsons provided one bridge between psychology   30
and sociology by introducing social forces as a variable in frustration–
aggression theory. He suggested that both the family and the occupational

[24]See Leonard Berkowitz, "Whatever Happened to the Frustration-Aggression Hypothesis?" *American Behavioral Scientist* 21 (1978): 691–708; L. Berkowitz, *Aggression: A Social Psychological Analysis* (New York: McGraw-Hill, 1962).

[25]D. Zillman, *Hostility and Aggression* (Hillsdale, N.J.: Laurence Erlbaum, 1979); R. A. Baron, *Human Aggression* (New York: Plenum Press, 1977); N. Pastore, "The Role of Arbitrariness in the Frustration-Aggression Hypothesis," *Journal of Abnormal and Social Psychology* 47 (1952): 728–31.

[26]A. H. Buss, "Instrumentality of Aggression, Feedback, and Frustration as Determinants of Physical Aggression," *Journal of Personality and Social Psychology* 3 (1966): 153–62.

[27]J. R. Averill, "Studies on Anger and Aggression: Implications for Theories of Emotion," *American Psychologist* 38 (1983): 1145–60.

structure may produce anxieties and insecurities that create frustration.[28] According to this view, the growing-up process (gaining parental affection and approval, identifying with and imitating sexual role models, and competing with others in adulthood) sometimes involves severe emotional strain. The result is an adult personality with a large reservoir of repressed aggression that becomes *free-floating*—susceptible to redirection against convenient scapegoats. Similarly, the occupational system is a source of frustration: its emphasis on competitiveness and individual achievement, its function of conferring status, its requirement that people inhibit their natural impulses at work, and its ties to the state of the economy are among the factors that generate emotional anxieties. Parsons pessimistically concluded that minorities fulfill a functional "need" as targets for displaced aggression and therefore will remain targets.[29]

Perhaps most influential in staking out the sociological position on prejudice was Herbert Blumer, who suggested that prejudice always involves the "sense of group position" in society. Agreeing with Kramer's delineation of three levels of prejudice, Blumer argued that prejudice can include beliefs, feelings, and a predisposition to action, thus motivating behavior that derives from the social hierarchy.[30] By emphasizing historically established group positions and relationships, Blumer shifted his focus away from the attitudes and personality compositions of individuals. As a social phenomenon, prejudice rises or falls according to issues that alter one group's position vis-à-vis that of another group.

Socialization. In the **socialization process,** individuals acquire the values, attitudes, beliefs, and perceptions of their culture or subculture, including religion, nationality, and social class. Generally, the child conforms to the parents' expectations in acquiring an understanding of the world and its people. Being impressionable and knowing of no alternative conceptions of the world, the child usually accepts these concepts without questioning. We thus learn the prejudices of our parents and others, which then become part of our values and beliefs. Even when based on false stereotypes, prejudices shape our perceptions of various peoples and influence our attitudes and actions toward particular groups. For example, if we develop negative attitudes about Jews because we are taught that they are shrewd, acquisitive, and clannish—all-too-familiar stereotypes—as adults we may refrain from business or social relationships with them. We may not even realize the reason for such avoidance, so subtle has been the prejudice instilled within us.

[28]Talcott Parsons, "Certain Primary Sources and Patterns of Aggression in the Social Structure of the Western World," in *Essays in Sociological Theory* (New York: Free Press, 1964), pp. 298–322.

[29]For an excellent review of Parsonian theory in this area, see Stanford M. Lyman, *The Black American in Sociological Thought: A Failure of Perspective* (New York: Putnam, 1972), pp. 145–69.

[30]Herbert Blumer, "Race Prejudice as a Sense of Group Position," *Pacific Sociological Review* 1 (1958): 3–7.

People may learn certain prejudices because of their pervasiveness. The cultural screen that we develop and through which we view the surrounding world is not always accurate, but it does permit transmission of shared values and attitudes, which are reinforced by others. Prejudice, like cultural values, is taught and learned through the socialization process. The prevailing prejudicial attitudes and actions may be deeply embedded in custom or law (e.g., the **Jim Crow laws** of the 1890s and the early twentieth century establishing segregated public facilities throughout the South, which subsequent generations accepted as proper, and maintained in their own adult lives).

Although socialization explains how prejudicial attitudes may be transmitted from one generation to the next, it does not explain their origin or why they intensify or diminish over the years. These aspects of prejudice must be explained in another way.

Economic Competition.   People tend to be more hostile toward others   35
when they feel that their security is threatened; thus many social scientists conclude that economic competition and conflict breed prejudice. Certainly, considerable evidence shows that negative stereotyping, prejudice, and discrimination increase markedly whenever competition for available jobs increases.

An excellent illustration relates to the Chinese sojourners in the nineteenth-century United States. Prior to the 1870s, the transcontinental railroad was being built, and the Chinese filled many of the jobs made available by this project in the sparsely populated West. Although they were expelled from the region's gold mines and schools and could obtain no redress of grievances in the courts, they managed to convey to some Whites the image of being a clean, hard-working, law-abiding people. The completion of the railroad, the flood of former Civil War soldiers into the job market, and the economic depression of 1873 worsened their situation. The Chinese became more frequent victims of open discrimination and hostility. Their positive stereotype among some Whites was widely displaced by a negative one: They were now "conniving," "crafty," "criminal," "the yellow menace." Only after they retreated into Chinatowns and entered specialty occupations that minimized their competition with Whites did the intense hostility abate.

One pioneer in the scientific study of prejudice, John Dollard, demonstrated how prejudice against the Germans, which had been virtually nonexistent, arose in a small U.S. industrial town when times got bad:

> Local Whites largely drawn from the surrounding farms manifested considerable direct aggression toward the newcomers. Scornful and derogatory opinions were expressed about the Germans, and the native Whites had a satisfying sense of superiority toward them.... The chief element in the permission to be aggressive against the Germans was rivalry for jobs and status in the local woodenware plants. The

native Whites felt definitely crowded for their jobs by the entering German groups and in case of bad times had a chance to blame the Germans who by their presence provided more competitors for the scarcer jobs. There seemed to be no traditional pattern of prejudice against Germans unless the skeletal suspicion of all out-groupers (always present) be invoked in this place.[31]

Both experimental studies and historical analyses have added credence to the economic-competition theory. Muzafer Sherif directed several experiments showing how intergroup competition at a boys' camp led to conflict and escalating hostility.[32] Donald Young pointed out that, throughout U.S. history, in times of high unemployment and thus intense job competition, nativist movements against minorities have flourished.[33] This pattern has held true regionally—against Asians on the West Coast, Italians in Louisiana, and French Canadians in New England—and nationally, with the antiforeign movements always peaking during periods of depression. So it was with the Native American Party in the 1830s, the Know-Nothing Party in the 1850s, the American Protective Association in the 1890s, and the Ku Klux Klan after World War I. Since the passage of civil rights laws on employment in the twentieth century, researchers have consistently detected the strongest antiblack prejudice among working-class and middle-class Whites who feel threatened by Blacks entering their socioeconomic group in noticeable numbers.[34] It seems that any group applying the pressure of job competition most directly on another group becomes a target of its prejudice.

Once again, a theory that offers some excellent insights into prejudice—in particular, that adverse economic conditions correlate with increased hostility toward minorities—also has some serious shortcomings. Not all groups that have been objects of hostility (e.g., Quakers and Mormons) have been economic competitors. Moreover, why is hostility against some groups greater than against others? Why do the negative feelings in some communities run against groups whose numbers are so small that they cannot possibly pose an economic threat? Evidently values besides economic ones cause people to be antagonistic to a group perceived as an actual or potential threat.

[31]John Dollard, "Hostility and Fear in Social Life," *Social Forces* 17 (1938): 15–26.

[32]Muzafer Sherif, O. J. Harvey, B. Jack White, William Hood, and Carolyn Sherif, *Intergroup Conflict and Cooperation: The Robbers Cave Experiment* (Norman: University of Oklahoma Institute of Intergroup Relations, 1961). See also M. Sherif, "Experiments in Group Conflict," *Scientific American* 195 (1956): 54–58.

[33]Donald Young, *Research Memorandum on Minority Peoples in the Depression* (New York: Social Science Research Council, 1937), pp. 133–41.

[34]Andrew Greeley and Paul Sheatsley, "The Acceptance of Desegregation Continues to Advance," *Scientific American* 210 (1971): 13–19; T. F. Pettigrew, "Three Issues in Ethnicity: Boundaries, Deprivations, and Perceptions," in M. Yinger and S. J. Cutler (eds.), *Major Social Issues: A Multidisciplinary View* (New York: Free Press, 1978); R. D. Vanneman and T. F. Pettigrew, "Race and Relative Deprivation in the United States," *Race* 13 (1972): 461–86.

Social Norms.   Some sociologists have suggested that a relationship   40
exists between prejudice and a person's tendency to conform to societal expectations.[35] **Social norms**—the norms of one's culture—form the generally shared rules defining what is and is not proper behavior. By learning
and automatically accepting the prevailing prejudices, an individual is
simply conforming to those norms.

This theory holds that a direct relationship exists between degree of
conformity and degree of prejudice. If so, people's prejudices should decrease or increase significantly when they move into areas where the prejudicial norm is lesser or greater. Evidence supports this view. Thomas
Pettigrew found that Southerners in the 1950s became less prejudiced
against Blacks when they interacted with them in the army, where the social
norms were less prejudicial.[36] In another study, Jeanne Watson found that
people moving into an anti-Semitic neighborhood in New York City became
more anti-Semitic.[37]

John Dollard's study, *Caste and Class in a Southern Town* (1937), provides an in-depth look at the emotional adjustment of Whites and Blacks to
rigid social norms.[38] In his study of the processes, functions, and maintenance of accommodation, Dollard detailed the "carrot-and-stick" method
social groups employed. Intimidation—sometimes even severe reprisals for
going against social norms—ensured compliance. However, reprisals usually were unnecessary. The advantages Whites and Blacks gained in psychological, economic, or behavioral terms served to perpetuate the caste order.
These gains in personal security and stability set in motion a vicious circle.
They encouraged a way of life that reinforced the rationale of the social system in this community.

Two 1994 studies provided further evidence of the powerful influence
of social norms. Joachim Krueger and Russell W. Clement found that consensus bias persisted despite the availability of statistical data and knowledge about such bias.[39] Michael R. Leippe and Donna Eisenstadt showed
that induced compliance can change socially significant attitudes and that
the change generalizes to broader beliefs.[40]

---

[35]See Harry H. L. Kitano, "Passive Discrimination in the Normal Person," *Journal of Social Psychology* 70 (1966): 23–31.

[36]Thomas Pettigrew, "Regional Differences in Anti-Negro Prejudice," *Journal of Abnormal and Social Psychology* 59 (1959): 28–36.

[37]Jeanne Watson, "Some Social and Psychological Situations Related to Change in Attitude," *Human Relations* 3 (1950): 15–56.

[38]John Dollard, *Caste and Class in a Southern Town*, 3d ed. (Garden City, N.Y.: Doubleday Anchor Books, 1957).

[39]Joachim Krueger and Russell W. Clement, "The Truly False Consensus Effect: An Ineradicable and Egocentric Bias in Social Perception," *Journal of Personality and Social Psychology* 67 (1994): 596–610.

[40]Michael R. Leippe and Donna Eisenstadt, "Generalization of Dissonance Reduction:
Decreasing Prejudice through Induced Compliance," *Journal of Personality and Social Psychology* 67 (1994): 395–414.

Although the social-norms theory explains prevailing attitudes, it does not explain either their origins or the reasons why new prejudices develop when other groups move into an area. In addition, the theory does not explain why prejudicial attitudes against a particular group rise and fall cyclically over the years.

Although many social scientists have attempted to identify the causes of   45
prejudice, no single factor provides an adequate explanation. Prejudice is a complex phenomenon, and it is most likely the product of more than one causal agent. Sociologists today tend either to emphasize multiple-cause explanations or to stress social forces encountered in specific and similar situations — forces such as economic conditions, stratification, and hostility toward an outgroup.

ENGAGING THE TEXT

1. Review Parrillo's discussion of the cognitive, emotional, and action-oriented levels of prejudice. Do you think it's possible for an individual to hold prejudiced beliefs that do *not* affect her feelings and actions? Why or why not?

2. How can prejudice arise from self-justification? Offer some examples of how a group can assume an attitude of superiority in order to justify ill-treatment of others.

3. How, according to Parrillo, might personal factors like authoritarian attitudes, low self-esteem, or frustration promote the growth of prejudice?

4. What is the "socialization process," according to Parrillo? In what different ways can socialization instill prejudice?

5. What is the relationship between economic competition and prejudice? Do you think prejudice would continue to exist if everyone had a good job with a comfortable income?

EXPLORING CONNECTIONS

6. Which of the theories Parrillo outlines, if any, might help to explain the attitudes toward blacks expressed by Thomas Jefferson (p. 551)? Which apply most clearly to the life story of C. P. Ellis (p. 591)?

7. Read or review Carmen Vázquez's "Appearances" (p. 489). How useful are the theories presented by Parrillo in analyzing prejudice against gays and lesbians? To what extent can concepts like levels of prejudice, self-justification, frustration, socialization, and economic competition help us understand antigay attitudes?

EXTENDING THE CRITICAL CONTEXT

8. List the various groups that you belong to (racial, economic, cultural, social, familial, and so forth) and arrange them in a status hierarchy. Which groups were you born into? Which groups did you join voluntarily? Which have

had the greatest impact on your socialization? Which groups isolate you the most from contact with outsiders?

9. Working in small groups, research recent news stories for examples of incidents involving racism or prejudice. Which of the theories described by Parrillo seem most useful for analyzing the motives underlying these events?

C. P. Ellis
STUDS TERKEL

The following oral history brings us uncomfortably close to unambiguous, deadly prejudice: C. P. Ellis is a former Ku Klux Klan member who claims to have overcome his racist (and sexist) attitudes; he speaks here as a union leader who feels an alliance to other workers, including blacks and women. Studs Terkel (b. 1912) is probably the best-known practitioner of oral history in the United States. He has compiled several books by interviewing dozens of widely varying people—ordinary people for the most part—about important subjects like work, social class, race, the Great Depression, and aging. The edited versions of these interviews are often surprisingly powerful crystallizations of American social history: Terkel's subjects give voice to the frustrations and hopes of whole generations of Americans. Terkel won a Pulitzer Prize in 1985 for "The Good War": An Oral History of World War II, *and in 1997 he received a National Humanities Medal from President Bill Clinton. Currently he serves as Distinguished Scholar-In-Residence at the Chicago Historical Society. "C. P. Ellis" first appeared in* American Dreams: Lost and Found *(1980).*

We're in his office in Durham, North Carolina. He is the business manager of the International Union of Operating Engineers. On the wall is a plaque: "Certificate of Service, in recognition to C. P. Ellis, for your faithful service to the city in having served as a member of the Durham Human Relations Council. February 1977."

At one time, he had been president (exalted cyclops) of the Durham chapter of the Ku Klux Klan....

He is fifty-two years old.

My father worked in a textile mill in Durham. He died at forty-eight years old. It was probably from cotton dust. Back then, we never heard of brown lung. I was about seventeen years old and had a mother and sister depending on somebody to make a livin'. It was just barely enough insurance to cover his burial. I had to quit school and go to work. I was about eighth grade when I quit.

My father worked hard but never had enough money to buy decent clothes. When I went to school, I never seemed to have adequate clothes to wear. I always left school late afternoon with a sense of inferiority. The other kids had nice clothes, and I just had what Daddy could buy. I still got some of those inferiority feelin's now that I have to overcome once in a while. 5

I loved my father. He would go with me to ball games. We'd go fishin' together. I was really ashamed of the way he'd dress. He would take this money and give it to me instead of putting it on himself. I always had the feeling about somebody looking at him and makin' fun of him and makin' fun of me. I think it had to do somethin' with my life.

My father and I were very close, but we didn't talk about too many intimate things. He did have a drinking problem. During the week, he would work every day, but weekends he was ready to get plastered. I can understand when a guy looks at his paycheck and looks at his bills, and he's worked hard all the week, and his bills are larger than his paycheck. He'd done the best he could the entire week, and there seemed to be no hope. It's an illness thing. Finally you just say: "The heck with it. I'll just get drunk and forget it."

My father was out of work during the depression, and I remember going with him to the finance company uptown, and he was turned down. That's something that's always stuck.

My father never seemed to be happy. It was a constant struggle with him just like it was for me. It's very seldom I'd see him laugh. He was just tryin' to figure out what he could do from one day to the next.

After several years pumping gas at a service station, I got married. We had to have children. Four. One child was born blind and retarded, which was a real additional expense to us. He's never spoken a word. He doesn't know me when I go to see him. But I see him, I hug his neck. I talk to him, tell him I love him. I don't know whether he knows me or not, but I know he's well taken care of. All my life, I had work, never a day without work, worked all the overtime I could get and still could not survive financially. I began to say there's somethin' wrong with this country. I worked my butt off and just never seemed to break even. 10

I had some real great ideas about this great nation. (Laughs.) They say to abide by the law, go to church, do right and live for the Lord, and everything'll work out. But it didn't work out. It just kept gettin' worse and worse.

I was workin' a bread route. The highest I made one week was seventy-five dollars. The rent on our house was about twelve dollars a week. I will never forget: outside of this house was a 265-gallon oil drum, and I never did get enough money to fill up that oil drum. What I would do every night, I would run up to the store and buy five gallons of oil and climb up the ladder and pour it in that 265-gallon drum. I could hear that five gallons when it hits the bottom of that oil drum, splatters, and it sounds like it's nothin' in there. But it would keep the house warm for the night. Next day you'd have to do the same thing.

I left the bread route with fifty dollars in my pocket. I went to the bank and borrowed four thousand dollars to buy the service station. I worked seven days a week, open and close, and finally had a heart attack. Just about two months before the last payments of that loan. My wife had done the best she could to keep it runnin'. Tryin' to come out of that hole, I just couldn't do it.

I really began to get bitter. I didn't know who to blame. I tried to find somebody. I began to blame it on black people. I had to hate somebody. Hatin' America is hard to do because you can't see it to hate it. You gotta have somethin' to look at to hate. (Laughs.) The natural person for me to hate would be black people, because my father before me was a member of the Klan. As far as he was concerned, it was the savior of the white people. It was the only organization in the world that would take care of the white people. So I began to admire the Klan.

I got active in the Klan while I was at the service station. Every Monday 15 night, a group of men would come by and buy a Coca-Cola, go back to the car, take a few drinks, and come back and stand around talkin'. I couldn't help but wonder: Why are these dudes comin' out every Monday? They said they were with the Klan and have meetings close-by. Would I be interested? Boy, that was an opportunity I really looked forward to! To be part of somethin'. I joined the Klan, went from member to chaplain, from chaplain to vice-president, from vice-president to president. The title is exalted cyclops.

The first night I went with the fellas, they knocked on the door and gave the signal. They sent some robed Klansmen to talk to me and give me some instructions. I was led into a large meeting room, and this was the time of my life! It was thrilling. Here's a guy who's worked all his life and struggled all his life to be something, and here's the moment to be something. I will never forget it. Four robed Klansmen led me into the hall. The lights were dim, and the only thing you could see was an illuminated cross. I knelt before the cross. I had to make certain vows and promises. We promised to uphold the purity of the white race, fight communism, and protect white womanhood.

After I had taken my oath, there was loud applause goin' throughout the building, musta been at least four hundred people. For this one little ol' person. It was a thrilling moment for C. P. Ellis.

It disturbs me when people who do not really know what it's all about are so very critical of individual Klansmen. The majority of 'em are low-income whites, people who really don't have a part in something. They have been shut out as well as the blacks. Some are not very well educated either. Just like myself. We had a lot of support from doctors and lawyers and police officers.

Maybe they've had bitter experiences in this life and they had to hate somebody. So the natural person to hate would be the black person. He's beginnin' to come up, he's beginnin' to learn to read and start votin' and run for political office. Here are white people who are supposed to be superior to them, and we're shut out.

I can understand why people join extreme right-wing or left-wing   20 groups. They're in the same boat I was. Shut out. Deep down inside, we want to be part of this great society. Nobody listens, so we join these groups.

At one time, I was state organizer of the National Rights party. I organized a youth group for the Klan. I felt we were getting old and our generation's gonna die. So I contacted certain kids in schools. They were havin' racial problems. On the first night, we had a hundred high school students. When they came in the door, we had "Dixie" playin'. These kids were just thrilled to death. I begin to hold weekly meetin's with 'em, teachin' the principles of the Klan. At that time, I believed Martin Luther King had Communist connections. I began to teach that Andy Young[1] was affiliated with the Communist party.

I had a call one night from one of our kids. He was about twelve. He said: "I just been robbed downtown by two niggers." I'd had a couple of drinks and that really teed me off. I go downtown and couldn't find the kid. I got worried. I saw two young black people. I had the .32 revolver with me. I said: "Nigger, you seen a little young white boy up here? I just got a call from him and was told that some niggers robbed him of fifteen cents." I pulled my pistol out and put it right at his head. I said: "I've always wanted to kill a nigger and I think I'll make you the first one." I nearly scared the kid to death, and he struck off.

This was the time when the civil rights movement was really beginnin' to peak. The blacks were beginnin' to demonstrate and picket downtown stores. I never will forget some black lady I hated with a purple passion. Ann Atwater. Every time I'd go downtown, she'd be leadin' a boycott. How I hated—pardon the expression, I don't use it much now—how I just hated the black nigger. (Laughs.) Big, fat, heavy woman. She'd pull about eight demonstrations, and first thing you know they had two, three blacks at the checkout counter. Her and I have had some pretty close confrontations.

I felt very big, yeah. (Laughs.) We're more or less a secret organization. We didn't want anybody to know who we were, and I began to do some

---

[1]*Andy Young:* Andrew Jackson Young, Jr. (b. 1932), prominent black leader and politician. Young was a friend and adviser of Martin Luther King, Jr., and served as President Jimmy Carter's ambassador to the United Nations. In the 1980s, he was twice elected mayor of Atlanta.

thinkin'. What am I hidin' for? I've never been convicted of anything in my life. I don't have any court record. What am I, C. P. Ellis, as a citizen and a member of the United Klansmen of America? Why can't I go the city council meeting and say: "This is the way we feel about the matter? We don't want you to purchase mobile units to set in our schoolyards. We don't want niggers in our schools."

We began to come out in the open. We would go to the meetings, and   25 the blacks would be there and we'd be there. It was a confrontation every time. I didn't hold back anything. We began to make some inroads with the city councilmen and county commissioners. They began to call us friend. Call us at night on the telephone: "C. P., glad you came to that meeting last night." They didn't want integration either, but they did it secretively, in order to get elected. They couldn't stand up openly and say it, but they were glad somebody was sayin' it. We visited some of the city leaders in their home and talked to 'em privately. It wasn't long before councilmen would call me up: "The blacks are comin' up tonight and makin' outrageous demands. How about some of you people showin' up and have a little balance?" I'd get on the telephone. "The niggers is comin' to the council meeting tonight. Persons in the city's called me and asked us to be there."

We'd load up our cars and we'd fill up half the council chambers, and the blacks the other half. During these times, I carried weapons to the meetings, outside my belt. We'd go there armed. We would wind up just hollerin' and fussin' at each other. What happened? As a result of our fightin' one another, the city council still had their way. They didn't want to give up control to the blacks nor the Klan. They were usin' us.

I began to realize this later down the road. One day I was walkin' downtown and a certain city council member saw me comin'. I expected him to shake my hand because he was talkin' to me at night on the telephone. I had been in his home and visited with him. He crossed the street. Oh shit, I began to think, somethin's wrong here. Most of 'em are merchants or maybe an attorney, an insurance agent, people like that. As long as they kept low-income whites and low-income blacks fightin', they're gonna maintain control.

I began to get that feeling after I was ignored in public. I thought: Bullshit, you're not gonna use me any more. That's when I began to do some real serious thinkin'.

The same thing is happening in this country today. People are being used by those in control, those who have all the wealth. I'm not espousing communism. We got the greatest system of government in the world. But those who have it simply don't want those who don't have it to have any part of it. Black and white. When it comes to money, the green, the other colors make no difference. (Laughs.)

I spent a lot of sleepless nights. I still didn't like blacks. I didn't want to   30 associate with 'em. Blacks, Jews, or Catholics. My father said: "don't have anything to do with 'em." I didn't until I met a black person and talked with him, eyeball to eyeball, and met a Jewish person and talked to him, eyeball to eyeball. I found out they're people just like me. They cried, they cussed, they prayed, they had desires. Just like myself. Thank God, I got to the point where I can look past labels. But at that time, my mind was closed.

I remember one Monday night Klan meeting. I said something was wrong. Our city fathers were using us. And I didn't like to be used. The reactions of the others was not too pleasant: "Let's just keep fightin' them niggers."

I'd go home at night and I'd have to wrestle with myself. I'd look at a black person walkin' down the street, and the guy'd have ragged shoes or his clothes would be worn. That began to do somethin' to me inside. I went through this for about six months. I felt I just had to get out of the Klan. But I wouldn't get out.

Then something happened. The state AFL–CIO[2] received a grant from the Department of HEW,[3] a $78,000 grant: how to solve racial problems in the school system. I got a telephone call from the president of the state AFL–CIO. "We'd like to get some people together from all walks of life." I said: "All walks of life? Who you talkin' about?" He said: "Blacks, whites, liberals, conservatives, Klansmen, NAACP[4] people."

I said: "No way am I comin' with all those niggers. I'm not gonna be associated with those type of people." A White Citizens Council guy said: "Let's go up there and see what's goin' on. It's tax money bein' spent." I walk in the door, and there was a large number of blacks and white liberals. I knew most of 'em by face 'cause I seen 'em demonstratin' around town. Ann Atwater was there. (Laughs.) I just forced myself to go in and sit down.

The meeting was moderated by a great big black guy who was bushy-headed. (Laughs.) That turned me off. He acted very nice. He said: "I want you all to feel free to say anything you want to say." Some of the blacks stand up and say it's white racism. I took all I could take. I asked for the floor and cut loose. I said: "No, sir, it's black racism. If we didn't have niggers in the schools, we wouldn't have the problems we got today."   35

I will never forget. Howard Clements, a black guy, stood up. He said: "I'm certainly glad C. P. Ellis come because he's the most honest man here tonight." I said: "What's that nigger tryin' to do?" (Laughs.) At the end of that meeting, some blacks tried to come up shake my hand, but I wouldn't do it. I walked off.

Second night, same group was there. I felt a little more easy because I got some things off my chest. The third night, after they elected all the com-

[2]*AFL–CIO:* American Federation of Labor and Congress of Industrial Organizations—a huge federation of independent labor unions in the United States, Canada, Mexico, Panama, and elsewhere.

[3]*HEW:* Health, Education, and Welfare—at the time, a department of the federal government.

[4]*NAACP:* National Association for the Advancement of Colored People.

mittees, they want to elect a chairman. Howard Clements stood up and said: "I suggest we elect two co-chairpersons." Joe Beckton, executive director of the Human Relations Commission, just as black as he can be, he nominated me. There was a reaction from some blacks. Nooo. And, of all things, they nominated Ann Atwater, that big old fat black gal that I had just hated with a purple passion, as co-chairman. I thought to myself: Hey, ain't no way I can work with that gal. Finally, I agreed to accept it, 'cause at this point, I was tired of fightin', either for survival or against black people or against Jews or against Catholics.

A Klansman and a militant black woman, co-chairmen of the school committee. It was impossible. How could I work with her? But after about two or three days, it was in our hands. We had to make it a success. This give me another sense of belongin', a sense of pride. This helped this inferiority feelin' I had. A man who has stood up publicly and said he despised black people, all of a sudden he was willin' to work with 'em. Here's a chance for a low-income white man to be somethin'. In spite of all my hatred for blacks and Jews and liberals, I accepted the job. Her and I began to reluctantly work together. (Laughs.) She had as many problems workin' with me as I had workin' with her.

One night, I called her: "Ann, you and I should have a lot of differences and we got 'em now. But there's somethin' laid out here before us, and if it's gonna be a success, you and I are gonna have to make it one. Can we lay aside some of these feelin's?" She said: "I'm willing if you are." I said: "Let's do it."

My old friends would call me at night: "C. P., what the hell is wrong   40
with you? You're sellin' out the white race." This begin to make me have guilt feelin's. Am I doin' right? Am I doin' wrong? Here I am all of a sudden makin' an about-face and tryin' to deal with my feelin's, my heart. My mind was beginnin' to open up. I was beginnin' to see what was right and what was wrong. I don't want the kids to fight forever.

We were gonna go ten nights. By this time, I had went to work at Duke University, in maintenance. Makin' very little money. Terry Sanford give me this ten days off with pay. He was president of Duke at the time. He knew I was a Klansman and realized the importance of blacks and whites getting along.

I said: "If we're gonna make this thing a success, I've got to get to my kind of people." The low-income whites. We walked the streets of Durham, and we knocked on doors and invited people. Ann was goin' into the black community. They just wasn't respondin' to us when we made these house calls. Some of 'em were cussin' us out. "You're sellin' us out, Ellis, get out of my door. I don't want to talk to you." Ann was gettin' the same response from blacks. "What are you doin' messin' with that Klansman?"

One day, Ann and I went back to the school and we sat down. We began to talk and just reflect. Ann said: "My daughter came home cryin' every day. She said her teacher was makin' fun of me in front of the other kids." I said: "Boy, the same thing happened to my kid. White liberal teacher was makin' fun of Tim Ellis's father, the Klansman. In front of other peoples. He came home cryin'." At this point—(he pauses, swallows hard, stifles a sob)—I begin to see, here we are, two people from the far ends of the fence, havin' identical problems, except hers bein' black and me bein' white. From that moment on, I tell ya, that gal and I worked together good. I begin to love the girl, really. (He weeps.)

The amazing thing about it, her and I, up to that point, had cussed each other, bawled each other, we hated each other. Up to that point, we didn't know each other. We didn't know we had things in common.

We worked at it, with the people who came to these meetings. They   45
talked about racism, sex education, about teachers not bein' qualified. After seven, eight nights of real intense discussion, these people, who'd never talked to each other before, all of a sudden came up with resolutions. It was really somethin', you had to be there to get the tone and feelin' of it.

At that point, I didn't like integration, but the law says you do this and I've got to do what the law says, okay? We said: "Let's take these resolutions to the school board." The most disheartening thing I've ever faced was the school system refused to implement any one of these resolutions. These were recommendations from the people who pay taxes and pay their salaries. (Laughs.)

I thought they were good answers. Some of 'em I didn't agree with, but I been in this thing from the beginning, and whatever comes of it, I'm gonna support it. Okay, since the school board refused, I decided I'd just run for the school board.

I spent eighty-five dollars on the campaign. The guy runnin' against me spent several thousand. I really had nobody on my side. The Klan turned against me. The low-income whites turned against me. The liberals didn't particularly like me. The blacks were suspicious of me. The blacks wanted to support me, but they couldn't muster up enough to support a Klansman on the school board. (Laughs.) But I made up my mind that what I was doin' was right, and I was gonna do it regardless what anybody said.

It bothered me when people would call and worry my wife. She's always supported me in anything I wanted to do. She was changing, and my boys were too. I got some of my youth corps kids involved. They still followed me.

I was invited to the Democratic women's social hour as a candidate.   50
Didn't have but one suit to my name. Had it six, seven, eight years. I had it cleaned, put on the best shirt I had and a tie. Here were all these high-class wealthy candidates shakin' hands. I walked up to the mayor and stuck out my hand. He give me that handshake with that rag type of hand. He said: "C. P., I'm glad to see you." But I could tell by his handshake he was lyin' to me. This was botherin' me. I know I'm a low-income person. I know I'm not wealthy. I know they were sayin': "What's this little ol' dude runnin' for school board?" Yet they had to smile and make like they're glad to see me. I

begin to spot some black people in that room. I automatically went to 'em and that was a firm handshake. They said: "I'm glad to see you, C. P." I knew they meant it—you can tell about a handshake.

Every place I appeared, I said I will listen to the voice of the people. I will not make a major decision until I first contacted all the organizations in the city. I got 4,640 votes. The guy beat me by two thousand. Not bad for eighty-five bucks and no constituency.

The whole world was openin' up, and I was learnin' new truths that I had never learned before. I was beginnin' to look at a black person, shake hands with him, and see him as a human bein'. I hadn't got rid of all this stuff, I've still got a little bit of it. But somethin' was happenin' to me.

It was almost like bein' born again. It was a new life. I didn't have these sleepless nights I used to have when I was active in the Klan and slippin' around at night. I could sleep at night and feel good about it. I'd rather live now than at any other time in history. It's a challenge.

Back at Duke, doin' maintenance, I'd pick up my tools, fix the commode, unstop the drains. But this got in my blood. Things weren't right in this country, and what we done in Durham needs to be told. I was so miserable at Duke, I could hardly stand it. I'd go to work every morning just hatin' to go.

My whole life had changed. I got an eighth-grade education, and I wanted to complete high school. Went to high school in the afternoons on a program called PEP—Past Employment Progress. I was about the only white in class, and the oldest. I begin to read about biology. I'd take my books home at night, 'cause I was determined to get through. Sure enough, I graduated. I got the diploma at home.

I come to work one mornin' and some guy says: "We need a union." At this time I wasn't pro-union. My daddy was anti-labor, too. We're not gettin' paid much, we're havin' to work seven days in a row. We're all starvin' to death. The next day, I meet the international representative of the Operating Engineers. He give me authorization cards. "Get these cards out and we'll have an election." There was eighty-eight for the union and seventeen no's. I was elected chief steward for the union.

Shortly after, a union man come down from Charlotte and says we need a full-time rep. We've got only two hundred people at the two plants here. It's just barely enough money comin' in to pay your salary. You'll have to get out and organize more people. I didn't know nothin' about organizin' unions, but I knew how to organize people, stir people up. (Laughs.) That's how I got to be business agent for the union.

When I began to organize, I began to see far deeper. I began to see people again bein' used. Blacks against whites. I say this without any hesitancy: management is vicious. There's two things they want to keep: all the money and all the say-so. They don't want these poor workin' folks to have none of that. I begin to see management fightin' me with everything they had. Hire anti-union law firms, badmouth unions. The people were makin' a dollar ninety-five an hour, barely able to get through weekends. I worked as a business rep for five years and was seein' all this.

Last year, I ran for business manager of the union. He's elected by the workers. The guy that ran against me was black, and our membership is seventy-five percent black. I thought: Claiborne, there's no way you can beat that black guy. People know your background. Even though you've made tremendous strides, those black people are not gonna vote for you. You know how much I beat him? Four to one. (Laughs.)

The company used my past against me. They put out letters with a picture of a robe and a cap: would you vote for a Klansman? They wouldn't deal with the issues. I immediately called for a mass meeting. I met with the ladies at an electric component plant. I said: "Okay, this is Claiborne Ellis. This is where I come from. I want you to know right now, you black ladies here, I was at one time a member of the Klan. I want you to know, because they'll tell you about it." 60

I invited some of my old black friends. I said: "Brother Joe, Brother Howard, be honest now and tell these people how you feel about me." They done it. (Laughs.) Howard Clements kidded me a little bit. He said: "I don't know what I'm doin' here, supportin' an ex-Klansman." (Laughs.) He said: "I know what C. P. Ellis come from. I knew him when he was. I knew him as he grew, and growed with him. I'm tellin' you now: follow, follow this Klansman." (He pauses, swallows hard.) "Any questions?" "No," the black ladies said. "Let's get on with the meeting, we need Ellis." (He laughs and weeps.) Boy, black people sayin' that about me. I won one thirty-four to forty-one. Four to one.

It makes you feel good to go into a plant and butt heads with professional union busters. You see black people and white people join hands to defeat the racist issues they use against people. They're tryin' the same things with the Klan. It's still happenin' today. Can you imagine a guy who's got an adult high school diploma runnin' into professional college graduates who are union busters? I gotta compete with 'em. I work seven days a week, nights and on Saturday and Sunday. The salary's not that great, and if I didn't care, I'd quit. But I care and I can't quit. I got a taste of it. (Laughs.)

I tell people there's a tremendous possibility in this country to stop wars, the battles, the struggles, the fights between people. People say: "That's an impossible dream. You sound like Martin Luther King." An ex-Klansman who sounds like Martin Luther King. (Laughs.) I don't think it's an impossible dream. It's happened in my life. It's happened in other people's lives in America.

I don't know what's ahead of me. I have no desire to be a big union official. I want to be right out here in the field with the workers. I want to walk through their factory and shake hands with that man whose hands are dirty. I'm gonna do all that one little ol' man can do. I'm fifty-two years old, and I ain't got many years left, but I want to make the best of 'em.

When the news came over the radio that Martin Luther King was assas-   65
sinated, I got on the telephone and begin to call other Klansmen. We just
had a real party at the service station. Really rejoicin' 'cause that son of a
bitch was dead. Our troubles are over with. They say the older you get, the
harder it is for you to change. That's not necessarily true. Since I changed,
I've set down and listened to tapes of Martin Luther King. I listen to it and
tears come to my eyes 'cause I know what he's sayin' now. I know what's
happenin'.

POSTSCRIPT:
The phone rings. A conversation.
*"This was a black guy who's director of Operation Breakthrough in
Durham. I had called his office. I'm interested in employin' some young
black person who's interested in learnin' the labor movement. I want somebody who's never had an opportunity, just like myself. Just so he can read
and write, that's all."*

ENGAGING THE TEXT

1. How does Ellis battle the racism he finds in himself? What gives him the
   motivation and strength to change? What specific changes does he un-
   dergo, and how successful is he in abandoning racist attitudes?

2. Would Ellis say that economic class is more important than race in determining job placement and occupational mobility? Find specific passages
   that reveal Ellis's beliefs about the connections between economic class,
   race, and success in American society. What do you believe?

3. How well does Ellis seem to understand himself, his feelings, his motives?
   Give evidence for your assertions.

4. What is Terkel's role in this selection? Is he unconsciously helping to rationalize or justify the actions of the Ku Klux Klan?

5. Does Ellis's story offer a credible way of overcoming misunderstanding and
   hatred between races? Do you think such a "solution" would be workable
   on a large scale? Why or why not?

EXPLORING CONNECTIONS

6. To what extent does Ellis's experience illustrate the theories of prejudice
   described by Vincent N. Parrillo in the previous selection (p. 577)? Which
   of these theories best account for Ellis's racism and for his eventual transformation?

7. Review the account of Malcolm X's self-education (p. 243). How does the
   dramatic self-transformation he experiences compare with C. P. Ellis's rebirth? What relationships can you find between the circumstances that led to
   their initial attitudes, the conditions or events that fostered their transformations, and the effects that these transformations had on their characters?

EXTENDING THE CRITICAL CONTEXT

8. Interview a friend, family member, or fellow student in another class to create your own oral history on the subject of racial attitudes. Ask your subject to describe a time when he or she was forced to re-evaluate his or her thoughts or feelings about someone from a different racial or ethnic group. Try to include as many relevant details as possible in your retelling of the story. Share and edit these oral histories in small groups, and then assemble them into a class anthology.

I'm Black, You're White, Who's Innocent?

SHELBY STEELE

This essay comes from one of the most controversial American books of the 1980s — The Content of Our Character: A New Vision of Race in America. *Shelby Steele (b. 1946) believes that black Americans have failed to seize opportunities that would lead to social equality; he is also an outspoken critic of affirmative action, arguing that instead of promoting equality it locks its recipients into second-class status. Critics have accused him of underestimating the power of racism, of blaming victims for their predicament, of being a traitor to his race. In this selection, Steele offers his observations on why black and white Americans have not been able to sustain the kind of dialogue that would make mutual understanding possible. Steele's second book,* A Dream Deferred: The Second Betrayal of Black Freedom in America *(1998), elaborates the critique of innocence and guilt laid out in this essay. In his new work, Steele argues that programs—like affirmative action—that were devised to reduce racial inequality have actually harmed rather than helped most African Americans, and have benefitted only guilty white liberals and a black "grievance elite." Steele's essays have garnered a number of awards and have appeared in* Harper's, The American Scholar, The New Republic, *and many other journals and magazines. He is a research fellow at the Hoover Institution, Stanford University.*

It is a warm, windless California evening, and the dying light that covers the redbrick patio is tinted pale orange by the day's smog. Eight of us, not close friends, sit in lawn chairs sipping chardonnay. A black engineer and I (we had never met before) integrate the group. A psychologist is also among us, and her presence encourages a surprising openness. But not until well after the lovely twilight dinner has been served, when the sky has turned to deep black and the drinks have long since changed to scotch, does the subject of race spring awkwardly upon us. Out of nowhere the engineer announces, with a coloring of accusation in his voice, that it bothers him to send his daughter to a school where she is one of only three black children. "I didn't realize my ambition to get ahead would pull me into a world where my daughter would lose touch with her blackness," he says.

Over the course of the evening we have talked about money, past and present addictions, child abuse, even politics. Intimacies have been revealed, fears named. But this subject, race, sinks us into one of those shaming silences where eye contact terrorizes. Our host looks for something in the bottom of his glass. Two women stare into the black sky as if to locate the Big Dipper and point it out to us. Finally, the psychologist seems to gather herself for a challenge, but it is too late. "Oh, I'm sure she'll be just fine," says our hostess, rising from her chair. When she excuses herself to get the coffee, the psychologist and two sky gazers offer to help.

With four of us now gone, I am surprised to see the engineer still silently holding his ground. There is a willfulness in his eyes, an inner pride. He knows he has said something awkward, but he is determined not to give a damn. His unwavering eyes intimidate even me. At last the host's head snaps erect. He has an idea. "The hell with coffee," he says. "How about some of the smoothest brandy you've ever tasted?" An idea made exciting by the escape it offers. Gratefully, we follow him back into the house, quickly drink his brandy, and say our good-byes.

An autopsy of this party might read: death induced by an abrupt and lethal injection of the American race issue. An accurate if superficial assessment. Since it has been my fate to live a rather integrated life, I have often witnessed sudden deaths like this. The threat of them, if not the reality, is a part of the texture of integration. In the late 1960s, when I was just out of college, I took a delinquent's delight in playing the engineer's role, and actually developed a small reputation for playing it well. Those were the days of flagellatory white guilt: it was such great fun to pinion some professor or housewife or, best of all, a large group of remorseful whites, with the knowledge of both their racism and their denial of it. The adolescent impulse to sneer at convention, to startle the middle-aged with doubt, could be indulged under the guise of racial indignation. And how could I lose? My victims—earnest liberals for the most part—could no more crawl out from under my accusations than Joseph K. in Kafka's *Trial*[1] could escape the amorphous charges brought against him. At this odd moment in history the world was aligned to facilitate my immaturity.

[1]*Kafka's* Trial: Czech writer Franz Kafka (1883–1924) is famous for his dreamlike and ominous stories. In his novel *The Trial,* the character known only as Joseph K. battles an intricate legal and police system that never specifies his alleged crime.

About a year of this was enough: the guilt that follows most cheap   5
thrills caught up to me, and I put myself in check. But the impulse to do it
faded more slowly. It was one of those petty talents that is tied to vanity,
and when there were ebbs in my self-esteem the impulse to use it would
come alive again. In integrated situations I can still feel the faint itch. But
then there are many youthful impulses that still itch and now, just inside the
door of midlife, this one is least precious to me.

In the literature classes I teach I often see how the presence of whites
all but seduces some black students into provocation. When we come to a
novel by a black writer, say Toni Morrison, the white students can easily discuss the human motivations of the black characters. But, inevitably, a black
student, as if by reflex, will begin to set in relief the various racial problems
that are the background of these characters' lives. This student's tone will
carry a reprimand: the class is afraid to confront the reality of racism.
Classes cannot be allowed to die like dinner parties, however. My latest
strategy is to thank that student for his or her moral vigilance and then ap-
point the young man or woman as the class's official racism monitor. But
even if I get a laugh—I usually do, but sometimes the student is particularly indignant, and it gets uncomfortable—the strategy never quite works.
Our racial division is suddenly drawn in neon. Overcaution spreads like
spilled paint. And, in fact, the black student who started it all does become a
kind of monitor. The very presence of this student imposes a new accountability on the class.

I think those who provoke this sort of awkwardness are operating out of
a black identity that obliges them to badger white people about race almost
on principle. Content hardly matters. (For example, it made little sense for
the engineer to expect white people to anguish terribly much over his decision to send his daughter to school with *white* children.) Race indeed remains a source of white shame; the goal of these provocations is to put
whites, no matter how indirectly, in touch with this collective guilt. In other
words, these provocations I speak of are *power* moves, little shows of power
that try to freeze the "enemy" in self-consciousness. They gratify and inflate
the provocateur. They are the underdog's bite. And whites, far more secure
in their power, respond with self-contained and tolerant silence that is itself
a show of power. What greater power than that of nonresponse, the power
to let a small enemy sizzle in his own juices, to even feel a little sad at his
frustration just as one is also complimented by it. Black anger always, in a
way, flatters white power. In America, to know that one is not black is to
feel an extra grace, a little boost of impunity.

I think the real trouble between the races in America is that the races
are not just races but competing power groups —a fact that is easily minimized, perhaps because it is so obvious. What is not so obvious is that this is
true quite apart from the issue of class. Even the well-situated middle-class
(or wealthy) black is never completely immune to that peculiar contest of
power that his skin color subjects him to. Race is a separate reality in Amer-

ican society, an entity that carries its own potential for power, a mark of fate that class can soften considerably but not eradicate.

The distinction of race has always been used in American life to sanction each race's pursuit of power in relation to the other. The allure of race as a human delineation is the very shallowness of the delineation it makes. Onto this shallowness—mere skin and hair—men can project a false depth, a system of dismal attributions, a series of malevolent or ignoble stereotypes that skin and hair lack the substance to contradict. These dark projections then rationalize the pursuit of power. Your difference from me makes you bad, and your badness justifies, even demands, my pursuit of power over you—the oldest formula for aggression known to man. Whenever much importance is given to race, power is the primary motive.

But the human animal almost never pursues power without first convincing himself that he is *entitled* to it. And this feeling of entitlement has its own precondition: to be entitled one must first believe in one's innocence, at least in the area where one wishes to be entitled. By innocence I mean a feeling of essential goodness in relation to others and, therefore, superiority to others. Our innocence always inflates us and deflates those we seek power over. Once inflated we are entitled; we are in fact licensed to go after the power our innocence tells us we deserve. In this sense, *innocence is power.* Of course, innocence need not be genuine or real in any objective sense, as the Nazis demonstrated not long ago. Its only test is whether or not we can convince ourselves of it.

I think the racial struggle in America has always been primarily a struggle for innocence. White racism from the beginning has been a claim of white innocence and therefore of white entitlement to subjugate blacks. And in the sixties, as went innocence so went power. Blacks used the innocence that grew out of their long subjugation to seize more power, while whites lost some of their innocence and so lost a degree of power over blacks. Both races instinctively understand that to lose innocence is to lose power (in relation to each other). To be innocent someone else must be guilty, a natural law that leads the races to forge their innocence on each other's backs. The inferiority of the black always makes the white man superior; the evil might of whites makes blacks good. This pattern means that both races have a hidden investment in racism and racial disharmony despite their good intentions to the contrary. Power defines their relations, and power requires innocence, which, in turn, requires racism and racial division.

I believe it was his hidden investment that the engineer was protecting when he made his remark—the white "evil" he saw in a white school "depriving" his daughter of her black heritage confirmed his innocence. Only the logic of power explained his emphasis—he bent reality to show that he was once again a victim of the white world and, as a victim, innocent. His determined eyes insisted on this. And the whites, in their silence, no doubt protected their innocence by seeing him as an ungracious troublemaker, his bad behavior underscoring their goodness. What none of us saw was the underlying game of power and innocence we were trapped in, or how much we needed a racial impasse to play that game.

When I was a boy of about twelve, a white friend of mine told me one day that his uncle, who would be arriving the next day for a visit, was a racist. Excited by the prospect of seeing such a man, I spent the following afternoon hanging around the alley behind my friend's house, watching from a distance as this uncle worked on the engine of his Buick. Yes, here was evil and I was compelled to look upon it. And I saw evil in the sharp angle of his elbow as he pumped his wrench to tighten nuts. I saw it in the blade-sharp crease of his chinos, in the pack of Lucky Strikes that threatened to slip from his shirt pocket as he bent, and in the way his concentration seemed to shut out the human world. He worked neatly and efficiently, wiping his hands constantly, and I decided that evil worked like this.

I felt a compulsion to have this man look upon me so that I could see evil—so that I could see the face of it. But when he noticed me standing beside his toolbox, he said only, "If you're looking for Bobby, I think he went up to the school to play baseball." He smiled nicely and went back to work. I was stunned for a moment, but then I realized that evil could be sly as well, could smile when it wanted to trick you.

Need, especially hidden need, puts a strong pressure on perception, and my need to have this man embody white evil was stronger than any contravening evidence. As a black person you always hear about racists but rarely meet any who will let you know them as such. And I needed to incarnate this odious category of humanity, those people who hated Martin Luther King, Jr., and thought blacks should "go slow" or not at all. So, in my mental dictionary, behind the term "white racist," I inserted this man's likeness. I would think of him and say to myself, "There is no reason for him to hate black people. Only evil explains unmotivated hatred." And this thought soothed me; I felt innocent. If I hated white people, which I did not, at least I had a reason. His evil commanded me to assert in the world the goodness he made me confident of in myself.

In looking at this man I was *seeing for innocence*—a form of seeing that has more to do with one's hidden need for innocence (and power) than with the person or group one is looking at. It is quite possible, for example, that the man I saw that day was not a racist. He did absolutely nothing in my presence to indicate that he was. I invested an entire afternoon in seeing not the man but in seeing my innocence through the man. *Seeing for innocence* is, in this way, the essence of racism—the use of others as a means to our own goodness and superiority.

The loss of innocence has always to do with guilt, Kierkegaard[2] tells us, and it has never been easy for whites to avoid guilt where blacks are concerned. For whites, *seeing for innocence* means seeing themselves and

15

---

[2]*Kierkegaard:* Danish philosopher and religious thinker Søren Kierkegaard (1813–1855).

blacks in ways that minimize white guilt. Often this amounts to a kind of white revisionism,[3] as when President Reagan declared himself "color-blind" in matters of race. The President, like many of us, may have aspired to racial color blindness, but few would grant that he ever reached this sublimely guiltless state. His statement clearly revised reality, moved it forward into some heretofore unknown America where all racial determinism would have vanished. I do not think that Ronald Reagan was a racist, as that term is commonly used, but neither do I think that he was capable of seeing color without making attributions, some of which may have been negative—nor am I, or anyone else I've ever met.

So why make such a statement? I think Reagan's claim of color blindness with regard to race was really a claim of racial innocence and guiltlessness—the preconditions for entitlement and power. This was the claim that grounded Reagan's campaign against special entitlement programs—affirmative action, racial quotas, and so on—that black power had won in the sixties. Color blindness was a strategic assumption of innocence that licensed Reagan's use of government power against black power. . . .

Black Americans have had to find a way to handle white society's presumption of racial innocence whenever they have sought to enter the American mainstream. Louis Armstrong's[4] exaggerated smile honored the presumed innocence of white society—*I will not bring you your racial guilt if you will let me play my music.* Ralph Ellison[5] calls this "masking"; I call it bargaining. But whatever it's called, it points to the power of white society to enforce its innocence. I believe this power is greatly diminished today. Society has reformed and transformed—Miles Davis[6] never smiles. Nevertheless, this power has not faded altogether and blacks must still contend with it.

Historically, blacks have handled white society's presumption of innocence in two ways: they have bargained with it, granting white society its innocence in exchange for entry into the mainstream, or they have challenged it, holding that innocence hostage until their demand for entry (or other concessions) was met. A bargainer says, *I already believe you are innocent (good, fair-minded) and have faith that you will prove it.* A challenger says, *If you are innocent, then prove it.* Bargainers *give* in hope of receiving; challengers *withhold* until they receive. Of course, there is risk in both approaches, but in each case the black is negotiating his own self-interest against the presumed racial innocence of the larger society.

Clearly, the most visible black bargainer on the American scene today is Bill Cosby. His television show has been a perfect formula for black

20

---

[3]*revisionism:* The reinterpretation or revising of reality to suit one's current purposes.

[4]*Louis Armstrong:* American jazz trumpet virtuoso and singer (1900–1971).

[5]*Ralph Ellison:* American novelist (1914–1994), best known for *Invisible Man,* the account of a nameless black youth coming of age in a hostile society.

[6]*Miles Davis:* Jazz musician and trumpeter (1926–1991).

bargaining in the eighties. The remarkable Huxtable family—with its doctor/lawyer parent combination, its drug-free, college-bound children, and its wise yet youthful grandparents—is a blackface version of the American dream. Cosby is a subscriber to the American identity, and his subscription confirms his belief in its fair-mindedness. His vast audience knows this, knows that Cosby will never assault their innocence with racial guilt. Racial controversy is all but banished from the show. The Huxtable family never discusses affirmative action.

The bargain Cosby offers his white viewers—*I will confirm your racial innocence if you accept me*—is a good deal for all concerned. Not only does it allow whites to enjoy Cosby's humor with no loss of innocence, but it actually enhances their innocence by implying that race is not the serious problem for blacks that it once was. If anything, the success of this handsome, affluent black family points to the fair-mindedness of whites who, out of their essential goodness, changed society so that black families like the Huxtables could succeed. Whites can watch *The Cosby Show* and feel complimented on a job well done.

The power that black bargainers wield is the power of absolution. On Thursday nights, Cosby, like a priest, absolves his white viewers, forgives and forgets the sins of the past. And for this he is rewarded with an almost sacrosanct[7] status. Cosby benefits from what might be called the gratitude factor. His continued number-one rating may have something to do with the (white) public's gratitude at being offered a commodity so rare in our time; he tells his white viewers each week that they are okay, and that this black man is not going to challenge them.

When a black bargains, he may invoke the gratitude factor and find himself cherished beyond the measure of his achievement; when he challenges, he may draw the dark projections of whites and become a source of irritation to them. If he moves back and forth between these two options, as I think many blacks do today, he will likely baffle whites. It is difficult for whites either to accept or reject such blacks. It seems to me that Jesse Jackson is such a figure—many whites see Jackson as a challenger by instinct and a bargainer by political ambition. They are uneasy with him, more than a little suspicious. His powerful speech at the 1984 Democratic Convention was a masterpiece of bargaining. In it he offered a King-like[8] vision of what America could be, a vision that presupposed Americans had the fair-mindedness to achieve full equality—an offer in hope of a return. A few days after this speech, looking for rest and privacy at a lodge in Big Sur,[9] he and his wife were greeted with standing ovations three times a day when they entered the dining room for meals. So much about Jackson is deeply American—this underdog striving, his irrepressible faith in himself, the

---

[7]*sacrosanct:* Sacred.

[8]*King-like:* Like that of Martin Luther King, Jr.

[9]*Big Sur:* Section of the California coast known for its natural beauty.

daring of his ambition, and even his stubbornness. These qualities point to his underlying faith that Americans can respond to him despite race, and this faith is a compliment to Americans, an offer of innocence.

But Jackson does not always stick to the terms of his bargain as Cosby   25
does on TV. When he hugs Arafat,[10] smokes cigars with Castro,[11] refuses to repudiate Farrakhan,[12] threatens a boycott of major league baseball, or, more recently, talks of "corporate barracudas," "pension-fund socialism," and "economic violence," he looks like a challenger in bargainer's clothing, and his positions on the issues look like familiar protests dressed in white-paper formality. At these times he appears to be revoking the innocence so much else about him seems to offer. The old activist seems to come out of hiding once again to take white innocence hostage until whites prove they deserve to have it. In his candidacy there is a suggestion of protest, a fierce insistence on his *right* to run, that sends whites a message that he may secretly see them as a good bit less than innocent. His dilemma is to appear the bargainer while his campaign itself seems to be a challenge.

There are, of course, other problems that hamper Jackson's bid for the Democratic presidential nomination. He has held no elective office, he is thought too flamboyant and opportunistic by many, there are rather loud whispers of "character" problems. As an individual, he may not be the best test of a black man's chances for winning so high an office. Still, I believe it is the aura of challenge surrounding him that hurts him most. Whether it is right or wrong, fair or unfair, I think no black candidate will have a serious chance at his party's nomination, much less the presidency, until he can convince white Americans that he can be trusted to preserve their sense of racial innocence. Such a candidate will have to use his power of absolution; he will have to flatly forgive and forget. He will have to bargain with white innocence out of genuine belief that it really exists. There can be no faking it. He will have to offer a vision that is passionately raceless, a vision that strongly condemns any form of racial politics. This will require the most courageous kind of leadership, leadership that asks all the people to meet a new standard.

Now the other side of America's racial impasse: how do blacks lay claim to their racial innocence?

The most obvious and unarguable source of black innocence is the victimization that blacks endured for centuries at the hands of a race that insisted on black inferiority as a means to its own innocence and power. Like all victims, what blacks lost in power they gained in innocence—innocence that, in turn, entitled them to pursue power. This was the innocence that

---

[10]*Arafat:* Yasir Arafat (b. 1929), leader of the Palestine Liberation Organization, or PLO.

[11]*Castro:* Fidel Castro (b. 1926), president of Cuba.

[12]*Farrakhan:* Louis Farrakhan (b. 1933), Nation of Islam leader, often accused of making anti-Semitic remarks. Many African American politicians carefully distance themselves from Farrakhan.

fueled the civil rights movement of the sixties and that gave blacks their first real power in American life—victimization metamorphosed into power via innocence. But this formula carries a drawback that I believe is virtually as devastating to blacks today as victimization once was. It is a formula that binds the victim to his victimization by linking his power to his status as a victim. And this, I'm convinced, is the tragedy of black power in America today. It is primarily a victim's power, grounded too deeply in the entitlement derived from past injustice and in the innocence that Western/Christian tradition has always associated with poverty.

Whatever gains this power brings in the short run through political action, it undermines in the long run. Social victims may be collectively entitled, but they are all too often individually demoralized. Since the social victim has been oppressed by society, he comes to feel that his individual life will be improved more by changes in society than by his own initiative. Without realizing it, he makes society rather than himself the agent of change. The power he finds in his victimization may lead him to collective action against society, but it also encourages passivity within the sphere of his personal life.

Not long ago, I saw a television documentary that examined life in Detroit's inner city on the twentieth anniversary of the riots there in which forty-three people were killed. A comparison of the inner city then and now showed a decline in the quality of life. Residents feel less safe, drug trafficking is far worse, crimes by blacks against blacks are more frequent, housing remains substandard, and the teenage pregnancy rate has skyrocketed. Twenty years of decline and demoralization, even as opportunities for blacks to better themselves have increased. This paradox is not peculiar to Detroit. By many measures, the majority of blacks—those not yet in the middle class—are further behind whites today than before the victories of the civil rights movement. But there is a reluctance among blacks to examine this paradox, I think, because it suggests that racial victimization is not our real problem. If conditions have worsened for most of us as racism has receded, then much of the problem must be of our own making. To admit this fully would cause us to lose the innocence we derive from our victimization. And we would jeopardize the entitlement we've always had to challenge society. We are in the odd and self-defeating position in which taking responsibility for bettering ourselves feels like a surrender to white power. 30

So we have a hidden investment in victimization and poverty. These distressing conditions have been the source of our own real power, and there is an unconscious sort of gravitation toward them, a complaining celebration of them. One sees evidence of this in the near happiness with which certain black leaders recount the horror of Howard Beach,[13] Bensonhurst,[14] and other recent instances of racial tension. As one is saddened by these

---

[13]*Howard Beach:* Scene in Queens, New York, of a December 1986 racial confrontation in which several young African American men were severely beaten and one died.

[14]*Bensonhurst:* Location in Brooklyn, New York, where the racially motivated murder of sixteen-year-old Yusuf Hawkins took place in August 1989.

tragic events, one is also repelled at the way some black leaders—agitated to near hysteria by the scent of victim power inherent in them—leap forward to exploit them as evidence of black innocence and white guilt. It is as though they sense the decline of black victimization as a loss of standing and dive into the middle of these incidents as if they were reservoirs of pure black innocence swollen with potential power.

Seeing for innocence pressures blacks to focus on racism and to neglect the individual initiative that would deliver them from poverty—the only thing that finally delivers *anyone* from poverty. With our eyes on innocence we see racism everywhere and miss opportunity even as we stumble over it. About 70 percent of black students at my university[15] drop out before graduation—a flight from opportunity that racism cannot explain. It is an injustice that whites can see for innocence with more impunity than blacks can. The price whites pay is a certain blindness to themselves. Moreover, for whites seeing for innocence continues to engender the bad faith of a long-disgruntled minority. But the price blacks pay is an ever-escalating poverty that threatens to make the worst off a permanent underclass. Not fair, but real.

Challenging works best for the collective, while bargaining is more the individual's suit. From this point on, the race's advancement will come from the efforts of its individuals. True, some challenging will be necessary for a long time to come. But bargaining is now—today—a way for the black individual to *join* the larger society, to make a place for himself or herself.

"Innocence is ignorance," Kierkegaard says, and if this is so, the claim of innocence amounts to an insistence on ignorance, a refusal to know. In their assertions of innocence both races carve out very functional areas of ignorance for themselves—territories of blindness that license a misguided pursuit of power. Whites gain superiority by not knowing blacks; blacks gain entitlement by not seeing their own responsibility for bettering themselves. The power each race seeks in relation to the other is grounded in a double-edged ignorance of the self as well as of the other.

The original sin that brought us to an impasse at the dinner party I mentioned occurred centuries ago, when it was first decided to exploit racial difference as a means to power. It was a determinism that flowed karmically from this sin that dropped over us like a net that night. What bothered me most was our helplessness. Even the engineer did not know how to go forward. His challenge hadn't worked, and he'd lost the option to bargain. The marriage of race and power depersonalized us, changed us from eight people to six whites and two blacks. The easiest thing was to let silence blanket our situation, our impasse. . . . 35

What both black and white Americans fear are the sacrifices and risks that true racial harmony demands. This fear is the measure of our racial

---

[15]*my university:* Refers to San Jose State University where Steele was then teaching.

FEIFFER®

chasm. And though fear always seeks a thousand justifications, none is ever good enough, and the problems we run from only remain to haunt us. It would be right to suggest courage as an antidote to fear, but the glory of the word might only intimidate us into more fear. I prefer the word *effort* — relentless effort, moral effort. What I like most about this word are its connotations of everydayness, earnestness, and practical sacrifice. No matter how badly it might have gone for us that warm summer night, we should have talked. We should have made the effort.

ENGAGING THE TEXT

1. What does Steele mean by "innocence" and by "seeing for innocence"? How does he apply these terms to racial conflict and struggles for power in the United States? How do blacks and whites claim innocence through racial conflict? What does Steele mean when he says "innocence is power"?

2. According to Steele, what strategies have African Americans employed to handle "white society's presumption of racial innocence" (para. 19)? How does he account for public reactions to figures like Bill Cosby and Jesse Jackson in terms of these strategies? Are there other possible explanations of their appeal?

3. Steele believes that "bargaining is now—today—a way for the black individual to *join* the larger society" (para. 33). Do you agree? Is bargaining an available and acceptable alternative for all African Americans?

4. Steele writes that when the issue of race comes up in classes, "overcaution spreads like spilled paint" (para. 6). If you have observed this phenomenon

in class or in other circumstances, write a journal entry describing one such incident and analyzing the behavior of the people involved.

EXPLORING CONNECTIONS

5. How might Ken Hamblin (p. 384), Vincent N. Parrillo (p. 577), George M. Fredrickson (p. 632), and Paul L. Wachtel (p. 613) evaluate Steele's assertion that racism grows out of the desire to claim "innocence"? Imagine that they are all participating in a panel discussion and role-play the conversation that would ensue.

6. Write an imaginary conversation among C. P. Ellis (p. 591), Malcolm X (p. 243), Randall Robinson (p. 557), and Steele on American racism. What might they each say about the causes of racist thinking and behavior? About the chances for curbing racism? How would they respond to each other's ideas and strategies for change?

7. What does Jules Feiffer's cartoon on this page suggest about the ways that black and white Americans see the world? How does Feiffer's view of the psychology of race compare to Steele's?

EXTENDING THE CRITICAL CONTEXT

8. At the end of this essay, Steele writes, "No matter how badly it might have gone for us...we should have talked. We should have made the effort." Working in groups, role-play the conversation that might have occurred that night. How might you initiate such conversations on your campus? Is talk the only or best solution to the kinds of tensions Steele describes?

Talking about Racism: How Our Dialogue Gets Short-Circuited

PAUL L. WACHTEL

In the following selection, eminent psychotherapist Paul L. Wachtel suggests that racial conflicts are often aggravated by problems of communication. African Americans' legitimate grievances need to be heard and addressed by whites, who often resist listening. In an effort to break through this resistance, blacks may hurl charges of racism that make whites even more defensive, which in turn shuts down conversation. In order to address America's race problem, Wachtel argues, we must learn to break these unproductive patterns of behavior. Wachtel (b. 1940) is CUNY Distinguished

Professor in clinical psychology at City University of New York Graduate Center and at City College of New York, where he also served as Acting Director of the Colin Powell Center for Policy Studies. He has written and edited many books on psychotherapy and has applied his psychological training to the analysis of social issues in such well-received works as The Poverty of Affluence *(1983),* Action and Insight *(1987), and* Race in the Mind of America *(1999), from which this passage is taken.*

Racism: A Term with a Host of Meanings

Consider the following scenarios—some tragic and dramatic, some mundane, but all sadly recognizable features of the racial landscape in America:

- A KKK mob burns a cross on the lawn of a black family that has moved into a formerly white neighborhood.
- A white person crosses the street to avoid encountering several black teenagers walking toward him.
- A black couple looking for an apartment is told that it is rented, but a white couple sent by a civil rights group to test for discrimination is shown the apartment an hour later and told it is available.
- A white person says he supports fair housing laws because he believes it is unfair and unjust to discriminate on the basis of race, but confesses that he himself would be afraid to live in a neighborhood that was not mostly white.
- A professor claims he has data proving that blacks are inferior in intelligence.
- A sports commentator comments that blacks are more naturally gifted as athletes.
- A white resident in an expensive co-op makes a friendly comment to a black woman riding in the elevator with her, but the comment makes it clear she has erroneously assumed that the black woman, who is in fact editor of a leading magazine, is a maid.
- The owner of a jewelry store does not buzz in a well-dressed black man for fear he is a robber.
- Two middle-class whites discuss their annoyance when a black youth passes by with a boom box loudly blaring rap music, saying, "Kids like that have no consideration; they think they own the streets."
- An employer interviewed by a researcher says that he has experienced repeatedly that blacks are more frequently late to work and tend to have an "attitude."
- A museum holds an exhibit of leading contemporary artists and none of the artists chosen are black.
- A literature survey course on the greatest works of world literature from Homer to the present has no black authors on the reading list.

- A candidate for office states that this country was founded as a white Christian nation and that is how it should remain.
- A high school institutes a writing requirement for graduation that requires mastery of standard English.
- A test is given for a civil service job and whites score higher on the test than blacks.
- A search committee for a faculty job at a prestigious university refuses to modify its criteria in considering a black applicant who has published few papers in leading professional journals.
- A black woman shopping in a department store that has had many robberies is watched more closely by the store detective than are the white women around her.
- A black child attends a school that has large classes, few books or study aids, and not nearly enough desks and chairs to go around.
- A teacher in that school says she is no longer as idealistic as she was when she began and that no matter how hard she tries, the kids don't seem to learn.
- A study reveals that garbage pickups in poor black neighborhoods are less frequent than in middle-class white neighborhoods.
- An activist for global environmental preservation advocates increasing efforts at promoting birth control in third world countries, where population increase is greatest.

These scenarios differ in a multitude of ways, but they have one significant thing in common: All have been labeled as instances of racism.

Do they all embody racism? Some of them seem to me clearly to merit the use of that term, but whether they all do is a virtually impossible question to answer. The platinum meter rod that lies in the International Bureau of Weights and Measures and defines for all of us just what a meter is has no real equivalent in the realm of language; no one owns a platinum dictionary that is the final arbiter of what the word racism should refer to. A word with such powerful emotional connotations, that is used to describe events and attitudes so close to the heart of our society's most basic afflictions, is bound to be a source of contention. "Looking it up in the dictionary" is utterly beside the point when a central issue is who gets to write the dictionary, who defines the terms of the debate. (Several of the black participants in our interracial dialogue groups contended that blacks cannot be racist "by definition" because the word racism means discrimination by the majority against an oppressed minority. Some of the whites, in turn, asked where they got that definition, and were convinced that most dictionaries did not define racism in that way—to which one black participant responded, "What color are the people who write the dictionaries?" This is at once a politically astute observation and an implicit acknowledgment that there is an element of arbitrariness that undermines *any* effort to assert in an absolute manner what racism "is.")[1]

But if we cannot really settle in any definitive or "objective" way what is and is not racism, we *can* ask what the *consequences* are of one or another way of using the term. Those consequences, I believe, point to the conclusion that we have seriously overused the words "racism" and "racist," to the detriment of the clarity and precision of our language and of our ability to overcome our racial divisions.

I make this suggestion not because I believe racism has disappeared in   5 American life, nor out of a view that our racial problems have become less severe, therefore meriting our use of "milder" terms. Racism remains a central fact of our life together, and in certain respects our racial divisions have become more rather than less intractable in recent years. What I wish to introduce is not a "milder" vocabulary, not a list of euphemisms, but rather a more *precise* and *differentiated* vocabulary. My aim is not to sweep racism under the rug, but to understand more clearly the experiences and attitudes to which the term is usually applied.

The terms racism and racist have been so stretched and extended in contemporary dialogue on race and inequality that their usage has become a serious impediment to our efforts to come to grips with problems that are difficult enough to begin with. There are many instances in which words like prejudice, bias, discrimination, stereotyping, ethnocentrism, insensitivity, inequality, injustice, indifference, and even ignorance, denote far more accurately the social and psychological reality of events now depicted almost reflexively as "racist." Moreover, not only does the use of these alternative terms provide a sharper and more differentiated analytic tool for understanding our society's dilemmas, it also enables us to avoid falling into a number of costly pitfalls embedded in our current linguistic habits.

One key problem is that the words "racism" and "racist" tend to be conversation stoppers. When "I disagree" or "You don't understand" or "You don't know the facts" or even "You're wrong" becomes "You're racist," real dialogue ceases. And it ceases regardless of whether what is evoked is an angry retort or a deferential and ultimately insincere genuflection. When whites walk on eggshells in their interactions with blacks, fearing that to express their views in all their complexity would leave them open to the accusation of being racists, all that results is a covering over of real issues and

---

[1]On another occasion, a white participant pointed out that blacks are not a minority in South Africa and asked, "Does that mean that by definition South African whites can't be racist?" The black participant then amended her claim, saying that *any* oppressed group, even if a majority, could not be racist; only the oppressor could. This then led to a discussion about whether whites were in fact oppressors in American society (everyone in the group was in agreement about South Africa). Here the debate was not so much about definitions (though the contention about that remained) as about the facts. Was it so cut and dried that whites are oppressors and blacks oppressed? Not surprisingly, there were significant differences between whites and blacks with regard to this question. [All notes are author's, except 4.]

feelings that are essential to address if any progress in race relations is to be made. In this respect, blacks may actually not appreciate how guilty many whites feel about the inequalities that exist in our society (even if that guilt is frequently repressed or insufficiently a source of remedial action). The use of a term that feels to blacks merely descriptive, simply an account of what they encounter every day of their lives, can create in whites a defensive attitude that stifles honest communication. And while there may be short-term advantage to blacks in being able to intimidate whites in this way, and a kind of poetic justice in being able to turn the tables in certain respects, there is, as I shall elaborate below, a high cost ultimately to be paid for whatever satisfaction is thereby achieved.

Moreover, overextension of the terms "racism" and "racist" actually can serve to obscure rather than make clearer the degree of racial injustice that pervades our society. "Racism" is a strong word, and part of the rationale for its use is that it takes a forceful message to break through strong denial: euphemisms permit continuing evasion. But volume is not the only determinant of what gets heard. After a while one habituates to—or "tunes out"—even the loudest noise if it is unvarying. Indeed, at times a silence that replaces a steady noise is a more attention-getting stimulus than the noise itself. A varied vocabulary is not just an aesthetic virtue; it also counters the tendency to tune out. Conveying the message in a language about which the intended hearer is set to be defensive is likely to have less impact than doing so in a language that is straightforward and pulls no punches, but is not needlessly provocative.

In a 1992 panel discussion on the *MacNeil-Lehrer NewsHour,* black journalist Joseph Boyce lamented the fact that

> at one time the last thing anyone wanted to be called was a racist, whether they were or not. It was a mark to be avoided. And today I don't think people really care that much, some of them, you know. They'll say, "Yeah, I'm a racist, so what, so what are you going to do about it?"[2]

This is indeed a regrettable state of affairs, but I believe that one reason for it is that the word racist has been bandied about so much that for some people it has lost its impact, lost its power to shock, to evoke guilt or revulsion. A term that once referred to the most deplorable and shameful of traits and actions has been extended to include virtually universal human characteristics and to include within its purview practically everyone in our society.

It should *not* be easy and common to say with equanimity "Yes, I'm a   10
racist, so what?" But if we are told in essence that *every* white person is a

[2]*The MacNeil-Lehrer NewsHour,* Thursday, June 11, 1992. Transcript provided by WNET and WETA. Page 14.

racist,[3] then it *becomes* a matter to which a ho-hum response becomes possible. Racism *is* a strong word (or at least it *was* a strong word), and it should remain one. It should *not* be a word whose power habituates. We are much the worse off when people can acknowledge racism with impunity, as a simple, familiar fact of life rather than a terrible aberration.

Bull Connor or Joe Next Door?

The phenomenon painfully noted by Boyce was certainly not intended or expected by those whose rhetoric first created the expansion of the word's usage. In large measure the expansion developed as a response to the changing challenges of the civil rights movement as it moved from the South to the North. As long as the South persisted in a particularly explicit and ugly form of racial segregation and disparagement of blacks, the subtler, but often no less persistent or destructive segregation of the North was effectively shrouded. Especially combined with the earlier close association of the South with outright slavery, this pattern of difference between North and South enabled the rest of the country to externalize its own quite considerable racial prejudices by holding to a fantasy of the "bad" South and the "good" North. When the most egregious features of racial discrimination in the South gave way in the 1960s, it became increasingly apparent that the North differed much less from the South than it had thought. Workers for change were confronted with a set of prejudices and institutional constraints that were more difficult to confront than those of the South precisely because they were more subtle, disguised, and unacknowledged.

In response to this, and in an effort to communicate to whites in the North that "you're not as different as you think from the Southerners you have been smugly criticizing," writers and activists began increasingly to employ a term that had once stood in the national imagination for such violent acts of lynchings or the vicious use of police dogs by Birmingham police chief Bull Connor.[4] Their aim was to break through the numbing denial, to confront Northerners with the need for changes as radical in their own way as the opening of schools, lunch counters, and other public facilities to blacks in the South. But in the process, a term that had largely pointed toward the most serious and heinous offenses against human dignity began, in effect, to be watered down to stand for more common human foibles. As a consequence, subtle but powerful changes in connotation were set in motion: On the one hand, the special emotional impact of the word "racism" was diminished; if it is not a term referring to violence and the extremes of

[3]See, among many examples, "Are you a racist?", by Peter Noel, *Village Voice*, February 11, 1992, pp. 34–35.

[4]*Bull Connor:* T. Eugene "Bull" Connor directed police to use dogs and water hoses to quell antisegregation demonstrations in Birmingham, Alabama, in 1963. TV broadcasts of these violent images actually strengthened the civil rights movement.

inhumanity, but rather to what the folks down the block do, then it's not really so bad. On the other hand, if the Bull Connors of the world are no different really from you or I or Joe next door, then an unfortunate covert link of solidarity is subtly fostered between flawed but decent people and people who deserve nothing but contempt.

The Paradoxes of Guilt

It may seem inconsistent to point out that "racist" is such a strong word that it stops meaningful dialogue and invokes defensiveness in whites, and simultaneously to contend that its overuse has desensitized us to the real horror the term should connote and enabled people to accept with equanimity the description of them as racist. The inconsistency, however, is more apparent than real. At the simplest level, we may note that different responses to the term can be manifested by different people; some may be intimidated or defensive while others are inured and desensitized. Moreover, even for the same person, the accusation of racism may sometimes be experienced as an intimidating conversation-stopper and sometimes as a tiresome harangue that has little real impact whatever formal obeisance may or may not be paid. Whether one or the other response is evoked will depend on many factors: who is making the accusation; how it is presented; with what mood or set the accused enters the encounter; the number of people present and the ratio of blacks and whites among them; and a host of other aspects of context and personality.

Moreover, the two seemingly antithetical reactions can often be but two sides of the same response. Both the defiant embrace of the term referred to by Boyce ("Yeah, I'm racist. So what?") and the reaction of boredom or disinterest that mutes the impact of a message that needs to be heard ("Here we go again! More rhetoric!") can be defensive responses to having been made to feel guilty. In these instances, it is *because* the impact of the accusation is so strong that its conscious acknowledgment is so minimal.

Guilt is a complex emotion and does not always produce the response   15
we might wish or expect. Sometimes, to be sure, it leads to efforts to right the wrong one has done. But very often, especially if guilt threatens to be overwhelming, the response to guilt can be paradoxical: still *further* insensitivity to those we have harmed, and anger at them for confronting us with our inadequacies and iniquities. Conveying the bad news is a subtle art. Whether in a marriage or friendship or in a larger social context, it is far from universal that when we succeed in making the person we think has wronged us feel guilty we end up pleased with the results.

Salutary responses to feelings of guilt are most likely to occur when there is something productive and reparative the individual can do to relieve the guilt. Global and overextended depictions of white racism block this healthy and useful response. If whites are left feeling they are going to be seen as racist no matter what they do—"if I'm not an overt racist, I'm a covert one"—then the response is likely to be one of "why bother?" or some other defensive reaction. Ritualistic acknowledgments of "racism" may be offered, but they will be *in place of* effective action to heal our social wounds rather than a harbinger of such actions.

"Institutional Racism"

Different problems are introduced by another way in which the use of the term racism has been expanded over the years. Increasingly, discourse on racism has stressed its *institutional* nature rather than simply the attitudes of individuals, and the concept of "institutional racism" has become a central feature of contemporary dialogue on issues of race.

As James M. Jones, a leading African American writer on racism and prejudice, has delineated the distinction, "The critical aspect of institutional racism that distinguished it from prejudice and from individual racism was the notion that institutions can produce racist consequences *whether they do so intentionally or not.*"[5] Robert Miles, a British sociologist who has written a comprehensive examination of the manifold ways in which the concept of racism is employed in contemporary discourse, offers a closely related definition of how the term is used—"all processes which, *intentionally or not,* result in the continued exclusion of a subordinated group."[6] In contrast with Jones, however, Miles sees serious difficulties with the concept. Although he views racism as indeed a central problem in contemporary society and regards the dissection of racism as a crucial task for social analysis, he decries the "conceptual inflation" that leads the term racism to be overused and overextended and its original sharp meaning to be significantly blurred. As the concept of racism is extended into the terminology of *institutional* racism the role of the motivations and attitudes of actual human beings becomes increasingly confused, and a highly abstract and impersonal conception becomes mischievously merged with one of the most emotionally charged words in our vocabulary.

The original use of the term institutional racism by Stokely Carmichael and Charles Hamilton in their influential book, *Black Power,*[7] was not as divorced from intentionality. They did depict two different kinds of racism—individual and institutional—and they noted how the latter, *seemingly* impersonal, can allow "respectable" individuals to dissociate themselves from the acts of those with the poor taste to be overtly racist, while continuing to benefit from the ways in which our institutions maintain the inequalities between blacks and whites. But Carmichael and Hamilton's conception of in-

[5]James M. Jones, Racism in black and white, in P. Katz & D. Taylor (Eds.), *Eliminating Racism: Profiles in Controversy,* New York: Plenum, 1986, p. 129. Emphasis added.
[6]Robert Miles, *Racism,* London: Routledge, 1989, p. 50.
[7]Stokely Carmichael and Charles V. Hamilton, *Black Power,* New York: Vintage, 1967.

stitutional racism does not eliminate motivation or intention. They state quite explicitly that

> Institutional racism relies on the active and pervasive operation of anti-black attitudes and practices. A sense of superior group position prevails: whites are "better" than blacks; therefore blacks should be subordinated to whites. This is a racist attitude and it permeates the society, on both the individual and institutional level, covertly and overtly.[8]

I believe that Carmichael and Hamilton accurately identified an atti-   20
tude that continues to prevail in America to a disturbing degree, and I agree as well that it merits the description as racist. But as the idea of institutional racism evolved over the years, it has increasingly come to be evoked whenever differences between the races are found, *regardless* of whether there is any evidence of racist intent. The outcome itself is taken as proof that racism *must* underlie the differences.[9]

It is indeed crucially important to understand how our institutional arrangements maintain inequalities and place continuing burdens on a people who already have a long history of oppression. But the labeling of these processes as institutional "racism" has muddled as much as it clarifies. The confusion arises because a term replete with connotations of intention is used to denote a process *outside* of specific intentions, a process almost mechanical in its impersonality and inexorability. To the white who says, "That's *not* how I feel; that's not what I want," the proponent of the concept of institutional racism can say, "You're misunderstanding what I'm saying. I'm not saying *you* want this to happen, I'm saying that the whole society is set up in such a way that certain outcomes inevitably result, and those outcomes are consistently to the detriment of people of color in comparison to whites."

This distinction is logically coherent (and, in my view, it is rooted in a largely accurate perception of how our society works). But it is couched in terms that fail to take into account how real people think and react. As a consequence, it injects into our public discourse a terminology that is misleading and inflammatory. No matter what disclaimers may be offered by the speaker, it is extremely difficult for whites (or blacks for that matter, though with a different set of reactions likely) to hear the term institutional *racism* without other, more sinister connotations of the word racism seeping in.

As a consequence, the concept of "institutional racism" can contribute to obscuring the very phenomenon it was designed to highlight. Because

---

[8]Carmichael & Hamilton, *Black Power*, p. 5.

[9]Many of these extensions of the meaning of racism are reviewed in Miles and depicted by him as an instance of "conceptual inflation." See also R. Blauner, *Racial Oppression in America*, New York: Harper & Row, 1972; D. Wellman, *Portraits of White Racism*, Cambridge: Cambridge University Press; and S. Steinberg, *The Ethnic Myth*, Boston: Beacon, 1989.

the terms "racism" and "racist" are likely to evoke in the hearer connotations of motivated rather than impersonal and systemic outcomes, whites who do not recognize racist *intent* in the operations of our dominant institutions or in the outcomes they yield are likely as a consequence to find claims of "institutional racism" implausible. In the process, they are enabled to avoid coming to grips with how the workings of our society do disadvantage blacks and other minorities even when there is no specific intention that that be the outcome.

As obvious as it ought to be that our social arrangements have a predictably differential overall impact on blacks and whites, it is easy not to see it, *and one need not be a racist not to.* For our society's customary way of thinking leads us to look away from predictable group differences and to emphasize instead individual choice and responsibility. This tendency is not limited to our perceptions with regard to minorities. It obscures as much about the differences in income and access among whites as it does about blacks. Part of the system we live under is that we are systematically trained not to see the system. That is, we are taught to understand the differences in income and influence that result from the way we organize our society as solely the result of individual choices and individual merit; and we are taught *not* to notice the statistical probabilities that make the bright child of a truck driver or a manual laborer less likely to go to college than the child of a doctor or lawyer.

Instead, we are trained to notice the *exceptions.* Since there are some children of truck drivers and manual laborers who do go to college—indeed, a sizable enough group to be noticeable—we affirm that we are a "land of opportunity," and essentially ignore the fact that we can predict with virtual statistical certainty the differential life courses of the children of the two groups.[10]

In similar fashion, we may use the existence of a growing black middle class to obscure the reality that blacks remain greatly overrepresented among those who receive the least of our society's rewards. Here again, the exceptions obscure the rule. The roots of the confusion lie in the fact that the effects of institutional arrangements are statistical rather than universal. That is, it is not the case that *no* blacks are able to succeed in our society or that all whites do better than the average black. Rather, what is predictable is that, all in all, the status and station of blacks is likely to be lower than that of whites; or, put differently, that the circumstances most blacks encounter from birth on are likely to make it harder for them to succeed than are the circumstances most whites encounter. Since there are fairly numerous exceptions—blacks who make it anyhow, through noteworthy talent, drive, or persistence—it is easy to overlook the way the cards are stacked against this

25

---

[10]A great deal of evidence demonstrating the powerful effects of parental income and social class on children's prospects is reviewed by Richard Kahlenberg in *The Remedy: Class, Race, and Affirmative Action,* New York: Basic Books, 1997. See especially pages 86–94.

happening. Instead, the very fact that *some* blacks have made it leads many whites to conclude that those who haven't simply do not try hard enough, are not sufficiently meritorious, or in some other way "deserve" the deprivation they endure.

If we are to transcend this superficial and censorious way of understanding the disparities that haunt our society, we will indeed have to make clearer the *institutional* aspects of what has been called institutional racism. The rhetoric of institutional racism can impede such understanding, leading people to focus on personal attitudes in a way that obscures precisely the institutional dimension. What results are responses such as, "This talk about institutional racism is nonsense. It's just an excuse. I'm not a racist. I judge people as individuals. I don't care if they are black, white, green, or purple. If they work hard and follow the rules, I respect them, and if they expect special favors, I say 'life's hard for me too.' "

I've certainly had enough psychoanalytic training to know that such a response *might* be covering over "unconscious racism." But I've also had enough psychoanalytic training to know that such an automatic assumption is a misuse of psychoanalysis. What is more obvious and definite is that such a response reflects highly *individualistic* assumptions that obscure the way social conditions influence people's behavior and aspirations. When people believe that everyone makes his or her own fate, and ignore the role of circumstance, they are unlikely to be sympathetic to those who do not make it, regardless of race.

This is not to imply that racial feelings play no part in our society's readiness to accept institutional arrangements that leave so many people of color disadvantaged. Rather, the question is whether "racism" is the best way of understanding those racial feelings. I turn now to an alternative conceptualization that I believe is both more accurate and more likely to contribute to the sense of recognition that is an essential precursor of change.

"Otherness" and Indifference

A more useful way, I suggest, to conceptualize the broad commonality   30
among the diverse experiences typically labeled as "racist" is to focus our attention on the sense of "otherness" that is central to these experiences. "Otherness" is not as sexy a word as racism. It is unlikely to come into widespread use as a catch-all term, and indeed, that is one of its great advantages. It points us toward an understanding of the underlying foundations of these various problematic features of our life as a society without co-opting the differentiations.

There are subtle differences among the words that depict the attitudes increasingly lumped together under the global rubric of racism. Some whites, for example, may be able to hear and consider a claim that they have been *prejudiced* in some situation or other but will reject (or only give superficial lip service to) the claim that they were being racist. What is the difference? Prejudice implies jumping to a quick, and even unfair, conclusion, but for many people it does not imply hostility and brutality as does racism.[11] While it is not pleasant to acknowledge the former, it is still a far cry from being guilty of the latter.

In similar fashion, for a white to be confronted with having been *insensitive* in some remark he might have made can be a quite different experience from having the remark described as racist. Once again, although both are likely to be painful to acknowledge, the first characterization is much more likely to get through than the second.

What is perhaps most important of all for whites to acknowledge and understand is *indifference*. A great deal of what is often characterized as racism can be more precisely and usefully described as indifference. Perhaps no other feature of white attitudes, and of the underlying attitudinal structure of white society as a whole, is as cumulatively responsible for the pain and privation experienced by our nation's black minority at this point in our history as is indifference. At the same time, perhaps no feature is as misunderstood or overlooked.

"Otherness" is at work in all of the destructive ways in which people of different groups interact. Prejudices, biases, stereotypes, and the like would have no objects were not some people experienced as "other." But "otherness" is perhaps especially germane to the role of indifference, which in a sense can be viewed as a pure culture of otherness. That is, in prejudice, stereotyping, ethnocentrism, and other such obviously problematic features of how groups of human beings interact, something is *added* to otherness. There is something more active in these behaviors and attitudes that makes them a bit more able to be detected. Indifference, in contrast, is a *quiet* toxin. It severs the sinews and nerves of society without announcing itself. Its effects are devastating, but its tracks are hidden in the overall attitude of "each man for himself" that is so prominent a part of our society's ethos.

Further obscuring the central role of indifference in our social problems is that highly immediate and visible tragedy can transcend the sense of otherness. Few white Americans would fail to rescue a black child trapped in a well or a black man pinned under the wreckage of a building collapse. At such moments the sense of human solidarity takes center stage, not the sense of differentness. And indeed, this is one of the reasons that most white Americans do not really believe in their heart of hearts that they are racist. 35

But when it comes to the slow bleeding that daily drains the spirit and hope from life in our nation's inner cities, indifference shows itself in full measure. We tolerate the misery in the midst of our affluent society because of the strong sense of "them" that attaches to the miserable, the sense that "they" are not like "us," that they are different. And so most whites,

[11]James M. Jones, for example, in a prominent textbook on racism and prejudice, depicts racism as something "far more sinister and deep" than prejudice (Jones, *Racism and Prejudice*, p. 196).

who are aware of little feeling of outright hostility, who believe in fair play and equal opportunity, see little that has to do with them in the painful realities of our inner cities. In both (ironically almost opposite) meanings of the phrase, what is happening there is "too bad." But for all too many whites, it is not perceived as their responsibility.

Of course, what I am describing comes very close in certain ways to what is often addressed under the rubric of institutional racism. Indifference, however, comes much closer to the unacknowledged core of truth in white America's guilty conscience. "Institutional racism" is unlikely to become a part of the phenomenological experience of white Americans; indifference can. It is indifference that whites can potentially recognize and acknowledge within themselves, and it is in combating indifference that the fulcrum of change may be most effectively placed.

Indifference and the sense of otherness are not experiences that are limited to issues of race. We may see them operating every time there is a plane crash abroad and the newscaster announces how many Americans are aboard. The likelihood, for any listener, that any American victim of the crash will be someone they actually know is exceedingly small; there are, after all, a quarter of a billion Americans. Yet this information is always supplied, for it defines whether the victim was "one of us," and, if truth be told, it defines to a significant degree whether we should *care*.[12]

---

[12]I assume that something similar happens when a plane crash is announced on the news in other countries as well. The phenomenon I am describing is by no means uniquely American.

This is precisely the issue that most burdens race relations in our society as well. The real meaning of race comes down largely to this: *Is this someone I should care about?* This is a terrible and shameful truth, and in its full impact it will not be easy for white America to face. But it points much more precisely, I believe, to the true source of white guilt than does the label of racism. As a consequence, it has a better chance both of leading us to examine what is in our hearts and of generating the concrete social and economic changes that are essential for real justice and equality to be achieved.

Summary and Conclusion

Accusing a guilty man of the wrong crime is one of the greatest gifts 40 one can bestow upon him. It fosters an orgy of self-righteous conviction of innocence, and conveniently diverts his attention from the offense of which he is truly guilty. In a similar fashion, the ubiquitous claim that racism is the cause of the grievous circumstances of life in our inner cities is, ironically, enabling white America to slough off its responsibility for the shameful neglect of the least privileged members of our society.

The real crime of which white America is now most guilty is not racism. It is indifference. Understanding the difference between the two is a crucial step in liberating ourselves from the sterile and unproductive impasse that has characterized the dialogue on race relations in recent years.

Distinguishing between racism and indifference is not a semantic quibble. The constant invocation of racism, often in ever more forced, abstract, and symbolic senses, can have the counterproductive effect of causing listeners to filter out potentially important arguments because they sound repetitive, rhetorical, and, most important, contrary to their experience. Racism is such a loaded word, so tinged with associations to lynchings and unprintable racial epithets, that many whites experience a sharp distinction between their own attitudes and what they believe is implied by such a word. As a consequence, accused of a crime of which their self-examination tells them they are innocent, they can go to bed with an undisturbed conscience.

But in fact there is little ground for a clear conscience in the relations of white America to its black minority. Many whites who can quite honestly claim that they hold no hatred for blacks, that they do not wish them harm or disparage them as a group—in short, that they are not "racist"—must acknowledge that it *is* true that almost daily news reports of the terrors and privations of growing up in the inner city leave them with the feeling, "That's not my problem." Such an attitude may be justified (or rationalized) by the claim that "Maybe there once were obstacles to blacks getting into college or getting good jobs, but times have changed. Now the opportunities are there if they'll only apply themselves."

And although there is a certain amount of truth in such a view, it fails not only to acknowledge the continuing discrimination that does still exist, but even more importantly, it fails to take into account how hard it is to *see* the new opportunities from the vantage point of the typical block in our poorest neighborhoods. Boarded-up buildings, drug pushers, gang members with guns, and the ubiquitous presence of unemployed men and women tend rather effectively to block the view of the wider world of opportunity readily visible from the suburbs. Few children, white or black, have the capacity to see past such a compellingly bleak immediate reality.

To some in the black community, describing the predominant white attitude as indifference rather than racism may seem like a kind of plea-bargaining in which a lesser offense is acknowledged instead of the real crime. I disagree. For most white Americans the crime of which they are most guilty *is* indifference, *not* racism. Moreover, and even more important, indifference in the face of severe human suffering is not a minor offense.   45

Our society is deeply flawed by racial inequalities, but the unswerving emphasis on racism as the explanation has become part of the problem rather than part of the solution. It is time to retire the rhetoric of racism, not because white neglect has become benign, but because it is essential for the well-being of all of us, white *and* black, that that neglect be recognized and addressed.

ENGAGING THE TEXT

1. Wachtel proposes that "words like prejudice, bias, discrimination, stereotyping, ethnocentrism, insensitivity, inequality, injustice, indifference, and even ignorance, denote far more accurately the social and psychological reality of events now depicted almost reflexively as 'racist'" (para. 6). How does each of these alternative terms differ in denotation or connotation from "racism"? Working in groups, draft definitions for these terms, and compare your results with those of your classmates.

2. Examine the scenarios at the beginning of this selection and discuss which ones illustrate true racism and which are instances of prejudice, insensitivity, indifference, ignorance, etc. How easy or difficult is it to agree on the interpretation of the scenarios?

3. Define "institutional racism." Why does Wachtel believe that the term is counterproductive although the concept itself is valid?

4. Define "otherness" and summarize the relationship Wachtel sees between otherness and indifference. Do you agree that white Americans, in general, are indifferent to the suffering of those they perceive as unlike themselves? If so, how might people in the United States behave differently if they cared deeply about the problems of "others," both within their own country and in the world? If not, what evidence do you see that contradicts Wachtel's claim?

5. In Wachtel's view, what role does the American ideal of individualism play in perpetuating racial misunderstanding and conflict?

EXPLORING CONNECTIONS

6. Write or act out imaginary dialogue between Randall Robinson (p. 557) and Wachtel on how best to achieve reparations for slavery.

7. Read the anecdote about the cocktail party at the beginning of Shelby Steele's essay (p. 602). To what extent does Wachtel's analysis of cross-racial communication seem relevant or useful in understanding what happened? Could his advice about how to talk about racial issues have helped in the case of the stalled conversation Steele describes? Why or why not?

8. Review the racial encounters described by Stephen Cruz (p. 348), Cora Tucker (p. 353), C. P. Ellis (p. 591), and Ralph Temple (p. 798). Which of these, if any, would you describe as instances of racism? Which would more accurately be defined by one of the alternative terms Wachtel proposes?

9. Compare Wachtel's discussion of individualism and race to Ken Hamblin's (p. 384). Which view do you find more compelling, and why?

10. What does the Ted Rall cartoon on page 625 suggest about whites' behavior and attitudes toward blacks? To what extent is the cartoonist's view of race relations consistent or inconsistent with Wachtel's?

EXTENDING THE CRITICAL CONTEXT

11. If you have witnessed or been involved in a confrontation about race, write a journal entry describing the conflict in detail. What was said and how did each participant react? Was the interaction productive? If so, for whom, and in what way(s)? If not, what made it frustrating or upsetting, and for whom? After reading Wachtel's analysis, do you understand the experience any differently? Why or why not?

Visual Portfolio
READING IMAGES OF THE MELTING POT

1. What is the significance of making the ad for the American Civil Liberties Union look like a "Wanted" poster from the wild West? What is the purpose of pairing the photos of Dr. Martin Luther King Jr. and Charles Manson? What values does the ad associate with the ACLU, and how does it communicate those values? Do you find the ad effective? Why or why not?

2. The second image in the portfolio shows construction workers erecting a segment of the fence that marks the border between the U.S. and Mexico. Freewrite for ten minutes about what you think the wall means to the people on each side. What sense does the picture give you of the photographer's perspective on the fence? What details of the picture itself—angle, lighting, proportion—suggest that perspective?

3. How many different ways could you describe the ethnic or cultural identity of each of the four friends on page 631 based on the visual cues provided by the photo? What knowledge or assumptions about race, ethnicity, and culture underlie your interpretations?

Models of American Ethnic Relations: A Historical Perspective
GEORGE M. FREDRICKSON

Are Irish Americans white? The answer is so self-evident that the question seems absurd, but as historian George Fredrickson notes, the idea of "whiteness" has in the past excluded many Europeans, including the Irish. A survey of ethnic and racial categories in American history shows how much they change with the politics and prejudices of the time. Yet citizenship, civil rights, even human status have been granted or withheld on the basis of these shifting definitions. Fredrickson examines four models of ethnic relations—hierarchy, assimilation, pluralism, and separatism—that have defined how groups perceived as different from each other should interact. Fredrickson (b. 1934) has written extensively about race in the history of the United States and South Africa and is a past president of the Organization for American Historians. His books include The Inner Civil War *(1965),* The Black Image in the White Mind *(1972),* White Supremacy *(1981),* Black Liberation *(1995), and* Racism: A Short History *(2002). He is the Edgar E. Robinson Professor Emeritus of U.S. History at Stanford University.*

Throughout its history, the United States has been inhabited by a variety of interacting racial or ethnic groups. In addition to the obvious "color line" structuring relationships between dominant whites and lower-status blacks, Indians, and Asians, there have at times been important social distinctions among those of white or European ancestry. Today we think of the differences between white Anglo-Saxon Protestants and Irish, Italian, Polish, and Jewish Americans as purely cultural or religious, but in earlier times these groups were sometimes thought of as "races" or "subraces"—people possessing innate or inborn characteristics and capabilities that affected their fitness for American citizenship. Moreover, differences apparently defined as cultural have sometimes been so reified[1] as to serve as the functional equivalent of physical distinctions. Indians, for example, were viewed by most nineteenth-century missionaries and humanitarians as potentially equal and similar to whites. Their status as noncitizens was not attributed to skin color or physical appearance; it was only their obdurate adherence to "savage ways" that allegedly stood in the way of their possessing equal rights and being fully assimilated. Analogously, conservative opponents of affirmative action and other antiracist policies in the 1990s may provide a "rational" basis for prejudice and discrimination by attributing the disadvantages and alleged shortcomings of African Americans to persistent cultural "pathology" rather than to genetic deficiencies (D'Souza 1995).

It can therefore be misleading to make a sharp distinction between race and ethnicity when considering intergroup relations in American history. As I have argued extensively elsewhere, ethnicity is "racialized" whenever distinctive group characteristics, however defined or explained, are used as the basis for a status hierarchy of groups who are thought to differ in ancestry or descent (Fredrickson 1997, ch. 5).

Four basic conceptions of how ethnic or racial groups should relate to each other have been predominant in the history of American thought about group relations—ethnic hierarchy, one-way assimilation, cultural pluralism, and group separatism. This [essay] provides a broad outline of the historical career of each of these models of intergroup relations, noting some of the changes in how various groups have defined themselves or been defined by others.

Ethnic Hierarchy

Looking at the entire span of American history, we find that the most influential and durable conception of the relations among those American racial or ethnic groups viewed as significantly dissimilar has been

---

[1]*reified:* Treated as if real, concrete, but actually abstract.

hierarchical. A dominant group—conceiving of itself as society's charter membership—has claimed rights and privileges not to be fully shared with outsiders or "others," who have been characterized as unfit or unready for equal rights and full citizenship. The hierarchical model has its deepest roots and most enduring consequences in the conquest of Indians and the enslavement of blacks during the colonial period (Axtell 1981; Jordan 1968). But it was also applied in the nineteenth century to Asian immigrants and in a less severe and more open-ended way to European immigrants who differed in culture and religion from old-stock Americans of British origin (Higham 1968; Miller 1969). The sharpest and most consequential distinction was always between "white" and "nonwhite." The first immigration law passed by Congress in 1790 specified that only white immigrants were eligible for naturalization. This provision would create a crucial difference in the mid-nineteenth century between Chinese "sojourners," who could not become citizens and voters, and Irish immigrants, who could.

Nevertheless, the Irish who fled the potato famine of the 1840s by emigrating to the United States also encountered discrimination. Besides being Catholic and poor, the refugees from the Emerald Isle were Celts rather than Anglo-Saxons, and a racialized discourse,[2] drawing on British precedents, developed as an explanation for Irish inferiority to Americans of English ancestry (Knobel 1986). The dominant group during the nineteenth and early twentieth centuries was not simply white but also Protestant and Anglo-Saxon. Nevertheless, the Irish were able to use their right to vote and the patronage they received from the Democratic Party to improve their status, an option not open to the Chinese. Hence, they gradually gained the leverage and respectability necessary to win admission to the dominant caste, a process that culminated in Al Smith's nomination for the presidency in 1928 and John F. Kennedy's election in 1960.

The mass immigration of Europeans from eastern and southern Europe in the late nineteenth and early twentieth centuries inspired new concerns about the quality of the American stock. In an age of eugenics,[3] scientific racism,[4] and social Darwinism,[5] the notion that northwestern Europeans were innately superior to those from the southern and eastern parts of the continent—to say nothing of those light-skinned people of actual or presumed west Asian origin (such as Jews, Syrians, and Armenians)—

[2]*racialized discourse:* Language that defines a group of people as a race and attributes distinctive "racial" characteristics to them.

[3]*eugenics:* Movement that advocated improving the human race by encouraging genetically "superior" people to reproduce and promoting the sterilization of "undesirables," including minorities, poor people, and those with mental and physical disorders.

[4]*scientific racism:* Refers to various efforts to find some scientific basis for white superiority, the results of which were inevitably bad science.

[5]*social Darwinism:* The belief that Darwin's theory of evolution and natural selection applies to society; thus the existence of extreme wealth and poverty (whether of individuals or nations) is rationalized as a "natural" result of competition and the survival of the fittest.

gained wide currency. A determined group of nativists, encouraged by the latest racial "science," fought for restrictive immigration policies that discriminated against those who were not of "Nordic" or "Aryan" descent (Higham 1968). In the 1920s the immigration laws were changed to reflect these prejudices. Low quotas were established for white people from nations or areas outside of those that had supplied the bulk of the American population before 1890. In the minds of many, true Americans were not merely white but also northern European. In fact, some harbored doubts about the full claim to "whiteness" of swarthy immigrants from southern Italy.

After immigration restriction had relieved ethnic and racial anxieties, the status of the new immigrants gradually improved as a result of their political involvement, their economic and professional achievement, and a decline in the respectability of the kind of scientific racism that had ranked some European groups below others. World War II brought revulsion against the genocidal anti-Semitism and eugenic experiments of the Nazis, dealing a coup de grâce to the de facto hierarchy that had placed Anglo-Saxons, Nordics, or Aryans at the apex of American society. All Americans of European origin were now unambiguously white and, for most purposes, ethnically equal to old-stock Americans of Anglo-Saxon, Celtic, and Germanic ancestry. Hierarchy was now based exclusively on color. Paradoxically, it might be argued, the removal of the burden of "otherness" from virtually all whites made more striking and salient than ever the otherness of people of color, especially African Americans.

The civil rights movement of the 1960s was directed primarily at the legalized racial hierarchy of the southern states. The Civil Rights Acts of 1964 and 1965 brought an end to government-enforced racial segregation and the denial of voting rights to blacks in that region. But the legacy of four centuries of white supremacy survives in the disadvantaged social and economic position of blacks and other people of color in the United States. The impoverished, socially deprived, and physically unsafe ghettos, barrios, and Indian reservations of this nation are evidence that ethnic hierarchy in a clearly racialized form persists in practice if not in law.

One-Way Assimilation

Policies aimed at the assimilation of ethnic groups have usually assumed that there is a single and stable American culture of European, and especially English, origin to which minorities are expected to conform as the price of admission to full and equal participation in the society and polity of the United States (Gordon 1964, ch. 4). Assimilationist thinking is not racist in the classic sense: it does not deem the outgroups in question to be innately or biologically inferior to the ingroup. The professed goal is equality—but on terms that presume the superiority, purity, and unchanging character of the dominant culture. Little or nothing in the cultures of the groups being invited to join the American mainstream is presumed

worthy of preserving. When carried to its logical conclusion, the assimilationist project demands what its critics have described—especially in reference to the coercive efforts to "civilize" Native Americans—as "cultural genocide."

Estimates of group potential and the resulting decisions as to which   10 groups are eligible for assimilation have varied in response to changing definitions of race. If an ethnic group is definitely racialized, the door is closed because its members are thought to possess ineradicable traits (biologically or culturally determined) that make them unfit for inclusion. At times there have been serious disagreements within the dominant group about the eligibility of particular minorities for initiation into the American club.

Although one-way assimilationism was mainly a twentieth-century ideology, it was anticipated in strains of nineteenth-century thinking about Irish immigrants, Native Americans, and even blacks. Radical white abolitionists and even some black antislavery activists argued that prejudice against African Americans was purely and simply a result of their peculiarly degraded and disadvantaged circumstances and that emancipation from slavery would make skin color irrelevant and open the way to their full equality and social acceptability (Fredrickson 1987, ch. 1). These abolitionists had little or no conception that there was a rich and distinctive black culture that could become the source of a positive group identity, and that African modes of thought and behavior had been adapted to the challenge of surviving under slavery.

If the hope of fully assimilating blacks into a color-blind society was held by only a small minority of whites, a majority probably supposed that the Irish immigrants of the 1840s and 1850s could become full-fledged Americans, if they chose to do so, simply by changing their behavior and beliefs. The doctrine of the innate inferiority of Celts to Anglo-Saxons was not even shared by all of the nativists who sought to slow down the process of Irish naturalization (Knobel 1986). A more serious problem for many of them was the fervent Catholicism of the Irish; Anglo-Protestant missionaries hoped to convert them en masse. The defenders of unrestricted Irish immigration came mostly from the ranks of the Democratic Party, which relied heavily on Irish votes. Among them were strong believers in religious toleration and a high wall of separation between church and state. They saw religious diversity as no obstacle to the full and rapid Americanization of all white-skinned immigrants.

The most sustained and serious nineteenth-century effort to assimilate people who differed both culturally and phenotypically[6] from the majority was aimed at American Indians. Frontier settlers, military men who fought Indians, and many other whites had no doubts that Indians were members of an inherently inferior race that was probably doomed to total extinction as a result of the conquest of the West. Their views were graphically expressed by General Philip Sheridan when he opined that "the only good Indian is a dead Indian." But an influential group of eastern philanthropists, humanitarian reformers, and government officials thought of the Indians as having been "noble savages" whose innate capacities were not inferior to those of whites. Thomas Jefferson, who had a much dimmer view of black potentialities, was one of the first to voice this opinion (Koch and Peden 1944, 210–11). For these ethnocentric humanitarians, the "Indian problem" was primarily cultural rather than racial, and its solution lay in civilizing the "savages" rather than exterminating them. Late in the century, the assimilationists adopted policies designed to force Indians to conform to Euro-American cultural norms; these included breaking up communally held reservations into privately owned family farms and sending Indian children to boarding schools where they were forbidden to speak their own languages and made to dress, cut their hair, and in every possible way act and look like white people. The policy was a colossal failure; most Native Americans refused to abandon key aspects of their traditional cultures, and venal whites took advantage of the land reforms to strip Indians of much of their remaining patrimony[7] (Berkhofer 1978; Hoxie 1984; Mardock 1971).

In the early twentieth century, the one-way assimilation model was applied to the southern and eastern European immigrants who had arrived in massive numbers before the discriminatory quota system of the 1920s was implemented. While some nativists called for their exclusion on the grounds of their innate deficiencies, other champions of Anglo-American cultural homogeneity hoped to assimilate those who had already arrived through education and indoctrination. The massive "Americanization" campaigns of the period just prior to World War I produced the concept of America as a "melting pot" in which cultural differences would be obliterated. The metaphor might have suggested that a new mixture would result—and occasionally it did have this meaning—but a more prevalent interpretation was that non-Anglo-American cultural traits and inclinations would simply disappear, making the final brew identical to the original one (Gordon 1964, ch. 5).

Before the 1940s, people of color, and especially African Americans, were generally deemed ineligible for assimilation because of their innate

15

---

[6]*phenotypically:* Physically.
[7]*patrimony:* Inheritance.

inferiority to white ethnics, who were now thought capable of being culturally reborn as Anglo-Americans. Such factors as the war-inspired reaction
against scientific racism and the gain in black political power resulting from
mass migration from the South (where blacks could not vote) to the urban
North (where the franchise was again open to them) led to a significant re-
consideration of the social position of African Americans and threw a spotlight on the flagrant denial in the southern states of the basic constitutional
rights of African Americans. The struggle for black civil rights that emerged
in the 1950s and came to fruition in the early 1960s was premised on a conviction that white supremacist laws and policies violated an egalitarian
"American Creed"—as Gunnar Myrdal had argued in his influential
wartime study *An American Dilemma* (1944). The war against Jim Crow[8] was
fought under the banner of "integration," which, in the minds of white liberals at least, generally meant one-way assimilation. Blacks, deemed by Myrdal
and others as having no culture worth saving, would achieve equal status by
becoming just like white Americans in every respect except pigmentation.

When it became clear that the civil rights legislation of the 1960s had
failed to improve significantly the social and economic position of blacks in
the urban ghettos of the North, large numbers of African Americans rejected the integrationist ideal on the grounds that it had been not only a
false promise but an insult to the culture of African Americans for ignoring
or devaluing their distinctive experience as a people. The new emphasis on
"black power" and "black consciousness" conveyed to those whites who
were listening that integration had to mean something other than one-way
assimilation to white middle-class norms if it was to be a solution to the
problem of racial inequality in America (Marable 1991; Van Deburg 1992).

It should be obvious by now that the one-way assimilation model has not
proved to be a viable or generally acceptable way of adjusting group differences in American society. It is based on an ethnocentric ideal of cultural homogeneity that has been rejected by Indians, blacks, Asians, Mexican Americans, and even many white ethnics. It reifies and privileges one cultural
strain in what is in fact a multicultural society. It should be possible to advocate the incorporation of all ethnic or racial groups into a common civic society without requiring the sacrifice of cultural distinctiveness and diversity.

Cultural Pluralism

Unlike assimilationists, cultural pluralists celebrate differences among
groups rather than seek to obliterate them. They argue that cultural diversity is a healthy and normal condition that does not preclude equal rights
and the mutual understandings about civic responsibilities needed to sustain a democratic nation-state. This model for American ethnic relations is a
twentieth-century invention that would have been virtually inconceivable at

---

[8]*Jim Crow:* Collective term for southern segregation laws.

an earlier time. The eighteenth and nineteenth centuries lacked the essential concept of the relativity of cultures. The model of cultural development during this period was evolutionary, progressive, and universalistic. People were either civilized or they were not. Mankind was seen as evolving from a state of "savagery" or "barbarism" to "civilization," and all cultures at a particular level were similar in every way that mattered. What differentiated nations and ethnic groups was their ranking on the scale of social evolution. Modern Western civilization stood at the apex of this universal historical process. Even nineteenth-century black nationalists accepted the notion that there were universal standards of civilization to which people of African descent should aspire. They differed from white supremacists in believing that blacks had the natural capability to reach the same heights as Caucasians if they were given a chance (Moses 1978).

The concept of cultural pluralism drew on the new cultural anthropology of the early twentieth century, as pioneered by Franz Boas. Boas and his disciples attempted to look at each culture they studied on its own terms and as an integrated whole. They rejected theories of social evolution that ranked cultures in relation to a universalist conception of "civilization." But relativistic cultural anthropologists were not necessarily cultural pluralists in their attitude toward group relations within American society. Since they generally believed that a given society or community functioned best with a single, integrated culture, they could favor greater autonomy for Indians on reservations but also call for the full assimilation of new immigrants or even African Americans. Boas himself was an early supporter of the National Association for the Advancement of Colored People (NAACP) and a pioneering advocate of what would later be called racial integration.

An effort to use the new concept of culture to validate ethnic diversity within the United States arose from the negative reaction of some intellectuals to the campaign to "Americanize" the new immigrants from eastern and southern Europe in the period just before and after World War I. The inventors of cultural pluralism were cosmopolitan critics of American provincialism or representatives of immigrant communities, especially Jews, who valued their cultural distinctiveness and did not want to be melted down in an Americanizing crucible. The Greenwich Village intellectual Randolph Bourne described his ideal as a "transnational America" in which various ethnic cultures would interact in a tolerant atmosphere to create an enriching variety of ideas, values, and lifestyles (Bourne 1964, ch. 8). The Jewish philosopher Horace Kallen, who coined the phrase "cultural pluralism," compared the result to a symphony, with each immigrant group represented as a section of the orchestra (Higham 1984, ch. 9; Kallen 1924). From a different perspective, W. E. B. DuBois celebrated a distinctive black culture rooted in the African and slave experiences and heralded its unacknowledged contributions to American culture in general (Lewis 1993). But the dominant version advocated by Kallen and Bourne stopped, for all practical purposes, at the color line. Its focus was on making America safe for a variety of European cultures. As a Zionist, Kallen was especially concerned with the preservation of Jewish distinctiveness and identity.

Since it was mainly the viewpoint of ethnic intellectuals who resisted the assimilationism of the melting pot, cultural pluralism was a minority persuasion in the twenties, thirties, and forties. A modified version reemerged in the 1950s in Will Herberg's (1960) conception of a "triple melting pot" of Protestants, Catholics, and Jews. The revulsion against Nazi anti-Semitism and the upward mobility of American Jews and Catholics inspired a synthesis of cultural pluralism and assimilationism that made religious persuasion the only significant source of diversity among white Americans. Herberg conceded, however, that black Protestants constituted a separate group that was not likely to be included in the Protestant melting pot. He therefore sharpened the distinction between race or color and ethnicity that was central to postwar thinking about group differences. Nevertheless, Herberg's view that significant differences between, say, Irish and Italian Catholics were disappearing was challenged in the 1960s and later, especially in the "ethnic revival" of the 1970s, which proclaimed that differing national origins among Euro-Americans remained significant and a valuable source of cultural variations.

The "multiculturalism" of the 1980s operated on assumptions that were similar to those of the cultural pluralist tradition, except that the color line was breached and the focus was shifted from the cultures and contributions of diverse European ethnic groups to those of African Americans, Mexican Americans, Asian Americans, and Native Americans. Abandonment of the earlier term "multiracialism" signified a desire to escape from the legacy of biological or genetic determinism and to affirm that the differences among people who happened to differ in skin color or phenotype were the result of their varying cultural and historical experiences. Under attack was the doctrine, shared by assimilationists and most earlier proponents of cultural pluralism, that the cultural norm in the United States was inevitably European in origin and character. Parity was now sought for groups of Asian, African, and American Indian ancestry. This ideal of cultural diversity and democracy was viewed by some of its critics as an invitation to national disunity and ethnic conflict (Schlesinger 1992). But its most thoughtful proponents argued that it was simply a consistent application of American democratic values and did not preclude the interaction and cooperation of groups within a common civic society (Hollinger 1995). Nevertheless, the mutual understandings upon which national unity and cohesion could be based needed to be negotiated rather than simply imposed by a Euro-American majority.

Group Separatism

Sometimes confused with the broadened cultural pluralism described here is the advocacy of group separatism. It originates in the desire of a culturally distinctive or racialized group to withdraw as much as possible from American society and interaction with other groups. Its logical outcome, autonomy in a separate, self-governing community, might conceivably be achieved either in an ethnic confederation like Switzerland or in the dissolution of the United States into several ethnic nations. But such a general theory is a logical construction rather than a program that has been explicitly advocated. Group separatism emanates from ethnocentric concerns about the status and destiny of particular groups, and its advocates rarely if ever theorize about what is going to happen to other groups. Precedents for group separatism based on cultural differences can be found in American history in the toleration of virtually autonomous religious communities like the Amish and the Hutterites[9] and in the modicum of self-government and immunity from general laws accorded to Indian tribes and reservations since the 1930s.

The most significant and persistent assertion of group separatism in American history has come from African Americans disillusioned with the prospects for equality within American society. In the nineteenth century, several black leaders and intellectuals called on African Americans to emigrate from the United States in order to establish an independent black republic elsewhere; Africa was the most favored destination. In the 1920s, Marcus Garvey created a mass movement based on the presumption that blacks had no future in the United States and should identify with the independence and future greatness of Africa, ultimately by emigrating there. More recently, the Nation of Islam has proposed that several American states be set aside for an autonomous black nation (Fredrickson 1995, chs. 2, 4, 7). At the height of the black power movement of the 1960s and early 1970s, a few black nationalists even called for the establishment of a noncontiguous federation of black urban ghettos—a nation of islands like Indonesia or the Philippines, but surrounded by white populations rather than the Pacific Ocean.

The current version of black separatism—"Afrocentrism"[10]—has not as yet produced a plan for political separation. Its aim is a cultural and spiritual secession from American society rather than the literal establishment of a black nation. Advocates of total separation could be found among other disadvantaged groups. In the late 1960s and 1970s Mexican American militants called for the establishment of the independent Chicano nation of Aztlán[11] in the American Southwest (Gutierrez 1995, 184–85) and some Native American radicals sought the reestablishment of truly independent tribal nations.

Group separatism might be viewed as a utopian vision or rhetorical device expressing the depths of alienation felt by the most disadvantaged

25

---

[9]*the Amish and the Hutterites:* Religious groups that reject the values and technology of contemporary society, living in relatively isolated, self-sufficient farming communities.

[10]*Afrocentrism:* An academic movement intended to counter the dominant European bias of Western scholarship; Afrocentric scholars seek to show the influence of African cultures, languages, and history on human civilization.

[11]*Aztlán:* Includes those parts of the United States once governed by Mexico.

racial or ethnic groups in American society. The extreme unlikelihood of realizing such visions has made their promulgation more cathartic than politically efficacious. Most members of groups exposed to such separatist appeals have recognized their impracticality, and the clash between the fixed and essentialist[12] view of identity that such projects entail and the fluid and hybrid quality of group cultures in the United States has become increasingly evident to many people of color, as shown most dramatically by the recent movement among those of mixed parentage to affirm a biracial identity. Few African Americans want to celebrate the greater or lesser degree of white ancestry most of them possess, but many have acknowledged not only their ancestral ties to Africa but their debt to Euro-American culture (and its debt to them). Most Mexican Americans value their cultural heritage but do not have the expectation or even the desire to establish an independent Chicano nation in the Southwest. Native Americans have authentic historical and legal claims to a high degree of autonomy but generally recognize that total independence on their current land base is impossible and would worsen rather than improve their circumstances. Asian Americans are proud of their various cultures and seek to preserve some of their traditions but have shown little or no inclination to separate themselves from other Americans in the civic, professional, and economic life of the nation. Afrocentrism raises troubling issues for American educational and cultural life but hardly represents a serious threat to national unity.

Ethnic separatism, in conclusion, is a symptom of racial injustice and a call to action against it, but there is little reason to believe that it portends "the disuniting of America." It is currently a source of great anxiety to many Euro-Americans primarily because covert defenders of ethnic hierarchy or one-way assimilation have tried to confuse the broad-based ideal of democratic multiculturalism with the demands of a relatively few militant ethnocentrists for thoroughgoing self-segregation and isolation from the rest of American society.

Of the four models of American ethnic relations, the one that I believe offers the best hope for a just and cohesive society is a cultural pluralism that is fully inclusive and based on the free choices of individuals to construct or reconstruct their own ethnic identities. We are still far from achieving the degree of racial and ethnic tolerance that realization of such an ideal requires. But with the demographic shift that is transforming the overwhelmingly Euro-American population of thirty or forty years ago into one that is much more culturally and phenotypically heterogeneous, a more democratic form of intergroup relations is a likely prospect, unless there is a desperate reversion to overt ethnic hierarchicalism by the shrinking Euro-American majority. It that were to happen, national unity and cohesion would indeed be hard to maintain. If current trends continue, minorities of

---

[12]*essentialist:* Refers to the idea that group characteristics are innate, or "essential," rather than cultural.

non-European ancestry will constitute a new majority sometime in the next century. Well before that point is reached, they will have the numbers and the provocation to make the country virtually ungovernable if a resurgent racism brings serious efforts to revive the blatantly hierarchical policies that have prevailed in the past.

References

Axtell, James. (1981). *The European and the Indian: Essays in the Ethnohistory of Colonial North America.* New York: Oxford University Press.

Berkhofer, Robert F., Jr. (1978). *The White Man's Indian: Image of the American Indian from Columbus to the Present.* New York: Alfred A. Knopf.

Bourne, Randolph S. (1964). *War and the Intellectuals: Collected Essays, 1915–1919.* New York: Harper Torch.

D'Souza, Dinesh. (1995). *The End of Racism: Principles for a Multiracial Society.* New York: Free Press.

Fredrickson, George M. (1987). *The Black Image in the White Mind: The Debate on Afro-American Character and Destiny, 1817–1914.* Middletown, Conn.: Wesleyan University Press.

———. (1995). *Black Liberation: A Comparative History of Black Ideologies in the United States and South Africa.* New York: Oxford University Press.

———. (1997). *The Comparative Imagination: On the History of Racism, Nationalism, and Social Movements.* Berkeley: University of California Press.

Gordon, Milton M. (1964). *Assimilation in American Life: The Role of Race, Religion, and National Origins.* New York: Oxford University Press.

Gutierrez, David. (1995). *Walls and Mirrors: Mexican Americans, Mexican Immigrants, and the Politics of Ethnicity.* Berkeley: University of California Press.

Herberg, Will. (1960). *Protestant-Catholic-Jew: An Essay in American Religious Sociology.* Garden City, N.Y.: Anchor Books.

Higham, John. (1968). *Strangers in the Land: Patterns of American Nativism, 1860–1925.* New York: Atheneum.

———. (1984). *Send These to Me: Jews and Other Immigrants in Urban America.* Baltimore: Johns Hopkins University Press.

Hollinger, David. (1995). *Postethnic America: Beyond Multiculturalism.* New York: Basic Books.

Hoxie, Frederick E. (1984). *A Final Promise: The Campaign to Assimilate the Indians, 1880–1920.* Lincoln: University of Nebraska Press.

Jordan, Winthrop D. (1968). *White Over Black: American Attitudes Toward the Negro, 1550–1812.* New York: University of North Carolina Press.

Kallen, Horace. (1924). *Culture and Democracy in the United States: Studies in the Group Psychology of American Peoples.* New York: Boni & Liveright.

Koch, Adrienne, and Peden, William. (Eds.). (1944). *The Life and Selected Writings of Thomas Jefferson.* New York: Modern Library.

Knobel, Dale T. (1986). *Paddy and the Republic: Ethnicity and Nationality in Antebellum America.* Middletown, Conn.: Wesleyan University Press.

Lewis, David Levering. (1993). *W. E. B. DuBois: Biography of a Race, 1868–1919.* New York: Henry Holt.

Marable, Manning. (1991). *Race, Reform, and Rebellion: The Second Reconstruction in Black America.* Jackson, Miss.: University of Mississippi Press.

Mardock, Robert W. (1971). *The Reformers and the American Indian.* Columbia: University of Missouri Press.

Miller, Stuart Creighton. (1969). *The Unwelcome Immigrant: The American Image of the Chinese, 1785–1882.* Berkeley: University of California Press.

Moses, Wilson Jeremiah. (1978). *The Golden Age of Black Nationalism, 1850–1925.* Hamden, Conn.: Archon Books.

Myrdal, Gunnar. (1944). *An American Dilemma.* New York: Harper and Row.

Schlesinger, Arthur M., Jr. (1992). *The Disuniting of America.* New York: Norton.

Van Deburg, William L. (1992). *New Day in Babylon: The Black Power Movement and American Culture, 1965–1975.* Chicago: University of Chicago Press.

ENGAGING THE TEXT

1. How does Fredrickson distinguish between race and ethnicity? How and under what circumstances can ethnicity become "racialized" (para. 2)?

2. What does Fredrickson mean by "the burden of 'otherness' "? Summarize the ways in which racial categories and definitions of "whiteness" have changed during the course of American history.

3. What are some of the ways that ethnic hierarchy has been eliminated? In what ways does it persist, according to Fredrickson? What evidence can you think of that would support or challenge this contention?

4. Fredrickson writes that "assimilationist thinking is not racist in the classic sense" (para. 9)—thereby implying that such thinking may be racist in some other sense. What does he mean by this? Do you agree?

5. How does Fredrickson distinguish cultural pluralism from assimilation? How did earlier forms of pluralism differ from the current concept of multiculturalism?

6. Why does Fredrickson reject the claim that an emphasis on ethnic identity threatens the unity and stability of American society? Why does a Euro-American backlash against ethnic diversity pose a greater risk in his view? Have you observed any recent examples of either divisiveness or backlash? Compare your observations with those of classmates.

EXPLORING CONNECTIONS

7. Write an essay examining the ways in which various models of ethnic relations can be seen operating in one or more of the following selections:

> Richard Rodriguez, "The Achievement of Desire" (p. 214)
> Malcolm X, "Learning to Read" (p. 243)
> Studs Terkel, "Stephen Cruz" (p. 348)
> Judith Ortiz Cofer, "The Story of My Body" (p. 433)
> Paula Gunn Allen, "Where I Come From Is Like This" (p. 443)
> Thomas Jefferson, from "Notes on the State of Virginia" (p. 551)
> Studs Terkel, "C. P. Ellis" (p. 591)
> Eric Liu, "Notes of a Native Speaker" (p. 660)
> Sherman Alexie, "Assimilation" (p. 674)

8. Based on the selections in this chapter by Randall Robinson (p. 557), Leonard Steinhorn and Barbara Diggs-Brown (p. 646), Eric Liu (p. 660), and Leon E. Wynter (p. 688), debate the extent to which cultural pluralism has been achieved in the United States.

9. What model or models of ethnic relations do you see represented in the cartoon by Lalo Alcaraz on page 636?

10. Examine the Visual Portfolio on pages 629–31. Identify the model of ethnic relations you see embodied in each image and explain your reasoning.

EXTENDING THE CRITICAL CONTEXT

11. If your campus or community is involved in a debate concerning affirmative action, immigration, bilingual education, multiculturalism, or ethnic studies, analyze several opinion pieces or position papers on the issue. What models of ethnic relations are expressed or assumed by each side of the debate?

Virtual Integration: How the Integration of Mass Media Undermines Integration

LEONARD STEINHORN AND
BARBARA DIGGS-BROWN

According to their own description, the coauthors of this selection epit-omize both the success and failure of integration in this country. Leonard Steinhorn, who is white, once worked for a black member of Congress; Barbara Diggs-Brown is the first black woman to win tenure in her department at American University in Washington, D.C. However, they grew up and continue to live in segregated neighborhoods and socialize al-most exclusively with people of their own race. They maintain that this same disjunction—between the ideal of integration and the reality of continued segregation—is pervasive in the United States today. Television helps to perpetuate the divide by presenting us with a racially idealized world that makes us complacent about the real problems of race. Steinhorn and Diggs-Brown are colleagues at American University's School of Communication. This selection is taken from their book, By the Color of Our Skin: The Illu-sion of Integration and the Reality of Race *(1999).*

The *Time* magazine cover called it "a death in the family." The *New York Times* described the outpouring of grief "as if it were a death in the family. In a way it was." Americans black and white, from every region and social standing, grieved with Bill Cosby at the tragic loss of his son, Ennis, who was gunned down on the side of a freeway in January 1997. Few Amer-icans knew much if anything about Ennis Cosby before his death, but we reacted almost as if we knew the family personally. And in a way we did. Seven months later we grieved again when Britain's Princess Diana lost her life in a sad and gruesome car accident. She was Diana to us, someone we felt we knew, a constant presence in our lives, a woman whose wedding we vicariously attended and whose intimacies seemed more familiar to us than those of our closest friends. For many of us the loss was profound and deeply personal. It reminded us of the shared national mourning for a dead president more than three decades earlier, when we felt the pain of a griev-ing widow and her two small children who were too young to comprehend the enormity of their loss. Since those poignant days in November 1963, the Kennedy family has become our own.

For half a century now people like Princess Diana and Bill Cosby have entered our lives and homes through the remarkable medium of television.

Television has brought us national leaders and fictional characters, personalities and eccentrics, Kennedys and Seinfelds, Oprah Winfrey and Dan Rather, Beaver Cleaver and Mr. Whipple, Ronald Reagan and Michael Jordan, Barbara Walters and Bart Simpson—a list so long yet so personal that it is almost dazzling to think of the many names and faces, celebrities and entertainers who have become part of our conversations and lives. What they all have in common is the power of television to project them into our living rooms and turn them into neighbors, friends, extended family, into people we truly believe we have come to know. Television is an intimate medium that creates a bond between actor and viewer, between a character and the public. It offers what two communications scholars call a "synthetic experience," a substitute for reality that feels very real.[1] An actor who plays a doctor on television becomes a doctor; a television lawyer becomes our model for the real thing, and a fictional character—Murphy Brown[2]—engages a real vice president in a national debate. And so we ascribe personality traits to the images on the screen, we track every career move and romance of our favorite actors, and we discuss their lives and futures as if they were connected to our own. The name of the popular show *Friends* describes more than just the fictional friendship among the characters portrayed in the show—it is also a metaphor for the relationship we have with these and so many other actors on television, people who visit us weekly in our homes and whose lives are finely detailed in the mass media that wallpapers our lives.

Ours is an unsettled nation of people constantly on the move. The westward spirit of the nineteenth century remains alive today in a restlessness that constantly seeks new frontiers and challenges. These very dynamics of American society have weakened ties both to family and to the geographically defined communities of old. We reach out and touch someone not over a table breaking bread but over fiber-optic phone lines and in cyberspace. In the modern American era, we yearn for a sense of community that in reality has become more and more elusive. And so television has stepped in to fill the void. It has become our virtual community, a stable presence in the living room that packs our lives with characters that in an earlier age we might have met in the union hall or town square. Americans today spend more time watching television than doing any other activity besides sleeping. By the time the average American teenager graduates from high school, he or she will have logged more hours in front of the television than in front of the teacher. Television viewing has become a surrogate for civic activity,

[1]The "synthetic experience" of television is described in G. Funkhouser and F. Shaw, "How Synthetic Experience Shapes Reality," *Journal of Communication* vol. 42; no. 2 (1990), pp. 75–87. [All notes except 2 are Steinhorn and Diggs-Brown's.]

[2]*Murphy Brown:* In 1992, then–Vice President Dan Quayle attacked the TV sitcom character Murphy Brown as an affront to "family values" because of her decision to have a baby outside marriage. Writers for the show made the issue, and Quayle himself, an ongoing source of humor in subsequent episodes.

a chance to participate in the lives of others in what has become our electronic village.

Now think of the average American, whose daily life usually consists of clicking the garage door open in the morning, driving to work, putting in the eight hours, getting back in the car, stopping at the store, and driving back home for what will likely be a comfortable evening in front of the television set. On a typical evening in the late 1990s, close to half of all American households are watching TV, and one network alone—NBC—holds the attention of more than one in five households every Thursday night. Now think more specifically of the average white American family. They may not watch the same prime-time series as most blacks.... But even on the shows they do watch they see more blacks beamed into their living room on a typical evening than they have seen at any other time or place during the day. It could be Michael Jordan or James Earl Jones pitching a product, Bill Cosby or Della Reese starring in a show, Whoopi Goldberg or Denzel Washington doing the celebrity interview, Ed Bradley or Bryant Gumbel describing a news story, or any combination of black newscasters, reporters, athletes, entertainers, or actors who populate the airwaves hour after hour, day after day. Some of them we think we know, like Bill Cosby or Bryant Gumbel, while others simply pass through our lives, like the blacks featured in advertisements, but they are all there in our living rooms, joining us in the intimacy of our own homes, creating the impression that the world is more integrated than it truly is.

For whites generally unaccustomed to interacting with blacks, who   5
walk out their front doors and see few black faces in the neighborhood, the mere presence of black images in their homes blurs the line between what is imagined and what is real about race relations in America. It also helps, as author Benjamin DeMott points out in his book *The Trouble with Friendship: Why Americans Can't Think Straight About Race*, that most of the blacks whom whites see on television either work with whites, have white friends, or operate in a predominantly white context. They have been tested, they are safe, and they fit in.[3] So what television has done is to give white Americans the sensation of having meaningful, repeated contact with blacks without actually having it. Black people have become part of white people's lives, virtually. We call this phenomenon "virtual integration," and it is a primary reason why the integration illusion—the belief that we are moving toward a color-blind nation—has such a powerful influence over race relations in America today.[4]

---

[3]Benjamin DeMott, *The Trouble with Friendship: Why Americans Can't Think Straight About Race* (New York: Atlantic Monthly Press, 1995).

[4]We developed the phrase "virtual integration" in 1995 when discussing ideas for this book and did not know that another author, John Hoberman, was planning to use the same phrase in his 1997 book, *Darwin's Athletes*.

So powerful is this virtual integration that it seems to promote a color-blindness toward black celebrities almost unattainable for blacks in the real world. Columnist Clarence Page, a former television reporter in Chicago, describes how he used to be greeted warmly in the same white ethnic neighborhoods that once pelted Martin Luther King with rocks and bottles. "You're not black anymore, Clarence," a white producer explained. "You're on television now."[5] The rise of black media images over the last three decades has come at precisely the same time that celebrity has become the measure of individual success in America. And being on television automatically confers celebrity, whether to a Frank Perdue who hawks his own brand of chickens, or to a low-paid weathercaster stuck in a small-market television station who nonetheless becomes a local personality. So whites have made room in their lives for black celebrities, indeed for almost any black they see on television, and have embraced them as evidence of their own open-mindedness and as proof that the nation isn't so hard on blacks after all. Blacks like O. J. Simpson, before his fall, are welcomed not only into the virtual neighborhood but into the actual neighborhood as well, as if their celebrity erases any negatives that whites otherwise would associate with their color. "I'm not black, I'm famous," the black lead singer of the rock group Fine Young Cannibals once said. Or, as the redneck rapist tells the black sheriff in the film of John Grisham's book *A Time to Kill*, "I seen you play for the Rams. The way I figured a nigger sheriff's okay, been on TV and all. No offense."[6]

Television has certainly come a long way since the days when stations in the South were deluged with complaints because white singer Petula Clark innocently put her hand on Harry Belafonte's arm during a music special, and NBC couldn't find a sponsor for *The Nat "King" Cole Show* and had to cancel it after one year. Until Bill Cosby broke the color line in 1965 as costar of the secret-agent show *I Spy*, there had never been a black star of a dramatic series. Until Lever Brothers featured black and white children playing together in a 1963 commercial for the detergent *Wisk*, no black had ever been on a nationwide television ad in a nonstereotypical role. At that time the only blacks who appeared regularly on television came via live sports telecasts. As recently as the early 1980s, advertisers approached by Michael Jordan's agent responded by saying "What on earth are we going to do with a black basketball player?"[7] So it would be difficult to argue that the change in television has been anything but deep and profound.

[5]Clarence Page, *Showing My Color: Impolite Essays on Race and Identity* (New York: HarperCollins, 1996), p. 252.
[6]The singer's quote is from Henry Louis Gates, Jr., "Thirteen Ways of Looking at a Black Man," *The New Yorker*, October 23, 1995, p. 63.
[7]The Michael Jordan reference is found in Lynn Hirschberg, "The Big Man Can Deal," *New York Times Magazine*, November 17, 1996, p. 49.

Yet there are some who claim that the medium has a much longer way to go than most of the viewing public might believe. They say there are no dramas on television built around a black family or protagonist, that most comedies are segregated, that too many black-oriented comedies reinforce clownish or sexual stereotypes, that the networks have few black programming executives with the power to green-light projects, and that there should be more ads featuring blacks other than athletes or entertainers. During the 1996–97 season, they point out, only three comedies on the top three networks featured more than one regular black character, and some high-profile shows — *Seinfeld, Friends, Ellen,* and *Cybill* — had none at all. Of the 245 made-for-TV movies on the four major networks in 1995 and 1996, only about twenty had blacks in leading roles.[8] These are serious, valid criticisms and must be addressed. But from the white perspective they may seem irrelevant or off base because the cumulative presence of blacks on television already provides such a contrast to their predominantly white lives that their virtual world seems thoroughly integrated as is. A black regular on *Seinfeld* or *Friends* probably wouldn't make much of a difference to whites, who believe, courtesy of television, that the world already is fully integrated.

Nothing better illustrates our virtually integrated world than the two prime-time specials aired by ABC on Sunday, November 2, 1997. More than one out of every four TV sets in use at the time was tuned into these shows. In the first, a Walt Disney update of Rodgers & Hammerstein's *Cinderella,* the future princess looks very different from the blond, blue-eyed Cinderella of the Disney animated version and the many storybooks that have followed. This Cinderella is played by the black actress Brandy, and the entire production is a bold and striking example of a new highbrow trend in the arts called color-blind casting. Cinderella's stepmother is white, one stepsister is white and the other black, the fairy godmother is black, the prince is of Filipino descent, his valet is white, the king is white, the queen is black, and the multi-ethnic cast of extras interact seamlessly in a fairy-tale kingdom of harmonious diversity broadcast right there in our own living rooms. Immediately following *Cinderella* that night was a well-publicized made-for-TV movie starring Oprah Winfrey, *Before Women Had Wings.* Again, the audience welcomed a black into their homes as Winfrey, who also produced the film, played the role of friend and savior to two white children abused and neglected by their mother. Also note that these two shows aired after a full afternoon of televised football with its many black sportscasters and players. In short, much of white America spent the afternoon and evening in a virtually integrated environment. Although Monday morning at school or work might not come close to resembling the living

---

[8]These and other facts can be found in Greg Braxton, "Roots Plus 20," *Los Angeles Times,* January 26, 1997, p. 8. See also Jacqueline Trescott, "'Roots,' Wrapped Around the American Psyche," *Washington Post,* February 16, 1997, p. G5.

room integration the night before, that might not matter in a virtually integrated America in which the image becomes the norm and the reality is made to feel like the exception. For whites whose lives are virtually integrated, the power of the image makes the racial reality all the more difficult to believe.

With the possible exception of the military, the television screen may   10
be the most integrated part of American life. We tracked three days of television programming in the fall of 1997 and found that black faces, personalities, newscasters, athletes, actors, and entertainers were intricately woven throughout the shows that most whites watch. To illustrate, we offer a snapshot of one evening, at this writing the highest rated on television, Thursday night on NBC.[9]

First up on October 2, 1997, was the local news at six, which featured one black anchor and four black reporters. We both live in the Washington metropolitan area, home to a large black population, so here one might expect a well-integrated local news team. In fact, though, throughout the country a racial mix on the news is fairly common. There are black men and women anchoring, reporting, forecasting the weather, and discussing sports on stations in every other market we checked: New York, Houston, Boston, Cincinnati, Kansas City, Omaha, Raleigh, and San Francisco. One scholar who viewed news programs on twenty-eight stations nationwide found that blacks made up 11 percent of the journalists he saw, a number almost equal to the percentage of blacks in America. As public opinion pollster Geoffrey Garin put it, there are so many black anchors and reporters on television that even Southern whites "never think twice about it" anymore.[10] In this respect, then, our Washington sample seems no different from the rest of the nation. Nor are the network news broadcasts any different. The *NBC Nightly News with Tom Brokaw,* the top-rated network news show during our viewing period, featured two black reporters doing major stories on the night we watched. A check of the other network news programs found a similar black presence.

The NBC prime-time schedule that Thursday night featured four sit-coms —*Friends, Union Square, Seinfeld,* and *Veronica's Closet*—and one dramatic series, *ER*. Although *Seinfeld* and *Friends* attract few black viewers, they have for a number of years been among the most highly rated comedies on television, which means their audience is almost exclusively white. *Friends* began the evening at eight o'clock. Although set in ethnically diverse New York City, the show has no black regulars. In a previous season one of the characters on *Friends* had a pet chimpanzee, which led a critic to

---

[9]We also tracked ABC on Tuesday, September 30, 1997, and channel-surfed through all three networks on Monday, October 6, 1997.

[10]The 11 percent figure comes from Christopher P. Campbell, *Race, Myth and the News* (Thousand Oaks, Calif.: Sage Publications, 1995), p. 38; Geoffrey Garin is quoted in Ronald Brownstein, "4 Decades Later, Legacy of *Brown vs. Topeka* Is Cloudy," *Los Angeles Times,* May 15, 1994, p. A1.

quip that monkeys had a better shot at getting on the show than blacks. But *Friends* may simply be more honest than many shows about the way we lead racially isolated lives, even in the big city. The token black cast member on the periphery of some other sitcoms can seem very contrived at times, leading one stand-up comedian to imagine network executives in a story meeting insisting that "three of the Klansmen in that sketch need to be black."[11] On the evening we watched, *Friends* was true to form, the only blacks being two extras sitting in a restaurant. But that doesn't mean the half hour was devoid of visible blacks. Commercials consume about 25 percent of all television time, and blacks played key roles in four ads during the show, including one for McDonald's showing a black male airline passenger and a black female car rental agent, and another for an NBC show that included a black female attorney. In other words, even during a show like *Friends,* the white audience welcomed a number of virtual blacks into their living rooms.

After *Friends* came a show called *Union Square,* whose six regulars include a black West Indian man who runs a diner that has a racially mixed staff and clientele. Again, blacks played prominent roles in the commercials, this time in five of them. Next up was *Seinfeld,* like *Friends* a show set in New York with an exclusive cast of white regulars, although this particular episode included a scene with a black female university dean. Four commercials included blacks, most of them professionals. On the following show, *Veronica's Closet,* a black male plays a regular though somewhat marginal part, and that night a few other blacks were visible as supporting cast and extras. Only one ad included blacks. Finally came the crown jewel of the evening, the number-one show in America, *ER.* The show features two prominent black members of the ensemble cast, a doctor and a physician's assistant, as well as seven blacks in recurring roles. That evening, as with most episodes of *ER,* there were a number of black extras serving as hospital employees, patients, and visitors. Of the twenty-four commercials interspersed throughout the hour-long show, ten featured blacks, including a number that portrayed black executives.

Think about the cumulative number of blacks on television that Thursday evening. The black characters on *ER* alone exceeded the number of blacks with whom many white Americans interact meaningfully each week. The other blacks on the commercials, the news, or the other shows further embroidered the integrated image they saw. Rarely did the typical viewer go for more than a few minutes without seeing a black face on the screen, even if one or two shows didn't include blacks. Over three or four hours of television that night, whites saw blacks on news shows, entertainment shows, promos, and commercials—as anchors, reporters, stars, supporting cast, walk-ons, extras, and product endorsers. Nor was there anything un-

---

[11]The comedian Patton Oswalt was quoted in the *New York Times,* March 4, 1997, p. C11.

usual about it. The presence of blacks in the living room has become a normal part of our virtual lives. Television represents reality, even if it doesn't represent mine, right?

Channel-surf through the rest of television and you'll find much the same thing. Whether in prime time or daytime, children's hour or late at night, the typical white American will have an integrated viewing experience. According to the Center for Media and Public Affairs, a research organization, blacks played 17 percent of all characters in prime-time entertainment shows in 1992, up from half a percent in the early 1960s.[12] Today you see blacks on the morning shows doing the news and the weather, blacks reporting stories for the newsmagazines, blacks playing and announcing sports, blacks interviewing or being interviewed, blacks on the cop shows investigating homicides, and blacks offering up opinions on the political talk-show circuit. Black TV surgeons treat white TV patients and black TV lawyers represent white TV clients in far greater proportion than they do in real life. Blacks are likewise well represented in commercials, constituting more than 12 percent of on-camera actors and more than 17 percent of all the extras in ads produced in 1995, according to the Screen Actors Guild. A 1989 study found that blacks appeared in 26 percent of all prime-time ads, though they were less likely than whites to be the main focus of an ad and more likely to be part of a group, a sequence, or the background cast.[13] Ads feature high-profile black celebrities, entertainers, and athletes as well as black professionals, families, and blue-collar workers. The advertising images of blacks are so common they cascade one on top of another: clips of Will Smith and Tommy Lee Jones promoting their movie *Men in Black,* a black construction worker waiting for his white colleague in a spot for Tylenol Extra Strength, athletes Shaquille O'Neil and Deion Sanders drinking Pepsi while hanging out in a white kid's bedroom, a group of white guys and their one black buddy ogling women in a bar on behalf of Bud Lite, a black man playing one of the Three Musketeers in an ad for the candy bar, a group of black and white kids warming up the image of the Chevy Astro van, a FedEx spot featuring a black business owner interacting with black and white employees. The list could consume this book.

On children's shows like *Wishbone, Barney,* and *Magic School Bus,* almost every group of cartoon characters or kids looks like the United Nations. A few teen and twenty-something shows are pushing the color line even further: MTV's dating game, *Singled Out,* is fully interracial, and Fox's *Party of Five* featured an ongoing interracial romantic relationship. Then there are the daytime soaps, faithfully watched by millions of college students and

[12]The Center for Media and Public Affairs statistic is cited in Rick Du Brow, "Portrayals of Latinos on Television Regressing," *Los Angeles Times,* September 7, 1994, p. A5.

[13]We are grateful to the Screen Actors Guild for supplying these figures on advertising. For the 1989 study, see Robert E. Wilkes and Humberto Valencia, "Hispanics and Blacks in Television Commercials," *Journal of Advertising,* vol. 18, no. 1 (1989), pp. 19–25.

stay-at-home moms. Almost every soap opera features at least two regular black characters, including doctors, cops, musicians, lawyers, nurses, nannies, reporters, executives, models, photographers, and just plain people. Behind them are plenty of black extras who stroll the beach, shop at the malls, attend social events, and work at hospitals. Interracial friendships are common and a few soaps have shown interracial relationships and marriages. As with most (though not all) television shows targeted to a predominantly white audience, soaps take color-blindness to the absurd point that the black and white characters, even those in interracial relationships, rarely discuss race. The audience may want realistic portrayals, but not when it comes to black and white. In the virtually integrated world of our living rooms, the last thing we want is the discomfort of reality intruding on the illusion.

Let us not be mistaken: the rise of black images on television and throughout the visual media is an extraordinarily positive development. Television may not be truly color-blind, but if it can help increase interracial familiarity, shatter some stereotypes, fortify the comfort zone, and multiply the number of black role models for everyone in America, then it has served an important goal that most other institutions in society have not been willing or able to accomplish. To suggest, as we do, that television undermines real integration—that it enables whites to lead virtually integrated lives without having much real contact with blacks—is not meant to condemn the visibility of blacks on TV but rather to explain its impact. Indeed, the only academic study to look at the phenomenon we call "virtual integration" tested black viewers and found that they, like whites, "more frequently perceived that racial integration is more prevalent, that blacks and whites were more similar, and that blacks were middle-class."[14]

By its very nature television creates imaginary or virtual relationships among people. What makes its impact on race unique is that for most whites their television contact with blacks is the closest they will ever come to crossing the color line. More than half of all whites in one survey say that what they know about blacks they get from the media.[15] "You sure gotta hand it to 'em," the Edith Bunker character said about blacks on the show *All in the Family*, "I mean, two years ago they was nothing but servants and janitors. Nowadays they're teachers and doctors and lawyers. They've come a long way on TV." Certainly it is ironic that one of the few visible institutions where black participation has advanced so far may also provide whites with an excuse not to move much beyond the status quo. If the world is so integrated, then my all-white neighborhood or social club just happens to be an exception, so it's not that big a deal. If the world is so integrated, if a

---

[14]P. W. Matabane, "Television and the Black Audience: Cultivating Moderate Perspectives on Racial Integration," *Journal of Communication,* vol. 38, no. 4 (1988), p. 26.

[15]For the survey showing that a majority of whites get their information about blacks from the media, see Matthew P. Smith, "Bridging the Gulf Between Blacks and Whites," *Pittsburgh Post-Gazette,* April 7, 1996, p. 1.

black person can become famous, make so much money, and appear on television, then it is they who push us away through all their whining and self-righteous anger. How can I be part of the problem if my kids idolize Michael Jordan and Barry Sanders and if I watch Bill Cosby and Della Reese every week on TV?

In New York City there had never been a black female news director at a local television station until 1996, when Vassar College graduate Paula Walker took the job at the NBC affiliate. Almost immediately she grasped how local news perpetuates the fear of black crime. Typically, a reporter describing a crime will dutifully draw on the police report, which might list the suspect as a black male, five-eight, 160 pounds. On the surface there seems nothing wrong with this description. But, as Walker told us, there are thousands upon thousands of people in the viewing area who fit it. Given that the purpose of putting out a description is to help the public finger the criminal, Walker sees no point in broadcasting such useless information when the only tangible impact will be to increase suspicion of blacks. "What you're doing is making all those women who are walking down the street clutch their pocketbooks closer to them," she said. To her, there would be nothing wrong with including race if the description also mentioned specific clothing, hair style, identifying characteristics such as a scar or a limp, and the neighborhood in which the suspect was last seen. Skin color then becomes relevant and serves a purpose.[16]

If the televised image of black actors, athletes, and entertainers leads   20 whites to think the world is integrated, the portrayal of black crime on television news helps keep real integration from ever happening. There is no irony in this aspect of television. Whether by accident or unconscious design, the face of crime on TV, especially on local news, tends to be black. It is true that blacks commit a disproportionate share of violent crimes, especially in urban areas, but it is also true that blacks are identified with criminal acts on television all out of proportion to the number they commit. Advertisers have long known that repetition, not to mention saturation, sells on television. The relentless association between blacks and crime on the news has colored white perceptions of blacks and has seriously undermined any hope for racial integration in America.

Years ago in the segregated South it was not uncommon for local newspapers to run all sex-crime accusations against blacks on page one, even if the incident took place on the other side of the country.[17] Today there are few if any in television news with such an intent to malign—yet in many ways the result is the same: crime in general is associated with blacks.

---

[16]Personal interview with Paula Walker, March 10, 1997.

[17]Ben H. Bagdikian, "Editorial Responsibility in Times of Urban Disorder," in *The Media and the Cities*, ed. Charles U. Daily (Chicago: University of Chicago Center for Policy Study, 1968), p. 15.

Findings from a number of research studies clearly document the distortion.[18] Even though most violent crimes are committed by people the same race as their victims, one 1994 study of local TV newscasts in Chicago found that the majority of perpetrators portrayed in the news were black or persons of color, while the majority of victims shown were white. A study of Philadelphia newscasts found that nonwhites were almost twice as likely to be shown as perpetrators than as victims of crime, almost the reverse of the portrayal of whites. Another study found that the percentage of blacks shown as suspects on one Los Angeles station far exceeded the percentage of violent crimes committed by blacks in Los Angeles County. This distortion is also evident in reality-based television programs, such as *COPS* and *America's Most Wanted.* According to one study, half of all the blacks who appear in these shows are criminals, versus 10 percent of all whites, while another found that stories about white victims lasted 74 percent longer than stories about black victims. Furthermore, research shows that blacks accused of the same crime as whites tend to be portrayed as more threatening and intimidating on television news. Whites arrested for crimes might be shown next to their attorneys, if they are shown at all, whereas blacks tend to be shown in handcuffs, on police walks, or being physically restrained by the police. News reports also provide the names of black suspects less often than they do for white suspects, leading one scholar to conclude that the individual identity of black suspects is less important than their race.

Put all these studies together and the composite is clear: whites are vulnerable to crime, blacks are responsible for it. So powerful is this image that when Charles Stuart, a white, killed his wife in Boston and Susan Smith, white, killed her children in South Carolina, both were able to point a finger at an imaginary though vaguely described black killer, knowing full well that the public would almost reflexively believe them. According to research by two University of California–Los Angeles professors, Shanto Iyengar and

---

[18]We have drawn on the following research studies for our information: Robert M. Entman, "Modern Racism and the Images of Blacks in Local Television News," *Critical Studies in Mass Communication,* vol. 7 (1990), pp. 332–345; Robert M. Entman, "Blacks in the News: Television, Modern Racism, and Cultural Change," *Journalism Quarterly,* Summer 1992, pp. 341–361; Robert M. Entman, "Representation and Reality in the Portrayal of Blacks on Network Television News," *Journalism Quarterly,* Autumn 1994, pp. 509–520; Robert M. Entman, *Violence on Television: News and "Reality" Programming in Chicago* (Chicago: Chicago Council on Urban Affairs, 1994); George Gerbner, "Women and Minorities on Television: A Study of Casting and Fate," *Report to the Screen Actors Guild and the American Federation of Television and Radio Artists,* June 1993; Daniel Romer, Kathleen H. Jamieson, and Nicole DeCoteau, "Differential Standards of Newsworthiness and Ethnic Blame Discourse on Television News: A Study of Crime Reporting in Philadelphia," unpublished paper sent to us by its authors. Research on the Los Angeles station is described in Howard Kurtz, "A Guilty Verdict on Crime, Race Bias," *Washington Post,* April 28, 1997, pp. 1, 4, who cites the findings of University of California, Los Angeles, professors Shanto Iyengar and Franklin Gilliam, Jr. See also Du Brow, "Portrayals of Latinos on Television Regressing"; and Mark Lorando, "TV's 'Average' Reveals Double Standard," *New Orleans Times-Picayune,* September 13, 1993, p. A9.

Franklin Gilliam, Jr., even when news reports of a crime made no reference to a suspect, 42 percent of viewers later remembered seeing a perpetrator, and two thirds of these viewers recalled this phantom criminal as black. When the news report did show a perpetrator, viewers disproportionately recalled him as black. Nor were white viewers the only ones making this mistake. Black viewers did as well, though to a lesser extent, further attesting to the power of racial images in televised reports of crime.[19]

The black criminal image on the news is also part of a larger problem with the news media. Television news feeds on a dramatic structure in which every report must have a plot, an emotional story line, and a moral. Crime fits the mold perfectly: there's a villain, a victim, fear, and human interest. As the entertainment programmers have learned, it's simply good and gripping television. Although the emphasis on crime distorts the portrayal of daily life, this is incidental to the imperative of holding the audience and getting a good story—so much so that coverage of murders on network evening news increased 721 percent since 1993, even though the nationwide homicide rate declined by 20 percent.[20] Blacks are simply caught in this media vise, their image held hostage to the very nature of TV news and its focus on the seamy side of reality. When the *New Orleans Times-Picayune* surveyed local evening news broadcasts for one week in 1993, it found that more than 42.1 percent of the total black images were crime-related and only 18.5 percent involved political or community issues—this in a heavily black city with blacks in charge of city hall.[21] In part this may be due to television's overemphasis on black crime; it is also likely due to television's overall fixation on crime. Because television news plays up crime regardless of color, and because the white majority has little or no contact with blacks except for what they see on television, even an accurate portrayal of crime—one showing how whites victimize mostly whites and blacks victimize mostly blacks—will still likely magnify the role of the black criminal among whites. The fact that the information is frequently reported by a black reporter or anchor validates it further.

Compounding the problem is that people take what they see on the news personally, as if the reality they see is the reality of their lives. By its very dependence on graphic images and compelling visuals, television news evokes emotions and creates impressions. People don't just think about the news—they feel it. That may be why surveys show that the public has more trust in the local TV news than the local newspaper. Surveys also show that up to two-thirds of Americans say their attitudes about crime are stirred by

---

[19]Research by the University of California, Los Angeles, professors Shanto Iyengar and Franklin Gilliam, Jr., is reported in Kurtz, "A Guilty Verdict on Crime, Race Bias."

[20]The murder-coverage statistics are from the Center for Media and Public Affairs press release, "In 1990s TV News Turns to Violence and Show Biz," August 12, 1997; for the drop in the nationwide homicide rate, see Vincent Schiraldi, "The Latest Trend in Juvenile Crime," *Washington Post*, January 11, 1998, p. C5.

[21]Mark Lorando, "Mass Media Wields Power That Reinforces Prejudice," *New Orleans Times-Picayune*, September 13, 1993, p. A7.

the media rather than their own experiences or those of friends.[22] Now add up all of these factors: the disproportionate portrayal of black crime, the emphasis on crime in the local news, the emotive power of the medium, the accumulation of images, the proximate reality of what's reported, the lack of real contact with blacks among the white audience, and the implicit validation provided by black journalists reporting the news. The result is a generalized fear of crime that translates to a generalized fear of blacks. It is a sad commentary to suggest that the only way to eliminate white fright is to eliminate the reporting of black crime altogether, not merely to make the reporting more accurate. But there may be no other way to change the defining image of crime that so profoundly shapes white Americans' view of their fellow black citizens.

For most white Americans, the only kind of integration they know is the virtual kind, and it may be the only kind they want. Virtual integration enables whites to live in a world with blacks without having to do so in fact. It provides a form of safe intimacy without any of the risks. It offers a clean and easy way for whites to establish and nourish what they see as their bona fide commitment to fairness, tolerance, and color-blindness. White Americans may genuinely feel they are open to blacks, as long as blacks—with their criminal tendencies—don't move into the neighborhood. So television giveth, in the form of the virtual community that transcends race, and it taketh away, by reinforcing an association between blacks and crime that makes real community building all but impossible. This curious television dynamic explains how, as Harvard Medical School psychiatrist Dr. Alvin Poussaint told us, "white kids who worship Michael Jordan will beat up black kids who come into their neighborhoods." It is another sad and tragic irony of race relations in America, brought to you in living color.

ENGAGING THE TEXT

1. What is "virtual integration," according to the authors? What evidence do they present to support their claim that television presents an integrated world? Think for a moment about the shows you watch regularly: Do you see any evidence that would contradict this view?

2. What potential benefits do Steinhorn and Diggs-Brown see in the increased visibility of blacks in mass media? What are its hazards? To what extent do you agree with their assessment?

3. How does news coverage misrepresent life in black communities? What are the effects of these distortions? What relationship do the authors see between the images of African Americans in the news and those in other forms of programming?

[22]The public's reliance on TV news for information on crime is described in Stephen Braun and Judy Pasternak, "With Terror on Its Mind," *Los Angeles Times*, February 13, 1994, p. A16.

THE BOONDOCKS   **by AARON MCGRUDER**

4. How has the representation of blacks changed since the early days of television? Do you see equally dramatic changes in the ways that other minorities are depicted?

EXPLORING CONNECTIONS

5. Compare Shelby Steele's analysis of black entertainers and white audiences (p. 602) to that of Steinhorn and Diggs-Brown. How do they explain the popularity of performers like Bill Cosby? What influence do they believe black celebrities have on race relations? Which view do you find more persuasive, and why?

6. Compare Leon E. Wynter's discussion of "transracial America" (p. 688) to Steinhorn and Diggs-Brown's analysis of "virtual integration." Evaluate the evidence each essay offers that current media images either do or do not reflect the reality of American race relations.

7. What does the cartoon on this page suggest about the images of African Americans in film, about movie audiences, and about racial understanding? To what extent do you think the cartoonist would agree with Steinhorn and Diggs-Brown's contention that our virtual world is more integrated than our real lives?

EXTENDING THE CRITICAL CONTEXT

8. Steinhorn and Diggs-Brown offer a "snapshot" of an evening's worth of programming and advertising on one network to illustrate the idea of virtual integration. As a class, do a similar analysis: working in groups, assign one or two people to take notes on each hour of programming for one evening (6 P.M.–11 P.M.). How often and in what roles do actors, newscasters, and citizens of each race or ethnicity appear? Pool your results and discuss the extent to which your class's "snapshot" reflects a virtually integrated world.

9. Do an informal survey to investigate integration and segregation on your campus. How often do students talk to people of different ethnicities in their classes? How many of their close friends belong to their own ethnic

group and how many to other groups? Do they live or work with people of different ethnicities? Do they participate in multi-ethnic clubs or service organizations? Do they belong to clubs or organizations focused on the interests of their own ethnic group? What are the ethnicities of their favorite musicians, actors, and athletes? To what extent do your survey results support the notion that we remain more segregated in our social lives than in our virtual lives?

10. The journal *Poverty and Race* devoted several issues to a discussion of Steinhorn and Diggs-Brown's book, with essays and responses by many noteworthy thinkers and writers on race. The journal is available online at www.prrac.org/topics (on the menu, select the issues from November 1999, January 2000, and March 2000). Read the excerpted passage from *By the Color of Our Skin* and at least three of the commentaries by other writers, then develop your own paper topic on the subject of integration.

Notes of a Native Speaker

Eric Liu

The son of Chinese immigrant parents, Eric Liu is an unrepentant assimilationist. As he details in this essay, he has worked hard to master the codes of the dominant culture. By any measure, he has succeeded, having graduated from an Ivy League university and worked in the U.S. Senate, the State Department, and the White House, where he served as a speech writer for President Clinton. He concedes that he has neglected or lost some measure of Chinese culture along the way, but rejects the idea that this makes him a "traitor" to his heritage. Instead, he suggests that his experience represents a much larger process that is transforming the face of America as a new, multi-ethnic generation comes into its own. "America is white no longer," he concludes, "and it will never be white again." Liu (b. 1968) founded the political journal The Next Progressive *and has edited an anthology titled* Next: Young American Writers on the New Generation *(1994). Currently he is a Visiting Fellow at the New American Foundation and teaches public policy at the University of Washington.*

1

Here are some of the ways you could say I am "white":

I listen to National Public Radio.
I wear khaki Dockers.

I own brown suede bucks.

I eat gourmet greens.

I have few close friends "of color."

I married a white woman.

I am a child of the suburbs.

I furnish my condo à la Crate & Barrel.

I vacation in charming bed-and-breakfasts.

I have never once been the victim of blatant discrimination.

I am a member of several exclusive institutions.

I have been in the inner sanctums of political power.

I have been there as something other than an attendant.

I have the ambition to return.

I am a producer of the culture.

I expect my voice to be heard.

I speak flawless, unaccented English.

I subscribe to *Foreign Affairs*.

I do not mind when editorialists write in the first person plural.

I do not mind how white television casts are.

I am not too ethnic.

I am wary of minority militants.

I consider myself neither in exile nor in opposition.

I am considered "a credit to my race."

I never asked to be white. I am not literally white. That is, I do not have white skin or white ancestors. I have yellow skin and yellow ancestors, hundreds of generations of them. But like so many other Asian Americans of the second generation, I find myself now the bearer of a strange new status: white, by acclamation. Thus it is that I have been described as an "honorary white," by other whites, and as a "banana,"[1] by other Asians. Both the honorific and the epithet take as a given this idea: to the extent that I have moved away from the periphery and toward the center of American life, I have become white inside. *Some are born white, others achieve whiteness, still others have whiteness thrust upon them.* This, supposedly, is what it means to assimilate.

There was a time when assimilation did quite strictly mean whitening. In fact, well into the first half of this century, mimicry of the stylized standards of the WASP[2] gentry was the proper, dominant, perhaps even sole method of ensuring that your origins would not be held against you. You "made it" in society not only by putting on airs of anglitude, but also by assiduously bleaching out the marks of a darker, dirtier past. And this bargain,

[1]*"banana"*: Derogatory term for an assimilated Asian American who is seen as a sellout, "yellow on the outside and white on the inside."
[2]*WASP:* Acronym for "White Anglo-Saxon Protestant."

stifling as it was, was open to European immigrants almost exclusively; to blacks, only on the passing occasion; to Asians, hardly at all.

Times have changed, and I suppose you could call it progress that a Chinaman, too, may now aspire to whiteness. But precisely because the times have changed, that aspiration—and the *imputation* of the aspiration—now seems astonishingly outmoded. The meaning of "American" has undergone a revolution in the twenty-nine years I have been alive, a revolution of color, class, and culture. Yet the vocabulary of "assimilation" has remained fixed all this time: fixed in whiteness, which is still our metonym for power; and fixed in shame, which is what the colored are expected to feel for embracing the power.

I have assimilated. I am of the mainstream. In many ways I fit the psychological profile of the so-called banana: imitative, impressionable, rootless, eager to please. As I will admit in this essay, I have at times gone to great lengths to downplay my difference, the better to penetrate the "establishment" of the moment. Yet I'm not sure that what I did was so cut-and-dried as "becoming white." I plead guilty to the charges above: achieving, learning the ways of the upper middle class, distancing myself from radicals of any hue. But having confessed, I still do not know my crime.

To be an accused banana is to stand at the ill-fated intersection of class   5
and race. And because class is the only thing Americans have more trouble talking about than race, a minority's climb up the social ladder is often willfully misnamed and wrongly portrayed. There is usually, in the portrayal, a strong whiff of betrayal: the assimilist is a traitor to his kind, to his class, to his own family. He cannot gain the world without losing his soul. To be sure, something *is* lost in any migration, whether from place to place or from class to class. But something is gained as well. And the result is always more complicated than the monochrome language of "whiteness" and "authenticity" would suggest.

My own assimilation began long before I was born. It began with my parents, who came here with an appetite for Western ways already whetted by films and books and music and, in my mother's case, by a father who'd been to the West. My parents, who traded Chinese formality for the more laissez-faire stance of this country. Who made their way by hard work and quiet adaptation. Who fashioned a comfortable life in a quiet development in a second-tier suburb. Who, unlike your "typical" Chinese parents, were not pushy, status-obsessed, rigid, disciplined, or prepared. Who were haphazard about passing down ancestral traditions and "lessons" to their children. Who did pass down, however, the sense that their children were entitled to mix and match, as they saw fit, whatever aspects of whatever cultures they encountered.

I was raised, in short, to assimilate, to claim this place as mine. I don't mean that my parents told me to act like an American. That's partly the point: they didn't tell me to do anything except to be a good boy. They trusted I would find my way, and I did, following their example and navigating by the lights of the culture that encircled me like a dome. As a function of my parents' own half-conscious, half-finished acculturation, I grew up feeling that my life was Book II of an ongoing saga. Or that I was running the second leg of a relay race. *Slap!* I was out of the womb and sprinting, baton in hand. Gradually more sure of my stride, my breathing, the feel of the track beneath me. Eyes forward, never backward.

Today, nearly seven years after my father's death and two years after my marriage into a large white family, it is as if I have come round a bend and realized that I am no longer sure where I am running or why. My sprint slows to a trot. I scan the unfamiliar vista that is opening up. I am somewhere else now, somewhere far from the China that yielded my mother and father; far, as well, from the modest horizons I knew as a boy. I look at my limbs and realize I am no longer that boy; my gait and grasp exceed his by an order of magnitude. Now I want desperately to see my face, to see what time has marked and what it has erased. But I can find no mirror except the people who surround me. And they are mainly pale, powerful.

How did I end up here, standing in what seems the very seat of whiteness, gazing from the promontory of social privilege? How did I cover so much ground so quickly? What was it, in my blind journey, that I felt I should leave behind? And what *did* I leave behind? This, the jettisoning of one mode of life to send another aloft, is not only the immigrant's tale; it is the son's tale, too. By coming to America, my parents made themselves into citizens of a new country. By traveling the trajectory of an assimilist, so did I.

2

As a child, I lived in a state of "amoebic bliss," to borrow the felicitous   10 phrase of the author of *Nisei Daughter,* Monica Sone. The world was a gossamer web of wonder that began with life at home, extended to my friendships, and made the imaginary realm of daydream seem as immediate as the real. If something or someone was in my personal web of meaning, then color or station was irrelevant. I made no distinctions in fourth grade between my best friend, a black boy named Kimathi, and my next-best friend, a white boy named Charlie—other than the fact that one was number one, the other number two. I did not feel, or feel for, a seam that separated the textures of my Chinese life from those of my American life. I was not "bicultural" but omnicultural, and omnivorous, too. To my mind, I differed from others in only two ways that counted: I was a faster runner than most, and a better student. Thus did work blend happily with play, school with home, Western culture with Eastern: it was all the same to a self-confident boy who believed he'd always be at the center of his own universe.

As I approached adolescence, though, things shifted. Suddenly, I could no longer subsume the public world under my private concept of self. Suddenly, the public world was more complicated than just a parade of smiling teachers and a few affirming friends. Now I had to contend with the unstated, inchoate, but inescapable standards of *cool*. The essence of cool was the ability to conform. The essence of conformity was the ability to anticipate what was cool. And I wasn't so good at that. For the first time, I had found something that did not come effortlessly to me. No one had warned me about this transition from happy amoeboid to social animal; no one had prepared me for the great labors of fitting in.

And so in three adjoining arenas — my looks, my loves, my manners — I suffered a bruising adolescent education. I don't mean to overdramatize: there was, in these teenage banalities, usually something humorous and nothing particularly tragic. But in each of these realms, I came to feel I was not normal. And obtusely, I ascribed the difficulties of that age not to my age but to my color. I came to suspect that there was an order to things, an order that I, as someone Chinese, could perceive but not quite crack. I responded not by exploding in rebellion but by dedicating myself, quietly and sometimes angrily, to learning the order as best I could. I was never ashamed of being Chinese; I was, in fact, rather proud to be linked to a great civilization. But I was mad that my difference should matter now. And if it had to matter, I did not want it to defeat me.

Consider, if you will, my hair. For the first eleven years of my life, I sported what was essentially the same hairstyle: a tapered bowl cut, the handiwork of my mother. For those eleven joyful years, this low-maintenance do was entirely satisfactory. But in my twelfth year, as sixth grade got under way, I became aware — gradually at first, then urgently — that bangs were no longer the look for boys. This was the year when certain early bloomers first made the height-weight-physique distribution in our class seem startlingly wide — and when I first realized that I was lingering near the bottom. It was essential that I compensate for my childlike mien by cultivating at least a patina of teenage style.

This is where my hair betrayed me. For some readers the words "Chinese hair" should suffice as explanation. For the rest, particularly those who have spent all your lives with the ability to comb back, style, and part your hair *at will*, what follows should make you count your blessings. As you may recall, 1980 was a vintage year for hair that was parted straight down the middle, then feathered on each side, feathered so immaculately that the ends would meet in the back like the closed wings of angels. I dreamed of such hair. I imagined tossing my head back casually, to ease into place the one or two strands that had drifted from their positions. I dreamed of wearing the fluffy, tailored locks of the blessed.

Instead, I was cursed. My hair was straight, rigid, and wiry. Not only   15 did it fail to feather back; it would not even bend. Worse still, it grew the wrong way. That is, it all emanated from a single swirl near the rear edge of my scalp. Parting my hair in any direction except back to front, the way certain balding men stage their final retreat, was a physical impossibility. It should go without saying that this was a disaster. For the next three years, I experimented with a variety of hairstyles that ranged from the ridiculous to the sublimely bad. There was the stringy pothead look. The mushroom do. Helmet head. Bangs folded back like curtains. I enlisted a blow-dryer, a Conair set on high heat, to force my hair into stiff postures of submission. The results, though sometimes innovative, fell always far short of cool.

I feigned nonchalance, and no one ever said anything about it. But make no mistake: this was one of the most consuming crises of my inner life as a young teen. Though neither of my parents had ever had such troubles, I blamed this predicament squarely on my Chinese genes. And I could not abide my fate. At a time when homogeneity was the highest virtue, I felt I stood out like a pigtailed Manchu.

My salvation didn't come until the end of junior high, when one of my buddies, in an epiphany as we walked past the Palace of Hair Design, dared me to get my head shaved. Without hesitation, I did it—to the tearful laughter of my friends and, soon afterward, the tearful horror of my mother. Of course, I had moments of doubt the next few days as I rubbed my peach-fuzzed skull. But what I liked was this: I had managed, without losing face, to rid myself of my greatest social burden. What's more, in the eyes of some classmates, I was now a bold (if bald) iconoclast. I've worn a crew cut ever since.

Well-styled hair was only one part of a much larger preoccupation during the ensuing years: wooing girls. In this realm I experienced a most frustrating kind of success. I was the boy that girls always found "sweet" and "funny" and "smart" and "nice." Which, to my highly sensitive ear, sounded like "leprous." Time and again, I would charm a girl into deep friendship. Time and again, as the possibility of romance came within reach, I would smash into what I took to be a glass ceiling.

The girls were white, you see; such were the demographics of my school. I was Chinese. And I was convinced that this was the sole obstacle to my advancement. It made sense, did it not? I was, after all, sweet and funny and smart and nice. Hair notwithstanding, I was not unattractive, at least compared with some of the beasts who had started "going out" with girls. There was simply no other explanation. Yet I could never say this out loud: it would have been the whining of a loser. My response, then, was to secretly scorn the girls I coveted. It was *they* who were subpar, whose small-mindedness and veiled prejudice made them unworthy.

My response, too, was to take refuge in my talents. I made myself into a   20 Renaissance boy, playing in the orchestra but also joining the wrestling team, winning science prizes but also editing the school paper. I thought I was defying the stereotype of the Asian American male as a one-dimensional nerd. But in the eyes of some, I suppose, I was simply another "Asian overachiever."

In hindsight, it's hard to know exactly how great a romantic penalty I paid for being Chinese. There may have been girls who would have had nothing to do with me on account of my race, but I never knew them. There were probably girls who, race aside, simply didn't like me. And then there were girls who liked me well enough but who also shied from the prospect of being part of an interracial couple. With so many boys out there, they probably reasoned, why take the path of greater resistance? Why risk so many status points? Why not be "just friends" with this Chinese boy?

Maybe this stigma was more imagined than real. But being an ABC ("American-born Chinese," as our parents called us) certainly affected me another way. It made me feel like something of a greenhorn, a social immigrant. I wanted so greatly to be liked. And my earnestness, though endearing, was not the sort of demeanor that won girls' hearts. Though I was observant enough to notice how people talked when flirting, astute enough to mimic the forms, I was oblivious to the subterranean levels of courtship, blind to the more subtle rituals of "getting chicks" by spurning them. I held the view that if you were manifestly a good person, eventually someone of the opposite sex would do the rational thing and be smitten with you. I was clueless. Many years would pass before I'd wise up.

It wasn't just dating rituals that befuddled me as a youth. It was ritual of all kinds. Ceremony, protocol, etiquette—all these made me feel like an awkward stranger. Things that came as second nature to many white kids were utterly exotic to me. American-style manners, for instance. Chinese families often have their own elaborate etiquette, but "please" and "may I" weren't the sort of words ever heard around my house. That kind of formality seemed so beside the point. I was never taught by my parents to write thank-you notes. I didn't even have the breeding to *say* "Thank you" after sleeping over at a friend's house. I can recall the awful, sour feeling in my stomach when this friend told me his mother had been offended by my impoliteness. (At that point, I expressed my thanks.)

Eating dinner at the home of a *yangren* could be especially trying. The oaken furniture seemed scaled-up, chairs like thrones. The meal would begin with someone, usually the father, mumbling grace. Furtively, I'd steal a glance at the heads bowed in prayer. What if they asked me to say something? I looked back down and kept my mouth shut. Next was the question of silverware: which pieces to use, in which order, and so forth. I'd realize then that at home I ate by using chopsticks to shove rice and meat straight from bowl to slurping mouth. Then the whole thing about passing platters of food around the table, instead of just reaching over and getting what you wanted. I would hear myself ask, in too-high tones, "Would you please pass the carrots, please?" It was usually at that point that I would notice that my napkin was the only one still folded neatly on the table.

All this, of course, was in the context of being with my friends and having a nice time. But something made me feel vaguely sad while I sat there, swallowing huge servings of gravy-drenched food with this other family. These were the moments when I realized I was becoming something other than my parents. I wanted so badly then just to be home, in my own kitchen, taking in the aroma of stir-fry on the wok and the chattery sounds of Chinglish. And yet, like an amphibian that has just breached the shore, I

25

could not stop inhaling this wondrous new atmosphere. My moist, blinking eyes opened wide, observing and recording the customs and predilections of these "regular" Americans. The more time I spent in their midst, the more I learned to be like them. To make their everyday idioms and idiosyncrasies familiar. To possess them.

This, the mundane, would be the locus of my conversion. It was through the small things that I made myself over. I wish, if only for story-telling purposes, that I could offer a more dramatic tale, a searing incident of racism that sent me into deep, self-abnegating alienation. The truth is, I can't. I was sometimes uncomfortable, but never really alienated. There were one or two occasions in seventh grade when the toughs in the back of the bus taunted me, called me *chink,* shot spitballs at me. I didn't like it. But each time, one of my friends—one of my white friends, in whose house I'd later eat dinner—would stand with me and fire back both spitballs and insults. Our insults were mean, too: scornful references to the trailer parks where these kids lived or the grubby clothes they wore or the crummy jobs their parents had. These skirmishes weren't just about race; they were also about mobility.

The same could be said, ultimately, about my own assimilation. To say simply that I became a banana, that I became white-identified, is somewhat simplistic. As an impressionable teen, I came to identify not with white people in general but with that subset of people, most of them white, who were educated, affluent: *going places.* It was their cues that I picked up, their judgments that I cared about. It was in their presence that old patterns of thought began to fall away like so much scaffolding around my psyche. It was in their presence that I began to imagine myself beyond race.

3

I recently dug up a photograph of myself from freshman year of college that made me smile. I have on the wrong shoes, the wrong socks, the wrong checkered shirt tucked the wrong way into the wrong slacks. I look like what I was: a boy sprung from a middlebrow burg who affected a secondhand preppiness. I look nervous. Compare that image to one from my senior-class dinner: now I am attired in a gray tweed jacket with a green plaid bow tie and a sensible button-down shirt, all purchased at the Yale Co-op. I look confident, and more than a bit contrived.

What happened in between those two photographs is that I experienced, then overcame, what the poet Meena Alexander has called "the shock of arrival." When I was deposited at the wrought-iron gates of my residential college as a freshman, I felt more like an outsider than I'd thought possible. It wasn't just that I was a small Chinese boy standing at a grand WASP temple; nor simply that I was a hayseed neophyte puzzled by the refinements of college style. It was *both:* color and class were all twisted together in a double helix of felt inadequacy.

For a while I coped with the shock by retreating to a group of my own 30 kind—not fellow Asians, but fellow marginal public-school grads who resented the rah-rah Yalies to whom everything came so effortlessly. Aligning myself this way was bearable—I was hiding, but at least I could place myself in a long tradition of underdog exiles at Yale. Aligning myself by race, on the other hand, would have seemed too inhibiting.

I know this doesn't make much sense. I know also that college, in the multicultural era, is supposed to be where the deracinated minority youth discovers the "person of color" inside. To a point, I did. I studied Chinese, took an Asian American history course, a seminar on race politics. But ultimately, college was where the unconscious habits of my adolescent assimilation hardened into self-conscious strategy.

I still remember the moment, in the first week of school, when I came upon a table in Yale Station set up by the Asian American Student Association. The upperclassman staffing the table was pleasant enough. He certainly did not strike me as a fanatic. Yet, for some reason, I flashed immediately to a scene I'd witnessed days earlier, on the corner outside. Several Lubavitcher Jews, dressed in black, their faces bracketed by dangling side curls, were looking for fellow travelers at this busy crossroads. Their method was crude but memorable. As any vaguely Jewish-looking male walked past, the zealots would quickly approach, extend a pamphlet, and ask, "Excuse me, sir, are you Jewish?" Since most were not, and since those who weren't about to stop, the result was a frantic, nervous, almost comical buzz all about the corner: Excuse me, are you Jewish? Are you Jewish? Excuse me. Are you Jewish?

I looked now at the clean-cut Korean boy at the AASA table (I think I can distinguish among Asian ethnicities as readily as those Hasidim thought they could tell Gentile from Jew), and though he had merely offered an introductory hello and was now smiling mutely at me, in the back of my mind I heard only this: *Excuse me, are you Asian? Are you Asian? Excuse me. Are you Asian?* I took one of the flyers on the table, even put my name on a mailing list, so as not to appear impolite. But I had already resolved not to be active in any Asians-only group. I thought then: I would never *choose* to be so pigeonholed.

This allergic sensitivity to "pigeonholing" is one of the unhappy hallmarks of the banana mentality. What does the banana fear? That is, what did *I* fear? The possibility of being mistaken for someone more Chinese. The possibility of being known only, or even primarily, for being Asian. The possibility of being written off by whites as a self-segregating ethnic clumper. These were the threats—unseen and, frankly, unsubstantiated—that I felt I should keep at bay.

I didn't avoid making Asian friends in college or working with Asian 35 classmates; I simply never went out of my way to do so. This distinction seemed important—it marked, to my mind, the difference between self-hate and self-respect. That the two should have been so proximate in the first place never struck me as odd, or telling. Nor did it ever occur to me that the reasons I gave myself for dissociating from Asians as a group—that I didn't want to be part of a clique, that I didn't want to get absorbed and lose my individuality—were the very developments that marked my own assimilation. I simply hewed to my ideology of race neutrality and self-reliance. I didn't need that crutch, I told myself nervously, that crutch of racial affinity. What's more, I was vaguely insulted by the presumption that I might.

But again: Who was making the presumption? Who more than I was taking the mere existence of Korean volleyball leagues or Taiwanese social sets or pan-Asian student clubs to mean that *all* people of Asian descent, myself, included, needed such quasi-kinship groups? And who more than I interpreted this need as infirmity, as a failure to fit in? I resented the faintly sneering way that some whites regarded Asians as an undifferentiated mass. But whose sneer, really, did I resent more than my own?

I was keenly aware of the unflattering mythologies that attach to Asian Americans: that we are indelibly foreign, exotic, math and science geeks, numbers people rather than people people, followers and not leaders, physically frail but devious and sneaky, unknowable and potentially treacherous. These stereotypes of Asian otherness and inferiority were like immense blocks of ice sitting before me, challenging me to chip away at them. And I did, tirelessly. All the while, though, I was oblivious to rumors of my *own* otherness and inferiority, rumors that rose off those blocks like a fog, wafting into my consciousness and chilling my sense of self.

As I had done in high school, I combated the stereotypes in part by trying to disprove them. If Asians were reputed to be math and science geeks, I would be a student of history and politics. If Asians were supposed to be feeble subalterns, I'd lift weights and go to Marine officer candidate school. If Asians were alien, I'd be ardently patriotic. If Asians were shy and retiring, I'd try to be exuberant and jocular. If they were narrow-minded specialists, I'd be a well-rounded generalist. If they were perpetual outsiders, I'd join every establishment outfit I could and show that I, too, could run with the swift.

I overstate, of course. It wasn't that I chose to do all these things with no other purpose than to cut against a supposed convention. I was neither so Pavlovian nor so calculating that I would simply remake myself into the opposite of what people expected. I actually *liked* history, and wasn't especially good at math. As the grandson of a military officer, I *wanted* to see what officer candidates school would be like, and I enjoyed it, at least once I'd finished. I am *by nature* enthusiastic and allegiant, a joiner, and a bit of a jingo.

At the same time, I was often aware, sometimes even hopeful, that others might think me "exceptional" for my race. I derived satisfaction from   40 being the "atypical" Asian, the only Chinese face at OCS or in this club or that.

The irony is that in working so duteously to defy stereotype, I became a slave to it. For to act self-consciously against Asian "tendencies" is not to break loose from the cage of myth and legend; it is to turn the very key that locks you inside. What spontaneity is there when the value of every act is measured, at least in part, by its power to refute a presumption about why you act? The *typical Asian* I imagined, and the *atypical Asian* I imagined myself to be, were identical in this sense: neither was as much a creature of free will as a human being ought to be.

Let me say it plainly, then: I am not proud to have had this mentality. I believe I have outgrown it. And I expose it now not to justify it but to detoxify it, to prevent its further spread.

Yet it would be misleading, I think, to suggest that my education centered solely on the discomfort caused by race. The fact is, when I first got to college I felt deficient compared with people of *every* color. Part of why I believed it so necessary to achieve was that I lacked the connections, the wealth, the experience, the sophistication that so many of my classmates seemed to have. I didn't get the jokes or the intellectual references. I didn't have the canny attitude. So in addition to all my coursework, I began to puzzle over this, the culture of the influential class.

Over time, I suppose, I learned the culture. My interests and vocabulary became ever more worldly. I made my way onto what Calvin Trillin once described as the "magic escalator" of a Yale education. Extracurriculars opened the door to an alumni internship, which brought me to Capitol Hill, which led to a job and a life in Washington after commencement. Gradually, very gradually, I found that I was not so much of an outsider anymore. I found that by almost any standard, but particularly by the standards of my younger self, I was actually beginning to "make it."

It has taken me until now, however, to appraise the thoughts and acts   45
of that younger self. I can see now that the straitening path I took was not the only or even the best path. For while it may be possible to transcend race, *it is not always necessary to try.* And while racial identity is sometimes a shackle, it is not *only* a shackle. I could have spared myself a great deal of heartache had I understood this earlier, that the choice of race is not simply "embrace or efface."

I wonder sometimes how I would have turned out had I been, from the start, more comfortable in my own skin. What did I miss by distancing myself from race? What friendships did I forgo, what self-knowledge did I defer? Had certain accidents of privilege been accidents of privation or exclusion, I might well have developed a different view of the world. But I do not know just how my view would have differed.

What I know is that through all those years of shadow-dancing with my identity, something happened, something that had only partially to do with color. By the time I left Yale I was no longer the scared boy of that freshman photo. I had become more sure of myself and of my place—sure enough, indeed, to perceive the folly of my fears. And in the years since, I have assumed a sense of expectation, of access and *belonging,* that my younger self could scarcely have imagined. All this happened incrementally. There was no clear tipping point, no obvious moment of mutation. The shock of arrival, it would seem, is simply that I arrived.

4

"The world is white no longer, and it will never be white again." So wrote James Baldwin after having lived in a tiny Swiss village where, to his knowledge, no black man had ever set foot. It was there, in the icy heart of whiteness, that the young expatriate began to comprehend the desire of so many of his countrymen to return to some state of nature where only white people existed. It was there too that he recognized just how impossible that was, just how intertwined were the fates and identities of the races in America. "No road whatever will lead Americans back to the simplicity of this European village where white men still have the luxury of looking on me as a stranger," he wrote. "I am not, really, a stranger any longer for any American alive."

That is precisely how I feel when I consider my own journey, my own family's travels. For here I am now, standing in a new country. Not as an expatriate or a resident alien, but as a citizen. And as I survey this realm—this Republic of Privilege—I realize certain things, things that my mother and father might also have realized about *their* new country a generation ago. I realize that my entry has yielded me great opportunities. I realize, as well, that my route of entry has taken a certain toll. I have neglected my ancestral heritage. I have lost something. Yes, I can speak some Mandarin and stir-fry a few easy dishes. I have been to China and know something of its history. Still, I could never claim to be Chinese at the core.

Yet neither would I claim, as if by default, to be merely "white inside." I do not want to be white. I only want to be integrated. When I identify with white people who wield economic and political power, it is not for their whiteness but for their power. When I imagine myself among white people who influence the currents of our culture, it is not for their whiteness but for their influence. When I emulate white people who are at ease with the world, it is not for their whiteness but for their ease. I don't like it that the people I should learn from tend so often to be white, for it says something damning about how opportunity is still distributed. But it helps not at all to call me white for learning from them. It is cruel enough that the least privileged Americans today have colored skin, the most privileged fair. It is crueler still that by our very language we should help convert this fact into rule. The time has come to describe assimilation as something other than the White Way of Being.

50

"Gosh, it kills me to do this to you, Worthington, but you're not turning out to be as black as we had hoped."

The time has also come, I think, to conceive of assimilation as more than a series of losses—and to recognize that what is lost is not necessarily sacred. I have, as I say, allowed my Chinese ethnicity to become diluted. And I often resolve to do more to preserve, to conserve, my inheritance. But have my acts of neglect thus far, my many omissions, been inherently wrong? G. K. Chesterton once wrote that "conservatism is based upon the idea that if you leave things alone, you leave them as they are. But you do not. If you leave a thing alone, you leave it to a torrent of change." I may have been born a Chinese baby, but it would have taken unremitting reinforcement, by my parents and by myself, for me to have remained Chinese. Instead, we left things alone. And a torrent of change washed over me.

This, we must remember, has been an act of creation as much as destruction. Something new is emerging from the torrent, in my case and the many millions like it. Something undeveloped, speaking the unformed tongue of an unformed nation. Something not white, and probably more Chinese than I know. Whatever it is that I am becoming, is it any less authentic for being an amalgam? Is it intrinsically less meaningful than what I might otherwise have been? In every assimilation, there is a mutiny against history—but there is also a destiny, which is to redefine history. What it means to be American—in spirit, in blood—is something far more borrowed and commingled than anything previous generations ever knew. Alongside the pain of migration, then, and the possibility, there is this truth: America is white no longer, and it will never be white again.

ENGAGING THE TEXT

1. Liu opens his essay with a list of the ways in which he could be seen as "white." What does each item on his list suggest about the characteristics of "whiteness"? Do you share these assumptions about what it means to be white? Why or why not?

2. What is Liu's reaction to being called a "banana"? What does he mean when he comments that the process of assimilation is "more complicated than the monochrome language of 'whiteness' and 'authenticity' would suggest" (para. 5)?

3. How do Liu's motives for conforming as a teenager differ from his motives as a college student? What efforts does he make to fit in, and to what extent does he succeed in each of these phases of his life?

4. How do you explain Liu's comment that he became a slave to stereotypes even as he conscientiously worked to disprove stereotypical beliefs about Asians? What does he mean by saying that he wants to expose his former mentality in order to "detoxify it" (para. 42)?

5. What does Liu believe he has lost and gained by assimilating? How and why does he believe the idea of assimilation is changing in the United States?

6. In the final paragraph of the essay, Liu observes that a new "borrowed and commingled" American identity is emerging. What indications of this trend, if any, have you observed?

EXPLORING CONNECTIONS

7. Compare Liu's experience of assimilation to that of Richard Rodriguez (p. 214). What similarities and differences do you see in the process of change each man goes through? How does each assess his gains and losses? How do you explain the differences in their perspectives?

8. What role does education play for Liu, Rodriguez (p. 214), Malcolm X (p. 243), and Judith Ortiz Cofer (p. 433) as they struggle to define their identities within a context of racial or cultural conflict?

9. How would Liu respond to George Fredrickson's (p. 632) assertion that "when carried to its logical conclusion, the assimilationist project demands what its critics have described...as 'cultural genocide'"? Write an imaginary conversation in which these two writers discuss the meaning of assimilation.

EXTENDING THE CRITICAL CONTEXT

10. If you have ever consciously attempted to disprove a stereotype or stereotypes about a group that you're a part of, write a journal entry describing

that experience. Why did you feel the need to refute the stereotype, how did you go about combatting it, and what was the result of your efforts, if any?

11. Liu writes that in college he deliberately avoided joining any groups associated with Asian identity but that he now sees this behavior as foolish and immature. As a group or class project, interview students of various ethnic backgrounds about why they have chosen to join or not to join campus organizations based on ethnicity. What are the benefits and drawbacks of such groups, according to your survey?

Assimilation

SHERMAN ALEXIE

Sherman Alexie won the 1999 World Heavyweight Championship Poetry Bout by improvising, in thirty seconds, a poetic riff on the word "dumbass." The poem, according to one reporter, was both humorous and poignant. Alexie's performance captured his sense of humor, his inventiveness, and his ability to wring insight from unlikely material. True to form, this story—about a Coeur d'Alene Indian woman who decides to cheat on her white husband—is a comedy that poses serious questions about race, class, culture, deception, and love. Alexie (b. 1966) grew up on the Spokane Indian Reservation in Washington State, but attended a high school where, in his words, he was "the only Indian ... except the school mascot." He claims not to believe in writer's block, and has the publications to prove it: two novels, Reservation Blues *(1995) and* Indian Killer *(1996); twelve volumes of poems and short stories; many essays and reviews. He coauthored the script for the award-winning film* Smoke Signals *(1998) and both wrote and directed* The Business of Fancydancing *(2002). "Assimilation" comes from Alexie's short story collection,* The Toughest Indian in the World *(2000).*

Regarding love, marriage, and sex, both Shakespeare and Sitting Bull knew the only truth: treaties get broken. Therefore, Mary Lynn wanted to have sex with any man other than her husband. For the first time in her life, she wanted to go to bed with an Indian man only because he was Indian. She was a Coeur d'Alene Indian married to a white man; she was a wife who wanted to have sex with an indigenous stranger. She didn't care about the stranger's job or his hobbies, or whether he was due for a Cost of Living raise, or owned ten thousand miles of model railroad track. She didn't care if he was handsome or ugly, mostly because she wasn't sure exactly what those terms meant anymore and how much relevance they truly had when it came to choosing sexual partners. Oh, she'd married a very handsome man, there was no doubt about that, and she was still attracted to her husband, to his long, graceful fingers, to his arrogance and utter lack of fear in social situations — he'd say anything to anybody — but lately, she'd been forced to concentrate too hard when making love to him. If she didn't focus completely on him, on the smallest details of his body, then she would drift away from the bed and float around the room like a bored angel. Of course, all this made her feel like a failure, especially since it seemed that her husband had yet to notice her growing disinterest. She wanted to be a good lover, wife, and partner, but she'd obviously developed some form of sexual dyslexia or had picked up a mutant, contagious, and erotic strain of Attention Deficit Disorder. She felt baffled by the complications of sex. She haunted the aisles of bookstores and desperately paged through every book in the self-help section and studied every diagram and chart in the human sensuality encyclopedias. She wanted answers. She wanted to feel it again, whatever *it* was.

A few summers ago, during Crow Fair, Mary Lynn had been standing in a Montana supermarket, in the produce aisle, when a homely white woman, her spiky blond hair still wet from a trailer-house shower, walked by in a white t-shirt and blue jeans, and though Mary Lynn was straight — having politely declined all three lesbian overtures thrown at her in her life — she'd felt a warm breeze pass through her DNA in that ugly woman's wake, and had briefly wanted to knock her to the linoleum and do beautiful things to her. Mary Lynn had never before felt such lust — in Montana, of all places, for a white woman who was functionally illiterate and underemployed! — and had not since felt that sensually about any other woman or man.

Who could explain such things, these vagaries of love? There were many people who would blame Mary Lynn's unhappiness, her dissatisfaction, on her ethnicity. God, she thought, how simple and earnest was that particular bit of psychotherapy! Yes, she was most certainly a Coeur d'Alene — she'd grown up on the rez, had been very happy during her time there, and had left without serious regrets or full-time enemies — but that wasn't the only way to define her. She wished that she could be called Coeur d'Alene as a description, rather than as an excuse, reason, prescription, placebo, prediction, or diminutive. She only wanted to be understood as eccentric and complicated!

Her most cherished eccentricity: when she was feeling her most lonely, she'd put one of the Big Mom Singers' powwow CDs on the stereo (*I'm not afraid of death, hey, ya, hey, death is my cousin, hey, ya, ha, ha*) and read from Emily Dickinson's poetry (*Because I could not stop for Death — / He kindly stopped for me —*).

Her most important complication: she was a woman in a turbulent marriage that was threatening to go bad, or had gone bad and might get worse.   5

Yes, she was a Coeur d'Alene woman, passionately and dispassionately, who wanted to cheat on her white husband because he was white. She wanted to find an anonymous lover, an Indian man who would fade away into the crowd when she was done with him, a man whose face could appear on the back of her milk carton. She didn't care if he was the kind of man who knew the punch lines to everybody's dirty jokes, or if he was the kind of man who read Zane Grey before he went to sleep, or if he was both of those men simultaneously. She simply wanted to find the darkest Indian in Seattle—the man with the greatest amount of melanin—and get naked with him in a cheap motel room. Therefore, she walked up to a flabby Lummi Indian man in a coffee shop and asked him to make love to her.

"Now," she said. "Before I change my mind."

He hesitated for a brief moment, wondering why he was the chosen one, and then took her by the hand. He decided to believe he was a handsome man.

"Don't you want to know my name?" he asked before she put her hand over his mouth.

"Don't talk to me," she said. "Don't say one word. Just take me to the closest motel and fuck me." 10

The obscenity bothered her. It felt staged, forced, as if she were an actress in a three-in-the-morning cable-television movie. But she was acting, wasn't she? She was not an adulteress, was she?

Why exactly did she want to have sex with an Indian stranger? She told herself it was because of pessimism, existentialism, even nihilism, but those reasons—*those words*—were a function of her vocabulary and not of her motivations. If forced to admit the truth, or some version of the truth, she'd testify she was about to go to bed with an Indian stranger because she wanted to know how it would feel. After all, she'd slept with a white stranger in her life, so why not include a Native American? Why not practice a carnal form of affirmative action? By God, her infidelity was a political act! Rebellion, resistance, revolution!

In the motel room, Mary Lynn made the Indian take off his clothes first. Thirty pounds overweight, with purple scars crisscrossing his pale chest and belly, he trembled as he undressed. He wore a wedding ring on his right hand. She knew that some Europeans wore their wedding bands on the right hand—so maybe this Indian was married to a French woman—but Mary Lynn also knew that some divorced Americans wore rings on their right hands as symbols of pain, of mourning. Mary Lynn didn't care if he was married or not, or whether he shared custody of the sons and daughters, or whether he had any children at all. She was grateful that he was plain and desperate and lonely.

Mary Lynn stepped close to him, took his hand, and slid his thumb into her mouth. She sucked on it and felt ridiculous. His skin was salty and oily, the taste of a working man. She closed her eyes and thought about her husband, a professional who had his shirts laundered. In one hour, he was going to meet her at a new downtown restaurant.

She walked a slow, tight circle around the Indian. She stood behind   15
him, reached around his thick waist, and held his erect penis. He moaned and she decided that she hated him. She decided to hate all men. Hate, hate, hate, she thought, and then let her hate go.

She was lovely and intelligent, and had grown up with Indian women who were more lovely and more intelligent, but who also had far less ambition and mendacity. She'd once read in a book, perhaps by Primo Levi or Elie Wiesel, that the survivors of the Nazi death camps were the Jews who lied, cheated, murdered, stole, and subverted. You must remember, said Levi or Wiesel, that the best of us did not survive the camps. Mary Lynn felt the same way about the reservation. Before she'd turned ten, she'd attended the funerals of seventeen good women—the best of the Coeur d'Alenes—and had read about the deaths of eighteen more good women since she'd left the rez. But what about the Coeur d'Alene men—those liars, cheats, and thieves—who'd survived, even thrived? Mary Lynn wanted nothing to do with them, then or now. As a teenager, she'd dated only white boys. As an adult, she'd only dated white men. God, she hated to admit it, but white men — her teachers, coaches, bosses, and lovers—had always been more dependable than the Indian men in her life. White men had rarely disappointed her, but they'd never surprised her either. White men were neutral, she thought, just like Belgium! And when has Belgium ever been sexy? When has Belgium caused a grown woman to shake with fear and guilt? She didn't want to feel Belgian; she wanted to feel dangerous.

In the cheap motel room, Mary Lynn breathed deeply. The Indian smelled of old sweat and a shirt worn twice before washing. She ran her finger along the ugly scars on his belly and chest. She wanted to know the scars' creation story—she hoped this Indian man was a warrior with a history of knife fighting—but she feared he was only carrying the transplanted heart and lungs of another man. She pushed him onto the bed, onto the scratchy comforter. She'd once read that scientists had examined a hotel-room comforter and discovered four hundred and thirty-two different samples of sperm. God, she thought, those scientists obviously had too much time on their hands and, in the end, had failed to ask the most important questions: Who left the samples? Spouses, strangers? Were these exchanges of money, tenderness, disease? Was there love?

"This has to be quick," she said to the stranger beside her.

Jeremiah, her husband, was already angry when Mary Lynn arrived thirty minutes late at the restaurant and he nearly lost all of his self-control when they were asked to wait for the next available table. He often raged at strangers, though he was incredibly patient and kind with their four children. Mary Lynn had seen that kind of rage in other white men when their

wishes and desires were ignored. At ball games, in parking lots, and especially in airports, white men demanded to receive the privileges whose very
existence they denied. White men could be so predictable, thought Mary
Lynn. She thought: O, Jeremiah! O, season ticket holder! O, monthly
parker! O, frequent flyer! She dreamed of him out there, sitting in the airplane with eighty-seven other white men wearing their second-best suits, all
of them traveling toward small rooms in the Ramadas, Radissons, and sometimes the Hyatts, where they all separately watched the same pay-per-view
porno that showed everything except penetration. What's the point of porno
without graphic penetration? Mary Lynn knew it only made these lonely
men feel all that more lonely. And didn't they deserve better, these white
salesmen and middle managers, these twenty-first-century Willy Lomans,[1]
who only wanted to be better men than their fathers had been? Of course,
thought Mary Lynn, these sons definitely deserved better—they were
smarter and more tender and generous than all previous generations of
white American men—but they'd never receive their just rewards, and thus
their anger was justified and banal.

"Calm down," Mary Lynn said to her husband as he continued to rage   20
at the restaurant hostess.

Mary Lynn said those two words to him more often in their marriage
than any other combination of words.

"It could be twenty, thirty minutes," said the hostess. "Maybe longer."

"We'll wait outside," said Jeremiah. He breathed deeply, remembering
some mantra that his therapist had taught him.

Mary Lynn's mantra: I cheated on my husband, I cheated on my husband.

"We'll call your name," said the hostess, a white woman who was tired   25
of men no matter what their color. "When."

Their backs pressed against the brick wall, their feet crossed on the
sidewalk, on a warm Seattle evening, Mary Lynn and Jeremiah smoked faux
cigarettes filled with some foul-tasting, overwhelmingly organic herb substance. For years they had smoked unfiltered Camels, but had quit after all
four of their parents had simultaneously suffered through at least one form
of cancer. Mary Lynn had called them the Mormon Tabernacle Goddamn
Cancer Choir, though none of them was Mormon and all of them were
altos. With and without grace, they had all survived the radiation,
chemotherapy, and in-hospital cable-television bingo games, with their bodies reasonably intact, only to resume their previously self-destructive habits.
After so many nights spent in hospital corridors, waiting rooms, and arm-
chairs, Mary Lynn and Jeremiah hated doctors, all doctors, even the ones on

---

[1]*Willy Lomans:* Willy Loman, the protagonist of Arthur Miller's play *Death of a Salesman,* is an ordinary but driven man struggling to find meaning in his work and family life; he
becomes a symbol of the problems and despair faced by the "little guy" in an increasingly impersonal world.

television, especially the ones on television. United in their obsessive hatred, Mary Lynn and Jeremiah resorted to taking vitamins, eating free-
range chicken, and smoking cigarettes rolled together and marketed by six
odoriferous white liberals in Northern California.

As they waited for a table, Mary Lynn and Jeremiah watched dozens of
people arrive and get seated immediately.

"I bet they don't have reservations," he said.

"I hate these cigarettes," she said.

"Why do you keep buying them?"   30

"Because the cashier at the health-food store is cute."

"You're shallow."

"Like a mud puddle."

Mary Lynn hated going out on weeknights. She hated driving into the
city. She hated waiting for a table. Standing outside the downtown restaurant, desperate to hear their names, she decided to hate Jeremiah for a few
seconds. Hate, hate, hate, she thought, and then she let her hate go. She
wondered if she smelled like sex, like indigenous sex, and if a white man
could recognize the scent of an enemy. She'd showered, but the water pressure had been weak and the soap bar too small.

"Let's go someplace else," she said.   35

"No. Five seconds after we leave, they'll call our names."

"But we won't know they called our names."

"But I'll feel it."

"It must be difficult to be psychic and insecure."

"I knew you were going to say that."   40

Clad in leather jackets and black jeans, standing inches apart but never
quite touching, both handsome to the point of distraction, smoking crappy
cigarettes that appeared to be real cigarettes, they could have been the subjects of a Schultz photograph or a Runnette poem.

The title of the photograph: "Infidelity."

The title of the poem: "More Infidelity."

Jeremiah's virtue was reasonably intact, though he'd recently been involved in a flirtatious near-affair with a coworker. At the crucial moment,
when the last button was about to be unbuttoned, when consummation was
just a fingertip away, Jeremiah had pushed his potential lover away and said
I can't, I just can't, I love my marriage. He didn't admit to love for his
spouse, partner, wife. No, he confessed his love for marriage, for the
blessed union, for the legal document, for the shared mortgage payments,
and for their four children.

Mary Lynn wondered what would happen if she grew pregnant with   45
the Lummi's baby. Would this full-blood baby look more Indian than her
half-blood sons and daughters?

"Don't they know who I am?" she asked her husband as they waited
outside the downtown restaurant. She wasn't pregnant; there would be no
paternity tests, no revealing of great secrets. His secret: he was still in love

with a white woman from high school he hadn't seen in decades. What Mary Lynn knew: he was truly in love with the idea of a white woman from a mythical high school, with a prom queen named *If Only* or a homecoming princess named *My Life Could Have Been Different.*

"I'm sure they know who you are," he said. "That's why we're on the wait list. Otherwise, we'd be heading for McDonald's or Denny's."

"Your kinds of places."

"Dependable. The Big Mac you eat in Hong Kong or Des Moines tastes just like the Big Mac in Seattle."

"Sounds like colonialism to me."   50

"Colonialism ain't all bad."

"Put that on a bumper sticker."

This place was called Tan Tan, though it would soon be trendy enough to go by a nickname: Tan's. Maybe Tan's would become T's, and then T's would be identified only by a slight turn of the head or a certain widening of the eyes. After that, the downhill slide in reputation would be inevitable, whether or not the culinary content and quality of the restaurant remained exactly the same or improved. As it was, Tan Tan was a pan-Asian restaurant whose ownership and chefs—head, sauce, and line—were white, though most of the wait staff appeared to be one form of Asian or another.

"Don't you hate it?" Jeremiah asked. "When they have Chinese waiters in sushi joints? Or Korean dishwashers in a Thai noodle house?"

"I hadn't really thought about it," she said.   55

"No, think about it, these restaurants, these Asian restaurants, they hire Asians indiscriminately because they think white people won't be able to tell the difference."

"White people can't tell the difference."

"I can."

"Hey, Geronimo, you've been hanging around Indians too long to be white."

"Fucking an Indian doesn't make me Indian."   60

"So, that's what we're doing now? Fucking?"

"You have a problem with fucking?"

"No, not with the act itself, but I do have a problem with your sexual thesaurus."

Mary Lynn and Jeremiah had met in college, when they were still called Mary and Jerry. After sleeping together for the first time, after her first orgasm and his third, Mary had turned to Jerry and said, with absolute seriousness: If this thing is going to last, we have to stop the end rhyme. She had majored in Milton and Blake. He'd been a chemical engineer since the age of seven, with the degree being only a matter of formality, so he'd had plenty of time to wonder how an Indian from the reservation could be so smart. He still wondered how it had happened, though he'd never had the courage to ask her.

Now, a little more than two decades after graduating with a useless de-   65
gree, Mary Lynn worked at Microsoft for a man named Dickinson. Jeremiah didn't know his first name, though he hoped it wasn't Emery, and had
never met the guy, and didn't care if he ever did. Mary Lynn's job title and
responsibilities were vague, so vague that Jeremiah had never asked her to
elaborate. She often worked sixty-hour weeks and he didn't want to reward
that behavior by expressing an interest in what specific tasks she performed
for Bill Gates.

Waiting outside Tan Tan, he and she could smell ginger, burned rice,
beer.

"Are they ever going to seat us?" she asked.

"Yeah, don't they know who you are?"

"I hear this place discriminates against white people."

"Really?"   70

"Yeah, I heard once, these lawyers, bunch of white guys in Nordstrom's
suits, had to wait, like, two hours for a table."

"Were those billable hours?"

"It's getting hard for a white guy to find a place to eat."

"Damn affirmative action is what it is."

Their first child had been an accident, the result of a broken condom   75
and a missed birth control pill. They named her Antonya, Toni for short.
The second and third children, Robert and Michael, had been on purpose,
and the fourth, Ariel, came after Mary Lynn thought she could no longer
get pregnant.

Toni was fourteen, immature for her age, quite beautiful and narcissistic, with her translucent skin, her long blond hair, and eight-ball eyes. Botti-
celli eyes, she bragged after taking an Introduction to Art class. She never
bothered to tell anybody she was Indian, mostly because nobody asked.

Jeremiah was quite sure that his daughter, his Antonya, had lost her vir-
ginity to the pimply quarterback of the junior varsity football team. He
found the thought of his daughter's adolescent sexuality both curious and
disturbing. Above all else, he believed that she was far too special to sleep
with a cliché, let alone a junior varsity cliché.

Three months out of every year, Robert and Michael were the same
age. Currently, they were both eleven. Dark-skinned, with their mother's
black hair, strong jawline, and endless nose, they looked Indian, very Indian. Robert, who had refused to be called anything other than Robert, was
the smart boy, a math prodigy, while Mikey was the basketball player.

When Mary Lynn's parents called from the reservation, they always
asked after the boys, always invited the boys out for the weekend, the holidays, and the summer, and always sent the boys more elaborate gifts than
they sent the two girls.

When Jeremiah had pointed out this discrepancy to Mary Lynn, she   80
had readily agreed, but had made it clear that his parents also paid more

attention to the boys. Jeremiah never mentioned it again, but had silently vowed to love the girls a little more than he loved the boys.

As if love were a thing that could be quantified, he thought.

He asked himself: What if I love the girls more because they look more like me, because they look more white than the boys?

Towheaded Ariel was two, and the clay of her personality was just beginning to harden, but she was certainly petulant and funny as hell, with the ability to sleep in sixteen-hour marathons that made her parents very nervous. She seemed to exist in her own world, enough so that she was periodically monitored for incipient autism. She treated her siblings as if they somehow bored her, and was the kind of kid who could stay alone in her crib for hours, amusing herself with all sorts of personal games and imaginary friends.

Mary Lynn insisted that her youngest daughter was going to be an artist, but Jeremiah didn't understand the child, and despite the fact that he was her father and forty-three years older, he felt inferior to Ariel.

He wondered if his wife was ever going to leave him because he was 85 white.

When Tan Tan's doors swung open, laughter and smoke rolled out together.

"You got another cigarette?" he asked.

"Quit calling them cigarettes. They're not cigarettes. They're more like rose bushes. Hell, they're more like the shit that rose bushes grow in."

"You think we're going to get a table?"

"By the time we get a table, this place is going to be very unpopular." 90

"Do you want to leave?"

"Do you?"

"If you do."

"We told the baby-sitter we'd be home by ten."

They both wished that Toni were responsible enough to baby-sit her 95 siblings, rather than needing to be sat along with them.

"What time is it?" she asked.

"Nine."

"Let's go home."

Last Christmas, when the kids had been splayed out all over the living room, buried to their shoulders in wrapping paper and expensive toys, Mary Lynn had studied her children's features, had recognized most of her face in her sons' faces and very little of it in her daughters', and had decided, quite facetiously, that the genetic score was tied.

We should have another kid, she'd said to Jeremiah, so we'll know if 100 this is a white family or an Indian family.

It's a family family, he'd said, without a trace of humor.

Only a white guy would say that, she'd said.

Well, he'd said, you married a white guy.

The space between them had grown very cold at that moment, in that silence, and perhaps one or both of them might have said something truly destructive, but Ariel had started crying then, for no obvious reason, relieving both parents of the responsibility of finishing that particular conversation. During the course of their relationship, Mary Lynn and Jeremiah had often discussed race as a concept, as a foreign country they occasionally visited, or as an enemy that existed outside their house, as a destructive force they could fight against as a couple, as a family. But race was also a constant presence, a houseguest and permanent tenant who crept around all the rooms in their shared lives, opening drawers, stealing utensils and small articles of clothing, changing the temperature.

Before he'd married Mary Lynn, Jeremiah had always believed there   105 was too much talk of race, that white people were all too willing to be racist and that brown people were just as willing and just as racist. As a rational scientist, he'd known that race was primarily a social construct, illusionary, but as the husband of an Indian woman and the father of Indian children, he'd since learned that race, whatever its construction, was real. Now, there were plenty of white people who wanted to eliminate the idea of race, to cast it aside as an unwanted invention, but it was far too late for that. If white people are the mad scientists who created race, thought Jeremiah, then we created race so we could enslave black people and kill Indians, and now race has become the Frankenstein monster that has grown beyond our control. Though he'd once been willfully blind, Jeremiah had learned how to recognize that monster in the faces of whites and Indians and in their eyes.

Long ago, Jeremiah and Mary Lynn had both decided to challenge those who stared by staring back, by flinging each other against walls and tongue-kissing with pornographic élan.

Long ago, they'd both decided to respond to any questions of why, how, what, who, or when by simply stating: Love is Love. They knew it was romantic bullshit, a simpleminded answer only satisfying for simpleminded people, but it was the best available defense.

Listen, Mary Lynn had once said to Jeremiah, asking somebody why they fall in love is like asking somebody why they believe in God.

You start asking questions like that, she had added, and you're either going to start a war or you're going to hear folk music.

You think too much, Jeremiah had said, rolling over and falling asleep.   110

Then, in the dark, as Jeremiah slept, Mary Lynn had masturbated while fantasizing about an Indian man with sundance scars on his chest.

After they left Tan Tan, they drove a sensible and indigenous Ford Taurus over the 520 bridge, back toward their house in Kirkland, a five-bedroom rancher only ten blocks away from the Microsoft campus. Mary Lynn walked to work. That made her feel privileged. She estimated there were twenty-two American Indians who had ever felt even a moment of privilege.

"We still have to eat," she said as she drove across the bridge. She felt strange. She wondered if she was ever going to feel normal again.

"How about Taco Bell drive-thru?" he asked.

"You devil, you're trying to get into my pants, aren't you?"   115

Impulsively, he dropped his head into her lap and pressed his lips against her black-jeaned crotch. She yelped and pushed him away. She wondered if he could smell her, if he could smell the Lummi Indian. Maybe he could, but he seemed to interpret it as something different, as something meant for him, as he pushed his head into her lap again. What was she supposed to do? She decided to laugh, so she did laugh as she pushed his face against her pubic bone. She loved the man for reasons she could not always explain. She closed her eyes, drove in that darkness, and felt dangerous.

Halfway across the bridge, Mary Lynn slammed on the brakes, not because she'd seen anything—her eyes were still closed—but because she'd felt something. The car skidded to a stop just inches from the bumper of a truck that had just missed sliding into the row of cars stopped ahead of it.

"What the hell is going on?" Jeremiah asked as he lifted his head from her lap.

"Traffic jam."

"Jesus, we'll never make it home by ten. We better call."   120

"The cell phone is in the glove."

Jeremiah dialed the home number but received only a busy signal.

"Toni must be talking to her boyfriend," she said.

"I don't like him."

"He doesn't like you."   125

"What the hell is going on? Why aren't we moving?"

"I don't know. Why don't you go check?"

Jeremiah climbed out of the car.

"I was kidding," she said as he closed the door behind him.

He walked up to the window of the truck ahead of him.   130

"You know what's going on?" Jeremiah asked the truck driver.

"Nope."

Jeremiah walked farther down the bridge. He wondered if there was a disabled car ahead, what the radio liked to call a "blocking accident." There was also the more serious "injury accident" and the deadly "accident with fatality involved." He had to drive this bridge ten times a week. The commute. White men had invented the commute, had deepened its meaning, had diversified its complications, and now spent most of the time trying to shorten it, reduce it, lessen it.

In the car, Mary Lynn wondered why Jeremiah always found it necessary to insert himself into every situation. He continually moved from the passive to the active. The man was kinetic. She wondered if it was a white thing. Possibly. But more likely, it was a Jeremiah thing. She remembered Mikey's third-grade-class's school play, an edited version of *Hamlet*.

Jeremiah had walked onto the stage to help his son drag the unconscious Polonius, who had merely been clubbed over the head rather than stabbed to death, from the stage. Mortally embarrassed, Mikey had cried himself to sleep that night, positive that he was going to be an elementary-school pariah, while Jeremiah vainly tried to explain to the rest of the family why he had acted so impulsively.

I was just trying to be a good father, he had said.   135

Mary Lynn watched Jeremiah walk farther down the bridge. He was just a shadow, a silhouette. She was slapped by the brief, irrational fear that he would never return.

Husband, come back to me, she thought, and I will confess.

Impatient drivers honked their horns. Mary Lynn joined them. She hoped Jeremiah would recognize the specific sound of their horn and return to the car.

Listen to me, listen to me, listen to me, she thought as she pounded the steering wheel.

Jeremiah heard their car horn, but only as one note in the symphony of   140 noise playing on the bridge. He walked through that noise, through an ever-increasing amount of noise, until he pushed through a sudden crowd of people and found himself witnessing a suicide.

Illuminated by headlights, the jumper was a white woman, pretty, wearing a sundress and good shoes. Jeremiah could see that much as she stood on the bridge railing, forty feet above the cold water.

He could hear sirens approaching from both sides of the bridge, but they would never make it through the traffic in time to save this woman.

The jumper was screaming somebody's name.

Jeremiah stepped closer, wanting to hear the name, wanting to have that information so that he could use it later. To what use, he didn't know, but he knew that name had value, importance. That name, the owner of that name, was the reason why the jumper stood on the bridge.

"Aaron," she said. The jumper screamed, "Aaron."   145

In the car, Mary Lynn could not see either Jeremiah or the jumper, but she could see dozens of drivers leaving their cars and running ahead.

She was suddenly and impossibly sure that her husband was the reason for this commotion, this emergency. He's dying, thought Mary Lynn, he's dead. This is not what I wanted, she thought, this is not why I cheated on him, this is not what was supposed to happen.

As more drivers left their cars and ran ahead, Mary Lynn dialed 911 on the cell phone and received only a busy signal.

She opened her door and stepped out, placed one foot on the pavement, and stopped.

The jumper did not stop. She turned to look at the crowd watching her.   150 She looked into the anonymous faces, into the maw, and then looked back down at the black water.

Then she jumped.

Jeremiah rushed forward, along with a few others, and peered over the edge of the bridge. One brave man leapt off the bridge in a vain rescue attempt. Jeremiah stopped a redheaded young man from jumping.

"No," said Jeremiah. "It's too cold. You'll die too."

Jeremiah stared down into the black water, looking for the woman who'd jumped and the man who'd jumped after her.

In the car, or rather with one foot still in the car and one foot placed on   155
the pavement outside of the car, Mary Lynn wept. Oh, God, she loved him, sometimes because he was white and often despite his whiteness. In her fear, she found the one truth Sitting Bull never knew: there was at least one white man who could be trusted.

The black water was silent.

Jeremiah stared down into that silence.

"Jesus, Jesus," said a lovely woman next to him. "Who was she? Who was she?"

"I'm never leaving," Jeremiah said.

"What?" asked the lovely woman, quite confused.   160

"My wife," said Jeremiah, strangely joyous. "I'm never leaving her." Ever the scientist and mathematician, Jeremiah knew that his wife was a constant. In his relief, he found the one truth Shakespeare never knew: gravity is overrated.

Jeremiah looked up through the crossbeams above him, as he stared at the black sky, at the clouds that he could not see but knew were there, the invisible clouds that covered the stars. He shouted out his wife's name, shouted it so loud that he could not speak in the morning.

In the car, Mary Lynn pounded the steering wheel. With one foot in the car and one foot out, she honked and honked the horn. She wondered if this was how the world was supposed to end, with everybody trapped on a bridge, with the black water pushing against their foundations.

Out on the bridge, four paramedics arrived far too late. Out of breath, exhausted from running across the bridge with medical gear and stretchers, the paramedics could only join the onlookers at the railing.

A boat, a small boat, a miracle, floated through the black water. They   165
found the man, the would-be rescuer, who had jumped into the water after the young woman, but they could not find her.

Jeremiah pushed through the crowd, as he ran away from the place where the woman had jumped. Jeremiah ran across the bridge until he could see Mary Lynn. She and he loved each other across the distance.

ENGAGING THE TEXT

1. What is the significance of the title "Assimilation" in the context of this story? How do you interpret the "truths" that Mary Lynn and Jeremiah discover at the end of the story? Do you think that Alexie is endorsing assimilation in this story? Why or why not?

2. What is the purpose and effect of the paired cultural references—to Shakespeare and Sitting Bull, the Big Mom Singers and Emily Dickinson— that Alexie includes in the story?

3. What glimpses does Alexie give us of reservation life and of Indians less privileged than Mary Lynn? What do these allusions tell us about her character and motives? What do they suggest about the nature of the "white" culture she is immersed in?

4. Mary Lynn and the narrator make a number of observations about white men—that they are dependable but "neutral ... like Belgium," that they invented the commute, and so forth. What overall portrait of white men emerges from these comments and from the character of Jeremiah? Explain why you think that Alexie is being fair or unfair in his characterization of white men.

5. What attitudes, behavior, and cultural phenomena does Alexie make fun of, and why? What values and ideas does he appear to take seriously? Are these categories mutually exclusive? Why or why not?

EXPLORING CONNECTIONS

6. Review the passages in the story that speak specifically about race. To what extent would Alexie endorse George Fredrickson's (p. 632) assertion that "ethnic hierarchy in a clearly racialized form persists in practice if not in law" in the United States?

7. If Mary Lynn were to list some of the ways that she could be seen as "white," as Eric Liu does at the beginning of the previous essay (p. 660), what characteristics and details of her life could be included in the list? To what extent is she, like Liu, a citizen of the "Republic of Privilege"? How does Alexie's treatment of the issues of assimilation and class privilege compare to Liu's?

EXTENDING THE CRITICAL CONTEXT

8. Watch a film written and directed by Native American artists (e.g., *Smoke Signals, Skins, The Business of Fancydancing*) and compare it to any recent film that portrays, but was not created by, Indians (e.g., *Pocahontas, Windtalkers*). What differences, if any, do you see in the way the films depict Indian/white cultures and relationships?

Transracial America Sells

LEON E. WYNTER

What do Queen Latifah, Home Depot, and white teens with dreadlocks have in common? According to Leon E. Wynter, they represent a phenomenon he calls "transracial America." The United States has always been more multi-ethnic and multiracial than the whitebread image it cultivated as an ideal. Now, says Wynter, consumer culture has begun to reflect and celebrate this diverse reality: nonwhite actors and celebrities have become mainstream, ethnic fashions and music are freely borrowed, racial categories are redefined. In all this he sees "a vision of the American dream in which we are liberated from the politics of race," with "free-market capitalist democracy" as the engine powering this profound social change. As a longtime columnist for the Wall Street Journal, *Wynter (b. 1952) originated its "Business and Race" feature; he has contributed essays on business, race, and culture to the* New York Times, Washington Post, *and* New York Newsday *and is often heard on National Public Radio.*

Ask yourself a few questions about race and marketing in America. Why is Muhammad Ali, once typecast as an overbearing, anti-American, draft-dodging acolyte of the Nation of Islam, now a national treasure and goldplated name that major marketers would kill to rent? Why has his one-time nemesis George Foreman, once the embodiment of a crude bone-crushing black man, been reinvented as the guy everyone trusts for everything from auto repair to home appliance choices? How is it that in commercials for Chevrolet cars, the wheels with the most red-white-and-blue product image in the industry, you're almost guaranteed to see non-whites included behind the wheel? Why have most successful action movies since the early 1990s relied on a black-white buddy relationship (or two) near the center of the plot? Why are nonwhite performers like actress Halle Berry, singer/actress Jennifer Lopez, singer Beyoncé Knowles, and Brandy fronting cosmetics commercials that until recently featured only "natural" (read: white) blonds? Why do more openly multiracial performers and athletes—from Mariah Carey to Tiger Woods to Yankee Derek Jeter to Halle Berry to Jimmy Smits—seem to be on fast tracks to a kind of superstardom once reserved only for "pure" whites? And how on earth do you explain Dennis Rodman and RuPaul getting away with their race- *and* gender-bending commercial success?

The simplest answer is that Transracial America[1] sells. Transracial America, in the marketplace, is a vision of the American dream in which we are liberated from the politics of race to openly embrace any style, cultural trope, or image of beauty that attracts us regardless of its origin. Executing the Transracial American vision requires retrofitting and reinventing the mythologies of what Lind calls Euro-America[2] to reflect a new reality. Or rather, Transracial American marketing revises the myths of American identity to reflect what was always real. So, for example, the Übermensch,[3] blue-collar man delivering the new half-ton Chevy pickup truck to some industrial site in a shower of welding sparks and testosterone, in the 2000 season of that commercial series, is a strapping African-American who stirs the collective-unconscious memory of John Henry, the original steel-driving black man of nineteenth-century American legend.

The selling of Transracial America is really the result of thousands of discrete and seemingly unconnected creative decisions in casting, marketing, and advertising. Individually they include mixing races in casting; using blues, gospel, salsa, or merengue as an aural bed; depicting a nonwhite as the prototypical consumer or "star" of a commercial; and expanding the use of nonwhite celebrity icons. But taken together, these individual decisions represent more than a fashion or even a trend. They add up to a paradigm shift in mainstream marketing based on a new principle in global marketing: Blackness (or nonwhiteness) now suffers less and less of a discount in the marketplace, while whiteness commands less and less of a premium.

In more and more commercial media, from print ads to movies to television shows and especially television ads, the stigma attached to people and cultures of color that once kept nonwhites out of the commercial mainstream is in permanent decline. The new transracial marketing principle rests in part on demographic necessities. The incomes and rates of consumption in most categories of goods and services are growing much faster for racial minorities than for whites, and marketers now routinely respond to that fact. Demographic reality has created a direct economic incentive to broaden the racial and ethnic appeal of mainstream product advertising and entertainment. . . . But the imperative pushing transracial marketing also flows from deeper truths about the place of race in American identity that are now bubbling to the surface. There's a little bit of a black Cinderella in all of us, because the story of innocence abused and faith rewarded is both the quintessential minority experience in America and an archetype of American identity. As a culture, we've been searching for a way to embrace our inner John Henrys for more than a hundred years. Nonwhiteness,

---

[1] In the sense of the term coined by Michael Lind in *The Next American Nation* (New York: Free Press, 1995). [Notes are author's, except 3–5, 8, 11–12, 14–15, and 17.]

[2] Ibid.

[3] *Übermensch:* Superman (German).

especially blackness, bears a historical-cultural taboo, but as with all forbidden fruit, the taboo has always been alloyed with allure. As this taboo melts in the marketplace, whether as a reflection of social reality or in spite of it, the underlying energy of desire associated with racial prohibition is being liberated for exploitation by commercial marketers.

As the impediment of color declines, so does the premium on whiteness. To be sure, whites in general and blonds in particular still "have more fun" in these commercial spaces, and they still tend to predominate. But they no longer rule by divine right, as they did as recently as the early 1980s; their undisputed hegemony is over. For example, a hair-color campaign with the tag line "Is it true blonds have more fun?" would be inconceivable today, unless perhaps it took care to include black, Latina, and Asian "blonds," too. In today's market whites share more and more foreground space with nonwhite others. Their very whiteness is subtly being redefined. Their lips are fuller (see Calista Flockhart in *Ally McBeal*) and so are their behinds (see singer Britney Spears and actress Jeri Ryan). The shapes of their eyes, noses, and cheekbones are expanding in range to reflect the genetic inheritances of models and icons of Hispanic and Middle Eastern descent who effectively "pass" for white, like supermodel Christy Turlington, singer Ricky Martin, and most unavoidably Jennifer Lopez. They channel Aretha Franklin, like the little white girl Hallie Eisenberg in the hot-selling 1999 Pepsi campaign. In the 2001 version, little white Hallie morphs into big black (or half-black) Halle Berry, all to the delight and amazement of a young black male. In the wake of her very public affair with Dennis Rodman, Madonna lost no whiteness premium, though many questioned her taste, because Madonna, the prototypical race-bending pop icon of the 1980s, had very little whiteness to lose.

High-status fictional characters, real-life role models, and icons of the month, year, or decade don't have to be exclusively white anymore: among these newly colorful characters are police detectives, lawyers, judges, doctors, military officers, fashion models, and especially computer geeks. It's not about altruism, it's about television ratings and box-office take. My favorite daily read on the transracial marketing paradigm is what I call the Macy's-Bloomingdale's Index, an unofficial survey you can take every day in the *New York Times*. Now New York, our teachers always warned us, is not America. It's only the preeminent center of finance, fashion, publishing, print and broadcast news, and fine and performing arts. The city gets its spirit from a polyglot[4] people whose distinct cultural, racial, and ethnic backgrounds are somehow ultimately subsumed by a larger identity, "New Yorker," that supersedes "American." New Yorkers, the mythology holds, are not real Americans in the cultural sense. We are individually too "ethnic," too yellow, brown, or black, to be average Americans. Even our hair comes in too many combinations of colors, textures, and lengths. Collec-

[4]*polyglot:* Speaking many languages; multilingual.

tively we need too many spices in our food, too many beats per second in our music, and too many sources of stimulation in our lifestyles to be genuine "heartland" Americans.

But while New York may not seem to be America, America, it seems, is always becoming New York (when it's not becoming southern California). The *New York Times* is America's paper of record for news, for editorial copy, and for public notice through its advertising. It is far from infallible or comprehensive in either capacity, and television is still the primary source of news and information for most Americans. But the paper published in Times Square (the address itself is as good a proxy for ground zero[5] in global pop culture as it gets) is agreed upon by people and institutions of influence as the single most important arbiter of mainstream culture. Most national and global media take the *Times* as a baseline for what is important, relevant, and agenda setting on a given day. And as the reporters, editors, producers, bankers, and brokers of the world turn its broadsheet pages, the display advertising in the *Times* becomes received wisdom in their minds.

As recently as the early 1980s, images of people of color were so few and far between in *Times* ads that none could be counted for months at a time.[6] Marketers, particularly fashion retailers whose ads were most likely to use pictures or illustrations of people, clearly saw no need to represent the real New York mixture of races and ethnicities to America, to the world, or even to the New Yorkers who were the core of the *Times's* circulation.

In an admittedly unscientific marking of the transracial tide, let's skim the *Times's* display ads during 1999. Leave aside the entertainment and arts sections for the moment, because nonwhites are already likely to appear in ads for movies, records, and live performances.[7] Entertainment and lifestyle sections of the paper are also skewed toward the preferences of younger readers, who are a special case when it comes to race. Skip too the (admittedly few) ads for packaged goods and electronic gadgets that show people with the products, because they are likely to deliberately reflect the demographics of the target consumer. (It should surprise no one when Pampers ads feature black or Hispanic babies and mothers.) And hold consideration of the business section ads until a little later in this chapter.

Let's just focus on what historically has been the "whitest only" category of advertising in America's most influential paper: the fashion ads that run on the high-priced pages near the front of the A section and on the expensive leaves of the Sunday magazine. They are key barometers for the

10

---

[5]*ground zero:* The center or origin of rapid or intense activity or change.

[6]A sampling of thirteen issues of the *Times* between November 1979 and December 1980 found just five images of color in display advertising in all sections excluding entertainment (movie, music, and performance ads). Interestingly, three of the five were media celebrities — television journalists Ed Bradley and Lem Tucker and then–Yankee star Reggie Jackson — and all appeared in the same July 14, 1980, issue.

[7]That is, nonwhites are already represented in ads for movies, music, theater, and live performance in New York in proportion to their share of the U.S. population.

mainstreaming of color because unlike ads for, say, motor oil, personal computers, or laundry detergent, ads for fashion apparel, accessories, and cosmetics represent objects of aspiration and desire for all segments of adult society. Women, whether they are file clerks, lawyers, restaurant servers, editors, or pampered suburban homemakers all dream themselves into the shifts and sweaters and scarves in a Saks Fifth Avenue ad. Men with dress-white shirt-sleeves, grease under their nails, or sweat under their blue-collar uniforms will linger on the feminine forms—especially those modeling bathing suits or lingerie—for their own fantasy pleasures as well as for cues as to what is desirable in a high-status gift for a wife, daughter, or sweetheart.

Thumbing through twenty-five days of A and Sunday magazine sections of the *Times* selected at random during April, May, and June 1999, I found people of color prominently represented in classy fashion ads on eighteen days. Most were in full-page ads, mainly in the magazine; many used people of color as the sole image. They ranged from lifestyle-action photographs, the kind that look like stills from a television commercial, to classic fashion illustrations in which the racial characteristics themselves are part physiology and part aesthetic imagination. An example from the lifestyle genre is a double-truck (two consecutive full pages) Bloomingdale's spread for designer khaki shorts. On the left-hand page, four hunky "boy next door" white guys and one dark-brown-skinned African-American lean shoulder to shoulder on one another on a windswept deserted beach in knee-length shorts. The black model's shorts are from the Sean John sportswear line of rapper-mogul Sean "Puffy" Combs, but they look no less preppy than the Kenneth Cole, Nautica, and Tommy Hilfiger styles on either side. On the right-hand page, the clean-shaven, clean-cut studs bare their chests and chiseled stomachs. The full-color ad plays on the razor-sharp contrast among blue sky, white sand, tan shorts, and pink and brown skin. Like metal to a magnet, the viewer's eyes are drawn to the black body in the middle, which is just a bit more strapping and posed full front than the rest, as if he were the anchor keeping the entire scene from blowing away.

In another example, a Sunday magazine full-page ad for a Liz Claiborne sweater uses a black woman, also on a beach, on her belly as if she has just slid into second base headfirst. Her pretty, short-Afro-ed face is tilted up, laughing as if only the devil would care about the sand getting all over the expensive knit. "Get comfortable," it says below her chin. The look typifies the racial transformation of the "all-American" image in fashion marketing. Even cosmetics, long considered to be as racially personal and particular as skin itself, are now sold in general-market television ads using models of different races. "Cinderella" Brandy[8] also represents Procter and Gamble's Cover Girl brand, one of the largest mass-market makeup lines in the United States. Many observers, including journalists who ought to know

---

[8]*"Cinderella" Brandy:* Brandy Norwood played Cinderella in *Rodgers & Hammerstein's Cinderella* (Disney 1997).

better, merely chalk the increasing number of black, Hispanic, and Asian women representing American beauty to demographics and target marketing; that is, they're there to sell products to the growing numbers of their own kind in the marketplace. Wrong. Nonwhite "Cover Girls," are very much on display in general market (read: predominantly white readership) magazines like *Glamour, Seventeen,* or *Cosmopolitan,* as well as in minority-targeted books like *Essence.* Even I was stunned to see Queen Latifah, a beautiful but somewhat plus-size black woman, back to back with white country superstar Faith Hill on the back page of the February 2002 *Cosmopolitan.* The Cover Girls were selling foundation, just different shades of beautiful skin.

"What is considered 'all-American' has changed," said Kimberly Stewart, a spokesperson for Cover Girl cosmetics in a 1996 interview. "All-American now means everybody; the most all-American brand is the most inclusive brand," not the whitest one anymore. What was socially unthinkable as recently as 1980 is now economically inescapable: "Black lips can sell lipstick to white women," Stewart said.

A 1997 study of race and marketing trends found minorities depicted in more than 25 percent of ads in the thirteen most popular mass-circulation magazines that had people in them at all.[9] The survey, based on a one-month sampling, found that automobile ads had the highest use, with minorities depicted in 19 percent of *all* the car ads. (Bear in mind that some 45 percent of the ads do not depict people at all.)

What goes for print fashion ads goes double for general-market televi-   15
sion advertising, because unlike niche-targeted magazines like *Vogue, Essence,* and *Vanity Fair,* network television spots generally aim for a broad cross-section of the entire market. It's hard to name a category of product pushed on television today that doesn't prominently include minority actors or celebrity endorsers. From the high-profile Michael Jordan multiproduct marketing machine that was at its height before his second retirement (Gatorade, Nike, MCI), to the pushy black woman in the Phillips' Milk of Magnesia commercials, to the hot salsa-dancing Latinos in a popular 1999 Visa card campaign, to that incongruously mixed group of apparently black, Hispanic, Asian, and white folks whooping it up on some country porch with Garth Brooks for Dr. Pepper, people of color are now a fixture in commercials selling most goods and services. According to the Screen Actors Guild, nonwhite actors doubled their share of jobs in TV commercials between 1985 and 1994.[10] Black, Hispanic, and Asian actors got 21 percent of all commercial jobs in 1995, compared with 10.8 percent in 1985. Of these jobs, African-Americans filled more than half the roles in 1995, or

---

[9]Minority Markets Alert, *Mass Circulation Magazine Ads Reflect Minority Population, Lifestyle Shifts* (New York: EPM Communications, March 1997).

[10]Screen Actors Guild surveys of television, theatrical, and commercial casting, 1996 and 1998.

12 percent of all roles. Twenty-one percent is not quite parity—the three groups constituted about 26 percent of the population in 1995—but it's close, and the direction of the trend is unambiguous.

"It's not that the mainstream is being replaced by multiracialism. The mainstream is becoming multiracial," says Bill Katz.[11] . . .

Advertising is created in a decidedly nonpolitical process, experts say. The transracial vision has acquired an aspirational value in the broad market not because it's politically correct but because it's how America wants to see itself: as a unified multiracial culture. That's why blues music, for example, in all its variations, is now so ubiquitous in commercials as a sound track for the American dream. B. B. King and his talking blues guitar Lucille have plugged McDonald's hamburgers. In 1996 Reebok teamed bluesman Buddy Guy with Chicago White Sox slugger Frank "The Big Hurt" Thomas to confess the hitter's career heartbreaks along the way to stardom. The punch line: "If the blues don't kill you, brother, it'll make you mighty mighty mad." A Pepsi campaign that same year featured John Lee Hooker.

Now in the real world between 1989 and 1996, the number of blues festivals and clubs actually doubled and *Billboard* established a separate blues chart to track booming sales. Yet Reebok insisted its move had nothing to do with hitching its mainstream product to the up-trend in blues consumption. Reebok may have come to the conclusion honestly, said Bill Ferris, former chairman of the National Endowment for the Humanities under President Clinton and longtime director of the Center for the Study of Southern Culture at the University of Mississippi, because the rise of the blues in marketing is more a case of the trend overtaking the mainstream than the other way around.

Quite simply, Ferris told me, the blues sells products to the mass of consumers who will never buy a blues album or go to a blues club, because it unifies Americans at a gut cultural level.

In a way, it's a quest by America to discover its own roots, to find meaning in their lives at a time when such meaning is hard to locate. It

[11]*Bill Katz:* President and CEO of BBDO New York, a large advertising agency.

goes back to Huck and Jim on the raft, the attempt by white America to try to bridge the eternal divide on race. For many whites the division is a tragedy, something we seek to reach out and touch to change. Blues is one way that happens.

Transracial sells in advertising because, with the triumph of big-box re-   20
tail chains coast to coast, that's how people buy. The arrival of a "Big K" Kmart or Home Depot or Wal-Mart in an area instantly offsets, to some degree, decades of local residential racial segregation, at least on weekend afternoons, because the patronage area of the typical gigantic store crosses most neighborhood boundaries, drawing clientele from a range of races and income groups. Older chains have increased their size and retrofitted their images where necessary to compete. Brand-new chains like Old Navy have successfully burst onto the market with a quirky kind of transracial populism built in. As writer Cynthia Joyce discovered:

> Old Navy store displays announce that it's the '50s all over again — but this time around, both American patriots and their one-time proletarian adversaries are united in a populist rhetoric of low-cost fashion. Big old American cars are incorporated into merchandise displays; star-spangled nail polish comes in red white and blue. . . .
>
> Old Navy brand allegiance is [a] classic case study in what historians call an invented tradition. The print ads . . . suggest that the three-year-old chain is actually an old American institution in the midst of a renaissance. But however confusing the messages of the chain's ad campaigns may be, Old Navy does fill a genuine market niche.
>
> The populist rhetoric, it turns out, isn't just rhetoric — Old Navy is where the locals shop. It seems like the only time you are likely to encounter a socioeconomically diverse group of people is either at the Department of Motor Vehicles or in the self-consciously prole[12] precincts of Old Navy. The last time I tried on a pair of jeans in Old Navy's co-ed dressing room, I emerged to find a heated button-fly vs. zipper debate taking place among the young Asian salesgirl, a middle-aged black man, and a Mexican mother of three. And as I examined my prospective purchase in the three-panel mirror, each of them freely offered their opinion of the fit. These aren't the most momentous breakthroughs in democratic culture, to be sure. But Old Navy's success has reversed a long-standing disdain for anything Middle American.[13]

Or, rather, Old Navy and the rest of the big-box retailers, have given "middle American" a long overdue redefinition to reflect transracial reality.

---

[12]*prole:* short for proletarian.

[13]Cynthia Joyce, "The Strange New Stirrings of Old Navy Nation," *Newsday,* July 12, 1998.

No matter how many times or ways I asked experts to explain exactly how and why Transracial America sells, the answer always boiled down to the belief that Transracial America is real. As BBDO's Katz put it:

> There may be this sociopolitical division [between races and ethnic groups]. They may have these thoughts [of racism, alienation, ethnic chauvinism]. But they are still living the way they are living. Their environment is as it is. The images they see are the images they see, and the malls they go to are the malls they go to.
>
> The reality is that this is the gestalt[14] of society. Advertising is not interested in recognizing the sociopolitical issues. It is only interested in realizing [consumer] reality, the gestalt. It can't affect sociopolitics, it doesn't want to go near it; it avoids it like the plague.

Color in advertising is especially reflective of reality for younger consumers, the so-called Gen-X (born between about 1965 and 1978) and Gen-Next or Echo Boomers (the late children of the baby boomers, born since 1978), because, as with science fiction devotees, it meets their expectation of what's next. One of the most salient psychographic markers of under-thirty-five consumers is their expectation that as they mature they will be immersed in an increasingly multiracial world. Remember those striking ads for Schick razors in which the faces of the shavers magically "morphed" from white to Asian to black and back to white? The goal was to capture the attention of eighteen-to-thirty-five-year-old shavers by combining what were then cutting-edge special effects with the leading edge of the Gen-X worldview, according to Dave McSpadden, who created the long-running ads for the J. Walter Thompson agency in 1993.

> We decided to tap into the mind-set of younger people—how they see the world. . . . In all the casting we had people who were realistic looking, not necessarily the perfect upscale ideal. We wanted to have a range of ethnicities; we thought it was truer to the marketplace and truer to younger people's perception that they are living in a multicultural world. We saw immediate sales growth when we introduced it. There are two things consumers like about it. One is the morphing technique—and as a group the characters seem approachable and likable.

The depth of this transracial perception for younger consumers was brought home for me by a full-page Jordache Jeans ad in 1995 in *Vibe* magazine. A chiseled, chest-naked, blue-black man hoists a very blond bra-clad model off her feet up to his shoulder and peels her prominently labeled jeans from her behind like a banana. She gazes toward the ceiling in near rapture. Flaunting taboo and provoking stereotypes, the ad seemed to break every rule of mass marketing. But Jordache's advertising director, Kaaryn Denig, told me that when it comes to consumers of a certain age, the rules are being changed.

---

[14]*gestalt:* Pattern or system of organization (German).

We've always done sexy images—but it's the first time we've brought
a black person into the imagery. With the youth of today, I think the
walls between the races are breaking down. They've grown up in [an]
atmosphere where everyone is considered equal and interracial dating
is no big deal.

Denig said she did get some calls complaining about the image, but not   25
from people in her target age group. *Their* calls were enthusiastic. "I got a
call from a girl in Utah in her early twenties. She loves the image—wanted
to blow it up and put it on her wall," Denig said. . . .

People of color, primarily blacks and Hispanics, sell well beyond expectations based on social status because of what I call the *heat factor*. Black
and brown skin stands out and warms up any scene before the cameras, especially when it's reflecting the energy of a "down home" black or Latino
cultural style. That's why black actor Cuba Gooding Jr. was seen pushing
white men out of airplanes to launch the new one-calorie cola Pepsi-One in
1998. Or at least that's how it looked to me. "Actually he's not pushing white
people out of an airplane," explained Katz of BBDO, which made the spot.
"He takes the product, throws it out, and induces white people to go after it.
It has nothing to do with race."

Which means the BBDO did not see either Gooding's race or the audience connection to his most recent film roles, which could generally be described as "over the top." But, Katz told me, they did feel Gooding's heat.

> He delivers the spirit, the intensity—he delivers the kind of entertain-
> ment value that you need when you're simply telling people there's a
> new product out there that tastes as good as any regular cola. We
> chose him as a person . . . [for] the energy that comes out. You want to
> watch him. You buy his act. You don't say he's going too far; there's an
> infectious quality to him.

Transracial sells because it is often more efficient to market and promote a unified brand image to consumers of all races than to ignore nonwhites in the general market, as many firms once did, or to create entirely
separate campaigns confined to minority-targeted media. This principle can
hold even for a product line that has been to some extent racially particular,
like cosmetics and beauty products. Lipstick, makeup, eye-color, and hair-
care products, categories once thought to be inherently segregated by race,
are now commonly advertised using models of all races to reach all races. . . .

Commenting on mainstream style in 1994, *New York Times* columnist
Molly O'Neill said that in the 1960s and 1970s she could count on a trip to
the mall in middle-American Columbus, Ohio, to make her feel culturally
smug and superior to the "whitebread crossroads of the status quo," where
the arc of American cultural diversity was neatly bracketed by "the fashionable Lazarus department store at one end . . . to the sensible Sears,
Roebuck at the other.

So imagine my discomfort seeing a young woman with a blond head full of dreadlocks selling cosmetics at a mall in Columbus recently. Today you don't know where you stand. Hip-hop has unbalanced the cultural compass. When white girls wear dreadlocks and black girls go blond, another distinction is being teased apart, hair by hair.

O'Neill went on to call this fashion transracialism a pose, a fad that while temporary and superficial was not "hopeless," since it was "weaving together formerly polarized segments of society." But . . . transracial style has proven to be more than a passing fancy to the industry. O'Neill only skimmed the truth in crediting hip-hop with weaving the races together. Hip-hop and the larger trends in American popular culture today do not actually weave black, white, Hispanic, Asian, and other adherents together. . . . Rather, the success of the transracial marketing style reveals the cultural stitching across race and ethnic lines that already existed. The slave/colored/Negro/black servant/blues shouter/rock-and-roll singer/Rastafarian princess has always lurked inside the stereotyped Ohio blond girl of O'Neill's imagination, whether she knew it or not, and Miss Anne's[15] sense of blond femininity-as-privilege has always been part of the American black girl. In transracial marketing America, the distinctions between so-called races are not just being teased; they're being humiliated by history. As Michael Lind declared in *The Next American Nation:*

> We Americans . . . are defined by a common language and culture; and as long as these unite us, we will constitute an ethnocultural nation, no matter what the composition of our gene pool, no matter what the political entity in which our people reside, or what its ultimate borders might be. There was an American cultural nation on the Atlantic seaboard before there was a republic called the United States; and, we may hope, there will be a flourishing American cultural nation in its North American homeland when the U.S. Constitution has long been scrapped or amended beyond recognition.[16]

Black blonds and white dreadlocks. All-American mulattoes. Black Cinderella and her white sisters. Dr. Dolittle in an Afro. White men who can jump, and hump Latinas, too. The part-Asian Superman and the little white girl channeling Aretha Franklin. Bill Cosby as Father Knows Best. Transracial drag queens riding into a sleepy middle-American town like the Earp brothers[17] and cleaning up its contradictions. A syndicated television judiciary where white petitioners volunteer to let black judges rule. All these things, and permutations to come that we can't even imagine, sell, and each dollar of profit accrues to the proof of Lind's theory of American identity

[15]*Miss Anne:* A white woman (slang); the term alludes to the relationship of mistress and servant/slave, and thus connotes a white woman with an air of entitlement.

[16]Lind, *Next American Nation*, 259–60.

[17]*Earp brothers:* Old West lawmen best known for their role in the gunfight at the O.K. Corral in Tombstone, Arizona, in 1881.

and prediction of a transracial American ethnicity freeing itself from the shackles of centuries-old political constructions of race. As he puts it:

> [T]he overwhelming majority of Americans—whatever their arbitrarily defined "race"—already belong, not just to a single citizenry, but to a single people, a single cultural nation, defined by common language, folkways, memories, and mores. Centuries of white supremacy have not prevented the formulation of a transracial American culture blending elements of the cultures of many European, African, American Indian, Latin American and Asian peoples with innovations unique to North America. Nor were white supremacist laws against miscegenation able to prevent a substantial degree of racial amalgamation, paralleling the fusion of cultures.[18]

The manifestation of Transracial American identity in the marketplace is perhaps the most unheralded consequence of the triumph of free-market capitalist democracy at the dawn of the twenty-first century. If Lind is right, as I believe he is, then the basis for the transracial commercial mainstream has always been in place, but its emergence was something less than inevitable. It still required a critical mass of competition for the imagination of consumers, a competition too brisk to be fettered by the past. No one will ever be able to mark the exact point on the time line where Transracial America became an absolute commercial reality, says Katz of BBDO. It's more like a successive revelation of a truth that, with each application in the marketplace, becomes a self-fulfilling prophecy. Katz describes a simple, powerful circular logic connecting the transracial imperative at work in advertising and the reality of who Americans are and how we live:

> It wouldn't be done if it weren't true. And if it weren't true, it wouldn't work. And if it didn't work, it wouldn't be done.

ENGAGING THE TEXT

1. What is "transracial America," according to Wynter? To what extent is it a reality in his view, and to what extent is it simply a desirable image used as a marketing tool?
2. Examine Wynter's use of the "Macy's-Bloomingdale's Index" (para. 6): Does he make a convincing case that the Index reflects mainstream American attitudes? Why or why not?
3. What reasons does Wynter offer to explain the appeal of transracial advertising (for instance, why does he believe that the blues "sell")? What kinds of evidence does he present to support each claim? Which parts of his analysis seem more compelling, which seem weaker, and why?
4. Debate Wynter's assertion that "big-box" chain stores like Wal-Mart and Home Depot offer an antidote to neighborhood segregation.

[18]Ibid., 260.

5. Wynter's analysis often plays with stereotypes: for example, he asserts that white Americans long to get in touch with their "inner John Henrys" (para. 4), that black women harbor "Miss Anne's sense of blond femininity-as-privilege" (para. 29), and that nonwhite models create a "heat factor" in ads (para. 25). Do you think that such arguments perpetuate stereotypes, undercut them, or both? Explain your reasoning.

EXPLORING CONNECTIONS

6. Write an imaginary letter to Wynter from Leonard Steinhorn and Barbara Diggs-Brown (p. 646) in which they discuss their research on "virtual integration" and comment on Wynter's concept of a transracial America.
7. Do you think that cultural borrowing and blending is likely to increase, decrease, or have no impact on the attitude of indifference to "otherness" discussed by Paul L. Wachtel (p. 613)? What evidence supports your prediction?
8. Wynter contends that transracial marketing is socially beneficial—that it not only reflects America's diversity but also helps to promote integration and racial harmony. Compare this vision of marketing and consumer culture to those of Benjamin Barber (p. 283), Jean Kilbourne (p. 455), Michael A. Messner (p. 477), Tim Kasser (p. 364), and cartoonist Lalo Alcarza (p. 694). Do you think that corporate advertising is more harmful than beneficial or vice versa? Why?

EXTENDING THE CRITICAL CONTEXT

9. Analyze the racial/cultural imagery in the current issue of a mainstream magazine or on your favorite TV show: How much evidence do you find of the transracial America that Wynter describes?
10. Write a journal entry or essay examining the extent to which you personally experience "transracial America" in your daily life. What are the ethnic or cultural origins of the music you listen to? Do you wear clothing, jewelry, makeup, or a hairstyle associated with a racial group other than your own? Who are your heroes and role models? Who do you socialize with? How do you define your own racial or ethnic heritage? To what extent do you think your experience represents the "mainstream"?

Child of the Americas
AURORA LEVINS MORALES

This poem concentrates on the positive aspects of a multicultural heritage, as Morales celebrates her uniqueness, her diversity, and her wholeness. It's an up-to-date and sophisticated reinterpretation of the melting pot myth. As this autobiographical poem states, Aurora Levins Morales (b. 1954) was the child of a Puerto Rican mother and a Jewish father. She moved to the United States when she was thirteen and now writes, performs, and teaches in the San Francisco Bay Area. "Child of the Americas" is from the collection Getting Home Alive *(1986), which she coauthored with her mother, Rosario Morales. Her mother has written that the book "began in long, budget-breaking telephone calls stretched across the width of this country . . . the phone line strung between us like a 3,000-mile umbilical cord from navel to navel, mine to hers, hers to mine, each of us mother and daughter by turns, feeding each other the substance of our dreams."* Morales has taught Jewish studies and women's studies at Berkeley and is a history educator and program historian for the Latino History Project at the Oakland Museum of California. She is the author of* Remedios: Stories of Earth and Iron from the History of Puertorriqueñas *(1998) and* Medicine Stories: History, Culture, and the Politics of Integrity *(1998).*

I am a child of the Americas,
a light-skinned mestiza of the Caribbean,
a child of many diaspora,[1] born into this continent at a crossroads.

I am a U.S. Puerto Rican Jew,
a product of the ghettos of New York I have never known.   5
An immigrant and the daughter and granddaughter of immigrants.
I speak English with passion: it's the tongue of my consciousness,
a flashing knife blade of crystal, my tool, my craft.

I am Caribeña,[2] island grown. Spanish is in my flesh,
ripples from my tongue, lodges in my hips: 10
the language of garlic and mangoes,

---

[1]*diaspora:* Scattered colonies. The word originally referred to Jews scattered outside Palestine after the Babylonian exile; it is now used to refer to African and other peoples scattered around the world.
[2]*Caribeña:* Caribbean woman.

the singing in my poetry, the flying gestures of my hands.
I am of Latinoamerica, rooted in the history of my continent:
I speak from that body.

I am not african. Africa is in me, but I cannot return.   15
I am not taína.³ Taíno is in me, but there is no way back.
I am not european. Europe lives in me, but I have no home there.

I am new. History made me. My first language was spanglish.⁴
I was born at the crossroads
and I am whole.   20

ENGAGING THE TEXT

1. Does this poem do more to challenge or to promote the myth of the melting pot? Explain.
2. Why does the poet list elements of her background that she scarcely knows ("the ghettos of New York" and Taíno)? How can they be part of her?
3. How do you interpret the last stanza? Rephrase its messages in more complete, more explicit statements.

EXPLORING CONNECTIONS

4. What similarities and differences do you see between Morales's celebration of her diverse heritage and Leon E. Wynter's vision of "transracial America" (p. 688)?
5. Many of the writers in this book express a sense of internal fragmentation or cultural conflict. How does the speaker of this poem avoid the feeling of cultural schizophrenia? How does her response compare to those of Richard Rodriguez (p. 214), Judith Ortiz Cofer (p. 433), Paula Gunn Allen (p. 443), and Eric Liu (p. 660)? Which responses do you find most appealing or most realistic, and why?

EXTENDING THE CRITICAL CONTEXT

6. Write your own version of "Child of the Americas," following Morales's structure but substituting ideas and images from your own heritage. Read it to the class.

---

³*taína:* Describing the Taíno, an aboriginal people of the Greater Antilles and Bahamas.
⁴*spanglish:* Spanish and English combined.

6

Land of Liberty

*American Mythology
in a "New World Order"*

The events of September 11, 2001, came as a shock to most Americans. As a nation, we were stunned by the violence of the assaults on New York's World Trade Center and the Pentagon, and appalled by the senseless loss of life. But what confounded so many Americans was the fact that we, as a nation, could inspire the kind of insane rage that motivated our attackers. As observers across the country were quick to point out, America lost its innocence on 9/11: as if overnight we found ourselves the object of hatred in a world teeming with potential enemies.

The idea of our essential "innocence" in relation to other nations is a central feature of America's cultural mythology. It has played an important role in shaping our national identity, and it is inextricably bound up with another powerful cultural myth—the notion of American freedom. Even before Columbus sailed for India in 1492, Europeans had long idealized the mythic lands they believed lay beyond the western horizon. In the Classical era, Greeks and Romans had envisioned a utopian realm to the west inhabited by "fabulous races" unlike any other people in the known world. Trying to describe the promise of this uncharted land, the poet and orator Horace encouraged his fellow Romans to

> See, see before us the distant glow,
> Through the thin dawn-mists of the West,
> Rich sunlit plains and hilltops gemmed with snow,
> The islands of the Blest!

To European minds straining to imagine what eyes could not see, the world beyond the curve of the Atlantic was an enchanted place. It was Atlantis, Avalon, the Garden of the Hesperides, the Seven Cities of Antillia, the New Eden, the promised land of Canaan. It was Elysium, the "happy land," where the weather was always gentle and people lived forever "untouched by sorrow." It was Eldorado, the mythic city where the streets were paved with gold, and precious jewels littered the earth like stones.

The Puritans who founded Plymouth Plantation in 1620 spiritualized this mythic vision of the meaning of the New World. Puritan fantasies of America were shaped by the stories that dominated the Protestant imagination—the legends of suffering and redemption related in the Bible. Persecuted by what they saw as a corrupt and authoritarian church in Europe, the Pilgrims viewed America through Old Testament stories of exile, enslavement, and salvation. They came to see themselves as the new "children of Israel," a "chosen people" destined to embark on an "errand in the wilderness" in search of the New Jerusalem, a new Promised Land. From the start, European colonizers were convinced that America was a place apart, a land that was sanctified by God and preordained to fulfill a special destiny in the history of the world. Colonial poets Philip Freneau and Hugh Brackenridge celebrated this biblical vision of America's destiny in their "Poem on the Rising Glory of America":

A new Jerusalem, sent down from heaven
Shall grace our happy earth. . . .
Paradise anew
Shall flourish, by no second Adam lost . . .
Another Canaan shall excel the old . . .

In the space of two generations, the Puritan fantasy of America as the cradle of the world's spiritual rebirth would collapse into the mass hysteria of the Salem witch trials and genocidal warfare against the same Native Americans who helped the original Pilgrims survive their first winter. But the Puritan contribution to America's cultural mythology would live on. From the founding of the Massachusetts Bay Colony to the present day, America has seen itself as a nation with a special role to play on the stage of world history. The New World has long dreamed itself the home of the "New Adam," a new kind of human being, capable of rising above the sins and weaknesses of the old "fallen" world of Europe. Growing directly from the Puritan religious vision of the New World as a place of personal rebirth, this belief in America's "exceptionalism" would become one of the central tenets in our national ideology.

By 1776, the Puritan vision of American exceptionalism had been thoroughly secularized. Americans no longer expected to create, in literal terms, a "New Jerusalem" on earth, but we hadn't given up on the idea that America itself was a place with a special meaning and destiny in the world. For the Founders of the Republic, freedom is what made America special, and the love of freedom is what distinguished America from all previous civilizations. Writing in 1769, the French immigrant farmer and social observer J. Hector St. John Crèvecoeur celebrated this special commitment to the spirit of liberty in his *Letters from an American Farmer*. American society, according to Crèvecoeur, was difficult to describe because it differed so radically from the authoritarian societies of Europe:

> It is not composed, as in Europe, of great lords, who possess every thing, and of a herd of people who have nothing. Here are no aristocratical families, no courts, no kings, no bishops, no ecclesiastical dominion, no invincible power. . . . The rich and the poor are not so far removed from each other as they are in Europe. . . .We have no princes, for whom we toil, starve, and bleed: we are the most perfect society now existing in the world. Here man is free as he ought to be. . . .

This vision of a new race of free human beings, liberated from the shackles of government, aristocracy, and religious domination, fueled the American Revolution. It found expression in the Declaration of Independence, which proclaims "that all men are created equal, that they are endowed by their Creator with certain unalienable Rights, that among these are Life, Liberty, and the pursuit of Happiness." And it is similarly enshrined in the Constitution—both in the preamble which asserts that the

Constitution itself was framed in order "to secure the blessings of liberty to ourselves and our posterity" and, of course, in the Bill of Rights.

Little wonder then that Americans were shocked by 9/11. After all, who would lash out against the country that symbolizes liberty and freedom to the rest of the world? And little wonder, too, that the president of the United States would respond to 9/11 by invoking the myth of freedom. As President Bush reminded us in his 2002 State of the Union address, America is synonymous with the ideal of liberty, and Americans, unlike the terrorists who attacked us, are a proud and free people:

> Our enemies send other people's children on missions of suicide and murder. They embrace tyranny and death as a cause and a creed. We stand for a different choice, made long ago, on the day of our founding. We affirm it again today. We choose freedom and the dignity of every life.
>
> Steadfast in our purpose, we now press on. We have known freedom's price. We have shown freedom's power. And in this great conflict, my fellow Americans, we will see freedom's victory.

From the perspective of American mythology, the events of 9/11 may be tragic and shocking, but they are easily explained. The United States stands for freedom in the world, and because we're a good and free people we inspire hatred among those who are either "evil," as the president has put it, or so backward as to oppose civilization's inevitable march toward liberty. Seen in this light, we're a peace-loving nation, whose only interest is to spread the gospel of democracy and respect for human rights. The problem, of course, is that a good deal of American history seems to challenge this glowing self-estimate. The principles of "Life, Liberty, and the pursuit of Happiness" that we as a nation extolled in the Declaration of Independence clearly didn't apply to the Native Americans who were systematically deprived of all three of these benefits during the first three hundred years of the American experiment. Nor did the rights guaranteed under the Constitution extend to all Americans. Indeed, the Constitution itself didn't ban the practice of slavery until the Fourteenth Amendment was adopted at the end of the Civil War, and another century would pass before equal treatment under the law was extended to African Americans during the civil rights movement of the 1960s.

Unfortunately, the American record on freedom abroad is even more problematic. Yes, the United States supported the cause of world freedom in World Wars I and II, but did we make the world a safer and more democratic place by allying ourselves with well-known tyrants like Francisco Franco in Spain, Ferdinand Marcos in the Philippines, Augusto Pinochet in Chili, Reza Shah Pahlavi in Iran, Roberto D'Aubuisson in El Salvador, and Mohamed Suharto in Indonesia? Moreover, as critics of American foreign policy have repeatedly pointed out, we've made a habit of demonizing tyrants who were once ardent American allies. After all, we trained Manuel

Noriega at our CIA-sponsored School of the Americas and helped him rise to power in Panama before deciding that he represented such a threat to liberty that he had to be driven by force from his country. In similar fashion, before we declared Iraq's Saddam Hussein an enemy of democratic values, we provided him and his Baathist followers both monetary and military assistance in abundance. Most astonishingly, we were even once the principal ally of Osama bin Laden — back in the days when the U.S. government portrayed him as a freedom fighter, and not as the embodiment of evil.

And since 9/11, our relation to the principle of liberty has become increasingly ambiguous, as well. As we send U.S. troops off to fight the enemies of freedom abroad, our leaders have begun to restrict American liberties at home. Arab Americans, Arab immigrants, and anyone who looks even vaguely "Middle Eastern" are now fair game at American airports as we embrace a campaign of ethnic profiling that echoes the anti-Japanese excesses of World War II. In the name of "homeland security" we've passed legislation that threatens to undermine the most fundamental of our civil liberties, including the right to privacy, the right of free speech, and the right to due process. It's even become acceptable today to debate whether torture or state-sponsored assassination are reasonable weapons in the war against terror.

Perhaps even more amazing is the fact that little more than two centuries after winning our own freedom from the British Empire, the prospect of an "American Empire" has moved to the forefront of U.S. foreign policy. The original founders of the United States took pains to warn against the temptations of empire building. In his "Farewell Address of 1797," George Washington cautioned his countrymen against becoming enmeshed in the intrigues and entanglements of foreign governments. In 1812, John Quincy Adams echoed Washington when he warned that if America were to "become the dictatress of the world, she would be no longer the ruler of her own spirit." Yet today the prospect of an American empire is no longer unthinkable. In an age of unilateral invasions, preemptive first strikes, regime change, and U.S.-sponsored "nation building," the idea that America might someday rule the world seems more and more like a real possibility.

But can the United States dominate world affairs and still lay claim to innocence? Can we pursue a policy of empire building and still take pride in the fact that we represent freedom to the rest of the world? These are just a few of the questions you'll encounter in this chapter. Our exploration of America's meaning in the new world order begins with two examples of the myth of freedom at work in the service of U.S. foreign policy. Written on the brink of America's war with Spain in 1898, Albert J. Beveridge's "The March of the Flag" is one of the best examples of modern American colonialist thinking. Published a little more than a century later, Dinesh D'Souza's "America the Beautiful" demonstrates just how powerful the ideology of American freedom continues to be as a justification for our attitudes toward the rest of the world. The next four selections challenge the notion of American innocence. In "The Oblivious Empire," journalist Mark Hertsgaard offers a critical perspective on why "America Fascinates and Infuriates the World" as he explores the contradictions of recent U.S. foreign relations. Joel Andreas's graphic exposé "The War on Terrorism" complements Hertsgaard by raising questions about how the United States has responded to the events of 9/11 and how these responses relate to the role we've played in the Middle East. In her "Poem for Benjamin Franklin" veteran activist June Jordan discovers a direct connection between the racist and sexist violence she sees in American society and the kind of violence that we as a nation have inflicted on the "others" around us. Novelist Walter Mosley rounds off this section by arguing that because of their experience with racism at home, African Americans are particularly well-prepared to serve as America's diplomats to the rest of the world during these difficult times.

The visual portfolio that follows offers you the chance to explore images that comment on the myth of freedom and America's meaning in the world. These images challenge some of our most deeply held assumptions about the way America is perceived by peoples in other nations. Next, you'll find a pair of essays on the worldwide impact of American popular culture. Michael Medved's "That's Entertainment? Hollywood's Contribution to Anti-Americanism Abroad" argues that the movie industry is responsible for the contempt that much of the world feels toward America today. Todd Gitlin offers a more optimistic analysis of the meaning of America's "fun" culture in "Under the Sign of Mickey Mouse & Co." The chapter closes with a quartet of readings focusing on the present state of freedom in American society. In her "By Any Means Necessary," Patricia Williams challenges us to think about the ways that the U.S. Patriot Act and other homeland security measures threaten the very liberties they are meant to protect. Civil libertarian Ralph Temple follows by examining how the war against terrorism is normalizing antidemocratic practices like racial profiling. In "Easy in the Harness," attorney Gerry Spence wonders what it means to be free in contemporary America and invites us to assess the depth of our own understanding of personal liberty. The chapter and book conclude with Langston Hughes's impassioned appeal to make America a land that lives up to its finest myths:

> The land that never has been yet —
> And yet must be — the land where *every* man is free.

Sources

George W. Bush, 2002 State of the Union Address, available at www
.whitehouse.gov/news/releases/2002/01/20020129-11.html.
Noam Chomsky, *9-11*. New York: Seven Stories Press, 2002.
J. Hector St. John de Crèvecoeur, *Letters from an American Farmer*. New
York: Dolphin Books, 1961. First published in London, 1782.

Michael Ignatieff, "The American Empire." *New York Times,* January 5, 2003, Section 6, p. 22.

Anne Taylor Fleming, "Aftermath: Innocence Lost; A Tragedy for an Optimistic Land." *New York Times,* September 23, 2001, Section 4, p. 4.

Krishan Kumar, *Utopia and Anti-Utopia in Modern Times.* Oxford: Basil Blackwell, 1987.

Howard Zinn, *A People's History of the United States.* New York: Harper and Row, 1980.

Howard Zinn, *Terrorism and War.* New York: Seven Stories Press, 2002.

BEFORE READING

- Using the picture at the beginning of this chapter as a point of departure, write about how you think America has changed since September 11, 2001. In what ways have American freedoms been restricted since 9/11? How has the threat of terrorism changed the way we see ourselves? How has it changed our way of life?

- Working in small groups, discuss what you think America represents to peoples in other countries. What values, ideas, and attitudes do you think America represents abroad? What misconceptions might people in other lands have about life in the United States? Why?

- Compare notes with your classmates about how well your own education has prepared you to cope with issues like U.S. foreign policy, globalization, and terrorism. How were these topics addressed in your prior educational experience? Test your own international literacy by working in pairs to sketch a rough map of the world with as many countries and capitals filled in as possible. How well do your results compare with those of your fellow students?

The March of the Flag

ALBERT J. BEVERIDGE

On September 16, 1898, during a political rally in Indianapolis, Indiana, a relatively unknown twenty-five-year-old lawyer offered a spirited defense of the United States in relation to the impending Spanish-American War. In "The March of the Flag," Albert Jeremiah Beveridge (1862–1927) argued for America's right to seize and maintain possession of the Philippines—a radical idea for a nation that had, until then, resisted the idea of meddling in the affairs of other countries. Within months, Beveridge's speech sold more than 300,000 copies and was well on its way to becoming one of the most important documents in twentieth-century American foreign policy. Beveridge himself was elected to the U.S. Senate a year later, where he served until 1911. In addition to his career in politics, Beveridge was a trained historian who published biographies of Abraham Lincoln and John Marshall, fourth chief justice of the United States.

It is a noble land that God has given us; a land that can feed and clothe the world; a land whose coastlines would inclose half the countries of Europe; a land set like a sentinel between the two imperial oceans of the globe, a greater England with a nobler destiny.

It is a mighty people that He has planted on this soil; a people sprung from the most masterful blood of history; a people perpetually revitalized by the virile, man-producing working-folk of all the earth; a people imperial by virtue of their power, by right of their institutions, by authority of their Heaven-directed purposes—the propagandists and not the misers of liberty.

It is a glorious history our God has bestowed upon His chosen people; a history heroic with faith in our mission and our future; a history of statesmen who flung the boundaries of the Republic out into unexplored lands and savage wilderness; a history of soldiers who carried the flag across blazing deserts and through the ranks of hostile mountains, even to the gates of sunset; a history of a multiplying people who overran a continent in half a century; a history of prophets who saw the consequences of evils inherited from the past and of martyrs who died to save us from them; a history divinely logical, in the process of whose tremendous reasoning we find ourselves to-day.

Therefore, in this campaign,[1] the question is larger than a party question. It is an American question. It is a world question. Shall the American people continue their march toward the commercial supremacy of the world? Shall free institutions broaden their blessed reign as the children of liberty wax in strength, until the empire of our principles is established over the hearts of all mankind?

Have we no mission to perform, no duty to discharge to our fellowman? 5 Has God endowed us with gifts beyond our deserts and marked us as the people of His peculiar favor, merely to rot in our own selfishness, as men and nations must, who take cowardice for their companion and self for their deity—as China has, as India has, as Egypt has?

Shall we be as the man who had one talent and hid it, or as he who had ten talents and used them until they grew to riches? And shall we reap the reward that waits on our discharge of our high duty; shall we occupy new mar-

[1]*this campaign:* This may refer to the Spanish-American War of 1898.

kets for what our farmers raise, our factories make, our merchants sell—aye, and, please God, new markets for what our ships shall carry?

Hawaii is ours; Porto Rico is to be ours; at the prayer of her people Cuba finally will be ours; in the islands of the East, even to the gates of Asia, coaling stations are to be ours at the very least; the flag of a liberal government is to float over the Philippines, and may it be the banner that Taylor[2] unfurled in Texas and Fremont[3] carried to the coast.

The Opposition tells us that we ought not to govern a people without their consent. I answer, The rule of liberty that all just government derives its authority from the consent of the governed, applies only to those who are capable of self-government. We govern the Indians without their consent, we govern our territories without their consent, we govern our children without their consent. How do they know that our government would be without their consent? Would not the people of the Philippines prefer the just, humane, civilizing government of this Republic to the savage, bloody rule of pillage and extortion from which we have rescued them?

And, regardless of this formula of words made only for enlightened, self-governing people, do we owe no duty to the world? Shall we turn these peoples back to the reeking hands from which we have taken them? Shall we abandon them, with Germany, England, Japan, hungering for them? Shall we save them from those nations, to give them a self-rule of tragedy?

They ask us how we shall govern these new possessions. I answer: Out   10 of local conditions and the necessities of the case methods of government will grow. If England can govern foreign lands, so can America. If Germany can govern foreign lands, so can America. If they can supervise protectorates, so can America. Why is it more difficult to administer Hawaii than New Mexico or California? Both had a savage and an alien population; both were more remote from the seat of government when they came under our dominion than the Philippines are to-day.

Will you say by your vote that American ability to govern has decayed; that a century's experience in self-rule has failed of a result? Will you affirm by your vote that you are an infidel to American power and practical sense? Or will you say that ours is the blood of government; ours the heart of dominion; ours the brain and genius of administration? Will you remember that we do but what our fathers did—we but pitch the tents of liberty farther westward, farther southward—we only continue the march of the flag?

The march of the flag! In 1789 the flag of the Republic waved over 4,000,000 souls in thirteen states, and their savage territory which stretched to the Mississippi, to Canada, to the Floridas. The timid minds of that day

---

[2]*Taylor:* Zachary Taylor (1784–1850), twelfth president of the United States, famous for the role he played in the U.S. war against Mexico (1846–1848) which led to the annexation of Texas and other western states.

[3]*Fremont:* John Charles Frémont (1813–1890), U.S. explorer, soldier, and politician who sparked a revolt against Mexican authorities in California in 1846.

said that no new territory was needed, and, for the hour, they were right. But Jefferson, through whose intellect the centuries marched; Jefferson, who dreamed of Cuba as an American state; Jefferson, the first Imperialist of the Republic—Jefferson acquired that imperial territory which swept from the Mississippi to the mountains, from Texas to the British possessions, and the march of the flag began!

The infidels to the gospel of liberty raved, but the flag swept on! The title to that noble land out of which Oregon, Washington, Idaho, and Montana have been carved was uncertain; Jefferson, strict constructionist of constitutional power though he was, obeyed the Anglo-Saxon impulse within him, whose watchword then and whose watchword throughout the world to-day is, "Forward!": another empire was added to the Republic, and the march of the flag went on!

Those who deny the power of free institutions to expand urged every argument, and more, that we hear, to-day; but the people's judgment approved the command of their blood, and the march of the flag went on!

A screen of land from New Orleans to Florida shut us from the Gulf, and over this and the Everglade Peninsula[4] waved the saffron flag of Spain; Andrew Jackson[5] seized both, the American people stood at his back, and, under Monroe,[6] the Floridas came under the dominion of the Republic, and the march of the flag went on! The Cassandras[7] prophesied every prophecy of despair we hear, to-day, but the march of the flag went on!

Then Texas responded to the bugle calls of liberty, and the march of the flag went on! And, at last, we waged war with Mexico, and the flag swept over the southwest, over peerless California, past the Gate of Gold to Oregon on the north, and from ocean to ocean its folds of glory blazed.

And, now, obeying the same voice that Jefferson heard and obeyed, that Jackson heard and obeyed, that Monroe heard and obeyed, that Seward[8] heard and obeyed, that Grant[9] heard and obeyed, that Harrison[10] heard and obeyed, our President[11] to-day plants the flag over the islands of

15

---

[4]*the Everglade Peninsula:* Florida.

[5]*Andrew Jackson:* Jackson (1767–1845), seventh president of the United States, extended U.S. claims to Florida in 1818 by crossing into Spanish territory and seizing Pensacola while carrying out reprisals against Seminole Indians.

[6]*Monroe:* James Monroe (1758–1831), fifth president of the United States and author of the Monroe Doctrine of 1823, which laid the groundwork for later U.S. imperialism in the Caribbean and Latin America by asserting that the U.S. has a special interest in maintaining the independence of all nations in the Americas.

[7]*the Cassandras:* In Greek legend, Cassandra is given the power of prophecy but is also cursed so that all of her prophesies remain unbelieved.

[8]*Seward:* William Henry Seward (1801–1872), American statesman and secretary of state under the administration of Abraham Lincoln.

[9]*Grant:* Ulysses Simpson Grant (1822–1885), eighteenth president of the United States.

[10]*Harrison:* William Henry Harrison (1773–1841), ninth president of the United States.

[11]*our President:* William McKinley (1843–1901), twenty-fifth president of the United States, who oversaw the expansion of American interests during the Spanish-American War (1898) and the Philippine Insurrection (1899–1901).

the seas, outposts of commerce, citadels of national security, and the march of the flag goes on!

Distance and oceans are no arguments. The fact that all the territory our fathers bought and seized is contiguous, is no argument. In 1819 Florida was farther from New York than Porto Rico is from Chicago today; Texas, farther from Washington in 1845 than Hawaii is from Boston in 1898; California, more inaccessible in 1847 than the Philippines are now. Gibraltar is farther from London than Havana is from Washington; Melbourne is farther from Liverpool than Manila is from San Francisco.

The ocean does not separate us from lands of our duty and desire—the oceans join us, rivers never to be dredged, canals never to be repaired. Steam joins us; electricity joins us—the very elements are in league with our destiny. Cuba not contiguous! Porto Rico not contiguous! Hawaii and the Philippines not contiguous! The oceans make them contiguous. And our navy will make them contiguous.

But the Opposition is right—there is a difference. We did not need the western Mississippi Valley when we acquired it, nor Florida, nor Texas, nor California, nor the royal provinces of the far northwest. We had no emigrants to people this imperial wilderness, no money to develop it, even no highways to cover it. No trade awaited us in its savage vastnesses. Our productions were not greater than our trade. There was not one reason for the land-lust of our statesmen from Jefferson to Grant, other than the prophet and the Saxon within them. But, to-day, we are raising more than we can consume, making more than we can use. Therefore we must find new markets for our produce. 20

And so, while we did not need the territory taken during the past century at the time it was acquired, we do need what we have taken in 1898, and we need it now. The resources and the commerce of these immensely rich dominions will be increased as much as American energy is greater than Spanish sloth. In Cuba, alone, there are 15,000,000 acres of forest unacquainted with the ax, exhaustless mines of iron, priceless deposits of manganese, millions of dollars' worth of which we must buy, to-day, from the Black Sea districts. There are millions of acres yet unexplored.

The resources of Porto Rico have only been trifled with. The riches of the Philippines have hardly been touched by the finger-tips of modern methods. And they produce what we consume, and consume what we produce—the very predestination of reciprocity—a reciprocity "not made with hands, eternal in the heavens." They sell hemp, sugar, cocoanuts, fruits of the tropics, timber of price like mahogany; they buy flour, clothing, tools, implements, machinery, and all that we can raise and make. Their trade will be ours in time. Do you indorse that policy with your vote?

Cuba is as large as Pennsylvania, and is the richest spot on the globe. Hawaii is as large as New Jersey; Porto Rico half as large as Hawaii; the Philippines larger than all New England, New York, New Jersey and Delaware combined. Together they are larger than the British Isles, larger than France, larger than Germany, larger than Japan.

If any man tells you that trade depends on cheapness and not on government influence, ask him why England does not abandon South Africa, Egypt, India. Why does France seize South China, Germany the vast region whose port is Kaouchou?

Our trade with Porto Rico, Hawaii, and the Philippines must be as free   25
as between the states of the Union, because they are American territory, while every other nation on earth must pay our tariff before they can compete with us. Until Cuba shall ask for annexation, our trade with her will, at the very least, be like the preferential trade of Canada with England. That, and the excellence of our goods and products; that, and the convenience of traffic; that, and the kinship of interests and destiny, will give the monopoly of these markets to the American people.

The commercial supremacy of the Republic means that this Nation is to be the sovereign factor in the peace of the world. For the conflicts of the future are to be conflicts of trade—struggles for markets—commercial wars for existence. And the golden rule of peace is impregnability of position and invincibility of preparedness. So, we see England, the greatest strategist of history, plant her flag and her cannon on Gibraltar, at Quebec, in the Bermudas, at Vancouver, everywhere.

So Hawaii furnished us a naval base in the heart of the Pacific; the Ladrones another, a voyage further on; Manila another, at the gates of Asia— Asia, to the trade of whose hundreds of millions American merchants, manufacturers, farmers, have as good right as those of Germany or France or Russia or England; Asia, whose commerce with the United Kingdom alone amounts to hundreds of millions of dollars every year; Asia, to whom Germany looks to take her surplus products; Asia, whose doors must not be shut against American trade. Within five decades the bulk of Oriental commerce will be ours.

Wonderfully has God guided us. Yonder at Bunker Hill[12] and Yorktown[13] His providence was above us. At New Orleans[14] and on ensanguined seas His hand sustained us. Abraham Lincoln was His minister and His was the altar of freedom the Nation's soldiers set up on a hundred battle-fields. His power directed Dewey[15] in the East and delivered the Spanish fleet into our hands, as He delivered the elder Armada into the hands of our English sires two centuries ago. . . . We can not fly from our world duties; it is ours to execute the purpose of a fate that has driven us to be greater than our small intentions. We can not retreat from any soil where

[12]*Bunker Hill:* Site of the first successful colonial resistance against British forces at the outbreak of the American Revolution in 1775.

[13]*Yorktown:* Site of the British surrender to American forces at the end of the American Revolution in 1781.

[14]*New Orleans:* Site of Andrew Jackson's decisive defeat of British forces at the end of the War of 1812 (1812–1815).

[15]*Dewey:* George Dewey (1837–1917), American admiral, who defeated the Spanish fleet at Manila at the outbreak of the Spanish-American War.

Providence has unfurled our banner; it is ours to save that soil for liberty and civilization.

ENGAGING THE TEXT

1. What is America's mission, according to Beveridge? What assumptions are embedded in this notion of a national "mission"? How, for example, does the idea of a national mission differ from a strategic goal or national interest? What is the source of this sense of mission?

2. How does Beveridge view America and Americans in relation to other peoples and nations? How would you describe his attitude toward other cultures and countries?

3. What arguments, stated or implied, does Beveridge offer to justify American imperialism? What role do history, economic forces, and American ideology play in this justification?

EXPLORING CONNECTIONS

4. How might the ideas expressed in Ronald Takaki's "Race at the End of History" (p. 393) complicate Beveridge's view of America's historical mission? To what extent does the current multicultural reality of America challenge the idea that we, as a nation, have a particular mission to fulfill in the world?

5. To what extent do the images in the Visual Portfolio for this chapter (p. 763) support Beveridge's claim that American society has a special destiny to fulfill in the world?

EXTENDING THE CRITICAL CONTEXT

6. Research the history of any of the U.S. territories or protectorates that Beveridge mentions in this selection. How have the original inhabitants of these nations fared under America's influence? To what extent has history borne out Beveridge's claims about the benefits of American civilization and administration?

7. Research statements made by contemporary U.S. politicians and foreign policy experts about America's role in relation to the rest of the world to see how they compare with Beveridge's view of America's international mission. To what extent does Beveridge's early argument for imperialism prefigure current trends in U.S. foreign policy?

America the Beautiful: What We're Fighting For

DINESH D'SOUZA

Before 9/11, most Americans probably hadn't given a lot of thought to how we, as a people, are viewed by the rest of the world. Of course, many of us were aware of the negative image of "the ugly American" that developed as the power and prestige of the United States grew after World War II. But nothing had prepared us for the idea that others hated the United States so much they'd gladly die to do us damage. In this selection, conservative thinker Dinesh D'Souza suggests that we're despised by much of the rest of the world precisely because we're so good: our freedom itself, according to D'Souza, lies at the root of the most toxic forms of anti-Americanism in the world today. The Robert and Karen Rishwain Fellow at the Stanford-based Hoover Institution, D'Souza (b. 1961) served as senior domestic policy analyst at the White House during the Reagan administration, has written extensively for the Wall Street Journal, *the* New York Times, *the* Boston Globe, *and the* Washington Post, *and appears regularly on news programs like* Nightline, Crossfire, Firing Line, *and* Good Morning America. *He has also written a number of best-selling books on politics and current events, including* Illiberal Education *(1991),* The End of Racism *(1995), and the source of this selection,* What's So Great About America? *(2002).*

> We have it in our power to begin the world all over again.
> —THOMAS PAINE

America represents a new way of being human and thus presents a radical challenge to the world. On the one hand, Americans have throughout their history held that they are special: that their country has been blessed by God, that the American system is unique, that Americans are not like people everywhere else. This set of beliefs is called "American exceptionalism." At the same time, Americans have also traditionally insisted that they provide a model for the world, that theirs is a formula that others can follow, and that there is no better life available elsewhere. Paradoxically enough, American exceptionalism leads to American universalism.

Both American exceptionalism and American universalism have come under fierce attack from the enemies of America, both at home and abroad. The critics of America deny that there is anything unique about America, and they ridicule the notion that the American model is one that others should seek to follow. Indeed, by chronicling the past and present crimes of America, they hope to extract apologies and financial reparations out of Americans. Some even seek to justify murderous attacks against America on the grounds that what America does, and what she stands for, invites such attacks.

These critics are aiming their assault on America's greatest weakness: her lack of moral self-confidence. Americans cannot effectively fight a war without believing that it is a just war. That's why America has only lost once, in Vietnam, and that was because most Americans did not know what they were fighting for. The enemies of America understand this vulnerability. At the deepest level their assault is moral: they seek to destroy America's belief in herself, knowing that if this happens, America is finished. By the same token, when Americans rally behind a good cause, as in World War II, they are invincible. The outcome of America's engagements abroad is usually determined by a single factor: America's will to prevail. In order to win, Americans need to believe that they are on the side of the angels. The good news is that they usually are.

The triumph of American ideas and culture in the global marketplace, and the fact that most immigrants from around the world choose to come to the United States, would seem to be sufficient grounds for establishing the superiority of American civilization. But this is not entirely so, because we have not shown that the people of the world are *justified* in preferring the American way of life to any other. We must contend with the Islamic fundamentalists' argument that their societies are based on high principles while America is based on low principles. The Islamic critics are happy to concede the attractions of America, but they insist that these attractions are base. America, they say, appeals to what is most degraded about human nature; by contrast, Islamic societies may be poor and "backward," but they at least aspire to virtue. Even if they fall short, they are trying to live by God's law.

Americans usually have a hard time answering this argument, in part because they are bewildered by its theological cadences. The usual tendency is to lapse into a kind of unwitting relativism. "You are following what you believe is right, and we are living by the values that we think are best." This pious buncombe usually concludes with a Rodney King–style[1] plea for tolerance, "So why don't we learn to appreciate our differences? Why don't we just get along?" To see why this argument fails completely, imagine that you are living during the time of the Spanish Inquisition.[2] The Grand Inquisitor is just starting to pull out your fingernails. You make the Rodney King move on him. "Torquemada,[3] please stop pulling out my fingernails. Why don't we

[5]

---

[1]*Rodney King:* Los Angeles resident whose apparently unprovoked beating by police was videotaped and televised, sparking riots across the city in 1992. [Notes 9, 12, and 13 are D'Souza's.]

[2]*Spanish Inquisition:* Tribunal of the Catholic Church in Spain from 1478 until 1510, famous for its cruelty and intolerance.

[3]*Torquemada:* Tomás de Torquemada (1420–1498), Spanish churchman who led the Inquisition and earned infamy for his brutal persecution of Spanish Jews.

learn to appreciate our differences?" Most of us probably realize that Torquemada would not find this persuasive. But it is less obvious why he would not. Let me paraphrase Torquemada's argument: "You think I am taking away your freedom, but I am concerned with your immortal soul. Ultimately virtue is far more important than freedom. Our lives last for a mere second in the long expanse of eternity. What measure of pleasure or pain we experience in our short life is trivial compared to our fate in the never ending life to come. I am trying to save your soul from damnation. Who cares if you have to let out a few screams in the process? My actions are entirely for your own benefit. You should be *thanking me* for pulling out your fingernails."

I have recalled the Spanish Inquisition to make the point that the Islamic argument is one that we have heard before. We should not find it so strange that people think this way; it is the way that many in our own civilization used to think not so very long ago. The reason that most of us do not think this way now is that Western history has taught us a hard lesson. That lesson is that when the institutions of religion and government are one, and the secular authority is given the power to be the interpreter and enforcer of God's law, then horrible abuses of power are perpetrated in God's name. This is just what we saw in Afghanistan with the Taliban,[4] and what we see now in places like Iran. This is not to suggest that Islam's historical abuses are worse than those of the West. But the West, as a consequence of its experience, learned to disentangle the institutions of religion and government—a separation that was most completely achieved in the United States. As we have seen, the West also devised a new way of organizing society around the institutions of science, democracy, and capitalism. The Renaissance, the Reformation, the Enlightenment, and the Scientific Revolution were some of the major signposts on Western civilization's road to modernity.

By contrast, the Islamic world did not have a Renaissance or a Reformation. No Enlightenment or Scientific Revolution either. Incredible though it may seem to many in the West, Islamic societies today are in some respects not very different from how they were a thousand years ago. Islam has been around for a long time. This brings us to a critical question: why are we seeing this upsurge of Islamic fundamentalism and Islamic fanaticism now?

To answer this question, we should recall that Islam was once one of the greatest and most powerful civilizations in the world. Indeed, there was a time when it seemed as if the whole world would fall under Islamic rule. Within a century of the prophet Muhammad's[5] death, his converts had overthrown the Sassanid dynasty in Iran and conquered large tracts of territory from the Byzantine dynasty. Soon the Muslims had established an empire greater than that of Rome at its zenith. Over the next several centuries, Islam made deep inroads into Africa, Southeast Asia, and southern Europe. The crusades were launched to repel the forces of Islam, but the crusades

---

[4]*the Taliban:* Radical Islamic sect that came to power in Afghanistan in 1996.

[5]*Muhammad:* The prophet of Islam (570?–632), whose collected visions and revelations compose the Koran.

ended in failure. By the sixteenth century, there were no fewer than five Islamic empires, unified by political ties, a common religion, and a common culture: the Mamluk sultans in Egypt, the Safavid dynasty in Iran, the Mughal empire in India, the empire of the Great Khans in Russia and Central Asia, and the Ottoman Empire based in Turkey. Of these, the Ottomans were by far the most formidable. They ruled most of North Africa, and threatened Mediterranean Europe and Austria. Europe was terrified that they might take over all the lands of Christendom. In all of history, Islam is the only non-Western civilization to pose a mortal threat to the West.

Then it all went wrong. Starting in the late seventeenth century, when the West was able to repel the Ottoman siege of Vienna, the power of Islam began a slow but steady decline. By the nineteenth century the Ottoman Empire was known as the "sick man of Europe," and it collapsed completely after World War I, when the victorious European powers carved it up and parceled out the pieces. Not only did the Muslims lose most of the territory they had conquered, but they also found themselves being ruled, either directly or indirectly, by the West. Today, even though colonialism has ended, the Islamic world is in a miserable state. Basically all that it has to offer is oil, and as technology opens up alternative sources of energy, even that will not amount to much. Without its oil revenues, the Islamic world will find itself in the position of sub-Saharan Africa: it will cease to matter. Even now it does not matter very much. The only reason it makes the news is by killing people. When is the last time you opened the newspaper to read about a great Islamic discovery or invention? While China and India, two other empires that were eclipsed by the West, have embraced Western technology and even assumed a leadership role in some areas, Islam's contribution to modern science and technology is negligible.

In addition to these embarrassments, the Islamic world faces a formidable threat from the United States. This is not the threat of American force or of American support for Israel. Israel is an irritant, but it does not threaten the existence of Islamic society. By contrast, America stands for an idea that is fully capable of transforming the Islamic world by winning the hearts of Muslims. The subversive American idea is one of shaping your own life, of making your own destiny, of following a path illumined not by external authorities but by your inner self. This American idea endangers the sanctity of the Muslim home, as well as the authority of Islamic society. It empowers women and children to assert their prerogatives against the male head of the household. It also undermines political and religious hierarchies. Of all American ideas, the "inner voice" is the most dangerous because it rivals the voice of Allah as a source of moral allegiance. So Islam is indeed, as bin Laden[6] warned, facing the greatest threat to its survival since the days of Muhammad.

10

---

[6]*bin Laden:* Osama bin Laden (b. 1957), son of one of Saudi Arabia's wealthiest families and founder of the international terrorist organization al-Qaeda, which has been linked to numerous attacks on U.S. targets around the world, including the assaults on September 11, 2001.

In recent decades, a great debate has broken out in the Muslim world to account for Islamic decline and to formulate a response to it. One response—let us call it the reformist or classical liberal response—is to acknowledge that the Islamic world has been left behind by modernity. The reformers' solution is to embrace science, democracy, and capitalism. This would mean adaptation—at least selective adaptation—to the ways of the West. The liberal reformers have an honorable intellectual tradition, associated with such names as Muhammad Abduh, Jamal al-Afghani, Muhammad Iqbal, and Taha Husayn. This group also enjoys a fairly strong base of support in the Muslim middle class. In the past two decades, however, the reformers have been losing the argument in the Islamic world to their rival group, the fundamentalists.

Here, in short, is the fundamentalist argument. The Koran promises that if Muslims are faithful to Allah, they will enjoy prosperity in this life and paradise in the next life. According to the fundamentalists, the Muslims were doing this for centuries, and they were invincible. But now, the fundamentalists point out, Islam is not winning any more; in fact, it is losing. What could be the reason for this? From the fundamentalist point of view, the answer is obvious: Muslims are not following the true teaching of Allah! The fundamentalists allege that Muslims have fallen away from the true faith and are mindlessly pursuing the ways of the infidel. The fundamentalists also charge that Islamic countries are now ruled by self-serving despots who serve as puppets for America and the West. The solution, the fundamentalists say, is to purge American troops and Western influence from the Middle East; to overthrow corrupt, pro-Western regimes like ones in Pakistan, Egypt, and Saudi Arabia; and to return to the pure, original teachings of the Koran. Only then, the fundamentalists insist, can Islam recover its lost glory.

One can see, from this portrait, that the fundamentalists are a humiliated people who are seeking to recover ancestral greatness. They are not complete "losers": they are driven by an awareness of moral superiority, combined with political, economic, and military inferiority. Their argument has a powerful appeal to proud Muslims who find it hard to come to terms with their contemporary irrelevance. And so the desert wind of fundamentalism has spread throughout the Middle East. It has replaced Arab nationalism as the most powerful political force in the region.

The success of the fundamentalists in the Muslim world should not blind us from recognizing that their counterattack against America and the West is fundamentally defensive. The fundamentalists know that their civilization does not have the appeal to expand outside its precinct. It's not as if the Muslims were plotting to take, say, Australia. It is the West that is making incursions into Islamic territory, winning converts, and threatening to subvert ancient loyalties and transform a very old way of life. So the fundamentalists are lashing out against this new, largely secular, Western "crusade." Terrorism, their weapon of counterinsurgency, is the weapon of the weak. Terrorism is the international equivalent of that domestic weapon of discontent: the riot. Political scientist Edward Banfield once observed that a riot is a failed revolution. People who know how to take over the government don't throw stones at a bus. Similarly terrorism of the bin Laden variety is a desperate strike against a civilization that the fundamentalists know they have no power to conquer.

But they do have the power to disrupt and terrify the people of America and the West. This is one of their goals, and their attack on September 11, 2001, was quite successful in this regard. But there is a second goal: to unify the Muslim world behind the fundamentalist banner and to foment uprisings against pro-Western regimes. Thus the bin Ladens of the world are waging a two-front war: against Western influence in the Middle East and against pro-Western governments and liberal influences within the Islamic world. So the West is not faced with a pure "clash of civilizations."[7] It is not "the West" against "Islam." It is a clash of civilizations within the Muslim world. One side or the other will prevail.   15

So what should American policy be toward the region? It is a great mistake for Americans to believe that their country is hated because it is misunderstood. It is hated because it is understood only too well. Sometimes people say to me, "But the mullahs have a point about American culture. They are right about Jerry Springer."[8] Yes, they are right about Springer. If we could get them to agree to stop bombing our facilities in return for us shipping them Jerry Springer to do with as they like, we should make the deal tomorrow, and throw in some of Springer's guests. But the Islamic fundamentalists don't just object to the excesses of American liberty: they object to liberty itself. Nor can we appease them by staying out of their world. We live in an age in which the flow of information is virtually unstoppable. We do not have the power to keep our ideals and our culture out of their lives.

Thus there is no alternative to facing their hostility. First, we need to destroy their terrorist training camps and networks. This is not easy to do, because some of these facilities are in countries like Iraq, Iran, Libya, and the Sudan. The U.S. should demand that those countries dismantle their terror networks and stop being incubators of terrorism. If they do not, we should work to get rid of their governments. How this is done is a matter of prudence. In some cases, such as Iraq, the direct use of force might be the answer. In others, such as Iran, the U.S. can capitalize on widespread popular dissatisfaction with the government.[9] Iran has a large middle class, with

---

[7]*"clash of civilizations"*: The title of Samuel P. Huntington's controversial 1996 book, based on a 1993 article published in *Foreign Affairs* magazine, which argues that the culture of the Western democracies, founded on "individualism, liberalism, constitutionalism, human rights, equality, liberty, [and] the rule of law," will inevitably come into conflict with the non-Western cultures across the globe.

[8]*Jerry Springer:* Talk show host known for featuring sexually explicit and violent themes and for instigating brawls among his guests.

[9]See, for example, Amy Waldman, "In Iran, an Angry Generation Longs for Jobs, More Freedom, and Power," *New York Times,* 7 December 2001.

strong democratic and pro-American elements. But the dissenters are sorely in need of leadership, resources, and an effective strategy to defeat the ruling theocracy.

The U.S. also has to confront the fact that regimes allied with America, such as Pakistan, Egypt, and Saudi Arabia, are undemocratic, corrupt, and repressive. Indeed, the misdoings and tyranny of these regimes strengthen the cause of the fundamentalists, who are able to tap deep veins of popular discontent. How do the regimes deal with this fundamentalist resistance? They subsidize various religious and educational programs administered by the fundamentalists that teach terrorism and hatred of America. By focusing the people's discontent against a foreign target, the United States, the regimes of Saudi Arabia, Egypt, and Pakistan hope to divert attention from their own failings. The United States must make it clear to its Muslim allies that this "solution" is unacceptable. If they want American aid and American support, they must stop funding mosques and schools that promote terrorism and anti-Americanism. Moreover, they must take steps to reduce corruption, expand civil liberties, and enfranchise their people.

In the long term, America's goal is a large and difficult one: to turn Muslim fundamentalists into classical liberals. This does not mean that we want them to stop being Muslims. It does mean, however, that we want them to practice their religion *in the liberal way*. Go to a Promise Keepers[10] meeting in Washington, D.C., or another of America's big cities. You will see tens of thousands of men singing, praying, hugging, and pledging chastity to their wives. A remarkable sight. These people are mostly evangelical and fundamentalist Christians. They are apt to approach you with the greeting, "Let me tell you what Jesus Christ has meant to my life." They want you to accept Christ, but their appeal is not to force but to consent. They do not say, "Accept Christ or I am going to plunge a dagger into your chest." Even the fundamentalist Christians in the West are liberals: they are practicing Christianity "in the liberal way."

The task of transforming Muslim fundamentalists into classical liberals 20 will not be an easy one to perform in the Islamic world, where there is no tradition of separating religion and government. We need not require that Islamic countries adopt America's strict form of separation, which prohibits any government involvement in religion. But it is indispensable that Muslim fundamentalists relinquish the use of force for the purpose of spreading Islam. They, too, should appeal to consent. If this seems like a ridiculous thing to ask of Muslims, let us remember that millions of Muslims are already living this way. These are, of course, the Muslim immigrants to Europe and the United States. They are following the teachings of their faith, but most of them understand that they must respect the equal rights

---

[10]*Promise Keepers:* Nationwide organization of Christian men.

of others. They have renounced the *jihad*[11] of the sword and confine themselves to the *jihad* of the pen and the *jihad* of the heart. In general, the immigrants are showing the way for Islam to change in the same way that
Christianity changed in order to survive and flourish in the modern world.

Whether America can succeed in the mammoth enterprises of stopping
terrorism and liberalizing the Islamic world depends a good deal on the
people in the Middle East and a great deal on us. Fundamentalist Islam has
now succeeded Soviet communism as the organizing theme of American
foreign policy. Thus our newest challenge comes from a very old adversary.
The West has been battling Islam for more than a thousand years. It is possible that this great battle has now been resumed, and that over time we will
come to see the seventy-year battle against communism as a short detour.
    But are we up to the challenge? There are some who think we are not.
They believe that Americans are a divided people: not even a nation, but a
collection of separate tribes. The multiculturalists actually proclaim this to
be a good thing, and they strive to encourage people to affirm their differences. If, however, the multiculturalists are right in saying that "all we have
in common is our diversity," then it follows that we have *nothing* in common. This does not bode well for the national unity that is a prerequisite to
fighting against a determined foe. If the ethnic group is the primary unit of
allegiance, why should we make sacrifices for people who come from ethnic
groups other than our own? Doesn't a nation require a loyalty that transcends ethnic particularity?
    Of course it does. And fortunately America does command such a loy-
alty. The multiculturalists are simply wrong about America, and despite their
best efforts to promote a politics of difference, Americans remain a united
people with shared values and a common way of life. There are numerous
surveys of national attitudes that confirm this,[12] but it is most easily seen
when Americans are abroad. Hang out at a Parisian café, for instance, and
you can easily pick out the Americans: they dress the same way, eat the same
food, listen to the same music, and laugh at the same jokes. However different their personalities, Americans who run into each other in remote places
always become fast friends. And even the most jaded Americans who spend
time in other countries typically return home with an intense feeling of relief
and a newfound appreciation for the routine satisfactions of American life.
    It is easy to forget the cohesiveness of a free people in times of peace
and prosperity. New York is an extreme example of the great pandemonium

---

[11]*jihad:* Arabic for "struggle," denoting the kind of spiritual effort required of Muslims by
the teachings of the Koran, and today frequently misinterpreted as being synonymous with the
notion of holy war.
    [12]See, for example, John Fetto and Rebecca Gardyn, "An All-American Melting Pot,"
American Demographics, July 2001, 8. The survey was conducted by Maritz Marketing Research.

that results when countless individuals and groups pursue their diverse interests in the normal course of life. In a crisis, however, the national tribe comes together, and this is exactly what happened in New York and the rest of America following the terrorist attack. Suddenly political, regional, and racial differences evaporated; suddenly Americans stood as one. This surprised many people, including many Americans, who did not realize that, despite the centrifugal forces that pull us in different directions, there is a deep national unity that holds us together.

Unity, however, is not sufficient for the challenges ahead. America also needs the moral self-confidence to meet its adversary. This is the true lesson of Vietnam: Americans cannot succeed unless they are convinced that they are fighting on behalf of the good. There are some, as we have seen, who fear that America no longer stands for what is good. They allege that American freedom produces a licentious, degenerate society that is scarcely worth defending. We return, therefore, to the question of what America is all about, and whether this country, in its dedication to the principle of freedom, subverts the higher principle of virtue.

So what about virtue? The fundamental difference between the society that the Islamic fundamentalists want and the society that Americans have is that the Islamic activists seek a country where the life of the citizens is *directed by others*, while Americans live in a nation where the life of the citizens is largely *self-directed*. The central goal of American freedom is self-reliance: the individual is placed in the driver's seat of his own life. The Islamic fundamentalists presume the moral superiority of the externally directed life on the grounds that it is aimed at virtue. The self-directed life, however, also seeks virtue—virtue realized not through external command but, as it were, "from within." The real question is: which type of society is more successful in achieving the goal of virtue?

Let us concede at the outset that, in a free society, freedom will frequently be used badly. Freedom, by definition, includes freedom to do good or evil, to act nobly or basely. Thus we should not be surprised that there is a considerable amount of vice, licentiousness, and vulgarity in a free society. Given the warped timber of humanity, freedom is simply an expression of human flaws and weaknesses. But if freedom brings out the worst in people, it also brings out the best. The millions of Americans who live decent, praiseworthy lives deserve our highest admiration because they have opted for the good when the good is not the only available option. Even amidst the temptations that a rich and free society offers, they have remained on the straight path. Their virtue has special luster because it is freely chosen. The free society does not guarantee virtue any more than it guarantees happiness. But it allows for the pursuit of both, a pursuit rendered all the more meaningful and profound because success is not guaranteed: it has to be won through personal striving.

By contrast, the externally directed life that Islamic fundamentalists seek undermines the possibility of virtue. If the supply of virtue is insufficient in self-directed societies, it is almost nonexistent in externally directed societies because coerced virtues are not virtues at all. Consider the woman who is required to wear a veil. There is no modesty in this, because the woman is being compelled. Compulsion cannot produce virtue: it can only produce the outward semblance of virtue. And once the reins of coercion are released, as they were for the terrorists who lived in the United States, the worst impulses of human nature break loose. Sure enough, the deeply religious terrorists spent their last days in gambling dens, bars, and strip clubs, sampling the licentious lifestyle they were about to strike out against.[13] In this respect they were like the Spartans,[14] who—Plutarch[15] tells us—were abstemious in public but privately coveted wealth and luxury. In externally directed societies, the absence of freedom signals the absence of virtue. Thus the free society is not simply richer, more varied, and more fun: it is also morally superior to the externally directed society. There is no reason for anyone, least of all the cultural conservatives, to feel hesitant about rising to the defense of our free society.

Even if Americans possess the necessary unity and self-confidence, there is also the question of nerve. Some people, at home and abroad, are skeptical that America can endure a long war against Islamic fundamentalism because they consider Americans to be, well, a little bit soft. As one of bin Laden's lieutenants put it, "Americans love life, and we love death." His implication was that Americans do not have the stomach for the kind of deadly, drawn-out battle that the militant Muslims are ready to fight. This was also the attitude of the Taliban. "Come and get us," they taunted America. "We are ready for *jihad*. Come on, you bunch of weenies." And then the Taliban was hit by a juggernaut of American firepower that caused their regime to disintegrate within a couple of weeks. Soon the Taliban leadership had headed for the caves, or for Pakistan, leaving their captured soldiers to beg for their lives. Even the call of *jihad* and the promise of martyrdom could not stop these hard men from—in the words of Mullah Omar[16] himself—"running like chickens with their heads cut off." This is not to say that Americans should expect all its battles against terrorism and Islamic fundamentalism to be so short and so conclusive. But neither should America's enemies expect Americans to show any less firmness or fierceness than they themselves possess.

. . . The firefighters and policemen who raced into the burning towers   30 of the World Trade Center showed that their lives were dedicated to something higher than "self-fulfillment." The same can be said of Todd Beamer and his fellow passengers who forced the terrorists to crash United Airlines

[13]Diane McWhorter, "Terrorists Tasted Lusty Lifestyle They So Despised," *USA Today,* 26 September 2001, 11-A.

[14]*Spartans:* In Classical Greece, the nondemocratic adversaries of the Athenians.

[15]*Plutarch:* Greek essayist and biographer (46–119).

[16]*Mullah Omar:* Leader of the Taliban (b. 1959).

Flight 93 in the woods of western Pennsylvania rather than flying on to Camp David or the White House. . . . The military has its own culture, which is closer to that of the firefighters and policemen, and also bears an affinity with the culture of the "greatest generation."[17] Only now are those Americans who grew up during the 1960s coming to appreciate the virtues—indeed the indispensability—of this older, sturdier culture of courage, nobility, and sacrifice. It is this culture that will protect the liberties of all Americans. . . .

As the American founders knew, America is a new kind of society that produces a new kind of human being. That human being—confident, self-reliant, tolerant, generous, future oriented—is a vast improvement over the wretched, servile, fatalistic, and intolerant human being that traditional societies have always produced, and that Islamic societies produce now. In America, the life we are given is not as important as the life we make. Ultimately, America is worthy of our love and sacrifice because, more than any other society, it makes possible the good life, and the life that is good.

American is the greatest, freest, and most decent society in existence. It is an oasis of goodness in a desert of cynicism and barbarism. This country, once an experiment unique in the world, is now the last best hope for the world. By making sacrifices for America, and by our willingness to die for her, we bind ourselves by invisible cords to those great patriots who fought at Yorktown, Gettysburg, and Iwo Jima,[18] and we prove ourselves worthy of the blessings of freedom. By defeating the terrorist threat posed by Islamic fundamentalism, we can protect the American way of life while once again redeeming humanity from a global menace. History will view America as a great gift to the world, a gift that Americans today must preserve and cherish.

ENGAGING THE TEXT

1. What, according to D'Souza, is meant by the terms American "exceptionalism" and American "universalism"? What makes the United States "exceptional" in his view? To what extent do you agree with the contention that our civilization is superior to the cultures of other countries?

2. Would you agree with D'Souza's claim that America's greatest weakness is "her lack of moral self-confidence"? Why, in his view, is it so important for Americans to believe in the moral superiority of our way of life? Do most Americans strike you as lacking this kind of self-confidence?

3. Why do Islamic peoples "hate" the United States, in D'Souza's view? What other possible reasons might be offered to explain the antipathy that some Islamic groups feel toward America? How does D'Souza view the criticisms

---

[17]*the "greatest generation":* Refers to the generation that fought in World War II, supposedly distinguished from following generations by their spirit of service and self-sacrifice.

[18]*Yorktown, Gettysburg, and Iwo Jima:* Sites of famous American victories during, respectively, the American Revolution, the Civil War, and World War II.

that Islamic fundamentalists level at American society and American
values? To what extent do you believe that we "don't have the power to
keep our ideals and our culture out of their lives"?

4. Would you agree that Christian fundamentalism is more "liberal" than its
Islamic counterpart? In what sense can Christian fundamentalist attitudes
toward issues like gay marriage, censorship, abortion, and the distinction
between church and state be viewed as liberal?

EXPLORING CONNECTIONS

5. Compare D'Souza's view of America's relation to other nations and cultures with that expressed by Albert J. Beveridge in "The March of the Flag"

(p. 709). Is D'Souza, like Beveridge, arguing for the establishment of a worldwide empire? What differences do you see between these two articulations of the myth of American exceptionalism?

6. How might Paul L. Wachtel (p. 613) interpret D'Souza's depictions of "other" cultures and civilizations? To what extent, if any, do D'Souza's views of Islamic nations echo racist stereotypes? Is it possible to move beyond such stereotypes while still acknowledging the differences between different world cultures? Why or why not?

7. Write a brief imaginary dialogue between D'Souza, John Taylor Gatto (p. 173), and/or Michael Moore (p. 153) on the importance of freedom in American culture. Would these critics of the American educational system be likely to agree that American civilization has created a "new way of being human" that is essentially superior to and more free than the ways of human beings found in "traditional societies"? Why or why not?

EXTENDING THE CRITICAL CONTEXT

8. Locate and examine statements made by political leaders or members of the Bush administration justifying the U.S. invasion of Afghanistan and Iraq or any other relatively unilateral U.S. military action. To what extent do such statements echo ideas expressed in D'Souza's assessment of the United States and our meaning in the world?

9. Working in groups, debate whether or not you agree with the notion of U.S. exceptionalism. Do you believe, as D'Souza does, that the United States is "an oasis of goodness in a desert of cynicism and barbarism" — or that "America is a new kind of society that produces a new kind of human being"? Is there a basis in fact for such claims, or are they simply a matter of nationalism or prejudice?

10. Research the traditions, values, and attitudes associated with Islam. How does the information you gather substantiate or challenge D'Souza's depiction of Islamic cultures and their attitudes toward the West?

The Oblivious Empire

MARK HERTSGAARD

The idea that America is an "exceptional" country that produces a unique kind of human being is as old as the concept of America itself. Belief in American "exceptionalism" goes all the way back to the Pilgrims, who came to the "New World" to liberate themselves from what they saw as the decadent civilizations of "old" Europe. During the colonial period and the nineteenth century, this belief in the uniqueness of the American mission was repeatedly invoked to justify the destruction of Native American tribes and military

*interventions against other sovereign nations in the Western Hemisphere.
Today, political observers note the emergence of a "new exceptionalism"—the
rebirth of the conviction that America has a special mission and meaning in
world affairs. But as Mark Hertsgaard suggests in this selection, America's
sense of superiority may well be the very thing that's feeding the flames of
anti-Americanism around the world. A broadcaster and journalist who contributes regularly to* The New Yorker, The Atlantic, Vanity Fair, Harpers, *the*
New York Times, *and the* Washington Post, *Hertsgaard has also authored five
books, including* Earth Odyssey: Around the World in Search of Our Environmental Future *(1999) and the source of this selection,* The Eagle's Shadow:
Why America Fascinates and Infuriates the World *(2001).*

"Texans are the worst," said the London cabbie. It was a fine late summer morning and we were waiting for the light to change so we could cross
the Thames.[1] "I had one in the cab a few weeks ago, must have been in his
thirties. We were driving past the London Eye[2] and he says, 'What's 'at?' I
tell him it's the London Eye, the tallest Ferris wheel in the world. He says,
'We got one bigger than that.' I thought, 'Uh-oh, one of those.' I mean, I
don't care if the Eye is the tallest in the world or not, maybe there is a bigger one in Texas for all I know. It's the bragging and the arrogance that put
me off. No matter what he saw, Texas had more. I forget what we passed
next, a double-decker bus, maybe, or Big Ben[3]—something totally unique
to London. He says, 'What's 'at?' I tell him. He says, 'We got one bigger
than that.' After that I couldn't be bothered."

The light went green, the cabbie hit the accelerator. "I like most Americans," he added, "but it is quite amazing how they don't know anything
about other places in the world"—he shot me a sly glance through the
rearview mirror—"unless they're invading them."

The cabbie delivered that little jab on September 10, 2001, but I doubt
he would have repeated it two days later. In the immediate aftermath of
September 11, the mood in Europe was one of shock and deep sympathy
for Americans. "We are very sorry," friends in Paris told me, as if I myself
had been attacked. A couple of days later, in Prague, I happened to walk by
the United States embassy one night on the way to dinner. The entire block
was softly lit by candles well-wishers had left, along with hundreds of flowers and notes of condolence and encouragement. I found more flowers and
notes at one of Prague's most revered public places: the monument on
Wenceslas Square where the student Jan Palach set himself on fire to

---

[1]*Thames:* River running through central London. [All notes are author's, except 1–3, 7, 8,
11, 15–18, 23–26, and 30.]

[2]*London Eye:* Gigantic Ferris wheel built on the south bank of the Thames as part of the
millennial celebrations in 2002.

[3]*Big Ben:* London landmark clock located on the main tower of Parliament.

protest the Soviet crackdown of 1968. "No Terrorism" read one message spray-painted onto the concrete. Newspapers across the Continent ran articles reporting similar acts of solidarity in Japan, Russia, and elsewhere, as well as commentaries declaring, "We are all Americans now."

The sympathy was genuine and genuinely touching, but as I continued in the following weeks to talk with people across Europe and to survey the local media, it was also clear that the terror attacks had not caused Europeans to forget whatever they had once believed about the United States. Good manners might have restrained the London cabbie from repeating his remark, but it didn't mean he'd stopped thinking Americans were arrogant know-nothings. History did not begin on September 11.

Horrified as they were by the tragedy in the United States, many foreigners were not exactly surprised. Most of them knew the reasons why the United States was resented, even hated, in parts of the world, and they usually had complaints of their own. A high school teacher in Spain offered condolences for the September 11 victims and their families, but he told me he hoped Americans would recognize that the tragedy was "a consequence of U.S. foreign policy," especially its one-sided approach to the Israeli-Palestinian conflict. Some Europeans went so far as to cite America's conduct overseas as a virtual justification for the attacks. Even those who rejected the argument that the United States had brought September 11 on itself admitted that America could be infuriating at times.

Perhaps nothing irritates foreigners more than America's habit of thinking it has all the answers, and the right to impose them on everyone else. An outstanding example was President Bush's first major speech after the terror attacks. Speaking before Congress on September 20, Bush declared that foreign nations had to understand that, in the impending U.S.-led war against terrorism, "either you are with us, or you are with the terrorists." Like Bush's declaration that he wanted bin Laden "dead or alive," this was more cowboy talk, the Wild West sheriff warning, "Do as I say or get out of town"—the very attitude that had irritated America's friends and enemies alike for decades. Never mind that many nations already had their own painful experiences with terrorism; they would follow Washington's orders or else.

The United States would never accept such ultimatums itself, yet the arrogance of Bush's remark went unnoticed by America's political and journalistic elite. The *International Herald Tribune,* the overseas daily published by the *New York Times* and the *Washington Post,* did not even mention Bush's statement until the twentieth paragraph of its story, deep inside the paper. By contrast, the French daily *Le Monde* highlighted it three times on its front page, including in the headline and first paragraph. If opinion polls can be trusted, ordinary Americans also saw nothing wrong

5

with their president's stance toward the rest of the world. Throughout the autumn of 2001, Bush's approval rating remained at above 75 percent.[4]

But I would plead ignorance rather than venality on behalf of my fellow Americans. The embarrassing truth is that most of us know little about the outside world, and we are particularly ill-informed about what our government is doing in our name overseas. For example, Americans are ceaselessly, and accurately, reminded that Saddam Hussein is an evil man, but not that American-enforced economic sanctions have, since 1991, caused the deaths of at least 350,000[5] Iraqi children and impoverished a once prosperous Iraqi middle class. The bloody violence between Israelis and Palestinians that raged throughout March and April of 2002 got plenty of media coverage in the United States. Nevertheless, many Americans remained uninformed about basic aspects of the conflict. A poll conducted in early May by the University of Maryland's Program on International Policy Attitudes revealed, for example, that only 32 percent of Americans were aware that more Palestinians than Israelis had died in the fighting; only 43 percent knew that most other countries in the world disapproved of America's Middle East policies; and a mere 27 percent knew that most countries were more sympathetic to the Palestinian than to the Israeli side of the dispute.[6]

In the wake of September 11, the question obsessing Americans about the Muslim world was "Why do they hate us?" But Muslims had long wondered the same about Americans. In a sparkling exception to most American news coverage, Sandy Tolan reported on National Public Radio in January 2002 that nearly everyone he had interviewed during six weeks of recent travel through the Middle East resented the negative stereotypes attached to Muslims and Arabs by American movies, television, and news coverage. In Europe, stretching back to the novels of Goethe[7] and the operas of Mozart,[8] there had long been respect for the great achievements of Islamic civilization in culture, astronomy, architecture, and more. America, by contrast, regarded Muslims as primitive, untrustworthy fanatics, worth dealing with only because they had oil.

"You are dealing here with people who are almost childlike in their understanding of what is going on in the world," Gerald Celente, director of the Trends Research Institute in Rhinebeck, New York, told the *Financial*   10

---

[4]Bush's 77 percent approval rating was reported in *Time*, February 4, 2002.

[5]The justification for the 350,000 figure, which is considerably lower than some frequently cited estimates, is discussed in "A Hard Look at Iraq Sanctions," by David Cortright, *The Nation*, December 3, 2001.

[6]Americans' views of the Middle East conflict were examined in a poll conducted by the Program on International Policy Attitudes of the University of Maryland, released to the media on May 8, 2002, and available via the program's web site at www.pipa.org.

[7]*Goethe:* Johann Wolfgang von Goethe (1749–1832), German poet, novelist, and dramatist.

[8]*Mozart:* Wolfgang Amadeus Mozart (1756–1791), German composer.

Times shortly after September 11.[9] "It's all: 'We never did anything to anybody, so why are they doing this to us?'"

Some Americans have taken refuge in the obvious answer: they envy our wealth and resent our power. There is truth in this, as I'll discuss, but it barely scratches the surface. The reason many foreigners don't share Americans' high opinion of themselves is simple: they dislike both how America behaves overseas and its attitude about that behavior.

America, foreigners say, is a trigger-happy bully that is both out for itself and full of itself. It feels no obligation to obey international law; it often pushes other countries around, forcing on them policies and sometimes tyrannical leaders that serve only American interests, and then, if they resist too much, it may bomb obedience into them with cruise missiles. Only an American would blink to hear the United States called the most bellicose major power in the world; to foreigners, the observation is obvious to the point of banality. America's high-handed behavior puzzles admirers of its domestic freedoms: how to explain the inconsistency? Less sentimental observers point out that this is how the strong have treated the weak throughout history. But, they add, what makes the United States uniquely annoying is its self-righteous insistence that it does nothing of the kind, that it is the epitome of evenhanded virtue and selfless generosity—the Beacon of Democracy that other nations should thank and emulate.

On November 10, 2001, President Bush made his first appearance before the United Nations General Assembly and, in a speech praised by the *New York Times* for its "plain-spoken eloquence,"[10] told the rest of the world it wasn't doing enough to help the United States fight terrorism. "Every nation in the world has a stake in this cause," declared Bush before lecturing his audience that the responsibility to fight terrorism was "binding on every nation with a place in this chamber." Yet on the same day—indeed, at the very moment—that Bush was admonishing others about their international responsibilities, his own administration was shunning negotiations in Morocco to finalize the Kyoto protocol[11] on global warming. Talk about an issue that every nation has a stake in! Already the earth's glaciers are melting, sea levels are rising, and catastrophic storms are becoming more severe and frequent—this after a mere 1 degree Fahrenheit increase in temperatures over the past century. The scientific consensus predicts 3 to 10.5 degrees of additional warming by 2100, bringing more violent weather, flooded coastlines, and social havoc. Yet the Bush administration insists on doing nothing to lower U.S. greenhouse gas emissions. No wonder foreigners resent us.

---

[9]Gerald Celente's quote appeared in the *Financial Times* of September 29–30, 2001.

[10]Bush's speech was reported, and praised, in the November 11 edition of the *New York Times*.

[11]*Kyoto protocol:* U.S. refusal to ratify the 1997 United Nations–sponsored Kyoto protocol which aimed at reducing greenhouse gas emissions below 1990 levels worldwide has been seen as an example of American arrogance and unilateralism.

American elites sometimes talk of our nation's isolationist tendencies, but the correct adjective is unilateralist. The United States has hardly shunned overseas involvement over the years; we simply insist on setting our own terms. This tendency has become especially pronounced since victory in the Cold War left us the only remaining superpower. Determined to keep it that way, senior officials in the first Bush administration drafted a grand strategy for the new era (which got leaked to the *New York Times*):[12] henceforth the goal of American foreign policy would be to prevent any other nation or alliance from becoming a superpower; the United States would rule supreme. This strategy lives on under George W. Bush—which is no surprise, since Vice President Dick Cheney and other key advisers were the ones who devised the strategy for Bush's father. Shortly after taking office, the administration of Bush II announced it was going to withdraw from the Anti-Ballistic Missile Treaty, a cornerstone of nuclear arms control for the past thirty years, in an assertion of unilateralism that evoked dismay not just from treaty partner Russia but from the entire global community. Bush's oddest rejection of global cooperation was his refusal to join, even retroactively, the accord against bioterrorism reached in July 2001 that could hinder future anthrax attacks. The United States delegation walked out of the negotiations because the Bush administration refused to accept the same rules it demands for Iraq and other "rogue states": international inspections of potential weapons production sites.[13]

I don't mean to pick on Mr. Bush. Double standards have a long bipartisan pedigree in American foreign policy. Bush's father uttered one of the most feverish declarations of American prerogative in 1988, while serving as Ronald Reagan's vice president. Five years earlier, when the Soviet Union shot down a Korean Airlines passenger jet over the Pacific, killing all 276 people on board, the United States had condemned the attack as further evidence of the "evil empire's" true nature, rejecting the Soviet explanation that the jet was acting like a military aircraft. Now the tables were turned: the United States had shot down an Iranian civilian jet it mistakenly believed was a military craft. All 290 passengers died. When Bush senior was asked if an apology was in order, he replied, "I will never apologize for the United States. I don't care what the facts are."

Democrats have been just as bad about this kind of thing. In 1998 critics at home and abroad were condemning the Clinton administration's launch of cruise missiles against Iraq as at best unnecessary and at worst a self-serving ploy to weaken impeachment proceedings against the president. But no, Secretary of State Madeleine Albright modestly explained, "if we have to use force, it is because we are America. We are the

[12]The first Bush administration's grand strategy is described in *The New Yorker* of April 1, 2002.
    [13]Bush's rejection of the verification protocol for biological weapons was analyzed by Milton Leitenberg in the *Los Angeles Times Book Review*, October 28, 2001.

indispensable nation. . . . We see farther into the future." As Rupert Corn-well, the Washington correspondent for the British newspaper *The Independent,* observed on another occasion, "No one wraps self-interest in moral superiority quite like the Americans do."[14]

Americans are a fair-minded people, however, and I doubt that a majority of us would support such hypocrisy if we were truly aware of it. I believe most of us would instead urge that the United States bring its global behavior into accord with its domestic principles. But that might threaten what Washington considers vital national interests, so the powers that be resist. Since America is the land of both Hollywood and Madison Avenue, our official response has instead been to hire public relations experts to do a better job of "getting our message out" overseas. Brilliant touch, no? After all, the problem couldn't possibly be our policies themselves.

Americans will continue to misunderstand the world, and our place within it, until we face the full truth of how our government has acted over-seas—a fact made powerfully clear to me in South Africa, where . . . enthusiasm for America . . . is balanced by the anger of those who recall that the United States was a firm, long-standing supporter of apartheid.[15]

Why Don't They Love Us?

The ferry from Cape Town takes forty minutes to reach Robben Island, the notorious prison where Nelson Mandela[16] and other South African free-dom fighters were jailed during their struggle for freedom. The ferry lands at a jetty two hundred yards from a complex of low buildings with corrugated tin roofs that is the prison proper. A sign retained from apartheid days reads, in English and Afrikaans, "Robben Island. Welcome. We Serve with Pride."

There are now guided tours of the island, and what makes them especially   20
compelling is that they are conducted by a thin man in a white windbreaker named Siphiwo Sobuwa. Speaking in a flat, deliberate tone, Sobuwa said he had been imprisoned at age seventeen after being captured smuggling arms for the ANC's[17] military wing. Interrogated, beaten, denied a lawyer, he was sentenced to forty-eight years in jail. He served fifteen years, all on Robben Island, before the crumbling of apartheid enabled his release in 1991.

As he ushered us into the prison's entry hall, Sobuwa recalled how he spent his first two years in solitary confinement because he didn't speak Afrikaans. A warden told his group of arriving prisoners that no talking was allowed, but since Sobuwa didn't understand Afrikaans, he asked another

[14]Rupert Cornwell's remark appeared in *The Independent* on July 27, 2001.

[15]*apartheid:* The South African government policy of racial segregation, abolished in 1992.

[16]*Nelson Mandela:* Nelson Rolihlahla Mandela (b. 1918), South African political leader, elected president in the nation's first post-apartheid multiracial elections in 1994.

[17]*ANC:* The African National Congress, a South African political organization, led by Nelson Mandela from 1991 until 1994, prominent for its opposition to apartheid.

inmate what was going on. The warden decided to make an example of Sobuwa. "I was sent to A section, the torture section," he told us. "I could not write or receive letters. I could not speak, sing, or whistle. Food was slipped underneath the grille of my cell. Those two years were the hardest."

We pushed through a door into an open-air courtyard, where we listened to Sobuwa recount other punishments common on Robben Island. Most humiliating was the guards' game of ordering an inmate buried in the ground up to his neck and then leaving him there all day to roast in the sun while guards took turns urinating on him. More gruesome was the practice of hanging a prisoner upside down from a tree and waiting as the hours passed for him to pass out and, in one case, to perish as the body's blood supply gradually accumulated in the brain, starving it of oxygen. But of all the deprivations—punishing physical labor, numbing boredom, inedible food, lack of heat—Sobuwa said the blackout on news was the hardest to bear. Inmates did their best to compensate. "The guard towers had no toilets," he explained, "so guards would relieve themselves in newspapers, then throw the papers down to the ground. We would retrieve those papers, scrape them off, and read the news they contained. We didn't care what kind of mess was inside, we wanted that news."

Hearing about such abominations firsthand makes visiting Robben Island as unforgettable as a pilgrimage to Dachau or Hiroshima.[18] And talking with a man like Sobuwa rescues foreign policy from its usual abstractions, making concrete the implications of such diplomatic double-talk as "constructive engagement," the Reagan administration's justification for its unswerving support for apartheid. When I interviewed Sobuwa at his cinder-block house in a Cape Town township, he said his work had taught him to distinguish between Americans as people and the American government. He had little good to say about the latter. Washington, he pointed out, as well as Israel, had supported apartheid—and thus the oppression on Robben Island—until the very end. Furthermore, he said, "it is a trend among United States presidents that so-called Third World countries must be destabilized. America believes in solving problems not by negotiations but through military pressure."

But his tour guide conversations had made Sobuwa realize that not all Americans supported their goverment's policy. He was grateful for those who had joined the protests that eventually forced Western governments, including that of the United States, to endorse apartheid's demise. He was unaware that America's new vice president had, as a U.S. congressman in 1985, voted against urging Mandela's release from jail,[19] but then neither

[18]*Dachau or Hiroshima:* Respectively, site of a World War II–era Nazi "death camp" and the Japanese city that, along with Nagasaki, was the first populated area to be targeted by nuclear weapons.

[19]Dick Cheney was one of only eight members of Congress who voted against the resolution urging the government of South Africa to release Mandela from jail and initiate negotiations with the African National Congress. See Joe Conason's story in Salon.com., August 1, 2000.

were most Americans aware of this aspect of Dick Cheney's past. What
Sobuwa did know was that Bill Clinton had a lot of nerve. "He came here a
couple years ago to visit Mandela and speak to our Parliament, and he told
us South Africa should cut its ties to Cuba because Cuba was a bad government. Well, when we needed help during our liberation struggle, Cuba gave
it. When we needed food, Cuba provided it. For someone who did not help
our struggle to come now and ask us to distance ourselves from someone
who did, that is very arrogant behavior."

Arrogant but, alas, not atypical. The United States has long pressed   25
South American nations to cut ties with the Castro government. Likewise,
in June 2002 George W. Bush announced that Yasir Arafat had to go as the
Palestinian leader. Free elections had to be held, said Bush, but Washing-
ton would push for a Palestinian state only if those "free" elections got rid of
Arafat.

Washington's might-makes-right view of such matters was succinctly
expressed by Henry Kissinger when, as President Richard Nixon's national
security adviser, he privately defended overthrowing the elected government of Chile by saying he saw no reason why the United States had to
allow Chile to "go Marxist" simply because "its people are irresponsible."[20]
Testifying before the U.S. Senate on the day of the coup, Kissinger claimed
the United States had played no role in the 1973 coup that toppled Allende.
But voluminous government documents show that Kissinger, as head of the
so-called Forty Committee that supervised U.S. covert actions between
1969 and 1976, was well-informed about how the CIA had ordered a coup
in 1970 that had failed to thwart Allende and, in 1973, had at least con-
doned if not actively aided the Chilean military men who, under future dic-
tator General Augusto Pinochet, imposed martial law and eventually killed
3,197 Chilean citizens.[21]

Note the date of the U.S.-sponsored assault on democratic government
in Chile: September 11, 1973. Note the estimated Chilean death toll—exe-
cutions plus military casualties—of 3,197 people. Is not the congruence between that coup and the World Trade Center attack striking? True, one was
authored by religious fanatics and the other by a state, and the events were
separated in time by twenty-eight years, yet both took place on the same
date and caused comparable numbers of deaths. Nevertheless, this eerie co-
incidence passed virtually unremarked in the United States.

This is self-defeating. It's no secret to Chileans that the United States
helped bring to power the dictatorship that ruled them for seventeen years.

---

[20]Kissinger's quote about Chile and his activities with the Forty Committee are described
in "The Case Against Henry Kissinger," by Christopher Hitchens, in *Harper's Magazine*, February and March 2001.
    [21]The death toll resulting from the 1973 coup in Chile is documented by John Dinges in
The Condor Years: How Pinochet and His Allies Brought Terrorism to Three Continents (New
York: New Press, 2003), chapter 1.

Nor are the people of El Salvador and Guatemala unaware that the United States gave money, weapons, and training to the military governments that killed so many of their fellow citizens in recent decades. In Guatemala, a truth commission sponsored by the United Nations concluded in 1999 that "American training of the officer corps in counterinsurgency techniques" was a "key factor" in a "genocide" that included the killing of 200,000 peasants.

Switch to Asia[22] or the Middle East and the same point applies. Virtually every one of Washington's allies in the Middle East is an absolute monarchy where democracy and human rights are foreign concepts and women in particular are second-class citizens. But they have oil, so all is forgiven. Likewise, in South Korea everyone knows that the United States chose the generals that ruled their country from the end of World War II until 1993; the facts came out during a trial that found two of the surviving dictators guilty of state terrorism. Ferdinand Marcos of the Philippines, General Suharto of Indonesia, General Lon Nol of Cambodia—the list of tyrants that Washington has supported in Asia is widely known, except in the United States.

Again, what offends is not simply the ruthlessness of American policies but their hypocrisy. The United States insists on the sanctity of United Nations resolutions when they punish enemies like Iraq with arms inspections, but not when they oblige its number-one foreign aid recipient, Israel, to withdraw from occupation of Palestinian territories in the West Bank and Gaza. On trade policy, Washington demands that poor countries honor World Trade Organization rules against subsiding domestic farmers or industries because these rules enable U.S.-based multinational firms to invade those countries' economies. Without blushing, Washington then lavishes billions of dollars in subsidies on our own agriculture sector (dominated, by the way, by those same multinationals) and imposes tariffs against foreign steel imports. Why do we violate fair play so brazenly? Because we can. "The United States can hurt us a lot worse than we can hurt them," grumbled one Canadian trade official. 30

Then there is our self-serving definition of "terrorism," a concept America's political and media elites never apply to the United States or its allies, only to enemies or third parties. No one disputes that the September 11 attacks against the United States were acts of terrorism; that is, they targeted innocent civilians to advance a political or military agenda. When the Irish Republican Army exploded bombs inside London subway stations and department stores in the mid-1990s, that, too, was terrorism. So were the Palestinian suicide bombings in Israel in early 2002, and Saddam Hussein's

---

[22]The findings of the United Nations–sponsored Commission for Historical Clarification, as well as American support for Asian dictators, were summarized in *Blowback: The Costs and Consequences of American Empire*, by Chalmers Johnson (New York: Henry Holt, Owl Books, 2001), pages 14 and 25–27, respectively.

use of poison gas against Kurds in Iraq in 1988. But when Israel attacked Palestinian refugee camps in April 2002, demolishing buildings and killing or wounding many civilians, was that not also terrorism? When the United States lobbed Volkswagen-sized shells into Lebanese villages in 1983 and dropped "smart bombs" on Baghdad in 1991, many innocent civilians perished while Washington sent its geopolitical message. The napalm dropped during the Vietnam War, the bombing of Dresden,[23] and the annihilation of Hiroshima and Nagasaki in World War II—these acts all pursued military or political objectives by killing vast numbers of civilians, just as the September 11 attacks did. Yet in mainstream American discourse, the United States is never the perpetrator of terrorism, only its victim and implacable foe.

These and other unsavory aspects of America's overseas dealings are not completely unknown in the United States. Academic specialists, human rights activists, and partisans of the political left are familiar with this history. Glimpses of the truth appear (very) occasionally in mainstream press coverage, and the CIA's role in subverting democracies and overthrowing governments was documented by congressional investigations in 1975. In 2002 Samantha Powers published a book, *A Problem from Hell*, that meticulously documented how Washington deliberately chose not to intervene against some of the worst acts of genocide in the twentieth century, including Pol Pot's[24] rampages in Cambodia, ethnic cleansing in Bosnia,[25] and tribal slaughter in Rwanda.[26] The book received considerable attention within media circles; its message got out. But in general, critical perspectives on American actions are given nowhere near the same prominence or repetition in government, media, and public discussion as is the conventional view of the United States as an evenhanded champion of democracy and freedom. Thus the basic direction of American foreign policy rarely shifts, and Washington creates for itself what the late *Wall Street Journal* reporter Jonathan Kwitny called "endless enemies"[27] around the world. Worse, average Americans are left unaware that this is happening, and so are shocked when foreigners don't love us as much as we think they should.

[23]*Dresden:* One of the world's most beautiful cities before World War II, Dresden, Germany, was the site of a particularly violent attack by Allied bombers in 1945 that resulted in 35,000 to 135,000 casualties and destroyed many of the city's original buildings.

[24]*Pol Pot:* Communist leader (1925–1998) who seized the government of Cambodia in 1975 and instituted a repressive regime that became infamous for its policy of systematic murder of rival groups and forced labor in the "killing fields" until Vietnam invaded in 1979. Pol Pot retired in 1985.

[25]*ethnic cleansing in Bosnia:* After Bosnia and Hercegovina declared their independence from Yugoslavia in 1992, Serbian and Croat Christian forces in Bosnia began a systematic campaign of "ethnic cleansing" to exterminate the majority Muslim population.

[26]*Rwanda:* In 1994, the Hutu tribe joined Rwandan government troops in a genocidal attack on their longtime rivals, the Tutsi clan, that resulted in between 500,000 and 800,000 casualties.

[27]Kwitny's phrase was the title of his illuminating and comprehensive book *Endless Enemies: The Making of an Unfriendly World* (New York: Congdon & Weed, 1984).

Ignorance is an excuse, but it is no shield. "Although most Americans may be largely ignorant of what was, and still is, being done in their names, all are likely to pay a steep price . . . for their nation's continued efforts to dominate the global scene," veteran Asian affairs analyst Chalmers Johnson wrote in his fierce book, *Blowback*. America's tendency to bully, warns Johnson, will "build up reservoirs of resentment against all Americans— tourists, students, and businessmen, as well as members of the armed forces—that can have lethal results."

"Blowback" is a CIA term for how foreign policy can come back to haunt a country years later in unforeseen ways, especially after cases of secret operations. Thus Johnson quotes a 1997 report by the Pentagon's Defense Science Board: "Historical data show a strong correlation between U.S. involvement in international situations and an increase in terrorist attacks against the United States." A glaring example is the Iranian hostage crisis of 1979. To protect American oil interests, the CIA in 1953 overthrew the elected government of Iran and installed Shah Reza Pahlavi (an act a subsequent CIA director, William Colby, described as the CIA's "proudest moment").[28] The shah ruled with an iron hand, murdered thousands, duly became widely hated, and was forced from power in 1979. Residual Iranian anger led to an attack on the United States embassy in Tehran and seizure of fifty-four hostages, a crisis that doomed Jimmy Carter's presidency.[29]

Because Johnson's book was published in 2000, it was unable to address the most spectacular of all cases of blowback: the September 11 terror attacks. But in the October 15 and December 10, 2001, issues of *The Nation*, Johnson explained how the CIA supported Osama bin Laden[30] from at least 1984 as part of its funding of the mujahideen, the Islamic resistance to the Soviet Union's occupation of Afghanistan. The CIA funneled its support for bin Laden and other mujahideen, including building the complex where bin Laden trained some thirty-five thousand followers, through Pakistan's intelligence service. But bin Laden turned against the United States after the 1991 Persian Gulf War, when "infidel" American troops were stationed on the Islamic holy ground of Saudi Arabia to prop up its authoritarian regime. The September 11 attacks, Johnson concludes, were the blowback from America's covert action in Afghanistan in the 1970s, and the cycle is probably not over: "The Pentagon's current response of 'bouncing the rubble' in Afghanistan [is] setting the stage for more rounds to come."

35

[28]The quotes from Johnson, *Blowback*, are from pages 33 and 4, respectively.

[29]The definitive account of America's actions in Iran, including the help that the local *New York Times* correspondent gave to the coup plotters, is found in Kwitny, *Endless Enemies*, pages 161–78.

[30]*Osama bin Laden:* Son of one of Saudi Arabia's wealthiest families, Osama bin Laden (b. 1957) founded the international terrorist organization al-Qaeda in 1988, which has since been linked to numerous attacks on U.S. targets around the world, including the assaults of September 11, 2001.

ENGAGING THE TEXT

1. How does the rest of the world view America, according to Hertsgaard? To what extent would you agree that we are a particularly "oblivious" nation when it comes to our relationships with other peoples?

2. What is the difference between American "isolationism" and what Hertsgaard terms American "unilateralism"? What examples does he offer of the new American unilateral approach to world affairs? How might recent events support or challenge this view?

3. Why does Hertsgaard object to the way our government defines terrorism? Does the idea of terrorism have a clear definition, or is it a purely political term used to demonize our enemies and justify our own national policies?

4. What is "blowback," and how does it account, in Hertsgaard's view, for much of the anti-American feeling in the world today? Do you think it's appropriate to speculate about the motives of terrorists, or does this kind of analysis amount to sympathizing with the enemy?

5. What would be required for the United States to "bring its global behavior into accord with its domestic principles" (para. 17)? How would the U.S. have to change its current approach to foreign affairs to do this?

EXPLORING CONNECTIONS

6. How does the historical context provided by Albert J. Beveridge's "The March of the Flag" (p. 709) help account for current American attitudes toward other nations, as described by Hertsgaard? How does it complicate Hertsgaard's claim that American unilateralism is a relatively recent development?

7. Compare Hertsgaard's analysis of anti-Americanism with that offered by Dinesh D'Souza (p. 716). Which strikes you as the more plausible? Why? Are these conflicting explanations mutually exclusive, or might they both have some merit?

8. How might Benjamin Barber's critique of education in the United States (p. 283) support Hertsgaard's claim that we Americans are dismally ignorant of our role in foreign affairs? What do you think might be done to make the United States less "oblivious" as a nation?

EXTENDING THE CRITICAL CONTEXT

9. Working in small groups, research the history of any of the examples Hertsgaard offers of U.S. "unilateralism," including American involvement in South Africa, Chile, El Salvador, Guatemala, the Philippines, Indonesia, Cambodia, Bosnia, Rwanda, Iran, and any other nation you might think a good candidate. Report your findings in class and discuss how the results of your research confirm or challenge Hertsgaard's view of American attitudes toward the rest of the world.

10. Test Hertsgaard's belief in our national ignorance by creating a survey of five to ten questions based on facts he provides in this selection or on your

own knowledge of U.S. foreign policy. Administer the survey to fellow students, friends, relatives, or members of your local community, and report your results in class. Do your findings suggest that we are, in fact, as "oblivious" as Hertsgaard suggests?

11. Do further research on the concept of "blowback" by reading the articles by Chalmers Johnson that Hertsgaard mentions in this selection, originally appearing in *The Nation* magazine on October 15 and December 10, 2001, or by consulting additional articles written by Johnson or those written in response to his 2000 book *Blowback: The Costs and Consequences of American Empire*. What might the idea of "blowback" suggest in relation to assessing the long-term consequences of U.S. actions in nations like Afghanistan and Iraq?

12. Since the formulation of the Defense Planning Guidance draft in 1992, which first articulated the case for American military domination in the post–Cold War era, the idea of a new American "empire" has been growing in popularity. Research the idea of American empire and related concepts like "the Bush Doctrine" to learn more about what Hertsgaard terms the new "grand strategy of American foreign policy." What, if anything, might be wrong with the idea of establishing an "empire" as a goal for America in its dealings with the rest of the world?

The War on Terrorism

Joel Andreas

You might think that comics are all about teenage superheroes or ducks in short jackets, but not if you've ever encountered the source of this selection. Joel Andreas's Addicted to War: Why the U.S. Can't Kick Militarism *(2002) is a cultural phenomenon — a comic book with a deadly serious subject that, in an era of ever increasing international tensions, has emerged as a nationwide best-seller. Joel Andreas (b. 1956) became a committed political activist while attending antiwar demonstrations with his parents in Vietnam-era Detroit. He completed his Ph.D. in sociology at UCLA and now teaches at Johns Hopkins University. In addition to* Addicted to War, *Andreas has published two other "illustrated exposés":* The Incredible Rocky, *an unauthorized biography of the Rockefeller family and* Made with Pure Rocky Mountain Scab Labor *(1977), a comic broadside in support of a strike by Coors Brewery workers.*

Chapter 4
The
"War on Terrorism"

After the horrific **September 11 terrorist attacks** on the World Trade Center and the Pentagon, **one question** was so **sensitive** it was seldom seriously addressed by the U.S. news media.

To find out, it makes sense to ask the **prime suspect** himself. As U.S. warplanes began bombing Afghanistan, **Osama bin Laden** released a videotaped message. He **praised** the **September 11 attacks** and called for more attacks on the United States. Then he spelled out his **motivations** quite clearly.

"What America is tasting now is something insignificant compared to what we have tasted for scores of years. Our nation (the Islamic world) has been tasting this **humiliation** and **degradation** for more than **80 years**. Its sons are killed, its **blood is shed**, its sanctuaries are attacked and no one hears and no one heeds. Millions of innocent children are being killed as I speak. They are being killed in **Iraq** without committing any sins.... To **America**, I say only a few words to it and its people. I swear to God, who has elevated the skies without pillars, **neither America nor the people** who live in it will **dream of security** before we live it here in **Palestine** and not before all the **infidel armies leave the land of Muhammad,** peace be upon him." (1)

Osama bin Laden Oct. 7, 2001

Mom, **why** did they do it?

[1]Bin Laden cited in *Wall Street Journal* online, October 7, 2001.

Over the last several decades the **true costs** of the wars the U.S. has waged overseas have been largely **hidden**. We have had to **pay the military bills** but few Americans have died. The **death** and **destruction** was all **overseas**. That changed on **September 11**.

> The **violence reached the United States**

The September 11 attacks, however, were not simply acts of **retribution**. They were also **provocation**. Bin Laden expected the U.S. to respond with **massive violence**, knowing this would bring him **new recruits**. Ultimately, he hoped to win the majority of the Muslim world to support his **holy war on the U.S.**

> More **martyrs**, more **recruits**.

The Bush Administration responded according to **bin Laden's script**. George W. Bush declared a "**War on Terrorism**," using "good vs. evil" rhetoric that mirrored bin Laden's. Bush and his advisors were ready, **even eager**, for the war bin Laden wanted. They saw the September 11 attacks as a **grand opportunity** to boost military spending and demonstrate U.S. military power.

(2)

> "This will be a monumental struggle of **good versus evil** ... This **crusade**, this **war on terrorism**, is going to take a while"

G.W. Bush, Sept. 12 and 16, 2001

Bush's "**War on Terrorism**" began with U.S. warplanes **bombing Afghanistan**. The Bush Administration refused to negotiate or consider any **alternatives to war**. When the Afghan government asked for evidence against bin Laden, a reasonable request that might have made it possible to cooperate with the U.S., Bush replied:

> I said - **no negotiations! Cough up** bin Laden now or **die** along with him!

Relatives prepare the bodies of four small children for burial after a U.S. airstrike. Kabul, October 2001.

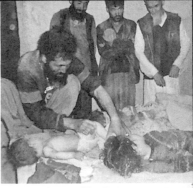

The people of Afghanistan **suffered the consequences**. **U.S. bombing** killed many civilians and the war cut off relief supplies to millions already **facing starvation**. The total number of deaths will never be known, but it's likely there will be many times more **civilian deaths** in Afghanistan than in the World Trade Center.

[2]Bush cited in "The President's Words," *Los Angeles Times*, September 22, 2001.

[3]Millions were endangered because the war cut off relief supplies (http://www .observer.co.uk/afghanistan/story/0,1501,577996,00.html). Analyzing media reports, Marc Herold of the University of New Hampshire estimated that U.S. bombs killed 3100 to 3700 Afghan civilians (http://www.pubpages.unh.edu/~mwherold). The *New York Times* estimated that 3086 people died in the Sept. 11 terrorist attacks (February 9, 2002, p. A7).

As warplanes of the world's **richest and most powerful** country bombed people in one of the **poorest and most miserable** countries on earth, the streets of cities throughout the Muslim world filled with **angry demonstrations**. Not only religious radicals were angry Almost everybody in the Muslim world **opposed the war.**

USA THE REAL TERRORIST

The war **added fuel** to simmering anti-American sentiments in the Middle East. Bombing Muslim countries and sending U.S. troops into this volatile region will only inspire more hatred for the United States and **more terrorist attacks** on Americans. Bush surely knows this, yet he decided to go ahead and **place us in greater danger** anyway.

We **never said** this war was not going to have **costs!**

The War on Terrorism **cannot possibly end terrorism.** Even if bin Laden is killed, **new converts will rally** to join his war to drive the U.S. out of the Middle East. The **spiral of violence** is escalating dangerously.

And the warmakers on both sides are **itching to escalate!**

The self-righteous **"good vs. evil"** rhetoric of the War on Terrorism sharpens ironies that have long shadowed U.S. pronouncements against **state-sponsored terrorism.** President Bush, for instance, promises to scour the globe in search of **states** that **harbor terrorists.**

He could start in the **State of Florida**

What do you mean?

For over forty years, **Miami** has served as the base of operations for well-financed groups of **Cuban exiles** that have carried out violent **terrorist attacks on Cuba.**

Most recently, they **bombed** a number of Havana tourist spots in 1997, killing an Italian tourist, and they tried to **assassinate** Fidel Castro in Panama in 2000.

It would not be difficult for the government to find evidence involving these terrorist organizations because the **CIA** and the **Pentagon trained** many of their **members**. Take, for instance, **Luis Posada Carriles** and **Orlando Bosch**, suspected masterminds of the **bombing** of a **Cuban passenger airliner** that claimed the lives of **73 people**.

④ "All of Castro's planes are **warplanes**"

Orlando Bosch, 1987, defending the bombing of the civilian Cuban plane

Before Posada Carriles could be tried for the airline bombing, he **escaped** from a **prison** in Venezuela and found a job **supplying arms** to the CIA-backed **Nicaraguan contras**.

My **experience** in the **CIA** gave me the **right credentials** for the job

⑤

Posada's accomplice, Orlando Bosch, has long been **protected from extradition** by the U.S. government. Although Bosch was convicted of carrying out a **bazooka attack** on a ship in **Miami harbor**, President Bush's father, George H., at the urging of his brother, Jeb, prevented his expulsion from the country. He signed an **executive pardon** providing Bosch with **safe haven** in Florida. Bosch promised he would...

⑥

"Rejoin **the struggle!**"

⑦

Hold on! Let me set the record straight. I **pardon** only **freedom fighters**, not terrorists!

If the younger Bush were serious about going after **all** states that **harbor terrorists**, he might issue his **next ultimatum** to **his brother**, the governor of Florida.

Listen Jeb, you're going to have to **cough up** the terrorists or we start **bombing Miami** tomorrow!

Posada, Bosch and their friends are **only a few** of the violent characters whose activities have been sponsored by the CIA. Many of the CIA's "**covert operations**" – bombings, **assassinations, sabotage, paramilitary massacres** – are terrorism by any definition. Many of the shadowy figures involved in these activities are still working with the CIA around the world. But others – including **Osama bin Laden** – have **turned on their former partners**.

⑧

It's **too bad**. They made such a **good team**.

[4]Bosch cited in Alexander Cockburn, "The Tribulations of Joe Doherty," *Wall Street Journal*, reprinted in the *Congressional Record*, page E2639.

[5]Cockburn; John Rice, "Man with CIA Links Accused of Plotting to Kill Castro," Associated Press, November 18, 2000; Frances Robles and Glenn Garvin, "Four Held in Plot Against Castro," *Miami Herald*, November 19, 2000; Jill Mullin, "The Burden of a Violent History," *Miami New Times*, April 20, 2000.

[6]Joe Conason, "The Bush Pardons," http://www.salon.com/news/col/cona/2001/02/27/pardons/print.html.

[7]Bosch cited in Cockburn.

[8]William Blum, *Killing Hope: U.S. Military and CIA Interventions Since World War II* (Monroe, Maine: Common Courage Press, 1995).

[9]Post-9-11 restrictions on Civil liberties: American Civil Liberties Union, http://www.aclu.org/safeandfree.

[10]Joshua Cohen, "An Interview with Ted Postol: What's Wrong with Missile Defense," *Boston Review,* October/November 2001; David E. Sanger, "Washington's New Freedom, and New Worries, in the Post-ABM-Treaty Era," *New York Times,* December 15, 2001.

[11]Submarine-based missiles: htto://no-nukes.org/nukewatch/.

[12]R. Jeffrey Smith, "U.S. Urged to Cut 50% of A-Arms: Soviet Breakup Is Said to Allow Radical Shift in Strategic Targeting," *Washington Post, January* 6, 1991, p. A1.

[13]Judith Miller, "U.S. Seeks Changes in Germ War Pact," *New York Times*, November 1, 2001; William Broad and Judith Miller, "U.S. Recently Produced Anthrax in a Highly Lethal Powder Form," *New York Times*, December 13, 2001.

[14]William Broad, Judith Miller, *Germs: Biological Weapons and America's Secret War*, (New York: Simon & Schuster, 2001); William Blum.

[15]Center for Defense Information, http://www.cdi.organization/isssues/wme/.

ENGAGING THE TEXT

1. How does Andreas explain the motives behind the 9/11 attacks? Why, in his view, is it crucial to understand that these were acts of provocation and not merely acts of retribution or revenge?

2. How does Andreas view the Bush administration's response to September 11? What does he see as the real motive behind the war on terrorism? What problems does he see with the notion of the United States declaring a war against terror?

3. Why, according to Andreas, would strengthening the U.S. military actually make us less safe? To what extent would you agree that the war on terror will actually end by making the world more dangerous? Who, from Andreas's perspective, is the greater threat to the world—terrorists like Osama bin Laden, or militaristic superpowers like the United States? Why?

4. Why do you think Andreas chose to present his views in comic book form? How do the images work here to support his argument? How, for example, does he portray military and political figures, and how do these portrayals compare with the mother and son figures who clearly speak for Andreas? Would Andreas's ideas and claims have been less persuasive if presented in the form of a traditional essay? Why or why not?

EXPLORING CONNECTIONS

5. How might Dinesh D'Souza (p. 716) respond to Andreas's depiction of American foreign policy? According to D'Souza, what does such thinking do to the United States? To what extent would you agree with him?

6. How does the information provided by Andreas challenge or support Mark Hertsgaard's claims about recent directions in U.S. foreign policy (p. 728)? Would Andreas be likely to agree with Hertsgaard that America is an "oblivious empire"? Which of these selections did you find the more persuasive? The more informative? Why?

EXTENDING THE CRITICAL CONTEXT

7. Do some research to test Andreas's depiction of the U.S. military. How has the size of the armed forces varied over the past 100 years? How has the level of military spending changed over the same period? How have the functions of the armed services evolved? To what extent do the results of your research support or challenge Andreas's depiction of the United States as an aggressively militaristic nation?

8. Research the accuracy of Andreas's claims about Afghanistan. How many military and civilian casualties resulted from the U.S.-led "liberation" of this country? What were the economic, cultural, and political impacts of military intervention? Overall, would you say that the United States achieved its goals in Afghanistan? How has "liberation" affected the lives of the Afghani people? If you wish, you might extend your research to Iraq as well.

9. Research the claim that our government has frequently been involved in acts of state terrorism. What can you learn about the "covert operations"

engaged in by the CIA over the past fifty years? What role, for example, did the U.S. play in the early careers of Osama bin Laden and Saddam Hussein? To what extent do you feel it is justifiable for the United States to engage in activities like assassinations, illegal traffic in weapons, sabotage, and support for "paramilitaries," in pursuit of its foreign policy goals?

Poem for Benjamin Franklin
JUNE JORDAN

The first "foreign" nations the fledgling United States had to contend with were here long before the colonists arrived. America's sense of its own "Manifest Destiny" in relation to the rest of the world developed as the United States expanded westward, systematically dispossessing the tribal peoples who once lived at liberty across the continent. Perhaps that's why June Jordan dedicated this angry poem to Benjamin Franklin—one of the most mythic of America's cultural heroes and a central figure in the founding of the Republic. Jordan's unusual treatment of Franklin reminds us that domination has long been a part of the American agenda, and that the struggle between the strong and weak can be just as bitter in personal as it is in foreign affairs. Born of West Indian parents in Harlem in 1936, Jordan was a prolific poet, essayist, journalist, teacher, and activist until her death in 2002. Her publications include On Call *(1985),* Technical Difficulties *(1992),* Affirmative Acts: Political Essays *(1998), and* Soldier: A Poet's Childhood *(2000). This selection originally appeared in* Naming Our Destiny: New and Selected Poems *(1989).*

Poem for Benjamin Franklin
Who said,
"I do not believe we shall ever have a firm peace with the Indians,
till we have well-drubbed them."

My Daddy, Mr. Franklin, my truculent
no-paunch
crack a coconut with one whack
of a handy homeowner's hammer-axe/my
Daddy, Mr. Franklin, my fastidious
first runaway from a true calypso/my[1]

5

---

[1] *from a true calypso:* "Calypso" here is both a type of West Indian music famous for its lively rhythms and a veiled allusion to "Kalypso," a young goddess who seduces Odysseus and keeps him from returning home in Homer's *Odyssey.*

Daddy, Mr. Franklin, my Daddy give this
little girl
your glorified life story she
must read   10
or else
when she didn't know much better than to trust
some pontiff-politician talk about save pennies/
take a stitch in time

anyway   15

you the one gone out there in the lightning
with a kite?

Let me electrify the ghost
of your redoubtable achievements!

The Indians been well drubbed   20
The Palestinians been well drubbed

firm peace prevails
in 2 out of every 3 American bedrooms
and
on the nighttime city sidewalks   25
Firm peace prevails

and
underneath the hanging tree
and
moaning down at Wounded Knee²   30
and north of Ocatál³
and
east of Ilopongo⁴
and
censored in the sandpits of an occupied West Bank⁵   35
and

---

²*Wounded Knee:* More than 200 disarmed Sioux Indians—men, women, and children—
were massacred at Wounded Knee Creek, South Dakota, on December 29, 1890, during the
last major confrontation between Native Americans and U.S. troops.

³*Ocatál:* Ocatál, Nicaragua, site of the first aerial bombing of a civilian population, carried
out by a U.S. Marine squadron on July 17, 1927.

⁴*Ilopongo:* During the Reagan administration in 1982, the air force base in Ilopongo, El
Salvador, was reputedly used with CIA knowledge as a transshipment point in an "arms-for-
drugs" scheme that supplied the anti-Communist Nicaraguan "Contras" with weapons funded
through cocaine sold on the streets of U.S. cities.

⁵*West Bank:* The predominantly Palestinian area along the western edge of the River Jordan, occupied by Israel since its seizure during the 1967 Arab-Israeli War, which has been the
site of the Palestinian "Intifada," or resistance movement, since 1993.

all around Johannesburg[6] where boiling water in a tin can
has become a crime

Firm peace prevails
Mr. Franklin   40
Firm peace prevails

We been well drubbed
but
like my Daddy could have told you/my
Daddy whistling in the ghetto   45
of your legacy/my
Daddy could have told you after he done beat me
how I laid real low but didn't hardly overlook to pay him
back
(big men must sleep sometime)   50
My Daddy/Mr. Franklin/my Daddy could have told you
firm peace ain' peace it's truce
and truce don't last
but temporarily

ENGAGING THE TEXT

1. What can you infer about the speaker of Jordan's poem from her subject,
   tone, and attitude? How do you picture her? How old do you think she is?
   What is her background?

2. What is the speaker of this poem saying about Benjamin Franklin? Why
   does she connect Franklin with her father? What connects Franklin to
   places like Wounded Knee, Ocatál, Ilopango, and Johannesburg? What
   mythic ideas in American culture are associated with the figure of Ben
   Franklin?

3. What overall is the theme of this poem? Is it primarily about domestic violence? Who does Jordan's speaker represent?

EXPLORING CONNECTIONS

4. In what sense might Jordan's poem be seen as a response or rebuttal to
   Albert J. Beveridge's "The March of the Flag" (p. 709)? What alternative
   vision of America's relation with other countries does Jordan offer in her
   poem?

5. How might Mark Hertsgaard (p. 728) interpret the threat that closes
   Jordan's poem? To what extent does Jordan's account of personal hatred
   and revenge help you to appreciate the kind of anti-American rage that
   Hertsgaard discusses in his essay?

---

[6]*Johannesburg:* Largest city in South Africa, identified in the past with apartheid, South
Africa's official policy of racial segregation, until its repeal in 1992.

Extending the Critical Context

6. Read more about Benjamin Franklin and his famous autobiography. What values and attitudes are typically associated with Franklin? What controversies surround this heroic American figure?

7. Do additional research to learn more about how other major American "Founding Fathers" like George Washington, Thomas Jefferson, and John Adams viewed Native Americans. Did they share Franklin's apparent disdain for the continent's original inhabitants? Did Franklin himself actually take such a brutal view of Native Americans and Yankee superiority?

An African-American Appeal for Peace

Walter Mosley

Despite slavery, Jim Crow discrimination, and lingering racism, African Americans enjoy a long and distinguished history of serving the United States in times of warfare. From Crispus Attucks, one of the first colonists killed by the British at the Boston Massacre in 1770, to Colin Powell, chairman of the Joint Chiefs of Staff during the 1991 "Desert Storm" campaign against Iraq, African Americans have played an important role in defending the United States. But according to Walter Mosley, African Americans should be playing a far different part. As Mosley sees it, African Americans are supremely equipped to bear the message of America to the rest of the world. Mosley is best known as the creator of Easy Rawlins, the black L.A.-based private eye featured in a series of six enormously popular detective novels that include Devil in a Blue Dress *(1990),* Black Betty *(1994), and most recently* Bad Boy Brawly Brown *(2002). Mosley's twelve novels and numerous short stories have won him a series of honors, including an O'Henry Award for fiction in 1996 and the Anisfield Wolf Award in 1998 for "works that increase the appreciation and understanding of race in America. Since 1996, Mosley has served as the first "Artist-in-Residence" at the Africana Studies Institute of New York University.*

On the morning of September 11, 2001, I was talking on the phone and looking down on the Hudson River from my southward-facing Greenwich Village apartment window. I heard a concussion, felt it almost. I looked around but saw nothing until my eyes rose up and caught sight of the World Trade Center. The gash on the upper side of the north tower was black and spewing smoke. There was also a trail of smoke down the left side of the building that went all the way to the street.

I was confused about that trail of smoke. I tried to figure out how it fit with the smoking wound. It wasn't until some time later, when the second jetliner crashed into the southern tower, that I understood that downward trail of dark vapor.

That cascading column came to mean to me everything about the war that was forming in people's minds around the world. It was a sign that I couldn't read clearly, but still I knew there were deadly ramifications to its manifestation.

I won't belabor the story here. We all went through it: our own planes raining death and destruction down upon our nation's most identifiable and important cities and structures. The towers falling, the heroic struggles, the war being waged upon our one-time allies against the USSR—all of this presaged in that dense black column that dissipated within minutes of its inception.

For months after this event, I, like so many Americans, was lost in a kind of anxiety-ridden daze. I worried about world war, about radical religious extremists wresting the reins of power from some nation with nuclear capabilities. I worried about air travel and subway cars, about doomsday plagues and about my nation falling under the sway of fascist rule. There was a deep disquiet in my heart, and I didn't know how to get at it except by worrying about nebulous issues far beyond my immediate control.   5

This is, of course, how the human mind works. When we feel menaced, we try to protect ourselves by considering every possible threat that might arise. The problem in this case, however, was that there was no defense against falling jetliners, religious hard-liners and the resort to unqualified nationalism.

The thing I feared most was the healing quality that time has on the human heart. I knew that after a while I would fall back into complacency—that I would learn to accept that which I knew was unacceptable.

Thousands of dark people are dying daily in the towns and villages and cities of Africa. We in the United States know this, but it doesn't seem to matter to us any more than a popular television show coming to the end of its run. Millions of people, maybe more than ever in the history of the world, are languishing in slavery and forced labor in Sudan and Haiti and many other countries. There are even slaves here in the United States, men and women trapped in the modern growth industry of private prisons, not to mention those caught in the traffic of forced prostitution.

Every night on every station there is some sitcom that makes a joke about what happens to young men in prison—but still we do nothing. Not only are these men raped, humiliated, and emotionally shattered, but they become infected with AIDS and hepatitis C, diseases that they bring home to our communities. And we, literally, just laugh.

War and poverty, disease and hopelessness are ravaging half the world,   10 while the other half wonders how long it will be able to stay out of the maelstrom.

All this is our responsibility. Every child wasting away under his mother's powerless gaze. Every Muslim burned by a Hindu. Every innocent citizen blown up by a suicide bomber or crushed by an onrushing, revenge-drunk tank. I know we are responsible because US dollars have found their way into, and out of, every battlefield, every hospital bed and every pocket of every terrorist in the world.

We—black men and women in every stratum of American society—live in and are part of an ecosystem of terror. We, descendants of human suffering, are living in a fine mansion at the edge of a precipice. And the ground is caving in under the weight of our wealth and privilege.

All this I saw in that column of smoke.

It is time for this nation to come up with a new program: a new notion of civil rights and peaceful negotiation, an international concept of harmony among the wide variety of humanity extant in the world of the twenty-first century. And who is better qualified than African-Americans for this task?

We know from bitter experience what it is to be shortchanged every   15 day, from cradle to grave. We know the lies propagated by the media, law enforcement, and even our own government. We know that the concepts of equality and fairness are actually only commodities distributed by the institutions of capital. We know because when we went to the store for our fair share, we were told, for centuries, that there was a shortage and that we'd have to wait until there was an increase in production.

It wasn't until we shouted, "No more!" and demanded our share that things began, no matter how slowly, to change.

The world today is caught in a paroxysm of violent upheaval. In order to contain and lessen the chaotic spiral of carnage and bloodshed, we must make a commitment to peace. We must declare what it is we feel that all people in the world should expect and conversely what we all deserve.

I'm not sure that there should be one set of expectations, however. All of us have a different view of the world, but I would like to put forward the following universal ideas as the rules of fair treatment that I personally would like to live by:

- First, I cannot be free while my neighbor is wearing chains.
- Second, I cannot know happiness while others are forced to live in despair.
- Third, I cannot know health if plague and famine thrive outside my door.

- And last, but not least, I cannot expect to know peace if war rides forward under my flag and with my consent.

I believe the institution of these simple statements would halt the rampant onslaught of the haves — in whose numbers many of us are counted — against the have-nots. Murdered and enslaved children, no matter what their color or gender or faith, suffer because of our failings. Starving millions go hungry so that we may dine in comfort, creating new enemies.

How do we know that someone is our enemy?   20

This is the first question we must answer. Who poses a threat to us? Who hates us to the degree that they are ready to do us harm? Who has contempt for our security and peace of mind?

For many people, the answer is quick and easy. It's the secret terrorist, the suicide bomber, the foreign religious radical who whips up the masses into a frenzy of hatred for America, its citizenry and all who ally themselves with us.

And certainly there is some validity to this answer. When innocent American blood is shed upon our streets, when intricate conspiracies are being hatched, even as you read these words, that are aimed at disrupting, disabling, and even destroying the American way of life, then we have every right to consider these schemers our enemies.

I would push this definition even further, however. Not only are those who plot against us the enemy, but any assassin, any murderer is our enemy. We represent civilization and sophistication, while they stand for chaos. We cannot say that murder is wrong only within our borders or if committed against our citizens. If some Peruvian woman or Nigerian child is assassinated by political zealots, then that assassin is also our foe. He has to be because once we accept, condone, or excuse the wrongful death of any human being, we have negated our own right to expect justice and respect. This is why there was an executive order that America cannot participate in the assassination of foreign leaders. If we can kill them, then they have the right to kill us.

Our enemies are the lawless dregs of a world gone half-mad. It doesn't   25
matter if they feel in their hearts that the crimes they commit are somehow justified. It doesn't matter if they are exonerated by their peers or religious leaders or by the moral interpretation of some government official. Murder in our realm is wrong, and anyone committing this crime is The Enemy of mankind — no exceptions allowed.

The Enemy is the same to all people, all nations. He is not a soldier, a law unto himself, or, sadly, unknown among our own number. He lives here among us and over there with them. He is a man, or woman, who has denied the common morality accepted by people everywhere in the world. He is not just my enemy, but The Enemy of everyone, everywhere.

If you accept this argument, then identifying those with whom we are allied is simple and straightforward: Our allies are those who do not accept murder, terrorism, and assassination as valid political discourse.

Our enemies are all persons involved in causing the death of others—either actively or from a consciously passive posture—for political, nationalistic, or economic ends. If Osama bin Laden[1] ordered the deaths of the Americans in the tragedy of September 11, then he is The Enemy. If our agents caused the deaths of innocent Kurds, Panamanians, or Guatemalans, then they are The Enemy. We can't have it one way and not the other. We can't say that an American life is worth more than a Sudanese life. We can't condone the violent actions of our armies and secret police if we condemn the actions of others who use violence, torture, and intimidation to obtain their ends.

Human life is sacred. We African-Americans know what it is like to be treated as less than human, as inferior to our white counterparts. We know the extent of abuse that can be heaped upon people because they are not seen as part of the human race. How can we stand by as our nation, while claiming peaceful intentions, wages war on people who may not have played any part in the crimes against us?

Even if we condone military actions, we might at least claim some culpability for the havoc visited upon a mostly innocent population. The death of innocent children is not "collateral damage." The wartime death of children is the murder of innocents. And if we commit these murders, then we are also The Enemy of civilization. 30

This is a tough argument, because it runs against the grain of present-day American nationalism and fear. America has clearly identified its enemies. They are mostly the dusky-skinned or black zealots of the Islamic religion. They are almost all Arabic and, coincidentally, they sit on some of the greatest oil reserves in the world today. We believe they are a threat because their religion is different from that of most Americans, because their religion is the fastest-growing faith in the world today, because their population tops the billion mark, and because many millions of this billion hate us.

That hatred, we believe, has led to terrorist attacks on us and our allies. Maybe this is true. Maybe their hatred is being expressed in religious terms. Maybe there are even those who believe in the sanctity of their violent acts against us. But the gods are put in place to protect their acolytes. If Middle Eastern religions speak out against America, I doubt that it is because our women don't cover their faces or that we practice another religion. They have been pressed into poverty and ruled by the whims of the almighty dollar; the cult of hatred against us is founded (I believe) in capitalism, not upon ancient texts or cultural differences. We Americans are seen as economic invaders who attempt to control everything that many people elsewhere in the world see as sacred.

---

[1]*Osama bin Laden:* Son of one of Saudi Arabia's wealthiest families (b. 1957) and founder of the international terrorist organization al-Qaeda, which has been linked to numerous attacks on U.S. targets around the world, including the assaults on September 11, 2001.

The Middle Eastern populations are our neighbors, our fellow human beings. It is paramount that we make peace with them if it is at all possible. And not peace on our terms, but a just and equitable peace.

In order to do this, we have to look beyond the TV shows and the newspapers, past our fears and doubts. We must redefine our notion of The Enemy, taking into account the role and actions of our own political and economic systems.

The entrance of the United States into the global struggle, which includes terrorism, has caused some permanent changes in our national psyche. One of these changes is the dawning realization that we are hated by so many people in the world at large.

We African-Americans have been living with people who have hated and despised us since the day we were first taken from our homelands and carted off to the plantation. The White Citizens Council, the Ku Klux Klan, the American Nazi Party, the Supreme Court, and many others have taken venomous swipes at our inherent rights. We've been kept out of neighborhoods, voting booths, country clubs, and educational institutions because of our skin. No one person had to do something wrong in order for us all to be vilified and hated.

But all that time, we only wanted to be free members of the American society. You could hate us all you want, but just let us have freedom and equality!

African-Americans know how to live with hatred. We've been stopped for walking in the wrong neighborhood, lynched for looking up the wrong skirt. We never liked the mistreatment, but we never gave up the dream, either. We know in our hearts that all people are equal and essentially good. We hold that goal to our breasts and move ahead without hesitation. Let's keep that up during this crisis. Our backs are strong enough to bear up under the weight of the hate people have for us. And let's critique the fainthearted other Americans who feel they can't bear living in a world where they are despised.

The problems the world faces today cannot be solved by superior strength alone. We Americans must use our hearts if we want to face the hatred confronting us. And we must be able to look critically at our own actions and motivations if we want to understand our enemies.

This kind of empathy comes hard for most Americans, because we have such a fuzzy understanding of our own history. Our past has always been depicted by images of upstanding white men conquering nature and "heathen foes." From the so-called primitive red man to Adolf Hitler, we've always seen ourselves as standing strong against the enemies of freedom and modernity. Sometimes our cause has been just, and often it has not. But never has an American campaign been so complex. Today we need more than John Wayne and the Winchester rifle. Today we need the subtle compassion of Black America, with its fine-honed attention to the etiquette of liberation.

Our collective freedom, fellow Americans, depends on our ability to defend the rights of others. All Americans should understand this concept, but I fear that it might only be Black America that has the historical perspective to move this notion from an idea into action. We, of all Americans, know what it's like to lose everything in order to come into alignment with the American Dream. Not only do we have a moral stake in protecting the innocent victims of the present war against terrorism, but we stand to profit, spiritually, from the process of working for peace.

Some of the greatest ambassadors representing American culture in the twentieth century have been black people. Louis Armstrong, Muhammad Ali, Martin Luther King Jr., Josephine Baker, and many others have gone abroad, with or without our government's blessings, to show the world the beauty they have found here. They were men and women of peace. For more than a century, African-Americans have represented America's culture and its high moral ideals, not its penchant for economic domination. While the American government was selling arms to the world, we were delivering jazz. While US Presidents waged war on foreign ideals, African-Americans spoke of peace.

Today is just a continuation of that history. We have to get out there and work for peace. We have to reject the fearmongers and the profiteers. Certainly, we have to protect America. Certainly, we have to arrest and monitor those who have made it their express desire to harm our nation. But we must also remember that there will be no defense if the whole world hates us.

We must remember, the only true defense is peace.

ENGAGING THE TEXT

1. Compare your own reaction to the destruction of the World Trade Center with those reported by Mosley. Would you agree that most Americans have returned to a state of "complacency," just as Mosley feared he would after 9/11? How would he like us to respond to this tragic event?

2. Why does Mosley feel that we are all personally responsible for the suffering that afflicts people in other nations across the globe? Would you agree? Why or why not?

3. Why does Mosley think that African Americans should play a leading role in establishing a "new notion of civil rights" for all nations and a new "international concept of harmony"? Why would the perspective of African Americans be particularly valuable, according to Mosley, in this undertaking? What other groups might also offer valuable insights on the nature of peace and the struggle for liberation? Is it "racist" of Mosley to suggest that one particular group of Americans is particularly well suited for the role of peacemaker? Why or why not?

4. Who, according to Mosley, is "the enemy"? Would you agree that we, as a nation, shouldn't value an American life more than we do a Sudanese life? Would you agree that "once we accept, condone, or excuse the wrongful death of any human being, we have negated our own right to expect justice and respect" (para. 24)? How would this principle change the current direction of U.S. foreign policy?

EXPLORING CONNECTIONS

5. How might Mosley interpret June Jordan's "Poem for Benjamin Franklin" (p. 752)? How, for example, might he explain Jordan's choice of speaker or the connections she makes between domestic violence, the treatment of Native Americans, and U.S. foreign policy? How might Jordan respond to Mosley's claim that African Americans are particularly well qualified to represent America to the world?
6. Write a brief dialogue between Mosley and Dinesh D'Souza (p. 716) on the meaning of freedom in America. How would Mosley and D'Souza each view America's relation to the concept of freedom in the past and the state of freedom in America today?
7. Revisit Randall Robinson's "Thoughts About Restitution" (p. 557) to explore how this argument in favor of reparations for slavery might provide a historical context for understanding Mosley's thesis. In your view, would reparations — direct compensation for past suffering caused by colonialism, capitalist exploitation, or foreign invasion — do more to liberate the world's peoples than America's current foreign policy?

EXTENDING THE CRITICAL CONTEXT

8. Mosley offers a list of African Americans who have served as America's "ambassadors" in recent times to the rest of the world. What do you think each of these figures has meant to the world? Working in groups, create your own list of famous Americans and discuss the message that each of them conveys to the world about American values and attitudes.
9. Working in groups, brainstorm a list of things you think that the average American might do to address the problems of war, poverty, and hopelessness that Mosley sees afflicting most of the world. How could you personally contribute to the effort of making America a safer — and more peaceful — nation?

Visual Portfolio

READING IMAGES OF AMERICA'S MEANING
IN A "NEW WORLD ORDER"

Visual Portfolio

READING IMAGES OF AMERICA'S MEANING IN A "NEW WORLD ORDER"

1. What do you think the images of Rambo and Colonel Sanders mean to the people in the first two photos in this Visual Portfolio? What do you think such advertising images say to people in other lands about America and American society?

2. How might the image of Afghani prisoners at Guantánamo Bay, Cuba, challenge the myth of the United States as the land of the free? How would you feel if you saw a photo that showed American prisoners of war held by another country in similar circumstances?

3. What does the photo of the American Marine Corps doctor comforting an Iraqi girl during "Operation Iraqi Freedom" suggest about Americans and the values of the Untied States? Why do you think it was featured so prominently in major U.S. newspapers and magazines at the beginning of the war?

4. In what countries might you expect to see the kind of anti-American protest that is represented on page 767? Why might South Koreans feel negatively toward the United States? What aspects of U.S. culture seem to be singled out for criticism in this protest?

5. How do you think the woman in the photo on page 768 feels about traveling since 9/11? How effective do you think the National Guardsmen in this photo are as a deterrent to terrorism? In what ways has the war on terror changed your own life since 9/11?

That's Entertainment? Hollywood's Contribution to Anti-Americanism Abroad

MICHAEL MEDVED

Remember the last time you took in a movie at the local Cineplex? You probably thought you were just out for an evening of fun, but according to Michael Medved you were actually exposing yourself to a dose of dangerous anti-American propaganda. For Medved, the local Cineplex is really a "Sin-aplex," because, as he sees it, Hollywood is bent on portraying America as a land seething with vice and violence. A film critic, radio talk show host, and best-selling author, Medved has written eight books on current events, politics, and mass media, including What Really Happened to the Class of '65 *(1976),* The Shadow Presidents: The Secret History of the Chief Executives and Their Top Aides *(1979), and* Hollywood Vs. America: Popular Culture and the War on Traditional Values *(1992).*

"THINK AMERICA: WHY THE HOLE WORLD HATES YOU?"

This message, proudly proclaimed in a hand-lettered sign held aloft by a scowling, bearded Pakistani protestor during one of the angry demonstrations that followed September 11, continues to challenge the world's dominant power. In responding to such disturbing questions about the origins of anti-Americanism, glib commentators may cite the imperial reach of U.S. corporations, or Washington's support for Israel, or sheer envy for the freedom and prosperity of American life. But they must also contend with the profound impact of the lurid Hollywood visions that penetrate every society on earth. The vast majority of people in Pakistan or Peru, Poland or Papua New Guinea, may never visit the United States or ever meet an American face to face, but they inevitably encounter images of L.A. and New York in the movies, television programs, and popular songs exported everywhere by the American entertainment industry.

Those images inevitably exert a more powerful influence on overseas consumers than they do on the American domestic audience. If you live in Seattle or Cincinnati, you understand that the feverish media fantasies provided by a DMX music video or a *Dark Angel* TV episode do not represent everyday reality for you or your neighbors. If you live in Indonesia or Nigeria, however, you will have little or no first-hand experience to balance the negative impressions provided by American pop culture, with its intense emphasis on violence, sexual adventurism, and every inventive variety of anti-social behavior that the most overheated imagination could concoct. No wonder so many Islamic extremists (and so many others) look upon America as a cruel, Godless, vulgar society—a "Great Satan," indeed.

During violent anti-American riots in October 2001, mobs in Quetta, Pakistan, specifically targeted five movie theaters showing U.S. imports and offered their negative review of this cinematic fare by burning each of those theaters to the ground. "Look what they did!" wailed Chaudary Umedali amid the smoking ruins of his cinema. He said that a thousand rioters smashed the doors of his theater and threw firebombs inside because "they didn't like our showing American films." Ironically, the last movie he had offered his Quetta customers was *Desperado*—a hyper-violent, R-rated 1995 shoot-em-up with Antonio Banderas and Salma Hayek, specifically designed by its Texas-born director Robert Rodriguez for export outside the United States (in this case, to worldwide Hispanic audiences).

Even the President of the United States worries publicly about the distorted view of this embattled nation that Hollywood conveys to the rest of the world. In his eloquent but uncelebrated address to students at Beijing's

Tsinghua University on February 22, George W. Bush declared: "As America learns more about China, I am concerned that the Chinese people do not always see a clear picture of my country. This happens for many reasons, and some of them of our own making. Our movies and television shows often do not portray the values of the real America I know."

Ironically, the President assumed in his remarks that the Beijing students he addressed felt repulsed by the messages they received from American entertainment—despite abundant evidence that hundreds of millions of Chinese, and in particular the nation's most ambitious young people, enthusiastically embrace our pop culture. During the tragic Tiananmen Square rebellion[1] more than a decade ago, pro-democracy reformers not only seized on the Statue of Liberty as a symbol of their movement, but indulged their taste for the music and fashions identified everywhere as part of American youth culture. American conservatives may abhor the redoubtable Madonna and all her works, but the youthful activists who brought about the Velvet Revolution in Prague[2] reveled in her cultural contributions.

This contradiction highlights the major dispute over the worldwide influence of Hollywood entertainment. Do the spectacularly successful exports from the big show business conglomerates inspire hatred and resentment of the United States, or do they advance the inevitable, End-of-History triumph of American values? Does the near-universal popularity of national icons from Mickey Mouse to Michael Jackson represent the power of our ideals of free expression and free markets, or do the dark and decadent images we broadcast to the rest of the world hand a potent weapon to American-haters everywhere?

Telling It Like It Isn't

Of course, apologists for the entertainment industry decry all attempts to blame Hollywood for anti-Americanism, insisting that American pop culture merely reports reality, accurately reflecting the promise and problems of the United States, and allowing the worldwide audience to respond as they may to the best and worst aspects of our society. During a forum on movie violence sponsored by a group of leading liberal activists, movie director Paul Verhoeven (author of such worthy ornaments to our civilization as *Robocop* and *Basic Instinct*) insisted: "Art is a reflection of the world. If the world is horrible, the reflection in the mirror is horrible." In other words, if people in developing countries feel disgusted by the Hollywood imagery so aggressively marketed in their homelands, then the problem

[1]*Tiananmen Square rebellion:* The 1989 demonstration in Beijing's central plaza by more than a million Chinese students, intellectuals, workers, and civil servants demanding democratic reforms, which lasted for more than a month until being brutally repressed by Chinese authorities.

[2]*Velvet Revolution in Prague:* Between November 17 and December 29, 1989, a six-week-long peaceful protest caused the bloodless overthrow of Czechoslovakia's communist government.

cannot be pinned on the shapers of show business but rather arises from the authentic excesses of American life.

This argument runs counter to every statistical analysis of the past twenty years on the distorted imagery of American society purveyed by the entertainment industry. All serious evaluations of movie and television versions of American life suggest that the pop culture portrays a world that is far more violent, dangerous, sexually indulgent (and, of course, dramatic) than everyday American reality. George Gerbner, a leading analyst of media violence at the Annenberg School of Communications at the University of Pennsylvania, concluded after thirty years of research that characters on network television fall victim to acts of violence *at least fifty times more frequently* than citizens of the real America.

If anything, the disproportionate emphasis on violent behavior only intensifies with the export of American entertainment. For many years, so-called action movies have traveled more effectively than other genres, since explosions and car crashes do not require translation. This leads to the widespread assumption abroad that the United States, despite the dramatically declining crime rate of the last decade, remains a dangerous and insecure society. On a recent trip to England, I encountered sophisticated and thoughtful Londoners who refused to travel across the Atlantic because of their wildly exaggerated fear of American street crime—ignoring recent statistics showing unequivocally that muggings and assaults are now more common in London than in New York. On a similar note, a recent traveler in rural Indonesia met a ten-year-old boy who, discovering the American origins of the visitor, asked to see her gun. When she insisted that she didn't carry any firearms, the child refused to believe her: he knew that all Americans carried guns because he had seen them perpetually armed on TV and at the movies.

The misleading media treatment of sexuality has proven similarly unreliable in its oddly altered version of American life. Analysis by Robert and Linda Lichter at the Center for Media and Public Affairs in Washington, DC reveals that on television, depictions of sex outside of marriage are nine to fourteen times more common than dramatizations of marital sex. This odd emphasis on non-marital intercourse leads to the conclusion that the only sort of sexual expression frowned upon by Hollywood involves physical affection between husband and wife. In reality, all surveys of intimate behavior (including the famous, sweeping 1994 national study by the University of Chicago) suggest that among the more than two-thirds of American adults who are currently married, sex is not only more satisfying, but significantly more frequent, than it is among their single counterparts. One of pop culture's most celebrated representatives of the "swinging singles" lifestyle today, Kim Cattrall[3] of *Sex and the City*, recently published a best-selling

10

---

[3]*Kim Cattrall:* Star of the television series *Sex and the City*, who has separated from her husband since publication of this selection.

book full of revealing confessions. In *Satisfaction: The Art of the Female Orgasm,* Cattrall describes a life dramatically different from the voracious and promiscuous escapades of the character she portrays on television. In the intimate arena, she felt frustrated and unfulfilled—as do nearly half of American females, she maintains—until the loving ministrations of her husband, Mark Levinson, finally enabled her to experience gratification and joy.

Even without Cattrall's revelations, anyone acquainted with actual unattached individuals could confirm that *Friends* and *Ally McBeal* hardly represent the common lot of American singles. On television and at the movies, the major challenge confronted by most unmarried characters is trying to decide among a superficially dazzling array of sexual alternatives. The entertainments in question may suggest that these explorations will prove less than wholly satisfying, but to most American viewers, single or married, they still look mightily intriguing. To most viewers in more traditional societies, by contrast, they look mightily decadent and disrespectful.

Consider, too, the emphasis on homosexuality in contemporary television and movies. In less than a year between 2001 and 2002, three major networks (NBC, HBO, MTV) offered different, competing dramatizations of the murder of Matthew Shepherd—the gay Wyoming college student beaten to death by two thugs. No other crime in memory—not even the murder of Nicole Brown Simpson[4]—has received comparable attention by major entertainment companies. The message to the world at large not only calls attention to homosexual alternatives in American life, but focuses on our brutal and criminal underclass.

The Gay and Lesbian Alliance Against Defamation (GLAAD) publishes an annual scorecard in which it celebrates the number of openly gay characters who appear regularly on national television series, and recently counted more than thirty. This trendy fascination with homosexuality (as illustrated by the worshipful attention given to Rosie O'Donnell's[5] hugely publicized "coming out") obviously overstates the incidence of out-of-the-closet gay identity; all scientific studies suggest that less than 3 percent of adults unequivocally see themselves as gay.

For purposes of perspective, it is useful to contrast the pop culture focus on gay orientation with media indifference to religious commitment. A handful of successful television shows such as *Touched By An Angel* and *Seventh Heaven* may invoke elements of conventional faith, if often in simplistic, childlike form, but ardent and mature believers remain rare on television and at the movies. The Gallup Poll and other surveys suggest that

---

[4]*Nicole Brown Simpson:* Along with friend Ronald Goldman, the victim of a brutal murder in 1994 that resulted in the much publicized trial and acquittal of her celebrity husband, O. J. Simpson.

[5]*Rosie O'Donnell:* Celebrity talk show host and actress who "came out" about her lesbian sexual orientation in a 1992 *People* magazine story.

some 40 percent of Americans attend religious services on a weekly basis—
more than four times the percentage who go to the movies in any given
week. Church or synagogue attendance, however, hardly ever appears in
Hollywood or television portrayals of contemporary American society, while
mass media feature gay references far more frequently than religious ones.
This is hardly an accurate representation of mainstream America, and the
distortion plays directly into the hands of some of our most deadly enemies.
In October 2001, an "official" press spokesman for Osama bin Laden's[6] al-
Qaeda terror network summarized the struggle between Islamic fanatics
and the United States as part of the eternal battle "between faith and atheism." Since the United States represents by far the most religiously committed, church-going nation in the Western world, this reference to the nation's godlessness gains credibility abroad only because of Hollywood's
habitual denial or downplaying of the faith-based nature of our civilization.

The ugly media emphasis on the dysfunctional nature of our national   15
life transcends examples of widely decried, tacky and exploitative entertainment, and pointedly includes the most prodigiously praised products of the
popular culture. In recent years, some 1.5 billion people around the world
watch at least part of Hollywood's annual Oscar extravaganza, and in April
2000 they saw the Motion Picture Academy confer all of its most prestigious
awards (Best Picture, Best Actor, Best Director, Best Screenplay) on a
puerile pastiche called *American Beauty*. This embittered assault on suburban family life shows a frustrated father (Kevin Spacey) who achieves redemption only through quitting his job, lusting after a teenaged cheer-
leader, insulting his harridan wife, compulsively exercising, and smoking
marijuana. The only visibly loving and wholesome relationship in this sur-
real middle class nightmare flourishes between two clean-cut gay male
neighbors. The very title, *American Beauty*, ironically invokes the name of
an especially cherished flower to suggest that all is not, well, rosy with the
American dream. If the entertainment establishment chooses to honor this
cinematic effort above all others, then viewers in Kenya or Kuala Lumpur
might understandably assume that it offers a mordantly accurate assessment
of the emptiness and corruption of American society.

Explaining Media Masochism

This prominent example of overpraised artistic ambition suggests that
the persistent problems in Hollywood's view of America go far beyond the
normal pursuit of profit. While *American Beauty* director Sam Mendes and
screenwriter Alan Ball might well aspire to critical acclaim, the movie's producers always understood that this tale of suburban dysfunction probably

[6]*Osama bin Laden:* Son of one of Saudi Arabia's wealthiest families (b. 1957) and founder
of the international terrorist organization al-Qaeda, which has been linked to numerous attacks
on U.S. targets around the world, including the assaults on September 11, 2001.

would not be a slam-dunk box office blockbuster (though the Oscars ensured that it did quite well commercially). The most common excuse for the ferocious focus on violence and bizarre behavior—the argument that the "market made me do it" and that public demands leave entertainment executives no choice—falls apart in the face of the most rudimentary analysis.

Every year, the American movie industry releases more than 300 films, with a recent average of 65 percent of those titles rated "R"—or adults only—by the Motion Picture Association of America. Conventional wisdom holds that the big studios emphasize such disturbing, edgy R-rated releases precisely because they perform best at the box office, but an abundance of recent studies proves that the public prefers feel-good, family fare. A recent comprehensive analysis confirms the conclusions on this point in my 1992 book, *Hollywood Vs. America.* Two economists, Arthur DeVany of the University of California at Irvine and W. David Walls of the University of Hong Kong, summarized their research: "This paper shows that Medved is right: there are too many R-rated movies in Hollywood's portfolio. . . . We show that, as Medved claimed, R-rated movies are dominated by G, PG, and PG-13 movies in all three dimensions of revenues, costs, return on production cost, and profits."

The other argument in defense of the entertainment emphasis on troubled aspects of American life involves the inherently dramatic nature of social dysfunction. According to the celebrated Tolstoyan[7] aphorism, "All happy families are the same; every unhappy family is unhappy in its own way." This logic suggests an inevitable tendency to highlight the same sort of unpleasant but gripping situations so memorably brought to life by eminent pre-cinematic screenwriters like Sophocles[8] and Shakespeare. Divorce and adultery offer more obvious entertainment value than marital bliss; criminality proves more instantly compelling than good citizenship. In an intensely competitive international marketplace, the dark—even deviant— obsessions of the present potentates of pop culture may seem to make a crude sort of sense.

This approach, however, ignores the striking lessons of Hollywood's own heritage and the wholesome basis on which our star-spangled entertainment industry came to conquer the world. In the 1920s and 1930s, the American movie business faced formidable competition from well-developed production centers in Italy, France, Germany, England, and even Russia. Obvious political disruptions (including the brutal intrusion of fascist and communist tyranny) helped U.S. corporations triumph over their European rivals, and drove many of the most talented individuals to seek refuge across the Atlantic. But even more than the historic circumstances that undermined America's competitors, Hollywood managed to dominate

[7]*Tolstoyan:* In an epic style reminiscent of the nineteenth-century Russian novelist, Count Lev Nikolayevich Tolstoy (1828–1910).
[8]*Sophocles:* (ca. 496–406 B.C.E.) Greek tragedian and author of *Oedipus the King.*

international markets because of a worldwide infatuation with the America it both exploited and promoted. Without question, iconic homegrown figures such as Jimmy Stewart, Mae West, Henry Fonda, Shirley Temple, Clark Gable, Jimmy Cagney, and John Wayne, in addition to charismatic imports like Charlie Chaplin, Cary Grant, and Greta Garbo, projected qualities on screen that came to seem quintessentially, irresistibly American. As film critic Richard Grenier aptly commented during a March 1992 symposium:

> Aside from the country's prominence, there seems to have been an irresistible magnetism about a whole assemblage of American attitudes—optimism, hope, belief in progress, profound assumptions of human equality, informality—often more apparent to foreigners than to Americans themselves, that the outside world has found compelling. Over many decades these attitudes became so entrenched in world opinion as "American" that in recent times, when certain Hollywood films have taken on a distinctly negative tone, America has still retained its dramatic power, Hollywood, as it were, living on its spiritual capital.

In other words, in its so-called Golden Age, the entertainment industry   20
found a way to make heroism look riveting, even fashionable, and to make decency dramatic. In contrast to the present day, when most of the world watches American pop culture with the sort of guilty fascination we might lavish on a particularly bloody car crash, people in every corner of the globe once looked to our entertainment exports as a source of inspiration, even enlightenment. As the English producer David Puttnam revealed in an eloquent 1989 interview with Bill Moyers, he cherished the days of his childhood when

> the image that was being projected overseas was of a society of which I wanted to be a member. Now cut to twenty years later—the image that America began projecting in the 1970s, of a self-loathing, very violent society, antagonistic within itself—that patently isn't a society that any thinking person in the Third World or Western Europe or Eastern Europe would wish to have anything to do with. America has for some years been exporting an extremely negative notion of itself.

The change came about in part because of a change in the people running the major studios and television networks. As movie historian Neal Gabler perceptively observed in his influential book, *An Empire of Their Own,* Hollywood's founding generation consisted almost entirely of East European immigrant Jews who craved American acceptance so powerfully that they used celluloid fantasies to express their ongoing adoration for their adopted country. Their successors, on the other hand, came from far more "respectable" backgrounds—in some cases as the privileged children and grandchildren of the founders themselves. In the 1960s and 1970s, they sought to establish their independence and artistic integrity by burnishing their countercultural credentials. To illustrate the magnitude and speed of the change, the 1965 Academy Award for Best Picture went to the delightful and traditionally romantic musical, *The Sound of Music.* A mere four years later, that same coveted Oscar went to *Midnight Cowboy*—the gritty story of a down-and-out male hustler in New York City, and the only X-rated feature ever to win Best Picture.

From the beginning and through to the present day, the leaders of the entertainment community have felt a powerful need to be taken seriously. The creators of the industry were born outsiders who earned that respect by expressing affection for America; the moguls of the later generations have been for the most part born insiders who earned their respect by expressing their alienation. This negativity naturally found an eager international audience during the Vietnam War era and in the waning years of the Cold War with the widespread dismissal of the "cowboy culture" of Reaganism.[9] Even after the collapse of the Soviet Empire, anti-Americanism remained fashionable among taste-setting elites in much of the world, appealing with equal fervor to critics from the Right and the Left. In Afghanistan in the 1980s, for example, the beleaguered Russian Communists and the indefatigable *mujaheddin*[10] might agree on very little—but they both felt powerful contempt for the freewheeling and self-destructive mores of American culture as promoted everywhere by the Hollywood entertainment machine.

Even as post–Cold War globalization enhanced the economic power and political influence of the United States, it helped the entertainment industry sustain its anti-American attitudes. With the removal of the Iron Curtain, vast new markets opened up for Hollywood entertainment, with developing economies in Asia and Latin America, too, providing hundreds of millions of additional customers. Between 1985 and 1990, inflation-adjusted revenues from overseas markets for U.S. feature films rose 124 percent at a time when domestic proceeds remained relatively flat. As a result, the portion of all movie income derived from foreign distribution rose from 30 percent in 1980 to more than 50 percent in 2000. James G. Robinson, influential chairman of Morgan Creek Productions, was right to have predicted to the *Los Angeles Times* in March 1992: "All of the real growth in the coming years will be overseas."

The fulfillment of his forecast has served to further detach today's producers from any sense of patriotic or parochial identification, encouraging their pose as Americans who have nobly transcended their own Americanism. A current captain of the entertainment industry need not ask whether a putative project will "play in Peoria"—so long as it plays in Paris, St. Petersburg,

[9]*the "cowboy culture" of Reaganism:* Former governor of California and fortieth president of the United States, Ronald Wilson Reagan (b. 1911) was famous for his simplistic "cowboy" style when dealing with complex issues of foreign affairs.
[10]*mujaheddin:* Islamic rebel group organized in the 1980s to resist the Soviet occupation of Afghanistan.

and Panama City. As I argued in the pages of *Hollywood Vs. America* in 1992: "While the populist products of Hollywood's Golden Age most certainly encouraged the world's love affair with America, today's nihilistic and degrading attempts at entertainment may, in the long run, produce the opposite effect, helping to isolate this country as a symbol of diseased decadence."

Why Do They Watch It?

With that isolation increasingly apparent after the unprecedented as-   25
sault of 9/11, the question remains: Why does so much of the world still seem so single-mindedly obsessed with American entertainment, for all its chaotic and unrepresentative elements?

The most likely answer involves what might be descried as the "*National Enquirer* appeal" of Hollywood's vision of life in the United States. While waiting in the supermarket checkout lines, we turn to the scandal-ridden tabloids not because of our admiration for the celebrities they expose, but because of our uncomfortable combination of envy and resentment toward them. The tabloids compel our attention because they allow us to feel superior to the rich and famous. For all their wealth and glamour and power, they cannot stay faithful to their spouses, avoid drug addiction, or cover up some other guilty secret. We may privately yearn to change places with some star of the moment, but the weekly revelations of the *National Enquirer* actually work best to reassure us that we are better off as we are.

In much the same way, Hollywood's unpleasant images of America enable the rest of the world to temper inevitable envy with a sense of their own superiority. The United States may be rich in material terms (and movies and television systematically overstate that wealth), but the violence, cruelty, injustice, corruption, arrogance, and degeneracy so regularly included in depictions of American life allow viewers abroad to feel fortunate by comparison. Like the *Enquirer* approach to the private peccadilloes of world-striding celebrities, you are supposed to feel fascinated by their profligate squandering of opportunity and power.

In this sense, American pop culture is not so much liberating as it is anarchic and even nihilistic. Our entertainment offerings do not honor our freedom and liberty as political or cultural values so much as they undermine all restraints and guidelines, both the tyrannical and the traditional. As Dwight Macdonald wrote in his celebrated 1953 essay, "A Theory of Mass Culture": "Like 19th century capitalism, Mass Culture is a dynamic, revolutionary force, breaking down the old barriers of class, tradition, taste, and dissolving all cultural distinctions." Amplifying Macdonald's work, Edward Rothstein of the *New York Times* wrote in March 2002: "There is something inherently disruptive about popular culture. It undermines the elite values of aristocratic art, displaces the customs of folk culture, and opposes any limitation on art's audiences or subjects. It asserts egalitarian tastes, encourages dissent, and does not shun desire." It should come as no surprise, then, that even those who embrace the symbols and themes of American entertainment may feel little gratitude toward a force that casts them loose from all traditional moorings, but offers no organized system of ideas or values by way of replacement.

Patriotism and Profit

In 1994, I participated in an international conference on the family in Warsaw and listened to the plaintive recollections of a troubled Polish priest. He recalled the days of the Cold War, "when we listened in basements to illegal radios to Radio Free Europe so we could get a little bit of hope, a little bit of truth, from the magical land of America." After the collapse of Communism, however, America's message seemed dangerous and decadent rather than hopeful. "All of a sudden, we're struggling against drugs and free sex and AIDS and crime—and all of that seems to be an import from America. It's like the message of freedom that we heard before was only the freedom to destroy ourselves."

On a similar note, an American businessman of my acquaintance traveling in Beirut struck up a conversation with the proprietor of a falafel stand who announced himself an enthusiastic supporter of the radical, pro-Iranian terrorist group, Hizballah. Ironically, his small business featured a faded poster showing a bare-chested, machine-gun toting Sylvester Stallone as Rambo. My friend asked about the place of honor provided to an American movie hero. "We all like Rambo," the Hizballah supporter unblushingly declared. "He is a fighter's fighter." But wouldn't that make the Lebanese dissident more favorably inclined toward the United States, the visitor inquired. "Not at all," was the response. "We will use Rambo's methods to destroy the evil America." 30

This love-hate relationship with Hollywood's twisted imagery also characterized the 19 conspirators who made such a notable attempt to "destroy evil America" with their September 11 atrocities. During their months and years in the United States, Mohammed Atta and his colleagues savored the popular culture—renting action videos and visiting bars, peep shows, lap dancing parlors, and Las Vegas—immersing themselves in Western degradation to stiffen their own hatred (and self-hatred?) of it.

In response to the terrorist attacks and to the onset of the war that followed, leaders of the Hollywood community expressed some dawning awareness that they may have indeed contributed to some of the hatred of America expressed around the world. Beyond a brief flurry of flag-waving, and the generous contributions to the 9/11 fund by leading celebrities from Julia Roberts to Jim Carrey, members of the entertainment elite showed a new willingness to cooperate with the defense establishment. Working through the Institute for Creative Technologies at USC (originally created to enlist Hollywood talent for shaping virtual reality simulators for military training), creators of movies like *Die Hard, Fight Club,* and even *Being John Malkovich* brainstormed with Pentagon brass. Their purpose, according to several press reports, involved an attempt to concoct the next possible plot that might be launched against the United States, and then to devise strategies to counteract it.

In a sense, this unconventional program acknowledged the fact that violent, demented, anti-social, and conspiratorial thinking has come to characterize a major segment of the entertainment establishment. How else could an objective observer interpret the idea that the military turned first to millionaire screenwriters in order to understand the thought processes of mass-murdering terrorists?

Beyond this strange collaboration, top show business executives met with Karl Rove, political representative of President Bush, in an attempt to mobilize Hollywood creativity to serve America in the war against terror. The well-publicized "summit" discussed public service ads to discourage bigotry against Muslims in America and additional productions to give the United States a more benign image in the Islamic world. A handful of top directors, including William Friedkin (*The French Connection, The Exorcist,* and the excellent *Rules of Engagement*) expressed their willingness to drop all their pressing projects and enlist full-time to help the American war effort. In this determination, these pop culture patriots hoped to follow the example of the great Golden Age director Frank Capra, who served his country during World War II through the creation of the epic *Why We Fight* series.

Alas, the White House and the Pentagon failed to take advantage of the self-sacrificing spirit of the moment, or to pursue the entertainment industry opportunities that presented themselves after September 11. As the trauma of terrorist attacks gradually recedes into memory and the nation loses focus on its sense of patriotic purpose, the popular culture is displaying few long-term changes. Perhaps a more positive attitude toward the military may be the chief legacy of the deadly attacks — an attitude publicly celebrated so far in a handful of movies (*Behind Enemy Lines, Black Hawk Down, We Were Soldiers*), incidentally, all produced before the September 11 catastrophe. More significant changes, involving a new sense of responsibility for the images of America that pop culture transmits around the world, never even merited serious discussion in Hollywood. For the top entertainment conglomerates, this may count as an unseized opportunity for public service, but also a missed chance for corporate profit.

In his February speech in Beijing, President Bush held the Chinese students transfixed with a picture of America that departed dramatically from the visions they had received from made-in-USA music, movies, and television. "America is a nation guided by faith," the President declared. "Someone once called us 'a nation with the soul of a church.' This may interest you — 95 percent of Americans say they believe in God, and I'm one of them." Bush went on to appeal to the family priorities that have characterized Chinese culture for more than 3,000 years: "Many of the values that guide our life in America are first shaped in our families, just as they are in your country. American moms and dads love their children and work hard and sacrifice for them because we believe life can always be better for the next generation. In our families, we find love and learn responsibility and character."

If Hollywood's leaders placed themselves within the context of the wider American family, they might also learn responsibility and character—and discover that a more wholesome, loving, and balanced portrayal of the nation they serve could enhance rather than undermine their worldwide popularity.

ENGAGING THE TEXT

1. What messages do Hollywood films convey to foreign audiences about life in the United States, according to Medved? To what extent might his choice of "typical" Hollywood films influence his judgment?

2. What arguments does Medved anticipate from defenders of the Hollywood film industry against his claims? How does he rebut each of these counterarguments? Overall, how persuasive is his case against Hollywood? To what extent do you think it's reasonable to attribute anti-Americanism abroad to the impact of the entertainment industry?

3. How does Medved explain the change that he believes occurred between the "Golden Age" of Hollywood movies and the "dark and decadent" sensibility of the current generation of Hollywood directors? What other historical events or cultural developments over the past fifty years might have influenced the tone of Hollywood cinema?

4. How appropriate would it be, in your view, for film and television producers to coordinate with government representatives and Pentagon advisers, as Medved suggests, in order to ensure that future Hollywood projects strike a more positive tone?

EXPLORING CONNECTIONS

5. How might Mark Hertsgaard (p. 728) and Joel Andreas (p. 741) respond to Medved's assertion that Islamic nations view America as a godless society "only because of Hollywood's habitual denial or downplaying of the faith-based nature of our civilization" (para. 14)? What other political, social, or historical factors might these writers cite to explain why Islamic peoples sometimes question American moral standards?

6. To what extent is it possible to reconcile Medved's assault on what he sees as the "nihilistic freedom" of American cinema with the kind of personal freedom that Dinesh D'Souza (p. 716) celebrates as the hallmark of American democracy? Is Medved suggesting that being true to traditional American values requires us to be less free?

EXTENDING THE CRITICAL CONTEXT

7. As a class, brainstorm a list of recent Hollywood movies you're familiar with, and try to list the attitudes and values that you think each of these films might convey to a foreign audience. What messages, for example, would the movies on your list communicate to the average Indonesian viewer about American society and culture? To what extent does your own analysis of the current state of Hollywood support or challenge Medved's thesis?

8. Screen the film *American Beauty* to test Medved's claim that it exemplifies Hollywood's degenerate tendencies. Would you agree that it presents a distorted view of American society? Why or why not? Should we expect all films—and all works of art—to present a "realistic" or even a "moral" depiction of society?

9. Compare notes in class on all the foreign films you're familiar with. What messages do these movies convey about life in their country of origin? To what extent can you assume that foreign films accurately reflect the social conditions, values, and attitudes of foreign cultures?

Under the Sign of Mickey Mouse & Co.

TODD GITLIN

Walt Disney's "Magic Kingdom" bills itself as the "Happiest Place on Earth," and that's exactly the way America's mass media present the United States, according to Todd Gitlin. Over the past twenty years American culture has been infiltrating nations all over the world, homogenizing traditional cultures into the kind of global "fun" culture that Disney is famous for. The question, of course, is whether it's good for Uzbek kids to spurn their parents' ways for Western styles or for American teens to groove to the beat of Third World music as they "shimmy" through the local mall. A nationally recognized authority on mass media, Todd Gitlin (b. 1943) has authored a novel and five works of nonfiction on popular culture and American society, including Inside Prime Time *(1983),* The Twilight of Common Dreams: Why America is Wracked by Culture Wars *(1995), and* Media Unlimited: How the Torrent of Images and Sounds Overwhelms Our Lives *(2001), the source of this selection. He is also the North American editor of* openDemocracy, *a member of the editorial board of* Dissent *magazine, and a faculty member of Columbia University's Graduate School of Journalism.*

Everywhere, the media flow defies national boundaries. This is one of its obvious, but at the same time amazing, features. A global torrent is not, of course, the master metaphor to which we have grown accustomed. We're more accustomed to Marshall McLuhan's *global village*.[1] Those who resort to this metaphor casually often forget that if the world is a global village, some live in mansions on the hill, others in huts. Some dispatch images and sounds around town at the touch of a button; others collect them at the touch of *their* buttons. Yet McLuhan's image reveals an indispensable half-truth. If there is a village, it speaks American. It wears jeans, drinks Coke, eats at the golden arches, walks on swooshed shoes, plays electric guitars, recognizes Mickey Mouse, James Dean, E.T., Bart Simpson, R2-D2, and Pamela Anderson.

At the entrance to the champagne cellar of Piper-Heidsieck[2] in Reims, in eastern France, a plaque declares that the cellar was dedicated by Marie Antoinette. The tour is narrated in six languages, and at the end you walk back upstairs into a museum featuring photographs of famous people drinking champagne. And who are they? Perhaps members of today's royal houses, presidents or prime ministers, economic titans or Nobel Prize winners? Of course not. They are movie stars, almost all of them American — Marilyn Monroe to Clint Eastwood. The symmetry of the exhibition is obvious, the premise unmistakable: Hollywood stars, champions of consumption, are the royalty of this century, more popular by far than poor doomed Marie.

Hollywood is the global cultural capital — capital in both senses. The United States presides over a sort of World Bank of styles and symbols, an International Cultural Fund of images, sounds, and celebrities. The goods may be distributed by American-, Canadian-, European-, Japanese-, or Australian-owned multinational corporations, but their styles, themes, and images do not detectably change when a new board of directors takes over. Entertainment is one of America's top exports.[3] In 1999, in fact, film, television, music, radio, advertising, print publishing, and computer software together *were* the top export, almost $80 billion worth, and while software alone accounted for $50 billion of the total, some of that category also qualifies as entertainment — video games and pornography, for example. Hardly anyone is exempt from the force of American images and sounds. French resentment of Mickey Mouse, Bruce Willis, and the rest of American civilization is well known. Less well known, and rarely acknowledged by the

---

[1]*Marshall McLuhan's global village:* Canadian communications theorist and educator, Herbert Marshall McLuhan (1911–1980) believed that the modern electronic media would eventually blur regional and cultural differences and unite the world in a single global culture or community. [All notes are author's, except 1, 2, 5, 15, 18, 20, 29, and 30.]

[2]*Piper-Heidsieck:* Brand of French champagne.

[3]*America's top exports:* Economists Incorporated for the International Intellectual Property Alliance, Executive Summary, 2000_SIWEK_EXEC.pdf. Thanks to Siva Vaidhyanathan for his discerning analysis of these statistics.

French, is the fact that *Terminator 2* sold 5 million tickets in France during the month it opened—with no submachine guns at the heads of the customers. The same culture minister, Jack Lang, who in 1982 achieved a moment of predictable notoriety in the United States for declaring that *Dallas* amounted to cultural imperialism, also conferred France's highest honor in the arts on Elizabeth Taylor and Sylvester Stallone. The point is not hypocrisy pure and simple but something deeper, something obscured by a single-minded emphasis on American power: dependency. American popular culture is the nemesis that hundreds of millions—perhaps billions—of people love, and love to hate. The antagonism and the dependency are inseparable, for the media flood—essentially American in its origin, but virtually unlimited in its reach—represents, like it or not, a common imagination.

How shall we understand the Hong Kong T-shirt that says "I Feel Coke"? Or the little Japanese girl who asks an American visitor in all innocence, "Is there really a Disneyland in America?" (She knows the one in Tokyo.) Or the experience of a German television reporter[4] sent to Siberia to film indigenous life, who after flying out of Moscow and then traveling for days by boat, bus, and jeep, arrives near the Arctic Sea where live a tribe of Tungusians known to ethnologists for their bearskin rituals. In the community store sits a grandfather with his grandchild on his knee. Grandfather is dressed in traditional Tungusian clothing. Grandson has on his head a reversed baseball cap.

American popular culture is the closest approximation today to a global lingua franca,[5] drawing the urban and young in particular into a common cultural zone where they share some dreams of freedom, wealth, comfort, innocence, and power—and perhaps most of all, youth as a state of mind. In general, despite the rhetoric of "identity," young people do not live in monocultures. They are not monocular. They are both local and cosmopolitan. Cultural bilingualism is routine. Just as their "cultures"[6] are neither hard-wired nor uniform, so there is no simple way in which they are "Americanized," though there are American tags on their experience—low-cost links to status and fun. Everywhere, fun lovers, efficiency seekers, Americaphiles, and Americaphobes alike pass through the portals of Disney and the arches of McDonald's wearing Levi's jeans and Gap jackets. Mickey Mouse and Donald Duck, John Wayne, Marilyn Monroe, James Dean, Bob Dylan, Michael Jackson, Madonna, Clint Eastwood, Bruce Willis, the multicolor chorus of Coca-Cola, and the next flavor of the month or the universe are the icons of a curious sort of one-world sensibility, a global semiculture. America's bid for global unification surpasses in reach that of the Romans,

[4]*a German television reporter:* This story is told by Berndt Ostendorf in "What Makes American Popular Culture So Popular: A View from Europe" (Odense, Denmark: Oasis, 2000).

[5]*lingua franca:* The commonly used language of trade or business.

[6]*Just as their "cultures":* I benefited from a discussion about the overuse of the term *culture* with Kevin Robins, March 2, 2001.

the British, the Catholic, or Islam; though without either an army or a God, it requires less. The Tungusian boy with the reversed cap on his head does not automatically think of it as "American," let alone side with the U.S. Army.

The misleadingly easy answer to the question of how American images and sounds became omnipresent is: American imperialism. But the images are not even faintly force-fed by American corporate, political, or military power. The empire strikes from inside the spectator as well as from outside. This is a conundrum that deserves to be approached with respect if we are to grasp the fact that Mickey Mouse and Coke are everywhere recognized and often enough *enjoyed*. In the peculiar unification at work throughout the world, there is surely a supply side, but there is not only a supply side. Some things are true even if multinational corporations claim so: there is demand.

What do American icons and styles mean to those who are not American? We can only imagine—but let us try. What young people graced with disposable income encounter in American television shows, movies, soft drinks, theme parks, and American-labeled (though not American-manufactured) running shoes, T-shirts, baggy pants, ragged jeans, and so on, is a way of being in the world, the experience of a flow of ready feelings and sensations bobbing up, disposable, dissolving, segueing to the next and the next after that. . . . It is a quality of immediacy and casualness not so different from what Americans desire. But what the young experience in the video game arcade or the music megastore is more than the flux of sensation. They flirt with a loose sort of social membership that requires little but a momentary (and monetary) surrender. Sampling American goods, images, and sounds, they affiliate with an empire of informality. Consuming a commodity, wearing a slogan or a logo, you affiliate with disaffiliation. You make a limited-liability connection, a virtual one. You borrow some of the effervescence that is supposed to emanate from this American staple, and hope to be recognized as one of the elect. When you wear the Israeli version that spells *Coca-Cola* in Hebrew, you express some worldwide connection with unknown peers, or a sense of irony, or both—in any event, a marker of membership. In a world of ubiquitous images, of easy mobility and casual tourism, you get to feel not only local or national but global—without locking yourself in a box so confining as to deserve the name "identity."

We are seeing on a world scale the familiar infectious rhythm of modernity. The money economy extends its reach, bringing with it a calculating mentality. Even in the poor countries it stirs the same hunger for private feeling, the same taste for disposable labels and sensations on demand, the same attention to fashion, the new and the now, that cropped up earlier in the West. Income beckons; income rewards. The taste for the marketed spectacle and the media-soaked way of life spreads. The culture consumer may not like the American goods in particular but still acquires a taste for the media's speed, formulas, and frivolity. Indeed, the lightness of American-sponsored "identity" is central to its appeal. It imposes few burdens. Attachments and affiliations coexist, overlap, melt together, form, and re-form.

Marketers, like nationalists and fundamentalists, promote "identities," but for most people, the mélange is the message. Traditional bonds bend under pressure from imports. Media from beyond help you have your "roots" and eat them, too. You can watch Mexican television in the morning and American in the afternoon, or graze between Kurdish and English. You can consolidate family ties with joint visits to Disney World—making Orlando, Florida, the major tourist destination in the United States, and the Tokyo and Marne-la-Vallée spin-offs massive attractions in Japan and France. You can attach to your parents, or children, by playing oldie music and exchanging sports statistics. You plunge back into the media flux, looking for—what? Excitement? Some low-cost variation on known themes? Some next new thing? You don't know just what, but you will when you see it—or if not, you'll change channels.

As devotees of Japanese video games, Hong Kong movies, and Mexican *telenovelas* would quickly remind us, the blends, juxtapositions, and recombinations of popular culture are not just American. American and American-based models, styles, and symbols are simply the most far-flung, successful, and consequential. In the course of a century, America's entertainment corporations succeeded brilliantly in cultivating popular expectations for entertainment—indeed, the sense of a *right* to be entertained, a right that belongs to the history of modernity, the rise of market economies, and individualism. The United States, which began as Europe's collective fantasy, built a civilization to deliver the goods for playing, feeling, and meaning. Competitors ignore its success at their own peril, financial and otherwise.

The Supply Side

About the outward thrust of the American culture industry there is no mystery. The mainspring is the classic drive to expand markets. In the latter half of the 1980s,[7] with worldwide deregulation, export sales increased from 30 percent to 40 percent of Hollywood's total revenue for television and film. Since then, the percentages have stabilized. In 2000,[8] total foreign revenues for all film and video revenue streams averaged 37 percent—for theatrical releases, 51 percent; for television, 41 percent; and for video, 27 percent.

Exporters benefit from the economies of scale afforded by serial production. American industrialists have long excelled at efficiencies, first anticipating and later developing the standardized production techniques of Henry Ford's assembly line. Early in the nineteenth century, minstrel

---

[7]*In the latter half of the 1980s:* National Technical Information Service, *Globalization of the Mass Media* (Washington, D.C.: Department of Commerce, 1993), pp. 1–2, cited in Edward S. Herman and Robert W. McChesney, *The Global Media: The New Missionaries of Corporate Capitalism* (London: Cassell, 1997), p. 39.

[8]*In 2000:* Calculated from *Schroder's International Media and Entertainment Report 2000*, p. 37. Courtesy of David Lieberman, media business editor of *USA Today*.

shows[9] were already being assembled from standardized components. Such efficiencies were later applied to burlesque, melodrama, vaudeville, radio soap opera, comic books, genre literature, musical comedy, and Hollywood studio productions. Cultural formula is not unique to the United States, but Americans were particularly adept at mass-producing it, using centralized management to organize road shows and coordinate local replicas.

If the American culture industry has long depended on foreign markets, foreign markets now also depend on American formulas: Westerns, action heroes, rock music, hip-hop. Globalized distribution expedites imitation. The American way generates proven results. Little imagination is required to understand why global entertainment conglomerates copy proven recipes or why theater owners outside the United States (many of whom are themselves American) want to screen them, even if they exaggerate the degree to which formula guarantees success. In a business freighted with uncertainty, the easiest decision is to copy. Individuals making careers also want to increase their odds of success.

It's a mistake to exaggerate the power of central supply to generate audiences, but the financial rewards of imitation are potentially so great, legions of entrepreneurs everywhere make the effort. All over the world, young filmmakers aspire to become the next Steven Spielberg or George Lucas, with their blatant emotional payoffs and predictable lines.

Around the world, as in the United States itself, America fabricated the templates, first, for Italian and Spanish Westerns, later for Hong Kong kung fu and "action," Europop, French soap operas, and so on. The Hollywood star system also came in for imitation everywhere. Even if, when faced with a choice,[10] people tend to prefer domestically produced television to Hollywood goods, competitors in television, as in film and music, are pulled[11] into America's gravitational field. 15

The Demand Side

But the supply-side argument won't suffice to explain global cultural dominance. American popular culture is not uniquely formulaic or transportable. (Indeed, in 1900, 142 special trains[12] transported touring companies of actors and musicians throughout England and Wales every Sunday.) Moreover,

---

[9]*minstrel shows:* Ostendorf, "What Makes American Popular Culture So Popular?" pp. 16–18, 47.

[10]*when faced with a choice:* Herman and McChesney, *Global Media,* p. 42. See also Tapio Varis, "Values and the Limits of the Global Media in the Age of Cyberspace," in Michael Prosser and K.S. Sitaram, eds., *Civic Discourse: Intercultural, International, and Global Media* (Stamford, CT: Ablex, 1999), vol. 2, pp. 5–17. During one week in the spring of 2001, not one of the fifty top-rated British TV shows was American.

[11]*competitors . . . are pulled:* Jeremy Tunstall, *The Media Are American: Anglo-American Media in the World* (New York: Columbia University Press, 1977), pp. 50–51.

[12]*142 special trains:* Cyril Ehrlich, *The Music Profession in Britain Since the Eighteenth Century* (London: Oxford University Press, 1985), p. 56. Thanks to Peter Mandler for this reference.

availability is not popularity. No one forced Danes to watch *Dallas,* however cheaply purchased. In fact, when a new television entertainment chief took charge in 1981–82 and proceeded to cancel the show, thirty thousand protest letters[13] poured in, and hundreds of Danes (mostly women, many rural) demonstrated in Copenhagen. When the chief's superiors told him he had better rethink his decision, he passed a sleepless night, bowed, and reversed himself. The dominance of American popular culture is a soft dominance—a collaboration. In the words of media analyst James Monaco, "American movies and TV are popular because they're *popular.*"[14]

That popularity has much to do with the fusion of market-mindedness and cultural diversity. The United States has the advantages of a polyglot, multirooted (or rather, uprooted) society that celebrates its compound nature and common virtues (and sins) with remarkable energy. Popular culture, by the time it ships from American shores, has already been "pretested" on a heterogeneous public—a huge internal market with variegated tastes. American popular culture is, after all, the rambunctious child of Europe and Africa. Our popular music and dance derive from the descendants of African slaves, among others. Our comic sense derives principally from the English, East European Jews, and, again, African-Americans, with growing Hispanic infusions. Our stories come from everywhere; consider Ralph Waldo Ellison's *Invisible Man,* inspired jointly by Dostoyevsky,[15] African-American folktales, and jazz. American culture is spongy, or in James Monaco's happy term, *promiscuous.*[16] He adds, "American culture simply doesn't exist without its African and European progenitors, and despite occasional outbursts of 'Americanism' it continues to accept almost any input."

To expand in the United States, popular culture had a clear avenue. It did not have to squeeze up against an aristocratic model, there being no wealthy landowning class to nourish one except in the plantation South—and there, slaves were the population that produced the most influential popular culture. Outside the South, from the early nineteenth century on, the market enjoyed prestige; it was no dishonor to produce culture for popular purposes. Ecclesiastical rivals were relatively weak. From the early years of the Republic, American culture was driven[17] by a single overriding

---

[13]*thirty thousand protest letters:* Personal communication, Henrik Christiansen, former chief of entertainment for Danish television (and previously head of news), September 1998.

[14]*James Monaco:* "Images and Sounds as Cultural Commodities," p. 231, from an article I clipped a long time ago but without noting from which magazine I'd clipped it.

[15]*Dostoyevsky:* Fyoder Michaylovich Dostoyevsky (1821–1881), Russian novelist.

[16]*Monaco's happy term:* Monaco, p. 231.

[17]*American culture was driven:* Library shelves groan with histories of popular American culture, but fundamental works worth singling out include Henry Nash Smith, *Virgin Land: The American West as Symbol and Myth* (Cambridge, Mass.: Harvard University Press, 1950); Richard Slotkin, *Regeneration Through Violence: The Mythology of the American Frontier, 1600–1860* (Middletown, Conn.: Wesleyan University Press, 1973); John G. Cawelti, *Adventure, Mystery, and Romance: Formula Stories as Art and Popular Culture* (Chicago: University of Chicago Press, 1976); and Michael Denning, *Mechanic Accents: Dime Novels and Working-Class Culture in America* (London: Verso, 1987).

purpose: to entertain the common man and woman. Hence Tocqueville's[18] recognition that American artists cultivated popularity, not elevation; fun, not refinement. As Daniel Dayan[19] has put it with only slight exaggeration, European (and traditional) cultures have a superego,[20] American culture does not. What is the market for entertainment if not a market for id?

Think about possible sources of competition, and the American advantage stands out. In the global market, bottom-up outsells top-down. Despite a tradition of popular culture, the main British model was classbound—culture as cultivation, culture as good for you. The head of the BBC's General Overseas Service[21] complained in 1944 that "if any hundred British troops are invited to choose their own records 90 per cent of the choice will be of American stuff," and from then onward Americanization came in for much high-minded abuse. As for Soviet Russia, when it was a major world power, its culture was mainly didactic. (In 1972, Soviet film exports[22] to its captive market in eastern and central Europe were still weaker, proportionately, than Hollywood's exports everywhere else in the world.) Who could produce fun like Americans? Who believed so fervently in colorful spectacle? In 1992, as France debated the establishment of Euro Disneyland outside Paris, as the theatrical director Arianne Mnouchkin denounced this "cultural Chernobyl" and French intellectuals joined her protest, it was not completely disingenuous for a Disney official[23] to deny the charge of American cultural imperialism by saying: "It's not America, it's Disney. . . . We're not trying to sell anything but fun, entertainment."

It is to America's advantage as well that commercial work emerges from Hollywood, New York, and Nashville in the principal world language. Thanks to the British Empire-cum-Commonwealth, English is the second most commonly spoken native language in the world, and the most international. (The vast majority of those who speak the leading language, Chinese, live in a single country, and their language, tonal in speech and ideographic on paper, is not well adapted for export.) English is spoken and read as a second language more commonly than any other. Increasingly, the English   20

---

[18]*Tocqueville:* Alexis de Tocqueville (1805–1859), French politician and writer, renowned for his observations on U.S. society and culture in *Democracy in America* (1835–40).

[19]*Daniel Dayan:* Personal communication, July 20, 2000.

[20]*superego:* Austrian psychiatrist Sigmund Freud (1856–1939) divided the human personality into three functional parts: the id, which is dominated by the pleasure principle and the quest for immediate gratification; the superego, which internalizes the role of the parent and thus embodies social expectations that "censor" the urges of the id; and the ego, which results from the interaction of id and superego with the external world.

[21]*The head of the BBC's General Overseas Service:* Quoted in Asa Briggs, *The War of Words* (London: Oxford University Press, 1970), p. 567–68. *Americanization:* Dick Hebdige, *Hiding in the Light* (London: Routledge/Comedia, 1988), pp. 52–76. There were exceptions, however. In the Noel Coward–David Lean film *Brief Encounter* (1946), the Trevor Howard character raves about the merits of Donald Duck as a distraction from the war.

[22]*Soviet film exports:* Tunstall, *Media Are American,* p. 62.

[23]*a Disney official:* Quoted in Todd Gitlin, "World Leaders: Mickey, et al." *New York Times,* Arts and Leisure Section, May 3, 1992, p. 1.

that is taught and learned, the language in demand, is American, not British. It is the language of business and has acquired the cachet of international media. Of the major world languages, English is the most compressed; partly because of its Anglo-Saxon origins, the English version of any text is almost always shorter than translations in other languages. English is grammatically simple. American English in particular[24] is pungent, informal, absorptive, evolving, precise when called upon to be precise, transferable between written and verbal forms, lacking in sharp distinctions between "high" and "low" forms, and all in all, well adapted for slogans, headlines, comic strips, song lyrics, jingles, slang, dubbing, and other standard features of popular culture. English is, in a word, the most torrential language.

Moreover, the American language of images is even more accessible than the American language of words. The global popularity of Hollywood product often depends less on the spoken word, even when kept elementary (non-English-speakers everywhere could understand Arnold Schwarzenegger without difficulty), than on crackling edits, bright smiles, the camera tracking and swooping, the cars crashing off cliffs or smashing into other cars, the asteroids plunging dramatically toward earth. In action movies, as in the Westerns that preceded them, speech is a secondary mode of expression. European competitors cannot make this claim, though Hong Kong can.

It is also an export advantage that "American" popular culture is frequently not so American at all. "Hollywood" is an export platform that happens to be located on the Pacific coast of the United States but uses capital, hires personnel, and depicts sites from many countries. Disney casually borrows mythologies from Britain, Germany, France, Italy, Denmark, China, colonial America, the Old Testament, anywhere. Any myth can get the Disney treatment: simplified, smoothed down, prettified. Pavilions as emblems of foreign countries, sites as replicas of sites, *Fantasia, Pinocchio, Song of the South, Pocahontas, Mulan* — Disney takes material where it can, as long as it comes out Disney's industrialized fun.

Moreover, to sustain market advantages, the Hollywood multinationals, ever thirsting for novelty, eagerly import, process, and export styles and practitioners from abroad. Consider, among directors, Alfred Hitchcock, Charlie Chaplin, Douglas Sirk, Michael Curtiz, Billy Wilder, Otto Preminger, Ridley Scott, Peter Weir, Bruce Beresford, Paul Verhoeven, John Woo, Ang Lee. (The big Hollywood movie of 1996, *Independence Day*, with its rousing nationalist features, was directed by the German Roland Emmerich — a Hollywood fact reminiscent of Louis B. Mayer's decision[25] to celebrate his birthday on July 4.) Consider, among stars, Greta Garbo, Ingrid Bergman, Cary Grant, Anthony Quinn, Sean Connery, Arnold Schwarzenegger, Jean-Claude

[24]*American English in particular:* Tunstall, *Media Are American*, pp. 127–8.
[25]*Louis B. Mayer's decision:* Neal Gabler, *An Empire of Their Own: How the Jews Invented Hollywood* (New York: Crown, 1988), p. 3.

Van Damme, Mel Gibson, Hugh Grant, Jackie Chan, Kate Winslet, Michelle Yeoh, Chow Yun-Fat, Catherine Zeta-Jones, Antonio Banderas, Penelope Cruz. Hollywood is the global magnet—and (to mix metaphors) the acid bath into which, often enough, talent dissolves. Even the locales come from everywhere, or nowhere. It is striking how many blockbusters take place in outer space (the *Star Wars*, *Alien*, and *Star Trek* series), in the prenational past (the *Jurassic Park* series), in the post-national future (the *Planet of the Apes* series, the two *Terminator* films, *The Matrix*), at sea (*Titanic*, *The Perfect Storm*—the latter also directed by a German, Wolfgang Petersen), or on an extended hop-skip-and-jump around the world (the James Bond series, *Mission: Impossible*).

In music, cultural import-export relations can be intricate. What exactly is an "American" style anyway? In the art critic Harold Rosenberg's phrase, the great American tradition is "the tradition of the new."[26] The cultural gates are poorly guarded and swing both ways. American rhythm and blues influenced Jamaican ska, which evolved into reggae, which in turn was imported to the United States, mainly via Britain. "Musicians in the Kingston tenement yards[27] picked up poor reception of New Orleans radio stations," writes music journalist Vivien Goldman, "and retransmitted boogie woogie piano, horn sections, and strolling, striding bass into Jamaica's insidious one drop groove and scratchy skanga-skanga guitar." The Jamaican custom of "toasting," with the disc jockey talking over prerecorded rhythm tracks (a style that in turn derived from African griot "chats"), led to "dub," in which the DJ remixed the song, which in turn evolved into American rap. The "trance-like quality" of dub's "thudding bass" led to "the incantatory, undulating repetitions of ambient and rave music." American punks[28] who imported ska from London in the 1990s were not necessarily aware that it was Jamaican. Mambo, tango, bossa nova, techno—dancing America puts up no obstacles to imported energies. The result is not an American equivalent of France's *mission civilisatrice*;[29] arguably it is the opposite, in which American teenagers shimmy through the malls to the rhythms of the wretched of the earth.

---

[26]*Harold Rosenberg: The Tradition of the New* (New York: Grove, 1961). Rosenberg was referring to modernism in the arts, but he might equally well have meant popular culture.

[27]*"Musicians in the Kingston tenement yards":* Vivien Goldman, "One Drop of Mighty Dread: How Jamaica Changed the World's Music," *CommonQuest* 4, no. 3 (2000), pp. 23, 22, 25.

[28]*American punks:* Ibid., p. 27. American food has been and continues to be shaped by a similar hybridization, which is the point of the joke about the tourist who walks up to a stranger in New York and asks where he can get a pizza. The stranger points to a Chinese restaurant. Perplexed, the tourist walks into the restaurant and says hesitantly to a waiter, "Is it really true that you serve pizza?" "Of course," is the answer, "what size would you like, and what topping? We have mushroom, pepperoni—" "Excuse me," says the tourist, "but I don't understand why a Chinese restaurant serves pizza." The waiter replies, "For all our Jewish customers!"

[29]*mission civilisatrice:* French for "civilizing mission."

No matter. Of Americanized popular culture, nothing more or less is 25
asked but that it be *interesting,* a portal into the pleasure dome. In the
main, an all-too-bearable lightness[30] is what the traffic will bear. Not for
American culture the televisual intricacies of Rainer Werner Fassbinder's
Berlin Alexanderplatz or Dennis Potter's *The Singing Detective,* or the sub-
tlety and inwardness of the great European filmmakers, or the historical
scale of Latin Americans, Japanese, and Chinese. Not for American popular
culture the presumption of Art with a capital *A,* known colloquially as *arti-
ness.* Playful, expressive, comfortably uplifting—a host of styles and themes
converge in what the psychologist Martha Wolfenstein called a *fun morality:* Thou Shalt Have Fun.[31]

ENGAGING THE TEXT

1. What specific qualities, values, and attitudes does Gitlin identify with
   American culture? Why, in his view, are these aspects of American culture
   so attractive to people in other countries? To what extent do these qualities
   and attitudes strike you as particularly "American"? Are there any others
   that you would add to Gitlin's list?

2. What does American global media do to local cultures and regional identities, according to Gitlin? What takes the place of local identity in the
   media-dominated world that Gitlin describes? What, in your estimation, is
   gained or lost in this transaction?

3. What is Gitlin suggesting when he says that American culture is "spongy"
   or "promiscuous"—or when he says that American popular culture produces entertainment for the "id" and not for the "superego"? What does he
   mean when he claims that, unlike traditional cultures, American culture is
   "bottom-up" instead of "top-down"? To what extent would you agree with
   these depictions of U.S. popular culture? Why?

4. In what way has the English language itself contributed to the worldwide
   dominance of American culture, according to Gitlin? Why, in this view, is
   English particularly well suited to a commercial culture built on advertising, slogans, headlines, and comic strips?

5. Overall, how would you characterize Gitlin's attitude toward American
   popular culture? Does he see it as a threat to the rest of the world, as an invitation to freedom, or simply as a source of pleasure? What concerns or
   limitations do you see in the "fun morality" that Gitlin identifies with America's cultural influence across the world? Is it in any way distasteful, for example, for American teens to "shimmy through the malls to the rhythms of
   the wretched of the earth" (para. 24)?

---

[30] *all-too-bearable lightness:* An allusion to the title of Czech author Milan Kundera's
(b. 1929) novel *The Unbearable Lightness of Being* (1984).

[31] *Martha Wolfenstein:* "The Emergence of Fun Morality," in Eric Larrabee, ed., *Mass
Leisure* (Glencoe, IL: Free Press, 1958), p. 86.

EXPLORING CONNECTIONS

6. How might Gitlin's analysis of American culture help explain the "transracial populism" that Leon E. Wynter (p. 688) sees emerging as the new dominant type in U.S. media and advertising? In your view, does the emergence of this new multi-ethnic model of beauty suggest a profound change in American cultural and racial attitudes? Or is it just a matter of expanding the market for advertisers' goods? To what extent might simple market forces underlie most of the qualities that Gitlin associates with American culture?

7. Compare Gitlin's assessment of American popular culture with that offered by Michael Medved (p. 769). How might Gitlin be expected to reply to Medved's indictment of Hollywood? Which of these portrayals of American mass media strikes you as the more valid? Why?

8. To what extent might Gitlin's analysis of American culture be seen as supporting Dinesh D'Souza's view of what America represents to the rest of the world (p. 716)? How would you expect people who live in "traditional" Middle Eastern, Asian, or African societies to respond to a foreign culture that respects only "the tradition of the new"?

EXTENDING THE CRITICAL CONTEXT

9. Research the topic of cultural imperialism in relation to globalization and the influence of American mass media abroad. How have peoples in other countries responded to the "Americanization" of their societies over the past few decades? What concerns are raised about the spread of American cultural influences abroad? To what extent does your research confirm or challenge Gitlin's claim that American culture is not a matter of "imperialism" but merely a matter of "fun"?

10. Using Gitlin's and Michael Medved's (p. 769) selections as a point of departure, as well as your own knowledge of film, music, and television programming, write your own analysis of the meaning of American popular culture. Do you generally see American mass media as dramatizing the violence and decadence of U.S. society? Or do you tend to see more positive messages in American music, film, and television shows about American life? What, in your view, does American pop culture tell the rest of the world about us as a people and as a nation?

11. Pool your knowledge of American pop music to test Gitlin's claims about how it has been influenced by other cultures from around the world. What specific "foreign" influences can you identify in recent pop music hits? What types or styles of popular music seem to be most open to non-American influences? Would you agree, as Gitlin suggests, that it's difficult to define what "American style" amounts to in relation to contemporary music?

By Any Means Necessary
PATRICIA J. WILLIAMS

> Six weeks after the assault on the Pentagon and the World Trade Center, Congress passed the U.S. Patriot Act—a sweeping "homeland security" bill aimed at thwarting future terrorist acts. Covering more than 340 pages and adopted almost without debate, the Patriot Act dramatically expanded the surveillance and law-enforcement powers of federal agencies like the FBI and the CIA. In fact, as Patricia Williams argues in this editorial, the Patriot Act may strengthen federal law enforcement to the point that it undermines the very freedoms it was designed to protect. Since graduating from Harvard Law School in 1975, Williams (b. 1951) has taught at the University of Wisconsin, City University of New York, Harvard, Stanford, Dartmouth, and Duke. Currently, she is on the faculty at Columbia Law School, where she continues to publish widely in scholarly journals and national magazines on issues of race, gender, and law. Her books include The Alchemy of Race and Rights (1991) and Seeing a Color-Blind Future: The Paradox of Race (1997). This selection originally appeared as one of Williams's regular columns in The Nation.

The new USA Patriot Act has brought into being an unprecedented merger between the functions of intelligence agencies and law enforcement. What this means might be clearer if we used the more straightforward term for intelligence—that is, spying. Law enforcement agents can now spy on us, "destabilizing" citizens, not just noncitizens. They can gather information with few checks or balances from the judiciary.

Morton Halperin, a defense expert who worked with the National Security Council under Henry Kissinger, worried in *The New Yorker* that if a government intelligence agency "thinks you're under the control of a foreign government, they can wiretap you and never tell you, search your house and never tell you, break into your home, copy your hard drive, and never tell you that they've done it." Moreover, says Halperin, on whose phone Kissinger placed a tap, "Historically, the government has often believed that anyone who is protesting government policy is doing it at the behest of a foreign government and opened counterintelligence investigations of them."

This expansion of domestic spying highlights the distinction between punishing what has already occurred and preventing what might happen in the future. In a very rough sense, agencies like the FBI have been primarily concerned with catching criminals who have already done their dirty work, while agencies like the CIA have been involved in predicting or manipulating future outcomes—activities of prior restraint, in other words, from which the Constitution generally protects citizens.

The events of September 11 were a tremendous failure of intelligence, as well as a monumental embarrassment for law enforcement. At the same time, we must not allow our sense of helplessness in a teetering, unruly world to distort us. In startling numbers, Americans suddenly seem willing to embrace profiling based on looks and ethnicity; detention without charges; searches without warrants; and even torture and assassination. We want to open up the hearts of those all around us, peer in and see for ourselves what evil lurks in the hearts of men, women, and neighbors. But the difficult reality is that no such measures were apt to have revealed the World Trade Center hijackers; no such measures were likely to have prevented Timothy McVeigh's[1] bombing of the federal building in Oklahoma City.

Prophesying wrongdoing, particularly of those with no history of mental illness or violent criminality, is guesswork at best. No one foresaw the attacks on the World Trade Center because well-financed, professionally trained operatives spent years planning, strategizing, and coordinating that effort. The sad and unpalatable truth is that preventing surprise attacks of that sophistication may never be possible. If the risk ever could be reduced, it will require not so much the identification of "suspect" profiles but the kind of cross-cultural fluency and diplomatic skill of which the intelligence community has confessed it has an unfortunately short supply.

Yet in recent weeks, student demonstrators, global justice workers, civil libertarians, animal rights and peace activists have been characterized as terrorist sympathizers. More than 1,000 people have been arrested and held, approximately 800 with no disclosure of identities or location or charges against them. This is "frighteningly close to the practice of 'disappearing' people in Latin America," according to Kate Martin, the director of the Center for National Security Studies. And neighborhood watch groups have geared themselves up with troubling expressions of vigilantism.

Most alarming of all, a recent CNN poll has revealed that 45 percent of Americans would not object to torturing someone if it would provide information about terrorism. Callers to radio programs say that we don't always have the "luxury of following all the rules"; that given recent events, people are "more understanding" of the necessity for a little behind-the-scenes roughing up. The unanimity of international conventions against torture notwithstanding, one hears authoritative voices—for example, Robert Litt, a former Justice Department official—arguing that while torture should not be "authorized," perhaps it could be used in an "emergency," as long as the person who tortures then presents himself to "take the consequences." The free enterprise version of torture, I guess we'd have to call it.

5

---

[1]*Timothy McVeigh:* Timothy McVeigh was executed in 2001 for the murder of 168 people in the 1995 bombing of the Federal Building in Oklahoma City.

While fully acknowledging the stakes of this new war, I worry that this righteous lawlessness is not new but has been practiced in oppressed communities for years. It is a habit that has produced cynicism, riots and bloodshed. The always urgently felt convenience of torture has left us with civic calamities ranging from Abner Louima in New York City to Jacobo Timerman in Argentina to Alexander Solzhenitsyn[2] in the Soviet Union—all victims of physical force and mental manipulation, all people who were "known" to know something.

The problem with this kind of "preventive" measure is that we are not mind-readers. Even with sodium pentothal, whose use some have suggested recently, we don't and we can't know every last thought of those who remain silent. Torture is an investment in the right to be all-knowing, in the certitude of what appears "obvious." It is the essence of totalitarianism. Those who justify it with confident proclamations of "I have nothing to hide, why should they?" overlap substantially with the class of those who have never been the persistent object of suspect profiling, never been harassed, never been stigmatized just for the way they look.

The human mind is endlessly inventive. People create enemies as much as fear real ones. We are familiar with stories of wrongheaded projections heaped upon the maid accused of taking something that the lady of the house simply misplaced or the wayward child stole. Stoked by tragedy and dread, the creativity of our paranoia is in overdrive right now. We must take a deep collective breath and be wary of persecuting those who conform to our fears instead of prosecuting foes who were and will be smart enough to play against such prejudices.

ENGAGING THE TEXT

1. What are Williams's objections to the U.S.A. Patriot Act? What assumptions does she make about this piece of antiterror legislation? How sound are her fears, in your opinion? Why?

2. Would you agree that no measure like the Patriot Act would have stopped the 9/11 terrorists? What could be done, in your opinion, to thwart future terrorist threats?

3. How far would you be willing to "bend the rules" of the law in order to safeguard U.S. citizens against the threat of terrorism? For example, which of the following measures would you be willing to condone:

   - National identification cards for all American citizens
   - Regular reporting to the INS for all foreign nationals in the United States

[2]*Abner Louima . . . Jacobo Timerman . . . Alexander Solzhenitsyn:* Abner Louima was a Haitian immigrant terrorized by the New York City police in 1997 after being arrested outside a Brooklyn nightclub; Jacobo Timerman (1923–1999) was an Argentine journalist who gained international fame by publicizing the brutality and corruption of the Argentine government during the 1970s and 80s; Alexander Solzhenitsyn (b. 1918) is a Russian novelist who won the Nobel Prize for his literary protests against Soviet Communism.

*"Look, you've got to accept some curtailment of your freedom
in exchange for increased security."*

- Racial profiling at airports
- Wiretaps without formal judicial approval
- Random computer surveillance of shopping, phone, and library records
- Secret "tip" hot lines for suspicious behaviors
- Detention and interrogation of "suspicious persons" without formal indictments
- Secret or military trials of suspected terrorists

4. If there were reason to believe that a suspect might have information that would lead to the apprehension of a terrorist cell, would you condone the use of torture to save innocent lives? Why or why not? Can torture even be practiced within the context of a democratic state?

EXPLORING CONNECTIONS

5. What difference is there, if any, between the kind of freedom that Williams is concerned about in this essay and the "fun" freedoms that Todd Gitlin describes in "Under the Sign of Mickey Mouse & Co." (p. 782)? How is it possible for American culture to be so obsessed with "fun" and indulge in the kind of "totalitarian" excesses that Williams warns of in this essay?

6. Write a brief imaginary conversation among Williams, Mark Hertsgaard (p. 728), and Joel Andreas (p. 741) on the future direction of America and the myth of freedom. To what extent would you agree with the picture each of these writers presents of the future of American civilization?

EXTENDING THE CRITICAL CONTEXT

7. Research concerns that have arisen in response to the U.S. Patriot Act and other measures aimed at strengthening homeland security since 9/11. How have the powers of U.S. law enforcement agencies grown during the ongoing war against terrorism? What specific concerns do critics cite in relation to homeland security legislation? How valid do these concerns seem to you?

8. Working in groups, find out as much as you can about Abner Louima, Jacobo Timerman, and Alexander Solzhenitsyn. What similarities or differences do you note among the cases of these three men? What does each of their stories suggest about the abuse of state power?

The Sorrow and the Pity of Racial Profiling
RALPH TEMPLE

Since the beginning of the war on terrorism, thousands of Arab Americans and Arab immigrants have been detained for questioning or subject to heightened security measures at U.S. airports—often for no other reason than the fact that they simply "looked suspicious." American courts and law enforcement agencies only recently began to reject the use of racial profiling of African Americans and other minority groups as a tool of law enforcement. Yet today, we're seeing a resurgence of racial profiling in relation to people who look Middle Eastern—a practice that evokes memories of the Japanese internment during World War II. In the view of long-time civil libertarian Ralph Temple, this return to the practice of racial profiling threatens to undermine the most central of all American principles—the principle of individual liberty. Temple served as Legal Director of the District of Columbia American Civil Liberties Union from 1966 until his retirement in 1980. Today, he lives in Ashland, Oregon, where he continues to speak and write on issues of civil liberties. This essay originally appeared in It's a Free Country: Personal Freedoms in America After September 11 *(2002).*

If Jewish extremists, like Yigal Amir who assassinated Israeli Prime Minister Yitzakh Rabin in 1995, ever engaged in acts of terrorism in the United States, a roundup of foreign Jews would be likely to follow. There is an echo of lynchings and pogroms in the indiscriminate arrests of over eleven hundred Middle Eastern men following the September 11 terrorist attacks. Such raids are an atavistic yet time-honored response. The dragnet of Arabs and Muslims has not yielded results, any more than did the 1920 Palmer raids,[1] the 1940s internment of Japanese-Americans, or the 1979 crackdown on Iranians during the hostage crisis. But the roundups reassure the public.

For Muhammad Rafiq Butt, a fifty-five-year-old working-class Pakistani free of any links to terrorism whose only offense was an expired visa, the experience meant death. The first fatality of the racial profiling of Arabs and Muslims following the September 11 attacks, Butt, arrested by the FBI, died of a heart attack after languishing for thirty-three days in a New Jersey county jail. In *The Gulag Archipelago*, Aleksandr Solzhenitsyn[2] characterizes that experience: "Arrest! Need it be said that it is a breaking point in your life, a bolt of lightning which has scored a direct hit on you? That it is an unassimilable spiritual earthquake not every person can cope with . . ."

Many other accounts of broken lives have emerged from the sweep arrests, and, as of this writing nine months later, hundreds are still being held. The arrests were followed by the Justice Department's program to interrogate another five thousand Arabs and Muslims, and in March 2002 several thousand more were added to the interrogation list. In June 2002 the department announced that it planned to fingerprint and photograph an additional 100,000. Middle Eastern people boarding airliners are being specially screened, and harassed.

The public, identifying with the three thousand murdered in the September 11 attacks, has not concerned itself much with the implications of this broadscale targeting of an ethnic minority. Bombarded on our own soil for the first time in two centuries, Americans are desperately afraid that one of us may be next—on an airliner, in a building, on the street. The traumatized political atmosphere has encouraged a vast expansion of government powers at the expense of traditional rights, and is reflected most dramatically in the public's embrace of racial profiling of Muslims.

Some liberals have joined the stampede. Journalist Michael Kinsley, in   5
a September 30, 2001, article in the *Washington Post*, argues, "[T]oday we're at war with a terror network that just killed six thousand innocents and has anonymous agents in our country planning more slaughter. Are we really supposed to ignore the one identifiable fact we know about them? That may be asking too much."

Kinsley reasons that "an Arab-looking man heading toward a plane is statistically more likely to be a terrorist." Stuart Taylor, Jr., in the conservative *National Journal*, similarly invokes "statistics," arguing that "one hundred percent of the people who have hijacked airliners for the purpose of

---

[1]*1920 Palmer raids:* Between 1919 and 1921, a series of well-publicized reprisals led by then U.S. Attorney General A. Mitchell Palmer against unionists, immigrants, and members of the American Communist and Socialist Parties.

[2]*Aleksandr Solzhenitsyn:* Russian novelist (b. 1918), who won the Nobel Prize for his literary protests against Soviet Communism.

mass-murdering Americans have been Arab men." These arguments have no basis in the science of statistics. Statistical validity requires more than the likelihood that the suspect is of one race rather than another; it requires that the selected group contains a sufficient probability of return to justify the selection. As these pundits acknowledge, the statistical yield of terrorists from screening all young Arab men is likely to be "tiny" or "infinitesimal."

The very occurrence of September 11 demonstrated the profound incompetence of the FBI, the CIA, and the Immigration and Naturalization Service (INS). Yet America, in denial, seems incapable even now of facing the extent to which years of spectacular bungling by these agencies has left us dangerously exposed. The ethnicity, age, and sex were in fact *not* the "one identifiable fact" known about the nineteen September 11 terrorists. Some were already on watch-lists but were missed anyway, while the conduct of others should have aroused suspicions. Even six months after the attacks, the INS unwittingly extended the visas of two of the dead September 11 terrorists. Congress has responded to the colossal failures of the FBI and the CIA by throwing more money into their already bloated budgets. The country thus reaches not for real security but for the habitual bromide of racial profiling, which diffuses and squanders investigative resources, undermining rather than enhancing public safety. Racial profiling is invoked, not for any proven effectiveness nor for lack of more sharply focused alternatives, but as a pacifier for a frightened public.

The notion that all members of the perpetrators' race or ethnic group are suspect, and therefore may be separated out for special treatment, has a familiar ring from an earlier era:

> [W]e cannot reject as unfounded the judgment . . . that there were disloyal members of that population whose number and strength could not be precisely and quickly ascertained. We cannot say that the . . . government did not have ground for believing that in a critical hour such persons could not readily be isolated and separately dealt with, and constituted a menace to the national defense and safety . . .

So did the Supreme Court, in *Korematsu vs. United States,* justify the World War II evacuation into concentration camps of 120,000 Japanese-Americans, an action for which the nation later confessed error and paid reparations. It is an all-too-common reaction to regard with fear and hostility all those of another racial or ethnic group. Reflexive actions, however, are not always beneficial. Civility and decency, not to say our genuine safety, frequently demand that we rise above our reactive fears and inclinations. That is in large part the function in a society of the rule of law.

The Rule of Law

The Constitution was intended to limit the public's misguided passions   10
against individuals and minorities by defining certain rights that are intrinsic. As Jefferson expressed it in the opening lines of the Declaration of

Independence: "We hold these truths to be self-evident, that all men are created equal, that they are endowed by their Creator with certain unalienable rights, that among these are Life, Liberty and the pursuit of Happiness."

Civil liberties are the gift, the endowment, given us by "the Creator," not by the ACLU,[3] not by the happenstance of "legal technicalities," not even by the Founding Fathers or John Locke's social compact.[4] In short, and in less sectarian terms, certain fundamental rights come with the condition of being human—they come with the skin—and no one, no group, no sovereign, not even the people as sovereign, has the moral, the social, or the political right to deprive any one of us of those rights. Any effort to do so is illegitimate. It was the very purpose of our constitutional system and the Bill of Rights to establish a form of government in which the autonomy and integrity of the individual would predominate over the interests of the state, the collective society—the public. The philosophy is that the state exists for the preservation and advancement of the liberty of the individual, not the other way around.

The people retain ample means to protect themselves from dangerous individuals and groups. But the means must be within the confines of law— law which makes certain rights of the individual ironclad, no matter what the collective temptation to violate them. Moreover, the equality principle —won at the cost of a Civil War in which more American lives were lost than in all other wars combined—provides a baseline solution: If the threat is so great that the restrictions to be imposed on liberty are truly necessary and worth the hardships they entail, let them be borne by all, equally, regardless of race. If Arabs are to be questioned and frisked at airports, let us all be questioned and frisked in the same way. Equality has the built-in virtue that, if all are similarly burdened, the public will not tolerate unnecessary and excessive measures.

The Anti-Democratic Nature of the Bill of Rights

In late October 2001, six weeks after the terrorist attacks, I attended a presentation by Professor Arthur Miller at the forty-fifth reunion of my Harvard Law School class, in which a television journalist on a panel answered each issue on how to reconcile liberty with security by applying his "MOS" standard: What would the Man on the Street say? Unsurprisingly, on his scorecard, individual rights lost out to collective security every time. The man on the street will almost always say that he believes in civil liberties, *"but."* "I am all for civil liberties, *but,"* is the argument for racial

---

[3]*ACLU:* American Civil Liberties Union.

[4]*John Locke's social compact:* English philosopher John Locke (1632–1704) theorized that governments were originally formed by "social contract" when individuals voluntarily surrendered some of their natural liberties in order to enjoy the benefits of the order and security of an organized state.

profiling, the argument always made when rights are asserted in hard cases. People are in favor of the presumption of innocence, *but* against the pretrial release of suspects; in favor of freedom of speech and assembly, *but* against allowing Nazis to march in Skokie, Illinois; in favor of freedom of religion, *but* against permitting a Ku Klux Klan rally around a fiery cross.

The argument that civil liberties and racial equality are good, *but* not in times like these, reflects an ignorance or lack of faith in the very purpose of the Bill of Rights. The Bill of Rights is by design anti-democratic, intended to restrain reactions to the offensive, the unpopular, and the threatening; intended to stand as a bulwark against popular will when the public is most agitated; intended for stormy times, groups, and people, which is when the rights are most needed. Its purpose is to protect the individual and minorities from a tyrannical majority.

The question of whether the anti-democratic nature of the Bill of Rights is a sound and just concept is addressed in philosopher John Rawls's 1971 work, *A Theory of Justice*. Rawls asks what rights people would vote for if they had to work out such rights and laws under a "Veil of Ignorance." Under this veil of ignorance, Rawls theorizes, each person would have to decide, in a group vote, on the rights each of them would have, and what steps the collective group might take against each of them, without knowing in advance what his or her status and power would be in the society that would follow and function under these rules. Thus, each person would have to vote on the rules without knowing whether he or she would, for example, be in a racial, ethnic, or political minority, would be rich or poor, talented or untalented, highly intelligent or not, physically strong or weak, etc. 15

To protect self-interest one is thus forced to contemplate such potential vulnerabilities as being in an unpopular minority, or being erroneously accused of a crime, or otherwise being disliked or targeted by the group for punishment, restriction, or other action. Everyone is therefore impelled to gauge the best distribution of power and rights between the group and the individual, looking at it from both points of view. Rawls concludes that a rational person going through this process is most likely to end up where the Founders did, with a set of individual rights approximating those in the Bill of Rights.

The Shoe on the Other Foot: Who Will Be Profiled Next?

Supporters of racial profiling need the Rawls "Veil of Ignorance" perspective. It is potentially dangerous to many of us to establish the precedent that members of a racial or ethnic minority may be treated differently. Being called out of line at the airport and sent to a separate area with all other members of one's ethnic group is of course not in the same league as being sent to a concentration camp. But surely it is more than the "pretty small imposition" and mere "inconvenience and embarrassment" with which Michael Kinsley dismisses it in his *Washington Post* article.

Consider the atmosphere generated around the lives of an ethnic group that is sorted out in public for special treatment. Dr. Martin Luther King, Jr., in *Letter From Birmingham City Jail*, spoke of the black person's "being harried by day and haunted by night by the fact that you are a Negro, living constantly at tip-toe stance never quite knowing what to expect next, and plagued with inner fears and outer resentments." We are seeing and hearing the anguish of Arab- and Muslim-Americans, sudden pariahs in a hostile atmosphere currently driving some to change their family names. Consider, too, proposals for national identification cards as another security measure; surely, if Arabs are a special category, such cards would prominently identify the bearer's ethnicity. Given racial profiling and a terrorized public subjected to a few more bombings, how far would we be from requiring Arabs to wear yellow crescents, as Jews in Nazi Germany were once made to wear yellow stars?

This is a path we should not follow. It is appalling to contemplate that, after an act of Jewish terrorism in the United States, all young Jews would be specially screened at airports, or that, just because the suspect is white, all white people would be subjected to special screening in cities like Washington, D.C., where they are in the minority. Racial profiling is a dangerous standard, hazardous to us all.

The National Spirit: What Is America?

Americans could benefit from looking at how another society responded when an ethnic group in its midst was targeted. Marcel Ophuls's 1970 documentary film, *The Sorrow and The Pity*, chronicles the shameful complicity of the French during the German occupation of the 1940s, including their cooperation in rounding up Jews for deportations to death camps. Another documentary film, *Weapons of the Spirit*, tells the story of Le Chambon-sur-Lignon, a small agricultural village in the mountains of Southern France, where five thousand Jews fleeing the Nazis were taken in and sheltered by five thousand Christians. This occurred organically, without a plan: Jewish families just started showing up, and the Huguenots of Le Chambon, with a history of persecution and concern for the scapegoat, took them in, one family at a time.

Forty years later, Pierre Sauvage, born in the town in 1944 to Jewish parents hiding there, returned to make the film. He asks villagers, now in their eighties, who had provided refuge, "What made you take in these people? Weren't you putting yourself in danger?" On camera we see an elderly lady shrug self-effacingly and answer, "We were used to it." A former school director explains, "It was the human thing to do." Eventually, the local Vichy prefect and the German army commander became aware of the presence of fugitive Jews, but for some unknown reason, both looked the other way. The Jews of Le Chambon escaped the Holocaust. Sauvage speculates that even the French prefect and the Nazi commander may have

20

been caught up in the contagious goodness of Le Chambon. Bill Moyers,[5] introducing the film, asks us to consider what each of us would have done if this had happened in America.

Of course, the anti-democratic and counterintuitive nature of civil liberties makes them unpopular. Opinion polls usually show that if the question is cast in a controversial context, about two-thirds of the public are opposed to any particular provision of the Bill of Rights. "Eternal vigilance is the price of liberty" is the adopted motto of the American Civil Liberties Union, and eternal vigilance—that is, an awareness by our political leaders, by our teachers, by our public commentators—has been lacking for a long time. The notion prevails that "civil libertarians" are a special interest group, and that civil liberties are an expendable luxury suitable only for calm times. Pierre Sauvage comments near the beginning of *Weapons of the Spirit* that when the crisis of the Nazi occupation came, Le Chambon found that it had the quality of leaders it needed and deserved. Our leaders, pundits, and other sculptors of the culture would do well to revisit the Jefferson Memorial and ponder the great man's warning, engraved on one of the walls: "Can the liberties of a nation be secure when the people have lost the conviction that those liberties are the gift of God?"

The system of civil liberties represents the highest qualities in law and government to which humans can aspire. As the philosopher Martin Buber maintains in his classic work, *I and Thou,* the challenge of being human is to rise above seeing people different from us as "the other," an object, a thing, an "it," and to see them instead as a part of an "I and Thou," a part of our very selves.

The Bill of Rights, civil liberties, and the primacy of the individual over the state are our most valuable heritage, our most unique and exalted national quality. They, more than mountains and free markets and consumerism, are what define our highest character as a people. We have shown in Afghanistan that we can defend our lives with weapons of war. Hopefully we can also preserve what we live *for* with weapons of the spirit.

ENGAGING THE TEXT

1. What arguments are commonly advanced in support of racial profiling, according to Temple? Why does he feel that racial profiling is bound to fail as a security strategy? Would you agree? Why or why not?

2. How would you characterize Temple's view of the average American—or, as he says, "the man on the street"? Why does he feel that the Bill of Rights is an "anti-democratic" document? Would you agree that the individual is always at odds with "the collective society"? Why or why not?

3. Why does Temple believe that we must work out our concepts of individual rights "under a veil of ignorance," as recommended by philosopher John Rawls? What are the benefits of this approach? Do you think it's possible to be unbiased when making decisions about individual rights?

[5]*Bill Moyers:* American television journalist and author (b. 1934).

4. Temple suggests that civil liberties are less "popular" in American society than are concepts like consumer rights or the free market. To what extent would you agree that civil liberties are relatively unimportant to most Americans? What leads you to this conclusion?

EXPLORING CONNECTIONS

5. Compare Temple's understanding of liberty with that offered by Dinesh D'Souza (p. 716). Which of these two views of freedom seems the more compelling or attractive to you? Why?
6. How might Walter Mosley (p. 755) respond to Temple's claim that in order to protect your own self-interest you have to see yourself in the shoes of a vulnerable minority? How does Temple's view of civil rights and American democracy support Mosley's claim that African Americans are particularly well prepared to wage peace in the name of the United States?
7. How might concepts like institutional racism and scapegoating as discussed in Chapter Five by Paul L. Wachtel (p. 613) and Vincent N. Parrillo (p. 577) help to explain why racial profiling appears, as Temple suggests, to be relatively acceptable to "the man on the street"?

EXTENDING THE CRITICAL CONTEXT

8. As a class, view Pierre Sauvage's *Weapons of the Spirit* and discuss what motivates the people in this documentary to risk their own lives to protect the rights of others. Do you think the average American would do the same under similar circumstances? Why or why not?
9. Do some Internet research to find out how many people have been detained for questioning by U.S. authorities since 9/11. What is the nationality of those who have been detained? How long have detainees been held on average? How many remain in custody? How has racial profiling disrupted the lives of Arab Americans? How can we tell if it has actually been effective in the "war on terrorism"?

Easy in the Harness:
The Tyranny of Freedom
GERRY SPENCE

As one of America's most outspoken and successful trial lawyers, Gerry Spence has more than a passing acquaintance with issues of freedom. In 1979 Spence came to national attention when he took on and defeated one of the largest nuclear power companies in the United States; representing

*Karen Silkwood, a power-plant employee exposed to lethal doses of radia-
tion, Spence won fame as a champion of individual rights and as a relentless
critic of corporate excess. In this selection, Spence wonders if Americans
understand the meaning of freedom and claims that genuine freedom is, in
fact, too painful for most of us to bear. The author of several books on justice
and injustice in American society, Spence (b. 1929) continues to practice
law in Jackson Hole, Wyoming. His most recent publication is a novel,* Half-
Moon and Empty Stars *(2001).* "Easy in the Harness" *originally appeared
in* From Freedom to Slavery: The Rebirth of Tyranny in America *(1994).*

"What is freedom?" an enlightened teacher asked her class.

"It's when you can leave home and go wherever you want, and do whatever you want, and your parents can't tell you what to do," a child replied.

"But what if you get hungry? Are you now free to starve?"

"I would go home," the child says.

We are not free. Nor have we ever been. Perfect freedom demands a   5
perfect vision of reality, one too painful for the healthy to endure. It requires that we be alive, alert, and exquisitely aware of our raw being. Faced
with the pain of freedom, man begs for his shackles. Afraid of death, he
seeks the stultifying boundaries of religion. Afraid of loneliness, he imprisons himself in relationships. Afraid of want, he accepts the bondage of employment. Afraid of rejection, he conforms to the commands of society. If
our knowledge of freedom were perfect we would not choose it. Pure freedom is pure terror.

Freedom is like a blank, white canvas when no commitments, no relationships, no plans, no values, no moral restraints have been painted on the
free soul. A state of perfect freedom is a state of nothingness. When we care
for another, when we make room for another's wants and needs, we have
lost an equal portion of our freedom, but in the bargain we are freed of
loneliness. When we take on marriage and a family, we are bound by our
vows, the law, and our moral commitments to spouse and child, but our bargain frees us of detachment and meaninglessness. When we live in the
country we can drive our trucks across the prairies, but when we join a community we cannot drive our cars across our neighbors' lawns. We can abide
by no moral values without being limited by them. We can belong to no
clubs without agreeing to their rules, or to a neighborhood without recognizing the rights of our neighbors. When we become residents of a village, a
state, or a nation, we must obey its laws. In short, when we join into any relationship our dues are always paid in freedom.

Robert Frost[1] understood freedom and expressed its essence in a typical Frostian metaphor: "Freedom is when you are easy in the harness." Easy

---

[1]*Robert Frost:* American poet (1874–1963).

in the harness. I used to sit behind a team of good horses, Star and Spiffy, and together we mowed the meadow hay. Their flanks foamed with sweat and after struggling for weeks at their tugs, sores developed on their necks from their rubbing collars. I remember a deep, sad look in the eyes of the horses. I liked to touch the horses, to feel their softer-than-velvet noses against my cheek. I liked their smell. I loved old Star and Spiffy.

I suppose that team of horses was mostly "easy in the harness." Willingly they would trudge up and down the field all day, their heads down, their tugs tight, their flanks digging like the pistons of engines, and at the end of the day when I lifted the wet harnesses from their backs they would run for the corral and lie down in the deep dust and roll, and roll again. Then they would get up and shake the dust from their backs and wait for me to open the corral gate to the pasture.

One spring when I returned to the ranch I found Star and Spiffy gone. Nobody wanted to talk about it. "They're just gone," the old rancher said.

"But where?" I asked. 10

"Gone," was all he would say, and the way he said it with such finality made it clear that was to be the end of it. Later I learned that each fall a horse buyer visited the neighboring ranches to buy the ranchers' worn-out nags. They brought a few cents a pound for dog meat. Some claimed the meat was shipped to Europe where horse meat was allegedly a delicacy, especially with the French, but I never confirmed it.

As I look back on it the horses were as easy in their harnesses as we. And their deaths were perhaps better than our own. I could see in my mind's eye the old team being shipped off, the eyes of the old horses as sad as ever. But it was only another ride to them. They were not being trucked to their execution. Their bellies were not gripped with fear. There was no sadness, no regrets. And as the truck rumbled down the highway toward the slaughterhouse, the fall air must have blown through their manes and made their old tired eyes water, and they must have felt joy.

Every day we spend our freedom like careless children with too many pennies. In exchange for acceptance by our friends we give up the right to say what we think. Being socially proper is more important than possessing a fresh, uncompromised soul. Being acceptable to our neighbors is often more important than being acceptable to ourselves. For nearly two hundred years slavery thrived in America over the silent protestations of decent citizens enslaved themselves by the tyranny of convention. The price of freedom is often rejection, even banishment.

I knew an old rancher who lived on the Wind River in Wyoming. People didn't have much good to say about old Jack. His chief crime was that he told the truth as he saw it and laughed at things we were all afraid to laugh at. Every once in a while I'd stop by to see him. He was usually in his garden. That day he was hoeing his corn, a special hybrid variety he had developed for our short growing season, and he was also locally famous for his high-altitude peas and potatoes.

"Well, what has God wrought today?" I asked, knowing full well my 15
question would engender a strong response.

"You talkin' 'bout *me*," he replied. "I'm my own god."

"Jack, aren't you afraid of going to hell for saying such irreligious
things?"

"There ain't no hell 'cept on earth." He went on hoeing. His shirt was
wet with good fresh summer sweat.

"Suppose God heard you say that," I said prodding him a little. "What if
he condemned you to burn in hell for an eternity for such heresy?" I'd been
introduced to such horrors as a child in Sunday school.

"No just god would condemn ya fer usin' the power of reason he give 20
ya," he said, "and the idea of hell is plumb unreasonable." He stopped,
leaned on his hoe handle, and squinted at me. "Besides, who would want ta
worship a god that would send yer ass to hell forever fer such a triflin' trans-
gression as not believin' somethin' that is unreasonable? That would be no
just god, and if he ain't just I don't want nothin' ta do with him."

The old boy was already well past eighty and he knew that by all odds
his days were numbered. "How you been feeling, Jack?" I asked, trying to
change the subject.

"Feel just perty perfect," he said. Then he went back to hoeing. "But I
may not make it another winter."

The following spring I stopped by. He was on his hands and knees
planting his garden.

"Well, Jack, I see you make it through another winter."

"Yep," he said. "See ya done the same." 25

"God willing," I said.

"God didn't have nothin' to do with it," he said.

"How come you're so tough on God?" I asked.

"On accounta those kinda ideas hurt a lotta innocent folks," he said. He
never looked up from his planting while he talked. He dropped the brown
bean seeds about an inch apart in the shallow furrow. "Christ taught that
love is the supreme law. But they got it all mixed up. I got a lotta neighbors
that love God and hate each other. I say if yer gonna love, ya oughta love
something ya can see, say, yer neighbor fer instance."

He had radical ideas for his time, for instance his views on birth con- 30
trol, about which he spoke often and freely. "This here earth is overrun with
people. The multitudes is starving everywhere. Now when I can't feed no
more cows on this little ranch I sure don't raise no more calves. There ain't
no starvin' calves here," he said. He covered the seed with his old crooked
fingers and tamped the fresh, moist soil over them with the heels of his
hands. "So how come my cows has got better rights than people? What kind
of a god would want ya to raise up kids ta starve?"

When he got to the end of the row he stood up, stretched his old stiff
back, and looked at me for the first time. "Why them churchgoin' neighbors
a mine claim to love the fetus in the womb. But as soon as the kid is born,

they say it's all right if it's left ta starve. I never could figure out why little kids who never done nothin' ta nobody should be punished by bein' sentenced ta starve ta death fer no worse crime than being born in the first place." When he looked at me I never saw a kinder set of eyes. I never knew a more honest man. I never knew a man who was more free than old Jack. But I think Jack was lonely sometimes. And, to the wonder and secret disappointment of some of his neighbors who were put off by his harsh and unedited comments on religion, and who thought for sure he'd never make it another winter, he lived through a dozen more after that.

Sometimes when I think of old Jack I realize how unfree I am, how afraid, how timid and intimidated and how the bargains I make sometimes leave me feeling cheated, how I sometimes trade honest convictions for silence to gain acceptance by those around me. Yet, in the end, I doubt that my neighbors love me any more than Jack's loved him. They respected him, that much I know, and maybe Jack valued their respect more than their love. Yet respect and love are sometimes hard to separate.

Jack's neighbors all came to his funeral, and some who had been his most severe critics had tears in their eyes. I doubt that Jack would have been surprised. I think he knew.

They buried old Jack out behind his garden where he wanted, close to the creek. As they lowered the pine box into the ground I could hear his creaky old voice arguing away. "Why, Spence," he said, "we kick our dogs if they shit in the house, but we shit all over this beautiful planet like a herd a hogs sufferin' from terminal diarrhea. Baby owls are smarter'n that. Ya never seen a baby owl that ever fouled its nest. These human bein's ain't too smart a species."

And I thought, Well, Jack, your old bones won't pollute this little plot behind your garden, that's for sure. Next spring you'll turn into fresh buds on the cottonwood trees, and maybe you won't think that's too bad a place to be. Maybe that's eternity after all. Earth to earth. 35

"Beats hell outta hell," I could hear old Jack reply. And then I turned away before the neighbors could catch up with me to tell me all about how old Jack was. One thing I knew: old Jack was free. Always had been.

The notion of "being American" is heavily laden with ideas of freedom. Being American and being free are often thought synonymous. As Americans we envision Washington's battered patriots marching to the beat of the boy drummer. We see Washington crossing the Delaware. We think of the Constitution and the Bill of Rights, and remember the Civil War, Lincoln and the Gettysburg Address, the freeing of the slaves, the great world wars "to keep America free." We see the billowing smoke of the ships sinking at Pearl Harbor and our American heroes raising the flag at Iwo Jima. And we remember the marches of Martin Luther King, Jr. We believe we are free in the same way we believe in God. Freedom is an article of faith, not a fact, not a condition. True, the freedom we enjoy in America, when set against the freedom of peoples in other lands, is emblazoned like a single candle lighting the gloom.

Law and order and rules, although antithetical to freedom, provide us with safeguards by which we are free to live with reasonable safety among those who are stronger. But the strong impose themselves upon us nevertheless. Although our younger, stronger neighbor is not free to force us out of our homes, the bank can do so if we fail to pay it its tribute of green flesh. Although we argue we are free to labor where we please for whomever we please, unless we show up in the morning, unless like old Star and Spiffy, we take our places in our stanchions and consent to the harness, we will be free to join the depressed and desperate masses of the unemployed who become harnessed to yet another master — fear.

If we are American, we believe in an American religion called "free enterprise," the principal tenet of which holds that it is not only moral but divine to reserve for the corporate oligarchy substantially all the wealth — leaving to the people the blessed right to obtain whatever, if any, dribbles down. The religion called "free enterprise" holds that in exchange for corporate America's right to squash and squeeze from all below it, the next in power possess the right to squash and squeeze those below them, and so on down the line until there is nothing left but the empty dredges of humanity. Some of these we discard on the streets, where they are free to die of hunger, disease, and shame. Those who rebel are at last housed — in prisons. . . .

Today we are more concerned with extracting freedom from our ene-   40
mies than in preserving our own. We wish into prison those who terrorize us in the streets and who break into our cars and homes. We wish the executioner's hand against those who kill our innocent without just cause. At last we wish to eliminate all those from our society who threaten us and frighten us and injure and kill us, and we seem willing to diminish or release our constitutional rights, indeed, our freedom, to be safer. In truth, we long for a more successful domestication of the human species.

I recall a certain white heifer at the ranch, a full-blown renegade. When she was disturbed in the slightest she would run bellowing and bawling and wildly kicking at everything and anything, including the air. To get her from one pasture to another took half a dozen good men on good horses half a day. I would have sent her to the butcher but for the fact that I had paid a pretty price for her one crazy afternoon at a fancy purebred sale that had been held in the lobby of the Hilton Hotel in Denver.

When her calf came, the calf was just like her. The little renegade wasn't more than a few days old when it kicked the old dog and broke his jaw. But for the fact that the calf in all other respects was quite a beautiful specimen and would bring a good price, I would have rid the ranch of her as well. But the calf's calf was even worse. Finally I realized I was breeding back to the wildebeest, and that unless I abandoned that bloodline, I would end up with an utterly unmanageable herd of cattle that would eventually do me in.

Domestication has been the specialty of man from the beginning. He domesticated the wolf into the dog, the wildcat into the lap pussy, the wild horse into the plow horse, the wildebeest into the Hereford and the Holstein. He has also been busily domesticating himself. As in the domestication of animals he has been selecting the most compliant members of his species and eliminating the least.

Today, America imprisons more people than any nation in the world. Those who occupy our prisons have been our noncomplying social deviants, whom we have removed from the reproductive cycle. In recent times we have become more willing to impose the death penalty against our own for a broader assortment of crimes. Facing proof that the death penalty has no deterring effect on crime whatsoever, we nevertheless encourage its imposition out of our true purpose, not to punish, not to prevent future crimes, but to further domesticate the species by eliminating those who are less compliant than we.

Something about servitude stills. Something about domestication stifles.   45
The wolf, now the poodle, no longer howls. The wild boar lies on its side in the hog pen and grunts. The wildebeest stands in her stall placidly chewing her cud while she's milked dry. Domestication of man and beast muffles the cry of freedom and suffocates the spirit of liberty.

As we continue to domesticate the species, we tend toward the creation of a mass of mankind that is as easily herded as a flock of dead-eyed sheep. This amorphous glob faithfully mumbles the liturgy demanded by the corporate oligarchy, which holds that it is moral to take first and most from the weakest and the poorest. The dogma also holds that it is laudable to create classes of people based on wealth, not virtue, that is to say, it makes no difference how miserly, how greedy, how uncaring and spiteful the individual may be, if he has wealth he is of a different and better class than the virtuous without wealth. This religion to which the people are bound delivers to the corporate oligarchy the prerogative to ply its enormous powers against the people in order to become yet more powerful. And so it has been throughout human history as man struggles for his freedom, fights and dies for it, but having once achieved it, squanders it or casts it aside as too naked, too frightening, too painful to long possess.

I think of the wars that have been fought, allegedly for freedom. More often the blood and suffering and death were sacrificed so that massively powerful moneyed interests might remain free to use us up in our harnesses. I think of the endless list of the dead who were said to have given their lives so that we might be free. But after the wars nothing much changed. As usual we arose every morning, slipped into our harnesses, plodded to our work, and believed we were free. Then we died.

We all wear our harnesses, and if we are easy in them, if we feel free, is not the illusion of freedom as satisfactory as freedom itself? Should we fret over our servitudes, petty or grand, when the fictions of freedom we embrace often serve as satisfactorily? Is not a shackled slave who cannot see or feel his chains as free as if he had no chains at all? Should we free the happy slave and cast him into the chaos and horrors of pure freedom? Indeed, have we not at last achieved the prediction of *Brave New World*,[2] in which Aldous Huxley observed that the "really efficient totalitarian state would be one in which the all-powerful executive of political bosses and their army of managers control a population of slaves who do not have to be coerced, because they love their servitude"? Huxley argued that, "To make them love it [their bondage] is the task assigned, in present-day totalitarian states. . . ." Ought we not consider the possibility that the *1984*[3] of George Orwell has come and gone and that his once chilling oracle is the culture of our time, one in which we do, in fact, love our bondage, one where, in fact, we happily accept the clichés, the images, the fables, and the fictions of freedom in the place of freedom itself?

Freedom, "that sweet bondage," as Shelley[4] called it, is a marvelous thing in small doses. Not to be afraid of our government is blessed. Not to be lied to, not to be cheated, not to be exploited and poisoned and hurt for corporate greed, not to be used up like old rags; to be heard, to be respected, to grow and to discover our uniqueness — these are the freedoms we most cherish, freedoms we, by reason of our occupancy of this earth, are entitled to enjoy.

Yet most of our freedoms lie within. As the poem goes, "Stone walls do 50 not a prison make, nor iron bars a cage." Most freedoms cannot be given, except as we give them to ourselves.

I think of old Jack who cherished his freedom above all. He is, at last, free, totally free, since freedom, by common definition, is a condition in which the individual may do what he wants, and since the dead have no wants they are, are they not, totally free? Or perhaps as the Greeks argued, "Only Zeus is free."

And I also think of old Star and Spiffy, and of their freedom. Were I as successful, as free. Were I able to mow the meadows of my life and live by my own work as well. Were I able to remove the harness from within — such is freedom. And when finally the legs have given out, when the bones are old and brittle and crooked, and at last the shoulders too crippled to pull the load, I should hope that on the way to wherever it is that old horses and old men go I feel the wind through my hair, and that my eyes do not water from tears, but from having felt the joy of the trip, the trip to the last and only freedom.

---

[2]*Brave New World:* A 1932 novel by Aldous Huxley (1894–1963) portraying a future technocratic society in which life is completely controlled from cradle to grave.

[3]*1984:* A 1949 novel by George Orwell (1903–1950) portraying life in an imagined totalitarian state.

[4]*Shelley:* Percy Bysshe Shelley (1792–1822), English Romantic poet also known for his radical politics, atheism, and advocacy of sexual freedom.

ENGAGING THE TEXT

1. What, according to Spence, is perfect freedom, and why is it so hard to bear?

2. Explain the point of the story Spence tells about Star and Spiffy. How does he feel about these horses and their fate? What does their story say about freedom?

3. Spence says that each American wears a "harness" within. What forces and institutions, according to Spence, impose this invisible harness? What other social forces or institutions would you add to this list? To what extent do you agree with Spence that "we long for a more successful domestication of the human species" (para. 40)?

4. What's particularly free about "old Jack"? Do you think it's inevitable that a genuinely free human being must also be offensive? Why?

EXPLORING CONNECTIONS

5. Review two or more selections involving the following individuals or characters:

   Richard Rodriguez (p. 214)   C. P. Ellis (p. 591)
   Mary Lynn in "Assimilation" (p. 674)   Gary Soto (p. 26)
   Malcolm X (p. 243)   Paula Gunn Allen (p. 443)
   Stephen Cruz (p. 348)   Judith Ortiz Cofer in "The Story
   Kathleen Boatwright (p. 498)   of My Body" (p. 433)
   Sylvia in "The Lesson" (p. 404)

   Which of these individuals or characters seem the most free to you in Spence's sense of the word? Which seem most "domesticated"? Which challenge or complicate Spence's definition of what it means to be free?

6. How does Spence's notion of freedom compare with those offered by Dinesh D'Souza (p. 716) and Todd Gitlin (p. 782)? When people in other lands think of freedom in America, do you suppose they have in mind the kind of freedom that Spence refers to in this essay?

7. To what extent would Ralph Temple (p. 798) be likely to agree with Spence about the average American's understanding of freedom? How would Temple probably view someone like Spence's "old Jack"?

EXTENDING THE CRITICAL CONTEXT

8. Make an inventory of the "deals," "bargains," or "trades" that you make with your friends, family, employer, school, and society every day. How do these implied agreements limit your freedom? What do you get in return for honoring them? Which of these "deals" impinge most on your freedom?

9. Write a profile of a person you've known who, as Jack does for Spence, symbolizes freedom for you. In this portrait, try to clarify how this person expresses her freeness and how her freedom has affected others.

10. Spence suggests America is more concerned with the "illusion" of freedom than with its reality. Working in groups, survey a number of music videos and print ads for contemporary images of freedom. How is it portrayed in American culture? What costs or consequences are associated with it?

Let America Be America Again

LANGSTON HUGHES

Our survey of American culture closes with a reflection on the power that the myth of freedom has to inspire hope, even in the face of despair. Written nine years into the great Depression, "Let America Be America Again" (1938) offers a stinging indictment of the hypocrisy that Langston Hughes perceived everywhere in American life. Yet Hughes transcends his rage and dares to hope for America's future; in so doing he pays homage to ideals that retain their potency even in the twenty-first century. James Langston Hughes (1902–1967) was a major figure in the Harlem Renaissance — a flowering of African American artists, musicians, and writers in New York City in the 1920s. His poems, often examining the experiences of urban African American life, use the rhythms of jazz, spirituals, and the blues. Among the most popular of his works today are The Ways of White Folks *(1934), a collection of short stories, and* Montage of a Dream Deferred *(1951), a selection of his poetry.*

Let America be America again.
Let it be the dream it used to be.
Let it be the pioneer on the plain
Seeking a home where he himself is free.

(America never was America to me.)   5

Let America be the dream the dreamers dreamed —
Let it be that great strong land of love
Where never kings connive nor tyrants scheme
That any man be crushed by one above.

(It never was America to me.)   10

O, let my land be a land where Liberty
Is crowned with no false patriotic wreath,
But opportunity is real, and life is free,
Equality is in the air we breathe.

(There's never been equality for me,   15
Nor freedom in this "homeland of the free.")

Say who are you that mumbles in the dark?
And who are you that draws your veil across the stars?

I am the poor white, fooled and pushed apart,
I am the red man driven from the land.   20
I am the refugee clutching the hope I seek —

But finding only the same old stupid plan
Of dog eat dog, of mighty crush the weak.
I am the Negro, "problem" to you all.
I am the people, humble, hungry, mean —   25
Hungry yet today despite the dream.
Beaten yet today — O, Pioneers!
I am the man who never got ahead.
The poorest worker bartered through the years.
Yet I'm the one who dreamt our basic dream   30
In that Old World while still a serf of kings,
Who dreamt a dream so strong, so brave, so true,
That even yet its mighty daring sings
In every brick and stone, in every furrow turned
That's made America the land it has become.   35
O, I'm the man who sailed those early seas
In search of what I meant to be my home —
For I'm the one who left dark Ireland's shore,
And Poland's plain, and England's grassy lea,
And torn from Black Africa's strand I came   40
To build a "homeland of the free."

The free?
Who said the free? Not me?
Surely not me? The millions on relief today?
The millions who have nothing for our pay   45
For all the dreams we've dreamed
And all the songs we sung
And all the hopes we've held
And all the flags we've hung,
The millions who have nothing for our pay —   50
Except the dream we keep alive today.

O, let America be America again —
The land that never has been yet —
And yet must be — the land where *every* man is free.
The land that's mine — the poor man's, Indian's, Negro's, ME —   55
Who made America,
Whose sweat and blood, whose faith and pain,
Whose hand at the foundry, whose plow in the rain,
Must bring back our mighty dream again.

        O, yes,   60
        I say it plain,
        America never was America to me,
        And yet I swear this oath —
        America will be!

ENGAGING THE TEXT

1. Explain the two senses of the word "America" as Hughes uses it in the title and refrain of the poem.
2. According to Hughes, who must rebuild the dream, and why?
3. Why does Hughes reaffirm the dream of an ideal America in the face of so much evidence to the contrary?
4. Explain the irony of lines 40–41 ("And torn from Black Africa's strand I came / To build a 'homeland of the free'").
5. Examine the way Hughes uses line length, repetition, stanza breaks, typography, and indentation to call attention to particular lines of the poem. Why does he emphasize these passages?

EXPLORING CONNECTIONS

6. Write an imaginary conversation among Hughes, Gerry Spence (p. 805), Dinesh D'Souza (p. 716), Todd Gitlin (p. 782), and Patricia Williams (p. 794) on the state of freedom in America. What would freedom mean to each of these writers? Which would have the most optimistic view of the future of freedom in America?
7. Compare the views of America that are presented in this poem and June Jordan's "Poem for Benjamin Franklin" (p. 752). How would you describe the tone of each poem? What are Jordan and Hughes saying about America and American cultural ideals?
8. Review some or all of the poems in *Rereading America*:

   Melvin Dixon, "Aunt Ida Pieces a Quilt" (p. 131)
   June Jordan, "Poem for Benjamin Franklin" (p. 752)
   Sharon Olds, "From Seven Floors Up" (p. 381)
   Dana Gioia, "Money" (p. 382)
   Aurora Levins Morales, "Child of the Americas" (p. 701)
   Inés Hernández-Ávila, "Para Teresa" (p. 227)
   Langston Hughes, "Let America Be America Again" (p. 814)

   Then discuss the role of poetry as a form of social action. What are the characteristics of this type of poetry? How does it differ from the poetry you have read before in school?

EXTENDING THE CRITICAL CONTEXT

9. Working in groups, "stage" a reading of the poem, using multiple speakers. Consider carefully how to divide up the lines for the most effective presentation. After the readings, discuss the choices made by the different groups in the class.
10. Working in pairs or in small groups, write prose descriptions of the two versions of America Hughes evokes. Read these aloud and discuss which description more closely matches your own view of the United States.

Text Acknowledgments

Horatio Alger. "Assimilation." From *Ragged Dick and Mark the Match Boy* by Horatio Alger. Copyright © 1962 by Macmillan Publishing Company. Reprinted with the permission of Scribner, a Division of Simon & Schuster Adult Publishing Group.

Sherman Alexie. "Assimilation." From *The Toughest Indian in the World* by Sherman Alexie. Copyright © 2000 by Sherman Alexie. Used by permission of Grove/Atlantic, Inc.

Paula Gunn Allen. "Where I Come From Is Like This." From *The Sacred Hoop* by Paula Gunn Allen. Copyright © 1986, 1992 by Paula Gunn Allen. Reprinted by permission of Beacon Press, Boston.

Joel Andreas. "The War on Terrorism." Reprinted with the permission of the author.

Jean Anyon. "Social Class and the Hidden Curriculum of Work." From *Journal of Education*, Boston University School of Education (1980), Volume 162, No. 1. Copyright © 1980 by the Trustees of Boston University. Reprinted with permission from the Trustees of Boston University and the author.

Judy Root Aulette. Excerpt from *Changing American Families* by Judy Root Aulette. Copyright © 2002 by Pearson Education. Published by Allyn and Bacon, Boston, MA. Reprinted by permission of the publisher.

Toni Cade Bambara. "The Lesson." From *Gorilla, My Love* by Toni Cade Bambara. Copyright © 1972 by Toni Cade Bambara. Used by permission of Random House, Inc.

Benjamin R. Barber. "The Educated Student: Global Citizen or Global Consumer?" Published originally in the *Liberal Education* (Association of American Colleges and Universities: Spring 2002, vol. 88, i2, p. 22). Copyright © 2002 by Benjamin R. Barber. Reprinted with the permission of the author.

Bebe Moore Campbell. "Envy." Chapter 5 from *Sweet Summer* by Bebe Moore Campbell. Copyright © 1989 by Bebe Moore Campbell. Used by permission of GP Putnam's Sons, a division of Penguin Putnam, Inc.

Judith Ortiz Cofer. "The Story of My Body." From *The Latin Deli: Prose and Poetry* by Judith Ortiz Cofer. Copyright © 1993 by Judith Ortiz Cofer. Used by permission of The University of Georgia Press.

Stephanie Coontz. "What We Really Miss About the 1950s." From *The Way We Really Are* by Stephanie Coontz. Copyright © 1997 by Basic Books, a division of HarperCollins Publishers, Inc. Reprinted by permission of Basic Books, a member of Perseus Books, L.L.C.

Anne Crittenden. "The Truly Invisible Hand." From *The Price of Motherhood: Why the Most Important Job in the World is Still the Least Valued* by Anne Crittenden. Copyright © 2001 by Anne Crittenden. Reprinted by permission of Henry Holt and Company, L.L.C.

Danielle Crittenden. "About Marriage." From *What Our Mothers Didn't Tell Us: Why Happiness Eludes the Modern Woman* by Danielle Crittenden. Copyright © 1999 by Danielle Crittenden. Reprinted by permission of Simon & Schuster Adult Publishing Group. All rights reserved.

Harlon L. Dalton. "Horatio Alger." From *Racial Healing* by Harlon L. Dalton. Copyright © 1995 by Harlon L. Dalton. Used by permission of Doubleday, a division of Random House, Inc.

Francesca Delbanco. "The Progressive Basics." From *Tales Out of School*, edited by Susan Richards Shreve and Porter Shreve. Copyright © Francesca Delbanco. Reprinted with the permission of Russell and Volkening Agency, on behalf of the author.

Holly Devor. "Becoming Members of Society: Learning the Social Meanings of Gender." From *Gender Blending: Confronting the Limits of Duality* by Holly

Devor. Copyright © 1998 by Indiana University Press. Reprinted with the permission of the publisher.

Melvin Dixon. "Aunt Ida Pieces a Quilt." From *Love's Instruments* by Melvin Dixon. Originally published by Tia Churcha Press. Reprinted with permission of the Estate of Melvin Dixon.

Dinesh D'Souza. "America the Beautiful: What We're Fighting For." From *What's So Great About America* by Dinesh D'Souza. Copyright © 2002 by Dinesh D'Souza. Reprinted with permission of Regnery Publishing.

Barbara Ehrenreich. "Serving in Florida." From *Nickel and Dimed* by Barbara Ehrenreich. Copyright © 2001 by Barbara Ehrenreich. Reprinted by permission of Henry Holt and Company, L.L.C.

Susan Faludi. "Girls Have All the Power: What's Troubling Troubled Boys." From *Stiffed: The Betrayal of the American Man* by Susan Faludi. Copyright © 1999 by Susan Faludi. Reprinted by permission of HarperCollins Publishers, Inc.

George M. Fredrickson. "Models of American Ethnic Relations: A Historical Perspective." From *Cultural Divides: Understanding and Overcoming Group Conflict*, edited by Deborah A. Prentice and Dale T. Miller. Copyright © 1999 Russell Sage Foundation. Reprinted with the permission of the Russell Sage Foundation.

Joshua Gamson. "Talking Freaks: Lesbian, Gay, Bisexual, and Transgender Families on Daytime Talk TV." From *Queer Families, Queer Politics: Challenging Culture and the State*, edited by Mary Bernstein and Renate Reimann. Copyright © 2001, Reprinted with the permission of Columbia University Press.

Anne Witte Garland. "Good Noise: Cora Tucker." From *Women Activists: Challenging the Abuse of Power* by Anne Witte Garland. Foreward by Ralph Nader. Introduction by Francis T. Farenthold. Published by the Feminist Press at the City University of New York. Copyright © 1988 by the Center for the Study of Responsive Law. Reprinted by permission of the Feminist Press at the City University of New York. www.feministpress.org.

John Taylor Gatto. "The Seven-Lesson Schoolteacher." From *Dumbing Us Down: The Hidden Curriculum of Compulsory Schooling* by John Taylor Gatto. Copyright © 1992. Published by New Society Publishers. www.newsociety.com. 1-800-567-6772. Reprinted by permission.

Dana Gioia. "Money." From *The Gods of Winter* by Dana Gioia. Copyright © 1991 by Dana Gioia. Reprinted with the permission of Graywolf Press, Saint Paul, Minnesota.

Todd Gitlin. "Under the Sign of Mickey Mouse & Company." From *Media Unlimited: How the Torrent of Images and Sounds Overwhelms Our Lives* by Todd Gitlin. Copyright © 2001 by Todd Gitlin. Reprinted by permission of Henry Holt and Company, L.L.C.

Google website screen shots. © 2003 Google. Courtesy of www.Google.com.

Ken Hamblin. "The Black Avenger." From *Pick a Better Country* by Ken Hamblin. Copyright © 1996 by Ken Hamblin. Reprinted with the permission of Simon & Schuster Adult Publishing Group.

Ines Hernandez-Avila. "Para Teresa." From *Con Razon, Corazon* by Ines Hernandez-Avila. Copyright © 1987 by Ines Hernandez-Avila. Reprinted by permission of the author, Ines Hernandez-Avila, Professor of Native American Studies at the University of California, Davis.

Mark Hertsgaard. "The Oblivious Empire." From *The Eagle's Shadow: Why America Fascinated and Infuriates the World* by Mark Hertsgaard. Copyright © 2002 by Mark Hertsgaard. Reprinted by permission of Farrar, Straus and Giroux, LLC.

Langston Hughes. "Let America Be America Again." From *Collected Poems* by Langston Hughes. Copyright © 1994 by the Estate of Langston Hughes. Used by permission of Alfred A. Knopf, a division of Random House, Inc.

Vincent N. Parrillo. "Causes of Prejudice." From *Strangers to These Shores*, Third Edition by Vincent N. Parrillo. Copyright © 1990 by Pearson Education. Reprinted by permission of the author.

Dan Rather. "Trug Dung." From *The American Dream: Stories from the Heart of Our Nation* by Dan Rather. Copyright © 2001 by Dan Rather. Reprinted by permission of HarperCollins Publishers, Inc.

Randall Robinson. "Thoughts about Restitution." From *The Debt: What America Owes to Blacks* by Randall Robinson. Copyright © 2000 by Randall Robinson. Used by permission of Dutton, a division of Penguin Group (USA) Inc.

Richard Rodriguez. "The Achievement of Desire." From *Hunger of Memory* by Richard Rodriguez. Copyright © 1982 by Richard Rodriguez. Reprinted by permission of David R. Godine, Publisher, Inc.

Mike Rose. "I Just Wanna Be Average." From *Lives on the Boundary: The Struggles and Achievements of America's Underprepared* by Mike Rose. Copyright © 1989 by Mike Rose. Reprinted with the permission of The Free Press, a Division of Simon & Schuster Adult Publishing Group.

Christina Hoff Sommers. "Save the Males." From *The War Against Boys* by Christina Hoff Summers. Copyright © 2001 by Christina Hoff Sommers. Reprinted with the permission of Simon & Schuster Adult Publishing Group. All rights reserved.

Gary Soto. "Looking for Work." From *Living Up the Street: Narrative Recollections* by Gary Soto. Copyright © 1985 by Gary Soto. Used by permission of the author.

Gerry Spence. "Easy in the Harness." From *Freedom to Slavery* by Gerry Spence. Copyright © 1993 by Gerry Spence. Reprinted by permission of St. Martin's Press, LLC.

Claude M. Steele. "Thin Ice: Stereotype Threat and Black College Students." Originally published as "Race and the Schooling of Black Americans" in *The Atlantic Monthly*. Copyright © 1992 by Claude M. Steele. Reprinted with the permission of the author.

Shelby Steele. "I'm Black, You're White, Who's Innocent?" From *The Content of Character* by Shelby Steele. Copyright © 1990 by Shelby Steele. Reprinted by permission of St. Martin's Press, LLC.

Leonard Steinhorn and Barbara Diggs-Brown. "Virtual Integration: How the Integration of Mass Media Undermines Integration." From *By the Color of Our Skin* by Leonard Steinhorn and Barbara Diggs-Brown. Copyright © 1999 by Leonard Steinhorn and Barbara Diggs-Brown. Used by permission of Dutton, a division of Penguin Group (USA) Inc.

Ronald Takaki. "Race at the End of History." From *Good Citizen* by Ronald Takaki. Copyright © 1990 by Ronald Takaki. Reproduced by permission of Routledge/Taylor & Francis Books, Inc.

Deborah Tannen. "The Roots of Debate in Education and the Hope of Dialogue." From *The Argument Culture* by Deborah Tannen. Copyright © 1997 by Deborah Tannen. Used with permission of Random House, Inc.

Ralph Temple. "The Sorrow and the Pity of Racial Profiling." By Ralph Temple, Legal Director of the Washington, DC, chapter of the American Civil Liberties Union from 1966 to 1980, now living in Ashland, Oregon. First published in *It's A Free Country: Personal Freedom in America After September 11*, edited by Danny Goldberg, Robert Greenwald, and Victor Goldberg (hardcover: September 2002, RDV Books/Akashic Books; paperback: September 2003, Nation Books).

Studs Terkel. "C. P. Ellis" and "Stephen Cruz." From *American Dreams: Lost and Found* by Studs Terkel. Copyright © 1980 by Studs Terkel. Reprinted by permission of Donadio & Olson, Inc.

Carmen Vasquez. "Appearances." From *Homophibia* by Warren J. Blumenfeld. Copyright © 1992 by Warren J. Blumenfeld. Reprinted with permission of Beacon Press, Boston.

Michele Wallace. Epigraph from "When Black Feminism Faces the Music, and the Music Is Rap." From *The New York Times*, July 29, 1990. Copyright © 1990 by The New York Times Company. Reprinted with permission.

Paul L. Wachtel. "Talking About Racism." From *Race in the Mind of America: Breaking the Vicious Circle between Blacks and Whites* by Paul L. Wachtel. Copyright © 1999 by Paul L. Wachtel. Reproduced by permission of Routledge/Taylor & Francis Books, Inc.

Patricia J. Williams. "By Any Means Necessary." From *The Nation*, November 26, 2001, vol. 273, No. 117, page 11. Copyright © 2001 The Nation Company L.P. Reprinted with permission of the publisher.

Leon E. Wynter. Excerpts from *American Skin: Pop Culture, Big Business, and the End of White America* by Leon E. Wynter. Copyright © 2002 by Leon E. Wynter. Reprinted with permission of Crown Publishers, a division of Random House, Inc.

Art Acknowledgments

CHAPTER 1: HARMONY AT HOME

17, Archive Photos/Getty Images.

22–24, Printed by permission of the Norman Rockwell Family Agency. Copyright © 2004 the Norman Rockwell Family Entities.

35, Copyright © 1988, Andrew Struthers. Used with permission.

50, © The New Yorker Collection 1997 Bruce Eric Kaplan from cartoonbank.com. All rights reserved.

78, © The New Yorker Collection 1992 Roz Chast from cartoonbank.com. All rights reserved.

84, James Newberry, the Elder.

85, © Erica Berger/Corbis Outline.

86, Nicole Bengiveno.

87, © Peter M. Fisher/Corbis.

88, Tony O'Brien/The Image Works.

89, Used by permission of Samsung Electronics.

CHAPTER 2: LEARNING POWER

135, Copyright © Charles Agel. Used with permission.

152, Copyright © Lloyd Dangle/Troubletown. Used with permission.

172, From *School Is Hell*. Copyright © 1987 Matt Groening. All rights reserved. Reprinted by permission of Pantheon Books, a division of Random House, Inc., NY.

181, From *Love Is Hell*. Copyright © 1986 Matt Groening. All rights reserved. Reprinted by permission of Pantheon Books, a division of Random House, Inc., NY.

211–213, Printed by permission of the Norman Rockwell Family Agency. Copyright © 2004 the Norman Rockwell Family Entities.

252, *Boondocks* © 2000 Aaron McGruder. Reprinted with permission of Universal Press Syndicate. Reprinted with permission. All rights reserved.

272, *Doonesbury* © 1992 G. B. Trudeau. Reprinted with permission of Universal Press Syndicate. All rights reserved.

283, 9 *Chickweed Lane* reprinted by permission of United Feature Syndicate, Inc.

CHAPTER 3: MONEY AND SUCCESS

293, Steven Weinrebe/Index Stock.

307, *Boondocks* © Aaron McGruder. Distributed By Universal Press Syndicate. Reprinted with permission. All rights reserved.

344, Copyright © Lloyd Dangle/Troubletown. Used with permission.

Index of Authors and Titles